THE
HISTORIES AND
POEMS

The Complete Works of William Shakespeare

VOLUME II

* * * * *

The Histories and Poems

Wordsworth Editions

The Complete Works of William Shakespeare
Volume II : The Histories and Poems

First published in 2002
by Wordsworth Editions Limited
Cumberland House, Crib Street, Ware,
Hertfordshire SG12 9ET

ISBN 1 84022 038 4

Printed and bound in the United States of America

CONTENTS

THE PLAYS

THE POEMS

THE PLAYS

THE FIRST PART OF
KING HENRY THE SIXTH

DRAMATIS PERSONAE

KING HENRY THE SIXTH.
DUKE OF GLOSTER, *uncle to the King, and Protector.*
DUKE OF BEDFORD, *uncle to the King, and Regent of France.*
THOMAS BEAUFORT, *Duke of Exeter, great-uncle to the King.*
HENRY BEAUFORT, *great-uncle to the King, Bishop of Winchester, and afterwards Cardinal.*
JOHN BEAUFORT, *Earl of Somerset, afterwards Duke.*
RICHARD PLANTAGENET, *son of Richard late Earl of Cambridge, afterwards Duke of York.*
EARL OF WARWICK.
EARL OF SALISBURY.
EARL OF SUFFOLK.
LORD TALBOT, *afterwards Earl of Shrewsbury.*
JOHN TALBOT, *his son.*
EDMUND MORTIMER, *Earl of March.*
SIR JOHN FASTOLFE.
SIR WILLIAM LUCY.
SIR WILLIAM GLANSDALE.
SIR THOMAS GARGRAVE.
MAYOR OF LONDON.
WOODVILLE, *Lieutenant of the Tower.*
VERNON, *of the White-Rose or York faction.*

BASSET, *of the Red-Rose or Lancaster faction.*
A LAWYER.—MORTIMER'S KEEPERS.

CHARLES, *Dauphin, and afterwards King, of France.*
REIGNIER, *Duke of Anjou, and titular King of Naples.*
DUKE OF BURGUNDY.
DUKE OF ALENÇON.
BASTARD OF ORLEANS.
GOVERNOR OF PARIS.
MASTER-GUNNER OF ORLEANS, *and his* SON.
GENERAL *of the French forces in Bourdeaux.*
A FRENCH SERGEANT.   A PORTER.
AN OLD SHEPHERD, *father to Joan la Pucelle.*

MARGARET, *daughter to Reignier, afterwards married to King Henry.*
COUNTESS OF AUVERGNE.
JOAN LA PUCELLE, *commonly called Joan of Arc.*
LORDS, WARDERS OF THE TOWER, HERALDS, OFFICERS, SOLDIERS, MESSENGERS *and* ATTENDANTS.
FIENDS *appearing to La Pucelle.*

SCENE—*Partly in England, and partly in France.*

ACT I. SCENE I.

Westminster Abbey.

Dead march.   Enter the Funeral of KING HENRY THE FIFTH, *attended on by the* DUKE OF BEDFORD, *Regent of France; the* DUKE OF GLOSTER, *Protector; the* DUKE OF EXETER, *the* EARL OF WARWICK, *the* BISHOP OF WINCHESTER, HERALDS, &c.

DUKE OF BEDFORD.

HUNG be the heavens with black, yield day to night!
Comets, importing change of times and states,
Brandish your crystal tresses in the sky,
And with them scourge the bad revolting stars
That have consented unto Henry's death!
Henry the Fifth, too famous to live long!
England ne'er lost a king of so much worth.

DUKE OF GLOSTER.

England ne'er had a king until his time.
Virtue he had, deserving to command:
His brandisht sword did blind men with his beams;
His arms spread wider than a dragon's wings;
His sparkling eyes, replete with wrathful fire,
More dazzled and drove back his enemies
Than mid-day sun fierce bent against their faces.
What should I say? his deeds exceed all speech.
He ne'er lift up his hand, but conquered.

DUKE OF EXETER.

We mourn in black: why mourn we not in blood?
Henry is dead, and never shall revive:

Upon a wooden coffin we attend;
And death's dishonourable victory
We with our stately presence glorify,
Like captives bound to a triumphant car.
What! shall we curse the planets of mishap
That plotted thus our glory's overthrow?
Or shall we think the subtle-witted French
Conjurers and sorcerers, that, afraid of him,
By magic verses have contrived his end?

BISHOP OF WINCHESTER.

He was a king blest of the King of kings.
Unto the French the dreadful judgement-day
So dreadful will not be as was his sight.
The battles of the Lord of hosts he fought:
The church's prayers made him so prosperous.

DUKE OF GLOSTER.

The church! where is it? Had not churchmen pray'd,
His thread of life had not so soon decay'd:
None do you like but an effeminate prince,
Whom, like a schoolboy, you may overawe.

BISHOP OF WINCHESTER.

Gloster, whate'er we like, thou art Protector,
And lookest to command the prince and realm.
Thy wife is proud; she holdeth thee in awe,
More than God or religious churchmen may.

DUKE OF GLOSTER.

Name not religion, for thou lovest the flesh;
And ne'er throughout the year to church thou go'st,
Except it be to pray against thy foes.

I

DUKE OF BEDFORD.

Cease, cease these jars, and rest your minds in
peace!
Let's to the altar:—heralds, wait on us:—
Instead of gold, we'll offer up our arms;
Since arms avail not, now that Henry's dead.—
Posterity, await for wretched years,
When at their mothers' moist eyes babes shall
suck;
Our isle be made a marish of salt tears,
And none but women left to wail the dead.—
Henry the Fifth! thy ghost I invocate;
Prosper this realm, keep it from civil broils!
Combat with adverse planets in the heavens!
A far more glorious star thy soul will make
Than Julius Cæsar or bright—

Enter a MESSENGER.

MESSENGER.

My honourable lords, health to you all!
Sad tidings bring I to you out of France,
Of loss, of slaughter, and discomfiture:
Guienne, Champagne, Rheims, Rouen, Orleans,
Paris, Guysors, Poictiers, are all quite lost.

DUKE OF BEDFORD.

What say'st thou, man! before dead Henry's corse
Speak softly, or the loss of those great towns
Will make him burst his lead, and rise from death.

DUKE OF GLOSTER.

Is Paris lost? is Rouen yielded up?
If Henry were recall'd to life again,
These news would cause him once more yield the
ghost.

DUKE OF EXETER.

How were they lost? what treachery was used?

MESSENGER.

No treachery; but want of men and money.
Amongst the soldiers this is muttered,
That here you maintain several factions;
And, whilst a field should be dispatcht and fought,
You are disputing of your generals:
One would have lingering wars, with little cost;
Another would fly swift, but wanteth wings;
A third thinks, without expense at all,
By guileful fair words peace may be obtain'd.
Awake, awake, English nobility!
Let not sloth dim your honours new-begot;
Cropt are the flower-de-luces in your arms;
Of England's coat one half is cut away.

DUKE OF EXETER.

Were our tears wanting to this funeral,
These tidings would call forth their flowing tides.

DUKE OF BEDFORD.

Me they concern; Regent I am of France.—
Give me my steeled coat! I'll fight for France.
Away with these disgraceful wailing robes!
Wounds will I lend the French, instead of eyes,
To weep their intermissive miseries.

Enter a SECOND MESSENGER.

SECOND MESSENGER.

Lords, view these letters, full of bad mischance.
France is revolted from the English quite,
Except some petty towns of no import:
The Dauphin Charles is crowned king in Rheims;
The Bastard of Orleans with him is join'd;
Reignier, duke of Anjou, doth take his part;
The Duke of Alençon flieth to his side.

DUKE OF EXETER.

The Dauphin crowned king! all fly to him!
O, whither shall we fly from this reproach?

DUKE OF GLOSTER.

We will not fly, but to our enemies' throats:—
Bedford, if thou be slack, I'll fight it out.

DUKE OF BEDFORD.

Gloster, why doubt'st thou of my forwardness?
An army have I muster'd in my thoughts,
Wherewith already France is overrun.

Enter a THIRD MESSENGER.

THIRD MESSENGER.

My gracious lords, to add to your laments,
Wherewith you now bedew King Henry's
hearse,
I must inform you of a dismal fight
Betwixt the stout Lord Talbot and the French.

BISHOP OF WINCHESTER.

What! wherein Talbot overcame? is't so?

THIRD MESSENGER.

O, no; wherein Lord Talbot was o'erthrown:
The circumstance I'll tell you more at large.
The tenth of August last, this dreadful lord,
Retiring from the siege of Orleans,
Having full scarce six thousand in his troop,
By three-and-twenty thousand of the French
Was round encompassed and set upon.
No leisure had he to enrank his men;
He wanted pikes to set before his archers;
Instead whereof, sharp stakes, pluckt out of
hedges,
They pitched in the ground confusedly,
To keep the horsemen off from breaking in.
More than three hours the fight continued;
Where valiant Talbot, above human thought,
Enacted wonders with his sword and lance:
Hundreds he sent to hell, and none durst stand
him;
Here, there, and every where, enraged he flew:
The French exclaim'd, the devil was in arms;
All the whole army stood agazed on him:
His soldiers, spying his undaunted spirit,
'A Talbot! a Talbot!' cried out amain,
And rusht into the bowels of the battle.
Here had the conquest fully been seal'd up,
If Sir John Fastolfe had not play'd the coward:
He, being in the vaward,—placed behind,
With purpose to relieve and follow them,—
Cowardly fled, not having struck one stroke.
Hence grew the general wrack and massacre;
Enclosed were they with their enemies:
A base Walloon, to win the Dauphin's grace,
Thrust Talbot with a spear into the back;
Whom all France, with their chief assembled
strength,
Durst not presume to look once in the face.

DUKE OF BEDFORD.

Is Talbot slain? then I will slay myself,
For living idly here in pomp and ease,
Whilst such a worthy leader, wanting aid,
Unto his dastard foemen is betray'd.

THIRD MESSENGER.

O, no, he lives; but is took prisoner,
And Lord Scales with him, and Lord Hunger-
ford:
Most of the rest slaughter'd or took likewise.

2

DUKE OF BEDFORD.

His ransom there is none but I shall pay:
I'll hale the Dauphin headlong from his throne,—
His crown shall be the ransom of my friend;
Four of their lords I'll change for one of ours.—
Farewell, my masters; to my task will I;
Bonfires in France forthwith I am to make,
To keep our great Saint George's feast withal:
Ten thousand soldiers with me I will take,
Whose bloody deeds shall make all Europe quake.

THIRD MESSENGER.

So you had need; for Orleans is besieged;
The English army is grown weak and faint:
The Earl of Salisbury craveth supply,
And hardly keeps his men from mutiny,
Since they, so few, watch such a multitude.

DUKE OF EXETER.

Remember, lords, your oaths to Henry sworn,
Either to quell the Dauphin utterly,
Or bring him in obedience to your yoke.

DUKE OF BEDFORD.

I do remember it; and here take my leave,
To go about my preparation.   [Exit.

DUKE OF GLOSTER.

I'll to the Tower, with all the haste I can,
To view th' artillery and munition;
And then I will proclaim young Henry king.
                                      [Exit.

DUKE OF EXETER.

To Eltham will I, where the young king is,
Being ordain'd his special governor;
And for his safety there I'll best devise.   [Exit.

BISHOP OF WINCHESTER.

Each hath his place and function to attend:
I am left out; for me nothing remains.
But long I will not be Jack-out-of-office:
The king from Eltham I intend to steal,
And sit at chiefest stern of public weal.   [Exit.

SCENE II.

France. Before Orleans.

Sound a flourish. Enter CHARLES, ALENÇON,
and REIGNIER, *marching with drum and* SOL-
DIERS.

CHARLES.

MARS his true moving, even as in the heavens,
So in the earth, to this day is not known:
Late did he shine upon the English side;
Now we are victors, upon us he smiles.
What towns of any moment but we have?
At pleasure here we lie, near Orleans;
Otherwhiles the famisht English, like pale ghosts,
Faintly besiege us one hour in a month.

DUKE OF ALENÇON.

They want their porridge and their fat bull-
beeves:
Either they must be dieted like mules,
And have their provender tied to their mouths,
Or piteous they will look, like drowned mice.

REIGNIER.

Let's raise the siege: why lie we idly here?
Talbot is taken, whom we wont to fear;
Remaineth none but mad-brain'd Salisbury;
And he may well in fretting spend his gall,—
Nor men nor money hath he to make war.

CHARLES.

Sound, sound alarum! we will rush on them.
Now for the honour of the forlorn French!—
Him I forgive my death that killeth me
When he sees me go back one foot or fly. [Exeunt.
*Here alarum; they are beaten back by the English
with great loss. Enter* CHARLES, ALENÇON,
REIGNIER, *and others.*

CHARLES.

Who ever saw the like? what men have I!—
Dogs! cowards! dastards!—I would ne'er have
fled,
But that they left me midst my enemies.

REIGNIER.

Salisbury is a desperate homicide;
He fighteth as one weary of his life.
The other lords, like lions wanting food,
Do rush upon us as their hungry prey.

DUKE OF ALENÇON.

Froissart, a countryman of ours, records,
England all Olivers and Rowlands bred
During the time Edward the Third did reign.
More truly now may this be verified;
For none but Samsons and Goliases
It sendeth forth to skirmish. One to ten!
Lean raw-boned rascals! who would e'er suppose
They had such courage and audacity?

CHARLES.

Let's leave this town; for they are hare-brain'd
slaves,
And hunger will enforce them be more eager:
Of old I know them; rather with their teeth
The walls they'll tear down than forsake the siege.

REIGNIER.

I think, by some odd gimmers or device,
Their arms are set like clocks, still to strike on;
Else ne'er could they hold out so as they do.
By my consent, we'll even let them alone.

DUKE OF ALENÇON.

Be it so.
                Enter the BASTARD OF ORLEANS.

BASTARD OF ORLEANS.

Where's the Prince Dauphin? I have news for
him.

CHARLES.

Bastard of Orleans, thrice welcome to us.

BASTARD OF ORLEANS.

Methinks your looks are sad, your cheer appall'd:
Hath the late overthrow wrought this offence?
Be not dismay'd, for succour is at hand:
A holy maid hither with me I bring,
Which, by a vision sent to her from heaven,
Ordained is to raise this tedious siege,
And drive the English forth the bounds of France.
The spirit of deep prophecy she hath,
Exceeding the nine sibyls of old Rome:
What's past and what's to come she can descry.
Speak, shall I call her in? Believe my words,
For they are certain and unfallible.

CHARLES.

Go, call her in. [Exit BASTARD.] But first, to try
her skill,
Reignier, stand thou as Dauphin in my place:
Question her proudly; let thy looks be stern:
By this means shall we sound what skill she hath.
                                      [Retires.

Enter the BASTARD OF ORLEANS, *with* JOAN
LA PUCELLE.
REIGNIER.
Fair maid, is't thou wilt do these wondrous feats?
JOAN LA PUCELLE.
Reignier, is't thou that thinkest to beguile me?
Where is the Dauphin?—Come, come from be-
hind;
I know thee well, though never seen before.
Be not amazed, there's nothing hid from me:
In private will I talk with thee apart.—
Stand back, you lords, and give us leave awhile.
REIGNIER.
She takes upon her bravely at first dash.
JOAN LA PUCELLE.
Dauphin, I am by birth a shepherd's daughter,
My wit untrain'd in any kind of art.
Heaven and our Lady gracious hath it pleased
To shine on my contemptible estate:
Lo, whilst I waited on my tender lambs,
And to sun's parching heat display'd my cheeks,
God's mother deigned to appear to me,
And, in a vision full of majesty,
Will'd me to leave my base vocation,
And free my country from calamity:
Her aid she promised, and assured success:
In complete glory she reveal'd herself;
And, whereas I was black and swart before,
With those clear rays which she infused on me
That beauty am I blest with which you see.
Ask me what question thou canst possible,
And I will answer unpremeditated:
My courage try by combat, if thou darest,
And thou shalt find that I exceed my sex.
Resolve on this,—thou shalt be fortunate,
If thou receive me for thy warlike mate.
CHARLES.
Thou hast astonisht me with thy high terms:
Only this proof I'll of thy valour make,—
In single combat thou shalt buckle with me;
And if thou vanquishest, thy words are true;
Otherwise I renounce all confidence.
JOAN LA PUCELLE.
I am prepared: here is my keen-edged sword,
Deckt with five flower-de-luces on each side;
The which at Touraine, in Saint Katharine's
churchyard,
Out of a deal of old iron I chose forth.
CHARLES.
Then come, o' God's name; I fear no woman.
JOAN LA PUCELLE.
And, while I live, I'll ne'er fly from a man.
[*Here they fight and* JOAN LA PUCELLE
overcomes.
CHARLES.
Stay, stay thy hands! thou art an Amazon,
And fightest with the sword of Deborah.
JOAN LA PUCELLE.
Christ's mother helps me, else I were too weak.
CHARLES.
Whoe'er helps thee, 'tis thou that must help me:
Impatiently I burn with thy desire;
My heart and hands thou hast at once subdued.
Excellent Pucelle, if thy name be so,
Let me thy servant, and not sovereign, be:
'Tis the French Dauphin sueth to thee thus.

JOAN LA PUCELLE.
I must not yield to any rites of love,
For my profession's sacred from above:
When I have chased all thy foes from hence,
Then will I think upon a recompense.
CHARLES.
Meantime look gracious on thy prostrate thrall.
REIGNIER.
My lord, methinks, is very long in talk.
DUKE OF ALENÇON.
Doubtless he shrives this woman to her smock;
Else ne'er could he so long protract his speech.
REIGNIER.
Shall we disturb him, since he keeps no mean?
DUKE OF ALENÇON.
He may mean more than we poor men do know:
These women are shrewd tempters with their
tongues.
REIGNIER.
My lord, where are you? what devise you on?
Shall we give over Orleans, or no?
JOAN LA PUCELLE.
Why, no, I say, distrustful recreants!
Fight till the last gasp; I will be your guard.
CHARLES.
What she says, I'll confirm: we'll fight it out.
JOAN LA PUCELLE.
Assign'd am I to be the English scourge.
This night the siege assuredly I'll raise:
Expect Saint Martin's summer, halcyon days,
Since I have entered into these wars.
Glory is like a circle in the water,
Which never ceaseth to enlarge itself,
Till, by broad spreading, it disperse to naught.
With Henry's death the English circle ends;
Dispersed are the glories it included.
Now am I like that proud-insulting ship
Which Cæsar and his fortune bare at once.
CHARLES.
Was Mahomet inspired with a dove?
Thou with an eagle art inspired, then.
Helen, the mother of great Constantine,
Nor yet Saint Philip's daughters, were like thee.
Bright star of Venus, faln down on the earth,
How may I ever worship thee enough?
DUKE OF ALENÇON.
Leave off delays, and let us raise the siege.
REIGNIER.
Woman, do what thou canst to save our honours;
Drive them from Orleans, and be immortalized.
CHARLES.
Presently we'll try:—come, let's away about it:—
No prophet will I trust, if she prove false. [*Exeunt.*

SCENE III.
London.　Before the Tower.

Enter the DUKE OF GLOSTER, *with his* SERVING-
MEN *in blue coats.*

DUKE OF·GLOSTER.
I AM come to survey the Tower this day:
Since Henry's death, I fear, there is convey-
ance.—
Where be these warders, that they wait not here?
Open the gates; 'tis Gloucester that calls.
[*Servants knock.*

4

FIRST WARDER [*within*].
Who's there that knocks so imperiously?
FIRST SERVING-MAN.
It is the noble Duke of Gloucester.
SECOND WARDER [*within*].
Whoe'er he be, you may not be let in.
FIRST SERVING-MAN.
Villains, answer you so the lord Protector?
FIRST WARDER [*within*].
The Lord protect him! so we answer him:
We do no otherwise than we are will'd.
DUKE OF GLOSTER.
Who willed you? or whose will stands but mine?
There's none Protector of the realm but I.—
Break up the gates, I'll be your warrantize:
Shall I be flouted thus by dunghill grooms?
[GLOSTER'S *men rush at the Tower-gates,
and* WOODVILLE, *the Lieutenant, speaks
within.*
WOODVILLE.
What noise is this? what traitors have we here?
DUKE OF GLOSTER.
Lieutenant, is it you whose voice I hear?
Open the gates; here's Gloster that would enter.
WOODVILLE.
Have patience, noble duke; I may not open;
The Cardinal of Winchester forbids:
From him I have express commandement
That thou nor none of thine shall be let in.
DUKE OF GLOSTER.
Faint-hearted Woodville, prizest him 'fore me,—
Arrogant Winchester, that haughty prelate,
Whom Henry, our late sovereign, ne'er could
brook?
Thou art no friend to God or to the king:
Open the gates, or I'll shut thee out shortly.
SERVING-MEN.
Open the gates unto the lord Protector:
Or we'll burst them open, if that you come not
quickly.
Enter to the PROTECTOR *at the Tower-gates* WIN-
CHESTER, *and his* MEN *in tawny coats.*
BISHOP OF WINCHESTER.
How now, ambitious Humphrey! what means this?
DUKE OF GLOSTER.
Peel'd priest, dost thou command me to be shut
out?
BISHOP OF WINCHESTER.
I do, thou most usurping proditor,
And not Protector, of the king or realm.
DUKE OF GLOSTER.
Stand back, thou manifest conspirator,
Thou that contrivedst to murder our dead lord;
Thou that givest whores indulgences to sin:
I'll canvass thee in thy broad cardinal's hat.
If thou proceed in this thy insolence.
BISHOP OF WINCHESTER.
Nay, stand thou back; I will not budge a foot:
This be Damascus, be thou cursed Cain,
To slay thy brother Abel, if thou wilt.
DUKE OF GLOSTER.
I will not slay thee, but I'll drive thee back.
Thy scarlet robes as a child's bearing-cloth
I'll use to carry thee out of this place.
BISHOP OF WINCHESTER.
Do what thou darest; I beard thee to thy face.

DUKE OF GLOSTER.
What! am I dared, and bearded to my face?—
Draw, men, for all this privileged place;
Blue-coats to tawny-coats.—Priest, beware your
beard;
I mean to tug it, and to cuff you soundly:
Under my feet I'll stamp thy cardinal's hat;
In spite of Pope or dignities of church,
Here by the cheeks I'll drag thee up and down.
BISHOP OF WINCHESTER.
Gloster, thou wilt answer this before the Pope.
DUKE OF GLOSTER.
Winchester goose! I cry, a rope! a rope!—
Now beat them hence; why do you let them
stay?—
Thee I'll chase hence, thou wolf in sheep's
array.—
Out, tawny-coats!—out, scarlet hypocrite!
Here GLOSTER'S *men beat out the* CARDINAL'S
men, and enter in the hurly-burly the MAYOR OF
LONDON *and his* OFFICERS.
MAYOR OF LONDON.
Fie, lords! that you, being supreme magistrates,
Thus contumeliously should break the peace!
DUKE OF GLOSTER.
Peace, mayor! thou know'st little of my wrongs:
Here's Beaufort, that regards nor God nor king,
Hath here distrain'd the Tower to his use.
BISHOP OF WINCHESTER.
Here's Gloucester, a foe to citizens;
One that still motions war, and never peace,
O'ercharging your free purses with large fines;
That seeks to overthrow religion,
Because he is Protector of the realm;
And would have armour here out of the Tower,
To crown himself king, and suppress the prince.
DUKE OF GLOSTER.
I will not answer thee with words, but blows.
[*Here they skirmish again.*
MAYOR OF LONDON.
Naught rests for me, in this tumultuous strife,
But to make open proclamation:—
Come, officer; as loud as e'er thou canst.
OFFICER [*cries*].
All manner of men assembled here in arms this
day against God's peace and the king's, we
charge and command you, in his highness' name,
to repair to your several dwelling-places; and not
to wear, handle, or use any sword, weapon, or
dagger, henceforward, upon pain of death.
DUKE OF GLOSTER.
Cardinal, I'll be no breaker of the law:
But we shall meet, and break our minds at large.
BISHOP OF WINCHESTER.
Gloster, we'll meet; to thy dear cost, be sure:
Thy heart-blood I will have for this day's work.
MAYOR OF LONDON.
I'll call for clubs, if you will not away:—
This cardinal's more haughty than the devil.
DUKE OF GLOSTER.
Mayor, farewell: thou dost but what thou mayst.
BISHOP OF WINCHESTER.
Abominable Gloster! guard thy head;
For I intend to have it ere long.
[*Exeunt, severally,* GLOSTER *and* WIN-
CHESTER *with their* SERVING-MEN.

5

MAYOR OF LONDON.
See the coast clear'd, and then we will depart.—
Good God, these nobles should such stomachs
      bear!
I myself fight not once in forty year.   [*Exeunt.*

SCENE IV.

France. Before Orleans.

Enter, on the walls, the MASTER-GUNNER OF
ORLEANS, *and his* BOY.

MASTER-GUNNER OF ORLEANS.
Sirrah, thou know'st how Orleans is besieged,
And how the English have the suburbs won.

BOY.
Father, I know; and oft have shot at them,
Howe'er unfortunate I miss'd my aim.

MASTER-GUNNER OF ORLEANS.
But now thou shalt not. Be thou ruled by me:
Chief master-gunner am I of this town;
Something I must do to procure me grace.
The prince's espials have informed me
How the English, in the suburbs close intrencht,
Wont, through a secret grate of iron bars
In yonder tower, to overpeer the city;
And thence discover how with most advantage
They may vex us with shot or with assault.
To intercept this inconvenience,
A piece of ordnance 'gainst it I have placed;
And even these three days have I watcht, if I
Could see them.
Now do thou watch, for I can stay no longer.
If thou spy'st any, run and bring me word;
And thou shalt find me at the governor's.   [*Exit.*

BOY.
Father, I warrant you; take you no care;
I'll never trouble you, if I may spy them.   [*Exit.*

Enter SALISBURY *and* TALBOT *on the turrets, with*
SIR WILLIAM GLANSDALE, SIR THOMAS GAR-
GRAVE, *and others.*

EARL OF SALISBURY.
Talbot, my life, my joy, again return'd!
How wert thou handled being prisoner,
Or by what means got'st thou to be released,
Discourse, I prithee, on this turret's top.

LORD TALBOT.
The Duke of Bedford had a prisoner
Called the brave Lord Ponton de Santrailles;
For him was I exchanged and ransomed.
But with a baser man-of-arms by far,
Once, in contempt, they would have barter'd me:
Which I, disdaining, scorn'd; and craved death
Rather than I would be so vile-esteem'd.
In fine, redeem'd I was as I desired.
But, O, the treacherous Fastolfe wounds my heart!
Whom with my bare fists I would execute,
If I now had him brought into my power.

EARL OF SALISBURY.
Yet tell'st thou not how thou wert entertain'd.

LORD TALBOT.
With scoffs, and scorns, and contumelious taunts,
In open market-place produced they me,
To be a public spectacle to all:
Here, said they, is the terror of the French,
The scarecrow that affrights our children so.
Then broke I from the officers that led me,

And with my nails digg'd stones out of the
To hurl at the beholders of my shame: [ground,
My grisly countenance made others fly;
None durst come near for fear of sudden death.
In iron walls they deem'd me not secure;   [spread,
So great fear of my name 'mongst them was
That they supposed I could rend bars of steel,
And spurn in pieces posts of adamant:
Wherefore a guard of chosen shot I had,
That walkt about me every minute-while;
And if I did but stir out of my bed,
Ready they were to shoot me to the heart.

Enter the BOY *with a linstock.*

EARL OF SALISBURY.
I grieve to hear what torments you endured;
But we will be revenged sufficiently.
Now it is supper-time in Orleans:
Here, through this grate, I count each one,
And view the Frenchmen how they fortify:
Let us look in; the sight will much delight thee.—
Sir Thomas Gargrave and Sir William Glansdale,
Let me have your express opinions
Where is best place to make our battery next.

SIR THOMAS GARGRAVE.
I think, at the north gate; for there stand lords.

SIR WILLIAM GLANSDALE.
And I, here, at the bulwark of the bridge.

LORD TALBOT.
For aught I see, this city must be famisht,
Or with light skirmishes enfeebled.

[*Here they shoot.* SALISBURY *and* SIR
THOMAS GARGRAVE *fall down.*

EARL OF SALISBURY.
O Lord, have mercy on us, wretched sinners!

SIR THOMAS GARGRAVE.
O Lord, have mercy on me, woful man!

LORD TALBOT.
What chance is this that suddenly hath crost us?
Speak, Salisbury; at least, if thou canst speak:
How farest thou, mirror of all martial men?
One of thy eyes and thy cheek's side struck off!—
Accursed tower! accursed fatal hand
That hath contrived this woful tragedy!
In thirteen battles Salisbury o'ercame;
Henry the Fifth he first train'd to the wars;
Whilst any trump did sound, or drum struck up,
His sword did ne'er leave striking in the field.—
Yet livest thou, Salisbury? though thy speech
      doth fail,
One eye thou hast, to look to heaven for grace:
The sun with one eye vieweth all the world.—
Heaven, be thou gracious to none alive,
If Salisbury wants mercy at thy hands!—
Bear hence his body; I will help to bury it.—
Sir Thomas Gargrave, hast thou any life?
Speak unto Talbot; nay, look up to him.—
Salisbury, cheer thy spirit with this comfort;
Thou shalt not die whiles—
He beckons with his hand, and smiles on me,
As who should say, 'When I am dead and gone,
Remember to avenge me on the French.'—
Plantagenet, I will; and, like thee, Nero,
Play on the lute, beholding the towns burn:
Wretched shall France be only in my name.
      [*Here an alarum, and it thunders and
      lightens.*

6

What stir is this? what tumult's in the heavens?
Whence cometh this alarum and this noise?

Enter a MESSENGER.

MESSENGER.

My lord, my lord, the French have gather'd head:
The Dauphin, with one Joan la Pucelle join'd,—
A holy prophetess new risen up,—
Is come with a great power to raise the siege.

[*Here* SALISBURY *lifteth himself up and groans.*

LORD TALBOT.

Hear, hear how dying Salisbury doth groan!
It irks his heart he cannot be revenged.—
Frenchmen, I'll be a Salisbury to you:—
Pucelle or puzzel, dolphin or dogfish,
Your hearts I'll stamp out with my horse's heels,
And make a quagmire of your mingled brains.—
Convey me Salisbury into his tent:
And then try what these dastard Frenchmen dare.

[*Alarum. Exeunt.*

SCENE V.

The same.

Here an alarum again: and TALBOT *pursueth the* DAUPHIN, *and driveth him: then enter* JOAN LA PUCELLE, *driving Englishmen before her, and exit after them: then enter* TALBOT.

LORD TALBOT.

WHERE is my strength, my valour, and my force?
Our English troops retire, I cannot stay them;
A woman clad in armour chaseth them.
Here, here she comes.

Enter LA PUCELLE.

I'll have a bout with thee;
Devil or devil's dam, I'll conjure thee:
Blood will I draw on thee,—thou art a witch,—
And straightway give thy soul to him thou servest.

JOAN LA PUCELLE.

Come, come, 'tis only I that must disgrace thee.

[*They fight.*

LORD TALBOT.

Heavens, can you suffer hell so to prevail?
My breast I'll burst with straining of my courage,
And from my shoulders crack my arms asunder,
But I will chastise this high-minded strumpet.

[*They fight again.*

JOAN LA PUCELLE.

Talbot, farewell; thy hour is not yet come:
I must go victual Orleans forthwith.

[*A short alarum: then enter the town, with* SOLDIERS.

O'ertake me, if thou canst; I scorn thy strength.
Go, go cheer up thy hunger-starved men;
Help Salisbury to make his testament:
This day is ours, as many more shall be.   [*Exit.*

LORD TALBOT.

My thoughts are whirled like a potter's wheel;
I know not where I am, nor what I do;
A witch by fear, not force, like Hannibal,
Drives back our troops, and conquers as she lists:
So bees with smoke, and doves with noisome stench,
Are from their hives and houses driven away.

They call'd us, for our fierceness, English dogs;
Now, like to whelps, we crying run away.

[*A short alarum.*

Hark, countrymen! either renew the fight,
Or tear the lions out of England's coat;
Renounce your soil, give sheep in lions' stead:
Sheep run not half so timorous from the wolf,
Or horse or oxen from the leopard,
As you fly from your oft-subdued slaves.

[*Alarum. Here another skirmish.*

It will not be:—retire into your trenches:
You all consented unto Salisbury's death,
For none would strike a stroke in his revenge.—
Pucelle is enter'd into Orleans,
In spite of us or aught that we could do.
O, would I were to die with Salisbury!
The shame hereof will make me hide my head.

[*Exit* TALBOT. *Alarum, retreat.*

SCENE VI.

The same.

Flourish. Enter, on the walls, LA PUCELLE, CHARLES, REIGNIER, ALENÇON, *and* SOLDIERS.

JOAN LA PUCELLE.

ADVANCE our waving colours on the walls;
Rescued is Orleans from the English:—
Thus Joan la Pucelle hath perform'd her word.

CHARLES.

Divinest creature, Astræa's daughter,
How shall I honour thee for this success?
Thy promises are like Adonis' gardens,
That one day bloom'd, and fruitful were the next.—
France, triumph in thy glorious prophetess!—
Recover'd is the town of Orleans:
More blessed hap did ne'er befall our state.

REIGNIER.

Why ring not out the bells aloud throughout the town?
Dauphin, command the citizens make bonfires,
And feast and banquet in the open streets,
To celebrate the joy that God hath given us.

DUKE OF ALENÇON.

All France will be replete with mirth and joy,
When they shall hear how we have play'd the men.

CHARLES.

'Tis Joan, not we, by whom the day is won;
For which I will divide my crown with her;
And all the priests and friars in my realm
Shall in procession sing her endless praise.
A statelier pyramis to her I'll rear
Than Rhodope's of Memphis ever was:
In memory of her when she is dead,
Her ashes, in an urn more precious
Than the rich-jewell'd coffer of Darius,
Transported shall be at high festivals
Before the kings and queens of France.
No longer on Saint Denis will we cry,
But Joan la Pucelle shall be France's saint.
Come in, and let us banquet royally,
After this golden day of victory.

[*Flourish. Exeunt.*

ACT II. SCENE I.

France. Before Orleans.

Enter a SERGEANT *of a band, with two* SEN-
TINELS.

SERGEANT.

SIRS, take your places, and be vigilant:
If any noise or soldier you perceive
Near to the walls, by some apparent sign
Let us have knowledge at the court-of-guard.

FIRST SENTINEL.

Sergeant, you shall. [*Exit* SERGEANT.] Thus are
  poor servitors—
When others sleep upon their quiet beds—
Constrain'd to watch in darkness, rain, and cold.

Enter TALBOT, BEDFORD, BURGUNDY, *and*
FORCES, *with scaling-ladders, their drums beating a dead march.*

LORD TALBOT.

Lord regent, and redoubted Burgundy,—
By whose approach the regions of Artois,
Walloon, and Picardy are friends to us,—
This happy night the Frenchmen are secure,
Having all day caroused and banqueted:
Embrace we, then, this opportunity,
As fitting best to quittance their deceit,
Contrived by art and baleful sorcery.

DUKE OF BEDFORD.

Coward of France!—how much he wrongs his
  fame,
Despairing of his own arm's fortitude,
To join with witches and the help of hell!

DUKE OF BURGUNDY.

Traitors have never other company.—
But what's that Pucelle, whom they term so
  pure?

LORD TALBOT.

A maid, they say.

DUKE OF BEDFORD.

       A maid! and be so martial!

DUKE OF BURGUNDY.

Pray God she prove not masculine ere long;
If underneath the standard of the French
She carry armour, as she hath begun.

LORD TALBOT.

Well, let them practise and converse with spirits:
God is our fortress, in whose conquering name
Let us resolve to scale their flinty bulwarks.

DUKE OF BEDFORD.

Ascend, brave Talbot; we will follow thee.

LORD TALBOT.

Not all together: better far, I guess,
That we do make our entrance several ways;
That, if it chance the one of us do fail,
The other yet may rise against their force.

DUKE OF BEDFORD.

Agreed: I'll to yond corner.

DUKE OF BURGUNDY.

          And I to this.

LORD TALBOT.

And here will Talbot mount, or make his
  grave.—
Now, Salisbury, for thee, and for the right
Of English Henry, shall this night appear
How much in duty I am bound to both.

        [*Cry,* St. George! A Talbot!

SENTINEL.

Arm! arm! the enemy doth make assault!

*The French leap o'er the walls in their shirts. Enter,
several ways, the* BASTARD OF ORLEANS,
ALENÇON, *and* REIGNIER, *half ready and half
unready.*

DUKE OF ALENÇON.

How now, my lords! what, all unready so?

BASTARD.

Unready! ay, and glad we scaped so well.

REIGNIER.

'Twas time, I trow, to wake and leave our beds,
Hearing alarums at our chamber-doors.

DUKE OF ALENÇON.

Of all exploits since first I follow'd arms,
Ne'er heard I of a warlike enterprise
More venturous or desperate than this.

BASTARD.

I think this Talbot be a fiend of hell.

REIGNIER.

If not of hell, the heavens, sure, favour him.

DUKE OF ALENÇON.

Here cometh Charles: I marvel how he sped.

BASTARD.

Tut, holy Joan was his defensive guard.

Enter CHARLES *and* LA PUCELLE.

CHARLES.

Is this thy cunning, thou deceitful dame?
Didst thou at first, to flatter us withal,
Make us partakers of a little gain,
That now our loss might be ten times so much?

JOAN LA PUCELLE.

Wherefore is Charles impatient with his friend?
At all times will you have my power alike?
Sleeping or waking, must I still prevail,
Or will you blame and lay the fault on me?
Improvident soldiers! had your watch been good,
This sudden mischief never could have faln.

CHARLES.

Duke of Alençon, this was your default,
That, being captain of the watch to-night,
Did look no better to that weighty charge.

DUKE OF ALENÇON.

Had all your quarters been as safely kept
As that whereof I had the government,
We had not been thus shamefully surprised.

BASTARD.

Mine was secure.

REIGNIER.

        And so was mine, my lord.

CHARLES.

And, for myself, most part of all this night,
Within her quarter and mine own precinct
I was employ'd in passing to and fro,
About relieving of the sentinels:
Then how or which way should they first break
  in?

JOAN LA PUCELLE.

Question, my lords, no further of the case,
How or which way: 'tis sure they found some
  place
But weakly guarded, where the breach was
  made.
And now there rests no other shift but this,—
To gather our soldiers, scatter'd and dispersed,
And lay new platforms to endamage them.

Alarums. Enter an English SOLDIER, *crying,* A
Talbot! a Talbot! *They fly, leaving their clothes
behind.*

SOLDIER.

I'll be so bold to take what they have left.
The cry of Talbot serves me for a sword;
For I have loaden me with many spoils,
Using no other weapon but his name.   [*Exit.*

SCENE II.

Orleans. Within the town.

Enter TALBOT, BEDFORD, BURGUNDY, *a* CAP-
TAIN, *and others.*

DUKE OF BEDFORD.

THE day begins to break, and night is fled,
Whose pitchy mantle over-veil'd the earth.
Here sound retreat, and cease our hot pursuit.
    [*Retreat sounded.*

LORD TALBOT.

Bring forth the body of old Salisbury,
And here advance it in the market-place,
The middle centre of this cursed town.
Now have I paid my vow unto his soul;
For every drop of blood was drawn from him,
There hath at least five Frenchmen died to-night.
And that hereafter ages may behold
What ruin happen'd in revenge of him,
Within their chiefest temple I'll erect
A tomb, wherein his corpse shall be interr'd:
Upon the which, that every one may read,
Shall be engraved the sack of Orleans,
The treacherous manner of his mournful death,
And what a terror he had been to France.
But, lords, in all our bloody massacre,
I muse we met not with the Dauphin's Grace,
His new-come champion, virtuous Joan of Arc,
Nor any of his false confederates.

DUKE OF BEDFORD.

'Tis thought, Lord Talbot, when the fight began,
Roused on the sudden from their drowsy beds,
They did, amongst the troops of armed men,
Leap o'er the walls for refuge in the field.

DUKE OF BURGUNDY.

Myself—as far as I could well discern
For smoke and dusky vapours of the night—
Am sure I scared the Dauphin and his trull,
When arm in arm they both came swiftly running,
Like to a pair of loving turtle-doves,
That could not live asunder day or night.
After that things are set in order here,
We'll follow them with all the power we have.

Enter a MESSENGER.

MESSENGER.

All hail, my lords! Which of this princely train
Call ye the warlike Talbot, for his acts
So much applauded through the realm of France?

LORD TALBOT.

Here is the Talbot: who would speak with him?

MESSENGER.

The virtuous lady, Countess of Auvergne,
With modesty admiring thy renown,
By me entreats, great lord, thou wouldst vouchsafe
To visit her poor castle where she lies,
That she may boast she hath beheld the man
Whose glory fills the world with loud report.

DUKE OF BURGUNDY.

Is it even so? Nay, then, I see our wars
Will turn unto a peaceful comic sport,
When ladies crave to be encounter'd with.—
You may not, my lord, despise her gentle suit.

LORD TALBOT.

Ne'er trust me, then; for when a world of men
Could not prevail with all their oratory,
Yet hath a woman's kindness over-ruled:—
And therefore tell her I return great thanks,
And in submission will attend on her.—
Will not your honours bear me company?

DUKE OF BEDFORD.

No, truly; it is more than manners will:
And I have heard it said, unbidden guests
Are often welcomest when they are gone.

LORD TALBOT.

Well then, alone, since there's no remedy,
I mean to prove this lady's courtesy.—
Come hither, captain. [*Whispers.*] You perceive
my mind?

CAPTAIN.

I do, my lord, and mean accordingly.   [*Exeunt.*

SCENE III.

Auvergne. Court of the Castle.

Enter the COUNTESS *and her* PORTER.

COUNTESS OF AUVERGNE.

PORTER, remember what I gave in charge;
And when you've done so, bring the keys to me.

PORTER.

Madam, I will.   [*Exit.*

COUNTESS OF AUVERGNE.

The plot is laid: if all things fall out right,
I shall as famous be by this exploit
As Scythian Tomyris by Cyrus' death.
Great is the rumour of this dreadful knight,
And his achievements of no less account:
Fain would mine eyes be witness with mine
    ears,
To give their censure of these rare reports.

Enter MESSENGER *and* TALBOT.

MESSENGER.

Madam,
According as your ladyship desired,
By message craved, so is Lord Talbot come.

COUNTESS OF AUVERGNE.

And he is welcome. What! is this the man?

MESSENGER.

Madam, it is.

COUNTESS OF AUVERGNE.

       Is this the scourge of France?
Is this the Talbot, so much fear'd abroad,
That with his name the mothers still their babes?
I see report is fabulous and false:
I thought I should have seen some Hercules,
A second Hector, for his grim aspect
And large proportion of his strong-knit limbs.
Alas, this is a child, a silly dwarf!
It cannot be this weak and writhled shrimp
Should strike such terror to his enemies.

LORD TALBOT.

Madam, I have been bold to trouble you;
But since your ladyship is not at leisure,
I'll sort some other time to visit you.   [*Going.*

9

COUNTESS OF AUVERGNE.
What means he now?—Go ask him whither he
  goes.
MESSENGER.
Stay, my Lord Talbot; for my lady craves
To know the cause of your abrupt departure.
LORD TALBOT.
Marry, for that she's in a wrong belief,
I go to certify her Talbot's here.
    Enter PORTER with keys.
COUNTESS OF AUVERGNE.
If thou be he, then art thou prisoner.
LORD TALBOT.
Prisoner! to whom?
COUNTESS OF AUVERGNE.
        To me, blood-thirsty lord;
And for that cause I train'd thee to my house.
Long time thy shadow hath been thrall to me,
For in my gallery thy picture hangs:.
But now the substance shall endure the like;
And I will chain these legs and arms of thine,
That hast by tyranny, these many years,
Wasted our country, slain our citizens,
And sent our sons and husbands captive.
LORD TALBOT.
Ha, ha, ha!
COUNTESS OF AUVERGNE.
Laughest thou, wretch? thy mirth shall turn to
  moan.
LORD TALBOT.
I laugh to see your ladyship so fond
To think that you have aught but Talbot's
  shadow
Whereon to practise your severity.
COUNTESS OF AUVERGNE.
Why, art not thou the man?
LORD TALBOT.
        I am, indeed.
COUNTESS OF AUVERGNE.
Then have I substance too.
LORD TALBOT.
No, no, I am but shadow of myself;
You are deceived, my substance is not here;
For what you see is but the smallest part
And least proportion of humanity:
I tell you, madam, were the whole frame here,
It is of such a spacious lofty pitch,
Your roof were not sufficient to contain 't.
COUNTESS OF AUVERGNE.
This is a riddling merchant for the nonce;
He will be here, and yet he is not here:
How can these contrarieties agree?
LORD TALBOT.
That will I show you presently.
    [*Winds his horn. Drums strike up: a peal
      of ordnance. Enter SOLDIERS.*
How say you, madam? are you now persuaded
That Talbot is but shadow of himself?
These are his substance, sinews, arms, and
  strength,
With which he yoketh your rebellious necks,
Razeth your cities, and subverts your towns,
And in a moment makes them desolate.
COUNTESS OF AUVERGNE.
Victorious Talbot! pardon my abuse:
I find thou art no less than fame hath bruited,

And more than may be gather'd by thy shape.
Let my presumption not provoke thy wrath;
For I am sorry that with reverence
I did not entertain thee as thou art.
LORD TALBOT.
Be not dismay'd, fair lady; nor misconster
The mind of Talbot, as you did mistake
The outward composition of his body.
What you have done hath not offended me:
Nor other satisfaction do I crave,
But only, with your patience, that we may
Taste of your wine, and see what cates you have;
For soldiers' stomachs always serve them well.
COUNTESS OF AUVERGNE.
With all my heart; and think me honoured
To feast so great a warrior in my house.   [*Exeunt.*

SCENE IV.
London. The Temple-garden.

Enter the EARLS OF SOMERSET, SUFFOLK, *and*
  WARWICK; RICHARD PLANTAGENET, VER-
  NON, *and a* LAWYER.
RICHARD PLANTAGENET.
GREAT lords and gentlemen, what means this
    silence?
Dare no man answer in a case of truth?
EARL OF SUFFOLK.
Within the Temple-hall we were too loud;
The garden here is more convenient.
RICHARD PLANTAGENET.
Then say at once if I maintain'd the truth;
Or else was wrangling Somerset in th' error?
EARL OF SUFFOLK.
Faith, I have been a truant in the law,
And never yet could frame my will to it;
And therefore frame the law unto my will.
EARL OF SOMERSET.
Judge you, my Lord of Warwick, then, between
  us.
EARL OF WARWICK.
Between two hawks, which flies the higher pitch;
Between two dogs, which hath the deeper mouth;
Between two blades, which bears the better
  temper;
Between two horses, which doth bear him best;
Between two girls, which hath the merriest eye;—
I have, perhaps, some shallow spirit of judge-
  ment:
But in these nice sharp quillets of the law,
Good faith, I am no wiser than a daw.
RICHARD PLANTAGENET.
Tut, tut, here is a mannerly forbearance:
The truth appears so naked on my side,
That any purblind eye may find it out.
EARL OF SOMERSET.
And on my side it is so well apparell'd,
So clear, so shining, and so evident,
That it will glimmer through a blind man's eye.
RICHARD PLANTAGENET.
Since you are tongue-tied and so loth to speak,
In dumb significants proclaim your thoughts:
Let him that is a true-born gentleman,
And stands upon the honour of his birth,
If he suppose that I have pleaded truth,
From off this brier pluck a white rose with me.

EARL OF SOMERSET.
Let him that is no coward nor no flatterer,
But dare maintain the party of the truth,
Pluck a red rose from off this thorn with me.
EARL OF WARWICK.
I love no colours; and, without all colour
Of base-insinuating flattery,
I pluck this white rose with Plantagenet.
EARL OF SUFFOLK.
I pluck this red rose with young Somerset;
And say withal, I think he held the right.
VERNON.
Stay, lords and gentlemen, and pluck no more,
Till you conclude that he, upon whose side
The fewest roses are cropt from the tree,
Shall yield the other in the right opinion.
EARL OF SOMERSET.
Good Master Vernon, it is well objected:
If I have fewest, I subscribe in silence.
RICHARD PLANTAGENET.
And I.
VERNON.
Then, for the truth and plainness of the case,
I pluck this pale and maiden blossom here,
Giving my verdict on the white rose side.
EARL OF SOMERSET.
Prick not your finger as you pluck it off,
Lest, bleeding, you do paint the white rose
red,
And fall on my side so, against your will.
VERNON.
If I, my lord, for my opinion bleed,
Opinion shall be surgeon to my hurt,
And keep me on the side where still I am.
EARL OF SOMERSET.
Well, well, come on: who else?
A LAWYER [to SOMERSET].
Unless my study and my books be false,
The argument you held was wrong in you;
In sign whereof I pluck a white rose too.
RICHARD PLANTAGENET.
Now, Somerset, where is your argument?
EARL OF SOMERSET.
Here in my scabbard; meditating that
Shall dye your white rose in a bloody red.
RICHARD PLANTAGENET.
Meantime your cheeks do counterfeit our
roses;
For pale they look with fear, as witnessing
The truth on our side.
EARL OF SOMERSET.
                No, Plantagenet,
'Tis not for fear; but anger that thy cheeks
Blush for pure shame to counterfeit our roses,
And yet thy tongue will not confess thy error.
RICHARD PLANTAGENET.
Hath not thy rose a canker, Somerset?
EARL OF SOMERSET.
Hath not thy rose a thorn, Plantagenet?
RICHARD PLANTAGENET.
Ay, sharp and piercing, to maintain his truth;
Whiles thy consuming canker eats his falsehood.
EARL OF SOMERSET.
Well, I'll find friends to wear my bleeding roses,
That shall maintain what I have said is true,
Where false Plantagenet dare not be seen.

RICHARD PLANTAGENET.
Now, by this maiden blossom in my hand,
I scorn thee and thy faction, peevish boy.
EARL OF SUFFOLK.
Turn not thy scorns this way, Plantagenet.
RICHARD PLANTAGENET.
Proud Pole, I will; and scorn both him and thee.
EARL OF SUFFOLK.
I'll turn my part thereof into thy throat.
EARL OF SOMERSET.
Away, away, good William de la Pole!
We grace the yeoman by conversing with him.
EARL OF WARWICK.
Now, by God's will, thou wrong'st him, Somer-
set;
His grandfather was Lionel Duke of Clarence,
Third son to the third Edward King of England:
Spring crestless yeomen from so deep a root?
RICHARD PLANTAGENET.
He bears him on the place's privilege,
Or durst not, for his craven heart, say thus.
EARL OF SOMERSET.
By Him that made me, I'll maintain my words
On any plot of ground in Christendom.
Was not thy father, Richard Earl of Cambridge,
For treason executed in our late king's days?
And, by his treason, stand'st not thou attainted,
Corrupted, and exempt from ancient gentry?
His trespass yet lives guilty in thy blood;
And, till thou be restored, thou art a yeoman.
RICHARD PLANTAGENET.
My father was attached, not attainted;
Condemn'd to die for treason, but no traitor;
And that I'll prove on better men than Somerset,
Were growing time once ripen'd to my will.
For your partaker Pole, and you yourself,
I'll note you in my book of memory,
To scourge you for this apprehension:
Look to it well, and say you are well warn'd.
EARL OF SOMERSET.
Ah, thou shalt find us ready for thee still;
And know us, by these colours, for thy foes,—
For these my friends, in spite of thee, shall wear.
RICHARD PLANTAGENET.
And, by my soul, this pale and angry rose,
As cognizance of my blood-drinking hate,
Will I for ever, and my faction, wear,
Until it wither with me to my grave,
Or flourish to the height of my degree.
EARL OF SUFFOLK.
Go forward, and be choked with thy ambition!
And so, farewell, until I meet thee next.   [Exit.
EARL OF SOMERSET.
Have with thee, Pole.—Farewell, ambitious
Richard.   [Exit.
RICHARD PLANTAGENET.
How I am braved, and must perforce endure it!
EARL OF WARWICK.
This blot, that they object against your house,
Shall be wiped out in the next parliament,
Call'd for the truce of Winchester and Gloster:
And if thou be not then created York,
I will not live to be accounted Warwick.
Meantime, in signal of my love to thee,
Against proud Somerset and William Pole,
Will I upon thy party wear this rose:

And here I prophesy,—this brawl to-day,
Grown to this faction, in the Temple-garden,
Shall send, between the red rose and the white,
A thousand souls to death and deadly night.
RICHARD PLANTAGENET.
Good Master Vernon, I am bound to you,
That you on my behalf would pluck a flower.
VERNON.
In your behalf still will I wear the same.
A LAWYER.
And so will I.
RICHARD PLANTAGENET.
Thanks, gentle sir.
Come, let us four to dinner: I dare say
This quarrel will drink blood another day.
[*Exeunt.*

SCENE V.

The Tower of London.

Enter MORTIMER, *brought in a chair, and*
GAOLERS.

EDMUND MORTIMER.

KIND keepers of my weak decaying age,
   Let dying Mortimer here rest himself.—
Even like a man new-haled from the rack,
So fare my limbs with long imprisonment;
And these grey locks, the pursuivants of death,
Nestor-like aged, in an age of care,
Argue the end of Edmund Mortimer:
These eyes—like lamps whose wasting oil is
   spent—
Wax dim, as drawing to their exigent:
Weak shoulders, overborne with burdening grief;
And pithless arms, like to a wither'd vine
That droops his sapless branches to the ground:
Yet are these feet—whose strengthless stay is
   numb,
Unable to support this lump of clay—
Swift-winged with desire to get a grave,
As witting I no other comfort have.—
But tell me, keeper, will my nephew come?
FIRST GAOLER.
Richard Plantagenet, my lord, will come:
We sent unto the Temple, unto his chamber;
And answer was return'd that he will come.
EDMUND MORTIMER.
Enough: my soul shall then be satisfied.—
Poor gentleman! his wrong doth equal mine.
Since Henry Monmouth first began to reign,
Before whose glory I was great in arms,
This loathsome sequestration have I had;
And even since then hath Richard been obscured,
Deprived of honour and inheritance.
But now, the arbitrator of despairs,
Just death, kind umpire of men's miseries,
With sweet enlargement doth dismiss me hence:
I would his troubles likewise were expired,
That so he might recover what was lost.
Enter RICHARD PLANTAGENET.
FIRST GAOLER.
My lord, your loving nephew now is come.
EDMUND MORTIMER.
Richard Plantagenet, my friend, is he come?
RICHARD PLANTAGENET.
Ay, noble uncle, thus ignobly used,
Your nephew, late-despised Richard, comes.

EDMUND MORTIMER.
Direct mine arms I may embrace his neck,
And in his bosom spend my latter gasp:
O, tell me when my lips do touch his cheeks,
That I may kindly give one fainting kiss.—
And now declare, sweet stem from York's great
   stock,
Why didst thou say, of late thou wert despised?
RICHARD PLANTAGENET.
First, lean thine aged back against mine arm;
And, in that ease, I'll tell thee my disease.
This day, in argument upon a case,
Some words there grew 'twixt Somerset and
   me;
Among which terms he used his lavish tongue,
And did upbraid me with my father's death:
Which obloquy set bars before my tongue,
Else with the like I had requited him.
Therefore, good uncle, for my father's sake,
In honour of a true Plantagenet,
And for alliance sake, declare the cause
My father, Earl of Cambridge, lost his head.
EDMUND MORTIMER.
That cause, fair nephew, that imprison'd me,
And hath detain'd me all my flowering youth
Within a loathsome dungeon, there to pine,
Was cursed instrument of his decease.
RICHARD PLANTAGENET.
Discover more at large what cause that was;
For I am ignorant, and cannot guess.
EDMUND MORTIMER.
I will, if that my fading breath permit,
And death approach not ere my tale be done.
Henry the Fourth, grandfather to this king,
Deposed his nephew Richard,—Edward's son,
The first-begotten and the lawful heir
Of Edward king, the third of that descent:
During whose reign, the Percies of the north,
Finding his usurpation most unjust,
Endeavour'd my advancement to the throne:
The reason moved these warlike lords to this
Was, for that—young King Richard thus re-
   moved,
Leaving no heir begotten of his body—
I was the next by birth and parentage;
For by my mother I derived am
From Lionel Duke of Clarence, the third son
To King Edward the Third; whereas he
From John of Gaunt doth bring his pedigree,
Being but fourth of that heroic line.
But mark: as, in this haughty-great attempt,
They laboured to plant the rightful heir,
I lost my liberty, and they their lives.
Long after this, when Henry the Fifth,
Succeeding his father Bolingbroke, did reign,
Thy father, Earl of Cambridge, then derived
From famous Edmund Langley, duke of York,
Marrying my sister, that thy mother was,
Again, in pity of my hard distress,
Levied an army, weening to redeem
And have install'd me in the diadem:
But, as the rest, so fell that noble earl,
And was beheaded. Thus the Mortimers,
In whom the title rested, were supprest.
RICHARD PLANTAGENET.
Of which, my lord, your honour is the last.

12

EDMUND MORTIMER.
True; and thou seest that I no issue have,
And that my fainting words do warrant death:
Thou art my heir; the rest I wish thee gather:
And yet be wary in thy studious care.
RICHARD PLANTAGENET.
Thy grave admonishments prevail with me:
But yet, methinks, my father's execution
Was nothing less than bloody tyranny.
EDMUND MORTIMER.
With silence, nephew, be thou politic:
Strong-fixed is the house of Lancaster,
And, like a mountain, not to be removed.
But now thy uncle is removing hence;
As princes do their courts, when they are cloy'd
With long continuance in a settled place.
RICHARD PLANTAGENET.
O, uncle, would some part of my young years
Might but redeem the passage of your age!
EDMUND MORTIMER.
Thou dost, then, wrong me,—as that slaughterer
doth
Which giveth many wounds when one will kill.
Mourn not, except thou sorrow for my good;
Only, give order for my funeral:
And so, farewell; and fair be all thy hopes,
And prosperous be thy life in peace and war!
[Dies.
RICHARD PLANTAGENET.
And peace, no war, befall thy parting soul!
In prison hast thou spent a pilgrimage,
And like a hermit overpast thy days.—
Well, I will lock his counsel in my breast;
And what I do imagine, let that rest.—
Keepers, convey him hence; and I myself
Will see his burial better than his life.
[Exeunt GAOLERS, bearing out the body of
MORTIMER.
Here dies the dusky torch of Mortimer,
Choked with ambition of the meaner sort:—
And for those wrongs, those bitter injuries,
Which Somerset hath offer'd to my house,
I doubt not but with honour to redress;
And therefore haste I to the parliament,
Either to be restored to my blood,
Or make my ill th' advantage of my good. [Exit.

ACT III. SCENE I.

London. The Parliament House.

Flourish. Enter KING HENRY, EXETER, GLOS-
TER, WARWICK, SOMERSET, and SUFFOLK;
the BISHOP OF WINCHESTER, RICHARD
PLANTAGENET, and others. GLOSTER offers
to put up a bill; WINCHESTER snatches it,
tears it.

BISHOP OF WINCHESTER.
COMEST thou with deep-premeditated lines,
With written pamphlets studiously devised,
Humphrey of Gloster? If thou canst accuse,
Or aught intend'st to lay unto my charge,
Do it without invention, suddenly;
As I with sudden and extemporal speech
Purpose to answer what thou canst object.

DUKE OF GLOSTER.
Presumptuous priest! this place commands my
patience,
Or thou shouldst find thou hast dishonour'd me.
Think not, although in writing I preferr'd
The manner of thy vile outrageous crimes,
That therefore I have forged, or am not able
Verbatim to rehearse the method of my pen:
No, prelate; such is thy audacious wickedness,
Thy lewd, pestiferous, and dissentious pranks,
As very infants prattle of thy pride.
Thou art a most pernicious usurer;
Froward by nature, enemy to peace;
Lascivious, wanton, more than well bescems
A man of thy profession and degree;
And for thy treachery, what's more manifest,—
In that thou laid'st a trap to take my life,
As well at London-bridge as at the Tower?
Beside, I fear me, if thy thoughts were sifted,
The king, thy sovereign, is not quite exempt
From envious malice of thy swelling heart.
BISHOP OF WINCHESTER.
Gloster, I do defy thee.—Lords, vouchsafe
To give me hearing what I shall reply.
If I were covetous, ambitious, or perverse,
As he will have me, how am I so poor?
Or how haps it I seek not to advance
Or raise myself, but keep my wonted calling?
And for dissension, who preferreth peace
More than I do,—except I be provoked?
No, my good lords, it is not that offends;
It is not that that hath incensed the duke:
It is, because no one should sway but he;
No one but he should be about the king;
And that engenders thunder in his breast,
And makes him roar these accusations forth.
But he shall know I am as good—
DUKE OF GLOSTER.
As good!
Thou bastard of my grandfather!—
BISHOP OF WINCHESTER.
Ay, lordly sir; for what are you, I pray,
But one imperious in another's throne?
DUKE OF GLOSTER.
Am I not lord Protector, saucy priest?
BISHOP OF WINCHESTER.
And am not I a prelate of the church?
DUKE OF GLOSTER.
Yes, as an outlaw in a castle keeps,
And useth it to patronage his theft.
BISHOP OF WINCHESTER.
Unreverent Gloster!
DUKE OF GLOSTER.
Thou art reverent
Touching thy spiritual function, not thy life.
BISHOP OF WINCHESTER.
This Rome shall remedy.
EARL OF WARWICK.
Roam thither, then.
EARL OF SOMERSET.
My lord, it were your duty to forbear.
EARL OF WARWICK.
Ay, see the bishop be not overborne.
EARL OF SOMERSET.
Methinks my lord should be religious,
And know the office that belongs to such.

.13

EARL OF WARWICK.
Methinks his lordship should be humbler;
It fitteth not a prelate so to plead.
EARL OF SOMERSET.
Yes, when his holy state is toucht so near.
EARL OF WARWICK.
State holy or unhallow'd, what of that?
Is not his Grace Protector to the king?
RICHARD PLANTAGENET [*aside*].
Plantagenet, I see, must hold his tongue,
Lest it be said, 'Speak, sirrah, when you should;
Must your bold verdict enter talk with lords?'
Else would I have a fling at Winchester.
KING HENRY.
Uncles of Gloster and of Winchester,
The special watchmen of our English weal,
I would prevail, if prayers might prevail,
To join your hearts in love and amity.
O, what a scandal is it to our crown,
That two such noble peers as ye should jar!
Believe me, lords, my tender years can tell
Civil dissension is a viperous worm
That gnaws the bowels of the commonwealth.
[*A noise within*, 'Down with the tawny-coats!'
What tumult's this?
EARL OF WARWICK.
        An uproar, I dare warrant,
Begun through malice of the bishop's men.
[*A noise again within*, 'Stones! stones!'
Enter MAYOR.
MAYOR.
O, my good lords,—and virtuous Henry,—
Pity the city of London, pity us!
The bishop and the Duke of Gloster's men,
Forbidden late to carry any weapon,
Have fill'd their pockets full of pebble-stones,
And, banding themselves in contrary parts,
Do pelt so fast at one another's pate,
That many have their giddy brains knockt out:
Our windows are broke down in every street,
And we, for fear, compell'd to shut our shops.
Enter SERVING-MEN, *in skirmish, with bloody
pates.*
KING HENRY.
We charge you, on allegiance to ourself,
To hold your slaughtering hands and keep the
        peace.—
Pray, uncle Gloster, mitigate this strife.
FIRST SERVING-MAN.
Nay, if we be forbidden stones, we'll fall to it
with our teeth.
SECOND SERVING-MAN.
Do what ye dare, we are as resolute.
        [*Skirmish again.*
DUKE OF GLOSTER.
You of my household, leave this peevish broil,
And set this unaccustom'd fight aside.
THIRD SERVING-MAN.
My lord, we know your Grace to be a man
Just and upright; and, for your royal birth,
Inferior to none but to his majesty:
And, ere that we will suffer such a prince,
So kind a father of the commonweal,
To be disgraced by an inkhorn mate,
We, and our wives, and children, all will fight,
And have our bodies slaughter'd by thy foes.

FIRST SERVING-MAN.
Ay, and the very parings of our nails
Shall pitch a field when we are dead. [*Begin again.*
DUKE OF GLOSTER.
        Stay, stay, I say!
An if you love me, as you say you do,
Let me persuade you to forbear awhile.
KING HENRY.
O, how this discord doth afflict my soul!—
Can you, my Lord of Winchester, behold
My sighs and tears, and will not once relent?
Who should be pitiful, if you be not?
Or who should study to prefer a peace,
If holy churchmen take delight in broils?
EARL OF WARWICK.
Yield, my lord Protector; yield, Winchester;
Except you mean, with obstinate repulse,
To slay your sovereign, and destroy the realm.
You see what mischief, and what murder too,
Hath been enacted through your enmity;
Then be at peace, except ye thirst for blood.
BISHOP OF WINCHESTER.
He shall submit, or I will never yield.
DUKE OF GLOSTER.
Compassion on the king commands me stoop;
Or I would see his heart out, ere the priest
Should ever get that privilege of me.
EARL OF WARWICK.
Behold, my Lord of Winchester, the duke
Hath banisht moody discontented fury,
As by his smoothed brows it doth appear:
Why look you still so stern and tragical?
DUKE OF GLOSTER.
Here, Winchester, I offer thee my hand.
KING HENRY.
Fie, uncle Beaufort! I have heard you preach
That malice was a great and grievous sin;
And will not you maintain the thing you teach,
But prove a chief offender in the same?
EARL OF WARWICK.
Sweet king!—the bishop hath a kindly gird.—
For shame, my Lord of Winchester, relent!
What, shall a child instruct you what to do?
BISHOP OF WINCHESTER.
Well, Duke of Gloster, I will yield to thee;
Love for thy love, and hand for hand I give.
DUKE OF GLOSTER [*aside*].
Ay, but, I fear me, with a hollow heart.
See here, my friends and loving countrymen;
This token serveth for a flag of truce
Betwixt ourselves and all our followers:
So help me God, as I dissemble not!
BISHOP OF WINCHESTER [*aside*].
So help me God, as I intend it not!
KING HENRY.
O loving uncle, kind Duke of Gloucester,
How joyful am I made by this contract!—
Away, my masters! trouble us no more;
But join in friendship, as your lords have done.
FIRST SERVING-MAN.
Content: I'll to the surgeon's.
SECOND SERVING-MAN.
        And so will I.
THIRD SERVING-MAN.
And I will see what physic the tavern affords.
        [*Exeunt* SERVING-MEN, MAYOR, &c.

EARL OF WARWICK.
Accept this scroll, most gracious sovereign,
Which in the right of Richard Plantagenet
We do exhibit to your majesty.
DUKE OF GLOSTER.
Well urged, my Lord of Warwick:—for, sweet
    prince,
An if your Grace mark every circumstance,
You have great reason to do Richard right;
Especially for those occasions
At Eltham-place I told your majesty.
KING HENRY.
And those occasions, uncle, were of force:
Therefore, my loving lords, our pleasure is,
That Richard be restored to his blood.
EARL OF WARWICK.
Let Richard be restored to his blood;
So shall his father's wrongs be recompensed.
BISHOP OF WINCHESTER.
As will the rest, so willeth Winchester.
KING HENRY.
If Richard will be true, not that alone,
But all the whole inheritance I give
That doth belong unto the house of York,
From whence you spring by lineal descent.
RICHARD PLANTAGENET.
Thy humble servant vows obedience
And humble service till the point of death.
KING HENRY.
Stoop, then, and set your knee against my foot;
And, in reguerdon of that duty done,
I girt thee with the valiant sword of York:
Rise, Richard, like a true Plantagenet,
And rise created princely Duke of York.
RICHARD PLANTAGENET.
And so thrive Richard as thy foes may fall!
And as my duty springs, so perish they
That grudge one thought against your majesty!
ALL.
Welcome, high prince, the mighty Duke of York!
EARL OF SOMERSET [aside].
Perish, base prince, ignoble Duke of York!
DUKE OF GLOSTER.
Now will it best avail your majesty
To cross the seas, and to be crown'd in France:
The presence of a king engenders love
Amongst his subjects and his loyal friends,
As it disanimates his enemies.
KING HENRY.
When Gloster says the word, King Henry goes;
For friendly counsel cuts off many foes.
DUKE OF GLOSTER.
Your ships already are in readiness.
    [Sennet. Flourish. Exeunt all except EXETER.
DUKE OF EXETER.
Ay, we may march in England or in France,
Not seeing what is likely to ensue.
This late dissension grown betwixt the peers
Burns under feigned ashes of forged love,
And will at last break out into a flame:
As fester'd members rot but by degree,
Till bones and flesh and sinews fall away,
So will this base and envious discord breed.
And now I fear that fatal prophecy
Which in the time of Henry named the Fifth
Was in the mouth of every sucking babe,—

That Henry born at Monmouth should win all,
And Henry born at Windsor should lose all:
Which is so plain, that Exeter doth wish
His days may finish ere that hapless time.   [Exit.

SCENE II.
France. Before Rouen.
Enter LA PUCELLE *disguised, with four* SOL-
DIERS, *with sacks upon their backs.*
JOAN LA PUCELLE.
THESE are the city-gates, the gates of Rouen,
    Through which our policy must make a
    breach:
Take heed, be wary how you place your words;
Talk like the vulgar sort of market-men
That come to gather money for their corn.
If we have entrance,—as I hope we shall,—
And that we find the slothful watch but weak,
I'll by a sign give notice to our friends,
That Charles the Dauphin may encounter them.
FIRST SOLDIER.
Our sacks shall be a mean to sack the city,
And we be lords and rulers over Rouen;
Therefore we'll knock.   [Knocks.
WATCHMAN [within].
Qui va là?
JOAN LA PUCELLE.
Paysans, pauvres gens de France,—
Poor market-folks, that come to sell their corn.
WATCHMAN [opening the gates].
Enter, go in; the market-bell is rung.
JOAN LA PUCELLE.
Now, Rouen, I'll shake thy bulwarks to the
    ground.   [LA PUCELLE, &c., enter the town.
Enter CHARLES, *the* BASTARD OF ORLEANS,
    ALENÇON, REIGNIER, *and* FORCES.
CHARLES.
Saint Denis bless this happy stratagem!
And once again we'll sleep secure in Rouen.
BASTARD OF ORLEANS.
Here enter'd Pucelle and her practisants;
Now she is there, how will she specify
Where is the best and safest passage in?
REIGNIER.
By thrusting out a torch from yonder tower; [is,—
Which, once discern'd, shows that her meaning
No way to that, for weakness, which she enter'd.
Enter LA PUCELLE *on the top, thrusting out a
    torch burning.*
JOAN LA PUCELLE.
Behold, this is the happy wedding-torch
That joineth Rouen unto her countrymen,
But burning fatal to the Talbotites.   [Exit.
BASTARD OF ORLEANS.
See, noble Charles, the beacon of our friend;
The burning torch in yonder turret stands.
CHARLES.
Now shine it like a comet of revenge,
A prophet to the fall of all our foes!
REIGNIER.
Defer no time, delays have dangerous ends;
Enter, and cry 'The Dauphin!' presently,
And then do execution on the watch.
    [Alarum. They enter.
An alarum. Enter TALBOT *in an excursion.*

LORD TALBOT.
France, thou shalt rue this treason with thy tears,
If Talbot but survive thy treachery.—
Pucelle, that witch, that damned sorceress,
Hath wrought this hellish mischief unawares,
That hardly we escaped the pride of France.
[Exit.
An alarum: excursions. BEDFORD *brought in sick
in a chair.* Enter TALBOT *and* BURGUNDY
without: within LA PUCELLE, CHARLES, *the*
BASTARD OF ORLEANS, ALENÇON, *and* REI-
GNIER, *on the walls.*
JOAN LA PUCELLE.
Good morrow, gallants! want ye corn for bread?
I think the Duke of Burgundy will fast,
Before he'll buy again at such a rate:
'Twas full of darnel;—do you like the taste?
DUKE OF BURGUNDY.
Scoff on, vile fiend and shameless courtezan!
I trust ere long to choke thee with thine own,
And make thee curse the harvest of that corn.
CHARLES.
Your Grace may starve, perhaps, before that
time.
DUKE OF BEDFORD.
O, let no words, but deeds, revenge this treason!
JOAN LA PUCELLE.
What will you do, good greybeard? break a lance,
And run a tilt at death within a chair?
LORD TALBOT.
Foul fiend of France, and hag of all despite,
Encompast with thy lustful paramours!
Becomes it thee to taunt his valiant age,
And twit with cowardice a man half dead?
Damsel, I'll have a bout with you again,
Or else let Talbot perish with his shame.
JOAN LA PUCELLE.
Are ye so hot, sir?—yet, Pucelle, hold thy peace;
If Talbot do but thunder, rain will follow.
[TALBOT *and the rest whisper together in
counsel.* [speaker?
God speed the parliament! who shall be the
LORD TALBOT.
Dare ye come forth and meet us in the field?
JOAN LA PUCELLE.
Belike your lordship takes us, then, for fools,
To try if that our own be ours or no.
LORD TALBOT.
I speak not to that railing Hecate,
But unto thee, Alençon, and the rest;
Will ye, like soldiers, come and fight it out?
DUKE OF ALENÇON.
Signior, no.
LORD TALBOT.
Signior, hang!—base muleters of France!
Like peasant foot-boys do they keep the walls,
And dare not take up arms like gentlemen.
JOAN LA PUCELLE.
Away, captains! let's get us from the walls;
For Talbot means no goodness by his looks.—
God b' wi' you, my lord! we came but to tell you
That we are here.
[*Exeunt* LA PUCELLE, &c., *from the walls.*
LORD TALBOT.
And there will we be too, ere it be long,
Or else reproach be Talbot's greatest fame!—

Vow, Burgundy, by honour of thy house—
Prickt on by public wrongs sustain'd in France—
Either to get the town again or die;
And I,—as sure as English Henry lives,
And as his father here was conqueror,—
As sure as in this late-betrayed town
Great Cœur-de-lion's heart was buried,—
So sure I swear to get the town or die.
DUKE OF BURGUNDY.
My vows are equal partners with thy vows.
LORD TALBOT.
But, ere we go, regard this dying prince,
The valiant Duke of Bedford.—Come, my lord,
We will bestow you in some better place,
Fitter for sickness and for crazy age.
DUKE OF BEDFORD.
Lord Talbot, do not so dishonour me:
Here will I sit before the walls of Rouen,
And will be partner of your weal or woe.
DUKE OF BURGUNDY.
Courageous Bedford, let us now persuade you.
DUKE OF BEDFORD.
Not to be gone from hence; for once I read,
That stout Pendragon, in his litter, sick,
Came to the field, and vanquished his foes:
Methinks I should revive the soldiers' hearts,
Because I ever found them as myself.
LORD TALBOT.
Undaunted spirit in a dying breast!—
Then be it so:—heavens keep old Bedford safe!—
And now no more ado, brave Burgundy,
But gather we our forces out of hand,
And set upon our boasting enemy.
[*Exeunt all but* BEDFORD *and* ATTEN-
DANTS.
An alarum: excursions. Enter SIR JOHN FAS-
TOLFE *and a* CAPTAIN.
CAPTAIN.
Whither away, Sir John Fastolfe, in such haste?
SIR JOHN FASTOLFE.
Whither away! to save myself by flight:
We are like to have the overthrow again.
CAPTAIN.
What! will you fly, and leave Lord Talbot?
SIR JOHN FASTOLFE.
Ay,
All the Talbots in the world, to save my life.
[*Exit.*
CAPTAIN.
Cowardly knight! ill fortune follow thee! [*Exit.*
Retreat: excursions. LA PUCELLE, ALENÇON,
and CHARLES *fly.*
DUKE OF BEDFORD.
Now, quiet soul, depart when heaven please,
For I have seen our enemies' overthrow.
What is the trust or strength of foolish man?
They that of late were daring with their scoffs,
Are glad and fain by flight to save themselves.
[BEDFORD *dies and is carried in by two in
his chair.*
An alarum. Enter TALBOT, BURGUNDY, *and
the rest.*
LORD TALBOT.
Lost and recover'd in a day again!
This is a double honour, Burgundy:
Yet heavens have glory for this victory!

DUKE OF BURGUNDY.

Warlike and martial Talbot, Burgundy
Enshrines thee in his heart, and there erects
Thy noble deeds, as valour's monuments.

LORD TALBOT.

Thanks, gentle duke. But where is Pucelle now?
I think her old familiar is asleep:
Now where's the Bastard's braves, and Charles
his gleeks?
What, all amort? Rouen hangs her head for grief,
That such a valiant company are fled.
Now will we take some order in the town,
Placing therein some expert officers;
And then depart to Paris to the king,
For there young Henry with his nobles lie.

DUKE OF BURGUNDY.

What wills Lord Talbot pleaseth Burgundy.

LORD TALBOT.

But yet, before we go, let's not forget
The noble Duke of Bedford late deceased,
But see his exequies fulfill'd in Rouen:
A braver soldier never couched lance,
A gentler heart did never sway in court:
But kings and mightiest potentates must die,
For that's the end of human misery.   [*Exeunt.*

SCENE III.

The plains near Rouen.

Enter CHARLES, *the* BASTARD OF ORLEANS,
ALENÇON, LA PUCELLE, *and* FORCES.

JOAN LA PUCELLE.

DISMAY not, princes, at this accident,
Nor grieve that Rouen is so recovered:
Care is no cure, but rather corrosive,
For things that are not to be remedied.
Let frantic Talbot triumph for a while,
And like a peacock sweep along his tail;
We'll pull his plumes, and take away his train,
If Dauphin and the rest will be but ruled.

CHARLES.

We have been guided by thee hitherto,
And of thy cunning had no diffidence:
One sudden foil shall never breed distrust.

BASTARD OF ORLEANS.

Search out thy wit for secret policies,
And we will make thee famous through the
world.

DUKE OF ALENÇON.

We'll set thy statue in some holy place,
And have thee reverenced like a blessed saint:
Employ thee, then, sweet virgin, for our good.

JOAN LA PUCELLE.

Then thus it must be; this doth Joan devise:
By fair persuasions, mixt with sugar'd words,
We will entice the Duke of Burgundy
To leave the Talbot and to follow us.

CHARLES.

Ay, marry, sweeting, if we could do that,
France were no place for Henry's warriors;
Nor should that nation boast it so with us,
But be extirped from our provinces.

DUKE OF ALENÇON.

For ever should they be expulsed from France,
And not have title of an earldom here.

JOAN LA PUCELLE.

Your honours shall perceive how I will work
To bring this matter to the wished end.
[*Drum sounds afar off.*
Hark! by the sound of drum you may perceive
Their powers are marching unto Paris-ward.
*Here sound an English march.   Enter, and pass over
at a distance,* TALBOT *and his* FORCES.
There goes the Talbot, with his colours spread,
And all the troops of English after him.
French march.   Enter the DUKE OF BURGUNDY
and his FORCES.
Now in the rearward comes the duke and his:
Fortune in favour makes him lag behind.
Summon a parley; we will talk with him.
[*Trumpets sound a parley.*

CHARLES.

A parley with the Duke of Burgundy!

DUKE OF BURGUNDY.

Who craves a parley with the Burgundy?

JOAN LA PUCELLE.

The princely Charles of France, thy countryman.

DUKE OF BURGUNDY.

What say'st thou, Charles? for I am marching
hence.

CHARLES.

Speak, Pucelle, and enchant him with thy words.

JOAN LA PUCELLE.

Brave Burgundy, undoubted hope of France!
Stay, let thy humble handmaid speak to thee.

DUKE OF BURGUNDY.

Speak on; but be not over-tedious.

JOAN LA PUCELLE.

Look on thy country, look on fertile France,
And see the cities and the towns defaced
By wasting ruin of the cruel foe!
As looks the mother on her lowly babe
When death doth close his tender dying eyes,
See, see the pining malady of France;
Behold the wounds, the most unnatural wounds,
Which thou thyself hast given her woful breast!
O, turn thy edged sword another way;
Strike those that hurt, and hurt not those that
help!
One drop of blood drawn from thy country's
bosom
Should grieve thee more than streams of foreign
gore:
Return thee, therefore, with a flood of tears,
And wash away thy country's stained spots.

DUKE OF BURGUNDY [*aside*].

Either she hath bewitcht me with her words,
Or nature makes me suddenly relent.

JOAN LA PUCELLE.

Besides, all French and France exclaim on
thee,
Doubting thy birth and lawful-progeny,
Who join'st thou with, but with a lordly nation,
That will not trust thee but for profit's sake?
When Talbot hath set footing once in France,
And fashion'd thee that instrument of ill,
Who then but English Henry will be lord,
And thou be thrust out like a fugitive?
Call we to mind,—and mark but this for proof,—
Was not the Duke of Orleans thy foe?
And was he not in England prisoner?

But when they heard he was thine enemy,
They set him free, without his ransom paid,
In spite of Burgundy and all his friends.
See, then, thou fight'st against thy countrymen,
And join'st with them will be thy slaughter-men.
Come, come, return; return, thou wandering
    lord;
Charles and the rest will take thee in their arms.
              DUKE OF BURGUNDY [aside].
I'm vanquished; these haughty words of hers
Have batter'd me like roaring cannon-shot,
And made me almost yield upon my knees.—
Forgive me, country, and sweet countrymen!
And, lords, accept this hearty kind embrace:
My forces and my power of men are yours:—
So, farewell, Talbot; I'll no longer trust thee.
              JOAN LA PUCELLE [aside].
Done like a Frenchman: turn, and turn again!
                       CHARLES.
Welcome, brave duke! thy friendship makes us
    fresh.
              BASTARD OF ORLEANS.
And doth beget new courage in our breasts.
              DUKE OF ALENÇON.
Pucelle hath bravely play'd her part in this,
And doth deserve a coronet of gold.
                       CHARLES.
Now let us on, my lords, and join our powers;
And seek how we may prejudice the foe. [Exeunt.

SCENE IV.

Paris.   The palace.

Enter the KING, GLOSTER, WINCHESTER,
YORK, SUFFOLK, SOMERSET, WARWICK,
EXETER, VERNON, BASSET, *etc. To them, with
his* SOLDIERS, TALBOT.

                  LORD TALBOT.
MY gracious prince,—and honourable peers,—
    Hearing of your arrival in this realm,
I have awhile given truce unto my wars,
To do my duty to my sovereign:
In sign whereof, this arm—that hath reclaim'd
To your obedience fifty fortresses,
Twelve cities, and seven walled towns of strength,
Beside five hundred prisoners of esteem—
Lets fall his sword before your highness' feet,
                              [Kneeling.
And with submissive loyalty of heart
Ascribes the glory of his conquest got
First to my God, and next unto your Grace.
                  KING HENRY.
Is this the Lord Talbot, uncle Gloster,
That hath so long been resident in France?
              DUKE OF GLOSTER.
Yes, if it please your majesty, my liege.
                  KING HENRY.
Welcome, brave captain and victorious lord!
When I was young,—as yet I am not old,—
I do remember how my father said
A stouter champion never handled sword.
Long since we were resolved of your truth,
Your faithful service, and your toil in war;
Yet never have you tasted our reward,

Or been reguerdon'd with so much as thanks,
Because till now we never saw your face:
Therefore, stand up; and, for these good deserts,
We here create you Earl of Shrewsbury;
And in our coronation take your place.
          [Sennet. Flourish. Exeunt all except VER-
              NON and BASSET.
                  VERNON.
Now, sir, to you, that were so hot at sea,
Disgracing of these colours that I wear
In honour of my noble Lord of York,—
Darest thou maintain the former words thou
    spakest?
                  BASSET.
Yes, sir; as well as you dare patronage
The envious barking of your saucy tongue
Against my lord the Duke of Somerset.
                  VERNON.
Sirrah, thy lord I honour as he is.
                  BASSET.
Why, what is he? as good a man as York.
                  VERNON.
Hark ye; not so: in witness, take ye that.
                              [Strikes him.
                  BASSET.
Villain, thou know'st the law of arms is such,
That whoso draws a sword, 'tis present death,
Or else this blow should broach thy dearest
    blood.
But I'll unto his majesty, and crave
I may have liberty to venge this wrong;
When thou shalt see I'll meet thee to thy cost.
                  VERNON.
Well, miscreant, I'll be there as soon as you;
And, after, meet you sooner than you would.
                              [Exeunt.

ACT IV. SCENE I.

Paris.   A room of state in the palace.

Enter the KING, GLOSTER, EXETER, YORK,
SUFFOLK, SOMERSET, WINCHESTER, WAR-
WICK, TALBOT, *the* GOVERNOR OF PARIS,
and others.

              DUKE OF GLOSTER.
LORD bishop, set the crown upon his head.
              BISHOP OF WINCHESTER.
God save King Henry, of that name the sixth!
              DUKE OF GLOSTER.
Now, governor of Paris, take your oath,—
                         [GOVERNOR kneels.
That you elect no other king but him;
Esteem none friends but such as are his friends,
And none your foes but such as shall pretend
Malicious practices against his state:
This shall ye do, so help you righteous God!
              [Exeunt GOVERNOR and his TRAIN.
          Enter SIR JOHN FASTOLFE.
                  SIR JOHN FASTOLFE.
My gracious sovereign, as I rode from Calais,
To haste unto your coronation,
A letter was deliver'd to my hands,
Writ to your Grace from th' Duke of Burgundy.
                  LORD TALBOT.
Shame to the Duke of Burgundy and thee!

I vow'd, base knight, when I did meet thee next,
To tear the garter from thy craven's leg,—
                                        [*Plucks it off.*
Which I have done,—because unworthily
Thou wast installed in that high degree.—
Pardon me, princely Henry, and the rest:
This dastard, at the battle of Patay,
When but in all I was six thousand strong,
And that the French were almost ten to one,—
Before we met, or that a stroke was given,
Like to a trusty squire, did run away:
In which assault we lost twelve hundred men;
Myself, and divers gentlemen beside,
Were there surprised and taken prisoners.
Then judge, great lords, if I have done amiss;
Or whether that such cowards ought to wear
This ornament of knighthood, yea or no.

DUKE OF GLOSTER.
To say the truth, this fact was infamous,
And ill beseeming any common man,
Much more a knight, a captain, and a leader.

LORD TALBOT.
When first this order was ordain'd, my lords,
Knights of the Garter were of noble birth,
Valiant and virtuous, full of haughty courage,
Such as were grown to credit by the wars;
Not fearing death, nor shrinking for distress,
But always resolute in most extremes.
He, then, that is not furnisht in this sort
Doth but usurp the sacred name of knight,
Profaning this most honourable order,
And should—if I were worthy to be judge—
Be quite degraded, like a hedge-born swain
That doth presume to boast of gentle blood.

KING HENRY.
Stain to thy countrymen, thou hear'st thy doom!
Be packing, therefore, thou that wast a knight:
Henceforth we banish thee, on pain of death.
                                [*Exit* FASTOLFE.
And now, my lord Protector, view the letter
Sent from our uncle Duke of Burgundy.

DUKE OF GLOSTER.
What means his Grace, that he hath changed his
  style?
No more but, plain and bluntly, 'To the king'?
Hath he forgot he is his sovereign?
Or doth this churlish superscription
Pretend some alteration in good will?
What's here?—[*Reads*] 'I have, upon especial,
  cause,—
Moved with compassion of my country's wrack,
Together with the pitiful complaints
Of such as your oppression feeds upon,—
Forsaken your pernicious faction,
And join'd with Charles, the rightful King of
  France.'
O monstrous treachery! can this be so,—
That in alliance, amity, andoaths,
There should be found such false dissembling
  guile?

KING HENRY.
What! doth my uncle Burgundy revolt?

DUKE OF GLOSTER.
He doth, my lord; and is become your foe.

KING HENRY.
Is that the worst this letter doth contain?

DUKE OF GLOSTER.
It is the worst, and all, my lord, he writes.

KING HENRY.
Why, then, Lord Talbot there shall talk with him,
And give him chastisement for this abuse.—
How say you, my lord? are you not content?

LORD TALBOT.
Content, my liege! yes, but that I am prevented,
I should have begg'd I might have been employ'd.

KING HENRY.
Then gather strength, and march unto him
  straight:
Let him perceive how ill we brook his treason,
And what offence it is to flout his friends.

LORD TALBOT.
I go, my lord; in heart desiring still
You may behold confusion of your foes.   [*Exit.*
     Enter VERNON AND BASSET.

VERNON.
Grant me the combat, gracious sovereign!

BASSET.
And me, my lord, grant me the combat too!

DUKE OF YORK.
This is my servant: hear him, noble prince!

EARL OF SOMERSET.
And this is mine: sweet Henry, favour him!

KING HENRY.
Be patient, lords; and give them leave to speak.—
Say, gentlemen, what makes you thus exclaim?
And wherefore crave you combat? or with whom?

VERNON.
With him, my lord; for he hath done me wrong.

BASSET.
And I with him; for he hath done me wrong.

KING HENRY.
What is that wrong whereof you both complain?
First let me know, and then I'll answer you.

BASSET.
Crossing the sea from England into France,
This fellow here, with envious carping tongue,
Upbraided me about the rose I wear;
Saying, the sanguine colour of the leaves
Did represent my master's blushing cheeks,
When stubbornly he did repugn the truth
About a certain question in the law
Argued betwixt the Duke of York and him;
With other vile and ignominious terms;
In confutation of which rude reproach,
And in defence of my lord's worthiness,
I crave the benefit of law of arms.

VERNON.
And that is my petition, noble lord:
For though he seem with forged quaint conceit
To set a gloss upon his bold intent,
Yet know, my lord, I was provoked by him;
And he first took exceptions at this badge,
Pronouncing that the paleness of this flower
Bewray'd the faintness of my master's heart.

DUKE OF YORK.
Will not this malice, Somerset, be left?

EARL OF SOMERSET.
Your private grudge, my Lord of York, will out,
Though ne'er so cunningly you smother it.

KING HENRY.
Good Lord, what madness rules in brain-sick
  men,

When for so slight and frivolous a cause
Such factious emulations shall arise!—
Good cousins both, of York and Somerset,
Quiet yourselves, I pray, and be at peace.

DUKE OF YORK.

Let this dissension first be tried by fight,
And then your highness shall command a peace.

EARL OF SOMERSET.

The quarrel toucheth none but us alone;
Betwixt ourselves let us decide it, then.

DUKE OF YORK.

There is my pledge; accept it, Somerset.

VERNON.

Nay, let it rest where it began at first.

BASSET.

Confirm it so, mine honourable lord.

DUKE OF GLOSTER.

Confirm it so! Confounded be your strife!
And perish ye, with your audacious prate!
Presumptuous vassals, are you not ashamed
With this immodest clamorous outrage
To trouble and disturb the king and us?—
And you, my lords,—methinks you do not well
To bear with their perverse objections;
Much less to take occasion from their mouths
To raise a mutiny betwixt yourselves:
Let me persuade you take a better course.

DUKE OF EXETER.

It grieves his highness:—good my lords, be
  friends.

KING HENRY.

Come hither, you that would be combatants:
Henceforth I charge you, as you love our favour,
Quite to forget this quarrel and the cause.—
And you, my lords, remember where we are;
In France, amongst a fickle wavering nation:
If they perceive dissension in our looks,
And that within ourselves we disagree,
How will their grudging stomachs be provoked
To wilful disobedience, and rebel!
Beside, what infamy will there arise,
When foreign princes shall be certified
That for a toy, a thing of no regard,
King Henry's peers and chief nobility
Destroy'd themselves, and lost the realm of
  France!
O, think upon the conquest of my father;
My tender years; and let us not forgo
That for a trifle that was bought with blood!
Let me be umpire in this doubtful strife.
I see no reason, if I wear this rose,
             [Putting on a red rose.
That any one should therefore be suspicious
I more incline to Somerset than York:
Both are my kinsmen, and I love them both:
As well they may upbraid me with my crown,
Because, forsooth, the King of Scots is crown'd.
But your discretions better can persuade
Than I am able to instruct or teach:
And therefore, as we hither came in peace,
So let us still continue peace and love.—
Cousin of York, we institute your Grace
To be our regent in these parts of France:—
And, good my Lord of Somerset, unite
Your troops of horsemen with his bands of foot:—
And, like true subjects, sons of your progenitors,

Go cheerfully together, and digest
Your angry choler on your enemies.
Ourself, my lord Protector, and the rest,
After some respite, will return to Calais;
From thence to England; where I hope ere long
To be presented, by your victories,
With Charles, Alençon, and that traitorous rout.
    [Flourish. Exeunt KING, GLOSTER, SOM-
      ERSET, WINCHESTER, SUFFOLK, and
      BASSET.

EARL OF WARWICK.

My Lord of York, I promise you, the king
Prettily, methought, did play the orator.

DUKE OF YORK.

And so he did; but yet I like it not,
In that he wears the badge of Somerset.

EARL OF WARWICK.

Tush, that was but his fancy, blame him not;
I dare presume, sweet prince, he thought no
  harm.

DUKE OF YORK.

An if I wist he did,—but let it rest;
Other affairs must now be managed.
    [Exeunt YORK, WARWICK, and VERNON.

DUKE OF EXETER.

Well didst thou, Richard, to suppress thy voice;
For, had the passions of thy heart burst out,
I fear we should have seen decipher'd there
More rancorous spite, more furious raging broils,
Than yet can be imagined or supposed.
But howsoe'er, no simple man that sees
This jarring discord of nobility,
This shouldering of each other in the court,
This factious bandying of their favourites,
But that he doth presage some ill event.
'Tis much when sceptres are in children's hands;
But more when envy breeds unkind division;
There comes the ruin, there begins confusion.
                    [Exit.

SCENE II.

Before Bourdeaux.

Enter TALBOT, with trump and drum.

LORD TALBOT.

GO to the gates of Bourdeaux, trumpeter;
  Summon their general unto the wall.
Trumpet sounds. Enter GENERAL and others aloft.
English John Talbot, captains, calls you forth,
Servant in arms to Harry King of England;
And thus he would,—Open your city-gates;
Be humble to us: call my sovereign yours,
And do him homage as obedient subjects;
And I'll withdraw me and my bloody power:
But, if you frown upon this proffer'd peace,
You tempt the fury of my three attendants,
Lean famine, quartering steel, and climbing fire;
Who, in a moment, even with the earth
Shall lay your stately and air-braving towers,
If you forsake the offer of our love.

GENERAL.

Thou ominous and fearful owl of death,
Our nation's terror, and their bloody scourge!
The period of thy tyranny approacheth.
On us thou canst not enter but by death;
For, I protest, we are well fortified,
And strong enough to issue out and fight:

If thou retire, the Dauphin, well appointed,
Stands with the snares of war to tangle thee:
On either hand thee there are squadrons pitcht,
To wall thee from the liberty of flight;
And no way canst thou turn thee for redress,
But death doth front thee with apparent spoil,
And pale destruction meets thee in the face.
Ten thousand French have ta'en the sacrament
To rive their dangerous artillery
Upon no Christian soul but English Talbot.
Lo, there thou stand'st, a breathing valiant man,
Of an invincible unconquer'd spirit!
This is the latest glory of thy praise
That I, thy enemy, due thee withal;
For ere the glass, that now begins to run,
Finish the process of his sandy hour,
These eyes, that see thee now well-coloured,
Shall see thee wither'd, bloody, pale, and dead.
[_Drum afar off._
Hark! hark! the Dauphin's drum, a warning bell,
Sings heavy music to thy timorous soul;
And mine shall ring thy dire departure out.
[_Exeunt_ GENERAL, _etc._
LORD TALBOT.
He fables not; I hear the enemy:—
Out, some light horsemen, and peruse their
    wings.—
O, negligent and heedless discipline!
How are we parkt and bounded in a pale,—
A little herd of England's timorous deer,
Mazed with a yelping kennel of French curs!
If we be English deer, be, then, in blood;
Not rascal-like, to fall down with a pinch,
But rather, moody-mad and desperate stags,
Turn on the bloody hounds with heads of steel,
And make the cowards stand aloof at bay:
Sell every man his life as dear as mine,
And they shall find dear deer of us, my friends.—
God and Saint George, Talbot and England's
    right,
Prosper our colours in this dangerous fight!
[_Exeunt._

SCENE III.

Plains in Gascony.

Enter a MESSENGER _that meets_ YORK. _Enter_
YORK _with trumpet and many_ SOLDIERS.

DUKE OF YORK.
ARE not the speedy scouts return'd again,
    That dogg'd the mighty army of the Dau-
MESSENGER.   [phin?
They are return'd, my lord; and give it out
That he is marcht to Bourdeaux with his power,
To fight with Talbot: as he marcht along,
By your espials were discovered
Two mightier troops than that the Dauphin
    led;
Which join'd with him, and made their march for
    Bourdeaux.
DUKE OF YORK.
A plague upon that villain Somerset,
That thus delays my promised supply
Of horsemen, that were levied for this siege!
Renowned Talbot doth expect my aid;
And I am louted by a traitor villain,
And cannot help the noble chevalier:

God comfort him in this necessity!
If he miscarry, farewell wars in France.
Enter SIR WILLIAM LUCY.
SIR WILLIAM LUCY.
Thou princely leader of our English strength,
Never so needful on the earth of France,
Spur to the rescue of the noble Talbot,
Who now is girdled with a waist of iron,
And hemm'd about with grim destruction:
To Bourdeaux, warlike duke! to Bourdeaux, York!
Else, farewell Talbot, France, and England's
    honour.
DUKE OF YORK.
O God, that Somerset—who in proud heart
Doth stop my cornets—were in Talbot's place!
So should we save a valiant gentleman
By forfeiting a traitor and a coward.
Mad ire and wrathful fury make me weep,
That thus we die, while remiss traitors sleep.
SIR WILLIAM LUCY.
O, send some succour to the distrest lord!
DUKE OF YORK.
He dies, we lose; I break my warlike word;
We mourn, France smiles; we lose, they daily
    get;
All long of this vile traitor Somerset.
SIR WILLIAM LUCY.
Then God take mercy on brave Talbot's soul;
And on his son young John, who two hours since
I met in travel toward his warlike father!
This seven years did not Talbot see his son;
And now they meet where both their lives are
    done.
DUKE OF YORK.
Alas, what joy shall noble Talbot have
To bid his young son welcome to his grave?
Away! vexation almost stops my breath,
That sunder'd friends greet in the hour of
    death.—
Lucy, farewell: no more my fortune can,
But curse the cause I cannot aid the man.
Maine, Blois, Poictiers, and Tours, are won away,
Long all of Somerset and his delay.
[_Exit with_ FORCES.
SIR WILLIAM LUCY.
Thus, while the vulture of sedition
Feeds in the bosom of such great commanders,
Sleeping neglection doth betray to loss
The conquest of our scarce-cold conqueror,
That ever-living man of memory,
Henry the Fifth:—whiles they each other cross,
Lives, honours, land, and all, hurry to loss. [_Exit._

SCENE IV.

Other plains in Gascony.

Enter SOMERSET, _with his_ ARMY; _an_ OFFICER _of_
TALBOT'S _with him._

EARL OF SOMERSET.
IT is too late: I cannot send them now:
    This expedition was by York and Talbot
Too rashly plotted; all our general force
Might with a sally of the very town
Be buckled with: the over-daring Talbot
Hath sullied all his gloss of former honour
By this unheedful, desperate, wild adventure:

York set him on to fight and die in shame,
That, Talbot dead, great York might bear the
name.
OFFICER.
Here is Sir William Lucy, who with me
Set from our o'er-matcht forces forth for aid.
Enter SIR WILLIAM LUCY.
EARL OF SOMERSET.
How now, Sir William! whither were you sent?
SIR WILLIAM LUCY.
Whither, my lord? from bought and sold Lord
Talbot;
Who, ring'd about with bold adversity,
Cries out for noble York and Somerset,
To beat assailing death from his weak legions:
And whiles the honourable captain there
Drops bloody sweat from his war-wearied limbs,
And, in advantage lingering, looks for rescue,
You, his false hopes, the trust of England's
honour,
Keep off aloof with worthless emulation.
Let not your private discord keep away
The levied succours that should lend him aid,
While he, renowned noble gentleman,
Yields up his life unto a world of odds:
Orleans the Bastard, Charles, Burgundy,
Alençon, Reignier, compass him about,
And Talbot perisheth by your default.
EARL OF SOMERSET.
York set him on, York should have sent him aid.
SIR WILLIAM LUCY.
And York as fast upon your Grace exclaims;
Swearing that you withhold his levied host,
Collected for this expedition.
EARL OF SOMERSET.
York lies; he might have sent and had the horse;
I owe him little duty, and less love;
And take foul scorn to fawn on him by sending.
SIR WILLIAM LUCY.
The fraud of England, not the force of France,
Hath now entrapt the noble-minded Talbot:
Never to England shall he bear his life;
But dies, betray'd to fortune by your strife.
EARL OF SOMERSET.
Come, go; I will dispatch the horsemen straight;
Within six hours they will be at his aid.
SIR WILLIAM LUCY.
Too late comes rescue; he is ta'en or slain:
For fly he could not, if he would have fled;
And fly would Talbot never, though he might.
EARL OF SOMERSET.
If he be dead, brave Talbot, then, adieu!
SIR WILLIAM LUCY.
His fame lives in the world, his shame in you.
[*Exeunt.*

SCENE V.

The English camp near Bourdeaux.

Enter TALBOT *and* JOHN *his son.*

LORD TALBOT.
O YOUNG John Talbot! I did send for thee
To tutor thee in stratagems of war,
That Talbot's name might be in thee revived
When sapless age and weak unable limbs
Should bring thy father to his drooping chair.
But,—O malignant and ill-boding stars!—

Now thou art come unto a feast of death,
A terrible and unavoided danger:
Therefore, dear boy, mount on my swiftest horse;
And I'll direct thee how thou shalt escape
By sudden flight: come, dally not, be gone.
JOHN TALBOT.
Is my name Talbot? and am I your son?
And shall I fly? O, if you love my mother,
Dishonour not her honourable name,
To make a bastard and a slave of me!
The world will say, he is not Talbot's blood,
That basely fled when noble Talbot stood.
LORD TALBOT.
Fly, to revenge my death, if I be slain.
JOHN TALBOT.
He that flies so will ne'er return again.
LORD TALBOT.
If we both stay, we both are sure to die.
JOHN TALBOT.
Then let me stay; and, father, do you fly:
Your loss is great, so your regard should be;
My worth unknown, no loss is known in me.
Upon my death the French can little boast;
In yours they will, in you all hopes are lost.
Flight cannot stain the honour you have won;
But mine it will, that no exploit have done:
You fled for vantage, every one will swear;
But, if I bow, they'll say it was for fear.
There is no hope that ever I will stay,
If, the first hour, I shrink and run away.
Here, on my knee, I beg mortality,
Rather than life preserved with infamy.
LORD TALBOT.
Shall all thy mother's hopes lie in one tomb?
JOHN TALBOT.
Ay, rather than I'll shame my mother's womb.
LORD TALBOT.
Upon my blessing, I command thee go.
JOHN TALBOT.
To fight I will, but not to fly the foe.
LORD TALBOT.
Part of thy father may be saved in thee.
JOHN TALBOT.
No part of him but will be shamed in me.
LORD TALBOT.
Thou never hadst renown, nor canst not lose it.
JOHN TALBOT.
Yes, your renowned name: shall flight abuse it?
LORD TALBOT.
Thy father's charge shall clear thee from that
stain.
JOHN TALBOT.
You cannot witness for me, being slain.
If death be so apparent, then both fly.
LORD TALBOT.
And leave my followers here, to fight and die?
My age was never tainted with such shame.
JOHN TALBOT.
And shall my youth be guilty of such blame?
No more can I be sever'd from your side
Than can yourself yourself in twain divide:
Stay, go, do what you will, the like do I;
For live I will not, if my father die.
LORD TALBOT.
Then here I take my leave of thee, fair son,
Born to eclipse thy life this afternoon.

Come, side by side together live and die;
And soul with soul from France to heaven fly.
[*Exeunt.*

SCENE VI.

A field of battle.

Alarum: excursions, wherein TALBOT'S SON *is hemm'd about, and* TALBOT *rescues him.*

LORD TALBOT.

SAINT George and victory! fight, soldiers, fight:
The regent hath with Talbot broke his word,
And left us to the rage of France his sword.
Where is John Talbot?—Pause, and take thy
breath;
I gave thee life, and rescued thee from death.

JOHN TALBOT.

O, twice my father, twice am I thy son!
The life thou gavest me first was lost and done,
Till with thy warlike sword, despite of fate,
To my determined time thou gavest new date.

LORD TALBOT.

When from the Dauphin's crest thy sword struck
fire,
It warm'd thy father's heart with proud desire
Of bold-faced victory. Then leaden age,
Quicken'd with youthful spleen and warlike rage,
Beat down Alençon, Orleans, Burgundy,
And from the pride of Gallia rescued thee.
The ireful bastard Orleans—that drew blood
From thee, my boy, and had the maidenhood
Of thy first fight—I soon encountered,
And, interchanging blows, I quickly shed
Some of his bastard blood; and, in disgrace,
Bespoke him thus,—'Contaminated, base,
And misbegotten blood I spill of thine,
Mean and right poor, for that pure blood of mine
Which thou didst force from Talbot, my brave
boy:'—
Here, purposing the Bastard to destroy,
Came in strong rescue. Speak, thy father's
care,—
Art thou not weary, John? how dost thou fare?
Wilt thou yet leave the battle, boy, and fly,
Now thou art seal'd the son of chivalry?
Fly, to revenge my death when I am dead:
The help of one stands me in little stead.
O, too much folly is it, well I wot,
To hazard all our lives in one small boat!
If I to-day die not with Frenchmen's rage,
To-morrow I shall die with mickle age:
By me they nothing gain, an if I stay,—
'Tis but the shortening of my life one day:
In thee thy mother dies, our household's name,
My death's revenge, thy youth, and England's
fame:
All these, and more, we hazard by thy stay;
All these are saved, if thou wilt fly away.

JOHN TALBOT.

The sword of Orleans hath not made me smart;
These words of yours draw life-blood from my
heart:
On that advantage, bought with such a shame,—
To save a paltry life, and slay bright fame,—
Before young Talbot from old Talbot fly,
The coward horse that bears me fall and die!
And like me to the peasant boys of France,

To be shame's scorn and subject of mischance!
Surely, by all the glory you have won,
An if I fly, I am not Talbot's son:
Then talk no more of flight, it is no boot;
If son to Talbot, die at Talbot's foot.

LORD TALBOT.

Then follow thou thy desperate sire of Crete,
Thou Icarus; thy life to me is sweet:
If thou wilt fight, fight by thy father's side;
And, commendable proved, let's die in pride.
[*Exeunt.*

SCENE VII.

Another part of the field.

Alarum: excursions. Enter old TALBOT *led by a*
SERVANT.

LORD TALBOT.

WHERE is my other life?—mine own is
gone;—
O, where's young Talbot? where is valiant
John?—
Triumphant death, smear'd with captivity,
Young Talbot's valour makes me smile at thee:—
When he perceived me shrink and on my knee,
His bloody sword he brandisht over me,
And, like a hungry lion, did commence
Rough deeds of rage and stern impatience;
But when my angry guardant stood alone,
Tendering my ruin, and assail'd of none,
Dizzy-eyed fury and great rage of heart
Suddenly made him from my side to start
Into the clustering battle of the French;
And in that sea of blood my boy did drench
His over-mounting spirit; and there died
My Icarus, my blossom, in his pride.

SERVANT.

O my dear lord, lo, where your son is borne!
Enter SOLDIERS, *with* JOHN TALBOT *borne.*

LORD TALBOT.

Thou antic death, which laugh'st us here to
scorn,
Anon, from thy insulting tyranny,
Coupled in bonds of perpetuity,
Two Talbots, winged through the lither sky,
In thy despite, shall scape mortality.—
O thou whose wounds become hard-favour'd
death,
Speak to thy father, ere thou yield thy breath!
Brave death by speaking, whether he will or no;
Imagine him a Frenchman and thy foe.—
Poor boy! he smiles, methinks, as who should say,
Had death been French, then death had died
to-day.—
Come, come, and lay him in his father's arms:
My spirit can no longer bear these harms.
Soldiers, adieu! I have what I would have,
Now my old arms are young John Talbot's grave.
[*Dies.*

Enter CHARLES, ALENÇON, BURGUNDY, BAS-
TARD, LA PUCELLE, *and* FORCES.

CHARLES.

Had York and Somerset brought rescue in,
We should have found a bloody day of this.

BASTARD OF ORLEANS.

How the young whelp of Talbot's, raging-wood,
Did flesh his puny sword in Frenchmen's blood!

23

JOAN LA PUCELLE.
Once I encounter'd him, and thus I said,
'Thou maiden youth, be vanquisht by a maid':
But, with a proud majestical high scorn,
He answer'd thus, 'Young Talbot was not born
To be the pillage of a giglot wench':
So, rushing in the bowels of the French,
He left me proudly, as unworthy fight.

DUKE OF BURGUNDY.
Doubtless he would have made a noble knight:
See, where he lies inhearsed in the arms
Of the most bloody nurser of his harms!

BASTARD OF ORLEANS.
Hew them to pieces, hack their bones asunder,
Whose life was England's glory, Gallia's wonder.

CHARLES.
O, no, forbear! for that which we have fled
During the life, let us not wrong it dead.

Enter SIR WILLIAM LUCY, *attended; a French*
HERALD *preceding.*

SIR WILLIAM LUCY.
Herald, conduct me to the Dauphin's tent,
To know who hath obtain'd the glory of the day.

CHARLES.
On what submissive message art thou sent?

SIR WILLIAM LUCY.
Submission, Dauphin! 'tis a mere French word;
We English warriors wot not what it means.
I come to know what prisoners thou hast ta'en,
And to survey the bodies of the dead.

CHARLES.
For prisoners ask'st thou? hell our prison is.
But tell me whom thou seek'st.

SIR WILLIAM LUCY.
Where is the great Alcides of the field,
Valiant Lord Talbot, Earl of Shrewsbury,—
Created, for his rare success in arms,
Great Earl of Washford, Waterford, and Valence;
Lord Talbot of Goodrig and Urchinfield,
Lord Strange of Blackmere, Lord Verdun of
    Alton,
Lord Cromwell of Wingfield, Lord Furnival of
    Sheffield,
The thrice-victorious Lord of Falconbridge;
Knight of the noble order of Saint George,
Worthy Saint Michael, and the Golden Fleece;
Great Marshal to Henry the Sixth
Of all his wars within the realm of France?

JOAN LA PUCELLE.
Here is a silly-stately style indeed!
The Turk, that two-and-fifty kingdoms hath,
Writes not so tedious a style as this.—
Him that thou magnifiest with all these titles,
Stinking and fly-blown, lies here at our feet.

SIR WILLIAM LUCY.
Is Talbot slain,—the Frenchmen's only scourge,
Your kingdom's terror and black Nemesis?
O, were mine eyeballs into bullets turn'd,
That I, in rage, might shoot them at your faces!
O, that I could but call these dead to life!
It were enough to fright the realm of France:
Were but his picture left amongst you here,
It would amaze the proudest of you all.
Give me their bodies, that I may bear them
    hence,
And give them burial as beseems their worth.

JOAN LA PUCELLE.
I think this upstart is old Talbot's ghost,
He speaks with such a proud-commanding spirit.
For God's sake, let him have 'em; to keep them
    here,
They would but stink, and putrefy the air.

CHARLES.
Go, take their bodies hence.

SIR WILLIAM LUCY.
I'll bear them hence: but from their ashes shall be
    rear'd
A phœnix that shall make all France afeard.

CHARLES.
So we be rid of them, do with 'em what thou
    wilt.—
And now to Paris, in this conquering vein:
All will be ours, now bloody Talbot's slain.

[*Exeunt.*

ACT V. SCENE I.

London. The palace.

Enter KING, GLOSTER, *and* EXETER.

KING HENRY.
HAVE you perused the letters from the Pope,
The emperor, and the Earl of Armagnac?

DUKE OF GLOSTER.
I have, my lord: and their intent is this,—
They humbly sue unto your excellence
To have a godly peace concluded of
Between the realms of England and of France.

KING HENRY.
How doth your Grace affect their motion?

DUKE OF GLOSTER.
Well, my good lord; and as the only means
To stop effusion of our Christian blood,
And stablish quietness on every side.

KING HENRY.
Ay, marry, uncle; for I always thought
It was both impious and unnatural
That such immanity and bloody strife
Should reign among professors of one faith.

DUKE OF GLOSTER.
Beside, my lord, the sooner to effect
And surer bind this knot of amity,
The Earl of Armagnac—near kin to Charles,
A man of great authority in France—
Proffers his only daughter to your Grace
In marriage, with a large and sumptuous dowry.

KING HENRY.
Marriage, uncle! alas, my years are young!
And fitter is my study and my books
Than wanton dalliance with a paramour.
Yet, call th' ambassadors; and, as you please,
So let them have their answers, every one:
I shall be well content with any choice
Tends to God's glory and my country's weal.

Enter a LEGATE *and two* AMBASSADORS, *with*
WINCHESTER *in a Cardinal's habit.*

DUKE OF EXETER [*aside*].
What! is my Lord of Winchester install'd,
And call'd unto a cardinal's degree?
Then I perceive that will be verified
Henry the Fifth did sometime prophesy,—
'If once he come to be a cardinal,
He'll make his cap co-equal with the crown.'

KING HENRY.

My lords ambassadors, your several suits
Have been consider'd and debated on.
Your purpose is both good and reasonable;
And therefore are we certainly resolved
To draw conditions of a friendly peace;
Which by my Lord of Winchester we mean
Shall be transported presently to France.

DUKE OF GLOSTER.

And for the proffer of my lord your master,
I have inform'd his highness so at large,
As, liking of the lady's virtuous gifts,
Her beauty, and the value of her dower,
He doth intend she shall be England's queen.

KING HENRY [to the AMBASSADORS].

In argument and proof of which contract,
Bear her this jewel, pledge of my affection.—
And so, my lord Protector, see them guarded,
And safely brought to Dover; where, inshipt,
Commit them to the fortune of the sea.

[Exeunt KING, GLOSTER, EXETER, and
AMBASSADORS.

CARDINAL.

Stay, my lord legate: you shall first receive
The sum of money which I promised
Should be deliver'd to his holiness
For clothing me in these grave ornaments.

LEGATE.

I will attend upon your lordship's leisure.

CARDINAL [aside].

Now Winchester will not submit, I trow,
Or be inferior to the proudest peer.
Humphrey of Gloster, thou shalt well perceive
That neither in birth or for authority
The bishop will be overborne by thee:
I'll either make thee stoop and bend thy knee,
Or sack this country with a mutiny.   [Exeunt.

SCENE II.

France. Plains in Anjou.

Enter CHARLES, BURGUNDY, ALENÇON, BAS-
TARD, LA PUCELLE, and FORCES.

CHARLES.

THESE news, my lords, may cheer our droop-
ing spirits:
'Tis said the stout Parisians do revolt,
And turn again unto the warlike French.

DUKE OF ALENÇON.

Then march to Paris, royal Charles of France,
And keep not back your powers in dalliance.

JOAN LA PUCELLE.

Peace be amongst them, if they turn to us;
Else, ruin combat with their palaces!

Enter a MESSENGER.

MESSENGER.

Success unto our valiant general,
And happiness to his accomplices!

CHARLES.

What tidings send our scouts? I prithee, speak.

MESSENGER.

The English army, that divided was
Into two parties, is now conjoin'd in one,
And means to give you battle presently.

CHARLES.

Somewhat too sudden, sirs, the warning is;
But we will presently provide for them.

DUKE OF BURGUNDY.

I trust the ghost of Talbot is not there:
Now he is gone, my lord, you need not fear.

JOAN LA PUCELLE.

Of all base passions, fear is most accurst:—
Command the conquest, Charles, it shall be
thine;
Let Henry fret, and all the world repine.

CHARLES.

Then on, my lords; and France be fortunate!
[Exeunt.

SCENE III.

Before Angiers.

Alarum: excursions. Enter LA PUCELLE.

JOAN LA PUCELLE.

THE regent conquers, and the Frenchmen fly.—
Now help, ye charming spells and periapts;
And ye choice spirits that admonish me,
And give me signs of future accidents,—
You speedy helpers, that are substitutes
Under the lordly monarch of the north,
Appear, and aid me in this enterprise!   [Thunder.

Enter FIENDS.

This speedy and quick appearance argues proof
Of your accustom'd diligence to me.
Now, ye familiar spirits, that are cull'd
Out of the powerful legions under earth,
Help me this once, that France may get the field.
[They walk, and speak not.
O, hold me not with silence over-long!
Where I was wont to feed you with my blood,
I'll lop a member off, and give it you,
In earnest of a further benefit,
So you do condescend to help me now.
[They hang their heads.
No hope to have redress?—My body shall
Pay recompense, if you will grant my suit.
[They shake their heads.
Cannot my body nor blood-sacrifice
Entreat you to your wonted furtherance?
Then take my soul,—my body, soul, and all,
Before that England give the French the foil.
[They depart.
See, they forsake me! Now the time is come,
That France must vail her lofty-plumed crest,
And let her head fall into England's lap.
My ancient incantations are too weak.
And hell too strong for me to buckle with:
Now, France, thy glory droopeth to the dust.
[Exit.
Excursions. LA PUCELLE and YORK fight hand to
hand: LA PUCELLE is taken. The French fly.

DUKE OF YORK.

Damsel of France, I think I have you fast:
Unchain your spirits now with spelling charms,
And try if they can gain your liberty.—
A goodly prize, fit for the devil's grace!
See, how the ugly witch doth bend her brows,
As if, with Circe, she would change my shape!

JOAN LA PUCELLE.

Changed to a worser shape thou canst not be.

DUKE OF YORK.
O, Charles the Dauphin is a proper man;
No shape but his can please your dainty eye.
JOAN LA PUCELLE.
A plaguing mischief light on Charles and thee!
And may ye both be suddenly surprised
By bloody hands, in sleeping on your beds!
DUKE OF YORK.
Fell banning hag, enchantress, hold thy tongue!
JOAN LA PUCELLE.
I prithee, give me leave to curse awhile.
DUKE OF YORK.
Curse, miscreant, when thou comest to the
   stake.
                              [Exeunt.
Alarum. Enter SUFFOLK, *with* MARGARET *in his
                     hand.*
EARL OF SUFFOLK.
Be what thou wilt, thou art my prisoner.
                              [*Gazes on her.*
O fairest beauty, do not fear nor fly!
For I will touch thee but with reverent hands,
And lay them gently on thy tender side.
I kiss these fingers for eternal peace.
                       [*Kissing her hand.*
Who art thou? say, that I may honour thee.
MARGARET.
Margaret my name, and daughter to a king,
The King of Naples,—whosoe'er thou art.
EARL OF SUFFOLK.
An earl I am, and Suffolk am I call'd.
Be not offended, nature's miracle,
Thou art allotted to be ta'en by me:
So doth the swan her downy cygnets save,
Keeping them prisoner underneath her wings.
Yet, if this servile usage once offend,
Go, and be free again as Suffolk's friend.
                              [*She is going.*
O, stay!—[*aside*] I have no power to let her
   pass;
My hand would free her, but my heart says
   no.
As plays the sun upon the glassy streams,
Twinkling another counterfeited beam,
So seems this gorgeous beauty to mine eyes.
Fain would I woo her, yet I dare not speak:
I'll call for pen and ink, and write my mind:—
Fie, de la Pole! disable not thyself;
Hast not a tongue? is she not here thy prisoner?
Wilt thou be daunted at a woman's sight?
Ay, beauty's princely majesty is such,
Confounds the tongue, and makes the senses
   rough.
MARGARET.
Say, Earl of Suffolk,—if thy name be so,—
What ransom must I pay before I pass?
For I perceive I am thy prisoner.
EARL OF SUFFOLK [*aside*].
How canst thou tell she will deny thy suit
Before thou make a trial of her love?
MARGARET.
Why speak'st thou not? what ransom must I
   pay?
EARL OF SUFFOLK [*aside*].
She's beautiful, and therefore to be woo'd;
She is a woman, therefore to be won.

MARGARET.
Wilt thou accept of ransom—yea or no?
EARL OF SUFFOLK [*aside*].
Fond man, remember that thou hast a wife;
Then how can Margaret be thy paramour?
MARGARET.
I were best to leave him, for he will not hear.
EARL OF SUFFOLK [*aside*].
There all is marr'd; there lies a cooling-card.
MARGARET.
He talks at random; sure, the man is mad.
EARL OF SUFFOLK [*aside*].
And yet a dispensation may be had.
MARGARET.
And yet I would that you would answer me.
EARL OF SUFFOLK [*aside*].
I'll win this Lady Margaret. For whom?
Why, for my king: tush, that's a wooden
   thing!
MARGARET.
He talks of wood: it is some carpenter.
EARL OF SUFFOLK [*aside*].
Yet so my fancy may be satisfied,
And peace established between these realms.
But there remains a scruple in that too;
For though her father be the King of Naples,
Duke of Anjou and Maine, yet is he poor,
And our nobility will scorn the match.
MARGARET.
Hear ye, captain,—are you not at leisure?
EARL OF SUFFOLK.
It shall be so, disdain they ne'er so much:
Henry is youthful, and will quickly yield.—
Madam, I have a secret to reveal.
MARGARET [*aside*].
What though I be enthrall'd? he seems a
   knight,
And will not any way dishonour me.
EARL OF SUFFOLK.
Lady, vouchsafe to listen what I say.
MARGARET [*aside*].
Perhaps I shall be rescued by the French;
And then I need not crave his courtesy.
EARL OF SUFFOLK.
Sweet madam, give me hearing in a cause—
MARGARET [*aside*].
Tush, women have been captivate ere now.
EARL OF SUFFOLK.
I prithee, lady, wherefore talk you so?
MARGARET.
I cry you mercy, 'tis but *quid* for *quo*.
EARL OF SUFFOLK.
Say, gentle princess, would you not suppose
Your bondage happy, to be made a queen?
MARGARET.
To be a queen in bondage is more vile
Than is a slave in base servility;
For princes should be free.
EARL OF SUFFOLK.
                              And so shall you,
If happy England's royal king be free.
MARGARET.
Why, what concerns his freedom unto me?
EARL OF SUFFOLK.
I'll undertake to make thee Henry's queen;
To put a golden sceptre in thy hand,

26

And set a precious crown upon thy head,
If thou wilt condescend to be my—
MARGARET.
                          What?
EARL OF SUFFOLK.
His love.
MARGARET.
I am unworthy to be Henry's wife.
EARL OF SUFFOLK.
No, gentle madam; I unworthy am
To woo so fair a dame to be his wife,
And have no portion in the choice myself.
How say you, madam,—are ye so content?
MARGARET.
An if my father please, I am content.
EARL OF SUFFOLK.
Then call our captains and our colours forth!—
                [*Troops come forward.*
And, madam, at your father's castle-walls
We'll crave a parley, to confer with him.
  A parley sounded. Enter REIGNIER *on the walls.*
See, Reignier, see, thy daughter prisoner!
REIGNIER.
To whom?
EARL OF SUFFOLK.
  To me.
REIGNIER.
        Suffolk, what remedy?
I am a soldier, and unapt to weep
Or to exclaim on fortune's fickleness.
EARL OF SUFFOLK.
Yes, there is remedy enough, my lord:
Consent—and, for thy honour, give consent—
Thy daughter shall be wedded to my king;
Whom I with pain have woo'd and won thereto;
And this her easy-held imprisonment
Hath gain'd thy daughter princely liberty.
REIGNIER.
Speaks Suffolk as he thinks?
EARL OF SUFFOLK.
             Fair Margaret knows
That Suffolk doth not flatter, face, or feign.
REIGNIER.
Upon thy princely warrant, I descend
To give thee answer of thy just demand.
EARL OF SUFFOLK.
And here I will expect thy coming.
           [*Exit* REIGNIER *from the walls.*
  Trumpets sound. Enter REIGNIER, *below.*
REIGNIER.
Welcome, brave earl, into our territories:
Command in Anjou what your honour pleases.
EARL OF SUFFOLK.
Thanks, Reignier, happy for so sweet a child,
Fit to be made companion with a king;
What answer makes your Grace unto my suit?
REIGNIER.
Since thou dost deign to woo her little worth
To be the princely bride of such a lord;
Upon condition I may quietly
Enjoy mine own, the counties Maine and Anjou,
Free from oppression or the stroke of war,
My daughter shall be Henry's, if he please.
EARL OF SUFFOLK.
That is her ransom,—I deliver her;

And those two counties I will undertake
Your Grace shall well and quietly enjoy.
REIGNIER.
And I again, in Henry's royal name,
As deputy unto that gracious king,
Give thee her hand, for sign of plighted faith.
EARL OF SUFFOLK.
Reignier of France, I give thee kingly thanks,
Because this is in traffic of a king:—
[*aside*] And yet, methinks, I could be well content
To be mine own attorney in this case.—
I'll over, then, to England with this news,
And make this marriage to be solemnized.
So, farewell, Reignier: set this diamond safe
In golden palaces, as it becomes.
REIGNIER.
I do embrace thee, as I would embrace
The Christian prince King Henry, were he here.
MARGARET.
Farewell, my lord: good wishes, praise, and
  prayers
Shall Suffolk ever have of Margaret.   [*Going.*

EARL OF SUFFOLK.
Farewell, sweet madam: but, hark you, Margaret,—
No princely commendations to my king?
MARGARET.
Such commendations as becomes a maid,
A virgin, and his servant, say to him.
EARL OF SUFFOLK.
Words sweetly placed and modestly directed.
But, madam, I must trouble you again,—
No loving token to his majesty?
MARGARET.
Yes, my good lord,—a pure unspotted heart,
Never yet taint with love, I send the king.
EARL OF SUFFOLK.
And this withal.   [*Kisses her.*
MARGARET.
That for thyself:—I will not so presume
To send such peevish tokens to a king.
       [*Exeunt* REIGNIER *and* MARGARET.
EARL OF SUFFOLK.
O, wert thou for myself!—But, Suffolk, stay;
Thou mayst not wander in that labyrinth;
There Minotaurs and ugly treasons lurk.
Solicit Henry with her wondrous praise:
Bethink thee on her virtues that surmount,
And natural graces that extinguish art;
Repeat their semblance often on the seas,
That, when thou comest to kneel at Henry's feet,
Thou mayst bereave him of his wits with wonder.
                      [*Exit.*

SCENE IV.

Camp of the DUKE OF YORK *in Anjou.*

Enter YORK, WARWICK, *and others.*

DUKE OF YORK.
BRING forth that sorceress condemn'd to burn.
    Enter LA PUCELLE, *guarded,*
       and a SHEPHERD.
SHEPHERD.
Ah, Joan, this kills thy father's heart outright!
Have I sought every country far and near,
And, now it is my chance to find thee out,

27

Must I behold thy timeless-cruel death?
Ah, Joan, sweet daughter Joan, I'll die with thee!

JOAN LA PUCELLE.
Decrepit miser! base ignoble wretch!
I am descended of a gentler blood:
Thou art no father nor no friend of mine.

SHEPHERD.
Out, out!—My lords, an please you, 'tis not so;
I did beget her, all the parish knows:
Her mother liveth yet, can testify
She was the first fruit of my bachelorship.

EARL OF WARWICK.
Graceless! wilt thou deny thy parentage?

DUKE OF YORK.
This argues what her kind of life hath been,—
Wicked and vile; and so her death concludes.

SHEPHERD.
Fie, Joan, that thou wilt be so obstacle!
God knows thou art a collop of my flesh;
And for thy sake have I shed many a tear:
Deny me not, I prithee, gentle Joan.

JOAN LA PUCELLE.
Peasant, avaunt!—You have suborn'd this man,
Of purpose to obscure my noble birth.

SHEPHERD.
'Tis true, I gave a noble to the priest
The morn that I was wedded to her mother.—
Kneel down and take my blessing, good my girl.
Wilt thou not stoop? Now cursed be the time
Of thy nativity! I would the milk
Thy mother gave thee when thou suck'dst her
   breast,
Had been a little ratsbane for thy sake!
Or else, when thou didst keep my lambs a-field,
I wish some ravenous wolf had eaten thee!
Dost thou deny thy father, cursed drab?
O, burn her, burn her! hanging is too good. [Exit.

DUKE OF YORK.
Take her away; for she hath lived too long,
To fill the world with vicious qualities.

JOAN LA PUCELLE.
First, let me tell you whom you have condemn'd:
Not one begotten of a shepherd swain,
But issued from the progeny of kings;
Virtuous and holy; chosen from above,
By inspiration of celestial grace,
To work exceeding miracles on earth.
I never had to do with wicked spirits:
But you,—that are polluted with your lusts,
Stain'd with the guiltless blood of innocents,
Corrupt and tainted with a thousand vices,—
Because you want the grace that others have,
You judge it straight a thing impossible
To compass wonders but by help of devils.
No, misconceived! Joan of Arc hath been
A virgin from her tender infancy,
Chaste and immaculate in very thought;
Whose maiden blood, thus rigorously effused,
Will cry for vengeance at the gates of heaven.

DUKE OF YORK.
Ay, ay:—away with her to execution!

EARL OF WARWICK.
And hark ye, sirs; because she is a maid,
Spare for no fagots; let there be enow:
Place barrels of pitch upon the fatal stake,
That so her torture may be shortened.

JOAN LA PUCELLE.
Will nothing turn your unrelenting hearts?—
Then, Joan, discover thine infirmity,
That warranteth by law to be thy privilege.—
I am with child, ye bloody homicides:
Murder not, then, the fruit within my womb,
Although ye hale me to a violent death.

DUKE OF YORK.
Now heaven forfend! the holy maid with child!

EARL OF WARWICK.
The greatest miracle that e'er ye wrought:
Is all your strict preciseness come to this?

DUKE OF YORK.
She and the Dauphin have been juggling:
I did imagine what would be her refuge.

EARL OF WARWICK.
Well, go to; we'll have no bastards live;
Especially since Charles must father it.

JOAN LA PUCELLE.
You are deceived; my child is none of his;
It was Alençon that enjoy'd my love.

DUKE OF YORK.
Alençon! that notorious Machiavel!
It dies, an if it had a thousand lives.

JOAN LA PUCELLE.
O, give me leave, I have deluded you:
'Twas neither Charles, nor yet the duke I named,
But Reignier, king of Naples, that prevail'd.

EARL OF WARWICK.
A married man! that's most intolerable.

DUKE OF YORK.
Why, here's a girl! I think she knows not well,
There were so many, whom she may accuse.

EARL OF WARWICK.
It's sign she hath been liberal and free.

DUKE OF YORK.
And yet, forsooth, she is a virgin pure.—
Strumpet, thy words condemn thy brat and thee:
Use no entreaty, for it is in vain.

JOAN LA PUCELLE.
Then lead me hence—with whom I leave my
   curse;
May never glorious sun reflex his beams
Upon the country where you make abode;
But darkness and the gloomy shade of death
Environ you, till mischief and despair
Drive you to break your necks or hang yourselves!
                              [Exit, guarded.

DUKE OF YORK.
Break thou in pieces, and consume to ashes,
Thou foul accursed minister of hell!

Enter CARDINAL BEAUFORT, attended.

CARDINAL BEAUFORT.
Lord regent, I do greet your excellence
With letters of commission from the king.
For know, my lords, the states of Christendom,
Moved with remorse of these outrageous broils,
Have earnestly implored a general peace
Betwixt our nation and the aspiring French;
And here at hand the Dauphin and his train
Approacheth, to confer about some matter.

DUKE OF YORK.
Is all our travail turn'd to this effect?
After the slaughter of so many peers,
So many captains, gentlemen, and soldiers,
That in this quarrel have been overthrown,

28

And sold their bodies for their country's benefit,
Shall we at last conclude effeminate peace?
Have we not lost most part of all the towns,
By treason, falsehood, and by treachery,
Our great progenitors had conquered?—
O, Warwick, Warwick! I foresee with grief
The utter loss of all the realm of France.

          EARL OF WARWICK.
Be patient, York: if we conclude a peace,
It shall be with such strict and severe covenants
As little shall the Frenchmen gain thereby.

    Enter CHARLES, ALENÇON, BASTARD, REI-
        GNIER, and others.

          CHARLES.
Since, lords of England, it is thus agreed
That peaceful truce shall be proclaim'd in
   France,
We come to be informed by yourselves
What the conditions of that league must be.

          DUKE OF YORK.
Speak, Winchester; for boiling choler chokes
The hollow passage of my prison'd voice,
By sight of these our baleful enemies.

          CARDINAL BEAUFORT.
Charles, and the rest, it is enacted thus:
That, in regard King Henry gives consent,
Of mere compassion and of lenity,
To ease your country of distressed war,
And suffer you to breathe in fruitful peace,—
You shall become true liegemen to his crown:
And, Charles, upon condition thou wilt swear
To pay him tribute, and submit thyself,
Thou shalt be placed as viceroy under him,
And still enjoy thy regal dignity.

          DUKE OF ALENÇON.
Must he be, then, a shadow of himself?
Adorn his temples with a coronet,
And yet, in substance and authority,
Retain but privilege of a private man?
This proffer is absurd and reasonless.

          CHARLES.
'Tis known already that I am possest
With more than half the Gallian territories,
And therein reverenced for their lawful king:
Shall I, for lucre of the rest unvanquisht,
Detract so much from that prerogative,
As to be call'd but viceroy of the whole?
No, lord ambassador; I'll rather keep
That which I have than, coveting for more,
Be cast from possibility of all.

          DUKE OF YORK.
Insulting Charles! hast thou by secret means
Used intercession to obtain a league,
And, now the matter grows to compromise,
Stand'st thou aloof upon comparison?
Either accept the title thou usurp'st,
Of benefit proceeding from our king,
And not of any challenge of desert,
Or we will plague thee with incessant wars.

       REIGNIER [aside to CHARLES].
My lord, you do not well in obstinacy
To cavil in the course of this contract:
If once it be neglected, ten to one
We shall not find like opportunity.

     DUKE OF ALENÇON [aside to CHARLES].
To say the truth, it is your policy

To save your subjects from such massacre
And ruthless slaughters as are daily seen
By our proceeding in hostility;
And therefore take this compact of a truce,
Although you break it when your pleasure serves.

          EARL OF WARWICK.
How say'st thou, Charles? shall our condition
   stand?

          CHARLES.
It shall;
Only reserved, you claim no interest
In any of our towns of garrison.

          DUKE OF YORK.
Then swear allegiance to his majesty;
As thou art knight, never to disobey
Nor be rebellious to the crown of England,—
Thou, nor thy nobles, to the crown of England.
So, now dismiss your army when ye please;
Hang up your ensigns, let your drums be still,
For here we entertain a solemn peace.   [Exeunt.

          SCENE V.

     London.   The royal palace.

  Enter SUFFOLK in conference with the KING;
      GLOSTER and EXETER.

          KING HENRY.
YOUR wondrous rare description, noble earl,
   Of beauteous Margaret hath astonisht me:
Her virtues, graced with external gifts,
Do breed love's settled passions in my heart:
And like as rigour of tempestuous gusts
Provokes the mightiest hulk against the tide,
So am I driven, by breath of her renown,
Either to suffer shipwrack, or arrive
Where I may have fruition of her love.

          EARL OF SUFFOLK.
Tush, my good lord,—this superficial tale
Is but a preface of her worthy praise;
The chief perfections of that lovely dame—
Had I sufficient skill to utter them—
Would make a volume of enticing lines,
Able to ravish any dull conceit:
And, which is more, she is not so divine,
So full-replete with choice of all delights,
But, with as humble lowliness of mind,
She is content to be at your command;
Command, I mean, of virtuous chaste intents,
To love and honour Henry as her lord.

          KING HENRY.
And otherwise will Henry ne'er presume.
Therefore, my lord Protector, give consent
That Margaret may be England's royal queen.

          DUKE OF GLOSTER.
So should I give consent to flatter sin.
You know, my lord, your highness is betroth'd
Unto another lady of esteem:
How shall we, then, dispense with that contract,
And not deface your honour with reproach?

          EARL OF SUFFOLK.
As doth a ruler with unlawful oaths;
Or one that, at a triumph having vow'd
To try his strength, forsaketh yet the lists
By reason of his adversary's odds:
A poor earl's daughter is unequal odds,
And therefore may be broke without offence.

DUKE OF GLOSTER.
Why, what, I pray, is Margaret more than that?
Her father is no better than an earl,
Although in glorious titles he excel.

EARL OF SUFFOLK.
Yes, my lord, her father is a king,
The King of Naples and Jerusalem;
And of such great authority in France,
As his alliance will confirm our peace,
And keep the Frenchmen in allegiance.

DUKE OF GLOSTER.
And so the Earl of Armagnac may do,
Because he is near kinsman unto Charles.

DUKE OF EXETER.
Beside, his wealth doth warrant a liberal dower,
Where Reignier sooner will receive than give.

EARL OF SUFFOLK.
A dower, my lords! disgrace not so your king,
That he should be so abject, base, and poor,
To choose for wealth and not for perfect love.
Henry is able to enrich his queen,
And not to seek a queen to make him rich:
So worthless peasants bargain for their wives,
As market-men for oxen, sheep, or horse.
Marriage is a matter of more worth
Than to be dealt in by attorneyship;
Not whom we will, but whom his Grace affects,
Must be companion of his nuptial bed:
And therefore, lords, since he affects her most,
It most of all these reasons bindeth us,
In our opinions she should be preferr'd.
For what is wedlock forced but a hell,
An age of discord and continual strife?
Whereas the contrary bringeth bliss,
And is a pattern of celestial peace.
Whom should we match with Henry, being a king,
But Margaret, that is daughter of a king?
Her peerless feature, joined with her birth,
Approves her fit for none but for a king:
Her valiant courage and undaunted spirit—
More than in women commonly is seen—
Will answer our hope in issue of a king;

For Henry, son unto a conqueror,
Is likely to beget more conquerors,
If with a lady of so high resolve
As is fair Margaret he be linkt in love.
Then yield, my lords; and here conclude with me
That Margaret shall be queen, and none but she.

KING HENRY.
Whether it be through force of your report,
My noble Lord of Suffolk, or for that
My tender youth was never yet attaint
With any passion of inflaming love,
I cannot tell; but this I am assured,
I feel such sharp dissension in my breast,
Such fierce alarums both of hope and fear,
As I am sick with working of my thoughts.
Take, therefore, shipping; post, my lord, to
   France;
Agree to any covenants; and procure
That Lady Margaret do vouchsafe to come
To cross the seas to England, and be crown'd
King Henry's faithful and anointed queen:
For your expenses and sufficient charge,
Among the people gather up a tenth.
Be gone, I say; for, till you do return,
I rest perplexed with a thousand cares.—
And you, good uncle, banish all offence:
If you do censure me by what you were,
Not what you are, I know it will excuse
This sudden execution of my will.
And so, conduct me where, from company,
I may revolve and ruminate my grief.   [*Exit.*

DUKE OF GLOSTER.
Ay, grief, I fear me, both at first and last.
            [*Exeunt* GLOSTER *and* EXETER.

EARL OF SUFFOLK.
Thus Suffolk hath prevail'd; and thus he goes,
As did the youthful Paris once to Greece,
With hope to find the like event in love,
But prosper better than the Trojan did.
Margaret shall now be queen, and rule the king;
But I will rule both her, the king, and realm.
                                        [*Exit.*

THE SECOND PART OF
KING HENRY THE SIXTH

DRAMATIS PERSONAE

KING HENRY THE SIXTH.
HUMPHREY, *Duke of Gloster, his uncle.*
CARDINAL BEAUFORT, *Bishop of Winchester, great-uncle to the King.*
RICHARD PLANTAGENET, *Duke of York.*
EDWARD *and* RICHARD, *his sons.*
DUKE OF SOMERSET.
DUKE OF SUFFOLK.
DUKE OF BUCKINGHAM.
LORD CLIFFORD.
YOUNG CLIFFORD, *his son.*
EARL OF SALISBURY.
EARL OF WARWICK.
LORD SCALES.
LORD SAY.
SIR HUMPHREY STAFFORD, *and* WILLIAM STAFFORD, *his brother.*
SIR JOHN STANLEY.
VAUX.
MATTHEW GOUGH.
A SEA-CAPTAIN, MASTER, *and* MASTER'S-MATE, *and* WALTER WHITMORE.
TWO GENTLEMEN, *prisoners with Suffolk.*
ALEXANDER IDEN, *a Kentish gentleman.*

JOHN HUME *and* JOHN SOUTHWELL, *two priests.*
ROGER BOLINGBROKE, *a conjurer.*
THOMAS HORNER, *an armorer.* PETER, *his man.*
CLERK OF CHATHAM.
MAYOR OF SAINT ALBAN'S.
SAUNDER SIMPCOX, *an impostor.*
JACK CADE, *a rebel.*
GEORGE BEVIS, JOHN HOLLAND, DICK *the butcher,* SMITH *the weaver,* MICHAEL, *&c., his followers.*
TWO MURDERERS.

MARGARET, *Queen to King Henry.*
ELEANOR, *Duchess of Gloster.*
MARGERY JOURDAIN, *a witch.*
WIFE *to Simpcox.*

LORDS, LADIES, *and* ATTENDANTS, PETITIONERS, ALDERMEN, *a* HERALD, *a* BEADLE, SHERIFF, *and* OFFICERS, CITIZENS, PRENTICES, FALCONERS, GUARDS, SOLDIERS, MESSENGERS, *&c.*
A SPIRIT.

SCENE—*In various parts of England.*

ACT I. SCENE I.

London. A room of state in the palace.

Flourish of trumpets: then hautboys. Enter the KING, DUKE OF GLOSTER, SALISBURY, WARWICK, *and* CARDINAL BEAUFORT, *on the one side; the* QUEEN, SUFFOLK, YORK, SOMERSET, *and* BUCKINGHAM, *on the other.*

DUKE OF SUFFOLK.
AS by your high imperial majesty
I had in charge at my depart for France,
As procurator to your excellence,
To marry Princess Margaret for your Grace;
So, in the famous ancient city Tours,
In presence of the Kings of France and Sicil,
The Dukes of Orleans, Calaber, Bretagne, and
Alençon,
Seven earls, twelve barons, and twenty reverend
bishops,
I have perform'd my task, and was espoused:
And humbly now, upon my bended knee,
In sight of England and her lordly peers,
Deliver up my title in the queen
To your most gracious hands, that are the sub-
stance
Of that great shadow I did represent;
The happiest gift that ever marquess gave,
The fairest queen that ever king received.
KING HENRY.
Suffolk, arise.—Welcome, Queen Margaret:
I can express no kinder sign of love
Than this kind kiss.—O Lord, that lends me life,
Lend me a heart replete with thankfulness!

For Thou hast given me, in this beauteous face,
A world of earthly blessings to my soul,
If sympathy of love unite our thoughts.
QUEEN MARGARET.
Great King of England, and my gracious lord,—
The mutual conference that my mind hath had,
By day, by night, waking and in my dreams,
In courtly company or at my beads,
With you, mine alder-liefest sovereign,
Makes me the bolder to salute my king
With ruder terms, such as my wit affords
And over-joy of heart doth minister.
KING HENRY.
Her sight did ravish; but her grace in speech,
Her words yclad with wisdom's majesty,
Make me from wondering fall to weeping joys;
Such is the fulness of my heart's content.—
Lords, with one cheerful voice welcome my love.
ALL [*kneeling*].
Long live Queen Margaret, England's happiness!
[*Flourish.*
QUEEN MARGARET.
We thank you all.
DUKE OF SUFFOLK.
My lord Protector, so it please your Grace,
Here are the articles of contracted peace
Between our sovereign and the French king
Charles.
For eighteen months concluded by consent.
DUKE OF GLOSTER [*reads*].
Imprimis, It is agreed between the French king
Charles, and William de la Pole, marquess of
Suffolk, ambassador for Henry King of England,

—that the said Henry shall espouse the Lady
Margaret, daughter unto Reignier King of Naples,
Sicilia, and Jerusalem; and crown her Queen of
England ere the thirtieth of May next ensuing.
Item, that the duchy of Anjou and the county of
Maine shall be released and deliver'd to the king
her father—　　　　　　　[*Lets the paper fall.*

KING HENRY.
Uncle, how now!

DUKE OF GLOSTER.
　　　　　Pardon me, gracious lord;
Some sudden qualm hath struck me at the heart,
And dimm'd mine eyes, that I can read no further.

KING HENRY.
Uncle of Winchester, I pray, read on.

CARDINAL BEAUFORT [*reads*].
Item, It is further agreed between them, that the
duchies of Anjou and Maine shall be released
and deliver'd over to the king her father; and
she sent over of the King of England's own
proper cost and charges, without having any
dowry.

KING HENRY.
They please us well.—Lord marquess, kneel
　　down:
We here create thee the first Duke of Suffolk,
And girt thee with the sword.—Cousin of York,
We here discharge your Grace from being regent
I' th' parts of France, till term of eighteen months
Be full expired.—Thanks, uncle Winchester,
Gloster, York, Buckingham, Somerset,
Salisbury, and Warwick;
We thank you all for this great favour done,
In entertainment to my princely queen.
Come, let us in; and with all speed provide
To see her coronation be perform'd.
　　　　[*Exeunt* KING, QUEEN, *and* SUFFOLK.

DUKE OF GLOSTER.
Brave peers of England, pillars of the state,
To you Duke Humphrey must unload his grief,—
Your grief, the common grief of all the land.
What! did my brother Henry spend his youth,
His valour, coin, and people in the wars?
Did he so often lodge in open field
In winter's cold and summer's parching heat,
To conquer France, his true inheritance?
And did my brother Bedford toil his wits,
To keep by policy what Henry got?
Have you yourselves, Somerset, Buckingham,
Brave York, Salisbury, and victorious Warwick,
Received deep scars in France and Normandy?
Or hath mine uncle Beaufort and myself,
With all the learned council of the realm,
Studied so long, sat in the council-house
Early and late, debating to and fro
How France and Frenchmen might be kept in
　　awe?
And was his highness in his infancy
Crowned in Paris in despite of foes?
And shall these labours and these honours die?
Shall Henry's conquest, Bedford's vigilance,
Your deeds of war, and all our counsel die?
O peers of England, shameful is this league!
Fatal this marriage! cancelling your fame,
Blotting your name from books of memory,
Razing the characters of your renown,

Defacing monuments of conquer'd France,
Undoing all, as all had never been!

CARDINAL BEAUFORT.
Nephew, what means this passionate discourse,
This peroration with such circumstance?
For France, 'tis ours; and we will keep it still.

DUKE OF GLOSTER.
Ay, uncle, we will keep it, if we can;
But now it is impossible we should:
Suffolk, the new-made duke that rules the roast,
Hath given the duchies of Anjou and Maine
Unto the poor King Reignier, whose large style
Agrees not with the leanness of his purse.

EARL OF SALISBURY.
Now, by the death of Him that died for all,
These counties were the keys of Normandy:—
But wherefore weeps Warwick, my valiant son?

EARL OF WARWICK.
For grief that they are past recovery:
For, were there hope to conquer them again,
My sword should shed hot blood, mine eyes no
　　tears.
Anjou and Maine! myself did win them both;
Those provinces these arms of mine did conquer:
And are the cities, that I got with wounds,
Deliver'd up again with peaceful words?
Mort Dieu!

DUKE OF YORK.
For Suffolk's duke, may he be suffocate,
That dims the honour of this warlike isle!
France should have torn and rent my very heart,
Before I would have yielded to this league.
I never read but England's kings have had
Large sums of gold and dowries with their wives;
And our King Henry gives away his own,
To match with her that brings no vantages.

DUKE OF GLOSTER.
A proper jest, and never heard before,
That Suffolk should demand a whole fifteenth
For costs and charges in transporting her!
She should have stay'd in France, and starved in
　　France,
Before—

CARDINAL BEAUFORT.
My Lord of Gloster, now ye grow too hot:
It was the pleasure of my lord the king.

DUKE OF GLOSTER.
My Lord of Winchester, I know your mind;
'Tis not my speeches that you do mislike,
But 'tis my presence that doth trouble ye.
Rancour will out: proud prelate, in thy face
I see thy fury: if I longer stay,
We shall begin our ancient bickerings.—
Lordings, farewell; and say, when I am gone,
I prophesied—France will be lost ere long. [*Exit.*

CARDINAL BEAUFORT.
So, there goes our Protector in a rage.
'Tis known to you he is mine enemy;
Nay, more, an enemy unto you all;
And no great friend, I fear me, to the king.
Consider, lords, he is the next of blood,
And heir-apparent to the English crown:
Had Henry got an empire by his marriage,
And all the wealthy kingdoms of the west,
There's reason he should be displeased at it.
Look to it, lords; let not his smoothing words

Bewitch your hearts; be wise and circumspect.
What though the common people favour him,
Calling him 'Humphrey, the good Duke of
    Gloster;'
Clapping their hands, and crying with loud
    voice,
'Jesu maintain your royal excellence!'
With 'God preserve the good Duke Humphrey!'
I fear me, lords, for all this flattering gloss,
He will be found a dangerous Protector.

DUKE OF BUCKINGHAM.

Why should he, then, protect our sovereign,
He being of age to govern of himself?—
Cousin of Somerset, join you with me,
And all together, with the Duke of Suffolk,
We'll quickly hoise Duke Humphrey from his
    seat.

CARDINAL BEAUFORT.

This weighty business will not brook delay;
I'll to the Duke of Suffolk presently.   [*Exit.*

DUKE OF SOMERSET.

Cousin of Buckingham, though Humphrey's
    pride
And greatness of his place be grief to us,
Yet let us watch the haughty cardinal:
His insolence is more intolerable
Than all the princes in the land beside:
If Gloster be displaced, he'll be Protector.

DUKE OF BUCKINGHAM.

Or thou or I, Somerset, will be Protector,
Despite Duke Humphrey or the cardinal.
    [*Exeunt* BUCKINGHAM *and* SOMERSET.

EARL OF SALISBURY.

Pride went before, ambition follows him.
While these do labour for their own preferment,
Behoves it us to labour for the realm.
I never saw but Humphrey duke of Gloster
Did bear him like a noble gentleman.
Oft have I seen the haughty cardinal—
More like a soldier than a man o' th' church,
As stout and proud as he were lord of all—
Swear like a ruffian, and demean himself
Unlike the ruler of a commonweal.—
Warwick, my son, the comfort of my age,
Thy deeds, thy plainness, and thy housekeep-
    ing,
Have won the greatest favour of the commons,
Excepting none but good Duke Humphrey:—
And, brother York, thy acts in Ireland,
In bringing them to civil discipline;
Thy late exploits done in the heart of France,
When thou wert regent for our sovereign,
Have made thee fear'd and honour'd of the
    people:—
Join we together, for the public good,
In what we can, to bridle and suppress
The pride of Suffolk and the cardinal,
With Somerset's and Buckingham's ambition;
And, as we may, cherish Duke Humphrey's
    deeds,
While they do tend the profit of the land.

EARL OF WARWICK.

So God help Warwick, as he loves the land,
And common profit of his country!

DUKE OF YORK [*aside*].

And so says York, for he hath greatest cause.

EARL OF SALISBURY.

Then let's make haste away, and look unto the
    main.

EARL OF WARWICK.

Unto the main! O father, Maine is lost,—
That Maine which by main force Warwick did
    win,
And would have kept so long as breath did last!
Main chance, father, you meant; but I meant
    Maine,—
Which I will win from France, or else be slain.
    [*Exeunt* WARWICK *and* SALISBURY.

DUKE OF YORK.

Anjou and Maine are given to the French;
Paris is lost; the state of Normandy
Stands on a tickle point, now they are gone:
Suffolk concluded on the articles;
The peers agreed; and Henry was well pleased
To change two dukedoms for a duke's fair
    daughter.
I cannot blame them all: what is't to them?
'Tis thine they give away, and not their own.
Pirates may make cheap pennyworths of their
    pillage,
And purchase friends, and give to courtezans,
Still revelling, like lords, till all be gone;
While as the silly owner of the goods
Weeps over them, and wrings his hapless hands,
And shakes his head, and trembling stands aloof,
While all is shared, and all is borne away,
Ready to starve, and dare not touch his own:
So York must sit, and fret, and bite his tongue,
While his own lands are bargain'd for and sold.
Methinks the realms of England, France, and
    Ireland
Bear that proportion to my flesh and blood
As did the fatal brand Althæa burn'd
Unto the prince's heart of Calydon.
Anjou and Maine, both given unto the French!
Cold news for me; for I had hope of France,
Even as I have of fertile England's soil.
A day will come when York shall claim his own;
And therefore I will take the Nevils' parts,
And make a show of love to proud Duke Hum-
    phrey,
And, when I spy advantage, claim the crown,
For that's the golden mark I seek to hit:
Nor shall proud Lancaster usurp my right,
Nor hold the sceptre in his childish fist,
Nor wear the diadem upon his head,
Whose church-like humours fits not for a crown.
Then, York, be still awhile, till time do serve:
Watch thou and wake, when others be asleep,
To pry into the secrets of the state;
Till Henry, surfeiting in joys of love,
With his new bride and England's dear-bought
    queen,
And Humphrey with the peers be faln at jars:
Then will I raise aloft the milk-white rose,
With whose sweet smell the air shall be perfumed;
And in my standard bear the arms of York,
To grapple with the house of Lancaster;
And, force perforce, I'll make him yield the
    crown,
Whose bookish rule hath pull'd fair England
    down.   [*Exit.*

SCENE II.

The same.   *The* DUKE OF GLOSTER'S *house.*

Enter DUKE HUMPHREY *and his Wife* ELEANOR.

DUCHESS OF GLOSTER.

WHY droops my lord, like over-ripen'd corn
    Hanging the head at Ceres' plenteous load?
Why doth the great Duke Humphrey knit his
    brows,
As frowning at the favours of the world?
Why are thine eyes fixt to the sullen earth,
Gazing on that which seems to dim thy sight?
What seest thou there? King Henry's diadem,
Enchased with all the honours of the world?
If so, gaze on, and grovel on thy face,
Until thy head be circled with the same.
Put forth thy hand, reach at the glorious gold:—
What, is't too short? I'll lengthen it with mine;
And, having both together heaved it up,
We'll both together lift our heads to heaven,
And never more abase our sight so low
As to vouchsafe one glance unto the ground.

DUKE OF GLOSTER.

O Nell, sweet Nell, if thou dost love thy lord,
Banish the canker of ambitious thoughts!
And may that thought, when I imagine ill
Against my king and nephew, virtuous Henry,
Be my last breathing in this mortal world!
My troublous dream this night doth make me sad.

DUCHESS OF GLOSTER.

What dream'd my lord? tell me, and I'll requite
    it
With sweet rehearsal of my morning's dream.

DUKE OF GLOSTER.

Methought this staff, mine office-badge in court,
Was broke in twain; by whom I have forgot,
But, as I think, 'twas by the cardinal;
And on the pieces of the broken wand
Were placed the heads of Edmund duke of
    Somerset,
And William de la Pole, first duke of Suffolk.
This was my dream: what it doth bode, God
    knows.

DUCHESS OF GLOSTER.

Tut, this was nothing but an argument
That he that breaks a stick of Gloster's grove
Shall lose his head for his presumption.
But list to me, my Humphrey, my sweet duke:
Methought I sat in seat of majesty
In the cathedral church of Westminster,
And in that chair where kings and queens are
    crown'd;
Where Henry and Dame Margaret kneel'd to
    me,
And on my head did set the diadem.

DUKE OF GLOSTER.

Nay, Eleanor, then must I chide outright:
Presumptuous dame, ill-nurtured Eleanor!
Art thou not second woman in the realm,
And the Protector's wife, beloved of him?
Hast thou not worldly pleasure at command,
Above the reach or compass of thy thought?
And wilt thou still be hammering treachery,
To tumble down thy husband and thyself
From top of honour to disgrace's feet?
Away from me, and let me hear no more!

DUCHESS OF GLOSTER.

What, what, my lord! are you so choleric
With Eleanor, for telling but her dream?
Next time I'll keep my dreams unto myself,
And not be checkt.

DUKE OF GLOSTER.

Nay, be not angry, I am pleased again.

Enter a MESSENGER.

MESSENGER.

My lord Protector, 'tis his highness' pleasure
You do prepare to ride unto Saint Alban's,
Whereas the king and queen do mean to hawk.

DUKE OF GLOSTER.

I go.—Come, Nell,—thou wilt ride with us, I'm
    sure.

DUCHESS OF GLOSTER.

Yes, my good lord, I'll follow presently.

    [*Exeunt* GLOSTER *and* MESSENGER.

Follow I must; I cannot go before,
While Gloster bears this base and humble mind.
Were I a man, a duke, and next of blood,
I would remove these tedious stumbling-blocks,
And smooth my way upon their headless necks;
And, being a woman, I will not be slack
To play my part in Fortune's pageant.—
Where are you there, Sir John? nay, fear not, man,
We are alone; here's none but thee and I.

Enter HUME.

JOHN HUME.

Jesus preserve your royal majesty!

DUCHESS OF GLOSTER.

What say'st thou? majesty! I am but grace.

JOHN HUME.

But, by the grace of God, and Hume's advice,
Your Grace's title shall be multiplied.

DUCHESS OF GLOSTER.

What say'st thou, man? hast thou as yet con-
    ferr'd
With Margery Jourdain, the cunning witch,
With Roger Bolingbroke, the conjurer?
And will they undertake to do me good?

JOHN HUME.

This they have promised,—to show your high-
    ness
A spirit raised from depth of under-ground,
That shall make answer to such questions
As by your Grace shall be propounded him.

DUCHESS OF GLOSTER.

It is enough; I'll think upon the questions:
When from Saint Alban's we do make return,
We'll see these things effected to the full.
Here, Hume, take this reward; make merry, man,
With thy confederates in this weighty cause.
    [*Exit.*

JOHN HUME.

Hume must make merry with the duchess' gold;
Marry, and shall. But, how now, Sir John Hume!
Seal up your lips, and give no words but mum:
The business asketh silent secrecy.
Dame Eleanor gives gold to bring the witch:
Gold cannot come amiss, were she a devil.
Yet have I gold flies from another coast:—
I dare not say, from the rich cardinal,
And from the great and new-made Duke of
    Suffolk;
Yet I do find it so: for, to be plain,

34

They, knowing Dame Eleanor's aspiring humour,
Have hired me to undermine the duchess,
And buzz these conjurations in her brain.
They say,—A crafty knave does need no broker;
Yet am I Suffolk and the cardinal's broker.
Hume, if you take not heed, you shall go near
To call them both a pair of crafty knaves.
Well, so it stands; and thus, I fear, at last
Hume's knavery will be the duchess' wrack,
And her attainture will be Humphrey's fall:
Sort how it will, I shall have gold for all.   [*Exit.*

SCENE III.

The same. The palace.

Enter PETER, *and other* PETITIONERS.

FIRST PETITIONER.
MY masters, let's stand close: my lord Protector will come this way by and by, and
then we may deliver our supplications in the quill.

SECOND PETITIONER.
Marry, the Lord protect him, for he's a good
man! Jesu bless him!

PETER.
Here 'a comes, methinks, and the queen with him.
I'll be the first, sure.

Enter SUFFOLK *and* QUEEN.

SECOND PETITIONER.
Come back, fool; this is the Duke of Suffolk, and
not my lord Protector.

DUKE OF SUFFOLK.
How now, fellow! wouldst any thing with me?

FIRST PETITIONER.
I pray, my lord, pardon me; I took ye for my lord
Protector.

QUEEN MARGARET.
For my lord Protector! Are your supplications to
his lordship? Let me see them:—what is thine?

FIRST PETITIONER.
Mine is, an't please your Grace, against John
Goodman, my lord cardinal's man, for keeping
my house, and lands, and wife and all, from me.

DUKE OF SUFFOLK.
Thy wife too! that's some wrong, indeed.—
What's yours?—What's here! [*reads*] 'Against
the Duke of Suffolk, for enclosing the commons
of Melford.'—How now, sir knave!

SECOND PETITIONER.
Alas, sir, I am but a poor petitioner of our whole
township.

PETER [*presenting his petition*].
Against my master, Thomas Horner, for saying
that the Duke of York was rightful heir to the
crown.

QUEEN MARGARET.
What say'st thou? did the Duke of York say he
was rightful heir to the crown?

PETER.
That my master was? no, forsooth: my master
said that he was; and that the king was an usurper.

DUKE OF SUFFOLK.
Who is there? [*Enter* SERVANT.]—Take this
fellow in, and send for his master with a pursuivant presently.—We'll hear more of your
matter before the king.

[*Exit* SERVANT *with* PETER.

QUEEN MARGARET.
And as for you, that love to be protected
Under the wings of our Protector's Grace,
Begin your suits anew, and sue to him.
[*Tears the supplications.*
Away, base cullions!—Suffolk, let them go.

ALL.
Come, let's be gone.   [*Exeunt* PETITIONERS.

QUEEN MARGARET.
My Lord of Suffolk, say, is this the guise,
Is this the fashion in the court of England?
Is this the government of Britain's isle,
And this the royalty of Albion's king?
What, shall King Henry be a pupil still,
Under the surly Gloster's governance?
Am I a queen in title and in style,
And must be made a subject to a duke?
I tell thee, Pole, when in the city Tours
Thou rann'st a tilt in honour of my love,
And stolest away the ladies' hearts of France,
I thought King Henry had resembled thee
In courage, courtship, and proportion:
But all his mind is bent to holiness,
To number *Ave-Maries* on his beads:
His champions are the prophets and apostles;
His weapons, holy saws of sacred writ;
His study is his tilt-yard, and his loves
Are brazen images of canonized saints.
I would the college of the cardinals
Would choose him Pope, and carry him to Rome,
And set the triple crown upon his head:—
That were a state fit for his holiness.

DUKE OF SUFFOLK.
Madam, be patient: as I was cause
Your highness came to England, so will I
In England work your Grace's full content.

QUEEN MARGARET.
Beside the haught Protector, have we Beaufort
The imperious churchman, Somerset, Bucking-
ham,
And grumbling York; and not the least of these
But can do more in England than the king.

DUKE OF SUFFOLK.
And he of these that can do most of all
Cannot do more in England than the Nevils:
Salisbury and Warwick are no simple peers.

QUEEN MARGARET.
Not all these lords do vex me half so much
As that proud dame, the lord Protector's wife.
She sweeps it through the court with troops of
ladies,
More like an empress than Duke Humphrey's
wife:
Strangers in court do take her for the queen:
She bears a duke's revenues on her back,
And in her heart she scorns our poverty:
Shall I not live to be avenged on her?
Contemptuous base-born callet as she is,
She vaunted 'mongst her minions t' other day,
The very train of her worst wearing gown
Was better worth than all my father's lands,
Till Suffolk gave two dukedoms for his daughter.

DUKE OF SUFFOLK.
Madam, myself have limed a bush for her,
And placed a quire of such enticing birds,
That she will light to listen to the lays,

And never mount to trouble you again.
So, let her rest: and, madam, list to me;
For I am bold to counsel you in this.
Although we fancy not the cardinal,
Yet must we join with him and with the lords,
Till we have brought Duke Humphrey in dis-
grace.
As for the Duke of York,—this late complaint
Will make but little for his benefit.
So, one by one, we'll weed them all at last,
And you yourself shall steer the happy helm.
Sound a sennet.   Enter the KING, DUKE HUM-
PHREY, CARDINAL BEAUFORT, BUCKING-
HAM, YORK, SOMERSET, SALISBURY, WAR-
WICK, *and the* DUCHESS OF GLOSTER.
KING HENRY.
For my part, noble lords, I care not which;
Or Somerset or York, all's one to me.
DUKE OF YORK.
If York have ill demean'd himself in France,
Then let him be denay'd the regentship.
DUKE OF SOMERSET.
If Somerset be unworthy of the place,
Let York be regent; I will yield to him.
EARL OF WARWICK.
Whether your Grace be worthy, yea or no,
Dispute not that: York is the worthier.
CARDINAL BEAUFORT.
Ambitious Warwick, let thy betters speak.
EARL OF WARWICK.
The cardinal's not my better in the field.
DUKE OF BUCKINGHAM.
All in this presence are thy betters, Warwick.
EARL OF WARWICK.
Warwick may live to be the best of all.
EARL OF SALISBURY.
Peace, son!—and show some reason, Bucking-
ham,
Why Somerset should be preferr'd in this.
QUEEN MARGARET.
Because the king, forsooth, will have it so.
DUKE OF GLOSTER.
Madam, the king is old enough himself
To give his censure: these are no women's
matters.
QUEEN MARGARET.
If he be old enough, what needs your Grace
To be Protector of his excellence?
DUKE OF GLOSTER.
Madam, I am Protector of the realm;
And, at his pleasure, will resign my place.
DUKE OF SUFFOLK.
Resign it, then, and leave thine insolence.
Since thou wert king,—as who is king but thou?—
The commonwealth hath daily run to wrack;
The Dauphin hath prevail'd beyond the seas;
And all the peers and nobles of the realm
Have been as bondmen to thy sovereignty.
CARDINAL BEAUFORT.
The commons hast thou rackt; the clergy's bags
Are lank and lean with thy extortions.
DUKE OF SOMERSET.
Thy sumptuous buildings, and thy wife's attire,
Have cost a mass of public treasury.
DUKE OF BUCKINGHAM.
Thy cruelty in execution

Upon offenders hath exceeded law,
And left thee to the mercy of the law.
QUEEN MARGARET.
Thy sale of offices and towns in France—
If they were known, as the suspect is great—
Would make thee quickly hop without thy head.
[*Exit* GLOSTER.   *The* QUEEN *drops her fan.*
Give me my fan: what, minion! can ye not?
[*She gives the* DUCHESS *a box on the ear.*
I cry you mercy, madam; was it you?
DUCHESS OF GLOSTER.
Was't I! yea, I it was, proud Frenchwoman:
Could I come near your beauty with my nails,
I'ld set my ten commandments in your face.
KING HENRY.
Sweet aunt, be quiet; 'twas against her will.
DUCHESS OF GLOSTER.
Against her will! good king, look to 't in time;
She'll hamper thee, and dandle thee like a baby:
Though in this place most master wear no
breeches,
She shall not strike Dame Eleanor unrevenged.
[*Exit.*
DUKE OF BUCKINGHAM.
Lord cardinal, I will follow Eleanor,
And listen after Humphrey, how he proceeds:
She's tickled now; her fury needs no spurs,
She'll gallop fast enough to her destruction.
[*Exit.*
Enter GLOSTER.
DUKE OF GLOSTER.
Now, lords, my choler being over-blown
With walking once about the quadrangle,
I come to talk of commonwealth affairs.
As for your spiteful false objections,
Prove them, and I lie open to the law:
But God in mercy so deal with my soul,
As I in duty love my king and country!
But, to the matter that we have in hand:—
I say, my sovereign, York is meetest man
To be your regent in the realm of France.
DUKE OF SUFFOLK.
Before we make election, give me leave
To show some reason, of no little force,
That York is most unmeet of any man.
DUKE OF YORK.
I'll tell thee, Suffolk, why I am unmeet:
First, for I cannot flatter thee in pride;
Next, if I be appointed for the place,
My Lord of Somerset will keep me here,
Without discharge, money, or furniture,
Till France be won into the Dauphin's hands:
Last time, I danced attendance on his will
Till Paris was besieged, famisht, and lost.
EARL OF WARWICK.
That can I witness; and a fouler fact
Did never traitor in the land commit.
DUKE OF SUFFOLK.
Peace, headstrong Warwick!
EARL OF WARWICK.
Image of pride, why should I hold my peace?
Enter HORNER, *the Armourer, and his man* PETER,
guarded.
DUKE OF SUFFOLK.
Because here is a man accused of treason:
Pray God the Duke of York excuse himself!

DUKE OF YORK.
Doth any one accuse York for a traitor?
KING HENRY.
What mean'st thou, Suffolk? tell me, what are
these?
DUKE OF SUFFOLK.
Please it your majesty, this is the man
That doth accuse his master of high treason:
His words were these,—that Richard duke of
York
Was rightful heir unto the English crown,
And that your majesty was an usurper.
KING HENRY.
Say, man, were these thy words?
THOMAS HORNER.
An 't shall please your majesty, I never said nor
thought any such matter: God is my witness, I
am falsely accused by the villain.
PETER [holding up his hands].
By these ten bones, my lords, he did speak them
to me in the garret one night, as we were scouring
my Lord of York's armour.
DUKE OF YORK.
Base dunghill villain and mechanical,
I'll have thy head for this thy traitor's speech.—
I do beseech your royal majesty,
Let him have all the rigour of the law.
THOMAS HORNER.
Alas, my lord, hang me, if ever I spake the words.
My accuser is my prentice; and when I did cor-
rect him for his fault the other day, he did vow
upon his knees he would be even with me: I have
good witness of this; therefore, I beseech your
majesty, do not cast away an honest man for a
villain's accusation.
KING HENRY.
Uncle, what shall we say to this in law?
DUKE OF GLOSTER.
This is my doom, my lord, if I may judge:
Let Somerset be regent o'er the French,
Because in York this breeds suspicion;
And let these have a day appointed them
For single combat in convenient place,
For he hath witness of his servant's malice:
This is the law, and this Duke Humphrey's
doom.
KING HENRY.
Then be it so.—My Lord of Somerset,
We make your Grace regent over the French.
DUKE OF SOMERSET.
I humbly thank your royal majesty.
THOMAS HORNER.
And I accept the combat willingly.
PETER.
Alas, my lord, I cannot fight; for God's sake, pity
my case! The spite of man prevaileth against me.
O Lord, have mercy upon me! I shall never be
able to fight a blow: O Lord, my heart!
DUKE OF GLOSTER.
Sirrah, or you must fight, or else be hang'd.
KING HENRY.
Away with them to prison; and the day
Of combat shall be the last of the next
month.—
Come, Somerset, we'll see thee sent away.
[Exeunt.

SCENE IV.

The same. GLOSTER'S *garden.*

Enter MARGERY JOURDAIN, HUME, SOUTH-
WELL, *and* BOLINGBROKE.

JOHN HUME.
COME, my masters; the duchess, I tell you,
expects performance of your promises.
ROGER BOLINGBROKE.
Master Hume, we are therefore provided: will her
ladyship behold and hear our exorcisms?
JOHN HUME.
Ay, what else? fear you not her courage.
ROGER BOLINGBROKE.
I have heard her reported to be a woman of an
invincible spirit: but it shall be convenient,
Master Hume, that you be by her aloft, while we
be busy below; and so, I pray you, go in God's
name, and leave us. [Exit HUME.] Mother Jour-
dain, be you prostrate, and grovel on the earth;—
John Southwell, read you;—and let us to our
work.
Enter DUCHESS *aloft;* HUME *following.*
DUCHESS OF GLOSTER.
Well said, my masters; and welcome all. To this
gear,—the sooner the better.
ROGER BOLINGBROKE.
Patience, good lady; wizards know their times:
Deep night, dark night, the silent of the night,
The time of night when Troy was set on fire;
The time when screech-owls cry, and ban-dogs
howl,
And spirits walk, and ghosts break up their
graves,—
That time best fits the work we have in hand.
Madam, sit you, and fear not: whom we raise,
We will make fast within a hallow'd verge.
[Here do the ceremonies belonging, and make
the circle; BOLINGBROKE or SOUTH-
WELL reads, Conjuro te, &c. It thun-
ders and lightens terribly; then the SPIRIT
riseth.
SPIRIT.
Adsum.
MARGERY JOURDAIN.
Asmath,
By the eternal God, whose name and power
Thou tremblest at, answer that I shall ask;
For, till thou speak, thou shalt not pass from
hence.
SPIRIT.
Ask what thou wilt:—that I had said and done!
ROGER BOLINGBROKE [reading out of a
paper].
'First of the king: what shall of him become?'
SPIRIT.
The duke yet lives that Henry shall depose;
But him outlive, and die a violent death.
[As the SPIRIT speaks, SOUTHWELL
writes the answer.
ROGER BOLINGBROKE.
'What fates await the Duke of Suffolk?'
SPIRIT.
By water shall he die, and take his end.
ROGER BOLINGBROKE.
'What shall befall the Duke of Somerset?'

SPIRIT.
Let him shun castles;
Safer shall he be upon the sandy plains
Than where castles mounted stand.—
Have done, for more I hardly can endure.
ROGER BOLINGBROKE.
Descend to darkness and the burning lake!
False fiend, avoid!
[*Thunder and lightning. Exit* SPIRIT.
Enter the DUKE OF YORK *and the* DUKE OF
BUCKINGHAM, *with their* GUARD, *and break in.*
DUKE OF YORK.
Lay hands upon these traitors and their trash.—
Beldam, I think we watcht you at an inch.—
What, madam, are you there? the king and
commonweal
Are deeply indebted for this piece of pains:
My lord Protector will, I doubt it not,
See you well guerdon'd for these good deserts.
DUCHESS OF GLOSTER.
Not half so bad as thine to England's king.
Injurious duke, that threatest where's no cause.
DUKE OF BUCKINGHAM.
True, madam, none at all:—what call you this?—
[*Showing her the papers.*
Away with them! let them be clapt up close,
And kept asunder.—You, madam, shall with us.—
Stafford, take her to thee.—
We'll see your trinkets here all forthcoming.—
Away!
[*Exeunt, above,* DUCHESS *and* HUME,
guarded. Exeunt, below, SOUTHWEL,
BOLINGBROKE, &c., *guarded.*
DUKE OF YORK.
Lord Buckingham, methinks you watcht her
well:
A pretty plot, well chosen to build upon!
Now, pray, my lord, let's see the devil's writ.
What have we here?   [*Reads.*
'The duke yet lives that Henry shall depose;
But him outlive, and die a violent death.'
Why, this is just
Aio te, Æacida, Romanos vincere posse.
Well, to the rest:
'Tell me what fate awaits the Duke of Suffolk?
By water shall he die, and take his end.—
What shall betide the Duke of Somerset?
Let him shun castles;
Safer shall he be upon the sandy plains
Than where castles mounted stand.'
Come, come, my lords;
These oracles are hardly attain'd,
And hardly understood.
The king is now in progress towards Saint
Alban's,
With him the husband of this lovely lady:
Thither goes these news, as fast as horse can
carry them,—
A sorry breakfast for my lord Protector.
DUKE OF BUCKINGHAM.
Your Grace shall give me leave, my Lord of
York,
To be the post, in hope of his reward.
DUKE OF YORK.
At your pleasure, my good lord.—Who's within
there, ho!

Enter a SERVANT.
Invite my Lords of Salisbury and Warwick
To sup with me to-morrow night.—Away!
[*Exeunt.*

ACT II. SCENE I.
Saint Alban's.

Enter the KING, QUEEN, GLOSTER, CARDINAL,
and SUFFOLK, *with* FALCONERS *hallooing.*
QUEEN MARGARET.
BELIEVE me, lords, for flying at the brook,
I saw not better sport these seven years' day:
Yet, by your leave, the wind was very high;
And, ten to one, old Joan had not gone out.
KING HENRY.
But what a point, my lord, your falcon made,
And what a pitch she flew above the rest!—
To see how God in all His creatures works!
Yea, man and birds are fain of climbing high.
DUKE OF SUFFOLK.
No marvel, an it like your majesty,
My lord Protector's hawks do tower so well;
They know their master loves to be aloft,
And bears his thoughts above his falcon's pitch.
DUKE OF GLOSTER.
My lord, 'tis but a base ignoble mind
That mounts no higher than a bird can soar.
CARDINAL BEAUFORT.
I thought as much: he would be above the
clouds.
DUKE OF GLOSTER.
Ay, my lord cardinal,—how think you by that?
Were it not good your Grace could fly to heaven?
KING HENRY.
The treasury of everlasting joy!
CARDINAL BEAUFORT.
Thy heaven is on earth; thine eyes and thoughts
Beat on a crown, the treasure of thy heart;
Pernicious Protector, dangerous peer,
That smooth'st it so with king and commonweal!
DUKE OF GLOSTER.
What, cardinal, is your priesthood grown per-
emptory?
Tantæne animis cælestibus iræ?
Churchmen so hot? good uncle, hide such malice;
With such holiness can you not do it?
DUKE OF SUFFOLK.
No malice, sir; no more than well becomes
So good a quarrel and so bad a peer.
DUKE OF GLOSTER.
As who, my lord?
DUKE OF SUFFOLK.
Why, as you, my lord,
An 't like your lordly lord-Protectorship.
DUKE OF GLOSTER.
Why, Suffolk, England knows thine insolence.
QUEEN MARGARET.
And thy ambition, Gloster.
KING HENRY.
I prithee, peace,
Good queen, and whet not on these furious peers;
For blessed are the peacemakers on earth.
CARDINAL BEAUFORT.
Let me be blessed for the peace I make,
Against this proud Protector, with my sword!

38

DUKE OF GLOSTER [*aside to* CARDINAL].
Faith, holy uncle, would 'twere come to that!
CARDINAL BEAUFORT [*aside to* GLOSTER].
Marry, when thou darest.
DUKE OF GLOSTER [*aside to* CARDINAL].
Make up no factious numbers for the matter;
In thine own person answer thy abuse.
CARDINAL BEAUFORT [*aside to* GLOSTER].
Ay, where thou darest not peep: an if thou
    darest,
This evening on the east side of the grove.
KING HENRY.
How now, my lords!
CARDINAL BEAUFORT.
                Believe me, cousin Gloster,
Had not your man put up the fowl so suddenly,
We had had more sport.—[*aside to* GLOSTER]
    Come with thy two-hand sword.
DUKE OF GLOSTER.
True, uncle.
CARDINAL BEAUFORT [*aside to* GLOSTER].
Are ye advised?—the east side of the grove?
DUKE OF GLOSTER [*aside to* CARDINAL].
Cardinal, I am with you.
KING HENRY.
Why, how now, uncle Gloster!
DUKE OF GLOSTER.
Talking of hawking; nothing else, my lord.—
[*aside to* CARDINAL] Now, by God's mother,
    priest, I'll shave your crown for this,
Or all my fence shall fail.
CARDINAL BEAUFORT [*aside to* GLOSTER].
                Medice, teipsum;
Protector, see to 't well, protect yourself.
KING HENRY.
The winds grow high; so do your stomachs,
    lords.
How irksome is this music to my heart!
When such strings jar, what hope of harmony?
I pray, my lords, let me compound this strife.
    Enter a TOWNSMAN *of St. Alban's, crying,*
            A miracle!
DUKE OF GLOSTER.
What means this noise?
Fellow, what dost thou proclaim?
TOWNSMAN.
A miracle! a miracle!
DUKE OF SUFFOLK.
Come to the king, and tell him what miracle.
TOWNSMAN.
Forsooth, a blind man at Saint Alban's shrine,
Within this half-hour, hath received his
    sight;
A man that ne'er saw in his life before.
KING HENRY.
Now, God be praised, that to believing souls
Gives light in darkness, comfort in despair!
Enter the MAYOR *of St. Alban's and his brethren,
    bearing* SIMPCOX, *between two in a chair, his*
    WIFE *and a multitude following.*
CARDINAL BEAUFORT.
Here comes the townsmen on procession,
To present your highness with the man.
KING HENRY.
Great is his comfort in this earthly vale,
Although by his sight his sin be multiplied.

DUKE OF GLOSTER.
Stand by, my masters:—bring him near the
    king;
His highness' pleasure is to talk with him.
KING HENRY.
Good fellow, tell us here the circumstance,
That we for thee may glorify the Lord.
What, hast thou been long blind, and now re-
    stored?
SAUNDER SIMPCOX.
Born blind, an't please your Grace.
WIFE.
                Ay, indeed was he.
DUKE OF SUFFOLK.
What woman is this?
WIFE.
                His wife, an't like your worship.
DUKE OF GLOSTER.
Hadst thou been his mother, thou couldst have
    better told.
KING HENRY.
Where wert thou born?
SAUNDER SIMPCOX.
At Berwick in the north, an't like your Grace.
KING HENRY.
Poor soul, God's goodness hath been great to
    thee:
Let never day nor night unhallow'd pass,
But still remember what the Lord hath done.
QUEEN MARGARET.
Tell me, good fellow, camest thou here by
    chance,
Or of devotion, to this holy shrine?
SAUNDER SIMPCOX.
God knows, of pure devotion; being call'd
A hundred times and oftener, in my sleep,
By good Saint Alban; who said, 'Simpcox,
    come,—
Come, offer at my shrine, and I will help
    thee.'
WIFE.
Most true, forsooth; and many time and oft
Myself have heard a voice to call him so.
CARDINAL BEAUFORT.
What, art thou lame?
SAUNDER SIMPCOX.
                Ay, God Almighty help me!
DUKE OF SUFFOLK.
How camest thou so?
SAUNDER SIMPCOX.
                A fall off of a tree.
WIFE.
A plum-tree, master.
DUKE OF GLOSTER.
                How long hast thou been blind?
SAUNDER SIMPCOX.
O, born so, master.
DUKE OF GLOSTER.
                What, and wouldst climb a tree?
SAUNDER SIMPCOX.
But that in all my life, when I was a youth.
WIFE.
Too true; and bought his climbing very dear.
DUKE OF GLOSTER.
Mass, thou lovedst plums well, that wouldst
    venture so.

SAUNDER SIMPCOX.
Alas, good master, my wife desired some damsons,
And made me climb, with danger of my life.
DUKE OF GLOSTER.
A subtle knave! but yet it shall not serve.—
Let me see thine eyes: wink now; now open
them:—
In my opinion yet thou see'st not well.
SAUNDER SIMPCOX.
Yes, master, clear as day, I thank God and Saint
Alban.
DUKE OF GLOSTER.
Say'st thou me so? What colour is this cloak of?
SAUNDER SIMPCOX.
Red, master; red as blood.
DUKE OF GLOSTER.
Why, that's well said. What colour is my gown
of?
SAUNDER SIMPCOX.
Black, forsooth; coal-black as jet.
KING HENRY.
Why, then, thou know'st what colour jet is of?
DUKE OF SUFFOLK.
And yet, I think, jet did he never see.
DUKE OF GLOSTER.
But cloaks and gowns, before this day, a many.
WIFE.
Never, before this day, in all his life.
DUKE OF GLOSTER.
Tell me, sirrah, what's my name?
SAUNDER SIMPCOX.
Alas, master, I know not.
DUKE OF GLOSTER.
What's his name?
SAUNDER SIMPCOX.
I know not.
DUKE OF GLOSTER.
Nor his?
SAUNDER SIMPCOX.
No, indeed, master.
DUKE OF GLOSTER.
What's thine own name?
SAUNDER SIMPCOX.
Saunder Simpcox, an if it please you, master.
DUKE OF GLOSTER.
Then, Saunder, sit there, the lyingest knave in
Christendom. If thou hadst been born blind,
thou mightst as well have known all our names as
thus to name the several colours we do wear.
Sight may distinguish of colours; but suddenly to
nominate them all, it is impossible.—My lords,
Saint Alban here hath done a miracle; and would
ye not think his cunning to be great that could
restore this cripple to his legs again?
SAUNDER SIMPCOX.
O master, that you could!
DUKE OF GLOSTER.
My masters of Saint Alban's, have you not
beadles in your town, and things call'd whips?
MAYOR OF ST. ALBAN'S.
Yes, my lord, if it please your Grace.
DUKE OF GLOSTER.
Then send for one presently.
MAYOR OF ST. ALBAN'S.
Sirrah, go fetch the beadle hither straight.
[Exit an ATTENDANT.

DUKE OF GLOSTER.
Now fetch me a stool hither by and by. [A stool
brought out.] Now, sirrah, if you mean to save
yourself from whipping, leap me over this stool
and run away.
SAUNDER SIMPCOX.
Alas, master, I am not able to stand alone:
You go about to torture me in vain.
Enter a BEADLE with whips.
DUKE OF GLOSTER.
Well, sir, we must have you find your legs.—
Sirrah beadle, whip him till he leap over that
same stool.
BEADLE.
I will, my lord.—Come on, sirrah; off with your
doublet quickly.
SAUNDER SIMPCOX.
Alas, master, what shall I do? I am not able to
stand.
[After the BEADLE hath hit him once, he
leaps over the stool and runs away; and
they follow and cry, A miracle!
KING HENRY.
O God, seest Thou this, and bearest so long?
QUEEN MARGARET.
It made me laugh to see the villain run.
DUKE OF GLOSTER.
Follow the knave; and take this drab away.
WIFE.
Alas, sir, we did it for pure need.
DUKE OF GLOSTER.
Let them be whipt through every market-town
till they come to Berwick, from whence they came.
[Exeunt MAYOR, BEADLE, WIFE, &c.
CARDINAL BEAUFORT.
Duke Humphrey has done a miracle to-day.
DUKE OF SUFFOLK.
True; made the lame to leap and fly away.
DUKE OF GLOSTER.
But you have done more miracles than I;
You made in a day, my lord, whole towns to fly.
Enter BUCKINGHAM.
KING HENRY.
What tidings with our cousin Buckingham?
DUKE OF BUCKINGHAM.
Such as my heart doth tremble to unfold.
A sort of naughty persons, lewdly bent,—
Under the countenance and confederacy
Of Lady Eleanor, the Protector's wife,
The ringleader and head of all this rout,—
Have practised dangerously against your state,
Dealing with witches and with conjurers:
Whom we have apprehended in the fact;
Raising up wicked spirits from under ground,
Demanding of King Henry's life and death,
And other of your highness' privy-council,
As more at large your Grace shall understand.
CARDINAL BEAUFORT.
And so, my lord Protector, by this means
Your lady is forthcoming yet at London.
[aside to GLOSTER] This news, I think, hath
turn'd your weapon's edge;
'Tis like, my lord, you will not keep your hour.
DUKE OF GLOSTER.
Ambitious churchman, leave to afflict my heart:
Sorrow and grief have vanquisht all my powers;

40

And, vanquisht as I am, I yield to thee,
Or to the meanest groom.
KING HENRY.
O God, what mischiefs work the wicked ones,
Heaping confusion on their own heads thereby!
QUEEN MARGARET.
Gloster, see here the tainture of thy nest;
And look thyself be faultless, thou wert best.
DUKE OF GLOSTER.
Madam, for myself, to heaven I do appeal,
How I have loved my king and commonweal:
And, for my wife, I know not how it stands;
Sorry I am to hear what I have heard:
Noble she is; but if she have forgot
Honour and virtue, and conversed with such
As, like to pitch, defile nobility,
I banish her my bed and company,
And give her, as a prey, to law and shame,
That hath dishonour'd Gloster's honest name.
KING HENRY.
Well, for this night we will repose us here:
To-morrow toward London back again,
To look into this business thoroughly,
And call these foul offenders to their answers;
And poise the cause in justice' equal scales,
Whose beam stands sure, whose rightful cause
    prevails.   [*Flourish. Exeunt.*

SCENE II.

London.   The DUKE OF YORK'S *garden.*

Enter YORK, SALISBURY, *and* WARWICK.

DUKE OF YORK.   [wick,
NOW, my good Lords of Salisbury and War-
    Our simple supper ended, give me leave,
In this close walk, to satisfy myself,
In craving your opinion of my title,
Which is infallible, to England's crown.
EARL OF SALISBURY.
My lord, I long to hear it at full.
EARL OF WARWICK.
Sweet York, begin: and if thy claim be good,
The Nevils are thy subjects to command.
DUKE OF YORK.
Then thus:—
Edward the Third, my lords, had seven sons:
The first, Edward the Black Prince, Prince of
    Wales;
The second, William of Hatfield; and the third,
Lionel duke of Clarence; next to whom
Was John of Gaunt, the duke of Lancaster;
The fifth was Edmund Langley, duke of York;
The sixth was Thomas of Woodstock, duke of
    Gloster;
William of Windsor was the seventh and last.
Edward the Black Prince died before his father;
And left behind him Richard, his only son, [king;
Who, after Edward the Third's death, reign'd as
Till Henry Bolingbroke, duke of Lancaster,
The eldest son and heir of John of Gaunt,
Crown'd by the name of Henry the Fourth,
Seized on the realm, deposed the rightful king,
Sent his poor queen to France, from whence she
    came,
And him to Pomfret,—where, as all you know,
Harmless Richard was murder'd traitorously.

EARL OF WARWICK.
Father, the duke hath told the truth;
Thus got the house of Lancaster the crown.
DUKE OF YORK.
Which now they hold by force, and not by right;
For Richard, the first son's heir, being dead,
The issue of the next son should have reign'd.
EARL OF SALISBURY.
But William of Hatfield died without an heir.
DUKE OF YORK.
The third son, Duke of Clarence,—from whose
    line   [daughter,
I claim the crown,—had issue, Philippe, a
Who married Edmund Mortimer, earl of March:
Edmund had issue, Roger earl of March;
Roger had issue, Edmund, Anne, and Eleanor.
EARL OF SALISBURY.
This Edmund, in the reign of Bolingbroke,
As I have read, laid claim unto the crown;
And, but for Owen Glendower, had been king,
Who kept him in captivity till he died.
But, to the rest.
DUKE OF YORK.
                His eldest sister, Anne,
My mother, being heir unto the crown,
Married Richard earl of Cambridge; who was son
To Edmund Langley, Edward the Third's fifth
    son.
By her I claim the kingdom: she was heir
To Roger earl of March; who was the son
Of Edmund Mortimer; who married Philippe,
Sole daughter unto Lionel duke of Clarence:
So, if the issue of the elder son
Succeed before the younger, I am king.
EARL OF WARWICK.
What plain proceeding is more plain than this?
Henry doth claim the crown from John of Gaunt,
The fourth son; York doth claim it from the third.
Till Lionel's issue fails, his should not reign:
It fails not yet, but flourishes in thee,
And in thy sons, fair slips of such a stock.—
Then, father Salisbury, kneel we together;
And, in this private plot, be we the first
That shall salute our rightful sovereign
With honour of his birthright to the crown.
BOTH.
Long live our sovereign Richard, England's king!
DUKE OF YORK.
We thank you, lords. But I am not your king
Till I be crown'd, and that my sword be stain'd
With heart-blood of the house of Lancaster;
And that's not suddenly to be perform'd,
But with advice and silent secrecy.
Do you as I do in these dangerous days:
Wink at the Duke of Suffolk's insolence,
At Beaufort's pride, at Somerset's ambition,
At Buckingham, and all the crew of them,
Till they have snared the shepherd of the flock,
That virtuous prince, the good Duke Humphrey:
'Tis that they seek; and they, in seeking that,
Shall find their deaths, if York can prophesy.
EARL OF SALISBURY.
My lord, break we off; we know your mind at full.
EARL OF WARWICK.
My heart assures me that the Earl of Warwick
Shall one day make the Duke of York a king.

DUKE OF YORK.

And, Nevil, this I do assure myself,—
Richard shall live to make the Earl of Warwick
The greatest man in England but the king.

[*Exeunt.*

SCENE III.

A hall of justice.

Sound trumpets. Enter the KING, *the* QUEEN,
GLOSTER, YORK, SUFFOLK, *and* SALISBURY;
the DUCHESS OF GLOSTER, MARGERY JOUR-
DAIN, SOUTHWELL, HUME, *and* BOLING-
BROKE, *under guard.*

KING HENRY.

STAND forth, Dame Eleanor Cobham, Glos-
ter's wife:
In sight of God and us, your guilt is great:
Receive the sentence of the law, for sins
Such as by God's book are adjudg'd to death.—
[*to* JOURDAIN, &c.] You four, from hence to
prison back again;
From thence unto the place of execution:
The witch in Smithfield shall be burnt to ashes,
And you three shall be strangled on the gallows.—
You, madam, for you are more nobly born,
Despoiled of your honour in your life,
Shall, after three days' open penance done,
Live in your country here, in banishment,
With Sir John Stanley, in the Isle of Man.

DUCHESS OF GLOSTER.

Welcome is banishment; welcome were my death.

DUKE OF GLOSTER.

Eleanor, the law, thou seest, hath judged thee:
I cannot justify whom the law condemns.—
[*Exeunt the* DUCHESS *and the other
prisoners, guarded.*
Mine eyes are full of tears, my heart of grief.
Ah, Humphrey, this dishonour in thine age
Will bring thy head with sorrow to the ground!—
I beseech your majesty, give me leave to go;
Sorrow would solace, and mine age would ease.

KING HENRY.

Stay, Humphrey duke of Gloster: ere thou go,
Give up thy staff: Henry will to himself
Protector be; and God shall be my hope,
My stay, my guide, and lantern to my feet:
And go in peace, Humphrey,—no less beloved
Than when thou wert Protector to thy king.

QUEEN MARGARET.

I see no reason why a king of years
Should be to be protected like a child.—
God and King Henry govern England's helm!—
Give up your staff, sir, and the king his realm.

DUKE OF GLOSTER.

My staff! here, noble Henry, is my staff:
As willingly do I the same resign
As e'er thy father Henry made it mine;
And even as willingly at thy feet I leave it
As others would ambitiously receive it.
Farewell, good king: when I am dead and gone,
May honourable peace attend thy throne!   [*Exit.*

QUEEN MARGARET.

Why, now is Henry king, and Margaret queen;
And Humphrey duke of Gloster scarce himself,
That bears so shrewd a maim; two pulls at once,—
His lady banisht, and a limb lopt off:

This staff of honour raught, there let it stand
Where it best fits to be,—in Henry's hand.

DUKE OF SUFFOLK.

Thus droops this lofty pine, and hangs his
sprays;
Thus Eleanor's pride dies in her youngest days.

DUKE OF YORK.

Lords, let him go.—Please it your majesty,
This is the day appointed for the combat;
And ready are the appellant and defendant,
The armourer and his man, to enter the lists,
So please your highness to behold the fight.

QUEEN MARGARET.

Ay, good my lord; for purposely therefore
Left I the court, to see this quarrel tried.

KING HENRY.

O' God's name, see the lists and all things fit:
Here let them end it; and God defend the right!

DUKE OF YORK.

I never saw a fellow worse bested,
Or more afraid to fight, than is the appellant,
The servant of this armourer, my lords.

Enter, at one door, HORNER, *the Armourer, and
his* NEIGHBOURS, *drinking to him so much that
he is drunk: and he enters with a drum before
him and his staff with a sandbag fasten'd to it;
and at the other door* PETER, *his man, with a
drum and sandbag, and* PRENTICES *drinking
to him.*

FIRST NEIGHBOUR.

Here, neighbour Horner, I drink to you in a cup
of sack: and fear not, neighbour, you shall do well
enough.

SECOND NEIGHBOUR.

And here, neighbour, here's a cup of charneco.

THIRD NEIGHBOUR.

And here's a pot of good double-beer, neighbour:
drink, and fear not your man.

THOMAS HORNER.

Let it come, i' faith, and I'll pledge you all; and
a fig for Peter!

FIRST PRENTICE.

Here, Peter, I drink to thee: and be not afraid.

SECOND PRENTICE.

Be merry, Peter, and fear not thy master: fight
for credit of the prentices.

PETER.

I thank you all: drink, and pray for me, I pray
you; for I think I have taken my last draught in
this world.—Here, Robin, an if I die, I give thee
my apron:—and, Will, thou shalt have my hammer:—and here, Tom, take all the money that I
have.—O Lord bless me, I pray God! for I am
never able to deal with my master, he hath learnt
so much fence already.

EARL OF SALISBURY.

Come, leave your drinking, and fall to blows.—
Sirrah, what's thy name?

PETER.

Peter, forsooth.

EARL OF SALISBURY.

Peter! what more?

PETER.

Thump.

EARL OF SALISBURY.

Thump! then see thou thump thy master well.

THOMAS HORNER.

Masters, I am come hither, as it were, upon my
man's instigation, to prove him a knave, and myself an honest man: and touching the Duke of
York, I will take my death, I never meant him
any ill, nor the king, nor the queen: and therefore,
Peter, have at thee with a downright blow!

DUKE OF YORK.

Dispatch:—this knave's tongue begins to double.
—Sound, trumpets, alarum to the combatants!

     [*Alarum. They fight, and* PETER *strikes
him down.*

THOMAS HORNER.

Hold, Peter, hold! I confess, I confess treason.

     [*Dies.*

DUKE OF YORK.

Take away his weapon.—Fellow, thank God, and
the good wine in thy master's way.

PETER.

O God, have I overcome mine enemy in this presence? O Peter, thou hast prevail'd in right!

KING HENRY.

Go, take hence that traitor from our sight;
For by his death we do perceive his guilt:
And God in justice hath reveal'd to us
The truth and innocence of this poor fellow,
Which he had thought to have murder'd wrong-
     fully.—
Come, fellow, follow us for thy reward.

     [*Sound a flourish. Exeunt.*

SCENE IV.

A street.

Enter GLOSTER *and his* MEN, *in mourning
cloaks.*

DUKE OF GLOSTER.   [cloud;

THUS sometimes hath the brightest day a
     And after summer evermore succeeds
Barren winter, with his wrathful nipping cold:
So cares and joys abound, as seasons fleet.—
Sirs, what's o'clock?

SERVING-MAN.

     'Tis almost ten, my lord.

DUKE OF GLOSTER.

Ten is the hour that was appointed me
To watch the coming of my punisht duchess:
Uneath may she endure the flinty streets,
To tread them with her tender-feeling feet.
Sweet Nell, ill can thy noble mind abrook
The abject people gazing on thy face
With envious looks, still laughing at thy shame,
That erst did follow thy proud chariot-wheels
When thou didst ride in triumph through the
     streets.
But, soft! I think she comes; and I'll prepare
My tear-stain'd eyes to see her miseries.

Enter the DUCHESS *of* GLOSTER *barefoot, in a
white sheet, with verses pinn'd on her back, and
a taper burning in her hand; with* SIR JOHN
STANLEY, *the* SHERIFF, *and* OFFICERS.

SERVING-MAN.

So please your Grace, we'll take her from the
sheriff.

DUKE OF GLOSTER.

No, stir not, for your lives; let her pass by.

DUCHESS OF GLOSTER.

Come you, my lord, to see my open shame?
Now thou dost penance too. Look how they
     gaze!
See how the giddy multitude do point,
And nod their heads, and throw their eyes on
     thee!
Ah, Gloster, hide thee from their hateful looks,
And, in thy closet pent up, rue my shame,
And ban thine enemies, both mine and thine!

DUKE OF GLOSTER.

Be patient, gentle Nell; forget this grief.

DUCHESS OF GLOSTER.

Ah, Gloster, teach me to forget myself!
For, whilst I think I am thy married wife,
And thou a prince, Protector of this land,
Methinks I should not thus be led along,
Mail'd up in shame, with papers on my back,
And follow'd with a rabble, that rejoice
To see my tears and hear my deep-fet groans.
The ruthless flint doth cut my tender feet;
And when I start, the envious people laugh,
And bid me be advised how I tread.
Ah, Humphrey, can I bear this shameful yoke?
Trow'st thou that e'er I'll look upon the world,
Or count them happy that enjoy the sun?
No; dark shall be my light, and night my day;
To think upon my pomp shall be my hell.
Sometime I'll say, I am Duke Humphrey's wife;
And he a prince, and ruler of the land:
Yet so he ruled, and such a prince he was,
As he stood by, whilst I, his forlorn duchess,
Was made a wonder and a pointing-stock
To every idle rascal follower.
But be thou mild, and blush not at my shame:
Nor stir at nothing, till the axe of death
Hang over thee, as, sure, it shortly will;
For Suffolk,—he that can do all in all
With her that hateth thee and hates us all,—
And York, and impious Beaufort, that false priest,
Have all limed bushes to betray thy wings,
And, fly thou how thou canst, they'll tangle thee:
But fear not thou, until thy foot be snared,
Nor never seek prevention of thy foes.

DUKE OF GLOSTER.

Ah, Nell, forbear! thou aimest all awry;
I must offend before I be attainted:
And had I twenty times so many foes,
And each of them had twenty times their power,
All these could not procure me any scathe,
So long as I am loyal, true, and crimeless.
Wouldst have me rescue thee from this reproach?
Why, yet thy scandal were not wiped away,
But I in danger for the breach of law.
Thy greatest help is quiet, gentle Nell:
I pray thee, sort thy heart to patience;
These few days' wonder will be quickly worn.

Enter a HERALD.

HERALD.

I summon your Grace to his majesty's parliament,
Holden at Bury the first of this next month.

DUKE OF GLOSTER.

And my consent ne'er askt herein before!
This is close dealing.—Well, I will be there.

     [*Exit* HERALD.,

My Nell, I take my leave:—and, master sheriff,
Let not her penance exceed the king's commission.

SHERIFF.
An't please your Grace, here my commission
stays;
And Sir John Stanley is appointed now
To take her with him to the Isle of Man.

DUKE OF GLOSTER.
Must you, Sir John, protect my lady here?

SIR JOHN STANLEY.
So am I given in charge, may't please your Grace.

DUKE OF GLOSTER.
Entreat her not the worse, in that I pray
You use her well: the world may laugh again;
And I may live to do you kindness, if
You do it her: and so, Sir John, farewell.

DUCHESS OF GLOSTER.
What, gone, my lord, and bid me not farewell!

DUKE OF GLOSTER.
Witness my tears, I cannot stay to speak.
[Exeunt GLOSTER and his MEN.

DUCHESS OF GLOSTER.
Art thou gone too? all comfort go with thee!
For none abides with me: my joy is death,—
Death, at whose name I oft have been afeard,
Because I wisht this world's eternity.—
Stanley, I prithee, go, and take me hence;
I care not whither, for I beg no favour,
Only convey me where thou art commanded.

SIR JOHN STANLEY.
Why, madam, that is to the Isle of Man;
There to be used according to your state.

DUCHESS OF GLOSTER.
That's bad enough, for I am but reproach,—
And shall I, then, be used reproachfully?

SIR JOHN STANLEY.
Like to a duchess, and Duke Humphrey's lady;
According to that state you shall be used.

DUCHESS OF GLOSTER.
Sheriff, farewell, and better than I fare,—
Although thou hast been conduct of my shame.

SHERIFF.
It is my office; and, madam, pardon me.

DUCHESS OF GLOSTER.
Ay, ay, farewell; thy office is discharged.—
Come, Stanley, shall we go?

SIR JOHN STANLEY.
Madam, your penance done, throw off this sheet,
And go we to attire you for our journey.

DUCHESS OF GLOSTER.
My shame will not be shifted with my sheet:
No, it will hang upon my richest robes,
And show itself, attire me how I can.
Go, lead the way; I long to see my prison.
[Exeunt.

ACT III. SCENE I.
The Abbey at Bury St. Edmund's.

Sound a sennet. Enter KING, QUEEN, CARDINAL
BEAUFORT, SUFFOLK, YORK, BUCKINGHAM,
SALISBURY, *and* WARWICK *to the Parliament.*

KING HENRY.
I MUSE my Lord of Gloster is not come:
'Tis not his wont to be the hindmost man,
Whate'er occasion keeps him from us now.

QUEEN MARGARET.
Can you not see? or will ye not observe
The strangeness of his alter'd countenance?
With what a majesty he bears himself;
How insolent of late he is become,
How proud, how peremptory, and unlike him-
self?
We know the time since he was mild and affable;
And, if we did but glance a far-off look,
Immediately he was upon his knee,
That all the court admired him for submission:
But meet him now, and, be it in the morn,
When every one will give the time of day,
He knits his brow, and shows an angry eye,
And passeth by with stiff unbowed knee,
Disdaining duty that to us belongs.
Small curs are not regarded when they grin;
But great men tremble when the lion roars,—
And Humphrey is no little man in England.
First note, that he is near you in descent;
And, should you fall, he is the next will mount.
Me seemeth, then, it is no policy,—
Respecting what a rancorous mind he bears,
And his advantage following your decease,—
That he should come about your royal person,
Or be admitted to your highness' council.
By flattery hath he won the commons' hearts;
And when he please to make commotion,
'Tis to be fear'd they all will follow him.
Now 'tis the spring, and weeds are shallow-
rooted;
Suffer them now, and they'll o'ergrow the garden,
And choke the herbs for want of husbandry.
The reverent care I bear unto my lord
Made me collect these dangers in the duke.
If it be fond, call it a woman's fear;
Which fear if better reasons can supplant,
I will subscribe, and say I wrong'd the duke.
My Lord of Suffolk, Buckingham, and York,
Reprove my allegation, if you can;
Or else conclude my words effectual.

DUKE OF SUFFOLK.
Well hath your highness seen into this duke;
And, had I first been put to speak my mind,
I think I should have told your Grace's tale.
The duchess, by his subornation,
Upon my life, began her devilish practices:
Or, if he were not privy to those faults,
Yet, by reputing of his high descent,—
As, next the king, he was successive heir,
And such high vaunts of his nobility,—
Did instigate the bedlam brain-sick duchess
By wicked means to frame our sovereign's fall.
Smooth runs the water where the brook is deep;
And in his simple show he harbours treason.
The fox barks not when he would steal the lamb.
No, no, my sovereign; Gloster is a man
Unsounded yet, and full of deep deceit.

CARDINAL BEAUFORT.
Did he not, contrary to form of law,
Devise strange deaths for small offences done?

DUKE OF YORK.
And did he not, in his Protectorship,
Levy great sums of money through the realm
For soldiers' pay in France, and never sent it?
By means whereof the towns each day revolted.

44

DUKE OF BUCKINGHAM.
Tut, these are petty faults to faults unknown,
Which time will bring to light in smooth Duke
  Humphrey.
KING HENRY.
My lords, at once:—the care you have of us,
To mow down thorns that would annoy our foot,
Is worthy praise: but—shall I speak my con-
  science?—
Our kinsman Gloster is as innocent
From meaning treason to our royal person
As is the sucking lamb or harmless dove:
The duke is virtuous, mild, and too well given
To dream on evil, or to work my downfall.
QUEEN MARGARET.
Ah, what's more dangerous than this fond
  affiance!
Seems he a dove? his feathers are but borrow'd,
For he's disposed as the hateful raven:
Is he a lamb! his skin is surely lent him,
For he's inclined as is the ravenous wolf.
Who cannot steal a shape that means deceit?
Take heed, my lord; the welfare of us all
Hangs on the cutting short that fraudful man.
Enter SOMERSET.
DUKE OF SOMERSET.
All health unto my gracious sovereign!
KING HENRY.
Welcome, Lord Somerset. What news from
  France?
DUKE OF SOMERSET.
That all your interest in those territories
Is utterly bereft you; all is lost.
KING HENRY.
Cold news, Lord Somerset: but God's will be
  done!
DUKE OF YORK [*aside*].
Cold news for me; for I had hope of France
As firmly as I hope for fertile England.
Thus are my blossoms blasted in the bud,
And caterpillars eat my leaves away:
But I will remedy this gear ere long,
Or sell my title for a glorious grave.
Enter GLOSTER.
DUKE OF GLOSTER.
All happiness unto my lord the king!
Pardon, my liege, that I have stay'd so long.
DUKE OF SUFFOLK.
Nay, Gloster, know that thou art come too soon,
Unless thou wert more loyal than thou art:
I do arrest thee of high treason here.
DUKE OF GLOSTER.
Well, Suffolk, well, thou shalt not see me blush
Nor change my countenance for this arrest:
A heart unspotted is not easily daunted.
The purest spring is not so free from mud
As I am clear from treason to my sovereign:
Who can accuse me? wherein am I guilty?
DUKE OF YORK.
'Tis thought, my lord, that you took bribes of
  France,
And, being Protector, stay'd the soldiers' pay;
By means whereof his highness hath lost France.
DUKE OF GLOSTER.
Is it but thought so? what are they that think it?
I never robb'd the soldiers of their pay,

Nor ever had one penny bribe from France.
So help me God, as I have watcht the night,—
Ay, night by night,—in studying good for
  England!
That doit that e'er I wrested from the king,
Or any groat I hoarded to my use,
Be brought against me at my trial-day!
No; many a pound of mine own proper store,
Because I would not tax the needy commons,
Have I dispursed to the garrisons,
And never askt for restitution.
CARDINAL BEAUFORT.
It serves you well, my lord, to say so much.
DUKE OF GLOSTER.
I say no more than truth, so help me God!
DUKE OF YORK.
In your Protectorship you did devise
Strange tortures for offenders, never heard of,
That England was defamed by tyranny.
DUKE OF GLOSTER.
Why, 'tis well known that, whiles I was Pro-
  tector,
Pity was all the fault that was in me;
For I should melt at an offender's tears,
And lowly words were ransom for their fault.
Unless it were a bloody murderer,
Or foul felonious thief that fleeced poor pas-
  sengers,
I never gave them condign punishment:
Murder, indeed, that bloody sin, I tortured
Above the felon or what trespass else.
DUKE OF SUFFOLK.
My lord, these faults are easy, quickly answer'd:
But mightier crimes are laid unto your charge,
Whereof you cannot easily purge yourself.
I do arrest you in his highness' name;
And here commit you to my lord cardinal
To keep, until your further time of trial.
KING HENRY.
My Lord of Gloster, 'tis my special hope
That you will clear yourself from all suspect:
My conscience tells me you are innocent.
DUKE OF GLOSTER.
Ah, gracious lord, these days are dangerous!
Virtue is choked with foul ambition,
And charity chased hence by rancour's hand;
Foul subornation is predominant,
And equity exiled your highness' land.
I know their complot is to have my life;
And, if my death might make this island happy,
And prove the period of their tyranny,
I would expend it with all willingness:
But mine is made the prologue to their play;
For thousands more, that yet suspect no peril,
Will not conclude their plotted tragedy.
Beaufort's red sparkling eyes blab his heart's
  malice,
And Suffolk's cloudy brow his stormy hate;
Sharp Buckingham unburdens with his tongue
The envious load that lies upon his heart;
And dogged York, that reaches at the moon,
Whose overweening arm I have pluckt back,
By false accuse doth level at my life:—
And you, my sovereign lady, with the rest,
Causeless have laid disgraces on my head,
And with your best endeavour have stirr'd up

My liefest liege to be mine enemy:—
Ay, all of you have laid your heads together—
Myself had notice of your conventicles—
And all to make away my guiltless life.
I shall not want false witness to condemn me,
Nor store of treasons to augment my guilt;
The ancient proverb will be well effected,—
A staff is quickly found to beat a dog.

CARDINAL BEAUFORT.
My liege, his railing is intolerable:
If those that care to keep your royal person
From treason's secret knife and traitors' rage
Be thus upbraided, chid, and rated at,
And the offender granted scope of speech,
'Twill make them cool in zeal unto your Grace.

DUKE OF SUFFOLK.
Hath he not twit our sovereign lady here
With ignominious words, though clerkly couch'd,
As if she had suborned some to swear
False allegations to o'erthrow his state?

QUEEN MARGARET.
But I can give the loser leave to chide.

DUKE OF GLOSTER.
Far truer spoke than meant: I lose, indeed;—
Beshrew the winners, for they play'd me false!
And well such losers may have leave to speak.

DUKE OF BUCKINGHAM.
He'll wrest the sense, and hold us here all day:—
Lord cardinal, he is your prisoner.

CARDINAL BEAUFORT.
Sirs, take away the duke, and guard him sure.

DUKE OF GLOSTER.
Ah, thus King Henry throws away his crutch,
Before his legs be firm to bear his body!
Thus is the shepherd beaten from thy side,
And wolves are gnarling who shall gnaw thee first.
Ah, that my fear were false! ah, that it were!
For, good King Henry, thy decay I fear.
                    [Exit GLOSTER, guarded.

KING HENRY.
My lords, what to your wisdoms seemeth best
Do or undo, as if ourself were here.

QUEEN MARGARET.
What, will your highness leave the parliament?

KING HENRY.
Ay, Margaret; my heart is drown'd with grief,
Whose flood begins to flow within mine eyes;
My body round engirt with misery,—
For what's more miserable than discontent?—
Ah, uncle Humphrey, in thy face I see
The map of honour, truth, and loyalty!
And yet, good Humphrey, is the hour to come
That e'er I proved thee false, or fear'd thy faith.
What louring star now envies thy estate,
That these great lords, and Margaret our queen,
Do seek subversion of thy harmless life?
Thou never didst them wrong, nor no man
  wrong:
And as the butcher takes away the calf,
And binds the wretch, and beats it when it strays,
Bearing it to the bloody slaughter-house;
Even so, remorseless, have they borne him hence:
And as the dam runs lowing up and down,
Looking the way her harmless young one went,
And can do naught but wail her darling's loss;
Even so myself bewails good Gloster's case

With sad unhelpful tears; and with dimm'd eyes
Look after him, and cannot do him good,—
So mighty are his vowed enemies.
His fortunes I will weep; and, 'twixt each groan,
Say, 'Who's a traitor, Gloster he is none.'   [Exit.

QUEEN MARGARET.
Fair lords, cold snow melts with the sun's hot
  beams.
Henry my lord is cold in great affairs,
Too full of foolish pity: and Gloster's show
Beguiles him, as the mournful crocodile
With sorrow snares relenting passengers;
Or as the snake, roll'd in a flowering bank,
With shining checker'd slough, doth sting a
  child,
That for the beauty thinks it excellent.
Believe me, lords, were none more wise than I,—
And yet herein I judge mine own wit good,—
This Gloster should be quickly rid the world,
To rid us from the fear we have of him.

CARDINAL BEAUFORT.
That he should die is worthy policy;
But yet we want a colour for his death:
'Tis meet he be condemn'd by course of law.

DUKE OF SUFFOLK.
But, in my mind, that were no policy:
The king will labour still to save his life;
The commons haply rise to save his life;
And yet we have but trivial argument,
More than mistrust, that shows him worthy
  death.

DUKE OF YORK.
So that, by this, you would not have him die.

DUKE OF SUFFOLK.
Ah, York, no man alive so fain as I!

DUKE OF YORK [aside].
'Tis York that hath more reason for his death.—
But, my lord cardinal, and you, my Lord of
  Suffolk,—
Say as you think, and speak it from your souls,—
Were't not all one, an empty eagle were set
To guard the chicken from a hungry kite,
As place Duke Humphrey for the king's Pro-
  tector?

QUEEN MARGARET.
So the poor chicken should be sure of death.

DUKE OF SUFFOLK.
Madam, 'tis true; and were't not madness, then,
To make the fox surveyor of the fold?
Who being accused a crafty murderer,
His guilt should be but idly posted over,
Because his purpose is not executed.
No; let him die, in that he is a fox,
By nature proved an enemy to the flock,
Before his chaps be stain'd with crimson blood,
As Humphrey, proved by reasons, to my liege,
And do not stand on quillets how to slay him:
Be it by gins, by snares, by subtlety,
Sleeping or waking, 'tis no matter how,
So he be dead; for that is good deceit
Which mates him first that first intends deceit.

QUEEN MARGARET.
Thrice-noble Suffolk, 'tis resolutely spoke.

DUKE OF SUFFOLK.
Not resolute, except so much were done;
For things are often spoke, and seldom meant:

46

But, that my heart accordeth with my tongue,—
Seeing the deed is meritorious,
And to preserve my sovereign from his foe,—
Say but the word, and I will be his priest.
CARDINAL BEAUFORT.
But I would have him dead, my Lord of Suffolk,
Ere you can take due orders for a priest:
Say you consent, and censure well the deed,
And I'll provide his executioner,—
I tender so the safety of my liege.
DUKE OF SUFFOLK.
Here is my hand, the deed is worthy doing.
QUEEN MARGARET.
And so say I.
DUKE OF YORK.
And I: and now we three have spoke it,
It skills not greatly who impugns our doom.
Enter a POST.
POST.
Great lords, from Ireland am I come amain,
To signify that rebels there are up,
And put the Englishmen unto the sword:
Send succours, lords, and stop the rage betime,
Before the wound do grow uncurable;
For, being green, there is great hope of help.
CARDINAL BEAUFORT.
A breach that craves a quick expedient stop!
What counsel give you in this weighty cause?
DUKE OF YORK.
That Somerset be sent as regent thither:
'Tis meet that lucky ruler be employ'd;
Witness the fortune he hath had in France.
DUKE OF SOMERSET.
If York, with all his far-fet policy,
Had been the regent there instead of me,
He never would have stay'd in France so long.
DUKE OF YORK.
No, not to lose it all, as thou hast done:
I rather would have lost my life betimes
Than bring a burden of dishonour home
By staying there so long till all were lost.
Show me one scar character'd on thy skin:
Men's flesh preserved so whole do seldom win.
QUEEN MARGARET.
Nay, then, this spark will prove a raging fire,
If wind and fuel be brought to feed it with:—
No more, good York;—sweet Somerset, be
still:—
Thy fortune, York, hadst thou been regent there,
Might happily have proved far worse than his.
DUKE OF YORK.
What, worse than naught? nay, then, a shame
take all!
DUKE OF SOMERSET.
And, in the number, thee that wishest shame!
CARDINAL BEAUFORT.
My Lord of York, try what your fortune is.
Th' uncivil kerns of Ireland are in arms,
And temper clay with blood of Englishmen:
To Ireland will you lead a band of men,
Collected choicely, from each county some,
And try your hap against the Irishmen?
DUKE OF YORK.
I will, my lord, so please his majesty.
DUKE OF SUFFOLK.
Why, our authority is his consent;

And what we do establish he confirms:
Then, noble York, take thou this task in hand.
DUKE OF YORK.
I am content: provide me soldiers, lords,
Whiles I take order for mine own affairs.
DUKE OF SUFFOLK.
A charge, Lord York, that I will see perform'd.
But now return we to the false Duke Humphrey.
CARDINAL BEAUFORT.
No more of him; for I will deal with him,
That henceforth he shall trouble us no more.
And so break off; the day is almost spent:
Lord Suffolk, you and I must talk of that event.
DUKE OF YORK.
My Lord of Suffolk, within fourteen days
At Bristol I expect my soldiers;
For there I'll ship them all for Ireland.
DUKE OF SUFFOLK.
I'll see it truly done, my Lord of York.
[Exeunt all except YORK.
DUKE OF YORK.
Now, York, or never, steel thy fearful thoughts,
And change misdoubt to resolution:
Be that thou hopest to be; or what thou art
Resign to death,—it is not worth th' enjoying:
Let pale-faced fear keep with the mean-born
man,
And find no harbour in a royal heart.
Faster than spring-time showers comes thought
on thought;
And not a thought but thinks on dignity.
My brain, more busy than the labouring spider,
Weaves tedious snares to trap mine enemies.
Well, nobles, well, 'tis politicly done,
To send me packing with an host of men:
I fear me you but warm the starved snake,
Who, cherisht in your breasts, will sting your
hearts.
'Twas men I lackt, and you will give them me:
I take it kindly; yet be well assured
You put sharp weapons in a madman's hands.
Whiles I in Ireland nourish a mighty band,
I will stir up in England some black storm,
Shall blow ten thousand souls to heaven or hell;
And this fell tempest shall not cease to rage
Until the golden circuit on my head,
Like to the glorious sun's transparent beams,
Do calm the fury of this mad-bred flaw.
And for a minister of my intent
I have seduced a headstrong Kentishman,
John Cade of Ashford,
To make commotion, as full well he can,
Under the title of John Mortimer.
In Ireland have I seen this stubborn Cade
Oppose himself against a troop of kerns,
And fought so long, till that his thighs with darts
Were almost like a sharp-quill'd porpentine;
And, in the end being rescued, I have seen
Him caper upright like a wild Morisco,
Shaking the bloody darts as he his bells.
Full often, like a shag-hair'd crafty kern,
Hath he conversed with the enemy,
And, undiscover'd, come to me again,
And given me notice of their villainies.
This devil here shall be my substitute;
For that John Mortimer, which now is dead,

In face, in gait, in speech, he doth resemble:
By this I shall perceive the commons' mind,
How they affect the house and claim of York.
Say he be taken, rackt, and tortured,
I know no pain they can inflict upon him
Will make him say I moved him to those arms.
Say that he thrive,—as 'tis great like he will,—
Why, then from Ireland come I with my strength,
And reap the harvest which that rascal sow'd;
For, Humphrey being dead, as he shall be,
And Henry put apart, the next for me.   [*Exit.*

SCENE II.

Bury St. Edmund's.   A room of state.

*Enter two or three running over the stage, from the
murder of* DUKE HUMPHREY.

FIRST MURDERER.

RUN to my Lord of Suffolk; let him know
We have dispatcht the duke, as he command-
     SECOND MURDERER.   [ed.
O, that it were to do!—What have we done?
Didst ever hear a man so penitent?
     FIRST MURDERER.
Here comes my lord.

Enter SUFFOLK.

DUKE OF SUFFOLK.

Now, sirs, have you dispatcht this thing?
     FIRST MURDERER.
Ay, my good lord, he's dead.
     DUKE OF SUFFOLK.
Why, that's well said. Go, get you to my house;
I will reward you for this venturous deed.
The king and all the peers are here at hand:—
Have you laid fair the bed? is all things well,
According as I gave directions?
     FIRST MURDERER.
'Tis, my good lord.
     DUKE OF SUFFOLK.
Away! be gone.   [*Exeunt* MURDERERS.
Sound trumpets.   Enter the KING, *the* QUEEN,
CARDINAL BEAUFORT, SOMERSET, LORDS,
and others.

KING HENRY.

Go, call our uncle to our presence straight;
Say we intend to try his Grace to-day,
If he be guilty, as 'tis published.
     DUKE OF SUFFOLK.
I'll call him presently, my noble lord.   [*Exit.*
     KING HENRY.
Lords, take your places; and, I pray you all,
Proceed no straiter 'gainst our uncle Gloster
Than from true evidence of good esteem
He be approved in practice culpable.
     QUEEN MARGARET.
God forbid any malice should prevail,
That faultless may condemn a nobleman!
Pray God he may acquit him of suspicion!
     KING HENRY.
I thank thee, Meg; these words content me much.
       Enter SUFFOLK.
How now! why look'st thou pale? why tremblest
thou?
Where is our uncle? what's the matter, Suffolk?
     DUKE OF SUFFOLK.
Dead in his bed, my lord; Gloster is dead.

QUEEN MARGARET.
Marry, God forfend!
     CARDINAL BEAUFORT.
God's secret judgement:—I did dream to-night
The duke was dumb, and could not speak a word.
       [*The* KING *swoons.*
     QUEEN MARGARET.
How fares my lord?—Help, lords! the king is
dead.
     DUKE OF SOMERSET.
Rear up his body; wring him by the nose.
     QUEEN MARGARET.
Run, go, help, help!—O Henry, ope thine eyes!
     DUKE OF SUFFOLK.
He doth revive again:—madam, be patient.
     KING HENRY.
O heavenly God!
     QUEEN MARGARET.
       How fares my gracious lord?
     DUKE OF SUFFOLK.
Comfort, my sovereign! gracious Henry, com-
fort!
     KING HENRY.
What, doth my Lord of Suffolk comfort me?
Came he right now to sing a raven's note,
Whose dismal tune bereft my vital powers;
And thinks he that the chirping of a wren,
By crying comfort from a hollow breast,
Can chase away the first-conceived sound?
Hide not thy poison with such sugar'd words:
Lay not thy hands on me; forbear, I say;
Their touch affrights me as a serpent's sting.
Thou baleful messenger, out of my sight!
Upon thy eyeballs murderous tyranny
Sits in grim majesty, to fright the world.
Look not upon me, for thine eyes are wound-
   ing:—
Yet do not go away:—come, basilisk,
And kill the innocent gazer with thy sight;
For in the shade of death I shall find joy,—
In life but double death, now Gloster's dead.
     QUEEN MARGARET.
Why do you rate my Lord of Suffolk thus?
Although the duke was enemy to him,
Yet he, most Christian-like, laments his death:
And for myself,—foe as he was to me,—
Might liquid tears, or heart-offending groans,
Or blood-consuming sighs recall his life,
I would be blind with weeping, sick with groans,
Look pale as primrose with blood-drinking sighs,
And all to have the noble duke alive.
What know I how the world may deem of me?
For it is known we were but hollow friends:
It may be judged I made the duke away;
So shall my name with slander's tongue be
   wounded,
And princes' courts be fill'd with my reproach.
This get I by his death: ay me, unhappy!
To be a queen, and crown'd with infamy!
     KING HENRY.
Ah, woe is me for Gloster, wretched man!
     QUEEN MARGARET.
Be woe for me, more wretched than he is.
What, dost thou turn away, and hide thy face?
I am no loathsome leper?—look on me.
What, art thou, like the adder, waxen deaf?

Be poisonous too, and kill thy forlorn queen.
Is all thy comfort shut in Gloster's tomb?
Why, then, Dame Margaret was ne'er thy joy:
Erect his statua, and worship it,
And make my image but an alehouse sign.
Was I for this nigh wrackt upon the sea,
And twice by awkward winds from England's
    bank
Drove back again unto my native clime?
What boded this but well-forewarning winds
Did seem to say,—'Seek not a scorpion's nest,
Nor set no footing on this unkind shore'?
What did I then but cursed the gentle gusts,
And he that loosed them forth their brazen caves;
And bid them blow towards England's blessed
    shore,
Or turn our stern upon a dreadful rock?
Yet Æolus would not be a murderer,
But left that hateful office unto thee:
The pretty-vaulting sea refused to drown me;
Knowing that thou wouldst have me drown'd on
    shore,
With tears as salt as sea, through thy unkindness:
The splitting rocks cower'd in the sinking sands,
And would not dash me with their ragged sides;
Because thy flinty heart, more hard than they,
Might in thy palace perish Margaret.
As far as I could ken the chalky cliffs,
When from thy shore the tempest beat us back,
I stood upon the hatches in the storm;
And when the dusky sky began to rob
My earnest-gaping sight of thy land's view,
I took a costly jewel from my neck,—
A heart it was, bound in with diamonds,—   [it;
And threw it towards thy land:—the sea received
And so I wisht thy body might my heart:
And even with this I lost fair England's view,
And bid mine eyes be packing with my heart,
And call'd them blind and dusky spectacles,
For losing ken of Albion's wished coast.
How often have I tempted Suffolk's tongue—
The agent of thy foul inconstancy—
To sit and witch me, as Ascanius did
When he to madding Dido would unfold
His father's acts commenced in burning Troy!
Am I not witcht like her? or thou not false like
    him?
Ay me, I can no more! die, Margaret!
For Henry weeps that thou dost live so long.
    Noise within. *Enter* WARWICK, SALISBURY,
        and many COMMONS.
EARL OF WARWICK.
It is reported, mighty sovereign,
That good Duke Humphrey traitorously is mur-
    der'd
By Suffolk and the Cardinal Beaufort's means.
The commons, like an angry hive of bees
That want their leader, scatter up and down,
And care not who they sting in his revenge.
Myself have calm'd their spleenful mutiny,
Until they hear the order of his death.
    KING HENRY.
That he is dead, good Warwick, 'tis too true;
But how he died God knows, not Henry:
Enter his chamber, view his breathless corpse,
And comment then upon his sudden death.

EARL OF WARWICK.
That shall I do, my liege.—Stay, Salisbury,
With the rude multitude till I return.   [*Exit.*
    KING HENRY.
O Thou that judgest all things, stay my
    thoughts,—
My thoughts, that labour to persuade my soul
Some violent hands were laid on Humphrey's life!
If my suspect be false, forgive me, God;
For judgement only doth belong to Thee.
Fain would I go to chafe his paly lips
With twenty thousand kisses, and to rain
Upon his face an ocean of salt tears,
To tell my love unto his dumb deaf trunk,
And with my fingers feel his hand unfeeling:
But all in vain are these mean obsequies;
And to survey his dead and earthy image
What were it but to make my sorrow greater?
    [WARWICK *draws the curtains and shows*
        DUKE HUMPHREY *in his bed.*
    EARL OF WARWICK.
Come hither, gracious sovereign, view this body.
    KING HENRY.
That is to see how deep my grave is made;
For with his soul fled all my worldly solace,
And seeing him, I see my life in death.
    EARL OF WARWICK.
As surely as my soul intends to live   [Him
With that dread King that took our state upon
To free us from His Father's wrathful curse,
I do believe that violent hands were laid
Upon the life of this thrice-famed duke.
    DUKE OF SUFFOLK.
A dreadful oath, sworn with a solemn tongue!
What instance gives Lord Warwick for his vow?
    EARL OF WARWICK.
See how the blood is settled in his face!
Oft have I seen a timely-parted ghost,
Of ashy semblance, meagre, pale, and bloodless,
Being all descended to the labouring heart;
Who, in the conflict that it holds with death,
Attracts the same for aidance 'gainst the enemy;
Which with the heart there cools, and ne'er re-
    turneth
To blush and beautify the cheek again.
But see, his face is black and full of blood;
His eyeballs further out than when he lived,
Staring full ghastly like a strangled man;
His hair uprear'd, his nostrils stretcht with
    struggling;
His hands abroad display'd, as one that graspt
And tugg'd for life, and was by strength subdued:
Look, on the sheets his hair, you see, is sticking;
His well-proportion'd beard made rough and
    rugged,
Like to the summer's corn by tempest lodged.
It cannot be but he was murder'd here;
The least of all these signs were probable.
    DUKE OF SUFFOLK.
Why, Warwick, who should do the duke to
    death?
Myself and Beaufort had him in protection;
And we, I hope, sir, are no murderers.
    EARL OF WARWICK.
But both of you were vow'd Duke Humphreys'
    foes;

49

And you, forsooth, had the good duke to keep:
'Tis like you would not feast him like a friend;
And 'tis well seen he found an enemy.
QUEEN MARGARET.
Then you, belike, suspect these noblemen
As guilty of Duke Humphrey's timeless death.
EARL OF WARWICK.
Who finds the heifer dead and bleeding fresh,
And sees fast by a butcher with an axe,
But will suspect 'twas he that made the slaughter?
Who finds the partridge in the puttock's nest,
But may imagine how the bird was dead,
Although the kite soar with unbloodied beak?
Even so suspicious is this tragedy.
QUEEN MARGARET.
Are you the butcher, Suffolk?—where's your
knife?
Is Beaufort term'd a kite?—where are his talons?
DUKE OF SUFFOLK.
I wear no knife to slaughter sleeping men;
But here's a vengeful sword, rusted with ease,
That shall be scoured in his rancorous heart
That slanders me with murder's crimson
badge:—
Say, if thou darest, proud Lord of Warwickshire,
That I am faulty in Duke Humphrey's death.
[Exeunt CARDINAL, SOMERSET, and others.
EARL OF WARWICK.
What dares not Warwick, if false Suffolk dare
him?
QUEEN MARGARET.
He dares not calm his contumelious spirit,
Nor cease to be an arrogant controller,
Though Suffolk dare him twenty thousand times.
EARL OF WARWICK.
Madam, be still,—with reverence may I say;
For every word you speak in his behalf
Is slander to your royal dignity.
DUKE OF SUFFOLK.
Blunt-witted lord, ignoble in demeanour!
If ever lady wrong'd her lord so much,
Thy mother took into her blameful bed
Some stern untutor'd churl, and noble stock
Was graft with crab-tree slip; whose fruit thou
art,
And never of the Nevils' noble race.
EARL OF WARWICK.
But that the guilt of murder bucklers thee,
And I should rob the deathsman of his fee,
Quitting thee thereby of ten thousand shames,
And that my sovereign's presence makes me mild,
I would, false murderous coward, on thy knee
Make thee beg pardon for thy passed speech,
And say it was thy mother that thou meant'st,—
That thou thyself wast born in bastardy;
And, after all this fearful homage done,
Give thee thy hire, and send thy soul to hell,
Pernicious blood-sucker of sleeping men!
DUKE OF SUFFOLK.
Thou shalt be waking while I shed thy blood,
If from this presence thou darest go with me.
EARL OF WARWICK.
Away even now, or I will drag thee hence:
Unworthy though thou art, I'll cope with thee,
And do some service to Duke Humphrey's ghost.
[Exeunt SUFFOLK and WARWICK.

KING HENRY.
What stronger breastplate than a heart untainted!
Thrice is he arm'd that hath his quarrel just;
And he but naked, though lockt up in steel,
Whose conscience with injustice is corrupted.
[A noise within.
QUEEN MARGARET.
What noise is this?
Enter SUFFOLK and WARWICK, with their
weapons drawn.
KING HENRY.
Why, how now, lords! your wrathful weapons
drawn
Here in our presence! dare you be so bold?—
Why, what tumultuous clamour have we here?
DUKE OF SUFFOLK.
The traitorous Warwick, with the men of Bury,
Set all upon me, mighty sovereign.
EARL OF SALISBURY [to the COMMONS at
the door].
Sirs, stand apart; the king shall know your
mind.—
Dread lord, the commons send you word by me,
Unless false Suffolk straight be done to death
Or banished fair England's territories,
They will by violence tear him from your palace,
And torture him with grievous lingering death.
They say, by him the good Duke Humphrey
died;
They say, in him they fear your highness' death;
And mere instinct of love and loyalty—
Free from a stubborn opposite intent,
As being thought to contradict your liking—
Makes them thus forward in his banishment.
They say, in care of your most royal person,
That if your highness should intend to sleep,
And charge that no man should disturb your
rest,
In pain of your dislike, or pain of death;
Yet, notwithstanding such a strait edict,
Were there a serpent seen, with forked tongue,
That slily glided towards your majesty,
It were but necessary you were waked;
Lest, being suffer'd in that harmful slumber,
The mortal worm might make the sleep eternal:
And therefore do they cry, though you forbid,
That they will guard you, whe'r you will or no,
From such fell serpents as false Suffolk is;
With whose envenomed and fatal sting,
Your loving uncle, twenty times his worth,
They say, is shamefully bereft of life.
COMMONS [within].
An answer from the king, my Lord of Salisbury!
DUKE OF SUFFOLK.
'Tis like the commons, rude unpolish'd hinds,
Could send such message to their sovereign:
But you, my lord, were glad to be employ'd,
To show how quaint an orator you are:
But all the honour Salisbury hath won
Is, that he was the lord ambassador
Sent from a sort of tinkers to the king.
COMMONS [within].
An answer from the king, or we will all break in!
KING HENRY.
Go, Salisbury, and tell them all from me,
I thank them for their tender loving care;

And had I not been cited so by them,
Yet did I purpose as they do entreat;
For, sure, my thoughts do hourly prophesy
Mischance unto my state by Suffolk's means:
And therefore,—by His majesty I swear,
Whose far unworthy deputy I am,—
He shall not breathe infection in this air
But three days longer, on the pain of death.
                              [*Exit* SALISBURY.
                QUEEN MARGARET.
O Henry, let me plead for gentle Suffolk!
                KING HENRY.
Ungentle queen, to call him gentle Suffolk!
No more, I say: if thou dost plead for him,
Thou wilt but add increase unto my wrath.
Had I but said, I would have kept my word;
But when I swear, it is irrevocable.—
If after three days' space thou here be'st found
On any ground that I am ruler of,
The world shall not be ransom for thy life.—
Come, Warwick, come, good Warwick, go with
    me;
I have great matters to impart to thee.
        [*Exeunt all except* QUEEN *and* SUFFOLK.
                QUEEN MARGARET.
Mischance and sorrow go along with you!
Heart's discontent and sour affliction
Be playfellows to keep you company!
There's two of you; the devil make a third!
And threefold vengeance tend upon your steps!
                EARL OF SUFFOLK.
Cease, gentle queen, these execrations,
And let thy Suffolk take his heavy leave.
                QUEEN MARGARET.
Fie, coward woman, and soft-hearted wretch!
Hast thou not spirit to curse thine enemies?
                DUKE OF SUFFOLK.
A plague upon them! wherefore should I curse
    them?
Would curses kill, as doth the mandrake's groan,
I would invent as bitter-searching terms,
As curst, as harsh, and horrible to hear,
Deliver'd strongly through my fixed teeth,
With full as many signs of deadly hate,
As lean-faced Envy in her loathsome cave:
My tongue should stumble in mine earnest
    words;
Mine eyes should sparkle like the beaten flint;
Mine hair be fixt on end, as one distract;
Ay, every joint should seem to curse and ban:
And even now my burden'd heart would break,
Should I not curse them. Poison be their drink!
Gall, worse than gall, the dainties that they
    taste!
Their sweetest shade a grove of cypress-trees!
Their chiefest prospect murdering basilisks!
Their softest touch as smart as lizards' stings!
Their music frightful as the serpent's hiss,
And boding screech-owls make the consort full!
All the foul terrors in dark-seated hell—
                QUEEN MARGARET.
Enough, sweet Suffolk; thou torment'st thyself;
And these dread curses—like the sun 'gainst
    glass,
Or like an overcharged gun—recoil,
And turn the force of them upon thyself.

                EARL OF SUFFOLK.
You bade me ban, and will you bid me leave?
Now, by the ground that I am banisht from,
Well could I curse away a winter's night,
Though standing naked on a mountain-top,
Where biting cold would never let grass grow,
And think it but a minute spent in sport.
                QUEEN MARGARET.
O, let me entreat thee, cease! Give me thy hand,
That I may dew it with my mournful tears;
Nor let the rain of heaven wet this place,
To wash away my woful monuments.
O, could this kiss be printed in thy hand,
                              [*Kisses his hand.*
That thou mightst think upon these by the seal,
Through whom a thousand sighs are breath'd for
    thee!
So, get thee gone, that I may know my grief;
'Tis but surmised whiles thou art standing by,
As one that surfeits thinking on a want.
I will repeal thee, or, be well assured,
Adventure to be banished myself:
And banished I am, if but from thee.
Go; speak not to me; even now be gone.—
O, go not yet!—Even thus two friends condemn'd
Embrace, and kiss, and take ten thousand leaves,
Lother a hundred times to part than die.
Yet now farewell; and farewell life with thee!
                DUKE OF SUFFOLK.
Thus is poor Suffolk ten times banished,—
Once by the king, and three times thrice by thee.
'Tis not the land I care for, wert thou thence;
A wilderness is populous enough,
So Suffolk had thy heavenly company:
For where thou art, there is the world itself,
With every several pleasure in the world;
And where thou art not, desolation.
I can no more:—live thou to joy thy life;
Myself no joy in naught but that thou livest.
                Enter VAUX.
                QUEEN MARGARET.
Whither goes Vaux so fast? what news, I prithee?
                VAUX.
To signify unto his majesty
That Cardinal Beaufort is at point of death;
For suddenly a grievous sickness took him,
That makes him gasp, and stare, and catch the
    air,
Blaspheming God, and cursing men on earth.
Sometime he talks as if Duke Humphrey's
    ghost
Were by his side; sometimes he calls the king,
And whispers to his pillow, as to him,
The secrets of his overcharged soul:
And I am sent to tell his majesty
That even now he cries aloud for him.
                QUEEN MARGARET.
Go tell this heavy message to the king.
                              [*Exit* VAUX.
Ay me! what is this world! what news are these!
But wherefore grieve I at an hour's poor loss,
Omitting Suffolk's exile, my soul's treasure?
Why only, Suffolk, mourn I not for thee,
And with the southern clouds contend in tears,—
Theirs for the earth's increase, mine for my
    sorrows?

51

Now get thee hence: the king, thou know'st, is
  coming;—
If thou be found by me, thou art but dead.
DUKE OF SUFFOLK.
If I depart from thee, I cannot live;
And in thy sight to die, what were it else
But like a pleasant slumber in thy lap?
Here could I breathe my soul into the air,
As mild and gentle as the cradle-babe
Dying with mother's dug between its lips:
Where, from thy sight, I should be raging mad,
And cry out for thee to close up mine eyes,
To have thee with thy lips to stop my mouth;
So shouldst thou either turn my flying soul,
Or I should breathe it so into thy body,
And then it lived in sweet Elysium.
To die by thee were but to die in jest;
From thee to die were torture more than death:
O, let me stay, befall what may befall!
QUEEN MARGARET.
Away! though parting be a fretful corrosive,
It is applied to a deathful wound.
To France, sweet Suffolk: let me hear from thee;
For wheresoe'er thou art in this world's globe,
I'll have an Iris that shall find thee out.
DUKE OF SUFFOLK.
I go.
QUEEN MARGARET.
        And take my heart with thee.
DUKE OF SUFFOLK.
A jewel, lockt into the wofull'st cask
That ever did contain a thing of worth.
Even as a splitted bark, so sunder we:
This way fall I to death.
QUEEN MARGARET.
        This way for me.
        [Exeunt severally.

SCENE III.
The CARDINAL's bedchamber.
*Enter the KING, SALISBURY, and WARWICK to
the CARDINAL in bed.*
KING HENRY.
HOW fares my lord? speak, Beaufort, to thy
    sovereign.
CARDINAL BEAUFORT.
If thou be'st Death, I'll give thee England's
  treasure,
Enough to purchase such another island,
So thou wilt let me live, and feel no pain.
KING HENRY.
Ah, what a sign it is of evil life,
Where death's approach is seen so terrible!
EARL OF WARWICK.
Beaufort, it is thy sovereign speaks to thee.
CARDINAL BEAUFORT.
Bring me unto my trial when you will.
Died he not in his bed? where should he die?
Can I make men live, whe'r they will or no?
O, torture me no more! I will confess.—
Alive again? then show me where he is:
I'll give a thousand pound to look upon him.—
He hath no eyes, the dust hath blinded them.—
Comb down his hair; look, look! it stands upright,
Like lime-twigs set to catch my winged soul!—

Give me some drink; and bid the apothecary
Bring the strong poison that I bought of him.
KING HENRY.
O Thou eternal Mover of the heavens,
Look with a gentle eye upon this wretch!
O, beat away the busy-meddling fiend
That lays strong siege unto this wretch's soul,
And from his bosom purge this black despair!
EARL OF WARWICK.
See how the pangs of death do make him grin!
EARL OF SALISBURY.
Disturb him not, let him pass peaceably.
KING HENRY.
Peace to his soul, if God's good pleasure be!—
Lord cardinal, if thou think'st on heaven's bliss,
Hold up thy hand, make signal of thy hope.—
He dies, and makes no sign:—O God, forgive
  him!
EARL OF WARWICK.
So bad a death argues a monstrous life.
KING HENRY.
Forbear to judge, for we are sinners all.—
Close up his eyes, and draw the curtain close;
And let us all to meditation.   [Exeunt.

ACT IV. SCENE I.
The coast of Kent.
*Alarum. Fight at sea. Ordnance goes off. Enter
a CAPTAIN, a MASTER, a MASTER'S-MATE,
WALTER WHITMORE, and others; with them
SUFFOLK and others, prisoners.*
CAPTAIN.
THE gaudy, blabbing, and remorseful day
    Is crept into the bosom of the sea;
And now loud-howling wolves arouse the jades
That drag the tragic melancholy night;
Who, with their drowsy, slow, and flagging wings,
Clip dead men's graves, and from their misty jaws
Breathe foul contagious darkness in the air.
Therefore bring forth the soldiers of our prize;
For, whilst our pinnace anchors in the Downs,
Here shall they make their ransom on the sand,
Or with their blood stain this discolour'd shore.—
Master, this prisoner freely give I thee;—
And thou that art his mate, make boot of this;—
The other [*pointing to* SUFFOLK], Walter Whit-
  more, is thy share.
FIRST GENTLEMAN.
What is my ransom, master? let me know.
MASTER.
A thousand crowns, or else lay down your head.
MASTER'S-MATE.
And so much shall you give, or off goes yours.
CAPTAIN.
What, think you much to pay two thousand
  crowns,
And bear the name and port of gentlemen?—
Cut both the villains' throats;—for die you
  shall:—
The lives of those which we have lost in fight
Be counterpoised with such a petty sum!
FIRST GENTLEMAN.
I'll give it, sir; and therefore spare my life.
SECOND GENTLEMAN.
And so will I, and write home for it straight.

WALTER WHITMORE.
I lost mine eye in laying the prize aboard,
[*to* SUFFOLK] And therefore, to revenge it, shalt
  thou die;
And so should these, if I might have my will.
CAPTAIN.
Be not so rash; take ransom, let him live.
DUKE OF SUFFOLK.
Look on my George,—I am a gentleman:
Rate me at what thou wilt, thou shalt be paid.
WALTER WHITMORE.
And so am I; my name is Walter Whitmore.
How now! why start'st thou? what, doth death
  affright?
DUKE OF SUFFOLK.
Thy name affrights me, in whose sound is death.
A cunning man did calculate my birth,
And told me that by *water* I should die:
Yet let this not make thee be bloody-minded;
Thy name is *Gualtier*, being rightly sounded.
WALTER WHITMORE.
Gualtier or *Walter*, which it is, I care not:
Never yet did base dishonour blur our name,
But with our sword we wiped away the blot;
Therefore, when merchant-like I sell revenge,
Broke be my sword, my arms torn and defaced,
And I proclaim'd a coward through the world!
              [*Lays hold on* SUFFOLK.
DUKE OF SUFFOLK.
Stay, Whitmore; for thy prisoner is a prince,
The Duke of Suffolk, William de la Pole.
WALTER WHITMORE.
The Duke of Suffolk muffled up in rags!
DUKE OF SUFFOLK.
Ay, but these rags are no part of the duke:
Jove sometime went disguised, and why not I?
CAPTAIN.
But Jove was never slain, as thou shalt be.
DUKE OF SUFFOLK.
Obscure and lowly swain, King Henry's blood,
The honourable blood of Lancaster,
Must not be shed by such a jaded groom.
Hast thou not kist thy hand, and held my stirrup?
Bare-headed plodded by my foot-cloth mule,
And thought thee happy when I shook my head?
How often hast thou waited at my cup,
Fed from my trencher, kneel'd down at the
  board,
When I have feasted with Queen Margaret?
Remember it, and let it make thee crest-faln,
Ay, and allay this thy abortive pride:
How in our voiding-lobby hast thou stood,
And duly waited for my coming forth?
This hand of mine hath writ in thy behalf,
And therefore shall it charm thy riotous tongue.
WALTER WHITMORE.
Speak, captain, shall I stab the forlorn swain?
CAPTAIN.
First let my words stab him, as he hath me.
DUKE OF SUFFOLK.
Base slave, thy words are blunt, and so art thou.
CAPTAIN.
Convey him hence, and on our long-boat's side
Strike off his head.
DUKE OF SUFFOLK.
        Thou darest not, for thy own.

CAPTAIN.
Yes, Pole.
DUKE OF SUFFOLK.
Pole!
CAPTAIN.
Pole! Sir Pole! lord!
Ay, kennel, puddle, sink; whose filth and dirt
Troubles the silver spring where England drinks.
Now will I dam up this thy yawning mouth
For swallowing the treasure of the realm:
Thy lips, that kist the queen, shall sweep the
  ground;
And thou, that smiledst at good Duke Hum-
  phrey's death,
Against the senseless winds shalt grin in vain,
Who, in contempt, shall hiss at thee again:
And wedded be thou to the hags of hell,
For daring to affy a mighty lord
Unto the daughter of a worthless king,
Having neither subject, wealth, nor diadem.
By devilish policy art thou grown great,
And, like ambitious Sylla, overgorged
With gobbets of thy mother's bleeding heart.
By thee Anjou and Maine were sold to France;
The false revolting Normans thorough thee
Disdain to call us lord; and Picardy
Hath slain their governors, surprised our forts,
And sent the ragged soldiers wounded home.
The princely Warwick, and the Nevils all,—
Whose dreadful swords were never drawn in
  vain,—
As hating thee, are rising up in arms: [crown
And now the house of York—thrust from the
By shameful murder of a guiltless king
And lofty proud-encroaching tyranny—
Burns with revenging fire; whose hopeful colours
Advance our half-faced sun, striving to shine,
Under the which is writ *Invitis nubibus*.
The commons here in Kent are up in arms:
And, to conclude, reproach and beggary
Is crept into the palace of our king,
And all by thee.—Away! convey him hence.
DUKE OF SUFFOLK.
O, that I were a god, to shoot forth thunder
Upon these paltry, servile, abject drudges!
Small things make base men proud: this villain
  here,
Being captain of a pinnace, threatens more
Than Bargulus, the strong Illyrian pirate.
Drones suck not eagles' blood, but rob bee-hives:
It is impossible that I should die
By such a lowly vassal as thyself.
Thy words move rage and not remorse in me:
I go of message from the queen to France;
I charge thee waft me safely cross the Channel.
CAPTAIN.
Walter,—
WALTER WHITMORE.
Come, Suffolk, I must waft thee to thy death.
DUKE OF SUFFOLK.
Gelidus timor occupat artus:—it is thee I fear.
WALTER WHITMORE.
Thou shalt have cause to fear before I leave thee.
What, are ye daunted now? now will ye stoop?
FIRST GENTLEMAN.
My gracious lord, entreat him, speak him fair.

53

DUKE OF SUFFOLK.
Suffolk's imperial tongue is stern and rough,
Used to command, untaught to plead for
  favour.
Far be it we should honour such as these
With humble suit: no, rather let my head
Stoop to the block than these knees bow to
  any,
Save to the God of heaven and to my king;
And sooner dance upon a bloody pole
Than stand uncover'd to the vulgar groom.
True nobility is exempt from fear:—
More can I bear than you dare execute.

CAPTAIN.
Hale him away, and let him talk no more.

DUKE OF SUFFOLK.
Come, soldiers, show what cruelty ye can,
That this my death may never be forgot!—
Great men oft die by vile besonians:
A Roman sworder and banditto slave
Murder'd sweet Tully; Brutus' bastard hand
Stabb'd Julius Cæsar; savage islanders
Pompey the Great; and Suffolk dies by pirates.
          [*Exeunt* WHITMORE *and others with* SUF-
          FOLK.

CAPTAIN.
And as for these whose ransom we have set,
It is our pleasure one of them depart:—
Therefore come you with us, and let him go.
          [*Exeunt all except the* FIRST GENTLEMAN.
          Enter WHITMORE *with* SUFFOLK'S *body*.

WALTER WHITMORE.
There let his head and lifeless body lie,
Until the queen his mistress bury it.   [*Exit*.

FIRST GENTLEMAN.
O barbarous and bloody spectacle!
His body will I bear unto the king:
If he revenge it not, yet will his friends;
So will the queen, that living held him dear.
          [*Exit with the body*.

SCENE II.

Blackheath.

Enter GEORGE BEVIS *and* JOHN HOLLAND.

GEORGE BEVIS.
COME, and get thee a sword, though made
  of a lath: they have been up these two days.

JOHN HOLLAND.
They have the more need to sleep now, then.

GEORGE BEVIS.
I tell thee, Jack Cade the clothier means to dress
the commonwealth, and turn it, and set a new nap
upon it.

JOHN HOLLAND.
So he had need, for 'tis threadbare. Well, I say it
was never merry world in England since gentlemen came up.

GEORGE BEVIS.
O miserable age! virtue is not regarded in handi-
crafts-men.

JOHN HOLLAND.
The nobility think scorn to go in leather aprons.

GEORGE BEVIS.
Nay, more, the king's council are no good workmen.

JOHN HOLLAND.
True; and yet it is said,—labour in thy vocation;
which is as much to say as,—let the magistrates
be labouring men; and therefore should we be
magistrates.

GEORGE BEVIS.
Thou hast hit it; for there's no better sign of a
brave mind than a hard hand.

JOHN HOLLAND.
I see them! I see them! There's Best's son, the
tanner of Wingham,—

GEORGE BEVIS.
He shall have the skins of our enemies, to make
dog's-leather of.

JOHN HOLLAND.
And Dick the butcher,—

GEORGE BEVIS.
Then is sin struck down like an ox, and iniquity's
throat cut like a calf.

JOHN HOLLAND.
And Smith the weaver,—

GEORGE BEVIS.
Argo, their thread of life is spun.

JOHN HOLLAND.
Come, come, let's fall in with them.
Drum. Enter CADE, DICK *Butcher*, SMITH *the
Weaver, and a* SAWYER, *with infinite numbers*.

JACK CADE.
We John Cade, so term'd of our supposed
father,—

DICK [*aside*].
Or rather, of stealing a cade of herrings.

JACK CADE.
For our enemies shall fall before us,—inspired
with the spirit of putting down kings and princes,
—Command silence.

DICK.
Silence!

JACK CADE.
My father was a Mortimer,—

DICK [*aside*].
He was an honest man, and a good bricklayer.

JACK CADE.
My mother a Plantagenet,—

DICK [*aside*].
I knew her well; she was a midwife.

JACK CADE.
My wife descended of the Lacies,—

DICK [*aside*].
She was, indeed, a pedler's daughter, and sold
many laces.

SMITH [*aside*].
But now of late, not able to travel with her furr'd
pack, she washes bucks here at home.

JACK CADE.
Therefore am I of an honourable house.

DICK [*aside*].
Ay, by my faith, the field is honourable; and there
was he born, under a hedge,—for his father had
never a house but the cage.

JACK CADE.
Valiant I am.

SMITH [*aside*].
'A must needs; for beggary is valiant.

JACK CADE.
I am able to endure much.

54

DICK [*aside*].
No question of that; for I have seen him whipt
three market-days together.
JACK CADE.
I fear neither sword nor fire.
SMITH [*aside*].
He need not fear the sword; for his coat is of
proof.
DICK [*aside*].
But methinks he should stand in fear of fire, being
burnt i' th' hand for stealing of sheep.
JACK CADE.
Be brave, then; for your captain is brave, and
vows reformation. There shall be in England
seven half-penny loaves sold for a penny: the
three-hoop'd pot shall have ten hoops; and I will
make it felony to drink small beer: all the realm
shall be in common; and in Cheapside shall my
palfrey go to grass: and when I am king,—as king
I will be,—
ALL.
God save your majesty!
JACK CADE.
I thank you, good people:—there shall be no
money; all shall eat and drink on my score; and I
will apparel them all in one livery, that they may
agree like brothers, and worship me their lord.
DICK.
The first thing we do, let's kill all the lawyers.
JACK CADE.
Nay, that I mean to do. Is not this a lamentable
thing, that of the skin of an innocent lamb should
be made parchment? that parchment, being
scribbled o'er, should undo a man? Some say the
bee stings: but I say, 'tis the bee's wax; for I did
but seal once to a thing, and I was never mine
own man since.—How now! who's there?
Enter some, bringing in the CLERK OF CHATHAM.
SMITH.
The clerk of Chatham: he can write and read and
cast accompt.
JACK CADE.
O monstrous!
SMITH.
We took him setting of boys' copies.
JACK CADE.
Here's a villain!
SMITH.
'Has a book in his pocket with red letters in't.
JACK CADE.
Nay, then, he is a conjurer.
DICK.
Nay, he can make obligations, and write court-
hand.
JACK CADE.
I am sorry for't: the man is a proper man, of mine
honour; unless I find him guilty, he shall not die.
—Come hither, sirrah, I must examine thee: what
is thy name?
CLERK OF CHATHAM.
Emmanuel.
DICK.
They use to write it on the top of letters:—'twill
go hard with you.
JACK CADE.
Let me alone.—Dost thou use to write thy name?

or hast thou a mark to thyself, like an honest
plain-dealing man?
CLERK OF CHATHAM.
Sir, I thank God, I have been so well brought up
that I can write my name.
ALL.
He hath confest: away with him! he's a villain and
a traitor.
JACK CADE.
Away with him, I say! hang him with his pen and
inkhorn about his neck.
[*Exit one with the* CLERK.
Enter MICHAEL.
MICHAEL.
Where's our general?
JACK CADE.
Here I am, thou particular fellow.
MICHAEL.
Fly, fly, fly! Sir Humphrey Stafford and his
brother are hard by, with the king's forces.
JACK CADE.
Stand, villain, stand, or I'll fell thee down. He
shall be encounter'd with a man as good as him-
self: he is but a knight, is 'a?
MICHAEL.
No.
JACK CADE.
To equal him, I will make myself a knight
presently. [*Kneels.*] Rise up Sir John Mortimer.
[*Rises.*] Now have at him!
Enter SIR HUMPHREY STAFFORD *and his*
BROTHER, *with drum and* SOLDIERS.
SIR HUMPHREY STAFFORD.
Rebellious hinds, the filth and scum of Kent,
Markt for the gallows, lay your weapons down;
Home to your cottages, forsake this groom:—
The king is merciful, if you revolt.
BROTHER.
But angry, wrathful, and inclined to blood,
If you go forward; therefore yield, or die.
JACK CADE.
As for these silken-coated slaves, I pass not:
It is to you, good people, that I speak,
Over whom, in time to come, I hope to reign;
For I am rightful heir unto the crown.
SIR HUMPHREY STAFFORD.
Villain, thy father was a plasterer;
And thou thyself a shearman,—art thou not?
JACK CADE.
And Adam was a gardener.
BROTHER.
And what of that?
JACK CADE.
Marry, thus:—Edmund Mortimer, Earl of
March,
Married the Duke of Clarence' daughter,—did
he not?
SIR HUMPHREY STAFFORD.
Ay, sir.
JACK CADE.
By her he had two children at one birth.
BROTHER.
That's false.
JACK CADE.
Ay, there's the question; but I say 'tis true:
The elder of them, being put to nurse,

Was by a beggar-woman stoln away;
And, ignorant of his birth and parentage,
Became a bricklayer when he came to age:
His son am I; deny it, if you can.
DICK.
Nay, 'tis too true; therefore he shall be king.
SMITH.
Sir, he made a chimney in my father's house, and
the bricks are alive at this day to testify it; there-
fore deny it not.
SIR HUMPHREY STAFFORD.
And will you credit this base drudge's words,
That speaks he knows not what?
ALL.
Ay, marry, will we; therefore get ye gone.
BROTHER.
Jack Cade, the Duke of York hath taught you this.
JACK CADE [aside].
He lies, for I invented it myself.
Go to, sirrah, tell the king from me, that, for his
father's sake, Henry the Fifth, in whose time boys
went to span-counter for French crowns, I am
content he shall reign; but I'll be Protector over
him.
DICK.
And furthermore, we'll have the Lord Say's head
for selling the dukedom of Maine.
JACK CADE.
And good reason; for thereby is England main'd,
and fain to go with a staff, but that my puissance
holds it up. Fellow kings, I tell you that that Lord
Say hath gelded the commonwealth, and made it
an eunuch: and more than that, he can speak
French; and therefore he is a traitor.
SIR HUMPHREY STAFFORD.
O gross and miserable ignorance!
JACK CADE.
Nay, answer, if you can:—the Frenchmen are our
enemies; go to, then, I ask but this,—can he that
speaks with the tongue of an enemy be a good
counsellor, or no?
ALL.
No, no; and therefore we'll have his head.
BROTHER.
Well, seeing gentle words will not prevail,
Assail them with the army of the king.
SIR HUMPHREY STAFFORD.
Herald, away; and throughout every town
Proclaim them traitors that are up with Cade;
That those which fly before the battle ends
May, even in their wives' and children's sight,
Be hang'd up for example at their doors:—
And you that be the king's friends, follow me.
    [Exeunt the two STAFFORDS and SOLDIERS.
JACK CADE.
And you that love the commons, follow me.
Now show yourselves men; 'tis for liberty.
We will not leave one lord, one gentleman:
Spare none but such as go in clouted shoon;
For they are thrifty honest men, and such
As would—but that they dare not—take our parts.
DICK.
They are all in order, and march toward us.
JACK CADE.
But then are we in order when we are most out of
order. Come, march forward!   [Exeunt.

SCENE III.
Another part of Blackheath.

Alarums to the fight, wherein both the STAFFORDS
are slain. Enter CADE *and the rest.*
JACK CADE.
WHERE'S Dick, the butcher of Ashford?
DICK.
Here, sir.
JACK CADE.
They fell before thee like sheep and oxen, and
thou behavedst thyself as if thou hadst been in
thine own slaughter-house: therefore thus will I
reward thee,—the Lent shall be as long again as
it is; and thou shalt have a licence to kill for a
hundred lacking one a week.
DICK.
I desire no more.
JACK CADE.
And, to speak truth, thou deservest no less. This
monument of the victory will I bear [*putting on*
SIR HUMPHREY'S *brigandine*]; and the bodies
shall be dragg'd at my horse heels till I do come
to London, where we will have the mayor's sword
borne before us.
DICK.
If we mean to thrive and do good, break open the
gaols, and let out the prisoners.
JACK CADE.
Fear not that, I warrant thee.—Come, let's
march towards London.   [Exeunt.

SCENE IV.
London. The palace.

Enter the KING *with a supplication, and the*
QUEEN *with* SUFFOLK'S *head; the* DUKE OF
BUCKINGHAM *and the* LORD SAY.
QUEEN MARGARET.
OFT have I heard that grief softens the mind,
    And makes it fearful and degenerate;
Think therefore on revenge, and cease to weep.
But who can cease to weep, and look on this?
Here may his head lie on my throbbing breast:
But where's the body that I should embrace?
DUKE OF BUCKINGHAM.
What answer makes your Grace to the rebels'
    supplication?
KING HENRY.
I'll send some holy bishop to entreat;
For God forbid so many simple souls
Should perish by the sword! And I myself,
Rather than bloody war shall cut them short,
Will parley with Jack Cade their general:—
But stay, I'll read it over once again.
QUEEN MARGARET.
Ah, barbarous villains! hath this lovely face
Ruled, like a wandering planet, over me,
And could it not enforce them to relent,
That were unworthy to behold the same?
KING HENRY.
Lord Say, Jack Cade hath sworn to have thy head.
LORD SAY.
Ay, but I hope your highness shall have his.
KING HENRY.
How now, madam!

56

Still lamenting, and mourning for Suffolk's death?
I fear me, love, if that I had been dead,
Thou wouldest not have mourn'd so much for me.

QUEEN MARGARET.
No, my love, I should not mourn, but die for
thee.

Enter a MESSENGER.

KING HENRY.
How now! what news? why comest thou in such
haste?

MESSENGER.
The rebels are in Southwark; fly, my lord!
Jack Cade proclaims himself Lord Mortimer,
Descended from the Duke of Clarence' house;
And calls your Grace usurper openly,
And vows to crown himself in Westminster.
His army is a ragged multitude
Of hinds and peasants, rude and merciless:
Sir Humphrey Stafford and his brother's death
Hath given them heart and courage to proceed:
All scholars, lawyers, courtiers, gentlemen,
They call false caterpillars, and intend their death.

KING HENRY.
O graceless men! they know not what they do.

DUKE OF BUCKINGHAM.
My gracious lord, retire to Killingworth,
Until a power be raised to put them down.

QUEEN MARGARET.
Ah, were the Duke of Suffolk now alive,
These Kentish rebels would be soon appeased!

KING HENRY.
Lord Say, the traitor hateth thee;
Therefore away with us to Killingworth.

LORD SAY.
So might your Grace's person be in danger;
The sight of me is odious in their eyes:
And therefore in this city will I stay,
And live alone as secret as I may.

Enter a second MESSENGER.

SECOND MESSENGER.
Jack Cade hath gotten London-bridge;
The citizens fly and forsake their houses:
The rascal people, thirsting after prey,
Join with the traitor; and they jointly swear
To spoil the city and your royal court.

DUKE OF BUCKINGHAM.
Then linger not, my lord; away, take horse.

KING HENRY.
Come, Margaret; God, our hope, will succour us.

QUEEN MARGARET.
My hope is gone, now Suffolk is deceased.

KING HENRY [*to* LORD SAY].
Farewell, my lord: trust not the Kentish rebels.

DUKE OF BUCKINGHAM.
Trust nobody, for fear you be betray'd.

LORD SAY.
The trust I have is in mine innocence,
And therefore am I bold and resolute.   [*Exeunt.*

SCENE V.

The same.   The Tower.

Enter LORD SCALES *upon the Tower, walking.
Then enter two or three* CITIZENS *below.*

LORD SCALES.
How now! is Jack Cade slain?

FIRST CITIZEN.
No, my lord, nor likely to be slain; for they have
won the bridge, killing all those that withstand
them: the lord mayor craves aid of your honour
from the Tower, to defend the city from the
rebels.

LORD SCALES.
Such aid as I can spare, you shall command;
But I am troubled here with them myself,—
The rebels have assay'd to win the Tower,
But get you to Smithfield, and gather head,
And thither I will send you Matthew Gough:
Fight for your king, your country, and your lives;
And so, farewell, for I must hence again. [*Exeunt.*

SCENE VI.

The same.   Cannon-street.

Enter JACK CADE *and the rest, and strikes his staff
on London-stone.*

JACK CADE.
NOW is Mortimer lord of this city. And here,
sitting upon London-stone, I charge and
command, that, of the city's cost, the pissing-
conduit run nothing but claret wine this first
year of our reign. And now henceforward it shall
be treason for any that calls me other than Lord
Mortimer.

Enter a SOLDIER, *running.*

SOLDIER.
Jack Cade! Jack Cade!

JACK CADE.
Knock him down there.   [*They kill him.*

SMITH.
If this fellow be wise, he'll never call ye Jack
Cade more: I think he hath a very fair warning.

DICK.
My lord, there's an army gather'd together in
Smithfield.

JACK CADE.
Come, then, let's go fight with them: but first,
go and set London-bridge on fire; and, if you can,
burn down the Tower too. Come, let's away.
                                           [*Exeunt.*

SCENE VII.

The same.   Smithfield.

Alarums. MATTHEW GOUGH *is slain, and all the
rest.   Then enter* JACK CADE, *with his company.*

JACK CADE.
SO, sirs:—now go some and pull down the
Savoy; others to the inns of court; down
with them all.

DICK.
I have a suit unto your lordship.

JACK CADE.
Be it a lordship, thou shalt have it for that word.

DICK.
Only, that the laws of England may come out of
your mouth.

JOHN HOLLAND [*aside*].
Mass, 'twill be sore law, then; for he was thrust
in the mouth with a spear, and 'tis not whole yet.

SMITH [*aside*].
Nay, John, it will be stinking law; for his breath
stinks with eating toasted cheese.

JACK CADE.
I have thought upon it, it shall be so. Away, burn all the records of the realm: my mouth shall be the parliament of England.

JOHN HOLLAND [aside].
Then we are like to have biting statutes, unless his teeth be pull'd out.

JACK CADE.
And henceforward all things shall be in common.

Enter a MESSENGER.

MESSENGER.
My lord, a prize, a prize! here's the Lord Say, which sold the towns in France; he that made us pay one-and-twenty fifteens, and one shilling to the pound, the last subsidy.

Enter GEORGE BEVIS, with the LORD SAY.

JACK CADE.
Well, he shall be beheaded for it ten times.—Ah, thou say, thou serge, nay, thou buckram lord! now art thou within point-blank of our jurisdiction regal. What canst thou answer to my majesty for giving up of Normandy unto Monsieur Basimecu, the dauphin of France? Be it known unto thee by these presence, even the presence of Lord Mortimer, that I am the besom that must sweep the court clean of such filth as thou art. Thou hast most traitorously corrupted the youth of the realm in erecting a grammar-school: and whereas, before, our forefathers had no other books but the score and the tally, thou hast caused printing to be used; and, contrary to the king, his crown, and dignity, thou hast built a paper-mill. It will be proved to thy face that thou hast men about thee that usually talk of a noun and a verb, and such abhominable words as no Christian ear can endure to hear. Thou hast appointed justices of peace, to call poor men before them about matters they were not able to answer. Moreover, thou hast put them in prison; and because they could not read, thou hast hang'd them; when, indeed, only for that cause they have been most worthy to live. Thou dost ride in a foot-cloth, dost thou not?

LORD SAY.
What of that?

JACK CADE.
Marry, thou ought'st not to let thy horse wear a cloak, when honester men than thou go in their hose and doublets.

DICK.
And work in their shirt too; as myself, for example, that am a butcher.

LORD SAY.
You men of Kent,—

DICK.
What say you of Kent?

LORD SAY.
Nothing but this,—'tis bona terra, mala gens.

JACK CADE.
Away with him, away with him! he speaks Latin.

LORD SAY.
Hear me but speak, and bear me where you will.
Kent, in the Commentaries Cæsar writ,
Is term'd the civill'st place of all this isle:
Sweet is the country, beauteous, full of riches;
The people liberal, valiant, active, wealthy;

Which makes me hope you are not void of pity.
I sold not Maine, I lost not Normandy;
Yet, to recover them, would lose my life.
Justice with favour have I always done;
Prayers and tears have moved me, gifts could
    never.
When have I aught exacted at your hands,
But to maintain the king, the realm, and you?
Large gifts have I bestow'd on learned clerks,
Because my book preferr'd me to the king:
And, seeing ignorance is the curse of God,
Knowledge the wing wherewith we fly to heaven,
Unless you be possest with devilish spirits,
You cannot but forbear to murder me:
This tongue hath parley'd unto foreign kings
For your behoof,—

JACK CADE.
Tut, when struck'st thou one blow in the field?

LORD SAY.
Great men have reaching hands: oft have I struck
Those that I never saw, and struck them dead.

GEORGE BEVIS.
O monstrous coward! what, to come behind folks?

LORD SAY.
These cheeks are pale for watching for your good

JACK CADE.
Give him a box o' th' ear, and that will make 'em red again.

LORD SAY.
Long sitting to determine poor men's causes
Hath made me full of sickness and diseases.

JACK CADE.
Ye shall have a hempen caudle, then, and the help of hatchet.

DICK.
Why dost thou quiver, man?

LORD SAY.
It is the palsy, and not fear, provokes me.

JACK CADE.
Nay, he nods at us, as who should say, I'll be ever with you: I'll see if his head will stand steadier on a pole, or no. Take him away, and behead him.

LORD SAY.
Tell me wherein have I offended most?
Have I affected wealth or honour? speak.
Are my chests fill'd up with extorted gold?
Is my apparel sumptuous to behold?
Whom have I injured, that ye seek my death?
These hands are free from guiltless blood-shedding.
This breast from harbouring foul deceitful
    thoughts.
O, let me live!

JACK CADE [aside].
I feel remorse in myself with his words; but I'll bridle it: he shall die, an it be but for pleading so well for his life.—Away with him! he has a familiar under his tongue; he speaks not o God's name. Go, take him away, I say, and strike off his head presently; and then break into his son-in-law's house, Sir James Cromer, and strike off his head, and bring them both upon two poles hither.

ALL.
It shall be done.

LORD SAY.
Ah, countrymen! if when you make your prayers,
God should be so obdurate as yourselves,
How would it fare with your departed souls?
And therefore yet relent, and save my life.
JACK CADE.
Away with him! and do as I command ye.
[*Exeunt some with* LORD SAY.
The proudest peer in the realm shall not wear a
head on his shoulders, unless he pay me tribute;
there shall not a maid be married, but she shall
pay to me her maidenhead ere they have it: men
shall hold of me *in capite;* and we charge and
command that their wives be as free as heart can
wish or tongue can tell.
DICK.
My lord, when shall we go to Cheapside, and
take up commodities upon our bills?
JACK CADE.
Marry, presently.
ALL.
O, brave!
Enter one with the heads.
JACK CADE.
But is not this braver?—Let them kiss one another, for they loved well when they were alive.
Now part them again, lest they consult about
the giving-up of some more towns in France.
Soldiers, defer the spoil of the city until night:
for with these borne before us, instead of maces,
will we ride through the streets; and at every
corner have them kiss.—Away! [*Exeunt.*

SCENE VIII.

Southwark.

Alarum and retreat. Enter again CADE *and all his
rabblement.*

JACK CADE.
UP Fish-street! down Saint Magnus'-corner!
kill and knock down! throw them into
Thames!—[*Sound a parley.*] What noise is this I
hear? Dare any be so bold to sound retreat or
parley, when I command them kill?
Enter BUCKINGHAM *and* OLD CLIFFORD.
DUKE OF BUCKINGHAM.
Ay, here they be that dare and will disturb thee:
Know, Cade, we come ambassadors from the king
Unto the commons whom thou hast misled;
And here pronounce free pardon to them all
That will forsake thee and go home in peace.
OLD CLIFFORD.
What say ye, countrymen? will ye relent,
And yield to mercy whilst 'tis offer'd you;
Or let a rebel lead you to your deaths?
Who loves the king, and will embrace his pardon,
Fling up his cap, and say, 'God save his majesty!'
Who hateth him, and honours not his father,
Henry the Fifth, that made all France to quake,
Shake he his weapon at us, and pass by.
ALL.
God save the king! God save the king!
JACK CADE.
What, Buckingham and Clifford, are ye so
brave?—And you, base peasants, do ye believe
him? will you needs be hang'd with your pardons

about your necks? Hath my sword therefore broke
through London gates, that you should leave me
at the White Hart in Southwark? I thought ye
would never have given out these arms till you
had recover'd your ancient freedom: but ye are
all recreants and dastards, and delight to live in
slavery to the nobility. Let them break your backs
with burdens, take your houses over your heads,
ravish your wives and daughters before your
faces: for me, I will make shift for one; and so,
God's curse light upon you all!
ALL.
We'll follow Cade! we'll follow Cade!
OLD CLIFFORD.
Is Cade the son of Henry the Fifth,
That thus you do exclaim you'll go with him?
Will he conduct you through the heart of France,
And make the meanest of you earls and dukes?
Alas, he hath no home, no place to fly to;
Nor knows he how to live but by the spoil,
Unless by robbing of your friends and us.
Were't not a shame, that whilst you live at jar,
The fearful French, whom you late vanquished,
Should make a start o'er seas, and vanquish you?
Methinks already in this civil broil
I see them lording it in London streets,
Crying 'Viliago!' unto all they meet.
Better ten thousand base-born Cades miscarry
Than you should stoop unto a Frenchman's
mercy.
To France, to France, and get what you have lost;
Spare England, for it is your native coast:
Henry hath money, you are strong and manly;
God on our side, doubt not of victory.
ALL.
A Clifford! a Clifford! we'll follow the king and
Clifford.
JACK CADE[*aside*].
Was ever feather so lightly blown to and fro
as this multitude? the name of Henry the Fifth
hales them to an hundred mischiefs, and makes
them leave me desolate. I see them lay their heads
together to surprise me: my sword make way for
me, for here is no staying.——In despite of the
devils and hell, have through the very middest of
you! and heavens and honour be witness, that no
want of resolution in me, but only my followers'
base and ignominious treasons, makes me betake
me to my heels. [*Exit.*
DUKE OF BUCKINGHAM.
What, is he fled? Go some, and follow him;
And he that brings his head unto the king
Shall have a thousand crowns for his reward.——
[*Exeunt some of them.*
Follow me, soldiers: we'll devise a mean
To reconcile you all unto the king. [*Exeunt.*

SCENE IX.

Killingworth Castle.

Sound trumpets. Enter KING, QUEEN, *and*
SOMERSET, *on the terrace.*

KING HENRY.
WAS ever king that joy'd an earthly throne,
And could command no more content than
No sooner was I crept out of my cradle [I?

59

But I was made a king, at nine months old:
Was never subject long'd to be a king
As I do long and wish to be a subject.
Enter BUCKINGHAM *and* OLD CLIFFORD.
DUKE OF BUCKINGHAM.
Health and glad tidings to your majesty!
KING HENRY.
Why, Buckingham, is the traitor Cade surprised?
Or is he but retired to make him strong?
*Enter, below, multitudes, with halters about their
necks.*
OLD CLIFFORD.
He is fled, my lord, and all his powers do yield;
And humbly thus, with halters on their necks,
Expect your highness' doom, of life or death.
KING HENRY.
Then, heaven, set ope thy everlasting gates,
To entertain my vows of thanks and praise!—
Soldiers, this day have you redeem'd your lives,
And show'd how well you love your prince and
    country:
Continue still in this so good a mind,
And Henry, though he be infortunate,
Assure yourselves, will never be unkind:
And so, with thanks and pardon to you all,
I do dismiss you to your several countries.
ALL.
God save the king! God save the king!
Enter a MESSENGER.
MESSENGER.
Please it your Grace to be advertised
The Duke of York is newly come from Ireland;
And with a puissant and a mighty power
Of gallowglasses and stout kerns
Is marching hitherward in proud array;
And still proclaimeth, as he comes along,
His arms are only to remove from thee
The Duke of Somerset, whom he terms a traitor.
KING HENRY.
Thus stands my state, 'twixt Cade and York
    distrest;
Like to a ship that, having scaped a tempest,
Is straightway calm'd, and boarded with a
    pirate:
But now is Cade driven back, his men dispersed;
And now is York in arms to second him.—
I pray thee, Buckingham, go and meet him;
And ask him what's the reason of these arms.
Tell him I'll send Duke Edmund to the
    Tower;—
And, Somerset, we will commit thee thither,
Until his army be dismist from him.
DUKE OF SOMERSET.
My lord,
I'll yield myself to prison willingly,
Or unto death, to do my country good.
KING HENRY.
In any case, be not too rough in terms;
For he is fierce, and cannot brook hard language.
DUKE OF BUCKINGHAM.
I will, my lord; and doubt not so to deal
As all things shall redound unto your good.
KING HENRY.
Come, wife, let's in, and learn to govern better;
For yet may England curse my wretched reign.
[Flourish. Exeunt.

SCENE X.
Kent. IDEN'S *garden.*
Enter CADE.
JACK CADE.
FIE on ambition! fie on myself, that have a
sword, and yet am ready to famish! These five
days have I hid me in these woods; and durst not
peep out, for all the country is laid for me; but now
am I so hungry, that if I might have a lease of my
life for a thousand years, I could stay no longer.
Wherefore, on a brick-wall have I climb'd into
this garden, to see if I can eat grass, or pick a
sallet another while, which is not amiss to cool a
man's stomach this hot weather. And I think this
word 'sallet' was born to do me good: for many a
time, but for a sallet, my brain-pan had been
cleft with a brown bill; and many a time, when I
have been dry, and bravely marching, it hath
served me instead of a quart-pot to drink in; and
now the word 'sallet' must serve me to feed on.
Enter IDEN, *and his* MEN *behind.*
ALEXANDER IDEN.
Lord, who would live turmoiled in the court,
And may enjoy such quiet walks as these?
This small inheritance my father left me
Contenteth me, and worth a monarchy.
I seek not to wax great by others' waning;
Or gather wealth, I care not with what envy:
Sufficeth that I have maintains my state,
And sends the poor well pleased from my gate.
JACK CADE [*aside*].
Here's the lord of the soil come to seize me for
a stray, for entering his fee-simple without leave.
—Ah, villain, thou wilt betray me, and get a
thousand crowns of the king by carrying my
head to him! but I'll make thee eat iron like an
ostrich, and swallow my sword like a great pin,
ere thou and I part.
ALEXANDER IDEN.
Why, rude companion, whatsoe'er thou be,
I know thee not; why, then, should I betray thee?
Is't not enough to break into my garden,
And, like a thief, to come to rob my grounds,
Climbing my walls in spite of me the owner,
But thou wilt brave me with these saucy terms?
JACK CADE.
Brave thee! ay, by the best blood that ever was
broacht, and beard thee too. Look on me well:
I have eat no meat these five days; yet, come thou
and thy five men, and if I do not leave you all as
dead as a door-nail, I pray God I may never eat
grass more.
ALEXANDER IDEN.
Nay, it shall ne'er be said, while England stands,
That Alexander Iden, an esquire of Kent,
Took odds to combat a poor famisht man.
Oppose thy steadfast-gazing eyes to mine,
See if thou canst outface me with thy looks:
Set limb to limb, and thou art far the lesser;
Thy hand is but a finger to my fist;
Thy leg a stick compared with this truncheon;
My foot shall fight with all the strength thou
    hast;
And if mine arm be heaved in the air,
Thy grave is digg'd already in the earth.

As for words,—whose greatness answers words,
Let this my sword report what speech forbears.
JACK CADE.
By my valour, the most complete champion that
ever I heard!—Steel, if thou turn the edge, or cut
not out the burly-boned clown in chines of beef
ere thou sleep in thy sheath, I beseech God, on
my knees, thou mayst be turn'd to hobnails.
[*Here they fight.* CADE *falls.*] O, I am slain!
famine and no other hath slain me: let ten
thousand devils come against me, and give me
but the ten meals I have lost, and I'ld defy them
all. Wither, garden; and be henceforth a burying-
place to all that do dwell in this house, because
the unconquer'd soul of Cade is fled.
ALEXANDER IDEN.
Is't Cade that I have slain, that monstrous traitor?
Sword, I will hallow thee for this thy deed,
And hang thee o'er my tomb when I am dead:
Ne'er shall this blood be wiped from thy point;
But thou shalt wear it as a herald's coat,
To emblaze the honour that thy master got.
JACK CADE.
Iden, farewell; and be proud of thy victory.
Tell Kent from me, she hath lost her best man;
and exhort all the world to be cowards,—for I,
that never fear'd any, am vanquisht by famine,
not by valour.   [*Dies.*
ALEXANDER IDEN.
How much thou wrong'st me, heaven be my
  judge.   [thee!
Die, damned wretch, the curse of her that bare
And as I thrust thy body in with my sword,
So wish I, I might thrust thy soul to hell.
Hence will I drag thee headlong by the heels
Unto a dunghill, which shall be thy grave,
And there cut off thy most ungracious head;
Which I will bear in triumph to the king,
Leaving thy trunk for crows to feed upon.
[*Exeunt* IDEN, *dragging out the body, and*
SERVANTS.

ACT V. SCENE I.

Fields between Dartford and Blackheath.

Enter YORK *and his army of Irish, with drum
and colours.*

DUKE OF YORK.
FROM Ireland thus comes York to claim his
    right,
And pluck the crown from feeble Henry's head:
Ring, bells, aloud; burn, bonfires, clear and bright;
To entertain great England's lawful king.
Ah, *sancta majestas!* who would not buy thee dear?
Let them obey that know not how to rule;
This hand was made to handle naught but gold.
I cannot give due action to my words,
Except a sword or sceptre balance it:
A sceptre shall it have,—have I a soul,—
On which I'll toss the flower-de-luce of France.
Enter BUCKINGHAM [*aside*].
Whom have we here? Buckingham, to disturb
  me?
The king hath sent him, sure: I must dissemble.
DUKE OF BUCKINGHAM.
York, if thou meanest well, I greet thee well.

DUKE OF YORK.
Humphrey of Buckingham, I accept thy greeting.
Art thou a messenger, or come of pleasure?
DUKE OF BUCKINGHAM.
A messenger from Henry, our dread liege,
To know the reason of these arms in peace;
Or why thou, being a subject as I am,
Against thy oath and true allegiance sworn,
Should raise so great a power without his leave,
Cʳ dare to bring thy force so near the court.
DUKE OF YORK [*aside*].
Scarce can I speak, my choler is so great:
O, I could hew up rocks, and fight with flint,
I am so angry at these abject terms;
And now, like Ajax Telamonius,
On sheep or oxen could I spend my fury!
I am far better born than is the king,
More like a king, more kingly in my thoughts:
But I must make fair weather yet awhile,
Till Henry be more weak, and I more strong.—
Buckingham, I prithee, pardon me,
That I have given no answer all this while;
My mind was troubled with deep melancholy.
The cause why I have brought this army hither
Is, to remove proud Somerset from the king,
Seditious to his Grace and to the state.
DUKE OF BUCKINGHAM.
That is too much presumption on thy part:
But if thy arms be to no other end,
The king hath yielded unto thy demand;
The Duke of Somerset is in the Tower.
DUKE OF YORK.
Upon thine honour, is he prisoner?
DUKE OF BUCKINGHAM.
Upon mine honour, he is prisoner.
DUKE OF YORK.
Then, Buckingham, I do dismiss my powers.—
Soldiers, I thank you all; disperse yourselves;
Meet me to-morrow in Saint George's field,
You shall have pay and every thing you wish.—
And let my sovereign, virtuous Henry,
Command my eldest son, nay, all my sons,
As pledges of my fealty and love;
I'll send them all as willing as I live:
Lands, goods, horse, armour, any thing I have,
Is his to use, so Somerset may die.
DUKE OF BUCKINGHAM.
York, I commend this kind submission:
We twain will go into his highness' tent.
Enter KING HENRY *and* ATTENDANTS.
KING HENRY.
Buckingham, doth York intend no harm to us,
That thus he marcheth with thee arm in arm?
DUKE OF YORK.
In all submission and humility
York doth present himself unto your highness.
KING HENRY.
Then what intends these forces thou dost bring?
DUKE OF YORK.
To heave the traitor Somerset from hence;
And fight against that monstrous rebel Cade,
Who since I heard to be discomfited.
Enter IDEN, *with* CADE'S *head.*
ALEXANDER IDEN.
If one so rude and of so mean condition
May pass into the presence of a king,

61

Lo, I present your Grace a traitor's head,
The head of Cade, whom I in combat slew.
KING HENRY.
The head of Cade!—Great God, how just art
  Thou!—
O, let me view his visage, being dead,
That living wrought me such exceeding trouble.—
Tell me, my friend, art thou the man that slew
  him?
ALEXANDER IDEN.
I was, an't like your majesty.
KING HENRY.
How art thou call'd? and what is thy degree?
ALEXANDER IDEN.
Alexander Iden, that's my name;
A poor esquire of Kent, that loves his king.
DUKE OF BUCKINGHAM.
So please it you, my lord, 'twere not amiss
He were created knight for his good service.
KING HENRY.
Iden, kneel down. [He kneels.] Rise up a knight.
We give thee for reward a thousand marks;
And will that thou henceforth attend on us.
ALEXANDER IDEN.
May Iden live to merit such a bounty,
And never live but true unto his liege!
KING HENRY.
See, Buckingham! Somerset comes with the
  queen:
Go, bid her hide him quickly from the duke.
Enter QUEEN MARGARET and SOMERSET.
QUEEN MARGARET.
For thousand Yorks he shall not hide his head,
But boldly stand, and front him to his face.
DUKE OF YORK.
How now! is Somerset at liberty?   [thoughts,
Then, York, unloose thy long-imprison'd
And let thy tongue be equal with thy heart.
Shall I endure the sight of Somerset?—
False king! why hast thou broken faith with me,
Knowing how hardly I can brook abuse?
King did I call thee? no, thou art not king;
Not fit to govern and rule multitudes,
Which darest not, no, nor canst not rule a traitor.
That head of thine doth not become a crown;
Thy hand is made to grasp a palmer's staff,
And not to grace an awful princely sceptre.
That gold must round engirt these brows of
  mine;
Whose smile and frown, like to Achilles' spear,
Is able with the change to kill and cure.
Here is a hand to hold a sceptre up,
And with the same to act controlling laws.
Give place: by heaven, thou shalt rule no more
O'er him whom heaven created for thy ruler.
DUKE OF SOMERSET.
O monstrous traitor!—I arrest thee, York,
Of capital treason 'gainst the king and crown:
Obey, audacious traitor; kneel for grace.
DUKE OF YORK.
Wouldst have me kneel? first let me ask of these,
If they can brook I bow a knee to man.—
Sirrah, call in my sons to be my bail:
[Exit an ATTENDANT.
I know, ere they will have me go to ward,   [ment.
They'll pawn their swords for my enfranchise-

QUEEN MARGARET.
Call hither Clifford; bid him come amain,
To say if that the bastard boys of York
Shall be the surety for their traitor father.
[Exit BUCKINGHAM.
DUKE OF YORK.
O blood-bespotted Neapolitan,
Outcast of Naples, England's bloody scourge!
The sons of York, thy betters in their birth,
Shall be their father's bail; and bane to those
That for my surety will refuse the boys!
See where they come: I'll warrant they'll make it
  good.
Enter EDWARD and RICHARD.
QUEEN MARGARET.
And here comes Clifford to deny their bail.
Enter OLD CLIFFORD and his SON.
OLD CLIFFORD.
Health and all happiness to my lord the king!
[Kneels.
DUKE OF YORK.
I thank thee, Clifford: say, what news with thee?
Nay, do not fright us with an angry look:
We are thy sovereign, Clifford, kneel again;
For thy mistaking so, we pardon thee.
OLD CLIFFORD.
This is my king, York, I do not mistake;
But thou mistakest me much to think I do:—
To Bedlam with him! is the man grown mad?
KING HENRY.
Ay, Clifford; a bedlam and ambitious humour
Makes him oppose himself against his king.
OLD CLIFFORD.
He is a traitor; let him to the Tower,
And chop away that factious pate of his.
QUEEN MARGARET.
He is arrested, but will not obey;
His sons, he says, shall give their words for him.
DUKE OF YORK.
Will you not, sons?
EDWARD.
Ay, noble father, if our words will serve.
RICHARD.
And if words will not, then our weapons shall.
OLD CLIFFORD.
Why, what a brood of traitors have we here!
DUKE OF YORK.
Look in a glass, and call thy image so:
I am thy king, and thou a false-heart traitor.—
Call hither to the stake my two brave bears,
That with the very shaking of their chains
They may astonish these fell-lurking curs:
Bid Salisbury and Warwick come to me.
Enter the EARLS OF WARWICK and SALISBURY.
OLD CLIFFORD.
Are these thy bears? we'll bait thy bears to death,
And manacle the bear-ward in their chains,
If thou darest bring them to the baiting-place.
RICHARD.
Oft have I seen a hot o'erweening cur
Run back and bite, because he was withheld;
Who, being suffer'd with the bear's fell paw,
Hath clapt his tail between his legs and cried:
And such a piece of service will you do,
If you oppose yourselves to match Lord War-
wick.

OLD CLIFFORD.
Hence, heap of wrath, foul indigested lump,
As crooked in thy manners as thy shape!
DUKE OF YORK.
Nay, we shall heat you thoroughly anon.
OLD CLIFFORD.
Take heed, lest by your heat you burn yourselves.
KING HENRY.
Why, Warwick, hath thy knee forgot to bow?—
Old Salisbury,—shame to thy silver hair,
Thou mad misleader of thy brain-sick son!—
What, wilt thou on thy death-bed play the ruffian,
And seek for sorrow with thy spectacles?—
O, where is faith? O, where is loyalty?
If it be banish't from the frosty head,
Where shall it find a harbour in the earth?—
Wilt thou go dig a grave to find out war,
And shame thine honourable age with blood?
Why art thou old, and want'st experience?
Or wherefore dost abuse it, if thou hast it?
For shame! in duty bend thy knee to me,
That bows unto the grave with mickle age.
EARL OF SALISBURY.
My lord, I have consider'd with myself
The title of this most renowned duke;
And in my conscience do repute his Grace
The rightful heir to England's royal seat.
KING HENRY.
Hast thou not sworn allegiance unto me?
EARL OF SALISBURY.
I have.
KING HENRY.
Canst thou dispense with heaven for such an
　oath?
EARL OF SALISBURY.
It is great sin to swear unto a sin;
But greater sin to keep a sinful oath.
Who can be bound by any solemn vow
To do a murderous deed, to rob a man,
To force a spotless virgin's chastity,
To reave the orphan of his patrimony,
To wring the widow from her custom'd right;
And have no other reason for this wrong,
But that he was bound by a solemn oath?
QUEEN MARGARET.
A subtle traitor needs no sophister.
KING HENRY.
Call Buckingham, and bid him arm himself.
DUKE OF YORK.
Call Buckingham, and all the friends thou hast,
I am resolved for death or dignity.
OLD CLIFFORD.
The first I warrant thee, if dreams prove true.
EARL OF WARWICK.
You were best to go to bed and dream again,
To keep thee from the tempest of the field.
OLD CLIFFORD.
I am resolved to bear a greater storm
Than any thou canst conjure up to-day;
And that I'll write upon thy burgonet,
Might I but know thee by thy household badge.
EARL OF WARWICK.
Now, by my father's badge, old Nevil's crest,
The rampant bear chain'd to the ragged staff,
This day I'll wear aloft my burgonet,—
As on a mountain-top the cedar shows,

That keeps his leaves in spite of any storm,—
Even to affright thee with the view thereof.
OLD CLIFFORD.
And from thy burgonet I'll rend thy bear,
And tread it under foot with all contempt,
Despite the bear-ward that protects the bear.
YOUNG CLIFFORD.
And so to arms, victorious father,
To quell the rebels and their complices.
RICHARD.
Fie! charity, for shame! speak not in spite,
For you shall sup with Jesu Christ to-night.
YOUNG CLIFFORD.
Foul stigmatic, that's more than thou canst tell.
RICHARD.
If not in heaven, you'll surely sup in hell.
　　　　　　　　　　　　[Exeunt severally.

SCENE II.
Saint Alban's.

Alarums to the battle. Enter WARWICK.

EARL OF WARWICK.
CLIFFORD of Cumberland, 'tis Warwick calls!
　An if thou dost not hide thee from the bear,
Now,—when the angry trumpet sounds alarum,
And dead men's cries do fill the empty air,—
Clifford, I say, come forth and fight with me!
Proud northern lord, Clifford of Cumberland,
Warwick is hoarse with calling thee to arms.
Enter YORK.
How now, my noble lord! what, all a-foot?
DUKE OF YORK.
The deadly-handed Clifford slew my steed;
But match to match I have encounter'd him,
And made a prey for carrion kites and crows
Even of the bonny beast he loved so well.
Enter OLD CLIFFORD.
EARL OF WARWICK.
Of one or both of us the time is come.
DUKE OF YORK.
Hold, Warwick, seek thee out some other chase,
For I myself must hunt this deer to death.
EARL OF WARWICK.
Then, nobly, York; 'tis for a crown thou fight'st.—
As I intend, Clifford, to thrive to-day,
It grieves my soul to leave thee unassail'd.　[Exit.
OLD CLIFFORD.
What seest thou in me, York? why dost thou
　pause?
DUKE OF YORK.
With thy brave bearing should I be in love,
But that thou art so fast mine enemy.
OLD CLIFFORD.
Nor should thy prowess want praise and esteem,
But that 'tis shown ignobly and in treason.
DUKE OF YORK.
So let it help me now against thy sword,
As I in justice and true right express it!
OLD CLIFFORD.
My soul and body on the action both!
DUKE OF YORK.
A dreadful lay!—address thee instantly.
　　　　[They fight.　OLD CLIFFORD *falls.*
OLD CLIFFORD.
La fin couronne les œuvres.　　　　　[Dies.

DUKE OF YORK.
Thus war hath given thee peace, for thou art still.
Peace with his soul, heaven, if it be thy will! [*Exit.*
Enter YOUNG CLIFFORD.
YOUNG CLIFFORD.
Shame and confusion! all is on the rout;
Fear frames disorder, and disorder wounds
Where it should guard. O war, thou son of hell,
Whom angry heavens do make their minister,
Throw in the frozen bosoms of our part
Hot coals of vengeance!—Let no soldier fly:
He that is truly dedicate to war
Hath no self-love; nor he that loves himself
Hath not essentially, but by circumstance,
The name of valour.—O, let the vile world end,
[*Seeing his father's body.*
And the premised flames of the last day
Knit earth and heaven together!
Now let the general trumpet blow his blast,
Particularities and petty sounds
To cease!—Wast thou ordain'd, dear father,
To lose thy youth in peace, and to achieve
The silver livery of advised age,
And, in thy reverence and thy chair-days, thus
To die in ruffian battle?—Even at this sight
My heart is turn'd to stone: and while 'tis mine,
It shall be stony. York not our old men spares;
No more will I their babes: tears virginal
Shall be to me even as the dew to fire;
And beauty, that the tyrant oft reclaims,
Shall to my flaming wrath be oil and flax.
Henceforth I will not have to do with pity:
Meet I an infant of the house of York,
Into as many gobbets will I cut it,
As wild Medea young Absyrtus did:
In cruelty will I seek out my fame.—
Come, thou new ruin of old Clifford's house.
[*Taking up the body.*
As did Æneas old Anchises bear,
So bear I thee upon my manly shoulders;
But then Æneas bare a living load,
Nothing so heavy as these woes of mine. [*Exit.*
Enter RICHARD *and* SOMERSET *to fight.*
SOMERSET *is kill'd.*
RICHARD.
So, lie thou there;—
For underneath an alehouse' paltry sign,
The Castle in Saint Alban's, Somerset
Hath made the wizard famous in his death.—
Sword, hold thy temper; heart, be wrathful still:
Priests pray for enemies, but princes kill. [*Exit.*
Fight. Excursions. Enter KING, QUEEN, *and others.*
QUEEN MARGARET.
Away, my lord! you are slow; for shame, away!
KING HENRY.
Can we outrun the heavens? good Margaret, stay.
QUEEN MARGARET.
What are you made of? you'll nor fight nor fly:
Now is it manhood, wisdom, and defence,
To give the enemy way; and to secure us
By what we can, which can no more but fly.
[*Alarum afar off.*

If you be ta'en, we then should see the bottom
Of all our fortunes: but if we haply scape,—
As well we may, if not through your neglect,—
We shall to London get: where you are loved;
And where this breach, now in our fortunes made,
May readily be stopt.
Enter YOUNG CLIFFORD.
YOUNG CLIFFORD.
But that my heart's on future mischief set,
I would speak blasphemy ere bid you fly:
But fly you must; uncurable discomfit
Reigns in the hearts of all our present part.
Away, for your relief! and we will live
To see their day, and them our fortune give:
Away, my lord, away! [*Exeunt.*

SCENE III.
Fields near Saint Alban's.

Alarum. Retreat. Enter YORK, RICHARD, WARWICK, *and* SOLDIERS, *with drum and colours.*
DUKE OF YORK.
OLD Salisbury, who can report of him,—
    That winter lion, who in rage forgets
Aged contusions and all brush of time,
And, like a gallant in the brow of youth,
Repairs him with occasion? This happy day
Is not itself, nor have we won one foot,
If Salisbury be lost.
RICHARD.
        My noble father,
Three times to-day I holp him to his horse,
Three times bestrid him, thrice I led him off,
Persuaded him from any further act:
But still, where danger was, still there I met him;
And like rich hangings in a homely house,
So was his will in his old feeble body.
But, noble as he is, look where he comes.
Enter SALISBURY.
EARL OF SALISBURY.
Now, by my sword, well hast thou fought to-day;
By th' mass, so did we all.—I thank you, Richard:
God knows how long it is I have to live;
And it hath pleased him that three times to-day
You have defended me from imminent death.—
Well, lords, we have not got that which we have:
'Tis not enough our foes are this time fled,
Being opposites of such repairing nature.
DUKE OF YORK.
I know our safety is to follow them;
For, as I hear, the king is fled to London,
To call a present court of parliament.
Let us pursue him, ere the writs go forth:—
What says Lord Warwick? shall we after them?
EARL OF WARWICK.
After them! nay, before them, if we can.
Now, by my faith, lords, 'twas a glorious day:
Saint Alban's battle, won by famous York,
Shall be eternized in all age to come.—
Sound drums and trumpets;—and to London all:
And more such days as these to us befall! [*Exeunt.*

THE THIRD PART OF
KING HENRY THE SIXTH

DRAMATIS PERSONAE

KING HENRY THE SIXTH.
EDWARD, *Prince of Wales, his son.*
LOUIS XI., *King of France.*
DUKE OF SOMERSET.
DUKE OF EXETER.
EARL OF OXFORD.
EARL OF NORTHUMBERLAND.
EARL OF WESTMORELAND.
LORD CLIFFORD.
RICHARD PLANTAGENET, *Duke of York.*
EDWARD, *Earl of March, afterwards King Edward IV.,*
EDMUND, *Earl of Rutland,*
GEORGE, *afterwards Duke of Clarence,* } *his sons.*
RICHARD, *afterwards Duke of Gloster,*
DUKE OF NORFOLK.
MARQUESS OF MONTAGUE.
EARL OF WARWICK.
EARL OF PEMBROKE.
LORD HASTINGS.
LORD STAFFORD.

SIR JOHN MORTIMER, } *uncles to the Duke of*
SIR HUGH MORTIMER, } *York.*
HENRY, *Earl of Richmond, a youth.*
LORD RIVERS, *brother to Lady Grey.*
SIR WILLIAM STANLEY.
SIR JOHN MONTGOMERY.
SIR JOHN SOMERVILLE.
TUTOR TO RUTLAND. MAYOR OF YORK.
LIEUTENANT OF THE TOWER. A NOBLEMAN.
TWO KEEPERS. A HUNTSMAN.
A SON THAT HAS KILL'D HIS FATHER.
A FATHER THAT HAS KILL'D HIS SON.

QUEEN MARGARET.
LADY GREY, *afterwards Queen to Edward IV.*
BONA, *sister to the French Queen.*

SOLDIERS, ATTENDANTS, MESSENGERS,
WATCHMEN, &c.

SCENE—*During part of the third Act in France;
during the rest of the Play in England.*

ACT I. SCENE I.

London. The Parliament-house.

Alarum. Enter the DUKE OF YORK, EDWARD,
RICHARD, NORFOLK, MONTAGUE, WAR-
WICK, *and* SOLDIERS.

EARL OF WARWICK.

I WONDER how the king escaped our hands.
DUKE OF YORK.
While we pursued the horsemen of the north,
He slily stole away, and left his men:
Whereat the great Lord of Northumberland,
Whose warlike ears could never brook retreat,
Cheer'd up the drooping army; and himself,
Lord Clifford, and Lord Stafford, all a-breast,
Charged our main battle's front, and, breaking in,
Were by the swords of common soldiers slain.
EDWARD.
Lord Stafford's father, Duke of Buckingham,
Is either slain or wounded dangerous;
I cleft his beaver with a downright blow:
That this is true, father, behold his blood.
[*Showing his bloody sword.*
MARQUESS OF MONTAGUE [*to* YORK,
showing his].
And, brother, here's the Earl of Wiltshire's blood,
Whom I encounter'd as the battles join'd.
RICHARD.
Speak thou for me, and tell them what I did.
[*Throwing down the* DUKE OF SOMER-
SET'S *head.*
DUKE OF YORK.
Richard hath best deserved of all my sons.—
But, is your Grace dead, my Lord of Somerset?
DUKE OF NORFOLK.
Such hap have all the line of John of Gaunt!
RICHARD.
Thus do I hope to shake King Henry's head.

EARL OF WARWICK.
And so do I.—Victorious Prince of York,
Before I see thee seated in that throne
Which now the house of Lancaster usurps,
I vow by heaven these eyes shall never close.
This is the palace of the fearful king,
And this the regal seat: possess it, York;
For this is thine, and not King Henry's heirs'.
DUKE OF YORK.
Assist me, then, sweet Warwick, and I will;
For hither we have broken in by force.
DUKE OF NORFOLK.
We'll all assist you; he that flies shall die.
DUKE OF YORK.
Thanks, gentle Norfolk:—stay by me, my
lords;—
And, soldiers, stay, and lodge by me this night.
EARL OF WARWICK.
And when the king comes, offer him no violence,
Unless he seek to thrust you out perforce.
[*They go up*
DUKE OF YORK.
The queen, this day, here holds her parliament,
But little thinks we shall be of her council:
By words or blows here let us win our right.
RICHARD.
Arm'd as we are, let's stay within this house.
EARL OF WARWICK.
The bloody parliament shall this be call'd,
Unless Plantagenet, duke of York, be king,
And bashful Henry deposed, whose cowardice
Hath made us by-words to our enemies.
DUKE OF YORK.
Then leave me not, my lords; be resolute;
I mean to take possession of my right.
EARL OF WARWICK.
Neither the king, nor he that loves him best,
The proudest he that holds up Lancaster,
Dares stir a wing, if Warwick shake his bells.

C

I'll plant Plantagenet, root him up who dares:—
Resolve thee, Richard; claim the English crown.
Flourish. Enter KING HENRY, CLIFFORD,
    NORTHUMBERLAND,   WESTMORELAND,
    EXETER, *and the rest.*

KING HENRY.
My lords, look where the sturdy rebel sits,
Even in the chair of state! belike he means—
Backt by the power of Warwick, that false peer—
To aspire unto the crown, and reign as king.—
Earl of Northumberland, he slew thy father;
And thine, Lord Clifford; and you both have
    vow'd revenge
On him, his sons, his favourites, and his friends.

EARL OF NORTHUMBERLAND.
If I be not, heavens be revenged on me!

LORD CLIFFORD.
The hope thereof makes Clifford mourn in steel.

EARL OF WESTMORELAND.
What, shall we suffer this? let's pluck him down:
My heart for anger burns: I cannot brook it.

KING HENRY.
Be patient, gentle Earl of Westmoreland.

LORD CLIFFORD.
Patience is for poltroons, such as he:
He durst not sit there, had your father lived.
My gracious lord, here in the parliament
Let us assail the family of York.

EARL OF NORTHUMBERLAND.
Well hast thou spoken, cousin: be it so.

KING HENRY.
Ah, know you not the city favours them,
And they have troops of soldiers at their beck?

DUKE OF EXETER.
But when the duke is slain, they'll quickly fly.

KING HENRY.
Far be the thought of this from Henry's heart,
To make a shambles of the parliament-house!
Cousin of Exeter, frowns, words, and threats
Shall be the war that Henry means to use.
Thou factious Duke of York, descend my
    throne,
And kneel for grace and mercy at my feet;
I am thy sovereign.

DUKE OF YORK.
        Thou'rt deceived; I'm thine.

DUKE OF EXETER.
For shame, come down: he made thee Duke of
    York.

DUKE OF YORK.
'Twas my inheritance, as the earldom was.

DUKE OF EXETER.
Thy father was a traitor to the crown.

EARL OF WARWICK.
Exeter, thou art a traitor to the crown
In following this usurping Henry.

LORD CLIFFORD.
Whom should he follow but his natural king?

EARL OF WARWICK.
True, Clifford; and that's Richard duke of York.

KING HENRY.
And shall I stand, and thou sit in my throne?

DUKE OF YORK.
It must and shall be so: content thyself.

EARL OF WARWICK.
Be Duke of Lancaster; let him be king.

EARL OF WESTMORELAND.
He is both king and Duke of Lancaster;   [tain.
And that the Lord of Westmoreland shall main-

EARL OF WARWICK.
And Warwick shall disprove it. You forget
That we are those which chased you from the
    field,
And slew your fathers, and with colours spread
Marcht through the city to the palace-gates.

EARL OF NORTHUMBERLAND.
No, Warwick, I remember it to my grief;
And, by his soul, thou and thy house shall rue it.

EARL OF WESTMORELAND.
Plantagenet, of thee, and these thy sons,   [lives
Thy kinsmen, and thy friends, I'll have more
Than drops of blood were in my father's veins.

LORD CLIFFORD.
Urge it no more; lest that, instead of words,
I send thee, Warwick, such a messenger
As shall revenge his death before I stir.

EARL OF WARWICK.
Poor Clifford! how I scorn his worthless threats!

DUKE OF YORK.
Will you we show our title to the crown?
If not, our swords shall plead it in the field.

KING HENRY.
What title hast thou, traitor, to the crown?
Thy father was, as thou art, Duke of York;
Thy grandfather, Roger Mortimer, Earl of
    March:
I am the son of Henry the Fifth,
Who made the Dauphin and the French to stoop,
And seized upon their towns and provinces.

EARL OF WARWICK.
Talk not of France, sith thou hast lost it all.

KING HENRY.
The lord Protector lost it, and not I:
When I was crown'd I was but nine months old.

RICHARD.
You are old enough now, and yet, methinks, you
    lose.—
Father, tear the crown from the usurper's head.

EDWARD.
Sweet father, do so; set it on your head.

MARQUESS OF MONTAGUE [*to* YORK].
Good brother, as thou lovest and honourest
    arms,
Let's fight it out, and not stand cavilling thus.

RICHARD.
Sound drums and trumpets, and the king will fly.

DUKE OF YORK.
Sons, peace!

KING HENRY.
Peace thou! and give King Henry leave to speak.

EARL OF WARWICK.
Plantagenet shall speak first: hear him, lords;
And be you silent and attentive too,
For he that interrupts him shall not live.

KING HENRY.
Think'st thou that I will leave my kingly throne,
Wherein my grandsire and my father sat?
No; first shall war unpeople this my realm;
Ay, and their colours—often borne in France,
And now in England to our heart's great sorrow—
Shall be my winding-sheet.—Why faint you, lords?
My title's good, and better far than his.

EARL OF WARWICK.
Prove it, Henry, and thou shalt be king.
KING HENRY.
Henry the Fourth by conquest got the crown.
DUKE OF YORK.
'Twas by rebellion against his king.
KING HENRY [aside].
I know not what to say; my title's weak.—
Tell me, may not a king adopt an heir?
DUKE OF YORK.
What then?
KING HENRY.
An if he may, then am I lawful king;
For Richard, in the view of many lords,
Resign'd the crown to Henry the Fourth,
Whose heir my father was, and I am his.
DUKE OF YORK.
He rose against him, being his sovereign,
And made him to resign his crown perforce.
EARL OF WARWICK.
Suppose, my lords, he did it unconstrain'd,
Think you 'twere prejudicial to his crown?
DUKE OF EXETER.
No; for he could not so resign his crown
But that the next heir should succeed and reign.
KING HENRY.
Art thou against us, Duke of Exeter?
DUKE OF EXETER.
His is the right, and therefore pardon me.
DUKE OF YORK.
Why whisper you, my lords, and answer not?
DUKE OF EXETER.
My conscience tells me he is lawful king.
KING HENRY [aside].
All will revolt from me, and turn to him.
EARL OF NORTHUMBERLAND.
Plantagenet, for all the claim thou lay'st,
Think not that Henry shall be so deposed.
EARL OF WARWICK.
Deposed he shall be, in despite of all.
EARL OF NORTHUMBERLAND.
Thou art deceived: 'tis not thy southern power,
Of Essex, Norfolk, Suffolk, nor of Kent—
Which makes thee thus presumptuous and
    proud—
Can set the duke up, in despite of me.
LORD CLIFFORD.
King Henry, be thy title right or wrong,
Lord Clifford vows to fight in thy defence:
May that ground gape, and swallow me alive,
Where I shall kneel to him that slew my father!
KING HENRY.
O Clifford, how thy words revive my heart!
DUKE OF YORK.
Henry of Lancaster, resign thy crown.—
What mutter you, or what conspire you, lords?
EARL OF WARWICK.
Do right unto this princely Duke of York;
Or I will fill the house with armed men,
And over the chair of state, where now he sits,
Write up his title with usurping blood. ·
    [He stamps with his foot, and the SOLDIERS
    show themselves.
KING HENRY.
My Lord of Warwick, hear me but one word:—
Let me for this my life-time reign as king.

DUKE OF YORK.
Confirm the crown to me and to mine heirs,
And thou shalt reign in quiet while thou
    livest.
KING HENRY.
I am content: Richard Plantagenet,
Enjoy the kingdom after my decease.
LORD CLIFFORD.
What wrong is this unto the prince your son!
EARL OF WARWICK.
What good is this to England and himself!
EARL OF WESTMORELAND.
Base, fearful, and despairing Henry!
LORD CLIFFORD.
How hast thou injured both thyself and us!
EARL OF WESTMORELAND.
I cannot stay to hear these articles.
EARL OF NORTHUMBERLAND.
Nor I.
LORD CLIFFORD.
Come, cousin, let us tell the queen these news.
EARL OF WESTMORELAND.
Farewell, faint-hearted and degenerate king,
In whose cold blood no spark of honour bides.
EARL OF NORTHUMBERLAND.
Be thou a prey unto the house of York,
And die in bands, for this unmanly deed!
LORD CLIFFORD.
In dreadful war mayst thou be overcome,
Or live in peace, abandon'd and despised!
    [Exeunt NORTHUMBERLAND, CLIFFORD,
    and WESTMORELAND.
EARL OF WARWICK.
Turn this way, Henry, and regard them not.
DUKE OF EXETER.
They seek revenge, and therefore will not yield.
KING HENRY.
Ah, Exeter!
EARL OF WARWICK.
    Why should you sigh, my lord?
KING HENRY.
Not for myself, Lord Warwick, but my son,
Whom I unnaturally shall disinherit.
But, be it as it may:—I here entail
The crown to thee, and to thine heirs for ever;
Conditionally, that here thou take an oath
To cease this civil war, and, whilst I live,
To honour me as thy king and sovereign,
And neither by treason nor hostility
To seek to put me down, and reign thyself.
DUKE OF YORK.
This oath I willingly take, and will perform.
EARL OF WARWICK.
Long live King Henry!—Plantagenet, embrace
him.
KING HENRY.
And long live thou, and these thy forward sons!
DUKE OF YORK.
Now York and Lancaster are reconciled.
DUKE OF EXETER.
Accurst be he that seeks to make them foes!
    [Sennet.   Here they come down.
DUKE OF YORK.
Farewell, my gracious lord; I'll to my castle.
EARL OF WARWICK.
And I'll keep London with my soldiers.

DUKE OF NORFOLK.
And I to Norfolk with my followers.
MARQUESS OF MONTAGUE.
And I unto the sea, from whence I came.
[*Exeunt* YORK *and his* SONS, WARWICK,
NORFOLK, MONTAGUE, SOLDIERS,
and ATTENDANTS.
KING HENRY.
And I, with grief and sorrow, to the court.
DUKE OF EXETER.
Here comes the queen, whose looks bewray her
anger:
I'll steal away.   [*Going*.
KING HENRY.
Exeter, so will I.   [*Going*.
Enter QUEEN MARGARET *and the* PRINCE OF
WALES.
QUEEN MARGARET.
Nay, go not from me; I will follow thee.
KING HENRY.
Be patient, gentle queen, and I will stay.
QUEEN MARGARET.
Who can be patient in such extremes?
Ah, wretched man! would I had died a maid,
And never seen thee, never borne thee son,
Seeing thou hast proved so unnatural a father!
Hath he deserved to lose his birthright thus?
Hadst thou but loved him half so well as I,
Or felt that pain which I did for him once,
Or nourish him as I did with my blood,
Thou wouldst have left thy dearest heart-blood
there,
Rather than have made that savage duke thine
heir,
And disinherited thine only son.
PRINCE OF WALES.
Father, you cannot disinherit me:
If you be king, why should not I succeed?
KING HENRY.
Pardon me, Margaret;—pardon me, sweet son:—
The Earl of Warwick and the duke enforced me.
QUEEN MARGARET.
Enforced thee! art thou king, and wilt be forced?
I shame to hear thee speak. Ah, timorous wretch!
Thou hast undone thyself, thy son, and me;
And given unto the house of York such head,
As thou shalt reign but by their sufferance.
To entail him and his heirs unto the crown,
What is it, but to make thy sepulchre,
And creep into it far before thy time?
Warwick is chancellor, and the lord of Calais;
Stern Falconbridge commands the narrow seas;
The duke is made Protector of the realm;
And yet shalt thou be safe? such safety finds
The trembling lamb environed with wolves.
Had I been there, which am a silly woman,
The soldiers should have toss'd me on their pikes
Before I would have granted to that act.
But thou preferr'st thy life before thine honour:
And seeing thou dost, I here divorce myself
Both from thy table, Henry, and thy bed,
Until that act of Parliament be repeal'd,
Whereby my son is disinherited.
The northern lords that have forsworn thy colours
Will follow mine, if once they see them spread;
And spread they shall be,—to thy foul disgrace,

And utter ruin of the house of York.
Thus do I leave thee.—Come, son, let's away;
Our army is ready; come, we'll after them.
KING HENRY.
Stay, gentle Margaret, and hear me speak.
QUEEN MARGARET.
Thou hast spoke too much already; get thee gone.
KING HENRY.
Gentle son Edward, thou wilt stay with me?
QUEEN MARGARET.
Ay, to be murder'd by his enemies.
PRINCE OF WALES.
When I return with victory from the field,
I'll see your Grace: till then I'll follow her.
QUEEN MARGARET.
Come, son, away; we may not linger thus.
[*Exeunt* QUEEN MARGARET *and the*
PRINCE.
KING HENRY.
Poor queen! how love to me and to her son
Hath made her break out into terms of rage!
Revenged may she be on that hateful duke,
Whose haughty spirit, winged with desire,
Will cost my crown, and like an empty eagle
Tire on the flesh of me and of my son!
The loss of those three lords torments my heart:
I'll write unto them, and entreat them fair:—
Come, cousin, you shall be the messenger.
DUKE OF EXETER.
And I, I hope, shall reconcile them all.
[*Exeunt*.

SCENE II.
Sandal Castle, near Wakefield.
Enter RICHARD, EDWARD, *and* MONTAGUE.
RICHARD.
BROTHER, though I be youngest, give me leave.
EDWARD.
No, I can better play the orator.
MARQUESS OF MONTAGUE.
But I have reasons strong and forcible.
Enter the DUKE OF YORK.
DUKE OF YORK.
Why, how now, sons and brother! at a strife?
What is your quarrel? how began it first?
EDWARD.
No quarrel, but a slight contention.
DUKE OF YORK.
About what?
RICHARD.
About that which concerns your Grace and us,—
The crown of England, father, which is yours.
DUKE OF YORK.
Mine, boy? not till King Henry be dead.
RICHARD.
Your right depends not on his life or death.
EDWARD.
Now you are heir, therefore enjoy it now:
By giving the house of Lancaster leave to breathe,
It will outrun you, father, in the end.
DUKE OF YORK.
I took an oath that he should quietly reign.
EDWARD.
But, for a kingdom, any oath may be broken:
I would break a thousand oaths to reign one year.

RICHARD.
No; God forbid your Grace should be forsworn.
DUKE OF YORK.
I shall be, if I claim by open war.
RICHARD.
I'll prove the contrary, if you'll hear me speak.
DUKE OF YORK.
Thou canst not, son; it is impossible.
RICHARD.
An oath is of no moment, being not took
Before a true and lawful magistrate,
That hath authority over him that swears:
Henry had none, but did usurp the place;
Then, seeing 'twas he that made you to depose,
Your oath, my lord, is vain and frivolous.
Therefore, to arms! And, father, do but think
How sweet a thing it is to wear a crown;
Within whose circuit is Elysium,
And all that poets feign of bliss and joy.
Why do we linger thus? I cannot rest
Until the white rose that I wear be dyed
Even in the lukewarm blood of Henry's heart.
DUKE OF YORK.
Richard, enough; I will be king, or die.—
Brother, thou shalt to London presently,
And whet-on Warwick to this enterprise.—
Thou, Richard, shalt to the Duke of Norfolk,
And tell him privily of our intent.—
You, Edward, shall unto my Lord Cobham,
With whom the Kentishmen will willingly rise:
In them I trust; for they are soldiers,
Witty, courteous, liberal, full of spirit.
While you are thus employ'd, what resteth more,
But that I seek occasion how to rise,
And yet the king not privy to my drift,
Nor any of the house of Lancaster?
Enter a MESSENGER.
But, stay: what news?—Why comest thou in such
post?
MESSENGER.
The queen with all the northern earls and lords
Intend here to besiege you in your castle:
She is hard by with twenty thousand men;
And therefore fortify your hold, my lord.
DUKE OF YORK.
Ay, with my sword. What! think'st thou that we
fear them?—
Edward and Richard, you shall stay with me;—
My brother Montague shall post to London:
Let noble Warwick, Cobham, and the rest,
Whom we have left protectors of the king,
With powerful policy strengthen themselves,
And trust not simple Henry nor his oaths.
MARQUESS OF MONTAGUE.
Brother, I go; I'll win them, fear it not:
And thus most humbly I do take my leave.
        [Exit.
Enter SIR JOHN *and* SIR HUGH MORTIMER.
DUKE OF YORK.
Sir John and Sir Hugh Mortimer, mine uncles!
You are come to Sandal in a happy hour;
The army of the queen mean to besiege us.
SIR JOHN MORTIMER.
She shall not need, we'll meet her in the field.
DUKE OF YORK.
What, with five thousand men?

RICHARD.
Ay, with five hundred, father, for a need:
A woman's general; what should we fear?
        [A march afar off.
EDWARD.
I hear their drums: let's set our men in order,
And issue forth, and bid them battle straight.
DUKE OF YORK.
Five men to twenty!—though the odds be great,
I doubt not, uncle, of our victory.
Many a battle have I won in France,
Whenas the enemy hath been ten to one:
Why should I not now have the like success?
        [Alarum. Exeunt.

SCENE III.

Field of battle near Sandal Castle.

Alarums. Enter RUTLAND *and his* TUTOR.

EARL OF RUTLAND.
AH, whither shall I fly to scape their hands?
  Ah, tutor, look where bloody Clifford comes!
Enter CLIFFORD *and* SOLDIERS.
LORD CLIFFORD.
Chaplain, away! thy priesthood saves thy life.
As for the brat of this accursed duke,
Whose father slew my father,—he shall die.
TUTOR.
And I, my lord, will bear him company.
LORD CLIFFORD.
Soldiers, away with him!
TUTOR.
Ah, Clifford, murder not this innocent child,
Lest thou be hated both of God and man!
    [Exit, forced off by SOLDIERS.
LORD CLIFFORD.
How now! is he dead already? or is it fear
That makes him close his eyes?—I'll open them.
EARL OF RUTLAND.
So looks the pent-up lion o'er the wretch
That trembles under his devouring paws;
And so he walks, insulting o'er his prey,
And so he comes, to rend his limbs asunder.—
Ah, gentle Clifford, kill me with thy sword,
And not with such a cruel threatening look!
Sweet Clifford, hear me speak before I die!—
I am too mean a subject for thy wrath:
Be thou revenged on men, and let me live.
LORD CLIFFORD.
In vain thou speak'st, poor boy; my father's blood
Hath stopt the passage where thy words should
enter.
EARL OF RUTLAND.
Then let my father's blood open it again:
He is a man, and Clifford, cope with him.
LORD CLIFFORD.
Had I thy brethren here, their lives and thine
Were not revenge sufficient for me;
No, if I digg'd up thy forefathers' graves,
And hung their rotten coffins up in chains,
It could not slake mine ire nor ease my heart.
The sight of any of the house of York
Is as a fury to torment my soul;
And till I root out their accursed line,
And leave not one alive, I live in hell.
Therefore—   *[Lifting his hand.*

EARL OF RUTLAND.
O, let me pray before I take my death!—
To thee I pray; sweet Clifford, pity me!
LORD CLIFFORD.
Such pity as my rapier's point affords.
EARL OF RUTLAND.
I never did thee harm: why wilt thou slay me?
LORD CLIFFORD.
Thy father hath.
EARL OF RUTLAND.
        But 'twas ere I was born.
Thou hast one son,—for his sake pity me;
Lest in revenge thereof,—sith God is just,—
He be as miserably slain as I.
Ah, let me live in prison all my days;
And when I give occasion of offence,
Then let me die, for now thou hast no cause!
LORD CLIFFORD.
No cause!
Thy father slew my father; therefore, die.
                              [Stabs him.
EARL OF RUTLAND.
Di faciant, laudis summa sit ista tuæ!   [Dies.
LORD CLIFFORD.
Plantagenet! I come, Plantagenet!
And this thy son's blood cleaving to my blade
Shall rust upon my weapon, till thy blood,
Congeal'd with this, do make me wipe off both.
                              [Exit.

SCENE IV.

Another part of the field.

Alarums. Enter RICHARD, DUKE OF YORK.

DUKE OF YORK.
THE army of the queen hath got the field:
  My uncles both are slain in rescuing me;
And all my followers to the eager foe
Turn back, and fly, like ships before the wind,
Or lambs pursued by hunger-starved wolves.
My sons,—God knows what hath bechanced
    them:
But this I know, they have demean'd themselves
Like men born to renown by life or death.
Three times did Richard make a lane to me,
And thrice cried, 'Courage, father! fight it
    out!'
And full as oft came Edward to my side,
With purple falchion, painted to the hilt
In blood of those that had encounter'd him:
And when the hardiest warriors did retire,
Richard cried, 'Charge! and give no foot of
    ground!'
And cried, 'A crown, or else a glorious tomb!
A sceptre, or an earthly sepulchre!'
With this, we charged again: but, out, alas!
We bodged again: as I have seen a swan
With bootless labour swim against the tide,
And spend her strength with over-matching
    waves.   [A short alarum within.
Ah, hark! the fatal followers do pursue;
And I am faint, and cannot fly their fury:
And were I strong, I would not shun their fury:
The sands are number'd that make up my life;
Here must I stay, and here my life must end.

Enter the QUEEN, CLIFFORD, NORTHUMBER-
LAND, *and* SOLDIERS.

Come, bloody Clifford,—rough Northumber-
    land,—
I dare your quenchless fury to more rage:
I am your butt, and I abide your shot.
EARL OF NORTHUMBERLAND.
Yield to our mercy, proud Plantagenet.
LORD CLIFFORD.
Ay, to such mercy as his ruthless arm,
With downright payment, show'd unto my father.
Now Phaethon hath tumbled from his car,
And made an evening at the noontide prick.
DUKE OF YORK.
My ashes, as the phœnix, may bring forth
A bird that will revenge upon you all;
And in that hope I throw mine eyes to heaven,
Scorning whate'er you can afflict me with.
Why come you not? what! multitudes, and fear?
LORD CLIFFORD.
So cowards fight when they can fly no further;
So doves do peck the falcon's piercing talons;
So desperate thieves, all hopeless of their lives,
Breathe out invectives 'gainst the officers.
DUKE OF YORK.
O Clifford, but bethink thee once again,
And in thy thought o'er-run my former time;
And, if thou canst for blushing, view this face,
And bite thy tongue, that slanders him with
    cowardice
Whose frown hath made thee faint and fly ere this!
LORD CLIFFORD.
I will not bandy with thee word for word,
But buckle with thee blows, twice two for one.
                              [Draws.
QUEEN MARGARET.
Hold, valiant Clifford! for a thousand causes
I would prolong awhile the traitor's life.—
Wrath makes him deaf:—speak thou, Northum-
    berland.
EARL OF NORTHUMBERLAND.
Hold, Clifford! do not honour him so much
To prick thy finger, though to wound his heart:
What valour were it, when a cur doth grin,
For one to thrust his hand between his teeth,
When he might spurn him with his foot away?
It is war's prize to take all vantages;
And ten to one is no impeach of valour.
        [They lay hands on YORK, who struggles.
LORD CLIFFORD.
Ay, ay, so strives the woodcock with the gin.
EARL OF NORTHUMBERLAND.
So doth the cony struggle in the net.
DUKE OF YORK.
So triumph thieves upon their conquer'd booty;
So true men yield, with robbers so o'ermatcht.
EARL OF NORTHUMBERLAND.
What would your Grace have done unto him
    now?
QUEEN MARGARET.
Brave warriors, Clifford and Northumberland,
Come, make him stand upon this molehill here,
That raught at mountains with outstretched arms,
Yet parted but the shadow with his hand.—
What! was it you that would be England's king?
Was't you that revell'd in our parliament,

And made a preachment of your high descent?
Where are your mess of sons to back you now?
The wanton Edward, and the lusty George?
And where's that valiant crook-back prodigy,
Dicky your boy, that with his grumbling voice
Was wont to cheer his dad in mutinies?
Or, with the rest, where is your darling Rutland?
Look, York: I stain'd this napkin with the blood
That valiant Clifford, with his rapier's point,
Made issue from the bosom of the boy;
And if thine eyes can water for his death,
I give thee this to dry thy cheeks withal.
Alas, poor York! but that I hate thee deadly,
I should lament thy miserable state.
I prithee, grieve, to make me merry, York;
Stamp, rave, and fret, that I may sing and dance.
What! hath thy fiery heart so parcht thine
    entrails
That not a tear can fall for Rutland's death?
Why art thou patient, man? thou shouldst be
    mad;
And I, to make thee mad, do mock thee thus.
Thou wouldst be fee'd, I see, to make me sport:
York cannot speak, unless he wear a crown.—
A crown for York!—and, lords, bow low to
    him:—
Hold you his hands, whilst I do set it on.—
                [*Putting a paper crown on his head.*
Ay, marry, sir, now looks he like a king!
Ay, this is he that took King Henry's chair;
And this is he was his adopted heir.—
But how is it that great Plantagenet
Is crown'd so soon, and broke his solemn oath?
As I bethink me, you should not be king
Till our King Henry had shook hands with death.
And will you pale your head in Henry's glory,
And rob his temples of the diadem,
Now in his life, against your holy oath?
O, 'tis a fault too-too unpardonable!—
Off with the crown, and, with the crown, his head;
And, whilst we breathe, take time to do him dead.
            LORD CLIFFORD.
That is my office, for my father's sake.
            QUEEN MARGARET.
Nay, stay; let's hear the orisons he makes.
            DUKE OF YORK.
She-wolf of France, but worse than wolves of
    France,
Whose tongue more poisons than the adder's
    tooth!
How ill-beseeming is it in thy sex
To triumph, like an Amazonian trull,
Upon their woes whom fortune captivates!
But that thy face is, vizard-like, unchanging,
Made impudent with use of evil deeds,
I would assay, proud queen, to make thee blush:
To tell thee whence thou camest, of whom
    derived,
Were shame enough to shame thee, wert thou
    not shameless.
Thy father bears the type of King of Naples,
Of both the Sicils and Jerusalem;
Yet not so wealthy as an English yeoman.
Hath that poor monarch taught thee to insult?
It needs not, nor it boots thee not, proud queen;
Unless the adage must be verified,—

That beggars mounted run their horse to death.
'Tis beauty that doth oft make women proud;
But, God he knows, thy share thereof is small:
'Tis virtue that doth make them most admired;
The contrary doth make thee wonder'd at:
'Tis government that makes them seem divine;
The want thereof makes thee abominable:
Thou art as opposite to every good
As the Antipodes are unto us,
Or as the south to the septentrion.
O tiger's heart wrapt in a woman's hide!
How couldst thou drain the life-blood of the
    child,
To bid the father wipe his eyes withal,
And yet be seen to bear a woman's face?
Women are soft, mild, pitiful, and flexible;
Thou stern, obdurate, flinty, rough, remorseless.
Bidd'st thou me rage? why, now thou hast thy
    wish;
Wouldst have me weep? why, now thou hast thy
    will:
For raging wind blows up incessant showers,
And when the rage allays, the rain begins.
These tears are my sweet Rutland's obsequies;
And every drop cries vengeance for his death,
'Gainst thee, fell Clifford, and thee, false French-
    woman.
            EARL OF NORTHUMBERLAND.
Beshrew me, but his passion moves me so
That hardly can I check my eyes from tears.
            DUKE OF YORK.
That face of his the hungry cannibals
Would not have toucht, would not have stain'd
    with blood:
But you are more inhuman, more inexorable,—
O, ten times more,—than tigers of Hyrcania.
See, ruthless queen, a hapless father's tears:
This cloth thou dipp'dst in blood of my sweet
    boy,
And I with tears do wash the blood away.
Keep thou the napkin, and go boast of this:
And, if thou tell'st the heavy story right,
Upon my soul, the hearers will shed tears;
Yea, even my foes will shed fast-falling tears,
And say, 'Alas, it was a piteous deed!'—
There, take the crown, and, with the crown, my
    curse;
                [*Giving back the paper crown.*
And in thy need such comfort come to thee
As now I reap at thy too cruel hand!—
Hard-hearted Clifford, take me from the world:
My soul to heaven, my blood upon your heads!
            EARL OF NORTHUMBERLAND.
Had he been slaughter-man to all my kin,
I should not for my life but weep with him,
To see how inly sorrow gripes his soul.
            QUEEN MARGARET.
What, weeping-ripe, my Lord Northumberland?
Think but upon the wrong he did us all,
And that will quickly dry thy melting tears.
            LORD CLIFFORD.
Here's for my oath, here's for my father's death.
                [*Stabbing him.*
            QUEEN MARGARET.
And here's to right our gentle-hearted king.
                [*Stabbing him.*

71

DUKE OF YORK.
Open Thy gate of mercy, gracious God!
My soul flies through these wounds to seek out
   Thee.   [*Dies.*
        QUEEN MARGARET.
Off with his head, and set it on York gates;
So York may overlook the town of York.
               [*Flourish. Exeunt.*

ACT II. SCENE I.

A plain near Mortimer's Cross in Herefordshire.
A march. Enter EDWARD, RICHARD, *and their*
           POWER.
        EDWARD.
I WONDER how our princely father scaped,
   Or whether he be scaped away or no
From Clifford's and Northumberland's pursuit:
Had he been ta'en, we should have heard the
   news;
Had he been slain, we should have heard the
   news;
Or had he scaped, methinks we should have heard
The happy tidings of his good escape.—
How fares my brother? why is he so sad?
        RICHARD.
I cannot joy, until I be resolved
Where our right valiant father is become.
I saw him in the battle range about;
And watcht him how he singled Clifford forth.
Methought he bore him in the thickest troop
As doth a lion in a herd of neat;
Or as a bear, encompast round with dogs,—
Who having pincht a few, and made them cry,
The rest stand all aloof, and bark at him.
So fared our father with his enemies;
So fled his enemies my warlike father:
Methinks, 'tis prize enough to be his son.—
See how the morning opes her golden gates,
And takes her farewell of the glorious sun!
How well resembles it the prime of youth,
Trimm'd like a younker prancing to his love!
        EDWARD.
Dazzle mine eyes, or do I see three suns?
        RICHARD.
Three glorious suns, each one a perfect sun;
Not separated with the racking clouds,
But sever'd in a pale clear-shining sky.
See, see! they join, embrace, and seem to kiss,
As if they vow'd some league inviolable:
Now are they but one lamp, one light, one sun.
In this the heaven figures some event.
        EDWARD.
'Tis wondrous strange, the like yet never heard of.
I think it cites us, brother, to the field,—
That we, the sons of brave Plantagenet,
Each one already blazing by our meeds,
Should, notwithstanding, join our lights together,
And over-shine the earth, as this the world.
Whate'er it bodes, henceforward will I bear
Upon my target three fair-shining suns.
        RICHARD.
Nay, bear three daughters:—by your leave I
   speak it,
You love the breeder better than the male.

Enter one blowing.
But what art thou, whose heavy looks foretell
Some dreadful story hanging on thy tongue?
        MESSENGER.
Ah, one that was a woful looker-on
Whenas the noble Duke of York was slain,
Your princely father and my loving lord!
        EDWARD.
O, speak no more! for I have heard too much.
        RICHARD.
Say how he died, for I will hear it all.
        MESSENGER.
Environed he was with many foes;
And stood against them as the hope of Troy
Against the Greeks that would have enter'd Troy.
But Hercules himself must yield to odds;
And many strokes, though with a little axe,
Hew down and fell the hardest-timber'd oak.
By many hands your father was subdued;
But only slaughtered by the ireful arm
Of unrelenting Clifford and the queen,
Who crown'd the gracious duke in high despite;
Laugh'd in his face; and when with grief he wept,
The ruthless queen gave him to dry his cheeks
A napkin steeped in the harmless blood
Of sweet young Rutland, by rough Clifford slain:
And after many scorns, many foul taunts,
They took his head, and on the gates of York
They set the same; and there it doth remain,
The saddest spectacle that e'er I view'd.
        EDWARD.
Sweet Duke of York, our prop to lean upon,
Now thou art gone, we have no staff, no stay!—
O Clifford, boisterous Clifford, thou hast slain
The flower of Europe for his chivalry;
And treacherously hast thou vanquisht him,
For hand to hand he would have vanquisht
   thee!—
Now my soul's palace is become a prison:
Ah, would she break from hence, that this my
   body
Might in the ground be closed up in rest!
For never henceforth shall I joy again,
Never, O never, shall I see more joy!
        RICHARD.
I cannot weep; for all my body's moisture
Scarce serves to quench my furnace-burning
   heart: [*burden;*
Nor can my tongue unload my heart's great
For selfsame wind that I should speak withal
Is kindling coals that fires all my breast,
And burns me up with flames that tears would
   quench.
To weep is to make less the depth of grief:
Tears, then, for babes; blows and revenge for
   me!—
Richard, I bear thy name; I'll venge thy death,
Or die renowned by attempting it.
        EDWARD.
His name that valiant duke hath left with thee;
His dukedom and his chair with me is left.
        RICHARD.
Nay, if thou be that princely eagle's bird,
Show thy descent by gazing 'gainst the sun:
For chair and dukedom, throne and kingdom say;
Either that is thine, or else thou wert not his.

March. Enter WARWICK, MONTAGUE, *and their*
ARMY.
EARL OF WARWICK.
How now, fair lords! What fare? what news
   abroad?
RICHARD.
Great Lord of Warwick, if we should recount
Our baleful news, and at each word's deliverance
Stab poniards in our flesh till all were told,
The words would add more anguish than the
   wounds.
O valiant lord, the Duke of York is slain!
EDWARD.
O Warwick, Warwick! that Plantagenet,
Which held thee dearly as his soul's redemption,
Is by the stern Lord Clifford done to death.
EARL OF WARWICK.
Ten days ago I drown'd these news in tears;
And now, to add more measure to your woes,
I come to tell you things sith then befaln.
After the bloody fray at Wakefield fought,
Where your brave father breathed his latest gasp,
Tidings, as swiftly as the posts could run,
Were brought me of your loss and his depart.
I, then in London, keeper of the king,
Muster'd my soldiers, gather'd flocks of friends,
And very well appointed, as I thought,   [queen,
Marcht toward Saint Alban's to intercept the
Bearing the king in my behalf along;
For by my scouts I was advertised
That she was coming with a full intent
To dash our late decree in parliament
Touching King Henry's oath and your succession.
Short tale to make,—we at Saint Alban's met,
Our battles join'd, and both sides fiercely fought:
But whether 'twas the coldness of the king,
Who lookt full gently on his warlike queen,
That robb'd my soldiers of their heated spleen;
Or whether 'twas report of her success;
Or more than common fear of Clifford's rigour,
Who thunders to his captives blood and death,
I cannot judge: but, to conclude with truth,
Their weapons like to lightning came and went;
Our soldiers—like the night-owl's lazy flight,
Or like an idle thrasher with a flail—
Fell gently down, as if they struck their friends.
I cheer'd them up with justice of our cause,
With promise of high pay and great rewards:
But all in vain; they had no heart to fight,
And we, in them, no hope to win the day;
So that we fled; the king unto the queen;
Lord George your brother, Norfolk, and myself,
In haste, post-haste, are come to join with you;
For in the marches here we heard you were
Making another head to fight again.
EDWARD.
Where is the Duke of Norfolk, gentle Warwick?
And when came George from Burgundy to
   England?
EARL OF WARWICK.
Some six miles off the duke is with his power;
And for your brother, he was lately sent
From your kind aunt, Duchess of Burgundy,
With aid of soldiers to this needful war.
RICHARD.
'Twas odds, belike, when valiant Warwick fled:

Oft have I heard his praises in pursuit,
But ne'er till now his scandal of retire.
EARL OF WARWICK.
Nor now my scandal, Richard, dost thou hear;
For thou shalt know this strong right hand of
   mine
Can pluck the diadem from faint Henry's head,
And wring the awful sceptre from his fist,
Were he as famous and as bold in war
As he is famed for mildness, peace, and prayer.
RICHARD.
I know it well, Lord Warwick; blame me not:
'Tis love I bear thy glories makes me speak.
But in this troublous time what's to be done?
Shall we go throw away our coats of steel,
And wrap our bodies in black mourning-gowns,
Numbering our Ave-Maries with our beads?
Or shall we on the helmets of our foes
Tell our devotion with revengeful arms?
If for the last, say 'Ay,' and to it, lords.
EARL OF WARWICK.
Why, therefore Warwick came to seek you out;
And therefore comes my brother Montague.
Attend me, lords. The proud insulting queen,
With Clifford and the haught Northumberland,
And of their feather many moe proud birds,
Have wrought the easy-melting king like wax.
He swore consent to your succession,
His oath enrolled in the parliament;
And now to London all the crew are gone,
To frustrate both his oath, and what beside
May make against the house of Lancaster.
Their power, I think, is thirty thousand strong:
Now, if the help of Norfolk and myself,
With all the friends that thou, brave Earl of
   March,
Amongst the loving Welshmen canst procure,
Will but amount to five-and-twenty thousand,
Why, *Via!* to London will we march amain;
And once again bestride our foaming steeds,
And once again cry, 'Charge! upon our foes!'
But never once again turn back and fly.
RICHARD.
Ay, now methinks I hear great Warwick speak:
Ne'er may he live to see a sunshine day,
That cries, 'Retire,' if Warwick bid him stay.
EDWARD.
Lord Warwick, on thy shoulder will I lean;
And when thou faint'st,—as God forbid the
   hour!—
Must Edward fall, which peril heaven forfend!
EARL OF WARWICK.
No longer Earl of March, but Duke of York:
The next degree is England's royal throne;
For King of England shalt thou be proclaim'd
In every borough as we pass along;
And he that throws not up his cap for joy,
Shall for the fault make forfeit of his head.
King Edward,—valiant Richard,—Montague,—
Stay we no longer, dreaming of renown,
But sound the trumpets, and about our task.
RICHARD.
Then, Clifford, were thy heart as hard as
   steel,—
As thou hast shown it flinty by thy deeds,—
I come to pierce it, or to give thee mine.

EDWARD.
Then strike up drums:—God and Saint George
  for us!
Enter a MESSENGER.
EARL OF WARWICK.
How now! what news?
MESSENGER.
The Duke of Norfolk sends you word by me
The queen is coming with a puissant host,
And craves your company for speedy counsel.
EARL OF WARWICK.
Why, then it sorts, brave warriors: let's away.
                              [*Exeunt.*

SCENE II.

Before York.

Flourish.   Enter the KING, QUEEN, *the* PRINCE
OF WALES, CLIFFORD, *and* NORTHUMBER-
LAND, *with drum and trumpets.*

QUEEN MARGARET.
WELCOME, my lord, to this brave town of
  York.
Yonder's the head of that arch-enemy
That sought to be encompast with your crown:
Doth not the object cheer your heart, my lord?
KING HENRY.
Ay, as the rocks cheer them that fear their
  wrack:—
To see this sight, it irks my very soul.—
Withhold revenge, dear God! 'tis not my fault,
Nor wittingly have I infringed my vow.
LORD CLIFFORD.
My gracious liege, this too much lenity
And harmful pity must be laid aside.
To whom do lions cast their gentle looks?
Not to the beast that would usurp their den.
Whose hand is that the forest bear doth lick?
Not his that spoils her young before her face.
Who scapes the lurking serpent's mortal sting?
Not he that sets his foot upon her back.
The smallest worm will turn being trodden on,
And doves will peck in safeguard of their brood.
Ambitious York did level at thy crown,
Thou smiling while he knit his angry brows:
He, but a duke, would have his son a king,
And raise his issue, like a loving sire;
Thou, being a king, blest with a goodly son,
Didst yield consent to disinherit him,
Which argued thee a most unloving father.
Unreasonable creatures feed their young;
And though man's face be fearful to their eyes,
Yet, in protection of their tender ones,
Who hath not seen them, even with those wings
Which sometime they have used in fearful flight,
Make war with him that climb'd unto their nest,
Offering their own lives in their young's defence?
For shame, my liege, make them your precedent!
Were it not pity that this goodly boy
Should lose his birthright by his father's fault,
And long hereafter say unto his child,
'What my great-grandfather and grandsire got
My careless father fondly gave away'?
Ah, what a shame were this! Look on the boy;
And let his manly face, which promiseth
Successful fortune, steel thy melting heart
To hold thine own, and leave thine own with him.

KING HENRY.
Full well hath Clifford play'd the orator,
Inferring arguments of mighty force.
But, Clifford, tell me, didst thou never hear
That things ill-got had ever bad success?
And happy always was it for that son
Whose father for his hoarding went to hell?
I'll leave my son my virtuous deeds behind;
And would my father had left me no more!
For all the rest is held at such a rate
As brings a thousand-fold more care to keep
Than in possession any jot of pleasure.—
Ah, cousin York! would thy best friends did know
How it doth grieve me that thy head is here!
QUEEN MARGARET.
My lord, cheer up your spirits: our foes are nigh,
And this soft courage makes your followers faint.
You promised knighthood to our forward son:
Unsheathe your sword, and dub him presently.—
Edward, kneel down.
KING HENRY.
Edward Plantagenet, arise a knight;
And learn this lesson,—draw thy sword in right.
PRINCE OF WALES.
My gracious father, by your kingly leave,
I'll draw it as apparent to the crown,
And in that quarrel use it to the death.
LORD CLIFFORD.
Why, that is spoken like a toward prince.
Enter a MESSENGER.
MESSENGER.
Royal commanders, be in readiness:
For with a band of thirty thousand men
Comes Warwick, backing of the Duke of York;
And in the towns, as they do march along,
Proclaims him king, and many fly to him:
Darraign your battle, for they are at hand.
LORD CLIFFORD.
I would your highness would depart the field:
The queen hath best success when you are absent.
QUEEN MARGARET.
Ay, good my lord, and leave us to our fortune.
KING HENRY.
Why, that's my fortune too; therefore I'll stay.
EARL OF NORTHUMBERLAND.
Be it with resolution, then, to fight.
PRINCE OF WALES.
My royal father, cheer these noble lords,
And hearten those that fight in your defence:
Unsheathe your sword, good father; cry, 'Saint
  George!'
March.   Enter EDWARD, GEORGE, RICHARD,
  WARWICK, NORFOLK, MONTAGUE, *and*
  SOLDIERS.
EDWARD.
Now, perjured Henry! wilt thou kneel for grace,
And set thy diadem upon my head;
Or bide the mortal fortune of the field?
QUEEN MARGARET.
Go, rate thy minions, proud insulting boy!
Becomes it thee to be thus bold in terms
Before thy sovereign and thy lawful king?
EDWARD.
I am his king, and he should bow his knee;
I was adopted heir by his consent:
Since when, his oath is broke; for, as I hear,

74

You, that are king, though he do wear the crown,
Have caused him, by new act of Parliament,
To blot out me, and put his own son in.
LORD CLIFFORD.
And reason too:
Who should succeed the father but the son?
RICHARD.
Are you there, butcher?—O, I cannot speak!
LORD CLIFFORD.
Ay, crook-back, here I stand to answer thee,
Or any he the proudest of thy sort.
RICHARD.
'Twas you that kill'd young Rutland, was it not?
LORD CLIFFORD.
Ay, and old York, and yet not satisfied.
RICHARD.
For God's sake, lords, give signal to the fight.
EARL OF WARWICK.
What say'st thou, Henry, wilt thou yield the crown?
QUEEN MARGARET.
Why, how now, long-tongued Warwick! dare you speak?
When you and I met at Saint Alban's last,
Your legs did better service than your hands.
EARL OF WARWICK.
Then 'twas my turn to fly, and now 'tis thine.
LORD CLIFFORD.
You said so much before, and yet you fled.
EARL OF WARWICK.
'Twas not your valour, Clifford, drove me thence.
EARL OF NORTHUMBERLAND.
No, nor your manhood that durst make you stay.
RICHARD.
Northumberland, I hold thee reverently.—
Break off the parle; for scarce I can refrain
The execution of my big-swoln heart
Upon that Clifford there, that cruel child-killer.
LORD CLIFFORD.
I slew thy father,—call'st thou him a child?
RICHARD.
Ay, like a dastard and a treacherous coward,
As thou didst kill our tender brother Rutland;
But ere sun set I'll make thee curse the deed.
KING HENRY.
Have done with words, my lords, and hear me speak.
QUEEN MARGARET.
Defy them, then, or else hold close thy lips.
KING HENRY.
I prithee, give no limits to my tongue:
I am a king, and privileged to speak.
LORD CLIFFORD.
My liege, the wound that bred this meeting here
Cannot be cured by words; therefore be still.
RICHARD.
Then, executioner, unsheathe thy sword:
By Him that made us all, I am resolved
That Clifford's manhood lies upon his tongue.
EDWARD.
Say, Henry, shall I have my right, or no?
A thousand men have broke their fasts to-day
That ne'er shall dine unless thou yield the crown.
EARL OF WARWICK.
If thou deny, their blood upon thy head;
For York in justice puts his armour on.

PRINCE OF WALES.
If that be right which Warwick says is right,
There is no wrong, but every thing is right.
RICHARD.
Whoever got thee, there thy mother stands;
For, well I wot, thou hast thy mother's tongue.
QUEEN MARGARET.
But thou art neither like thy sire nor dam;
But like a foul mis-shapen stigmatic,
Markt by the Destinies to be avoided,
As venom toads, or lizards' dreadful stings.
RICHARD.
Iron of Naples hid with English gilt,
Whose father bears the title of a king,—
As if a channel should be call'd the sea,—
Shamest thou not, knowing whence thou art ex-
    traught,
To let thy tongue detect thy base-born heart?
EDWARD.
A wisp of straw were worth a thousand crowns,
To make this shameless callet know herself.—
Helen of Greece was fairer far than thou,
Although thy husband may be Menelaus;
And ne'er was Agamemnon's brother wrong'd
By that false woman as this king by thee.
His father revell'd in the heart of France,
And tamed the king, and made the dauphin stoop;
And had he matcht according to his state,
He might have kept that glory to this day;
But when he took a beggar to his bed,
And graced thy poor sire with his bridal-day,
Even then that sunshine brew'd a shower for him,
That washt his father's fortunes forth of France,
And heapt sedition on his crown at home.
For what hath broacht this tumult but thy pride?
Hadst thou been meek, our title still had slept;
And we, in pity of the gentle king,
Had slipt our claim unto another age.
GEORGE.
But when we saw our sunshine made thy spring,
And that thy summer bred us no increase,
We set the axe to thy usurping root;   [selves,
And though the edge hath something hit our-
Yet, know thou, since we have begun to strike,
We'll never leave till we have hewn thee down,
Or bathed thy growing with our heated bloods.
EDWARD.
And, in this resolution, I defy thee;
Not willing any longer conference,
Since thou deniest the gentle king to speak.—
Sound trumpets!—let our bloody colours wave!—
And either victory, or else a grave.
QUEEN MARGARET.
Stay, Edward.
EDWARD.
No, wrangling woman, we'll no longer stay;
These words will cost ten thousand lives this day.
[Exeunt.

SCENE III.

*A field of battle between Towton and Saxton, in
Yorkshire.*

Alarum.   Excursions.   Enter WARWICK.

EARL OF WARWICK.
FORSPENT with toil, as runners with a race,
I lay me down a little while to breathe;

75

For strokes received, and many blows repaid,
Have robb'd my strong-knit sinews of their
    strength,
And, spite of spite, needs must I rest awhile.
        Enter EDWARD, *running.*
EDWARD.
Smile, gentle heaven! or strike, ungentle death!
For this world frowns, and Edward's sun is
    clouded.
EARL OF WARWICK.
How now, my lord! what hap? what hope of good?
        Enter GEORGE.
GEORGE.
Our hap is loss, our hope but sad despair;
Our ranks are broke, and ruin follows us:
What counsel give you? whither shall we fly?
EDWARD.
Bootless is flight,—they follow us with wings;
And weak are we, and cannot shun pursuit.
        Enter RICHARD.
RICHARD.
Ah, Warwick, why hast thou withdrawn thyself?
Thy brother's blood the thirsty earth hath drunk,
Broacht with the steely point of Clifford's lance;
And, in the very pangs of death, he cried,
Like to a dismal clangor heard from far,
'Warwick, revenge! brother, revenge my death!'
So, underneath the belly of their steeds,
That stain'd their fetlocks in his smoking blood,
The noble gentleman gave up the ghost.
EARL OF WARWICK.
Then let the earth be drunken with our blood:
I'll kill my horse, because I will not fly.
Why stand we like soft-hearted women here,
Wailing our losses, whiles the foe doth rage;
And look upon, as if the tragedy
Were play'd in jest by counterfeiting actors?
Here on my knee I vow to God above,
I'll never pause again, never stand still,
Till either death hath closed these eyes of mine,
Or fortune given me measure of revenge.
EDWARD.
O Warwick, I do bend my knee with thine;
And in this vow do chain my soul to thine!—
And, ere my knee rise from the earth's cold face,
I throw my hands, mine eyes, my heart to Thee,
Thou setter-up and plucker-down of kings,—
Beseeching Thee, if with Thy will it stands
That to my foes this body must be prey,
Yet that Thy brazen gates of heaven may ope,
And give sweet passage to my sinful soul!—
Now, lords, take leave until we meet again,
Where'er it be, in heaven or in earth.
RICHARD.
Brother, give me thy hand;—and, gentle Warwick,
Let me embrace thee in my weary arms:
I, that did never weep, now melt with woe
That winter should cut off our spring-time so.
EARL OF WARWICK.
Away, away! Once more, sweet lords, farewell.
GEORGE.
Yet let us all together to our troops,
And give them leave to fly that will not stay;
And call them pillars that will stand to us;
And, if we thrive, promise them such rewards
As victors wear at the Olympian games:

This may plant courage in their quailing breasts;
For yet is hope of life and victory.—
Forslow no longer, make we hence amain.
        [*Exeunt.*

SCENE IV.
Another part of the field.
Excursions. Enter RICHARD *and* CLIFFORD.
RICHARD.
NOW, Clifford, I have singled thee alone:
   Suppose this arm is for the Duke of York,
And this for Rutland; both bound to revenge,
Wert thou environ'd with a brazen wall.
LORD CLIFFORD.
Now, Richard, I am with thee here alone:
This is the hand that stabb'd thy father York;
And this the hand that slew thy brother Rutland;
And here's the heart that triumphs in their death,
And cheers these hands that slew thy sire and
    brother,
To execute the like upon thyself;
And so, have at thee!
    [*They fight.* WARWICK *comes;* CLIFFORD
    flies.
RICHARD.
Nay, Warwick, single out some other chase;
For I myself will hunt this wolf to death.
        [*Exeunt.*

SCENE V.
Another part of the field.
Alarum. Enter KING HENRY *alone.*
KING HENRY.
THIS battle fares like to the morning's war,
   When dying clouds contend with growing
    light,
What time the shepherd, blowing of his nails,
Can neither call it perfect day nor night.
Now sways it this way, like a mighty sea
Forced by the tide to combat with the wind;
Now sways it that way, like the selfsame sea
Forced to retire by fury of the wind:
Sometime the flood prevails, and then the wind;
Now one the better, then another best;
Both tugging to be victors, breast to breast,
Yet neither conqueror nor conquered:
So is the equal poise of this fell war.
Here on this molehill will I sit me down.
To whom God will, there be the victory!
For Margaret my queen, and Clifford too,
Have chid me from the battle; swearing both
They prosper best of all when I am thence.
Would I were dead! if God's good will were so;
For what is in this world but grief and woe?
O God! methinks it were a happy life,
To be no better than a homely swain;
To sit upon a hill, as I do now,
To carve out dials quaintly, point by point,
Thereby to see the minutes how they run,—
How many makes the hour full complete;
How many hours brings about the day;
How many days will finish up the year;
How many years a mortal man may live.
When this is known, then to divide the times:—
So many hours must I tend my flock;
So many hours must I take my rest;

So many hours must I contemplate;
So many hours must I sport myself;
So many days my ewes have been with young;
So many weeks ere the poor fools will ean;
So many months ere I shall shear the fleece:
So minutes, hours, days, months, and years,
Past over to the end they were created,
Would bring white hairs unto a quiet grave.
Ah, what a life were this! how sweet! how lovely!
Gives not the hawthorn-bush a sweeter shade
To shepherds looking on their silly sheep,
Than doth a rich-embroider'd canopy
To kings that fear their subjects' treachery?
O, yes, it doth; a thousand-fold it doth.
And to conclude,—the shepherd's homely curds,
His cold thin drink out of his leather bottle,
His wonted sleep under a fresh tree's shade,
All which secure and sweetly he enjoys,
Is far beyond a prince's delicates,
His viands sparkling in a golden cup,
His body couched in a curious bed,
When care, mistrust, and treason waits on him.

Alarum. Enter a SON *that hath kill'd his father,*
bringing in the dead body.

SON.
Ill blows the wind that profits nobody.
This man, whom hand to hand I slew in fight,
May be possessed with some store of crowns;
And I, that haply take them from him now,
May yet ere night yield both my life and them
To some man else, as this dead man doth me.—
Who's this?—O God! it is my father's face,
Whom in this conflict I un'wares have kill'd.
O heavy times, begetting such events!
From London by the king was I prest forth;
My father, being the Earl of Warwick's man,
Came on the part of York, prest by his master;
And I, who at his hands received my life,
Have by my hands of life bereaved him.—
Pardon me, God, I knew not what I did!—
And pardon, father, for I knew not thee!—
My tears shall wipe away these bloody marks;
And no more words till they have flow'd their
fill.

KING HENRY.
O piteous spectacle! O bloody times!
Whiles lions war and battle for their dens,
Poor harmless lambs abide their enmity.—
Weep, wretched man, I'll aid thee tear for tear;
And let our hearts and eyes, like civil war,
Be blind with tears, and break o'ercharged with
grief.

Enter FATHER, *bearing of his son.*

FATHER.
Thou that so stoutly hast resisted me,
Give me thy gold, if thou hast any gold;
For I have bought it with an hundred blows.—
But let me see: is this our foeman's face?
Ah, no, no, no, it is mine only son!
Ah, boy, if any life be left in thee,
Throw up thine eye! see, see what showers arise,
Blown with the windy tempest of my heart,
Upon thy wounds, that kills mine eye and
heart!—
O, pity, God, this miserable age!—
What stratagems, how fell, how butcherly,

Erroneous, mutinous, and unnatural,
This deadly quarrel daily doth beget!
O boy, thy father gave thee life too soon,
And hath bereft thee of thy life too late!

KING HENRY.
Woe above woe! grief more than common grief!
O, that my death would stay these ruthful
deeds!—
O, pity, pity, gentle heaven, pity!—
The red rose and the white are on his face,
The fatal colours of our striving houses:
The one his purple blood right well resembles;
The other his pale cheeks, methinks, presenteth:
Wither one rose, and let the other flourish;
If you contend, a thousand lives must wither.

SON.
How will my mother for a father's death
Take on with me, and ne'er be satisfied!

FATHER.
How will my wife for slaughter of my son
Shed seas of tears, and ne'er be satisfied!

KING HENRY.
How will the country for these woful chances
Misthink the king, and not be satisfied!

SON.
Was ever son so rued a father's death?

FATHER.
Was ever father so bemoan'd his son?

KING HENRY.
Was ever king so grieved for subjects' woe?
Much is your sorrow; mine ten times so much.

SON.
I'll bear thee hence, where I may weep my fill.
                    [*Exit with the body.*

FATHER.
These arms of mine shall be thy winding-sheet;
My heart, sweet boy, shall be thy sepulchre,—
For from my heart thine image ne'er shall go;
My sighing breast shall be thy funeral bell;
And so obsequious will thy father be,
E'en for the loss of thee, having no more,
As Priam was for all his valiant sons.
I'll bear thee hence; and let them fight that will,
For I have murder'd where I should not kill.
                    [*Exit with the body.*

KING HENRY.
Sad-hearted men, much overgone with care,
Here sits a king more woful than you are.

Alarums. Excursions. Enter the QUEEN, *the*
PRINCE, *and* EXETER.

PRINCE OF WALES.
Fly, father, fly! for all your friends are fled,
And Warwick rages like a chafed bull:
Away! for death doth hold us in pursuit.

QUEEN MARGARET.
Mount you, my lord; towards Berwick post
amain:
Edward and Richard, like a brace of greyhounds
Having the fearful flying hare in sight,
With fiery eyes sparkling for very wrath,
And bloody steel graspt in their ireful hands,
Are at our backs; and therefore hence amain.

DUKE OF EXETER.
Away! for vengeance comes along with them:
Nay, stay not to expostulate,—make speed;
Or else come after: I'll away before.

77

KING HENRY.

Nay, take me with thee, good sweet Exeter:
Not that I fear to stay, but love to go
Whither the queen intends. Forward; away!
[*Exeunt.*

SCENE VI.

Another part of the field.

A loud alarum. Enter CLIFFORD, *wounded.*

LORD CLIFFORD.

HERE burns my candle out,—ay, here it dies,
    Which, whiles it lasted, gave King Henry
O Lancaster, I fear thy overthrow   [light.
More than my body's parting with my soul!
My love and fear glued many friends to thee;
And, now I fall, that tough commixture melts.
Impairing Henry, strengthening misproud York,
The common people swarm like summer flies;
And whither fly the gnats but to the sun?
And who shines now but Henry's enemies?
O Phœbus, hadst thou never given consent
That Phaethon should check thy fiery steeds,
Thy burning car never had scorcht the earth!
And, Henry, hadst thou sway'd as kings should
    do,
Or as thy father and his father did,
Giving no ground unto the house of York,
I and ten thousand in this luckless realm
Had left no mourning widows for our death;
And thou this day hadst kept thy chair in peace.
For what doth cherish weeds but gentle air?
And what makes robbers bold but too much
    lenity?—
Bootless are plaints, and cureless are my wounds;
No way to fly, nor strength to hold out flight:
The foe is merciless, and will not pity;
For at their hands I have deserved no pity.
The air hath got into my deadly wounds,
And much effuse of blood doth make me faint.—
Come, York and Richard, Warwick and the rest;
I stabb'd your fathers' bosoms,—split my breast.
[*Faints.*

Alarum and retreat. Enter EDWARD, GEORGE,
    RICHARD, MONTAGUE, WARWICK, *and* SOL-
    DIERS.

EDWARD.

Now breathe we, lords: good fortune bids us
    pause,
And smooth the frowns of war with peaceful
    looks.—
Some troops pursue the bloody-minded queen,
That led calm Henry, though he were a king,
As doth a sail, fill'd with a fretting gust,
Command an argosy to stem the waves.
But think you, lords, that Clifford fled with
    them?

EARL OF WARWICK.

No, 'tis impossible he should escape;
For, though before his face I speak the words,
Your brother Richard markt him for the grave:
And wheresoe'er he is, he's surely dead.
[CLIFFORD *groans, and dies.*

EDWARD.

Whose soul is that which takes her heavy leave?

RICHARD.

A deadly groan, like life and death's departing.

EDWARD.

See who it is: and, now the battle's ended,
If friend or foe, let him be gently used.

RICHARD.

Revoke that doom of mercy, for 'tis Clifford;
Who not contented that he lopt the branch
In hewing Rutland when his leaves put forth,
But set his murdering knife unto the root
From whence that tender spray did sweetly
    spring,—
I mean our princely father, Duke of York.

EARL OF WARWICK.

From off the gates of York fetch down the head,
Your father's head, which Clifford placed there;
Instead whereof let this supply the room:
Measure for measure must be answered.

EDWARD.

Bring forth that fatal screech-owl to our house,
That nothing sung but death to us and ours:
Now death shall stop his dismal-threatening
    sound,
And his ill-boding tongue no more shall speak.
[SOLDIERS *bring the body forward.*

EARL OF WARWICK.

I think his understanding is bereft.—
Speak, Clifford, dost thou know who speaks to
    thee?—
Dark cloudy death o'ershades his beams of life,
And he nor sees nor hears us what we say.

RICHARD.

O, would he did! and so, perhaps, he doth:
'Tis but his policy to counterfeit,
Because he would avoid such bitter taunts
Which in the time of death he gave our father.

GEORGE.

If so thou think'st, vex him with eager words.

RICHARD.

Clifford, ask mercy, and obtain no grace.

EDWARD.

Clifford, repent in bootless penitence.

EARL OF WARWICK.

Clifford, devise excuses for thy faults.

GEORGE.

While we devise fell tortures for thy faults.

RICHARD.

Thou didst love York, and I am son to York.

EDWARD.

Thou pitied'st Rutland; I will pity thee.

GEORGE.

Where's Captain Margaret, to fence you now?

EARL OF WARWICK.

They mock thee, Clifford: swear as thou wast
    wont.

RICHARD.

What, not an oath? nay, then the world goes hard
When Clifford cannot spare his friends an oath.—
I know by that he's dead; and, by my soul,
If this right hand would buy two hours' life,
That I in all despite might rail at him,
This hand should chop it off; and with the issuing
    blood
Stifle the villain whose unstanched thirst
York and young Rutland could not satisfy.

EARL OF WARWICK.

Ay, but he's dead: off with the traitor's head,
And rear it in the place your father's stands.—

And now to London with triumphant march,
There to be crowned England's royal king.
From whence shall Warwick cut the sea to France,
And ask the Lady Bona for thy queen:
So shalt thou sinew both these lands together;
And, having France thy friend, thou shalt not
    dread
The scatter'd foe that hopes to rise again;
For though they cannot greatly sting to hurt,
Yet look to have them buzz to offend thine ears.
First will I see the coronation;
And then to Brittany I'll cross the sea,
To effect this marriage, so it please my lord.
                    EDWARD.
Even as thou wilt, sweet Warwick, let it be;
For in thy shoulder do I build my seat,
And never will I undertake the thing
Wherein thy counsel and consent is wanting.—
Richard, I will create thee Duke of Gloster;—
And George, of Clarence:—Warwick, as ourself,
Shall do and undo as him pleaseth best.
                    RICHARD.
Let me be Duke of Clarence, George of Gloster;
For Gloster's dukedom is too ominous.
                EARL OF WARWICK.
Tut, that's a foolish observation:
Richard, be Duke of Gloster. Now to London,
To see these honours in possession.   [*Exeunt.*

ACT III. SCENE I.

A chase in the north of England.

Enter two KEEPERS, *with cross-bows in their
·hands.*

                FIRST KEEPER.
UNDER this thick-grown brake we'll shroud
    ourselves;
For through this laund anon the deer will come;
And in this covert will we make our stand,
Culling the principal of all the deer.
                SECOND KEEPER.
I'll stay above the hill, so both may shoot.
                FIRST KEEPER.
That cannot be; the noise of thy cross-bow
Will scare the herd, and so my shoot is lost.
Here stand we both, and aim we at the best:
And, for the time shall not seem tedious,
I'll tell thee what befell me on a day
In this self-place where now we mean to stand.
                SECOND KEEPER.
Here comes a man; let's stay till he be past.
Enter the KING, *with a prayer-book.*
                KING HENRY.
From Scotland am I stoln, even of pure love,
To greet mine own land with my wishful sight.
No, Harry, Harry, 'tis no land of thine;
Thy place is fill'd, thy sceptre wrung from thee,
Thy balm washt off wherewith thou wast
    anointed.
No bending knee will call thee Cæsar now,
No humble suitors press to speak for right,
No, not a man comes for redress of thee;
For how can I help them, and not myself?
                FIRST KEEPER.
Ay, here's a deer whose skin's a keeper's fee:
This is the *quondam* king; let's seize upon him.

                KING HENRY.
Let me embrace thee, sour adversity;
For wise men say it is the wisest course.
                SECOND KEEPER.
Why linger we? let us lay hands upon him.
                FIRST KEEPER.
Forbear awhile; we'll hear a little more.
                KING HENRY.
My queen and son are gone to France for aid;
And, as I hear, the great-commanding Warwick
Is thither gone, to crave the French king's sister
To wife for Edward: if this news be true,
Poor queen and son, your labour is but lost;
For Warwick is a subtle orator,
And Louis a prince soon won with moving
    words.
By this account, then, Margaret may win him;
For she's a woman to be pitied much:
Her sighs will make a battery in his breast;
Her tears will pierce into a marble heart;
The tiger will be mild whiles she doth mourn;
And Nero will be tainted with remorse,
To hear and see her plaints, her brinish tears.
Ay, but she's come to beg; Warwick, to give:
She, on his left side, craving aid for Henry;
He, on his right, asking a wife for Edward.
She weeps, and says her Henry is deposed;
He smiles, and says his Edward is install'd;
That she, poor wretch, for grief can speak no
    more;
Whiles Warwick tells his title, smooths the wrong,
Inferreth arguments of mighty strength,
And in conclusion wins the king from her,
With promise of his sister, and what else,
To strengthen and support King Edward's place.
O Margaret, thus 'twill be; and thou, poor soul,
Art then forsaken, as thou went'st forlorn!
                SECOND KEEPER.
Say, what art thou that talk'st of kings and
    queens?
                KING HENRY.
More than I seem, and less than I was born to:
A man at least, for less I should not be;
And men may talk of kings, and why not I?
                SECOND KEEPER.
Ay, but thou talk'st as if thou wert a king.
                KING HENRY.
Why, so I am—in mind; and that's enough.
                SECOND KEEPER.
But, if thou be a king, where is thy crown?
                KING HENRY.
My crown is in my heart, not on my head;
Not deckt with diamonds and Indian stones,
Nor to be seen: my crown is call'd content—
A crown it is that seldom kings enjoy.
                SECOND KEEPER.
Well, if you be a king crown'd with content,
Your crown content and you must be contented
To go along with us; for, as we think,
You are the king King Edward hath deposed;
And we his subjects, sworn in all allegiance,
Will apprehend you as his enemy.
                KING HENRY.
But did you never swear, and break an oath?
                SECOND KEEPER.
No, never such an oath; nor will not now.

79

KING HENRY.
Where did you dwell when I was king of England?
SECOND KEEPER.
Here in this country, where we now remain.
KING HENRY.
I was anointed king at nine months old;
My father and my grandfather were kings;
And you were sworn true subjects unto me:
And tell me, then, have you not broke your oaths?
FIRST KEEPER.
No;
For we were subjects but while you were king.
KING HENRY.
Why, am I dead? do I not breathe a man?
Ah, simple men, you know not what you
swear!
Look, as I blow this feather from my face,
And as the air blows it to me again,
Obeying with my wind when I do blow,
And yielding to another when it blows,
Commanded always by the greater gust;
Such is the lightness of you common men.
But do not break your oaths; for of that sin
My mild entreaty shall not make you guilty.
Go where you will, the king shall be commanded;
And be you kings; command, and I'll obey.
FIRST KEEPER.
We are true subjects to the king, King Edward.
KING HENRY.
So would you be again to Henry,
If he were seated as King Edward is.
FIRST KEEPER.
We charge you, in God's name, and the king's,
To go with us unto the officers.
KING HENRY.
In God's name, lead; your king's name be obey'd:
And what God will, that let your king perform;
And what he will, I humbly yield unto. [Exeunt.

SCENE II.

London. A room in the palace.

Enter KING EDWARD, GLOSTER, CLARENCE,
and LADY GREY.
KING EDWARD.
BROTHER of Gloster, at Saint Alban's field
This lady's husband, Sir Richard Grey, was
slain,
His lands then seized on by the conqueror:
Her suit is now to repossess those lands;
Which we in justice cannot well deny,
Because in quarrel of the house of York
The worthy gentleman did lose his life.
DUKE OF GLOSTER.
Your highness shall do well to grant her suit;
It were dishonour to deny it her.
KING EDWARD.
It were no less; but yet I'll make a pause.
DUKE OF GLOSTER [aside to CLARENCE].
Yea, is it so?
I see the lady hath a thing to grant,
Before the king will grant her humble suit.
DUKE OF CLARENCE [aside to GLOSTER].
He knows the game: how true he keeps the
wind!

DUKE OF GLOSTER [aside to CLARENCE].
Silence!
KING EDWARD.
Widow, we will consider of your suit;
And come some other time to know our mind.
LADY GREY.
Right gracious lord, I cannot brook delay:
May't please your highness to resolve me
now;
And what your pleasure is shall satisfy me.
DUKE OF GLOSTER [aside].
Ay, widow? then I'll warrant you all your
lands,
An if what pleases him shall pleasure you.
Fight closer, or, good faith, you'll catch a blow.
DUKE OF CLARENCE [aside to GLOSTER].
I fear her not, unless she chance to fall.
DUKE OF GLOSTER [aside to CLARENCE].
God forbid that! for he'll take vantages.
KING EDWARD.
How many children hast thou, widow? tell me.
DUKE OF CLARENCE [aside to GLOSTER].
I think he means to beg a child of her.
DUKE OF GLOSTER [aside to CLARENCE].
Nay, whip me, then; he'll rather give her two.
LADY GREY.
Three, my most gracious lord.
DUKE OF GLOSTER [aside].
You shall have four, if you'll be ruled by him.
KING EDWARD.
'Twere pity they should lose their father's lands.
LADY GREY.
Be pitiful, dread lord, and grant it, then.
KING EDWARD.
Lords, give us leave: I'll try this widow's wit.
DUKE OF GLOSTER [aside].
Ay, good leave have you; for you will have
leave,
Till youth take leave, and leave you to the
crutch. [Retires with CLARENCE
KING EDWARD.
Now tell me, madam, do you love your chil-
dren?
LADY GREY.
Ay, full as dearly as I love myself.
KING EDWARD.
And would you not do much to do them good?
LADY GREY.
To do them good, I would sustain some harm.
KING EDWARD.
Then get your husband's lands, to do them
good.
LADY GREY.
Therefore I came unto your majesty.
KING EDWARD.
I'll tell you how these lands are to be got.
LADY GREY.
So shall you bind me to your highness' service.
KING EDWARD.
What service wilt thou do me, if I give them?
LADY GREY.
What you command, that rests in me to do.
KING EDWARD.
But you will take exceptions to my boon.
LADY GREY.
No, gracious lord, except I cannot do it.

KING EDWARD.
Ay, but thou canst do what I mean to ask.
LADY GREY.
Why, then I will do what your Grace commands.
DUKE OF GLOSTER [aside to CLARENCE].
He plies her hard; and much rain wears the marble.
DUKE OF CLARENCE [aside to GLOSTER].
As red as fire! nay, then her wax must melt.
LADY GREY.
Why stops my lord? shall I not hear my task?
KING EDWARD.
An easy task; 'tis but to love a king.
LADY GREY.
That's soon perform'd, because I am a subject.
KING EDWARD.
Why, then, thy husband's lands I freely give thee.
LADY GREY.
I take my leave with many thousand thanks.
DUKE OF GLOSTER [aside to CLARENCE].
The match is made; she seals it with a curt'sy.
KING EDWARD.
But stay thee,—'tis the fruits of love I mean.
LADY GREY.
The fruits of love I mean, my loving liege.
KING EDWARD.
Ay, but, I fear me, in another sense.
What love, think'st thou, I sue so much to get?
LADY GREY.
My love till death, my humble thanks, my prayers;
That love which virtue begs, and virtue grants.
KING EDWARD.
No, by my troth, I did not mean such love.
LADY GREY.
Why, then you mean not as I thought you did.
KING EDWARD.
But now you partly may perceive my mind.
LADY GREY.
My mind will never grant what I perceive
Your highness aims at, if I aim aright.
KING EDWARD.
To tell thee plain, I aim to lie with thee.
LADY GREY.
To tell you plain, I had rather lie in prison.
KING EDWARD.
Why, then thou shalt not have thy husband's lands.
LADY GREY.
Why, then mine honesty shall be my dower;
For by that loss I will not purchase them.
KING EDWARD.
Therein thou wrong'st thy children mightily.
LADY GREY.
Herein your highness wrongs both them and me.
But, mighty lord, this merry inclination
Accords not with the sadness of my suit:
Please you dismiss me, either with 'ay' or 'no.'
KING EDWARD.
Ay, if thou wilt say 'ay' to my request;
No, if thou dost say 'no' to my demand.
LADY GREY.
Then, no, my lord. My suit is at an end.

DUKE OF GLOSTER [aside to CLARENCE].
The widow likes him not, she knits her brows.
DUKE OF CLARENCE [aside to GLOSTER].
He is the bluntest wooer in Christendom.
KING EDWARD [aside].
Her looks do argue her replete with modesty;
Her words do show her wit incomparable:
All her perfections challenge sovereignty;
One way or other, she is for a king;
And she shall be my love, or else my queen.—
Say that King Edward take thee for his queen?
LADY GREY.
'Tis better said than done, my gracious lord:
I am a subject fit to jest withal,
But far unfit to be a sovereign.
KING EDWARD.
Sweet widow, by my state I swear to thee
I speak no more than what my soul intends;
And that is, to enjoy thee for my love.
LADY GREY.
And that is more than I will yield unto:
I know I am too mean to be your queen,
And yet too good to be your concubine.
KING EDWARD.
You cavil, widow: I did mean, my queen.
LADY GREY.
'Twill grieve your Grace my sons should call you father.
KING EDWARD.
No more than when my daughters call thee mother.
Thou art a widow, and thou hast some children;
And, by God's mother, I, being but a bachelor,
Have other some: why, 'tis a happy thing
To be the father unto many sons.
Answer no more, for thou shalt be my queen.
DUKE OF GLOSTER [aside to CLARENCE].
The ghostly father now hath done his shrift.
DUKE OF CLARENCE [aside to GLOSTER].
When he was made a shriver, 'twas for shift.
KING EDWARD.
Brothers, you muse what chat we two have had.
DUKE OF GLOSTER.
The widow likes it not, for she looks sad.
KING EDWARD.
You'ld think it strange if I should marry her.
DUKE OF CLARENCE.
To whom, my lord?
KING EDWARD.
Why, Clarence, to myself.
DUKE OF GLOSTER.
That would be ten days' wonder at the least.
DUKE OF CLARENCE.
That's a day longer than a wonder lasts.
DUKE OF GLOSTER.
By so much is the wonder in extremes.
KING EDWARD.
Well, jest on, brothers: I can tell you both
Her suit is granted for her husband's lands.

Enter a NOBLEMAN.
NOBLEMAN.
My gracious lord, Henry your foe is taken,
And brought as prisoner to your palace-gate.
KING EDWARD.
See that he be convey'd unto the Tower:—
And go we, brothers, to the man that took him,
To question of his apprehension.—
Widow, go you along:—lords, use her honourably.
                    [*Exeunt all except* GLOSTER.
DUKE OF GLOSTER.
Ay, Edward will use women honourably.—
Would he were wasted, marrow, bones, and all,
That from his loins no hopeful branch may spring,
To cross me from the golden time I look for!
And yet, between my soul's desire and me—
The lustful Edward's title buried—
Is Clarence, Henry, and his son young Edward,
And all the unlookt-for issue of their bodies,
To take their rooms, ere I can place myself:
A cold premeditation for my purpose!
Why, then, I do but dream on sovereignty
Like one that stands upon a promontory,
And spies a far-off shore where he would tread,
Wishing his foot were equal with his eye;
And chides the sea that sunders him from thence,
Saying, he'll lade it dry to have his way:
So do I wish the crown, being so far off;
And so I chide the means that keeps me from it;
And so I say, I'll cut the causes off,
Flattering me with impossibilities.—
My eye 's too quick, my heart o'erweens too much,
Unless my hand and strength could equal them.
Well, say there is no kingdom, then, for Richard;
What other pleasure can the world afford?
I'll make my heaven in a lady's lap,
And deck my body in gay ornaments,
And witch sweet ladies with my words and looks.
O miserable thought! and more unlikely
Than to accomplish twenty golden crowns!
Why, love forswore me in my mother's womb:
And, for I should not deal in her soft laws,
She did corrupt frail nature with some bribe,
To shrink mine arm up like a wither'd shrub;
To make an envious mountain on my back,
Where sits deformity to mock my body;
To shape my legs of an unequal size;
To disproportion me in every part,
Like to a chaos, or an unlickt bear-whelp
That carries no impression like the dam.
And am I, then, a man to be beloved?
O monstrous fault, to harbour such a thought!
Then, since this earth affords no joy to me,
But to command, to check, to o'erbear such
As are of better person than myself,
I'll make my heaven to dream upon the crown,
And, whiles I live, t' account this world but hell,
Until my mis-shaped trunk that bears this head,
Be round impaled with a glorious crown.
And yet I know not how to get the crown,
For many lives stand between me and home:
And I—like one lost in a thorny wood,
That rents the thorns, and is rent with the thorns,
Seeking a way, and straying from the way;
Not knowing how to find the open air,
But toiling desperately to find it out—

Torment myself to catch the English crown:
And from that torment I will free myself,
Or hew my way out with a bloody axe.
Why, I can smile, and murder whiles I smile;
And cry 'Content' to that which grieves my
     heart;
And wet my cheeks with artificial tears,
And frame my face to all occasions:
I'll drown more sailors than the mermaid shall;
I'll slay more gazers than the basilisk;
I'll play the orator as well as Nestor;
Deceive more slily than Ulysses could;
And, like a Sinon, take another Troy:
I can add colours to the chameleon;
Change shapes with Proteus for advantages;
And set the murderous Machiavel to school.
Can I do this, and cannot get a crown?
Tut, were it further off, I'll pluck it down.   [*Exit.*

SCENE III.
France. The KING'S *palace.*

Flourish.   Enter LOUIS *the French king, his sister*
     BONA, *his Admiral call'd* BOURBON; PRINCE
     EDWARD, QUEEN MARGARET, *and the* EARL
     OF OXFORD.   LOUIS *sits and riseth up again.*
KING LOUIS.
FAIR Queen of England, worthy Margaret,
     Sit down with us: it ill befits thy state
And birth, that thou shouldst stand while Louis
     doth sit.
QUEEN MARGARET.
No, mighty King of France: now Margaret
Must strike her sail, and learn awhile to serve,
Where kings command. I was, I must confess,
Great Albion's queen in former golden days:
But now mischance hath trod my title down,
And with dishonour laid me on the ground;
Where I must take like seat unto my fortune,
And to my humble seat conform myself.
KING LOUIS.
Why, say, fair queen, whence springs this deep
     despair?
QUEEN MARGARET.
From such a cause as fills mine eyes with tears,
And stops my tongue, while heart is drown'd in
     cares.
KING LOUIS.
Whate'er it be, be thou still like thyself,
And sit thee by our side: yield not thy neck
                    [*Seats her by him.*
To fortune's yoke, but let thy dauntless mind
Still ride in triumph over all mischance.
Be plain, Queen Margaret, and tell thy grief;
It shall be eased, if France can yield relief.
QUEEN MARGARET.
Those gracious words revive my drooping
     thoughts,
And give my tongue-tied sorrows leave to speak.
Now, therefore, be it known to noble Louis,
That Henry, sole possessor of my love,
Is, of a king, become a banisht man,
And forced to live in Scotland a forlorn;
While proud ambitious Edward duke of York
Usurps the regal title and the seat
Of England's true-anointed lawful king.

This is the cause that I, poor Margaret,—
With this my son, Prince Edward, Henry's
    heir,—
Am come to crave thy just and lawful aid;
And if thou fail us, all our hope is done:
Scotland hath will to help, but cannot help;
Our people and our peers are both misled,
Our treasure seized, our soldiers put to flight,
And, as thou seest, ourselves in heavy plight.

KING LOUIS.

Renowned queen, with patience calm the storm,
While we bethink a means to break it off.

QUEEN MARGARET.

The more we stay, the stronger grows our foe.

KING LOUIS.

The more I stay, the more I'll succour thee.

QUEEN MARGARET.

O, but impatience waiteth on true sorrow:—
And see where comes the breeder of my sorrow!

Enter WARWICK, *attended.*

KING LOUIS.

What's he approacheth boldly to our presence?

QUEEN MARGARET.

Our Earl of Warwick, Edward's greatest friend.

KING LOUIS.

Welcome, brave Warwick! What brings thee to
    France?   [*He descends. She ariseth.*

QUEEN MARGARET [*aside*].

Ay, now begins a second storm to rise;
For this is he that moves both wind and tide.

EARL OF WARWICK.

From worthy Edward, king of Albion,
My lord and sovereign, and thy vowed friend,
I come, in kindness and unfeigned love,—
First, to do greetings to thy royal person;
And then to crave a league of amity; ¡
And lastly, to confirm that amity
With nuptial knot, if thou vouchsafe to grant
That virtuous Lady Bona, thy fair sister,
To England's king in lawful marriage.

QUEEN MARGARET [*aside*].

If that go forward, Henry's hope is done.

EARL OF WARWICK [*to* BONA].

And, gracious madam, in our king's behalf,
I am commanded, with your leave and favour,
Humbly to kiss your hand, and with my tongue
To tell the passion of my sovereign's heart;
Where fame, late entering at his heedful ears,
Hath placed thy beauty's image and thy virtue.

QUEEN MARGARET.

King Louis,—and Lady Bona,—hear me speak,
Before you answer Warwick. His demand
Springs not from Edward's well-meant honest
    love,
But from deceit bred by necessity;
For how can tyrants safely govern home,
Unless abroad they purchase great alliance?
To prove him tyrant this reason may suffice,—
That Henry liveth still; but were he dead,
Yet here Prince Edward stands, King Henry's son.
Look therefore, Louis, that by this league and
    marriage
Thou draw not on thy danger and dishonour;
For though usurpers sway the rule awhile,
Yet heavens are just, and time suppresseth
    wrongs.

EARL OF WARWICK.

Injurious Margaret!

PRINCE EDWARD.
            And why not queen?

EARL OF WARWICK.

Because thy father Henry did usurp;
And thou no more art prince than she is queen.

EARL OF OXFORD.

Then Warwick disannuls great John of Gaunt,
Which did subdue the greatest part of Spain;
And, after John of Gaunt, Henry the Fourth,
Whose wisdom was a mirror to the wisest;
And, after that wise prince, Henry the Fifth,
Who by his prowess conquered all France:
From these our Henry lineally descends.

EARL OF WARWICK.

Oxford, how haps it, in this smooth discourse,
You told not how Henry the Sixth hath lost
All that which Henry the Fifth had gotten?   [that.
Methinks these peers of France should smile at
But for the rest,—you tell a pedigree
Of threescore and two years; a silly time
To make prescription for a kingdom's worth.

EARL OF OXFORD.

Why, Warwick, canst thou speak against thy liege
Whom thou obeyed'st thirty and six years,
And not bewray thy treason with a blush?

EARL OF WARWICK.

Can Oxford, that did ever fence the right,
Now buckler falsehood with a pedigree?
For shame! leave Henry, and call Edward king.

EARL OF OXFORD.

Call him my king by whose injurious doom
My elder brother, the Lord Aubrey Vere,
Was done to death? and more than so, my father,
Even in the downfall of his mellow'd years,
When nature brought him to the door of death?
No, Warwick, no; while life upholds this arm,
This arm upholds the house of Lancaster.

EARL OF WARWICK.

And I the house of York.

KING LOUIS.

Queen Margaret, Prince Edward, and Oxford,
Vouchsafe, at our request, to stand aside,
While I use further conference with Warwick.

[*They stand aloof.*

QUEEN MARGARET.

Heavens grant that Warwick's words bewitch
    him not!

KING LOUIS.

Now, Warwick, tell me, even upon thy conscience,
Is Edward your true king? for I were loth
To link with him that were not lawful chosen.

EARL OF WARWICK.

Thereon I pawn my credit and mine honour.

KING LOUIS.

But is he gracious in the people's eye?

EARL OF WARWICK.

The more that Henry was unfortunate.

KING LOUIS.

Then further,—all dissembling set aside,
Tell me for truth the measure of his love
Unto our sister Bona.

EARL OF WARWICK.
            Such it seems
As may beseem a monarch like himself.

Myself have often heard him say and swear
That this his love was an eternal plant,
Whereof the root was fixt in virtue's ground,
The leaves and fruit maintain'd with beauty's sun;
Exempt from envy, but not from disdain,
Unless the Lady Bona quit his pain.
                    KING LOUIS.
Now, sister, let us hear your firm resolve.
                    BONA.
Your grant, or your denial, shall be mine:—
[to WARWICK] Yet I confess that often ere this
   day,
When I have heard your king's desert recounted,
Mine ear hath tempted judgement to desire.
                    KING LOUIS.
Then, Warwick, thus,—Our sister shall be
   Edward's;
And now forthwith shall articles be drawn
Touching the jointure that your king must make,
Which with her dowry shall be counterpoised.—
Draw near, Queen Margaret, and be a witness
That Bona shall be wife to the English king.
                    PRINCE EDWARD.
To Edward, but not to the English king.
                    QUEEN MARGARET.
Deceitful Warwick! it was thy device
By this alliance to make void my suit:
Before thy coming, Louis was Henry's friend.
                    KING LOUIS.
And still is friend to him and Margaret:
But if your title to the crown be weak,—
As may appear by Edward's good success,—
Then 'tis but reason that I be released
From giving aid which late I promised.
Yet shall you have all kindness at my hand
That your estate requires, and mine can yield.
                    EARL OF WARWICK.
Henry now lives in Scotland at his ease,
Where having nothing, nothing can he lose.
And as for you yourself, our *quondam* queen,
You have a father able to maintain you;
And better 'twere you troubled him than France.
                    QUEEN MARGARET.
Peace, impudent and shameless Warwick! peace,
Proud setter-up and puller-down of kings!
I will not hence till, with my talk and tears,
Both full of truth, I make King Louis behold
Thy sly conveyance and thy lord's false love;
For both of you are birds of selfsame feather.
              [POST *blowing a horn within.*
                    KING LOUIS.
Warwick, this is some post to us or thee.
              Enter the POST.
                    POST [*to* WARWICK].
My lord ambassador, these letters are for you,
Sent from your brother, Marquess Montague:—
[*to* LOUIS] These from our king unto your
   majesty:—
[*to* MARGARET] And, madam, these for you; from
   whom I know not.   [*They all read their letters.*
                    EARL OF OXFORD.
I like it well that our fair queen and mistress
Smiles at her news, while Warwick frowns at his.
                    PRINCE EDWARD.
Nay, mark how Louis stamps, as he were nettled:
I hope all's for the best.

                    KING LOUIS.
Warwick, what are thy news?—and yours, fair
   queen?
                    QUEEN MARGARET.
Mine such as fill my heart with unhoped joys.
                    EARL OF WARWICK.
Mine full of sorrow and heart's discontent.
                    KING LOUIS.
What! has your king married the Lady Grey?
And now, to soothe your forgery and his,
Sends me a paper to persuade me patience?
Is this th'alliance that he seeks with France?
Dare he presume to scorn us in this manner?
                    QUEEN MARGARET.
I told your majesty as much before: [honesty.
This proveth Edward's love and Warwick's
                    EARL OF WARWICK.
King Louis, I here protest, in sight of heaven,
And by the hope I have of heavenly bliss,
That I am clear from this misdeed of Edward's,—
No more my king, for he dishonours me,
But most himself, if he could see his shame.
Did I forget that by the house of York
My father came untimely to his death?
Did I let pass th' abuse done to my niece?
Did I impale him with the regal crown?
Did I put Henry from his native right?
And am I guerdon'd at the last with shame?
Shame on himself! for my desert is honour:
And, to repair my honour lost for him,
I here renounce him, and return to Henry.—
My noble queen, let former grudges pass,
And henceforth I am thy true servitor:
I will revenge his wrong to Lady Bona,
And replant Henry in his former state.
                    QUEEN MARGARET.
Warwick, these words have turn'd my hate to love;
And I forgive and quite forget old faults,
And joy that thou becomest King Henry's friend.
                    EARL OF WARWICK.
So much his friend, ay, his unfeigned friend,
That, if King Louis vouchsafe to furnish us
With some few bands of chosen soldiers,
I'll undertake to land them on our coast,
And force the tyrant from his seat by war.
'Tis not his new-made bride shall succour him:
And as for Clarence,—as my letters tell me,
He's very likely now to fall from him,
For matching more for wanton lust than honour,
Or than for strength and safety of our country.
                    BONA.
Dear brother, how shall Bona be revenged
But by thy help to this distressed queen?
                    QUEEN MARGARET.
Renowned prince, how shall poor Henry live,
Unless thou rescue him from foul despair?
                    BONA.
My quarrel and this English queen's are one.
                    EARL OF WARWICK.
And mine, fair Lady Bona, joins with yours.
                    KING LOUIS.
And mine with hers and thine and Margaret's:
Therefore, at last, I firmly am resolved
You shall have aid.
                    QUEEN MARGARET.
Let me give humble thanks for all at once.

KING LOUIS.
Then, England's messenger, return in post,
And tell false Edward, thy supposed king,
That Louis of France is sending over maskers
To revel it with him and his new bride:
Thou seest what's past,—go fear thy king withal.
BONA.
Tell him, in hope he'll prove a widower shortly,
I'll wear the willow-garland for his sake.
QUEEN MARGARET.
Tell him, my mourning-weeds are laid aside,
And I am ready to put armour on.
EARL OF WARWICK.
Tell him from me, that he hath done me wrong;
And therefore I'll uncrown him ere't be long.
There's thy reward: be gone.   [Exit POST.
KING LOUIS.
                    But, Warwick,
Thou and Oxford, with five thousand men,
Shall cross the seas, and bid false Edward battle;
And, as occasion serves, this noble queen
And prince shall follow with a fresh supply.
Yet, ere they go, but answer me one doubt,—
What pledge have we of thy firm loyalty?
EARL OF WARWICK.
This shall assure my constant loyalty,—
That if our queen and this young prince agree,
I'll join mine eldest daughter and my joy
To him forthwith in holy wedlock-bands.
QUEEN MARGARET.
Yes, I agree, and thank you for your motion.—
Son Edward, she is fair and virtuous;
Therefore delay not, give thy hand to Warwick;
And, with thy hand, thy faith irrevocable,
That only Warwick's daughter shall be thine.
PRINCE OF WALES.
Yes, I accept her, for she well deserves it;
And here, to pledge my vow, I give my hand.
                [He gives his hand to WARWICK.
KING LOUIS.
Why stay we now? These soldiers shall be levied;
And thou, Lord Bourbon, our high-admiral,
Shalt waft them over with our royal fleet.—
I long till Edward fall by war's mischance,
For mocking marriage with a dame of France.
                [Exeunt all except WARWICK.
EARL OF WARWICK.
I came from Edward as ambassador,
But I return his sworn and mortal foe:
Matter of marriage was the charge he gave me,
But dreadful war shall answer his demand.
Had he none else to make a stale but me?
Then none but I shall turn his jest to sorrow.
I was the chief that raised him to the crown,
And I'll be chief to bring him down again:
Not that I pity Henry's misery,
But seek revenge on Edward's mockery.   [Exit.

ACT IV. SCENE I.
London. The palace.
Enter GLOSTER, CLARENCE, SOMERSET, and
MONTAGUE.
DUKE OF GLOSTER.
NOW tell me, brother Clarence, what think you
Of this new marriage with the Lady Grey?
Hath not our brother made a worthy choice?

DUKE OF CLARENCE.
Alas, you know 'tis far from hence to France;
How could he stay till Warwick made return?
DUKE OF SOMERSET.
My lords, forbear this talk; here comes the king.
DUKE OF GLOSTER.
And his well-chosen bride.
DUKE OF CLARENCE.
I mind to tell him plainly what I think.
Flourish. Enter KING EDWARD, LADY GREY, as
    Queen; PEMBROKE, STAFFORD, HASTINGS:
    four stand on one side and four on the other.
KING EDWARD.
Now, brother of Clarence, how like you our
    choice,
That you stand pensive, as half malcontent?
DUKE OF CLARENCE.
As well as Louis of France or the Earl of War-
    wick;
Which are so weak of courage and in judgement,
That they'll take no offence at our abuse.
KING EDWARD.
Suppose they take offence without a cause,
They are but Louis and Warwick: I am Edward,
Your king and Warwick's, and must have my will.
DUKE OF GLOSTER.
Ay, and shall have your will, because our king:
Yet hasty marriage seldom proveth well.
KING EDWARD.
Yea, brother Richard, are you offended too?
DUKE OF GLOSTER.
Not I:
No, God forbid that I should wish them sever'd
Whom God hath join'd together; ay, and 'twere
    pity
To sunder them that yoke so well together.
KING EDWARD.
Setting your scorns and your mislike aside,
Tell me some reason why the Lady Grey
Should not become my wife and England's
    queen:—
And you too, Somerset and Montague,
Speak freely what you think.
DUKE OF CLARENCE.
Then this is mine opinion,—that King Louis
Becomes your enemy, for mocking him
About the marriage of the Lady Bona.
DUKE OF GLOSTER.
And Warwick, doing what you gave in charge,
Is now dishonoured by this new marriage.
KING EDWARD.
What if both Louis and Warwick be appeased
By such invention as I can devise?
MARQUESS OF MONTAGUE.
Yet, to have join'd with France in such alliance
Would more have strengthen'd this our
    commonwealth
'Gainst foreign storms than any home-bred
    marriage.
LORD HASTINGS.
Why, knows not Montague that of itself
England is safe, if true within itself?
MARQUESS OF MONTAGUE.
Yes; but the safer when 'tis backt with France.
LORD HASTINGS.
'Tis better using France than trusting France:

Let us be backt with God, and with the seas
Which He hath given for fence impregnable,
And with their helps only defend ourselves;
In them and in ourselves our safety lies.

DUKE OF CLARENCE.

For this one speech Lord Hastings well deserves
To have the heir of the Lord Hungerford.

KING EDWARD.

Ay, what of that? it was my will and grant;
And for this once my will shall stand for law.

DUKE OF GLOSTER.

And yet methinks your Grace hath not done
well,
To give the heir and daughter of Lord Scales
Unto the brother of your loving bride;
She better would have fitted me or Clarence:
But in your bride you bury brotherhood.

DUKE OF CLARENCE.

Or else you would not have bestow'd the heir
Of the Lord Bonville on your new wife's son,
And leave your brothers to go speed elsewhere.

KING EDWARD.

Alas, poor Clarence! is it for a wife
That thou art malcontent? I will provide thee.

DUKE OF CLARENCE.

In choosing for yourself, you show'd your judge-
ment,
Which being shallow, you shall give me leave
To play the broker in mine own behalf;
And to that end I shortly mind to leave you.

KING EDWARD.

Leave me, or tarry, Edward will be king,
And not be tied unto his brother's will.

QUEEN ELIZABETH.

My lords, before it pleased his majesty
To raise my state to title of a queen,
Do me but right, and you must all confess
That I was not ignoble of descent;
And meaner than myself have had like fortune.
But as this title honours me and mine,
So your dislikes, to whom I would be pleasing,
Doth cloud my joys with danger and with sorrow.

KING EDWARD.

My love, forbear to fawn upon their frowns:
What danger or what sorrow can befall thee,
So long as Edward is thy constant friend,
And their true sovereign, whom they must obey?
Nay, whom they shall obey, and love thee too,
Unless they seek for hatred at my hands;
Which if they do, yet will I keep thee safe,
And they shall feel the vengeance of my wrath.

DUKE OF GLOSTER [aside].

I hear, yet say not much, but think the more.

Enter a POST.

KING EDWARD.

Now, messenger, what letters or what news
From France?

POST.

My sovereign liege, no letters; and few words,
But such as I, without your special pardon,
Dare not relate.

KING EDWARD.

Go to, we pardon thee: therefore, in brief,
Tell me their words as near as thou canst guess
them.
What answer makes King Louis unto our letters?

POST.

At my depart, these were his very words:
'Go tell false Edward, thy supposed king,
That Louis of France is sending over maskers
To revel it with him and his new bride.'

KING EDWARD.

Is Louis so brave? belike he thinks me Henry.
But what said Lady Bona to my marriage?

POST.

These were her words, utter'd with mild disdain:
'Tell him, in hope he'll prove a widower shortly,
I'll wear the willow-garland for his sake.'

KING EDWARD.

I blame not her, she could say little less;
She had the wrong. But what said Henry's
queen?
For I have heard that she was there in place.

POST.

'Tell him,' quoth she, 'my mourning-weeds are
done,
And I am ready to put armour on.'

KING EDWARD.

Belike she minds to play the Amazon.
But what said Warwick to these injuries?

POST.

He, more incensed against your majesty
Than all the rest, discharged me with these words:
'Tell him from me, that he hath done me wrong,
And therefore I'll uncrown him ere't be long.'

KING EDWARD.

Ha! durst the traitor breathe out so proud words?
Well, I will arm me, being thus forewarn'd:
They shall have wars, and pay for their presump-
tion.
But say, is Warwick friends with Margaret?

POST.

Ay, gracious sovereign; they are so linkt in friendship,   [daughter.
That young Prince Edward marries Warwick's

DUKE OF CLARENCE.

Belike the elder; Clarence will have the younger.
Now, brother king, farewell, and sit you fast,
For I will hence to Warwick's other daughter;
That, though I want a kingdom, yet in marriage
I may not prove inferior to yourself.—
You that love me and Warwick, follow me.

[Exit CLARENCE, and SOMERSET follows.

DUKE OF GLOSTER [aside].

Not I:
My thoughts aim at a further matter; I
Stay not for the love of Edward, but the crown.

KING EDWARD.

Clarence and Somerset both gone to Warwick!
Yet am I arm'd against the worst can happen;
And haste is needful in this desperate case.—
Pembroke and Stafford, you in our behalf
Go levy men, and make prepare for war;
They are already, or quickly will be landed:
Myself in person will straight follow you.

[Exeunt PEMBROKE and STAFFORD.

But, ere I go, Hastings and Montague,
Resolve my doubt. You twain, of all the rest,
Are near to Warwick by blood and by alliance:
Tell me if you love Warwick more than me?
If it be so, then both depart to him;
I rather wish you foes than hollow friends:

But if you mind to hold your true obedience,
Give me assurance with some friendly vow,
That I may never have you in suspect.

MARQUESS OF MONTAGUE.

So God help Montague as he proves true!

LORD HASTINGS.

And Hastings as he favours Edward's cause!

KING EDWARD.

Now, brother Richard, will you stand by us?

DUKE OF GLOSTER.

Ay, in despite of all that shall withstand you.

KING EDWARD.

Why, so! then am I sure of victory.
Now therefore let us hence; and lose no hour,
Till we meet Warwick with his foreign power.

[Exeunt.

SCENE II.

A plain in Warwickshire.

Enter WARWICK *and* OXFORD, *with French*
SOLDIERS.

EARL OF WARWICK.

TRUST me, my lord, all hitherto goes well;
  The common people by numbers swarm to us.
But see where Somerset and Clarence comes!

Enter CLARENCE *and* SOMERSET.

Speak suddenly, my lords,—are we all friends?

DUKE OF CLARENCE.

Fear not that, my lord.

EARL OF WARWICK.

Then, gentle Clarence, welcome unto Warwick;—
And welcome, Somerset:—I hold it cowardice
To rest mistrustful where a noble heart
Hath pawn'd an open hand in sign of love;
Else might I think that Clarence, Edward's
  brother,
Were but a feigned friend to our proceedings:
But welcome, sweet Clarence; my daughter shall
  be thine.
And now what rests but, in night's coverture,
Thy brother being carelessly encampt,
His soldiers lurking in the towns about,
And but attended by a simple guard,
We may surprise and take him at our pleasure?
Our scouts have found the adventure very easy:
That as Ulysses and stout Diomede
With sleight and manhood stole to Rhesus' tents,
And brought from thence the Thracian fatal
  steeds;
So we, well cover'd with the night's black mantle,
At unawares may beat down Edward's guard,
And seize himself; I say not, slaughter him,
For I intend but only to surprise him.—
You that will follow me in this attempt
Applaud the name of Henry with your leader.

[They all cry, 'Henry!'

Why, then, let's on our way in silent sort:
For Warwick and his friends, God and Saint
  George!   [Exeunt.

SCENE III.

EDWARD'S *camp, near* Warwick.

Enter three WATCHMEN, *to guard the* KING'S *tent.*

FIRST WATCHMAN.

COME on, my masters, each man take his stand:
  The king, by this, is set him down to sleep.

SECOND WATCHMAN.

What, will he not to bed?

FIRST WATCHMAN.

Why, no; for he hath made a solemn vow
Never to lie and take his natural rest
Till Warwick or himself be quite supprest.

SECOND WATCHMAN.

To-morrow, then, belike shall be the day,
If Warwick be so near as men report.

THIRD WATCHMAN.

But say, I pray, what nobleman is that
That with the king here resteth in his tent?

FIRST WATCHMAN.

'Tis the Lord Hastings, the king's chiefest friend.

THIRD WATCHMAN.

O, is it so? But why commands the king
That his chief followers lodge in towns about
  him,
While he himself keeps here in the cold field?

SECOND WATCHMAN.

'Tis the more honour, because more dangerous.

THIRD WATCHMAN.

Ay, but give me worship and quietness;
I like it better than a dangerous honour.
If Warwick knew in what estate he stands,
'Tis to be doubted he would waken him.

FIRST WATCHMAN.

Unless our halberds did shut up his passage.

SECOND WATCHMAN.

Ay, wherefore else guard we his royal tent,
But to defend his person from night-foes?

Enter WARWICK, CLARENCE, OXFORD, SOMER-
SET, *and French* SOLDIERS, *silent all.*

EARL OF WARWICK.

This is his tent; and see where stand his guard.
Courage, my masters! honour now or never!
But follow me, and Edward shall be ours.

FIRST WATCHMAN.

Who goes there?

SECOND WATCHMAN.

Stay, or thou diest!

[WARWICK *and the rest cry all,* 'Warwick!
  Warwick!' *and set upon the* GUARD, *who
  fly, crying,* 'Arm! arm!' WARWICK *and
  the rest following them.*
The drum playing and trumpet sounding, enter
  WARWICK, SOMERSET, *and the rest, bringing*
  the KING *out in his gown, sitting in a chair.*
  RICHARD *and* HASTINGS *fly over the stage.*

DUKE OF SOMERSET.

What are they that fly there?

EARL OF WARWICK.

Richard and Hastings: let them go; here is the
duke.

KING EDWARD.

The duke! Why, Warwick, when we parted last
Thou call'dst me king.

EARL OF WARWICK.

                Ay, but the case is alter'd:
When you disgraced me in my embassade,
Then I degraded you from being king,
And come now to create you Duke of York.
Alas, how should you govern any kingdom,
That know not how to use ambassadors;
Nor how to be contented with one wife;
Nor how to use your brothers brotherly;

87

Nor how to study for the people's welfare;
Nor how to shroud yourself from enemies?
KING EDWARD.
Yea, brother of Clarence, art thou here too?
Nay, then I see that Edward needs must down.—
Yet, Warwick, in despite of all mischance,
Of thee thyself and all thy complices,
Edward will always bear himself as king:
Though fortune's malice overthrow my state,
My mind exceeds the compass of her wheel.
EARL OF WARWICK.
Then, for his mind, be Edward England's king:
[Takes off his crown.
But Henry now shall wear the English crown,
And be true king indeed; thou but the shadow.—
My Lord of Somerset, at my request,
See that forthwith Duke Edward be convey'd
Unto my brother, Archbishop of York.   [lows,
When I have fought with Pembroke and his fel-
I'll follow you, and tell the duke what answer
Louis and the Lady Bona send to him.—
Now, for a while farewell, good Duke of York.
KING EDWARD.
What fates impose, that men must needs abide;
It boots not to resist both wind and tide.
[They lead him out forcibly.
EARL OF OXFORD.
What now remains, my lords, for us to do,
But march to London with our soldiers?
EARL OF WARWICK.
Ay, that's the first thing that we have to do;
To free King Henry from imprisonment,
And see him seated in the regal throne. [Exeunt.

SCENE IV.

London. The palace.

Enter QUEEN ELIZABETH *and* RIVERS.

LORD RIVERS.
MADAM, what makes you in this sudden
change?
QUEEN ELIZABETH.
Why, brother Rivers, are you yet to learn
What late misfortune is befaln King Edward?
LORD RIVERS.
What, loss of some pitcht battle against Warwick?
QUEEN ELIZABETH.
No, but the loss of his own royal person.
LORD RIVERS.
Then, is my sovereign slain?
QUEEN ELIZABETH.
Ay, almost slain, for he is taken prisoner;
Either betray'd by falsehood of his guard,
Or by his foe surprised at unawares:
And, as I further have to understand,
Is new committed to the Bishop of York,
Fell Warwick's brother, and by that our foe.
LORD RIVERS.
These news, I must confess, are full of grief;
Yet, gracious madam, bear it as you may:
Warwick may lose, that now hath won the day.
QUEEN ELIZABETH.
Till then, fair hope must hinder life's decay.
And I the rather wean me from despair,
For love of Edward's offspring in my womb:
This is it that makes me bridle passion,

And bear with mildness my misfortune's cross;
Ay, ay, for this I draw-in many a tear,
And stop the rising of blood-sucking sighs,
Lest with my sighs or tears I blast or drown
King Edward's fruit, true heir to th' English
crown.
LORD RIVERS.
But, madam, where is Warwick, then, become?
QUEEN ELIZABETH.
I am inform'd that he comes towards London,
To set the crown once more on Henry's head:
Guess thou the rest; King Edward's friends must
down.
But, to prevent the tyrant's violence,—
For trust not him that hath once broken faith,—
I'll hence forthwith unto the sanctuary,
To save at least the heir of Edward's right:
There shall I rest secure from force and fraud.
Come, therefore, let us fly while we may fly:
If Warwick take us, we are sure to die.   [Exeunt.

SCENE V.

A park near Middleham Castle in Yorkshire.

Enter GLOSTER, HASTINGS, SIR WILLIAM
STANLEY, *and others.*

DUKE OF GLOSTER.
NOW, my Lord Hastings and Sir William
Stanley,
Leave off to wonder why I drew you hither,
Into this chiefest thicket of the park.
Thus stands the case: you know our king, my
brother,
Is prisoner to the bishop here, at whose hands
He hath good usage and great liberty;
And, often but attended with weak guard,
Comes hunting this way to disport himself.
I have advertised him by secret means,
That if about this hour he make this way,
Under the colour of his usual game,
He shall here find his friends, with horse and men,
To set him free from his captivity.
Enter KING EDWARD *and a* HUNTSMAN.
HUNTSMAN.
This way, my lord; for this way lies the game.
KING EDWARD.
Nay, this way, man: see where the huntsmen
stand.—   [rest,
Now, brother of Gloster, Lord Hastings, and the
Stand you thus close, to steal the bishop's deer?
DUKE OF GLOSTER.
Brother, the time and case requireth haste:
Your horse stands ready at the park-corner.
KING EDWARD.
But whither shall we then?
LORD HASTINGS.
To Lynn, my lord; and ship from thence to
Flanders.
DUKE OF GLOSTER.
Well guest, believe me; for that was my meaning.
KING EDWARD.
Stanley, I will requite thy forwardness.
DUKE OF GLOSTER.
But wherefore stay we? 'tis no time to talk.
KING EDWARD.
Huntsman, what say'st thou? wilt thou go along?

HUNTSMAN.
Better do so than tarry and be hang'd.
DUKE OF GLOSTER.
Come then, away; let's ha' no more ado.
KING EDWARD.
Bishop, farewell: shield thee from Warwick's
frown;
And pray that I may repossess the crown.
[*Exeunt.*

SCENE VI.

London. The Tower.

Enter KING HENRY, CLARENCE, WARWICK,
SOMERSET, *young* RICHMOND, OXFORD,
MONTAGUE, *and* LIEUTENANT OF THE
TOWER.

KING HENRY.
MASTER lieutenant, now that God and friends
Have shaken Edward from the regal seat,
And turn'd my captive state to liberty,
My fear to hope, my sorrows unto joys,—
At our enlargement what are thy due fees?
LIEUTENANT OF THE TOWER.
Subjects may challenge nothing of their sove-
reigns;
But if an humble prayer may prevail,
I then crave pardon of your majesty.
KING HENRY.
For what, lieutenant? for well-using me?
Nay, be thou sure I'll well requite thy kindness,
For that it made my imprisonment a pleasure;
Ay, such a pleasure as incaged birds
Conceive, when, after many moody thoughts,
At last, by notes of household harmony,
They quite forget their loss of liberty.—
But, Warwick, after God, thou sett'st me free,
And chiefly therefore I thank God and thee;
He was the author, thou the instrument.
Therefore, that I may conquer fortune's spite,
By living low, where fortune cannot hurt me,
And that the people of this blessed land
May not be punisht with my thwarting stars,—
Warwick, although my head still wear the crown,
I here resign my government to thee,
For thou art fortunate in all thy deeds.
EARL OF WARWICK.
Your Grace hath still been famed for virtuous;
And now may seem as wise as virtuous,
By spying and avoiding fortune's malice,
For few men rightly temper with the stars:
Yet in this one thing let me blame your Grace,
For choosing me when Clarence is in place.
DUKE OF CLARENCE.
No, Warwick, thou art worthy of the sway,
To whom the heavens, in thy nativity,
Adjudged an olive-branch and laurel-crown,
As likely to be blest in peace and war;
And therefore I yield thee my free consent.
EARL OF WARWICK.
And I choose Clarence only for Protector.
KING HENRY.
Warwick and Clarence, give me both your hands:
Now join your hands, and with your hands your
hearts,
That no dissension hinder government:
I make you both Protectors of this land;

While I myself will lead a private life,
And in devotion spend my latter days,
To sin's rebuke and my Creator's praise.
EARL OF WARWICK.
What answers Clarence to his sovereign's will?
DUKE OF CLARENCE.
That he consents, if Warwick yield consent;
For on thy fortune I repose myself.
EARL OF WARWICK.
Why, then, though loth, yet must I be content:
We'll yoke together, like a double shadow
To Henry's body, and supply his place;
I mean, in bearing weight of government,
While he enjoys the honour and his ease.
And, Clarence, now then it is more than needful
Forthwith that Edward be pronounced a traitor,
And all his lands and goods be confiscate.
DUKE OF CLARENCE.
What else? and that succession be determined.
EARL OF WARWICK.
Ay, therein Clarence shall not want his part.
KING HENRY.
But, with the first of all your chief affairs,
Let me entreat—for I command no more—
That Margaret your queen, and my son Edward,
Be sent for, to return from France with speed;
For, till I see them here, by doubtful fear
My joy of liberty is half eclipsed.
DUKE OF CLARENCE.
It shall be done, my sovereign, with all speed.
KING HENRY.
My Lord of Somerset, what youth is that,
Of whom you seem to have so tender care?
DUKE OF SOMERSET.
My liege, it is young Henry, earl of Richmond.
KING HENRY.
Come hither, England's hope.—If secret powers
[*Lays his hand on his head.*
Suggest but truth to my divining thoughts,
This pretty lad will prove our country's bliss.
His looks are full of peaceful majesty;
His head by nature framed to wear a crown,
His hand to wield a sceptre; and himself
Likely in time to bless a regal throne.
Make much of him, my lords, for this is he
Must help you more than you are hurt by me.
Enter a POST.
EARL OF WARWICK.
What news, my friend?
POST.
That Edward is escaped from your brother,
And fled, as he hears since, to Burgundy.
EARL OF WARWICK.
Unsavoury news! but how made he escape?
POST.
He was convey'd by Richard duke of Gloster,
And the Lord Hastings, who attended him
In secret ambush on the forest-side,
And from the bishop's huntsmen rescued him;
For hunting was his daily exercise.
EARL OF WARWICK.
My brother was too careless of his charge.—
But let us hence, my sovereign, to provide
A salve for any sore that may betide.
[*Exeunt all but* SOMERSET, RICHMOND,
and OXFORD.

DUKE OF SOMERSET.

My lord, I like not of this flight of Edward's;
For doubtless Burgundy will yield him help,
And we shall have more wars before 't be long.
As Henry's late presaging prophecy
Did glad my heart with hope of this young Richmond,
So doth my heart misgive me, in these conflicts
What may befall him, to his harm and ours:
Therefore, Lord Oxford, to prevent the worst,
Forthwith we'll send him hence to Brittany,
Till storms be past of civil enmity.

EARL OF OXFORD.

Ay, for if Edward repossess the crown,
'Tis like that Richmond with the rest shall down.

DUKE OF SOMERSET.

It shall be so; he shall to Brittany.
Come, therefore, let's about it speedily. [*Exeunt.*

SCENE VII.

Before York.

Flourish. Enter KING EDWARD, GLOSTER,
HASTINGS, *and* SOLDIERS.

KING EDWARD.

NOW, brother Richard, Lord Hastings, and
the rest,
Yet thus far fortune maketh us amends,
And says, that once more I shall interchange
My waned state for Henry's regal crown.
Well have we past and now repast the seas,
And brought desired help from Burgundy:
What, then, remains, we being thus arrived
From Ravenspurg haven before the gates of
York,
But that we enter, as into our dukedom?

DUKE OF GLOSTER.

The gates made fast!—Brother, I like not this;
For many men that stumble at the threshold
Are well foretold that danger lurks within.

KING EDWARD.

Tush, man, abodements must not now affright us:
By fair or foul means we must enter in,
For hither will our friends repair to us.

LORD HASTINGS.

My liege, I'll knock once more to summon them.
Enter, on the walls, the MAYOR OF YORK *and his*
BRETHREN.

MAYOR OF YORK.

My lords, we were forewarned of your coming,
And shut the gates for safety of ourselves;
For now we owe allegiance unto Henry.

KING EDWARD.

But, master mayor, if Henry be your king,
Yet Edward at the least is Duke of York.

MAYOR OF YORK.

True, my good lord; I know you for no less.

KING EDWARD.

Why, and I challenge nothing but my dukedom,
As being well content with that alone.

DUKE OF GLOSTER [*aside*].

But when the fox hath once got in his nose,
He'll soon find means to make the body follow.

LORD HASTINGS.

Why, master mayor, why stand you in a doubt?
Open the gates; we are King Henry's friends.

MAYOR OF YORK.

Ay, say you so? the gates shall then be open'd.
[*They descend.*

DUKE OF GLOSTER.

A wise stout captain, and soon persuaded!

LORD HASTINGS.

The good old man would fain that all were well,
So 'twere not 'long of him; but being enter'd,
I doubt not, I, but we shall soon persuade
Both him and all his brothers unto reason.
Enter the MAYOR *and two* ALDERMEN.

KING EDWARD.

So, master mayor: these gates must not be shut
But in the night or in the time of war.
What! fear not, man, but yield me up the keys;
[*Takes his keys.*
For Edward will defend the town and thee,
And all those friends that deign to follow me.
March.   Enter MONTGOMERY *with drum and*
SOLDIERS.

DUKE OF GLOSTER.

Brother, this is Sir John Montgomery,
Our trusty friend, unless I be deceived.

KING EDWARD.

Welcome, Sir John! But why come you in arms?

SIR JOHN MONTGOMERY.

To help King Edward in his time of storm,
As every loyal subject ought to do.

KING EDWARD.

Thanks, good Montgomery: but we now forget
Our title to the crown, and only claim
Our dukedom till God please to send the rest.

SIR JOHN MONTGOMERY.

Then fare you well, for I will hence again:
I came to serve a king, and not a duke.—
Drummer, strike up, and let us march away.
[*The drum begins to march.*

KING EDWARD.

Nay, stay, Sir John, awhile; and we'll debate
By what safe means the crown may be recover'd.

SIR JOHN MONTGOMERY.

What talk you of debating? in few words,—
If you'll not here proclaim yourself our king,
I'll leave you to your fortune, and be gone
To keep them back that come to succour you:
Why shall we fight, if you pretend no title?

DUKE OF GLOSTER.

Why, brother, wherefore stand you on nice
points?

KING EDWARD.

When we grow stronger, then we'll make our
claim:
Till then, 'tis wisdom to conceal our meaning.

LORD HASTINGS.

Away with scrupulous wit! now arms must
rule.

DUKE OF GLOSTER.

And fearless minds climb soonest unto crowns.
Brother, we will proclaim you out of hand;
The bruit thereof will bring you many friends.

KING EDWARD.

Then be it as you will: for 'tis my right,
And Henry but usurps the diadem.

SIR JOHN MONTGOMERY.

Ay, now my sovereign speaketh like himself;
And now will I be Edward's champion.

LORD HASTINGS.
Sound trumpet; Edward shall be here pro-
claim'd:—
Come, fellow-soldier, make thou proclamation.
[*Flourish.*

SOLDIER.
Edward the Fourth, by the grace of God, king of
England and France, and lord of Ireland, &c.

SIR JOHN MONTGOMERY.
And whosoe'er gainsays King Edward's right,
By this I challenge him to single fight.
[*Throws down his gauntlet.*

ALL.
Long live Edward the Fourth!

KING EDWARD.
Thanks, brave Montgomery;—and thanks unto
you all:
If fortune serve me, I'll requite this kindness.
Now, for this night, let's harbour here in York;
And when the morning sun shall raise his car
Above the border of this horizon,
We'll forward towards Warwick and his mates;
For well I wot that Henry is no soldier.—
Ah, froward Clarence! how evil it beseems thee
To flatter Henry, and forsake thy brother!
Yet, as we may, we'll meet both thee and War-
wick.—
Come on, brave soldiers: doubt not of the day;
And that once gotten, doubt not of large pay.
[*Exeunt.*

SCENE VIII.

London. The palace.

Flourish. Enter KING HENRY, WARWICK, MON-
TAGUE, CLARENCE, EXETER, *and* OXFORD.

EARL OF WARWICK.
WHAT counsel, lords? Edward from Belgia,
With hasty Germans and blunt Hollanders,
Hath past in safety through the narrow seas,
And with his troops doth march amain to London;
And many giddy people flock to him.

EARL OF OXFORD.
Let's levy men, and beat him back again.

DUKE OF CLARENCE.
A little fire is quickly trodden out;
Which, being suffer'd, rivers cannot quench.

EARL OF WARWICK.
In Warwickshire I have true-hearted friends,
Not mutinous in peace, yet bold in war;
Those will I muster up; and thou, son Clarence,
Shalt stir in Suffolk, Norfolk, and in Kent,
The knights and gentlemen to come with thee:
Thou, brother Montague, in Buckingham,
Northampton, and in Leicestershire, shalt find
Men well inclined to hear what thou command'st:
And thou, brave Oxford, wondrous well beloved,
In Oxfordshire shalt muster up thy friends.
My sovereign, with the loving citizens,—
Like to his island girt in with the ocean,
Or modest Dian circled with her nymphs,—
Shall rest in London till we come to him.
Fair lords, take leave, and stand not to reply.
Farewell, my sovereign.

KING HENRY.
Farewell, my Hector, and my Troy's true hope.

DUKE OF CLARENCE.
In sign of truth, I kiss your highness' hand.

KING HENRY.
Well-minded Clarence, be thou fortunate!

SIR JOHN MONTGOMERY.
Comfort, my lord; and so I take my leave.

EARL OF OXFORD [*kissing* HENRY'S *hand*].
And thus I seal my truth, and bid adieu.

KING HENRY.
Sweet Oxford, and my loving Montague,
And all at once, once more a happy farewell.

EARL OF WARWICK.
Farewell, sweet lords: let's meet at Coventry.
[*Exeunt all but* KING HENRY *and* EXETER.

KING HENRY.
Here at the palace will I rest awhile.
Cousin of Exeter, what thinks your lordship?
Methinks the power that Edward hath in field
Should not be able to encounter mine.

DUKE OF EXETER.
The doubt is that he will seduce the rest.

KING HENRY.
That's not my fear; my meed hath got me fame:
I have not stopt mine ears to their demands,
Nor posted off their suits with slow delays;
My pity hath been balm to heal their wounds,
My mildness hath allay'd their swelling griefs,
My mercy dried their water-flowing tears;
I have not been desirous of their wealth,
Nor much opprest them with great subsidies,
Nor forward of revenge, though they much err'd:
Then why should they love Edward more than
me?
No, Exeter, these graces challenge grace:
And, when the lion fawns upon the lamb,
The lamb will never cease to follow him.
[*Shout within,* 'A York! A York!'

DUKE OF EXETER.
Hark, hark, my lord! what shouts are these?
Enter KING EDWARD, GLOSTER, *and* SOLDIERS.

KING EDWARD.
Seize on the shame-faced Henry, bear him hence;
And once again proclaim us king of England.—
You are the fount that makes small brooks to flow:
Now stops thy spring; my sea shall suck them dry,
And swell so much the higher by their ebb.—
Hence with him to the Tower; let him not speak.
[*Exeunt some with* KING HENRY.
And, lords, towards Coventry bend we our course,
Where peremptory Warwick now remains:
The sun shines hot; and, if we use delay,
Cold-biting winter mars our hoped-for hay.

DUKE OF GLOSTER.
Away betimes, before his forces join,
And take the great-grown traitor unawares:
Brave warriors, march amain towards Coventry.
[*Exeunt.*

ACT V. SCENE I.

Coventry.

Enter WARWICK, *the* MAYOR OF COVENTRY,
two MESSENGERS, *and others upon the walls.*

EARL OF WARWICK.
WHERE is the post that came from valiant
Oxford?—
How far hence is thy lord, mine honest fellow?

FIRST MESSENGER.
By this at Dunsmore, marching hitherward.
EARL OF WARWICK.
How far off is our brother Montague?—
Where is the post that came from Montague?
SECOND MESSENGER.
By this at Daintry, with a puissant troop.
Enter SIR JOHN SOMERVILLE.
EARL OF WARWICK.
Say, Somerville, what says my loving son?
And, by thy guess, how nigh is Clarence now?
SIR JOHN SOMERVILLE.
At Southam I did leave him with his forces,
And do expect him here some two hours hence.
[*Drum heard.*
EARL OF WARWICK.
Then Clarence is at hand; I hear his drum.
SIR JOHN SOMERVILLE.
It is not his, my lord; here Southam lies:
The drum your honour hears marcheth from
Warwick.
EARL OF WARWICK.
Who should that be? belike, unlookt-for friends.
SIR JOHN SOMERVILLE.
They are at hand, and you shall quickly know.
[*Enters the city.*
March. Flourish. Enter KING EDWARD,
GLOSTER, *and* SOLDIERS.
KING EDWARD.
Go, trumpet, to the walls, and sound a parle.
DUKE OF GLOSTER.
See how the surly Warwick mans the wall!
EARL OF WARWICK.
O unbid spite! is sportful Edward come?
Where slept our scouts, or how are they seduced,
That we could hear no news of his repair?
KING EDWARD.
Now, Warwick, wilt thou ope the city-gates,
Speak gentle words, and humbly bend thy knee,
Call Edward king, and at his hands beg mercy?
And he shall pardon thee these outrages.
EARL OF WARWICK.
Nay, rather, wilt thou draw thy forces hence,
Confess who set thee up and pluckt thee down,
Call Warwick patron, and be penitent?
And thou shalt still remain the Duke of York.
DUKE OF GLOSTER.
I thought at least he would have said the king;
Or did he make the jest against his will?
EARL OF WARWICK.
Is not a dukedom, sir, a goodly gift?
DUKE OF GLOSTER.
Ay, by my faith, for a poor earl to give:
I'll do thee service for so good a gift.
EARL OF WARWICK.
'Twas I that gave the kingdom to thy brother.
KING EDWARD.
Why, then, 'tis mine, if but by Warwick's gift.
EARL OF WARWICK.
Thou art no Atlas for so great a weight:
And, weakling, Warwick takes his gift again;
And Henry is my king, Warwick his subject.
KING EDWARD.
But Warwick's king is Edward's prisoner:
And, gallant Warwick, do but answer this,—
What is the body when the head is off?

DUKE OF GLOSTER.
Alas, that Warwick had no more forecast,
But, whiles he thought to steal the single ten,
The king was slily finger'd from the deck!
You left poor Henry at the bishop's palace,
And, ten to one, you'll meet him in the Tower.
KING EDWARD.
'Tis even so; yet you are Warwick still.
DUKE OF GLOSTER.
Come, Warwick, take the time; kneel down, kneel
down:
Nay, when? strike now, or else the iron cools.
EARL OF WARWICK.
I had rather chop this hand off at a blow,
And with the other fling it at thy face,
Than bear so low a sail, to strike to thee.
KING EDWARD.
Sail how thou canst, have wind and tide thy
friend,
This hand, fast wound about thy coal-black hair,
Shall, whiles thy head is warm and new cut off,
Write in the dust this sentence with thy blood,—
'Wind-changing Warwick now can change no
more.'
Enter OXFORD, *with drum and colours.*
EARL OF WARWICK.
O cheerful colours! see where Oxford comes!
EARL OF OXFORD.
Oxford, Oxford, for Lancaster!
[*He and his* FORCES *enter the city.*
DUKE OF GLOSTER.
The gates are open, let us enter too.
KING EDWARD.
So other foes may set upon our backs.
Stand we in good array; for they no doubt
Will issue out again and bid us battle:
If not, the city being but of small defence,
We'll quickly rouse the traitors in the same.
EARL OF WARWICK.
O, welcome, Oxford! for we want thy help.
Enter MONTAGUE, *with drum and colours.*
MARQUESS OF MONTAGUE.
Montague, Montague, for Lancaster!
[*He and his* FORCES *enter the city.*
DUKE OF GLOSTER.
Thou and thy brother both shall buy this treason
Even with the dearest blood your bodies bear.
KING EDWARD.
The harder matcht, the greater victory:
My mind presageth happy gain and conquest.
Enter SOMERSET, *with drums and colours.*
DUKE OF SOMERSET.
Somerset, Somerset, for Lancaster!
[*He and his* FORCES *enter the city.*
DUKE OF GLOSTER.
Two of thy name both Dukes of Somerset,
Have sold their lives unto the house of York;
And thou shalt be the third, if this sword hold.
Enter CLARENCE, *with drum and colours.*
EARL OF WARWICK.
And lo, where George of Clarence sweeps along,
Of force enough to bid his brother battle;
With whom an upright zeal to right prevails
More than the nature of a brother's love!—
Come, Clarence, come; thou wilt, if Warwick
call.

[*Sound a parley; and* RICHARD *and*
CLARENCE *whisper together, and then*
CLARENCE *takes his red rose out of his
hat and throws it at* WARWICK.

DUKE OF CLARENCE.
Father of Warwick, know you what this means?
Look here, I throw my infamy at thee:
I will not ruinate my father's house,
Who have his blood to lime the stones together,
And set up Lancaster. Why, trow'st thou, War-
wick,
That Clarence is so harsh, so blunt, unnatural,
To bend the fatal instruments of war
Against his brother and his lawful king?
Perhaps thou wilt object my holy oath:
To keep that oath were more impiety
Than Jephtha's, when he sacrificed his daughter.
I am so sorry for my trespass made,
That, to deserve well at my brother's hands,
I here proclaim myself thy mortal foe;
With resolution, wheresoe'er I meet thee,—
As I will meet thee, if thou stir abroad,—
To plague thee for thy foul misleading me.
And so, proud-hearted Warwick, I defy thee,
And to my brother turn my blushing cheeks.—
Pardon me, Edward, I will make amends;
And, Richard, do not frown upon my faults,
For I will henceforth be no more unconstant.
KING EDWARD.
Now welcome more and ten times more beloved
Than if thou never hadst deserved our hate.
DUKE OF GLOSTER.
Welcome, good Clarence; this is brother-like.
EARL OF WARWICK.
O passing traitor, perjured and unjust!
KING EDWARD.
What, Warwick, wilt thou leave the town, and
fight?
Or shall we beat the stones about thine ears?
EARL OF WARWICK.
Alas, I am not coopt here for defence!
I will away towards Barnet presently,
And bid thee battle, Edward, if thou darest.
KING EDWARD.
Yes, Warwick, Edward dares, and leads the
way.—
Lords, to the field; Saint George and victory!
[*Exeunt* KING EDWARD *and his* COM-
PANY. *March.* WARWICK *and his*
COMPANY *follow.*

SCENE II.

A field of battle near Barnet.

Alarums and excursions. Enter KING EDWARD,
bringing forth WARWICK, *wounded.*

KING EDWARD.
SO, lie thou there: die thou, and die our fear;
For Warwick was a bug that fear'd us all.—
Now, Montague, sit fast; I seek for thee,
That Warwick's bones may keep thine company.
[*Exit.*
EARL OF WARWICK.
Ah, who is nigh? come to me, friend or foe,
And tell me who is victor, York or Warwick?
Why ask I that? my mangled body shows,

My blood, my want of strength, my sick heart
shows,
That I must yield my body to the earth,
And, by my fall, the conquest to my foe.
Thus yields the cedar to the axe's edge,
Whose arms gave shelter to the princely eagle,
Under whose shade the ramping lion slept,
Whose top-branch overpeer'd Jove's spreading
tree,
And kept low shrubs from winter's powerful
wind.
These eyes, that now are dimm'd with death's
black veil,
Have been as piercing as the mid-day sun,
To search the secret treasons of the world:
The wrinkles in my brows, now fill'd with blood,
Were liken'd oft to kingly sepulchres;
For who lived king, but I could dig his grave?
And who durst smile when Warwick bent his
brow?
Lo, now my glory smear'd in dust and blood!
My parks, my walks, my manors that I had,
Even now forsake me; and of all my lands
Is nothing left me but my body's length!
Why, what is pomp, rule, reign, but earth and dust?
And, live we how we can, yet die we must.
Enter OXFORD *and* SOMERSET.
DUKE OF SOMERSET.
Ah, Warwick, Warwick! wert thou as we are,
We might recover all our loss again: [power;
The queen from France hath brought a puissant
Even now we heard the news: ah, couldst thou fly!
EARL OF WARWICK.
Why, then, I would not fly.—Ah, Montague,
If thou be there, sweet brother, take my hand,
And with thy lips keep in my soul awhile!
Thou lovest me not; for, brother, if thou didst,
Thy tears would wash this cold congealed blood,
That glues my lips and will not let me speak.
Come quickly, Montague, or I am dead.
DUKE OF SOMERSET.
Ah, Warwick! Montague hath breath'd his last;
And to the latest gasp cried out for Warwick,
And said, 'Commend me to my valiant brother.'
And more he would have said; and more he spoke,
Which sounded like a clamour in a vault,
That mought not be distinguisht; but at last
I well might hear, deliver'd with a groan,
'O, farewell, Warwick!'
EARL OF WARWICK.
Sweet rest his soul!—Fly, lords, and save your-
selves.
For Warwick bids you all farewell, to meet in
heaven.   -   [*Dies.*
EARL OF OXFORD.
Away, away, to meet the queen's great power!
[*Here they bear away his body.   Exeunt.*

SCENE III.

Another part of the field.

Flourish.   Enter KING EDWARD *in triumph; with*
GLOSTER, CLARENCE, *and the rest.*

KING EDWARD.
THUS far our fortune keeps an upward course,
And we are graced with wreaths of victory.

But, in the midst of this bright-shining day,
I spy a black, suspicious, threatening cloud,
That will encounter with our glorious sun
Ere he attain his easeful western bed:
I mean, my lords, those powers that the queen
Hath raised in Gallia have arrived our coast,
And, as we hear, march on to fight with us.

DUKE OF CLARENCE.
A little gale will soon disperse that cloud,
And blow it to the source from whence it came:
Thy very beams will dry those vapours up;
For every cloud engenders not a storm.

DUKE OF GLOSTER.
The queen is valued thirty thousand strong,
And Somerset, with Oxford, fled to her:
If she have time to breathe, be well assured
Her faction will be full as strong as ours.

KING EDWARD.
We are advertised by our loving friends
That they do hold their course toward Tewks-
   bury:
We, having now the best at Barnet field,
Will thither straight, for willingness rids way;
And, as we march, our strength will be aug-
   mented
In every county as we go along.—
Strike up the drum; cry, 'Courage!' and away.
                                          [Exeunt.

SCENE IV.

Plains near Tewksbury.

Flourish. March. Enter QUEEN MARGARET,
PRINCE EDWARD, SOMERSET, OXFORD, *and*
SOLDIERS.

QUEEN MARGARET.
GREAT lords, wise men ne'er sit and wail their
   loss,
But cheerly seek how to redress their harms.
What though the mast be now blown overboard,
The cable broke, the holding-anchor lost,
And half our sailors swallow'd in the flood?
Yet lives our pilot still: is't meet that he
Should leave the helm, and, like a fearful lad,
With tearful eyes add water to the sea,
And give more strength to that which hath too
   much;
Whiles, in his moan, the ship splits on the rock,
Which industry and courage might have saved?
Ah, what a shame! ah, what a fault were this!
Say Warwick was our anchor; what of that?
And Montague our topmast; what of him?
Our slaughter'd friends the tackles; what of these?
Why, is not Oxford here another anchor?
And Somerset another goodly mast?
The friends of France our shrouds and tacklings?
And, though unskilful, why not Ned and I
For once allow'd the skilful pilot's charge?
We will not from the helm to sit and weep;   [no,
But keep our course, though the rough wind say
From shelves and rocks that threaten us with
   wrack.
As good to chide the waves as speak them fair.
And what is Edward but a ruthless sea?
What Clarence but a quicksand of deceit?
And Richard but a ragged fatal rock?
All these the enemies to our poor bark.

Say you can swim,—alas, 'tis but awhile!
Tread on the sand,—why, there you quickly sink;
Bestride the rock,—the tide will wash you off,
Or else you famish; that's a threefold death.
This speak I, lords, to let you understand,
If case some one of you would fly from us,
That there's no hoped-for mercy with the
   brothers,
More than with ruthless waves, with sands, and
   rocks.
Why, courage, then! what cannot be avoided
'Twere childish weakness to lament or fear.

PRINCE EDWARD.
Methinks a woman of this valiant spirit
Should, if a coward heard her speak these words,
Infuse his breast with magnanimity,
And make him naked foil a man-at-arms.
I speak not this as doubting any here;
For did I but suspect a fearful man,
He should have leave to go away betimes;
Lest in our need he might infect another,
And make him of like spirit to himself.
If any such be here,—as God forbid!—
Let him depart before we need his help.

EARL OF OXFORD.
Women and children of so high a courage,
And warriors faint! why, 'twere perpetual
   shame.—
O brave young prince! thy famous grandfather
Doth live again in thee: long mayst thou live
To bear his image and renew his glories!

DUKE OF SOMERSET.
And he that will not fight for such a hope,
Go home to bed, and, like the owl by day,
If he arise, be mockt and wonder'd at.

QUEEN MARGARET.
Thanks, gentle Somerset;—sweet Oxford, thanks.

PRINCE EDWARD.
And take his thanks that yet hath nothing else.

Enter a MESSENGER.

MESSENGER.
Prepare you, lords; for Edward is at hand,
Ready to fight; therefore be resolute.

EARL OF OXFORD.
I thought no less: it is his policy
To haste thus fast, to find us unprovided.

DUKE OF SOMERSET.
But he's deceived; we are in readiness.

QUEEN MARGARET.
This cheers my heart, to see your forwardness.

EARL OF OXFORD.
Here pitch our battle; hence we will not budge.

Flourish and march. Enter KING EDWARD,
GLOSTER, CLARENCE, *and* FORCES.

KING EDWARD.
Brave followers, yonder stands the thorny wood,
Which, by the heavens' assistance and your
   strength,
Must by the roots be hewn up yet ere night.
I need not add more fuel to your fire,
For well I wot ye blaze to burn them out:
Give signal to the fight, and to it, lords.

QUEEN MARGARET.
Lords, knights, and gentlemen, what I should say
My tears gainsay; for every word I speak,
Ye see, I drink the water of mine eyes.

94

Therefore, but no more but this:—Henry, your
  sovereign,
Is prisoner to the foe; his state usurpt,
His realm a slaughter-house, his subjects slain,
His statutes cancell'd, and his treasure spent;
And yonder is the wolf that makes this spoil.
You fight in justice: then, in God's name, lords,
Be valiant, and give signal to the fight.
    [*Alarum. Retreat. Excursions. Exeunt.*

SCENE V.

Another part of the field.

Flourish. Enter KING EDWARD, GLOSTER,
CLARENCE, *and* SOLDIERS; *with* QUEEN
MARGARET, OXFORD, *and* SOMERSET, *pri-
soners.*

KING EDWARD.
LO, here a period of tumultuous broils.
  Away with Oxford to Hames Castle straight:
For Somerset, off with his guilty head.
Go, bear them hence; I will not hear them speak.
       EARL OF OXFORD.
For my part, I'll not trouble thee with words.
      DUKE OF SOMERSET.
Nor I, but stoop with patience to my fortune.
    [*Exeunt* OXFORD *and* SOMERSET, *guarded.*
      QUEEN MARGARET.
So part we sadly in this troublous world,
To meet with joy in sweet Jerusalem.
      KING EDWARD.
Is proclamation made, that who finds Edward
Shall have a high reward, and he his life?
      DUKE OF GLOSTER.
It is: and lo, where youthful Edward comes!
  Enter SOLDIERS, *with* PRINCE EDWARD.
      KING EDWARD.
Bring forth the gallant, let us hear him speak.
What! can so young a thorn begin to prick?—
Edward, what satisfaction canst thou make
For bearing arms, for stirring up my subjects,
And all the trouble thou hast turn'd me to?
      PRINCE EDWARD.
Speak like a subject, proud ambitious York!
Suppose that I am now my father's mouth;
Resign thy chair, and where I stand kneel thou,
Whilst I propose the selfsame words to thee,
Which, traitor, thou wouldst have me answer to.
      QUEEN MARGARET.
Ah, that thy father had been so resolved!
      DUKE OF GLOSTER.
That you might still have worn the petticoat,
And ne'er have stol'n the breech from Lancaster.
      PRINCE EDWARD.
Let Aesop fable in a winter's night;
His currish riddles sort not with this place.
      DUKE OF GLOSTER.
By heaven, brat, I'll plague ye for that word.
      QUEEN MARGARET.
Ay, thou wast born to be a plague to men.
      DUKE OF GLOSTER.
For God's sake, take away this captive scold.
      PRINCE EDWARD.
Nay, take away this scolding crook-back rather.
      KING EDWARD.
Peace, wilful boy, or I will charm your tongue.

      DUKE OF CLARENCE.
Untutor'd lad, thou art too malapert.
      PRINCE EDWARD.
I know my duty; you are all undutiful: ·
Lascivious Edward,—and thou, perjured
  George,—
And thou, mis-shapen Dick,—I tell ye all
I am your better, traitors as ye are;—
And thou usurp'st my father's right and mine.
      KING EDWARD.
Take that, thou likeness of this railer here.
          [*Stabs him.*
      DUKE OF GLOSTER.   ·
Sprawl'st thou? take that, to end thy agony.
          [*Stabs him.*
      DUKE OF CLARENCE.
And there's for twitting me with perjury.
          [*Stabs him.*
      QUEEN MARGARET.
O, kill me too!
      DUKE OF GLOSTER.
Marry, and shall.   [*Offers to kill her.*
      KING EDWARD.
Hold, Richard, hold; for we have done too much.
      DUKE OF GLOSTER.
Why should she live, to fill the world with words?
      KING EDWARD.
What, doth she swoon? use means for her re-
  covery.
      DUKE OF GLOSTER.
Clarence, excuse me to the king my brother;
I'll hence to London on a serious matter:
Ere ye come there, be sure to hear some news.
      DUKE OF CLARENCE.
What? what? ·
      DUKE OF GLOSTER.
The Tower, man, the Tower!—I'll root 'em out.
          [*Exit.*
      QUEEN MARGARET.
O Ned, sweet Ned! speak to thy mother, boy!
Canst thou not speak? O traitors! murderers!
They that stabb'd Cæsar shed no blood at all,
Did not offend, nor were not worthy blame,
If this foul deed were by to equal it:
He was a man; this, in respect, a child,—
And men ne'er spend their fury on a child.
What's worse than murderer, that I may name it?
No, no, my heart will burst, an if I speak:
And I will speak, that so my heart may burst.
Butchers and villains! bloody cannibals!
How sweet a plant have you untimely cropt!
You have no children, butchers! if you had,
The thought of them would have stirr'd up
  remorse:
But if you ever chance to have a child,
Look in his youth to have him so cut off   [prince!
As, deathsmen, you have rid this sweet young
      KING EDWARD.
Away with her; go, bear her hence perforce.
      QUEEN MARGARET.
Nay, never bear me hence, dispatch me here;
Here sheathe thy sword, I'll pardon thee my
  death:
What, wilt thou not?—then, Clarence, do it thou.
      DUKE OF CLARENCE.
By heaven, I will not do thee so much ease.

QUEEN MARGARET.
Good Clarence, do; sweet Clarence, do thou do it.
DUKE OF CLARENCE.
Didst thou not hear me swear I would not do it?
QUEEN MARGARET.
Ay, but thou usest to forswear thyself:
'Twas sin before, but now 'tis charity.
What, wilt thou not?—Where is that devil's
   butcher,
Hard-favour'd Richard?—Richard, where art
   thou?
Thou art not here: murder is thy alms-deed;
Petitioners for blood thou ne'er putt'st back.
KING EDWARD.
Away, I say; I charge ye, bear her hence.
QUEEN MARGARET.
So come to you and yours, as to this prince!
                     [Exit, led out forcibly.
KING EDWARD.
Where's Richard gone?
DUKE OF CLARENCE.
To London, all in post; and, as I guess,
To make a bloody supper in the Tower.
KING EDWARD.
He's sudden, if a thing comes in his head.
Now march we hence: discharge the common sort
With pay and thanks, and let's away to London,
And see our gentle queen how well she fares,—
By this, I hope, she hath a son for me. [Exeunt.

SCENE VI.

London. The Tower.

Enter KING HENRY and GLOSTER, with the
   LIEUTENANT, *on the walls.*

DUKE OF GLOSTER.
GOOD day, my lord. What, at your book so
   hard?
KING HENRY.
Ay, my good lord:—my lord, I should say rather;
'Tis sin to flatter; 'good' was little better:
'Good Gloster' and 'good devil' were alike,
And both preposterous; therefore, not 'good
   lord.'
DUKE OF GLOSTER.
Sirrah, leave us to ourselves: we must confer.
                     [Exit LIEUTENANT.
KING HENRY.
So flies the reckless shepherd from the wolf;
So first the harmless sheep doth yield his fleece,
And next his throat unto the butcher's knife.—
What scene of death hath Roscius now to act?
DUKE OF GLOSTER.
Suspicion always haunts the guilty mind;
The thief doth fear each bush an officer.
KING HENRY.
The bird that hath been limed in a bush,
With trembling wings misdoubteth every bush;
And I, the hapless male to one sweet bird,
Have now the fatal object in my eye
Where my poor young was limed, was caught,
   and kill'd.
DUKE OF GLOSTER.
Why, what a peevish fool was that of Crete,
That taught his son the office of a fowl!
And yet, for all his wings, the fool was drown'd.

KING HENRY.
I, Dædalus; my poor boy, Icarus;
Thy father, Minos, that denied our course;
The sun, that sear'd the wings of my sweet boy,
Thy brother Edward; and thyself, the sea,
Whose envious gulf did swallow up his life.
Ah, kill me with thy weapon, not with words!
My breast can better brook thy dagger's point
Than can my ears that tragic history.
But wherefore dost thou come? is't for my life?
DUKE OF GLOSTER.
Think'st thou I am an executioner?
KING HENRY.
A persecutor, I am sure, thou art:
If murdering innocents be executing,
Why, then thou art an executioner.
DUKE OF GLOSTER.
Thy son I kill'd for his presumption.
KING HENRY.
Hadst thou been kill'd when first thou didst pre-
   sume,
Thou hadst not lived to kill a son of mine.
And thus I prophesy,—that many a thousand,
Which now mistrust no parcel of my fear,
And many an old man's sigh and many a widow's,
And many an orphan's water-standing eye—
Men for their sons, wives for their husbands'
   fate,
And orphans for their parents' timeless death—
Shall rue the hour that ever thou wast born.
The owl shriekt at thy birth,—an evil sign;
The night-crow cried, aboding luckless time;
Dogs howl'd, and hideous tempest shook down
   trees;
The raven rookt her on the chimney's top,
And chattering pies in dismal discord sung.
Thy mother felt more than a mother's pain,
And yet brought forth less than a mother's
   hope,—
An indigested and deformed lump,
Not like the fruit of such a goodly tree.
Teeth hadst thou in thy head when thou wast
   born,
To signify thou camest to bite the world:
And, if the rest be true which I have heard,
Thou camest—
DUKE OF GLOSTER.
I'll hear no more: die, prophet, in thy speech:
                     [Stabs him.
For this, amongst the rest, was I ordain'd.
KING HENRY.
Ay, and for much more slaughter after this.
O, God forgive my sins, and pardon thee! [Dies.
DUKE OF GLOSTER.
What, will the aspiring blood of Lancaster
Sink in the ground? I thought it would have
   mounted.
See how my sword weeps for the poor king's
   death!
O, may such purple tears be alway shed
From those that wish the downfall of our house!
If any spark of life be yet remaining,
Down, down to hell; and say I sent thee thither,
                     [Stabs him again.
I, that have neither pity, love, nor fear.
Indeed, 'tis true that Henry told me of;

For I have often heard my mother say
I came into the world with my legs forward:
Had I not reason, think ye, to make haste,
And seek their ruin that usurpt our right?
The midwife wonder'd; and the women cried,
'O, Jesus bless us, he is born with teeth!'
And so I was; which plainly signified
That I should snarl, and bite, and play the dog.
Then, since the heavens have shaped my body so,
Let hell make crookt my mind to answer it.
I have no brother, I am like no brother;
And this word 'love,' which greybeards call
    divine,
Be resident in men like one another,
And not in me: I am myself alone.—
Clarence, beware; thou keep'st me from the light:
But I will sort a pitchy day for thee;
For I will buzz abroad such prophecies,
That Edward shall be fearful of his life;
And then, to purge his fear, I'll be thy death.
King Henry and the prince his son are gone:
Clarence, thy turn is next, and then the rest;
Counting myself but bad till I be best.—
I'll throw thy body in another room,
And triumph, Henry, in thy day of doom.
                        [*Exit with the body.*

SCENE VII.

London.   The palace.

Flourish.   Enter KING EDWARD, QUEEN ELIZA-
BETH, GLOSTER, CLARENCE, HASTINGS, *a*
NURSE *with the young* PRINCE, *and* ATTEN-
DANTS.

KING EDWARD.

ONCE more we sit in England's royal throne,
    Re-purchased with the blood of enemies.
What valiant foemen, like to autumn's corn,
Have we mow'd down in tops of all their pride!
Three Dukes of Somerset, threefold renown'd
For hardy and undoubted champions;
Two Cliffords, as the father and the son;
And two Northumberlands,—two braver men
Ne'er spurr'd their coursers at the trumpet's
    sound;
With them, the two brave bears, Warwick and
    Montague,

That in their chains fetter'd the kingly lion,
And made the forest tremble when they roar'd.
Thus have we swept suspicion from our seat,
And made our footstool of security.—
Come hither, Bess, and let me kiss my boy.
Young Ned, for thee, thine uncles and myself
Have in our armours watcht the winter's night;
Went all afoot in summer's scalding heat,
That thou mightst repossess the crown in peace:
And of our labours thou shalt reap the gain.

DUKE OF GLOSTER [*aside*].

I'll blast his harvest, if your head were laid;
For yet I am not lookt on in the world.
This shoulder was ordain'd so thick to heave;
And heave it shall some weight, or break my
    back:—
Work thou the way,—and thou shalt execute.

KING EDWARD.

Clarence and Gloster, love my lovely queen;
And kiss your princely nephew, brothers both.

DUKE OF CLARENCE.

The duty that I owe unto your majesty
I seal upon the lips of this sweet babe.

QUEEN ELIZABETH.

Thanks, noble Clarence; worthy brother, thanks.

DUKE OF GLOSTER.

And, that I love the tree from whence thou
    sprang'st,
Witness the loving kiss I give the fruit.—
[*aside*] To say the truth, so Judas kist his Master,
And cried, 'All hail!' whenas he meant all harm.

KING EDWARD.

Now am I seated as my soul delights,
Having my country's peace and brothers' loves.

DUKE OF CLARENCE.

What will your Grace have done with Margaret?
Reignier, her father, to the king of France
Hath pawn'd the Sicils and Jerusalem,
And hither have they sent it for her ransom.

KING EDWARD.

Away with her, and waft her hence to France.
And now what rests, but that we spend the time
With stately triumphs, mirthful comic shows,
Such as befits the pleasure of the court?
Sound drums and trumpets! farewell sour annoy!
For here, I hope, begins our lasting joy.
                                    [*Exeunt.*

KING RICHARD THE THIRD

DRAMATIS PERSONAE

KING EDWARD THE FOURTH.
EDWARD, *Prince of Wales, afterwards King Edward V.*, } *sons to the King.*
RICHARD, *Duke of York*,
GEORGE, *Duke of Clarence*,
RICHARD, *Duke of Gloster, afterwards King Richard III.*, } *brothers to the King.*
A YOUNG SON OF CLARENCE.
HENRY, *Earl of Richmond, afterwards King Henry VII.*
CARDINAL BOURCHIER, *Archbishop of Canterbury.*
THOMAS ROTHERHAM, *Archbishop of York.*
JOHN MORTON, *Bishop of Ely.*
DUKE OF BUCKINGHAM.
DUKE OF NORFOLK.
EARL OF SURREY, *his son.*
EARL RIVERS, *brother to Elizabeth.*
MARQUESS OF DORSET *and* LORD GREY, *sons to Elizabeth.*
EARL OF OXFORD.
LORD HASTINGS.
LORD STANLEY, *call'd also Earl of Derby.*
LORD LOVEL.
SIR THOMAS VAUGHAN.
SIR RICHARD RATCLIFF.
SIR WILLIAM CATESBY.

SIR JAMES TYRREL.
SIR JAMES BLOUNT.
SIR WALTER HERBERT.
SIR ROBERT BRAKENBURY, *lieutenant of the Tower.*
CHRISTOPHER URSWICK, *a priest.* ANOTHER PRIEST.
LORD MAYOR OF LONDON. SHERIFF OF WILTSHIRE.
TRESSEL *and* BERKELEY, *attending on Lady Anne.*

ELIZABETH, *queen to King Edward IV.*
MARGARET, *widow of King Henry VI.*
DUCHESS OF YORK, *mother to King Edward IV., Clarence, and Gloster.*
LADY ANNE, *widow of Edward, Prince of Wales, son to King Henry VI.; afterwards married to Richard, Duke of Gloster.*
A YOUNG DAUGHTER OF CLARENCE (MARGARET PLANTAGENET).

LORDS *and other* ATTENDANTS; *a* PURSUIVANT, SCRIVENER, CITIZENS, MURDERERS, MESSENGERS, SOLDIERS, &c.

SCENE—*England.*

ACT I. SCENE I.

London. A street.

Enter RICHARD, DUKE OF GLOSTER, *solus.*

DUKE OF GLOSTER.

NOW is the winter of our discontent
Made glorious summer by this sun of York;
And all the clouds that lour'd upon our house
In the deep bosom of the ocean buried.
Now are our brows bound with victorious
  wreaths;
Our bruised arms hung up for monuments;
Our stern alarums changed to merry meetings,
Our dreadful marches to delightful measures.
Grim-visaged war hath smooth'd his wrinkled
  front;
And now—instead of mounting barbed steeds
To fright the souls of fearful adversaries—
He capers nimbly in a lady's chamber
To the lascivious pleasing of a lute.
But I, that am not shaped for sportive tricks,
Nor made to court an amorous looking-glass;
I, that am rudely stampt, and want love's majesty
To strut before a wanton ambling nymph;
I, that am curtail'd of this fair proportion,
Cheated of feature by dissembling nature,
Deform'd, unfinisht, sent before my time
Into this breathing world, scarce half made up,
And that so lamely and unfashionable
That dogs bark at me as I halt by them;—
Why, I, in this weak piping time of peace,
Have no delight to pass away the time,

Unless to spy my shadow in the sun,
And descant on mine own deformity:
And therefore, since I cannot prove a lover,
To entertain these fair well-spoken days,
I am determined to prove a villain,
And hate the idle pleasures of these days.
Plots have I laid, inductions dangerous,
By drunken prophecies, libels, and dreams,
To set my brother Clarence and the king
In deadly hate the one against the other:
And, if King Edward be as true and just
As I am subtle, false, and treacherous,
This day should Clarence closely be mew'd up,
About a prophecy, which says that G
Of Edward's heirs the murderer shall be.
Dive, thoughts, down to my soul:—here Clarence
  comes.

Enter CLARENCE, *guarded, and* BRAKENBURY.

Brother, good day: what means this armed guard
That waits upon your Grace?

DUKE OF CLARENCE.
                          His majesty,
Tendering my person's safety, hath appointed
This conduct to convey me to the Tower.

DUKE OF GLOSTER.
Upon what cause?

DUKE OF CLARENCE.
                Because my name is George.

DUKE OF GLOSTER.
Alack, my lord, that fault is none of yours;
He should, for that, commit your godfathers:—
O, belike his majesty hath some intent

98

That you shall be new-christen'd in the Tower.
But what's the matter, Clarence? may I know?
DUKE OF CLARENCE.
Yea, Richard, when I know; for I protest
As yet I do not: but, as I can learn,
He hearkens after prophecies and dreams;
And from the cross-row plucks the letter G,
And says a wizard told him that by G
His issue disinherited should be;
And, for my name of George begins with G,
It follows in his thought that I am he.
These, as I learn, and such-like toys as these,
Have moved his highness to commit me now.
DUKE OF GLOSTER.
Why, this it is, when men are ruled by women:—
'Tis not the king that sends you to the Tower;
My Lady Grey his wife, Clarence, 'tis she
That tempers him to this extremity.
Was it not she, and that good man of worship,
Antony Woodville, her brother there,
That made him send Lord Hastings to the Tower,
From whence this present day he is deliver'd?
We are not safe, Clarence; we are not safe.
DUKE OF CLARENCE.
By heaven, I think there's no man is secure
But the queen's kindred, and night-walking
   heralds
That trudge betwixt the king and Mistress Shore.
Heard ye not what an humble suppliant
Lord Hastings was to her for his delivery?
DUKE OF GLOSTER.
Humbly complaining to her deity
Got my lord chamberlain his liberty.
I'll tell you what,—I think it is our way,
If we will keep in favour with the king,
To be her men, and wear her livery:
The jealous o'erworn widow and herself,
Since that our brother dubb'd them gentlewomen,
Are mighty gossips in this monarchy.
SIR ROBERT BRAKENBURY.
I beseech your Graces both to pardon me;
His majesty hath straitly given in charge
That no man shall have private conference,
Of what degree soever, with his brother.
DUKE OF GLOSTER.
Even so; an please your worship, Brakenbury,
You may partake of any thing we say:
We speak no treason, man;—we say the king
Is wise and virtuous; and his noble queen
Well struck in years, fair, and not jealous;—
We say that Shore's wife hath a pretty foot,
A cherry lip, a bonny eye, a passing pleasing
   tongue;   [folks:
And that the queen's kindred are made gentle-
How say you, sir? can you deny all this?
SIR ROBERT BRAKENBURY.
With this, my lord, myself have naught to do.
DUKE OF GLOSTER.
Naught to do with Mistress Shore! I tell thee,
   fellow,
He that doth naught with her, excepting one,
Were best to do it secretly, alone.
SIR ROBERT BRAKENBURY.
What one, my lord?
DUKE OF GLOSTER.
Her husband, knave:—wouldst thou betray me?

SIR ROBERT BRAKENBURY.
I beseech your Grace to pardon me; and, withal,
Forbear your conference with the noble duke.
DUKE OF CLARENCE.
We know thy charge, Brakenbury, and will obey.
DUKE OF GLOSTER.
We are the queen's abjects, and must obey.—
Brother, farewell: I will unto the king;
And whatsoe'er you will employ me in,—
Were it to call King Edward's widow sister,—
I will perform it to enfranchise you.
Meantime, this deep disgrace in brotherhood
Touches me deeper than you can imagine.
DUKE OF CLARENCE.
I know it pleaseth neither of us well.
DUKE OF GLOSTER.
Well, your imprisonment shall not be long;
I will deliver you, or else lie for you:
Meantime, have patience.
DUKE OF CLARENCE.
                I must perforce: farewell.
   [*Exeunt* CLARENCE, BRAKENBURY, *and*
   GUARD.
DUKE OF GLOSTER.
Go, tread the path that thou shalt ne'er return,
Simple, plain Clarence!—I do love thee so,
That I will shortly send thy soul to heaven,
If heaven will take the present at our hands.—
But who comes here? the new-deliver'd
   Hastings?
         Enter HASTINGS.
LORD HASTINGS.
Good time of day unto my gracious lord!
DUKE OF GLOSTER.
As much unto my good lord chamberlain!
Well are you welcome to the open air.
How hath your lordship brookt imprisonment?
LORD HASTINGS.
With patience, noble lord, as prisoners must:
But I shall live, my lord, to give them thanks
That were the cause of my imprisonment.
DUKE OF GLOSTER.
No doubt, no doubt; and so shall Clarence too;
For they that were your enemies are his,
And have prevail'd as much on him as you.
LORD HASTINGS.
More pity that the eagle should be mew'd,
While kites and buzzards prey at liberty.
DUKE OF GLOSTER.
What news abroad?
LORD HASTINGS.
No news so bad abroad as this at home,—
The king is sickly, weak, and melancholy,
And his physicians fear him mightily.
DUKE OF GLOSTER.
Now, by Saint Paul, this news is bad indeed.
O, he hath kept an evil diet long,
And overmuch consumed his royal person:
'Tis very grievous to be thought upon.
What, is he in his bed?
LORD HASTINGS.
He is.
DUKE OF GLOSTER.
Go you before, and I will follow you.
                [*Exit* HASTINGS.
He cannot live, I hope; and must not die

Till George be packt with post-horse up to
   heaven.
I'll in, to urge his hatred more to Clarence,
With lies well steel'd with weighty arguments;
And, if I fail not in my deep intent,
Clarence hath not another day to live:
Which done, God take King Edward to His
   mercy,
And leave the world for me to bustle in!
For then I'll marry Warwick's youngest
   daughter:
What though I kill'd her husband and her father?
The readiest way to make the wench amends,
Is to become her husband and her father:
The which will I; not all so much for love
As for another secret close intent,
By marrying her which I must reach unto.
But yet I run before my horse to market:
Clarence still breathes; Edward still lives and
   reigns: .
When they are gone, then must I count my gains.
                                    [*Exit.*

SCENE II.

The same. Another street.

Enter the corse of HENRY THE SIXTH, *with halberds to guard it,* LADY ANNE *being the
mourner;* TRESSEL *and* BERKELEY.

LADY ANNE.

SET down, set down your honourable load,—
   If honour may be shrouded in a hearse,—
Whilst I awhile obsequiously lament
Th' untimely fall of virtuous Lancaster.
Poor key-cold figure of a holy king!
Pale ashes of the house of Lancaster!
Thou bloodless remnant of that royal blood!
Be it lawful that I invocate thy ghost,
To hear the lamentations of poor Anne,
Wife to thy Edward, to thy slaughter'd son,
Stabb'd by the selfsame hand that made these
   wounds!
Lo, in these windows that let forth thy life,
I pour the helpless balm of my poor eyes:—
O, cursed be the hand that made these holes!
Cursed the heart that had the heart to do it!
Cursed the blood that let this blood from hence!
More direful hap betide that hated wretch,
That makes us wretched by the death of thee,
Than I can wish to adders, spiders, toads,
Or any creeping venom'd thing that lives!
If ever he have child, abortive be it,
Prodigious, and untimely brought to light,
Whose ugly and unnatural aspect
May fright the hopeful mother at the view;
And that be heir to his unhappiness!
If ever he have wife, let her be made
More miserable by the death of him
Than I am made by my young lord and thee!—
Come, now towards Chertsey with your holy
   load,   ‘
Taken from Paul's to be interred there;
And still, as you are weary of the weight, ‘
Rest you, whiles I lament King Henry's corse.
               Enter GLOSTER.

DUKE OF GLOSTER.

Stay, you that bear the corse, and set it down.

LADY ANNE.

What black magician conjures up this fiend,
To stop devoted charitable deeds?

DUKE OF GLOSTER.

Villains, set down the corse; or, by Saint Paul,
I'll make a corse of him that disobeys!

FIRST GENTLEMAN.

My lord, stand back, and let the coffin pass.

DUKE OF GLOSTER.

Unmanner'd dog! stand thou, when I command:
Advance thy halberd higher than my breast,
Or, by Saint Paul, I'll strike thee to my foot,
And spurn upon thee, beggar, for thy boldness.

LADY ANNE.

What, do you tremble? are you all afraid?
Alas, I blame you not; for you are mortal,
And mortal eyes cannot endure the devil.—
Avaunt, thou dreadful minister of hell!
Thou hadst but power over his mortal body,—
His soul thou canst not have; therefore, be gone.

DUKE OF GLOSTER.

Sweet saint, for charity, be not so curst.

LADY ANNE.

Foul devil, for God's sake, hence, and trouble us
   not;
For thou hast made the happy earth thy hell,
Fill'd it with cursing cries and deep exclaims.
If thou delight to view thy heinous deeds,
Behold this pattern of thy butcheries.
O, gentlemen, see, see! dead Henry's wounds
Open their congeal'd mouths and bleed afresh!
Blush, blush, thou lump of foul deformity;
For 'tis thy presence that exhales this blood
From cold and empty veins, where no blood
   dwells;
Thy deed, inhuman and unnatural,
Provokes this deluge most unnatural.—
O God, which this blood mad'st, revenge his
   death!
O earth, which this blood drink'st, revenge his
   death!
Either heaven with lightning strike the murderer
   dead;
Or, earth, gape open wide, and eat him quick,
As thou dost swallow up this good king's blood,
Which his hell-govern'd arm hath butchered!

DUKE OF GLOSTER.

Lady, you know no rules of charity,
Which renders good for bad, blessings for curses.

LADY ANNE.

Villain, thou know'st no law of God nor man:
No beast so fierce but knows some touch of
   pity.

DUKE OF GLOSTER.

But I know none, and therefore am no beast.

LADY ANNE.

O wonderful, when devils tell the truth!

DUKE OF GLOSTER.

More wonderful, when angels are so angry.—
Vouchsafe, divine perfection of a woman,
Of these supposed evils, to give me leave,
By circumstance, but to acquit myself.

LADY ANNE.

Vouchsafe, defused infection of a man,
For these known evils, but to give me leave,
By circumstance, to curse thy cursed self.

DUKE OF GLOSTER.
Fairer than tongue can name thee, let me have
Some patient leisure to excuse myself.
LADY ANNE.
Fouler than heart can think thee, thou canst
make
No excuse current, but to hang thyself.
DUKE OF GLOSTER.
By such despair, I should accuse myself.
LADY ANNE.
And, by despairing, shouldst thou stand excused
For doing worthy vengeance on thyself,
That didst unworthy slaughter upon others.
DUKE OF GLOSTER.
Say that I slew them not?
LADY ANNE.
        Why, then, they are not dead:
But dead they are, and, devilish slave, by thee.
DUKE OF GLOSTER.
I did not kill your husband.
LADY ANNE.
        Why, then, he is alive.
DUKE OF GLOSTER.
Nay, he is dead; and slain by Edward's hand.
LADY ANNE.
In thy foul throat thou liest: Queen Margaret
saw
Thy murderous falchion smoking in his blood;
The which thou once didst bend against her
breast,
But that thy brothers beat aside the point.
DUKE OF GLOSTER.
I was provoked by her slanderous tongue,
That laid their guilt upon my guiltless shoulders.
LADY ANNE.
Thou wast provoked by thy bloody mind,
That never dreamt on aught but butcheries:
Didst thou not kill this king?
DUKE OF GLOSTER.
        I grant ye.
LADY ANNE.
Dost grant me, hedgehog? then, God grant me
too
Thou mayst be damned for that wicked deed!
O, he was gentle, mild, and virtuous!
DUKE OF GLOSTER.
The fitter for the King of heaven, that hath him.
LADY ANNE.
He is in heaven, where thou shalt never come.
DUKE OF GLOSTER.
Let him thank me, that holp to send him thither;
For he was fitter for that place than earth.
LADY ANNE.
And thou unfit for any place but hell.
DUKE OF GLOSTER.
Yes, one place else, if you will hear me name it.
LADY ANNE.
Some dungeon.
DUKE OF GLOSTER.
        Your bed-chamber.
LADY ANNE.
Ill rest betide the chamber where thou liest!
DUKE OF GLOSTER.
So will it, madam, till I lie with you.
LADY ANNE.
I hope so.

DUKE OF GLOSTER.
        I know so. But, gentle Lady Anne,—
To leave this keen encounter of our wits,
And fall somewhat into a slower method,—
Is not the causer of the timeless deaths
Of these Plantagenets, Henry and Edward,
As blameful as the executioner?
LADY ANNE.
Thou wast the cause and most accurst effect.
DUKE OF GLOSTER.
Your beauty was the cause of that effect;
Your beauty, that did haunt me in my sleep
To undertake the death of all the world,
So I might live one hour in your sweet bosom.
LADY ANNE.
If I thought that, I tell thee, homicide,   [cheeks.
These nails should rend that beauty from my
DUKE OF GLOSTER.
These eyes could not endure that beauty's
wrack;
You should not blemish it, if I stood by:
As all the world is cheered by the sun,
So I by that; it is my day, my life.
LADY ANNE.
Black night o'ershade thy day, and death thy life!
DUKE OF GLOSTER.
Curse not thyself, fair creature; thou art both.
LADY ANNE.
I would I were, to be revenged on thee.
DUKE OF GLOSTER.
It is a quarrel most unnatural,
To be revenged on him that loveth thee.
LADY ANNE.
It is a quarrel just and reasonable,
To be revenged on him that kill'd my husband.
DUKE OF GLOSTER.
He that bereft thee, lady, of thy husband,
Did it to help thee to a better husband.
LADY ANNE.
His better doth not breathe upon the earth.
DUKE OF GLOSTER.
He lives that loves thee better than he could.
LADY ANNE.
Name him.
DUKE OF GLOSTER.
        Plantagenet.
LADY ANNE.
        Why, that was he.
DUKE OF GLOSTER.
The selfsame name, but one of better nature.
LADY ANNE.
Where is he?
DUKE OF GLOSTER.
        Here. [She spits at him.] Why dost
thou spit at me?
LADY ANNE.
Would it were mortal poison, for thy sake!
DUKE OF GLOSTER.
Never came poison from so sweet a place.
LADY ANNE.
Never hung poison on a fouler toad.
Out of my sight! thou dost infect mine eyes.
DUKE OF GLOSTER.
Thine eyes, sweet lady, have infected mine.
LADY ANNE.
Would they were basilisks, to strike thee dead!

DUKE OF GLOSTER.
I would they were, that I might die at once;
For now they kill me with a living death.
Those eyes of thine from mine have drawn salt
    tears,
Shamed their aspects with store of childish drops:
These eyes, which never shed remorseful tear,
No, when my father York and Edward wept
To hear the piteous moan that Rutland made
When black-faced Clifford shook his sword at
    him;
Nor when thy warlike father, like a child,
Told the sad story of my father's death,
And twenty times made pause to sob and weep,
That all the standers-by had wet their cheeks,
Like trees bedasht with rain; in that sad time
My manly eyes did scorn an humble tear;
And what these sorrows could not thence exhale,
Thy beauty hath, and made them blind with
    weeping.
I never sued to friend nor enemy;
My tongue could never learn sweet smoothing
    words;
But, now thy beauty is proposed my fee,
My proud heart sues, and prompts my tongue to
    speak.   [She looks scornfully at him.
Teach not thy lips such scorn; for they were made
For kissing, lady, not for such contempt.
If thy revengeful heart cannot forgive,
Lo, here I lend thee this sharp-pointed sword;
Which if thou please to hide in this true breast,
And let the soul forth that adoreth thee,
I lay it naked to the deadly stroke,
And humbly beg the death upon my knee.
          [He lays his breast open; she offers at it with
          his sword.
Nay, do not pause; for I did kill King Henry,
But 'twas thy beauty that provoked me.
Nay, now dispatch; 'twas I that stabb'd young
    Edward,
But 'twas thy heavenly face that set me on.
                    [She falls the sword.
Take up the sword again, or take up me.
          LADY ANNE.
Arise, dissembler: though I wish thy death,
I will not be thy executioner.
          DUKE OF GLOSTER.
Then bid me kill myself, and I will do it.
          LADY ANNE.
I have already.
          DUKE OF GLOSTER.
          That was in thy rage:
Speak it again, and, even with the word,
This hand, which for thy love did kill thy love,
Shall for thy love kill a far truer love;
To both their deaths shalt thou be accessary.
          LADY ANNE.
I would I knew thy heart.
          DUKE OF GLOSTER.
'Tis figured in my tongue.
          LADY ANNE.
I fear me both are false.
          DUKE OF GLOSTER.
Then never man was true.
          LADY ANNE.
Well, well, put up your sword.

DUKE OF GLOSTER.
Say, then, my peace is made.
          LADY ANNE.
That shalt thou know hereafter.
          DUKE OF GLOSTER.
But shall I live in hope?
          LADY ANNE.
All men, I hope, live so.
          DUKE OF GLOSTER.
Vouchsafe to wear this ring.
          LADY ANNE.
To take, is not to give.
          DUKE OF GLOSTER.
Look, how this ring encompasseth thy finger,
Even so thy breast encloseth my poor heart;
Wear both of them, for both of them are thine.
And if thy poor devoted servant may
But beg one favour at thy gracious hand,
Thou dost confirm his happiness for ever.
          LADY ANNE.
What is it?
          DUKE OF GLOSTER.
That it may please you leave these sad designs
To him that hath more cause to be a mourner,
And presently repair to Crosby-place;
Where—after I have solemnly interr'd
At Chertsey monastery this noble king,
And wet his grave with my repentant tears—
I will with all expedient duty see you:
For divers unknown reasons, I beseech you,
Grant me this boon.
          LADY ANNE.
With all my heart; and much it joys me too
To see you are become so penitent.—
Tressel and Berkeley, go along with me.
          DUKE OF GLOSTER.
Bid me farewell.
          LADY ANNE.
          'Tis more than you deserve;
But since you teach me how to flatter you,
Imagine I have said farewell already.
          [Exeun LADY ANNE, TRESSEL, and
          BERKELEY.
          DUKE OF GLOSTER.
Sirs, take up the corse.
          GENTLEMEN.
          Towards Chertsey, noble lord?
          DUKE OF GLOSTER.
No, to White-Friars; there attend my coming.
          [Exeunt all, except GLOSTER.
Was ever woman in this humour woo'd?
Was ever woman in this humour won?
I'll have her;—but I will not keep her long.
What! I, that kill'd her husband and his father,
To take her in her heart's extremest hate;
With curses in her mouth, tears in her eyes,
The bleeding witness of her hatred by;
Having God, her conscience, and these bars
    against me,
And I no friends to back my suit withal
But the plain devil and dissembling looks,
And yet to win her,—all the world to nothing!
Ha!
Hath she forgot already that brave prince,
Edward, her lord, whom I, some three months
    since,

Stabb'd in my angry mood at Tewksbury?
A sweeter and a lovelier gentleman—
Framed in the prodigality of nature,
Young, valiant, wise, and, no doubt, right royal—
The spacious world cannot again afford:
And will she yet abase her eyes on me,
That cropt the golden prime of this sweet prince,
And made her widow to a woful bed?
On me, whose all not equals Edward's moiety?
On me, that halt and am mis-shapen thus?
My dukedom to a beggarly denier,
I do mistake my person all this while:
Upon my life, she finds, although I cannot,
Myself to be a marvellous proper man.
I'll be at charges for a looking-glass;
And entertain a score or two of tailors
To study fashions to adorn my body:
Since I am crept in favour with myself,
I will maintain it with some little cost.
But first I'll turn yon fellow in his grave;
And then return lamenting to my love.—
Shine out, fair sun, till I have bought a glass,
That I may see my shadow as I pass.   [*Exit.*

SCENE III.
The palace.

Enter QUEEN ELIZABETH, RIVERS, *and* GREY.
EARL RIVERS.
HAVE patience, madam: there's no doubt his majesty
Will soon recover his accustom'd health.
LORD GREY.
In that you brook it ill, it makes him worse:
Therefore, for God's sake, entertain good comfort,
And cheer his Grace with quick and merry words.
QUEEN ELIZABETH.
If he were dead, what would betide of me?
EARL RIVERS.
No other harm but loss of such a lord.
QUEEN ELIZABETH.
The loss of such a lord includes all harms.
LORD GREY.
The heavens have blest you with a goodly son,
To be your comforter when he is gone.
QUEEN ELIZABETH.
Ah, he is young; and his minority
Is put unto the trust of Richard Gloster,
A man that loves not me nor none of you.
EARL RIVERS.
Is it concluded he shall be Protector?
QUEEN ELIZABETH.
It is determined, not concluded yet:
But so it must be, if the king miscarry.

Enter BUCKINGHAM *and* DERBY.
LORD GREY.
Here come the lords of Buckingham and Derby.
DUKE OF BUCKINGHAM.
Good time of day unto your royal Grace!
EARL OF DERBY.
God make your majesty joyful as you have been!
QUEEN ELIZABETH.
The Countess Richmond, good my Lord of Derby,
To your good prayer will scarcely say amen.

Yet, Derby, notwithstanding she's your wife,
And loves not me, be you, good lord, assured
I hate not you for her proud arrogance.
EARL OF DERBY.
I do beseech you, either not believe
The envious slanders of her false accusers;
Or, if she be accused on true report,
Bear with her weakness, which, I think, proceeds
From wayward sickness, and no grounded malice.
EARL RIVERS.
Saw you the king to-day, my Lord of Derby?
EARL OF DERBY.
But now the Duke of Buckingham and I
Are come from visiting his majesty.
QUEEN ELIZABETH.
What likelihood of his amendment, lords?
DUKE OF BUCKINGHAM.
Madam, good hope; his Grace speaks cheerfully.
QUEEN ELIZABETH.
God grant him health! Did you confer with him?
DUKE OF BUCKINGHAM.
Ay, madam: he desires to make atonement
Between the Duke of Gloster and your brothers,
And betwixt them and my lord chamberlain;
And sent to warn them to his royal presence.
QUEEN ELIZABETH.
Would all were well!—but that will never be:
I fear our happiness is at the height.

Enter GLOSTER, HASTINGS, *and* DORSET.
DUKE OF GLOSTER.
They do me wrong, and I will not endure it:—
Who are they that complain unto the king
That I, forsooth, am stern, and love them not?
By holy Paul, they love his Grace but lightly
That fill his ears with such dissentious rumours.
Because I cannot flatter and speak fair,
Smile in men's faces, smooth, deceive, and cog,
Duck with French nods and apish courtesy,
I must be held a rancorous enemy.
Cannot a plain man live and think no harm,
But thus his simple truth must be abused
By silken, sly, insinuating Jacks?
EARL RIVERS.
To whom in all this presence speaks your Grace?
DUKE OF GLOSTER.
To thee, that hast nor honesty nor grace.
When have I injured thee? when done thee wrong?—
Or thee?—or thee?—or any of your faction?
A plague upon you all! His royal Grace—
Whom God preserve better than you would wish!—
Cannot be quiet scarce a breathing-while,
But you must trouble him with lewd complaints.
QUEEN ELIZABETH.
Brother of Gloster, you mistake the matter.
The king, of his own royal disposition,
And not provoked by any suitor else;
Aiming, belike, at your interior hatred,
That in your outward action shows itself
Against my children, brothers, and myself,
Makes him to send, that thereby he may gather
The ground of your ill-will, and so remove it.
DUKE OF GLOSTER.
I cannot tell: the world is grown so bad,
That wrens may prey where eagles dare not perch:

Since every Jack became a gentleman,
There's many a gentle person made a Jack.
QUEEN ELIZABETH.
Come, come, we know your meaning, brother
  Gloster;
You envy my advancement and my friends':
God grant we never may have need of you!
DUKE OF GLOSTER.
Meantime, God grants that we have need of you:
Our brother is imprison'd by your means,
Myself disgraced, and the nobility
Held in contempt; while great promotions
Are daily given to ennoble those
That scarce, some two days since, were worth
  a noble.
QUEEN ELIZABETH.
By Him that raised me to this careful height
From that contented hap which I enjoy'd,
I never did incense his majesty
Against the Duke of Clarence, but have been
An earnest advocate to plead for him.
My lord, you do me shameful injury,
Falsely to draw me in these vile suspects.
DUKE OF GLOSTER.
You may deny that you were not the cause
Of my Lord Hastings' late imprisonment.
EARL RIVERS.
She may, my lord; for—
DUKE OF GLOSTER.
She may, Lord Rivers!—why, who knows not so?
She may do more, sir, than denying that:
She may help you to many fair preferments;
And then deny her aiding hand therein,
And lay those honours on your high desert.
What may she not? She may,—ay, marry, may
  she,—
EARL RIVERS.
What, marry, may she?
DUKE OF GLOSTER.
What, marry, may she! marry with a king,
A bachelor, a handsome stripling too:
I wis your grandam had a worser match.
QUEEN ELIZABETH.
My Lord of Gloster, I have too long borne
Your blunt upbraidings and your bitter scoffs:
By heaven, I will acquaint his majesty
With those gross taunts I often have endured.
I had rather be a country servant-maid
Than a great queen, with this condition,—
To be so baited, scorn'd, and stormed at:
Enter QUEEN MARGARET, *behind.*
Small joy have I in being England's queen.
QUEEN MARGARET [*aside*].
And lessen'd be that small, God, I beseech
  Him!
Thy honour, state, and seat is due to me.
DUKE OF GLOSTER.
What! threat you me with telling of the king?
Tell him, and spare not: look, what I have said
I will avouch in presence of the king:
I dare adventure to be sent to th' Tower.
'Tis time to speak,—my pains are quite forgot.
QUEEN MARGARET [*aside*].
Out, devil! I remember them too well:
Thou kill'dst my husband Henry in the Tower,
And Edward, my poor son, at Tewksbury.

DUKE OF GLOSTER.
Ere you were queen, ay, or your husband king,
I was a pack-horse in his great affairs;
A weeder-out of his proud adversaries,
A liberal rewarder of his friends:
To royalize his blood I spilt mine own.
QUEEN MARGARET [*aside*].
Ay, and much better blood than his or thine.
DUKE OF GLOSTER.
In all which time you and your husband Grey
Were factious for the house of Lancaster;—
And, Rivers, so were you:—was not your husband
In Margaret's battle at Saint Alban's slain?
Let me put in your minds, if you forget,
What you have been ere now, and what you are;
Withal, what I have been, and what I am.
QUEEN MARGARET [*aside*].
A murderous villain, and so still thou art.
DUKE OF GLOSTER.
Poor Clarence did forsake his father, Warwick;
Ay, and forswore himself,—which Jesu pardon!—
QUEEN MARGARET [*aside*].
Which God revenge!
DUKE OF GLOSTER.
To fight on Edward's party, for the crown;
And for his meed, poor lord, he is mew'd up.
I would to God my heart were flint, like Ed-
  ward's;
Or Edward's soft and pitiful, like mine:
I am too childish-foolish for this world.
QUEEN MARGARET [*aside*].
Hie thee to hell for shame, and leave this
  world,
Thou cacodemon! there thy kingdom is.
EARL RIVERS.
My Lord of Gloster, in those busy days
Which here you urge to prove us enemies,
We follow'd then our lord, our lawful king:
So should we you, if you should be our king.
DUKE OF GLOSTER.
If I should be!—I had rather be a pedlar:
Far be it from my heart, the thought of it!
QUEEN ELIZABETH.
As little joy, my lord, as you suppose
You should enjoy, were you this country's
  king,—
As little joy may you suppose in me,
That I enjoy, being the queen thereof.
QUEEN MARGARET [*aside*].
As little joy enjoys the queen thereof;
For I am she, and altogether joyless.
I can no longer hold me patient.—   [*Advancing.*
Hear me, you wrangling pirates, that fall out
In sharing that which you have pill'd from me!
Which of you trembles not that looks on me?
If not, that, I being queen, you bow like subjects,
Yet that, by you deposed, you quake like rebels?—
Ah, gentle villain, do not turn away!
DUKE OF GLOSTER.
Foul wrinkled witch, what makest thou in my
  sight?
QUEEN MARGARET.
But repetition of what thou hast marr'd;
That will I make before I let thee go.
DUKE OF GLOSTER.
Wert thou not banished on pain of death?

QUEEN MARGARET.

I was;
But I do find more pain in banishment
Than death can yield me here by my abode.
A husband and a son thou owest to me,—
And thou a kingdom,—all of you allegiance:
The sorrow that I have, by right is yours;
And all the pleasures you usurp are mine.

DUKE OF GLOSTER.

The curse my noble father laid on thee,
When thou didst crown his warlike brows with
    paper,
And with thy scorns drew'st rivers from his eyes:
And then, to dry them, gavest the duke a clout
Steept in the faultless blood of pretty Rutland;—
His curses, then from bitterness of soul
Denounced against thee, are all faln upon thee;
And God, not we, hath plagued thy bloody deed.

QUEEN ELIZABETH.

So just is God, to right the innocent.

LORD HASTINGS.

O, 'twas the foulest deed to slay that babe,
And the most merciless that e'er was heard of!

EARL RIVERS.

Tyrants themselves wept when it was reported.

MARQUESS OF DORSET.

No man but prophesied revenge for it.

DUKE OF BUCKINGHAM.

Northumberland, then present, wept to see it.

QUEEN MARGARET.

What! were you snarling all before I came,
Ready to catch each other by the throat,
And turn you all your hatred now on me?
Did York's dread curse prevail so much with
    heaven,
That Henry's death, my lovely Edward's death,
Their kingdom's loss, my woful banishment,
Could all but answer for that peevish brat?
Can curses pierce the clouds and enter heaven?—
Why, then, give way, dull clouds, to my quick
    curses!—
Though not by war, by surfeit die your king,
As ours by murder, to make him a king!
Edward thy son, that now is Prince of Wales,
For Edward my son, that was Prince of Wales,
Die in his youth by like untimely violence!
Thyself a queen, for me that was a queen,
Outlive thy glory, like my wretched self!
Long mayst thou live to wail thy children's loss;
And see another, as I see thee now,
Deckt in thy rights, as thou art stall'd in mine!
Long die thy happy days before thy death;
And, after many lengthen'd hours of grief,
Die neither mother, wife, nor England's queen!—
Rivers and Dorset, you were standers by,—
And so wast thou, Lord Hastings,—when my
    son
Was stabb'd with bloody daggers: God, I pray
    Him,
That none of you may live his natural age,
But by some unlookt accident cut off!

DUKE OF GLOSTER.

Have done thy charm, thou hateful wither'd hag!

QUEEN MARGARET.

And leave out thee? stay, dog, for thou shalt hear
me.

If heaven have any grievous plague in store
Exceeding those that I can wish upon thee,
O, let them keep it till thy sins be ripe,
And then hurl down their indignation
On thee, the troubler of the poor world's peace!
The worm of conscience still begnaw thy soul!
Thy friends suspect for traitors while thou livest,
And take deep traitors for thy dearest friends!
No sleep close up that deadly eye of thine,
Unless it be while some tormenting dream
Affrights thee with a hell of ugly devils!
Thou elvish-markt, abortive, rooting hog!
Thou that wast seal'd in thy nativity
The slave of nature and the son of hell!
Thou slander of thy mother's heavy womb!
Thou loathed issue of thy father's loins!
Thou rag of honour! thou detested—

DUKE OF GLOSTER.

Margaret.

QUEEN MARGARET.

Richard!

DUKE OF GLOSTER.

Ha!

QUEEN MARGARET.

I call thee not.

DUKE OF GLOSTER.

I cry thee mercy, then; for did I think
That thou hadst call'd me all these bitter names.

QUEEN MARGARET.

Why, so I did; but lookt for no reply.
O, let me make the period to my curse!

DUKE OF GLOSTER.

'Tis done by me, and ends in—Margaret.

QUEEN ELIZABETH.

Thus have you breathed your curse against yourself.

QUEEN MARGARET.

Poor painted queen, vain flourish of my fortune!
Why strew'st thou sugar on that bottled spider,
Whose deadly web ensnareth thee about?
Fool, fool! thou whett'st a knife to kill thyself.
The day will come that thou shalt wish for me
To help thee curse that poisonous bunch-backt
    toad.

LORD HASTINGS.

False-boding woman, end thy frantic curse,
Lest to thy harm thou move our patience.

QUEEN MARGARET.

Foul shame upon you! you have all moved mine.

EARL RIVERS.

Were you well served, you would be taught your
    duty.

QUEEN MARGARET.

To serve me well, you all should do me duty,
Teach me to be your queen, and you my subjects:
O, serve me well, and teach yourselves that duty!

MARQUESS OF DORSET.

Dispute not with her,—she is lunatic.

QUEEN MARGARET.

Peace, master marquess, you are malapert:
Your fire-new stamp of honour is scarce current:
O, that your young nobility could judge
What 'twere to lose it, and be miserable!
They that stand high have many blasts to shake
    them;
And if they fall, they dash themselves to pieces.

DUKE OF GLOSTER.

Good counsel, marry:—learn it, learn it, marquess.

MARQUESS OF DORSET.

It touches you, my lord, as much as me.

DUKE OF GLOSTER.

Ay, and much more: but I was born so high,
Our aery buildeth in the cedar's top,
And dallies with the wind, and scorns the sun.

QUEEN MARGARET.

And turns the sun to shade;—alas! alas!—
Witness my son, now in the shade of death;
Whose bright out-shining beams thy cloudy
wrath
Hath in eternal darkness folded up.
Your aery buildeth in our aery's nest:—
O God, that seest it, do not suffer it;
As it was won with blood, lost be it so!

DUKE OF BUCKINGHAM.

Peace, peace, for shame, if not for charity.

QUEEN MARGARET.

Urge neither charity nor shame to me:
Uncharitably with me have you dealt,
And shamefully by you my hopes are butcher'd.
My charity is outrage, life my shame,—
And in that shame still live my sorrow's rage!

DUKE OF BUCKINGHAM.

Have done, have done.

QUEEN MARGARET.

O princely Buckingham, I'll kiss thy hand,
In sign of league and amity with thee:
Now fair befall thee and thy noble house!
Thy garments are not spotted with our blood,
Nor thou within the compass of my curse.

DUKE OF BUCKINGHAM.

Nor no one here; for curses never pass
The lips of those that breathe them in the air.

QUEEN MARGARET.

I'll not believe but they ascend the sky,
And there awake God's gentle-sleeping peace.
O Buckingham, take heed of yonder dog!
Look, when he fawns he bites; and when he bites,
His venom tooth will rankle to the death:
Have not to do with him, beware of him;
Sin, death, and hell have set their marks on him,
And all their ministers attend on him.

DUKE OF GLOSTER.

What doth she say, my Lord of Buckingham?

DUKE OF BUCKINGHAM.

Nothing that I respect, my gracious lord.

QUEEN MARGARET.

What, dost thou scorn me for my gentle counsel?
And soothe the devil that I warn thee from?
O, but remember this another day,
When he shall split thy very heart with sorrow,
And say, poor Margaret was a prophetess!—
Live each of you the subjects to his hate,
And he to yours, and all of you to God's!   [Exit.

LORD HASTINGS.

My hair doth stand on end to hear her curses.

EARL RIVERS.

And so doth mine: I muse why she's at liberty.

DUKE OF GLOSTER.

I cannot blame her: by God's holy mother,
She hath had too much wrong; and I repent
My part thereof that I have done to her.

QUEEN ELIZABETH.

I never did her any, to my knowledge.

DUKE OF GLOSTER.

Yet you have all the vantage of her wrong.
I was too hot to do somebody good
That is too cold in thinking of it now.
Marry, as for Clarence, he is well repaid;
He is frankt up to fatting for his pains;—
God pardon them that are the cause of it!

EARL RIVERS.

A virtuous and a Christian-like conclusion,
To pray for them that have done scathe to us.

DUKE OF GLOSTER [aside].

So do I ever, being well advised;
For had I cursed now, I had cursed myself.

Enter CATESBY.

SIR WILLIAM CATESBY

Madam, his majesty doth call for you,—
And for your Grace,—and you, my noble lords.

QUEEN ELIZABETH.

Catesby, I come.—Lords, will you go with me?

EARL RIVERS.

We wait upon your Grace.
[Exeunt all except GLOSTER.

DUKE OF GLOSTER.

I do the wrong, and first begin to brawl.
The secret mischiefs that I set abroach
I lay unto the grievous charge of others.   [ness,—
Clarence,—whom I, indeed, have laid in dark-
I do beweep to many simple gulls;
Namely, to Hastings, Derby, Buckingham;
And say it is the queen and her allies
That stir the king against the duke my brother.
Now, they believe it; and withal whet me
To be revenged on Rivers, Vaughan, Grey:
But then I sigh; and, with a piece of Scripture,
Tell them that God bids us do good for evil:
And thus I clothe my naked villainy
With old odd ends stoln out of holy writ;
And seem a saint, when most I play the devil.—
But, soft! here come my executioners.

Enter two MURDERERS.

How now, my hardy, stout-resolved mates!
Are you now going to dispatch this thing?

FIRST MURDERER.

We are, my lord; and come to have the warrant,
That we may be admitted where he is.

DUKE OF GLOSTER.

Well thought upon;—I have it here about me:
[Gives the warrant.
When you have done, repair to Crosby-place.
But, sirs, be sudden in the execution,
Withal obdurate, do not hear him plead;
For Clarence is well-spoken, and perhaps
May move your hearts to pity, if you mark him.

FIRST MURDERER.

Tut, tut, my lord, we will not stand to prate;
Talkers are no good doers: be assured
We go to use our hands, and not our tongues.

DUKE OF GLOSTER.

Your eyes drop millstones, when fools' eyes drop
tears:
I like you, lads;—about your business straight;
Go, go, dispatch.

FIRST MURDERER.

We will, my noble lord.   [Exeunt.

SCENE IV.

The Tower.

Enter CLARENCE *and* BRAKENBURY.

SIR ROBERT BRAKENBURY.

WHY looks your Grace so heavily to-day?

DUKE OF CLARENCE.

O, I have past a miserable night,
So full of fearful dreams, of ugly sights,
That, as I am a Christian faithful man,
I would not spend another such a night,
Though 'twere to buy a world of happy days,—
So full of dismal terror was the time!

SIR ROBERT BRAKENBURY.

What was your dream, my lord? I pray you, tell
me.

DUKE OF CLARENCE.

Methought that I had broken from the Tower,
And was embarkt to cross to Burgundy;
And, in my company, my brother Gloster;
Who from my cabin tempted me to walk
Upon the hatches: thence we lookt toward
    England,
And cited up a thousand heavy times,
During the wars of York and Lancaster,
That had befaln us. As we paced along
Upon the giddy footing of the hatches,
Methought that Gloster stumbled; and, in falling,
Struck me, that thought to stay him, overboard
Into the tumbling billows of the main.
Lord, Lord! methought, what pain it was to
    drown!
What dreadful noise of waters in mine ears!
What ugly sights of death within mine eyes!
Methought I saw a thousand fearful wracks;
Ten thousand men that fishes gnaw'd upon;
Wedges of gold, great anchors, heaps of pearl,
Inestimable stones, unvalued jewels,
All scatt'red in the bottom of the sea:
Some lay in dead men's skulls; and, in those holes
Where eyes did once inhabit, there were crept,
As 'twere in scorn of eyes, reflecting gems,
That woo'd the slimy bottom of the deep,
And mockt the dead bones that lay scatt'red by.

SIR ROBERT BRAKENBURY.

Had you such leisure in the time of death
To gaze upon the secrets of the deep?

DUKE OF CLARENCE.

Methought I had; and often did I strive
To yield the ghost: but still the envious flood
Kept in my soul, and would not let it forth
To seek the empty, vast, and wandering air;
But smother'd it within my panting bulk,
Which almost burst to belch it in the sea.

SIR ROBERT BRAKENBURY.

Awaked you not with this sore agony?

DUKE OF CLARENCE.

No, no, my dream was lengthen'd after life;
O, then began the tempest to my soul!
I past, methought, the melancholy flood,
With that grim ferryman which poets write of,
Unto the kingdom of perpetual night.
The first that there did greet my stranger soul,
Was my great father-in-law, renowned Warwick;
Who cried aloud, 'What scourge for perjury
Can this dark monarchy afford false Clarence?'

And so he vanisht: then came wandering by
A shadow like an angel, with bright hair
Dabbled in blood; and he shriekt out aloud,
'Clarence is come; false, fleeting, perjured
    Clarence,
That stabb'd me in the field by Tewksbury:
Seize on him, Furies, take him to your torments!'
With that, methought, a legion of foul fiends
Environ'd me, and howled in mine ears
Such hideous cries, that, with the very noise,
I trembling waked, and, for a season after,
Could not believe but that I was in hell,—
Such terrible impression made my dream.

SIR ROBERT BRAKENBURY.

No marvel, lord, though it affrighted you:
I am afraid, methinks, to hear you tell it.

DUKE OF CLARENCE.

O Brakenbury, I have done those things,
That now give evidence against my soul,
For Edward's sake; and see how he requites me!
O God! if my deep prayers cannot appease
    Thee,
But Thou wilt be avenged on my misdeeds,
Yet execute Thy wrath in me alone;
O, spare my guiltless wife and my poor chil-
    dren!—
I pray thee, gentle keeper, stay by me;
My soul is heavy, and I fain would sleep.

SIR ROBERT BRAKENBURY.

I will, my lord: God give your Grace good rest!—
                        [CLARENCE *sleeps.*
Sorrow breaks seasons and reposing hours,
Makes the night morning, and the noontide
    night.
Princes have but their titles for their glories,
An outward honour for an inward toil;
And, for unfelt imaginations,
They often feel a world of restless cares:
So that, betwixt their titles and low names,
There's nothing differs but the outward fame.

Enter the two MURDERERS.

FIRST MURDERER.

Ho! who's here?

SIR ROBERT BRAKENBURY.

What wouldst thou, fellow? and how camest thou
hither?

FIRST MURDERER.

I would speak with Clarence, and I came hither
on my legs.

SIR ROBERT BRAKENBURY.

What, so brief?

SECOND MURDERER.

'Tis better, sir, than to be tedious.—Let him see
our commission; and talk no more.
                    [BRAKENBURY *reads it.*

SIR ROBERT BRAKENBURY.

I am, in this, commanded to deliver
The noble Duke of Clarence to your hands:—
I will not reason what is meant hereby,
Because I will be guiltless of the meaning.
Here are the keys;—there sits the duke asleep:
I'll to the king; and signify to him
That thus I have resign'd to you my charge.

FIRST MURDERER.

You may, sir; 'tis a point of wisdom: fare you well.
                        [*Exit* BRAKENBURY.

SECOND MURDERER.
What, shall we stab him as he sleeps?
FIRST MURDERER.
No; he'll say 'twas done cowardly, when he wakes.
SECOND MURDERER.
When he wakes! why, fool, he shall never wake
till the judgement-day.
FIRST MURDERER.
Why, then he'll say we stabb'd him sleeping.
SECOND MURDERER.
The urging of that word 'judgement' hath bred
a kind of remorse in me.
FIRST MURDERER.
What, art thou afraid?
SECOND MURDERER.
Not to kill him, having a warrant for it; but to be
damn'd for killing him, from the which no warrant can defend me.
FIRST MURDERER.
I thought thou hadst been resolute.
SECOND MURDERER.
So I am, to let him live.
FIRST MURDERER.
I'll back to the Duke of Gloster, and tell him so.
SECOND MURDERER.
I pray thee, stay a while: I hope my holy humour
will change; 'twas wont to hold me but while one
tells twenty.
FIRST MURDERER.
How dost thou feel thyself now?
SECOND MURDERER.
Faith, some certain dregs of conscience are yet
within me.
FIRST MURDERER.
Remember our reward, when the deed is done.
SECOND MURDERER.
Zounds, he dies: I had forgot the reward.
FIRST MURDERER.
Where is thy conscience now?
SECOND MURDERER.
In the Duke of Gloster's purse.
FIRST MURDERER.
So, when he opens his purse to give us our reward,
thy conscience flies out.
SECOND MURDERER.
Let it go; there's few or none will entertain it.
FIRST MURDERER.
How if it come to thee again?
SECOND MURDERER.
I'll not meddle with it: it is a dangerous thing: it
makes a man a coward: a man cannot steal, but it
accuseth him; he cannot swear, but it checks him;
he cannot lie with his neighbour's wife, but it detects him: it is a blushing shame-faced spirit that
mutinies in a man's bosom; it fills one full of
obstacles: it made me once restore a purse of gold,
that by chance I found; it beggars any man that
keeps it: it is turn'd out of all towns and cities for
a dangerous thing; and every man that means to
live well endeavours to trust to himself and to live
without it.
FIRST MURDERER.
Zounds, it is even now at my elbow, persuading
me not to kill the duke.
SECOND MURDERER.
Take the devil in thy mind, and believe him not:

he would insinuate with thee but to make thee
sigh.
FIRST MURDERER.
Tut, I am strong-framed, he cannot prevail with
me, I warrant thee.
SECOND MURDERER.
Spoke like a tall fellow that respects his reputation.   Come, shall we to this gear?
FIRST MURDERER.
Take him over the costard with the hilts of thy
sword, and then we will chop him in the malmsey-butt in the next room.
SECOND MURDERER.
O excellent device! make a sop of him.
FIRST MURDERER.
Hark! he stirs: shall I strike?
SECOND MURDERER.
No, first let's reason with him.
DUKE OF CLARENCE [waking].
Where art thou, keeper? give me a cup of
wine.
FIRST MURDERER.
You shall have wine enough, my lord, anon.
DUKE OF CLARENCE.
In God's name, what art thou?
FIRST MURDERER.
A man, as you are.
DUKE OF CLARENCE.
But not, as I am, royal.
FIRST MURDERER.
Nor you, as we are, loyal.
DUKE OF CLARENCE.
Thy voice is thunder, but thy looks are humble.
FIRST MURDERER.
My voice is now the king's, my looks mine own.
DUKE OF CLARENCE.
How darkly and how deadly dost thou speak!
Your eyes do menace me: why look you pale?
Who sent you hither? Wherefore do you
come?
BOTH MURDERERS.
To, to, to—
DUKE OF CLARENCE.
To murder me?
BOTH MURDERERS.
Ay, ay.
DUKE OF CLARENCE.
You scarcely have the hearts to tell me so,
And therefore cannot have the hearts to do it.
Wherein, my friends, have I offended you?
FIRST MURDERER.
Offended us you have not, but the king.
DUKE OF CLARENCE.
I shall be reconciled to him again.
SECOND MURDERER.
Never, my lord; therefore prepare to die.
DUKE OF CLARENCE.
Are you call'd forth from out a world of men
To slay the innocent? What is my offence?
Where are the evidence that do accuse me?
What lawful quest have given their verdict
up
Unto the frowning judge? or who pronounced
The bitter sentence of poor Clarence' death?
Before I be convict by course of law,
To threaten me with death is most unlawful.

I charge you, as you hope to have redemption
By Christ's dear blood shed for our grievous sins,
That you depart, and lay no hands on me:
The deed you undertake is damnable.
FIRST MURDERER.
What we will do, we do upon command.
SECOND MURDERER.
And he that hath commanded is the king.
DUKE OF CLARENCE.
Erroneous vassal! the great King of kings
Hath in the tables of His law commanded
That thou shalt do no murder: will you, then,
Spurn at His edict, and fulfil a man's?
Take heed; for He holds vengeance in His hand,
To hurl upon their heads that break His law.
SECOND MURDERER.
And that same vengeance doth He hurl on thee,
For false forswearing, and for murder too:
Thou didst receive the sacrament to fight
In quarrel of the house of Lancaster.
FIRST MURDERER.
And, like a traitor to the name of God,   [blade
Didst break that vow; and with thy treacherous
Unripp'dst the bowels of thy sovereign's son.
SECOND MURDERER.
Whom thou wert sworn to cherish and defend.
FIRST MURDERER.
How canst thou urge God's dreadful law to us,
When thou hast broke it in so dear degree?
DUKE OF CLARENCE.
Alas! for whose sake did I that ill deed?
For Edward, for my brother, for his sake:
Why, sirs,
He sends ye not to murder me for this;
For in this sin he is as deep as I.
If God will be revenged for this deed,
O, know you yet, He doth it publicly:
Take not the quarrel from His powerful arm;
He needs no indirect nor lawless course
To cut off those that have offended Him.
FIRST MURDERER.
Who made thee, then, a bloody minister,
When gallant-springing brave Plantagenet,
That princely novice, was struck dead by thee?
DUKE OF CLARENCE.
My brother's love, the devil, and my rage.
FIRST MURDERER.
Thy brother's love, our duty, and thy fault,
Provoke us hither now to slaughter thee.
DUKE OF CLARENCE.
O, if you do love my brother, hate not me;
I am his brother, and I love him well.
If you be hired for meed, go back again,
And I will send you to my brother Gloster,
Who shall reward you better for my life
Than Edward will for tidings of my death.
SECOND MURDERER.
You are deceived, your brother Gloster hates you.
DUKE OF CLARENCE.
O, no, he loves me, and he holds me dear:
Go you to him from me.
BOTH MURDERERS.
    Ay, so we will.
DUKE OF CLARENCE.
Tell him, when that our princely father York
Blest his three sons with his victorious arm,

And charged us from his soul to love each other,
He little thought of this divided friendship:
Bid Gloster think of this, and he will weep.
FIRST MURDERER.
Ay, millstones; as he lesson'd us to weep.
DUKE OF CLARENCE.
O, do not slander him, for he is kind.
FIRST MURDERER.
Right.
As snow in harvest.—Thou deceivest thyself:
'Tis he that sent us hither now to slaughter thee.
DUKE OF CLARENCE.
It cannot be; for when I parted with him,
He hugg'd me in his arms, and swore, with sobs,
That he would labour my delivery.
FIRST MURDERER.
Why, so he doth, now he delivers thee
From this earth's thraldom to the joys of heaven.
SECOND MURDERER.
Make peace with God, for you must die, my lord.
DUKE OF CLARENCE.
Hast thou that holy feeling in thy soul,
To counsel me to make my peace with God,
And art thou yet to thy own soul so blind,
That thou wilt war with God by murdering
    me?—
Ah, sirs, consider, he that set you on
To do this deed will hate you for the deed.
SECOND MURDERER.
What shall we do?
DUKE OF CLARENCE.
    Relent, and save your souls.
Which of you, if you were a prince's son,
Being pent from liberty, as I am now,
If two such murderers as yourselves came to you,
Would not entreat for life? As you would beg,
Were you in my distress—
FIRST MURDERER.
Relent! 'tis cowardly and womanish.
DUKE OF CLARENCE.
Not to relent is beastly, savage, devilish.
My friend, I spy some pity in thy looks;
O, if thine eye be not a flatterer,
Come thou on my side, and entreat for me:
A begging prince what beggar pities not?
SECOND MURDERER.
Look behind you, my lord.
FIRST MURDERER.
Take that, and that [stabs him]: if all this will not
    do,
I'll drown you in the malmsey-butt within.
    [Exit, with the body.
SECOND MURDERER.
A bloody deed, and desperately dispatcht!
How fain, like Pilate, would I wash my hands
Of this most grievous guilty murder done!
Enter FIRST MURDERER.
FIRST MURDERER.
How now! what mean'st thou, that thou help'st
    me not?
By heaven, the duke shall know how slack thou
    art!
SECOND MURDERER.
I would he knew that I had saved his brother!
Take thou the fee, and tell him what I say;
For I repent me that the duke is slain.   [Exit.

FIRST MURDERER.
So do not I: go, coward as thou art.—
Well, I'll go hide the body in some hole,
Till that the duke give order for his burial:
And when I have my meed, I will away;
For this will out, and then I must not stay. [*Exit.*

ACT II. SCENE I.

London.   The palace.

Enter the KING, *sick, the* QUEEN, DORSET,
RIVERS, HASTINGS, BUCKINGHAM, GREY,
and others.

KING EDWARD.
WHY, so: now have I done a good day's work:
You peers, continue this united league:
I every day expect an embassage
From my Redeemer to redeem me hence;
And now in peace my soul shall part to heaven,
Since I have made my friends at peace on earth.
Rivers and Hastings, take each other's hand;
Dissemble not your hatred, swear your love.

EARL RIVERS.
By heaven, my soul is purged from grudging
hate;
And with my hand I seal my true heart's love.

LORD HASTINGS.
So thrive I, as I truly swear the like!

KING EDWARD.
Take heed you dally not before your king;
Lest He that is the supreme King of kings,
Confound your hidden falsehood, and award
Either of you to be the other's end.

LORD HASTINGS.
So prosper I, as I swear perfect love!

EARL RIVERS.
And I, as I love Hastings with my heart!

KING EDWARD.
Madam, yourself are not exempt in this,—
Nor you, son Dorset,—Buckingham, nor you;—
You have been factious one against the other.
Wife, love Lord Hastings, let him kiss your hand;
And what you do, do it unfeignedly.

QUEEN ELIZABETH.
There, Hastings; I will never more remember
Our former hatred, so thrive I and mine!

KING EDWARD.
Dorset, embrace him;—Hastings, love lord
marquess.

MARQUESS OF DORSET.
This interchange of love, I here protest,
Upon my part shall be inviolable.

LORD HASTINGS.
And so swear I.   [*They embrace.*

KING EDWARD.
Now, princely Buckingham, seal thou this league
With thy embracements to my wife's allies,
And make me happy in your unity.

DUKE OF BUCKINGHAM [*to the* QUEEN].
Whenever Buckingham doth turn his hate
Upon your Grace, but with all duteous love
Doth cherish you and yours, God punish me
With hate in those where I expect most love!
When I have most need to employ a friend,
And most assured that he is a friend,
Deep, hollow, treacherous, and full of guile,

Be he unto me!—this do I beg of God,
When I am cold in zeal to you or yours.
                                             [*They embrace.*

KING EDWARD.
A pleasing cordial, princely Buckingham,
Is this thy vow unto my sickly heart.
There wanteth now our brother Gloster here,
To make the perfect period of this peace.

DUKE OF BUCKINGHAM.
And, in good time, here comes the noble duke.

Enter GLOSTER.

DUKE OF GLOSTER.
Good morrow to my sovereign king and queen;
And, princely peers, a happy time of day!

KING EDWARD.
Happy, indeed, as we have spent the day.
Brother, we have done deeds of charity;
Made peace of enmity, fair love of hate,
Between these swelling wrong-incensed peers.

DUKE OF GLOSTER.
A blessed labour, my most sovereign liege.
Among this princely heap, if any here,
By false intelligence or wrong surmise,
Hold me a foe;
If I unwittingly, or in my rage,
Have aught committed that is hardly borne
By any in this presence, I desire
To reconcile me to his friendly peace:
'Tis death to me to be at enmity;
I hate it, and desire all good men's love.
First, madam, I entreat true peace of you,
Which I will purchase with my duteous service;
Of you, my noble cousin Buckingham,
If ever any grudge were lodged between us;
Of you, Lord Rivers, and, Lord Grey, of you,
That all without desert have frown'd on me;—
Dukes, earls, lords, gentlemen;—indeed, of all.
I do not know that Englishman alive
With whom my soul is any jot at odds
More than the infant that is born to-night:
I thank my God for my humility.

QUEEN ELIZABETH.
A holiday shall this be kept hereafter:
I would to God all strifes were well compounded.
My sovereign lord, I do beseech your highness
To take our brother Clarence to your grace.

DUKE OF GLOSTER.
Why, madam, have I offer'd love for this,
To be so flouted in this royal presence?
Who knows not that the gentle duke is dead?
                                             [*They all start.*
You do him injury to scorn his corse.

EARL RIVERS.
Who knows not he is dead! who knows he is?

QUEEN ELIZABETH.
All-seeing heaven, what a world is this!

DUKE OF BUCKINGHAM.
Look I so pale, Lord Dorset, as the rest?

MARQUESS OF DORSET.
Ay, my good lord; and no one in this presence
But his red colour hath forsook his cheeks.

KING EDWARD.
Is Clarence dead? the order was reversed.

DUKE OF GLOSTER.
But he, poor soul, by your order first died,
And that a winged Mercury did bear;

Some tardy cripple bore the countermand,
That came too lag to see him buried.
God grant that some, less noble and less loyal,
Nearer in bloody thoughts, but not in blood,
Deserve not worse than wretched Clarence did,
And yet go current from suspicion!
Enter DERBY.
EARL OF DERBY.
A boon, my sovereign, for my service done!
KING EDWARD.
I prithee, peace: my soul is full of sorrow.
EARL OF DERBY.
I will not rise, unless your highness hear me.
KING EDWARD.
Then say at once what is it thou request'st.
EARL OF DERBY.
The forfeit, sovereign, of my servant's life;
Who slew to-day a riotous gentleman
Lately attendant on the Duke of Norfolk.
KING EDWARD.
Have I a tongue to doom my brother's death,
And shall that tongue give pardon to a slave?
My brother kill'd no man,—his fault was
　thought,
And yet his punishment was bitter death.
Who sued to me for him? who, in my rage,
Kneel'd at my feet, and bade me be advised?
Who spoke of brotherhood? who spoke of love?
Who told me how the poor soul did forsake
The mighty Warwick, and did fight for me?
Who told me, in the field at Tewksbury,
When Oxford had me down, he rescued me,
And said, 'Dear brother, live, and be a king'?
Who told me, when we both lay in the field
Frozen almost to death, how he did lap me
Even in his garments, and did give himself,
All thin and naked, to the numb-cold night?
All this from my remembrance brutish wrath
Sinfully pluckt, and not a man of you
Had so much grace to put it in my mind.
But when your carters or your waiting-vassals
Have done a drunken slaughter, and defaced
The precious image of our dear Redeemer,
You straight are on your knees for pardon,
　pardon;
And I, unjustly too, must grant it you:
But for my brother not a man would speak,
Nor I, ungracious, speak unto myself
For him, poor soul. The proudest of you all
Have been beholding to him in his life;
Yet none of you would once plead for his life.—
O God, I fear Thy justice will take hold
On me, and you, and mine, and yours for this!—
Come, Hastings, help me to my closet.—Ah,
Poor Clarence!
　　　　[*Exeunt some with* KING *and* QUEEN.
DUKE OF GLOSTER.
This is the fruit of rashness!—Markt you not
How that the guilty kindred of the queen
Lookt pale when they did hear of Clarence'
　death?
O, they did urge it still unto the king!
God will revenge it.—Come, lords, will you go
To comfort Edward with our company?
DUKE OF BUCKINGHAM.
We wait upon your Grace.　　　　[*Exeunt.*

SCENE II.
The palace.

Enter the old DUCHESS OF YORK, *with the two*
CHILDREN *of* CLARENCE.
SON.
GOOD grandam, tell us, is our father dead?
DUCHESS OF YORK.
No, boy.
DAUGHTER.
Why do you weep so oft, and beat your breast,
And cry, 'O Clarence, my unhappy son!'
SON.
Why do you look on us, and shake your head,
And call us orphans, wretches, castaways,
If that our noble father be alive?
DUCHESS OF YORK.
My pretty cousins, you mistake me both;
I do lament the sickness of the king,
As loth to lose him, not your father's death;
It were lost sorrow to wail one that's lost.
SON.
Then, grandam, you conclude that he is dead.
The king my uncle is to blame for this:
God will revenge it; Whom I will importune
With daily prayers all to that effect.
DAUGHTER.
And so will I.
DUCHESS OF YORK.
Peace, children, peace! the king doth love you
　well:
Incapable and shallow innocents,
You cannot guess who caused your father's death.
SON.
Grandam, we can; for my good uncle Gloster
Told me, the king, provoked by the queen,
Devised impeachments to imprison him:
And when my uncle told me so, he wept,
And pitied me, and kindly kist my cheek;
Bade me rely on him as on my father,
And he would love me dearly as his child.
DUCHESS OF YORK.
Ah, that deceit should steal such gentle shapes,
And with a virtuous vizor hide deep vice!
He is my son; ay, and therein my shame;
Yet from my dugs he drew not this deceit.
SON.
Think you my uncle did dissemble, grandam?
DUCHESS OF YORK.
Ay, boy.
SON.
I cannot think it.—Hark! what noise is this?
Enter the QUEEN, *with her hair about her ears;*
RIVERS *and* DORSET *after her.*
QUEEN ELIZABETH.
O, who shall hinder me to wail and weep,
To chide my fortune, and torment myself?
I'll join with black despair against my soul,
And to myself become an enemy.
DUCHESS OF YORK.
What means this scene of rude impatience?
QUEEN ELIZABETH.
To make an act of tragic violence:—
Edward, my lord, thy son, our king, is dead!
Why grow the branches when the root is gone?
Why wither not the leaves that want their sap?

If you will live, lament; if die, be brief,
That our swift-winged souls may catch the king's,
Or, like obedient subjects, follow him
To his new kingdom of ne'er-changing night.

DUCHESS OF YORK.
Ah, so much interest have I in thy sorrow
As I had title in thy noble husband!
I have bewept a worthy husband's death,
And lived by looking on his images:
But now two mirrors of his princely semblance
Are crackt in pieces by malignant death,
And I for comfort have but one false glass,
That grieves me when I see my shame in him.
Thou art a widow; yet thou art a mother,
And hast the comfort of thy children left thee:
But death hath snatcht my husband from mine
  arms,
And pluckt two crutches from my feeble hands,—
Clarence and Edward. O, what cause have I—
Thine being but a moiety of my grief—
To over-go thy plaints and drown thy cries!

SON.
Ah, aunt, you wept not for our father's death!
How can we aid you with our kindred tears?

DAUGHTER.
Our fatherless distress was left unmoan'd;
Your widow-dolour likewise be unwept!

QUEEN ELIZABETH.
Give me no help in lamentation;
I am not barren to bring forth complaints:
All springs reduce their currents to mine eyes,
That I, being govern'd by the watery moon,
May send forth plenteous tears to drown the
  world!
Ah for my husband, for my dear lord Edward!

CHILDREN.
Ah for our father, for our dear lord Clarence!

DUCHESS OF YORK.
Alas for both, both mine, Edward and Clarence!

QUEEN ELIZABETH.
What stay had I but Edward? and he's gone.

CHILDREN.
What stay had we but Clarence? and he's gone.

DUCHESS OF YORK.
What stays had I but they; and they are gone.

QUEEN ELIZABETH.
Was never widow had so dear a loss!

CHILDREN.
Were never orphans had so dear a loss!

DUCHESS OF YORK.
Was never mother had so dear a loss!
Alas, I am the mother of these griefs!
Their woes are parcell'd, mine are general.
She for an Edward weeps, and so do I;
I for a Clarence weep, so doth not she:
These babes for Clarence weep, and so do I;
I for an Edward weep, so do not they:—
Alas, you three, on me, threefold distrest,
Pour all your tears! I am your sorrow's nurse,
And I will pamper it with lamentations.

MARQUESS OF DORSET.
Comfort, dear mother: God is much displeased
That you take with unthankfulness His doing:
In common worldly things 'tis call'd ungrateful
With dull unwillingness to repay a debt
Which with a bounteous hand was kindly lent;

Much more to be thus opposite with heaven,
For it requires the royal debt it lent you.

EARL RIVERS.
Madam, bethink you, like a careful mother,
Of the young prince your son: send straight for
  him;
Let him be crown'd; in him your comfort lives:
Drown desperate sorrow in dead Edward's grave,
And plant your joys in living Edward's throne.

Enter GLOSTER, BUCKINGHAM, DERBY, HAST-
 INGS, RATCLIFF, *and others.*

DUKE OF GLOSTER.
Sister, have comfort: all of us have cause
To wail the dimming of our shining star;
But none can cure their harms by wailing them.—
Madam, my mother, I do cry you mercy;
I did not see your Grace:—humbly on my knee
I crave your blessing.

DUCHESS OF YORK.
God bless thee; and put meekness in thy breast,
Love, charity, obedience, and true duty!

DUKE OF GLOSTER.
Amen;—[*aside*] and make me die a good old man!
That is the butt-end of a mother's blessing:
I marvel that her Grace did leave it out.

DUKE OF BUCKINGHAM.
You cloudy princes and heart-sorrowing peers,
That bear this mutual heavy load of moan,
Now cheer each other in each other's love:
Though we have spent our harvest of this king,
We are to reap the harvest of his son.
The broken rancour of your high-swoln hearts,
But lately splinter'd, knit and join'd together,
Must gently be preserved, cherisht, and kept:
Me seemeth good, that, with some little train,
Forthwith from Ludlow the young prince be fet
Hither to London, to be crown'd our king.

EARL RIVERS.
Why with some little train, my Lord of Buckingham?

DUKE OF BUCKINGHAM.
Marry, my lord, lest, by a multitude,
The new-heal'd wound of malice should break
  out;
Which would be so much the more dangerous,
By how much the estate is green and yet un-
  govern'd:
Where every horse bears his commanding rein,
And may direct his course as please himself,
As well the fear of harm as harm apparent,
In my opinion, ought to be prevented.

DUKE OF GLOSTER.
I hope the king made peace with all of us;
And the compact is firm and true in me.

EARL RIVERS.
And so in me; and so, I think, in all:
Yet, since it is but green, it should be put
To no apparent likelihood of breach,
Which haply by much company might be urged:
Therefore I say with noble Buckingham,
That it is meet so few should fetch the prince.

LORD HASTINGS.
And so say I.

DUKE OF GLOSTER.
Then be it so; and go we to determine [*Ludlow*
Who they shall be that straight shall post to

Madam,—and you, my mother,—will you go
To give your censures in this business?
QUEEN ELIZABETH *and* DUCHESS OF YORK.
With all our hearts.
          [*Exeunt all except* BUCKINGHAM *and*
                    GLOSTER.
          DUKE OF BUCKINGHAM.
My lord, whoever journeys to the prince,
For God's sake, let not us two stay at home;
For, by the way, I'll sort occasion,
As index to the story we late talkt of,
To part the queen's proud kindred from the
     prince.
          DUKE OF GLOSTER.
My other self, my counsel's consistory,
My oracle, my prophet!—my dear cousin,
I, as a child, will go by thy direction.
Towards Ludlow then, for we'll not stay behind.
                    [*Exeunt.*

SCENE III.

London.   A street.

Enter two CITIZENS, *meeting.*

          FIRST CITIZEN.
GOOD morrow, neighbour: whither away so
     fast?
          SECOND CITIZEN.
I promise you I scarcely know myself:
Hear you the news abroad?
          FIRST CITIZEN.
               Ay,—that the king is dead.
          SECOND CITIZEN.
Ill news, by 'r lady; seldom comes the better:
I fear, I fear 'twill prove a giddy world.
          Enter another CITIZEN.
          THIRD CITIZEN.
Neighbours, God speed!
          FIRST CITIZEN.
               Give you good morrow, sir.
          THIRD CITIZEN.
Doth the news hold of good King Edward's
     death?
          SECOND CITIZEN.
Ay, sir, it is too true; God help, the while!
          THIRD CITIZEN.
Then, masters, look to see a troublous world.
          FIRST CITIZEN.
No, no; by God's good grace his son shall reign.
          THIRD CITIZEN.
Woe to that land that's govern'd by a child!
          SECOND CITIZEN.
In him there is a hope of government,
That, in his nonage, council under him,
And, in his full and ripen'd years, himself,
No doubt, shall then, and till then, govern well.
          FIRST CITIZEN.
So stood the state when Henry the Sixth
Was crown'd in Paris but at nine months old.
          THIRD CITIZEN.
Stood the state so? No, no, good friends, God
     wot;
For then this land was famously enricht
With politic grave counsel; then the king
Had virtuous uncles to protect his Grace.
          FIRST CITIZEN.
Why, so hath this, both by his father and mother.

          THIRD CITIZEN.
Better it were they all came by his father,
Or by his father there were none at all;
For emulation now, who shall be nearest,
Will touch us all too near, if God prevent not.
O, full of danger is the Duke of Gloster!   [proud:
And the queen's sons and brothers haught and
And were they to be ruled, and not to rule,
This sickly land might solace as before.
          FIRST CITIZEN.
Come, come, we fear the worst; all will be well.
          THIRD CITIZEN.
When clouds are seen, wise men put on their
     cloaks;
When great leaves fall, then winter is at hand;
When the sun sets, who doth not look for night?
Untimely storms make men expect a dearth.
All may be well; but, if God sort it so,
'Tis more than we deserve, or I expect.
          SECOND CITIZEN.
Truly, the hearts of men are full of fear:
You cannot reason almost with a man
That looks not heavily and full of dread.
          THIRD CITIZEN.
Before the days of change, still is it so:
By a divine instinct men's minds mistrust
Ensuing danger; as, by proof, we see
The waters swell before a boisterous storm.
But leave it all to God.—Whither away?
          SECOND CITIZEN.
Marry, we were sent for to the justices.
          THIRD CITIZEN.
And so was I: I'll bear you company.   [*Exeunt.*

SCENE IV.

London.   The palace.

Enter the ARCHBISHOP OF YORK, *the young*
DUKE OF YORK, *the* QUEEN, *and the* DUCHESS
OF YORK.

          ARCHBISHOP OF YORK.
LAST night, I hear, they lay at Northampton;
     At Stony-Stratford will they be to-night;
To-morrow, or next day, they will be here.
          DUCHESS OF YORK.
I long with all my heart to see the prince:
I hope he is much grown since last I saw him.
          QUEEN ELIZABETH.
But I hear, no; they say my son of York
Has almost overta'en him in his growth.
          DUKE OF YORK.
Ay, mother; but I would not have it so.
          DUCHESS OF YORK.
Why, my young cousin, it is good to grow.
          DUKE OF YORK.
Grandam, one night, as we did sit at supper,
My uncle Rivers talkt how I did grow
More than my brother: 'Ay,' quoth my uncle
     Gloster,   [apace:'
'Small herbs have grace, great weeds do grow
And since, methinks, I would not grow so fast,
Because sweet flowers are slow, and weeds make
     haste.
          DUCHESS OF YORK.
Good faith, good faith, the saying did not hold
In him that did object the same to thee:

113

He was the wretched'st thing when he was young,
So long a-growing and so leisurely,
That, if his rule were true, he should be gracious.
　　　　　ARCHBISHOP OF YORK.
And so, no doubt, he is, my gracious madam.
　　　　　DUCHESS OF YORK.
I hope he is; but yet let mothers doubt.
　　　　　DUKE OF YORK.
Now, by my troth, if I had been remember'd,
I could have given my uncle's Grace a flout,
To touch his growth nearer than he toucht mine.
　　　　　DUCHESS OF YORK.
How, my young York? I prithee, let me hear it.
　　　　　DUKE OF YORK.
Marry, they say my uncle grew so fast
That he could gnaw a crust at two hours old:
'Twas full two years ere I could get a tooth.
Grandam, this would have been a biting jest.
　　　　　DUCHESS OF YORK.
I prithee, pretty York, who told thee this?
　　　　　DUKE OF YORK.
Grandam, his nurse.
　　　　　DUCHESS OF YORK.
His nurse! why, she was dead ere thou wast
　born.
　　　　　DUKE OF YORK.
If 'twere not she, I cannot tell who told me.
　　　　　QUEEN ELIZABETH.
A parlous boy:—go to, you are too shrewd.
　　　　　ARCHBISHOP OF YORK.
Good madam, be not angry with the child.
　　　　　QUEEN ELIZABETH.
Pitchers have ears.
　　　　　ARCHBISHOP OF YORK.
Here comes a messenger.
　　　　Enter a MESSENGER.
　　　　　　　　　What news?
　　　　　MESSENGER.
Such news, my lord, as grieves me to report.
　　　　　QUEEN ELIZABETH.
How doth the prince?
　　　　　MESSENGER.
　　　　　Well, madam, and in health.
　　　　　DUCHESS OF YORK.
What is thy news, then?
　　　　　MESSENGER.
Lord Rivers and Lord Grey are sent to Pomfret,
With them Sir Thomas Vaughan, prisoners.
　　　　　DUCHESS OF YORK.
Who hath committed them?
　　　　　MESSENGER.
　　　　　　　The mighty dukes
Gloster and Buckingham.
　　　　　QUEEN ELIZABETH.
　　　　　　For what offence?
　　　　　MESSENGER.
The sum of all I can I have disclosed;
Why or for what these nobles were committed
Is all unknown to me, my gracious lady.
　　　　　QUEEN ELIZABETH.
Ay me, I see the downfall of our house!
The tiger now hath seized the gentle hind;
Insulting tyranny begins to jet
Upon the innocent and aweless throne:
Welcome, destruction, blood, and massacre!
I see, as in a map, the end of all.

　　　　　DUCHESS OF YORK.
Accursed and unquiet wrangling days,
How many of you have mine eyes beheld!
My husband lost his life to get the crown;
And often up and down my sons were tost,
For me to joy and weep their gain and loss:
And being seated, and domestic broils
Clean over-blown, themselves, the conquerors,
Make war upon themselves; brother to brother,
Blood to blood, self against self:—O, prepos-
　terous
And frantic outrage, end thy damned spleen;
Or let me die, to look on death no more!
　　　　　QUEEN ELIZABETH.
Come, come, my boy; we will to sanctuary.—
Madam, farewell.
　　　　　DUCHESS OF YORK.
　　　　　Stay, I will go with you.
　　　　　QUEEN ELIZABETH.
You have no cause.
　　　　　ARCHBISHOP OF YORK [to the QUEEN].
　　　　　　My gracious lady, go;
And thither bear your treasure and your goods.
For my part, I'll resign unto your Grace
The seal I keep: and so betide to me
As well I tender you and all of yours!
Come, I'll conduct you to the sanctuary. [Exeunt.

ACT III.　SCENE I.

London.　A street.

The trumpets sound.　Enter the young PRINCE,
　GLOSTER, BUCKINGHAM, CARDINAL BOUR-
　CHIER, CATESBY, *and others.*
　　　　　DUKE OF BUCKINGHAM.
WELCOME, sweet prince, to London, to
　　　your chamber.
　　　　　DUKE OF GLOSTER.
Welcome, dear cousin, my thoughts' sovereign:
The weary way hath made you melancholy.
　　　　　PRINCE.
No, uncle; but our crosses on the way
Have made it tedious, wearisome, and heavy:
I want more uncles here to welcome me.
　　　　　DUKE OF GLOSTER.
Sweet prince, the untainted virtue of your years
Hath not yet dived into the world's deceit;
Nor more can you distinguish of a man
Than of his outward show; which, God He
　knows,
Seldom or never jumpeth with the heart.
Those uncles which you want were dangerous;
Your Grace attended to their sugar'd words,
But lookt not on the poison of their hearts:
God keep you from them, and from such false
　friends!
　　　　　PRINCE.
God keep me from false friends! but they were
　none.
　　　　　DUKE OF GLOSTER.
My lord, the mayor of London comes to greet
　you.
　　　　Enter the LORD MAYOR and his TRAIN.
　　　　　MAYOR.
God bless your Grace with health and happy
　days!

PRINCE.
I thank you, good my lord;—and thank you all.
        [MAYOR *and his* TRAIN *retire.*
I thought my mother, and my brother York,
Would long ere this have met us on the way:
Fie, what a slug is Hastings, that he comes not
To tell us whether they will come or no!
            DUKE OF BUCKINGHAM.
And, in good time, here comes the sweating lord.
        Enter HASTINGS.
            PRINCE.
Welcome, my lord: what, will our mother come?
            LORD HASTINGS.
On what occasion, God He knows, not I,
The queen your mother, and your brother York,
Have taken sanctuary: the tender prince
Would fain have come with me to meet your
    Grace,
But by his mother was perforce withheld.
        DUKE OF BUCKINGHAM.
Fie, what an indirect and peevish course
Is this of hers!—Lord Cardinal, will your Grace
Persuade the queen to send the Duke of York
Unto his princely brother presently?
If she deny, Lord Hastings, go with him,
And from her jealous arms pluck him perforce.
            CARDINAL BOURCHIER.
My Lord of Buckingham, if my weak oratory
Can from his mother win the Duke of York,
Anon expect him here; but if she be obdurate
To mild entreaties, God in heaven forbid
We should infringe the holy privilege
Of blessed sanctuary! not for all this land
Would I be guilty of so great a sin.
            DUKE OF BUCKINGHAM.
You are too senseless-obstinate, my lord,
Too ceremonious and traditional:
Weigh it but with the grossness of this age,
You break not sanctuary in seizing him.
The benefit thereof is always granted
To those whose dealings have deserved the place,
And those who have the wit to claim the place:
This prince hath neither claim'd it nor deserved
    it;
And therefore, in mine opinion, cannot have it:
Then, taking him from thence that is not there,
You break no privilege nor charter there.
Oft have I heard of sanctuary-men;
But sanctuary-children ne'er till now.
            CARDINAL BOURCHIER.
My lord, you shall o'er-rule my mind for once.—
Come on, Lord Hastings, will you go with me?
            LORD HASTINGS.
I go, my lord.
            PRINCE.
Good lords, make all the speedy haste you may.
        [*Exeunt* CARDINAL *and* HASTINGS.
Say, uncle Gloster, if our brother come,
Where shall we sojourn till our coronation?
            DUKE OF GLOSTER.
Where it seems best unto your royal self.
If I may counsel you, some day or two
Your highness shall repose you at the Tower;
Then where you please, and shall be thought
    most fit
For your best health and recreation.

PRINCE.
I do not like the Tower, of any place.—
Did Julius Cæsar build that place, my lord?
            DUKE OF BUCKINGHAM.
He did, my gracious lord, begin that place;
Which, since, succeeding ages have re-edified.
            PRINCE.
Is it upon record, or else reported
Successively from age to age, he built it?
            DUKE OF BUCKINGHAM.
Upon record, my gracious lord.
            PRINCE.
But say, my lord, it were not register'd,
Methinks the truth should live from age to
    age,
As 'twere retail'd to all posterity,
Even to the general all-ending day.
        DUKE OF GLOSTER [*aside*].
So wise so young, they say, do never live long.
            PRINCE.
What say you, uncle?
            DUKE OF GLOSTER.
I say, without characters, fame lives long.—
[*aside*] Thus, like the formal Vice, Iniquity,
I moralize two meanings in one word.
            PRINCE.
That Julius Cæsar was a famous man;
With what his valour did enrich his wit,
His wit set down to make his valour live:
Death makes no conquest of this conqueror;
For now he lives in fame, though not in life.
I'll tell you what, my cousin Buckingham,—
            DUKE OF BUCKINGHAM.
What, my gracious lord?
            PRINCE.
An if I live until I be a man,
I'll win our ancient right in France again,
Or die a soldier, as I lived a king.
        DUKE OF GLOSTER [*aside*].
Short summers lightly have a forward spring.
            DUKE OF BUCKINGHAM.
Now, in good time, here comes the Duke of
    York.
        Enter young YORK, HASTINGS, *and the*
            CARDINAL.
            PRINCE.
Richard of York! how fares our loving brother?
            DUKE OF YORK.
Well, my dread lord; so must I call you now.
            PRINCE.
Ay, brother,—to our grief, as it is yours:
Too late he died that might have kept that
    title,
Which by his death hath lost much majesty.
            DUKE OF GLOSTER.
How fares our cousin, noble Lord of York?
            DUKE OF YORK.
I thank you, gentle uncle. O, my lord,
You said that idle weeds are fast in growth:
The prince my brother hath outgrown me far.
            DUKE OF GLOSTER.
He hath, my lord.
            DUKE OF YORK.
            And therefore is he idle?
            DUKE OF GLOSTER.
O, my fair cousin, I must not say so.

DUKE OF YORK.
Then he is more beholding to you than I.
DUKE OF GLOSTER.
He may command me as my sovereign;
But you have power in me as in a kinsman.
DUKE OF YORK.
I pray you, uncle, give me this dagger.
DUKE OF GLOSTER.
My dagger, little cousin? with all my heart.
PRINCE.
A beggar, brother?
DUKE OF YORK.
Of my kind uncle, that I know will give;
And being but a toy, which is no grief to give.
DUKE OF GLOSTER.
A greater gift than that I'll give my cousin.
DUKE OF YORK.
A greater gift! O, that's the sword to it.
DUKE OF GLOSTER.
Ay, gentle cousin, were it light enough.
DUKE OF YORK.
O, then, I see you will part with but light gifts;
In weightier things you'll say a beggar nay.
DUKE OF GLOSTER.
It is too heavy for your Grace to wear.
DUKE OF YORK.
I weigh it lightly, were it heavier.
DUKE OF GLOSTER.
What, would you have my weapon, little lord?
DUKE OF YORK.
I would, that I might thank you as you call me.
DUKE OF GLOSTER.
How?
DUKE OF YORK.
Little.
PRINCE.
My Lord of York will still be cross in talk:—
Uncle, your Grace knows how to bear with
　him.
DUKE OF YORK.
You mean, to bear me, not to bear with me:—
Uncle, my brother mocks both you and me;
Because that I am little, like an ape,
He thinks that you should bear me on your
　shoulders.
DUKE OF BUCKINGHAM [aside to HASTINGS].
With what a sharp-provided wit he reasons!
To mitigate the scorn he gives his uncle,
He prettily and aptly taunts himself:
So cunning and·so young is wonderful.
DUKE OF GLOSTER.
My lord, will 't please you pass along?
Myself and my good cousin Buckingham
Will to your mother, to entreat of her
To meet you at the Tower and welcome you.
DUKE OF YORK.
What, will you go unto the Tower, my lord?
PRINCE.
My lord Protector needs will have it so.
DUKE OF YORK.
I shall not sleep in quiet at the Tower.
DUKE OF GLOSTER.
Why, what should you fear?
DUKE OF YORK.
Marry, my uncle Clarence' angry ghost:
My grandam told me he was murder'd there.

PRINCE.
I fear no uncles dead.
DUKE OF GLOSTER.
Nor none that live, I hope.
PRINCE.
An if they live, I hope I need not fear.
But come, my lord; and with a heavy heart,
Thinking on them, go I unto the Tower.
　　　[A sennet. Exeunt all but GLOSTER,
　　　　BUCKINGHAM, and CATESBY.
DUKE OF BUCKINGHAM.
Think you, my lord, this little prating York
Was not incensed by his subtle mother
To taunt and scorn you thus opprobriously?
DUKE OF GLOSTER.
No doubt, no doubt: O, 'tis a parlous boy,
Bold, quick, ingenious, forward, capable:
He is all the mother's, from the top to toe.
DUKE OF BUCKINGHAM.
Well, let them rest.—Come hither, Catesby.
　Thou
Art sworn as deeply to effect what we intend
As closely to conceal what we impart:
Thou know'st our reasons urged upon the way;—
What think'st thou? is it not an easy matter
To make William Lord Hastings of our mind,
For the instalment of this noble duke
In the seat royal of this famous isle?
SIR WILLIAM CATESBY.
He for his father's sake so loves the prince,
That he will not be won to aught against him.
DUKE OF BUCKINGHAM.
What think'st thou, then, of Stanley? will not he?
SIR WILLIAM CATESBY.
He will do all in all as Hastings doth.
DUKE OF BUCKINGHAM.
Well, then, no more but this: go, gentle Catesby,
And, as it were far off, sound thou Lord Hastings,
How he doth stand affected to our purpose;
And summon him to-morrow to the Tower,
To sit about the coronation.
If thou dost find him tractable to us,
Encourage him, and show him all our reasons:
If he be leaden, icy-cold, unwilling,
Be thou so too; and so break off your talk,
And give us notice of his inclination:
For we to-morrow hold divided councils,
Wherein thyself shalt highly be employ'd.
DUKE OF GLOSTER.
Commend me to Lord William: tell him,
　Catesby,
His ancient knot of dangerous adversaries
To-morrow are let blood at Pomfret-castle;
And bid my friend, for joy of this good news,
Give Mistress Shore one gentle kiss the more.
DUKE OF BUCKINGHAM.
Good Catesby, go, effect this business soundly.
SIR WILLIAM CATESBY.
My good lords both, with all the heed I can.
DUKE OF GLOSTER.
Shall we hear from you, Catesby, ere we sleep?
SIR WILLIAM CATESBY.
You shall, my lord.
DUKE OF GLOSTER.
At Crosby-place, there shall you find us both.
　　　　　　　　　　　　[Exit CATESBY.

DUKE OF BUCKINGHAM.

Now, my lord, what shall we do, if we perceive
Lord Hastings will not yield to our complots?

DUKE OF GLOSTER.

Chop off his head, man;—somewhat we will
do:—
And, look, when I am king, claim thou of me]
The earldom of Hereford, and the moveables
Whereof the king my brother stood possest.

DUKE OF BUCKINGHAM.

I'll claim that promise at your Grace's hand.

DUKE OF GLOSTER.¶

And look to have it yielded with all kindness.
Come, let us sup betimes, that afterwards
We may digest our complots in some form.

[Exeunt.

SCENE II.

Before LORD HASTINGS' house.

Enter a MESSENGER to the door of HASTINGS.

MESSENGER.

M Y lord! my lord!—   [Knocking.
   LORD HASTINGS [within].
Who knocks?

MESSENGER.

One from the Lord Stanley.

LORD HASTINGS [within].

What is 't o'clock?

MESSENGER.

Upon the stroke of four.

Enter HASTINGS.

LORD HASTINGS.

Cannot thy master sleep these tedious nights?

MESSENGER.

So it appears by that I have to say.
First, he commends him to your noble self.

LORD HASTINGS.

What then?

MESSENGER.

Then certifies your lordship, that this night
He dreamt the boar had razed off his helm:
Besides, he says there are two councils held;
And that may be determined at the one
Which may make you and him to rue at th' other.
Therefore he sends to know your lordship's
pleasure,—
If presently you will take horse with him,
And with all speed post with him toward the
north,
To shun the danger that his soul divines.

LORD HASTINGS.

Go, fellow, go, return unto thy lord;
Bid him not fear the separated councils:
His honour and myself are at the one,
And at the other is my good friend Catesby;
Where nothing can proceed that toucheth us
Whereof I shall not have intelligence.
Tell him his fears are shallow, wanting instance:
And for his dreams, I wonder he's so simple
To trust the mockery of unquiet slumbers:
To fly the boar before the boar pursues,
Were to incense the boar to follow us,
And make pursuit where he did mean no chase.
Go, bid thy master rise and come to me;
And we will both together to the Tower,
Where he shall see the boar will use us kindly.

MESSENGER.

I'll go, my lord, and tell him what you say. [Exit.

Enter CATESBY.

SIR WILLIAM CATESBY.

Many good morrows to my noble lord!

LORD HASTINGS.

Good morrow, Catesby; you are early stirring:
What news, what news, in this our tottering
state?

SIR WILLIAM CATESBY.

It is a reeling world, indeed, my lord;
And I believe will never stand upright
Till Richard wear the garland of the realm.

LORD HASTINGS.

How! wear the garland! dost thou mean the
crown?

SIR WILLIAM CATESBY.

Ay, my good lord.

LORD HASTINGS.

I'll have this crown of mine cut from my shoul-
ders
Before I'll see the crown so foul misplaced.
But canst thou guess that he doth aim at it?

SIR WILLIAM CATESBY.

Ay, on my life; and hopes to find you forward
Upon his party for the gain thereof:
And thereupon he sends you this good news,—
That this same very day your enemies,
The kindred of the queen, must die at Pomfret.

LORD HASTINGS.

Indeed, I am no mourner for that news,
Because they have been still my adversaries:
But, that I'll give my voice on Richard's side,
To bar my master's heirs in true descent,
God knows I will not do it to the death.

SIR WILLIAM CATESBY.

God keep your lordship in that gracious mind!

LORD HASTINGS.

But I shall laugh at this a twelve-month hence,—
That they who brought me in my master's hate,
I live to look upon their tragedy.
Well, Catesby, ere a fortnight make me older,
I'll send some packing that yet think not on 't.

SIR WILLIAM CATESBY.

'Tis a vile thing to die, my gracious lord,
When men are unprepared and look not for it.

LORD HASTINGS.

O monstrous, monstrous! and so falls it out
With Rivers, Vaughan, Grey: and so 'twill do
With some men else, that think themselves as safe
As thou and I; who, as thou know'st, are dear
To princely Richard and to Buckingham.

SIR WILLIAM CATESBY.

The princes both make high account of you,—
[aside] For they account his head upon the bridge.

LORD HASTINGS.

I know they do; and I have well deserved it.

Enter STANLEY.

Come on, come on; where is your boar-spear,
man?
Fear you the boar, and go so unprovided?

LORD STANLEY.

My lord, good morrow;—good morrow,
Catesby:—
You may jest on, but, by the holy rood,
I do not like these several councils, I.

LORD HASTINGS.

My lord,
I hold my life as dear as you do yours;
And never in my days, I do protest,
Was it more precious to me than 'tis now:
Think you, but that I know our state secure,
I would be so triumphant as I am?

LORD STANLEY.

The lords at Pomfret, when they rode from
    London,   [sure,—
Were jocund, and supposed their states were
And they, indeed, had no cause to mistrust;
But yet, you see, how soon the day o'ercast.
This sudden stab of rancour I misdoubt:
Pray God, I say, I prove a needless coward!
What, shall we toward the Tower? the day is
    spent.

LORD HASTINGS.

Come, come, have with you.—Wot you what, my
    lord?
To-day the lords you talk of are beheaded.

LORD STANLEY.

They, for their truth, might better wear their
    heads
Than some that have accused them wear their
    hats.—
But come, my lord, let us away.

Enter a PURSUIVANT.

LORD HASTINGS.

Go on before; I'll talk with this good fellow.
                    [*Exeunt* STANLEY *and* CATESBY.
How now, sirrah! how goes the world with thee?

PURSUIVANT.

The better that your lordship please to ask.

LORD HASTINGS.

I tell thee, man, 'tis better with me now   [meet:
Than when thou mett'st me last where now we
Then was I going prisoner to the Tower,
By the suggestion of the queen's allies;
But now, I tell thee—keep it to thyself—
This day those enemies are put to death,
And I in better state than e'er I was.

PURSUIVANT.

God hold it, to your honour's good content!

LORD HASTINGS.

Gramercy, fellow: there, drink that for me.
                    [*Throwing him his purse.*

PURSUIVANT.

God save your lordship!   [*Exit.*

Enter a PRIEST.

PRIEST.

Well met, my lord; I am glad to see your honour.

LORD HASTINGS.

I thank thee, good Sir John, with all my heart.
I am in your debt for your last exercise;
Come the next Sabbath, and I will content you.
                    [*He whispers in his ear.*

Enter BUCKINGHAM.

DUKE OF BUCKINGHAM.

What, talking with a priest, lord chamberlain!
Your friends at Pomfret, they do need the priest;
Your honour hath no shriving-work in hand.

LORD HASTINGS.

Good faith, and when I met this holy man,
The men you talk of came into my mind.—
What, go you toward the Tower?

DUKE OF BUCKINGHAM.

I do, my lord; but long I cannot stay there:
I shall return before your lordship thence.

LORD HASTINGS.

Nay, like enough, for I stay dinner there.

DUKE OF BUCKINGHAM [*aside*].

And supper too, although thou know'st it
    not.—
Come, will you go?

LORD HASTINGS.

                I'll wait upon your lordship.
                    [*Exeunt.*

SCENE III.

Pomfret Castle.

Enter SIR RICHARD RATCLIFF, *with halberds,*
carrying RIVERS, GREY, *and* VAUGHAN *to death.*

SIR RICHARD RATCLIFF.

COME, bring forth the prisoners.

EARL RIVERS.

Sir Richard Ratcliff, let me tell thee this,—
To-day shalt thou behold a subject die
For truth, for duty, and for loyalty.

LORD GREY.

God keep the prince from all the pack of you!
A knot you are of damned blood-suckers.

SIR THOMAS VAUGHAN.

You live that shall cry woe for this hereafter.

SIR RICHARD RATCLIFF.

Dispatch; the limit of your lives is out.

EARL RIVERS.

O Pomfret, Pomfret! O thou bloody prison,
Fatal and ominous to noble peers!
Within the guilty closure of thy walls
Richard the Second here was hackt to death;
And, for more slander to thy dismal seat,
We give thee up our guiltless blood to drink.

LORD GREY.

Now Margaret's curse is faln upon our heads,
When she exclaim'd on Hastings, you, and I,
For standing by when Richard stabb'd her son.

EARL RIVERS.

Then cursed she Richard, then cursed she Buck-
    ingham,
Then cursed she Hastings:—O, remember, God,
To hear her prayers for them, as now for us!
And for my sister and her princely sons,
Be satisfied, dear God, with our true blood,
Which, as Thou know'st, unjustly must be spilt.

SIR RICHARD RATCLIFF.

Make haste; the hour of death is expiate.

EARL RIVERS.

Come, Grey,—come, Vaughan,—let us here
    embrace:
Farewell, until we meet again in heaven. [*Exeunt.*

SCENE IV.

London. The Tower.

Enter BUCKINGHAM, DERBY, HASTINGS, *the*
BISHOP OF ELY, RATCLIFF, LOVEL, *with*
others, at a table.

LORD HASTINGS.

NOW, noble peers, the cause why we are met
Is, to determine of the coronation.
In God's name, speak,—when is the royal day?

DUKE OF BUCKINGHAM.
Are all things ready for that royal time?
EARL OF DERBY.
It is; and wants but nomination.
BISHOP OF ELY.
To-morrow, then, I judge a happy day.
DUKE OF BUCKINGHAM.
Who knows the lord Protector's mind herein?
Who is most inward with the noble duke?
BISHOP OF ELY.
Your Grace, we think, should soonest know his
    mind.
DUKE OF BUCKINGHAM.
Who, I, my lord? We know each other's faces,
But for our hearts, he knows no more of mine
Than I of yours; nor I no more of his
Than you of mine.
Lord Hastings, you and he are near in love.
LORD HASTINGS.
I thank his Grace, I know he loves me well;
But, for his purpose in the coronation,
I have not sounded him, nor he deliver'd
His gracious pleasure any way therein:
But you, my noble lords, may name the time;
And in the duke's behalf I'll give my voice,
Which, I presume, he'll take in gentle part.
BISHOP OF ELY.
In happy time, here comes the duke himself.
Enter GLOSTER.
DUKE OF GLOSTER.
My noble lords and cousins all, good morrow.
I have been long a sleeper: but, I trust,
My absence doth neglect no great design,
Which by my presence might have been con-
    cluded.
DUKE OF BUCKINGHAM.
Had you not come upon your cue, my lord,
William Lord Hastings had pronounced your
    part,—
I mean, your voice,—for crowning of the king.
DUKE OF GLOSTER.
Than my Lord Hastings no man might be
    bolder;
His lordship knows me well, and loves me
    well.
My Lord of Ely, when I was last in Holborn,
I saw good strawberries in your garden there:
I do beseech you send for some of them.
BISHOP OF ELY.
Marry, and will, my lord, with all my heart. [*Exit.*
DUKE OF GLOSTER.
Cousin of Buckingham, a word with you.
                  [*Takes him aside.*
Catesby hath sounded Hastings in our business,
And finds the testy gentleman so hot,
That he will lose his head ere give consent
His master's child, as worshipfully he terms it,
Shall lose the royalty of England's throne.
DUKE OF BUCKINGHAM.
Withdraw you hence, my lord; I'll follow you.
    [*Exit* GLOSTER, *follow'd by* BUCKINGHAM.
EARL OF DERBY.
We have not yet set down this day of triumph.
To-morrow, in my judgement, is too sudden;
For I myself am not so well provided
As else I would be, were the day prolong'd.

Enter BISHOP OF ELY.
BISHOP OF ELY.
Where is my lord the Duke of Gloucester?
I have sent for these strawberries.
His Grace looks cheerfully and smooth to-day;
There's some conceit or other likes him well,
When he doth bid good-morrow with such a
    spirit.
I think there's never a man in Christendom
That can less hide his love or hate than he;
For by his face straight shall you know his heart.
EARL OF DERBY.
What of his heart perceive you in his face
By any likelihood he show'd to-day?
LORD HASTINGS.
Marry, that with no man here he is offended;
For, were he, he had shown it in his looks.
EARL OF DERBY.
I pray God he be not, I say.
Enter GLOSTER *and* BUCKINGHAM.
DUKE OF GLOSTER.
I pray you all, tell me what they deserve
That do conspire my death with devilish plots
Of damned witchcraft, and that have prevail'd
Upon my body with their hellish charms?
LORD HASTINGS.
The tender love I bear your Grace, my lord,
Makes me most forward in this noble presence
To doom th' offenders: whosoe'er they be,
I say, my lord, they have deserved death.
DUKE OF GLOSTER.
Then be your eyes the witness of their evil:
Look how I am bewitcht; behold mine arm
Is, like a blasted sapling, wither'd up:
And this is Edward's wife, that monstrous witch,
Consorted with that harlot-strumpet Shore,
That by their witchcraft thus have marked me.
LORD HASTINGS.
If they have done this thing, my gracious lord,—
DUKE OF GLOSTER.
If! thou protector of this damned strumpet,
Talk'st thou to me of 'ifs'? Thou art a traitor:—
Off with his head!—now, by Saint Paul, I swear
I will not dine until I see the same.—
Lovel and Ratcliff, look that it be done:—
The rest, that love me, rise and follow me.
    [*Exeunt all, except* HASTINGS, LOVEL, *and*
          RATCLIFF.
LORD HASTINGS.
Woe, woe for England! not a whit for me;
For I, too fond, might have prevented this.
Stanley did dream the boar did raze his helm;
But I disdain'd it, and did scorn to fly: [stumble,
Three times to-day my foot-cloth horse did
And started when he lookt upon the Tower,
As loth to bear me to the slaughter-house.
O, now I need the priest that spake to me:
I now repent I told the pursuivant,
As too triumphing, how mine enemies
To-day at Pomfret bloodily were butcher'd,
And I myself secure in grace and favour.
O Margaret, Margaret, now thy heavy curse
Is lighted on poor Hastings' wretched head!
SIR RICHARD RATCLIFF.
Dispatch, my lord; the duke would be at dinner:
Make a short shrift; he longs to see your head.

LORD HASTINGS.

O momentary grace of mortal men,
Which we more hunt for than the grace of God!
Who builds his hope in air of your fair looks,
Lives like a drunken sailor on a mast,
Ready, with every nod, to tumble down
Into the fatal bowels of the deep.

LORD LOVEL.

Come, come, dispatch; 'tis bootless to exclaim.

LORD HASTINGS.

O bloody Richard!—miserable England!
I prophesy the fearfull'st time to thee
That ever wretched age hath lookt upon.—
Come, lead me to the block; bear him my head:
They smile at me who shortly shall be dead.

[*Exeunt.*

SCENE V.

The Tower-walls.

Enter GLOSTER *and* BUCKINGHAM, *in rotten
armour, marvellous ill-favour'd.*

DUKE OF GLOSTER.

COME, cousin, canst thou quake, and change
thy colour,
Murder thy breath in middle of a word,
And then begin again, and stop again,
As if thou wert distraught and mad with terror?

DUKE OF BUCKINGHAM.

Tut, I can counterfeit the deep tragedian;
Speak and look back, and pry on every side,
Tremble and start at wagging of a straw,
Intending deep suspicion: ghastly looks
Are at my service, like enforced smiles;
And both are ready in their offices,
At any time, to grace my stratagems.
But what, is Catesby gone?

DUKE OF GLOSTER.

He is; and, see, he brings the mayor along.

DUKE OF BUCKINGHAM.

Let me alone to entertain him.

Enter *the* MAYOR *and* CATESBY.

Lord mayor,—

DUKE OF GLOSTER.

Look to the drawbridge there!

DUKE OF BUCKINGHAM.

Hark! a drum.

DUKE OF GLOSTER.

Catesby, o'erlook the walls.

DUKE OF BUCKINGHAM.

Lord mayor, the reason we have sent,—

DUKE OF GLOSTER.

Look back, defend thee,—here are enemies.

DUKE OF BUCKINGHAM.

God and our innocency defend and guard us!

DUKE OF GLOSTER.

Be patient, they are friends,—Ratcliff and Lovel.

Enter LOVEL *and* RATCLIFF, *with* HASTINGS'
head.

LORD LOVEL.

Here is the head of that ignoble traitor,
The dangerous and unsuspected Hastings.

DUKE OF GLOSTER.

So dear I loved the man, that I must weep.
I took him for the plainest harmless creature
That breathed upon the earth a Christian;
Made him my book, wherein my soul recorded

The history of all her secret thoughts:
So smooth he daub'd his vice with show of virtue,
That, his apparent open guilt omitted,—
I mean, his conversation with Shore's wife,—
He lived from all attainder of suspect.

DUKE OF BUCKINGHAM.

Well, well, he was the covert'st shelter'd traitor
That ever lived.
Would you imagine, or almost believe,—
Were 't not that, by great preservation,
We live to tell it you,—the subtle traitor
This day had plotted, in the council-house,
To murder me and my good Lord of Gloster?

MAYOR OF LONDON.

What, had he so?

DUKE OF GLOSTER.

What, think you we are Turks or infidels?
Or that we would, against the form of law,
Proceed thus rashly in the villain's death,
But that the extreme peril of the case,
The peace of England and our persons' safety,
Enforc'd us to this execution?

MAYOR OF LONDON.

Now, fair befall you! he deserved his death;
And your good Graces both have well proceeded,
To warn false traitors from the like attempts.
I never lookt for better at his hands,
After he once fell in with Mistress Shore.

DUKE OF BUCKINGHAM.

Yet had we not determined he should die,
Until your lordship came to see his end;
Which now the loving haste of these our friends,
Somewhat against our meaning, have prevented;
Because, my lord, we would have had you heard
The traitor speak, and timorously confess
The manner and the purpose of his treason;
That you might well have signified the same
Unto the citizens, who haply may
Misconster us in him, and wail his death.

MAYOR OF LONDON.

But, my good lord, your Grace's word shall serve,
As well as I had seen, and heard him speak;
And do not doubt, right noble princes both,
But I'll acquaint our duteous citizens
With all your just proceedings in this case.

DUKE OF GLOSTER.

And to that end we wisht your lordship here,
T' avoid the censures of the carping world.

DUKE OF BUCKINGHAM.

But since you come too late of our intent,
Yet witness what you hear we did intend:
And so, my good lord mayor, we bid farewell.

[*Exit* MAYOR.

DUKE OF GLOSTER.

Go, after, after, cousin Buckingham.
The mayor towards Guildhall hies him in all
post:—
There, at your meetest vantage of the time,
Infer the bastardy of Edward's children:
Tell them how Edward put to death a citizen,
Only for saying he would make his son
Heir to the crown; meaning, indeed, his house,
Which, by the sign thereof, was termed so.
Moreover, urge his hateful luxury,
And bestial appetite in change of lust;   [wives,
Which stretcht unto their servants, daughters,

Even where his raging eye or savage heart,
Without control, listed to make a prey.
Nay, for a need, thus far come near my person:—
Tell them, when that my mother went with child
Of that insatiate Edward, noble York
My princely father then had wars in France;
And, by just computation of the time,
Found that the issue was not his begot;
Which well appeared in his lineaments,
Being nothing like the noble duke my father:
Yet touch this sparingly, as 'twere far off;
Because, my lord, you know my mother lives.

DUKE OF BUCKINGHAM.
Doubt not, my lord, I'll play the orator
As if the golden fee for which I plead
Were for myself: and so, my lord, adieu.

DUKE OF GLOSTER.
If you thrive well, bring them to Baynard's
Castle;
Where you shall find me well accompanied
With reverend fathers and well-learned bishops.

DUKE OF BUCKINGHAM.
I go; and towards three or four o'clock
Look for the news that the Guildhall affords.
[Exit.

DUKE OF GLOSTER.
Go, Lovel, with all speed to Doctor Shaw,—
[to CATESBY] Go thou to Friar Penker;—bid
them both
Meet me within this hour at Baynard's Castle.
[Exeunt LOVEL, CATESBY, and RATCLIFF.
Now will I in, to take some privy order, •
To draw the brats of Clarence out of sight;
And to give notice that no manner person
Have any time recourse unto the princes. [Exit.

SCENE VI.

The same. A street.

Enter a SCRIVENER, with a paper in his hand.

SCRIVENER.
HERE is th' indictment of the good Lord
    Hastings;
Which in a set hand fairly is engross'd,
That it may be to-day read o'er in Paul's.
And mark how well the sequel hangs together:
Eleven hours I have spent to write it over,
For yesternight by Catesby was it sent me;
The precedent was full as long a-doing:
And yet within these five hours Hastings lived,
Untainted, unexamined, free, at liberty. [gross
Here's a good world the while! Why, who's so
That cannot see this palpable device?
Yet who so bold but says he sees it not?
Bad is the world; and all will come to naught
When such ill dealing must be seen in thought.
[Exit.

SCENE VII.

Baynard's Castle.

Enter GLOSTER and BUCKINGHAM, meeting.

DUKE OF GLOSTER.
HOW now, how now! what say the citizens?

DUKE OF BUCKINGHAM.
Now, by the holy mother of our Lord,
The citizens are mum, say not a word.

DUKE OF GLOSTER.
Toucht you the bastardy of Edward's children?

DUKE OF BUCKINGHAM.
I did; with his contract with Lady Lucy,
And his contract by deputy in France,
Th' insatiate greediness of his desires,
And his enforcement of the city wives;
His tyranny for trifles, his own bastardy,—
As being got, your father then in France,
And his resemblance, being not like the duke:
Withal I did infer your lineaments,—
Being the right idea of your father,
Both in your form and nobleness of mind;
Laid open all your victories in Scotland,
Your discipline in war, wisdom in peace,
Your bounty, virtue, fair humility;
Indeed, left nothing fitting for the purpose
Untoucht, or slightly handled, in discourse:
And when my oratory drew toward end,
I bade them that did love their country's good
Cry, 'God save Richard, England's royal king!'

DUKE OF GLOSTER.
And did they so?

DUKE OF BUCKINGHAM.
No, so God help me, they spake not a word;
But, like dumb statuas or breathing stones,
Stared each on other, and lookt deadly pale.
Which when I saw, I reprehended them;
And askt the mayor what meant this wilful
silence:
His answer was,—the people were not used
To be spoke to but by the recorder.
Then he was urged to tell my tale again,—
'Thus saith the duke, thus hath the duke in-
ferr'd;'
But nothing spake in warrant from himself.
When he had done, some followers of mine own,
At lower end of the hall, hurl'd up their caps,
And some ten voices cried, 'God save King
Richard!'
And thus I took the vantage of those few,—
'Thanks, gentle citizens and friends,' quoth I;
'This general applause and cheerful shout
Argues your wisdom and your love to Richard:'
And even here brake off, and came away.

DUKE OF GLOSTER.
What tongueless blocks were they! would they
not speak?

DUKE OF BUCKINGHAM.
No, by my troth, my lord.

DUKE OF GLOSTER.
Will not the mayor, then, and his brethren,
come?

DUKE OF BUCKINGHAM.
The mayor is here at hand. Intend some fear;
Be not you spoke with but by mighty suit:
And look you get a prayer-book in your hand,
And stand between two churchmen, good my
lord;
For on that ground I'll make a holy descant:
And be not easily won to our request;
Play the maid's part,—still answer nay, and take it.

DUKE OF GLOSTER.
I go; and if you plead as well for them
As I can say nay to thee for myself,
No doubt we'll bring it to a happy issue.

DUKE OF BUCKINGHAM.
Go, go, up to the leads; the lord mayor knocks.
                              [*Exit* GLOSTER.
Enter the MAYOR, ALDERMEN, *and* CITIZENS.
Welcome, my lord: I dance attendance here;
I think the duke will not be spoke withal.
              Enter CATESBY.
Now, Catesby, what says your lord to my
  request?
          SIR WILLIAM CATESBY.
He doth entreat your Grace, my noble lord,
To visit him to-morrow or next day: .
He is within, with two right-reverend fathers,
Divinely bent to meditation:
And in no worldly suit would he be moved,
To draw him from his holy exercise.
          DUKE OF BUCKINGHAM.
Return, good Catesby, to the gracious duke;
Tell him, myself, the mayor and aldermen,
In deep designs and matters of great moment,
No less importing than our general good,
Are come to have some conference with his
  Grace.
          SIR WILLIAM CATESBY.
I'll signify so much unto him straight.   [*Exit.*
          DUKE OF BUCKINGHAM.
Ah, ha, my lord, this prince is not an Edward!
He is not lolling on a lewd day-bed,
But on his knees at meditation;
Not dallying with a brace of courtezans,
But meditating with two deep divines;
Not sleeping, to engross his idle body,
But praying, to enrich his watchful soul:
Happy were England, would this virtuous prince
Take on himself the sovereignty thereof;
But sure I fear we shall not win him to it.
          MAYOR OF LONDON.
Marry, God defend his Grace should say us nay!
          DUKE OF BUCKINGHAM.
I fear he will. Here Catesby comes again.
              Enter CATESBY.
Now, Catesby, what says his Grace?
          SIR WILLIAM CATESBY.
He wonders to what end you have assembled
Such troops of citizens to come to him,
His Grace not being warn'd thereof before:
He fears, my lord, you mean no good to him.
          DUKE OF BUCKINGHAM.
Sorry I am my noble cousin should
Suspect me, that I mean no good to him:
By heaven, we come to him in perfect love;
And so once more return and tell his Grace.
                              [*Exit* CATESBY.
When holy and devout religious men
Are at their beads, 'tis much to draw them
  thence,—
So sweet is zealous contemplation.
  Enter GLOSTER *aloft, between two* BISHOPS.
          CATESBY *returns.*
          MAYOR OF LONDON.
See, where his Grace stands 'tween two clergy-
  men!
          DUKE OF BUCKINGHAM.
Two props of virtue for a Christian prince,
To stay him from the fall of vanity:
And, see, a book of prayer in his hand,—

True ornaments to know a holy man.—
Famous Plantagenet, most gracious prince,
Lend favourable ear to our request;
And pardon us the interruption
Of thy devotion and right Christian zeal.
          DUKE OF GLOSTER.
My lord, there needs no such apology:
I rather do beseech you pardon me,
Who, earnest in the service of my God,
Neglect the visitation of my friends.
But, leaving this, what is your Grace's pleasure?
          DUKE OF BUCKINGHAM.
Even that, I hope, which pleaseth God above,
And all good men of this ungovern'd isle.
          DUKE OF GLOSTER.
I do suspect I have done some offence
That seems disgracious in the city's eye;
And that you come to reprehend my ignorance.
          DUKE OF BUCKINGHAM.
You have, my lord: would it might please your
  Grace,
On our entreaties, to amend your fault!
          DUKE OF GLOSTER.
Else wherefore breathe I in a Christian land?
          DUKE OF BUCKINGHAM.
Know, then, it is your fault that you resign
The supreme seat, the throne majestical,
The scepter'd office of your ancestors,
Your state of fortune and your due of birth,
The lineal glory of your royal house,
To the corruption of a blemisht stock:
Whilst in the mildness of your sleepy thoughts—
Which here we waken to our country's good—
This noble isle doth want her proper limbs;
Her face defaced with scars of infamy,
Her royal stock graft with ignoble plants,
And almost shoulder'd in the swallowing gulf
Of dark forgetfulness and deep oblivion.
Which to recure, we heartily solicit
Your gracious self to take on you the charge
And kingly government of this your land;—
Not as protector, steward, substitute,
Or lowly factor for another's gain;
But as successively, from blood to blood,
Your right of birth, your empery, your own.
For this, consorted with the citizens,
Your very worshipful and loving friends,
And by their vehement instigation,
In this just suit come I to move your Grace.
          DUKE OF GLOSTER.
I cannot tell, if to depart in silence,
Or bitterly to speak in your reproof,
Best fitteth my degree or your condition:
If not to answer, you might haply think
Tongue-tied ambition, not replying, yielded
To bear the golden yoke of sovereignty,
Which fondly you would here impose on me;
If to reprove you for this suit of yours,
So season'd with your faithful love to me,
Then, on the other side, I checkt my friends.
Therefore,—to speak, and to avoid the first,
And then, in speaking, not to incur the last,—
Definitively thus I answer you.
Your love deserves my thanks; but my desert
Unmeritable shuns your high request.
First, if all obstacles were cut away,

And that my path were even to the crown,
As the ripe revenue and due of birth;
Yet so much is my poverty of spirit,
So mighty and so many my defects,
That I would rather hide me from my greatness—
Being a bark to brook no mighty sea—
Than in my greatness covet to be hid,
And in the vapour of my glory smother'd.
But, God be thankt, there is no need of me;—
And much I need to help us, were there need;—
The royal tree hath left us royal fruit,
Which, mellow'd by the stealing hours of time,
Will well become the seat of majesty,
And make, no doubt, us happy by his reign.
On him I lay what you would lay on me,
The right and fortune of his happy stars;
Which God defend that I should wring from him!

DUKE OF BUCKINGHAM.
My lord, this argues conscience in your Grace;
But the respects thereof are nice and trivial,
All circumstances well considered.
You say that Edward is your brother's son:
So say we too, but not by Edward's wife;
For first he was contract to Lady Lucy,—
Your mother lives a witness to his vow,—
And afterward by substitute betroth'd
To Bona, sister to the King of France.
These both put by, a poor petitioner,
A care-crazed mother of a many children,
A beauty-waning and distressed widow,
Even in the afternoon of her best days,
Made prize and purchase of his wanton eye,
Seduced the pitch and height of his degree
To base declension and loath'd bigamy:
By her, in his unlawful bed, he got
This Edward, whom our manners call the prince.
More bitterly could I expostulate,
Save that, for reverence to some alive,
I give a sparing limit to my tongue.
Then, good my lord, take to your royal self
This proffer'd benefit of dignity;
If not to bless us and the land withal,
Yet to draw forth your noble ancestry
From the corruption of abusing time
Unto a lineal true-derived course.

MAYOR OF LONDON.
Do, good my lord; your citizens entreat you.

DUKE OF BUCKINGHAM.
Refuse not, mighty lord, this proffer'd love.

SIR WILLIAM CATESBY.
O, make them joyful, grant their lawful suit!

DUKE OF GLOSTER.
Alas, why would you heap these cares on me?
I am unfit for state and majesty:—
I do beseech you, take it not amiss;
I cannot nor I will not yield to you.

DUKE OF BUCKINGHAM.
If you refuse it,—as, in love and zeal,
Loth to depose the child, your brother's son;
As well we know your tenderness of heart,
And gentle, kind, effeminate remorse,
Which we have noted in you to your kindred,
And egally indeed to all estates,—
Yet whether you accept our suit or no,
Your brother's son shall never reign our king;
But we will plant some other in the throne,

To the disgrace and downfall of your house:
And in this resolution here we leave you.
Come, citizens: zounds, I'll entreat no more.

DUKE OF GLOSTER.
O, do not swear, my lord of Buckingham.
[*Exit* BUCKINGHAM *with the* CITIZENS.

SIR WILLIAM CATESBY.
Call him again, sweet prince, accept their suit:
If you deny them, all the land will rue it.

DUKE OF GLOSTER.
Will you enforce me to a world of cares?
Well, call them again. I am not made of stones,
But penetrable to your kind entreats,
Albeit against my conscience and my soul.

Enter BUCKINGHAM *and the others.*
Cousin of Buckingham, and you sage, grave
men,
Since you will buckle fortune on my back,
To bear her burden, whe'r I will or no,
I must have patience to endure the load:
But if black scandal or foul-faced reproach
Attend the sequel of your imposition,
Your mere enforcement shall acquittance me
From all the impure blots and stains thereof;
For God He knows, and you may partly see,
How far I am from the desire of this

MAYOR OF LONDON.
God bless your Grace! we see it, and will say it.

DUKE OF GLOSTER.
In saying so, you shall but say the truth.

DUKE OF BUCKINGHAM.
Then I salute you with this royal title,—
Long live King Richard, England's worthy king!

ALL.
Amen.

DUKE OF BUCKINGHAM.
To-morrow may it please you to be crown'd?

DUKE OF GLOSTER.
Even when you please, since you will have it so.

DUKE OF BUCKINGHAM.
To-morrow, then, we will attend your Grace:
And so, most joyfully, we take our leave.

DUKE OF GLOSTER [*to the* BISHOPS].
Come, let us to our holy work again.—
Farewell, good cousin; farewell, gentle friends.
[*Exeunt.*

ACT IV. SCENE I.

London.   Before the Tower.

Enter, on one side, QUEEN ELIZABETH, DUCHESS
OF YORK, *and* DORSET; *on the other,* ANNE,
DUCHESS OF GLOSTER, *leading* LADY MAR-
GARET PLANTAGENET, CLARENCE'S *young
daughter.*

DUCHESS OF YORK.
WHO meets us here? my niece Plantagenet,
Led in the hand of her kind aunt of Gloster?
Now, for my life, she's wandering to the Tower,
On pure heart's love, to greet the tender
princes.—
Daughter, well met.

LADY ANNE.
God give your Graces both
A happy and a joyful time of day!

QUEEN ELIZABETH.
As much to you, good sister! Whither away?

LADY ANNE.
No further than the Tower; and, as I guess,
Upon the like devotion as yourselves,
To gratulate the gentle princes there.
QUEEN ELIZABETH.
Kind sister, thanks: we'll enter all together:—
And, in good time, here the lieutenant comes.
Enter BRAKENBURY.
Master lieutenant, pray you, by your leave,
How doth the prince, and my young son of York?
SIR ROBERT BRAKENBURY.
Right well, dear madam. By your patience,
I may not suffer you to visit them;
The king hath straitly charged the contrary.
QUEEN ELIZABETH.
The king! who's that?
SIR ROBERT BRAKENBURY.
I mean the lord Protector.
QUEEN ELIZABETH.
The Lord protect him from that kingly title!
Hath he set bounds between their love and me?
I am their mother; who shall bar me from them?
DUCHESS OF YORK.
I am their father's mother; I will see them.
LADY ANNE.
Their aunt I am in law, in love their mother:
Then bring me to their sights; I'll bear thy
blame,
And take thy office from thee, on my peril.
SIR ROBERT BRAKENBURY.
No, madam, no,—I may not leave it so:
I'm bound by oath, and therefore pardon me.
[*Exit.*

Enter STANLEY.
LORD STANLEY.
Let me but meet you, ladies, one hour hence,
And I'll salute your Grace of York as mother,
And reverend looker-on, of two fair queens.—
[*to the* DUCHESS OF GLOSTER] Come, madam,
you must straight to Westminster,
There to be crowned Richard's royal queen.
QUEEN ELIZABETH.
Ah, cut my lace asunder,
That my pent heart may have some scope to beat,
Or else I swoon with this dead-killing news!
LADY ANNE.
Despiteful tidings! O unpleasing news!
MARQUESS OF DORSET.
Be of good cheer:—mother, how fares your
Grace?
QUEEN ELIZABETH.
O Dorset, speak not to me, get thee hence!
Death and destruction dog thee at the heels;
Thy mother's name is ominous to children.
If thou wilt outstrip death, go cross the seas,
And live with Richmond, from the reach of hell:
Go, hie thee, hie thee from this slaughter-house,
Lest thou increase the number of the dead;
And make me die the thrall of Margaret's curse,—
Nor mother, wife, nor England's counted queen.
LORD STANLEY.
Full of wise care is this your counsel, madam.—
Take all the swift advantage of the hours;
You shall have letters from me to my son
In your behalf, to meet you on the way:
Be not ta'en tardy by unwise delay.

DUCHESS OF YORK.
O ill-dispersing wind of misery!—
O my accursed womb, the bed of death!
A cockatrice hast thou hatcht to the world,
Whose unavoided eye is murderous.
LORD STANLEY.
Come, madam, come; I in all haste was sent.
LADY ANNE.
And I in all unwillingness will go.—
O, would to God that the inclusive verge
Of golden metal that must round my brow
Were red-hot steel, to sear me to the brain!
Anointed let me be with deadly venom;
And die, ere men can say, 'God save the queen!'
QUEEN ELIZABETH.
Go, go, poor soul, I envy not thy glory;
To feed my humour, wish thyself no harm.
LADY ANNE.
No! why?—When he that is my husband now
Came to me, as I follow'd Henry's corse;
When scarce the blood was well washt from his
hands
Which issued from my other angel husband,
And that dead saint which then I weeping
follow'd;
O, when, I say, I lookt on Richard's face,
This was my wish,—'Be thou,' quoth I, 'accurst,
For making me, so young, so old a widow!
And, when thou wedd'st, let sorrow haunt thy
bed;
And be thy wife—if any be so mad—
More miserable by the life of thee
Than thou hast made me by my dear lord's
death!'
Lo, ere I can repeat this curse again,
Even in so short a space, my woman's heart
Grossly grew captive to his honey words,
And proved the subject of mine own soul's
curse,—
Which ever since hath kept mine eyes from rest;
For never yet one hour in his bed
Have I enjoy'd the golden dew of sleep,
But have been waked by his timorous dreams.
Besides, he hates me for my father Warwick;
And will, no doubt, shortly be rid of me.
QUEEN ELIZABETH.
Poor heart, adieu! I pity thy complaining.
LADY ANNE.
No more than from my soul I mourn for yours.
QUEEN ELIZABETH.
Farewell, thou woful welcomer of glory!
LADY ANNE.
Adieu, poor soul, that takest thy leave of it!
DUCHESS OF YORK [*to* DORSET].
Go thou to Richmond, and good fortune guide
thee!—
[*to* ANNE] Go thou to Richard, and good angels
tend thee!—
[*to* QUEEN ELIZABETH] Go thou to sanctuary,
and good thoughts possess thee!—
I to my grave, where peace and rest lie with me!
Eighty odd years of sorrow have I seen,
And each hour's joy wrackt with a week of teen.
QUEEN ELIZABETH.
Stay yet, look back with me unto the Tower.
Pity, you ancient stones, those tender babes,

Whom envy hath immured within your walls!
Rough cradle for such little pretty ones!
Rude ragged nurse, old sullen playfellow
For tender princes, use my babies well!
So foolish sorrow bids your stones farewell.

[*Exeunt.*

SCENE II.

London. The Palace.

Sound a sennet. Enter RICHARD, *in pomp, crown'd;* BUCKINGHAM, CATESBY, *a* PAGE, *and others.*

KING RICHARD.

STAND all apart.—Cousin of Buckingham,—
    DUKE OF BUCKINGHAM.
My gracious sovereign?
    KING RICHARD.
Give me thy hand. [*Here he ascendeth the throne.*]
Thus high, by thy advice
And thy assistance, is King Richard seated:—
But shall we wear these honours for a day?
Or shall they last, and we rejoice in them?
    DUKE OF BUCKINGHAM.
Still live they, and for ever let them last!
    KING RICHARD.
Ah, Buckingham, now do I play the touch,
To try if thou be current gold indeed:—
Young Edward lives;—think now what I would
    speak.
    DUKE OF BUCKINGHAM.
Say on, my loving lord.
    KING RICHARD.
Why, Buckingham, I say, I would be king.
    DUKE OF BUCKINGHAM.
Why, so you are, my thrice-renowned liege.
    KING RICHARD.
Ha! am I king? 'tis so:—but Edward lives.
    DUKE OF BUCKINGHAM.
True, noble prince.
    KING RICHARD.
         O bitter consequence,
That Edward still should live! 'True, noble
    prince!'
Cousin, thou wert not wont to be so dull:
Shall I be plain?—I wish the bastards dead;
And I would have it suddenly perform'd.
What say'st thou now? speak suddenly, be brief.
    DUKE OF BUCKINGHAM.
Your Grace may do your pleasure.
    KING RICHARD.
Tut, tut, thou art all ice, thy kindness freezes:
Say, have I thy consent that they shall die?
    DUKE OF BUCKINGHAM.
Give me some breath, some little pause, my lord,
Before I positively speak herein:
I will resolve your Grace immediately.   [*Exit.*
    SIR WILLIAM CATESBY [*aside to another*].
The king is angry; see, he gnaws his lip.
    KING RICHARD.
I will converse with iron-witted fools
And unrespective boys: none are for me
That look into me with considerate eyes:
High-reaching Buckingham grows circumspect.
Boy!—
    PAGE.
My lord?

KING RICHARD.
Know'st thou not any whom corrupting gold
Would tempt unto a close exploit of death?
    PAGE.
I know a discontented gentleman,
Whose humble means match not his haughty
    mind:
Gold were as good as twenty orators,
And will, no doubt, tempt him to any thing.
    KING RICHARD.
What is his name?
    PAGE.
        His name, my lord, is Tyrrel.
    KING RICHARD.
I partly know the man: go call him hither.
               [*Exit* PAGE.
The deep-revolving witty Buckingham
No more shall be the neighbour to my counsels:
Hath he so long held out with me untired,
And stops he now for breath?—well, be it so.
    Enter STANLEY.
How now! what news with you?
    LORD STANLEY.
My lord, I hear the Marquess Dorset's fled
To Richmond, in those parts beyond the seas
Where he abides.
    KING RICHARD.
Come hither, Catesby:—rumour it abroad
That Anne, my wife, is very grievous sick;
I will take order for her keeping close.
Inquire me out some mean-born gentleman,
Whom I will marry straight to Clarence'
    daughter;—
The boy is foolish, and I fear not him.—
Look, how thou dream'st!—I say again, give out
That Anne my queen is sick, and like to die:
About it; for it stands me much upon,
To stop all hopes whose growth may damage me.
             [*Exit* CATESBY.
I must be married to my brother's daughter,
Or else my kingdom stands on brittle glass:—
Murder her brothers, and then marry her!
Uncertain way of gain! But I am in
So far in blood, that sin will pluck on sin:
Tear-falling pity dwells not in this eye.
    Enter PAGE, *with* TYRREL.
Is thy name Tyrrel?
    SIR JAMES TYRREL.
James Tyrrel, and your most obedient subject.
    KING RICHARD.
Art thou indeed?
    SIR JAMES TYRREL.
        Prove me, my gracious sovereign.
    KING RICHARD.
Darest thou resolve to kill a friend of mine?
    SIR JAMES TYRREL.
Ay, my lord;
But I had rather kill two enemies.
    KING RICHARD.
Why, then thou hast it: two deep enemies,
Foes to my rest and my sweet sleep's disturbers,
Are they that I would have thee deal upon:—
Tyrrel, I mean those bastards in the Tower.
    SIR JAMES TYRREL.
Let me have open means to come to them,
And soon I'll rid you from the fear of them.

KING RICHARD.
Thou sing'st sweet music. Hark, come hither,
Tyrrel:
Go, by this token:—rise, and lend thine ear:
                      [*Whispers.*
There is no more but so:—say it is done,
And I will love thee, and prefer thee for it.
       SIR JAMES TYRREL.
I will dispatch it straight.   [*Exit.*
      Enter BUCKINGHAM.
    DUKE OF BUCKINGHAM.
My lord, I have consider'd in my mind
The late demand that you did sound me in.
       KING RICHARD
Well, let that rest. Dorset is fled to Richmond.
    DUKE OF BUCKINGHAM.
I hear the news, my lord.
       KING RICHARD.
Stanley, he is your wife's son:—well, look to
it.
    DUKE OF BUCKINGHAM.
My lord, I claim the gift, my due by promise,
For which your honour and your faith is
pawn'd;
Th' earldom of Hereford, and the movables,
The which you promised I should possess.
       KING RICHARD.
Stanley, look to your wife: if she convey
Letters to Richmond, you shall answer it.
    DUKE OF BUCKINGHAM.
What says your highness to my just request?
       KING RICHARD.
I do remember me,—Henry the Sixth
Did prophesy that Richmond should be king,
When Richmond was a little peevish boy.
A king! perhaps, perhaps—
    DUKE OF BUCKINGHAM.
My lord,—
       KING RICHARD.
How chance the prophet could not at that time
Have told me, I being by, that I should kill
him?
    DUKE OF BUCKINGHAM.
My lord, your promise for the earldom,—
       KING RICHARD.
Richmond!—When last I was at Exeter,
The mayor in courtesy show'd me the castle,
And call'd it Rougemont: at which name I
started,
Because a bard of Ireland told me once,
I should not live long after I saw Richmond.
    DUKE OF BUCKINGHAM.
My lord,—
       KING RICHARD.
Ay, what's o'clock?
    DUKE OF BUCKINGHAM.
I am thus bold to put your Grace in mind
Of what you promised me.
       KING RICHARD.
          Well, but what's o'clock?
    DUKE OF BUCKINGHAM.
Upon the stroke of ten.
       KING RICHARD.
          Well, let it strike.
    DUKE OF BUCKINGHAM.
Why let it strike?

KING RICHARD.
Because that, like a Jack, thou keep'st the stroke
Betwixt thy begging and my meditation.
I am not in the giving vein to-day.
    DUKE OF BUCKINGHAM.
Why, then resolve me whether you will or no.
       KING RICHARD.
Tut, tut,
Thou troublest me; I am not in the vein.
      [*Exeunt all except* BUCKINGHAM.
    DUKE OF BUCKINGHAM.
Is it even so? rewards he my true service
With such contempt? made I him king for this?
O, let me think on Hastings, and be gone
To Brecknock, while my fearful head is on! [*Exit.*

       SCENE III.
        The same.
      Enter TYRREL.
     SIR JAMES TYRREL.
THE tyrannous and bloody act is done,—
   The most arch deed of piteous massacre
That ever yet this land was guilty of.
Dighton and Forrest, whom I did suborn
To do this ruthless piece of butchery,
Albeit they were flesht villains, bloody dogs,
Melting with tenderness and mild compassion,
Wept like two children in their death's sad story.
'Lo, thus,' quoth Dighton, 'lay the gentle
babes,'—
'Thus, thus,' quoth Forrest, 'girdling one another
Within their innocent alabaster arms:
Their lips were four red roses on a stalk,
Which in their summer beauty kist each other.
A book of prayers on their pillow lay;
Which once,' quoth Forrest, 'almost changed
my mind;
But, O, the devil'—there the villain stopt;
When Dighton thus told on,—'We smothered
The most replenished sweet work of nature,
That from the prime creation e'er she framed.'
Hence both are gone with conscience and remorse;
They could not speak; and so I left them both,
To bear this tidings to the bloody king:—
And here he comes.
      Enter KING RICHARD.
        All health, my sovereign lord!
       KING RICHARD.
Kind Tyrrel, am I happy in thy news?
     SIR JAMES TYRREL.
If to have done the thing you gave in charge
Beget your happiness, be happy then,
For it is done.
       KING RICHARD.
But didst thou see them dead?
     SIR JAMES TYRREL.
I did, my lord.
       KING RICHARD.
      And buried, gentle Tyrrel?
     SIR JAMES TYRREL.
The chaplain of the Tower hath buried them;
But where, to say the truth, I do not know.
       KING RICHARD.
Come to me, Tyrrel, soon at after supper,
When thou shalt tell the process of their death.

Meantime, but think how I may do thee good,
And be inheritor of thy desire.
Farewell till then.
                    SIR JAMES TYRREL.
                        I humbly take my leave. [*Exit.*
                    KING RICHARD.
The son of Clarence have I pent up close;
His daughter meanly have I matcht in marriage;
The sons of Edward sleep in Abraham's bosom,
And Anne my wife hath bid the world good night.
Now, for I know the Breton Richmond aims
At young Elizabeth, my brother's daughter,
And, by that knot, looks proudly on the crown,
To her go I, a jolly thriving wooer.
                    Enter CATESBY.
                    SIR WILLIAM CATESBY.
My lord,—
                    KING RICHARD.
Good news or bad, that thou comest in so
    bluntly?
                    SIR WILLIAM CATESBY.
Bad news, my lord: Ely is fled to Richmond;
And Buckingham, backt with the hardy Welsh-
    men,
Is in the field, and still his power increaseth.
                    KING RICHARD.
Ely with Richmond troubles me more near
Than Buckingham and his rash-levied strength.
Come,—I have learn'd that fearful commenting
Is leaden servitor to dull delay;
Delay leads impotent and snail-paced beggary:
Then fiery expedition be my wing,
Jove's Mercury, and herald for a king!
Go, muster men: my counsel is my shield;
We must be brief, when traitors brave the field.
                    [*Exeunt.*

SCENE IV.

Before the palace.

Enter QUEEN MARGARET.

                    QUEEN MARGARET.
So, now prosperity begins to mellow,
And drop into the rotten mouth of death.
Here in these confines slily have I lurkt,
To watch the waning of mine enemies.
A dire induction am I witness to,
And will to France; hoping the consequence
Will prove as bitter, black, and tragical.—
Withdraw thee, wretched Margaret: who comes
here?   [*Retires.*
Enter QUEEN ELIZABETH *and the* DUCHESS OF
                    YORK.
                    QUEEN ELIZABETH.
Ah, my poor princes! ah, my tender babes!
My unblown flowers, new-appearing sweets!
If yet your gentle souls fly in the air,
And be not fixt in doom perpetual,
Hover about me with your airy wings,
And hear your mother's lamentation!
                    QUEEN MARGARET [*aside*].
Hover about her; say, that right for right
Hath dimm'd your infant morn to aged night.
                    DUCHESS OF YORK.
So many miseries have crazed my voice,
That my woe-wearied tongue is still and mute.—
Edward Plantagenet, why art thou dead?

                    QUEEN MARGARET [*aside*].
Plantagenet doth quit Plantagenet,
Edward for Edward pays a dying debt.
                    QUEEN ELIZABETH.
Wilt Thou, O God, fly from such gentle lambs,
And throw them in the entrails of the wolf?
When didst Thou sleep, when such a deed was
    done?
                    QUEEN MARGARET [*aside*].
When holy Harry died, and my sweet son.
                    DUCHESS OF YORK.
Dead life, blind sight, poor mortal living ghost,
Woe's scene, world's shame, grave's due by life
    usurpt,
Brief abstract and record of tedious days,
Rest thy unrest on England's lawful earth,
                        [*Sitting down.*
Unlawfully made drunk with innocents' blood!
                    QUEEN ELIZABETH.
Ah, that thou wouldst as soon afford a grave
As thou canst yield a melancholy seat!
Then would I hide my bones, not rest them here.
Ah, who hath any cause to mourn but I?
                        [*Sitting down by her.*
                    QUEEN MARGARET [*coming forward*].
If ancient sorrow be most reverend,
Give mine the benefit of seniory,
And let my griefs frown on the upper hand.
If sorrow can admit society,
                        [*Sitting down with them.*
Tell o'er your woes again by viewing mine:—
I had an Edward, till a Richard kill'd him;
I had a Harry, till a Richard kill'd him;
Thou hadst an Edward, till a Richard kill'd
    him;
Thou hadst a Richard, till a Richard kill'd him.
                    DUCHESS OF YORK.
I had a Richard too, and thou didst kill him;
I had a Rutland too, thou holp'st to kill him.
                    QUEEN MARGARET.
Thou hadst a Clarence too, and Richard kill'd
    him.
From forth the kennel of thy womb hath crept
A hell-hound that doth hunt us all to death:
That dog, that had his teeth before his eyes,
To worry lambs, and lap their gentle blood;
That foul defacer of God's handiwork;
That excellent grand tyrant of the earth,
That reigns in galled eyes of weeping souls,—
Thy womb let loose, to chase us to our graves.—
O upright, just, and true-disposing God,
How do I thank thee, that this carnal cur
Preys on the issue of his mother's body,
And makes her pew-fellow with others' moan!
                    DUCHESS OF YORK.
O Harry's wife, triumph not in my woes!
God witness with me, I have wept for thine.
                    QUEEN MARGARET.
Bear with me; I am hungry for revenge,
And now I cloy me with beholding it.
Thy Edward he is dead, that kill'd my Edward;
Thy other Edward dead, to quit my Edward;
Young York he is but boot, because both they
Match not the high perfection of my loss:
Thy Clarence he is dead that stabb'd my
    Edward;

And the beholders of this tragic play,
Th' adulterate Hastings, Rivers, Vaughan, Grey,
Untimely smother'd in their dusky graves.
Richard yet lives, hell's black intelligencer;
Only reserved their factor, to buy souls,
And send them thither:—but at hand, at hand,
Ensues his piteous and unpitied end:
Earth gapes, hell burns, fiends roar, saints pray,
To have him suddenly convey'd from hence.—
Cancel his bond of life, dear God, I pray,
That I may live to say, 'The dog is dead!'

QUEEN ELIZABETH.
O, thou didst prophesy the time would come
That I should wish for thee to help me curse
That bottled spider, that foul bunch-backt toad!

QUEEN MARGARET.
I call'd thee then vain flourish of my fortune;
I call'd thee then poor shadow, painted queen;
The presentation of but what I was;
The flattering index of a direful pageant;
One heaved a-high, to be hurl'd down below;
A mother only mockt with two sweet babes;
A dream of what thou wast; a breath, a bubble;
A sign of dignity, a garish flag
To be the aim of every dangerous shot;
A queen in jest, only to fill the scene.   [brothers?
Where is thy husband now? where be thy
Where be thy two sons? wherein dost thou joy?
Who sues to thee, and cries, 'God save the
    queen'?
Where be the bending peers that flattered thee?
Where be the thronging troops that followed thee?
Decline all this, and see what now thou art:
For happy wife, a most distressed widow;
For joyful mother, one that wails the name;
For one being sued-to, one that humbly sues;
For queen, a very caitiff crown'd with care;
For one that scorn'd at me, now scorn'd of me:
For one being fear'd of all, now fearing one;
For one commanding all, obey'd of none;
Thus hath the course of justice wheel'd about,
And left thee but a very prey to time;
Having no more but thought of what thou wast,
To torture thee the more, being what thou art.
Thou didst usurp my place, and dost thou not
Usurp the just proportion of my sorrow?
Now thy proud neck bears half my burden'd yoke;
From which even here I slip my wearied head,
And leave the burden of it all on thee.
Farewell, York's wife; and queen of sad mischance:
These English woes will make me smile in France.

QUEEN ELIZABETH.
O thou well-skill'd in curses, stay awhile,
And teach me how to curse mine enemies!

QUEEN MARGARET.
Forbear to sleep the night, and fast the day;
Compare dead happiness with living woe;
Think that thy babes were fairer than they were,
And he that slew them fouler than he is:
Bettering thy loss makes the bad causer worse:
Revolving this will teach thee how to curse.

QUEEN ELIZABETH.
My words are dull; O, quicken them with thine!

QUEEN MARGARET.
Thy woes will make them sharp, and pierce like
    mine.   [Exit.

DUCHESS OF YORK.
Why should calamity be full of words?

QUEEN ELIZABETH.
Windy attorneys to their client woes,
Airy succeeders of intestate joys,
Poor breathing orators of miseries!
Let them have scope: though what they do impart
Help nothing else, yet do they ease the heart.

DUCHESS OF YORK.
If so, then be not tongue-tied: go with me,
And in the breath of bitter words let's smother
My damned son, that thy two sweet sons
    smother'd.   [Drum within.
I hear his drum:—be copious in exclaims.

Enter KING RICHARD and his TRAIN, marching,
    with drums and trumpets.

KING RICHARD.
Who intercepts me in my expedition?

DUCHESS OF YORK.
O, she that might have intercepted thee,
By strangling thee in her accursed womb,   [done!
From all the slaughters, wretch, that thou hast

QUEEN ELIZABETH.
Hidest thou that forehead with a golden crown,
Where should be branded, if that right were right,
The slaughter of the prince that owed that crown,
And the dire death of my poor sons and brothers?
Tell me, thou villain-slave, where are my children?

DUCHESS OF YORK.
Thou toad, thou toad, where is thy brother
    Clarence?
And little Ned Plantagenet, his son?

QUEEN ELIZABETH.
Where is the gentle Rivers, Vaughan, Grey?

DUCHESS OF YORK.
Where is kind Hastings?

KING RICHARD.
A flourish, trumpets! strike alarum, drums!
Let not the heavens hear these tell-tale women
Rail on the Lord's anointed: strike, I say!
    [Flourish.   Alarums.
Either be patient, and entreat me fair,
Or with the clamorous report of war
Thus will I drown your exclamations.

DUCHESS OF YORK.
Art thou my son?

KING RICHARD.
Ay, I thank God, my father, and yourself.

DUCHESS OF YORK.
Then patiently hear my impatience.

KING RICHARD.
Madam, I have a touch of your condition,
That cannot brook the accent of reproof.

DUCHESS OF YORK.
O, let me speak!

KING RICHARD.
    Do, then; but I'll not hear.

DUCHESS OF YORK.
I will be mild and gentle in my words.

KING RICHARD.
And brief, good mother; for I am in haste.

DUCHESS OF YORK.
Art thou so hasty? I have stay'd for thee,
God knows, in torment and in agony.

KING RICHARD.
And came I not at last to comfort you?

DUCHESS OF YORK.
No, by the holy rood, thou know'st it well,
Thou camest on earth to make the earth my hell.
A grievous burden was thy birth to me;
Tetchy and wayward was thy infancy;
Thy school-days frightful, desperate, wild, and
   furious;
Thy prime of manhood daring, bold, and ven-
   turous;
Thy age confirm'd, proud, subtle, bloody,
   treacherous,
More mild, but yet more harmful-kind in hatred:
What comfortable hour canst thou name,
That ever graced me in thy company?
     KING RICHARD.
Faith, none, but Humphrey Hour, that call'd
   your Grace
To breakfast once forth of my company.
If I be so disgracious in your eye,
Let me march on, and not offend you, madam.—
Strike up the drum.
     DUCHESS OF YORK.
        I prithee, hear me speak.
     KING RICHARD.
You speak too bitterly.
     DUCHESS OF YORK.
          Hear me a word;
For I shall never speak to thee again.
     KING RICHARD.
So.
     DUCHESS OF YORK.
Either thou wilt die, by God's just ordinance,
Ere from this war thou turn a conqueror;
Or I with grief and extreme age shall perish,
And never look upon thy face again.
Therefore take with thee my most heavy curse;
Which, in the day of battle, tire thee more
Than all the complete armour that thou wear'st!
My prayers on the adverse party fight;
And there the little souls of Edward's children
Whisper the spirits of thine enemies,
And promise them success and victory.
Bloody thou art, bloody will be thy end;
Shame serves thy life, and doth thy death attend.
                    [Exit.
     QUEEN ELIZABETH.
Though far more cause, yet much less spirit to
   curse
Abides in me; I say amen to her.   [Going.
     KING RICHARD.
Stay, madam; I must speak a word with you.
     QUEEN ELIZABETH.
I have no more sons of the royal blood
For thee to murder: for my daughters, Richard,—
They shall be praying nuns, not weeping queens;
And therefore level not to hit their lives.
     KING RICHARD.
You have a daughter call'd Elizabeth,
Virtuous and fair, royal and gracious.
     QUEEN ELIZABETH.
And must she die for this? O, let her live,
And I'll corrupt her manners, stain her beauty;
Slander myself as false to Edward's bed;
Throw over her the veil of infamy:
So she may live unscarr'd of bleeding slaughter,
I will confess she was not Edward's daughter.

     KING RICHARD.
Wrong not her birth, she is a royal princess.
     QUEEN ELIZABETH.
To save her life, I'll say she is not so.
     KING RICHARD.
Her life is safest only in her birth.
     QUEEN ELIZABETH.
And only in that safety died her brothers.
     KING RICHARD.
Lo, at their births good stars were opposite.
     QUEEN ELIZABETH.
No, to their lives ill friends were contrary.
     KING RICHARD.
All unavoided is the doom of destiny.
     QUEEN ELIZABETH.
True, when avoided grace makes destiny:
My babes were destined to a fairer death,
If grace had blest thee with a fairer life.
     KING RICHARD.
You speak as if that I had slain my cousins.
     QUEEN ELIZABETH.
Cousins, indeed; and by their uncle cozen'd
Of comfort, kingdom, kindred, freedom, life.
Whose hand soever lanced their tender hearts,
Thy head, all indirectly, gave direction:
No doubt the murderous knife was dull and blunt
Till it was whetted on thy stone-hard heart,
To revel in the entrails of my lambs.
But that still use of grief makes wild grief tame,
My tongue should to thy ears not name my boys
Till that my nails were anchor'd in thine eyes;
And I, in such a desperate bay of death,
Like a poor bark, of sails and tackling reft,
Rush all to pieces on thy rocky bosom.
     KING RICHARD.
Madam, so thrive I in my enterprise
And dangerous success of bloody wars,
As I intend more good to you and yours
Than ever you and yours by me were harm'd!
     QUEEN ELIZABETH.
What good is cover'd with the face of heaven,
To be discover'd, that can do me good?
     KING RICHARD.
Th' advancement of your children, gentle lady.
     QUEEN ELIZABETH.
Up to some scaffold, there to lose their heads?
     KING RICHARD.
No, to the dignity and height of honour,
The high imperial type of this earth's glory.
     QUEEN ELIZABETH.
Flatter my sorrows with report of it;
Tell me what state, what dignity, what honour,
Canst thou demise to any child of mine?
     KING RICHARD.
Even all I have; ay, and myself and all,
Will I withal endow a child of thine;
So in the Lethe of thy angry soul
Thou drown the sad remembrance of those
   wrongs
Which thou supposest I have done to thee.
     QUEEN ELIZABETH.
Be brief, lest that the process of thy kindness
Last longer telling than thy kindness' date.
     KING RICHARD.
Then know, that from my soul I love thy
   daughter.

QUEEN ELIZABETH.
My daughter's mother thinks it with her soul.
KING RICHARD.
What do you think?
QUEEN ELIZABETH.
That thou dost love my daughter from thy soul:
So, from thy soul's love, didst thou love her
    brothers;
And, from my heart's love, I do thank thee for it.
KING RICHARD.
Be not so hasty to confound my meaning:
I mean, that with my soul I love thy daughter,
And do intend to make her Queen of England.
QUEEN ELIZABETH.
Well, then, who dost thou mean shall be her king?
KING RICHARD.
Even he that makes her queen: who else should
    be?
QUEEN ELIZABETH.
What, thou?
KING RICHARD.
I, even I: what think you of it, madam?
QUEEN ELIZABETH.
How canst thou woo her?
KING RICHARD.
                That would I learn of you,
As one being best acquainted with her humour.
QUEEN ELIZABETH.
And wilt thou learn of me?
KING RICHARD.
            Madam, with all my heart.
QUEEN ELIZABETH.
Send to her, by the man that slew her brothers,
A pair of bleeding hearts; thereon engrave
'Edward and York;' then haply will she weep:
Therefore present to her—as sometime Margaret
Did to thy father, steept in Rutland's blood—
A handkerchief; which, say to her, did drain
The purple sap from her sweet brother's body,
And bid her dry her weeping eyes withal.
If this inducement move her not to love,
Send her a letter of thy noble deeds;
Tell her thou madest away her uncle Clarence,
Her uncle Rivers; ay, and, for her sake,
Madest quick conveyance with her good aunt
    Anne.
KING RICHARD.
You mock me, madam; this is not the way
To win your daughter.
QUEEN ELIZABETH.
                There is no other way;
Unless thou couldst put on some other shape,
And not be Richard that hath done all this.
KING RICHARD.
Say that I did all this for love of her?
QUEEN ELIZABETH.
Nay, then indeed she cannot choose but hear thee,
Having bought love with such a bloody spoil.
KING RICHARD.
Look, what is done cannot be now amended:
Men shall deal unadvisedly sometimes,
Which after-hours gives leisure to repent.
If I did take the kingdom from your sons,
To make amends, I'll give it to your daughter.
If I have kill'd the issue of your womb,
To quicken your increase, I will beget

Mine issue of your blood upon your daughter:
A grandam's name is little less in love
Than is the doting title of a mother;
They are as children but one step below,
Even of your mettle, of your very blood;
Of all one pain,—save for a night of groans
Endured of her, for whom you bid like sorrow.
Your children were vexation to your youth;
But mine shall be a comfort to your age.
The loss you have is but a son being king,
And by that loss your daughter is made queen.
I cannot make you what amends I would,
Therefore accept such kindness as I can.
Dorset your son, that with a fearful soul
Leads discontented steps in foreign soil,
This fair alliance quickly shall call home
To high promotions and great dignity:
The king, that calls your beauteous daughter
    wife,
Familiarly shall call thy Dorset brother;
Again shall you be mother to a king,
And all the ruins of distressful times
Repair'd with double riches of content.
What! we have many goodly days to see:
The liquid drops of tears that you have shed
Shall come again, transform'd to orient pearl,
Advantaging their loan with interest
Of ten-times-double gain of happiness.
Go, then, my mother, to thy daughter go;
Make bold her bashful years with your ex-
    perience;
Prepare her ears to hear a wooer's tale;
Put in her tender heart th' aspiring flame
Of golden sovereignty; acquaint the princess
With the sweet silent hours of marriage joys:
And when this arm of mine hath chastised
The petty rebel, dull-brain'd Buckingham,
Bound with triumphant garlands will I come,
And lead thy daughter to a conqueror's bed;
To whom I will retail my conquest won,
And she shall be sole victress, Cæsar's Cæsar.
QUEEN ELIZABETH.
What were I best to say? her father's brother
Would be her lord? or shall I say, her uncle?
Or, he that slew her brothers and her uncles?
Under what title shall I woo for thee,
That God, the law, my honour, and her love,
Can make seem pleasing to her tender years?
KING RICHARD.
Infer fair England's peace by this alliance.
QUEEN ELIZABETH.
Which she shall purchase with still-lasting war.
KING RICHARD.
Tell her, the king, that may command, entreats.
QUEEN ELIZABETH.
That at her hands which the king's King forbids.
KING RICHARD.
Say, she shall be a high and mighty queen.
QUEEN ELIZABETH.
To wail the title, as her mother doth.
KING RICHARD.
Say, I will love her everlastingly.
QUEEN ELIZABETH.
But how long shall that title 'ever' last?
KING RICHARD.
Sweetly in force unto her fair life's end.

QUEEN ELIZABETH.
But how long fairly shall her sweet life last?
KING RICHARD.
As long as heaven and nature lengthens it.
QUEEN ELIZABETH.
As long as hell and Richard likes of it.
KING RICHARD.
Say, I, her sovereign, am her subject love.
QUEEN ELIZABETH.
But she, your subject, loathes such sovereignty.
KING RICHARD.
Be eloquent in my behalf to her.
QUEEN ELIZABETH.
An honest tale speeds best being plainly told.
KING RICHARD.
Then, plainly to her tell my loving tale.
QUEEN ELIZABETH.
Plain and not honest is too harsh a style.
KING RICHARD.
Your reasons are too shallow and too quick.
QUEEN ELIZABETH.
O, no, my reasons are too deep and dead;—
Too deep and dead, poor infants, in their graves.
KING RICHARD.
Harp not on that string, madam; that is past.
QUEEN ELIZABETH.
Harp on it still shall I till heart-strings break.
KING RICHARD.
Now, by my George, my garter, and my
    crown,—
QUEEN ELIZABETH.
Profaned, dishonour'd, and the third usurpt.
KING RICHARD.
I swear—
QUEEN ELIZABETH.
        By nothing; for this is no oath:
Thy George, profaned, hath lost his holy honour;
Thy garter, blemisht, pawn'd his knightly virtue;
Thy crown, usurpt, disgraced his kingly glory.
If something thou wouldst swear to be believed,
Swear, then, by something that thou hast not
    wrong'd.
KING RICHARD.
Now, by the world,—
QUEEN ELIZABETH.
        'Tis full of thy foul wrongs.
KING RICHARD.
My father's death,—
QUEEN ELIZABETH.
        Thy life hath that dishonour'd.
KING RICHARD.
Then, by myself,—
QUEEN ELIZABETH.
        Thyself is self-misused.
KING RICHARD.
Why, then, by God,—
QUEEN ELIZABETH.
        God's wrong is most of all.
If thou hadst fear'd to break an oath by Him,
The unity the king thy brother made
Had not been broken, nor my brother slain:
If thou hadst fear'd to break an oath by Him,
Th' imperial metal, circling now thy head,
Had graced the tender temples of my child;
And both the princes had been breathing here,
Which now, two tender bedfellows for dust,

Thy broken faith hath made a prey for worms.
What canst thou swear by now?
KING RICHARD.
        The time to come.
QUEEN ELIZABETH.
That thou hast wronged in the time o'erpast;
For I myself have many tears to wash
Hereafter time, for time past wrong'd by thee.
The children live, whose parents thou hast
    slaughter'd,
Ungovern'd youth, to wail it in their age;
The parents live, whose children thou hast
    butcher'd,
Old wither'd plants, to wail it with their age.
Swear not by time to come; for that thou hast
Misused ere used, by time misused o'erpast.
KING RICHARD.
As I intend to prosper and repent,
So thrive I in my dangerous attempt
Of hostile arms! myself myself confound!
Heaven and fortune bar me happy hours!
Day, yield me not thy light; nor, night, thy
    rest!
Be opposite all planets of good luck
To my proceeding!—if, with pure heart's love,
Immaculate devotion, holy thoughts,
I tender not thy beauteous princely daughter!
In her consists my happiness and thine;
Without her, follows to myself and thee,
Herself, the land, and many a Christian soul,
Death, desolation, ruin, and decay:
It cannot be avoided but by this;
It will not be avoided but by this.
Therefore, dear mother,—I must call you so,—
Be the attorney of my love to her:
Plead what I will be, not what I have been;
Not my deserts, but what I will deserve:
Urge the necessity and state of times,
And be not peevish-fond in great designs.
QUEEN ELIZABETH.
Shall I be tempted of the devil thus?
KING RICHARD.
Ay, if the devil tempt thee to do good.
QUEEN ELIZABETH.
Shall I forget myself to be myself?
KING RICHARD.
Ay, if your self's remembrance wrong yourself.
QUEEN ELIZABETH.
But thou didst kill my children.
KING RICHARD.
But in your daughter's womb I'll bury them:
Where, in that nest of spicery, they shall breed
Selves of themselves, to your recomforture.
QUEEN ELIZABETH.
Shall I go win my daughter to thy will?
KING RICHARD.
And be a happy mother by the deed.
QUEEN ELIZABETH.
I go.—Write to me very shortly,
And you shall understand from me her mind.
KING RICHARD.
Bear her my true love's kiss; and so, farewell.
            [Exit QUEEN ELIZABETH.
Relenting fool, and shallow, changing woman!
    Enter RATCLIFF; CATESBY following.
How now! what news?

SIR RICHARD RATCLIFF.
My gracious sovereign, on the western coast
Rideth a puissant navy; to the shore
Throng many doubtful hollow-hearted friends,
Unarm'd, and unresolved to beat them back:
'Tis thought that Richmond is their admiral;
And there they hull, expecting but the aid
Of Buckingham to welcome them ashore.
KING RICHARD.
Some light-foot friend post to the Duke of
    Norfolk:—
Ratcliff, thyself,—or Catesby; where is he?
SIR WILLIAM CATESBY.
Here, my good lord.
KING RICHARD.
Fly to the duke.—[to RATCLIFF] Post thou to
    Salisbury:
When thou comest thither,—[to CATESBY] Dull,
    unmindful villain,
Why stay'st thou here, and go'st not to the duke?
SIR WILLIAM CATESBY.
First, mighty liege, tell me your highness'
    pleasure,
What from your Grace I shall deliver to him.
KING RICHARD.
O, true, good Catesby:—bid him levy straight
The greatest strength and power he can make,
And meet me suddenly at Salisbury.
SIR WILLIAM CATESBY.
I go.   [Exit.
SIR RICHARD RATCLIFF.
What, may it please you, shall I do at Salisbury?
KING RICHARD.
Why, what wouldst thou do there before I go?
SIR RICHARD RATCLIFF.
Your highness told me I should post before.
Enter STANLEY.
KING RICHARD.
My mind is changed.—Stanley, what news with
    you?
LORD STANLEY.   [ing;
None good, my liege, to please you with the hear-
Nor none so bad, but well may be reported.
KING RICHARD.
Hoyday, a riddle! neither good nor bad!
What need'st thou run so many miles about,
When thou mayst tell thy tale the nearest way?
Once more, what news?
LORD STANLEY.
                    Richmond is on the seas.
KING RICHARD.
There let him sink, and be the seas on him,
White-liver'd runagate! what doth he there?
LORD STANLEY.
I know not, mighty sovereign, but by guess.
KING RICHARD.
Well, as you guess?
LORD STANLEY.
Stirr'd up by Dorset, Buckingham, and Ely,
He makes for England, here, to claim the crown.
KING RICHARD.
Is the chair empty? is the sword unsway'd?
Is the king dead? the empire unpossest?
What heir of York is there alive but we?
And who is England's king but great York's heir?
Then, tell me, what makes he upon the seas?

LORD STANLEY.
Unless for that, my liege, I cannot guess.
KING RICHARD.
Unless for that he comes to be your liege,
You cannot guess wherefore the Welshman
    comes.
Thou wilt revolt, and fly to him, I fear.
LORD STANLEY.
No, mighty liege, therefore mistrust me not.
KING RICHARD.
Where is thy power, then, to beat him back?
Where be thy tenants and thy followers?
Are they not now upon the western shore,
Safe-conducting the rebels from their ships?
LORD STANLEY.
No, my good lord, my friends are in the north.
KING RICHARD.
Cold friends to me: what do they in the north,
When they should serve their sovereign in the
    west?
LORD STANLEY.
They have not been commanded, mighty king:
Pleaseth your majesty to give me leave,
I'll muster up my friends, and meet your Grace
Where and what time your majesty shall please.
KING RICHARD.
Ay, ay, thou wouldst be gone to join with
    Richmond:
I will not trust you, sir.
LORD STANLEY.
                    Most mighty sovereign,
You have no cause to hold my friendship doubt-
    ful:
I never was nor never will be false.
KING RICHARD.
Go, then, and muster men. But leave behind
Your son, George Stanley: look your faith be
    firm,
Or else his head's assurance is but frail.
LORD STANLEY.
So deal with him as I prove true to you.   [Exit.
Enter a MESSENGER.
MESSENGER.
My gracious sovereign, now in Devonshire,
As I by friends am well advertised,
Sir Edward Courtney, and the haughty prelate
Bishop of Exeter, his elder brother,
With many moe confederates, are in arms.
Enter a second MESSENGER.
SECOND MESSENGER.
In Kent, my liege, the Guildfords are in arms;
And every hour more competitors
Flock to the rebels, and their power grows strong.
Enter a third MESSENGER.
THIRD MESSENGER.
My lord, the army of great Buckingham—
KING RICHARD.
Out on ye, owls! nothing but songs of death?
                            [He striketh him.
There, take thou that, till thou bring better news.
THIRD MESSENGER.
The news I have to tell your majesty
Is, that by sudden floods and fall of waters,
Buckingham's army is dispersed and scatter'd;
And he himself wander'd away alone,
No man knows whither.

KING RICHARD.
         I cry thee mercy:
There is my purse to cure that blow of thine.
Hath any well-advised friend proclaim'd
Reward to him that brings the traitor in?
THIRD MESSENGER.
Such proclamation hath been made, my lord.
Enter a fourth MESSENGER.
FOURTH MESSENGER.
Sir Thomas Lovel and Lord Marquess Dorset,
'Tis said, my liege, in Yorkshire are in arms.
But this good comfort bring I to your highness,—
The Breton navy is dispersed by tempest:
Richmond, in Dorsetshire, sent out a boat
Unto the shore, to ask those on the banks
If they were his assistants, yea or no;
Who answer'd him, they came from Buckingham
Upon his party: he, mistrusting them,
Hoised sail, and made his course again for Bretagne.
KING RICHARD.
March on, march on, since we are up in arms;
If not to fight with foreign er.emies,
Yet to beat down these rebels here at home.
Enter CATESBY.
SIR WILLIAM CATESBY.
My liege, the Duke of Buckingham is taken,—
That is the best news: that the Earl of Richmond
Is with a mighty power landed at Milford,
Is colder tidings, yet they must be told.
KING RICHARD.
Away towards Salisbury! while we reason here,
A royal battle might be won and lost:—
Some one take order Buckingham be brought
To Salisbury; the rest march on with me.
         [*Flourish. Exeunt.*

SCENE V.
LORD DERBY'S *house.*
Enter DERBY *and* SIR CHRISTOPHER URSWICK.
EARL OF DERBY.
SIR Christopher, tell Richmond this from me:—
That, in the sty of this most bloody boar,
My son George Stanley is frankt up in hold:
If I revolt, off goes young George's head:
The fear of that withholds my present aid.
But, tell me, where is princely Richmond now?
SIR CHRISTOPHER URSWICK.
At Pembroke, or at Ha'rford-west, in Wales.
EARL OF DERBY.
What men of name resort to him?
SIR CHRISTOPHER URSWICK.
Sir Walter Herbert, a renowned soldier;
Sir Gilbert Talbot, Sir William Stanley;
Oxford, redoubted Pembroke, Sir James Blunt,
And Rice ap Thomas, with a valiant crew;
And many moe of noble fame and worth:
And towards London they do bend their course,
If by the way they be not fought withal.
EARL OF DERBY.
Return unto thy lord; commend me to him:
Tell him the queen hath heartily consented
He shall espouse Elizabeth her daughter.
These letters will resolve him of my mind.
Farewell.   [*Exeunt.*

ACT V.   SCENE I.
Salisbury. An open place.
Enter the SHERIFF, *and* BUCKINGHAM, *with halberds, led to execution.*
DUKE OF BUCKINGHAM.
WILL not King Richard let me speak with him?
SHERIFF.
No, my good lord; therefore be patient.
DUKE OF BUCKINGHAM.
Hastings, and Edward's children, Rivers, Grey,
Holy King Henry, and thy fair son Edward,
Vaughan, and all that have miscarried
By underhand corrupted foul injustice,—
If that your moody discontented souls
Do through the clouds behold this present hour,
Even for revenge mock my destruction!—
This is All-Souls' day, fellows, is it not?
SHERIFF.
It is, my lord.
DUKE OF BUCKINGHAM.
Why, then All-Souls' day is my body's doomsday.
This is the day that, in King Edward's time,
I wisht might fall on me, when I was found
False to his children or his wife's allies;
This is the day wherein I wisht to fall
By the false faith of him I trusted most;
This, this All-Souls' day to my fearful soul
Is the determined respite of my wrongs:
That high All-Seer that I dallied with
Hath turn'd my feigned prayer on my head,
And given in earnest what I begg'd in jest.
Thus doth He force the swords of wicked men
To turn their own points on their masters'
    bosoms:
Thus Margaret's curse falls heavy on my neck,—
'When he,' quoth she, 'shall split thy heart with
    sorrow,
Remember Margaret was a prophetess.'—
Come, sirs, convey me to the block of shame;
Wrong hath but wrong, and blame the due of
    blame.   [*Exeunt.*
SCENE II.
Plain near Tamworth.
Enter RICHMOND, OXFORD, BLUNT, *and others, with drum and colours.*
EARL OF RICHMOND.
FELLOWS in arms, and my most loving
    friends,
Bruised underneath the yoke of tyranny,
Thus far into the bowels of the land
Have we marcht on without impediment;
And here receive we from our father Stanley
Lines of fair comfort and encouragement.
The wretched, bloody, and usurping boar,
That spoil'd your summer fields and fruitful
    vines,   [trough
Swills your warm blood like wash, and makes his
In your embowell'd bosoms,—this foul swine
Lies now even in the centre of this isle,
Near to the town of Leicester, as we learn:
From Tamworth thither is but one day's march.
In God's name, cheerly on, courageous friends,
To reap the harvest of perpetual peace

By this one bloody trial of sharp war.

EARL OF OXFORD.

Every man's conscience is a thousand swords,
To fight against this guilty homicide.

SIR WALTER HERBERT.

I doubt not but his friends will turn to us.

SIR JAMES BLUNT.

He hath no friends but what are friends for fear,
Which in his dearest need will shrink from him.

EARL OF RICHMOND.

All for our vantage. Then, in God's name, march:
True hope is swift, and flies with swallow's wings;
Kings it makes gods, and meaner creatures kings.

[*Exeunt.*

SCENE III.

Bosworth field.

Enter KING RICHARD *in arms, with* NORFOLK, *the* EARL OF SURREY, *and others.*

KING RICHARD.

HERE pitch our tents, even here in Bosworth field.
My Lord of Surrey, why look you so sad?

EARL OF SURREY.

My heart is ten times lighter than my looks.

KING RICHARD.

My Lord of Norfolk,—

DUKE OF NORFOLK.

Here, most gracious liege.

KING RICHARD.

Norfolk, we must have knocks; ha! must we not?

DUKE OF NORFOLK.

We must both give and take, my loving lord.

KING RICHARD.

Up with my tent! here will I lie to-night;

[SOLDIERS *begin to set up the* KING'S *tent.*

But where to-morrow? Well, all's one for that.—
Who hath descried the number of the traitors?

DUKE OF NORFOLK.

Six or seven thousand is their utmost power.

KING RICHARD.

Why, our battalia trebles that account:
Besides, the king's name is a tower of strength,
Which they upon the adverse party want.—
Up with the tent!—Come, noble gentlemen,
Let us survey the vantage of the ground;—
Call for some men of sound direction:—
Let's lack no discipline, make no delay;
For, lords, to-morrow is a busy day.   [*Exeunt.*

Enter, on the other side of the field, RICHMOND, BRANDON, OXFORD, *and others. Some of the* SOLDIERS *pitch* RICHMOND'S *tent.*

EARL OF RICHMOND.

The weary sun hath made a golden set,
And, by the bright track of his fiery car,
Gives token of a goodly day to-morrow.—
Sir William Brandon, you shall bear my standard.—
Give me some ink and paper in my tent:
I'll draw the form and model of our battle,
Limit each leader to his several charge,
And part in just proportion our small power.—
My Lord of Oxford,—you, Sir William Brandon,—

And you, Sir Walter Herbert,—stay with me.—
The Earl of Pembroke keeps his regiment:—
Good Captain Blunt, bear my good-night to him,
And by the second hour in the morning
Desire the earl to see me in my tent:
Yet one thing more, good captain, do for me,—
Where is Lord Stanley quarter'd, do you know?

SIR JAMES BLUNT.

Unless I have mista'en his colours much,—
Which well I am assured I have not done,—
His regiment lies half a mile at least
South from the mighty power of the king.

EARL OF RICHMOND.

If without peril it be possible,   [him,
Sweet Blunt, make some good means to speak with
And give him from me this most needful note.

SIR JAMES BLUNT.

Upon my life, my lord, I'll undertake it;
And so, God give you quiet rest to-night!

EARL OF RICHMOND.

Good night, good Captain Blunt. [*Exit* BLUNT.]
Come, gentlemen,
Let us consult upon to-morrow's business:
In to my tent; the air is raw and cold.

[*They withdraw into the tent.*

Enter, to his tent, KING RICHARD, NORFOLK, RATCLIFF, CATESBY, *and others.*

KING RICHARD.

What is't o'clock?

SIR WILLIAM CATESBY.

It's supper-time, my lord;
It's nine o'clock.

KING RICHARD.

I will not sup to-night.—
Give me some ink and paper.—
What, is my beaver easier than it was?
And all my armour laid into my tent?

SIR WILLIAM CATESBY.

It is, my liege; and all things are in readiness.

KING RICHARD.

Good Norfolk, hie thee to thy charge;
Use careful watch, choose trusty sentinels.

DUKE OF NORFOLK.

I go, my lord.

KING RICHARD.

Stir with the lark to-morrow, gentle Norfolk.

DUKE OF NORFOLK.

I warrant you, my lord.   [*Exit.*

KING RICHARD.

Catesby,—

SIR WILLIAM CATESBY.

My lord?

KING RICHARD.

Send out a pursuivant-at-arms
To Stanley's regiment; bid him bring his power
Before sunrising, lest his son George fall
Into the blind cave of eternal night.

[*Exit* CATESBY.

Fill me a bowl of wine.—Give me a watch.—
Saddle white Surrey for the field to-morrow.—
Look that my staves be sound, and not too heavy.—
Ratcliff,—

SIR RICHARD RATCLIFF.

My lord?

134

KING RICHARD.
Saw'st thou the melancholy Lord Northumber-
    land?
                SIR RICHARD RATCLIFF.
Thomas the Earl of Surrey, and himself,
Much about cock-shut time, from troop to troop
Went through the army, cheering up the soldiers.
                KING RICHARD.
So, I am satisfied.—Give me a bowl of wine:
I have not that alacrity of spirit,
Nor cheer of mind, that I was wont to have.
                                [Wine brought.
Set it down.—Is ink and paper ready?
                SIR RICHARD RATCLIFF.
It is, my lord.
                KING RICHARD.
Bid my guard watch; leave me.—Ratcliff,
About the mid of night come to my tent
And help to arm me.—Leave me, I say.
                        [Exeunt RATCLIFF and others.

Enter DERBY to RICHMOND in his tent; LORDS
    and GENTLEMEN.
                EARL OF DERBY.
Fortune and victory sit on thy helm!
                EARL OF RICHMOND.
All comfort that the dark night can afford
Be to thy person, noble father-in-law!
Tell me, how fares our loving mother?
                EARL OF DERBY.
I, by attorney, bless thee from thy mother,
Who prays continually for Richmond's good:
So much for that. The silent hours steal on,
And flaky darkness breaks within the east.
In brief,—for so the season bids us be,—
Prepare thy battle early in the morning,
And put thy fortune to th' arbitrement
Of bloody strokes and mortal-staring war.
I, as I may,—that which I would I cannot,—
With best advantage will deceive the time,
And aid thee in this doubtful shock of arms:
But on thy side I may not be too forward,
Lest, being seen, thy brother, tender George,
Be executed in his father's sight.
Farewell: the leisure and the fearful time
Cuts off the ceremonious vows of love
And ample interchange of sweet discourse,
Which so-long-sunder'd friends should dwell
    upon:
God give us leisure for these rites of love!
Once more, adieu: be valiant, and speed well!
                EARL OF RICHMOND.
Good lords, conduct him to his regiment:
I'll strive, with troubled thoughts, to take a
    nap,
Lest leaden slumber peise me down to-morrow,
When I should mount with wings of victory:
Once more, good night, kind lords and gentle-
    men.   [Exeunt all but RICHMOND.
O Thou, whose captain I account myself,
Look on my forces with a gracious eye;
Put in their hands Thy bruising irons of
    wrath,
That they may crush down with a heavy fall
Th' usurping helmets of our adversaries!
Make us Thy ministers of chastisement,

That we may praise Thee in the victory!
To Thee I do commend my watchful soul,
Ere I let fall the windows of mine eyes:
Sleeping and waking, O, defend me still! [Sleeps.

Enter the GHOST of PRINCE EDWARD, son to
    KING HENRY THE SIXTH.
        GHOST [to KING RICHARD].
Let me sit heavy on thy soul to-morrow!
Think, how thou stabb'dst me in my prime of
    youth
At Tewksbury: despair, therefore, and die!
[to RICHMOND] Be cheerful, Richmond; for the
    wronged souls
Of butcher'd princes fight in thy behalf:
King Henry's issue, Richmond, comforts thee.
    Enter the GHOST of HENRY THE SIXTH.
        GHOST [to KING RICHARD].
When I was mortal, my anointed body
By thee was punched full of deadly holes:
Think on the Tower and me: despair, and die,
Harry the Sixth bids thee despair and die!
[to RICHMOND] Virtuous and holy, be thou con-
    queror!
Harry, that prophesied thou shouldst be king,
Doth comfort thee in thy sleep: live, and
    flourish!
        Enter the GHOST of CLARENCE.
        GHOST [to KING RICHARD].
Let me sit heavy on thy soul to-morrow!
I, that was washt to death with fulsome wine,
Poor Clarence, by thy guile betray'd to death!
To-morrow in the battle think on me,
And fall thy edgeless sword: despair, and die!
[to RICHMOND] Thou offspring of the house of
    Lancaster,
The wronged heirs of York do pray for thee:
Good angels guard thy battle! live, and flour-
    ish!
    Enter the GHOSTS of RIVERS, GREY, and
        VAUGHAN.
    GHOST OF RIVERS [to KING RICHARD].
Let me sit heavy on thy soul to-morrow,
Rivers, that died at Pomfret! despair, and die!
    GHOST OF GREY [to KING RICHARD].
Think upon Grey, and let thy soul despair!
    GHOST OF VAUGHAN [to KING RICHARD].
Think upon Vaughan, and, with guilty fear,
Let fall thy lance: despair, and die!
        ALL THREE [to RICHMOND].
Awake, and think our wrongs in Richard's
    bosom
Will conquer him!—awake, and win the day!
        Enter the GHOST of HASTINGS.
        GHOST [to KING RICHARD].
Bloody and guilty, guiltily awake,
And in a bloody battle end thy days!
Think on Lord Hastings: despair, and die.
[to RICHMOND] Quiet untroubled soul, awake,
    awake!
Arm, fight, and conquer, for fair England's
    sake!
Enter the GHOSTS of the two young PRINCES.
        GHOSTS [to KING RICHARD].
Dream on thy cousins smothered in the Tower:
Let us be lead within thy bosom, Richard,

And weigh thee down to ruin, shame, and death!
Thy nephews' souls bid thee despair and die!
[to RICHMOND] Sleep, Richmond, sleep in peace,
    and wake in joy;
Good angels guard thee from the boar's annoy!
Live, and beget a happy race of kings!
Edward's unhappy sons do bid thee flourish.
    Enter the GHOST *of* ANNE, *his wife.*
       GHOST [*to* KING RICHARD].
Richard, thy wife, that wretched Anne thy wife,
That never slept a quiet hour with thee,
Now fills thy sleep with perturbations:
To-morrow in the battle think on me,
And fall thy edgeless sword: despair, and die!
[to RICHMOND] Thou quiet soul, sleep thou a
    quiet sleep;
Dream of success and happy victory!
Thy adversary's wife doth pray for thee.
    Enter the GHOST *of* BUCKINGHAM.
       GHOST [*to* KING RICHARD].
The first was I that helpt thee to the crown;
The last was I that felt thy tyranny:
O, in the battle think on Buckingham,
And die in terror of thy guiltiness!
Dream on, dream on, of bloody deeds and death:
Fainting, despair; despairing, yield thy breath!
[to RICHMOND] I died for hope ere I could lend
    thee aid:
But cheer thy heart, and be thou not dismay'd:
God and good angels fight on Richmond's
    side;
And Richard falls in height of all his pride.
    [*The* GHOSTS *vanish.* KING RICHARD
      starts out of his dream.
       KING RICHARD.
Give me another horse,—bind up my wounds,—
Have mercy, Jesu!—Soft! I did but dream.
O coward conscience, how dost thou afflict me!
The lights burn blue. It is now dead midnight.
Cold fearful drops stand on my trembling
    flesh.
What do I fear? myself? there's none else by:
·Richard loves Richard; that is, I am I.
Is there a murderer here? No;—yes, I am:
Then fly. What, from myself? Great reason why:
Lest I revenge. What, myself upon myself?
Alack, I love myself. Wherefore? for any good
That I myself have done unto myself?
O, no! alas, I rather hate myself
For hateful deeds committed by myself!
I am a villain: yet I lie, I am not.
Fool, of thyself speak well:—fool, do not flatter.
My conscience hath a thousand several tongues,
And every tongue brings in a several tale,
And every tale condemns me for a villain.
Perjury, perjury, in the high'st degree;
Murder, stern murder, in the direst degree;
All several sins, all used in each degree,
Throng to the bar, crying all 'Guilty! guilty!'
I shall despair. There is no creature loves me;
And if I die, no soul shall pity me:
Nay, wherefore should they,—since that I myself
Find in myself no pity to myself?
       Enter RATCLIFF.
    SIR RICHARD RATCLIFF.
My lord,—

       KING RICHARD.
Who's there?
    SIR RICHARD RATCLIFF.
My lord, 'tis I. The early village-cock
Hath twice done salutation to the morn;
Your friends are up, and buckle on their arm-
    our.
       KING RICHARD.
O Ratcliff, I have dream'd a fearful dream!—
What thinkest thou,—will our friends prove all
    true?
    SIR RICHARD RATCLIFF.
No doubt, my lord.
       KING RICHARD.
       O Ratcliff, I fear, I fear!—
Methought the souls of all that I had murder'd
Came to my tent; and every one did threat
To-morrow's vengeance on the head of Richard.
    SIR RICHARD RATCLIFF.
Nay, good my lord, be not afraid of shadows.
       KING RICHARD.
By the apostle Paul, shadows to-night
Have struck more terror to the soul of Richard
Than can the substance of ten thousand soldiers
Armed in proof and led by shallow Richmond.
It is not yet near day. Come, go with me;
Under our tents I'll play the eaves-dropper,
To hear if any mean to shrink from me.
    [*Exeunt* KING RICHARD *and* RATCLIFF.

    Enter the LORDS *to* RICHMOND, *sitting in his tent.*
       LORDS.
Good morrow, Richmond!
    EARL OF RICHMOND [*waking*].
Cry mercy, lords and watchful gentlemen,
That you have ta'en a tardy sluggard here.
       LORDS.
How have you slept, my lord?
    EARL OF RICHMOND.
The sweetest sleep, and fairest-boding dreams
That ever enter'd in a drowsy head,
Have I since your departure had, my lords.
Methought their souls, whose bodies Richard
    murder'd,
Came to my tent, and cried on victory:
I promise you, my heart is very jocund
In the remembrance of so fair a dream.
How far into the morning is it, lords?
       LORDS.
Upon the stroke of four.
    EARL OF RICHMOND.
Why, then 'tis time to arm and give direction.
    His oration to his SOLDIERS.
More than I have said, loving countrymen,
The leisure and enforcement of the time
Forbids to dwell upon: yet remember this,—
God and our good cause fight upon our side;
The prayers of holy saints and wronged souls,
Like high-rear'd bulwarks, stand before our
    faces;
Richard except, those whom we fight against
Had rather have us win than him they follow:
For what is he they follow? truly, gentlemen,
A bloody tyrant and a homicide;
One rais'd in blood, and one in blood establisht;
One that made means to come by what he hath,

And slaughter'd those that were the means to
    help him;
A base foul stone, made precious by the foil
Of England's chair, where he is falsely set;
One that hath ever been God's enemy:
Then, if you fight against God's enemy,
God will, in justice, ward you as his soldiers;
If you do sweat to put a tyrant down,
You sleep in peace, the tyrant being slain;
If you do fight against your country's foes,
Your country's fat shall pay your pains the hire;
If you do fight in safeguard of your wives,
Your wives shall welcome home the conquerors;
If you do free your children from the sword,
Your children's children quit it in your age.
Then, in the name of God and all these rights,
Advance your standards, draw your willing
    swords.
For me, the ransom of my bold attempt
Shall be this cold corpse on the earth's cold face;
But if I thrive, the gain of my attempt
The least of you shall share his part thereof.
Sound drums and trumpets, boldly and cheer-
    fully;
God and Saint George! Richmond and victory!
                                        [*Exeunt.*
Enter KING RICHARD, RATCLIFF, ATTEN-
    DANTS, *and* FORCES.
                KING RICHARD.
What said Northumberland as touching Rich-
    mond?
            SIR RICHARD RATCLIFF.
That he was never trained up in arms.
                KING RICHARD.
He said the truth: and what said Surrey, then?
            SIR RICHARD RATCLIFF.
He smiled, and said, 'The better for our pur-
    pose.'
                KING RICHARD.
He was in the right; and so, indeed, it is.
                                    [*Clock strikes.*
Tell the clock there.—Give me a calendar.—
Who saw the sun to-day?
            SIR RICHARD RATCLIFF.
                            Not I, my lord.
                KING RICHARD.
Then he disdains to shine; for, by the book,
He should have braved the east an hour ago:
A black day will it be to somebody.—
Ratcliff,—
            SIR RICHARD RATCLIFF.
My lord?
                KING RICHARD.
        The sun will not be seen to-day;
The sky doth frown and lour upon our army.
I would these dewy tears were from the ground.
Not shine to-day! Why, what is that to me
More than to Richmond? for the selfsame heaven
That frowns on me looks sadly upon him.
            Enter NORFOLK.
                DUKE OF NORFOLK.
Arm, arm, my lord; the foe vaunts in the field.
                KING RICHARD.
Come, bustle, bustle;—caparison my horse;
Call up Lord Stanley, bid him bring his power:
I will lead forth my soldiers to the plain,

And thus my battle shall be ordered:—
My foreward shall be drawn out all in length,
Consisting equally of horse and foot;
Our archers shall be placed in the midst:
John Duke of Norfolk, Thomas Earl of Surrey,
Shall have the leading of this foot and horse.
They thus directed, we will follow
In the main battle; whose puissance on either side
Shall be well winged with our chiefest horse.
This, and Saint George to boot!—What think'st
    thou, Norfolk?
                DUKE OF NORFOLK.
A good direction, warlike sovereign.
This found I on my tent this morning.
                        [*He sheweth him a paper.*
            KING RICHARD [*reads*].
'Jockey of Norfolk, be not too bold,
For Dickon thy master is bought and sold.'
A thing devised by the enemy.—
Go, gentlemen, every man unto his charge:
Let not our babbling dreams affright our souls;
Conscience is but a word that cowards use,
Devised at first to keep the strong in awe:
Our strong arms be our conscience, swords our
    law.
March on, join bravely, let us to't pell-mell;
If not to heaven, then hand in hand to hell.—
            His oration to his ARMY.
What shall I say more than I have inferr'd?
Remember whom you are to cope withal;—
A sort of vagabonds, rascals, and runaways,
A scum of Bretons, and base lackey peasants,
Whom their o'er-cloyed country vomits forth
To desperate ventures and assured destruction.
You sleeping safe, they bring to you unrest;
You having lands, and blest with beauteous
    wives,
They would distrain the one, distain the other.
And who doth lead them but a paltry fellow,
Long kept in Bretagne at our mother's cost?
A milk-sop, one that never in his life
Felt so much cold as over shoes in snow?
Let's whip these stragglers o'er the seas again;
Lash hence these overweening rags of France,
These famisht beggars, weary of their lives;
Who, but for dreaming on this fond exploit,
For want of means, poor rats, had hang'd them-
    selves:
If we be conquer'd, let men conquer us,
And not these bastard Bretons; whom our fathers
Have in their own land beaten, bobb'd, and
    thumpt,
And, on record, left them the heirs of shame.
Shall these enjoy our lands? lie with our wives?
Ravish our daughters? [*Drum afar off.*] Hark! I
    hear their drum.
Fight, gentlemen of England! fight, bold yeomen!
Draw, archers, draw your arrows to the head!
Spur your proud horses hard, and ride in blood;
Amaze the welkin with your broken staves!
            Enter a MESSENGER.
What says Lord Stanley? will he bring his power?
                MESSENGER.
My lord, he doth deny to come.
                KING RICHARD.
Off with his son George's head!

DUKE OF NORFOLK.
My lord, the enemy is past the marsh:
After the battle let George Stanley die.
KING RICHARD.
A thousand hearts are great within my bosom:
Advance our standards, set upon our foes;
Our ancient word of courage, fair Saint George,
Inspire us with the spleen of fiery dragons!
Upon them! Victory sits on our helms.   [*Exeunt.*

SCENE IV.

Another part of the field.

Alarum: excursions. Enter NORFOLK *and*
FORCES; *to him* CATESBY.

SIR WILLIAM CATESBY.
RESCUE, my Lord of Norfolk, rescue, rescue!
The king enacts more wonders than a man,
Daring an opposite to every danger:
His horse is slain, and all on foot he fights,
Seeking for Richmond in the throat of death.
Rescue, fair lord, or else the day is lost!
Alarums. Enter KING RICHARD.
KING RICHARD.
A horse! a horse! my kingdom for a horse!
SIR WILLIAM CATESBY.
Withdraw, my lord; I'll help you to a horse.
KING RICHARD.
Slave, I have set my life upon a cast,
And I will stand the hazard of the die:
I think there be six Richmonds in the field;
Five have I slain to-day instead of him.
A horse! a horse! my kingdom for a horse!
    [*Exeunt.*

SCENE V.

Another part of the field.

Alarum. Enter RICHARD *and* RICHMOND; *they*
fight. RICHARD *is slain. Retreat and flourish.*
Re-enter RICHMOND, DERBY *bearing the*
crown, with divers other LORDS.

EARL OF RICHMOND.
GOD and your arms be praised, victorious
friends!
The day is ours, the bloody dog is dead.
EARL OF DERBY.
Courageous Richmond, well hast thou acquit thee.

Lo, here, this long-usurped royalty
From the dead temples of this bloody wretch
Have I pluckt off, to grace thy brows withal:
Wear it, enjoy it, and make much of it.
EARL OF RICHMOND.
Great God of heaven, say Amen to all!—
But, tell me, is young George Stanley living?
EARL OF DERBY.
He is, my lord, and safe in Leicester town;
Whither, if't please you, we may now withdraw
us.
EARL OF RICHMOND.
What men of name are slain on either side?
EARL OF DERBY.
John Duke of Norfolk, Walter Lord Ferrers,
Sir Robert Brakenbury, and Sir William Brand-
on.
EARL OF RICHMOND.
Inter their bodies as becomes their births:
Proclaim a pardon to the soldiers fled
That in submission will return to us:
And then, as we have ta'en the sacrament,
We will unite the white rose and the red.
Smile heaven upon this fair conjunction,
That long have frown'd upon their enmity!—
What traitor hears me, and says not Amen?
England hath long been mad and scarr'd herself;
The brother blindly shed the brother's blood,
The father rashly slaughter'd his own son,
The son, compell'd, been butcher to the sire:
All this divided York and Lancaster,
Divided in their dire division,
O, now let Richmond and Elizabeth,
The true succeeders of each royal house,
By God's fair ordinance conjoin together!
And let their heirs—God, if Thy will be so—
Enrich the time to come with smooth-faced peace,
With smiling plenty, and fair prosperous days!
Abate the edge of traitors, gracious Lord,
That would reduce these bloody days again,
And make poor England weep in streams of
blood!
Let them not live to taste this land's increase
That would with treason wound this fair land's
peace!
Now civil wounds are stopt, peace lives agen:
That she may long live here, God say Amen!
    [*Exeunt.*

KING JOHN

DRAMATIS PERSONAE

KING JOHN.

PRINCE HENRY, *his son; afterwards King Henry III.*

ARTHUR, *Duke of Bretagne, son to Geffrey, late Duke of Bretagne, the elder brother to King John.*

WILLIAM MARESHALL, *Earl of Pembroke.*

GEFFREY FITZ-PETER, *Earl of Essex, chief-justiciary of England.*

WILLIAM LONGSWORD, *Earl of Salisbury.*

ROBERT BIGOT, *Earl of Norfolk.*

HUBERT DE BURGH, *chamberlain to the King.*

ROBERT FAULCONBRIDGE, *son to Sir Robert Faulconbridge.*

PHILIP FAULCONBRIDGE, *his half-brother, bastard son to King Richard the First.*

JAMES GURNEY, *servant to Lady Faulconbridge.*

PETER *of Pomfret, a prophet.*

PHILIP, *King of France.*

LOUIS, *the Dauphin.*

ARCHDUKE OF AUSTRIA.

CARDINAL PANDULPH, *the Pope's legate.*

MELUN, *a French lord.*

CHATILLON, *ambassador from France to King John.*

ELINOR, *widow of King Henry II. and mother to King John.*

CONSTANCE, *mother to Arthur.*

BLANCH, *daughter to Alphonso, King of Castile, and niece to King John.*

LADY FAULCONBRIDGE, *mother to the Bastard and Robert Faulconbridge.*

LORDS, CITIZENS OF ANGIERS, SHERIFF, HER-ALDS, OFFICERS, SOLDIERS, MESSENGERS, *and other* ATTENDANTS.

SCENE—*Sometimes in England, and sometimes in France.*

ACT I. SCENE I.

KING JOHN'S *palace.*

Enter KING JOHN, QUEEN ELINOR, PEM-BROKE, ESSEX, SALISBURY, *and others, with* CHATILLON.

KING JOHN.

NOW, say, Chatillon, what would France with us?

CHATILLON.

Thus, after greeting, speaks the King of France,
In my behaviour, to the majesty,
The borrow'd majesty of England here.

QUEEN ELINOR.

A strange beginning:—borrow'd majesty!

KING JOHN.

Silence, good mother; hear the embassy.

CHATILLON.

Philip of France, in right and true behalf
Of thy deceased brother Geffrey's son,
Arthur Plantagenet, lays most lawful claim
To this fair island and the territories,—
To Ireland, Poictiers, Anjou, Touraine, Maine;
Desiring thee to lay aside the sword
Which sways usurpingly these several titles,
And put the same into young Arthur's hand,
Thy nephew and right royal sovereign.

KING JOHN.

What follows, if we disallow of this?

CHATILLON.

The proud control of fierce and bloody war,
To enforce these rights so forcibly withheld.

KING JOHN.

Here have we war for war, and blood for blood,
Controlment for controlment: so answer France.

CHATILLON.

Then take my king's defiance from my mouth,
The furthest limit of my embassy.

KING JOHN.

Bear mine to him, and so depart in peace:

Be thou as lightning in the eyes of France;
For ere thou canst report I will be there,
The thunder of my cannon shall be heard:
So, hence! Be thou the trumpet of our wrath,
And sullen presage of your own decay.—
An honourable conduct let him have:—
Pembroke, look to't.—Farewell, Chatillon.

[*Exeunt* CHATILLON *and* PEMBROKE.

QUEEN ELINOR.

What now, my son! have I not ever said
How that ambitious Constance would not cease
Till she had kindled France and all the world
Upon the right and party of her son?
This might have been prevented and made whole
With very easy arguments of love;
Which now the manage of two kingdoms must
With fearful bloody issue arbitrate.

KING JOHN.

Our strong possession and our right for us.

QUEEN ELINOR [*aside to* KING JOHN].

Your strong possession much more than your right,
Or else it must go wrong with you and me:
So much my conscience whispers in your ear,
Which none but heaven and you and I shall hear.

Enter a SHERIFF.

ESSEX.

My liege, here is the strangest controversy,
Come from the country to be judged by you,
That e'er I heard: shall I produce the men?

KING JOHN.

Let them approach.—— [*Exit* SHERIFF.
Our abbeys and our priories shall pay
This expedition's charge.

Enter SHERIFF, *with* ROBERT FAULCONBRIDGE, *and* PHILIP *his bastard brother.*

What men are you?

BASTARD.

Your faithful subject I, a gentleman
Born in Northamptonshire, and eldest son,

As I suppose, to Robert Faulconbridge,
A soldier, by the honour-giving hand
Of Cœur-de-lion knighted in the field.

KING JOHN.

What art thou?

ROBERT FAULCONBRIDGE.

The son and heir to that same Faulconbridge.

KING JOHN.

Is that the elder, and art thou the heir?
You came not of one mother, then, it seems.

BASTARD.

Most certain of one mother, mighty king;
That is well known; and, as I think, one father:
But for the certain knowledge of that truth,
I put you o'er to heaven and to my mother:
Of that I doubt, as all men's children may.

QUEEN ELINOR.

Out on thee, rude man! thou dost shame thy
    mother
And wound her honour with this diffidence.

BASTARD.

I, madam? no, I have no reason for it,—
That is my brother's plea, and none of mine;
The which if he can prove, a' pops me out
At least from fair five hundred pound a year:
Heaven guard my mother's honour and my land!

KING JOHN.

A good blunt fellow.—Why, being younger born,
Doth he lay claim to thine inheritance?

BASTARD.

I know not why, except to get the land.
But once he slander'd me with bastardy:
But whe'r I be as true begot or no,
That still I lay upon my mother's head;
But, that I am as well begot, my liege,—
Fair fall the bones that took the pains for me!—
Compare our faces, and be judge yourself.
If old Sir Robert did beget us both
And were our father and this son like him,
O old Sir Robert, father, on my knee
I give heaven thanks I was not like to thee!

KING JOHN.

Why, what a madcap hath heaven lent us here!

QUEEN ELINOR.

He hath a trick of Coeur-de-lion's face;
The accent of his tongue affecteth him:
Do you not read some tokens of my son
In the large composition of this man?

KING JOHN.

Mine eye hath well examined his parts,
And finds them perfect Richard.—Sirrah, speak,
What doth move you to claim your brother's land?

BASTARD.

Because he hath a half-face, like my father,
With that half-face would he have all my land:
A half-faced groat five hundred pound a year!

ROBERT FAULCONBRIDGE.

My gracious liege, when that my father lived,
Your brother did employ my father much,—

BASTARD.

Well, sir, by this you cannot get my land:
Your tale must be, how he employ'd my mother.

ROBERT FAULCONBRIDGE.

And once dispatcht him in an embassy
To Germany, there with the emperor
To treat of high affairs touching that time.

Th'advantage of his absence took the king,
And in the meantime sojourn'd at my father's;
Where how he did prevail, I shame to speak,
But truth is truth: large lengths of seas and shores
Between my father and my mother lay,—
As I have heard my father speak himself,—
When this same lusty gentleman was got.
Upon his death-bed he by will bequeath'd
His lands to me; and took it, on his death,
That this, my mother's son, was none of his;
And if he were, he came into the world
Full fourteen weeks before the course of time.
Then, good my liege, let me have what is mine,
My father's land, as was my father's will.

KING JOHN.

Sirrah, your brother is legitimate;
Your father's wife did after wedlock bear him;
And if she did play false, the fault was hers;
Which fault lies on the hazards of all husbands
That marry wives. Tell me, how if my brother,
Who, as you say, took pains to get this son,
Had of your father claim'd this son for his?
In sooth, good friend, your father might have
    kept
This calf, bred from his cow, from all the world;
In sooth, he might: then, if he were my brother's,
My brother might not claim him; nor your father,
Being none of his, refuse him: this concludes,—
My mother's son did get your father's heir;
Your father's heir must have your father's land.

ROBERT FAULCONBRIDGE.

Shall, then, my father's will be of no force
To dispossess that child which is not his?

BASTARD.

Of no more force to dispossess me, sir,
Than was his will to get me, as I think.

QUEEN ELINOR.

Whether hadst thou rather be a Faulconbridge,
And like thy brother, to enjoy thy land,
Or the reputed son of Cœur-de-lion,
Lord of thy presence, and no land beside?

BASTARD.

Madam, an if my brother had my shape,
And I had his, Sir Robert's his, like him;
And if my legs were two such riding-rods,
My arms such eel-skins stuft; my face so thin,
That in mine ear I durst not stick a rose,
Lest men should say, 'Look, where three-
    farthings goes!'
And, to his shape, were heir to all this land,—
Would I might never stir from off this place,
I'ld give it every foot to have this face;
I would not be Sir Nob in any case.

QUEEN ELINOR.

I like thee well: wilt thou forsake thy fortune,
Bequeath thy land to him, and follow me?
I am a soldier, and now bound to France.

BASTARD.

Brother, take you my land, I'll take my chance:
Your face hath got five hundred pound a year;
Yet sell your face for five pence, and 'tis dear.—
Madam, I'll follow you unto the death.

QUEEN ELINOR.

Nay, I would have you go before me thither.

BASTARD.

Our country manners give our betters way.

KING JOHN.
What is thy name?
                BASTARD.
Philip, my liege,—so is my name begun,—
Philip, good old Sir Robert's wife's eldest son.
                KING JOHN.
From henceforth bear his name whose form thou
      bear'st:
Kneel thou down Philip, but rise more great,—
Arise Sir Richard and Plantagenet.
                BASTARD.
Brother by the mother's side, give me your hand:
My father gave me honour, yours gave land.—
Now blessed be the hour, by night or day,
When I was got, Sir Robert was away!
                QUEEN ELINOR.
The very spirit of Plantagenet!—
I am thy grandam, Richard; call me so.
                BASTARD.
Madam, by chance, but not by truth: what
      though?
Something about, a little from the right,
   In at the window, or else o'er the hatch;
Who dares not stir by day must walk by night;
   And have is have, however men do catch;
Near or far off, well won is still well shot;
And I am I, howe'er I was begot.
                KING JOHN.
Go, Faulconbridge: now hast thou thy desire;
A landless knight makes thee a landed squire.—
Come, madam,—and come, Richard; we must
      speed
For France, for France; for it is more than need.
                BASTARD.
Brother, adieu: good fortune come to thee!
For thou wast got i' th' way of honesty.
            [Exeunt all but BASTARD.
A foot of honour better than I was;
But many a many foot of land the worse.
Well, now can I make any Joan a lady:—
'Good den, Sir Richard:'—'God-a-mercy,
      fellow;'—
And if his name be George, I'll call him Peter;
For new-made honour doth forget men's names,—
'Tis too respective and too sociable
For your conversion. Now your traveller,—
He and his toothpick at my worship's mess;
And when my knightly stomach is sufficed,
Why then I suck my teeth, and catechize
My picked man of countries:—'My dear sir,'
Thus, leaning on mine elbow, I begin,
'I shall beseech you'—that is question now;
And then comes answer like an Absey-book:—
'O sir,' says answer, 'at your best command;
At your employment; at your service, sir:'
'No, sir,' says question, 'I, sweet sir, at yours:'
And so, ere answer knows what question
      would,—
Saving in dialogue of compliment,
And talking of the Alps and Apennines,
The Pyrenean and the river Po,—
It draws toward supper in conclusion so.
But this is worshipful society,
And fits the mounting spirit like myself;
For he is but a bastard to the time,
That doth not smack of observation;

And so am I, whether I smack or no;
And not alone in habit and device,
Exterior form, outward accoutrement,
But from the inward motion to deliver
Sweet, sweet, sweet poison for the age's tooth:
Which, though I will not practise to deceive,
Yet to avoid deceit, I mean to learn;
For it shall strew the footsteps of my rising.—
But who comes in such haste in riding-robes?
What woman-post is this? hath she no husband,
That will take pains to blow a horn before her?
      Enter LADY FAULCONBRIDGE and JAMES
                GURNEY.
O me! it is my mother.—How now, good lady!
What brings you here to court so hastily?
            LADY FAULCONBRIDGE.
Where is that slave, thy brother? where is he,
That holds in chase mine honour up and down?
                BASTARD.
My brother Robert? old Sir Robert's son?
Colbrand the giant, that same mighty man?
Is it Sir Robert's son that you seek so?
            LADY FAULCONBRIDGE.
Sir Robert's son! Ay, thou unreverend boy,
Sir Robert's son: why scorn'st thou at Sir Robert?
He is Sir Robert's son; and so art thou.
                BASTARD.
James Gurney, wilt thou give us leave awhile?
                JAMES GURNEY.
Good leave, good Philip.
                BASTARD.
            Philip?—sparrow!—James,
There's toys abroad: anon I'll tell thee more.
                        [Exit GURNEY.
Madam, I was not old Sir Robert's son;
Sir Robert might have eat his part in me
Upon Good Friday, and ne'er broke his fast:
Sir Robert could do well: marry to confess,
Could he get me? Sir Robert could not do it,—
We know his handiwork:—therefore, good
      mother
To whom am I beholding for these limbs?
Sir Robert never holp to make this leg.
            LADY FAULCONBRIDGE.
Hast thou conspired with thy brother too,
That for thine own gain shouldst defend mine
      honour?
What means this scorn, thou most untoward
      knave?
                BASTARD.
Knight, knight, good mother,—Basilisco-like:
What! I am dubb'd; I have it on my shoulder.
But, mother, I am not Sir Robert's son;
I have disclaim'd Sir Robert and my land;
Legitimation, name, and all is gone:
Then, good my mother, let me know my father,—
Some proper man, I hope: who was it, mother?
            LADY FAULCONBRIDGE.
Hast thou denied thyself a Faulconbridge?
                BASTARD.
As faithfully as I deny the devil.
            LADY FAULCONBRIDGE.
King Richard Coeur-de-lion was thy father:
By long and vehement suit I was seduced
To make room for him in my husband's bed:—
Heaven lay not my transgression to my charge!—

Thou art the issue of my dear offence,
Which was so strongly urged, past my defence.
BASTARD.
Now, by this light, were I to get again,
Madam, I would not wish a better father.
Some sins do bear their privilege on earth,
And so doth yours; your fault was not your folly:
Needs must you lay your heart at his dispose,
Subjected tribute to commanding love,
Against whose fury and unmatched force
The aweless lion could not wage the fight,
Nor keep his princely heart from Richard's hand:
He that perforce robs lions of their hearts
May easily win a woman's. Ay, my mother,
With all my heart I thank thee for my father!
Who lives and dares but say, thou didst not well
When I was got, I'll send his soul to hell.
Come, lady, I will show thee to my kin;
   And they shall say, when Richard me begot,
If thou hadst said him nay, it had been sin:
   Who says it was, he lies; I say 'twas not.
                    [*Exeunt.*

ACT II. SCENE I.

France. Before the walls of Angiers.

Enter, on one side, PHILIP, *king of France,*
LOUIS, CONSTANCE, ARTHUR, *and* FORCES;
on the other, the ARCHDUKE OF AUSTRIA *and*
FORCES.

KING PHILIP.
BEFORE Angiers well met, brave Austria.—
Arthur, that great forerunner of thy blood,
Richard, that robb'd the lion of his heart,
And fought the holy wars in Palestine,
By this brave duke came early to his grave:
And, for amends to his posterity,
At our importance hither is he come,
To spread his colours, boy, in thy behalf;
And to rebuke the usurpation
Of thy unnatural uncle, English John:
Embrace him, love him, give him welcome hither.
ARTHUR.
God shall forgive you Cœur-de-lion's death
The rather that you give his offspring life,
Shadowing their right under your wings of war:
I give you welcome with a powerless hand,
But with a heart full of unstained love:
Welcome before the gates of Angiers, duke.
KING PHILIP.
A noble boy! Who would not do thee right?
ARCHDUKE OF AUSTRIA.
Upon thy cheek lay I this zealous kiss,
As seal to this indenture of my love;—
That to my home I will no more return,
Till Angiers, and the right thou hast in France,
Together with that pale, that white-faced shore,
Whose foot spurns back the ocean's roaring tides,
And coops from other lands her islanders,—
Even till that England, hedged in with the main,
That water-walled bulwark, still secure
And confident from foreign purposes,—
Even till that utmost corner of the west
Salute thee for her king: till then, fair boy,
Will I not think of home, but follow arms.

CONSTANCE.
O, take his mother's thanks, a widow's thanks,
Till your strong hand shall help to give him
   strength
To make a more requital to your love!
ARCHDUKE OF AUSTRIA.
The peace of heaven is theirs that lift their
   swords
In such a just and charitable war.
KING PHILIP.
Well, then, to work: our cannon shall be bent
Against the brows of this resisting town.—
Call for our chiefest men of discipline,
To cull the plots of best advantages:
We'll lay before this town our royal bones,
Wade to the market-place in Frenchmen's blood,
But we will make it subject to this boy.
CONSTANCE.
Stay for an answer to your embassy,
Lest unadvised you stain your swords with
   blood:
My Lord Chatillon may from England bring
That right in peace, which here we urge in war;
And then we shall repent each drop of blood
That hot rash haste so indirectly shed.
KING PHILIP.
A wonder, lady,—lo, upon thy wish,
Our messenger Chatillon is arrived!
Enter CHATILLON.
What England says, say briefly, gentle lord;
We coldly pause for thee; Chatillon, speak.
CHATILLON.
Then turn your forces from this paltry siege,
And stir them up against a mightier task.
England, impatient of your just demands,
Hath put himself in arms: the adverse winds,
Whose leisure I have stay'd, have given him
   time
To land his legions all as soon as I;
His marches are expedient to this town,
His forces strong, his soldiers confident.
With him along is come the mother-queen,
An Ate, stirring him to blood and strife;
With her her niece, the Lady Blanch of Spain;
With them a bastard of the king's deceased:
And all th' unsettled humours of the land,—
Rash, inconsiderate, fiery voluntaries,
With ladies' faces and fierce dragons' spleens,—
Have sold their fortunes at their native homes,
Bearing their birthrights proudly on their backs,
To make a hazard of new fortunes here:
In brief, a braver choice of dauntless spirits,
Than now the English bottoms have waft o'er,
Did never float upon the swelling tide,
To do offence and scathe in Christendom.
The interruption of their churlish drums
                  [*Drum beats.*
Cuts off more circumstance: they are at hand,
To parley or to fight; therefore prepare.
KING PHILIP.
How much unlookt for is this expedition!
ARCHDUKE OF AUSTRIA.
By how much unexpected, by so much
We must awake endeavour for defence;
For courage mounteth with occasion:
Let them be welcome, then; we are prepared.

Enter KING JOHN, ELINOR, BLANCH, BAS-
TARD, LORDS, *and* FORCES.

KING JOHN.

Peace be to France, if France in peace permit
Our just and lineal entrance to our own!
If not, bleed France, and peace ascend to heaven!
Whiles we, God's wrathful agent, do correct
Their proud contempt that beats His peace to
　heaven.

KING PHILIP.

Peace be to England, if that war return
From France to England, there to live in peace!
England we love; and for that England's sake
With burden of our armour here we sweat.
This toil of ours should be a work of thine;
But thou from loving England art so far,
That thou hast under-wrought his lawful king,
Cut off the sequence of posterity,
Out-faced infant state, and done a rape
Upon the maiden virtue of the crown.
Look here upon thy brother Geffrey's face;—
These eyes, these brows, were moulded out of his:
This little abstract doth contain that large
Which died in Geffrey; and the hand of time
Shall draw this brief into as huge a volume.
That Geffrey was thy elder brother born,
And this his son; England was Geffrey's right,
And this is Geffrey's: in the name of God,
How comes it, then, that thou art call'd a king,
When living blood doth in these temples beat,
Which owe the crown that thou o'ermasterest?

KING JOHN.

From whom hast thou this great commission,
To draw my answer from thy articles?　　[France,

KING PHILIP.

From that supernal judge, that stirs good thoughts
In any breast of strong authority,
To look into the blots and stains of right.
That judge hath made me guardian to this boy:
Under whose warrant I impeach thy wrong;
And by whose help I mean to chastise it.

KING JOHN.

Alack, thou dost usurp authority.

KING PHILIP.

Excuse,—it is to beat usurping down.

QUEEN ELINOR.

Who is it thou dost call usurper, France?

CONSTANCE.

Let me make answer;—thy usurping son.

QUEEN ELINOR.

Out, insolent! thy bastard shall be king,
That thou mayst be a queen, and check the world!

CONSTANCE.

My bed was ever to thy son as true
As thine was to thy husband; and this boy
Liker in feature to his father Geffrey
Than thou and John in manners,—being as like
As rain to water, or devil to his dam.
My boy a bastard! By my soul, I think
His father never was so true begot:
It cannot be, an if thou wert his mother.

QUEEN ELINOR.

There's a good mother, boy, that blots thy father.

CONSTANCE.

There's a good grandam, boy, that would blot
　thee.

ARCHDUKE OF AUSTRIA.

Peace!

BASTARD.

　　Hear the crier.

ARCHDUKE OF AUSTRIA.

　　　　　　What the devil art thou?

BASTARD.

One that will play the devil, sir, with you,
An a' may catch your hide and you alone:
You are the hare of whom the proverb goes,
Whose valour plucks dead lions by the beard:
I'll smoke your skin-coat, an I catch you right;
Sirrah, look to't; i'faith, I will, i'faith.

BLANCH.

O, well did he become that lion's robe
That did disrobe the lion of that robe!

BASTARD.

It lies as sightly on the back of him
As great Alcides' shows upon an ass:—
But, ass, I'll take that burden from your back,
Or lay on that shall make your shoulders crack.

ARCHDUKE OF AUSTRIA.

What cracker is this same that deafs our ears
With this abundance of superfluous breath?—
King Philip, determine what we shall do straight.

KING PHILIP.

Women and fools, break off your conference.
King John, this is the very sum of all,—
England and Ireland, Anjou, Touraine, Maine,
In right of Arthur do I claim of thee:
Wilt thou resign them, and lay down thy arms?

KING JOHN.

My life as soon:—I do defy thee, France.—
Arthur of Bretagne, yield thee to my hand;
And, out of my dear love, I'll give thee more
Than e'er the coward hand of France can win:
Submit thee, boy.

QUEEN ELINOR.

　　Come to thy grandam, child.

CONSTANCE.

Do, child, go to it grandam, child;
Give grandam kingdom, and it grandam will
Give it a plum, a cherry, and a fig:
There's a good grandam.

ARTHUR.

　　　　　　Good my mother, peace
I would that I were low laid in my grave:
I am not worth this coil that's made for me.

QUEEN ELINOR.

His mother shames him so, poor boy, he weeps.

CONSTANCE.

Now shame upon you, whe'r she does or no!
His grandam's wrongs, and not his mother's
　shames,
Draw those heaven-moving pearls from his poor
　eyes,
Which heaven shall take in nature of a fee;
Ay, with these crystal beads heaven shall be
　bribed
To do him justice, and revenge on you.

QUEEN ELINOR.

Thou monstrous slanderer of heaven and earth!

CONSTANCE.

Thou monstrous injurer of heaven and earth!
Call me not slanderer; thou and thine usurp
The dominations, royalties, and rights

Of this oppressed boy: this is thy eld'st son's son,
Infortunate in nothing but in thee:
Thy sins are visited in this ˉoor child;
The canon of the law is laid on him,
Being but the second generation
Removed from thy sin-conceiving womb.
> KING JOHN.
Bedlam, have done.
> CONSTANCE.
I have but this to say,—
That he is not only plagued for her sin,
But God hath made her sin and her the plague
On this removed issue, plagued for her,
And with her plague; her sin his injury,
Her injury the beadle to her sin;
All punisht in the person of this child,
And all for her; a plague upon her!
> QUEEN ELINOR.
Thou unadvised scold, I can produce
A will that bars the title of thy son.
> CONSTANCE.
Ay, who doubts that? a will! a wicked will;
A woman's will; a canker'd grandam's will!
> KING PHILIP.
Peace, lady! pause, or be more temperate:
It ill beseems this presence to cry aim
To these ill-tuned repetitions.—
Some trumpet summon hither to the walls
These men of Angiers: let us hear them speak,
Whose title they admit, Arthur's or John's.
Trumpet sounds.   Enter CITIZENS *upon the walls.*
> FIRST CITIZEN.
Who is it that hath warn'd us to the walls?
> KING PHILIP.
'Tis France, for England.
> KING JOHN.
England, for itself:—
You men of Angiers, and my loving subjects,—
> KING PHILIP.
You loving men of Angiers, Arthur's subjects,
Our trumpet call'd you to this gentle parle,—
> KING JOHN.
For our advantage; therefore hear us first.
These flags of France, that are advanced here
Before the eye and prospect of your town,
Have hither marcht to your endamagement:
The cannons have their bowels full of wrath,
And ready mounted are they to spit forth
Their iron indignation 'gainst your walls:
All preparation for a bloody siege
And merciless proceeding by these French
Confronts your city's eyes, your winking gates;
And, but for our approach, those sleeping stones,
That as a waist doth girdle you about,
By the compulsion of their ordinance
By this time from their fixed beds of lime
Had been dishabited, and wide havoc made
For bloody power to rush upon your peace.
But, on the sight of us, your lawful king,—
Who painfully, with much expedient march,
Have brought a countercheck before your gates,
To save unscratcht your city's threaten'd
    cheeks,—
Behold, the French, amazed, vouchsafe a parle;
And now, instead of bullets wrapt in fire,
To make a shaking fever in your walls,

They shoot but calm words, folded up in smoke,
To make a faithless error in your ears:
Which trust accordingly, kind citizens,
And let us in, your king; whose labour'd spirits,
Forwearied in this action of swift speed,
Crave harbourage within your city-walls.
> KING PHILIP.
When I have said, make answer to us both.
Lo, in this right hand, whose protection
Is most divinely vow'd upon the right
Of him it holds, stands young Plantagenet,
Son to the elder brother of this man,
And king o'er him, and all that he enjoys:
For this down-trodden equity, we tread
In warlike march these greens before your town;
Being no further enemy to you
Than the constraint of hospitable zeal
In the relief of this oppressed child
Religiously provokes. Be pleased, then,
To pay that duty which you truly owe
To him that owes it, namely, this young prince:
And then our arms, like to a muzzled bear,
Save in aspect, hath all offence seal'd up:
Our cannons' malice vainly shall be spent
Against th'invulnerable clouds of heaven;
And with a blessed and unvext retire,
With unhackt swords and helmets all unbruised,
We will bear home that lusty blood again,
Which here we came to spout against your town,
And leave your children, wives, and you in peace.
But if you fondly pass our proffer'd offer,
'Tis not the roundure of your old-faced walls
Can hide you from our messengers of war,
Though all these English, and their discipline,
Were harbour'd in their rude circumference.
Then, tell us, shall your city call us lord,
In that behalf which we have challenged it?
Or shall we give the signal to our rage,
And stalk in blood to our possession?
> FIRST CITIZEN.
In brief, we are the king of England's subjects:
For him, and in his right, we hold this town.
> KING JOHN.
Acknowledge, then, the king, and let me in.
> FIRST CITIZEN.
That can we not; but he that proves the king,
To him will we prove loyal: till that time
Have we ramm'd up our gates against the world.
> KING JOHN.
Doth not the crown of England prove the king?
And if not that, I bring you witnesses,
Twice fifteen thousand hearts of England's
    breed,—
> BASTARD.
Bastards, and else.
> KING JOHN.
To verify our title with their lives.
> KING PHILIP.
As many and as well-born bloods as those,—
> BASTARD.
Some bastards too.
> KING PHILIP.
Stand in his face, to contradict his claim.
> FIRST CITIZEN.
Till you compound whose right is worthiest,
We for the worthiest hold the right from both.

KING JOHN.

Then God forgive the sin of all those souls
That to their everlasting residence,
Before the dew of evening fall, shall fleet,
In dreadful trial of our kingdom's king!

KING PHILIP.

Amen, amen!--Mount, chevaliers! to arms!

BASTARD.

Saint George, that swinged the dragon, and e'er
    since
Sits on his horse back at mine hostess' door,
Teach us some fence!—[to AUSTRIA] Sirrah,
    were I at home,
At your den, sirrah, with your lioness,
I'ld set an ox-head to your lion's hide,
And make a monster of you.

ARCHDUKE OF AUSTRIA.

                Peace! no more.

BASTARD.

O, tremble, for you hear the lion roar!

KING JOHN.

Up higher to the plain; where we'll set forth
In best appointment all our regiments.

BASTARD.

Speed, then, to take advantage of the field.

KING PHILIP.

It shall be so;—[to LOUIS] and at the other hill
Command the rest to stand.—God and our right!

    [*Exeunt, severally, the English and French*
    KINGS, *&c.*
Here, after excursions, enter the HERALD OF
FRANCE, *with trumpets, to the gates.*

FRENCH HERALD.

You men of Angiers, open wide your gates,
And let young Arthur, Duke of Bretagne, in,
Who, by the hand of France, this day hath made
Much work for tears in many an English mother,
Whose sons lie scatter'd on the bleeding ground:
Many a widow's husband grovelling lies,
Coldly embracing the discolour'd earth;
And victory, with little loss, doth play
Upon the dancing banners of the French,
Who are at hand, triumphantly display'd,
To enter conquerors, and to proclaim
Arthur of Bretagne England's king and yours.

    Enter ENGLISH HERALD, *with trumpet.*

ENGLISH HERALD.

Rejoice, you men of Angiers, ring your bells;
King John, your king and England's, doth
    approach,
Commander of this hot malicious day:
Their armours, that marcht hence so silver-
    bright,
Hither return all gilt with Frenchmen's blood;
There stuck no plume in any English crest
That is removed by a staff of France;
Our colours do return in those same hands
That did display them when we first marcht
    forth;
And, like a jolly troop of huntsmen, come
Our lusty English, all with purpled hands,
Dyed in the dying slaughter of their foes:
Open your gates, and give the victors way.

FIRST CITIZEN.

Heralds, from off our towers we might behold,
From first to last, the onset and retire

Of both your armies; whose equality
By our best eyes cannot be censured:
Blood hath bought blood, and blows have
    answer'd blows;
Strength matcht with strength, and power con-
    fronted power:
Both are alike; and both alike we like.
One must prove greatest: while they weight so
    even,
We hold our town for neither; yet for both.

    Enter the two KINGS, *with their powers, severally.*

KING JOHN.

France, hast thou yet more blood to cast away?
Say, shall the current of our right run on?
Whose passage, vext with thy impediment,
Shall leave his native channel, and o'erswell
With course disturb'd even thy confining shores,
Unless thou let his silver water keep
A peaceful progress to the ocean.

KING PHILIP.

England, thou hast not saved one drop of blood,
In this hot trial, more than we of France;
Rather, lost more: and by this hand I swear,
That sways the earth this climate overlooks,
Before we will lay down our just-borne arms,
We'll put thee down, 'gainst whom these arms
    we bear,
Or add a royal number to the dead,
Gracing the scroll that tells of this war's loss
With slaughter coupled to the name of kings.

BASTARD.

Ha, majesty! how high thy glory towers,
When the rich blood of kings is set on fire!
O, now doth Death line his dead chaps with
    steel;
The swords of soldiers are his teeth, his fangs;
And now he feasts, mousing the flesh of men,
In undetermined differences of kings.—
Why stand these royal fronts amazed thus?
Cry 'havoc,' kings! back to the stained field,
You equal-potent, fiery-kindled spirits!
Then let confusion of one part confirm
The other's peace; till then, blows, blood, and
    death!

KING JOHN.

Whose party do the townsmen yet admit?

KING PHILIP.

Speak, citizens, for England; who's your king?

FIRST CITIZEN.

The king of England, when we know the king.

KING PHILIP.

Know him in us, that here hold up his right.

KING JOHN.

In us, that are our own great deputy,
And bear possession of our person here;
Lord of our presence, Angiers, and of you.

FIRST CITIZEN.

A greater power than we denies all this;
And till it be undoubted, we do lock
Our former scruple in our strong-barr'd gates;
King'd of our fears, until our fears, resolved,
Be by some certain king purged and deposed.

BASTARD.

By heaven, these scroyles of Angiers flout you,
    kings,
And stand securely on their battlements,

As in a theatre, whence they gape and point
At your industrious scenes and acts of death.
Your royal presences be ruled by me:—
Do like the mutines of Jerusalem,
Be friends a while, and both conjointly bend
Your sharpest deeds of malice on this town:
By east and west let France and England mount
Their battering cannon, charged to the mouths,
Till their soul-fearing clamours have brawl'd
    down
The flinty ribs of this contemptuous city:
I'ld play incessantly upon these jades,
Even till unfenced desolation
Leave them as naked as the vulgar air.
That done, dissever your united strengths,
And part your mingled colours once again;
Turn face to face, and bloody point to point;
Then, in a moment, Fortune shall cull forth
One of one side her happy minion,
To whom in favour she shall give the day,
And kiss him with a glorious victory.
How like you this wild counsel, mighty states?
Smacks it not something of the policy?
            KING JOHN.
Now, by the sky that hangs above our heads,
I like it well.—France, shall we knit our powers,
And lay this Angiers even with the ground;
Then, after, fight who shall be king of it?
            BASTARD.
An if thou hast the mettle of a king,—
Being wrong'd, as we are, by this peevish town,—
Turn thou the mouth of thy artillery,
As we will ours, against these saucy walls;
And when that we have dasht them to the
    ground,
Why, then defy each other, and, pell-mell,
Make work upon ourselves, for heaven or hell.
            KING PHILIP.
Let it be so.—Say, where will you assault?
            KING JOHN.
We from the west will send destruction
Into this city's bosom.
            ARCHDUKE OF AUSTRIA.
I from the north.
            KING PHILIP.
          Our thunder from the south
Shall rain their drift of bullets on this town.
            BASTARD [aside].
O prudent discipline! From north to south,—
Austria and France shoot in each other's mouth:
I'll stir them to it.—Come, away, away!
            FIRST CITIZEN.
Hear us, great kings: vouchsafe awhile to stay,
And I shall show you peace and fair-faced league;
Win you this city without stroke or wound;
Rescue those breathing lives to die in beds,
That here come sacrifices for the field:
Persever not, but hear me, mighty kings.
            KING JOHN.
Speak on, with favour; we are bent to hear.
            FIRST CITIZEN.
That daughter there of Spain, the Lady Blanch,
Is niece to England:—look upon the years
Of Louis the Dauphin and that lovely maid:
If lusty love should go in quest of beauty,
Where should he find it fairer than in Blanch?

If zealous love should go in search of virtue,
Where should he find it purer than in Blanch?
If love ambitious sought a match of birth,
Whose veins bound richer blood than Lady
    Blanch?
Such as she is, in beauty, virtue, birth,
Is the young Dauphin every way complete,—
If not complete, O, say he is not she;
And she again wants nothing, to name want,
If want it be not, that she is not he:
He is the half part of a blessed man,
Left to be finished by such a she;
And she a fair divided excellence,
Whose fulness of perfection lies in him.
O, two such silver currents, when they join,
Do glorify the banks that bound them in;
And two such shores to two such streams made
    one,
Two such controlling bounds shall you be, kings,
To these two princes, if you marry them.
This union shall do more than battery can
To our fast-closed gates; for, at this match,
With swifter spleen than powder can enforce,
The mouth of passage shall we fling wide ope,
And give you entrance: but without this match,
The sea enraged is not half so deaf,
Lions more confident, mountains and rocks
More free from motion; no, not Death himself
In mortal fury half so peremptory,
As we to keep this city.
            BASTARD.
          Here's a stay,
That shakes the rotten carcass of old Death
Out of his rags! Here's a large mouth, indeed,
That spits forth death and mountains, rocks and
    seas;
Talks as familiarly of roaring lions
As maids of thirteen do of puppy-dogs!
What cannoneer begot this lusty blood?
He speaks plain cannon,—fire and smoke and
    bounce;
He gives the bastinado with his tongue:
Our ears are cudgell'd; not a word of his
But buffets better than a fist of France:
Zounds, I was never so bethumpt with words
Since I first call'd my brother's father dad.
            QUEEN ELINOR [aside to KING JOHN].
Son, list to this conjunction, make this match;
Give with our niece a dowry large enough:
For by this knot thou shalt so surely tie
Thy now-unsured assurance to the crown,
That yon green boy shall have no sun to ripe
The bloom that promiseth a mighty fruit.
I see a yielding in the looks of France;
Mark, how they whisper: urge them while their
    souls
Are capable of this ambition,
Lest zeal, now melted by the windy breath
Of soft petitions, pity, and remorse,
Cool and congeal again to what it was.
            FIRST CITIZEN.
Why answer not the double majesties
This friendly treaty of our threaten'd town?
            KING PHILIP.
Speak England first, that hath been forward first
To speak unto this city: what say you?

KING JOHN.
If that the Dauphin there, thy princely son,
Can in this book of beauty read 'I love,'
Her dowry shall weigh equal with a queen:
For Anjou, and fair Touraine, Maine, Poictiers,
And all that we upon this side the sea—
Except this city now by us besieged—
Find liable to our crown and dignity,
Shall gild her bridal bed; and make her rich
In titles, honours, and promotions,
As she in beauty, education, blood,
Holds hand with any princess of the world.
KING PHILIP.
What say'st thou, boy? look in the lady's face.
LOUIS.
I do, my lord; and in her eye I find
A wonder, or a wondrous miracle,
The shadow of myself form'd in her eye;
Which, being but the shadow of your son,
Becomes a sun, and makes your son a shadow:
I do protest I never loved myself,
Till now infixed I beheld myself
Drawn in the flattering table of her eye.
                    [*Whispers with* BLANCH.
BASTARD [*aside*].
Drawn in the flattering table of her eye!—
   Hang'd in the frowning wrinkle of her brow!—
And quarter'd in her heart!—he doth espy
   Himself love's traitor:—this is pity now,
That, hang'd and drawn and quarter'd, there
In such a love so vile a lout as he.   [should be
BLANCH.
My uncle's will in this respect is mine:
If he see aught in you that makes him like,
That any thing he sees, which moves his liking,
I can with ease translate it to my will;
Or if you will, to speak more properly,
I will enforce it easily to my love.
Further I will not flatter you, my lord,
That all I see in you is worthy love,
Than this,—that nothing do I see in you,
Though churlish thoughts themselves should be
   your judge,
That I can find should merit any hate.
KING JOHN.
What say these young ones?—What say you, my
   niece?
BLANCH.
That she is bound in honour still to do
What you in wisdom still vouchsafe to say.
KING JOHN.
Speak then, Prince Dauphin; can you love this
   lady?
LOUIS.
Nay, ask me if I can refrain from love;
For I do love her most unfeignedly.
KING JOHN.
Then do I give Volquessen, Touraine, Maine,
Poictiers, and Anjou, these five provinces,
With her to thee; and this addition more,
Full thirty thousand marks of English coin.—
Philip of France, if thou be pleased withal,
Command thy son and daughter to join hands.
KING PHILIP.
It likes us well.—Young princes, close your
   hands.

ARCHDUKE OF AUSTRIA.
And your lips too; for I am well assured
That I did so when I was first assured.
KING PHILIP.
Now, citizens of Angiers, ope your gates,
Let in that amity which you have made;
For at Saint Mary's chapel presently
The rites of marriage shall be solemnized.—
Is not the Lady Constance in this troop?
I know she is not; for this match made up
Her presence would have interrupted much:
Where is she and her son? tell me, who knows.
LOUIS.
She is sad and passionate at your highness' tent.
KING PHILIP.
And, by my faith, this league that we have made
Will give her sadness very little cure.—
Brother of England, how may we content
This widow lady? In her right we came;
Which we, God knows, have turn'd another way,
To our own vantage.
KING JOHN.
         We will heal up all;
For we'll create young Arthur Duke of Bretagne
And Earl of Richmond; and this rich fair town
We make him lord of.—Call the Lady Constance;
Some speedy messenger bid her repair
To our solemnity:—I trust we shall,
If not fill up the measure of her will,
Yet in some measure satisfy her so
That we shall stop her exclamation.
Go we, as well as haste will suffer us,
To this unlookt-for, unprepared pomp.
                    [*Exeunt all but* BASTARD.
BASTARD.
Mad world! mad kings! mad composition!
John, to stop Arthur's title in the whole,
Hath willingly departed with a part;
And France,—whose armour conscience buckled
   on,
Whom zeal and charity brought to the field
As God's own soldier,—rounded in the ear
With that same purpose-changer, that sly devil;
That broker, that still breaks the pate of faith;
That daily break-vow; he that wins of all,
Of kings, of beggars, old men, young men,
   maids,—
Who having no external thing to lose
But the word 'maid,' cheats the poor maid of that;
That smooth-faced gentleman, tickling Com-
   modity,—
Commodity, the bias of the world;
The world, who of itself is peised well,
Made to run even upon even ground,
Till this advantage, this vile-drawing bias,
This sway of motion, this Commodity,
Makes it take head from all indifferency,
From all direction, purpose, course, intent:
And this same bias, this Commodity,
This bawd, this broker, this all-changing word,
Clapt on the outward eye of fickle France,
Hath drawn him from his own determined aid,
From a resolved and honourable war,
To a most base and vile-concluded peace.—
And why rail I on this Commodity?
But for because he hath not woo'd me yet:

Not that I have the power to clutch my hand,
When his fair angels would salute my palm;
But for my hand, as unattempted yet,
Like a poor beggar, raileth on the rich.
Well, whiles I am a beggar, I will rail,
And say, There is no sin but to be rich:
And being rich, my virtue then shall be,
To say, There is no vice but beggary:
Since kings break faith upon commodity,
Gain, be my lord,—for I will worship thee! [*Exit.*

ACT III. SCENE I.

France.   The French KING'S *tent.*

Enter CONSTANCE, ARTHUR, *and* SALISBURY.

CONSTANCE.

GONE to be married! gone to swear a peace!
False blood to false blood join'd! gone to be
friends!
Shall Louis have Blanch? and Blanch those
provinces?
It is not so; thou hast misspoke, misheard;
Be well advised, tell o'er thy tale again:
It cannot be; thou dost but say 'tis so:
I trust I may not trust thee; for thy word
Is but the vain breath of a common man:
Believe me, I do not believe thee, man;
I have a king's oath to the contrary.
Thou shalt be punisht for thus frighting me,
For I am sick, and capable of fears;
Opprest with wrongs, and therefore full of fears;
A widow, husbandless, subject to fears;
A woman, naturally born to fears;
And though thou now confess thou didst but jest,
With my vext spirits I cannot take a truce,
But they will quake and tremble all this day.
What dost thou mean by shaking of thy head?
Why dost thou look so sadly on my son?
What means that hand upon that breast of thine?
Why holds thine eye that lamentable rheum,
Like a proud river peering o'er his bounds?
Be these sad signs confirmers of thy words?
Then speak again,—not all thy former tale,
But this one word, whether thy tale be true.

EARL OF SALISBURY.

As true as I believe you think them false
That give you cause to prove my saying true.

CONSTANCE.

O, if thou teach me to believe this sorrow,
Teach thou this sorrow how to make me die;
And let belief and life encounter so
As doth the fury of two desperate men,
Which in the very meeting fall and die!—
Louis marry Blanch! O boy, then where art thou?
France friend with England! what becomes of
me?—
Fellow, be gone: I cannot brook thy sight;
This news hath made thee a most ugly man.

EARL OF SALISBURY.

What other harm have I, good lady, done,
But spoke the harm that is by others done?

CONSTANCE.

Which harm within itself so heinous is,
As it makes harmful all that speak of it.

ARTHUR.

I do beseech you, madam, be content.

CONSTANCE.

If thou, that bidd'st me be content, wert grim,
Ugly, and slanderous to thy mother's womb,
Full of unpleasing blots and sightless stains,
Lame, foolish, crooked, swart, prodigious,
Patcht with foul moles and eye-offending marks,
I would not care, I then would be content;
For then I should not love thee; no, nor thou
Become thy great birth, nor deserve a crown.
But thou art fair; and at thy birth, dear boy,
Nature and Fortune join'd to make thee great:
Of Nature's gifts thou mayst with lilies boast
And with the half-blown rose: but Fortune, O!
She is corrupted, changed, and won from thee;
Sh' adulterates hourly with thine uncle John;
And with her golden hand hath pluckt on
France
To tread down fair respect of sovereignty,
And made his majesty the bawd to theirs.
France is a bawd to Fortune and King John,
That strumpet Fortune, that usurping John!
Tell me, thou fellow, is not France forsworn?
Envenom him with words: or get thee gone,
And leave those woes alone which I alone
Am bound to under-bear.

EARL OF SALISBURY.

               Pardon me, madam,
I may not go without you to the kings.

CONSTANCE.

Thou mayst, thou shalt; I will not go with thee:
I will instruct my sorrows to be proud;
For grief is proud, and makes his owner stout,
To me, and to the state of my great grief,
Let kings assemble; for my grief's so great,
That no supporter but the huge firm earth
Can hold it up: here I and sorrows sit;
Here is my throne, bid kings come bow to it.
              [*Seats herself on the ground.*

Enter KING JOHN, KING PHILIP, LOUIS,
BLANCH, ELINOR, BASTARD, AUSTRIA, *and*
ATTENDANTS.

KING PHILIP.

'Tis true, fair daughter; and this blessed day
Ever in France shall be kept festival;
To solemnize this day the glorious sun
Stays in his course, and plays the alchemist,
Turning with splendour of his precious eye
The meagre cloddy earth to glittering gold:
The yearly course that brings this day about
Shall never see it but a holiday.

CONSTANCE.

A wicked day, and not a holy day!—   [*Rising.*
What hath this day deserved? what hath it done,
That it in golden letters should be set
Among the high tides in the calendar?
Nay, rather turn this day out of the week,
This day of shame, oppression, perjury:
Or, if it must stand still, let wives with child
Pray that their burdens may not fall this day,
Lest that their hopes prodigiously be crost:
But on this day let seamen fear no wrack;
No bargains break that are not this day made:
This day, all things begun come to ill end,—
Yes, faith itself to hollow falsehood change!

KING PHILIP.

By heaven, lady, you shall have no cause

148

To curse the fair proceedings of this day:
Have I not pawn'd to you my majesty?
CONSTANCE.
You have beguiled me with a counterfeit [tried,
Resembling majesty; which, being toucht and
Proves valueless: you are forsworn, forsworn;
You came in arms to spill mine enemies' blood,
But now in arms you strengthen it with yours:
The grappling vigour and rough frown of war
Is cold in amity and painted peace,
And our oppression hath made up this league.
Arm, arm, you heavens, against these perjured
  kings!
A widow cries; be husband to me, heavens!
Let not the hours of this ungodly day
Wear out the day in peace; but, ere sunset,
Set armed discord 'twixt these perjured kings!
Hear me, O, hear me!
ARCHDUKE OF AUSTRIA.
      Lady Constance, peace!
CONSTANCE.
War! war! no peace! peace is to me a war.
O Limoges! O Austria! thou dost shame [coward!
That bloody spoil: thou slave, thou wretch, thou
Thou little valiant, great in villainy!
Thou ever strong upon the stronger side!
Thou Fortune's champion that dost never fight
But when her humorous ladyship is by
To teach thee safety! thou art perjured too,
And sooth'st up greatness. What a fool art thou,
A ramping fool, to brag, and stamp, and swear,
Upon my party! Thou cold-blooded slave,
Hast thou not spoke like thunder on my side?
Been sworn my soldier? bidding me depend
Upon thy stars, thy fortune, and thy strength?
And dost thou now fall over to my foes?
Thou wear a lion's hide! doff it for shame,
And hang a calf's-skin on those recreant limbs.
ARCHDUKE OF AUSTRIA.
O, that a man should speak those words to me!
BASTARD.
And hang a calf's-skin on those recreant limbs.
ARCHDUKE OF AUSTRIA.
Thou darest not say so, villain, for thy life.
BASTARD.
And hang a calf's-skin on those recreant limbs.
KING JOHN.
We like not this; thou dost forget thyself.
KING PHILIP.
Here comes the holy legate of the Pope.
Enter PANDULPH, *attended.*
CARDINAL PANDULPH.
Hail, you anointed deputies of heaven!
To thee, King John, my holy errand is.
I Pandulph, of fair Milan cardinal,
And from Pope Innocent the legate here,
Do in his name religiously demand,
Why thou against the church, our holy mother,
So wilfully dost spurn, and, force perforce,
Keep Stephen Langton, chosen archbishop
Of Canterbury, from that holy see?
This, in our foresaid holy father's name,
Pope Innocent, I do demand of thee.
KING JOHN.
What earthly name to interrogatories
Can task the free breath of a sacred king?

Thou canst not, cardinal, devise a name
So slight, unworthy, and ridiculous,
To charge me to an answer, as the Pope.
Tell him this tale; and from the mouth of England
Add thus much more,—that no Italian priest
Shall tithe or toll in our dominions;
But as we, under heaven, are supreme head,
So, under Him, that great supremacy,
Where we do reign, we will alone uphold,
Without th'assistance of a mortal hand:
So tell the Pope; all reverence set apart
To him and his usurpt authority.
KING PHILIP.
Brother of England, you blaspheme in this.
KING JOHN.
Though you, and all the kings of Christendom,
Are led so grossly by this meddling priest,
Dreading the curse that money may buy out;
And by the merit of vile gold, dross, dust,
Purchase corrupted pardon of a man,
Who in that sale sells pardon from himself;
Though you and all the rest, so grossly led,
This juggling witchcraft with revenue cherish;
Yet I, alone, alone do me oppose
Against the Pope, and count his friends my foes.
CARDINAL PANDULPH.
Then, by the lawful power that I have,
Thou shalt stand cursed and excommunicate:
And blessed shall he be that doth revolt
From his allegiance to an heretic;
And meritorious shall that hand be call'd,
Canonized, and worship as a saint,
That takes away by any secret course
Thy hateful life.
CONSTANCE.
      O, lawful let it be
That I have room with Rome to curse awhile!
Good father cardinal, cry thou amen
To my keen curses; for without my wrong
There is no tongue hath power to curse him right.
CARDINAL PANDULPH.
There's law and warrant, lady, for my curse.
CONSTANCE.
And for mine too: when law can do no right,
Let it be lawful that law bar no wrong:
Law cannot give my child his kingdom here;
For he that holds his kingdom holds the law:
Therefore, since law itself is perfect wrong,
How can the law forbid my tongue to curse?
CARDINAL PANDULPH.
Philip of France, on peril of a curse,
Let go the hand of that arch-heretic;
And raise the power of France upon his head,
Unless he do submit himself to Rome.
QUEEN ELINOR.
Look'st thou pale, France? do not let go thy hand.
CONSTANCE.
Look to that, devil; lest that France repent,
And by disjoining hands, hell lose a soul.
ARCHDUKE OF AUSTRIA.
King Philip, listen to the cardinal.
BASTARD.
And hang a calf's-skin on his recreant limbs.
ARCHDUKE OF AUSTRIA.
Well, ruffian, I must pocket up these wrongs,
Because—

BASTARD.
Your breeches best may carry them.
KING JOHN.
Philip, what say'st thou to the cardinal?
CONSTANCE.
What should he say, but as the cardinal?
LOUIS.
Bethink you, father; for the difference
Is, purchase of a heavy curse from Rome,
Or the light loss of England for a friend:
Forgo the easier.
BLANCH.
That's the curse of Rome.
CONSTANCE.
O Louis, stand fast! the devil tempts thee here
In likeness of a new untrimmed bride.
BLANCH.
The Lady Constance speaks not from her faith,
But from her need.
CONSTANCE.
O, if thou grant my need,
Which only lives but by the death of faith,
That need must needs infer this principle,—
That faith would live again by death of need!
O, then, tread down my need, and faith mounts up;
Keep my need up, and faith is trodden down!
KING JOHN.
The king is moved, and answers not to this.
CONSTANCE.
O, be removed from him, and answer well!
ARCHDUKE OF AUSTRIA.
Do so, King Philip; hang no more in doubt.
BASTARD.
Hang nothing but a calf's-skin, most sweet lout.
KING PHILIP.
I am perplext, and know not what to say.
CARDINAL PANDULPH.
What canst thou say but will perplex thee more,
If thou stand excommunicate and cursed?
KING PHILIP.
Good reverend father, make my person yours,
And tell me how you would bestow yourself.
This royal hand and mine are newly knit,
And the conjunction of our inward souls
Married in league, coupled and linkt together
With all religious strength and sacred vows;
The latest breath that gave the sound of words
Was deep-sworn faith, peace, amity, true love
Between our kingdoms and our royal selves;
And even before this truce, but new before,—
No longer than we well could wash our hands,
To clap this royal bargain up of peace,—
Heaven knows, they were besmear'd and over-stain'd
With slaughter's pencil, where revenge did paint
The fearful difference of incensed kings:
And shall these hands, so lately purged of blood,
So newly join'd in love, so strong in both,
Unyoke this seizure and this kind regreet?
Play fast and loose with faith? so jest with heaven,
Make such unconstant children of ourselves,
As now again to snatch our palm from palm;
Unswear faith sworn; and on the marriage-bed
Of smiling peace to march a bloody host,
And make a riot on the gentle brow

Of true sincerity? O, holy sir,
My reverend father, let it not be so!
Out of your grace devise, ordain, impose
Some gentle order; and then we shall be blest
To do your pleasure, and continue friends.
CARDINAL PANDULPH.
All form is formless, order orderless,
Save what is opposite to England's love.
Therefore, to arms! be champion of our church!
Or let the church, our mother, breathe her curse,—
A mother's curse,—on her revolting son.
France, thou mayst hold a serpent by the tongue,
A chafed lion by the mortal paw,
A fasting tiger safer by the tooth,   [hold.
Than keep in peace that hand which thou dost
KING PHILIP.
I may disjoin my hand, but not my faith.
CARDINAL PANDULPH.
So makest thou faith an enemy to faith;
And, like a civil war, sett'st oath to oath,
Thy tongue against thy tongue. O, let thy vow
First made to heaven, first be to heaven per-form'd,—
That is, to be the champion of our church!
What since thou sworest is sworn against thyself,
And may not be performed by thyself:
For that which thou hast sworn to do amiss
Is not amiss when it is truly done;
And being not done, where doing tends to ill,
The truth is then most done, not doing it:
The better act of purposes mistook
Is to mistake again; though indirect,
Yet indirection thereby grows direct,
And falsehood falsehood cures; as fire cools fire
Within the scorched veins of one new-burn'd.
It is religion that doth make vows kept;
But thou hast sworn against religion:
By what thou swear'st against the thing thou swear'st;
And makest an oath the surety for thy truth
Against an oath: the truth thou art unsure
To swear, swears only not to be forsworn;
Else what a mockery should it be to swear!
But thou dost swear only to be forsworn;
And most forsworn, to keep what thou dost swear.
Therefore thy later vows against thy first
Is in thyself rebellion to thyself;
And better conquest never canst thou make
Than arm thy constant and thy nobler parts
Against these giddy loose suggestions:
Upon which better part our prayers come in,
If thou vouchsafe them; but if not, then know
The peril of our curses light on thee,
So heavy as thou shalt not shake them off,
But in despair die under their black weight.
ARCHDUKE OF AUSTRIA.
Rebellion, flat rebellion!
BASTARD.
Will't not be?
Will not a calf's-skin stop that mouth of thine?
LOUIS.
Father, to arms!
BLANCH.
Upon thy wedding day?
Against the blood that thou hast married?

150

What, shall our feast be kept with slaughter'd
　men?
Shall braying trumpets and loud churlish
　drums,—
Clamours of hell,—be measures to our pomp?
O husband, hear me!—ay, alack, how new
Is husband in my mouth!—even for that name,
Which till this time my tongue did ne'er pro-
　nounce,
Upon my knee I beg, go not to arms
Against mine uncle.
　　　　　CONSTANCE.
　　　　　　O, upon my knee,
Made hard with kneeling, I do pray to thee,
Thou virtuous Dauphin, alter not the doom
Forethought by heaven!
　　　　　BLANCH.
Now shall I see thy love: what motive may
Be stronger with thee than the name of wife?
　　　　　CONSTANCE.
That which upholdeth him that thee upholds,
His honour:—O, thine honour, Louis, thine
　honour!
　　　　　LOUIS.
I muse your majesty doth seem so cold,
When such profound respects do pull you on.
　　　　CARDINAL PANDULPH.
I will denounce a curse upon his head.
　　　　　KING PHILIP.
Thou shalt not need.—England, I will fall from
　thee.
　　　　　CONSTANCE.
O fair return of banisht majesty!
　　　　QUEEN ELINOR.
O foul revolt of French inconstancy!
　　　　　KING JOHN.
France, thou shalt rue this hour within this hour.
　　　　　BASTARD.
Old Time the clock-setter, that bald sexton
　Time,
Is it as he will? well, then, France shall rue.
　　　　　BLANCH.
The sun's o'ercast with blood: fair day, adieu!
Which is the side that I must go withal?
I am with both: each army hath a hand;
And in their rage, I having hold of both,
They whirl asunder and dismember me.
Husband, I cannot pray that thou mayst win;
Uncle, I needs must pray that thou mayst lose;
Father, I may not wish the fortune thine;
Grandam, I will not wish thy wishes thrive:
Whoever wins, on that side shall I lose;
Assured loss before the match be play'd.
　　　　　LOUIS.
Lady, with me; with me thy fortune lies.
　　　　　BLANCH.
There where my fortune lives, there my life dies.
　　　　　KING JOHN.
Cousin, go draw our puissance together.
　　　　　　　　　[Exit BASTARD.
France, I am burn'd up with inflaming wrath;
A rage whose heat hath this condition,
That nothing can allay, nothing but blood,—
The blood, the dearest-valued blood of France.
　　　　　KING PHILIP.
Thy rage shall burn thee up, and thou shalt turn

To ashes, ere our blood shall quench that fire:
Look to thyself, thou art in jeopardy.
　　　　　KING JOHN.
No more than he that threats.—To arms let's hie!
　　　　　　　　　[Exeunt.

SCENE II.

The same.　Plains near Angiers.

Alarums, excursions.　Enter BASTARD, *with*
AUSTRIA'S *head.*

　　　　　BASTARD.
NOW, by my life, this day grows wondrous hot;
　　Some airy devil hovers in the sky,
And pours down mischief.—Austria's head lie
　there,
While Philip breathes.
　　Enter KING JOHN, ARTHUR, *and* HUBERT.
　　　　　KING JOHN.
Hubert, keep this boy.—Philip, make up:
My mother is assailed in our tent,
And ta'en, I fear.
　　　　　BASTARD.
　　　　　My lord, I rescued her;
Her highness is in safety, fear you not:
But on, my liege; for very little pains
Will bring this labour to an happy end.　[Exeunt.

SCENE III.

The same.

Alarums, excursions, retreat.　Enter KING JOHN,
ELINOR, ARTHUR, BASTARD, HUBERT, *and*
LORDS.

　　　　　KING JOHN [*to* QUEEN ELINOR].
SO shall it be; your Grace shall stay behind,
　　So strongly guarded.—[*to* ARTHUR] Cousin,
　　look not sad:
Thy grandam loves thee; and thy uncle will
As dear be to thee as thy father was.
　　　　　ARTHUR.
O, this will make my mother die with grief!
　　　　　KING JOHN [*to* BASTARD].
Cousin, away for England: haste before:
And ere our coming, see thou shake the bags
Of hoarding abbots; their imprison'd angels
Set thou at liberty: the fat ribs of peace
Must by the hungry now be fed upon:
Use our commission in his utmost force.
　　　　　BASTARD.
Bell, book, and candle shall not drive me back,
When gold and silver becks me to come on.
I leave your highness.—Grandam, I will pray—
If ever I remember to be holy—
For your fair safety; so, I kiss your hand.
　　　　　QUEEN ELINOR.
Farewell, gentle cousin.
　　　　　KING JOHN.
　　　　　Coz, farewell.
　　　　　　　　　[Exit BASTARD.
　　　　　QUEEN ELINOR.
Come hither, little kinsman; hark, a word.
　　　　　　　　　[Takes ARTHUR aside.
　　　　　KING JOHN.
Come hither, Hubert. O my gentle Hubert,
We owe thee much! within this wall of flesh

There is a soul counts thee her creditor,
And with advantage means to pay thy love:
And, my good friend, thy voluntary oath
Lives in this bosom, dearly cherished.
Give me thy hand. I had a thing to say,—
But I will fit it with some better time.
By heaven, Hubert, I am almost ashamed
To say what good respect I have of thee.
HUBERT DE BURGH.
I am much bounden to your majesty.
KING JOHN.
Good friend, thou hast no cause to say so yet:
But thou shalt have; and creep time ne'er so slow,
Yet it shall come for me to do thee good.
I had a thing to say,—but let it go:
The sun is in the heaven, and the proud day,
Attended with the pleasures of the world,
Is all too wanton and too full of gauds
To give me audience:—if the midnight bell
Did, with his iron tongue and brazen mouth,
Sound one into the drowsy ear of night;
If this same were a churchyard where we stand,
And thou possessed with a thousand wrongs;
Or if that surly spirit, melancholy,
Had baked thy blood, and made it heavy-thick,
Which else runs tickling up and down the veins,
Making that idiot, laughter, keep men's eyes,
And strain their cheeks to idle merriment,—
A passion hateful to my purposes;
Or if that thou couldst see me without eyes,
Hear me without thine ears, and make reply
Without a tongue, using conceit alone,
Without eyes, ears, and harmful sound of words;
Then, in despite of brooded watchful day,
I would into thy bosom pour my thoughts:
But, ah, I will not!—yet I love thee well;
And, by my troth, I think thou lovest me well.
HUBERT DE BURGH.
So well, that what you bid me undertake,
Though that my death were adjunct to my act,
By heaven, I would do it.
KING JOHN.
Do not I know thou wouldst?
Good Hubert, Hubert, Hubert, throw thine eye
On yon young boy: I'll tell thee what, my friend,
He is a very serpent in my way;
And wheresoe'er this foot of mine doth tread,
He lies before me:—dost thou understand me?
Thou art his keeper.
HUBERT DE BURGH.
And I'll keep him so,
That he shall not offend your majesty.
KING JOHN.
Death.
HUBERT DE BURGH.
My lord?
KING JOHN.
A grave.
HUBERT DE BURGH.
He shall not live.
KING JOHN.
Enough.
I could be merry now. Hubert, I love thee;
Well, I'll not say what I intend for thee:
Remember.—Madam, fare you well:
I'll send these powers o'er to your majesty.

QUEEN ELINOR.
My blessing go with thee!
KING JOHN.
For England, cousin, go:
Hubert shall be your man, attend on you
With all true duty.—On toward Calais, ho!
[*Exeunt.*

SCENE IV.
The same.   The French KING'S *tent.*

Enter KING PHILIP, LOUIS, PANDULPH, *and*
ATTENDANTS.

KING PHILIP.
SO, by a roaring tempest on the flood,
A whole armado of convented sail
Is scatter'd and disjoin'd from fellowship.
CARDINAL PANDULPH.
Courage and comfort! all shall yet go well.
KING PHILIP.
What can go well, when we have run so ill?
Are we not beaten? Is not Angiers lost?
Arthur ta'en prisoner? divers dear friends slain?
And bloody England into England gone,
O'erbearing interruption, spite of France?
LOUIS.
What he hath won, that hath he fortified:
So hot a speed with such advice disposed,
Such temperate order in so fierce a course,
Doth want example: who hath read or heard
Of any kindred action like to this?
KING PHILIP.
Well could I bear that England had this praise,
So we could find some pattern of our shame.—
Look, who comes here! a grave unto a soul;
Holding th'eternal spirit, against her will,
In the vile prison of afflicted breath.
Enter CONSTANCE.
I prithee, lady, go away with me.
CONSTANCE.
Lo, now! now see the issue of your peace!
KING PHILIP.
Patience, good lady! comfort, gentle Constance!
CONSTANCE.
No, I defy all counsel, all redress,
But that which ends all counsel, true redress,
Death, death:—O amiable lovely death!
Thou odoriferous stench! sound rottenness!
Arise forth from the couch of lasting night,
Thou hate and terror to prosperity,
And I will kiss thy detestable bones;
And put my eyeballs in thy vaulty brows;
And ring these fingers with thy household
worms;
And stop this gap of breath with fulsome dust;
And be a carrion monster like thyself:
Come, grin on me; and I will think thou smilest,
And buss thee as thy wife! Misery's love,
O, come to me!
KING PHILIP.
O fair affliction, peace!
CONSTANCE.
No, no, I will not, having breath to cry:
O, that my tongue were in the thunder's mouth!
Then with a passion would I shake the world;
And rouse from sleep that fell anatomy

Which cannot hear a lady's feeble voice,
Which scorns a modern invocation.
           CARDINAL PANDULPH.
Lady, you utter madness, and not sorrow.
           CONSTANCE.
Thou art not holy to belie me so;
I am not mad: this hair I tear is mine;
My name is Constance; I was Geffrey's wife;
Young Arthur is my son, and he is lost:
I am not mad;—I would to heaven I were!
For then 'tis like I should forget myself:
O, if I could, what grief should I forget!—
Preach some philosophy to make me mad,
And thou shalt be canonized, cardinal;
For, being not mad, but sensible of grief,
My reasonable part produces reason
How I may be deliver'd of these woes,
And teaches me to kill or hang myself:
If I were mad, I should forget my son,
Or madly think a babe of clouts were he:
I am not mad; too well, too well I feel
The different plague of each calamity.
           KING PHILIP.
Bind up those tresses.—O, what love I note
In the fair multitude of those her hairs!
Where but by chance a silver drop hath fall'n,
Even to that drop ten thousand wiry friends
Do glue themselves in sociable grief;
Like true, inseparable, faithful loves,
Sticking together in calamity.
           CONSTANCE.
To England, if you will.
           KING PHILIP.
           Bind up your hairs.
           CONSTANCE.
Yes, that I will; and wherefore will I do it?
I tore them from their bonds, and cried aloud,
'O, that these hands could so redeem my son,
As they have given these hairs their liberty!'
But now I envy at their liberty,
And will again commit them to their bonds,
Because my poor child is a prisoner.—
And, father cardinal, I have heard you say
That we shall see and know our friends in heaven:
If that be true, I shall see my boy again;
For since the birth of Cain, the first male child,
To him that did but yesterday suspire,
There was not such a gracious creature born.
But now will canker-sorrow eat my bud,
And chase the native beauty from his cheek,
And he will look as hollow as a ghost,
As dim and meagre as an ague's fit;
And so he'll die; and, rising so again,
When I shall meet him in the court of heaven
I shall not know him: therefore never, never
Must I behold my pretty Arthur more.
           CARDINAL PANDULPH.
You hold too heinous a respect of grief.
           CONSTANCE.
He talks to me that never had a son.
           KING PHILIP.
You are as fond of grief as of your child.
           CONSTANCE.
Grief fills the room up of my absent child,
Lies in his bed, walks up and down with me,
Puts on his pretty looks, repeats his words,

Remembers me of all his gracious parts,
Stuffs out his vacant garments with his form;
Then have I reason to be fond of grief.
Fare you well: had you such a loss as I,
I could give better comfort than you do.—
I will not keep this form upon my head,
When there is such disorder in my wit.
O Lord! my boy, my Arthur, my fair son!
My life, my joy, my food, my all the world!
My widow-comfort, and my sorrows' cure! [Exit.
           KING PHILIP.
I fear some outrage, and I'll follow her.   [Exit.
           LOUIS.
There's nothing in this world can make me joy:
Life is as tedious as a twice-told tale
Vexing the dull ear of a drowsy man;
And bitter shame hath spoil'd the sweet world's
    taste,
That it yields naught but shame and bitterness.
           CARDINAL PANDULPH.
Before the curing of a strong disease,
Even in the instant of repair and health,
The fit is strongest; evils that take leave,
On their departure most of all show evil:
What have you lost by losing of this day?
           LOUIS.
All days of glory, joy, and happiness.
           CARDINAL PANDULPH.
If you had won it, certainly you had.
No, no; when Fortune means to men most good,
She looks upon them with a threatening eye.
'Tis strange to think how much King John hath
    lost
In this which he accounts so clearly won:
Are not you grieved that Arthur is his prisoner?
           LOUIS.
As heartily as he is glad he hath him.
           CARDINAL PANDULPH.
Your mind is all as youthful as your blood.
Now hear me speak with a prophetic spirit;
For even the breath of what I mean to speak
Shall blow each dust, each straw, each little rub,
Out of the path which shall directly lead
Thy foot to England's throne; and therefore
    mark.
John hath seized Arthur; and it cannot be,
That, whiles warm life plays in that infant's veins,
The misplaced John should entertain an hour,
One minute, nay, one quiet breath of rest:
A sceptre snatcht with an unruly hand
Must be as boisterously maintain'd as gain'd;
And he that stands upon a slippery place
Makes nice of no vile hold to stay him up:
That John may stand, then Arthur needs must
    fall;
So be it, for it cannot be but so.
           LOUIS.
But what shall I gain by young Arthur's fall?
           CARDINAL PANDULPH.
You, in the right of Lady Blanch your wife,
May then make all the claim that Arthur did.
           LOUIS.
And lose it, life and all, as Arthur did.
           CARDINAL PANDULPH.
How green you are, and fresh in this old world!
John lays you plots; the times conspire with you;

For he that steeps his safety in true blood
Shall find but bloody safety and untrue.
This act, so evilly borne, shall cool the hearts
Of all his people, and freeze up their zeal,
That none so small advantage shall step forth
To check his reign, but they will cherish it;
No natural exhalation in the sky,
No scape of nature, no distemper'd day,
No common wind, no customed event,
But they will pluck away his natural cause,
And call them meteors, prodigies, and signs,
Abortives, presages, and tongues of heaven,
Plainly denouncing vengeance upon John.

LOUIS.
May be he will not touch young Arthur's life,
But hold himself safe in his prisonment.

CARDINAL PANDULPH.
O, sir, when he shall hear of your approach,
If that young Arthur be not gone already,
Even at that news he dies; and then the hearts
Of all his people shall revolt from him,
And kiss the lips of unacquainted change;
And pick strong matter of revolt and wrath
Out of the bloody fingers' ends of John.
Methinks I see this hurly all on foot:
And, O, what better matter breeds for you
Than I have named!—The bastard Faulcon-
    bridge
Is now in England, ransacking the church,
Offending charity: if but a dozen French
Were there in arms, they would be as a call
To train ten thousand English to their side;
Or as a little snow, tumbled about,
Anon becomes a mountain. O noble Dauphin,
Go with me to the king:—'tis wonderful
What may be wrought out of their discontent,
Now that their souls are topful of offence:
For England go:—I will whet on the king.

LOUIS.
Strong reasons make strong actions: let us go:
If you say ay, the king will not say no. [*Exeunt.*

ACT IV. SCENE I.

A room in a castle.

Enter HUBERT *and* EXECUTIONERS.

HUBERT DE BURGH.
HEAT me these irons hot; and look thou stand
    Within the arras: when I strike my foot
Upon the bosom of the ground, rush forth,
And bind the boy which you shall find with me
Fast to the chair: be heedful: hence, and watch.

FIRST EXECUTIONER.
I hope your warrant will bear out the deed.

HUBERT DE BURGH.
Uncleanly scruples! fear not you: look to't.
    [*Exeunt* EXECUTIONERS.
Young lad, come forth; I have to say with you.

Enter ARTHUR.

ARTHUR.
Good morrow, Hubert.

HUBERT DE BURGH.
        Good morrow, little prince.

ARTHUR.
As little prince, having so great a title
To be more prince, as may be.—You are sad.

HUBERT DE BURGH.
Indeed, I have been merrier.

ARTHUR.
        Mercy on me!
Methinks no body should be sad but I:
Yet, I remember, when I was in France,
Young gentlemen would be as sad as night,
Only for wantonness. By my christendom,
So I were out of prison, and kept sheep,
I should be as merry as the day is long;
And so I would be here, but that I doubt
My uncle practises more harm to me:
He is afraid of me, and I of him:
Is it my fault that I was Geffrey's son?
No, indeed, is't not; and I would to heaven
I were your son, so you would love me, Hubert.

HUBERT DE BURGH [*aside*].
If I talk to him, with his innocent prate
He will awake my mercy, which lies dead:
Therefore I will be sudden and dispatch.

ARTHUR.
Are you sick, Hubert? you look pale to-day:
In sooth, I would you were a little sick,
That I might sit all night and watch with you:
I warrant I love you more than you do me.

HUBERT DE BURGH [*aside*].
His words do take possession of my bosom.—
Read here, young Arthur. [*Showing a paper.*
    [*Aside*] How now, foolish rheum!
Turning dispiteous torture out of door!
I must be brief, lest resolution drop
Out at mine eyes in tender womanish tears.—
Can you not read it, is it not fair writ?

ARTHUR.
Too fairly, Hubert, for so foul effect:
Must you with hot irons burn out both mine eyes?

HUBERT DE BURGH.
Young boy, I must.

ARTHUR.
    And will you?

HUBERT DE BURGH.
        And I will.

ARTHUR.
Have you the heart? When your head did but
    ache,
I knit my handkercher about your brows,—
The best I had, a princess wrought it me,—
And I did never ask it you again;
And with my hand at midnight held your head;
And like the watchful minutes to the hour,
Still and anon cheer'd up the heavy time, [grief?'
Saying, 'What lack you?' and, 'Where lies your
Or, 'What good love may I perform for you?'
Many a poor man's son would have lien still,
And ne'er have spoke a loving word to you;
But you at your sick service had a prince.
Nay, you may think my love was crafty love,
And call it cunning:—do, an if you will:
If heaven be pleased that you must use me ill,
Why, then you must.—Will you put out mine
    eyes?
These eyes that never did nor never shall
So much as frown on you?

HUBERT DE BURGH.
        I have sworn to do it;
And with hot irons must I burn them out.

ARTHUR.
Ah, none but in this iron age would do it!
The iron of itself, though heat red-hot,
Approaching near these eyes, would drink my
   tears,
And quench his fiery indignation
Even in the water of mine innocence;
Nay, after that, consume away in rust,
But for containing fire to harm mine eye.
Are you more stubborn-hard than hammer'd
   iron?
An if an angel should have come to me,
And told me Hubert should put out mine eyes,
I would not have believed him,—no tongue but
   Hubert's.

HUBERT DE BURGH.
Come forth!   [Stamps.
Enter EXECUTIONERS, with cord, irons, &c.
Do as I bid you do.

ARTHUR.
O, save me, Hubert, save me! my eyes are out
Even with the fierce looks of these bloody men.

HUBERT DE BURGH.
Give me the iron, I say, and bind him here.

ARTHUR.
Alas, what need you be so boisterous-rough?
I will not struggle, I will stand stone-still.
For heaven sake, Hubert, let me not be bound!
Nay, hear me, Hubert!—drive these men away,
And I will sit as quiet as a lamb;
I will not stir, nor wince, nor speak a word,
Nor look upon the iron angerly:
Thrust but these men away, and I'll forgive you,
Whatever torment you do put me to.

HUBERT DE BURGH.
Go, stand within; let me alone with him.

FIRST EXECUTIONER.
I am best pleased to be from such a deed.
                    [Exeunt EXECUTIONERS.

ARTHUR.
Alas, I then have chid away my friend!
He hath a stern look, but a gentle heart:—
Let him come back, that his compassion may
Give life to yours.

HUBERT DE BURGH.
         Come, boy, prepare yourself.

ARTHUR.
Is there no remedy?

HUBERT DE BURGH.
            None, but to lose your eyes.

ARTHUR.
O heaven!—that there were but a mote in yours,
A grain, a dust, a gnat, a wandering hair,
Any annoyance in that precious sense!
Then, feeling what small things are boisterous
   there,
Your vile intent must needs seem horrible.

HUBERT DE BURGH.
Is this your promise? go to, hold your tongue.

ARTHUR.
Hubert, the utterance of a brace of tongues
Must needs want pleading for a pair of eyes:
Let me not hold my tongue,—let me not, Hubert;
Or, Hubert, if you will, cut out my tongue,
So I may keep my eyes: O, spare mine eyes,
Though to no use but still to look on you!—

Lo, by my troth, the instrument is cold,
And would not harm me.

HUBERT DE BURGH.
            I can heat it, boy.

ARTHUR.
No, in good sooth; the fire is dead with grief,
Being create for comfort, to be used
In undeserved extremes: see else yourself;
There is no malice in this burning coal;
The breath of heaven hath blown his spirit out,
And strew'd repentant ashes on his head.

HUBERT DE BURGH.
But with my breath I can revive it, boy.

ARTHUR.
And if you do, you will but make it blush,
And glow with shame of your proceedings,
   Hubert:
Nay, it perchance will sparkle in your eyes;
And, like a dog that is compell'd to fight,
Snatch at his master that doth tarre him on.
All things that you should use to do me wrong
Deny their office: only you do lack
That mercy which fierce fire and iron extends,
Creatures of note for mercy-lacking uses.

HUBERT DE BURGH.
Well, see to live; I will not touch thine eye
For all the treasure that thine uncle owes:
Yet am I sworn, and I did purpose, boy,
With this same very iron to burn them out.

ARTHUR.
O, now you look like Hubert! all this while
You were disguised.

HUBERT DE BURGH.
            Peace; no more. Adieu.
Your uncle must not know but you are dead;
I'll fill these dogged spies with false reports:
And, pretty child, sleep doubtless and secure
That Hubert, for the wealth of all the world,
Will not offend thee.

ARTHUR.
            O heaven! I thank you, Hubert.

HUBERT DE BURGH.
Silence; no more: go closely in with me:
Much danger do I undergo for thee.   [Exeunt.

SCENE II.

KING JOHN'S palace.

Enter KING JOHN, PEMBROKE, SALISBURY,
            and other LORDS.

KING JOHN.
HERE once again we sit, once again crown'd,
   And lookt upon, I hope, with cheerful eyes.

EARL OF PEMBROKE.
This once again, but that your highness pleased,
Was once superfluous: you were crown'd before,
And that high royalty was ne'er pluckt off;
The faiths of men ne'er stained with revolt;
Fresh expectation troubled not the land
With any long'd-for change or better state.

EARL OF SALISBURY.
Therefore, to be possest with double pomp,
To guard a title that was rich before,
To gild refined gold, to paint the lily,
To throw a perfume on the violet,

155

To smooth the ice, or add another hue
Unto the rainbow, or with taper-light
To seek the beauteous eye of heaven to garnish,
Is wasteful and ridiculous excess.

EARL OF PEMBROKE.

But that your royal pleasure must be done,
This act is as an ancient tale new-told;
And in the last repeating troublesome,
Being urged at a time unseasonable.

EARL OF SALISBURY.

In this, the antique and well-noted face
Of plain old form is much disfigured;
And, like a shifted wind unto a sail,
It makes the course of thoughts to fetch about;
Startles and frights consideration;
Makes sound opinion sick, and truth suspected,
For putting on so new a fashion'd robe.

EARL OF PEMBROKE.

When workmen strive to do better than well,
They do confound their skill in covetousness;
And oftentimes excusing of a fault
Doth make the fault the worse by the excuse,—
As patches set upon a little breach
Discredit more in hiding of the fault
Than did the fault before it was so patcht.

EARL OF SALISBURY.

To this effect, before you were new-crown'd,
We breathed our counsel: but it pleased your
    highness
To overbear it; and we are all well pleased,
Since all and every part of what we would
Doth make a stand at what your highness will.

KING JOHN.

Some reasons of this double coronation
I have possest you with, and think them strong;
And more, more strong, then lesser is my fear,
I shall indue you with: meantime but ask
What you would have reform'd that is not well,
And well shall you perceive how willingly
I will both hear and grant you your requests.

EARL OF PEMBROKE.

Then I—as one that am the tongue of these,
To sound the purposes of all their hearts,
Both for myself and them, but, chief of all,
Your safety, for the which myself and them
Bend their best studies—heartily request
Th'enfranchisement of Arthur; whose restraint
Doth move the murmuring lips of discontent
To break into this dangerous argument,—
If what in rest you have in right you hold,
Why, then your fears—which, as they say, attend
The steps of wrong—should move you to mew up
Your tender kinsman, and to choke his days
With barbarous ignorance, and deny his youth
The rich advantage of good exercise.
That the time's enemies may not have this
To grace occasions, let it be our suit,
That you have bid us ask, his liberty;
Which for our goods we do no further ask
Than whereupon our weal, on you depending,
Counts it your weal he have his liberty.

KING JOHN.

Let it be so: I do commit his youth
To your direction.

Enter HUBERT.

Hubert, what news with you?

EARL OF PEMBROKE.

This is the man should do the bloody deed;
He show'd his warrant to a friend of mine:
The image of a wicked heinous fault
Lives in his eye; that close aspect of his
Does show the mood of a much-troubled breast;
And I do fearfully believe 'tis done,
What we so fear'd he had a charge to do.

EARL OF SALISBURY.

The colour of the king doth come and go
Between his purpose and his conscience.
Like heralds 'twixt two dreadful battles set:
His passion is so ripe, it needs must break.

EARL OF PEMBROKE.

And when it breaks, I fear will issue thence
The foul corruption of a sweet child's death.

KING JOHN.

We cannot hold mortality's strong hand:—
Good lords, although my will to give is living,
The suit which you demand is gone and dead:
He tells us Arthur is deceased to-night.

EARL OF SALISBURY.

Indeed, we fear'd his sickness was past cure.

EARL OF PEMBROKE.

Indeed, we heard how near his death he was
Before the child himself felt he was sick:
This must be answer'd either here or hence.

KING JOHN.

Why do you bend such solemn brows on me?
Think you I bear the shears of destiny?
Have I commandment on the pulse of life?

EARL OF SALISBURY.

It is apparent foul-play; and 'tis shame
That greatness should so grossly offer it:
So thrive it in your game! and so, farewell.

EARL OF PEMBROKE.

Stay yet, Lord Salisbury; I'll go with thee,
And find th'inheritance of this poor child,
His little kingdom of a forced grave.
That blood which owed the breadth of all this
    isle,
Three foot of it doth hold:—bad world the while!
This must not be thus borne: this will break out
To all our sorrows, and ere long I doubt.
                  [*Exeunt* LORDS.

KING JOHN.

They burn in indignation. I repent:
There is no sure foundation set on blood,
No certain life achieved by others' death.—

Enter a MESSENGER.

A fearful eye thou hast: where is that blood
That I have seen inhabit in those cheeks?
So foul a sky clears not without a storm:
Pour down thy weather: how goes all in France?

MESSENGER.

From France to England. Never such a power
For any foreign preparation
Was levied in the body of a land.
The copy of your speed is learn'd by them;
For when you should be told they do prepare,
The tidings comes that they are all arrived.

KING JOHN.

O, where hath our intelligence been drunk?
Where hath it slept? Where is my mother's ear,
That such an army could be drawn in France,
And she not hear of it?

MESSENGER.
My liege, her ear
Is stopt with dust; the first of April died
Your noble mother; and, as I hear, my lord,
The Lady Constance in a frenzy died
Three days before; but this from rumour's tongue
I idly heard; if true or false I know not.
KING JOHN.
Withhold thy speed, dreadful occasion!
O, make a league with me, till I have pleased
My discontented peers! What! mother dead!
How wildly, then, walks my estate in France!—
Under whose conduct came those powers of
France
That thou for truth givest out are landed here?
MESSENGER.
Under the Dauphin.
KING JOHN.
Thou hast made me giddy
With these ill tidings.
Enter BASTARD *and* PETER *of Pomfret.*
Now, what says the world
To your proceedings? do not seek to stuff
My head with more ill news, for it is full.
BASTARD.
But if you be afeard to hear the worst,
Then let the worst, unheard, fall on your head.
KING JOHN.
Bear with me, cousin; for I was amazed
Under the tide: but now I breathe again
Aloft the flood; and can give audience
To any tongue, speak it of what it will.
BASTARD.
How I have sped among the clergy-men,
The sums I have collected shall express.
But as I travell'd hither through the land,
I find the people strangely fantasied;
Possest with rumours, full of idle dreams,
Not knowing what they fear, but full of fear:
And here's a prophet, that I brought with me
From forth the streets of Pomfret, whom I found
With many hundreds treading on his heels;
To whom he sung, in rude harsh-sounding
rimes,
That, ere the next Ascension-day at noon,
Your highness should deliver up your crown.
KING JOHN.
Thou idle dreamer, wherefore didst thou so?
PETER.
Foreknowing that the truth will fall out so.
KING JOHN.
Hubert, away with him; imprison him;
And on that day at noon, whereon he says
I shall yield up my crown, let him be hang'd.
Deliver him to safety; and return,
For I must use thee. [*Exit* HUBERT *with* PETER.
O my gentle cousin,
Hear'st thou the news abroad, who are arrived?
BASTARD.
The French, my lord: men's mouths are full of
it:
Besides, I met Lord Bigot and Lord Salisbury
With eyes as red as new-enkindled fire,
And others more, going to seek the grave
Of Arthur, who, they say, is kill'd to-night
On your suggestion.

KING JOHN.
Gentle kinsman, go,
And thrust thyself into their companies:
I have a way to win their loves again;
Bring them before me.
BASTARD.
I will seek them out.
KING JOHN.
Nay, but make haste; the better foot before.
O, let me have no subject enemies,
When adverse foreigners affright my towns
With dreadful pomp of stout invasion!
Be Mercury, set feathers to thy heels,
And fly like thought from them to me again.
BASTARD.
The spirit of the time shall teach me speed.
KING JOHN.
Spoke like a sprightful noble gentleman.
[*Exit* BASTARD.
Go after him; for he perhaps shall need
Some messenger betwixt me and the peers;
And be thou he.
MESSENGER.
With all my heart, my liege. [*Exit.*
KING JOHN.
My mother dead!
Enter HUBERT.
HUBERT DE BURGH.
My lord, they say five moons were seen to-night;
Four fixed; and the fifth did whirl about
The other four in wondrous motion.
KING JOHN.
Five moons!
HUBERT DE BURGH.
Old men and beldams in the streets
Do prophesy upon it dangerously:
Young Arthur's death is common in their mouths:
And when they talk of him, they shake their
heads,
And whisper one another in the ear;
And he that speaks doth gripe the hearer's wrist;
Whilst he that hears makes fearful action,
With wrinkled brows, with nods, with rolling
eyes.
I saw a smith stand with his hammer, thus,
The whilst his iron did on the anvil cool,
With open mouth swallowing a tailor's news;
Who, with his shears and measure in his hand,
Standing on slippers, which his nimble haste
Had falsely thrust upon contrary feet,
Told of a many thousand warlike French
That were embattailed and rankt in Kent:
Another lean unwasht artificer
Cuts off his tale, and talks of Arthur's death.
KING JOHN.
Why seek'st thou to possess me with these fears?
Why urgest thou so oft young Arthur's death?
Thy hand hath murder'd him: I had a mighty
cause
To wish him dead, but thou hadst none to kill
him.
HUBERT DE BURGH.
No had, my lord! why, did you not provoke me?
KING JOHN.
It is the curse of kings to be attended
By slaves that take their humours for a warrant

To break within the bloody house of life;
And, on the winking of authority,
To understand a law; to know the meaning
Of dangerous majesty, when perchance it frowns
More upon humour than advised respect.
HUBERT DE BURGH.
Here is your hand and seal for what I did.
KING JOHN.
O, when the last account 'twixt heaven and earth
Is to be made, then shall this hand and seal
Witness against us to damnation!
How oft the sight of means to do ill deeds
Make deeds ill done! Hadst not thou been by,
A fellow by the hand of nature markt,
Quoted, and sign'd, to do a deed of shame,
This murder had not come into my mind:
But, taking note of thy abhorr'd aspect,
Finding thee fit for bloody villainy,
Apt, liable to be employ'd in danger,
I faintly broke with thee of Arthur's death;
And thou, to be endeared to a king,
Made it no conscience to destroy a prince.
HUBERT DE BURGH.
My lord,—
KING JOHN.
Hadst thou but shook thy head, or made a pause,
When I spake darkly what I purposed,
Or turn'd an eye of doubt upon my face,
As bid me tell my tale in express words,
Deep shame had struck me dumb, made me
    break off,
And those thy fears might have wrought fears in
    me:
But thou didst understand me by my signs,
And didst in signs again parley with sin;
Yea, without stop, didst let thy heart consent,
And consequently thy rude hand to act
The deed, which both our tongues held vile to
    name.—
Out of my sight, and never see me more!
My nobles leave me; and my state is braved,
Even at my gates, with ranks of foreign powers:
Nay, in the body of this fleshly land,
This kingdom, this confine of blood and breath,
Hostility and civil tumult reigns
Between my conscience and my cousin's death.
HUBERT DE BURGH.
Arm you against your other enemies,
I'll make a peace between your soul and you.
Young Arthur is alive: this hand of mine
Is yet a maiden and an innocent hand,
Not painted with the crimson spots of blood.
Within this bosom never enter'd yet
The dreadful motion of a murderous thought;
And you have slander'd nature in my form,
Which, howsoever rude exteriorly,
Is yet the cover of a fairer mind
Than to be butcher of an innocent child.
KING JOHN.
Doth Arthur live? O, haste thee to the peers,
Throw this report on their incensed rage,
And make them tame to their obedience!
Forgive the comment that my passion made
Upon thy feature; for my rage was blind,
And foul imaginary eyes of blood
Presented thee more hideous than thou art.

O, answer not; but to my closet bring
The angry lords with all expedient haste!
I conjure thee but slowly; run more fast. [*Exeunt.*

SCENE III.
Before a castle.

Enter ARTHUR *on the walls.*
ARTHUR.
THE wall is high, and yet will I leap down:
  Good ground, be pitiful, and hurt me not!
There's few or none do know me: if they did,
This ship-boy's semblance hath disguised me
I am afraid; and yet I'll venture it.   [quite.
If I get down, and do not break my limbs,
I'll find a thousand shifts to get away:
As good to die and go, as die and stay.
                  [*Leaps down.*
O me! my uncle's spirit is in these stones:
Heaven take my soul, and England keep my
    bones!   [*Dies.*
Enter PEMBROKE, SALISBURY, *and* BIGOT.
EARL OF SALISBURY.
Lords, I will meet him at Saint Edmund's-Bury:
It is our safety, and we must embrace
This gentle offer of the perilous time.
EARL OF PEMBROKE.
Who brought that letter from the cardinal?
EARL OF SALISBURY.
The Count Melun, a noble lord of France;
Whose private with me of the Dauphin's love
Is much more general than these lines import.
ROBERT BIGOT.
To-morrow morning let us meet him, then.
EARL OF SALISBURY.
Or rather then set forward; for 'twill be
Two long days' journey, lords, or e'er we meet.
·Enter BASTARD.
BASTARD.
Once more to-day well met, distemper'd lords!
The king by me requests your presence straight.
EARL OF SALISBURY.
The king hath dispossest himself of us:
We will not line his thin bestained cloak
With our pure honours, nor attend the foot
That leaves the print of blood where'er it walks.
Return and tell him so: we know the worst.
BASTARD.
Whate'er you think, good words, I think, were
    best.
EARL OF SALISBURY.
Our griefs, and not our manners, reason now.
BASTARD.
But there is little reason in your grief;
Therefore 'twere reason you had manners now.
EARL OF PEMBROKE.
Sir, sir, impatience hath his privilege.
BASTARD.
'Tis true,—to hurt his master, no man else.
EARL OF SALISBURY.
This is the prison:—what is he lies here?
             [*Seeing* ARTHUR.
EARL OF PEMBROKE.
O death, made proud with pure and princely
    beauty!
The earth had not a hole to hide this deed.

EARL OF SALISBURY.
Murder, as hating what himself hath done,
Doth lay it open to urge on revenge.
ROBERT BIGOT.
Or, when he doom'd this beauty to a grave,
Found it too precious-princely for a grave.
EARL OF SALISBURY.
Sir Richard, what think you? Have you beheld,
Or have you read or heard? or could you think?
Or do you almost think, although you see,
That you do see? could thought, without this
    object,
Form such another? This is the very top,
The height, the crest, or crest unto the crest,
Of murder's arms: this is the bloodiest shame,
The wildest savagery, the vilest stroke,
That ever wall-eyed wrath or staring rage
Presented to the tears of soft remorse.
EARL OF PEMBROKE.
All murders past do stand excused in this:
And this, so sole and so unmatchable,
Shall give a holiness, a purity,
To the yet-unbegotten sin of times;
And prove a deadly bloodshed but a jest,
Exampled by this heinous spectacle.
BASTARD.
It is a damned and a bloody work;
The graceless action of a heavy hand,—
If that it be the work of any hand.
EARL OF SALISBURY.
If that it be the work of any hand!—
We had a kind of light what would ensue:
It is the shameful work of Hubert's hand;
The practice and the purpose of the king:—
From whose obedience I forbid my soul,
Kneeling before this ruin of sweet life,
And breathing to his breathless excellence
The incense of a vow, a holy vow,
Never to taste the pleasures of the world,
Never to be infected with delight,
Nor conversant with ease and idleness,
Till I have set a glory to this hand,
By giving it the worship of revenge.
EARL OF PEMBROKE and ROBERT BIGOT.
Our souls religiously confirm thy words.
Enter HUBERT.
HUBERT DE BURGH.
Lords, I am hot with haste in seeking you:
Arthur doth live; the king hath sent for you.
EARL OF SALISBURY.
O, he is bold, and blushes not at death:—
Avaunt, thou hateful villain, get thee gone!
HUBERT DE BURGH.
I am no villain.
EARL OF SALISBURY.
Must I rob the law?
[Drawing his sword.
BASTARD.
Your sword is bright, sir; put it up again.
EARL OF SALISBURY.
Not till I sheathe it in a murderer's skin.
HUBERT DE BURGH.
Stand back, Lord Salisbury,—stand back, I say;
By heaven, I think my sword's as sharp as yours:
I would not have you, lord, forget yourself,
Nor tempt the danger of my true defence;

Lest I, by marking of your rage, forget
Your worth, your greatness, and nobility.
ROBERT BIGOT.
Out, dunghill! darest thou brave a nobleman?
HUBERT DE BURGH.
Not for my life: but yet I dare defend
My innocent life against an emperor.
EARL OF SALISBURY.
Thou art a murderer.
HUBERT DE BURGH.
Do not prove me so;
Yet I am none: whose tongue soe'er speaks false,
Not truly speaks; who speaks not truly, lies.
EARL OF PEMBROKE.
Cut him to pieces.
BASTARD.
Keep the peace, I say.
EARL OF SALISBURY.
Stand by, or I shall gall you, Faulconbridge.
BASTARD.
Thou wert better gall the devil, Salisbury:
If thou but frown on me, or stir thy foot,
Or teach thy hasty spleen to do me shame,
I'll strike thee dead. Put up thy sword betime;
Or I'll so maul you and your toasting-iron,
That you shall think the devil is come from hell.
ROBERT BIGOT.
What wilt thou do, renowned Faulconbridge?
Second a villain and a murderer?
HUBERT DE BURGH.
Lord Bigot, I am none.
ROBERT BIGOT.
Who kill'd this prince?
HUBERT DE BURGH.
'Tis not an hour since I left him well:
I honour'd him, I loved him; and will weep
My date of life out for his sweet life's loss.
EARL OF SALISBURY.
Trust not those cunning waters of his eyes,
For villainy is not without such rheum;
And he, long traded in it, makes it seem
Like rivers of remorse and innocency.
Away with me, all you whose souls abhor
Th'uncleanly savours of a slaughter-house;
For I am stifled with this smell of sin.
ROBERT BIGOT.
Away toward Bury, to the Dauphin there!
EARL OF PEMBROKE.
There, tell the king, he may inquire us out.
[Exeunt LORDS.
BASTARD.
Here's a good world!—Knew you of this fair
    work?
Beyond the infinite and boundless reach
Of mercy, if thou didst this deed of death,
Art thou damn'd, Hubert.
HUBERT DE BURGH.
Do but hear me, sir:—
BASTARD.
Ha! I'll tell thee what;
Thou'rt damn'd as black—nay, nothing is so black;
Thou art more deep damn'd than Prince Lucifer:
There is not yet so ugly a fiend of hell
As thou shalt be, if thou didst kill this child.
HUBERT DE BURGH.
Upon my soul,—

BASTARD.
If thou didst but consent
To this most cruel act, do but despair;
And if thou want'st a cord, the smallest thread
That ever spider twisted from her womb
Will serve to strangle thee; a rush will be a beam
To hang thee on; or wouldst thou drown thyself,
Put but a little water in a spoon,
And it shall be as all the ocean,
Enough to stifle such a villain up.
I do suspect thee very grievously.

HUBERT DE BURGH.
If I in act, consent, or sin of thought,
Be guilty of the stealing that sweet breath
Which was embounded in this beauteous clay,
Let hell want pains enough to torture me!
I left him well.

BASTARD.
    Go, bear him in thine arms.—
I am amazed, methinks; and lose my way
Among the thorns and dangers of this world.—
How easy dost thou take all England up!
From forth this morsel of dead royalty,
The life, the right, and truth of all this realm
Is fled to heaven; and England now is left
To tug and scamble, and to part by th' teeth
The unowed interest of proud-swelling state.
Now for the bare-pickt bone of majesty
Doth dogged war bristle his angry crest,
And snarleth in the gentle eyes of peace:
Now powers from home and discontents at home
Meet in one line; and vast confusion waits,
As doth a raven on a sick-fall'n beast,
The imminent decay of wrested pomp.
Now happy he whose cloak and cincture can
Hold out this tempest.—Bear away that child,
And follow me with speed: I'll to the king:
A thousand businesses are brief in hand,
And heaven itself doth frown upon the land.
                      [*Exeunt.*

ACT V. SCENE I.

KING JOHN'S *palace.*

Enter KING JOHN, PANDULPH *with the crown,*
and ATTENDANTS.

KING JOHN.
THUS have I yielded up into your hand
   The circle of my glory.

CARDINAL PANDULPH.
    Take again [*Giving back the crown.*
From this my hand, as holding of the Pope
Your sovereign greatness and authority.

KING JOHN.
Now keep your holy word: go meet the French;
And from his holiness use all your power
To stop their marches 'fore we are inflamed.
Our discontented counties do revolt;
Our people quarrel with obedience,
Swearing allegiance and the love of soul
To stranger blood, to foreign royalty.
This inundation of mistemper'd humour
Rests by you only to be qualified:
Then pause not; for the present time's so sick,
That present medicine must be minister'd,
Or overthrow incurable ensues.

CARDINAL PANDULPH.
It was my breath that blew this tempest up,
Upon your stubborn usage of the Pope:
But since you are a gentle convertite,
My tongue shall hush again this storm of war,
And make fair weather in your blustering land.
On this Ascension-day, remember well,
Upon your oath of service to the Pope,
Go I to make the French lay down their arms.
                      [*Exit.*

KING JOHN.
Is this Ascension-day? Did not the prophet
Say, that before Ascension-day at noon
My crown I should give off? Even so I have:
I did suppose it should be on constraint;
But, heaven be thankt, it is but voluntary.

Enter BASTARD.

BASTARD.
All Kent hath yielded; nothing there holds out
But Dover Castle: London hath received,
Like a kind host, the Dauphin and his powers:
Your nobles will not hear you, but are gone
To offer service to your enemy;
And wild amazement hurries up and down
The little number of your doubtful friends.

KING JOHN.
Would not my lords return to me again,
After they heard young Arthur was alive?

BASTARD.
They found him dead, and cast into the streets;
An empty casket, where the jewel of life
By some damn'd hand was robb'd and ta'en away.

KING JOHN.
That villain Hubert told me he did live.

BASTARD.
So, on my soul, he did, for aught he knew.
But wherefore do you droop? why look you sad?
Be great in act, as you have been in thought;
Let not the world see fear and sad distrust
Govern the motion of a kingly eye:
Be stirring as the time; be fire with fire;
Threaten the threatener, and outface the brow
Of bragging horror: so shall inferior eyes,
That borrow their behaviours from the great,
Grow great by your example, and put on
The dauntless spirit of resolution.
Away, and glister like the god of war,
When he intendeth to become the field:
Show boldness and aspiring confidence.
What, shall they seek the lion in his den,
And fright him there? and make him tremble
   there?
O, let it not be said!—Forage, and run
To meet displeasure further from the doors,
And grapple with him ere he come so nigh.

KING JOHN.
The legate of the Pope hath been with me,
And I have made a happy peace with him;
And he hath promised to dismiss the powers
Led by the Dauphin.

BASTARD.
    O inglorious league!
Shall we, upon the footing of our land,
Send fair-play orders, and make compromise,
Insinuation, parley, and base truce,
To arms invasive? shall a beardless boy,

A cocker'd silken wanton, brave our fields,
And flesh his spirit in a warlike soil,
Mocking the air with colours idly spread,
And find no check? Let us, my liege, to arms:
Perchance the cardinal cannot make your peace;
Or if he do, let it at least be said
They saw we had a purpose of defence.

KING JOHN.
Have thou the ordering of this present time.

BASTARD.
Away, then, with good courage! yet, I know,
Our party may well meet a prouder foe.   [*Exeunt.*

SCENE II.

Near St. Edmund's-Bury. The French camp.

Enter, in arms, LOUIS, SALISBURY, MELUN,
    PEMBROKE, BIGOT, *and* SOLDIERS.

LOUIS.
MY Lord Melun, let this be copied out,
And keep it safe for our remembrance:
Return the precedent to these lords again;
That, having our fair order written down,
Both they and we, perusing o'er these notes,
May know wherefore we took the sacrament,
And keep our faiths firm and inviolable.

EARL OF SALISBURY.
Upon our sides it never shall be broken.
And, noble Dauphin, albeit we swear
A voluntary zeal and unurged faith
To your proceedings; yet, believe me, prince,
I am not glad that such a sore of time
Should seek a plaster by contemn'd revolt,
And heal the inveterate canker of one wound
By making many. O, it grieves my soul,
That I must draw this metal from my side
To be a widow-maker! O, and there
Where honourable rescue and defence
Cries out upon the name of Salisbury!
But such is the infection of the time,
That, for the health and physic of our right,
We cannot deal but with the very hand
Of stern injustice and confused wrong.
And is't not pity, O my grieved friends,
That we, the sons and children of this isle,
Were born to see so sad an hour as this;
Wherein we step after a stranger, march
Upon her gentle bosom, and fill up
Her enemies' ranks,—I must withdraw and weep
Upon the spot of this enforced cause,—
To grace the gentry of a land remote,
And follow unacquainted colours here?
What, here? O nation, that thou couldst remove!
That Neptune's arms, who clippeth thee about,
Would bear thee from the knowledge of thyself,
And grapple thee unto a pagan shore;
Where these two Christian armies might combine
The blood of malice in a vein of league,
And not to spend it so unneighbourly!

LOUIS.
A noble temper dost thou show in this;
And great affections wrestling in thy bosom
Do make an earthquake of nobility.
O, what a noble combat hast thou fought
Between compulsion and a brave respect!
Let me wipe off this honourable dew

That silverly doth progress on thy cheeks:
My heart hath melted at a lady's tears,
Being an ordinary inundation;
But this effusion of such manly drops,
This shower, blown up by tempest of the soul,
Startles mine eyes, and makes me more amazed
Than had I seen the vaulty top of heaven
Figured quite o'er with burning meteors.
Lift up thy brow, renowned Salisbury,
And with a great heart heave away this storm:
Commend these waters to those baby eyes
That never saw the giant world enraged;
Nor met with fortune other than at feasts,
Full of warm blood, of mirth, of gossiping.
Come, come; for thou shalt thrust thy hand as
    deep
Into the purse of rich prosperity
As Louis himself:—so, nobles, shall you all,
That knit your sinews to the strength of mine.—
And even there, methinks, an angel spake:
Look, where the holy legate comes apace,
To give us warrant from the hand of heaven,
And on our actions set the name of right
With holy breath.

Enter PANDULPH, *attended.*

CARDINAL PANDULPH.
      Hail, noble Prince of France!
The next is this,—King John hath reconciled
Himself to Rome; his spirit is come in,
That so stood out against the holy church,
The great metropolis and see of Rome:
Therefore thy threatening colours now wind up;
And tame the savage spirit of wild war,
That, like a lion foster'd-up at hand,
It may lie gently at the foot of peace,
And be no further harmful than in show.

LOUIS.
Your Grace shall pardon me, I will not back:
I am too high-born to be propertied,
To be a secondary at control,
Or useful serving-man, and instrument,
To any sovereign state throughout the world.
Your breath first kindled the dead coal of wars
Between this chastised kingdom and myself,
And brought in matter that should feed this fire;
And now 'tis far too huge to be blown out
With that same weak wind which enkindled it.
You taught me how to know the face of right,
Acquainted me with interest to this land,
Yea, thrust this enterprise into my heart;
And come ye now to tell me John hath made
His peace with Rome? What is that peace to me?
I, by the honour of my marriage-bed,
After young Arthur, claim this land for mine;
And, now it is half-conquer'd, must I back
Because that John hath made his peace with
    Rome?
Am I Rome's slave? What penny hath Rome
    borne,
What men provided, what munition sent,
To underprop this action? Is't not I
That undergo this charge? who else but I,
And such as to my claim are liable,
Sweat in this business and maintain this war?
Have I not heard these islanders shout out,
Vive le roi! as I have bankt their towns?

Have I not here the best cards for the game,
To win this easy match play'd for a crown?
And shall I now give o'er the yielded set?
No, no, on my soul, it never shall be said.

CARDINAL PANDULPH.
You look but on the outside of this work.

LOUIS.
Outside or inside, I will not return
Till my attempt so much be glorified
As to my ample hope was promised
Before I drew this gallant head of war,
And cull'd these fiery spirits from the world,
To outlook conquest, and to win renown
Even in the jaws of danger and of death.—
                                    [Trumpet sounds.
What lusty trumpet thus doth summon us?
        Enter BASTARD, attended.

BASTARD.
According to the fair-play of the world,
Let me have audience; I am sent to speak:—
My holy lord of Milan, from the king
I come, to learn how you have dealt for him;
And, as you answer, I do know the scope
And warrant limited unto my tongue.

CARDINAL PANDULPH.
The Dauphin is too wilful-opposite,
And will not temporize with my entreaties;
He flatly says he'll not lay down his arms.

BASTARD.
By all the blood that ever fury breathed, [king;
The youth says well.—Now hear our English
For thus his royalty doth speak in me.
He is prepared; and reason too he should:
This apish and unmannerly approach,
This harness'd mask and unadvised revel,
This unhair'd sauciness and boyish troops,
The king doth smile at; and is well prepared
To whip this dwarfish war, these pigmy arms,
From out the circle of his territories. [door,
That hand which had the strength, even at your
To cudgel you, and make you take the hatch;
To dive, like buckets, in concealed wells;
To crouch in litter of your stable planks;
To lie, like pawns, lockt up in chests and trunks;
To hug with swine; to seek sweet safety out
In vaults and prisons; and to thrill and shake
Even at the crying of your nation's crow,
Thinking his voice an armed Englishman;—
Shall that victorious hand be feebled here,
That in your chambers gave you chastisement?
No: know the gallant monarch is in arms;
And, like an eagle o'er his aery, towers,
To souse annoyance that comes near his nest.—
And you degenerate, you ingrate revolts,
You bloody Neroes, ripping up the womb
Of your dear mother England, blush for shame;
For your own ladies and pale-visaged maids,
Like Amazons, come tripping after drums,
Their thimbles into armed gauntlets change,
Their needles to lances, and their gentle hearts
To fierce and bloody inclination.

LOUIS.
There end thy brave, and turn thy face in peace;
We grant thou canst outscold us: fare thee well;
We hold our time too precious to be spent
With such a brabbler.

CARDINAL PANDULPH.
                    Give me leave to speak.
BASTARD.
No, I will speak.
LOUIS.
            We will attend to neither.—
Strike up the drums; and let the tongue of war
Plead for our interest and our being here.
BASTARD.
Indeed, your drums, being beaten, will cry out;
And so shall you, being beaten: do but start
An echo with the clamour of thy drum,
And even at hand a drum is ready braced
That shall reverberate all as loud as thine;
Sound but another, and another shall,
As loud as thine, rattle the welkin's ear, [hand—
And mock the deep-mouth'd thunder: for at
Not trusting to this halting legate here,
Whom he hath used rather for sport than need—
Is warlike John; and in his forehead sits
A bare-ribb'd death, whose office is this day
To feast upon whole thousands of the French.
LOUIS.
Strike up our drums, to find this danger out.
BASTARD.
And thou shalt find it, Dauphin, do not doubt.
                                        [Exeunt.

SCENE III.
The field of battle.

Alarums. Enter KING JOHN *and* HUBERT.

KING JOHN.
HOW goes the day with us? O, tell me, Hubert.
HUBERT DE BURGH.
Badly, I fear. How fares your majesty?
KING JOHN.
This fever, that hath troubled me so long,
Lies heavy on me;—O, my heart is sick!
        Enter a MESSENGER.
MESSENGER.
My lord, your valiant kinsman, Faulconbridge,
Desires your majesty to leave the field,
And send him word by me which way you go.
KING JOHN.
Tell him, toward Swinstead, to the abbey there.
MESSENGER.
Be of good comfort; for the great supply,
That was expected by the Dauphin here,
Are wrackt three nights ago on Goodwin Sands.
This news was brought to Richard but even now:
The French fight coldly, and retire themselves.
KING JOHN.
Ay me, this tyrant fever burns me up,
And will not let me welcome this good news!—
Set on toward Swinstead: to my litter straight;
Weakness possesseth me, and I am faint.
                                        [Exeunt

SCENE IV.
Another part of the field.

Enter SALISBURY, PEMBROKE, *and* BIGOT.

EARL OF SALISBURY.
I DID not think the king so stored with friends.
EARL OF PEMBROKE.
Up once again; put spirit in the French:
If they miscarry, we miscarry too.

EARL OF SALISBURY.
That misbegotten devil, Faulconbridge,
In spite of spite, alone upholds the day.
EARL OF PEMBROKE.
They say King John sore-sick hath left the field.
Enter MELUN, *wounded.*
MELUN.
Lead me to the revolts of England here.
EARL OF SALISBURY.
When we were happy we had other names.
EARL OF PEMBROKE.
It is the Count Melun.
EARL OF SALISBURY.
                    Wounded to death.
MELUN.
Fly, noble English, you are bought and sold;
Unthread the rude eye of rebellion,
And welcome home again discarded faith.
Seek out King John, and fall before his feet;
For if the French be lords of this loud day,
He means to recompense the pains you take
By cutting off your heads: thus hath he sworn,
And I with him, and many moe with me,
Upon the altar at Saint Edmund's-Bury;
Even on that altar where we swore to you
Dear amity and everlasting love.
EARL OF SALISBURY.
May this be possible? may this be true?
MELUN.
Have I not hideous death within my view,
Retaining but a quantity of life,
Which bleeds away, even as a form of wax
Resolveth from his figure 'gainst the fire?
What in the world should make me now deceive,
Since I must lose the use of all deceit?
Why should I, then, be false, since it is true
That I must die here, and live hence by truth?
I say again, if Louis do win the day,
He is forsworn, if e'er those eyes of yours
Behold another day break in the east:
But even this night,—whose black contagious
    breath
Already smokes about the burning crest
Of the old, feeble, and day-wearied sun,—
Even this ill night, your breathing shall expire,
Paying the fine of rated treachery
Even with a treacherous fine of all your lives,
If Louis by your assistance win the day.
Commend me to one Hubert, with your king:
The love of him,—and this respect besides,
For that my grandsire was an Englishman,—
Awakes my conscience to confess all this.
In lieu whereof, I pray you, bear me hence
From forth the noise and rumour of the field;
Where I may think the remnant of my thoughts
In peace, and part this body and my soul
With contemplation and devout desires.
EARL OF SALISBURY.
We do believe thee:—and beshrew my soul
But I do love the favour and the form
Of this most fair occasion, by the which
We will untread the steps of damned flight;
And, like a bated and retired flood,
Leaving our rankness and irregular course,
Stoop low within those bounds we have o'er-
    lookt,

And calmly run on in obedience,
Even to our ocean, to our great King John.—
My arm shall give thee help to bear thee hence;
For I do see the cruel pangs of death
Right in thine eye.—Away, my friends! New
    flight;
And happy newness, that intends old right.
                    [*Exeunt, leading off* MELUN.

SCENE V.

The French camp.

Enter LOUIS *and his* TRAIN.

LOUIS.
THE sun of heaven methought was loth to
    set,
But stay'd, and made the western welkin blush,
When th'English measure backward their own
    ground
In faint retire. O, bravely came we off,
When with a volley of our needless shot,
After such bloody toil, we bid good night;
And wound our tottering colours clearly up,
Last in the field, and almost lords of it!
Enter a MESSENGER.
MESSENGER.
Where is my prince, the Dauphin?
LOUIS.
                    Here:—what news?
MESSENGER.
The Count Melun is slain; the English lords,
By his persuasion, are again fall'n off;
And your supply, which you have wisht so long,
Are cast away and sunk on Goodwin Sands.
LOUIS.
Ah, foul shrewd news!—beshrew thy very
    heart!—
I did not think to be so sad to-night
As this hath made me.—Who was he that said
King John did fly an hour or two before
The stumbling night did part our weary powers?
MESSENGER.
Whoever spoke it, it is true, my lord.
LOUIS.
Well; keep good quarter and good care to-night:
The day shall not be up so soon as I,
To try the fair adventure of to-morrow. [*Exeunt.*

SCENE VI.

An open place near Swinstead Abbey.

Enter BASTARD *and* HUBERT, *severally.*

HUBERT DE BURGH.
WHO'S there? speak, ho! speak quickly, or I
    shoot.
BASTARD.
A friend.—What art thou?
HUBERT DE BURGH.
                    Of the part of England.
BASTARD.
Whither dost thou go?
HUBERT DE BURGH.
What's that to thee? Why may not I demand
Of thine affairs, as well as thou of mine?
BASTARD.
Hubert, I think?

HUBERT DE BURGH.
            Thou hast a perfect thought:
I will, upon all hazards, well believe   [well.
Thou art my friend, thou know'st my tongue so
Who art thou?
BASTARD.
           Who thou wilt: an if thou please,
Thou mayst befriend me so much as to think
I come one way of the Plantagenets.
HUBERT DE BURGH.
Unkind remembrance! thou and eyeless night
Have done me shame:—brave soldier, pardon me,
That any accent breaking from thy tongue
Should scape the true acquaintance of mine ear.
BASTARD.
Come, come; sans compliment, what news abroad?
HUBERT DE BURGH.
Why, here walk I, in the black brow of night,
To find you out.
BASTARD.
         Brief, then; and what's the news?
HUBERT DE BURGH.
O, my sweet sir, news fitting to the night,—
Black, fearful, comfortless, and horrible.
BASTARD.
Show me the very wound of this ill news:
I am no woman, I'll not swound at it.
HUBERT DE BURGH.
The king, I fear, is poison'd by a monk:
I left him almost speechless; and broke out
To acquaint you with this evil, that you might
The better arm you to the sudden time,
Than if you had at leisure known of this.
BASTARD.
How did he take it? who did taste to him?
HUBERT DE BURGH.
A monk, I tell you; a resolved villain,
Whose bowels suddenly burst out: the king
Yet speaks, and peradventure may recover.
BASTARD.
Who didst thou leave to tend his majesty?
HUBERT DE BURGH.
Why, know you not the lords are all come back,
And brought Prince Henry in their company?
At whose request the king hath pardon'd them,
And they are all about his majesty.
BASTARD.
Withhold thine indignation, mighty heaven,
And tempt us not to bear above our power!—
I'll tell thee, Hubert, half my power this night,
Passing these flats, are taken by the tide,—
These Lincoln Washes have devoured them;
Myself, well-mounted, hardly have escaped.
Away, before! conduct me to the king;
I doubt he will be dead or e'er I come.   [Exeunt.

SCENE VII.

The orchard of Swinstead Abbey.

Enter PRINCE HENRY, SALISBURY, *and* BIGOT.

PRINCE HENRY.
IT is too late: the life of all his blood
Is toucht corruptibly; and his pure brain—
Which some suppose the soul's frail dwelling-
     house—

Doth, by the idle comments that it makes,
Foretell the ending of mortality.
Enter PEMBROKE.
EARL OF PEMBROKE.
His highness yet doth speak; and holds belief
That, being brought into the open air,
It would allay the burning quality
Of that fell poison which assaileth him.
PRINCE HENRY.
Let him be brought into the orchard here.—
Doth he still rage?   [*Exit* BIGOT.
EARL OF PEMBROKE.
           He is more patient
Than when you left him; even now he sung.
PRINCE HENRY.
O vanity of sickness! fierce extremes
In their continuance will not feel themselves.
Death, having prey'd upon the outward parts,
Leaves them invisible; and his siege is now
Against the mind, the which he pricks and wounds
With many legions of strange fantasies,
Which, in their throng and press to that last hold,
Confound themselves. 'Tis strange that death
     should sing.—
I am the cygnet to this pale faint swan,
Who chants a doleful hymn to his own death,
And from the organ-pipe of frailty sings
His soul and body to their lasting rest.
EARL OF SALISBURY.
Be of good comfort, prince; for you are born
To set a form upon that indigest
Which he hath left so shapeless and so rude.
KING JOHN *brought in.*
KING JOHN.
Ay, marry, now my soul hath elbow-room;
It would not out at windows nor at doors.
There is so hot a summer in my bosom,
That all my bowels crumble up to dust:
I am a scribbled form, drawn with a pen
Upon a parchment; and against this fire
Do I shrink up.
PRINCE HENRY.
         How fares your majesty?
KING JOHN.
Poison'd,—ill fare;—dead, forsook, cast off:
And none of you will bid the winter come,
To thrust his icy fingers in my maw;
Nor let my kingdom's rivers take their course
Through my burn'd bosom; nor entreat the north
To make his bleak winds kiss my parched lips,
And comfort me with cold:—I do not ask you
     much,
I beg cold comfort; and you are so strait,
And so ingrateful, you deny me that.
PRINCE HENRY.
O, that there were some virtue in my tears,
That might relieve you!
KING JOHN.
          The salt in them is hot.—
Within me is a hell; and there the poison
Is, as a fiend, confined to tyrannize
On unreprievable condemned blood.
Enter BASTARD.
BASTARD.
O, I am scalded with my violent motion,
And spleen of speed to see your majesty!

KING JOHN.
O cousin, thou art come to set mine eye:
The tackle of my heart is crackt and burn'd;
And all the shrouds, wherewith my life should
    sail,
Are turned to one thread, one little hair:
My heart hath one poor string to stay it by,
Which holds but till thy news be uttered;
And then all this thou see'st is but a clod,
And module of confounded royalty.
            BASTARD.
The Dauphin is preparing hitherward,
Where heaven he knows how we shall answer
    him;
For in a night the best part of my power,
As I upon advantage did remove,
Were in the Washes all unwarily
Devoured by the unexpected flood.
                    [KING JOHN dies.
        EARL OF SALISBURY.
You breathe these dead news in as dead an ear.—
My liege! my lord!—but now a king,—now thus.
            PRINCE HENRY.
Even so must I run on, and even so stop.
What surety of the world, what hope, what stay,
When this was now a king, and now is clay?
            BASTARD.
Art thou gone so? I do but stay behind
To do the office for thee of revenge,
And then my soul shall wait on thee to heaven,
As it on earth hath been thy servant still.—
Now, now, you stars that move in your right
    spheres,
Where be your powers? show now your mended
    faiths;
And instantly return with me again,
To push destruction and perpetual shame
Out of the weak door of our fainting land.
Straight let us seek, or straight we shall be
    sought;
The Dauphin rages at our very heels.
            EARL OF SALISBURY.
It seems you know not, then, so much as we:
The Cardinal Pandulph is within at rest,
Who half an hour since came from the Dauphin,

And brings from him such offers of our peace
As we with honour and respect may take,
With purpose presently to leave this war.
            BASTARD.
He will the rather do it when he sees
Ourselves well sinewed to our defence.
        EARL OF SALISBURY.
Nay, it is in a manner done already;
For many carriages he hath dispatcht
To the sea-side, and put his cause and quarrel
To the disposing of the cardinal:
With whom yourself, myself, and other lords,
If you think meet, this afternoon will post
To consummate this business happily.
            BASTARD.
Let it be so:—and you, my noble prince,
With other princes that may best be spared,
Shall wait upon your father's funeral.
            PRINCE HENRY.
At Worcester must his body be interr'd;
For so he will'd it.
            BASTARD.
                Thither shall it, then:
And happily may your sweet self put on
The lineal state and glory of the land!
To whom, with all submission, on my knee,
I do bequeath my faithful services
And true subjection everlastingly.
        EARL OF SALISBURY.
And the like tender of our love we make,
To rest without a spot for evermore.
            PRINCE HENRY.
I have a kind soul that would give you thanks,
And knows not how to do it but with tears.
            BASTARD.
O, let us pay the time but needful woe,
Since it hath been beforehand with our griefs.—
This England never did, nor never shall,
Lie at the proud foot of a conqueror,
But when it first did help to wound itself.
Now these her princes are come home again,
Come the three corners of the world in arms,
And we shall shock them; naught shall make us
    rue,
If England to itself do rest but true.   [Exeunt.

KING RICHARD THE SECOND

DRAMATIS PERSONAE

KING RICHARD THE SECOND.
JOHN OF GAUNT, *Duke of Lancaster,* ⎫
EDMUND OF LANGLEY, *Duke of York,* ⎬ *uncles to the King.*
HENRY, *surnamed* BOLINGBROKE, *Duke of Hereford, son to John of Gaunt; afterwards King Henry IV.*
DUKE OF AUMERLE, *son to the Duke of York.*
THOMAS MOWBRAY, *Duke of Norfolk.*
DUKE OF SURREY.
EARL OF SALISBURY.
LORD BERKLEY.
BUSHY, ⎫
BAGOT, ⎬ *creatures to King Richard.*
GREEN, ⎭
EARL OF NORTHUMBERLAND.
HENRY PERCY, *his son.*

LORD ROSS.
LORD WILLOUGHBY.
LORD FITZWATER.
BISHOP OF CARLISLE.
ABBOT OF WESTMINSTER.
LORD MARSHAL.
SIR STEPHEN SCROOP.
SIR PIERCE OF EXTON.
CAPTAIN OF A BAND OF WELSHMEN.

QUEEN *to King Richard.*
DUCHESS OF YORK.
DUCHESS OF GLOSTER.
LADIES *attending on the Queen.*

LORDS, HERALDS, OFFICERS, SOLDIERS, TWO GARDENERS, KEEPER, MESSENGER, GROOM, *and other* ATTENDANTS.

SCENE—*England and Wales.*

ACT I. SCENE I.

London. KING RICHARD'S *palace.*

Enter KING RICHARD, JOHN OF GAUNT, *with other* NOBLES *and* ATTENDANTS.

KING RICHARD.

OLD John of Gaunt, time-honour'd Lancaster,
Hast thou, according to thy oath and band,
Brought hither Henry Hereford thy bold son,
Here to make good the boisterous late appeal,
Which then our leisure would not let us hear,
Against the duke of Norfolk, Thomas Mowbray?

JOHN OF GAUNT.
I have, my liege.

KING RICHARD.
Tell me, moreover, hast thou sounded him,
If he appeal the duke on ancient malice;
Or worthily, as a good subject should,
On some known ground of treachery in him?

JOHN OF GAUNT.
As near as I could sift him on that argument,—
On some apparent danger seen in him
Aim'd at your highness,—no inveterate malice.

KING RICHARD.
Then call them to our presence: face to face,
And frowning brow to brow, ourselves will hear
Th'accuser and the accused freely speak:—
High-stomach'd are they both, and full of ire,
In rage deaf as the sea, hasty as fire.

Enter BOLINGBROKE *and* NORFOLK.

HENRY BOLINGBROKE.
Many years of happy days befall
My gracious sovereign, my most loving liege!

DUKE OF NORFOLK.
Each day still better other's happiness;
Until the heavens, envying earth's good hap,
Add an immortal title to your crown!

KING RICHARD.
We thank you both: yet one but flatters us,
As well appeareth by the cause you come;
Namely, to appeal each other of high treason.—
Cousin of Hereford, what dost thou object
Against the duke of Norfolk, Thomas Mowbray?

HENRY BOLINGBROKE.
First,—heaven be the record to my speech!—
In the devotion of a subject's love,
Tendering the precious safety of my prince,
And free from other misbegotten hate,
Come I appellant to this princely presence.—
Now, Thomas Mowbray, do I turn to thee,
And mark my greeting well; for what I speak
My body shall make good upon this earth,
Or my divine soul answer it in heaven.
Thou art a traitor and a miscreant,
Too good to be so, and too bad to live,—
Since the more fair and crystal is the sky,
The uglier seem the clouds that in it fly.
Once more, the more to aggravate the note,
With a foul traitor's name stuff I thy throat;
And wish,—so please my sovereign,—ere I move,
What my tongue speaks, my right-drawn sword
    may prove.

DUKE OF NORFOLK.
Let not my cold words here accuse my zeal:
'Tis not the trial of a woman's war,
The bitter clamour of two eager tongues,
Can arbitrate this cause betwixt us twain;
The blood is hot that must be cool'd for this:
Yet can I not of such tame patience boast
As to be husht, and naught at all to say:
First, the fair reverence of your highness curbs
    me
From giving reins and spurs to my free speech;
Which else would post until it had return'd
These terms of treason doubled down his throat.

Setting aside his high blood's royalty,
And let him be no kinsman to my liege,
I do defy him, and I spit at him;
Call him a slanderous coward and a villain:
Which to maintain, I would allow him odds;
And meet him, were I tied to run a-foot
Even to the frozen ridges of the Alps,
Or any other ground inhabitable,
Wherever Englishman durst set his foot.
Meantime let this defend my loyalty,—
By all my hopes, most falsely doth he lie.

         HENRY BOLINGBROKE.
Pale trembling coward, there I throw my gage,
Disclaiming here the kindred of the king;
And lay aside my high blood's royalty,
Which fear, not reverence, makes thee to except.
If guilty dread have left thee so much strength
As to take up mine honour's pawn, then stoop:
By that and all the rites of knighthood else,
Will I make good against thee, arm to arm,
What I have spoke, or thou canst worse devise.

         DUKE OF NORFOLK.
I take it up; and by that sword I swear,
Which gently laid my knighthood on my shoulder,
I'll answer thee in any fair degree,
Or chivalrous design of knightly trial:
And when I mount, alive may I not light,
If I be traitor or unjustly fight!

         KING RICHARD.
What doth our cousin lay to Mowbray's charge?
It must be great that can inherit us
So much as of a thought of ill in him.

         HENRY BOLINGBROKE.
Look, what I speak, my life shall prove it true:—
That Mowbray hath received eight thousand
    nobles
In name of lendings for your highness' soldiers,
The which he hath detain'd for lewd employ-
    ments,
Like a false traitor and injurious villain.
Besides, I say, and will in battle prove,—
Or here, or elsewhere to the furthest verge
That ever was survey'd by English eye,—
That all the treasons for these eighteen years
Complotted and contrived in this land   [spring.
Fetch from false Mowbray their first head and
Further, I say,—and further will maintain
Upon his bad life to make all this good,—
That he did plot the Duke of Gloster's death,
Suggest his soon-believing adversaries,
And consequently, like a traitor-coward,
Sluiced out his innocent soul through streams of
    blood:
Which blood, like sacrificing Abel's, cries,
Even from the tongueless caverns of the earth,
To me for justice and rough chastisement;
And, by the glorious worth of my descent,
This arm shall do it, or this life be spent.

         KING RICHARD.
How high a pitch his resolution soars!—
Thomas of Norfolk, what say'st thou to this?

         DUKE OF NORFOLK.
O, let my sovereign turn away his face,
And bid his ears a little while be deaf,
Till I have told this slander of his blood,
How God and good men hate so foul a liar!

         KING RICHARD.
Mowbray, impartial are our eyes and ears:
Were he my brother, nay, my kingdom's heir,—
As he is but my father's brother's son,—
Now, by my sceptre's awe, I make a vow,
Such neighbour-nearness to our sacred blood
Should nothing privilege him, nor partialize
The unstooping firmness of my upright soul:
He is our subject, Mowbray; so art thou:
Free speech and fearless I to thee allow.

         DUKE OF NORFOLK.
Then, Bolingbroke, as low as to thy heart,
Through the false passage of thy throat, thou
    liest!
Three parts of that receipt I had for Calais
Disbursed I duly to his highness' soldiers;
The other part reserved I by consent,
For that my sovereign liege was in my debt
Upon remainder of a dear account,
Since last I went to France to fetch his queen:
Now swallow down that lie.—For Gloster's
    death—
I slew him not; but, to my own disgrace,
Neglected my sworn duty in that case.—
For you, my noble Lord of Lancaster,
The honourable father to my foe,
Once did I lay an ambush for your life,—
A trespass that doth vex my grieved soul:
But, ere I last received the sacrament,
I did confess it; and exactly begg'd
Your Grace's pardon, and I hope I had it.
This is my fault: as for the rest appeal'd,
It issues from the rancour of a villain,
A recreant and most degenerate traitor:
Which in myself I boldly will defend;
And interchangeably hurl down my gage
Upon this overweening traitor's foot,
To prove myself a loyal gentleman
Even in the best blood chamber'd in his bosom.
In haste whereof, most heartily I pray
Your highness to assign our trial-day.

         KING RICHARD.
Wrath-kindled gentlemen, be ruled by me;
Let's purge this choler without letting blood:
This we prescribe, though no physician;
Deep malice makes too deep incision:
Forget, forgive; conclude and be agreed;
Our doctors say this is no month to bleed.—
Good uncle, let this end where it begun;
We'll calm the Duke of Norfolk, you your son.

         JOHN OF GAUNT.
To be a make-peace shall become my age:—
Throw down, my son, the Duke of Norfolk's
    gage.

         KING RICHARD.
And, Norfolk, throw down his.

         JOHN OF GAUNT.
               When, Harry? when?
Obedience bids I should not bid agen.

         KING RICHARD.
Norfolk, throw down; we bid; there is no boot.

         DUKE OF NORFOLK.
Myself I throw, dread sovereign, at thy foot.
My life thou shalt command, but not my shame:
The one my duty owes; but my fair name—
Despite of death, that lives upon my grave,—

To dark dishonour's use thou shalt not have.
I am disgraced, impeach'd, and baffled here;
Pierced to the soul with slander's venom'd spear,
The which no balm can cure but his heart-blood
Which breathed this poison.

KING RICHARD.
                    Rage must be withstood:—
Give me his gage:—lions make leopards tame.

DUKE OF NORFOLK.
Yea, but not change his spots: take but my shame,
And I resign my gage. My dear dear lord,
The purest treasure mortal times afford
Is spotless reputation; that away,
Men are but gilded loam or painted clay.
A jewel in a ten-times-barr'd-up chest
Is a bold spirit in a loyal breast.
Mine honour is my life; both grow in one;
Take honour from me, and my life is done:
Then, dear my liege, mine honour let me try;
In that I live, and for that will I die.

        KING RICHARD.
Cousin, throw down your gage; do you begin.

    HENRY BOLINGBROKE.
O, God defend my soul from such deep sin!
Shall I seem crest-fall'n in my father's sight?
Or with pale beggar-fear impeach my height
Before this outdared dastard? Ere my tongue
Shall wound my honour with such feeble wrong,
Or sound so base a parle, my teeth shall tear
The slavish motive of recanting fear,
And spit it bleeding in his high disgrace,
Where shame doth harbour, even in Mowbray's
    face.   [Exit GAUNT.

        KING RICHARD.
We were not born to sue, but to command;—
Which since we cannot do to make you friends,
Be ready, as your lives shall answer it,
At Coventry, upon Saint Lambert's day:
There shall your swords and lances arbitrate
The swelling difference of your settled hate:
Since we cannot atone you, we shall see
Justice design the victor's chivalry.—
Lord marshal, command our officers-at-arms
Be ready to direct these home-alarms.   [Exeunt.

SCENE II.

The same.   A room in the DUKE OF LANCAS-
TER'S *palace.*

Enter GAUNT *and* DUCHESS OF GLOSTER.

        JOHN OF GAUNT.
ALAS, the part I had in Woodstock's blood
    Doth more solicit me than your exclaims,
To stir against the butchers of his life!
But since correction lieth in those hands
Which made the fault that we cannot correct,
Put we our quarrel to the will of heaven;
Who, when they see the hours ripe on earth,
Will rain hot vengeance on offenders' heads.

    DUCHESS OF GLOSTER.
Finds brotherhood in thee no sharper spur?
Hath love in thy old blood no living fire?
Edward's seven sons, whereof thyself art one,
Were as seven vials of his sacred blood,
Or seven fair branches springing from one root:
Some of those seven are dried by nature's course,

Some of those branches by the Destinies cut;
But Thomas, my dear lord, my life, my Gloster,
One vial full of Edward's sacred blood,
One flourishing branch of his most royal root,
Is crackt, and all the precious liquor spilt,
Is hackt down, and his summer-leaves all faded,
By envy's hand and murder's bloody axe.
Ah, Gaunt, his blood was thine! that bed, that
    womb,
That metal, that self-mould, that fashion'd thee,
Made him a man; and though thou livest and
    breathest,
Yet art thou slain in him: thou dost consent
In some large measure to thy father's death,
In that thou seest thy wretched brother die,
Who was the model of thy father's life.
Call it not patience, Gaunt,—it is despair:
In suffering thus thy brother to be slaughter'd,
Thou show'st the naked pathway to thy life,
Teaching stern murder how to butcher thee:
That which in mean men we entitle patience,
Is pale cold cowardice in noble breasts.
What shall I say? to safeguard thine own life,
The best way is to venge my Gloster's death.

        JOHN OF GAUNT.
God's is the quarrel; for God's substitute,
His deputy anointed in His sight,
Hath caused his death: the which if wrongfully,
Let heaven revenge; for I may never lift
An angry arm against His minister.

    DUCHESS OF GLOSTER.
Where, then, alas, may I complain myself?

        JOHN OF GAUNT.
To God, the widow's champion and defence.

    DUCHESS OF GLOSTER.
Why, then, I will. Farewell, old Gaunt:
Thou go'st to Coventry, there to behold
Our cousin Hereford and fell Mowbray fight:
O, sit my husband's wrongs on Hereford's spear,
That it may enter butcher Mowbray's breast!
Or, if misfortune miss the first career,
Be Mowbray's sins so heavy in his bosom,
That they may break his foaming courser's back,
And throw the rider headlong in the lists,
A caitiff recreant to my cousin Hereford!
Farewell, old Gaunt: thy sometimes brother's wife
With her companion grief must end her life.

        JOHN OF GAUNT.
Sister, farewell; I must to Coventry:
As much good stay with thee as go with me!

    DUCHESS OF GLOSTER.
Yet one word more:—grief boundeth where it
    falls,
Not with the empty hollowness, but weight:
I take my leave before I have begun:
For sorrow ends not when it seemeth done.
Commend me to my brother, Edmund York.
Lo, this is all:—nay, yet depart not so;
Though this be all, do not so quickly go;
I shall remember more. Bid him—ah, what?—
With all good speed at Plashy visit me.
Alack, and what shall good old York there see,
But empty lodgings and unfurnisht walls,
Unpeopled offices, untrodden stones?   [groans?
And what cheer there for welcome, but my
Therefore commend me; let him not come there,

To seek out sorrow that dwells every where.
Desolate, desolate, will I hence and die:
The last leave of thee takes my weeping eye.
                                        [*Exeunt.*

SCENE III.

Gosford Green, near Coventry.

Lists set out, and a throne; with ATTENDANTS.
Enter the LORD MARSHAL *and* AUMERLE.

LORD MARSHAL.

MY Lord Aumerle, is Harry Hereford arm'd?
              DUKE OF AUMERLE.
Yea, at all points; and longs to enter in.
              LORD MARSHAL.
The Duke of Norfolk, sprightfully and bold,
Stays but the summons of the appellant's trumpet.
              DUKE OF AUMERLE.
Why, then, the champions are prepared, and stay
For nothing but his majesty's approach.
The trumpets sound, and the KING *enters with his
nobles,* GAUNT, BUSHY, BAGOT, GREEN, *and
others. When they are set, enter the* DUKE OF
NORFOLK *in arms, defendant, with a* HERALD.
              KING RICHARD.
Marshal, demand of yonder champion
The cause of his arrival here in arms:
Ask him his name; and orderly proceed
To swear him in the justice of his cause.
              LORD MARSHAL.
In God's name and the king's, say who thou art,
And why thou comest thus knightly clad in arms;
Against what man thou comest, and what thy
    quarrel:
Speak truly, on thy knighthood and thy oath;
As so defend thee heaven and thy valour!
              DUKE OF NORFOLK.
My name is Thomas Mowbray, duke of Norfolk;
Who hither come engaged by my oath,—
Which God defend a knight should violate!—
Both to defend my loyalty and truth
To God, my king, and my succeeding issue,
Against the Duke of Hereford that appeals me;
And, by the grace of God and this mine arm,
To prove him, in defending of myself,
A traitor to my God, my king, and me:
And as I truly fight, defend me heaven!
The trumpets sound.   Enter BOLINGBROKE, *appellant, in armour, with a* HERALD.
              KING RICHARD.   ·
Marshal, ask yonder knight in arms,
Both who he is, and why he cometh hither
Thus plated in habiliments of war;
And formally, according to our law,
Depose him in the justice of his cause.
              LORD MARSHAL.
What is thy name? and wherefore comest thou
    hither,
Before King Richard in his royal lists?
Against whom comest thou? and what's thy
    quarrel?
Speak like a true knight, so defend thee heaven!
              HENRY BOLINGBROKE.
Harry of Hereford, Lancaster, and Derby,
Am I; who ready here do stand in arms,
To prove, by God's grace, and my body's valour,

In lists, on Thomas Mowbray, duke of Norfolk,
That he is a traitor, foul and dangerous,
To God of heaven, King Richard, and to me:
And as I truly fight, defend me heaven!
              LORD MARSHAL.
On pain of death, no person be so bold
Or daring-hardy as to touch the lists,
Except the marshal and such officers
Appointed to direct these fair designs.
              HENRY BOLINGBROKE.
Lord marshal, let me kiss my sovereign's hand,
And bow my knee before his majesty:
For Mowbray and myself are like two men
That vow a long and weary pilgrimage;
Then let us take a ceremonious leave
And loving farewell of our several friends.
              LORD MARSHAL.
The appellant in all duty greets your highness,
And craves to kiss your hand and take his leave.
              KING RICHARD.
We will descend and fold him in our arms.—
Cousin of Hereford, as thy cause is right,
So be thy fortune in this royal fight!
Farewell, my blood; which if to-day thou shed,
Lament we may, but not revenge thee dead.
              HENRY BOLINGBROKE.
O, let no noble eye profane a tear
For me, if I be gored with Mowbray's spear:
As confident as is the falcon's flight
Against a bird, do I with Mowbray fight.—
[*to* LORD MARSHAL] My loving lord, I take my
    leave of you;—
Of you, my noble cousin, Lord Aumerle;
Not sick, although I have to do with death,
But lusty, young, and cheerly drawing breath.—
Lo, as at English feasts, so I regreet
The daintiest last, to make the end most sweet:
[*to* GAUNT] O thou, the earthly author of my
    blood,—
Whose youthful spirit, in me regenerate,
Doth with a twofold vigour lift me up
To reach at victory above my head,—
Add proof unto mine armour with thy prayers;
And with thy blessings steel my lance's point,
That it may enter Mowbray's waxen coat,
And furbish new the name of John o' Gaunt,
Even in the lusty haviour of his son.
              JOHN OF GAUNT.
God in thy good cause make thee prosperous!
Be swift like lightning in the execution;
And let thy blows, doubly redoubled,
Fall like amazing thunder on the casque
Of thy adverse pernicious enemy:
Rouse up thy youthful blood, be valiant and live.
              HENRY BOLINGBROKE.
Mine innocency and Saint George to thrive!
              DUKE OF NORFOLK.
However God or fortune cast my lot,
There lives or dies, true to King Richard's throne,
A loyal, just, and upright gentleman:
Never did captive with a freer heart
Cast off his chains of bondage, and embrace
His golden uncontroll'd enfranchisement,
More than my dancing soul doth celebrate
This feast of battle with mine adversary.—
Most mighty liege, and my companion peers,

Take from my mouth the wish of happy years:
As gentle and as jocund as to jest
Go I to fight: truth hath a quiet breast.
KING RICHARD.
Farewell, my lord: securely I espy
Virtue with valour couched in thine eye.—
Order the trial, marshal, and begin.
LORD MARSHAL.
Harry of Hereford, Lancaster, and Derby,
Receive thy lance; and God defend the right!
HENRY BOLINGBROKE.
Strong as a tower in hope, I cry amen.
LORD MARSHAL [to an OFFICER].
Go bear this lance to Thomas, duke of Norfolk.
FIRST HERALD.
Harry of Hereford, Lancaster, and Derby,
Stands here for God, his sovereign, and himself,
On pain to be found false and recreant,
To prove the duke of Norfolk, Thomas Mowbray,
A traitor to his God, his king, and him;
And dares him to set forward to the fight.
SECOND HERALD.
Here standeth Thomas Mowbray, duke of
Norfolk,
On pain to be found false and recreant,
Both to defend himself, and to approve
Henry of Hereford, Lancaster, and Derby,
To God, his sovereign, and to him disloyal;
Courageously, and with a free desire,
Attending but the signal to begin.
LORD MARSHAL.
Sound, trumpets; and set forward, combatants.
[A charge sounded.
Stay, the king hath thrown his warder down.
KING RICHARD.
Let them lay by their helmets and their spears,
And both return back to their chairs again:—
Withdraw with us:—and let the trumpets sound
While we return these dukes what we decree.—
[A long flourish.
Draw near,
And list what with our council we have done.
For that our kingdom's earth should not be soil'd
With that dear blood which it hath fostered;
And for our eyes do hate the dire aspect
Of civil wounds plough'd up with neighbours'
sword;
And for we think the eagle-winged pride
Of sky-aspiring and ambitious thoughts,
With rival-hating envy, set on you
To wake our peace, which in our country's cradle
Draws the sweet infant breath of gentle sleep;
Which so roused up with boisterous untuned
drums,
With harsh-resounding trumpets' dreadful bray,
And grating shock of wrathful iron arms,
Might from our quiet confines fright fair peace,
And make us wade even in our kindred's blood;—
Therefore we banish you our territories:
You, cousin Hereford, upon pain of life,
Till twice five summers have enrich'd our fields,
Shall not regreet our fair dominions,
But tread the stranger paths of banishment.
HENRY BOLINGBROKE.
Your will be done: this must my comfort be,—
That sun that warms you here shall shine on me;

And those his golden beams to you here lent
Shall point on me and gild my banishment.
KING RICHARD.
Norfolk, for thee remains a heavier doom,
Which I with some unwillingness pronounce:
The sly slow hours shall not determinate
The dateless limit of thy dear exile;—
The hopeless word of 'never to return'
Breathe I against thee, upon pain of life.
DUKE OF NORFOLK.
A heavy sentence, my most sovereign liege,
And all unlookt-for from your highness' mouth:
A dearer merit, not so deep a maim
As to be cast forth in the common air,
Have I deserved at your highness' hands.
The language I have learn'd these forty years,
My native English, now I must forgo:
And now my tongue's use is to me no more
Than an unstringed viol or a harp;
Or like a cunning instrument cased up,
Or, being open, put into his hands
That knows no touch to tune the harmony:
Within my mouth you have engaol'd my tongue,
Doubly portcullised with my teeth and lips;
And dull, unfeeling, barren ignorance
Is made my gaoler to attend on me.
I am too old to fawn upon a nurse,
Too far in years to be a pupil now:
What is thy sentence, then, but speechless
death,
Which robs my tongue from breathing native
breath?
KING RICHARD.
It boots thee not to be compassionate:
After our sentence plaining comes too late.
DUKE OF NORFOLK.
Then thus I turn me from my country's light,
To dwell in solemn shades of endless night.
KING RICHARD.
Return again, and take an oath with thee.
Lay on our royal sword your banisht hands;
Swear by the duty that you owe to God,—
Our part therein we banish with yourselves,—
To keep the oath that we administer:—
You never shall—so help you truth and God!—
Embrace each other's love in banishment;
Nor never look upon each other's face;
Nor never write, regreet, nor reconcile
This louring tempest of your home-bred
hate;
Nor never by advised purpose meet
To plot, contrive, or complot any ill
'Gainst us, our state, our subjects, or our land.
HENRY BOLINGBROKE.
I swear.
DUKE OF NORFOLK.
And I, to keep all this.
HENRY BOLINGBROKE.
Norfolk, so far as to mine enemy;—
By this time, had the king permitted us,
One of our souls had wander'd in the air,
Banisht this frail sepulchre of our flesh,
As now our flesh is banisht from this land:
Confess thy treasons, ere thou fly the realm;
Since thou hast far to go, bear not along
The clogging burden of a guilty soul.

DUKE OF NORFOLK.

No, Bolingbroke: if ever I were traitor,
My name be blotted from the book of life,
And I from heaven banisht, as from hence!
But what thou art, God, thou, and I do know;
And all too soon, I fear, the king shall rue.—
Farewell, my liege.—Now no way can I stray:
Save back to England, all the world's my way. [Exit.

KING RICHARD.

Uncle, even in the glasses of thine eyes
I see thy grieved heart: thy sad aspect
Hath from the number of his banisht years
Pluckt four away.—[to BOLINGBROKE] Six
    frozen winters spent,
Return with welcome home from banishment.

HENRY BOLINGBROKE.

How long a time lies in one little word!
Four lagging winters and four wanton springs
End in a word: such is the breath of kings.

JOHN OF GAUNT.

I thank my liege, that in regard of me
He shortens four years of my son's exile:
But little vantage shall I reap thereby;
For, ere the six years that he hath to spend
Can change their moons and bring their times
    about,
My oil-dried lamp and time-bewasted light
Shall be extinct with age and endless night;
My inch of taper will be burnt and done,
And blindfold death not let me see my son.

KING RICHARD.

Why, uncle, thou hast many years to live.

JOHN OF GAUNT.

But not a minute, king, that thou canst give:
Shorten my days thou canst with sullen sorrow,
And pluck nights from me, but not lend a
    morrow;
Thou canst help time to furrow me with age,
But stop no wrinkle in his pilgrimage;
Thy word is current with him for my death,
But dead, thy kingdom cannot buy my breath.

KING RICHARD.

Thy son is banisht upon good advice,
Whereto thy tongue a party-verdict gave:
Why at our justice seem'st thou, then, to lour?

JOHN OF GAUNT.

Things sweet to taste prove in digestion sour.
You urged me as a judge; but I had rather
You would have bid me argue like a father.
O, had it been a stranger, not my child,   [mild:
To smooth his fault I should have been more
A partial slander sought I to avoid,
And in the sentence my own life destroy'd.
Alas, I lookt when some of you should say,
I was too strict to make mine own away;
But you gave leave to my unwilling tongue
Against my will to do myself this wrong.

KING RICHARD.

Cousin, farewell;—and, uncle, bid him so:
Six years we banish him, and he shall go.
    [Flourish. Exeunt KING RICHARD and
    TRAIN.

DUKE OF AUMERLE.

Cousin, farewell: what presence must not know,
From where you do remain let paper show.

LORD MARSHAL.

My lord, no leave take I; for I will ride,
As far as land will let me, by your side.

JOHN OF GAUNT.

O, to what purpose dost thou hoard thy words,
That thou return'st no greeting to thy friends?

HENRY BOLINGBROKE.

I have too few to take my leave of you,
When the tongue's office should be prodigal
To breathe th'abundant dolour of the heart.

JOHN OF GAUNT.

Thy grief is but thy absence for a time.

HENRY BOLINGBROKE.

Joy absent, grief is present for that time.

JOHN OF GAUNT.

What is six winters? they are quickly gone.

HENRY BOLINGBROKE.

To men in joy; but grief makes one hour ten.

JOHN OF GAUNT.

Call it a travel that thou takest for pleasure.

HENRY BOLINGBROKE.

My heart will sigh when I miscall it so,
Which finds it an enforced pilgrimage.

JOHN OF GAUNT.

The sullen passage of thy weary steps
Esteem as foil, wherein thou art to set
The precious jewel of thy home-return.

HENRY BOLINGBROKE.

Nay, rather, every tedious stride I make
Will but remember me what deal of world
I wander from the jewels that I love.
Must I not serve a long apprenticehood
To foreign passages; and in the end,
Having my freedom, boast of nothing else
But that I was a journeyman to grief?

JOHN OF GAUNT.

All places that the eye of heaven visits
Are to a wise man ports and happy havens.
Teach thy necessity to reason thus;
There is no virtue like necessity.
Think not the king did banish thee,
But thou the king; woe doth the heavier sit,
Where it perceives it is but faintly borne.
Go say, I sent thee forth to purchase honour,
And not, the king exiled thee; or suppose
Devouring pestilence hangs in our air,
And thou art flying to a fresher clime:
Look, what thy soul holds dear, imagine it
To lie that way thou go'st, not whence thou
    comest:
Suppose the singing-birds musicians,
The grass whereon thou tread'st the presence
    strew'd,
The flowers fair ladies, and thy steps no more
Than a delightful measure or a dance;
For gnarling sorrow hath less power to bite
The man that mocks at it and sets it light.

HENRY BOLINGBROKE.

O, who can hold a fire in his hand
By thinking on the frosty Caucasus?
Or cloy the hungry edge of appetite
By bare imagination of a feast?
Or wallow naked in December snow
By thinking on fantastic summer's heat?
O, no! the apprehension of the good
Gives but the greater feeling to the worse:

Fell sorrow's tooth doth never rankle more
Than when he bites, but lanceth not the sore.
JOHN OF GAUNT.
Come, come, my son, I'll bring thee on thy way:
Had I thy youth and cause, I would not stay.
HENRY BOLINGBROKE.
Then, England's ground, farewell; sweet soil,
adieu;
My mother, and my nurse, that bears me yet!
Where'er I wander, boast of this I can,—
Though banisht, yet a true-born Englishman.
[*Exeunt.*

SCENE IV.

The court.

Enter, from one side, KING RICHARD, BAGOT,
and GREEN; *from the other,* AUMERLE.

KING RICHARD.
WE did observe.—Cousin Aumerle,
How far brought you high Hereford on his
way?
DUKE OF AUMERLE.
I brought high Hereford, if you call him so,
But to the next highway, and there I left him.
KING RICHARD.
And say, what store of parting tears were shed?
DUKE OF AUMERLE.
Faith, none for me; except the north-east wind,
Which then blew bitterly against our faces,
Awaked the sleeping rheum, and so by chance
Did grace our hollow parting with a tear.
KING RICHARD.
What said our cousin when you parted with him?
DUKE OF AUMERLE.
'Farewell;'
And, for my heart disdained that my tongue
Should so profane the word, that taught me craft
To counterfeit oppression of such grief,
That words seem'd buried in my sorrow's grave.
Marry, would the word 'farewell' have lengthen'd
hours,
And added years to his short banishment,
He should have had a volume of 'farewells;'
But since it would not, he had none of me.
KING RICHARD.
He is our cousin, cousin; but 'tis doubt,
When time shall call him home from banishment,
Whether our kinsman come to see his friends.
Ourself, and Bushy, Bagot here, and Green,
Observed his courtship to the common people;
How he did seem to dive into their hearts
With humble and familiar courtesy;
What reverence he did throw away on slaves;
Wooing poor craftsmen with the craft of smiles,
And patient underbearing of his fortune,
As 'twere to banish their affects with him.
Off goes his bonnet to an oyster-wench;
A brace of draymen bid God speed him well,
And had the tribute of his supple knee,
With 'Thanks, my countrymen, my loving
friends;'
As were our England in reversion his,
And he our subjects' next degree in hope.
GREEN.
Well, he is gone; and with him go these thoughts.
Now for the rebels which stand out in Ireland,—

Expedient manage must be made, my liege,
Ere further leisure yield them further means
For their advantage and your highness' loss.
KING RICHARD.
We will ourself in person to this war:
And, for our coffers, with too great a court
And liberal largess, are grown somewhat light,
We are enforced to farm our royal realm;
The revenue whereof shall furnish us
For our affairs in hand. If that come short,
Our substitutes at home shall have blank charters;
Whereto, when they shall know what men are
rich,
They shall subscribe them for large sums of gold,
And send them after to supply our wants;
For we will make for Ireland presently.
Enter BUSHY.
Bushy, what news?
BUSHY.
Old John of Gaunt is grievous sick, my lord,
Suddenly taken; and hath sent post-haste
To entreat your majesty to visit him.
KING RICHARD.
Where lies he?
BUSHY.
At Ely-house.
KING RICHARD.
Now put it, God, in the physician's mind
To help him to his grave immediately!
The lining of his coffers shall make coats
To deck our soldiers for these Irish wars.—
Come, gentlemen, let's all go visit him:
Pray God we may make haste, and come too late!
ALL.
Amen.   [*Exeunt.*

ACT II. SCENE I.

London. A room in Ely-house.

Enter GAUNT *sick, with the* DUKE OF YORK
and others.

JOHN OF GAUNT.
WILL the king come, that I may breathe my
last
In wholesome counsel to his unstaid youth?
DUKE OF YORK.
Vex not yourself, nor strive not with your breath;
For all in vain comes counsel to his ear.
JOHN OF GAUNT.
O, but they say the tongues of dying men
Enforce attention like deep harmony:
Where words are scarce, they are seldom spent
in vain;
For they breathe truth that breathe their words in
pain.
He that no more must say is listen'd more
Than they whom youth and ease have taught to
gloze;
More are men's ends markt than their lives
before:
The setting sun, and music at the close,
As the last taste of sweets, is sweetest last,
Writ in remembrance more than things long past:
Though Richard my life's counsel would not hear,
My death's sad tale may yet undeaf his ear.

DUKE OF YORK.

No; it is stopt with other flattering sounds,
As, praises of his state: then there are found
Lascivious metres, to whose venom sound
The open ear of youth doth always listen;
Report of fashions in proud Italy,
Whose manners still our tardy apish nation
Limps after in base imitation.
Where doth the world thrust forth a vanity,—
So it be new, there's no respect how vile,—
That is not quickly buzz'd into his ears?
Then all too late comes counsel to be heard,
Where will doth mutiny with wit's regard.
Direct not him, whose way himself will choose:
'Tis breath thou lack'st, and that breath wilt thou
    lose.

JOHN OF GAUNT.

Methinks I am a prophet new-inspired,
And thus, expiring, do foretell of him:
His rash fierce blaze of riot cannot last,
For violent fires soon burn out themselves;
Small showers last long, but sudden storms are
    short;
He tires betimes that spurs too fast betimes;
With eager feeding food doth choke the feeder:
Light vanity, insatiate cormorant,
Consuming means, soon preys upon itself.
This royal throne of kings, this scepter'd isle,
This earth of majesty, this seat of Mars,
This other Eden, demi-Paradise;
This fortress built by Nature for herself
Against infection and the hand of war;
This happy breed of men, this little world;
This precious stone set in the silver sea,
Which serves it in the office of a wall,
Or as a moat defensive to a house,
Against the envy of less happier lands;
This blessed plot, this earth, this realm, this
    England,
This nurse, this teeming womb of royal kings,
Fear'd by their breed, and famous by their
    birth,
Renowned for their deeds as far from home,—
For Christian service and true chivalry,—
As is the sepulchre, in stubborn Jewry,
Of the world's ransom, blessed Mary's Son;—
This land of such dear souls, this dear dear land,
Dear for her reputation through the world,
Is now leased out—I die pronouncing it—
Like to a tenement or pelting farm:
England, bound in with the triumphant sea,
Whose rocky shore beats back the envious siege
Of watery Neptune, is now bound in with shame,
With inky blots, and rotten parchment bonds:
That England, that was wont to conquer others,
Hath made a shameful conquest of itself.
Ah, would the scandal vanish with my life,
How happy then were my ensuing death!

Enter KING RICHARD *and* QUEEN, AUMERLE,
    BUSHY, GREEN, BAGOT, ROSS, *and* WIL-
    LOUGHBY.

DUKE OF YORK.

The king is come: deal mildly with his youth;
For young hot colts being raged do rage the more.

QUEEN.

How fares our noble uncle, Lancaster?

KING RICHARD.

What comfort, man? how is 't with aged Gaunt?

JOHN OF GAUNT.

O, how that name befits my composition!
Old Gaunt, indeed; and gaunt in being old:
Within me grief hath kept a tedious fast;
And who abstains from meat, that is not gaunt?
For sleeping England long time have I watcht;
Watching breeds leanness, leanness is all gaunt:
The pleasure that some fathers feed upon,
Is my strict fast,—I mean, my children's looks;
And therein fasting, hast thou made me gaunt:
Gaunt am I for the grave, gaunt as a grave,
Whose hollow womb inherits naught but bones.

KING RICHARD.

Can sick men play so nicely with their names?

JOHN OF GAUNT.

No, misery makes sport to mock itself:
Since thou dost seek to kill my name in me,
I mock my name, great king, to flatter thee.

KING RICHARD.

Should dying men flatter with those that live?

JOHN OF GAUNT.

No, no, men living flatter those that die.

KING RICHARD.

Thou, now a-dying, say'st thou flatter'st me.

JOHN OF GAUNT.

O, no! thou diest, though I the sicker be.

KING RICHARD.

I am in health, I breathe, and see thee ill.

JOHN OF GAUNT.

Now, He that made me knows I see thee ill;
Ill in myself to see, and in thee seeing ill.
Thy death-bed is no lesser than thy land,
Wherein thou liest in reputation sick;
And thou, too careless patient as thou art,
Committ'st thy 'nointed body to the cure
Of those physicians that first wounded thee:
A thousand flatterers sit within thy crown,
Whose compass is no bigger than thy head;
And yet, incaged in so small a verge,
The waste is no whit lesser than thy land.
O, had thy grandsire, with a prophet's eye,
Seen how his son's son should destroy his sons,
From forth thy reach he would have laid thy
    shame,
Deposing thee before thou wert possest,
Which art possest now to depose thyself.
Why, cousin, wert thou regent of the world,
It were a shame to let this land by lease;
But for thy world enjoying but this land,
Is it not more than shame to shame it so?
Landlord of England art thou now, not king:
Thy state of law is bond-slave to the law;
And thou—

KING RICHARD.

                A lunatic lean-witted fool,
Presuming on an ague's privilege,
Darest with thy frozen admonition
Make pale our cheek, chasing the royal blood
With fury from his native residence.
Now, by my seat's right royal majesty,
Wert thou not brother to great Edward's son,
This tongue that runs so roundly in thy head
Should run thy head from thy unreverent
    shoulders.

JOHN OF GAUNT.

O, spare me not, my brother Edward's son,
For that I was his father Edward's son;—
That blood already, like the pelican,
Hast thou tapt out, and drunkenly caroused:
My brother Gloster, plain well-meaning soul,—
Whom fair befall in heaven 'mongst happy
    souls!—
May be a precedent and witness good
That thou respect'st not spilling Edward's
    blood:
Join with the present sickness that I have;
And thy unkindness be like crooked age,
To crop at once a too-long wither'd flower.
Live in thy shame, but die not shame with thee!—
These words hereafter thy tormentors be!—
Convey me to my bed, then to my grave:
Love they to live that love and honour have.
        [Exit, borne out by his ATTENDANTS.

KING RICHARD.

And let them die that age and sullens have;
For both hast thou, and both become the grave.

DUKE OF YORK.

I do beseech your majesty, impute his words
To wayward sickliness and age in him:
He loves you, on my life, and holds you dear
As Harry, duke of Hereford, were he here.

KING RICHARD.

Right, you say true: as Hereford's love, so his;
As theirs, so mine; and all be as it is.

        Enter NORTHUMBERLAND.

EARL OF NORTHUMBERLAND.

My liege, old Gaunt commends him to your
    majesty.

KING RICHARD.

What says he?

EARL OF NORTHUMBERLAND.

        Nay, nothing; all is said:
His tongue is now a stringless instrument;
Words, life, and all, old Lancaster hath spent.

DUKE OF YORK.

Be York the next that must be bankrupt so!
Though death be poor, it ends a mortal woe.

KING RICHARD.

The ripest fruit first falls, and so doth he;
His time is spent, our pilgrimage must be:
So much for that.—Now for our Irish wars:
We must supplant these rough rug-headed kerns,
Which live like venom, where no venom else
But only they have privilege to live.
And for these great affairs do ask some charge,
Towards our assistance we do seize to us
The plate, coin, revenues, and movables,
Whereof our uncle Gaunt did stand possest.

DUKE OF YORK.

How long shall I be patient? ah, how long
Shall tender duty make me suffer wrong?
Not Gloster's death, nor Hereford's banishment,
Not Gaunt's rebukes, nor England's private
    wrongs,
Nor the prevention of poor Bolingbroke
About his marriage, nor my own disgrace,
Have ever made me sour my patient cheek,
Or bend one wrinkle on my sovereign's face.
I am the last of noble Edward's sons,
Of whom thy father, Prince of Wales, was first:

In war was never lion raged more fierce,
In peace was never gentle lamb more mild,
Than was that young and princely gentleman.
His face thou hast, for even so lookt he,
Accomplisht with the number of thy hours;
But when he frown'd, it was against the French,
And not against his friends: his noble hand
Did win what he did spend, and spent not that
Which his triumphant father's hand had won:
His hands were guilty of no kindred's blood,
But bloody with the enemies of his kin.
O Richard! York is too far gone with grief,
Or else he never would compare between.

KING RICHARD.

Why, uncle, what's the matter?

DUKE OF YORK.

        O my liege,
Pardon me, if you please; if not, I, pleased
Not to be pardon'd, am content withal.
Seek you to seize, and gripe into your hands,
The royalties and rights of banisht Hereford?
Is not Gaunt dead? and doth not Hereford live?
Was not Gaunt just? and is not Harry true?
Did not the one deserve to have an heir?
Is not his heir a well-deserving son?
Take Hereford's rights away, and take from
    Time
His charters and his customary rights;
Let not to-morrow, then, ensue to-day;
Be not thyself,—for how art thou a king
But by fair sequence and succession?
Now, afore God,—God forbid I say true!—
If you do wrongfully seize Hereford's rights,
Call in the letters-patents that he hath
By his attorneys-general to sue
His livery, and deny his offer'd homage,
You pluck a thousand dangers on your head,
You lose a thousand well-disposed hearts,
And prick my tender patience to those thoughts
Which honour and allegiance cannot think.

KING RICHARD.

Think what you will, we seize into our hands
His plate, his goods, his money, and his lands.

DUKE OF YORK.

I'll not be by the while: my liege, farewell:
What will ensue hereof, there's none can tell;
But by bad courses may be understood
That their events can never fall out good.   [Exit.

KING RICHARD.

Go, Bushy, to the Earl of Wiltshire straight:
Bid him repair to us to Ely-house
To see this business. To-morrow next
We will for Ireland; and 'tis time, I trow:
And we create, in absence of ourself,
Our uncle York lord governor of England;
For he is just, and always loved us well.—
Come on, our queen: to-morrow must we part;
Be merry, for our time of stay is short.
    [Flourish. Exeunt KING, QUEEN, AU-
        MERLE, BUSHY, GREEN, and BAGOT.

EARL OF NORTHUMBERLAND.

Well, lords, the Duke of Lancaster is dead.

LORD ROSS.

And living too; for now his son is duke.

LORD WILLOUGHBY.

Barely in title, not in revenues.

EARL OF NORTHUMBERLAND.
Richly in both, if justice had her right.
LORD ROSS.
My heart is great; but it must break with silence,
Ere't be disburden'd with a liberal tongue.
EARL OF NORTHUMBERLAND.
Nay, speak thy mind; and let him ne'er speak
more
That speaks thy words again to do thee harm!
LORD WILLOUGHBY.
Tends that thou wouldst speak to the Duke of
Hereford?
If it be so, out with it boldly, man;
Quick is mine ear to hear of good towards him.
LORD ROSS.
No good at all, that I can do for him;
Unless you call it good to pity him,
Bereft and gelded of his patrimony.
EARL OF NORTHUMBERLAND.
Now, afore God, 'tis shame such wrongs are
borne
In him, a royal prince, and many moe
Of noble blood in this declining land.
The king is not himself, but basely led
By flatterers; and what they will inform,
Merely in hate, 'gainst any of us all,
That will the king severely prosecute
'Gainst us, our lives, our children, and our heirs.
LORD ROSS.
The commons hath he pill'd with grievous taxes,
And quite lost their hearts: the nobles hath he
fined
For ancient quarrels, and quite lost their hearts.
LORD WILLOUGHBY.
And daily new exactions are devised,—
As blanks, benevolences, and I wot not what:
But what, o' God's name, doth become of this?
EARL OF NORTHUMBERLAND.
Wars have not wasted it, for warr'd he hath not,
But basely yielded upon compromise
That which his ancestors achieved with blows:
More hath he spent in peace than they in wars.
LORD ROSS.
The Earl of Wiltshire hath the realm in farm.
LORD WILLOUGHBY.
The king's grown bankrout, like a broken man.
EARL OF NORTHUMBERLAND.
Reproach and dissolution hangeth over him.
LORD ROSS.
He hath not money for these Irish wars,
His burdenous taxations notwithstanding,
But by the robbing of the banisht duke.
EARL OF NORTHUMBERLAND.
His noble kinsman:—most degenerate king!
But, lords, we hear this fearful tempest sing,
Yet seek no shelter to avoid the storm;
We see the wind sit sore upon our sails,
And yet we strike not, but securely perish.
LORD ROSS.
We see the very wrack that we must suffer;
And unavoided is the danger now,
For suffering so the causes of our wrack.
EARL OF NORTHUMBERLAND.
Not so; even through the hollow eyes of death
I spy life peering; but I dare not say
How near the tidings of our comfort is.

LORD WILLOUGHBY.
Nay, let us share thy thoughts, as thou dost ours.
LORD ROSS.
Be confident to speak, Northumberland:
We three are but thyself; and, speaking so,
Thy words are but as thoughts; therefore, be bold.
EARL OF NORTHUMBERLAND.
Then thus:—I have from Port le Blanc, a bay
In Brittany, received intelligence
That Harry, Duke of Hereford, Rainold, Lord
Cobham,
That late broke from the Duke of Exeter,
His brother, Archbishop late of Canterbury,
Sir Thomas Erpingham, Sir John Ramston,
Sir John Norbery, Sir Robert Waterton, and
Francis Quoint,—
All these well furnisht by the Duke of Bretagne,
With eight tall ships, three thousand men of war,
Are making hither with all due expedience,
And shortly mean to touch our northern shore:
Perhaps they had ere this, but that they stay
The first departing of the king for Ireland.
If, then, we shall shake off our slavish yoke,
Imp out our drooping country's broken wing,
Redeem from broking pawn the blemisht crown,
Wipe off the dust that hides our sceptre's gilt,
And make high majesty look like itself,
Away with me in post to Ravenspurg;
But if you faint, as fearing to do so,
Stay, and be secret, and myself will go.
LORD ROSS.
To horse, to horse! urge doubts to them that fear.
LORD WILLOUGHBY.
Hold out my horse, and I will first be there.
[Exeunt.

SCENE II.
The Court.

Enter QUEEN, BUSHY, and BAGOT.

BUSHY.
MADAM, your majesty is too much sad:
You promised, when you parted with the
king,
To lay aside life-harming heaviness,
And entertain a cheerful disposition.
QUEEN.
To please the king, I did; to please myself,
I cannot do it; yet I know no cause
Why I should welcome such a guest as grief,
Save bidding farewell to so sweet a guest
As my sweet Richard: yet, again, methinks
Some unborn sorrow, ripe in fortune's womb,
Is coming towards me; and my inward soul
With nothing trembles: at something it grieves,
More than with parting from my lord the king.
BUSHY.
Each substance of a grief hath twenty shadows,
Which shows like grief itself, but is not so;
For sorrow's eye, glazed with blinding tears,
Divides one thing entire to many objects;
Like perspectives, which rightly gazed upon,
Show nothing but confusion,—eyed awry,
Distinguish form: so your sweet majesty,
Looking awry upon your lord's departure,
Find shapes of grief, more than himself, to wail;

Which, lookt on as it is, is naught but shadows
Of what it is not. Then, thrice-gracious queen,
More than your lord's departure weep not,—
    more's not seen;
Or if it be, 'tis with false sorrow's eye,
Which for things true weeps things imaginary.
        QUEEN.
It may be so; but yet my inward soul
Persuades me it is otherwise: howe'er it be,
I cannot but be sad; so heavy sad,
As, though, on thinking, on no thought I think.
Makes me with heavy nothing faint and shrink.
        BUSHY.
'Tis nothing but conceit, my gracious lady.
        QUEEN.
'Tis nothing less: conceit is still derived
From some forefather grief; mine is not so,
For nothing hath begot my something grief;
Or something hath the nothing that I grieve:
'Tis in reversion that I do possess;
But what it is, that is not yet known; what
I cannot name; 'tis nameless woe, I wot.
        Enter GREEN.
        GREEN.
God save your majesty! and well met, gentlemen:
I hope the king is not yet shipt for Ireland.
        QUEEN.
Why hopest thou so? 'tis better hope he is;
For his designs crave haste, his haste good hope:
Then wherefore dost thou hope he is not shipt?
        GREEN.
That he, our hope, might have retired his power,
And driven into despair an enemy's hope,
Who strongly hath set footing in this land:
The banisht Bolingbroke repeals himself,
And with uplifted arms is safe arrived
At Ravenspurg.
        QUEEN.
        Now God in heaven forbid!
        GREEN.
Ah madam, 'tis too true: and that is worse,
The Lord Northumberland, his son young Henry
    Percy,
The Lords of Ross, Beaumond, and Willoughby,
With all their powerful friends, are fled to him.
        BUSHY.
Why have you not proclaim'd Northumberland
And all the rest revolted faction traitors?
        GREEN.
We have: whereupon the Earl of Worcester
Hath broke his staff, resign'd his stewardship,
And all the household servants fled with him
To Bolingbroke.
        QUEEN.
So, Green, thou art the midwife to my woe,
And Bolingbroke my sorrow's dismal heir:
Now hath my soul brought forth her prodigy;
And I, a gasping new-deliver'd mother,
Have woe to woe, sorrow to sorrow join'd.
        BUSHY.
Despair not, madam.
        QUEEN.
        Who shall hinder me?
I will despair, and be at enmity
With cozening hope,—he is a flatterer,
A parasite, a keeper-back of death,

Who gently would dissolve the bands of life,
Which false hope lingers in extremity.
        GREEN.
Here comes the Duke of York.
        QUEEN.
With signs of war about his aged neck:
O, full of careful business are his looks!
        Enter YORK.
Uncle, for God's sake, speak comfortable words.
        DUKE OF YORK.
Should I do so, I should belie my thoughts:
Comfort's in heaven; and we are on the earth,
Where nothing lives but crosses, cares, and grief.
Your husband, he is gone to save far off,
Whilst others come to make him lose at home:
Here am I left to underprop his land,
Who, weak with age, cannot support myself:
Now comes the sick hour that his surfeit made;
Now shall he try his friends that flatter'd him.
        Enter a SERVANT.
        SERVANT.
My lord, your son was gone before I came.
        DUKE OF YORK.
He was?—Why, so!—go all which way it will!—
The nobles they are fled, the commons they are
    cold,
And will, I fear, revolt on Hereford's side.—
Sirrah, get thee to Plashy, to my sister Gloster;
Bid her send me presently a thousand pound:—
Hold, take my ring.
        SERVANT.
My lord, I had forgot to tell your lordship,
To-day, as I came by, I called there;—
But I shall grieve you to report the rest.
        DUKE OF YORK.
What is it, knave?
        SERVANT.
An hour before I came, the duchess died.
        DUKE OF YORK.
God for his mercy! what a tide of woes
Comes rushing on this woful land at once!
I know not what to do:—I would to God,—
So my untruth had not provoked him to it,—
The king had cut off my head with my
    brother's.—
What, are there no posts dispatcht for Ire-
    land?—
How shall we do for money for these wars?—
Come, sister,—cousin, I would say,—pray, par-
    don me.—
Go, fellow, get thee home, provide some carts,
And bring away the armour that is there.
        [Exit SERVANT.
Gentlemen, will you go muster men? If I
Know how or which way to order these affairs,
Thus disorderly thrust into my hands,
Never believe me. Both are my kinsmen:—
Th'one is my sovereign, whom both my oath
And duty bids defend; th'other, again,
Is my kinsman, whom the king hath wrong'd,
Whom conscience and my kindred bids to right.
Well, somewhat we must do.—Come, cousin, I'll
Dispose of you.—Gentlemen, go muster up your
    men,
And meet me presently at Berkley.
I should to Plashy too;—

But time will not permit:—all is uneven,
And every thing is left at six and seven.
     [*Exeunt* YORK *and* QUEEN.
     BUSHY.
The wind sits fair for news to go to Ireland,
But none returns. For us to levy power
Proportionable to the enemy
Is all unpossible.
     GREEN.
Besides, our nearness to the king in love
Is near the hate of those love not the king.
     BAGOT.
And that's the wavering commons: for their love
Lies in their purses; and whoso empties them,
By so much fills their hearts with deadly hate.
     BUSHY.
Wherein the king stands generally condemn'd.
     BAGOT.
If judgement lie in them, then so do we,
Because we ever have been near the king.
     GREEN.
Well, I will for refuge straight to Bristol-castle:
The Earl of Wiltshire is already there.
     BUSHY.
Thither will I with you; for little office
The hateful commons will perform for us,
Except like curs to tear us all to pieces.—
Will you go along with us?
     BAGOT.
No; I will to Ireland to his majesty.
Farewell: if heart's presages be not vain,
We three here part that ne'er shall meet again.
     BUSHY.
That's as York thrives to beat back Bolingbroke.
     GREEN.
Alas, poor duke! the task he undertakes
Is numbering sands, and drinking oceans dry:
Where one on his side fights, thousands will fly.
Farewell at once,—for once, for all, and ever.
     BUSHY.
Well, we may meet again.
     BAGOT.
     I fear me, never.
         [*Exeunt.*

SCENE III.

The wilds in Glostershire.

Enter BOLINGBROKE *and* NORTHUMBER-
LAND, *with* FORCES.

     HENRY BOLINGBROKE.
HOW far is it, my lord, to Berkley now?
  EARL OF NORTHUMBERLAND.
Believe me, noble lord,
I am a stranger here in Glostershire:
These high wild hills and rough uneven ways
Draw out our miles, and make them wearisome;
And yet your fair discourse hath been as sugar,
Making the hard way sweet and delectable.
But I bethink me what a weary way
From Ravenspurg to Cotswold will be found
In Ross and Willoughby, wanting your company,
Which, I protest, hath very much beguiled
The tediousness and process of my travel:
But theirs is sweeten'd with the hope to have
The present benefit which I possess;
And hope to joy is little less in joy

Than hope enjoy'd: by this the weary lords
Shall make their way seem short; as mine hath
 done
By sight of what I have, your noble company.
     HENRY BOLINGBROKE.
Of much less value is my company
Than your good words.—But who comes here?
   EARL OF NORTHUMBERLAND.
It is my son, young Harry Percy,
Sent from my brother Worcester, whencesoever.
     Enter PERCY.
Harry, how fares your uncle?
     HENRY PERCY.
I had thought, my lord, to have learn'd his health
 of you.
   EARL OF NORTHUMBERLAND.
Why, is he not with the queen?
     HENRY PERCY.
No, my good lord; he hath forsook the court,
Broken his staff of office, and dispersed
The household of the king.
   EARL OF NORTHUMBERLAND.
      What was his reason?
He was not so resolved when last we spake to-
 gether.
     HENRY PERCY.
Because your lordship was proclaimed traitor.
But he, my lord, is gone to Ravenspurg,
To offer service to the Duke of Hereford;
And sent me over by Berkley, to discover
What power the Duke of York had levied there;
Then with directions to repair to Ravenspurg.
   EARL OF NORTHUMBERLAND.
Have you forgot the Duke of Hereford, boy?
     HENRY PERCY.
No, my good lord; for that is not forgot
Which ne'er I did remember: to my knowledge,
I never in my life did look on him.
   EARL OF NORTHUMBERLAND.
Then learn to know him now; this is the duke.
     HENRY PERCY.
My gracious lord, I tender you my service,
Such as it is, being tender, raw, and young;
Which elder days shall ripen, and confirm
To more approved service and desert.
     HENRY BOLINGBROKE.
I thank thee, gentle Percy; and be sure
I count myself in nothing else so happy
As in a soul remembering my good friends;
And, as my fortune ripens with thy love,
It shall be still thy true love's recompense:
My heart this covenant makes, my hand thus seals
 it.
   EARL OF NORTHUMBERLAND.
How far is it to Berkley? and what stir
Keeps good old York there with his men of war?
     HENRY PERCY.
There stands the castle, by yond tuft of trees,
Mann'd with three hundred men, as I have
 heard;
And in it are the Lords of York, Berkley, and
 Seymour,—
None else of name and noble estimate.
   EARL OF NORTHUMBERLAND.
Here come the Lords of Ross and Willoughby,
Bloody with spurring, fiery-red with haste.

Enter ROSS *and* WILLOUGHBY.
HENRY BOLINGBROKE.
Welcome, my lords. I wot your love pursues
A banisht traitor: all my treasury
Is yet but unfelt thanks, which, more enrich'd,
Shall be your love and labour's recompense.
LORD ROSS.
Your presence makes us rich, most noble lord.
LORD WILLOUGHBY.
And far surmounts our labour to attain it.
HENRY BOLINGBROKE.
Evermore thanks, the exchequer of the poor;
Which, till my infant fortune comes to years,
Stands for my bounty.—But who comes here?
EARL OF NORTHUMBERLAND.
It is my Lord of Berkley, as I guess.
Enter BERKLEY.
LORD BERKLEY.
My Lord of Hereford, my message is to you.
HENRY BOLINGBROKE.
My lord, my answer is—'to Lancaster;'
And I am come to seek that name in England;
And I must find that title in your tongue,
Before I make reply to aught you say.
LORD BERKLEY.
Mistake me not, my lord; 'tis not my meaning
To raze one title of your honour out:—
To you, my lord, I come,—what lord you will,—
From the most gracious regent of this land,
The Duke of York, to know what pricks you on
To take advantage of the absent time,
And fright our native peace with self-born arms.
HENRY BOLINGBROKE.
I shall not need transport my words by you;
Here comes his Grace in person.
Enter YORK *attended.*
          My noble uncle! [*Kneels.*
DUKE OF YORK.
Show me thy humble heart, and not thy knee,
Whose duty is deceivable and false.
HENRY BOLINGBROKE.
My gracious uncle!
DUKE OF YORK.
Tut, tut!
Grace me no grace, nor uncle me no uncle:
I am no traitor's uncle; and that word 'grace'
In an ungracious mouth is but profane.
Why have those banisht and forbidden legs
Dared once to touch a dust of England's ground?
But, then, more 'why?'—why have they dared to
So many miles upon her peaceful bosom, [march
Frighting her pale-faced villages with war
And ostentation of despised arms?
Comest thou because th' anointed king is hence?
Why, foolish boy, the king is left behind,
And in my loyal bosom lies his power.
Were I but now the lord of such hot youth
As when brave Gaunt thy father, and myself,
Rescued the Black Prince, that young Mars of men,
From forth the ranks of many thousand French,
O, then, how quickly should this arm of mine,
Now prisoner to the palsy, chastise thee,
And minister correction to thy fault!
HENRY BOLINGBROKE.
My gracious uncle, let me know my fault;
On what condition stands it and wherein?

DUKE OF YORK.
Even in condition of the worst degree,—
In gross rebellion and detested treason:
Thou art a banisht man; and here art come
Before the expiration of thy time,
In braving arms against thy sovereign.
HENRY BOLINGBROKE.
As I was banisht, I was banisht Hereford;
But as I come, I come for Lancaster.
And, noble uncle, I beseech your Grace
Look on my wrongs with an indifferent eye:
You are my father, for methinks in you
I see old Gaunt alive; O, then, my father,
Will you permit that I shall stand condemn'd
A wandering vagabond; my rights and royalties
Pluckt from my arms perforce, and given away
To upstart unthrifts? Wherefore was I born?
If that my cousin king be King of England,
It must be granted I am Duke of Lancaster.
You have a son, Aumerle, my noble cousin;
Had you first died, and he been thus trod down,
He should have found his uncle Gaunt a father,
To rouse his wrongs, and chase them to the bay.
I am denied to sue my livery here,
And yet my letters-patents give me leave:
My father's goods are all distrain'd and sold;
And these and all are all amiss employ'd.
What would you have me do? I am a subject,
And I challenge law: attorneys are denied me;
And therefore personally I lay my claim
To my inheritance of free descent.
EARL OF NORTHUMBERLAND.
The noble duke hath been too much abused.
LORD ROSS.
It stands your Grace upon to do him right.
LORD WILLOUGHBY.
Base men by his endowments are made great.
DUKE OF YORK.
My lords of England, let me tell you this:—
I have had feeling of my cousin's wrongs,
And labour'd all I could to do him right;
But in this kind to come, in braving arms,
Be his own carver, and cut out his way,
To find out right with wrong,—it may not be;
And you that do abet him in this kind
Cherish rebellion and are rebels all.
EARL OF NORTHUMBERLAND.
The noble duke hath sworn his coming is
But for his own; and for the right of that
We all have strongly sworn to give him aid;
And let him ne'er see joy that breaks that oath!
DUKE OF YORK.
Well, well, I see the issue of these arms;
I cannot mend it, I must needs confess,
Because my power is weak and all ill left:
But if I could, by Him that gave me life,
I would attach you all, and make you stoop
Unto the sovereign mercy of the king;
But since I cannot, be it known to you
I do remain as neuter. So, fare you well;—
Unless you please to enter in the castle,
And there repose you for this night.
HENRY BOLINGBROKE.
An offer, uncle, that we will accept:
But we must win your Grace to go with us
To Bristol-castle, which they say is held

By Bushy, Bagot, and their complices,
The caterpillars of the commonwealth,
Which I have sworn to weed and pluck away.
DUKE OF YORK.
It may be I will go with you:—but yet I'll pause;
For I am loth to break our country's laws.
Nor friends nor foes, to me welcome you are:
Things past redress are now with me past care.
[*Exeunt.*

SCENE IV.

A camp in Wales.

Enter SALISBURY *and a* CAPTAIN.

CAPTAIN.
MY Lord of Salisbury, we have stay'd ten days,
And hardly kept our countrymen together,
And yet we hear no tidings from the king;
Therefore we will disperse ourselves: farewell.
EARL OF SALISBURY.
Stay yet another day, thou trusty Welshman:
The king reposeth all his confidence in thee.
CAPTAIN.
'Tis thought the king is dead; we will not stay.
The bay-trees in our country all are wither'd,
And meteors fright the fixed stars of heaven;
The pale-faced moon looks bloody on the earth,
And leant-lookt prophets whisper fearful change;
Rich men look sad, and ruffians dance and
leap,—
The one in fear to lose what they enjoy,
The other to enjoy by rage and war:
These signs forerun the death or fall of kings.—
Farewell: our countrymen are gone and fled,
As well assured Richard their king is dead. [*Exit.*
EARL OF SALISBURY.
Ah, Richard, with the eyes of heavy mind,
I see thy glory, like a shooting star,
Fall to the base earth from the firmament!
Thy sun sets weeping in the lowly west,
Witnessing storms to come, woe, and unrest:
Thy friends are fled, to wait upon thy foes;
And crossly to thy good all fortune goes. [*Exit.*

ACT III.   SCENE I.

BOLINGBROKE'S *camp at Bristol.*

Enter BOLINGBROKE, YORK, NORTHUMBER-
LAND, PERCY, WILLOUGHBY, *with* BUSHY
and GREEN, *prisoners.*

HENRY BOLINGBROKE.
BRING forth these men.
Bushy and Green, I will not vex your souls—
Since presently your souls must part your
bodies—
With too much urging your pernicious lives,
For 'twere no charity; yet, to wash your blood
From off my hands, here, in the view of men,
I will unfold some causes of your deaths.
You have misled a prince, a royal king,
A happy gentleman in blood and lineaments,
By you unhappied and disfigured clean:
You have in manner with your sinful hours
Made a divorce betwixt his queen and him;
Broke the possession of a royal bed,
And stain'd the beauty of a fair queen's cheeks

With tears drawn from her eyes by your foul
wrongs.
Myself,—a prince by fortune of my birth,
Near to the king in blood, and near in love
Till you did make him misinterpret me,—
Have stoopt my neck under your injuries,
And sigh'd my English breath in foreign clouds,
Eating the bitter bread of banishment;
Whilst you have fed upon my signories,
Disparkt my parks, and fell'd my forest-woods,
From my own windows torn my household coat,
Razed out my imprese, leaving me no sign,
Save men's opinions and my living blood,
To show the world I am a gentleman.
This and much more, much more than twice all
this,
Condemns you to the death.—See them deliver'd
over
To execution and the hand of death.
BUSHY.
More welcome is the stroke of death to me
Than Bolingbroke to England.—Lords, farewell.
GREEN.
My comfort is, that heaven will take our souls,
And plague injustice with the pains of hell.
HENRY BOLINGBROKE.
My Lord Northumberland, see them dispatcht.
[*Exeunt* NORTHUMBERLAND *and others,*
with the PRISONERS.
Uncle, you say the queen is at your house;
For God's sake, fairly let her be entreated:
Tell her I send to her my kind commends;
Take special care my greetings be deliver'd.
DUKE OF YORK.
A gentleman of mine I have dispatcht
With letters of your love to her at large.
HENRY BOLINGBROKE.
Thanks, gentle uncle.—Come, lords, away,
To fight with Glendower and his complices:
Awhile to work, and after holiday. [*Exeunt.*

SCENE II.

The coast of Wales.   A castle in view.

Drums: flourish and colours.   Enter KING RICH-
ARD, *the* BISHOP OF CARLISLE, AUMERLE,
and SOLDIERS.

KING RICHARD.
BARKLOUGHLY-castle call they this at
hand?
DUKE OF AUMERLE.
Yea, my lord. How brooks your Grace the air,
After your late tossing on the breaking seas?
KING RICHARD.
Needs must I like it well: I weep for joy
To stand upon my kingdom once again.—
Dear earth, I do salute thee with my hand,
Though rebels wound thee with their horses'
hoofs:
As a long-parted mother with her child
Plays fondly with her tears and smiles in meeting,
So, weeping, smiling, greet I thee, my earth,
And do thee favours with my royal hands.
Feed not thy sovereign's foe, my gentle earth,
Nor with thy sweets comfort his ravenous sense;
But let thy spiders, that suck up thy venom,

And heavy-gaited toads, lie in their way,
Doing annoyance to the treacherous feet
Which with usurping steps do trample thee:
Yield stinging nettles to mine enemies;
And when they from thy bosom pluck a flower,
Guard it, I pray thee, with a lurking adder,
Whose double tongue may with a mortal touch
Throw death upon thy sovereign's enemies.—
Mock not my senseless conjuration, lords:
This earth shall have a feeling, and these stones
Prove armed soldiers, ere her native king
Shall falter under foul rebellion's arms.

BISHOP OF CARLISLE.
Fear not, my lord: that Power that made you
   king ·
Hath power to keep you king in spite of all.
The means that heaven yields must be embraced,
And not neglected; else, if heaven would,
And we will not, heaven's offer we refuse,
The proffer'd means of succour and redress.

DUKE OF AUMERLE.
He means, my lord, that we are too remiss;
Whilst Bolingbroke, through our security,
Grows strong and great in substance and in
   friends.

KING RICHARD.
Discomfortable cousin! know'st thou not
That when the searching eye of heaven is hid
Behind the globe, that lights the lower world,
Then thieves and robbers range abroad unseen,
In murders and in outrage, boldly here;
But when, from under this terrestrial ball,
He fires the proud tops of the eastern pines,
And darts his light through every guilty hole,
Then murders, treasons, and detested sins,
The cloak of night being pluckt from off their
   backs,
Stand bare and naked, trembling at themselves?
So when this thief, this traitor, Bolingbroke,—
Who all this while hath revell'd in the night,
Whilst we were wandering with the Antipodes,—
Shall see us rising in our throne, the east,
His treasons will sit blushing in his face,
Not able to endure the sight of day,
But self-affrighted tremble at his sin.
Not all the water in the rough rude sea
Can wash the balm from an anointed king;
The breath of worldly men cannot depose
The deputy elected by the Lord:
For every man that Bolingbroke hath prest
To lift shrewd steel against our golden crown,
God for his Richard hath in heavenly pay
A glorious angel: then, if angels fight,
Weak men must fall; for heaven still guards the
   right.

Enter SALISBURY.
Welcome, my lord: how far off lies your power?

EARL OF SALISBURY.
Not near nor further off, my gracious lord,
Than this weak arm: discomfort guides my
   tongue,
And bids me speak of nothing but despair.
One day too late, I fear me, noble lord,
Hath clouded all thy happy days on earth:
O, call back yesterday, bid time return,
And thou shalt have twelve thousand fighting men!

To-day, to-day, unhappy day, too late,
O'erthrows thy joys, friends, fortune, and thy
   state;
For all the Welshmen, hearing thou wert dead,
Are gone to Bolingbroke, dispersèd and fled.

DUKE OF AUMERLE.
Comfort, my liege: why looks your Grace so pale?

KING RICHARD.
But now the blood of twenty thousand men
Did triumph in my face, and they are fled;
And, till so much blood thither come agen,
Have I not reason to look pale and dead?
All souls that will be safe, fly from my side;
For time hath set a blot upon my pride.

DUKE OF AUMERLE.
Comfort, my liege; remember who you are.

KING RICHARD.
I had forgot myself: am I not king?
Awake, thou coward majesty! thou sleepest.
Is not the king's name twenty thousand names?
Arm, arm, my name! a puny subject strikes
At thy great glory.—Look not to the ground,
Ye favourites of a king: are we not high?
High be our thoughts: I know my uncle York
Hath power enough to serve our turn.—
But who comes here?

Enter SCROOP.
SIR STEPHEN SCROOP.
More health and happiness betide my liege
Than can my care-tuned tongue deliver him!

KING RICHARD.
Mine ear is open and my heart prepared:
The worst is worldly loss thou canst unfold.
Say, is my kingdom lost? why, 'twas my care;
And what loss is it to be rid of care?
Strives Bolingbroke to be as great as we?
Greater he shall not be; if he serve God,
We'll serve Him too, and be his fellow so:
Revolt our subjects? that we cannot mend;
They break their faith to God as well as us:
Cry woe, destruction, ruin, loss, decay;
The worst is death, and death will have his day.

SIR STEPHEN SCROOP.
Glad am I that your highness is so arm'd
To bear the tidings of calamity.
Like an unseasonable stormy day,
Which makes the silver rivers drown their shores,
As if the world were all dissolved to tears;
So high above his limits swells the rage
Of Bolingbroke, covering your fearful land
With hard bright steel, and hearts harder than
   steel.
White-beards have arm'd their thin and hairless
   scalps
Against thy majesty; boys with women's voices
Strive to speak big, and clap their female joints
In stiff unwieldy arms against thy crown;
The very beadsmen learn to bend their bows
Of double-fatal yew against thy state;
Yea, distaff-women manage rusty bills
Against thy seat: both young and old rebel,
And all goes worse than I have power to tell.

KING RICHARD.
Too well, too well thou tell'st a tale so ill.
Where is the Earl of Wiltshire? where is Bagot?
What is become of Bushy? where is Green?

That they have let the dangerous enemy
Measure our confines with such peaceful steps?
If we prevail, their heads shall pay for it:
I warrant they have made peace with Boling-
broke.

SIR STEPHEN SCROOP.
Peace have they made with him, indeed, my lord.

KING RICHARD.
O villains, vipers, damn'd without redemption!
Dogs, easily won to fawn on any man!
Snakes, in my heart-blood warm'd, that sting my
heart!
Three Judases, each one thrice worse than Judas!
Would they make peace? terrible hell make war
Upon their spotted souls for this offence!

SIR STEPHEN SCROOP.
Sweet love, I see, changing his property,
Turns to the sourest and most deadly hate:—
Again uncurse their souls; their peace is made
With heads: and not with hands: those whom you]
curse
Have felt the worst of death's destroying wound,
And lie full low, graved in the hollow ground.

DUKE OF AUMERLE.
Is Bushy, Green, and the Earl of Wiltshire dead?

SIR STEPHEN SCROOP.
Ay, all of them at Bristol lost their heads.

DUKE OF AUMERLE.
Where is the duke my father with his power?

KING RICHARD.
No matter where;—of comfort no man speak:
Let's talk of graves, of worms, and epitaphs;
Make dust our paper, and with rainy eyes
Write sorrow on the bosom of the earth.
Let's choose executors, and talk of wills:
And yet not so,—for what can we bequeath,
Save our deposed bodies to the ground?
Our lands, our lives, and all are Bolingbroke's,
And nothing can we call our own but death,
And that small model of the barren earth
Which serves as paste and cover to our bones.
For God's sake, let us sit upon the ground,
And tell sad stories of the death of kings:—
How some have been deposed; some slain in war;
Some haunted by the ghosts they have deposed;
Some poison'd by their wives; some sleeping
kill'd;
All murder'd:—for within the hollow crown
That rounds the mortal temples of a king
Keeps Death his court; and there the antick sits,
Scoffing his state, and grinning at his pomp;
Allowing him a breath, a little scene,
To monarchize, be fear'd, and kill with looks;
Infusing him with self and vain conceit,—
As if this flesh, which walls about our life,
Were brass impregnable; and humour'd thus,
Comes at the last, and with a little pin
Bores through his castle-wall, and—farewell
king!
Cover your heads, and mock not flesh and blood
With solemn reverence; throw away respect,
Tradition, form, and ceremonious duty;
For you have but mistook me all this while:
I live with bread like you, feel want,
Taste grief, need friends:—subjected thus,
How can you say to me, I am a king?

BISHOP OF CARLISLE.
My lord, wise men ne'er sit and wail their woes,
But presently prevent the ways to wail.
To fear the foe, since fear oppresseth strength,
Gives, in your weakness, strength unto your foe,
And so your follies fight against yourself.
Fear, and be slain; no worse can come to fight:
And fight and die is death destroying death;
Where fearing dying pays death servile breath.

DUKE OF AUMERLE.
My father hath a power; inquire of him;
And learn to make a body of a limb.

KING RICHARD.
Thou chidest me well:—proud Bolingbroke, I
come
To change blows with thee for our day of doom.
This ague-fit of fear is over-blown;
An easy task it is to win our own.—
Say, Scroop, where lies our uncle with his power?
Speak sweetly, man, although thy looks be sour.

SIR STEPHEN SCROOP.
Men judge by the complexion of the sky
   The state and inclination of the day;
So may you by my dull and heavy eye,
   My tongue hath but a heavier tale to say.
I play the torturer, by small and small
To lengthen out the worst that must be spoken:—
Your uncle York is join'd with Bolingbroke,
And all your northern castles yielded up,
And all your southern gentlemen in arms
Upon his party.

KING RICHARD.
            Thou hast said enough.—
[to AUMERLE] Beshrew thee, cousin, which didst
   lead me forth
Of that sweet way I was in to despair!
What say you now? what comfort have we now?
By heaven, I'll hate him everlastingly
That bids me be of comfort any more.
Go to Flint-castle: there I'll pine away;
A king, woe's slave, shall kingly woe obey.
That power I have, discharge; and let them go
To ear the land that hath some hope to grow,
For I have none:—let no man speak again
To alter this, for counsel is but vain.

DUKE OF AUMERLE.
My liege, one word.

KING RICHARD.
            He does me double wrong
That wounds me with the flatteries of his tongue.
Discharge my followers: let them hence away,
From Richard's night to Bolingbroke's fair day.
                                    [Exeunt.

SCENE III.

Wales. Before Flint-castle.

Enter, with drums and colours, BOLINGBROKE,
YORK, NORTHUMBERLAND, *and* FORCES.

HENRY BOLINGBROKE.
SO that by this intelligence we learn
  The Welshmen are dispersed; and Salisbury
Is gone to meet the king, who lately landed
With some few private friends upon this coast.

EARL OF NORTHUMBERLAND.
The news is very fair and good, my lord:
Richard not far from hence hath hid his head.

DUKE OF YORK.
It would beseem the Lord Northumberland
To say 'King Richard:'—alack the heavy day
When such a sacred king should hide his head!
EARL OF NORTHUMBERLAND.
Your Grace mistakes; only to be brief,
Left I his title out.
DUKE OF YORK.
          The time hath been,
Would you have been so brief with him, he would
Have been so brief with you, to shorten you,
For taking so the head, your whole head's length.
HENRY BOLINGBROKE.
Mistake not, uncle, further than you should.
DUKE OF YORK.
Take not, good cousin, further than you should,
Lest you mistake: the heavens are over our heads.
HENRY BOLINGBROKE.
I know it, uncle; and oppose not myself
Against their will.—But who comes here?
          Enter PERCY.
Welcome, Harry: what, will not this castle yield?
HENRY PERCY.
The castle royally is mann'd, my lord,
Against thy entrance.
HENRY BOLINGBROKE.
Royally!
Why, it contains no king?
HENRY PERCY.
          Yes, my good lord,
It doth contain a king; King Richard lies
Within the limits of yon lime and stone:
And with him are the Lord Aumerle, Lord Salis-
     bury,
Sir Stephen Scroop; besides a clergyman
Of holy reverence; who I cannot learn.
EARL OF NORTHUMBERLAND.
O, belike it is the Bishop of Carlisle.
HENRY BOLINGBROKE.
[to NORTHUMBERLAND] Noble lord,
Go to the rude ribs of that ancient castle;
Through brazen trumpet send the breath of
     parley
Into his ruin'd ears, and thus deliver:—
Henry Bolingbroke
On both his knees doth kiss King Richard's hand,
And sends allegiance and true faith of heart
To his most royal person; hither come
Even at his feet to lay my arms and power,
Provided that my banishment repeal'd
And lands restored again be freely granted:
If not, I'll use th' advantage of my power,
And lay the summer's dust with showers of blood
Rain'd from the wounds of slaughter'd English-
     men:
The which, how far off from the mind of Boling-
     broke
It is, such crimson tempest should bedrench
The fresh green lap of fair King Richard's land,
My stooping duty tenderly shall show.
Go, signify as much, while here we march
Upon the grassy carpet of this plain.
Let's march without the noise of threatening
     drum,
That from this castle's totter'd battlements
Our fair appointments may be well perused.

Methinks King Richard and myself should meet
With no less terror than the elements
Of fire and water, when their thundering shock
At meeting tears the cloudy cheeks of heaven.
Be he the fire, I'll be the yielding water:
The rage be his, while on the earth I rain
My waters,—on the earth and not on him.
March on, and mark King Richard how he looks.
Parle without, and answer within. Then a flourish.
     Enter, on the walls, KING RICHARD, *the*
     BISHOP OF CARLISLE, AUMERLE, SCROOP,
     and SALISBURY.
DUKE OF YORK.
See, see, King Richard doth himself appear,
As doth the blushing discontented sun
From out the fiery portal of the east,
When he perceives the envious clouds are bent
To dim his glory, and to stain the track
Of his bright passage to the occident.
Yet looks he like a king: behold, his eye,
As bright as is the eagle's, lightens forth
Controlling majesty:—alack, alack, for woe,
That any harm should stain so fair a show!
KING RICHARD [to NORTHUMBERLAND].
We are amazed; and thus long have we stood
To watch the fearful bending of thy knee,
Because we thought ourself thy lawful king:
And if we be, how dare thy joints forget
To pay their awful duty to our presence?
If we be not, show us the hand of God
That hath dismist us from our stewardship;
For well we know, no hand of blood and bone
Can gripe the sacred handle of our sceptre,
Unless he do profane, steal, or usurp.
And though you think that all, as you have done,
Have torn their souls by turning them from us,
And we are barren and bereft of friends;
Yet know,—my master, God omnipotent,
Is mustering in his clouds, on our behalf,
Armies of pestilence; and they shall strike
Your children yet unborn and unbegot,
That lift your vassal hands against my head,
And threat the glory of my precious crown.
Tell Bolingbroke,—for yond methinks he
     stands,—
That every stride he makes upon my land
Is dangerous treason: he is come to ope
The purple testament of bleeding war;
But ere the crown he looks for live in peace,
Ten thousand bloody crowns of mothers' sons
Shall ill become the flower of England's face,
Change the complexion of her maid-pale peace
To scarlet indignation, and bedew
Her pastures' grass with faithful English blood.
EARL OF NORTHUMBERLAND.
The king of heaven forbid our lord the king
Should so with civil and uncivil arms
Be rusht upon! Thy thrice-noble cousin
Harry Bolingbroke doth humbly kiss thy hand;
And by the honourable tomb he swears
That stands upon your royal grandsire's bones,
And by the royalties of both your bloods,—
Currents that spring from one most gracious
     head,—
And by the buried hand of warlike Gaunt,
And by the worth and honour of himself,

Comprising all that may be sworn or said,—
His coming hither hath no further scope
Than for his lineal royalties, and to beg
Enfranchisement immediate on his knees:
Which on thy royal party granted once,
His glittering arms he will commend to rust,
His barbed steeds to stables, and his heart
To faithful service of your majesty.
This swears he, as he is a prince, is just;
And, as I am a gentleman, I credit him.
   KING RICHARD.
Northumberland, say thus the king returns:—
His noble cousin is right welcome hither;
And all the number of his fair demands
Shall be accomplisht without contradiction:
With all the gracious utterance thou hast
Speak to his gentle hearing kind commends.—
[to AUMERLE] We do debase ourself, cousin, do
 we not,
To look so poorly, and to speak so fair?
Shall we call back Northumberland, and send
Defiance to the traitor, and so die?
   DUKE OF AUMERLE.
No, good my lord; let's fight with gentle words
Till time lend friends, and friends their helpful
 swords.
   KING RICHARD.
O God, O God! that e'er this tongue of mine,
That laid the sentence of dread banishment
On yond proud man, should take it off again
With words of sooth! O, that I were as great
As is my grief, or lesser than my name!
Or that I could forget what I have been!
Or not remember what I must be now!
Swell'st thou, proud heart? I'll give thee scope to
 beat,
Since foes have scope to beat both thee and me.
   DUKE OF AUMERLE.
Northumberland comes back from Bolingbroke.
   KING RICHARD.
What must the king do now? must he submit?
The king shall do it: must he be deposed?
The king shall be contented: must he lose
The name of king? o' God's name, let it go:
I'll give my jewels for a set of beads,
My gorgeous palace for a hermitage,
My gay apparel for an almsman's gown,
My figured goblets for a dish of wood,
My sceptre for a palmer's walking-staff,
My subjects for a pair of carved saints,
And my large kingdom for a little grave,
A little little grave, an obscure grave;—
Or I'll be buried in the king's highway,
Some way of common trade, where subjects' feet
May hourly trample on their sovereign's head;
For on my heart they tread now whilst I live;
And buried once, why not upon my head?—
Aumerle, thou weep'st,—my tender-hearted
 cousin!—
We'll make foul weather with despised tears;
Our sighs and they shall lodge the summer corn,
And make a dearth in this revolting land.
Or shall we play the wantons with our woes,
And make some pretty match with shedding
 tears?
As thus;—to drop them still upon one place,

Till they have fretted us a pair of graves
Within the earth; and, therein laid,—'There lies
Two kinsmen digg'd their graves with weeping
 eyes.'
Would not this ill do well?—Well, well, I see
I talk but idly, and you laugh at me.—
Most mighty prince, my Lord Northumberland,
What says King Bolingbroke? will his majesty
Give Richard leave to live till Richard die?
You make a leg, and Bolingbroke says ay.
   EARL OF NORTHUMBERLAND.
My lord, in the base court he doth attend
To speak with you;—may it please you to come
 down.
   KING RICHARD.
Down, down I come; like glistering Phaëton,
Wanting the manage of unruly jades.
In the base court? Base court, where kings grow
 base,
To come at traitors' calls, and do them grace.
In the base court? Come down? Down, court!
 down, king!
For night-owls shriek where mounting larks
 should sing.   [Exeunt above.
   HENRY BOLINGBROKE.
What says his majesty?
   EARL OF NORTHUMBERLAND.
      Sorrow and grief of heart
Makes him speak fondly, like a frantic man:
Yet he is come.
   Enter KING RICHARD attended, below.
   HENRY BOLINGBROKE.
Stand all apart,
And show fair duty to his majesty.—
My gracious lord,—   [Kneeling.
   KING RICHARD.
Fair cousin, you debase your princely knee
To make the base earth proud with kissing it:
Me rather had my heart might feel your love
Than my unpleased eye see your courtesy.
Up, cousin, up;—your heart is up, I know.
Thus high at least [touching his own head], al-
 though your knee be low.
   HENRY BOLINGBROKE.
My gracious lord, I come but for mine own.
   KING RICHARD.
Your own is yours, and I am yours, and all.
   HENRY BOLINGBROKE.
So far be mine, my most redoubted lord,
As my true service shall deserve your love.
   KING RICHARD.
Well you deserve:—they well deserve to have,
That know the strong'st and surest way to
 get.—
Uncle, give me your hand: nay, dry your eyes;
Tears show their love, but want their remedies.—
Cousin, I am too young to be your father,
Though you are old enough to be my heir.
What you will have, I'll give, and willing too;
For do we must what force will have us do.—
Set on towards London:—cousin, is it so?
   HENRY BOLINGBROKE.
Yea, my good lord.
   KING RICHARD.
     Then I must not say no.
      [Flourish. Exeunt.

SCENE IV.

Langley. The DUKE OF YORK'S *garden.*
Enter the QUEEN *and two* LADIES.

QUEEN.

WHAT sport shall we devise here in this
garden,
To drive away the heavy thought of care?

FIRST LADY.
Madam, we'll play at bowls.

QUEEN.
'Twill make me think the world is full of rubs,
And that my fortune runs against the bias.

FIRST LADY.
Madam, we'll dance.

QUEEN.
My legs can keep no measure in delight,
When my poor heart no measure keeps in grief:
Therefore, no dancing, girl; some other sport.

FIRST LADY.
Madam, we'll tell tales.

QUEEN.
Of sorrow of or joy?

FIRST LADY.
Of either, madam.

QUEEN.
Of neither, girl:
For if of joy, being altogether wanting,
It doth remember me the more of sorrow;
Or if of grief, being altogether had,
It adds more sorrow to my want of joy:
For what I have, I need not to repeat;
And what I want, it boots not to complain.

FIRST LADY.
Madam, I'll sing.

QUEEN.
'Tis well that thou hast cause;
But thou shouldst please me better, wouldst thou
weep.

FIRST LADY.
I could weep, madam, would it do you good.

QUEEN.
And I could weep, would weeping do me good,
And never borrow any tear of thee.—
But stay, here come the gardeners:
Let's step into the shadow of these trees.
My wretchedness unto a row of pins,
They'll talk of state; for every one doth so
Against a change: woe is forerun with woe.

[QUEEN *and* LADIES *retire.*
Enter a GARDENER *and two* SERVANTS.

GARDENER.
Go, bind thou up yon dangling apricocks,
Which, like unruly children, make their sire
Stoop with oppression of their prodigal weight:
Give some supportance to the bending twigs.—
Go thou, and, like an executioner,
Cut off the heads of too-fast-growing sprays,
That look too lofty in our commonwealth:
All must be even in our government.—
You thus employ'd, I will go root away
The noisome weeds, that without profit suck
The soil's fertility from wholesome flowers.

FIRST SERVANT.
Why should we, in the compass of a pale,
Keep law and form and due proportion,

Showing, as in a model, our firm estate,
When our sea-walled garden, the whole land,
Is full of weeds; her fairest flowers choked up,
Her fruit-trees all unpruned, her hedges ruin'd,
Her knots disorder'd, and her wholesome herbs
Swarming with caterpillars?

GARDENER.
Hold thy peace:—
He that hath suffer'd this disorder'd spring
Hath now himself met with the fall of leaf:
The weeds that his broad-spreading leaves did
shelter,
That seem'd in eating him to hold him up,
Are pluckt up root and all by Bolingbroke,—
I mean the Earl of Wiltshire, Bushy, Green.

FIRST SERVANT.
What, are they dead?

GARDENER.
They are; and Bolingbroke
Hath seized the wasteful king.—O, what pity is it
That he had not so trimm'd and drest his land
As we this garden! We at time of year
Do wound the bark, the skin of our fruit-trees,
Lest, being over-proud in sap and blood,
With too much riches it confound itself:
Had he done so to great and growing men,
They might have lived to bear, and he to taste
Their fruits of duty. All superfluous branches
We lop away, that bearing boughs may live:
Had he done so, himself had borne the crown,
Which waste of idle hours hath quite thrown
down.

FIRST SERVANT.
What, think you, then, the king shall be deposed?

GARDENER.
Deprest he is already; and deposed
'Tis doubt he will be: letters came last night
To a dear friend of the good Duke of York's,
That tell black tidings.

QUEEN.
O, I am prest to death through want of speak-
ing!—   [*Comes forward with* LADIES.
Thou, old Adam's likeness, set to dress this
garden,
How dares thy harsh rude tongue sound this un-
pleasing news?
What Eve, what serpent, hath suggested thee
To make a second fall of cursed man?
Why dost thou say King Richard is deposed?
Darest thou, thou little better thing than earth,
Divine his downfall? Say, where, when, and how,
Camest thou by this ill tidings? speak, thou
wretch.

GARDENER.
Pardon me, madam: little joy have I
To breathe this news: yet what I say is true.
King Richard, he is in the mighty hold
Of Bolingbroke: their fortunes both are weigh'd:
In your lord's scale is nothing but himself,
And some few vanities that make him light;
But in the balance of great Bolingbroke,
Besides himself, are all the English peers,
And with that odds he weighs King Richard
down.
Post you to London, and you will find it so;
I speak no more than every man doth know.

QUEEN.

Nimble mischance, that art so light of foot,
Doth not thy embassage belong to me,
And am I last that knows it? O, thou think'st
To serve me last, that I may longest keep
Thy sorrow in my breast.—Come, ladies, go,
To meet at London London's king in woe.—
What, was I born to this, that my sad look
Should grace the triumph of great Bolingbroke?
Gardener, for telling me this news of woe,
Pray God the plants thou graft'st may never
    grow.   [*Exeunt* QUEEN *and* LADIES.

GARDENER.

Poor queen! so that thy state might be no worse,
I would my skill were subject to thy curse.—
Here did she fall a tear; here, in this place,
I'll set a bank of rue, sour herb of grace:
Rue, even for ruth, here shortly shall be seen,
In the remembrance of a weeping queen.
                           [*Exeunt.*

ACT IV. SCENE I.

Westminster Hall.

Enter as to the Parliament BOLINGBROKE, AU-
MERLE, NORTHUMBERLAND, PERCY, FITZ-
WATER, SURREY, *another* LORD, *the* BISHOP
OF CARLISLE, *the* ABBOT OF WESTMINSTER,
and ATTENDANTS. HERALD, OFFICERS, *and*
BAGOT.

HENRY BOLINGBROKE.

CALL forth Bagot.
   Now, Bagot, freely speak thy mind;
What dost thou know of noble Gloster's death;
Who wrought it with the king, and who per-
    form'd
The bloody office of his timeless end.

BAGOT.

Then set before my face the Lord Aumerle.

HENRY BOLINGBROKE.

Cousin, stand forth, and look upon that man.

BAGOT.

My Lord Aumerle, I know your daring tongue
Scorns to unsay what once it hath deliver'd.
In that dead time when Gloster's death was
    plotted,
I heard you say,—'Is not my arm of length,
That reacheth from the restful English court
As far as Calais, to my uncle's head?'
Amongst much other talk, that very time,
I heard you say that you had rather refuse
The offer of an hundred thousand crowns
Than Bolingbroke's return to England;
Adding withal, how blest this land would be
In this your cousin's death.

DUKE OF AUMERLE.

             Princes, and noble lords,
What answer shall I make to this base man?
Shall I so much dishonour my fair stars,
On equal terms to give him chastisement?
Either I must, or have mine honour soil'd
With the attainder of his slanderous lips.—
There is my gage, the manual seal of death,
That marks thee out for hell: I say, thou liest,
And will maintain what thou hast said is false

In thy heart-blood, though being all too base
To stain the temper of my knightly sword.

HENRY BOLINGBROKE.

Bagot, forbear; thou shalt not take it up.

DUKE OF AUMERLE.

Excepting one, I would he were the best
In all this presence that hath moved me so.

LORD FITZWATER.

If that thy valour stand on sympathy,
There is my gage, Aumerle, in gage to thine:
By that fair sun which shows me where thou
    stand'st,
I heard thee say, and vauntingly thou spakest it,
That thou wert cause of noble Gloster's death.
If thou deny'st it twenty times, thou liest;
And I will turn thy falsehood to thy heart,
Where it was forged, with my rapier's point.

DUKE OF AUMERLE.

Thou darest not, coward, live to see that day.

LORD FITZWATER.

Now, by my soul, I would it were this hour.

DUKE OF AUMERLE.

Fitzwater, thou art damn'd to hell for this.

HENRY PERCY.

Aumerle, thou liest; his honour is as true
In this appeal as thou art all unjust;
And that thou art so, there I throw my gage,
To prove it on thee to th' extremest point
Of mortal breathing: seize it, if thou darest.

DUKE OF AUMERLE.

And if I do not, may my hands rot off,
And never brandish more revengeful steel
Over the glittering helmet of my foe!

ANOTHER LORD.

I task the earth to the like, forsworn Aumerle;
And spur thee on with full as many lies
As may be holla'd in thy treacherous ear
From sun to sun: there is my honour's pawn;
Engage it to the trial, if thou darest.

DUKE OF AUMERLE.

Who sets me else? by heaven, I'll throw at all:
I have a thousand spirits in one breast,
To answer twenty thousand such as you.

DUKE OF SURREY.

My Lord Fitzwater, I do remember well
The very time Aumerle and you did talk.

LORD FITZWATER.

'Tis very true: you were in presence then;
And you can witness with me this is true.

DUKE OF SURREY.

As false, by heaven, as heaven itself is true.

LORD FITZWATER.

Surrey, thou liest.

DUKE OF SURREY.

           Dishonourable boy!
That lie shall lie so heavy on my sword,
That it shall render vengeance and revenge
Till thou the lie-giver and that lie do lie
In earth as quiet as thy father's skull:
In proof whereof, there is my honour's pawn;
Engage it to the trial, if thou darest.

LORD FITZWATER.

How fondly dost thou spur a forward horse!
If I dare eat, or drink, or breathe, or live,
I dare meet Surrey in a wilderness,
And spit upon him, whilst I say he lies,

And lies, and lies: there is my bond of faith,
To tie thee to my strong correction.—
As I intend to thrive in this new world,
Aumerle is guilty of my true appeal:
Besides, I heard the banisht Norfolk say,
That thou, Aumerle, didst send two of thy men
To execute the noble duke at Calais.

DUKE OF AUMERLE.

Some honest Christian trust me with a gage,
That Norfolk lies: here do I throw down this,
If he may be repeal'd, to try his honour.

HENRY BOLINGBROKE.

These differences shall all rest under gage
Till Norfolk be repeal'd: repeal'd he shall be,
And, though mine enemy, restored again
To all his lands and signories: when he's return'd,
Against Aumerle we will enforce his trial.

BISHOP OF CARLISLE.

That honourable day shall ne'er be seen.
Many a time hath banisht Norfolk fought
For Jesu Christ in glorious Christian field,
Streaming the ensign of the Christian cross
Against black pagans, Turks, and Saracens;
And toil'd with works of war, retired himself
To Italy; and there, at Venice, gave
His body to that pleasant country's earth,
And his pure soul unto his captain Christ,
Under whose colours he had fought so long.

HENRY BOLINGBROKE.

Why, bishop, is Norfolk dead?

BISHOP OF CARLISLE.

As surely as I live, my lord.

HENRY BOLINGBROKE.

Sweet peace conduct his sweet soul to the bosom
Of good old Abraham!—Lords appellants,
Your differences shall all rest under gage
Till we assign you to your days of trial.

Enter YORK, *attended.*

DUKE OF YORK.

Great Duke of Lancaster, I come to thee
From plume-pluckt Richard; who with willing
    soul
Adopts thee heir, and his high sceptre yields
To the possession of thy royal hand:
Ascend his throne, descending now from him,—
And long live Henry, fourth of that name!

HENRY BOLINGBROKE.

In God's name, I'll ascend the regal throne.

BISHOP OF CARLISLE.

Marry, God forbid!—
Worst in this royal presence may I speak,
Yet best beseeming me to speak the truth.
Would God that any in this noble presence
Were enough noble to be upright judge
Of noble Richard! then true noblesse would
Learn him forbearance from so foul a wrong.
What subject can give sentence on his king?
And who sits here that is not Richard's subject?
Thieves are not judged but they are by to hear,
Although apparent guilt be seen in them;
And shall the figure of God's majesty,
His captain, steward, deputy elect,
Anointed, crowned, planted many years,
Be judged by subject and inferior breath,
And he himself not present? O, forfend it, God,
That in a Christian climate, souls refined

Should show so heinous, black, obscene a deed!
I speak to subjects, and a subject speaks,
Stirr'd up by God, thus boldly for his king.
My Lord of Hereford here, whom you call king,
Is a foul traitor to proud Hereford's king;
And if you crown him, let me prophesy,—
The blood of English shall manure the ground,
And future ages groan for this foul act;
Peace shall go sleep with Turks and infidels,
And in this seat of peace tumultuous wars
Shall kin with kin and kind with kind confound;
Disorder, horror, fear, and mutiny,
Shall here inhabit, and this land be call'd
The field of Golgotha and dead men's skulls.
O, if you raise this house against this house,
It will the wofullest division prove
That ever fell upon this cursed earth.
Prevent, resist it, let it not be so,
Lest child, child's children cry against you 'woe!'

EARL OF NORTHUMBERLAND.

Well have you argued, sir; and, for your pains,
Of capital treason we arrest you here.—
My Lord of Westminster, be it your charge
To keep him safely till his day of trial.—   [suit.
May it please you, lords, to grant the commons'

HENRY BOLINGBROKE.

Fetch hither Richard, that in common view
He may surrender; so we shall proceed
Without suspicion.

DUKE OF YORK.

           I will be his conduct.   [*Exit.*

HENRY BOLINGBROKE.

Lords, you that here are under our arrest,
Procure your sureties for your days of answer.—
Little are we beholding to your love,
                    [*to* CARLISLE.
And little lookt for at your helping hands.

Enter YORK, *with* KING RICHARD, *and*
    OFFICERS *bearing the crown,* &c.

KING RICHARD.

Alack, why am I sent for to a king,
Before I have shook off the regal thoughts
Wherewith I reign'd? I hardly yet have learn'd
To insinuate, flatter, bow, and bend my knee:
Give sorrow leave awhile to tutor me
To this submission. Yet I well remember
The favours of these men: were they not mine?
Did they not sometime cry, 'All hail!' to me?
So Judas did to Christ: but he, in twelve,
Found truth in all but one; I, in twelve thousand,
    none.
God save the king!—Will no man say amen?
Am I both priest and clerk? well then, amen.
God save the king! although I be not he;
And yet, amen, if heaven do think him me.—
To do what service am I sent for hither?

DUKE OF YORK.

To do that office of thine own good will
Which tired majesty did make thee offer,—
The resignation of thy state and crown
To Henry Bolingbroke.

KING RICHARD.

Give me the crown.—Here, cousin, seize the
    crown;
Here, cousin:
On this side my hand ,and on that side yours.

Now is this golden crown like a deep well
That owes two buckets, filling one another;
The emptier ever dancing in the air,
The other down, unseen, and full of water:
That bucket down and full of tears am I,
Drinking my griefs, whilst you mount up on high.

HENRY BOLINGBROKE.
I thought you had been willing to resign.

KING RICHARD.
My crown I am; but still my griefs are mine:
You may my glories and my state depose,
But not my griefs; still am I king of those.

HENRY BOLINGBROKE.
Part of your cares you give me with your crown.

KING RICHARD.
Your cares set up do not pluck my cares down.
My care is, loss of care, by old care done;
Your care is, gain of care, by new care won:
The cares I give, I have, though given away;
They tend the crown, yet still with me they stay.

HENRY BOLINGBROKE.
Are you contented to resign the crown?

KING RICHARD.
Ay, no;—no, ay; for I must nothing be;
Therefore no no, for I resign to thee.
Now mark me, how I will undo myself:—
I give this heavy weight from off my head,
And this unwieldy sceptre from my hand,
The pride of kingly sway from out my heart;
With mine own tears I wash away my balm,
With mine own hands I give away my crown,
With mine own tongue deny my sacred state,
With mine own breath release all duty's rites:
All pomp and majesty I do forswear;
My manors, rents, revenues I forgo;
My acts, decrees, and statutes I deny:
God pardon all oaths that are broke to me!
God keep all vows unbroke that swear to thee!
Make me, that nothing have, with nothing
  grieved,
And thou with all pleased, that hast all achieved!
Long mayst thou live in Richard's seat to sit,
And soon lie Richard in an earthy pit!
God save King Henry, unking'd Richard says,
And send him many years of sunshine days!—
What more remains?

EARL OF NORTHUMBERLAND.
              No more, but that you read
              [Offering a paper.
These accusations, and these grievous crimes
Committed by your person and your followers
Against the state and profit of this land;
That, by confessing them, the souls of men
May deem that you are worthily deposed.

KING RICHARD.
Must I do so? and must I ravel out
My weaved-up follies? Gentle Northumberland,
If thy offences were upon record,
Would it not shame thee in so fair a troop
To read a lecture of them? If thou wouldst,
There shouldst thou find one heinous article,—
Containing the deposing of a king,
And cracking the strong warrant of an oath,—
Markt with a blot, damn'd in the book of
  heaven:—
Nay, all of you that stand and look upon,

Whilst that my wretchedness doth bait myself,—
Though some of you, with Pilate, wash your
  hands,
Showing an outward pity; yet you Pilates
Have here deliver'd me to my sour cross,
And water cannot wash away your sin.

EARL OF NORTHUMBERLAND.
My lord, dispatch; read o'er these articles.

KING RICHARD.
Mine eyes are full of tears, I cannot see:
And yet salt water blinds them not so much
But they can see a sort of traitors here.
Nay, if I turn mine eyes upon myself,
I find myself a traitor with the rest;
For I have given here my soul's consent
T'undeck the pompous body of a king;
Made glory base, and sovereignty a slave,
Proud majesty a subject, state a peasant.

EARL OF NORTHUMBERLAND.
My lord,—

KING RICHARD.
No lord of thine, thou haught-insulting man,
Nor no man's lord; I have no name, no title,—
No, not that name was given me at the font,—
But 'tis usurpt:—alack the heavy day,
That I have worn so many winters out,
And know not now what name to call myself!
O, that I were a mockery-king of snow,
Standing before the sun of Bolingbroke,
To melt myself away in water-drops!—
Good king,—great king,—and yet not greatly
  good,—
An if my word be sterling yet in England,
Let it command a mirror hither straight,
That it may show me what a face I have,
Since it is bankrupt of his majesty.

HENRY BOLINGBROKE.
Go, some of you, and fetch a looking-glass.
              [Exit an ATTENDANT.

EARL OF NORTHUMBERLAND.
Read o'er this paper while the glass doth come.

KING RICHARD.
Fiend, thou torment'st me ere I come to hell!

HENRY BOLINGBROKE.
Urge it no more, my Lord Northumberland.

EARL OF NORTHUMBERLAND.
The commons will not, then, be satisfied.

KING RICHARD.
They shall be satisfied: I'll read enough,
When I do see the very book indeed
Where all my sins are writ, and that's myself.
       Enter ATTENDANT with a glass.
Give me the glass, and therein will I read.—
No deeper wrinkles yet? hath sorrow struck
So many blows upon this face of mine,
And made no deeper wounds!—O flattering glass
Like to my followers in prosperity,
Thou dost beguile me! Was this face the face
That every day under his household roof
Did keep ten thousand men? was this the face
That, like the sun, did make beholders wink?
Was this the face that faced so many follies,
And was at last out-faced by Bolingbroke?
A brittle glory shineth in this face:
As brittle as the glory is the face;
    [Dashes the glass against the ground

For there it is, crackt in a hundred shivers.—
Mark, silent king, the moral of this sport,—
How soon my sorrow hath destroy'd my face.
> HENRY BOLINGBROKE.
The shadow of your sorrow hath destroy'd
The shadow of your face.
> KING RICHARD.
          Say that again.
The shadow of my sorrow? ha! let 's see:—
'Tis very true, my grief lies all within;
And these external manners of lament
Are merely shadows to the unseen grief
That swells with silence in the tortured soul;
There lies the substance: and I thank thee, king,
For thy great bounty, that not only givest
Me cause to wail, but teachest me the way
How to lament the cause. I'll beg one boon,
And then be gone and trouble you no more.
Shall I obtain it?
> HENRY BOLINGBROKE.
          Name it, fair cousin.
> KING HENRY.
Fair cousin! I am greater than a king:
For when I was a king, my flatterers
Were then but subjects; being now a subject,
I have a king here to my flatterer.
Being so great, I have no need to beg.
> HENRY BOLINGBROKE.
Yet ask.
> KING RICHARD.
And shall I have?
> HENRY BOLINGBROKE.
You shall.
> KING RICHARD.
Then give me leave to go.
> HENRY BOLINGBROKE.
Whither?
> KING RICHARD.
Whither you will, so I were from your sights.
> HENRY BOLINGBROKE.
Go, some of you convey him to the Tower.
> KING RICHARD.
O, good! convey?—conveyers are you all,
That rise thus nimbly by a true king's fall.
> [*Exeunt* KING RICHARD, *some* LORDS,
> *and a* GUARD.
> HENRY BOLINGBROKE.
On Wednesday next we solemnly set down
Our coronation: lords, prepare yourselves.
> [*Exeunt all except the* BISHOP OF CAR-
> LISLE, *the* ABBOT OF WESTMINSTER,
> *and* AUMERLE.
> ABBOT OF WESTMINSTER.
A woful pageant have we here beheld.
> BISHOP OF CARLISLE.
The woe's to come; the children yet unborn
Shall feel this day as sharp to them as thorn.
> DUKE OF AUMERLE.
You holy clergymen, is there no plot
To rid the realm of this pernicious blot?
> ABBOT OF WESTMINSTER.
My lord,
Before I freely speak my mind herein,
You shall not only take the sacrament
To bury mine intents, but also to effect
Whatever I shall happen to devise.—

I see your brows are full of discontent,
Your hearts of sorrow, and your eyes of tears:
Come home with me to supper: I will lay
A plot shall show us all a merry day.   [*Exeunt.*

ACT V. SCENE I.

London. A street leading to the Tower.

Enter QUEEN *and* LADIES.

> QUEEN.
THIS way the king will come; this is the way
To Julius Caesar's ill-erected tower,
To whose flint bosom my condemned lord
Is doom'd a prisoner by proud Bolingbroke:
Here let us rest, if this rebellious earth
Have any resting for her true king's queen.—
But soft, but see, or rather do not see,
My fair rose wither: yet look up, behold,
That you in pity may dissolve to dew,
And wash him fresh again with true-love tears.
> *Enter* KING RICHARD *and* GUARDS.
Ah, thou, the model where old Troy did stand,
Thou map of honour, thou King Richard's tomb,
And not King Richard; thou most beauteous inn,
Why should hard-favour'd grief be lodged in
   thee,
When triumph is become an alehouse guest?
> KING RICHARD.
Join not with grief, fair woman, do not so,
To make my end too sudden: learn, good soul,
To think our former state a happy dream;
From which awaked, the truth of what we are
Shows us but this: I am sworn brother, sweet,
To grim Necessity; and he and I
Will keep a league till death. Hie thee to France,
And cloister thee in some religious house:
Our holy lives must win a new world's crown,
Which our profane hours here have stricken
   down.
> QUEEN.
What, is my Richard both in shape and mind
Transform'd and weaken'd? hath Bolingbroke
   deposed
Thine intellect? hath he been in thy heart?
The lion dying thrusteth forth his paw,
And wounds the earth, if nothing else, with rage
To be o'erpower'd; and wilt thou, pupil-like,
Take thy correction mildly, kiss the rod,
And fawn on rage with base humility,
Which art a lion and a king of beasts?
> KING RICHARD.
A king of beasts, indeed; if aught but beasts,
I had been still a happy king of men.
Good sometime queen, prepare thee hence for
   France:
Think I am dead; and that even here thou takest,
As from my death-bed, thy last living leave.
In winter's tedious nights sit by the fire
With good old folks, and let them tell thee tales
Of woful ages long ago betid;
And ere thou bid good night, to quit their griefs
Tell thou the lamentable tale of me,
And send the hearers weeping to their beds:
For why the senseless brands will sympathize
The heavy accent of thy moving tongue,
And in compassion weep the fire out;

And some will mourn in ashes, some coal-black,
For the deposing of a rightful king.

Enter NORTHUMBERLAND *attended.*

EARL OF NORTHUMBERLAND.

My lord, the mind of Bolingbroke is changed;
You must to Pomfret, not unto the Tower.—
And, madam, there is order ta'en for you;
With all swift speed you must away to France.

KING RICHARD.

Northumberland, thou ladder wherewithal
The mounting Bolingbroke ascends my throne,
The time shall not be many hours of age
More than it is, ere foul sin gathering head
Shall break into corruption: thou shalt think,
Though he divide the realm, and give thee half,
It is too little, helping him to all;
And he shall think, that thou, which know'st the
     way
To plant unrightful kings, wilt know again,
Being ne'er so little urged, another way
To pluck him headlong from the usurped throne.
The love of wicked friends converts to fear;
That fear to hate; and hate turns one or both
To worthy danger and deserved death.

EARL OF NORTHUMBERLAND.

My guilt be on my head, and there an end.
Take leave, and part; for you must part forth-
     with.

KING RICHARD.

Doubly divorced!—Bad men, you violate
A twofold marriage,—'twixt my crown and me,
And then betwixt me and my married wife.—
Let me unkiss the oath 'twixt thee and me;
And yet not so, for with a kiss 'twas made.—
Part us, Northumberland; I towards the north,
Where shivering cold and sickness pines the
     clime;
My wife to France,—from whence, set forth in
     pomp,
She came adorned hither like sweet May,
Sent back to Hallowmas or short'st of day.

QUEEN.

And must we be divided? must we part?

KING RICHARD.

Ay, hand from hand, my love, and heart from
     heart.

QUEEN.

Banish us both, and send the king with me.

EARL OF NORTHUMBERLAND.

That were some love, but little policy.

QUEEN.

Then whither he goes, thither let me go.

KING RICHARD.

So two, together weeping, make one woe.
Weep thou for me in France, I for thee here;
Better far off than, near, be ne'er the near.
Go, count thy way with sighs; I, mine with
     groans.

QUEEN.

So longest way shall have the longest moans.

KING RICHARD.

Twice for one step I'll groan, the way being
     short,
And piece the way out with a heavy heart.
Come, come, in wooing sorrow let's be brief,
Since, wedding it, there is such length in grief:

One kiss shall stop our mouths, and dumbly part;
Thus give I mine, and thus take I thy heart.

[*They kiss.*

QUEEN.

Give me mine own again; 'twere no good part
To take on me to keep and kill thy heart.

[*They kiss again.*

So, now I have mine own again, be gone,
That I may strive to kill it with a groan.

KING RICHARD.

We make woe wanton with this fond delay:
Once more, adieu; the rest let sorrow say.

[*Exeunt.*

SCENE II.

The DUKE OF YORK'S *palace.*

Enter YORK *and his* DUCHESS.

DUCHESS OF YORK.

MY lord, you told me you would tell the rest,
     When weeping made you break the story off
Of our two cousins coming into London.

DUKE OF YORK.

Where did I leave?

DUCHESS OF YORK.

                    At that sad stop, my lord,
Where rude misgovern'd hands from windows'
     tops
Threw dust and rubbish on King Richard's head.

DUKE OF YORK.

Then, as I said, the duke, great Bolingbroke,—
Mounted upon a hot and fiery steed,
Which his aspiring rider seem'd to know,—
With slow but stately pace kept on his course,
While all tongues cried, 'God save thee, Boling-
     broke!'
You would have thought the very windows spake,
So many greedy looks of young and old
Through casements darted their desiring eyes
Upon his visage; and that all the walls
With painted imagery had said at once,
'Jesu preserve thee! welcome, Bolingbroke!'
Whilst he, from one side to the other turning,
Bareheaded, lower than his proud steed's neck,
Bespake them thus,—'I thank you, countrymen:'
And thus still doing, thus he past along.

DUCHESS OF YORK.

Alack, poor Richard! where rode he the whilst?

DUKE OF YORK.

As in a theatre, the eyes of men,
After a well-graced actor leaves the stage,
Are idly bent on him that enters next,
Thinking his prattle to be tedious;
Even so, or with much more contempt, men's
     eyes
Did scowl on gentle Richard; no man cried, 'God
     save him!'
No joyful tongue gave him his welcome home:
But dust was thrown upon his sacred head;
Which with such gentle sorrow he shook off,—
His face still combating with tears and smiles,
The badges of his grief and patience,—
That had not God, for some strong purpose,
     steel'd
The hearts of men, they must perforce have
     melted,

And barbarism itself have pitied him.
But heaven hath a hand in these events,
To whose high will we bound our calm contents.
To Bolingbroke are we sworn subjects now,
Whose state and honour I for aye allow. ·
DUCHESS OF YORK.
Here comes my son Aumerle.
DUKE OF YORK.
                    Aumerle that was;
But that is lost for being Richard's friend,
And, madam, you must call him Rutland now:
I am in parliament pledge for his truth
And lasting fealty to the new-made king.
Enter AUMERLE.
DUCHESS OF YORK.
Welcome, my son: who are the violets now
That strew the green lap of the new-come
        spring?
DUKE OF AUMERLE.
Madam, I know not, nor I greatly care not:
God knows I had as lief be none as one.
DUKE OF YORK.
Well, bear you well in this new spring of time,
Lest you be cropt before you come to prime.
What news from Oxford?—hold those justs and
        triumphs?
DUKE OF AUMERLE.
For aught I know, my lord, they do.
DUKE OF YORK.
You will be there, I know.
DUKE OF AUMERLE.
If God prevent not, I do purpose so.
DUKE OF YORK.
What seal is that that hangs without thy bosom?
Yea, look'st thou pale? let me see the writing.
DUKE OF AUMERLE.
My lord, 'tis nothing.
DUKE OF YORK.
                    No matter, then, who see it:
I will be satisfied; let me see the writing.
DUKE OF AUMERLE.
I do beseech your Grace to pardon me:
It is a matter of small consequence,
Which for some reasons I would not have seen.
DUKE OF YORK.
Which for some reasons, sir, I mean to see.
I fear, I fear,—
DUCHESS OF YORK.
                    What should you fear?
'Tis nothing but some band that he is enter'd
        into
For gay apparel 'gainst the triumph-day.
DUKE OF YORK.
Bound to himself! what doth he with a bond
That he is bound to? Wife, thou art a fool.—
Boy, let me see the writing.
DUKE OF AUMERLE.
I do beseech you, pardon me; I may not show it.
DUKE OF YORK.
I will be satisfied: let me see 't, I say.
[He plucks it out of his bosom and reads it.
Treason! foul treason!—Villain! traitor! slave!
DUCHESS OF YORK.
What is the matter, my lord!
DUKE OF YORK.
Ho! who is within there? ho!

Enter a SERVANT.
                    Saddle my horse.—
God for his mercy, what treachery is here!
DUCHESS OF YORK.
Why, what is it, my lord?
DUKE OF YORK.
Give me my boots, I say; saddle my horse,—
                    [Exit SERVANT.
Now, by mine honour, by my life, by my troth,
I will appeach the villain.
DUCHESS OF YORK.
                    What is the matter?
DUKE OF YORK.
Peace, foolish woman.
DUCHESS OF YORK.
I will not peace.—What is the matter, Aumerle?
DUKE OF AUMERLE.
Good mother, be content; it is no more
Than my poor life must answer.
DUCHESS OF YORK.
                    Thy life answer!
DUKE OF YORK.
Bring me my boots:—I will unto the king.
His MAN enters with his boots.
DUCHESS OF YORK.
Strike him, Aumerle.—Poor boy, thou art
        amazed.—
Hence, villain! never more come in my sight.
DUKE OF YORK.
Give me my boots, I say.
DUCHESS OF YORK.
Why, York, what wilt thou do?
Wilt thou not hide the trespass of thine own?
Have we more sons? or are we like to have?
Is not my teeming date drunk up with time?
And wilt thou pluck my fair son from mine age,
And rob me of a happy mother's name?
Is he not like thee? is he not thine own?
DUKE OF YORK.
Thou fond mad woman,
Wilt thou conceal this dark conspiracy?
A dozen of them here have ta'en the sacrament,
And interchangeably set down their hands,
To kill the king at Oxford.
DUCHESS OF YORK.
                    He shall be none;
We'll keep him here: then what is that to him?
DUKE OF YORK.
Away, fond woman! were he twenty times my son,
I would appeach him.
DUCHESS OF YORK.
                    Hadst thou groan'd for him
As I have done, thou wouldst be more pitiful.
But now I know thy mind; thou dost suspect
That I have been disloyal to thy bed,
And that he is a bastard, not thy son:
Sweet York, sweet husband, be not of that mind:
He is as like thee as a man may be,
Not like to me, nor any of my kin,
And yet I love him.
DUKE OF YORK.
                    Make way, unruly woman!
                    [Exit.
DUCHESS OF YORK.
After, Aumerle, mount thee upon his horse;
Spur post, and get before him to the king,

And beg thy pardon ere he do accuse thee.
I'll not be long behind; though I be old,
I doubt not but to ride as fast as York;
And never will I rise up from the ground
Till Bolingbroke have pardon'd thee. Away, be
   gone!   [*Exeunt.*

SCENE III.

Windsor Castle.

Enter BOLINGBROKE, PERCY, *and other* LORDS.

HENRY BOLINGBROKE.

CAN no man tell me of my unthrifty son?
   'Tis full three months since I did see him
last:—
If any plague hang over us, 'tis he.
I would to God, my lords, he might be found:
Inquire at London, 'mongst the taverns there,
For there, they say, he daily doth frequent,
With unrestrained loose companions,—
Even such, they say, as stand in narrow lanes,
And beat our watch, and rob our passengers;
While he, young wanton and effeminate boy,
Takes on the point of honour to support
So dissolute a crew.

HENRY PERCY.

My lord, some two days since I saw the prince,
And told him of those triumphs held at Oxford.

HENRY BOLINGBROKE.

And what said the gallant?

HENRY PERCY.

His answer was,—he would unto the stews,
And from the common'st creature pluck a glove,
And wear it as a favour; and with that
He would unhorse the lustiest challenger.

HENRY BOLINGBROKE.

As dissolute as desperate; yet through both
I see some sparkles of a better hope,
Which elder days may happily bring forth.—
But who comes here?

Enter AUMERLE, *hastily.*

DUKE OF AUMERLE.

           Where is the king?

HENRY BOLINGBROKE.

                    What means
Our cousin, that he stares and looks so wildly?

DUKE OF AUMERLE.

God save your Grace! I do beseech your majesty,
To have some conference with your Grace alone.

HENRY BOLINGBROKE.

Withdraw yourselves, and leave us here alone.
           [*Exeunt* PERCY *and* LORDS.
What is the matter with our cousin now?

DUKE OF AUMERLE.

For ever may my knees grow to the earth,
                        [*Kneels.*
My tongue cleave to my roof within my mouth,
Unless a pardon ere I rise or speak.

HENRY BOLINGBROKE.

Intended or committed was this fault?
If on the first, how heinous e'er it be,
To win thy after-love I pardon thee.

DUKE OF AUMERLE.

Then give me leave that I may turn the key,
That no man enter till my tale be done.

HENRY BOLINGBROKE.

Have thy desire.

DUKE OF YORK [*within*].

My liege, beware; look to thyself;
Thou hast a traitor in thy presence there.

HENRY BOLINGBROKE.

Villain, I'll make thee safe.   [*Drawing.*

DUKE OF AUMERLE.

Stay thy revengeful hand; thou hast no cause to
   fear.

DUKE OF YORK [*within*].

Open the door, secure, foolhardy king:
Shall I, for love, speak treason to thy face?
Open the door, or I will break it open.

Enter YORK.

HENRY BOLINGBROKE.

What is the matter, uncle? speak;
Recover breath; tell us how near is danger,
That we may arm us to encounter it.

DUKE OF YORK.

Peruse this writing here, and thou shalt know
The treason that my haste forbids me show.

DUKE OF AUMERLE.

Remember, as thou read'st, thy promise past:
I do repent me; read not my name there;
My heart is not confederate with my hand.

DUKE OF YORK.

It was, villain, ere thy hand did set it down.—
I tore it from the traitor's bosom, king;
Fear, and not love, begets his penitence:
Forget to pity him, lest thy pity prove
A serpent that will sting thee to the heart.

HENRY BOLINGBROKE.

O heinous, strong, and bold conspiracy!—
O loyal father of a treacherous son!
Thou sheer, immaculate, and silver fountain,
From whence this stream through muddy
   passages
Hath held his current, and defiled himself!
Thy overflow of good converts to bad;
And thy abundant goodness shall excuse
This deadly blot in thy digressing son.

DUKE OF YORK.

So shall my virtue be his vice's bawd;
And he shall spend mine honour with his
   shame,
As thriftless sons their scraping fathers' gold.
Mine honour lives when his dishonour dies,
Or my shamed life in his dishonour lies:
Thou kill'st me in his life; giving him breath,
The traitor lives, the true man's put to death.

DUCHESS OF YORK [*within*].

What ho, my liege! for God's sake, let me in.

HENRY BOLINGBROKE.

What shrill-voiced suppliant makes this eager
   cry?

DUCHESS OF YORK [*within*].

A woman, and thy aunt, great king; 'tis I.
Speak with me, pity me, open the door:
A beggar begs that never begg'd before.

HENRY BOLINGBROKE.

Our scene is alter'd from a serious thing,
And now changed to 'The Beggar and the
   King.'—
My dangerous cousin, let your mother in:
I know she is come to pray for your foul sin.

DUKE OF YORK.
If thou do pardon, whosoever pray,
More sins, for this forgiveness, prosper may.
This fester'd joint cut off, the rest rest sound;
This let alone will all the rest confound.

Enter DUCHESS.

DUCHESS OF YORK.
O king, believe not this hard-hearted man!
Love, loving not itself, none other can.

DUKE OF YORK.
Thou frantic woman, what dost thou make here?
Shall thy old dugs once more a traitor rear?

DUCHESS OF YORK.
Sweet York, be patient.—Hear me, gentle liege.
[*Kneels.*

HENRY BOLINGBROKE.
Rise up, good aunt.

DUCHESS OF YORK.
                  Not yet, I thee beseech:
For ever will I walk upon my knees,
And never see day that the happy sees,
Till thou give joy; until thou bid me joy,
By pardoning Rutland, my transgressing boy.

DUKE OF AUMERLE.
Unto my mother's prayers I bend my knee.
[*Kneels.*

DUKE OF YORK.
Against them both my true joints bended be.
[*Kneels.*
Ill mayst thou thrive, if thou grant any grace!

DUCHESS OF YORK.
Pleads he in earnest? look upon his face;
His eyes do drop no tears, his prayers are in jest;
His words come from his mouth, ours from our
    breast:
He prays but faintly, and would be denied;
We pray with heart and soul, and all beside:
His weary joints would gladly rise, I know;
Our knees shall kneel till to the ground they grow:
His prayers are full of false hypocrisy;
Ours of true zeal and deep integrity.
Our prayers do out-pray his; then let them have
That mercy which true prayer ought to have.

HENRY BOLINGBROKE.
Good aunt, stand up.

DUCHESS OF YORK.
                  Nay, do not say 'stand up;'
But 'pardon' first, and afterwards 'stand up.'
An if I were thy nurse, thy tongue to teach,
'Pardon' should be the first word of thy speech.
I never long'd to hear a word till now;
Say 'pardon' king; let pity teach thee how:
The word is short, but not so short as sweet;
No word like 'pardon' for kings' mouths so meet.

DUKE OF YORK.
Speak it in French, king; say, *pardonne moi.*

DUCHESS OF YORK.
Dost thou teach pardon pardon to destroy?
Ah, my sour husband, my hard-hearted lord,
That sett'st the word itself against the word!—
Speak 'pardon' as 'tis current in our land;
The chopping French we do not understand.
Thine eye begins to speak, set thy tongue there:
Or in thy piteous heart plant thou thine ear;
That hearing how our plaints and prayers do
Pity may move thee 'pardon' to rehearse. [*pierce,*

HENRY BOLINGBROKE.
Good aunt, stand up.

DUCHESS OF YORK.
                  I do not sue to stand;
Pardon is all the suit I have in hand.

HENRY BOLINGBROKE.
I pardon him, as God shall pardon me.

DUCHESS OF YORK.
O happy vantage of a kneeling knee!
Yet am I sick for fear: speak it again;
Twice saying 'pardon' doth not pardon twain,
But makes one pardon strong.

HENRY BOLINGBROKE.
                  With all my heart
I pardon him.

DUCHESS OF YORK.
                  A god on earth thou art.

HENRY BOLINGBROKE.
But for our trusty brother-in-law, and the abbot,
With all the rest of that consorted crew,
Destruction straight shall dog them at the heels.—
Good uncle, help to order several powers
To Oxford, or where'er these traitors are:
They shall not live within this world, I swear,
But I will have them, if I once know where.
Uncle, farewell:—and, cousin too, adieu:
Your mother well hath pray'd, and prove you
    true.

DUCHESS OF YORK.
Come, my old son:—I pray God make thee new.
[*Exeunt.*

SCENE IV.

The same.

Enter SIR PIERCE OF EXTON *and a* SERVANT.

SIR PIERCE OF EXTON.
DIDST thou not mark the king, what words he
    spake,—
'Have I no friend will rid me of this living fear?'
Was it not so?

SERVANT.
Those were his very words.

SIR PIERCE OF EXTON.
'Have I no friend?' quoth he: he spake it twice,
And urged it twice together,—did he not?

SERVANT.
He did.

SIR PIERCE OF EXTON.
And speaking it, he wistly lookt on me;
As who should say,—'I would thou wert the man
That would divorce this terror from my heart,'—
Meaning the king at Pomfret.   Come, let's go:
I am the king's friend, and will rid his foe.
[*Exeunt.*

SCENE V.

Pomfret Castle.

Enter KING RICHARD.

KING RICHARD.
I HAVE been studying how I may compare
This prison where I live unto the world:
And, for because the world is populous,
And here is not a creature but myself,
I cannot do it;—yet I'll hammer it out.
My brain I'll prove the female to my soul,

My soul the father: and these two beget
A generation of still-breeding thoughts,
And these same thoughts people this little world;
In humours like the people of this world,
For no thought is contented. The better sort,—
As thoughts of things divine,—are intermixt
With scruples, and do set the word itself
Against the word:
As thus, 'Come, little ones;' and then again,
'It is as hard to come as for a camel
To thread the postern of a small needle's eye.'
Thoughts tending to ambition, they do plot
Unlikely wonders; how these vain weak nails
May tear a passage through the flinty ribs
Of this hard world, my ragged prison-walls;
And, for they cannot, die in their own pride.
Thoughts tending to content flatter themselves
That they are not the first of fortune's slaves,
Nor shall not be the last; like silly beggars,
Who, sitting in the stocks, refuge their shame,
That many have and others must sit there;
And in this thought they find a kind of ease,
Bearing their own misfortunes on the back
Of such as have before endured the like.
Thus play I, in one person, many people,
And none contented: sometimes am I king;
Then treason makes me wish myself a beggar,
And so I am: then crushing penury
Persuades me I was better when a king;
Then am I king'd again: and by and by
Think that I am unking'd by Bolingbroke,
And straight am nothing:—but whate'er I be,
Nor I, nor any man that but man is,
With nothing shall be pleased, till he be eased
With being nothing.—Music do I hear? [*Music.*
Ha, ha! keep time:—how sour sweet music is,
When time is broke and no proportion kept!
So is it in the music of men's lives.
And here have I the daintiness of ear
To check time broke in a disorder'd string;
But, for the concord of my state and time,
Had not an ear to hear my true time broke.
I wasted time, and now doth time waste me;
For now hath time made me his numbering
   clock;
My thoughts are minutes; and with sighs they
   jar
Their watches to mine eyes, the outward watch,
Whereto my finger, like a dial's point,
Is pointing still, in cleansing them from tears:
Now, sir, the sound that tells what hour it is,
Are clamorous groans, which strike upon my
   heart,
Which is the bell: so sighs and tears and groans
Show minutes, times, and hours:—but my time
Runs posting on in Bolingbroke's proud joy,
While I stand fooling here, his Jack o' th' clock.
This music mads me; let it sound no more;
For though it have holp madmen to their wits,
In me it seems it will make wise men mad.
Yet, blessing on his heart that gives it me!
For 'tis a sign of love; and love to Richard
Is a strange brooch in this all-hating world.
            Enter GROOM.
                  GROOM.
Hail, royal prince!

                KING RICHARD.
         Thanks, noble peer;
The cheapest of us is ten groats too dear.
What art thou? and how comest thou hither,
Where no man never comes, but that sad dog
That brings me food to make misfortune live?
                  GROOM.
I was a poor groom of thy stable, king,   [York,
When thou wert king; who, travelling towards
With much ado at length have gotten leave
To look upon my sometimes royal master's face.
O, how it yearn'd my heart, when I beheld,
In London streets, that coronation-day,
When Bolingbroke rode on roan Barbary,—
That horse that thou so often hast bestrid,
That horse that I so carefully have drest!
                KING RICHARD.
Rode he on Barbary? Tell me, gentle friend,
How went he under him?
                  GROOM.
So proudly as if he disdain'd the ground.
                KING RICHARD.
So proud that Bolingbroke was on his back!
That jade hath eat bread from my royal hand;
This hand hath made him proud with clapping
   him.
Would he not stumble? would he not fall down,—
Since pride must have a fall,—and break the neck
Of that proud man that did usurp his back?
Forgiveness, horse! why do I rail on thee,
Since thou, created to be awed by man,
Wast born to bear? I was not made a horse;
And yet I bear a burden like an ass,
Spur-gall'd and tired by jauncing Bolingbroke.
        Enter KEEPER, *with a dish.*
      KEEPER [*to the* GROOM].
Fellow, give place; here is no longer stay.
                KING RICHARD.
If thou love me, 'tis time thou wert away.
                  GROOM.
What my tongue dares not, that my heart shall
   say.   [*Exit.*
                  KEEPER.
My lord, will't please you to fall to?
                KING RICHARD.
Taste of it first, as thou art wont to do.
                  KEEPER.
My lord, I dare not. Sir Pierce of Exton,
Who lately came from th' king, commands the
   contrary.
                KING RICHARD.
The devil take Henry of Lancaster and thee!
Patience is stale, and I am weary of it.
                          [*Beats the* KEEPER.
                  KEEPER.
Help, help, help!
   Enter SIR PIERCE OF EXTON *and* SERVANTS,
                  arm'd.
                KING RICHARD.
How now! what means death in this rude assault?
Villain, thy own hand yields thy death's instru-
   ment.
      [*Snatching a weapon, and killing a* SERVANT.
Go thou, and fill another room in hell.
      [*He kills another* SERVANT. *Then* EXTON
         strikes him down.

That hand shall burn in never-quenching fire
That staggers thus my person.—Exton, thy fierce
　hand
Hath with the king's blood stain'd the king's own
　land.
Mount, mount, my soul! thy seat is up on high;
Whilst my gross flesh sinks downward, here to
　die. 　　　　　　　　　　　　　　　*[Dies.*

　　　　SIR PIERCE OF EXTON.
As full of valour as of royal blood:
Both have I spilt;—O, would the deed were
　good!
For now the devil, that told me I did well,
Says that this deed is chronicled in hell.
This dead king to the living king I'll bear:—
Take hence the rest, and give them burial here.
　　　　　　　　　　　　　　　　[Exeunt.

SCENE VI.

Windsor Castle.

Flourish. Enter BOLINGBROKE, YORK, LORDS,
and ATTENDANTS.

　　　　HENRY BOLINGBROKE.
KIND uncle York, the latest news we hear
　　Is that the rebels have consumed with fire
Our town of Cicester in Glostershire;
But whether they be ta'en or slain we hear not.
　　　　Enter NORTHUMBERLAND.
Welcome, my lord: what is the news?
　　　　EARL OF NORTHUMBERLAND.
First, to thy sacred state wish I all happiness.
The next news is, I have to London sent
The heads of Oxford, Salisbury, Blunt, and
　Kent:
The manner of their taking may appear
At large discoursed in this paper here.
　　　　HENRY BOLINGBROKE.
We thank thee, gentle Percy, for thy pains;
And to thy worth will add right worthy gains.
　　　　Enter FITZWATER.
　　　　LORD FITZWATER.
My lord, I have from Oxford sent to London
The heads of Brocas and Sir Bennet Seely,
Two of the dangerous consorted traitors
That sought at Oxford thy dire overthrow.

　　　　HENRY BOLINGBROKE.
Thy pains, Fitzwater, shall not be forgot;
Right noble is thy merit, well I wot.
　　Enter PERCY, *with the* BISHOP OF CARLISLE.
　　　　　　　HENRY PERCY.
The grand conspirator, Abbot of Westminster,
With clog of conscience and sour melancholy,
Hath yielded up his body to the grave;
But here is Carlisle living, to abide
Thy kingly doom and sentence of his pride.
　　　　HENRY BOLINGBROKE.
Carlisle, this is your doom:—
Choose out some secret place, some reverend
　room,
More than thou hast, and with it joy thy life;
So, as thou livest in peace, die free from strife:
For though mine enemy thou hast ever been,
High sparks of honour in thee have I seen.
　　　Enter SIR PIERCE OF EXTON, *with a coffin.*
　　　　SIR PIERCE OF EXTON.
Great king, within this coffin I present
Thy buried fear: herein all breathless lies
The mightiest of thy greatest enemies,
Richard of Bourdeaux, by me hither brought.
　　　　HENRY BOLINGBROKE.
Exton, I thank thee not; for thou hast wrought
A deed of slander, with thy fatal hand,
Upon my head and all this famous land.
　　　　SIR PIERCE OF EXTON.
From your own mouth, my lord, did I this deed.
　　　　HENRY BOLINGBROKE.
They love not poison that do poison need,
Nor do I thee: though I did wish him dead,
I hate the murderer, love him murdered.
The guilt of conscience take thou for thy labour,
But neither my good word nor princely favour:
With Cain go wander through the shades of
　night,
And never show thy head by day nor light.—
Lords, I protest, my soul is full of woe
That blood should sprinkle me to make me grow:
Come, mourn with me for that I do lament,
And put on sullen black incontinent:
I'll make a voyage to the Holy Land,
To wash this blood off from my guilty hand:—
March sadly after; grace my mournings here,
In weeping after this untimely bier. 　　*[Exeunt.*

THE FIRST PART OF
KING HENRY THE FOURTH

DRAMATIS PERSONAE

KING HENRY THE FOURTH.
HENRY, *Prince of Wales,* } *sons to the King.*
PRINCE JOHN *of Lancaster,*
EARL OF WESTMORELAND.
SIR WALTER BLUNT.
THOMAS PERCY, *Earl of Worcester.*
HENRY PERCY, *Earl of Northumberland.*
HENRY PERCY, *surnamed* HOTSPUR, *his son.*
EDMUND MORTIMER, *Earl of March.*
SCROOP, *Archbishop of York.*
ARCHIBALD, *Earl of Douglas.*
OWEN GLENDOWER.
SIR RICHARD VERNON.
SIR JOHN FALSTAFF.
SIR MICHAEL, *a friend to the Archbishop of York.*

POINTZ.
GADSHILL.
PETO.
BARDOLPH.

LADY PERCY, *wife to Hotspur, and sister to Mortimer.*
LADY MORTIMER, *daughter to Glendower, and wife to Mortimer.*
MISTRESS QUICKLY, *hostess of a tavern in East-cheap.*

LORDS, OFFICERS, SHERIFF, VINTNER, CHAMBERLAIN, DRAWERS, TWO CARRIERS, TRAVELLERS, *and* ATTENDANTS.

SCENE—*England.*

ACT I. SCENE I.
London.   The palace.

Enter KING HENRY, WESTMORELAND, SIR WALTER BLUNT, *and others.*

KING HENRY.

SO shaken as we are, so wan with care,
Find we a time for frighted peace to pant,
And breathe short-winded accents of new broils
To be commenced in stronds afar remote.
No more the thirsty entrance of this soil
Shall daub her lips with her own children's blood;
No more shall trenching war channel her fields,
Nor bruise her flowerets with the armed hoofs
Of hostile paces: those opposed eyes,
Which, like the meteors of a troubled heaven,
All of one nature, of one substance bred,
Did lately meet in the intestine shock
And furious close of civil butchery,
Shall now, in mutual well-beseeming ranks,
March all one way, and be no more opposed
Against acquaintance, kindred, and allies:
The edge of war, like an ill-sheathed knife,
No more shall cut his master. Therefore, friends,
As far as to the sepulchre of Christ,—
Whose soldier now, under whose blessed cross
We are impressed and engaged to fight,—
Forthwith a power of English shall we levy;
Whose arms were moulded in their mothers'
To chase these pagans in those holy fields [womb
Over whose acres walkt those blessed feet
Which fourteen hundred years ago were nail'd
For our advantage on the bitter cross.
But this our purpose now is twelve month old,
And bootless 'tis to tell you we will go:
Therefore we meet not now.—Then let me hear
Of you, my gentle cousin Westmoreland,
What yesternight our council did decree
In forwarding this dear expedience.
EARL OF WESTMORELAND.
My liege, this haste was hot in question,
And many limits of the charge set down

But yesternight: when, all athwart, there came
A post from Wales loaden with heavy news;
Whose worst was,—that the noble Mortimer,
Leading the men of Herefordshire to fight
Against the irregular and wild Glendower,
Was by the rude hands of that Welshman taken,
A thousand of his people butchered,
Upon whose dead corpse there was such misuse,
Such beastly, shameless transformation,
By those Welshwomen done, as may not be
Without much shame re-told or spoken of.
KING HENRY.
It seems, then, that the tidings of this broil
Brake off our business for the Holy Land.
EARL OF WESTMORELAND.
This, matcht with other, did, my gracious lord;
For more uneven and unwelcome news
Came from the north, and thus it did import:
On Holy-rood day, the gallant Hotspur there,
Young Harry Percy, and brave Archibald,
That ever-valiant and approved Scot,
At Holmedon met,
Where they did spend a sad and bloody hour;
As by discharge of their artillery,
And shape of likelihood, the news was told;
For he that brought them, in the very heat
And pride of their contention did take horse,
Uncertain of the issue any way.
KING HENRY.
Here is a dear, a true industrious friend,
Sir Walter Blunt, new lighted from his horse,
Stain'd with the variation of each soil
Betwixt that Holmedon and this seat of ours;
And he hath brought us smooth and welcome
news.
The Earl of Douglas is discomfited;
Ten thousand bold Scots, two-and-twenty
knights,
Balk'd in their own blood, did Sir Walter see
On Holmedon's plains: of prisoners, Hotspur
took
Mordake the Earl of Fife, and eldest son

To beaten Douglas; and the Earl of Athol,
Of Murray, Angus, and Menteith:
And is not this an honourable spoil,
A gallant prize? ha, cousin, is it not?

EARL OF WESTMORELAND.

In faith,
It is a conquest for a prince to boast of.

KING HENRY.

Yea, there thou makest me sad, and makest me sin
In envy that my Lord Northumberland
Should be the father to so blest a son,—
A son who is the theme of honour's tongue;
Amongst a grove, the very straightest plant;
Who is sweet Fortune's minion and her pride:
Whilst I, by looking on the praise of him,
See riot and dishonour stain the brow
Of my young Harry. O, that it could be proved
That some night-tripping fairy had exchanged
In cradle-clothes our children where they lay,
And call'd mine Percy, his Plantagenet!
Then would I have his Harry, and he mine:
But let him from my thoughts.—What think you,
      coz,
Of this young Percy's pride? the prisoners,
Which he in this adventure hath surprised,
To his own use he keeps; and sends me word
I shall have none but Mordake Earl of Fife.

EARL OF WESTMORELAND.

This is his uncle's teaching, this is Worcester,
Malevolent to you in all aspects;
Which makes him prune himself, and bristle up
The crest of youth against your dignity.

KING HENRY.

But I have sent for him to answer this;
And for this cause awhile we must neglect
Our holy purpose to Jerusalem.
Cousin, on Wednesday next our council we
Will hold at Windsor,—so inform the lords:
But come yourself with speed to us again;
For more is to be said and to be done
Than out of anger can be uttered.

EARL OF WESTMORELAND.

I will, my liege.   [Exeunt.

SCENE II.

London.   A tavern.

Enter PRINCE HENRY *and* FALSTAFF.

SIR JOHN FALSTAFF.

NOW, Hal, what time of day is it, lad?

PRINCE HENRY.

Thou art so fat-witted, with drinking of old sack,
and unbuttoning thee after supper, and sleeping
upon benches after noon, that thou hast forgotten
to demand that truly which thou wouldst truly
know. What a devil hast thou to do with the time
of the day? unless hours were cups of sack, and
minutes capons, and clocks the tongues of bawds,
and dials the signs of leaping-houses, and the
blessed sun himself a fair hot wench in flame-
colour'd taffeta,—I see no reason why thou
shouldst be so superfluous to demand the time of
the day.

SIR JOHN FALSTAFF.

Indeed, you come near me now, Hal; for we that
take purses go by the moon and the seven stars,

and not by Phœbus, he, 'that wandering knight
so fair.' And, I prithee, sweet wag, when thou art
king,—as, God save thy Grace,—majesty I should
say, for grace thou wilt have none,—

PRINCE HENRY.

What, none?

SIR JOHN FALSTAFF.

No, by my troth,—not so much as will serve to be
prologue to an egg and butter.

PRINCE HENRY.

Well, how then? come, roundly, roundly.

SIR JOHN FALSTAFF.

Marry, then, sweet wag, when thou art king, let
not us that are squires of the night's body be
call'd thieves of the day's beauty: let us be Diana's
foresters, gentlemen of the shade, minions of the
moon; and let men say we be men of good government, being govern'd, as the sea is, by our noble
and chaste mistress the moon, under whose countenance we steal.

PRINCE HENRY.

Thou say'st well, and it holds well too; for the
fortune of us that are the moon's men doth ebb
and flow like the sea, being govern'd, as the sea is,
by the moon. As, for proof, now: a purse of gold
most resolutely snatch'd on Monday night, and
most dissolutely spent on Tuesday morning; got
with swearing 'lay by,' and spent with crying
'bring in;' now in as low an ebb as the foot of the
ladder, and by and by in as high a flow as the
ridge of the gallows.

SIR JOHN FALSTAFF.

By the Lord, thou say'st true, lad. And is not my
hostess of the tavern a most sweet wench?

PRINCE HENRY.

As the honey of Hybla, my old lad of the castle.
And is not a buff jerkin a most sweet robe of
durance?

SIR JOHN FALSTAFF.

How now, how now, mad wag! what, in thy quips
and thy quiddities? what a plague have I to do
with a buff jerkin?

PRINCE HENRY.

Why, what a pox have I to do with my hostess of
the tavern?

SIR JOHN FALSTAFF.

Well, thou hast call'd her to a reckoning many a
time and oft.

PRINCE HENRY.

Did I ever call for thee to pay thy part?

SIR JOHN FALSTAFF.

No; I'll give thee thy due, thou hast paid all there.

PRINCE HENRY.

Yea, and elsewhere, so far as my coin would
stretch; and where it would not, I have used my
credit.

SIR JOHN FALSTAFF.

Yea, and so used it, that, were it not here apparent
that thou art heir apparent—But, I prithee,
sweet wag, shall there be gallows standing in
England when thou art king? and resolution thus
fobb'd as it is with the rusty curb of old father
antick the law? Do not thou, when thou art king,
hang a thief.

PRINCE HENRY.

No; thou shalt.

SIR JOHN FALSTAFF.
Shall I? O rare! By the Lord, I'll be a brave judge.
PRINCE HENRY.
Thou judgest false already: I mean, thou shalt have the hanging of the thieves, and so become a rare hangman.
SIR JOHN FALSTAFF.
Well, Hal, well; and in some sort it jumps with my humour as well as waiting in the court, I can tell you.
PRINCE HENRY.
For obtaining of suits?
SIR JOHN FALSTAFF.
Yea, for obtaining of suits, whereof the hangman hath no lean wardrobe. 'Sblood, I am as melancholy as a gib-cat or a lugg'd bear.
PRINCE HENRY.
Or an old lion, or a lover's lute.
SIR JOHN FALSTAFF.
Yea, or the drone of a Lincolnshire bagpipe.
PRINCE HENRY.
What say'st thou to a hare, or the melancholy of Moor-ditch?
SIR JOHN FALSTAFF.
Thou hast the most unsavoury similes, and art, indeed, the most comparative, rascalliest,—sweet young prince. But, Hal, I prithee, trouble me no more with vanity. I would to God thou and I knew where a commodity of good names were to be bought. An old lord of the council rated me the other day in the street about you, sir,—but I markt him not; and yet he talkt very wisely,—but I regarded him not; and yet he talkt wisely, and in the street too.
PRINCE HENRY.
Thou didst well; for wisdom cries out in the streets, and no man regards it.
SIR JOHN FALSTAFF.
O, thou hast damnable iteration, and art, indeed, able to corrupt a saint. Thou hast done much harm upon me, Hal,—God forgive thee for it! Before I knew thee, Hal, I knew nothing; and now am I, if a man should speak truly, little better than one of the wicked. I must give over this life, and I will give it over; by the Lord, an I do not, I am a villain: I'll be damn'd for never a king's son in Christendom.
PRINCE HENRY.
Where shall we take a purse to-morrow, Jack?
SIR JOHN FALSTAFF.
Zounds, where thou wilt, lad; I'll make one: an I do not, call me villain, and baffle me.
PRINCE HENRY.
I see a good amendment of life in thee,—from praying to purse-taking.
Enter POINTZ.
SIR JOHN FALSTAFF.
Why, Hal, 'tis my vocation, Hal; 'tis no sin for a man to labour in his vocation.—Pointz!—Now shall we know if Gadshill have set a match.—O, if men were to be saved by merit, what hole in hell were hot enough for him? This is the most omnipotent villain that ever cried 'stand' to a true man.
PRINCE HENRY.
Good morrow, Ned.

POINTZ.
Good morrow, sweet Hal.—What says Monsieur Remorse? what says Sir John Sack-and-sugar? Jack, how agrees the devil and thee about thy soul, that thou soldest him on Good-Friday last for a cup of Madeira and a cold capon's leg?
PRINCE HENRY.
Sir John stands to his word,—the devil shall have his bargain; for he was never yet a breaker of proverbs,—he will give the devil his due.
POINTZ.
Then art thou damn'd for keeping thy word with the devil.
PRINCE HENRY.
Else he had been damn'd for cozening the devil.
POINTZ.
But, my lads, my lads, to-morrow morning, by four o'clock, early at Gadshill! there are pilgrims going to Canterbury with rich offerings, and traders riding to London with fat purses: I have vizards for you all; you have horses for yourselves: Gadshill lies to-night in Rochester: I have bespoke supper to-morrow night in Eastcheap: we may do it as secure as sleep. If you will go, I will stuff your purses full of crowns; if you will not, tarry at home and be hang'd.
SIR JOHN FALSTAFF.
Hear ye, Yedward; if I tarry at home and go not, I'll hang you for going.
POINTZ.
You will, chops?
SIR JOHN FALSTAFF.
Hal, wilt thou make one?
PRINCE HENRY.
Who, I rob? I a thief? not I, by my faith.
SIR JOHN FALSTAFF.
There's neither honesty, manhood, nor good fellowship in thee, nor thou camest not of the blood royal, if thou darest not stand for ten shillings.
PRINCE HENRY.
Well, then, once in my days I'll be a madcap.
SIR JOHN FALSTAFF.
Why, that's well said.
PRINCE HENRY.
Well, come what will, I'll tarry at home.
SIR JOHN FALSTAFF.
By the Lord, I'll be a traitor, then, when thou art king.
PRINCE HENRY.
I care not.
POINTZ.
Sir John, I prithee, leave the prince and me alone: I will lay him down such reasons for this adventure, that he shall go.
SIR JOHN FALSTAFF.
Well, God give thee the spirit of persuasion, and him the ears of profiting, that what thou speakest may move, and what he hears may be believed, that the true prince may, for recreation sake, prove a false thief; for the poor abuses of the time want countenance. Farewell: you shall find me in Eastcheap.
PRINCE HENRY.
Farewell, thou latter spring! farewell, All-hallown summer!   [*Exit* FALSTAFF.

POINTZ.

Now, my good sweet honey lord, ride with us to-
morrow: I have a jest to execute that I cannot
manage alone. Falstaff, Bardolph, Peto, and Gadshill, shall rob those men that we have already
waylaid; yourself and I will not be there; and
when they have the booty, if you and I do not rob
them, cut this head from my shoulders.

PRINCE HENRY.

But how shall we part with them in setting forth?

POINTZ.

Why, we will set forth before or after them, and
appoint them a place of meeting, wherein it is at
our pleasure to fail; and then will they adventure
upon the exploit themselves; which they shall
have no sooner achieved, but we'll set upon them.

PRINCE HENRY.

Yea, but 'tis like that they will know us by our
horses, by our habits, and by every other appointment, to be ourselves.

POINTZ.

Tut! our horses they shall not see,—I'll tie them
in the wood; our vizards we will change, after we
leave them; and, sirrah, I have cases of buckram
for the nonce, to immask our noted outward garments.

PRINCE HENRY.

Yea, but I doubt they will be too hard for us.

POINTZ.

Well, for two of them, I know them to be as true-
bred cowards as ever turn'd back; and for the
third, if he fight longer than he sees reason, I'll
forswear arms. The virtue of this jest will be, the
incomprehensible lies that this same fat rogue
will tell us when we meet at supper: how thirty,
at least, he fought with; what wards, what blows,
what extremities he endured; and in the reproof
of this lies the jest.

PRINCE HENRY.

Well, I'll go with thee: provide us all things
necessary, and meet me to-night in Eastcheap;
there I'll sup. Farewell.

POINTZ.

Farewell, my lord.   [Exit.

PRINCE HENRY.

I know you all, and will awhile uphold
The unyoked humour of your idleness:
Yet herein will I imitate the sun,
Who doth permit the base contagious clouds
To smother up his beauty from the world,
That, when he please again to be himself,
Being wanted, he may be more wonder'd at,
By breaking through the foul and ugly mists
Of vapours that did seem to strangle him.
If all the year were playing holidays,
To sport would be as tedious as to work;
But when they seldom come, they wisht for
    come,
And nothing pleaseth but rare accidents.
So, when this loose behaviour I throw off,
And pay the debt I never promised,
By how much better than my word I am,
By so much shall I falsity men's hopes;
And, like bright metal on a sullen ground,
My reformation, glittering o'er my fault,
Shall show more goodly and attract more eyes

Than that which hath no foil to set it off.
I'll so offend, to make offence a skill;
Redeeming time, when men think least I will.
                                                [Exit.

SCENE III.

London.   The palace.

Enter KING HENRY, NORTHUMBERLAND, WOR-
    CESTER, HOTSPUR, SIR WALTER BLUNT, and
    others.

KING HENRY.

MY blood hath been too cold and temperate,
   Unapt to stir at these indignities,
And you have found me; for accordingly
You tread upon my patience: but be sure
I will from henceforth rather be myself,
Mighty and to be fear'd, than my condition;
Which hath been smooth as oil, soft as young
    down,
And therefore lost that title of respect
Which the proud soul ne'er pays but to the
    proud.

EARL OF WORCESTER.

Our house, my sovereign liege, little deserves
The scourge of greatness to be used on it;
And that same greatness too which our own hands
Have holp to make so portly.

EARL OF NORTHUMBERLAND.

My lord,—

KING HENRY.

Worcester, get thee gone; for I do see
Danger and disobedience in thine eye:
O, sir, your presence is too bold and peremptory,
And majesty might never yet endure
The moody frontier of a servant brow.
You have good leave to leave us: when we need
Your use and counsel, we shall send for you.
                              [Exit WORCESTER.
[to NORTHUMBERLAND] You were about to
    speak.

EARL OF NORTHUMBERLAND.

                    Yea, my good lord.
Those prisoners in your highness' name de-
    manded,
Which Harry Percy here at Holmedon took,
Were, as he says, not with such strength denied
As is deliver'd to your majesty:
Either envy, therefore, or misprision
Is guilty of this fault, and not my son.

HOTSPUR.

My liege, I did deny no prisoners.
But I remember, when the fight was done,
When I was dry with rage and extreme toil,
Breathless and faint, leaning upon my sword,
Came there a certain lord, neat, and trimly drest,
Fresh as a bridegroom; and his chin new reapt
Show'd like a stubble-land at harvest-home;
He was perfumed like a milliner;
And 'twixt his finger and his thumb he held
A pouncet-box, which ever and anon
He gave his nose, and took't away again;—
Who therewith angry, when it next came there,
Took it in snuff:—and still he smiled and talkt;
And as the soldiers bore dead bodies by,
He call'd them untaught knaves, unmannerly,
To bring a slovenly unhandsome corse

Betwixt the wind and his nobility.
With many holiday and lady terms
He question'd me; amongst the rest, demanded
My prisoners in your majesty's behalf.
I then, all smarting with my wounds being cold,
To be so pester'd with a popinjay,
Out of my grief and my impatience,
Answer'd neglectingly, I know not what,—
He should, or he should not; for he made me mad
To see him shine so brisk, and smell so sweet,
And talk so like a waiting-gentlewoman
Of guns and drums and wounds,—God save the
  mark!—
And telling me the sovereign'st thing on earth
Was parmaceti for an inward bruise;
And that it was great pity, so it was,
This villainous salt-petre should be digg'd
Out of the bowels of the harmless earth,
Which many a good tall fellow had destroy'd
So cowardly; and but for these vile guns,
He would himself have been a soldier.
This bald unjointed chat of his, my lord,
I answer'd indirectly, as I said;
And I beseech you, let not his report
Come current for an accusation
Betwixt my love and your high majesty.
            SIR WALTER BLUNT.
The circumstance consider'd, good my lord,
Whate'er Lord Harry Percy then had said
To such a person, and in such a place,
At such a time, with all the rest re-told,
May reasonably die, and never rise
To do him wrong, or any way impeach
What then he said, so he unsay it now.
            KING HENRY.
Why, yet he doth deny his prisoners,
But with proviso and exception,—
That we at our own charge shall ransom straight
His brother-in-law, the foolish Mortimer;
Who, on my soul, hath wilfully betray'd
The lives of those that he did lead to fight
Against the great magician, damn'd Glendower,
Whose daughter, as we hear, that Earl of March
Hath lately married. Shall our coffers, then,
Be emptied to redeem a traitor home?
Shall we buy treason? and indent with fears,
When they have lost and forfeited themselves?
No, on the barren mountains let him starve;
For I shall never hold that man my friend
Whose tongue shall ask me for one penny cost
To ransom home revolted Mortimer.
            HOTSPUR.
Revolted Mortimer!
He never did fall off, my sovereign liege,
But by the chance of war:—to prove that true
Needs no more but one tongue for all those
  wounds,
Those mouthed wounds, which valiantly he took,
When on the gentle Severn's sedgy bank,
In single opposition, hand to hand,
He did confound the best part of an hour
In changing hardiment with great Glendower:
Three times they breathed, and three times did
  they drink,
Upon agreement, of swift Severn's flood;
Who then, affrighted with their bloody looks,

Ran fearfully among the trembling reeds,
And hid his crisp head in the hollow bank
Blood-stained with these valiant combatants.
Never did base and rotten policy
Colour her working with such deadly wounds;
Nor never could the noble Mortimer
Receive so many, and all willingly:
Then let him not be slander'd with revolt.
            KING HENRY.
Thou dost belie him, Percy, thou dost belie him;
He never did encounter with Glendower:
I tell thee,
He durst as well have met the devil alone
As Owen Glendower for an enemy.
Art thou not ashamed? But, sirrah, henceforth
Let me not hear you speak of Mortimer:
Send me your prisoners with the speediest means,
Or you shall hear in such a kind from me
As will displease you.—My Lord Northumber-
  land,
We license your departure with your son.—
Send us your prisoners, or you will hear of it.
    [Exeunt KING HENRY, BLUNT, and TRAIN.
            HOTSPUR.
An if the devil come and roar for them,
I will not send them:—I will after straight
And tell him so: for I will ease my heart,
Albeit I make a hazard of my head.
            EARL OF NORTHUMBERLAND.
What, drunk with choler? stay, and pause awhile:
Here comes your uncle.
            Enter WORCESTER.
            HOTSPUR.
                    Speak of Mortimer!
Zounds, I will speak of him; and let my soul
Want mercy, if I do not join with him:
Yea, on his part I'll empty all these veins,
And shed my dear blood drop by drop i' th' dust,
But I will lift the down-trod Mortimer
As high i' th' air as this unthankful king,
As this ingrate and canker'd Bolingbroke.
            EARL OF NORTHUMBERLAND.
[to WORCESTER] Brother, the king hath made
  your nephew mad.
            EARL OF WORCESTER.
Who struck this heat up after I was gone?
            HOTSPUR.
He will, forsooth, have all my prisoners;
And when I urged the ransom once again
Of my wife's brother, then his cheek lookt pale,
And on my face he turn'd an eye of death,
Trembling even at the name of Mortimer.
            EARL OF WORCESTER.
I cannot blame him: was not he proclaim'd
By Richard that dead is the next of blood?
            EARL OF NORTHUMBERLAND.
He was; I heard the proclamation:
And then it was when the unhappy king—
Whose wrongs in us God pardon!—did set forth
Upon his Irish expedition;
From whence he intercepted did return
To be deposed, and shortly murdered.
            EARL OF WORCESTER.
And for whose death we in the world's wide
  mouth
Live scandalized and foully spoken of.

HOTSPUR.
But, soft, I pray you; did King Richard then
Proclaim my brother Edmund Mortimer
Heir to the crown?
EARL OF NORTHUMBERLAND.
He did; myself did hear it.
HOTSPUR.
Nay, then I cannot blame his cousin king,
That wisht him on the barren mountains starve.
But shall it be, that you, that set the crown
Upon the head of this forgetful man,
And for his sake wear the detested blot
Of murderous subornation,—shall it be,
That you a world of curses undergo,
Being the agents, or base second means,
The cords, the ladder, or the hangman rather?—
O, pardon me, that I descend so low,
To show the line and the predicament
Wherein you range under this subtle king;—
Shall it, for shame, be spoken in these days,
Or fill up chronicles in time to come,
That men of your nobility and power
Did gage them both in an unjust behalf,—
As both of you, God pardon it! have done,—
To put down Richard, that sweet lovely rose,
And plant this thorn, this canker, Bolingbroke?
And shall it, in more shame, be further spoken,
That you are fool'd, discarded, and shook off
By him for whom these shames ye underwent?
No; yet time serves, wherein you may redeem
Your banisht honours, and restore yourselves
Into the good thoughts of the world again;—
Revenge the jeering and disdain'd contempt
Of this proud king, who studies day and night
To answer all the debt he owes to you
Even with the bloody payment of your deaths:
Therefore, I say,—
EARL OF WORCESTER.
Peace, cousin, say no more:
And now I will unclasp a secret book,
And to your quick-conceiving discontents
I'll read you matter deep and dangerous;
As full of peril and adventurous spirit
As to o'er-walk a current roaring loud
On the unsteadfast footing of a spear.
HOTSPUR.
If he fall in, good night!—or sink or swim:—
Send danger from the east unto the west,
So honour cross it from the north to south,
And let them grapple:—O, the blood more stirs
To rouse a lion than to start a hare!
EARL OF NORTHUMBERLAND.
Imagination of some great exploit
Drives him beyond the bounds of patience.
HOTSPUR.
By heaven, methinks it were an easy leap,
To pluck bright honour from the pale-faced
moon;
Or dive into the bottom of the deep,
Where fadom-line could never touch the ground,
And pluck up drowned honour by the locks;
So he that doth redeem her thence might wear
Without corrival all her dignities;
But out upon this half-faced fellowship!
EARL OF WORCESTER.
He apprehends a world of figures here,

But not the form of what he should attend.—
Good cousin, give me audience for a while.
HOTSPUR.
I cry you mercy.
EARL OF WORCESTER.
Those same noble Scots
That are your prisoners,—
HOTSPUR.
I'll keep them all;
By God, he shall not have a Scot of them;
No, if a Scot would save his soul, he shall not:
I'll keep them, by this hand.
EARL OF WORCESTER.
You start away,
And lend no ear unto my purposes.—
Those prisoners you shall keep.
HOTSPUR.
Nay, I will; that's flat:—
He said he would not ransom Mortimer;
Forbad my tongue to speak of Mortimer;
But I will find him when he lies asleep,
And in his ear I'll holla 'Mortimer!'
Nay, I'll have a starling shall be taught to speak
Nothing but 'Mortimer,' and give it him,
To keep his anger still in motion.
EARL OF WORCESTER.
Hear you, cousin; a word.
HOTSPUR.
All studies here I solemnly defy,
Save how to gall and pinch this Bolingbroke:
And that same sword-and-buckler Prince of
Wales,—
But that I think his father loves him not,
And would be glad he met with some mischance,
I would have him poison'd with a pot of ale.
EARL OF WORCESTER.
Farewell, kinsman: I'll talk to you
When you are better temper'd to attend.
EARL OF NORTHUMBERLAND.
Why, what a wasp-stung and impatient fool
Art thou to break into this woman's mood,
Tying thine ear to no tongue but thine own!
HOTSPUR.
Why, look you, I am whipt and scourged with
rods,
Nettled, and stung with pismires, when I hear
Of this vile politician, Bolingbroke.
In Richard's time,—what do you call the
place?—
A plague upon 't—it is in Glostershire;—
'Twas where the madcap duke his uncle kept,—
His uncle York;—where I first bow'd my knee
Unto this king of smiles, this Bolingbroke,—
'Sblood!—
When you and he came back from Ravenspurg.
EARL OF NORTHUMBERLAND.
At Berkley-castle.
HOTSPUR.
You say true:—
Why, what a candy deal of courtesy
This fawning greyhound then did proffer me!
Look, 'when his infant fortune came to age,'
And, 'gentle Harry Percy,' and, 'kind cousin,'—
O, the devil take such cozeners!—God forgive
me!—
Good uncle, tell your tale; I have done.

EARL OF WORCESTER.
Nay, if you have not, to it again;
We will stay your leisure.

HOTSPUR.
I have done, i' faith.

EARL OF WORCESTER.
Then once more to your Scottish prisoners.
Deliver them up without their ransom straight,
And make the Douglas' son your only mean
For powers in Scotland; which, for divers
    reasons
Which I shall send you written, be assured,
Will easily be granted—. [to NORTHUMBER-
LAND] You, my lord,
Your son in Scotland being thus employ'd,
Shall secretly into the bosom creep
Of that same noble prelate, well beloved,
The archbishop.

HOTSPUR.
Of York, is it not?

EARL OF WORCESTER.
True; who bears hard
His brother's death at Bristol, the Lord Scroop.
I speak not this in estimation,
As what I think might be, but what I know
Is ruminated, plotted, and set down,
And only stays but to behold the face
Of that occasion that shall bring it on.

HOTSPUR.
I smell it: upon my life, it will do well.

EARL OF NORTHUMBERLAND.
Before the game is a-foot, thou still lett'st slip.

HOTSPUR.
Why, it cannot choose but be a noble plot:—
And then the power of Scotland and of York,—
To join with Mortimer, ha?

EARL OF WORCESTER.
And so they shall.

HOTSPUR.
In faith, it is exceedingly well aim'd.

EARL OF WORCESTER.
And 'tis no little reason bids us speed,
To save our heads by raising of a head;
For, bear ourselves as even as we can,
The king will always think him in our debt,
And think we think ourselves unsatisfied,
Till he hath found a time to pay us home:
And see already how he doth begin
To make us strangers to his looks of love.

HOTSPUR.
He does, he does; we'll be revenged on him.

EARL OF WORCESTER.
Cousin, farewell:—no further go in this
Than I by letters shall direct your course.
When time is ripe,—which will be suddenly,—
I'll steal to Glendower and Lord Mortimer;
Where you and Douglas, and our powers at once,
As I will fashion it, shall happily meet,
To bear our fortunes in our own strong arms,
Which now we hold at much uncertainty.

EARL OF NORTHUMBERLAND.
Farewell, good brother: we shall thrive, I trust.

HOTSPUR.
Uncle, adieu:—O, let the hours be short,
Till fields and blows and groans applaud our
    sport!   [Exeunt.

ACT II. SCENE I.

Rochester.   An inn-yard.

Enter a CARRIER *with a lantern in his hand.*

FIRST CARRIER.
HEIGH-HO! an't be not four by the day, I'll
be hang'd: Charles' wain is over the new
chimney, and yet our horse not packt.—What,
ostler!

OSTLER [within].
Anon, anon.

FIRST CARRIER.
I prithee, Tom, beat Cut's saddle, put a few
flocks in the point; poor jade is wrung in the
withers out of all cess.

Enter another CARRIER.

SECOND CARRIER.
Peas and beans are as dank here as a dog, and that is
the next way to give poor jades the bots: this house
is turn'd upside down since Robin ostler died.

FIRST CARRIER.
Poor fellow! never joy'd since the price of oats
rose; it was the death of him.

SECOND CARRIER.
I think this be the most villainous house in all
London road for fleas: I am stung like a tench.

FIRST CARRIER.
Like a tench! by the mass, there is ne'er a king
christen could be better bit than I have been since
the first cock.

SECOND CARRIER.
Why, they will allow us ne'er a jordan, and then
we leak in the chimney; and your chamber-lie
breeds fleas like a loach.

FIRST CARRIER.
What, ostler! come away, and be hang'd! come
away.

SECOND CARRIER.
I have a gammon of bacon and two razes of ginger, to be deliver'd as far as Charing-cross.

FIRST CARRIER.
God's body, the turkeys in my pannier are quite
starved.—What, ostler!—A plague on thee! hast
thou never an eye in thy head? canst not hear? An
'twere not as good a deed as drink, to break the
pate on thee, I am a very villain.—Come, and be
hang'd!—hast no faith in thee?

Enter GADSHILL.

GADSHILL.
Good morrow, carriers. What's o'clock?

FIRST CARRIER.
I think it be two o'clock.

GADSHILL.
I prithee, lend me thy lantern, to see my gelding
in the stable.

FIRST CARRIER.
Nay, by God, soft; I know a trick worth two of
that, i' faith.

GADSHILL.
I pray thee, lend me thine.

SECOND CARRIER.
Ay, when? canst tell?—Lend me thy lantern,
quoth a?—marry, I'll see thee hang'd first.

GADSHILL.
Sirrah carrier, what time do you mean to come to
London?

SECOND CARRIER.

Time enough to go to bed with a candle, I warrant thee.—Come, neighbour Mugs, we'll call up the gentlemen: they will along with company, for they have great charge. [*Exeunt* CARRIERS.

GADSHILL.

What, ho! chamberlain!

CHAMBERLAIN [*within*].

At hand, quoth pick-purse.

GADSHILL.

That's even as fair as—at hand, quoth the chamberlain; for thou variest no more from picking of purses than giving direction doth from labouring; thou lay'st the plot how.

Enter CHAMBERLAIN.

CHAMBERLAIN.

Good morrow, Master Gadshill. It holds current that I told you yesternight:—there's a franklin in the wild of Kent hath brought three hundred marks with him in gold: I heard him tell it to one of his company last night at supper; a kind of auditor; one that hath abundance of charge too, God knows what. They are up already, and call for eggs and butter; they will away presently.

GADSHILL.

Sirrah, if they meet not with Saint Nicholas' clerks, I'll give thee this neck.

CHAMBERLAIN.

No, I'll none of it: I prithee, keep that for the hangman; for I know thou worship'st Saint Nicholas as truly as a man of falsehood may.

GADSHILL.

What talkest thou to me of the hangman? if I hang, I'll make a fat pair of gallows; for if I hang, old Sir John hangs with me, and thou know'st he's no starveling! Tut! there are other Trojans that thou dream'st not of, the which, for sport sake, are content to do the profession some grace; that would, if matters should be lookt into, for their own credit sake, make all whole. I am join'd with no foot land-rakers, no long-staff sixpenny strikers, none of these mad mustachio purple-hued malt-worms; but with nobility and tranquillity, burgomasters and great oneyers, such as can hold in, such as will strike sooner than speak, and speak sooner than drink, and drink sooner than pray: and yet, zounds, I lie; for they pray continually to their saint, the commonwealth; or, rather, not pray to her, but prey on her,—for they ride up and down on her, and make her their boots.

CHAMBERLAIN.

What, the commonwealth their boots? will she hold out water in foul way?

GADSHILL.

She will, she will; justice hath liquor'd her. We steal as in a castle, cock-sure; we have the receipt of fern-seed,—we walk invisible.

CHAMBERLAIN.

Nay, by my faith, I think you are more beholding to the night than to fern-seed for your walking invisible.

GADSHILL.

Give me thy hand: thou shalt have a share in our purchase, as I am a true man.

CHAMBERLAIN.

Nay, rather let me have it, as you are a false thief.

GADSHILL.

Go to; *homo* is a common name to all men. Bid the ostler bring my gelding out of the stable. Farewell, you muddy knave. [*Exeunt*.

SCENE II.

The road by Gadshill.

Enter PRINCE HENRY *and* POINTZ; BARDOLPH *and* PETO *at some distance*.

POINTZ.

COME, shelter, shelter: I have removed Falstaff's horse, and he frets like a gumm'd velvet.

PRINCE HENRY.

Stand close. [*They retire*.

Enter FALSTAFF.

SIR JOHN FALSTAFF.

Pointz! Pointz, and be hang'd! Pointz!

PRINCE HENRY [*coming forward*].

Peace, ye fat-kidney'd rascal! what a brawling dost thou keep!

SIR JOHN FALSTAFF.

Where's Pointz, Hal?

PRINCE HENRY.

He is walkt up to the top of the hill: I'll go seek him. [*Retires*.

SIR JOHN FALSTAFF.

I am accurst to rob in that thief's company: the rascal hath removed my horse, and tied him I know not where. If I travel but four foot by the squier further a-foot, I shall break my wind. Well, I doubt not but to die a fair death for all this, if I scape hanging for killing that rogue. I have forsworn his company hourly any time this two-and-twenty year, and yet I am bewitcht with the rogue's company. If the rascal have not given me medicines to make me love him, I'll be hang'd; it could not be else; I have drunk medicines.—Pointz!—Hal!—a plague upon you both!—Bardolph!—Peto!—I'll starve, ere I'll rob a foot further. An 'twere not as good a deed as drink, to turn true man, and to leave these rogues, I am the veriest varlet that ever chew'd with a tooth. Eight yards of uneven ground is threescore and ten miles a-foot with me; and the stony-hearted villains know it well enough: a plague upon't, when thieves cannot be true one to another! [*They whistle*.] Whew!—A plague upon you all! Give me my horse, you rogues; give me my horse, and be hang'd!

PRINCE HENRY [*coming forward*].

Peace, ye fat-guts! lie down; lay thine ear close to the ground, and list if thou canst hear the tread of travellers.

SIR JOHN FALSTAFF.

Have you any levers to lift me up again, being down? 'Sblood, I'll not bear mine own flesh so far a-foot again for all the coin in thy father's exchequer. What a plague mean ye to colt me thus?

PRINCE HENRY.

Thou liest; thou art not colted, thou art uncolted.

SIR JOHN FALSTAFF.

I prithee, good Prince Hal, help me to my horse, good king's son.

PRINCE HENRY.

Out, ye rogue! shall I be your ostler?

SIR JOHN FALSTAFF.

Go, hang thyself in thine own heir-apparent garters! If I be ta'en, I'll peach for this. An I have not ballads made on you all, and sung to filthy tunes, let a cup of sack be my poison:—when a jest is so forward, and a-foot too!—I hate it.

Enter GADSHILL.

GADSHILL.

Stand!

SIR JOHN FALSTAFF.

So I do, against my will.

POINTZ.

O, 'tis our setter: I know his voice.

[*Coming forward with* BARDOLPH *and* PETO.

BARDOLPH.

What news?

GADSHILL.

Case ye, case ye; on with your vizards: there's money of the king's coming down the hill; 'tis going to the king's exchequer.

SIR JOHN FALSTAFF.

You lie, ye rogue; 'tis going to the king's tavern.

GADSHILL.

There's enough to make us all.

SIR JOHN FALSTAFF.

To be hang'd.

PRINCE HENRY.

Sirs, you four shall front them in the narrow lane; Ned Pointz and I will walk lower: if they scape from your encounter, then they light on us.

PETO.

How many be there of them?

GADSHILL.

Some eight or ten.

SIR JOHN FALSTAFF.

Zounds, will they not rob us?

PRINCE HENRY.

What, a coward, Sir John Paunch?

SIR JOHN FALSTAFF.

Indeed, I am not John of Gaunt, your grandfather; but yet no coward, Hal.

PRINCE HENRY.

Well, we leave that to the proof.

POINTZ.

Sirrah Jack, thy horse stands behind the hedge: when thou need'st him, there thou shalt find him. Farewell, and stand fast.

SIR JOHN FALSTAFF.

Now cannot I strike him, if I should be hang'd.

PRINCE HENRY [*aside to* POINTZ].

Ned, where are our disguises?

POINTZ [*aside to* PRINCE HENRY].

Here, hard by: stand close.

[*Exeunt* PRINCE HENRY *and* POINTZ.

SIR JOHN FALSTAFF.

Now, my masters, happy man be his dole, say I: every man to his business.

Enter TRAVELLERS.

FIRST TRAVELLER.

Come, neighbour: the boy shall lead our horses down the hill; we'll walk a-foot awhile, and ease our legs.

THIEVES.

Stand!

TRAVELLERS.

Jesus bless us!

SIR JOHN FALSTAFF.

Strike; down with them; cut the villains' throats: —ah, whoreson caterpillars! bacon-fed knaves! they hate us youth:—down with them; fleece them.

TRAVELLERS.

O, we are undone, both we and ours for ever!

SIR JOHN FALSTAFF.

Hang ye, gorbellied knaves, are ye undone? No, ye fat chuffs; I would your store were here! On, bacons, on! What, ye knaves! young men must live. You are grand-jurors, are ye? we'll jure ye, i' faith.

[*Here they rob them and bind them. Exeunt.*
Enter PRINCE HENRY *and* POINTZ *disguised.*

PRINCE HENRY.

The thieves have bound the true men. Now could thou and I rob the thieves, and go merrily to London, it would be argument for a week, laughter for a month, and a good jest for ever.

POINTZ.

Stand close: I hear them coming.   [*They retire.*
Enter THIEVES *again.*

SIR JOHN FALSTAFF.

Come, my masters, let us share, and then to horse before day. An the Prince and Pointz be not two arrant cowards, there's no equity stirring: there's no more valour in that Pointz than in a wild-duck.

PRINCE HENRY.

Your money!

POINTZ.

Villains!

[*As they are sharing, the* PRINCE *and* POINTZ *set upon them. They all run away, and* FALSTAFF *after a blow or two runs away too, leaving the booty behind them.*

PRINCE HENRY.

Got with much ease. Now merrily to horse:
The thieves are scatter'd, and possest with fear
So strongly that they dare not meet each other;
Each takes his fellow for an officer.
Away, good Ned. Falstaff sweats to death,
And lards the lean earth as he walks along:
Were't not for laughing, I should pity him.

POINTZ.

How the rogue roar'd!   [*Exeunt.*

SCENE III.

Warkworth Castle.

Enter HOTSPUR *solus, reading a letter.*

HOTSPUR.

'—BUT, for mine own part, my lord, I could be well contented to be there, in respect of the love I bear your house.'—He could be contented,—why is he not, then? In respect of the love he bears our house:—he shows in this, he loves his own barn better than he loves our house. Let me see some more. 'The purpose you undertake is dangerous:'—why, that's certain: 'tis dangerous to take a cold, to sleep, to drink; but I tell

you, my lord fool, out of this nettle, danger, we
pluck this flower, safety. 'The purpose you undertake is dangerous; the friends you have named
uncertain; the time itself unsorted; and your
whole plot too light for the counterpoise of so
great an opposition.'—Say you so, say you so? I
say unto you again, you are a shallow, cowardly
hind, and you lie. What a lack-brain is this! By
the Lord, our plot is a good plot as ever was laid;
our friends true and constant: a good plot, good
friends, and full of expectation; an excellent plot,
very good friends. What a frosty-spirited rogue
is this! Why, my Lord of York commends the
plot and the general course of the action. Zounds,
an I were now by this rascal, I could brain him
with his lady's fan. Is there not my father, my
uncle, and myself? Lord Edmund Mortimer, my
Lord of York, and Owen Glendower? is there not,
besides, the Douglas? have I not all their letters
to meet me in arms by the ninth of the next
month? and are they not some of them set forward already? What a pagan rascal is this! an
infidel! Ha! you shall see now, in very sincerity
of fear and cold heart, will he to the king, and lay
open all our proceedings. O, I could divide myself, and go to buffets, for moving such a dish of
skim milk with so honourable an action! Hang
him! let him tell the king: we are prepared. I will
set forward to-night.

Enter LADY PERCY.

How now, Kate! I must leave you within these
two hours.

LADY PERCY.

O, my good lord, why are you thus alone?
For what offence have I this fortnight been
A banisht woman from my Harry's bed?
Tell me, sweet lord, what is't that takes from
    thee
Thy stomach, pleasure, and thy golden sleep?
Why dost thou bend thine eyes upon the earth,
And start so often when thou sitt'st alone?
Why hast thou lost the fresh blood in thy cheeks;
And given my treasures and my rights of thee
To thick-eyed musing and curst melancholy?
In thy faint slumbers I by thee have watcht,
And heard thee murmur tales of iron wars;
Speak terms of manage to thy bounding steed;
Cry, 'Courage! to the field!'—and thou hast
    talkt
Of sallies and retires, of trenches, tents,
Of palisadoes, frontiers, parapets,
Of basilisks, of cannon, culverin,
Of prisoners' ransom, and of soldiers slain,
And all the currents of a heady fight.
Thy spirit within thee hath been so at war,
And thus hath so bestirr'd thee in thy sleep,
That beads of sweat have stood upon thy brow,
Like bubbles in a late-disturbed stream;
And in thy face strange motions have appear'd,
Such as we see when men restrain their breath
On some great sudden hest. O, what portents are
    these?
Some heavy business hath my lord in hand,
And I must know it, else he loves me not.

HOTSPUR.

What, ho!

Enter a SERVANT.

Is Gilliams with the packet gone?

SERVANT.

He is, my lord, an hour ago.

HOTSPUR.

Hath Butler brought those horses from the
    sheriff?

SERVANT.

One horse, my lord, he brought even now.

HOTSPUR.

What horse? a roan, a crop-ear, is it not?

SERVANT.

It is, my lord.

HOTSPUR.

That roan shall be my throne.
Well, I will back him straight: O *esperance!*—
Bid Butler lead him forth into the park.
                                    [*Exit* SERVANT.

LADY PERCY.

But hear you, my lord.

HOTSPUR.

                What say'st thou, my lady?

LADY PERCY.

What is it carries you away?

HOTSPUR.

                        Why, my horse,
My love,—my horse.

LADY PERCY.

                Out, you mad-headed ape!
A weasel hath not such a deal of spleen
As you are tost with. In faith,
I'll know your business, Harry,—that I will.
I fear my brother Mortimer doth stir
About his title, and hath sent for you
To line his enterprise: but if you go,—

HOTSPUR.

So far a-foot, I shall be weary, love.

LADY PERCY.

Come, come, you paraquito, answer me
Directly unto this question that I ask:
In faith, I'll break thy little finger, Harry,
An if thou wilt not tell me all things true.

HOTSPUR.

Away, away, you trifler!—Love?—I love thee
    not,
I care not for thee, Kate: this is no world
To play with mammets and to tilt with lips:
We must have bloody noses and crackt crowns,
And pass them current too.—God's me, my
    horse!—
What say'st thou, Kate? what wouldst thou have
    with me?

LADY PERCY.

Do you not love me? do you not, indeed?
Well, do not, then; for since you love me not,
I will not love myself. Do you not love me?
Nay, tell me if you speak in jest or no.

HOTSPUR.

Come, wilt thou see me ride?
And when I am o' horseback, I will swear
I love thee infinitely. But hark you, Kate;
I must not have you henceforth question me
Whither I go, nor reason whereabout:
Whither I must, I must; and, to conclude,
This evening must I leave you, gentle Kate.
I know you wise; but yet no further wise

Than Harry Percy's wife: constant you are;
But yet a woman: and for secrecy,
No lady closer; for I well believe
Thou wilt not utter what thou dost not know,—
And so far will I trust thee, gentle Kate.

LADY PERCY.

How! so far?

HOTSPUR.

Not an inch further. But hark you, Kate:
Whither I go, thither shall you go too;
To-day will I set forth, to-morrow you.—
Will this content you, Kate?

LADY PERCY.

It must of force.
[Exeunt.

SCENE IV.

Eastcheap. The Boar's-Head Tavern.

Enter PRINCE HENRY.

PRINCE HENRY.

NED, prithee, come out of that fat room, and
lend me thy hand to laugh a little.
Enter POINTZ.

POINTZ.

Where hast been, Hal?

PRINCE HENRY.

With three or four loggerheads amongst three or
fourscore hogsheads. I have sounded the very
base-string of humility. Sirrah, I am sworn
brother to a leash of drawers; and can tell them
all by their christen names, as,—Tom, Dick, and
Francis. They take it already upon their salvation,
that though I be but Prince of Wales, yet I am
the king of courtesy; and tell me flatly I am no
proud Jack, like Falstaff, but a Corinthian, a lad
of mettle, a good boy, by the Lord, so they call
me, and when I am king of England, I shall
command all the good lads in Eastcheap. They
call drinking deep, dyeing scarlet; and when you
breathe in your watering, they cry 'hem!' and bid
you play it off. To conclude, I am so good a pro-
ficient in one quarter of an hour, that I can drink
with any tinker in his own language during my
life. I tell thee, Ned, thou hast lost much honour,
that thou wert not with me in this action. But,
sweet Ned,—to sweeten which name of Ned, I
give thee this pennyworth of sugar, clapt even
now into my hand by an under-skinker, one that
never spake other English in his life than 'Eight
shillings and sixpence,' and 'You are welcome,'
with this shrill addition, 'Anon, anon, sir! Score
a pint of bastard in the Half-moon,' or so:—but,
Ned, to drive away the time till Falstaff come, I
prithee, do thou stand in some by-room, while I
question my puny drawer to what end he gave me
the sugar; and do thou never leave calling 'Francis,' that his tale to me may be nothing but 'anon.'
Step aside, and I'll show thee a precedent.
[Exit POINTZ.

POINTZ [within].

Francis!

PRINCE HENRY.

Thou art perfect.

POINTZ [within].

Francis!

Enter FRANCIS.

FRANCIS.

Anon, anon, sir.—Look down into the Pom-
garnet, Ralph.

PRINCE HENRY.

Come hither, Francis.

FRANCIS.

My lord?

PRINCE HENRY.

How long hast thou to serve, Francis?

FRANCIS.

Forsooth, five years, and as much as to—

POINTZ [within].

Francis!

FRANCIS.

Anon, anon, sir.

PRINCE HENRY.

Five years! by'r lady, a long lease for the clinking
of pewter. But, Francis, darest thou be so valiant
as to play the coward with thy indenture and
show it a fair pair of heels and run from it?

O Lord, sir, I'll be sworn upon all the books in
England, I could find in my heart—

POINTZ [within].

Francis!

FRANCIS.

Anon, anon, sir.

PRINCE HENRY.

How old art thou, Francis?

FRANCIS.

Let me see,—about Michaelmas next I shall
be—

POINTZ [within].

Francis!

FRANCIS.

Anon, sir.—Pray you, stay a little, my lord.

PRINCE HENRY.

Nay, but hark you, Francis: for the sugar thou
gavest me,—'twas a pennyworth, was't not?

FRANCIS.

O Lord, sir, I would it had been two!

PRINCE HENRY.

I will give thee for it a thousand pound: ask me
when thou wilt, and thou shalt have it.

POINTZ [within].

Francis!

FRANCIS.

Anon, anon.

PRINCE HENRY.

Anon, Francis? No, Francis; but to-morrow,
Francis; or, Francis, o' Thursday; or, indeed,
Francis, when thou wilt. But, Francis,—

FRANCIS.

My lord?

PRINCE HENRY.

Wilt thou rob this leathern-jerkin, crystal-button,
nott-pated, agate-ring, puke-stocking, caddis-
garter, smooth-tongue, Spanish-pouch,—

FRANCIS.

O Lord, sir, what do you mean?

PRINCE HENRY.

Why, then, your brown bastard is your only
drink; for, look you, Francis, your white canvas
doublet will sully: in Barbary, sir, it cannot come
to so much.

FRANCIS.

What, sir?

POINTZ [*within*].

Francis!

PRINCE HENRY.

Away, you rogue! dost thou not hear them call?
[*Here they both call him; the* DRAWER *stands
amazed, not knowing which way to go.*
Enter VINTNER.

VINTNER.

What, stand'st thou still, and hear'st such a calling? Look to the guests within. [*Exit* FRANCIS.]
My lord, old Sir John, with half-a-dozen more,
are at the door: shall I let them in?

PRINCE HENRY.

Let them alone awhile, and then open the door.
[*Exit* VINTNER.] Pointz!

Enter POINTZ.

POINTZ.

Anon, anon, sir.

PRINCE HENRY.

Sirrah, Falstaff and the rest of the thieves are at
the door: shall we be merry?

POINTZ.

As merry as crickets, my lad. But hark ye; what
cunning match have you made with this jest of
the drawer? come, what's the issue?

PRINCE HENRY.

I am now of all humours that have show'd themselves humours since the old days of goodman Adam to the pupil age of this present
twelve o'clock at midnight. — What's o'clock,
Francis?

FRANCIS [*within*].

Anon, anon, sir.

PRINCE HENRY.

That ever this fellow should have fewer words
than a parrot, and yet the son of a woman! His industry is up-stairs and down-stairs; his eloquence
the parcel of a reckoning. I am not yet of Percy's
mind, the Hotspur of the north; he that kills me
some six or seven dozen of Scots at a breakfast,
washes his hands, and says to his wife, "Fie upon
this quiet life! I want work.' 'O my sweet Harry,'
says she, 'how many hast thou kill'd to-day?'
'Give my roan horse a drench,' says he; and answers, 'Some fourteen,' an hour after,—'a trifle, a
trifle.' I prithee, call in Falstaff: I'll play Percy,
and that damn'd brawn shall play Dame Mortimer his wife. 'Rivo,' says the drunkard. Call in
ribs, call in tallow.

Enter FALSTAFF, GADSHILL, BARDOLPH, *and*
PETO; *followed by* FRANCIS *with wine.*

POINTZ.

Welcome, Jack: where hast thou been?

SIR JOHN FALSTAFF.

A plague of all cowards, I say, and a vengeance
too! marry, and amen!—Give me a cup of sack,
boy.—Ere I lead this life long, I'll sew nether-
stocks, and mend them and foot them too. A
plague of all cowards!—Give me a cup of
sack, rogue.—Is there no virtue extant?

[*Drinks.*

PRINCE HENRY.

Didst thou never see Titan kiss a dish of butter
(pitiful-hearted Titan!) that melted at the sweet

tale of the sun! if thou didst, then behold that
compound.

SIR JOHN FALSTAFF.

You rogue, here's lime in this sack too: there is
nothing but roguery to be found in villainous
man: yet a coward is worse than a cup of sack with
lime in it,—a villainous coward.—Go thy ways,
old Jack; die when thou wilt, if manhood, good
manhood, be not forgot upon the face of the
earth, then am I a shotten herring. There lives
not three good men unhang'd in England; and
one of them is fat, and grows old: God help the
while! a bad world, I say. I would I were a
weaver; I could sing psalms or any thing. A
plague of all cowards! I say still.

PRINCE HENRY.

How now, wool-sack! what mutter you?

SIR JOHN FALSTAFF.

A king's son! If I do not beat thee out of thy
kingdom with a dagger of lath, and drive all thy
subjects afore thee like a flock of wild-geese, I'll
never wear hair on my face more. You Prince of
Wales!

PRINCE HENRY.

Why, you whoreson round man, what's the
matter?

SIR JOHN FALSTAFF.

Are not you a coward? answer me to that:—and
Pointz there?

POINTZ.

Zounds, ye fat paunch, an ye call me coward, by
the Lord, I'll stab thee.

SIR JOHN FALSTAFF.

I call thee coward! I'll see thee damn'd ere I call
thee coward: but I would give a thousand pound,
I could run as fast as thou canst. You are straight
enough in the shoulders,—you care not who sees
your back: call you that backing of your friends?
A plague upon such backing! give me them that
will face me.—Give me a cup of sack:—I am a
rogue, if I drunk to-day.

PRINCE HENRY.

O villain! thy lips are scarce wiped since thou
drunk'st last.

SIR JOHN FALSTAFF.

All's one for that. A plague of all cowards! still
say I.   [*Drinks.*

PRINCE HENRY.

What's the matter?

SIR JOHN FALSTAFF.

What's the matter! there be four of us here have
ta'en a thousand pound this day morning.

PRINCE HENRY.

Where is it, Jack? where is it?

SIR JOHN FALSTAFF.

Where is it! taken from us it is: a hundred upon
poor four of us.

PRINCE HENRY.

What, a hundred, man?

SIR JOHN FALSTAFF.

I am a rogue, if I were not at half-sword with a
dozen of them two hours together. I have scaped
by miracle. I am eight times thrust through the
doublet, four through the hose; my buckler cut
through and through; my sword hackt like a hand-
saw,—*ecce signum!* I never dealt better since I was

a man: all would not do. A plague of all cowards!
—Let them speak: if they speak more or less than
truth, they are villains and the sons of darkness.

PRINCE HENRY.

Speak, sirs; how was it?

GADSHILL.

We four set upon some dozen,—

SIR JOHN FALSTAFF.

Sixteen at least, my lord.

GADSHILL.

And bound them.

PETO.

No, no, they were not bound.

SIR JOHN FALSTAFF.

You rogue, they were bound, every man of them;
or I am a Jew else, an Ebrew Jew.

GADSHILL.

As we were sharing, some six or seven fresh men
set upon us,—

SIR JOHN FALSTAFF.

And unbound the rest, and then come in the
other.

PRINCE HENRY.

What, fought you with them all?

SIR JOHN FALSTAFF.

All! I know not what you call all; but if I fought
not with fifty of them, I am a bunch of radish: if
there were not two or three and fifty upon poor
old Jack, then am I no two-legg'd creature.

PRINCE HENRY.

Pray God you have not murder'd some of them.

SIR JOHN FALSTAFF.

Nay, that's past praying for: I have pepper'd two
of them; two I am sure I have paid,—two rogues
in buckram suits. I tell thee what, Hal,—if I tell
thee a lie, spit in my face, call me horse. Thou
knowest my old ward;—here I lay, and thus I
bore my point. Four rogues in buckram let drive
at me,—

PRINCE HENRY.

What, four? thou saidst but two even now.

SIR JOHN FALSTAFF.

Four, Hal; I told thee four.

POINTZ.

Ay, ay, he said four.

SIR JOHN FALSTAFF.

These four came all a-front, and mainly thrust at
me. I made me no more ado but took all their
seven points in my target, thus.

PRINCE HENRY.

Seven? why, there were but four even now.

SIR JOHN FALSTAFF.

In buckram?

POINTZ.

Ay, four, in buckram suits.

SIR JOHN FALSTAFF.

Seven, by these hilts, or I am a villain else.

PRINCE HENRY.

Prithee, let him alone; we shall have more anon.

SIR JOHN FALSTAFF.

Dost thou hear me, Hal?

PRINCE HENRY.

Ay, and mark thee too, Jack.

SIR JOHN FALSTAFF.

Do so, for it is worth the listening to. These nine
in buckram that I told thee of,—

PRINCE HENRY.

So, two more already.

SIR JOHN FALSTAFF.

Their points being broken,—

POINTZ.

Down fell their hose.

SIR JOHN FALSTAFF.

Began to give me ground: but I follow'd me close,
came in foot and hand; and with a thought seven
of the eleven I paid.

PRINCE HENRY.

O monstrous! eleven buckram men grown out of
two!

SIR JOHN FALSTAFF.

But, as the devil would have it, three misbegotten
knaves in Kendal green came at my back and let
drive at me;—for it was so dark, Hal, that thou
couldst not see thy hand.

PRINCE HENRY.

These lies are like their father that begets them,—
gross as a mountain, open, palpable. Why, thou
clay-brain'd guts, thou nott-pated fool, thou
whoreson, obscene, greasy tallow-keech,—

SIR JOHN FALSTAFF.

What, art thou mad? art thou mad? is not the
truth the truth?

PRINCE HENRY.

Why, how couldst thou know these men in
Kendal green, when it was so dark thou couldst
not see thy hand? come, tell us your reason: what
say'st thou to this?

POINTZ.

Come, your reason, Jack, your reason.

SIR JOHN FALSTAFF.

What, upon compulsion? Zounds, an I were at
the strappado, or all the racks in the world, I
would not tell you on compulsion. Give you a
reason on compulsion! if reasons were as plentiful
as blackberries, I would give no man a reason
upon compulsion, I.

PRINCE HENRY.

I'll be no longer guilty of this sin; this sanguine
coward, this bed-presser, this horse-back-
breaker, this huge hill of flesh,—

SIR JOHN FALSTAFF.

Away, you starveling, you eel-skin, you dried
neat's-tongue, you bull's-pizzle, you stock-fish,—
O, for breath to utter what is like thee!—you
tailor's-yard, you sheath, you bow-case, you vile
standing-tuck,—

PRINCE HENRY.

Well, breathe awhile, and then to it again: and
when thou hast tired thyself in base comparisons,
hear me speak but this.

POINTZ.

Mark, Jack.

PRINCE HENRY.

We two saw you four set on four and bound
them, and were masters of their wealth.—Mark
now, how a plain tale shall put you down.—Then
did we two set on you four; and, with a word, out-
faced you from your prize, and have it; yea, and
can show it you here in the house:—and, Falstaff,
you carried your guts away as nimbly, with as
quick dexterity, and roar'd for mercy, and still
ran and roar'd, as ever I heard bull-calf. What a

slave art thou, to hack thy sword as thou hast done, and then say it was in fight! What trick, what device, what starting-hole, canst thou now find out to hide thee from this open and apparent shame?

POINTZ.

Come, let's hear, Jack; what trick hast thou now?

SIR JOHN FALSTAFF.

By the Lord, I knew ye as well as he that made ye. Why, hear you, my masters: was it for me to kill the heir-apparent? should I turn upon the true prince? why, thou knowest I am as valiant as Hercules: but beware instinct; the lion will not touch the true prince. Instinct is a great matter; I was a coward on instinct. I shall think the better of myself and thee during my life; I for a valiant lion, and thou for a true prince. But, by the Lord, lads, I am glad you have the money.—Hostess, clap-to the doors [to HOSTESS within]:—watch to-night, pray to-morrow.—Gallants, lads, boys, hearts of gold, all the titles of good fellowship come to you! What, shall we be merry? shall we have a play extempore?

PRINCE HENRY.

Content;—and the argument shall be thy running away.

SIR JOHN FALSTAFF.

Ah, no more of that, Hal, an thou lovest me!

Enter HOSTESS.

HOSTESS.

O Jesu, my lord the prince,—

PRINCE HENRY.

How now, my lady the hostess! what say'st thou to me?

HOSTESS.

Marry, my lord, there is a nobleman of the court at door would speak with you: he says he comes from your father.

PRINCE HENRY.

Give him as much as will make him a royal man, and send him back again to my mother.

SIR JOHN FALSTAFF.

What manner of man is he?

HOSTESS.

An old man.

SIR JOHN FALSTAFF.

What doth gravity out of his bed at midnight?—Shall I give him his answer?

PRINCE HENRY.

Prithee, do, Jack.

SIR JOHN FALSTAFF.

Faith, and I'll send him packing.   [Exit.

PRINCE HENRY.

Now, sirs:—by'r lady, you fought fair;—so did you, Peto;—so did you, Bardolph: you are lions too, you ran away upon instinct, you will not touch the true prince; no,—fie!

BARDOLPH.

Faith, I ran when I saw others run.

PRINCE HENRY.

Faith, tell me now in earnest, how came Falstaff's sword so hackt?

PETO.

Why, he hackt it with his dagger; and said he would swear truth out of England, but he would

make you believe it was done in fight; and persuaded us to do the like.

BARDOLPH.

Yea, and to tickle our noses with spear-grass to make them bleed; and then to beslubber our garments with it, and swear it was the blood of true men. I did that I did not this seven year before,—I blusht to hear his monstrous devices.

PRINCE HENRY.

O villain, thou stolest a cup of sack eighteen years ago, and wert taken with the manner, and ever since thou hast blusht extempore. Thou hadst fire and sword on thy side, and yet thou ran'st away: what instinct hadst thou for it?

BARDOLPH.

My lord, do you see these meteors? do you behold these exhalations?

PRINCE HENRY.

I do.

BARDOLPH.

What think you they portend?

PRINCE HENRY.

Hot livers and cold purses.

BARDOLPH.

Choler, my lord, if rightly taken.

PRINCE HENRY.

No, if rightly taken, halter.—Here comes lean Jack, here comes bare-bone.

Enter FALSTAFF.

How now, my sweet creature of bombast! How long is't ago, Jack, since thou saw'st thine own knee?

SIR JOHN FALSTAFF.

My own knee! when I was about thy years, Hal, I was not an eagle's talon in the waist; I could have crept into any alderman's thumb-ring: a plague of sighing and grief! it blows a man up like a bladder.—There's villainous news abroad: here was Sir John Bracy from your father; you must to the court in the morning. That same mad fellow of the north, Percy; and he of Wales, that gave Amaimon the bastinado, and made Lucifer cuckold, and swore the devil his true liegeman upon the cross of a Welsh hook,—what, a plague, call you him?—

POINTZ.

O, Glendower.

SIR JOHN FALSTAFF.

Owen, Owen,—the same; and his son-in-law, Mortimer; and old Northumberland; and that sprightly Scot of Scots, Douglas, that runs o' horseback up a hill perpendicular,—

PRINCE HENRY.

He that rides at high speed and with his pistol kills a sparrow flying.

SIR JOHN FALSTAFF.

You have hit it.

PRINCE HENRY.

So did he never the sparrow.

SIR JOHN FALSTAFF.

Well, that rascal hath good mettle in him; he will not run.

PRINCE HENRY.

Why, what a rascal art thou, then, to praise him so for running!

SIR JOHN FALSTAFF.

O' horseback, ye cuckoo; but a-foot he will not budge a foot.

PRINCE HENRY.

Yes, Jack, upon instinct.

SIR JOHN FALSTAFF.

I grant ye, upon instinct.—Well, he is there too, and one Mordake, and a thousand blue-caps more: Worcester is stolen away to-night; thy father's beard is turn'd white with the news: you may buy land now as cheap as stinking mackerel.

PRINCE HENRY.

Why, then, it is like, if there come a hot June, and this civil buffeting hold, we shall buy maiden-heads as they buy hob-nails, by the hundreds.

SIR JOHN FALSTAFF.

By the mass, lad, thou say'st true; it is like we shall have good trading that way.—But tell me, Hal, art thou not horrible afeard? thou being heir-apparent, could the world pick thee out three such enemies again as that fiend Douglas, that spirit Percy, and that devil Glendower? art thou not horribly afraid? doth not thy blood thrill at it?

PRINCE HENRY.

Not a whit, i' faith; I lack some of thy instinct.

SIR JOHN FALSTAFF.

Well, thou wilt be horribly chid to-morrow when thou comest to thy father: if thou love me, prac-tise an answer.

PRINCE HENRY.

Do thou stand for my father, and examine me upon the particulars of my life.

SIR JOHN FALSTAFF.

Shall I? content:—this chair shall be my state, this dagger my sceptre, and this cushion my crown.

PRINCE HENRY.

Thy state is taken for a joint-stool, thy golden sceptre for a leaden dagger, and thy precious rich crown for a pitiful bald crown!

SIR JOHN FALSTAFF.

Well, an the fire of grace be not quite out of thee, now shalt thou be moved.—Give me a cup of sack to make my eyes look red, that it may be thought I have wept; for I must speak in passion, and I will do it in King Cambyses' vein.

[Drinks.

PRINCE HENRY.

Well, here is my leg.

SIR JOHN FALSTAFF.

And here is my speech.—Stand aside, nobility.

HOSTESS.

O Jesu, this is excellent sport, i' faith!

SIR JOHN FALSTAFF.

Weep not, sweet queen; for trickling tears are vain.

HOSTESS.

O, the father, how he holds his countenance!

SIR JOHN FALSTAFF.

For God's sake, lords, convey my tristful queen; For tears do stop the flood-gates of her eyes.

HOSTESS.

O Jesu, he doth it as like one of these harlotry players as ever I see!

SIR JOHN FALSTAFF.

Peace, good pint-pot; peace, good tickle-brain.—

Harry, I do not only marvel where thou spendest thy time, but also how thou art accompanied: for though the camomile, the more it is trodden on, the faster it grows, yet youth, the more it is wasted, the sooner it wears. That thou art my son, I have partly thy mother's word, partly my own opinion; but chiefly a villainous trick of thine eye, and a foolish hanging of thy nether lip, that doth warrant me. If, then, thou be son to me, here lies the point;—why, being son to me, art thou so pointed at? Shall the blessed sun of heaven prove a micher, and eat blackberries? a question not to be askt. Shall the son of England prove a thief, and take purses? a question to be askt. There is a thing, Harry, which thou hast often heard of, and it is known to many in our land by the name of pitch: this pitch, as ancient writers do report, doth defile; so doth the com-pany thou keepest: for, Harry, now I do not speak to thee in drink, but in tears; not in pleasure, but in passion; not in words only, but in woes also:— and yet there is a virtuous man whom I have often noted in thy company, but I know not his name.

PRINCE HENRY.

What manner of man, an it like your majesty?

SIR JOHN FALSTAFF.

A goodly portly man, i' faith, and a corpulent; of a cheerful look, a pleasing eye, and a most noble carriage; and, as I think, his age some fifty, or, by'r lady, inclining to three-score; and now I re-member me, his name is Falstaff: if that man should be lewdly given, he deceiveth me; for, Harry, I see virtue in his looks. If, then, the tree may be known by the fruit, as the fruit by the tree, then, peremptorily I speak it, there is virtue in that Falstaff: him keep with, the rest banish. And tell me now, thou naughty varlet, tell me where hast thou been this month?

PRINCE HENRY.

Dost thou speak like a king? Do thou stand for me, and I'll play my father.

SIR JOHN FALSTAFF.

Depose me? if thou dost it half so gravely, so majestically, both in word and matter, hang me up by the heels for a rabbit-sucker or a poulter's hare.

PRINCE HENRY.

Well, here I am set.

SIR JOHN FALSTAFF.

And here I stand:—judge, my masters.

PRINCE HENRY.

Now, Harry, whence come you?

SIR JOHN FALSTAFF.

My noble lord, from Eastcheap.

PRINCE HENRY.

The complaints I hear of thee are grievous.

SIR JOHN FALSTAFF.

'Sblood, my lord, they are false:—nay, I'll tickle ye for a young prince, i' faith.

PRINCE HENRY.

Swearest thou, ungracious boy? henceforth ne'er look on me. Thou art violently carried away from grace: there is a devil haunts thee, in the likeness of an old fat man,—a tun of man is thy com-panion. Why dost thou converse with that trunk of humours, that bolting-hutch of beastliness, that swoll'n parcel of dropsies, that huge bombard of sack, that stuft cloakbag of guts, that roasted Manningtree ox with the pudding in his belly, that reverend vice, that gray iniquity, that father ruffian, that vanity in years? Wherein is he good, but to taste sack and drink it? wherein neat and cleanly, but to carve a capon and eat it? wherein cunning, but in craft? wherein crafty, but in villainy? wherein villainous, but in all things? wherein worthy, but in nothing?

SIR JOHN FALSTAFF.

I would your Grace would take me with you: whom means your Grace?

PRINCE HENRY.

That villainous abominable misleader of youth, Falstaff, that old white-bearded Satan.

SIR JOHN FALSTAFF.

My lord, the man I know.

PRINCE HENRY.

I know thou dost.

SIR JOHN FALSTAFF.

But to say I know more harm in him than in myself, were to say more than I know. That he is old,—the more the pity,—his white hairs do witness it; but that he is—saving your reverence —a whoremaster, that I utterly deny. If sack and sugar be a fault, God help the wicked! if to be old and merry be a sin, then many an old host that I know is damn'd: if to be fat be to be hated, then Pharaoh's lean kine are to be loved. No, my good lord; banish Peto, banish Bardolph, banish Pointz: but, for sweet Jack Falstaff, kind Jack Falstaff, true Jack Falstaff, valiant Jack Falstaff, and therefore more valiant, being, as he is, old Jack Falstaff, banish not him thy Harry's company, banish not him thy Harry's company:— banish plump Jack, and banish all the world.

PRINCE HENRY.

I do, I will.   [A knocking heard.

[Exeunt HOSTESS, FRANCIS, and BAR-DOLPH.

Enter BARDOLPH, running.

BARDOLPH.

O, my lord, my lord! the sheriff with a most monstrous watch is at the door.

SIR JOHN FALSTAFF.

Out, ye rogue!—Play out the play: I have much to say in the behalf of that Falstaff.

Enter HOSTESS, hastily.

HOSTESS.

O Jesu, my lord, my lord,—

PRINCE HENRY.

Heigh, heigh! the devil rides upon a fiddlestick: what's the matter?

HOSTESS.

The sheriff and all the watch are at the door: they are come to search the house. Shall I let them in?

SIR JOHN FALSTAFF.

Dost thou hear, Hal? never call a true piece of gold a counterfeit: thou art essentially mad, without seeming so.

PRINCE HENRY.

And thou a natural coward, without instinct.

SIR JOHN FALSTAFF.

I deny your major: if you will deny the sheriff, so; if not, let him enter: if I become not a cart as well as another man, a plague on my bringing up! I hope I shall as soon be strangled with a halter as another.

PRINCE HENRY.

Go, hide thee behind the arras:—the rest walk up above. Now, my masters, for a true face and good conscience.

SIR JOHN FALSTAFF.

Both which I have had; but their date is out, and therefore I'll hide me.

PRINCE HENRY.

Call in the sheriff.

[Exeunt all except the PRINCE and POINTZ.

Enter SHERIFF and CARRIER.

Now, master sheriff, what's your will with me?

SHERIFF.

First, pardon me, my lord. A hue and cry Hath follow'd certain men unto this house.

PRINCE HENRY.

What men?

SHERIFF.

One of them is well known, my gracious lord, A gross fat man.

CARRIER.

As fat as butter.

PRINCE HENRY.

The man, I do assure you, is not here; For I myself at this time have employ'd him. And, sheriff, I will engage my word to thee, That I will, by to-morrow dinner-time, Send him to answer thee, or any man, For any thing he shall be charged withal: And so, let me entreat you leave the house.

SHERIFF.

I will, my lord. There are two gentlemen Have in this robbery lost three hundred marks.

PRINCE HENRY.

It may be so: if he have robb'd these men, He shall be answerable; and so, farewell.

SHERIFF.

Good night, my noble lord.

PRINCE HENRY.

I think it is good morrow, is it not?

SHERIFF.

Indeed, my lord, I think it be two o'clock.

[Exeunt SHERIFF and CARRIER.

PRINCE HENRY.

This oily rascal is known as well as Paul's. Go, call him forth.

POINTZ.

Falstaff!—fast asleep behind the arras, and snorting like a horse.

PRINCE HENRY.

Hark, how hard he fetches breath. Search his pockets. [He searcheth his pockets and findeth certain papers.] What hast thou found?

POINTZ.

Nothing but papers, my lord.

PRINCE HENRY.

Let's see what they be: read them.

POINTZ [reads].

Item, A capon,	. . .	2s. 2d.
Item, Sauce,	. .	4d.
Item, Sack, two gallons,	. .	5s. 8d.
Item, Anchovies and sack after supper,		2s. 6d.
Item, Bread,	. . .	ob.

PRINCE HENRY.

O monstrous! but one half-pennyworth of bread
to this intolerable deal of sack!—What there is
else, keep close; we'll read it at more advantage:
there let him sleep till day. I'll to the court in the
morning. We must all to the wars, and thy place
shall be honourable. I'll procure this fat rogue a
charge of foot; and I know his death will be a
march of twelve-score. The money shall be paid
back again with advantage. Be with me betimes
in the morning; and so, good morrow, Pointz.

POINTZ.

Good morrow, good my lord.   [*Exeunt.*

ACT III. SCENE I.

Bangor.   The Archdeacon's house.

Enter HOTSPUR, WORCESTER, MORTIMER,
and GLENDOWER.

EDMUND MORTIMER.

THESE promises are fair, the parties sure,
And our induction full of prosperous hope.

HOTSPUR.

Lord Mortimer,—and cousin Glendower,—
Will you sit down?—
And uncle Worcester:—a plague upon it!
I have forgot the map.

OWEN GLENDOWER.

No, here it is.
Sit, cousin Percy;—sit, good cousin Hotspur,
For by that name as oft as Lancaster
Doth speak of you, his cheek looks pale, and with
A rising sigh he wisheth you in heaven.

HOTSPUR.

And you in hell, as oft as he hears Owen Glendower spoke of.

OWEN GLENDOWER.

I cannot blame him: at my nativity
The front of heaven was full of fiery shapes,
Of burning cressets; and at my birth
The frame and huge foundation of the earth
Shaked like a coward.

HOTSPUR.

Why, so it would have done at the same season, if
your mother's cat had but kitten'd, though yourself had never been born.

OWEN GLENDOWER.

I say the earth did shake when I was born.

HOTSPUR.

And I say the earth was not of my mind,
If you suppose as fearing you it shook.

OWEN GLENDOWER.

The heavens were all on fire, the earth did
tremble.

HOTSPUR.

O, then the earth shook to see the heavens on fire,
And not in fear of your nativity.
Diseased nature oftentimes breaks forth
In strange eruptions; oft the teeming earth
Is with a kind of colic pincht and vext
By the imprisoning of unruly wind
Within her womb; which, for enlargement
striving,
Shakes the old beldam earth, and topples down
Steeples and moss-grown towers. At your birth

Our grandam earth, having this distemperature,
In passion shook.

OWEN GLENDOWER.

Cousin, of many men
I do not bear these crossings. Give me leave
To tell you once again, that at my birth
The front of heaven was full of fiery shapes;
The goats ran from the mountains, and the herds
Were strangely clamorous to the frighted fields.
These signs have markt me extraordinary;
And all the courses of my life do show
I am not in the roll of common men.
Where is he living,—clipt in with the sea
That chides the banks of England, Scotland,
Wales,—
Which calls me pupil, or hath read to me?
And bring him out that is but woman's son
Can trace me in the tedious ways of art,
And hold me pace in deep experiments.

HOTSPUR.

I think there is no man speaks better Welsh.—
I'll to dinner.

EDMUND MORTIMER.

Peace, cousin Percy; you will make him mad.

OWEN GLENDOWER.

I can call spirits from the vasty deep.

HOTSPUR.

Why, so can I, or so can any man;
But will they come when you do call for them?

OWEN GLENDOWER.

Why, I can teach you, cousin, to command
The devil.

HOTSPUR.

And I can teach thee, coz, to shame the devil
By telling truth: tell truth, and shame the devil.—
If thou have power to raise him, bring him
hither,
And I'll be sworn I have power to shame him
hence.
O, while you live, tell truth, and shame the devil!

EDMUND MORTIMER.

Come, come, no more of this unprofitable chat.

OWEN GLENDOWER.

Three times hath Henry Bolingbroke made head
Against my power; thrice from the banks of Wye
And sandy-bottom'd Severn have I sent him
Bootless home and weather-beaten back.

HOTSPUR.

Home without boots, and in foul weather too!
How scapes he agues, in the devil's name?

OWEN GLENDOWER.

Come, here's the map: shall we divide our right
According to our threefold order ta'en?

EDMUND MORTIMER.

The archdeacon hath divided it
Into three limits very equally:—
England, from Trent and Severn hitherto,
By south and east is to my part assign'd:
All westward, Wales beyond the Severn shore,
And all the fertile land within that bound,
To Owen Glendower:—and, dear coz, to you
The remnant northward, lying off from Trent.
And our indentures tripartite are drawn;
Which being sealed interchangeably,—
A business that this night may execute,—
To-morrow, cousin Percy, you, and I,

And my good Lord of Worcester, will set forth
To meet your father and the Scottish power,
As is appointed us, at Shrewsbury.
My father Glendower is not ready yet,
Nor shall we need his help these fourteen days:—
[to GLENDOWER] Within that space you may have
  drawn together   [men.
Your tenants, friends, and neighbouring gentle-
                OWEN GLENDOWER.
A shorter time shall send me to you, lords:
And in my conduct shall your ladies come;
From whom you now must steal, and take no
  leave,
For there will be a world of water shed
Upon the parting of your wives and you.
                HOTSPUR.
Methinks my moiety, north from Burton here,
In quantity equals not one of yours:
See how this river comes me cranking in,
And cuts me from the best of all my land
A huge half-moon, a monstrous cantle out.
I'll have the current in this place damm'd up;
And here the smug and silver Trent shall run
In a new channel, fair and evenly:
It shall not wind with such a deep indent,
To rob me of so rich a bottom here.
                OWEN GLENDOWER.
Not wind? it shall, it must; you see it doth.
                EDMUND MORTIMER.
Yea, but
Mark how he bears his course, and runs me up
With like advantage on the other side;
Gelding the opposed continent as much
As on the other side it takes from you.
                EARL OF WORCESTER.
Yea, but a little charge will trench him here,
And on this north side win this cape of land;
And then he runs straight and even.
                HOTSPUR.
I'll have it so: a little charge will do it.
                OWEN GLENDOWER.
I'll not have it alter'd.
                HOTSPUR.
               Will not you?
                OWEN GLENDOWER.
No, nor you shall not.
                HOTSPUR.
               Who shall say me nay?
                OWEN GLENDOWER.
Why, that will I.
                HOTSPUR.
            Let me not understand you, then;
Speak it in Welsh.
                OWEN GLENDOWER.
I can speak English, lord, as well as you;
For I was train'd up in the English court;
Where, being but young, I framed to the harp
Many an English ditty lovely well,
And gave the tongue a helpful ornament,—
A virtue that was never seen in you.
                HOTSPUR.
Marry, and I am glad of it with all my heart:
I had rather be a kitten, and cry mew,
Than one of these same metre ballet-mongers;
I had rather hear a brazen canstick turn'd,
Or a dry wheel grate on the axletree;

And that would set my teeth nothing on edge,
Nothing so much as mincing poetry:—
'Tis like the forced gait of a shuffling nag.
                OWEN GLENDOWER.
Come, you shall have Trent turn'd.
                HOTSPUR.
I do not care: I'll give thrice so much land
To any well-deserving friend;
But in the way of bargain, mark ye me,
I'll cavil on the ninth part of a hair.
Are the indentures drawn? shall we be gone?
                OWEN GLENDOWER.
The moon shines fair; you may away by night:
I'll in and haste the writer, and withal
Break with your wives of your departure hence:
I am afraid my daughter will run mad,
So much she doteth on her Mortimer.   [Exit.
                EDMUND MORTIMER.
Fie, cousin Percy! how you cross my father!
                HOTSPUR.
I cannot choose: sometime he angers me
With telling me of the moldwarp and the ant,
Of the dreamer Merlin and his prophecies,
And of a dragon and a finless fish,
A clip-wing'd griffin and a moulten raven,
A couching lion and a ramping cat,
And such a deal of skimble-skamble stuff
As puts me from my faith. I tell you what,—
He held me last night at least nine hours
In reckoning up the several devils' names
That were his lackeys: I cried 'hum,' and 'well,
  go to,'
But markt him not a word. O, he is as tedious
As a tired horse, a railing wife;
Worse than a smoky house:—I had rather live
With cheese and garlic in a windmill, far,
Than feed on cates and have him talk to me
In any summer-house in Christendom.
                EDMUND MORTIMER.
In faith, he is a worthy gentleman;
Exceedingly well-read, and profited
In strange concealments; valiant as a lion,
And wondrous affable, and as bountiful
As mines of India. Shall I tell you, cousin?
He holds your temper in a high respect,
And curbs himself even of his natural scope
When you do cross his humour; faith, he does:
I warrant you, that man is not alive
Might so have tempted him as you have done,
Without the taste of danger and reproof:
But do not use it oft, let me entreat you.
                EARL OF WORCESTER.
In faith, my lord, you are too wilful-blame;
And since your coming hither have done enough
To put him quite beside his patience.
You must needs learn, lord, to amend this fault:
Though sometimes it show greatness, courage,
  blood,—
And that's the dearest grace it renders you,—
Yet oftentimes it doth present harsh rage,
Defect of manners, want of government,
Pride, haughtiness, opinion, and disdain:
The least of which haunting a nobleman
Loseth men's hearts, and leaves behind a stain
Upon the beauty of all parts besides,
Beguiling them of commendation.

HOTSPUR.
Well, I am school'd: good manners be your speed!
Here come our wives, and let us take our leave.
Enter GLENDOWER, *with the* LADIES.
EDMUND MORTIMER.
This is the deadly spite that angers me,—
My wife can speak no English, I no Welsh.
OWEN GLENDOWER.
My daughter weeps: she will not part with you;
She'll be a soldier too, she'll to the wars.
EDMUND MORTIMER.
Good father, tell her that she and my aunt Percy
Shall follow in your conduct speedily.
[GLENDOWER *speaks to her in Welsh, and*
she answers him in the same.
OWEN GLENDOWER.
She is desperate here; a peevish self-will'd har-
lotry, one that no persuasion can do good upon.
[*The* LADY *speaks in Welsh.*
EDMUND MORTIMER.
I understand thy looks: that pretty Welsh
Which thou pour'st down from these swelling
heavens
I am too perfect in; and, but for shame,
In such a parley should I answer thee.
[*The* LADY *speaks again in Welsh.*
I understand thy kisses, and thou mine,
And that's a feeling disputation:
But I will never be a truant, love,
Till I have learn'd thy language; for thy tongue
Makes Welsh as sweet as ditties highly penn'd,
Sung by a fair queen in a summer's bower,
With ravishing division, to her lute.
OWEN GLENDOWER.
Nay, if you melt, then will she run quite mad.
[*The* LADY *speaks again in Welsh.*
EDMUND MORTIMER.
O, I am ignorance itself in this!
OWEN GLENDOWER.
She bids you on the wanton rushes lay you down,
And rest your gentle head upon her lap,
And she will sing the song that pleaseth you,
And on your eyelids crown the god of sleep,
Charming your blood with pleasing heaviness;
Making such difference 'twixt wake and sleep,
As is the difference betwixt day and night,
The hour before the heavenly-harness'd team
Begins his golden progress in the east.
EDMUND MORTIMER.
With all my heart I'll sit and hear her sing:
By that time will our book, I think, be drawn.
OWEN GLENDOWER.
Do so;
And those musicians that shall play to you
Hang in the air a thousand leagues from hence;
And straight they shall be here: sit, and attend.
HOTSPUR.
Come, Kate, thou art perfect in lying down:
come, quick, quick, that I may lay my head in thy
lap.
LADY PERCY.
Go, ye giddy goose.   [*The music plays.*
HOTSPUR.
Now I perceive the devil understands Welsh;
And 'tis no marvel he is so humorous.
By 'r lady, he is a good musician.

LADY PERCY.
Then should you be nothing but musical; for you
are altogether govern'd by humours. Lie still, ye
thief, and hear the lady sing in Welsh.
HOTSPUR.
I had rather hear Lady, my brach, howl in Irish.
LADY PERCY.
Wouldst thou have thy head broken?
HOTSPUR.
No.
LADY PERCY.
Then be still.
HOTSPUR.
Neither; 'tis a woman's fault.
LADY PERCY.
Now God help thee!
HOTSPUR.
To the Welsh lady's bed.
LADY PERCY.
What's that?
HOTSPUR.
Peace! she sings.
[*Here the* LADY *sings a Welsh song.*
Come, Kate, I'll have your song too.
LADY PERCY.
Not mine, in good sooth.
HOTSPUR.
Not yours, in good sooth! Heart! you swear like a
comfit-maker's wife. 'Not you, in good sooth;' and
'as true as I live;' and 'as God shall mend me;' and
'as sure as day;'
And givest such sarcenet surety for thy oaths,
As if thou never walk'st further than Finsbury.
Swear me, Kate, like a lady as thou art,
A good mouth-filling oath; and leave 'in sooth,'
And such protest of pepper-gingerbread,
To velvet-guards and Sunday-citizens.
Come, sing.
LADY PERCY.
I will not sing.
HOTSPUR.
'Tis the next way to turn tailor, or be redbreast
teacher. An the indentures be drawn, I'll away
within these two hours; and so, come in when ye
will.   [*Exit.*
OWEN GLENDOWER.
Come, come, Lord Mortimer; you are as slow
As hot Lord Percy is on fire to go.
By this our book is drawn; we'll but seal, and then
To horse immediately.
EDMUND MORTIMER.
With all my heart. [*Exeunt.*

SCENE II.
London.   The palace.
Enter KING HENRY, PRINCE HENRY, *and*
LORDS.
KING HENRY.
LORDS, give us leave; the Prince of Wales
and I
Must have some private conference: but be near
at hand,
For we shall presently have need of you.
[*Exeunt* LORDS.

I know not whether God will have it so,
For some displeasing service I have done,
That, in his secret doom, out of my blood
He'll breed revengement and a scourge for me;
But thou dost, in thy passages of life,
Make me believe that thou art only markt
For the hot vengeance and the rod of heaven
To punish my mistreadings. Tell me else,
Could such inordinate and low desires,
Such poor, such base, such lewd, such mean at-
  tempts,
Such barren pleasures, rude society,
As thou art matcht withal and grafted to,
Accompany the greatness of thy blood,
And hold their level with thy princely heart?
             PRINCE HENRY.
So please your majesty, I would I could
Quit all offences with as clear excuse
As well as I am doubtless I can purge
Myself of many I am charged withal:
Yet such extenuation let me beg,
As, in reproof of many tales devised,—
Which oft the ear of greatness needs must hear,—
By smiling pick-thanks and base news-mongers,
I may, for some things true, wherein my youth
Hath faulty wander'd and irregular,
Find pardon on my true submission.
             KING HENRY.
God pardon thee!—yet let me wonder, Harry,
At thy affections, which do hold a wing
Quite from the flight of all thy ancestors.
Thy place in council thou hast rudely lost,
Which by thy younger brother is supplied;
And art almost an alien to the hearts
Of all the court and princes of my blood:
The hope and expectation of thy time
Is ruin'd; and the soul of every man
Prophetically do forethink thy fall.
Had I so lavish of my presence been,
So common-hackney'd in the eyes of men,
So stale and cheap to vulgar company,—
Opinion, that did help me to the crown,
Had still kept loyal to possession,
And left me in reputeless banishment,
A fellow of no mark nor likelihood.
By being seldom seen, I could not stir
But, like a comet, I was wonder'd at;
That men would tell their children, 'This is he;'
Others would say, 'Where, which is Bolingbroke?'
And then I stole all courtesy from heaven,
And drest myself in such humility
That I did pluck allegiance from men's hearts,
Loud shouts and salutations from their mouths,
Even in the presence of the crowned king.
Thus did I keep my person fresh and new;
My presence, like a robe pontifical,
Ne'er seen but wonder'd at: and so my state,
Seldom but sumptuous, show'd like a feast,
And won by rareness such solemnity.
The skipping king, he ambled up and down
With shallow jesters and rash bavin wits,
Soon kindled and soon burnt; carded his state;
Mingled his royalty with capering fools,
Had his great name profaned with their scorns;
And gave his countenance, against his name,
To laugh at gibing boys, and stand the push

Of every beardless vain comparative;
Grew a companion to the common streets,
Enfeoft himself to popularity;
That, being daily swallow'd by men's eyes,
They surfeited with honey, and began
To loathe the taste of sweetness, whereof a little
More than a little is by much too much.
So, when he had occasion to be seen,
He was but as the cuckoo is in June,
Heard, not regarded,—seen, but with such eyes
As, sick and blunted with community,
Afford no extraordinary gaze,
Such as is bent on sun-like majesty
When it shines seldom in admiring eyes;
But rather drowzed, and hung their eyelids down,
Slept in his face. and render'd such aspect
As cloudy men use to their adversaries,
Being with his presence glutted, gorged, and full.
And in that very line, Harry, stand'st thou;
For thou hast lost thy princely privilege
With vile participation: not an eye
But is a-weary of thy common sight,
Save mine, which hath desired to see thee more;
Which now doth that I would not have it do,—
Make blind itself with foolish tenderness.
             PRINCE HENRY.
I shall hereafter, my thrice-gracious lord,
Be more myself.
             KING HENRY.
         For all the world,
As thou art to this hour, was Richard then
When I from France set foot at Ravenspurg;
And even as I was then is Percy now.
Now, by my sceptre, and my soul to boot,
He hath more worthy interest to the state
Than thou, the shadow of succession;
For, of no right, nor colour like to right,
He doth fill fields with harness in the realm;
Turns head against the lion's armed jaws;
And, being no more in debt to years than thou,
Leads ancient lords and reverend bishops on
To bloody battles and to bruising arms.
What never-dying honour hath he got
Against renowned Douglas! whose high deeds,
Whose hot incursions, and great name in arms,
Holds from all soldiers chief majority
And military title capital
Through all the kingdoms that acknowledge
  Christ:
Thrice hath this Hotspur, Mars in swathling-
  clothes,
This infant warrior, in his enterprises
Discomfited great Douglas: ta'en him once,
Enlarged him, and made a friend of him,
To fill the mouth of deep defiance up,
And shake the peace and safety of our throne.
And what say you to this? Percy, Northumber-
  land,
The Archbishop's Grace of York, Douglas, Mor-
  timer,
Capitulate against us, and are up.
But wherefore do I tell these news to thee?
Why, Harry, do I tell thee of my foes,
Which art my near'st and dearest enemy?
Thou that art like enough,—through vassal fear,
Base inclination, and the start of spleen,—

To fight against me under Percy's pay,
To dog his heels, and court'sy at his frowns,
To show how much thou art degenerate.
PRINCE HENRY.
Do not think so; you shall not find it so:
And God forgive them that so much have sway'd
Your majesty's good thoughts away from me!
I will redeem all this on Percy's head,
And, in the closing of some glorious day,
Be bold to tell you that I am your son;
When I will wear a garment all of blood,
And stain my favours in a bloody mask,
Which, washt away, shall scour my shame with
    it:
And that shall be the day, whene'er it lights,
That this same child of honour and renown,
This gallant Hotspur, this all-praised knight,
And your unthought-of Harry, chance to meet.
For every honour sitting on his helm,
Would they were multitudes, and on my head
My shames redoubled! for the time will come,
That I shall make this northern youth exchange
His glorious deeds for my indignities.
Percy is but my factor, good my lord,
To engross up glorious deeds on my behalf;
And I will call him to so strict account,
That he shall render every glory up,
Yea, even the slightest worship of his time,
Or I will tear the reckoning from his heart.
This, in the name of God, I promise here:
The which if He be pleased I shall perform,
I do beseech your majesty, may salve
The long-grown wounds of my intemperance:
If not, the end of life cancels all bands;
And I will die a hundred thousand deaths
Ere break the smallest parcel of this vow.
KING HENRY.
A hundred thousand rebels die in this:—
Thou shalt have charge and sovereign trust
    herein.
Enter SIR WALTER BLUNT.
How now, good Blunt! thy looks are full of
    speed.
SIR WALTER BLUNT.
So hath the business that I come to speak of.
Lord Mortimer of Scotland hath sent word
That Douglas and the English rebels met
The eleventh of this month at Shrewsbury:
A mighty and a fearful head they are,
If promises be kept on every hand,
As ever offer'd foul play in a state.
KING HENRY.
The Earl of Westmoreland set forth to-day;
With him my son, Lord John of Lancaster;
For this advertisement is five days old:—
On Wednesday next, Harry, you shall set for-
    ward;
On Thursday we ourselves will march:
Our meeting is Bridgenorth: and, Harry, you
Shall march through Glostershire; by which ac-
    count,
Our business valued, some twelve days hence
Our general forces at Bridgenorth shall meet.
Our hands are full of business: let's away;
Advantage feeds him fat, while men delay.
[Exeunt.

SCENE III.
Eastcheap.   The Boar's-Head Tavern.
Enter FALSTAFF and BARDOLPH.
SIR JOHN FALSTAFF.
BARDOLPH, am I not fall'n away vilely since
this last action? do I not bate? do I not
dwindle? Why, my skin hangs about me like an
old lady's loose gown; I am wither'd like an old
apple-john. Well, I'll repent, and that suddenly,
while I am in some liking; I shall be out of heart
shortly, and then I shall have no strength to repent. An I have not forgotten what the inside of a
church is made of, I am a peppercorn, a brewer's
horse: the inside of a church! Company, villainous
company, hath been the spoil of me.
BARDOLPH.
Sir John, you are so fretful, you cannot live long.
SIR JOHN FALSTAFF.
Why, there is it:—come, sing me a bawdy song;
make me merry. I was as virtuously given as a
gentleman need to be; virtuous enough; swore
little; diced not above seven times a week; went to
a bawdy-house not above once in a quarter—of
an hour; paid money that I borrow'd—three or
four times; lived well, and in good compass: and
now I live out of all order, out of all compass. ·
BARDOLPH.
Why, you are so fat, Sir John, that you must
needs be out of all compass,—out of all reasonable compass, Sir John.
SIR JOHN FALSTAFF.
Do thou amend thy face, and I'll amend my life:
thou art our admiral, thou bearest the lantern in
the poop,—but 'tis in the nose of thee; thou art
the Knight of the Burning Lamp.
BARDOLPH.
Why, Sir John, my face does you no harm.
SIR JOHN FALSTAFF.
No, I'll be sworn; I make as good use of it as
many a man doth of a death's-head or a *memento
mori:* I never see thy face but I think upon hell-
fire, and Dives that lived in purple; for there he
is in his robes, burning, burning. If thou wert any
way given to virtue, I would swear by thy face;
my oath should be, 'By this fire, that's God's
angel:' but thou art altogether given over; and
wert indeed, but for the light in thy face, the son
of utter darkness. When thou ran'st up Gadshill
in the night to catch my horse, if I did not think
thou hadst been an *ignis fatuus* or a ball of wildfire, there's no purchase in money. O, thou art a
perpetual triumph, an everlasting bonfire-light!
Thou hast saved me a thousand marks in links and
torches, walking with thee in the night betwixt
tavern and tavern: but the sack that thou hast
drunk me would have bought me lights as good
cheap at the dearest chandler's in Europe. I have
maintain'd that salamander of yours with fire any
time this two-and-thirty years; God reward me
for it!
BARDOLPH.
'Sblood, I would my face were in your belly!
SIR JOHN FALSTAFF.
God-a-mercy! so should I be sure to be heart-
burn'd.

Enter HOSTESS.

How now, Dame Partlet the hen! have you inquired yet who pickt my pocket?

HOSTESS.

Why, Sir John, what do you think, Sir John? do you think I keep thieves in my house? I have searcht, I have inquired, so has my husband, man by man, boy by boy, servant by servant: the tithe of a hair was never lost in my house before.

SIR JOHN FALSTAFF.

Ye lie, hostess: Bardolph was shaved, and lost many a hair; and I'll be sworn my pocket was pickt. Go to, you are a woman, go.

HOSTESS.

Who, I? no; I defy thee: God's light, I was never call'd so in mine own house before.

SIR JOHN FALSTAFF.

Go to, I know you well enough.

HOSTESS.

No, Sir John; you do not know me, Sir John. I know you, Sir John: you owe me money, Sir John; and now you pick a quarrel to beguile me of it: I bought you a dozen of shirts to your back.

SIR JOHN FALSTAFF.

Dowlas, filthy dowlas: I have given them away to bakers' wives, and they have made bolters of them.

HOSTESS.

Now, as I am a true woman, holland of eight shillings an ell. You owe money here besides, Sir John, for your diet and by-drinkings, and money lent you, four-and-twenty pound.

SIR JOHN FALSTAFF.

He had his part of it; let him pay.

HOSTESS.

He? alas, he is poor; he hath nothing.

SIR JOHN FALSTAFF.

How! poor? look upon his face; what call you rich? let them coin his nose, let them coin his cheeks: I'll not pay a denier. What, will you make a younker of me? shall I not take mine ease in mine inn, but I shall have my pocket pickt? I have lost a seal-ring of my grandfather's worth forty mark.

HOSTESS.

O Jesu, I have heard the prince tell him, I know not how oft, that that ring was copper!

SIR JOHN FALSTAFF.

How! the prince is a Jack, a sneak-cup: 'sblood, an he were here, I would cudgel him like a dog, if he would say so.

Enter the PRINCE *and* POINTZ, *marching, and* FALSTAFF *meets them, playing on his truncheon like a fife.*

How now, lad! is the wind in that door, i' faith? must we all march?

BARDOLPH.

Yea, two and two, Newgate-fashion.

HOSTESS.

My lord, I pray you, hear me.

PRINCE HENRY.

What say'st thou, Mistress Quickly? How doth thy husband? I love him well; he is an honest man.

HOSTESS.

Good my lord, hear me.

SIR JOHN FALSTAFF.

Prithee, let her alone, and list to me.

PRINCE HENRY.

What say'st thou, Jack?

SIR JOHN FALSTAFF.

The other night I fell asleep here behind the arras, and had my pocket pickt: this house is turn'd bawdy-house; they pick pockets.

PRINCE HENRY.

What didst thou lose, Jack?

SIR JOHN FALSTAFF.

Wilt thou believe me, Hal? three or four bonds of forty pound a-piece, and a seal-ring of my grandfather's.

PRINCE HENRY.

A trifle, some eight-penny matter.

HOSTESS.

So I told him, my lord; and I said I heard your Grace say so: and, my lord, he speaks most vilely of you, like a foul-mouth'd man as he is; and said he would cudgel you.

PRINCE HENRY.

What! he did not?

HOSTESS.

There's neither faith, truth, nor womanhood in me else.

SIR JOHN FALSTAFF.

There's no more faith in thee than in a stew'd prune; nor no more truth in thee than in a drawn fox; and for womanhood, Maid Marian may be the deputy's wife of the ward to thee. Go, you thing, go.

HOSTESS.

Say, what thing? what thing?

SIR JOHN FALSTAFF.

What thing! why, a thing to thank God on.

HOSTESS.

I am no thing to thank God on, I would thou shouldst know it; I am an honest man's wife: and, setting thy knighthood aside, thou art a knave to call me so.

SIR JOHN FALSTAFF.

Setting thy womanhood aside, thou art a beast to say otherwise.

HOSTESS.

Say, what beast, thou knave, thou?

SIR JOHN FALSTAFF.

What beast! why, an otter.

PRINCE HENRY.

An otter, Sir John! why an otter?

SIR JOHN FALSTAFF.

Why, she's neither fish nor flesh; a man knows not where to have her.

HOSTESS.

Thou art an unjust man in saying so: thou or any man knows where to have me, thou knave, thou!

PRINCE HENRY.

Thou say'st true, hostess; and he slanders thee most grossly.

HOSTESS.

So he doth you, my lord; and said this other day you ought him a thousand pound.

PRINCE HENRY.

Sirrah, do I owe you a thousand pound?

SIR JOHN FALSTAFF.

A thousand pound, Hal! a million: thy love is worth a million; thou owest me thy love.

HOSTESS.

Nay, my lord, he call'd you Jack, and said he would cudgel you.

SIR JOHN FALSTAFF.

Did I, Bardolph?

BARDOLPH.

Indeed, Sir John, you said so.

SIR JOHN FALSTAFF.

Yea,—if he said my ring was copper.

PRINCE HENRY.

I say 'tis copper: darest thou be as good as thy word now?

SIR JOHN FALSTAFF.

Why, Hal, thou know'st, as thou art but man, I dare; but as thou art prince, I fear thee as I fear the roaring of the lion's whelp.

PRINCE HENRY.

And why not as the lion?

SIR JOHN FALSTAFF.

The king himself is to be fear'd as the lion: dost thou think I'll fear thee as I fear thy father? nay, an I do, I pray God my girdle break.

PRINCE HENRY.

O, if it should, how would thy guts fall about thy knees! But, sirrah, there's no room for faith, truth, nor honesty in this bosom of thine,—it is all fill'd up with guts and midriff. Charge an honest woman with picking thy pocket! why, thou whoreson, impudent, embost rascal, if there were anything in thy pocket but tavern-reckonings, memorandums of bawdy-houses, and one poor pennyworth of sugar-candy to make thee long-winded,—if thy pocket were enrich with any other injuries but these, I am a villain: and yet you will stand to it; you will not pocket-up wrong: art thou not ashamed?

SIR JOHN FALSTAFF.

Dost thou hear, Hal? thou know'st in the state of innocency Adam fell; and what should poor Jack Falstaff do in the days of villainy? Thou seest I have more flesh than another man; and therefore more frailty. You confess, then, you pickt my pocket?

PRINCE HENRY.

It appears so by the story.

SIR JOHN FALSTAFF.

Hostess, I forgive thee: go, make ready breakfast; love thy husband, look to thy servants, cherish thy guests: thou shalt find me tractable to any honest reason: thou seest I am pacified still.— Nay, prithee, be gone. [Exit Hostess.] Now, Hal, to the news at court: for the robbery, lad,—how is that answer'd?

PRINCE HENRY.

O, my sweet beef, I must still be good angel to thee:—the money is paid back again.

SIR JOHN FALSTAFF.

O, I do not like that paying back; 'tis a double labour.

PRINCE HENRY.

I am good friends with my father, and may do any thing.

SIR JOHN FALSTAFF.

Rob me the exchequer the first thing thou dost, and do it with unwasht hands too.

BARDOLPH.

Do, my lord.

PRINCE HENRY.

I have procured thee, Jack, a charge of foot.

SIR JOHN FALSTAFF.

I would it had been of horse. Where shall I find one that can steal well? O, for a fine thief, of the age of two-and-twenty or thereabouts! I am heinously unprovided. Well, God be thankt for these rebels,—they offend none but the virtuous: I laud them, I praise them.

PRINCE HENRY.

Bardolph,—

BARDOLPH.

My lord?

PRINCE HENRY.

Go bear this letter to Lord John of Lancaster, to my brother John; this to my Lord of Westmoreland. [Exit BARDOLPH.] Go, Pointz, to horse, to horse; for thou and I have thirty miles to ride yet ere dinner-time. [Exit POINTZ.] Jack, meet me to-morrow in the Temple-hall at two o'clock in the afternoon:

There shalt thou know thy charge; and there receive

Money and order for their furniture.

The land is burning; Percy stands on high;

And either we or they must lower lie. [Exit.

SIR JOHN FALSTAFF.

Rare words! brave world!—Hostess, my breakfast; come:—

O, I could wish this tavern were my drum! [Exit.

ACT IV. SCENE I.

The rebel camp near Shrewsbury.

Enter HOTSPUR, WORCESTER, *and* DOUGLAS.

HOTSPUR.

WELL said, my noble Scot: if speaking truth
In this fine age were not thought flattery,
Such attribution should the Douglas have,
As not a soldier of this season's stamp
Should go so general current through the world.
By God, I cannot flatter; I defy
The tongues of soothers; but a braver place
In my heart's love hath no man than yourself:
Nay, task me to my word; approve me, lord.

EARL OF DOUGLAS.

Thou art the king of honour:
No man so potent breathes upon the ground
But I will beard him.

HOTSPUR.

Do so, and 'tis well.—

Enter a MESSENGER *with letters.*

What letters hast thou there?—I can but thank you.

MESSENGER.

These letters come from your father.

HOTSPUR.

Letters from him! why comes he not himself?

MESSENGER.

He cannot come, my lord; he is grievous sick.

HOTSPUR.

Zounds! how has he the leisure to be sick
In such a justling time? Who leads his power?
Under whose government come they along?

MESSENGER.
His letters bear his mind, not I, my lord.
EARL OF WORCESTER.
I prithee, tell me, doth he keep his bed?
MESSENGER.
He did, my lord, four days ere I set forth;
And at the time of my departure thence
He was much fear'd by his physicians.
EARL OF WORCESTER.
I would the state of time had first been whole
Ere he by sickness had been visited:
His health was never better worth than now.
HOTSPUR.
Sick now! droop now! this sickness doth infect
The very life-blood of our enterprise;
'Tis catching hither, even to our camp.—
He writes me here, that inward sickness,—
And that his friends by deputation could not
So soon be drawn; nor did he think it meet
To lay so dangerous and dear a trust
On any soul removed, but on his own.
Yet doth he give us bold advertisement,
That with our small conjunction we should on,
To see how fortune is disposed to us;
For, as he writes, there is no quailing now,
Because the king is certainly possest
Of all our purposes. What say you to it?
EARL OF WORCESTER.
Your father's sickness is a maim to us.
HOTSPUR.
A perilous gash, a very limb lopt off:—
And yet, in faith, it is not; his present want
Seems more than we shall find it:—were it good
To set the exact wealth of all our states
All at one cast? to set so rich a main
On the nice hazard of one doubtful hour?
It were not good; for therein should we read
The very bottom and the soul of hope,
The very list, the very utmost bound
Of all our fortunes.
EARL OF DOUGLAS.
                    Faith, and so we should;
Where now remains a sweet reversion;
We may boldly spend upon the hope of what
Is to come in:
A comfort of retirement lives in this.
HOTSPUR.
A rendezvous, a home to fly unto,
If that the devil and mischance look big
Upon the maidenhead of our affairs.
EARL OF WORCESTER.
But yet I would your father had been here.
The quality and hair of our attempt
Brooks no division: it will be thought
By some, that know not why he is away,
That wisdom, loyalty, and mere dislike
Of our proceedings, kept the earl from hence:
And think how such an apprehension
May turn the tide of fearful faction,
And breed a kind of question in our cause;
For well you know we of the offering side
Must keep aloof from strict arbitrement,
And stop all sight-holes, every loop from
    whence
The eye of reason may pry in upon us:
This absence of your father's draws a curtain,

That shows the ignorant a kind of fear
Before not dreamt of.
HOTSPUR.
                    You strain too far.
I, rather, of his absence make this use:—
It lends a lustre and more great opinion,
A larger dare to our great enterprise,
Than if the earl were here; for men must think,
If we, without his help, can make a head
To push against a kingdom, with his help
We shall o'erturn it topsy-turvy down.—
Yet all goes well, yet all our joints are whole.
EARL OF DOUGLAS.
As heart can think: there is not such a word
Spoke of in Scotland as this term of fear.
Enter SIR RICHARD VERNON.
HOTSPUR.
My cousin Vernon! welcome, by my soul.
SIR RICHARD VERNON.
Pray God my news be worth a welcome, lord.
The Earl of Westmoreland, seven thousand
    strong,
Is marching hitherwards; with him Prince John.
HOTSPUR.
No harm:—what more?
SIR RICHARD VERNON.
                    And further, I have learn'd,
The king himself in person is set forth,
Or hitherwards intended speedily,
With strong and mighty preparation.
HOTSPUR.
He shall be welcome too. Where is his son,
The nimble-footed madcap Prince of Wales,
And his comrades, that daft the world aside,
And bid it pass?
SIR RICHARD VERNON.
                    All furnisht, all in arms;
All plumed like estridges that wing the wind;
Bated like eagles having lately bathed;
Glittering in golden coats, like images;
As full of spirit as the month of May,
And gorgeous as the sun at midsummer;
Wanton as youthful goats, wild as young bulls.
I saw young Harry,—with his beaver on,
His cuisses on his thighs, gallantly arm'd,—
Rise from the ground like feather'd Mercury,
And vaulted with such ease into his seat,
As if an angel dropt down from the clouds,
To turn and wind a fiery Pegasus,
And witch the world with noble horsemanship.
HOTSPUR.
No more, no more: worse than the sun in March,
This praise doth nourish agues. Let them come;
They come like sacrifices in their trim,
And to the fire-eyed maid of smoky war,
All hot and bleeding, will we offer them:
The mailed Mars shall on his altar sit
Up to the ears in blood. I am on fire
To hear this rich reprisal is so nigh,
And yet not ours.—Come, let me taste my horse,
Who is to bear me, like a thunderbolt,
Against the bosom of the Prince of Wales :
Harry to Harry shall, hot horse to horse,
Meet, and ne'er part till one drop down a
    corse.—
O, that Glendower were come!

SIR RICHARD VERNON.
                              There is more news:
I learn'd in Worcester, as I rode along,
He cannot draw his power this fourteen days.
                    EARL OF DOUGLAS.
That's the worst tidings that I hear of yet.
                    EARL OF WORCESTER.
Ay, by my faith, that bears a frosty sound.
                    HOTSPUR.
What may the king's whole battle reach unto?
                    SIR RICHARD VERNON.
To thirty thousand.
                    HOTSPUR.
                              Forty let it be:
My father and Glendower being both away,
The powers of us may serve so great a day.
Come, let us take a muster speedily:
Doomsday is near; die all, die merrily.
                    EARL OF DOUGLAS.
Talk not of dying: I am out of fear
Of death or death's hand for this one half-year.
                                        [*Exeunt.*

SCENE II.

A public road near Coventry.

Enter FALSTAFF *and* BARDOLPH.

                    SIR JOHN FALSTAFF.

BARDOLPH, get thee before to Coventry;
     fill me a bottle of sack: our soldiers shall
march through; we'll to Sutton-Co'fil' to-night.
                    BARDOLPH.
Will you give me money, captain?
                    SIR JOHN FALSTAFF.
Lay out, lay out.
                    BARDOLPH.
This bottle makes an angel.
                    SIR JOHN FALSTAFF.
An if it do, take it for thy labour; and if it make
twenty, take them all; I'll answer the coinage.
Bid my lieutenant Peto meet me at town's end.
                    BARDOLPH.
I will, captain: farewell.   [*Exit.*
                    SIR JOHN FALSTAFF.
If I be not ashamed of my soldiers, I am a soused
gurnet. I have misused the king's press damnably.
I have got, in exchange of a hundred and fifty
soldiers, three hundred and odd pounds. I press
me none but good householders, yeomen's sons;
inquire me out contracted bachelors, such as had
been askt twice on the banns; such a commodity
of warm slaves as had as lieve hear the devil as a
drum; such as fear the report of a caliver worse
than a struck fowl or a hurt wild-duck. I prest me
none but such toasts-and-butter, with hearts in
their bellies no bigger than pins'-heads, and they
have bought out their services; and now my whole
charge consists of ancients, corporals, lieutenants,
gentlemen of companies, slaves as ragged as
Lazarus in the painted cloth, where the glutton's
dogs lickt his sores; and such as, indeed, were
never soldiers, but discarded unjust serving-men,
younger sons to younger brothers, revolted tapsters, and ostlers trade-fall'n; the cankers of a
calm world and a long peace; ten times more dishonourable ragged than an old-faced ancient: and

such have I, to fill up the rooms of them that have
bought out their services, that you would think
that I had a hundred and fifty tatter'd prodigals
lately come from swine-keeping, from eating
draff and husks. A mad fellow met me on the way,
and told me I had unloaded all the gibbets, and
prest the dead bodies. No eye hath seen such
scarecrows. I'll not march through Coventry
with them, that's flat:—nay, and the villains
march wide betwixt the legs, as if they had gyves
on; for, indeed, I had the most of them out of
prison. There's but a shirt and a half in all my
company; and the half-shirt is two napkins tackt
together and thrown over the shoulders like a
herald's coat without sleeves; and the shirt, to say
the truth, stolen from my host at Saint Albans,
or the red-nose innkeeper of Daventry. But that's
all one; they'll find linen enough on every hedge.
Enter the PRINCE *and* WESTMORELAND.
                    PRINCE HENRY.
How now, blown Jack! how now, quilt!
                    SIR JOHN FALSTAFF.
What, Hal! how now, mad wag! what a devil dost
thou in Warwickshire?—My good Lord of Westmoreland, I cry you mercy: I thought your honour
had already been at Shrewsbury.
                    EARL OF WESTMORELAND.
Faith, Sir John, 'tis more than time that I were
there, and you too; but my powers are there already. The king, I can tell you, looks for us all:
we must away all night.
                    SIR JOHN FALSTAFF.
Tut, never fear me: I am as vigilant as a cat to
steal cream.
                    PRINCE HENRY.
I think, to steal cream, indeed; for thy theft hath
already made thee butter. But tell me, Jack,
whose fellows are these that come after?
                    SIR JOHN FALSTAFF.
Mine, Hal, mine.
                    PRINCE HENRY.
I did never see such pitiful rascals.
                    SIR JOHN FALSTAFF.
Tut, tut; good enough to toss; food for powder,
food for powder; they'll fill a pit as well as better:
tush, man, mortal men, mortal men.
                    EARL OF WESTMORELAND.
Ay, but, Sir John, methinks they are exceeding
poor and bare,—too beggarly.
                    SIR JOHN FALSTAFF.
Faith, for their poverty, I know not where they
had that; and for their bareness, I am sure they
never learn'd that of me.
                    PRINCE HENRY.
No, I'll be sworn; unless you call three fingers on
the ribs bare. But, sirrah, make haste: Percy is al-
ready in the field.   [*Exit.*
                    SIR JOHN FALSTAFF.
What, is the king encampt?
                    EARL OF WESTMORELAND.
He is, Sir John: I fear we shall stay too long.[*Exit.*
                    SIR JOHN FALSTAFF.
Well,
To the latter end of a fray and the beginning of a
     feast
Fits a dull fighter and a keen guest.   [*Exit.*

SCENE III.

The rebel camp near Shrewsbury.

Enter HOTSPUR, WORCESTER, DOUGLAS, *and* VERNON.

HOTSPUR.

WE'LL fight with him to-night.

EARL OF WORCESTER.
                         It may not be.

EARL OF DOUGLAS.
You give him, then, advantage.

SIR RICHARD VERNON.
                       Not a whit.

HOTSPUR.
Why say you so? looks he not for supply?

SIR RICHARD VERNON.
So do we.

HOTSPUR.
His is certain, ours is doubtful.

EARL OF WORCESTER.
Good cousin, be advised; stir not to-night.

SIR RICHARD VERNON.
Do not, my lord.

EARL OF DOUGLAS.
                 You do not counsel well:
You speak it out of fear and cold heart.

SIR RICHARD VERNON.
Do me no slander, Douglas: by my life,—
And I dare well maintain it with my life,—
If well-respected honour bid me on,
I hold as little counsel with weak fear
As you, my lord, or any Scot that this day lives:—
Let it be seen to-morrow in the battle
Which of us fears.

EARL OF DOUGLAS.
              Yea, or to-night.

SIR RICHARD VERNON.
                       Content.

HOTSPUR.
To-night, say I.

SIR RICHARD VERNON.
Come, come, it may not be. I wonder much,
Being men of such great leading as you are,
That you foresee not what impediments
Drag back our expedition: certain horse
Of my cousin Vernon's are not yet come up;
Your uncle Worcester's horse came but to-day;
And now their pride amd mettle is asleep,
Their courage with hard labour tame and dull,
That not a horse is half the half of himself.

HOTSPUR.
So are the horses of the enemy
In general, journey-bated and brought low:
The better part of ours are full of rest.

EARL OF WORCESTER.
The number of the king exceedeth ours:
For God's sake, cousin, stay till all come in.

[*The trumpet sounds a parley.*

Enter SIR WALTER BLUNT.

SIR WALTER BLUNT.
I come with gracious offers from the king,
If you vouchsafe me hearing and respect.

HOTSPUR.
Welcome, Sir Walter Blunt; and would to God
You were of our determination!
Some of us love you well; and even those some

Envy your great deservings and good name,
Because you are not of our quality,
But stand against us like an enemy.

SIR WALTER BLUNT.
And God defend but still I should stand so,
So long as out of limit and true rule
You stand against anointed majesty!
But, to my charge!—The king hath sent to know
The nature of your griefs; and whereupon
You conjure from the breast of civil peace
Such bold hostility, teaching his duteous land
Audacious cruelty. If that the king
Have any way your good deserts forgot,
Which he confesseth to be manifold,
He bids you name your griefs; and with all speed
You shall have your desires with interest,
And pardon absolute for yourself and these
Herein misled by your suggestion.

HOTSPUR.
The king is kind; and well we know the king
Knows at what time to promise, when to pay.
My father and my uncle and myself
Did give him that same royalty he wears;
And when he was not six-and-twenty strong,
Sick in the world's regard, wretched and low,
A poor unminded outlaw sneaking home,
My father gave him welcome to the shore;
And when he heard him swear and vow to God,
He came but to be Duke of Lancaster,
To sue his livery and beg his peace,
With tears of innocency and terms of zeal,—
My father, in kind heart and pity moved,
Swore him assistance, and perform'd it too.
Now, when the lords and barons of the realm
Perceived Northumberland did lean to him,
The more and less came in with cap and knee;
Met him in boroughs, cities, villages,
Attended him on bridges, stood in lanes,
Laid gifts before him, proffer'd him their oaths,
Gave him their heirs as pages, follow'd him
Even at the heels in golden multitudes.
He presently,—as greatness knows itself,—
Steps me a little higher than his vow
Made to my father, while his blood was poor,
Upon the naked shore at Ravenspurg;
And now, forsooth, takes on him to reform
Some certain edicts and some strait decrees
That lie too heavy on the commonwealth;
Cries out upon abuses, seems to weep
Over his country's wrongs; and, by this face,
This seeming brow of justice, did he win
The hearts of all that he did angle for:
Proceeded further; cut me off the heads
Of all the favourites, that the absent king
In deputation left behind him here
When he was personal in the Irish war.

SIR WALTER BLUNT.
Tut, I came not to hear this.

HOTSPUR.
                     Then to the point.
In short time after, he deposed the king;
Soon after that, deprived him of his life;
And, in the neck of that, taskt the whole state:
To make that worse, suffer'd his kinsman
     March,—
Who is, if every owner were well placed,

221

Indeed his king,—to be engaged in Wales,
There without ransom to lie forfeited;
Disgraced me in my happy victories,
Sought to entrap me by intelligence;
Rated my uncle from the council-board;
In rage dismiss'd my father from the court;
Broke oath on oath, committed wrong on wrong;
And, in conclusion, drove us to seek out
This head of safety; and withal to pry
Into his title, the which we find
Too indirect for long continuance.

SIR WALTER BLUNT.

Shall I return this answer to the king?

HOTSPUR.

Not so, Sir Walter: we'll withdraw awhile.
Go to the king; and let there be impawn'd
Some surety for a safe return again,
And in the morning early shall mine uncle
Bring him our purposes: and so, farewell.

SIR WALTER BLUNT.

I would you would accept of grace and love.

HOTSPUR.

And may be so we shall.

SIR WALTER BLUNT.

Pray God you do.

[Exeunt.

SCENE IV.

York. The ARCHBISHOP'S palace.

Enter the ARCHBISHOP OF YORK and
SIR MICHAEL.

ARCHBISHOP OF YORK.

HIE, good Sir Michael; bear this sealed brief
With winged haste to the lord marshal;
This to my cousin Scroop; and all the rest
To whom they are directed. If you knew [haste.
How much they do import, you would make

SIR MICHAEL.

My good lord,
I guess their tenour.

ARCHBISHOP OF YORK.

Like enough you do.
To-morrow, good Sir Michael, is a day
Wherein the fortune of ten thousand men
Must bide the touch; for, sir, at Shrewsbury,
As I am truly given to understand,
The king, with mighty and quick-raised power,
Meets with Lord Harry: and, I fear, Sir Michael,
What with the sickness of Northumberland,
Whose power was in the first proportion,
And what with Owen Glendower's absence
  thence,
Who with them was a rated sinew too,
And comes not in, o'er-ruled by prophecies,—
I fear the power of Percy is too weak
To wage an instant trial with the king.

SIR MICHAEL.

Why, my good lord, you need not fear;
There is Douglas and Lord Mortimer.

ARCHBISHOP OF YORK.

No, Mortimer is not there.

SIR MICHAEL.

But there is Mordake, Vernon, Lord Harry Percy,
And there is my Lord of Worcester; and a head
Of gallant warriors, noble gentlemen.

ARCHBISHOP OF YORK.

And so there is: but yet the king hath drawn
The special head of all the land together;—
The Prince of Wales, Lord John of Lancaster,
The noble Westmoreland, and warlike Blunt;
And many moe corrivals and dear men
Of estimation and command in arms.

SIR MICHAEL.

Doubt not, my lord, they shall be well opposed.

ARCHBISHOP OF YORK.

I hope no less, yet needful 'tis to fear;
And, to prevent the worst, Sir Michael, speed:
For if Lord Percy thrive not, ere the king
Dismiss his power, he means to visit us,
For he hath heard of our confederacy,—
And 'tis but wisdom to make strong against
  him:
Therefore make haste. I must go write again
To other friends; and so, farewell, Sir Michael.

[Exeunt.

ACT V. SCENE I.

The KING'S camp near Shrewsbury.

Enter the KING, PRINCE OF WALES, LORD
JOHN OF LANCASTER, SIR WALTER BLUNT,
and FALSTAFF.

KING HENRY.

HOW bloodily the sun begins to peer
Above yon busky hill! the day looks pale
At his distemperature.

PRINCE HENRY.

The southern wind
Doth play the trumpet to his purposes;
And by his hollow whistling in the leaves
Foretells a tempest and a blustering day.

KING HENRY.

Then with the losers let it sympathise,
For nothing can seem foul to those that win.

[The trumpet sounds.

Enter WORCESTER and VERNON.

How now, my Lord of Worcester! 'tis not well
That you and I should meet upon such terms
As now we meet. You have deceived our trust;
And made us doff our easy robes of peace,
To crush our old limbs in ungentle steel:
This is not well, my lord, this is not well.
What say you to it? will you again unknit
This churlish knot of all-abhorred war?
And move in that obedient orb again
Where you did give a fair and natural light;
And be no more an exhaled meteor,
A prodigy of fear, and a portent
Of broached mischief to the unborn times?

EARL OF WORCESTER.

Hear me, my liege:
For mine own part, I could be well content
To entertain the lag-end of my life
With quiet hours; for, I do protest,
I have not sought the day of this dislike.

KING HENRY.

You have not sought it! how comes it, then?

SIR JOHN FALSTAFF.

Rebellion lay in his way, and he found it.

PRINCE HENRY.

Peace, chewet, peace!

222

EARL OF WORCESTER.
It pleased your majesty to turn your looks
Of favour from myself and all our house;
And yet I must remember you, my lord,
We were the first and dearest of your friends.
For you my staff of office did I break
In Richard's time; and posted day and night
To meet you on the way, and kiss your hand,
When yet you were in place and in account
Nothing so strong and fortunate as I.
It was myself, my brother, and his son,
That brought you home, and boldly did out-
    dare
The dangers of the time. You swore to us,
And you did swear that oath at Doncaster,
That you did nothing purpose 'gainst the state;
Nor claim no further than your new-fall'n
    right,
The seat of Gaunt, dukedom of Lancaster:
To this we swore our aid. But in short space
It rain'd down fortune showering on your
    head;
And such a flood of greatness fell on you,—
What with our help, what with the absent
    king,
What with the injuries of a wanton time,
The seeming sufferances that you had borne,
And the contrarious winds that held the king
So long in his unlucky Irish wars
That all in England did repute him dead,—
And from this swarm of fair advantages
You took occasion to be quickly woo'd
To gripe the general sway into your hand;
Forgot your oath to us at Doncaster;
And, being fed by us, you used us so
As that ungentle gull, the cuckoo's bird,
Useth the sparrow,—did oppress our nest;
Grew by our feeding to so great a bulk,
That even our love durst not come near your
    sight
For fear of swallowing; but with nimble wing
We were enforced, for safety sake, to fly
Out of your sight, and raise this present head:
Whereby we stand opposed by such means
As you yourself have forged against yourself,
By unkind usage, dangerous countenance,
And violation of all faith and troth
Sworn to us in your younger enterprise.
              KING HENRY.
These things, indeed, you have articulate,
Proclaim'd at market-crosses, read in churches,
To face the garment of rebellion
With some fine colour that may please the eye
Of fickle changelings and poor discontents,
Which gape and rub the elbow at the news
Of hurlyburly innovation:
And never yet did insurrection want
Such water-colours to impaint his cause;
Nor moody beggars, starving for a time
Of pellmell havoc and confusion.
              PRINCE HENRY.
In both our armies there is many a soul
Shall pay full dearly for this encounter,
If once they join in trial. Tell your nephew,
The Prince of Wales doth join with all the
    world

In praise of Henry Percy: by my hopes,
This present enterprise set off his head,
I do not think a braver gentleman,
More active-valiant or more valiant-young,
More daring or more bold, is now alive
To grace this latter age with noble deeds.
For my part, I may speak it to my shame,
I have a truant been to chivalry;
And so I hear he doth account me too:
Yet this before my father's majesty,—
I am content that he shall take the odds
Of his great name and estimation,
And will, to save the blood on either side,
Try fortune with him in a single fight.
              KING HENRY.
And, Prince of Wales, so dare we venture thee,
Albeit considerations infinite
Do make against it.—No, good Worcester,
    no,
We love our people well; even those we love
That are misled upon your cousin's part;
And, will they take the offer of our grace,
Both he, and they, and you, yea, every man
Shall be my friend again, and I'll be his:
So tell your cousin, and bring me word
What he will do: but if he will not yield,
Rebuke and dread correction wait on us,
And they shall do their office. So, be gone;
We will not now be troubled with reply:
We offer fair; take it advisedly.
              [Exeunt WORCESTER and VERNON.
              PRINCE HENRY.
It will not be accepted, on my life:
The Douglas and the Hotspur both together
Are confident against the world in arms.
              KING HENRY.
Hence, therefore, every leader to his charge;
For, on their answer, will we set on them:
And God befriend us, as our cause is just!
              [Exeunt KING, BLUNT, and PRINCE JOHN.
              SIR JOHN FALSTAFF.
Hal, if thou see me down in the battle, and be-
stride me, so; 'tis a point of friendship.
              PRINCE HENRY.
Nothing but a colossus can do thee that friend-
ship. Say thy prayers, and farewell.
              SIR JOHN FALSTAFF.
I would 'twere bedtime, Hal, and all well.
              PRINCE HENRY.
Why, thou owest God a death.   [Exit.
              SIR JOHN FALSTAFF.
'Tis not due yet; I would be loth to pay him before his day. What need I be so forward with him
that calls not on me? Well, 'tis no matter; honour
pricks me on. Yea, but how if honour prick me
off when I come on? how then? Can honour set to
a leg? no: or an arm? no: or take away the grief of
a wound? no. Honour hath no skill in surgery,
then? no. What is honour? a word. What is that
word honour? air. A trim reckoning!—Who hath
it? he that died o' Wednesday. Doth he feel it? no.
Doth he hear it? no. 'Tis insensible, then? yea, to
the dead. But will it not live with the living? no.
Why? detraction will not suffer it. Therefore I'll
none of it: honour is a mere scutcheon:—and so
ends my catechism.   [Exit.

SCENE II.

The rebel camp.

Enter WORCESTER *and* VERNON.

EARL OF WORCESTER.

O, NO, my nephew must not know, Sir Richard,
The liberal and kind offer of the king.

SIR RICHARD VERNON.

'Twere best he did.

EARL OF WORCESTER.

Then are we all undone.
It is not possible, it cannot be,
The king should keep his word in loving us;
He will suspect us still, and find a time
To punish this offence in other faults:
Suspicion all our lives shall be stuck full of
  eyes;
For treason is but trusted like the fox,
Who, ne'er so tame, so cherisht, and lockt up,
Will have a wild trick of his ancestors.
Look how we can, or sad or merrily,
Interpretation will misquote our looks;
And we shall feed like oxen at a stall,
The better cherisht, still the nearer death.
My nephew's trespass may be well forgot,—
It hath the excuse of youth and heat of blood;
And an adopted name of privilege,—
A hare-brain'd Hotspur, govern'd by a spleen:
All his offences live upon my head
And on his father's: we did train him on;
And, his corruption being ta'en from us,
We, as the spring of all, shall pay for all.
Therefore, good cousin, let not Harry know,
In any case, the offer of the king.

SIR RICHARD VERNON.

Deliver what you will, I'll say 'tis so.
Here comes your cousin.

Enter HOTSPUR *and* DOUGLAS; OFFICERS *and*
SOLDIERS *behind.*

HOTSPUR.

My uncle is return'd:—
Deliver up, my Lord of Westmoreland.—
Uncle, what news?

EARL OF WORCESTER.

The king will bid you battle presently.

EARL OF DOUGLAS.

Defy him by the Lord of Westmoreland.

HOTSPUR.

Lord Douglas, go you and tell him so.

EARL OF DOUGLAS.

Marry, and shall, and very willingly.   [*Exit.*

EARL OF WORCESTER.

There is no seeming mercy in the king.

HOTSPUR.

Did you beg any? God forbid!

EARL OF WORCESTER.

I told him gently of our grievances,
Of his oath-breaking; which he mended thus,
By now forswearing that he is forsworn:
He calls us rebels, traitors; and will scourge
With haughty arms this hateful name in us.

Enter DOUGLAS.

EARL OF DOUGLAS.

Arm, gentlemen; to arms! for I have thrown
A brave defiance in King Henry's teeth,
And Westmoreland, that was engaged, did bear it;
Which cannot choose but bring him quickly on.

EARL OF WORCESTER.

The Prince of Wales stept forth before the king,
And, nephew challenged you to single fight.

HOTSPUR.

O, would the quarrel lay upon our heads;
And that no man might draw short breath to-day
But I and Harry Monmouth! Tell me, tell me,
How show'd his tasking? seem'd it in contempt?

SIR RICHARD VERNON.

No, by my soul; I never in my life
Did hear a challenge urged more modestly,
Unless a brother should a brother dare
To gentle exercise and proof of arms.
He gave you all the duties of a man;
Trimm'd up your praises with a princely tongue;
Spoke your deservings like a chronicle,
Making you ever better than his praise,
By still dispraising praise valued with you:
And, which became him like a prince indeed,
He made a blushing cital of himself;
And chid his truant youth with such a grace,
As if he master'd there a double spirit,
Of teaching and of learning instantly.
There did he pause: but let me tell the world,—
If he outlive the envy of this day,
England did never owe so sweet a hope,
So much misconstrued in his wantonness.

HOTSPUR.

Cousin, I think thou art enamoured
On his follies: never did I hear
Of any prince so wild a libertine.
But be he as he will, yet once ere night
I will embrace him with a soldier's arm,
That he shall shrink under my courtesy.—
Arm, arm with speed:—and, fellows, soldiers,
  friends,
Better consider what you have to do
Than I, that have not well the gift of tongue,
Can lift your blood up with persuasion.

Enter a MESSENGER.

MESSENGER.

My lord, here are letters for you.

HOTSPUR.

I cannot read them now.—
O gentlemen, the time of life is short!
To spend that shortness basely were too long,
If life did ride upon a dial's point,
Still ending at the arrival of an hour.
An if we live, we live to tread on kings;
If die, brave death, when princes die with us!
Now, for our consciences,—the arms are fair,
When the intent of bearing them is just.

Enter another MESSENGER.

MESSENGER.

My lord, prepare; the king comes on apace.

HOTSPUR.

I thank him, that he cuts me from my tale,
For I profess not talking; only this,—
Let each man do his best: and here draw I
A sword, whose temper I intend to stain
With the best blood that I can meet withal
In the adventure of this perilous day.
Now,—*Esperance!*—Percy!—and set on.—
Sound all the lofty instruments of war,

224

And by that music let us all embrace;
For, heaven to earth, some of us never shall
A second time do such a courtesy.
  [*The trumpets sound.   They embrace, and
    exeunt.*

SCENE III.

Plain between the camps.

The KING *enters with his Power.   Alarum to the
  battle.   Then enter* DOUGLAS *and* SIR WALTER
  BLUNT.

SIR WALTER BLUNT.

WHAT is thy name, that in the battle thus
  Thou crossest me? what honour dost thou
    seek
Upon my head?
      EARL OF DOUGLAS.
          Know, then, my name is Douglas;
And I do haunt thee in the battle thus
Because some tell me that thou art a king.
      SIR WALTER BLUNT.
They tell thee true.
      EARL OF DOUGLAS.
The Lord of Stafford dear to-day hath bought
Thy likeness; for, instead of thee, King Harry,
This sword hath ended him: so shall it thee,
Unless thou yield thee as my prisoner.
      SIR WALTER BLUNT.
I was not born a yielder, thou proud Scot;
And thou shalt find a king that will revenge
Lord Stafford's death.
      [*They fight,* DOUGLAS *kills* BLUNT.
          Enter HOTSPUR.
      HOTSPUR.
O Douglas, hadst thou fought at Holmedon thus,
I never had triumpht upon a Scot.
      EARL OF DOUGLAS.
All's done, all's won; here breathless lies the king.
      HOTSPUR.
Where?
      EARL OF DOUGLAS.
Here.
      HOTSPUR.
This, Douglas? no; I know this face full well:
A gallant knight he was, his name was Blunt;
Semblably furnisht like the king himself.
      EARL OF DOUGLAS.
A fool go with thy soul, whither it goes!
A borrow'd title hast thou bought too dear:
Why didst thou tell me that thou wert a king?
      HOTSPUR.
The king hath many masking in his coats.
      EARL OF DOUGLAS.
Now, by my sword, I will kill all his coats;
I'll murder all his wardrobe piece by piece,
Until I meet the king.
      HOTSPUR.
          Up, and away!
Our soldiers stand full fairly for the day.
      [*Exeunt.*
Alarum.   Enter FALSTAFF *solus.*
      SIR JOHN FALSTAFF.
Though I could scape shot-free at London, I fear
the shot here; here's no scoring but upon the
pate.—Soft! who are you? Sir Walter Blunt:—

there's honour for you! here's no vanity!—I am
as hot as molten lead, and as heavy too: God
keep lead out of me! I need no more weight than
mine own bowels.—I have led my ragamuffins
where they are pepper'd: there's but three of my
hundred and fifty left alive; and they are for the
town's end,—to beg during life.—But who comes
here?

      Enter PRINCE HENRY.
      PRINCE HENRY.
What, stand'st thou idle here? lend me thy sword:
Many a nobleman lies stark and stiff
Under the hoofs of vaunting enemies,
Whose deaths are yet unrevenged:
I prithee, lend me thy sword.
      SIR JOHN FALSTAFF.
O Hal, I prithee, give me leave to breathe awhile.
—Turk Gregory never did such deeds in arms as
I have done this day. I have paid Percy, I have
made him sure.
      PRINCE HENRY.
He is, indeed; and living to kill thee. I prithee,
lend me thy sword.
      SIR JOHN FALSTAFF.
Nay, before God, Hal, if Percy be alive, thou
gett'st not my sword; but take my pistol, if thou
wilt.
      PRINCE HENRY.
Give it me: what, is it in the case?
      SIR JOHN FALSTAFF.
Ay, Hal. 'Tis hot, 'tis hot: there's that will sack a
city.   [*The* PRINCE *draws it out, and finds it to
          be a bottle of sack.*
      PRINCE HENRY.
What, is it a time to jest and dally now?
        [*He throws the bottle at him.   Exit.*
      SIR JOHN FALSTAFF.
Well, if Percy be alive, I'll pierce him. If he do
come in my way, so; if he do not, if I come in his
willingly, let him make a carbonado of me. I like
not such grinning honour as Sir Walter hath: give
me life; which if I can save, so; if not, honour
comes unlookt for, and there's an end.   [*Exit.*

SCENE IV.

Another part of the field.

Alarum.   Excursions.   Enter KING, *the* PRINCE,
  LORD JOHN OF LANCASTER, *and* WESTMORE-
  LAND.

      KING HENRY.
I PRITHEE,
  Harry, withdraw thyself; thou bleed'st too
    much.—
Lord John of Lancaster, go you with him.
      PRINCE JOHN.
Not I, my lord, unless I did bleed too.
      PRINCE HENRY.
I beseech your majesty, make up,
Lest your retirement do amaze your friends.
      KING HENRY.
I will do so.—
My Lord of Westmoreland, lead him to his tent.
      EARL OF WESTMORELAND.
Come, my lord, I will lead you to your tent.

PRINCE HENRY.

Lead me, my lord? I do not need your help:
And God forbid, a shallow scratch should drive
The Prince of Wales from such a field as this,
Where stain'd nobility lies trodden on,
And rebels' arms triumph in massacres!

PRINCE JOHN.

We breathe too long:—come, cousin Westmore-
land,
Our duty this way lies; for God's sake, come.
[Exeunt PRINCE JOHN and WESTMORE-
LAND.

PRINCE HENRY.

By God, thou hast deceived me, Lancaster;
I did not think thee lord of such a spirit:
Before, I loved thee as a brother, John;
But now, I do respect thee as my soul.

KING HENRY.

I saw him hold Lord Percy at the point
With lustier maintenance than I did look for
Of such an ungrown warrior.

PRINCE HENRY.

O, this boy
Lends mettle to us all!   [Exit.

Enter DOUGLAS.

EARL OF DOUGLAS.

Another king! they grow like Hydra's heads:
I am the Douglas, fatal to all those
That wear those colours on them:—what art thou,
That counterfeit'st the person of a king?

KING HENRY.

The king himself; who, Douglas, grieves at heart,
So many of his shadows thou hast met,
And not the very king. I have two boys
Seek Percy and thyself about the field:
But, seeing thou fall'st on me so luckily,
I will assay thee: so, defend thyself.

EARL OF DOUGLAS.

I fear thou art another counterfeit;
And yet, in faith, thou bear'st thee like a king:
But mine I am sure thou art, whoe'er thou be,
And thus I win thee.

[They fight; the KING being in danger, enter
PRINCE OF WALES.

PRINCE HENRY.

Hold up thy head, vile Scot, or thou art like
Never to hold it up again! the spirits
Of valiant Shirley, Stafford, Blunt, are in my
arms:
It is the Prince of Wales that threatens thee;
Who never promiseth but he means to pay.
[They fight; DOUGLAS flies.
Cheerly, my lord: how fares your Grace?—
Sir Nicholas Gawsey hath for succour sent,
And so hath Clifton: I'll to Clifton straight.

KING HENRY.

Stay, and breathe awhile:—
Thou hast redeem'd thy lost opinion;
And show'd thou makest some tender of my life,
In this fair rescue thou hast brought to me.

PRINCE HENRY.

O God, they did me too much injury
That ever said I hearken'd for your death!
If it were so, I might have let alone
The insulting hand of Douglas over you,
Which would have been as speedy in your end

As all the poisonous potions in the world,
And saved the treacherous labour of your son.

KING HENRY.

Make up to Clifton: I'll to Sir Nicholas Gawsey.
[Exit.

Enter HOTSPUR.

HOTSPUR.

If I mistake not, thou art Harry Monmouth.

PRINCE HENRY.

Thou speak'st as if I would deny my name.

HOTSPUR.

My name is Harry Percy.

PRINCE HENRY.

Why, then I see
A very valiant rebel of the name.
I am the Prince of Wales; and think not, Percy,
To share with me in glory any more:
Two stars keep not their motion in one sphere;
Nor can one England brook a double reign,
Of Harry Percy and the Prince of Wales.

HOTSPUR.

Nor shall it, Harry, for the hour is come
To end the one of us; and would to God
Thy name in arms were now as great as mine!

PRINCE HENRY.

I'll make it greater ere I part from thee;
And all the budding honours on thy crest
I'll crop, to make a garland for my head.

HOTSPUR.

I can no longer brook thy vanities.   [They fight.

Enter FALSTAFF.

SIR JOHN FALSTAFF.

Well said, Hal! to it, Hal!—Nay, you shall find no
boy's play here, I can tell you.
Enter DOUGLAS; he fights with FALSTAFF, who
falls down as if he were dead, and exit DOUGLAS.
The PRINCE killeth PERCY.

HOTSPUR.

O Harry, thou hast robb'd me of my youth!
I better brook the loss of brittle life
Than those proud titles thou hast won of me;
They wound my thoughts worse than thy sword
my flesh:—
But thought's the slave of life, and life time's fool;
And time, that takes survey of all the world,
Must have a stop. O, I could prophesy,
But that the earthy and cold hand of death
Lies on my tongue:—no, Percy, thou art dust,
And food for—   [Dies.

PRINCE HENRY.

For worms, brave Percy: fare thee well, great
heart!—
Ill-weaved ambition, how much art thou shrunk!
When that this body did contain a spirit,
A kingdom for it was too small a bound;
But now two paces of the vilest earth
Is room enough:—this earth that bears thee
dead
Bears not alive so stout a gentleman.
If thou wert sensible of courtesy,
I should not make so dear a show of zeal:—
But let my favours hide thy mangled face;
And, even in thy behalf, I'll thank myself
For doing these fair rites of tenderness.
Adieu, and take thy praise with thee to heaven!
Thy ignomy sleep with thee in the grave,

But not remember'd in thy epitaph!—
   [*He spieth* FALSTAFF *on the ground.*
What, old acquaintance! could not all this flesh
Keep in a little life? Poor Jack, farewell!
I could have better spared a better man:
O, I should have a heavy miss of thee,
If I were much in love with vanity!
Death hath not struck so fat a deer to-day,
Though many dearer, in this bloody fray.
Embowell'd will I see thee by and by:
Till then in blood by noble Percy lie. [*Exit.*
   [FALSTAFF *riseth up.*
   SIR JOHN FALSTAFF.
Embowell'd! if thou embowel me to-day, I'll give
you leave to powder me and eat me too to-mor-
row. 'Sblood, 'twas time to counterfeit, or that
hot termagant Scot had paid me scot and lot too.
Counterfeit? I lie, I am no counterfeit: to die, is to
be a counterfeit; for he is but the counterfeit of a
man who hath not the life of a man: but to counterfeit dying, when a man thereby liveth, is to be
no counterfeit, but the true and perfect image of
life indeed. The better part of valour is discretion;
in the which better part I have saved my life.
Zounds, I am afraid of this gunpowder Percy,
though he be dead: how, if he should counterfeit
too, and rise? by my faith, I am afraid he would
prove the better counterfeit. Therefore I'll make
him sure; yea, and I'll swear I kill'd him. Why
may not he rise as well as I? Nothing confutes me
but eyes, and nobody sees me. Therefore, sirrah
[*stabbing him*], with a new wound in your thigh,
come you along with me.
   [*He takes up* HOTSPUR *on his back.*
Enter the PRINCE OF WALES *and* LORD JOHN
OF LANCASTER.
   PRINCE HENRY.
Come, brother John; full bravely hast thou flesht
Thy maiden sword.
   LORD JOHN OF LANCASTER.
     But, soft! whom have we here?
Did you not tell me this fat man was dead?
   PRINCE HENRY.
I did; I saw him dead,
Breathless and bleeding on the ground.—
Art thou alive? or is it fantasy
That plays upon our eyesight? I prithee, speak;
We will not trust our eyes without our ears:—
Thou art not what thou seem'st.
   SIR JOHN FALSTAFF.
No, that's certain; I am not a double man: but if
I be not Jack Falstaff, then am I a Jack. There is
Percy [*throwing the body down*]: if your father will
do me any honour, so; if not, let him kill the next
Percy himself. I look to be either earl or duke, I
can assure you.
   PRINCE HENRY.
Why, Percy I kill'd myself, and saw thee dead.
   SIR JOHN FALSTAFF.
Didst thou?—Lord, Lord, how this world is given
to lying!—I grant you I was down and out of
breath; and so was he: but we rose both at an instant, and fought a long hour by Shrewsbury
clock. If I may be believed, so; if not, let them
that should reward valour bear the sin upon their
own heads. I'll take it upon my death, I gave him

this wound in the thigh: if the man were alive,
and would deny it, zounds, I would make him eat
a piece of my sword.
   LORD JOHN OF LANCASTER.
This is the strangest tale that e'er I heard.
   PRINCE HENRY.
This is the strangest fellow, brother John.—
Come, bring your luggage nobly on your back:
For my part, if a lie may do thee grace,
I'll gild it with the happiest terms I have.
   [*A retreat is sounded.*
The trumpet sounds retreat; the day is ours.
Come, brother, let's to the highest of the field,
To see what friends are living, who are dead.
   [*Exeunt* PRINCES.
   SIR JOHN FALSTAFF.
I'll follow, as they say, for reward. He that re-
wards me, God reward him! If I do grow great,
I'll grow less; for I'll purge, and leave sack, and
live cleanly as a nobleman should do.
   [*Exit, bearing off the body.*

   SCENE V.
  Another part of the field.
The trumpets sound. Enter the KING, PRINCE
OF WALES, LORD JOHN OF LANCASTER,
WESTMORELAND, *and others, with* WORCES-
TER *and* VERNON *prisoners.*
   KING HENRY.
THUS ever did rebellion find rebuke.—
  Ill-spirited Worcester! did we not send grace,
Pardon, and terms of love to all of you?
And wouldst thou turn our offers contrary?
Misuse the tenour of thy kinsman's trust?
Three knights upon our party slain to-day,
A noble earl, and many a creature else,
Had been alive this hour,
If, like a Christian, thou hadst truly borne
Betwixt our armies true intelligence.
   EARL OF WORCESTER.
What I have done my safety urged me to;
And I embrace this fortune patiently,
Since not to be avoided it falls on me.
   KING HENRY.
Bear Worcester to the death, and Vernon too:
Other offenders we will pause upon.—
   [*Exeunt* WORCESTER *and* VERNON, *guarded.*
How goes the field?
   PRINCE HENRY.
The noble Scot, Lord Douglas, when he saw
The fortune of the day quite turn'd from him,
The noble Percy slain, and all his men
Upon the foot of fear,—fled with the rest;
And falling from a hill, he was so bruised
That the pursuers took him. At my tent
The Douglas is; and I beseech your Grace
I may dispose of him.
   KING HENRY.
    With all my heart.
   PRINCE HENRY.
Then, brother John of Lancaster, to you
This honourable bounty shall belong:
Go to the Douglas, and deliver him

Up to his pleasure, ransomless and free;
His valour, shown upon our crests to-day,
Hath taught us how to cherish such high deeds
Even in the bosom of our adversaries.
　　　　　LORD JOHN OF LANCASTER.
I thank your Grace for this high courtesy
Which I shall give away immediately.
　　　　　KING HENRY.
Then this remains,—that we divide our
　power.—
You, son John, and my cousin Westmoreland,
Towards York shall bend you with your dearest
　speed,
To meet Northumberland and the prelate Scroop,
Who, as we hear, are busily in arms:
Myself,—and you, son Harry,—will towards
　Wales,
To fight with Glendower and the Earl of March.
Rebellion in this land shall lose his sway,
Meeting the check of such another day:
And since this business so fair is done,
Let us not leave till all our own be won. [*Exeunt.*

THE SECOND PART OF
KING HENRY THE FOURTH

DRAMATIS PERSONAE

RUMOUR, *the Presenter.*
KING HENRY THE FOURTH.
PRINCE HENRY, *afterwards crown'd* KING
   HENRY THE FIFTH.
PRINCE JOHN *of Lan-* ⎫
  caster,   ⎪ *Sons to Henry the Fourth*
HUMPHREY *of Gloster,* ⎬ *and Brethren to Henry*
THOMAS *of Clarence,* ⎭ *the Fifth.*
NORTHUMBERLAND, ⎫
THE ARCHBISHOP OF ⎪
   YORK,   ⎪
MOWBRAY,   ⎬ *Opposites to the King.*
HASTINGS,   *Henry the Fourth.*
LORD BARDOLPH,   ⎪
TRAVERS,   ⎪
MORTON,   ⎭
COLEVILE,
WARWICK,   ⎫
WESTMORELAND, ⎪
SURREY,   ⎬ *Of the King's Priory.*
GOWER,   ⎪
HARCOURT,   ⎭
BLUNT,
LORD CHIEF JUSTICE,

POINTZ,
FALSTAFF,
BARDOLPH,
PISTOL,
PETO,
PAGE,
A SERVANT *of the Chief Justice.*
SHALLOW, ⎱ *both Country Justices.*
SILENCE, ⎰
DAVY, *servant to Shallow.*
FANG *and* SNARE, *two Sergeants.*
MOULDY, ⎫
SHADOW, ⎪
WART,   ⎬ *Recruits.*
FEEBLE, ⎪
BULLCALF,⎭
DRAWERS. BEADLES. GROOMS. PORTER.

NORTHUMBERLAND'S WIFE.
PERCY'S WIDOW.
HOSTESS QUICKLY.
DOLL TEARSHEET.
EPILOGUE.

SCENE—*England.*

INDUCTION.

Warkworth. Before the castle.

Enter RUMOUR, *painted full of tongues.*

RUMOUR.

OPEN your ears; for which of you will stop
  The vent of hearing when loud Rumour
    speaks?
I, from the orient to the drooping west,
Making the wind my post-horse, still unfold
The acts commenced on this ball of earth:
Upon my tongues continual slanders ride,
The which in every language I pronounce,
Stuffing the ears of men with false reports.
I speak of peace, while covert enmity,
Under the smile of safety, wounds the world:
And who but Rumour, who but only I,
Make fearful musters and prepared defence,
Whilst the big year, swoln with some other grief,
Is thought with child by the stern tyrant war,
And no such matter? Rumour is a pipe
Blown by surmises, jealousies, conjectures;
And of so easy and so plain a stop,
That the blunt monster with uncounted heads,
The still-discordant wavering multitude,
Can play upon it. But what need I thus
My well-known body to anatomise
Among my household? Why is Rumour here?
I run before King Harry's victory;
Who, in a bloody field by Shrewsbury,
Hath beaten down young Hotspur and his troops,
Quenching the flame of bold rebellion
Even with the rebels' blood. But what mean I
To speak so true at first? my office is
To noise abroad, that Harry Monmouth fell
Under the wrath of noble Hotspur's sword;
And that the king before the Douglas' rage
Stoopt his anointed head as low as death.
This have I rumour'd through the peasant towns
Between that royal field of Shrewsbury
And this worm-eaten hold of ragged stone,
Where Hotspur's father, old Northumberland,
Lies crafty-sick: the posts come tiring on,
And not a man of them brings other news
Than they have learn'd of me: from Rumour's
    tongues
They bring smooth comforts false, worse than
    true wrongs.   [*Exit.*

ACT I. SCENE I.

The same.

Enter LORD BARDOLPH; *the* PORTER *at the gate.*

LORD BARDOLPH.

WHO keeps the gate here, ho? Where is the
  earl?

PORTER.
What shall I say you are?

LORD BARDOLPH.
               Tell thou the earl
That the Lord Bardolph doth attend him here.

PORTER.
His lordship is walkt forth into the orchard:

Please it your honour, knock but at the gate,
And he himself will answer.

LORD BARDOLPH.
Here comes the earl.
[*Exit* PORTER.

Enter NORTHUMBERLAND.

NORTHUMBERLAND.
What news, Lord Bardolph? every minute now
Should be the father of some stratagem:
The times are wild; contention, like a horse
Full of high feeding, madly hath broke loose,
And bears down all before him.

LORD BARDOLPH.
Noble earl,
I bring you certain news from Shrewsbury.

NORTHUMBERLAND.
Good, an God will!

LORD BARDOLPH.
As good as heart can wish:—
The king is almost wounded to the death;
And, in the fortune of my lord your son,
Prince Harry slain outright; and both the Blunts
Kill'd by the hand of Douglas; young Prince John
And Westmoreland and Stafford fled the field;
And Harry Monmouth's brawn, the hulk Sir
    John,
Is prisoner to your son: O, such a day,
So fought, so follow'd, and so fairly won,
Came not till now to dignify the times,
Since Cæsar's fortunes !

NORTHUMBERLAND.
How is this derived?
Saw you the field? came you from Shrewsbury?

LORD BARDOLPH.
I spake with one, my lord, that came from thence,
A gentleman well bred and of good name,
That freely render'd me these news for true.

NORTHUMBERLAND.
Here comes my servant Travers, whom I sent
On Tuesday last to listen after news.

LORD BARDOLPH.
My lord, I over-rode him on the way;
And he is furnisht with no certainties
More than he haply may retail from me.

Enter TRAVERS.

NORTHUMBERLAND.
Now, Travers, what good tidings comes with you?

TRAVERS.
My lord, Sir John Umfrevile turn'd me back
With joyful tidings; and, being better horsed,
Out-rode me. After him came spurring hard
A gentleman, almost forspent with speed,
That stopt by me to breathe his bloodied horse.
He askt the way to Chester; and of him
I did demand what news from Shrewsbury:
He told me that rebellion had ill luck,
And that young Harry Percy's spur was cold.
With that, he gave his able horse the head,
And, bending forward, struck his armed heels
Against the panting sides of his poor jade
Up to the rowel-head; and starting so,
He seem'd in running to devour the way,
Staying no longer question.

NORTHUMBERLAND.
Ha!—Again:
Said he young Harry Percy's spur was cold?

Of Hotspur, Coldspur? that rebellion
Had met ill luck?

LORD BARDOLPH.
My lord, I'll tell you what;
If my young lord your son have not the day,
Upon mine honour, for a silken point
I'll give my barony: ne'er talk of it.

NORTHUMBERLAND.
Why should the gentleman that rode by Travers
Give, then, such instances of loss?

LORD BARDOLPH.
Who, he?
He was some hilding fellow, that had stoln
The horse he rode on; and, upon my life,
Spoke at a venture.—Look, here comes more
    news.

Enter MORTON.

NORTHUMBERLAND.
Yea, this man's brow, like to a title-leaf,
Foretells the nature of a tragic volume:
So looks the strond whereon the imperious flood
Hath left a witness'd usurpation.—
Say, Morton, didst thou come from Shrewsbury?

MORTON.
I ran from Shrewsbury, my noble lord;
Where hateful death put on his ugliest mask
To fright our party.

NORTHUMBERLAND.
How doth my son and brother?
Thou tremblest; and the whiteness in thy cheek
Is apter than thy tongue to tell thy errand.
Even such a man, so faint, so spiritless,
So dull, so dead in look, so woe-begone,
Drew Priam's curtain in the dead of night,
And would have told him half his Troy was
    burnt;
But Priam found the fire ere he his tongue,
And I my Percy's death ere thou report'st it.
This thou wouldst say, 'Your son did thus and
    thus;
Your brother thus; so fought the noble Douglas;'
Stopping my greedy ear with their bold deeds:
But in the end, to stop my ear indeed,
Thou hast a sigh to blow away this praise,
Ending with 'Brother, son, and all are dead.'

MORTON.
Douglas is living, and your brother, yet;
But, for my lord your son,—

NORTHUMBERLAND.
Why, he is dead.
See what a ready tongue suspicion hath!
He that but fears the thing he would not know
Hath by instinct knowledge from others' eyes,
That what he fear'd is chanced. Yet speak,
    Morton;
Tell thou thy earl his divination lies,
And I will take it as a sweet disgrace,
And make thee rich for doing me such wrong.

MORTON.
You are too great to be by me gainsaid:
Your spirit is too true, your fears too certain.

NORTHUMBERLAND.
Yet, for all this, say not that Percy's dead.
I see a strange confession in thine eye:
Thou shakest thy head, and hold'st it fear or sin
To speak a truth. If he be slain, say so;

The tongue offends not that reports his death:
And he doth sin that doth belie the dead;
Not he which says the dead is not alive.
Yet the first bringer of unwelcome news
Hath but a losing office; and his tongue
Sounds ever after as a sullen bell,
Remember'd tolling a departing friend.

LORD BARDOLPH.
I cannot think, my lord, your son is dead.

MORTON.
I am sorry I should force you to believe
That which I would to God I had not seen;
But these mine eyes saw him in bloody state,
Rendering faint quittance, wearied and out-
breathed,
To Harry Monmouth; whose swift wrath beat
down
The never-daunted Percy to the earth,
From whence with life he never more sprung up.
In few, his death—whose spirit lent a fire
Even to the dullest peasant in his camp—
Being bruited once, took fire and heat away
From the best-temper'd courage in his troops;
For from his metal was his party steel'd;
Which once in him abated, all the rest
Turn'd on themselves, like dull and heavy lead:
And as the thing that's heavy in itself,
Upon enforcement flies with greatest speed,
So did our men, heavy in Hotspur's loss,
Lend to this weight such lightness with their fear,
That arrows fled not swifter toward their aim
Than did our soldiers, aiming at their safety,
Fly from the field. Then was that noble Wor-
cester
Too soon ta'en prisoner; and that furious Scot,
The bloody Douglas, whose well-labouring sword
Had three times slain th'appearance of the king,
Gan vail his stomach, and did grace the shame
Of those that turn'd their backs; and in his flight,
Stumbling in fear, was took. The sum of all
Is, that the king hath won; and hath sent out
A speedy power to encounter you, my lord,
Under the conduct of young Lancaster
And Westmoreland. This is the news at full.

NORTHUMBERLAND.
For this I shall have time enough to mourn.
In poison there is physic; and these news,
Having been well, that would have made me sick,
Being sick, have in some measure made me well:
And as the wretch, whose fever-weaken'd joints,
Like strengthless hinges, buckle under life,
Impatient of his fit, breaks like a fire
Out of his keeper's arms; even so my limbs,
Weaken'd with grief, being now enraged with
grief,
Are thrice themselves. Hence, therefore, thou
nice crutch!
A scaly gauntlet now, with joints of steel,
Must glove this hand: and hence, thou sickly
quoif!
Thou art a guard too wanton for the head
Which princes, flesht with conquest, aim to hit.
Now bind my brows with iron; and approach
The ragged'st hour that time and spite dare bring
To frown upon th'enraged Northumberland!
Let heaven kiss earth! now let not Nature's hand

Keep the wild flood confined! let order die!
And let this world no longer be a stage
To feed contention in a lingering act;
But let one spirit of the first-born Cain
Reign in all bosoms, that, each heart being set
On bloody courses, the rude scene may end,
And darkness be the burier of the dead!

TRAVERS.
This strained passion doth you wrong, my lord.

LORD BARDOLPH.
Sweet earl, divorce not wisdom from your honour.

MORTON.
The lives of all your loving complices
Lean on your health; the which, if you give o'er
To stormy passion, must perforce decay.
You cast th'event of war, my noble lord,
And summ'd the account of chance, before you
said,
'Let us make head.' It was your presurmise
That, in the dole of blows, your son might drop;
You knew he walkt o'er perils on an edge,
More likely to fall in than to get o'er;
You were advised his flesh was capable
Of wounds and scars, and that his forward spirit
Would lift him where most trade of danger
ranged:
Yet did you say, 'Go forth;' and none of this,
Though strongly apprehended, could restrain
The stiff-borne action: what hath, then, befaln,
Or what hath this bold enterprise brought forth,
More than that being which was like to be?

LORD BARDOLPH.
We all that are engaged to this loss
Knew that we ventured on such dangerous seas,
That if we wrought out life, 'twas ten to one;
And yet we ventured, for the gain proposed
Choked the respect of likely peril fear'd;
And since we are o'erset, venture again.
Come, we will all put forth, body and goods.

MORTON.
'Tis more than time: and, my most noble lord,
I hear for certain, and do speak the truth,
The gentle Archbishop of York is up
With well-appointed powers: he is a man
Who with a double surety binds his followers.
My lord your son had only but the corpse,
But shadows and the shows of men, to fight;
For that same word, rebellion, did divide
The action of their bodies from their souls;
And they did fight with queasiness, constrain'd,
As men drink potions; that their weapons only
Seem'd on our side, but, for their spirits and
souls,
This word, rebellion, it had froze them up,
As fish are in a pond. But now the bishop
Turns insurrection to religion:
Supposed sincere and holy in his thoughts,
He's follow'd both with body and with mind;
And doth enlarge his rising with the blood
Of fair King Richard, scraped from Pomfret
stones;
Derives from heaven his quarrel and his cause;
Tells them he doth bestride a bleeding land,
Gasping for life under great Bolingbroke;
And more and less do flock to follow him.

NORTHUMBERLAND.
I knew of this before; but, to speak truth,
This present grief had wiped it from my mind.
Go in with me; and counsel every man
The aptest way for safety and revenge:
Get posts and letters, and make friends with
     speed,—
Never so few, and never yet more need.   [Ex unt.

SCENE II.

London. A street.

Enter FALSTAFF, *with his* PAGE *bearing his
sword and buckler.*

FALSTAFF.
SIRRAH, you giant, what says the doctor to
my water?

PAGE.
He said, sir, the water itself was a good healthy
water; but, for the party that owed it, he might
have moe diseases than he knew for.

FALSTAFF.
Men of all sorts take a pride to gird at me: the
brain of this foolish-compounded clay, man, is
not able to invent any thing that tends to laughter,
more than I invent or is invented on me: I am not
only witty in myself, but the cause that wit is in
other men. I do here walk before thee like a sow
that hath overwhelm'd all her litter but one. If the
prince put thee into my service for any other
reason than to set me off, why then I have no
judgement. Thou whoreson mandrake, thou art
fitter to be worn in my cap than to wait at my
heels. I was never mann'd with an agate till now:
but I will inset you neither in gold nor silver, but
in vile apparel, and send you back again to your
master, for a jewel,— the juvenal, the prince your
master, whose chin is not yet fledged. I will sooner
have a beard grow in the palm of my hand than
he shall get one on his cheek; and yet he will not
stick to say his face is a face-royal: God may
finish it when he will, 'tis not a hair amiss yet: he
may keep it still at a face-royal, for a barber shall
never earn sixpence out of it; and yet he'll be
crowing as if he had writ man ever since his father
was a bachelor. He may keep his own grace, but
he's almost out of mine, I can assure him.—
What said Master Dombledon about the satin for
my short cloak and my slops?

PAGE.
He said, sir, you should procure him better assurance than Bardolph: he would not take his bond
and yours; he liked not the security.

FALSTAFF.
Let him be damn'd, like the glutton! pray God
his tongue be hotter!—A whoreson Achitophel! a
rascally yea-forsooth knave! to bear a gentleman
in hand, and then stand upon security!—The
whoreson smooth-pates do now wear nothing but
high shoes, and bunches of keys at their girdles;
and if a man is through with them in honest
taking-up, then they must stand upon security. I
had as lief they would put ratsbane in my mouth
as offer to stop it with security. I lookt a' should
have sent me two-and-twenty yards of satin, as I
am a true knight, and he sends me security. Well,

he may sleep in security; for he hath the horn of
abundance, and the lightness of his wife shines
through it: and yet cannot he see, though he
have his own lantern to light him.—Where's
Bardolph?

PAGE.
He's gone into Smithfield to buy your worship a
horse.

FALSTAFF.
I bought him in Paul's, and he'll buy me a horse
in Smithfield: an I could get me but a wife in
the stews, I were mann'd, horsed, and wived.

PAGE.
Sir, here comes the nobleman that committed the
prince for striking him about Bardolph.

FALSTAFF.
Wait close; I will not see him.

Enter the LORD CHIEF JUSTICE *and* SERVANT.

LORD CHIEF JUSTICE.
What's he that goes there?

SERVANT.
Falstaff, an't please your lordship.

LORD CHIEF JUSTICE.
He that was in question for the robbery?

SERVANT.
He, my lord: but he hath since done good service
at Shrewsbury; and, as I hear, is now going with
some charge to the Lord John of Lancaster.

LORD CHIEF JUSTICE.
What, to York? Call him back again.

SERVANT.
Sir John Falstaff!

FALSTAFF.
Boy, tell him I am deaf.

PAGE.
You must speak louder; my master is deaf.

LORD CHIEF JUSTICE.
I am sure he is, to the hearing of any thing good.
—Go, pluck him by the elbow; I must speak with
him.

SERVANT.
Sir John,—

FALSTAFF.
What! a young knave, and begging! Is there not
wars? is there not employment? doth not the king
lack subjects? do not the rebels need soldiers?
Though it be a shame to be on any side but one,
it is worse shame to beg than to be on the worst
side, were it worse than the name of rebellion can
can tell how to make it.

SERVANT.
You mistake me, sir.

FALSTAFF.
Why, sir, did I say you were an honest man? setting my knighthood and my soldiership aside, I
had lied in my throat, if I had said so.

SERVANT.
I pray you, sir, then set your knighthood and your
soldiership aside; and give me leave to tell you,
you lie in your throat, if you say I am any other
than an honest man.

FALSTAFF.
I give thee leave to tell me so! I lay aside that
which grows to me! If thou gett'st any leave of
me, hang me; if thou takest leave, thou wert better
be hang'd. You hunt-counter: hence! avaunt!

SERVANT.
Sir, my lord would speak with you.
LORD CHIEF JUSTICE.
Sir John Falstaff, a word with you.
FALSTAFF.
My good lord!—God give your lordship good time of day. I am glad to see your lordship abroad: I heard say your lordship was sick: I hope your lordship goes abroad by advice. Your lordship, though not clean past your youth, hath yet some smack of age in you, some relish of the saltness of time; and I most humbly beseech your lordship to have a reverend care of your health.
LORD CHIEF JUSTICE.
Sir John, I sent for you before your expedition to Shrewsbury.
FALSTAFF.
An't please your lordship, I hear his majesty is return'd with some discomfort from Wales.
LORD CHIEF JUSTICE.
I talk not of his majesty:—you would not come when I sent for you.
FALSTAFF.
And I hear, moreover, his highness is faln into this same whoreson apoplexy.
LORD CHIEF JUSTICE.
Well, God mend him!—I pray you, let me speak with you.
FALSTAFF.
This apoplexy is, as I take it, a kind of lethargy, an't please your lordship; a kind of sleeping in the blood, a whoreson tingling.
LORD CHIEF JUSTICE.
What tell you me of it? be it as it is.
FALSTAFF.
It hath its original from much grief, from study, and perturbation of the brain: I have read the cause of his effects in Galen: it is a kind of deafness.
LORD CHIEF JUSTICE.
I think you are faln into the disease; for you hear not what I say to you.
FALSTAFF.
Very well, my lord, very well: rather, an't please you, it is the disease of not listening, the malady of not marking, that I am troubled withal.
LORD CHIEF JUSTICE.
To punish you by the heels would amend the attention of your ears; and I care not if I do become your physician.
FALSTAFF.
I am as poor as Job, my lord, but not so patient: your lordship may minister the potion of imprisonment to me in respect of poverty; but how I should be your patient to follow your prescriptions, the wise may make some dram of a scruple, or, indeed, a scruple itself.
LORD CHIEF JUSTICE.
I sent for you, when there were matters against you for your life, to come speak with me.
FALSTAFF.
As I was then advised by my learned counsel in the laws of this land-service, I did not come.
LORD CHIEF JUSTICE.
Well, the truth is, Sir John, you live in great infamy.

FALSTAFF.
He that buckles him in my belt cannot live in less.
LORD CHIEF JUSTICE.
Your means are very slender, and your waste is great.
FALSTAFF.
I would it were otherwise; I would my means were greater, and my waist slenderer.
LORD CHIEF JUSTICE.
You have misled the youthful prince.
FALSTAFF.
The young prince hath misled me: I am the fellow with the great belly, and he my dog.
LORD CHIEF JUSTICE.
Well, I am loth to gall a new-heal'd wound: your day's service at Shrewsbury hath a little gilded over your night's exploit on Gadshill: you may thank the unquiet time for your quiet o'er-posting that action.
FALSTAFF.
My lord,—
LORD CHIEF JUSTICE.
But since all is well, keep it so: wake not a sleeping wolf.
FALSTAFF.
To wake a wolf is as bad as to smell a fox.
LORD CHIEF JUSTICE.
What! you are as a candle, the better part burnt out.
FALSTAFF.
A wassail candle, my lord; all tallow: if I did say of wax, my growth would approve the truth.
LORD CHIEF JUSTICE.
There is not a white hair on your face but should have his effect of gravity.
FALSTAFF.
His effect of gravy, gravy, gravy.
LORD CHIEF JUSTICE.
You follow the young prince up and down, like his ill angel.
FALSTAFF.
Not so, my lord; your ill angel is light; but I hope he that looks upon me will take me without weighing: and yet, in some respects, I grant, I cannot go:—I cannot tell. Virtue is of so little regard in these costermonger times, that true valour is turn'd bear-herd: pregnancy is made a tapster, and hath his quick wit wasted in giving reckonings: all the other gifts appertinent to man, as the malice of this age shapes them, are not worth a gooseberry. You that are old consider not the capacities of us that are young; you measure the heat of our livers with the bitterness of your galls: and we that are in the vaward of our youth, I must confess, are wags too.
LORD CHIEF JUSTICE.
Do you set down your name in the scroll of youth, that are written down old with all the characters of age? Have you not a moist eye? a dry hand? a yellow cheek? a white beard? a decreasing leg? an increasing belly? is not your voice broken? your wind short? your chin double? your wit single? and every part about you blasted with antiquity? and will you yet call yourself young? Fie, fie, fie, Sir John!

FALSTAFF.

My lord, I was born about three of the clock in the afternoon, with a white head and something a round belly. For my voice,—I have lost it with hallooing, and singing of anthems. To approve my youth further, I will not: the truth is, I am only old in judgement and understanding; and he that will caper with me for a thousand marks, let him lend me the money, and have at him. For the box of th'ear that the prince gave you,—he gave it like a rude prince, and you took it like a sensible lord. I have checkt him for it; and the young lion repents,—marry, not in ashes and sackcloth, but in new silk and old sack.

LORD CHIEF JUSTICE.

Well, God send the prince a better companion!

FALSTAFF.

God send the companion a better prince! I cannot rid my hands of him.

LORD CHIEF JUSTICE.

Well, the king hath sever'd you and Prince Harry: I hear you are going with Lord John of Lancaster against the Archbishop and the Earl of Northumberland.

FALSTAFF.

Yea; I thank your pretty sweet wit for it. But look you pray, all you that kiss my lady Peace at home, that our armies join not in a hot day; for, by the Lord, I take but two shirts out with me, and I mean not to sweat extraordinarily: if it be a hot day, an I brandish any thing but a bottle, I would I might never spit white again. There is not a dangerous action can peep out his head, but I am thrust upon it: well, I cannot last ever: but it was alway yet the trick of our English nation, if they have a good thing, to make it too common. If ye will needs say I am an old man, you should give me rest. I would to God, my name were not so terrible to the enemy as it is: I were better to be eaten to death with a rust than to be scour'd to nothing with perpetual motion.

LORD CHIEF JUSTICE.

Well, be honest, be honest; and God bless your expedition!

FALSTAFF.

Will your lordship lend me a thousand pound to furnish me forth?

LORD CHIEF JUSTICE.

Not a penny, not a penny; you are too impatient to bear crosses. Fare you well: commend me to my cousin Westmoreland.

[Exeunt CHIEF JUSTICE and SERVANT.

FALSTAFF.

If I do, fillip me with a three-man beetle.—A man can no more separate age and covetousness than a' can part young limbs and lechery: but the gout galls the one, and the pox pinches the other; and so both the degrees prevent my curses.—Boy!

PAGE.

Sir?

FALSTAFF.

What money is in my purse?

PAGE.

Seven groats and two pence.

FALSTAFF.

I can get no remedy against this consumption of the purse: borrowing only lingers and lingers it out, but the disease is incurable.—Go bear this letter to my Lord of Lancaster; this to the prince; this to the Earl of Westmoreland; and this to old Mistress Ursula, whom I have weekly sworn to marry since I perceived the first white hair on my chin. About it: you know where to find me. [Exit PAGE.] A pox of this gout! or, a gout of this pox! for the one or the other plays the rogue with my great toe. 'Tis no matter if I do halt; I have the wars for my colour, and my pension shall seem the more reasonable. A good wit will make use of any thing: I will turn diseases to commodity.

[Exit.

SCENE III.

York. The ARCHBISHOP'S palace.

Enter the ARCHBISHOP, HASTINGS, MOWBRAY, and LORD BARDOLPH.

ARCHBISHOP OF YORK.

THUS have you heard our cause and know our means;
And, my most noble friends, I pray you all
Speak plainly your opinions of our hopes:—
And first, lord marshal, what say you to it?

MOWBRAY.

I well allow the occasion of our arms;
But gladly would be better satisfied
How, in our means, we should advance ourselves
To look with forehead bold and big enough
Upon the power and puissance of the king.

HASTINGS.

Our present musters grow upon the file
To five-and-twenty thousand men of choice;
And our supplies live largely in the hope
Of great Northumberland, whose bosom burns
With an incensed fire of injuries.

LORD BARDOLPH.

The question, then, Lord Hastings, standeth thus;—
Whether our present five-and-twenty thousand
May hold up head without Northumberland?

HASTINGS.

With him, we may.

LORD BARDOLPH.

Yea, marry, there's the point:
But if without him we be thought too feeble,
My judgement is, we should not step too far
Till we had his assistance by the hand;
For, in a theme so bloody-faced as this,
Conjecture, expectation, and surmise
Of aids incertain should not be admitted.

ARCHBISHOP OF YORK.

'Tis very true, Lord Bardolph; for, indeed,
It was young Hotspur's case at Shrewsbury.

LORD BARDOLPH.

It was, my lord; who lined himself with hope,
Eating the air on promise of supply,
Flattering himself with project of a power
Much smaller than the smallest of his thoughts:
And so, with great imagination,
Proper to madmen, led his powers to death,
And, winking, leapt into destruction.

HASTINGS.

But, by your leave, it never yet did hurt
To lay down likelihoods and forms of hope.

LORD BARDOLPH.
Yes, if this present quality of war;—
Indeed, the instant action—a cause on foot—
Lives so in hope, as in an early spring
We see th'appearing buds; which to prove fruit,
Hope gives not so much warrant, as despair
That frosts will bite them. When we mean to
    build,
We first survey the plot, then draw the model;
And when we see the figure of the house,
Then must we rate the cost of the erection;
Which if we find outweighs ability,
What do we then but draw anew the model
In fewer offices, or at last desist
To build at all? Much more, in this great work—
Which is almost to pluck a kingdom down,
And set another up—should we survey
The plot of situation and the model,
Consent upon a sure foundation,
Question surveyors, know our own estate,
How able such a work to undergo,
To weigh against his opposite; or else
We fortify in paper and in figures,
Using the names of men instead of men:
Like one that draws the model of a house
Beyond his power to build it; who, half through,
Gives o'er, and leaves his part-created cost
A naked subject to the weeping clouds,
And waste for churlish winter's tyranny.
            HASTINGS.
Grant that our hopes—yet likely of fair birth—
Should be still-born, and that we now possest
The utmost man of expectation;
I think we are a body strong enough,
Even as we are, to equal with the king.
            LORD BARDOLPH.
What, is the king but five-and-twenty thousand?
            HASTINGS.
To us no more; nay, not so much, Lord Bardolph.
For his divisions, as the times do brawl,
Are in three heads: one power against the French,
And one against Glendower; perforce a third
Must take up us: so is the unfirm king
In three divided; and his coffers sound
With hollow poverty and emptiness.
            ARCHBISHOP OF YORK.
That he should draw his several strengths to-
    gether,
And come against us in full puissance,
Need not be dreaded.
            HASTINGS.
            If he should do so,
He leaves his back unarm'd, the French and Welsh
Baying him at the heels: never fear that.
            LORD BARDOLPH.
Who is it like should lead his forces hither?
            HASTINGS.
The Duke of Lancaster and Westmoreland;
Against the Welsh, himself and Harry Mon-
    mouth:
But who is substituted 'gainst the French,
I have no certain notice.
            ARCHBISHOP OF YORK.
            Let us on,
And publish the occasion of our arms.
The commonwealth is sick of their own choice;

Their over-greedy love hath surfeited:
An habitation giddy and unsure
Hath he that buildeth on the vulgar heart.
O thou fond many! with what loud applause
Didst thou beat heaven with blessing Boling-
    broke,
Before he was what thou wouldst have him be!
And being now trimm'd in thine own desires,
Thou, beastly feeder, art so full of him,
That thou provokest thyself to cast him up.
So, so, thou common dog, didst thou disgorge
Thy glutton bosom of the royal Richard;
And now thou wouldst eat thy dead vomit up,
And howl'st to find it. What trust is in these
    times?
They that, when Richard lived, would have him
    die,
Are now become enamour'd on his grave:
Thou, that threw'st dust upon his goodly head
When through proud London he came sighing on
After th'admired heels of Bolingbroke,
Cry'st now, 'O earth, yield us that king again,
And take thou this!' O thoughts of men accurst!
Past, and to come, seems best; things present,
    worst.
            MOWBRAY.
Shall we go draw our numbers, and set on?
            HASTINGS.
We are time's subjects, and time bids be gone.
                        [Exeunt.

ACT II. SCENE I.

London. A street.

Enter HOSTESS, FANG *and his* BOY *with her,*
and SNARE *following.*

            HOSTESS.
MASTER Fang, have you enter'd the exion?
            FANG.
It is enter'd.
            HOSTESS.
Where's your yeoman? Is't a lusty yeoman? will
a' stand to't?
            FANG.
Sirrah, where's Snare?
            HOSTESS.
O Lord, ay! good Master Snare.
            SNARE.
Here, here.
            FANG.
Snare, we must arrest Sir John Falstaff.
            HOSTESS.
Yes, good Master Snare; I have enter'd him and
all.
            SNARE.
It may chance cost some of us our lives, for he
will stab.
            HOSTESS.
Alas the day! take heed of him; he stabb'd me in
mine own house, and that most beastly: in good
faith, a' cares not what mischief he doth, if his
weapon be out: he will foin like any devil; he will
spare neither man, woman, nor child.
            FANG.
If I can close with him, I care not for his thrust.
            HOSTESS.
No, nor I neither: I'll be at your elbow.

FANG.

An I but fist him once; an a' come but within my vice,—

HOSTESS.

I am undone by his going; I warrant you, he's an infinitive thing upon my score:—good Master Fang, hold him sure;—good Master Snare, let him not scape. A' comes continuantly to Piecorner—saving your manhoods—to buy a saddle; and he is indited to dinner to the Lubber's-head in Lumbert-street, to Master Smooth's the silkman: I pray ye, since my exion is enter'd, and my case so openly known to the world, let him be brought in to his answer. A hundred mark is a long one for a poor lone woman to bear: and I have borne, and borne, and borne; and have been fubb'd off, and fubb'd off, and fubb'd off, from this day to that day, that it is a shame to be thought on. There is no honesty in such dealing; unless a woman should be made an ass and a beast, to bear every knave's wrong.—Yonder he comes; and that arrant malmsey-nose knave Bardolph with him. Do your offices, do your offices, Master Fang and Master Snare; do me, do me, do me your offices.

Enter FALSTAFF, PAGE, *and* BARDOLPH.

FALSTAFF.

How now! whose mare's dead? what's the matter?

FANG.

Sir John, I arrest you at the suit of Mistress Quickly.

FALSTAFF.

Away, varlets!—Draw, Bardolph: cut me off the villain's head; throw the quean in the channel.

HOSTESS.

Throw me in the channel! I'll throw thee in the channel. Wilt thou? wilt thou? thou bastardly rogue!—Murder, murder! Ah, thou honey-suckle villain! wilt thou kill God's officers and the king's? Ah, thou honey-seed rogue! thou art a honeyseed, a man-queller, and a woman-queller.

FALSTAFF.

Keep them off, Bardolph.

FANG.

A rescue! a rescue!

HOSTESS.

Good people, bring a rescue or two.—Thou wo't, wo't thou? thou wo't, wo't ta? do, do, thou rogue! do, thou hemp-seed!

FALSTAFF.

Away, you scullion! you rampallian! you fustilarian! I'll tickle your catastrophe.

Enter the LORD CHIEF JUSTICE, *and his men.*

LORD CHIEF JUSTICE.

What is the matter? keep the peace here, ho!

HOSTESS.

Good my lord, be good to me! I beseech you, stand to me!

LORD CHIEF JUSTICE.

How now, Sir John! what are you brawling here? Doth this become your place, your time, and business? You should have been well on your way to York.— Stand from him, fellow: wherefore hang'st upon him?

HOSTESS.

O my most worshipful lord, an't please your Grace, I am a poor widow of Eastcheap, and he is arrested at my suit.

LORD CHIEF JUSTICE.

For what sum?

HOSTESS.

It is more than for some, my lord; it is for all,— all I have. He hath eaten me out of house and home; he hath put all my substance into that fat belly of his:—but I will have some of it out again, or I will ride thee o' nights like the mare.

FALSTAFF.

I think I am as like to ride the mare, if I have any vantage of ground to get up.

LORD CHIEF JUSTICE.

How comes this, Sir John? Fie! what man of good temper would endure this tempest of exclamation? Are you not ashamed to enforce a poor widow to so rough a course to come by her own?

FALSTAFF.

What is the gross sum that I owe thee?

HOSTESS.

Marry, if thou wert an honest man, thyself and the money too. Thou didst swear to me upon a parcel-gilt goblet, sitting in my Dolphin-chamber, at the round table, by a sea-coal fire, upon Wednesday in Wheeson-week, when the prince broke thy head for liking his father to a singingman of Windsor,—thou didst swear to me then, as I was washing thy wound, to marry me, and make me my lady thy wife. Canst thou deny it? Did not goodwife Keech, the butcher's wife, come in then, and call me gossip Quickly? coming in to borrow a mess of vinegar; telling us she had a good dish of prawns; whereby thou didst desire to eat some; whereby I told thee they were ill for a green wound? And didst thou not, when she was gone down stairs, desire me to be no more so familiar with such poor people; saying that ere long they should call me madam? And didst thou not kiss me, and bid me fetch thee thirty shillings? I put thee now to thy book-oath: deny it, if thou canst.

FALSTAFF.

My lord, this is a poor mad soul; and she says, up and down the town, that her eldest son is like you: she hath been in good case, and the truth is, poverty hath distracted her. But for these foolish officers, I beseech you I may have redress against them.

LORD CHIEF JUSTICE.

Sir John, Sir John, I am well acquainted with your manner of wrenching the true cause the false way. It is not a confident brow, nor the throng of words that come with such more than impudent sauciness from you, can thrust me from a level consideration: you have, as it appears to me, practised upon the easy-yielding spirit of this woman, and made her serve your uses both in purse and in person.

HOSTESS.

Yea, in truth, my lord.

LORD CHIEF JUSTICE.

Pray thee, peace.—Pay her the debt you owe her, and unpay the villany you have done her: the one you may do with sterling money, and the other with current repentance.

FALSTAFF.
My lord, I will not undergo this sneap without reply. You call honourable boldness impudent sauciness: if a man will make court'sy, and say nothing, he is virtuous:—no, my lord, my humble duty remember'd, I will not be your suitor. I say to you, I do desire deliverance from these officers, being upon hasty employment in the king's affairs.

LORD CHIEF JUSTICE.
You speak as having power to do wrong: but answer in the effect of your reputation, and satisfy the poor woman.

FALSTAFF.
Come hither, hostess.   [Takes her aside.
Enter GOWER.

LORD CHIEF JUSTICE.
Now, Master Gower, what news?

GOWER.
The king, my lord, and Harry Prince of Wales
Are near at hand: the rest the paper tells.
                              [Gives a letter.

FALSTAFF.
As I am a gentleman,—

HOSTESS.
Faith, you said so before.

FALSTAFF.
As I am a gentleman:—come, no more words of it.

HOSTESS.
By this heavenly ground I tread on, I must be fain to pawn both my plate and the tapestry of my dining-chambers.

FALSTAFF.
Glasses, glasses, is the only drinking: and for thy walls,—a pretty slight drollery, or the story of the Prodigal, or the German Hunting in water-work, is worth a thousand of these bed-hangings and these fly-bitten tapestries. Let it be ten pound, if thou canst. Come, an 'twere not for thy humours, there's not a better wench in England. Go, wash thy face, and draw the action. Come, thou must not be in this humour with me; dost not know me? come, come, I know thou wast set on to this.

HOSTESS.
Pray thee, Sir John, let it be but twenty nobles: i' faith, I am loth to pawn my plate, so God save me, la.

FALSTAFF.
Let it alone; I'll make other shift: you'll be a fool still.

HOSTESS.
Well, you shall have it, though I pawn my gown. I hope you'll come to supper. You'll pay me all together?

FALSTAFF.
Will I live?—[To BARDOLPH] Go, with her, with her; hook on, hook on.

HOSTESS.
Will you have Doll Tearsheet meet you at supper?

FALSTAFF.
No more words; let's have her.
        [Exeunt HOSTESS, BARDOLPH, OFFICERS,
        and BOY.

LORD CHIEF JUSTICE.
I have heard better news.

FALSTAFF.
What's the news, my lord?

LORD CHIEF JUSTICE.
Where lay the king last night?

GOWER.
At Basingstoke, my lord.

FALSTAFF.
I hope, my lord, all's well: what is the news, my lord?

LORD CHIEF JUSTICE.
Come all his forces back?

GOWER.
No; fifteen hundred foot, five hundred horse,
Are marcht up to my Lord of Lancaster,
Against Northumberland and the Archbishop.

FALSTAFF.
Comes the king back from Wales, my noble lord?

LORD CHIEF JUSTICE.
You shall have letters of me presently:
Come, go along with me, good Master Gower.

FALSTAFF.
My lord!

LORD CHIEF JUSTICE.
What's the matter?

FALSTAFF.
Master Gower, shall I entreat you with me to dinner?

GOWER.
I must wait upon my good lord here,—I thank you, good Sir John.

LORD CHIEF JUSTICE.
Sir John, you loiter here too long, being you are to take soldiers up in counties as you go.

FALSTAFF.
Will you sup with me, Master Gower?

LORD CHIEF JUSTICE.
What foolish master taught you these manners, Sir John?

FALSTAFF.
Master Gower, if they become me not, he was a fool that taught them me.—This is the right fencing grace, my lord; tap for tap, and so part fair.

LORD CHIEF JUSTICE.
Now, the Lord lighten thee! thou art a great fool.
                              [Exeunt.

SCENE II.
London.   Another Street.

Enter PRINCE HENRY and POINTZ.

PRINCE HENRY.
BEFORE God, I am exceeding weary.

POINTZ.
Is't come to that? I had thought weariness durst not have attach'd one of so high blood.

PRINCE HENRY.
Faith, it does me; though it discolours the complexion of my greatness to acknowledge it. Doth it not show vilely in me to desire small beer?

POINTZ.
Why, a prince should not be so loosely studied as to remember so weak a composition.

PRINCE HENRY.
Belike, then, my appetite was not princely got; for, by my troth, I do now remember the poor

creature, small beer. But, indeed, these humble considerations make me out of love with my greatness. What a disgrace is it to me to remember thy name! or to know thy face to-morrow! or to take note how many pair of silk stockings thou hast, viz. these, and those that were thy peach-colour'd ones! or to bear the inventory of thy shirts, as, one for superfluity, and one other for use!—but that the tennis-court-keeper knows better than I; for it is a low ebb of linen with thee when thou keepest not racket there; as thou hast not done a great while, because the rest of thy low-countries have made a shift to eat up thy holland: and God knows whether those that bawl out of the ruins of thy linen shall inherit his kingdom: but the midwives say the children are not in the fault; whereupon the world increases, and kindreds are mightily strengthen'd.

POINTZ.
How ill it follows, after you have labour'd so hard, you should talk so idly! Tell me, how many good young princes would do so, their fathers being so sick as yours at this time is?

PRINCE HENRY.
Shall I tell thee one thing, Pointz?

POINTZ.
Yes, faith; and let it be an excellent good thing.

PRINCE HENRY.
It shall serve among wits of no higher breeding than thine.

POINTZ.
Go to; I stand the push of your one thing that you will tell.

PRINCE HENRY.
Marry, I tell thee,—it is not meet that I should be sad, now my father is sick: albeit I could tell to thee,—as to one it pleases me, for fault of a better, to call my friend,—I could be sad, and sad indeed too.

POINTZ.
Very hardly upon such a subject.

PRINCE HENRY.
By this hand, thou think'st me as far in the devil's book as thou and Falstaff for obduracy and persistency: let the end try the man. But I tell thee, my heart bleeds inwardly that my father is so sick: and keeping such vile company as thou art hath in reason taken from me all ostentation of sorrow.

The reason?
POINTZ.

PRINCE HENRY.
What wouldst thou think of me, if I should weep?

POINTZ.
I would think thee a most princely hypocrite.

PRINCE HENRY.
It would be every man's thought; and thou art a blessed fellow to think as every man thinks: never a man's thought in the world keeps the road-way better than thine: every man would think me an hypocrite indeed. And what accites your most worshipful thought to think so?

POINTZ.
Why, because you have been so lewd, and so much engraft to Falstaff.

PRINCE HENRY.
And to thee.

POINTZ.
By this light, I am well spoke on; I can hear it with mine own ears: the worst that they can say of me is, that I am a second brother, and that I am a proper fellow of my hands; and those two things, I confess, I cannot help.—By the mass, here comes Bardolph.

PRINCE HENRY.
And the boy that I gave Falstaff: a' had him from me Christian; and look, if the fat villain have not transform'd him ape.

Enter BARDOLPH *and* PAGE.

BARDOLPH.
God save your Grace!

PRINCE HENRY.
And yours, most noble Bardolph!

BARDOLPH [*to the* PAGE].
Come, you virtuous ass, you bashful fool, must you be blushing? wherefore blush you now? What a maidenly man-at-arms are you become! Is't such a matter to get a pottle-pot's maidenhead?

PAGE.
A' calls me e'en now, my lord, through a red lattice, and I could discern no part of his face from the window: at last I spied his eyes; and methought he had made two holes in the alewife's new petticoat, and so peept through.

PRINCE HENRY.
Hath not the boy profited?

BARDOLPH.
Away, you whoreson upright rabbit, away!

PAGE.
Away, you rascally Althæa's dream, away!

PRINCE HENRY.
Instruct us, boy; what dream, boy?

PAGE.
Marry, my lord, Althæa dream'd she was deliver'd of a firebrand; and therefore I call him her dream.

PRINCE HENRY.
A crown's worth of good interpretation:—there 'tis, boy.   [*Gives money.*

POINTZ.
O, that this good blossom could be kept from cankers!—Well, there is sixpence to preserve thee.   [*Gives money.*

BARDOLPH.
An you do not make him hang'd among you, the gallows shall have wrong.

PRINCE HENRY.
And how doth thy master, Bardolph?

BARDOLPH.
Well, my lord. He heard of your Grace's coming to town; there's a letter for you.   [*Gives a letter.*

POINTZ.
Deliver'd with good respect.—And how doth the martlemas, your master?

BARDOLPH.
In bodily health, sir.

POINTZ.
Marry, the immortal part needs a physician; but that moves not him: though that be sick, it dies not.

PRINCE HENRY.
I do allow this wen to be as familiar with me as my dog: and he holds his place; for look you how he writes.

POINTZ [*reads*].

'John Falstaff, knight,'—every man must know that, as oft as he has occasion to name himself: even like those that are kin to the king; for they never prick their finger but they say, 'There's some of the king's blood spilt.' 'How comes that?' says he, that takes upon him not to conceive. The answer is as ready as a borrower's cap, 'I am the king's poor cousin, sir.'

PRINCE HENRY.

Nay, they will be kin to us, or they will fetch it from Japhet. But to the letter:—

POINTZ [*reads*].

'Sir John Falstaff, knight, to the son of the king, nearest his father, Harry Prince of Wales, greeting.'—Why, this is a certificate.

PRINCE HENRY.

Peace!

POINTZ [*reads*].

'I will imitate the honourable Roman in brevity:' —sure he means brevity in breath, short-winded. —'I commend me to thee, I commend thee, and I leave thee. Be not too familiar with Pointz; for he misuses thy favours so much, that he swears thou art to marry his sister Nell. Repent at idle times as thou may'st; and so, farewell.

'Thine, by yea and no (which is as much as to say, as thou usest him), JACK FALSTAFF with my familiars, JOHN with my brothers and sisters, and SIR JOHN with all Europe.'

My lord, I'll steep this letter in sack, and make him eat it.

PRINCE HENRY.

That's to make him eat twenty of his words. But do you use me thus, Ned? must I marry your sister?

POINTZ.

God send the wench no worse fortune! but I never said so.

PRINCE HENRY.

Well, thus we play the fools with the time; and the spirits of the wise sit in the clouds and mock us.—Is your master here in London?

BARDOLPH.

Yes, my lord.

PRINCE HENRY.

Where sups he? doth the old boar feed in the old frank?

BARDOLPH.

At the old place, my lord,—in Eastcheap.

PRINCE HENRY.

What company?

PAGE.

Ephesians, my lord,—of the old church.

PRINCE HENRY.

Sup any women with him?

PAGE.

None, my lord, but old Mistress Quickly and Mistress Doll Tearsheet.

PRINCE HENRY.

What pagan may that be?

PAGE.

A proper gentlewoman, sir, and a kinswoman of my master's.

PRINCE HENRY.

Even such kin as the parish heifers are to the town bull.—Shall we steal upon them, Ned, at supper?

POINTZ.

I am your shadow, my lord; I'll follow you.

PRINCE HENRY.

Sirrah, you boy,—and Bardolph,—no word to your master that I am yet come to town: there's for your silence.   [*Gives money*.

BARDOLPH.

I have no tongue, sir.

PAGE.

And for mine, sir,—I will govern it.

PRINCE HENRY.

Fare you well; go. [*Exeunt* BARDOLPH *and* PAGE.]—This Doll Tearsheet should be some road.

POINTZ.

I warrant you, as common as the way between Saint Alban's and London.

PRINCE HENRY.

How might we see Falstaff bestow himself tonight in his true colours, and not ourselves be seen?

POINTZ.

Put on two leathern jerkins and aprons, and wait upon him at his table as drawers.

PRINCE HENRY.

From a god to a bull? a heavy descension! it was Jove's case. From a prince to a prentice? a low transformation! that shall be mine; for in every thing the purpose must weigh with the folly. Follow me, Ned.   [*Exeunt*.

SCENE III.

Warkworth.   Before the castle.

Enter NORTHUMBERLAND, LADY NORTHUMBERLAND, *and* LADY PERCY.

NORTHUMBERLAND.

I PRAY thee, loving wife, and gentle daughter,
Give even way unto my rough affairs:
Put not you on the visage of the times,
And be, like them, to Percy troublesome.

LADY NORTHUMBERLAND.

I have given over, I will speak no more:
Do what you will; your wisdom be your guide.

NORTHUMBERLAND.

Alas, sweet wife, my honour is at pawn;
And, but my going, nothing can redeem it.

LADY PERCY.

O, yet, for God's sake, go not to these wars!
The time was, father, that you broke your word,
When you were more endear'd to it than now;
When your own Percy, when my heart's dear Harry,
Threw many a northward look to see his father
Bring up his powers; but he did long in vain.
Who then persuaded you to stay at home?
There were two honours lost,—yours and your son's.
For yours,—the God of heaven brighten it!
For his,—it stuck upon him, as the sun
In the gray vault of heaven; and by his light
Did all the chivalry of England move
To do brave acts: he was, indeed, the glass
Wherein the noble youth did dress themselves:

He had no legs that practised not his gait;
And speaking thick, which nature made his
    blemish,
Became the accents of the valiant;
For those that could speak low and tardily
Would turn their own perfection to abuse,
To seem like him: so that in speech, in gait,
In diet, in affections of delight,
In military rules, humours of blood,
He was the mark and glass, copy and book,
That fashion'd others. And him,—O wondrous
    him!
O miracle of men!—him did you leave—
Second to none, unseconded by you—
To look upon the hideous god of war
In disadvantage; to abide a field
Where nothing but the sound of Hotspur's name
Did seem defensible:—so you left him.
Never, O never, do his ghost the wrong
To hold your honour more precise and nice
With others than with him! let them alone:
The marshal and the archbishop are strong;
Had my sweet Harry had but half their numbers,
To-day might I, hanging on Hotspur's neck,
Have talkt of Monmouth's grave.

NORTHUMBERLAND.
               . Beshrew your heart,
Fair daughter, you do draw my spirits from me
With new lamenting ancient oversights.
But I must go, and meet with danger there;
Or it will seek me in another place,
And find me worse provided.

LADY NORTHUMBERLAND.
                  O, fly to Scotland,
Till that the nobles and the armed commons
Have of their puissance made a little taste.

LADY PERCY.
If they get ground and vantage of the king,
Then join you with them, like a rib of steel,
To make strength stronger; but, for all our loves,
First let them try themselves. So did your son;
He was so suffer'd: so came I a widow;
And never shall have length of life enough
To rain upon remembrance with mine eyes,
That it may grow and sprout as high as heaven,
For recordation to my noble husband.

NORTHUMBERLAND.
Come, come, go in with me. 'Tis with my mind
As with the tide swell'd up unto his height,
That makes a still-stand, running neither way:
Fain would I go to meet the archbishop,
But many thousand reasons hold me back.
I will resolve for Scotland: there am I,
Till time and vantage crave my company.
                           [Exeunt.

SCENE IV.

London.   The Boar's-Head Tavern in Eastcheap.

Enter two DRAWERS.

FIRST DRAWER.
WHAT the devil hast thou brought there?
apple-johns? thou know'st Sir John cannot
endure an apple-john.

SECOND DRAWER.
Mass, thou say'st true. The prince once set a dish
of apple-johns before him, and told him there
were five more Sir Johns; and, putting off his hat,
said, 'I will now take my leave of these six dry,
round, old, wither'd knights.' It anger'd him to
the heart: but he hath forgot that.

FIRST DRAWER.
Why, then, cover, and set them down: and see if
thou canst find out Sneak's noise; Mistress Tearsheet would fain hear some music. Dispatch:—
the room where they supt is too hot; they'll come
in straight.

SECOND DRAWER.
Sirrah, here will be the prince and Master Pointz
anon; and they will put on two of our jerkins and
aprons; and Sir John must not know of it: Bardolph hath brought word.

FIRST DRAWER.
By the mass, here will be old utis: it will be an
excellent stratagem.

SECOND DRAWER.
I'll see if I can find out Sneak.   [Exit.
    Enter HOSTESS *and* DOLL TEARSHEET.

HOSTESS.
I'faith, sweetheart, methinks now you are in an
excellent good temperality: your pulsidge beats
as extraordinarily as heart would desire; and your
colour, I warrant you, is as red as any rose, in
good truth, la: but, i'faith, you have drunk too
much canaries; and that's a marvellous searching
wine, and it perfumes the blood ere one can say
'What's this?'—How do you now?

DOLL TEARSHEET.
Better than I was:—hem.

HOSTESS.
Why, that's well said; a good heart's worth gold.
—Lo, here comes Sir John.
              Enter FALSTAFF.

FALSTAFF [*singing*].
'When Arthur first in court'—Empty the jordan.
[*Exit* FIRST DRAWER.]—[*singing*] 'And was a
worthy king.'—How now, Mistress Doll!

HOSTESS.
Sick of a calm; yea, good faith.

FALSTAFF.
So is all her sect; an they be once in a calm, they
are sick.

DOLL TEARSHEET.
You muddy rascal, is that all the comfort you give
me?

FALSTAFF.
You make fat rascals, Mistress Doll.

DOLL TEARSHEET.
I make them! gluttony and diseases make them; I
make them not.

FALSTAFF.
If the cook help to make the gluttony, you help to
make the diseases, Doll; we catch of you, Doll,
we catch of you; grant that, my poor virtue, grant
that.

DOLL TEARSHEET.
Yea, joy,—our chains and our jewels.

FALSTAFF.
'Your brooches, pearls, and ouches:'—for to
serve bravely is to come halting off, you know:
to come off the breach with his pike bent bravely, and
to surgery bravely; to venture upon the charged
chambers bravely,—

DOLL TEARSHEET.

Hang yourself, you muddy conger, hang yourself!

HOSTESS.

By my troth, this is the old fashion; you two never meet but you fall to some discord: you are both, i' good truth, as rheumatic as two dry toasts; you cannot one bear with another's confirmities. What the good-year! one must bear, and that must be you [to DOLL TEARSHEET]: you are the weaker vessel, as they say, the emptier vessel.

DOLL TEARSHEET.

Can a weak empty vessel bear such a huge full hogshead? there's a whole merchant's venture of Bourdeaux stuff in him; you have not seen a hulk better stuft in the hold.—Come, I'll be friends with thee, Jack: thou art going to the wars; and whether I shall ever see thee again or no, there is nobody cares.

Enter FIRST DRAWER.

FIRST DRAWER.

Sir, Ancient Pistol's below, and would speak with you.

DOLL TEARSHEET.

Hang him, swaggering rascal! let him not come hither: it is the foul-mouth'dst rogue in England.

HOSTESS.

If he swagger, let him not come here: no, by my faith; I must live among my neighbours; I'll no swaggerers: I am in good name and fame with the very best:—shut the door;—there comes no swaggerers here: I have not lived all this while, to have swaggering now:—shut the door, I pray you.

FALSTAFF.

Dost thou hear, hostess?—

HOSTESS.

Pray ye, pacify yourself, Sir John: there comes no swaggerers here.

FALSTAFF.

Dost thou hear? it is mine ancient.

HOSTESS.

Tilly-fally, Sir John, ne'er tell me: your ancient swaggerer comes not in my doors. I was before Master Tisick, the deputy, t'other day; and, as he said to me, 'twas no longer ago than Wednesday last, 'I' good faith, neighbour Quickly,' says he;—Master Dumbe, our minister, was by then;—'neighbour Quickly,' says he, 'receive those that are civil; for,' saith he, 'you are in an ill name:'—now a' said so, I can tell whereupon; 'for,' says he, 'you are an honest woman, and well thought on; therefore take heed what guests you receive: receive,' says he, 'no swaggering companions.' There comes none here: you would bless you to hear what he said: no, I'll no swaggerers.

FALSTAFF.

He's no swaggerer, hostess; a tame cheater, i' faith; you may stroke him as gently as a puppy greyhound; he'll not swagger with a Barbary hen, if her feathers turn back in any show of resistance. —Call him up, drawer.   [*Exit* FIRST DRAWER.

HOSTESS.

Cheater, call you him? I will bar no honest man my house, nor no cheater: but I do not love swaggering; by my troth, I am the worse when one says 'swagger': feel, masters, how I shake; look you, I warrant you.

DOLL TEARSHEET.

So you do, hostess.

HOSTESS.

Do I? yea, in very truth, do I, an 'twere an aspen-leaf: I cannot abide swaggerers.

Enter PISTOL, BARDOLPH, *and* PAGE.

PISTOL.

God save you, Sir John!

FALSTAFF.

Welcome, Ancient Pistol. Here, Pistol, I charge you with a cup of sack: do you discharge upon mine hostess.

PISTOL.

I will discharge upon her, Sir John, with two bullets.

FALSTAFF.

She is pistol-proof, sir; you shall hardly offend her.

HOSTESS.

Come, I'll drink no proofs nor no bullets: I'll drink no more than will do me good, for no man's pleasure, I.

PISTOL.

Then to you, Mistress Dorothy; I will charge you.

DOLL TEARSHEET.

Charge me! I scorn you, scurvy companion. What! you poor, base, rascally, cheating, lacklinen mate! Away, you mouldy rogue, away! I am meat for your master.

PISTOL.

I know you, Mistress Dorothy.

DOLL TEARSHEET.

Away, you cut-purse rascal! you filthy bung, away! by this wine, I'll thrust my knife in your mouldy chaps, an you play the saucy cuttle with me. Away, you bottle-ale rascal! you basket-hilt stale juggler, you!—Since when, I pray you, sir? —God's light, with two points on your shoulder? much!

PISTOL.

God let me not live, but I will murder your ruff for this.

FALSTAFF.

No more, Pistol; I would not have you go off here, discharge yourself of our company, Pistol.

HOSTESS.

No, good Captain Pistol; not here, sweet captain.

DOLL TEARSHEET.

Captain! thou abominable damn'd cheater, art thou not ashamed to be call'd captain? An captains were of my mind, they would truncheon you out, for taking their names upon you before you have earn'd them. You a captain! you slave, for what? for tearing a poor whore's ruff in a bawdy-house!—He a captain! hang him, rogue! he lives upon mouldy stew'd prunes and dried cakes. A captain! God's light, these villains will make the word as odious as the word 'occupy;' which was an excellent good word before it was ill sorted: therefore captains had need look to't.

BARDOLPH.

Pray thee, go down, good ancient.

FALSTAFF.

Hark thee hither, Mistress Doll.

PISTOL.

Not I: I tell thee what, Corporal Bardolph,—I could tear her: I'll be revenged of her.

PAGE.
Pray thee, go down.

PISTOL.
I'll see her damned first;—to Pluto's damned lake, by this hand, to the infernal deep, with Erebus and tortures vile also. Hold hook and line, say I. Down, down, dogs! down, faitors! Have we not Hiren here?

HOSTESS.
Good Captain Peesel, be quiet; 'tis very late, i' faith: I beseek you now, aggravate your choler.

PISTOL.
These be good humours, indeed! Shall pack-horses,
And hollow pamper'd jades of Asia,
Which cannot go but thirty mile a-day,
Compare with Cæsars, and with Cannibals,
And Trojan Greeks? nay, rather damn them with King Cerberus; and let the welkin roar.
Shall we fall foul for toys?

HOSTESS.
By my troth, captain, these are very bitter words.

BARDOLPH.
Be gone, good ancient: this will grow to a brawl anon.

PISTOL.
Die men like dogs! give crowns like pins! Have we not Hiren here?

HOSTESS.
O' my word, captain, there's none such here. What the good-year! do you think I would deny her? For God's sake, be quiet.

PISTOL.
Then feed, and be fat, my fair Calipolis.
Come, give's some sack.
Si fortune me tormente, sperato me contento.—
Fear we broadsides? no, let the fiend give fire:
Give me some sack:—and, sweetheart, lie thou there.   [*Laying down his sword.*
Come we to full points here, and are etceteras nothing?

FALSTAFF.
Pistol, I would be quiet.

PISTOL.
Sweet knight, I kiss thy neif: what! we have seen the seven stars.

DOLL TEARSHEET.
For God's sake, thrust him down stairs: I cannot endure such a fustian rascal.

PISTOL.
Thrust him down stairs! know we not Galloway nags?

FALSTAFF.
Quoit him down, Bardolph, like a shove-groat shilling: nay, an a' do nothing but speak nothing, a' shall be nothing here.

BARDOLPH.
Come, get you down stairs.

PISTOL.
What! shall we have incision? shall we imbrue?—   [*Snatching up his sword.*
Then death rock me asleep, abridge my doleful days!
Why, then, let grievous, ghastly, gaping wounds Untwine the Sisters Three! Come, Atropos, I say!

HOSTESS.
Here's goodly stuff toward!

FALSTAFF.
Give me my rapier, boy.

DOLL TEARSHEET.
I pray thee, Jack, I pray thee, do not draw.

FALSTAFF.
Get you down stairs.
          [*Drawing, and driving* PISTOL *out.*

HOSTESS.
Here's a goodly tumult! I'll forswear keeping house, afore I'll be in these tirrits and frights. So; murder, I warrant now.—Alas, alas! put up your naked weapons, put up your naked weapons.
          [*Exeunt* PISTOL *and* BARDOLPH.

DOLL TEARSHEET.
I pray thee, Jack, be quiet; the rascal's gone. Ah, you whoreson little valiant villain, you!

HOSTESS.
Are you not hurt i' th' groin? methought a' made a shrewd thrust at your belly.

Enter BARDOLPH.

FALSTAFF.
Have you turn'd him out o' doors?

BARDOLPH.
Yes, sir. The rascal's drunk; you have hurt him, sir, i' th' shoulder.

FALSTAFF.
A rascal! to brave me!

DOLL TEARSHEET.
Ah, you sweet little rogue, you! Alas, poor ape, how thou sweat'st! come, let me wipe thy face; come on, you whoreson chops:—ah, rogue! i' faith, I love thee: thou art as valorous as Hector of Troy, worth five of Agamemnon, and ten times better than the Nine Worthies: ah, villain!

FALSTAFF.
A rascally slave! I will toss the rogue in a blanket.

DOLL TEARSHEET.
Do, an thou darest for thy heart: an thou dost, I'll canvass thee between a pair of sheets.

Enter MUSICIANS.

PAGE.
The music is come, sir.

FALSTAFF.
Let them play:—play, sirs.—Sit on my knee, Doll. [*Music.*] A rascal bragging slave! the rogue fled from me like quicksilver.

DOLL TEARSHEET.
I'faith, and thou followdst him like a church. Thou whoreson little tidy Bartholomew boar-pig, when wilt thou leave fighting o' days and foining o' nights, and begin to patch up thine old body for heaven?

Enter, behind, PRINCE HENRY *and* POINTZ *disguised as* DRAWERS.

FALSTAFF.
Peace, good Doll! do not speak like a death's-head; do not bid me remember mine end.

DOLL TEARSHEET.
Sirrah, what humour's the prince of?

FALSTAFF.
A good shallow young fellow: a' would have made a good pantler, a' would ha' chipt bread well.

DOLL TEARSHEET.
They say Pointz has a good wit.

FALSTAFF.
He a good wit? hang him, baboon! his wit's as thick as Tewkesbury mustard; there's no more conceit in him than is in a mallet.

DOLL TEARSHEET.
Why does the prince love him so, then?

FALSTAFF.
Because their legs are both of a bigness; and a' plays at quoits well; and eats conger and fennel; and drinks off candles' ends for flap-dragons; and rides the wild-mare with the boys; and jumps upon joint-stools; and swears with a good grace; and wears his boots very smooth, like unto the sign of the leg; and breeds no bate with telling of discreet stories; and such other gambol faculties a' has, that show a weak mind and an able body, for the which the prince admits him: for the prince himself is such another; the weight of a hair will turn the scales between their avoirdupois.

PRINCE HENRY.
Would not this nave of a wheel have his ears cut off?

POINTZ.
Let's beat him before his whore.

PRINCE HENRY.
Look, whether the wither'd elder hath not his poll claw'd like a parrot.

POINTZ.
Is it not strange that desire should so many years outlive performance?

FALSTAFF.
Kiss me, Doll.

PRINCE HENRY.
Saturn and Venus this year in conjunction! what says the almanac to that?

POINTZ.
And, look, whether the fiery Trigon, his man, be not lisping to his master's own tables, his note-book, his counsel-keeper.

FALSTAFF.
Thou dost give me flattering busses.

DOLL TEARSHEET.
By my troth, I kiss thee with a most constant heart.

FALSTAFF.
I am old, I am old.

DOLL TEARSHEET.
I love thee better than I love e'er a scurvy young boy of them all.

FALSTAFF.
What stuff wilt have a kirtle of? I shall receive money o' Thursday: shalt have a cap to-morrow. A merry song, come: it grows late; we'll to bed. Thou'lt forget me when I am gone.

DOLL TEARSHEET.
By my troth, thou'lt set me a-weeping, an thou say'st so: prove that ever I dress myself handsome till thy return:—well, hearken the end.

FALSTAFF.
Some sack, Francis.

PRINCE HENRY and POINTZ.
Anon, anon, sir.   [Advancing.

FALSTAFF.
Ha! a bastard son of the king's?—And art not thou Pointz his brother?

PRINCE HENRY.
Why, thou globe of sinful continents, what a life dost thou lead!

FALSTAFF.
A better than thou: I am a gentleman; thou art a drawer.

PRINCE HENRY.
Very true, sir; and I come to draw you out by the ears.

HOSTESS.
O, the Lord preserve thy good Grace! by my troth, welcome to London. Now, the Lord bless that sweet face of thine! O Jesu, are you come from Wales?

FALSTAFF.
Thou whoreson mad compound of majesty,—by this light flesh and corrupt blood, thou art welcome.

[Leaning his hand upon DOLL TEARSHEET.

DOLL TEARSHEET.
How, you fat fool! I scorn you.

POINTZ.
My lord, he will drive you out of your revenge, and turn all to a merriment, if you take not the heat.

PRINCE HENRY.
You whoreson candle-mine, you, how vilely did you speak of me even now before this honest, virtuous, civil gentlewoman!

HOSTESS.
God's blessing of your good heart! and so she is, by my troth.

FALSTAFF.
Didst thou hear me?

PRINCE HENRY.
Yea; and you knew me, as you did when you ran away by Gadshill: you knew I was at your back, and spoke it on purpose to try my patience.

FALSTAFF.
No, no, no; not so; I did not think thou wast within hearing.

PRINCE HENRY.
I shall drive you, then, to confess the wilful abuse; and then I know how to handle you.

FALSTAFF.
No abuse, Hal, o' mine honour; no abuse.

PRINCE HENRY.
Not,—to dispraise me, and call me pantler, and bread-chipper, and I know not what!

FALSTAFF.
No abuse, Hal!

POINTZ.
No abuse!

FALSTAFF.
No abuse, Ned, i' th' world; honest Ned, none. I dispraised him before the wicked, that the wicked might not fall in love with him;—in which doing, I have done the part of a careful friend and a true subject, and thy father is to give me thanks for it. No abuse, Hal;—none, Ned, none;—no, faith, boys, none.

PRINCE HENRY.
See now, whether pure fear and entire cowardice doth not make thee wrong this virtuous gentle-woman to close with us. Is she of the wicked? is thine hostess here of the wicked? or is thy boy of

the wicked? or honest Bardolph, whose zeal burns in his nose, of the wicked?

POINTZ.

Answer, thou dead elm, answer.

FALSTAFF.

The fiend hath prickt down Bardolph irrecoverable; and his face is Lucifer's privy-kitchen, where he doth nothing but roast malt-worms. For the boy,—there is a good angel about him; but the devil outbids him too.

PRINCE HENRY.

For the women?

FALSTAFF.

For one of them,—she is in hell already, and burns, poor soul! For the other,—I owe her money; and whether she be damn'd for that, I know not.

HOSTESS.

No, I warrant you.

FALSTAFF.

No, I think thou art not; I think thou art quit for that. Marry, there is another indictment upon thee, for suffering flesh to be eaten in thy house, contrary to the law; for the which I think thou wilt howl.

HOSTESS.

All victuallers do so: what's a joint of mutton or two in a whole Lent?

PRINCE HENRY.

You, gentlewoman,—

DOLL TEARSHEET.

What says your Grace?

FALSTAFF.

His grace says that which his flesh rebels against.

[Knocking within.

HOSTESS.

Who knocks so loud at door?—Look to the door there, Francis.

Enter PETO.

PRINCE HENRY.

Peto, how now! what news?

PETO.

The king your father is at Westminster;
And there are twenty weak and wearied posts
Come from the north: and, as I came along,
I met and overtook a dozen captains,
Bare-headed, sweating, knocking at the taverns,
And asking every one for Sir John Falstaff.

PRINCE HENRY.

By heaven, Pointz, I feel me much to blame,
So idly to profane the precious time;
When tempest of commotion, like the south,
Borne with black vapour, doth begin to melt,
And drop upon our bare unarmed heads.   [night.
Give me my sword and cloak.—Falstaff, good-

[Exeunt PRINCE HENRY, POINTZ, PETO,
and BARDOLPH.

FALSTAFF.

Now comes in the sweetest morsel of the night, and we must hence, and leave it unpickt. [Knocking within.] More knocking at the door!

Enter BARDOLPH.

How now! what's the matter?

BARDOLPH.

You must away to court, sir, presently;
A dozen captains stay at door for you.

FALSTAFF [to the PAGE].

Pay the musicians, sirrah.—Farewell, hostess;—farewell, Doll.—You see, my good wenches, how men of merit are sought after: the undeserver may sleep, when the man of action is call'd on. Farewell, good wenches: if I be not sent away post, I will see you again ere I go.

DOLL TEARSHEET.

I cannot speak;—if my heart be not ready to burst,—well, sweet Jack, have a care of thyself.

FALSTAFF.

Farewell, farewell.

[Exeunt FALSTAFF and BARDOLPH.

HOSTESS.

Well, fare thee well: I have known thee these twenty-nine years, come peascod-time; but an honester and truer-hearted man,—well, fare thee well.

BARDOLPH [within].

Mistress Tearsheet!

HOSTESS.

What's the matter?

BARDOLPH [within].

Bid Mistress Tearsheet come to my master.

HOSTESS.

O, run, Doll, run; run, good Doll: come [she comes blubber'd]; yea, will you come, Doll?

[Exeunt.

ACT III. SCENE I.

Westminster. A room in the palace.

Enter KING HENRY *in his nightgown, with a*
PAGE.

KING HENRY.

GO call the Earls of Surrey and of Warwick;
But, ere they come, bid them o'er-read these letters,
And well consider of them: make good speed.

[Exit PAGE.

How many thousand of my poorest subjects
Are at this hour asleep!—O sleep, O gentle sleep,
Nature's soft nurse, how have I frighted thee,
That thou no more wilt weigh my eyelids down,
And steep my senses in forgetfulness?
Why rather, sleep, liest thou in smoky cribs,
Upon uneasy pallets stretching thee,
And husht with buzzing night-flies to thy
   slumber,
Than in the perfumed chambers of the great,
Under the canopies of costly state,
And lull'd with sound of sweetest melody?
O thou dull god, why liest thou with the vile
In loathsome beds, and leavest the kingly couch
A watch-case or a common 'larum-bell?
Wilt thou upon the high and giddy mast
Seal up the ship-boy's eyes, and rock his brains
In cradle of the rude imperious surge,
And in the visitation of the winds,
Who take the ruffian billows by the top,
Curling their monstrous heads, and hanging them
With deafening clamour in the slippery shrouds,
That, with the hurly, death itself awakes?—
Cansy thou, O partial sleep, give thy repose
To the wet sea-boy in an hour so rude;
And in the calmest and most stillest night,

With all appliances and means to boot,
Deny it to a king? Then, happy low, lie down!
Uneasy lies the head that wears a crown.

Enter WARWICK *and* SURREY.

WARWICK.
Many good morrows to your majesty!

KING HENRY.
Is it good morrow, lords?

WARWICK.
'Tis one o'clock, and past.

KING HENRY.
Why, then, good morrow to you all, my lords.
Have you read o'er the letters that I sent you?

WARWICK.
We have, my liege.

KING HENRY.
Then you perceive the body of our kingdom
How foul it is; what rank diseases grow,
And with what danger, near the heart of it.

WARWICK.
It is but as a body yet distemper'd;
Which to his former strength may be restored
With good advice and little medicine:
My Lord Northumberland will soon be cool'd.

KING HENRY.
O God! that one might read the book of fate,
And see the revolution of the times
Make mountains level, and the continent,
Weary of solid firmness, melt itself
Into the sea! and, other times, to see
The beachy girdle of the ocean
Too wide for Neptune's hips; how chances mock,
And changes fill the cup of alteration
With divers liquors! O, if this were seen,
The happiest youth,—viewing his progress
    through,
What perils past, what crosses to ensue,—
Would shut the book, and sit him down and die.
'Tis not ten years gone   [friends,
Since Richard and Northumberland, great
Did feast together, and in two years after
Were they at wars: it is but eight years since
This Percy was the man nearest my soul;
Who like a brother toil'd in my affairs,
And laid his love and life under my foot;
Yea, for my sake, even to the eyes of Richard
Gave him defiance. But which of you was by—
[*to* WARWICK] You, cousin Nevil, as I may re-
    member,—
When Richard,—with his eye brimful of tears,
Then checkt and rated by Northumberland,—
Did speak these words, now proved a prophecy?
'Northumberland, thou ladder by the which
My cousin Bolingbroke ascends my throne,'—
Though then, God knows, I had no such intent,
But that necessity so bow'd the state,
That I and greatness were compell'd to kiss:—
'The time shall come,' thus did he follow it,
'The time will come, that foul sin, gathering
    head,
Shall break into corruption:'—so went on,
Foretelling this same time's condition,
And the division of our amity.

WARWICK.
There is a history in all men's lives,
Figuring the nature of the times deceased;

The which observed, a man may prophesy,
With a near aim, of the main chance of things
As yet not come to life, which in their seeds
And weak beginnings lie intreasured.
Such things become the hatch and brood of time;
And, by the necessary form of this,
King Richard might create a perfect guess,
That great Northumberland, then false to him,
Would of that seed grow to a greater falseness;
Which should not find a ground to root upon,
Unless on you.

KING HENRY.
Are these things, then, necessities?
Then let us meet them like necessities;—
And that same word even now cries out on us:
They say the bishop and Northumberland
Are fifty thousand strong.

WARWICK.
It cannot be, my lord;
Rumour doth double, like the voice and echo,
The numbers of the fear'd. Please it your Grace
To go to bed. Upon my soul, my lord,
The powers that you already have sent forth
Shall bring this prize in very easily.
To comfort you the more, I have received
A certain instance that Glendower is dead.
Your majesty hath been this fortnight ill;
And these unseason'd hours perforce must add
Unto your sickness.

KING HENRY.
I will take your counsel:
And were these inward wars once out of hand,
We would, dear lords, unto the Holy Land.
                                        [*Exeunt.*

SCENE II.

Glostershire.   Court before JUSTICE
SHALLOW'S *house.*

Enter SHALLOW *and* SILENCE; MOULDY,
SHADOW, WART, FEEBLE, BULLCALF, *and*
SERVANTS, *behind.*

SHALLOW.
COME on, come on, come on, sir; give me
your hand, sir, give me your hand, sir: an
early stirrer, by the rood! And how doth my good
cousin Silence?

SILENCE.
Good morrow, good cousin Shallow.

SHALLOW.
And how doth my good cousin, your bedfellow?
and your fairest daughter and mine, my god-
daughter Ellen?

SILENCE.
Alas, a black ousel, cousin Shallow!

SHALLOW.
By yea and nay, sir, I dare say my cousin William
is become a good scholar: he is at Oxford still, is
he not?

SILENCE.
Indeed, sir, to my cost.

SHALLOW.
A' must, then, to the inns o' court shortly: I was
once of Clement's-inn, where I think they will
talk of mad Shallow yet.

SILENCE.
You were call'd 'lusty Shallow' then, cousin.

SHALLOW.

By the mass, I was call'd any thing; and I would have done any thing indeed too, and roundly too. There was I, and little John Doit of Staffordshire, and black George Barnes, and Francis Pickbone, and Will Squele a Cotsall man,—you had not four such swinge-bucklers in all the inns o' court again: and, I may say to you, we knew where the bona-robas were, and had the best of them all at commandment. Then was Jack Falstaff, now Sir John, a boy, and page to Thomas Mowbray, duke of Norfolk.

SILENCE.

This Sir John, cousin, that comes hither anon about soldiers?

SHALLOW.

The same Sir John, the very same. I see him break Skogan's head at the court-gate, when a' was a crack not thus high: and the very same day did I fight with one Sampson Stockfish, a fruiterer, behind Gray's-inn. Jesu, Jesu, the mad days that I have spent! and to see how many of my old acquaintance are dead!

SILENCE.

We shall all follow, cousin.

SHALLOW.

Certain, 'tis certain; very sure, very sure: death, as the Psalmist saith, is certain to all; all shall die.—How a good yoke of bullocks at Stamford fair?

SILENCE.

Truly, cousin, I was not there.

SHALLOW.

Death is certain.—Is old Double of your town living yet?

SILENCE.

Dead, sir.

SHALLOW.

Jesu, Jesu, dead!—a' drew a good bow;—and dead!—a' shot a fine shoot:—John o' Gaunt loved him well, and betted much money on his head. Dead!—a' would have clapt i' th' clout at twelve score; and carried you a forehand shaft a fourteen and fourteen and a half, that it would have done a man's heart good to see.—How a score of ewes now?

SILENCE.

Thereafter as they be: a score of good ewes may be worth ten pounds.

SHALLOW.

And is old Double dead?

SILENCE.

Here come two of Sir John Falstaff's men, as I think.

Enter BARDOLPH and one with him.

BARDOLPH.

Good morrow, honest gentlemen: I beseech you, which is Justice Shallow?

SHALLOW.

I am Robert Shallow, sir; a poor esquire of this county, and one of the king's justices of the peace: what is your good pleasure with me?

BARDOLPH.

My captain, sir, commends him to you; my captain, Sir John Falstaff,—a tall gentleman, by heaven, and a most gallant leader.

SHALLOW.

He greets me well, sir. I knew him a good backsword man. How doth the good knight? may I ask how my lady his wife doth?

BARDOLPH.

Sir, pardon; a soldier is better accommodated than with a wife.

SHALLOW.

It is well said, in faith, sir; and it is well said indeed too. Better accommodated!—it is good; yea, indeed, is it: good phrases are surely, and ever were, very commendable. Accommodated!—it comes of *accommodo:* very good; a good phrase.

BARDOLPH.

Pardon, sir; I have heard the word. Phrase call you it? by this good day, I know not the phrase; but I will maintain the word with my sword to be a soldier-like word, and a word of exceeding good command, by heaven. Accommodated; that is, when a man is, as they say, accommodated; or when a man is, being, whereby a' may be thought to be accommodated; which is an excellent thing.

SHALLOW.

It is very just.—Look, here comes good Sir John.

Enter FALSTAFF.

Give me your good hand, give me your worship's good hand: by my troth, you like well, and bear your years very well: welcome, good Sir John.

FALSTAFF.

I am glad to see you well, good Master Robert Shallow:—Master Surecard, as I think?

SHALLOW.

No, Sir John; it is my cousin Silence, in commission with me.

FALSTAFF.

Good Master Silence, it well befits you should be of the peace.

SILENCE.

Your good worship is welcome.

FALSTAFF.

Fie! this is hot weather, gentlemen. Have you provided me here half a dozen sufficient men?

SHALLOW.

Marry, have we, sir. Will you sit?

FALSTAFF.

Let me see them, I beseech you.

SHALLOW.

Where's the roll? where's the roll? where's the roll?—Let me see, let me see, let me see. So, so, so, so, so, so, so: yea, marry, sir:—Ralph Mouldy! —let them appear as I call; let them do so, let them do so.—Let me see; where is Mouldy?

MOULDY.

Here, an't please you.

SHALLOW.

What think you, Sir John? a good-limb'd fellow; young, strong, and of good friends.

FALSTAFF.

Is thy name Mouldy?

MOULDY.

Yea, an't please you.

FALSTAFF.

'Tis the more time thou wert used.

SHALLOW.

Ha, ha, ha! most excellent, i'faith! things that are

mouldy lack use: very singular good!—in faith, well said, Sir John; very well said.

FALSTAFF [*to* SHALLOW].

Prick him.

MOULDY.

I was prickt well enough before, an you could have let me alone: my old dame will be undone now, for one to do her husbandry and her drudgery; you need not to have prickt me; there are other men fitter to go out than I.

FALSTAFF.

Go to: peace, Mouldy; you shall go. Mouldy, it is time you were spent.

MOULDY.

Spent!

SHALLOW.

Peace, fellow, peace; stand aside: know you where you are?—For th'other, Sir John:—let me see;—Simon Shadow!

FALSTAFF.

Yea, marry, let me have him to sit under: he's like to be a cold soldier.

SHALLOW.

Where's Shadow?

SHADOW.

Here, sir.

FALSTAFF.

Shadow, whose son art thou?

SHADOW.

My mother's son, sir.

FALSTAFF.

Thy mother's son! like enough; and thy father's shadow: so the son of the female is the shadow of the male: it is often so, indeed; but much of the father's substance!

SHALLOW.

Do you like him, Sir John?

FALSTAFF.

Shadow will serve for summer,—prick him; for we have a number of shadows to fill up the muster-book.

SHALLOW.

Thomas Wart!

FALSTAFF.

Where's he?

WART.

Here, sir.

FALSTAFF.

Is thy name Wart?

WART.

Yea, sir.

FALSTAFF.

Thou art a very ragged wart.

SHALLOW.

Shall I prick him, Sir John?

FALSTAFF.

It were superfluous; for his apparel is built upon his back, and the whole frame stands upon pins: prick him no more.

SHALLOW.

Ha, ha, ha!—you can do it, sir; you can do it: I commend you well—Francis Feeble!

FEEBLE.

Here, sir.

FALSTAFF.

What trade art thou, Feeble?

FEEBLE.

A woman's tailor, sir.

SHALLOW.

Shall I prick him, sir?

FALSTAFF.

You may: but if he had been a man's tailor, he'ld ha' prickt you.—Wilt thou make as many holes in an enemy's battle as thou hast done in a woman's petticoat?

FEEBLE.

I will do my good will, sir; you can have no more.

FALSTAFF.

Well said, good woman's tailor! well said, courageous Feeble! thou wilt be as valiant as the wrathful dove or most magnanimous mouse.—Prick the woman's tailor well, Master Shallow; deep, Master Shallow.

FEEBLE.

I would Wart might have gone, sir.

FALSTAFF.

I would thou wert a man's tailor, that thou mightst mend him, and make him fit to go. I cannot put him to a private soldier, that is the leader of so many thousands: let that suffice, most forcible Feeble.

FEEBLE.

It shall suffice, sir.

FALSTAFF.

I am bound to thee, reverend Feeble.—Who is next?

SHALLOW.

Peter Bullcalf o' th' green!

FALSTAFF.

Yea, marry, let's see Bullcalf.

BULLCALF.

Here, sir.

FALSTAFF.

'Fore God, a likely fellow!—Come, prick me Bullcalf till he roar again.

BULLCALF.

O Lord! good my lord captain,—

FALSTAFF.

What, dost thou roar before thou art prickt?

BULLCALF.

O Lord, sir! I am a diseased man.

FALSTAFF.

What disease hast thou?

BULLCALF.

A whoreson cold, sir,—a cough, sir,—which I caught with ringing in the king's affairs upon his coronation-day, sir.

FALSTAFF.

Come, thou shalt go to the wars in a gown; we will have away thy cold; and I will take such order, that thy friends shall ring for thee.—Is here all?

SHALLOW.

Here is two more call'd than your number; you must have but four here, sir:—and so, I pray you, go in with me to dinner.

FALSTAFF.

Come, I will go drink with you, but I cannot tarry dinner. I am glad to see you, by my troth, Master Shallow.

SHALLOW.

O, Sir John, do you remember since we lay all night in the windmill in Saint George's field?

FALSTAFF.

No more of that, good Master Shallow, no more of that.

SHALLOW.

Ha, 'twas a merry night. And is Jane Nightwork alive?

FALSTAFF.

She lives, Master Shallow.

SHALLOW.

She never could away with me.

FALSTAFF.

Never, never; she would always say she could not abide Master Shallow.

SHALLOW.

By the mass, I could anger her to the heart. She was then a bona-roba. Doth she hold her own well?

FALSTAFF.

Old, old, Master Shallow.

SHALLOW.

Nay, she must be old; she cannot choose but be old; certain she's old; and had Robin Nightwork by old Nightwork before I came to Clement's-inn.

SILENCE.

That's fifty-five year ago.

SHALLOW.

Ha, cousin Silence, that thou hadst seen that that this knight and I have seen!—Ha, Sir John, said I well?

FALSTAFF.

We have heard the chimes at midnight, Master Shallow.

SHALLOW.

That we have, that we have, that we have; in faith, Sir John, we have: our watch-word was, 'Hem, boys!'—Come, let's to dinner; come, let's to dinner:—Jesus, the days that we have seen!—come, come.

[*Exeunt* FALSTAFF, SHALLOW, *and* SILENCE.

BULLCALF.

Good master corporate Bardolph, stand my friend; and here's four Harry ten shillings in French crowns for you. In very truth, sir, I had as lief be hang'd, sir, as go: and yet, for mine own part, sir, I do not care; but rather, because I am unwilling, and, for mine own part, have a desire to stay with my friends; else, sir, I did not care, for mine own part, so much.

BARDOLPH.

Go to; stand aside.

MOULDY.

And, good master corporal captain, for my old dame's sake, stand my friend: she has nobody to do any thing about her when I am gone; and she is old, and cannot help herself: you shall have forty, sir.

BARDOLPH.

Go to; stand aside.

FEEBLE.

By my troth, I care not; a man can die but once;—we owe God a death: I'll ne'er bear a base mind: an't be my destiny, so; an't be not, so: no man's too good to serve's prince; and let it go which way it will, he that dies this year is quit for the next.

BARDOLPH.

Well said; thou'rt a good fellow.

FEEBLE.

Faith, I'll bear no base mind.

Enter FALSTAFF, SHALLOW, *and* SILENCE.

FALSTAFF.

Come, sir, which men shall I have?

SHALLOW.

Four of which you please.

BARDOLPH.

Sir, a word with you:—I have three pound to free Mouldy and Bullcalf.

FALSTAFF.

Go to; well.

SHALLOW.

Come, Sir John, which four will you have?

FALSTAFF.

Do you choose for me.

SHALLOW.

Marry, then,—Mouldy, Bullcalf, Feeble, and Shadow.

FALSTAFF.

Mouldy and Bullcalf:—for you, Mouldy, stay at home till you are past service:—and for your part, Bullcalf, grow till you come unto it:—I will none of you.

SHALLOW.

Sir John, Sir John, do not yourself wrong: they are your likeliest men, and I would have you served with the best.

FALSTAFF.

Will you tell me, Master Shallow, how to choose a man? Care I for the limb, the thews, the stature, bulk, and big assemblance of a man! Give me the spirit, Master Shallow.—Here's Wart;—you see what a ragged appearance it is: a' shall charge you, and discharge you, with the motion of a pewterer's hammer; come off, and on, swifter than he that gibbets-on the brewer's bucket. And this same half-faced fellow, Shadow,—give me this man: he presents no mark to the enemy,—the foeman may with as great aim level at the edge of a penknife. And, for a retreat,—how swiftly will this Feeble, the woman's tailor, run off! O, give me the spare men, and spare me the great ones.—Put me a caliver into Wart's hand, Bardolph.

BARDOLPH.

Hold, Wart, traverse; thus, thus, thus.

FALSTAFF.

Come, manage me your caliver. So:—very well —go to:—very good:—exceeding good.—O, give me always a little, lean, old, chapt, bald shot.—Well said, i'faith, Wart: thou'rt a good scab: hold, there's a tester for thee.

SHALLOW.

He is not his craft's-master; he doth not do it right. I remember at Mile-end Green,—when I lay at Clement's-inn,—I was then Sir Dagonet in Arthur's show,—there was a little quiver fellow, and a' would manage you his piece thus; and a' would about and about, and come you in and come you in: 'rah, tah, tah,' would a' say; 'bounce' would a' say; and away again would a' go, and again would a' come:—I shall ne'er see such a fellow.

FALSTAFF.

These fellows will do well, Master Shallow.—
God keep you, Master Silence: I will not use
many words with you.—Fare you well, gentlemen
both: I thank you: I must a dozen mile to-night.
—Bardolph, give the soldiers coats.

SHALLOW.

Sir John, the Lord bless you! God prosper your
affairs! God send us peace! As you return, visit
our house; let our old acquaintance be renew'd:
peradventure I will with ye to the court.

FALSTAFF.

'Fore God, I would you would, Master Shallow.

SHALLOW.

Go to; I have spoke at a word; God keep you.

FALSTAFF.

Fare you well, gentle gentlemen. [*Exeunt* SHAL-
LOW *and* SILENCE.] On, Bardolph; lead the men
away. [*Exeunt* BARDOLPH, RECRUITS, &c.] As I
return, I will fetch off these justices: I do see the
bottom of Justice Shallow. Lord, Lord, how subject we old men are to this vice of lying! This
same starved justice hath done nothing but prate
to me of the wildness of his youth, and the feats
he hath done about Turnbull-street; and every
third word a lie, duer paid to the hearer than the
Turk's tribute. I do remember him at Clement's-
inn, like a man made after supper of a cheese-
paring: when a' was naked, he was, for all the
world, like a forkt radish, with a head fantastically
carved upon it with a knife; a' was so forlorn, that
his dimensions to any thick sight were invisible:
a' was the very genius of famine; yet lecherous as
a monkey, and the whores call'd him mandrake:
a' came ever in the rearward of the fashion; and
sung those tunes to the overscutcht huswives that
he heard the carmen whistle, and sware they were
his Fancies or his Good-nights. And now is this
Vice's dagger become a squire, and talks as familiarly of John o' Gaunt as if he had been sworn
brother to him; and I'll be sworn a' ne'er saw him
but once in the Tilt-yard; and then he burst his
head for crowding among the marshal's men. I
saw it, and told John o' Gaunt he beat his own
name; for you might have thrust him and all his
apparel into an eel-skin; the case of a treble haut-
boy was a mansion for him, a court:—and now
has he land and beefs. Well, I'll be acquainted
with him, if I return; and it shall go hard but I'll
make him a philosopher's two stones to me: if the
young dace be a bait for the old pike, I see no
reason, in the law of nature, but I may snap at
him. Let time shape, and there an end. [*Exit.*

ACT IV. SCENE I.

Yorkshire. Gaultree Forest.

Enter the ARCHBISHOP OF YORK, MOWBRAY,
HASTINGS, *and others.*

ARCHBISHOP OF YORK.

WHAT is this forest call'd?

HASTINGS.

'Tis Gaultree Forest, an't shall please your
Grace.

ARCHBISHOP OF YORK.

Here stand, my lords; and send discoverers forth
To know the numbers of our enemies.

HASTINGS.

We have sent forth already.

ARCHBISHOP OF YORK.

'Tis well done.
My friends and brethren in these great affairs,
I must acquaint you that I have received
New-dated letters from Northumberland;
Their cold intent, tenour, and substance, thus:—
Here doth he wish his person, with such powers
As might hold sortance with his quality,
The which he could not levy; whereupon
He is retired, to ripe his growing fortunes,
To Scotland; and concludes in hearty prayers
That your attempts may overlive the hazard
And fearful meeting of their opposite.

MOWBRAY.

Thus do the hopes we have in him touch ground,
And dash themselves to pieces.

Enter a MESSENGER.

HASTINGS.
Now, what news?

MESSENGER.

West of this forest, scarcely off a mile,
In goodly form comes on the enemy;
And, by the ground they hide, I judge their
    number
Upon or near the rate of thirty thousand.

MOWBRAY.

The just proportion that we gave them out.
Let us sway on, and face them in the field.

ARCHBISHOP OF YORK.

What well-appointed leader fronts us here?

MOWBRAY.

I think it is my Lord of Westmoreland.

Enter WESTMORELAND.

WESTMORELAND.

Health and fair greeting from our general,
The prince, Lord John and Duke of Lancaster.

ARCHBISHOP OF YORK.

Say on, my Lord of Westmoreland, in peace:
What doth concern your coming?

WESTMORELAND.
Then, my lord,
Unto your Grace do I in chief address
The substance of my speech.   If that rebellion
Came like itself, in base and abject routs,
Led on by heady youth, guarded with rags,
And countenanced by boys and beggary,—
I say, if damn'd commotion so appear'd,
In his true, native, and most proper shape,
You, reverend father, and these noble lords,
Had not been here, to dress the ugly form
Of base and bloody insurrection
With your fair honours. You, lord archbishop,—
Whose see is by a civil peace maintain'd;
Whose beard the silver hand of peace hath toucht;
Whose learning and good letters peace hath tu-
    tor'd;
Whose white investments figure innocence,
The dove and very blessed spirit of peace,—
Wherefore do you so ill translate yourself
Out of the speech of peace, that bears such grace,
Into the harsh and boisterous tongue of war;

249

Turning your books to greaves, your ink to blood,
Your pens to lances, and your tongue divine
To a loud trumpet and a point of war?
ARCHBISHOP OF YORK.
Wherefore do I this?—so the question stands.
Briefly to this end:—we are all diseased:
And with our surfeiting and wanton hours
Have brought ourselves into a burning fever,
And we must bleed for it: of which disease
Our late king, Richard, being infected, died.
But, my most noble Lord of Westmoreland,
I take not on me here as a physician;
Nor do I, as an enemy to peace,
Troop in the throngs of military men;
But, rather, show awhile like fearful war,
To diet rank minds sick of happiness,
And purge th'obstructions which begin to stop
Our very veins of life. Hear me more plainly.
I have in equal balance justly weigh'd
What wrongs our arms may do, what wrongs we
    suffer,
And find our griefs heavier than our offences.
We see which way the stream of time doth run,
And are enforced from our most quiet sphere
By the rough torrent of occasion;
And have the summary of all our griefs,
When time shall serve, to show in articles;
Which long ere this we offer'd to the king,
And might by no suit gain our audience:
When we are wrong'd, and would unfold our
    griefs,
We are denied access unto his person
Even by those men that most have done us wrong.
The dangers of the days but newly gone,
Whose memory is written on the earth
With yet-appearing blood, and the examples
Of every minute's instance, present now,
Have put us in these ill-beseeming arms;
Not to break peace, or any branch of it,
But to establish here a peace indeed,
Concurring both in name and quality.
WESTMORELAND.
When ever yet was your appeal denied?
Wherein have you been galled by the king?
What peer hath been suborn'd to grate on you;—
That you should seal this lawless bloody book
Of forged rebellion with a seal divine,
And consecrate commotion's bitter edge?
ARCHBISHOP OF YORK.
My brother general, the commonwealth,
To brother born an household cruelty,
I make my quarrel in particular.
WESTMORELAND.
There is no need of any such redress;
Or if there were, it not belongs to you.
MOWBRAY.
Why not to him in part, and to us all
That feel the bruises of the days before,
And suffer the condition of these times
To lay a heavy and unequal hand
Upon our honours?
WESTMORELAND.
        O, my good Lord Mowbray,
Construe the times to their necessities,
And you shall say indeed, it is the time,
And not the king, that doth you injuries.

Yet, for your part, it not appears to me,
Either from the king, or in the present time,
That you should have an inch of any ground
To build a grief on: were you not restored
To all the Duke of Norfolk's signiories,
Your noble and right-well-remember'd father's?
MOWBRAY.
What thing, in honour, had my father lost,
That need to be revived and breathed in me?
The king, that loved him, as the state stood then,
Was, force perforce, compell'd to banish him:
And then that Henry Bolingbroke and he—
Being mounted and both roused in their seats,
Their neighing coursers daring of the spur,
Their armed staves in charge, their beavers
    down,
Their eyes of fire sparkling through sights of steel,
And the loud trumpet blowing them together,—
Then, then, when there was nothing could have
    stay'd
My father from the breast of Bolingbroke,
O, when the king did throw his warder down,
His own life hung upon the staff he threw:
Then threw he down himself, and all their lives
That by indictment and by dint of sword
Have since miscarried under Bolingbroke.
WESTMORELAND.
You speak, Lord Mowbray, now you know not
    what.
The Earl of Hereford was reputed then
In England the most valiant gentleman:
Who knows on whom fortune would then have
    smiled?
But if your father had been victor there,
He ne'er had borne it out of Coventry:
For all the country, in a general voice,
Cried hate upon him; and all their prayers and
    love
Were set on Hereford, whom they doted on,
And blest and graced indeed, more than the king.
But this is mere digression from my purpose.—
Here come I from our princely general
To know your griefs; to tell you from his Grace
That he will give you audience; and wherein
It shall appear that your demands are just,
You shall enjoy them,—every thing set off
That might so much as think you enemies.
MOWBRAY.
But he hath forced us to compel this offer;
And it proceeds from policy, not love.
WESTMORELAND.
Mowbray, you overween to take it so;
This offer comes from mercy, not from fear:
For, lo! within a ken our army lies;
Upon mine honour, all too confident
To give admittance to a thought of fear.
Our battle is more full of names than yours,
Our men more perfect in the use of arms,
Our armour all as strong, our cause the best;
Then reason will our hearts should be as good:
Say you not, then, our offer is compell'd.
MOWBRAY.
Well, by my will we shall admit no parley.
WESTMORELAND.
That argues but the shame of your offence:
A rotten case abides no handling.

HASTINGS.
Hath the Prince John a full commission,
In very ample virtue of his father,
To hear and absolutely to determine
Of what conditions we shall stand upon?
WESTMORELAND.
That is intended in the general's name:
I muse you make so slight a question.
ARCHBISHOP OF YORK.
Then take, my Lord of Westmoreland, this
schedule,
For this contains our general grievances:
Each several article herein redrest,
All members of our cause, both here and hence,
That are insinew'd to this action,
Acquitted by a true substantial form
And present execution of our wills
To us and to our purposes consign'd,—
We come within our awful banks again,
And knit our powers to the arm of peace.
WESTMORELAND.
This will I show the general. Please you, lords,
In sight of both our battles we may meet;
And either end in peace,—which God so
frame!—
Or to the place of difference call the swords
Which must decide it.
ARCHBISHOP OF YORK.
My lord, we will do so.
[Exit WESTMORELAND.
MOWBRAY.
There is a thing within my bosom tells me
That no conditions of our peace can stand.
HASTINGS.
Fear you not that: if we can make our peace
Upon such large terms and so absolute
As our conditions shall consist upon,
Our peace shall stand as firm as rocky mountains.
MOWBRAY.
Yea, but our valuation shall be such,
That every slight and false-derived cause,
Yea, every idle, nice, and wanton reason
Shall to the king taste of this action;
That, were our royal faiths martyrs in love,
We shall be winnow'd with so rough a wind,
That even our corn shall seem as light as chaff,
And good from bad find no partition.
ARCHBISHOP OF YORK.
No, no, my lord. Note this,—the king is weary
Of dainty and such picking grievances:
For he hath found, to end one doubt by death
Revives two greater in the heirs of life;
And therefore will he wipe his tables clean,
And keep no tell-tale to his memory,
That may repeat and history his loss
To new remembrance: for full well he knows
He cannot so precisely weed this land
As his misdoubts present occasion:
His foes are so enrooted with his friends,
That, plucking to unfix an enemy,
He doth unfasten so and shake a friend.
So that this land, like an offensive wife
That hath enraged him on to offer strokes,
As he is striking, holds his infant up,
And hangs resolved correction in the arm
That was uprear'd to execution.

HASTINGS.
Besides, the king hath wasted all his rods
On late offenders, that he now doth lack
The very instruments of chastisement:
So that his power, like to a fangless lion,
May offer, but not hold.
ARCHBISHOP OF YORK.
'Tis very true:
And therefore be assured, my good lord marshal,
If we do now make our atonement well,
Our peace will, like a broken limb united,
Grow stronger for the breaking.
MOWBRAY.
Be it so.
Here is return'd my Lord of Westmoreland.
Enter WESTMORELAND.
WESTMORELAND.
The prince is here at hand: pleaseth your lordship
To meet his Grace just distance 'tween our
armies.
MOWBRAY.
Your Grace of York, in God's name, then, set
forward.
ARCHBISHOP OF YORK.
Before, and greet his Grace:—my lord, we come.
[Exeunt.

SCENE II.

Another part of the forest.

Enter, from one side, MOWBRAY, *the* ARCH-
BISHOP, HASTINGS, *and others; from the
other side,* PRINCE JOHN OF LANCASTER,
WESTMORELAND, OFFICERS, *and* ATTEND-
ANTS.

PRINCE JOHN OF LANCASTER.
YOU are well encounter'd here, my cousin
Mowbray:—
Good day to you, gentle lord archbishop;—
And so to you, Lord Hastings,—and to all.—
My Lord of York, it better show'd with you,
When that your flock, assembled by the bell,
Encircled you to hear with reverence
Your exposition on the holy text,
Than now to see you here an iron man,
Cheering a rout of rebels with your drum,
Turning the word to sword, and life to death.
That man that sits within a monarch's heart,
And ripens in the sunshine of his favour,
Would he abuse the countenance of the king,
Alack, what mischiefs might he set abroach,
In shadow of such greatness! With you, lord
bishop,
It is even so. Who hath not heard it spoken,
How deep you were within the books of God?
To us the speaker in his parliament;
To us th' imagined voice of God himself;
The very opener and intelligencer
Between the grace, the sanctities of heaven
And our dull workings. O, who shall believe,
But you misuse the reverence of your place,
Employ the countenance and grace of heaven,
As a false favourite doth his prince's name,
In deeds dishonourable? You have ta'en up,
Under the counterfeited zeal of God,
The subjects of his substitute, my father,

And both against the peace of heaven and him
Have here up-swarm'd them.
ARCHBISHOP OF YORK.
Good my Lord of Lancaster,
I am not here against your father's peace;
But, as I told my Lord of Westmoreland,
The time misorder'd doth, in common sense,
Crowd us and crush us to this monstrous form,
To hold our safety up. I sent your Grace
The parcels and particulars of our grief,—
The which hath been with scorn shoved from
the court,—
Whereon this Hydra son of war is born;
Whose dangerous eyes may well be charm'd
asleep
With grant of our most just and right desires,
And true obedience, of this madness cured,
Stoop tamely to the foot of majesty.
MOWBRAY.
If not, we ready are to try our fortunes
To the last man.
HASTINGS.
And though we here fall down,
We have supplies to second our attempt:
If they miscarry, theirs shall second them;
And so success of mischief shall be born,
And heir from heir shall hold this quarrel up,
Whiles England shall have generation.
PRINCE JOHN OF LANCASTER.
You are too shallow, Hastings, much too shallow,
To sound the bottom of the after-times.
WESTMORELAND.
Pleaseth your Grace to answer them directly,
How far-forth you do like their articles.
PRINCE JOHN OF LANCASTER.
I like them all, and do allow them well;
And swear here, by the honour of my blood,
My father's purposes have been mistook;
And some about him have too lavishly
Wrested his meaning and authority.—
My lord, these griefs shall be with speed re-
drest;
Upon my soul, they shall. If this may please you,
Discharge your powers unto their several
counties,
As we will ours: and here, between the armies,
Let's drink together friendly and embrace,
That all their eyes may bear those tokens home
Of our restored love and amity.
ARCHBISHOP OF YORK.
I take your princely word for these redresses.
PRINCE JOHN OF LANCASTER.
I give it you, and will maintain my word:
And thereupon I drink unto your Grace. [Drinks.
HASTINGS [to an OFFICER].
Go, captain, and deliver to the army
This news of peace: let them have pay, and part:
I know it will well please them. Hie thee, captain.
[Exit OFFICER.
ARCHBISHOP OF YORK.
To you, my noble Lord of Westmoreland.
[Drinks.
WESTMORELAND.
I pledge your Grace [Drinks]; and, if you knew
what pains
I have bestow'd to breed this present peace,

You would drink freely: but my love to ye
Shall show itself more openly hereafter.
ARCHBISHOP OF YORK.
I do not doubt you.
WESTMORELAND.
I am glad of it.—
Health to my lord and gentle cousin, Mowbray.
[Drinks.
MOWBRAY.
You wish me health in very happy season;
For I am, on the sudden, something ill.
ARCHBISHOP OF YORK.
Against ill chances men are ever merry;
But heaviness foreruns the good event.
WESTMORELAND.
Therefore be merry, coz; since sudden sorrow
Serves to say thus, 'Some good thing comes to-
morrow.'
ARCHBISHOP OF YORK.
Believe me, I am passing light in spirit.
MOWBRAY.
So much the worse, if your own rule be true.
[Shouts within.
The word of peace is render'd: hark, how they
shout!
MOWBRAY.
This had been cheerful after victory.
ARCHBISHOP OF YORK.
A peace is of the nature of a conquest;
For then both parties nobly are subdued,
And neither party loser.
PRINCE JOHN OF LANCASTER.
Go, my lord,
And let our army be discharged too.
[Exit WESTMORELAND.
And, good my lord, so please you, let our trains
March by us, that we may peruse the men
We should have coped withal.
ARCHBISHOP OF YORK.
Go, good Lord Hastings,
And, ere they be dismiss'd, let them march by.
[Exit HASTINGS.
PRINCE JOHN OF LANCASTER.
I trust, lords, we shall lie to-night together.
Enter WESTMORELAND.
Now, cousin, wherefore stands our army still?
WESTMORELAND.
The leaders, having charge from you to stand,
Will not go off until they hear you speak.
PRINCE JOHN OF LANCASTER.
They know their duties.
Enter HASTINGS.
HASTINGS.
My lord, our army is dispersed already:
Like youthful steers unyoked, they take their
courses
East, west, north, south; or, like a school broke
up,
Each hurries toward his home and sporting-
place.
WESTMORELAND.
Good tidings, my Lord Hastings; for the which
I do arrest thee, traitor, of high treason:—
And you, lord archbishop,—and you, Lord
Mowbray,—
Of capital treason I attach you both.

MOWBRAY.
Is this proceeding just and honourable?
WESTMORELAND.
Is your assembly so?
ARCHBISHOP OF YORK.
Will you thus break your faith!
PRINCE JOHN OF LANCASTER.
　　　　　　　　I pawn'd thee none:
I promised you redress of these same grievances
Whereof you did complain; which, by mine
　honour,
I will perform with a most Christian care.
But for you, rebels,—look to taste the due
Meet for rebellion and such acts as yours.
Most shallowly did you these arms commence,
Fondly brought here, and foolishly sent hence.—
Strike up our drums, pursue the scatter'd stray:
God, and not we, hath safely fought to-day.—
Some guard these traitors to the block of death,
Treason's true bed and yielder-up of breath.
　　　　　　　　　　　　　　[Exeunt.

SCENE III.

Another part of the forest.

Alarums: excursions.　Enter FALSTAFF *and*
　　COLEVILE, *meeting.*

FALSTAFF.
WHAT'S your name, sir? of what condition
are you, and of what place, I pray?
COLEVILE.
I am a knight, sir; and my name is Colevile of the
dale.
FALSTAFF.
Well, then, Colevile is your name, a knight is
your degree, and your place the dale: Colevile
shall be still your name, a traitor your degree, and
the dungeon your place,—a dale deep enough; so
shall you be still Colevile of the dale.
COLEVILE.
Are not you Sir John Falstaff?
FALSTAFF.
As good a man as he, sir, whoe'er I am. Do ye
yield, sir? or shall I sweat for you? If I do sweat,
they are the drops of thy lovers, and they weep
for thy death: therefore rouse up fear and trembling, and do observance to my mercy.
COLEVILE.
I think you are Sir John Falstaff; and in that
thought yield me.
FALSTAFF.
I have a whole school of tongues in this belly of
mine; and not a tongue of them all speaks any
other word but my name. An I had but a belly of
any indifferency, I were simply the most active
fellow in Europe: my womb, my womb, my
womb, undoes me.—Here comes our general.
Enter PRINCE JOHN OF LANCASTER, WEST-
　　MORELAND, BLUNT, *and others.*
PRINCE JOHN OF LANCASTER.
The heat is past; follow no further now:—
Call in the powers, good cousin Westmoreland.
　　　　　　　　　　　[*Exit* WESTMORELAND.
Now, Falstaff, where have you been all this
　while?
When every thing is ended, then you come:

These tardy tricks of yours will, on my life,
One time or other break some gallows' back.
FALSTAFF.
I would be sorry, my lord, but it should be thus:
I never knew yet but rebuke and check was the
reward of valour. Do you think me a swallow,
an arrow, or a bullet? have I, in my poor and
old motion, the expedition of thought? I have
speeded hither with the very extremest inch of
possibility; I have founder'd nine-score and odd
posts: and here, travel-tainted as I am, have, in
my pure and immaculate valour, taken Sir John
Colevile of the dale, a most furious knight and
valorous enemy. But what of that? he saw me,
and yielded; that I may justly say with the hook-
nosed fellow of Rome,—I came, saw, and overcame.
PRINCE JOHN OF LANCASTER.
It was more of his courtesy than your deserving.
FALSTAFF.
I know not:—here he is, and here I yield him:
and I beseech your Grace, let it be bookt with
the rest of this day's deeds; or, by the Lord, I will
have it in a particular ballad else, with mine own
picture on the top of it, Colevile kissing my foot:
to the which course if I be enforced, if you do
not all show like gilt twopences to me, and I, in
the clear sky of fame, o'ershine you as much as
the full moon doth the cinders of the element,
which show like pins' heads to her, believe not
the word of the noble: therefore let me have right,
and let desert mount.
PRINCE JOHN OF LANCASTER.
Thine's too heavy to mount.
FALSTAFF.
Let it shine, then.
PRINCE JOHN OF LANCASTER.
Thine's too thick to shine.
FALSTAFF.
Let it do something, my good lord, that may do
me good, and call it what you will.
PRINCE JOHN OF LANCASTER.
Is thy name Colevile?
COLEVILE.
It is, my lord.
PRINCE JOHN OF LANCASTER.
A famous rebel art thou, Colevile.
FALSTAFF.
And a famous true subject took him.
COLEVILE.
I am, my lord, but as my betters are,
That led me hither: had they been ruled by me,
You should have won them dearer than you
　have.
FALSTAFF.
I know not how they sold themselves: but thou,
like a kind fellow, gavest thyself away gratis; and
I thank thee for thee.
　　　　　　　　Enter WESTMORELAND.
PRINCE JOHN OF LANCASTER.
Now, have you left pursuit?
WESTMORELAND.
Retreat is made, and execution stay'd.
PRINCE JOHN OF LANCASTER.
Send Colevile, with his confederates,
To York, to present execution:—

253

Blunt, lead him hence; and see you guard him
sure.
[*Exeunt* BLUNT *and others with* COLEVILE.
And now dispatch we toward the court, my
lords:
I hear the king my father is sore sick:
Our news shall go before us to his majesty,—
Which, cousin, you shall bear,—to comfort him;
And we with sober speed will follow you.

FALSTAFF.
My lord, I beseech you, give me leave to go
Through Glostershire: and, when you come to
court,
Stand my good lord, pray, in your good report.

PRINCE JOHN OF LANCASTER.
Fare you well, Falstaff: I, in my condition,
Shall better speak of you than you deserve.
[*Exeunt all except* FALSTAFF.

FALSTAFF.
I would you had but the wit: 'twere better than
your dukedom.—Good faith, this same young
sober-blooded boy doth not love me; nor a man
cannot make him laugh;—but that's no marvel,
he drinks no wine. There's never none of these
demure boys come to any proof; for thin drink
doth so over-cool their blood, and making many
fish-meals, that they fall into a kind of male
green-sickness; and then, when they marry, they
get wenches: they are generally fools and cowards;
—which some of us should be too, but for in-
flammation. A good sherris-sack hath a twofold
operation in it. It ascends me into the brain; dries
me there all the foolish and dull and crudy vapours
which environ it; makes it apprehensive, quick,
forgetive, full of nimble, fiery, and delectable
shapes; which, deliver'd o'er to the voice, the
tongue, which is the birth, becomes excellent wit.
The second property of your excellent sherris is,
the warming of the blood; which, before cold and
settled, left the liver white and pale, which is
the badge of pusillanimity and cowardice; but
the sherris warms it, and makes it course from the
inwards to the parts extreme: it illumineth the
face, which, as a beacon, gives warning to all
the rest of this little kingdom, man, to arm; and
then the vital commoners and inland petty spirits
muster me all to their captain, the heart, who,
great and puft up with this retinue, doth any deed
of courage: and this valour comes of sherris. So
that skill in the weapon is nothing without sack,
for that sets it a-work; and learning, a mere hoard
of gold kept by a devil, till sack commences it,
and sets it in act and use. Hereof comes it, that
Prince Harry is valiant; for the cold blood he did
naturally inherit of his father, he hath, like lean,
sterile, and bare land, manured, husbanded, and
till'd, with excellent endeavour of drinking good
and good store of fertile sherris, that he is become
very hot and valiant. If I had a thousand sons,
the first humane principle I would teach them
should be,—to forswear thin potations, and to
addict themselves to sack.
Enter BARDOLPH.
How now, Bardolph!

BARDOLPH.
The army is discharged all, and gone.

FALSTAFF.
Let them go. I'll through Glostershire; and there
will I visit Master Robert Shallow, esquire: I have
him already tempering between my finger and my
thumb, and shortly will I seal with him. Come
away. [*Exeunt.*

SCENE IV.

Westminster.   The Jerusalem Chamber.

Enter the KING, THOMAS DUKE OF CLARENCE,
HUMPHREY OF GLOSTER, WARWICK, *and
others.*

KING HENRY.
NOW, lords, if God doth give successful end
To this debate that bleedeth at our doors,
We will our youth lead on to higher fields,
And draw no swords but what are sanctified.
Our navy is addrest, our power collected,
Our substitutes in absence well invested,
And every thing lies level to our wish:
Only, we want a little personal strength;
And pause us, till these rebels, now afoot,
Come underneath the yoke of government.

WARWICK.
Both which we doubt not but your majesty
Shall soon enjoy.

KING HENRY.
                    Humphrey, my son of Gloster,
Where is the prince your brother?

GLOSTER.
I think he's gone to hunt, my lord, at Windsor.

KING HENRY.
And how accompanied?

GLOSTER.
                    I do not know, my lord.

KING HENRY.
Is not his brother, Thomas of Clarence, with
him?

GLOSTER.
No, my good lord; he is in presence here.

CLARENCE.
What would my lord and father?

KING HENRY.
Nothing but well to thee, Thomas of Clarence.
How chance thou art not with the prince thy
brother?
He loves thee, and thou dost neglect him,
Thomas;
Thou hast a better place in his affection
Than all thy brothers: cherish it, my boy;
And noble offices thou mayst effect
Of mediation, after I am dead,
Between his greatness and thy other brethren:
Therefore omit him not; blunt not his love,
Nor lose the good advantage of his grace
By seeming cold or careless of his will;
For he is gracious, if he be observed:
He hath a tear for pity, and a hand
Open as day for melting charity:
Yet notwithstanding, being incensed, he's flint;
As humorous as winter, and as sudden
As flaws congealed in the spring of day.
His temper, therefore, must be well observed:
Chide him for faults, and do it reverently,
When you perceive his blood inclined to mirth;

254

But, being moody, give him line and scope,
Till that his passions, like a whale on ground,
Confound themselves with working. Learn this, Thomas,
And thou shalt prove a shelter to thy friends;
A hoop of gold to bind thy brothers in,
That the united vessel of their blood,
Mingled with venom of suggestion—
As, force perforce, the age will pour it in—
Shall never leak, though it do work as strong
As aconitum or rash gunpowder.

CLARENCE.
I shall observe him with all care and love.

KING HENRY.
Why art thou not at Windsor with him, Thomas?

CLARENCE.
He is not there to-day; he dines in London.

KING HENRY.
And how accompanied? canst thou tell that?

CLARENCE.
With Pointz, and other his continual followers.

KING HENRY.
Most subject is the fattest soil to weeds;
And he, the noble image of my youth,
Is overspread with them: therefore my grief
Stretches itself beyond the hour of death:
The blood weeps from my heart, when I do shape,
In forms imaginary, th'unguided days
And rotten times that you shall look upon
When I am sleeping with my ancestors.
For when his headstrong riot hath no curb,
When rage and hot blood are his counsellors,
When means and lavish manners meet together,
O, with what wings shall his affections fly
Towards fronting peril and opposed decay!

WARWICK.
My gracious lord, you look beyond him quite:
The prince but studies his companions,   [guage,
Like a strange tongue; wherein, to gain the lan-
'Tis needful that the most immodest word
Be lookt upon and learn'd; which once attain'd
Your highness knows, comes to no further use
But to be known and hated. So, like gross terms,
The prince will, in the perfectness of time,
Cast off his followers; and their memory
Shall as a pattern or a measure live,
By which his grace must mete the lives of others,
Turning past evils to advantages.

KING HENRY.
'Tis seldom when the bee doth leave her comb
In the dead carrion.

Enter WESTMORELAND.
                    Who's here? Westmoreland?

WESTMORELAND.
Health to my sovereign, and new happiness
Added to that that I am to deliver!
Prince John, your son, doth kiss your Grace's hand:
Mowbray, the Bishop Scroop, Hastings, and all,
Are brought to the correction of your law;
There is not now a rebel's sword unsheathed,
But Peace puts forth her olive every where:
The manner how this action hath been borne,
Here at more leisure may your highness read,
With every course in his particular.

                    [*Giving packet.*

KING HENRY.
O Westmoreland, thou art a summer bird,
Which ever in the haunch of winter sings
The lifting-up of day.—Look, here's more news.

Enter HARCOURT.

HARCOURT.
From enemies heaven keep your majesty;
And, when they stand against you, may they fall
As those that I am come to tell you of!
The Earl Northumberland and the Lord Bardolph,
With a great power of English and of Scots,
Are by the shrieve of Yorkshire overthrown:
The manner and true order of the fight,
This packet, please it you, contains at large.

                    [*Giving packet.*

KING HENRY.
And wherefore should these good news make me sick?
Will Fortune never come with both hands full,
But write her fair words still in foulest letters?
She either gives a stomach, and no food,—
Such are the poor, in health; or else a feast,
And takes away the stomach,—such are the rich,
That have abundance, and enjoy it not.
I should rejoice now at this happy news;
And now my sight fails, and my brain is giddy:—
O me! come near me; now I am much ill.

                    [*Falls back.*

GLOSTER.
Comfort, your majesty!

CLARENCE.
                    O my royal father!

WESTMORELAND.
My sovereign lord, cheer up yourself, look up.

WARWICK.
Be patient, princes; you do know, these fits
Are with his highness very ordinary.
Stand from him, give him air; he'll straight be well.

CLARENCE.
No, no, he cannot long hold out these pangs:
Th'incessant care and labour of his mind
Hath wrought the mure, that should confine it in,
So thin that life looks through and will break out.

GLOSTER.
The people fear me; for they do observe
Unfather'd heirs and loathly births of nature:
The seasons change their manners, as the year
Had found some months asleep, and leapt them over.

CLARENCE.
The river hath thrice flow'd, no ebb between;
And the old folk, time's doting chronicles,
Say it did so a little time before
That our great-grandsire, Edward, sick'd and died.

WARWICK.
Speak lower, princes, for the king recovers.

GLOSTER.
This apoplex will certain be his end.

KING HENRY.
I pray you, take me up, and bear me hence
Into some other chamber: softly, pray.

          [*They lay the* KING *on a bed in an inner room.*

Let there be no noise made, my gentle friends;

Unless some dull and favourable hand
Will whisper music to my weary spirit.
WARWICK.
Call for the music in the other room.
KING HENRY.
Set me the crown upon my pillow here.
CLARENCE.
His eye is hollow, and he changes much.
WARWICK.
Less noise, less noise!
Enter PRINCE HENRY.
PRINCE HENRY.
Who saw the Duke of Clarence?
CLARENCE.
I am here, brother, full of heaviness.
PRINCE HENRY.
How now! rain within doors, and none abroad!
How doth the king?
GLOSTER.
Exceeding ill.
PRINCE HENRY.
Heard he
The good news yet? tell it him.
GLOSTER.
He alter'd much
Upon the hearing it.
PRINCE HENRY.
If he be sick with joy, he'll recover without physic.
WARWICK.
Not so much noise, my lords:—sweet prince,
speak low;
The king your father is disposed to sleep.
CLARENCE.
Let us withdraw into the other room.
WARWICK.
Will't please your Grace to go along with us?
PRINCE HENRY.
No; I will sit and watch here by the king.
[*Exeunt all except* PRINCE HENRY.
Why doth the crown lie there upon his pillow,
Being so troublesome a bedfellow?
O polisht perturbation! golden care!
That keep'st the ports of slumber open wide
To many a watchful night!—sleep with it now!
Yet not so sound and half so deeply sweet
As he whose brow with homely biggen bound
Snores out the watch of night. O majesty!
When thou dost pinch thy bearer, thou dost sit
Like a rich armour worn in heat of day,
That scalds with safety. By his gates of breath
There lies a downy feather which stirs not:
Did he suspire, that light and weightless down
Perforce must move.—My gracious lord! my
father!—
This sleep is sound indeed; this is a sleep,
That from this golden rigol hath divorced
So many English kings. Thy due from me
Is tears and heavy sorrows of the blood,
Which nature, love, and filial tenderness,
Shall, O dear father, pay thee plenteously:
My due from thee is this imperial crown,
Which, as immediate from thy place and blood,
Derives itself to me. Lo, here it sits,—
[*Putting it on his head.*
Which God shall guard: and put the world's
whole strength

Into one giant arm, it shall not force
This lineal honour from me: this from thee
Will I to mine leave, as 'tis left to me.   [*Exit.*
KING HENRY.
Warwick! Gloster! Clarence!
Enter WARWICK *and the rest.*
CLARENCE.
Doth the king call?
WARWICK.
What would your majesty? how fares your Grace?
KING HENRY.
Why did you leave me here alone, my lords?
CLARENCE.
We left the prince my brother here, my liege,
Who undertook to sit and watch by you.
KING HENRY.
The Prince of Wales! Where is he? let me see him:
He is not here.
WARWICK.
This door is open; he is gone this way.
GLOSTER.
He came not through the chamber where we
stay'd.
KING HENRY.
Where is the crown? who took it from my pillow?
WARWICK.
When we withdrew, my liege, we left it here.
KING HENRY.
The prince hath ta'en it hence:—go, seek him
out.
Is he so hasty, that he doth suppose
My sleep my death?—
Find him, my Lord of Warwick; chide him hither.
[*Exit* WARWICK.
This part of his conjoins with my disease,
And helps to end me.—See, sons, what things you
are!
How quickly nature falls into revolt
When gold becomes her object!
For this the foolish over-careful fathers
Have broke their sleeps with thought, their brains
with care,
Their bones with industry;
For this they have engrossed and piled up
The canker'd heaps of strange-achieved gold;
For this they have been thoughtful to invest
Their sons with arts and martial exercises:
When, like the bee, culling from every flower
The virtuous sweets,
Our thighs packt with wax, our mouths with
honey,
We bring it to the hive; and, like the bees,
Are murder'd for our pains. This bitter taste
Yield his engrossments to the ending father.
Enter WARWICK.
Now, where is he that will not stay so long
Till his friend sickness hath determined me?
WARWICK.
My lord, I found the prince in the next room,
Washing with kindly tears his gentle cheeks;
With such a deep demeanour in great sorrow,
That tyranny, which never quaff'd but blood,
Would, by beholding him, have washt his knife
With gentle eye-drops. He is coming hither.
KING HENRY.
But wherefore did he take away the crown?

Enter PRINCE HENRY.

Lo, where he comes.—Come hither to me,
  Harry.—
Depart the chamber, leave us here alone.
   [*Exeunt all except* KING HENRY *and*
   PRINCE HENRY.
       PRINCE HENRY.
I never thought to hear you speak again.
       KING HENRY.
Thy wish was father, Harry, to that thought:
I stay too long by thee, I weary thee.
Dost thou so hunger for mine empty chair,
That thou wilt needs invest thee with my honours
Before thy hour be ripe? O foolish youth!
Thou seek'st the greatness that will overwhelm
  thee.
Stay but a little; for my cloud of dignity
Is held from falling with so weak a wind
That it will quickly drop: my day is dim.
Thou hast stoln that which, after some few
  hours,
Were thine without offence; and at my death
Thou hast seal'd up my expectation:
Thy life did manifest thou loved'st me not,
And thou wilt have me die assured of it.
Thou hidest a thousand daggers in thy thoughts,
Which thou hast whetted on thy stony heart,
To stab at half an hour of my life.
What! canst thou not forbear me half an hour?
Then, get thee gone, and dig my grave thyself;
And bid the merry bells ring to thine ear,
That thou art crowned, not that I am dead.
Let all the tears that should bedew my hearse
Be drops of balm to sanctify thy head:
Only compound me with forgotten dust;
Give that which gave thee life unto the worms.
Pluck down my officers, break my decrees;
For now a time is come to mock at form:—
Harry the Fifth is crown'd:—up, vanity!
Down, royal state! all you sage counsellors, hence!
And to the English court assemble now,
From every region, apes of idleness!
Now, neighbour confines, purge you of your
  scum:
·Have you a ruffian that will swear, drink, dance,
Revel the night, rob, murder, and commit
The oldest sins the newest kind of ways?
Be happy, he will trouble you no more;
England shall double-gild his treble guilt,—
England shall give him office, honour, might;
For the Fifth Harry from curb'd licence plucks
The muzzle of restraint, and the wild dog
Shall flesh his tooth in every innocent.
O my poor kingdom, sick with civil blows!
When that my care could not withhold thy riots,
What wilt thou do when riot is thy care?
O, thou wilt be a wilderness again,
Peopled with wolves, thy old inhabitants!
       PRINCE HENRY.
O, pardon me, my liege! but for my tears,
            [*Kneeling.*
The moist impediments unto my speech,
I had forestall'd this dear and deep rebuke,
Ere you with grief had spoke, and I had heard
The course of it so far. There is your crown;
And He that wears the crown immortally

Long guard it yours! If I affect it more
Than as your honour and as your renown,
Let me no more from this obedience rise,—
Which my most inward true and duteous spirit
Teacheth,—this prostrate and exterior bending!
God witness with me, when I here came in,
            [*Rising.*
And found no course of breath within your
  majesty,
How cold it struck my heart! If I do feign,
O, let me in my present wildness die,
And never live to show th'incredulous world
The noble change that I have purposed!
Coming to look on you, thinking you dead,—
And dead almost, my liege, to think you were,—
I spake unto this crown as having sense,
And thus upbraided it: 'The care on thee depend-
  ing
Hath fed upon the body of my father;
Therefore, thou, best of gold, art worst of gold:
Other, less fine in carat, is more precious,
Preserving life in medicine potable;
But thou, most fine, most honour'd, most re-
  nown'd,
Hast eat thy bearer up.' Thus, my most royal
  liege,
Accusing it, I put it on my head,
To try with it—as with an enemy
That had before my face murder'd my father—
The quarrel of a true inheritor.
But if it did infect my blood with joy,
Or swell my thoughts to any strain of pride;
If any rebel or vain spirit of mine
Did with the least affection of a welcome
Give entertainment to the might of it,—
Let God for ever keep it from my head,
And make me as the poorest vassal is,
That doth with awe and terror kneel to it!
       KING HENRY.
O my son,
God put it in thy mind to take it hence,
That thou mightst win the more thy father's love,
Pleading so wisely in excuse of it!
Come hither, Harry, sit thou by my bed;
And hear, I think, the very latest counsel
That ever I shall breathe. God knows, my son,
By what by-paths and indirect crookt ways
I met this crown; and I myself know well
How troublesome it sat upon my head:
To thee it shall descend with better quiet,
Better opinion, better confirmation;
For all the soil of the achievement goes
With me into the earth. It seem'd in me
But as an honour snatcht with boisterous hand;
And I had many living to upbraid
My gain of it by their assistances;
Which daily grew to quarrel and to bloodshed,
Wounding supposed peace: all these bold fears
Thou see'st with peril I have answered;
For all my reign hath been but as a scene
Acting that argument: and now my death
Changes the mode; for what in me was purchased,
Falls upon thee in a more fairer sort:
So thou the garland wear'st successively.
Yet, though thou stand'st more sure than I could
  do,

Thou art not firm enough, since griefs are green;
And all my foes, which thou must make thy
   friends,
Have but their stings and teeth newly ta'en out;
By whose fell working I was first advanced,
And by whose power I well might lodge a fear
To be again displaced: which to avoid,
I cut some off, and had a purpose now
To lead out many to the Holy Land,
Lest rest and lying still might make them look
Too near unto my state. Therefore, my Harry,
Be it thy course to busy giddy minds   [out,
With foreign quarrels; that action, hence borne
May waste the memory of the former days.
More would I, but my lungs are wasted so
That strength of speech is utterly denied me.
How I came by the crown, O God forgive;
And grant it may with thee in true peace live!
           PRINCE HENRY.
My gracious liege,
You won it, wore it, kept it, gave it me;
Then plain and right must my possession be:
Which I with more than with a common pain
'Gainst all the world will rightfully maintain.
           KING HENRY.
Look, look, here comes my John of Lancaster.
  Enter PRINCE JOHN OF LANCASTER, WAR-
    WICK, LORDS, *and others.*
   PRINCE JOHN OF LANCASTER.
Health, peace, and happiness to my royal father!
           KING HENRY.
Thou bring'st me happiness and peace, son John;
But health, alack, with youthful wings is flown
From this bare wither'd trunk: upon thy sight
My worldly business makes a period.—
Where is my Lord of Warwick?
       PRINCE HENRY.
             My Lord of Warwick!
           KING HENRY.
Doth any name particular belong
Unto the lodging where I first did swoon?
           WARWICK.
'Tis call'd Jerusalem, my noble lord.
           KING HENRY.
Laud be to God!—even there my life must end.
It hath been prophesied to me many years,
I should not die but in Jerusalem;
Which vainly I supposed the Holy Land:—
But bear me to that chamber; there I'll lie;
In that Jerusalem shall Harry die.   [*Exeunt.*

ACT V. SCENE I.

Glostershire. SHALLOW'S *house.*

Enter SHALLOW, FALSTAFF, BARDOLPH, *and*
        PAGE.
          SHALLOW.
BY cock and pie, sir, you shall not away to-night.
  —What, Davy, I say!
          FALSTAFF.
You must excuse me, Master Robert Shallow.
          SHALLOW.
I will not excuse you; you shall not be excused;
excuses shall not be admitted; there is no excuse
shall serve; you shall not be excused.—Why,
Davy!

       Enter DAVY.
        DAVY.
Here, sir.
         SHALLOW.
Davy, Davy, Davy, Davy,—let me see, Davy; let
me see, Davy; let me see:—yea, marry, William
cook, bid him come hither.—Sir John, you shall
not be excused.
         DAVY.
Marry, sir, thus; those precepts cannot be served:
and again, sir,—shall we sow the headland with
wheat?
         SHALLOW.
With red wheat, Davy. But for William cook:—
are there no young pigeons?
         DAVY.
Yes, sir.—Here is now the smith's note for shoe-
ing and plough-irons.
         SHALLOW.
Let it be cast, and paid.—Sir John, you shall not
be excused.
         DAVY.
Now, sir, a new link to the bucket must needs be
had:—and, sir, do you mean to stop any of
William's wages, about the sack he lost the other
day at Hinckley fair?
         SHALLOW.
A' shall answer it.—Some pigeons, Davy, a
couple of short-legg'd hens, a joint of mutton, and
any pretty little tiny kickshaws, tell William cook.
         DAVY.
Doth the man of war stay all night, sir?
          SHALLOW.
Yea, Davy. I will use him well: a friend i'th'
court is better than a penny in purse. Use his men
well, Davy; for they are arrant knaves, and will
backbite.
         DAVY.
No worse than they are backbitten, sir; for they
have marvellous foul linen.
          SHALLOW.
Well conceited, Davy:—about thy business, Davy.
         DAVY.
I beseech you, sir, to countenance William Visor
of Woncot against Clement Perkes o'th' hill.
         SHALLOW.
There is many complaints, Davy, against that
Visor: that Visor is an arrant knave, on my knowledge.
         DAVY.
I grant your worship that he is a knave, sir; but
yet, God forbid, sir, but a knave should have
some countenance at his friend's request. An
honest man, sir, is able to speak for himself, when
a knave is not. I have served your worship truly,
sir, this eight years; and if I cannot once or twice
in a quarter bear out a knave against an honest
man, I have but a very little credit with your worship. The knave is mine honest friend, sir; therefore, I beseech your worship, let him be countenanced.
         SHALLOW.
Go to; I say he shall have no wrong. Look about,
Davy. [*Exit* DAVY.] Where are you, Sir John?
Come, come, come, off with your boots.—Give
me your hand, Master Bardolph.

BARDOLPH.

I am glad to see your worship.

SHALLOW.

I thank thee with all my heart, kind Master Bardolph:—[*to the* PAGE] and welcome, my tall fellow.—Come, Sir John.

FALSTAFF.

I'll follow you, good Master Robert Shallow. [*Exit* SHALLOW.] Bardolph, look to our horses. [*Exeunt* BARDOLPH *and* PAGE.] If I were saw'd into quantities, I should make four dozen of such bearded hermits'-staves as Master Shallow. It is a wonderful thing to see the semblable coherence of his men's spirits and his: they, by observing of him, do bear themselves like foolish justices; he, by conversing with them, is turn'd into a justice-like serving-man: their spirits are so married in conjunction with the participation of society, that they flock together in consent, like so many wild-geese. If I had a suit to Master Shallow, I would humour his men with the imputation of being near their master: if to his men, I would curry with Master Shallow, that no man could better command his servants. It is certain that either wise bearing or ignorant carriage is caught, as men take diseases, one of another: therefore let men take heed of their company. I will devise matter enough out of this Shallow to keep Prince Harry in continual laughter the wearing-out of six fashions,—which is four terms, or two actions,—and a' shall laugh without *intervallums*. O, it is much that a lie with a slight oath, and a jest with a sad brow, will do with a fellow that never had the ache in his shoulders! O, you shall see him laugh till his face be like a wet cloak ill laid up!

SHALLOW [*within*].

Sir John!

FALSTAFF.

I come, Master Shallow; I come, Master Shallow.
[*Exit.*

SCENE II.

Westminster.   The palace.

Enter WARWICK *and the* LORD CHIEF JUSTICE, *meeting.*

WARWICK.

HOW now, my lord chief justice! whither away?

LORD CHIEF JUSTICE.

How doth the king?

WARWICK.

Exceeding well; his cares are now all ended.

LORD CHIEF JUSTICE.

I hope, not dead.

WARWICK.

He's walkt the way of nature;
And, to our purposes, he lives no more.

LORD CHIEF JUSTICE.

I would his majesty had call'd me with him:
The service that I truly did his life
Hath left me open to all injuries.

WARWICK.

Indeed I think the young king loves you not.

LORD CHIEF JUSTICE.

I know he doth not; and do arm myself

To welcome the condition of the time;
Which cannot look more hideously upon me
Than I have drawn it in my fantasy.

WARWICK.

Here come the heavy issue of dead Harry:
O, that the living Harry had the temper
Of him, the worst of these three gentlemen!
How many nobles then should hold their places,
That must strike sail to spirits of vile sort!

LORD CHIEF JUSTICE.

O God, I fear all will be overturn'd!

Enter JOHN OF LANCASTER, CLARENCE, GLOSTER, WESTMORELAND, *and others.*

PRINCE JOHN OF LANCASTER.

Good morrow, cousin Warwick, good morrow.

GLOSTER *and* CLARENCE.

Good morrow, cousin.

PRINCE JOHN OF LANCASTER.

We meet like men that had forgot to speak.

WARWICK.

We do remember; but our argument
Is all too heavy to admit much talk.

PRINCE JOHN OF LANCASTER.

Well, peace be with him that hath made us heavy!

LORD CHIEF JUSTICE.

Peace be with us, lest we be heavier!

GLOSTER.

O, good my lord, you've lost a friend indeed;
And I dare swear you borrow not that face
Of seeming sorrow,—it is sure your own.

PRINCE JOHN OF LANCASTER.

Though no man be assured what grace to find,
You stand in coldest expectation:
I am the sorrier; would 'twere otherwise.

CLARENCE.

Well, you must now speak Sir John Falstaff fair;
Which swims against your stream of quality.

LORD CHIEF JUSTICE.

Sweet princes, what I did, I did in honour,
Led by th'impartial conduct of my soul;
And never shall you see that I will beg
A ragged and forestall'd remission.
If truth and upright innocency fail me,
I'll to the king my master that is dead,
And tell him who hath sent me after him.

WARWICK.

Here comes the prince.

Enter KING HENRY THE FIFTH, *attended.*

LORD CHIEF JUSTICE.

Good morrow; and God save your majesty!

KING HENRY THE FIFTH.

This new and gorgeous garment, majesty,
Sits not so easy on me as you think.—
Brothers, you mix your sadness with some fear:
This is the English, not the Turkish court;
Not Amurath an Amurath succeeds,
But Harry Harry. Yet be sad, good brothers,
For, by my faith, it very well becomes you:
Sorrow so royally in you appears,
That I will deeply put the fashion on,
And wear it in my heart: why, then, be sad;
But entertain no more of it, good brothers,
Than a joint burden laid upon us all.
For me, by heaven, I bid you be assured,
I'll be your father and your brother too;
Let me but bear your love, I'll bear your cares:

Yet weep that Harry's dead; and so will I;
But Harry lives, that shall convert those tears,
By number, into hours of happiness.

CLARENCE, PRINCE JOHN OF LANCASTER,
and GLOSTER.

We hope no other from your majesty.

KING HENRY THE FIFTH.

You all look strangely on me:—and you most;
[*To the* CHIEF JUSTICE.
You are, I think, assured I love you not.

LORD CHIEF JUSTICE.

I am assured, if I be measured rightly,
Your majesty hath no just cause to hate me.

KING HENRY THE FIFTH.

No!
How might a prince of my great hopes forget
So great indignities you laid upon me?
What! rate, rebuke, and roughly send to prison
Th'immediate heir of England? Was this easy?
May this be washt in Lethe and forgotten?

LORD CHIEF JUSTICE.

I then did use the person of your father;
The image of his power lay then in me:
And in th'administration of his law,
Whiles I was busy for the commonwealth,
Your highness pleased to forget my place,
The majesty and power of law and justice,
The image of the king whom I presented,
And struck me in my very seat of judgement;
Whereon, as an offender to your father,
I gave bold way to my authority,
And did commit you. If the deed were ill,
Be you contented, wearing now the garland,
To have a son set your decrees at naught,
To pluck down justice from your awful bench,
To trip the course of law, and blunt the sword
That guards the peace and safety of your person;
Nay, more, to spurn at your most royal image,
And mock your workings in a second body.
Question your royal thoughts, make the case
yours;
Be now the father, and propose a son:
Hear your own dignity so much profaned,
See your most dreadful laws so loosely slighted,
Behold yourself so by a son disdain'd;
And then imagine me taking your part,
And, in your power, soft silencing your son:
After this cold consideration, sentence me;
And, as you are a king, speak in your state
What I have done that misbecame my place,
My person, or my liege's sovereignty.

KING HENRY THE FIFTH.

You are right, justice, and you weigh this well;
Therefore still bear the balance and the sword:
And I do wish your honours may increase,
Till you do live to see a son of mine
Offend you, and obey you, as I did.
So shall I live to speak my father's words:
'Happy am I, that have a man so bold
That dares do justice on my proper son;
And not less happy, having such a son
That would deliver up his greatness so
Into the hands of justice.'—You did commit me:
For which, I do commit into your hand
Th'unstained sword that you have used to bear;
With this remembrance,—that you use the same

With the like bold, just, and impartial spirit
As you have done 'gainst me. There is my hand.
You shall be as a father to my youth:
My voice shall sound as you do prompt mine
ear;
And I will stoop and humble my intents
To your well-practised wise directions.—
And, princes all, believe me, I beseech you;—
My father is gone wild into his grave,
For in his tomb lie my affections;
And with his spirit sadly I survive,
To mock the expectation of the world,
To frustrate prophecies, and to raze out
Rotten opinion, who hath writ me down
After my seeming. The tide of blood in me
Hath proudly flow'd in vanity till now:
Now doth it turn, and ebb back to the sea,
Where it shall mingle with the state of floods,
And flow henceforth in formal majesty.
Now call we our high court of parliament:
And let us choose such limbs of noble counsel,
That the great body of our state may go
In equal rank with the best-govern'd nation;
That war, or peace, or both at once, may be
As things acquainted and familiar to us;
In which you, father, shall have foremost hand.
Our coronation done, we will accite,
As I before remember'd, all our state:
And, God consigning to my good intents,
No prince nor peer shall have just cause to say,
God shorten Harry's happy life one day! [*Exeunt.*

SCENE III.

Glostershire. SHALLOW'S *orchard.*

Enter FALSTAFF, SHALLOW, SILENCE, BAR-
DOLPH, *the* PAGE, *and* DAVY.

SHALLOW.

NAY, you shall see my orchard, where, in an
arbour, we will eat a last year's pippin of
my own graffing, with a dish of caraways, and so
forth:—come, cousin Silence:—and then to bed.

FALSTAFF.

'Fore God, you have here a goodly dwelling and
a rich.

SHALLOW.

Barren, barren, barren; beggars all, beggars all,
Sir John:—marry, good air.—Spread, Davy;
spread, Davy: well said, Davy.

FALSTAFF.

This Davy serves you for good uses; he is your
serving-man and your husband.

SHALLOW.

A good varlet, a good varlet, a very good varlet,
Sir John:—by the mass, I have drunk too much
sack at supper:—a good varlet. Now sit down,
now sit down:—come, cousin.

SILENCE.

Ah, sirrah! quoth-a,—we shall
[*Singing.*
Do nothing but eat, and make good cheer,
And praise God for the merry year;
When flesh is cheap and females dear,
And lusty lads roam here and there
So merrily,
And ever among so merrily.

FALSTAFF.
There's a merry heart!—Good Master Silence,
I'll give you a health for that anon.
SHALLOW.
Give Master Bardolph some wine, Davy.
DAVY.
Sweet sir, sit; I'll be with you anon; most sweet
sir, sit.—Master page, good master page, sit.—
Proface! What you want in meat, we'll have in
drink: but you must bear;—the heart's all.
[Exit.
SHALLOW.
Be merry, Master Bardolph;—and, my little
soldier there, be merry.
SILENCE [singing].
Be merry, be merry, my wife has all;
For women are shrews, both short and tall:
'Tis merry in hall when beards wag all,
And welcome merry Shrove-tide.
Be merry, be merry.
FALSTAFF.
I did not think Master Silence had been a man of
this mettle.
SILENCE.
Who, I? I have been merry twice and once ere
now.
Enter DAVY.
DAVY.
There's a dish of leather-coats for you.
[Setting them before BARDOLPH.
SHALLOW.
Davy,—
DAVY.
Your worship?—[to BARDOLPH] I'll be with you
straight.—A cup of wine, sir?
SILENCE [singing].
A cup of wine that's brisk and fine,
And drink unto the leman mine;
And a merry heart lives long-a.
FALSTAFF.
Well said, Master Silence.
SILENCE.
And we shall be merry;—now comes in the sweet
o' th' night.
FALSTAFF.
Health and long life to you, Master Silence!
SILENCE [singing].
Fill the cup, and let it come;
I'll pledge you a mile to the bottom.
SHALLOW.
Honest Bardolph, welcome: if thou want'st any
thing, and wilt not call, beshrew thy heart.—[to
the PAGE] Welcome, my little tiny thief, and wel-
come indeed too.—I'll drink to Master Bardolph,
and to all the cavaleroes about London.
DAVY.
I hope to see London once ere I die.
BARDOLPH.
An I might see you there, Davy,—
SHALLOW.
By the mass, you'll crack a quart together,—ha!
will you not, Master Bardolph?
BARDOLPH.
Yea, sir, in a pottle-pot.
SHALLOW.
By God's liggens, I thank thee:—the knave will

stick by thee, I can assure thee that: a' will not
out; he is true bred.
BARDOLPH.
And I'll stick by him, sir.
SHALLOW.
Why, there spoke a king. Lack nothing: be merry.
[Knocking within.] Look who's at door there, ho!
who knocks?   [Exit DAVY.
FALSTAFF.
Why, now you have done me right.
[To SILENCE, who has drunk a bumper.
SILENCE [singing].
Do me right,
And dub me knight:
Samingo.
Is't not so?
FALSTAFF.
'Tis so.
SILENCE.
Is't so? Why, then, say an old man can do some-
what.
Enter DAVY.
DAVY.
An't please your worship, there's one Pistol come
from the court with news.
FALSTAFF.
From the court! let him come in.
Enter PISTOL.
How now, Pistol!
PISTOL.
Sir John, God save you!
FALSTAFF.
What wind blew you hither, Pistol?
PISTOL.
Not the ill wind which blows no man to good.—
Sweet knight, thou art now one of the greatest
men in the realm.
SILENCE.
By'r lady, I think a' be, but goodman Puff of
Barson.
PISTOL.
Puff!
Puff in thy teeth, most recreant coward base!—
Sir John, I am thy Pistol and thy friend,
And helter-skelter have I rode to thee;
And tidings do I bring, and lucky joys,
And golden times, and happy news of price.
FALSTAFF.
I pray thee, now, deliver them like a man of this
world.
PISTOL.
A foutre for the world and worldlings base!
I speak of Africa and golden joys.
FALSTAFF.
O base Assyrian knight, what is thy news?
Let King Cophetua know the truth thereof.
SILENCE [singing].
And Robin Hood, Scarlet, and John.
PISTOL.
Shall dunghill curs confront the Helicons?
And shall good news be baffled?
Then, Pistol, lay thy head in Furies' lap.
SHALLOW.
Honest gentleman, I know not your breeding.
PISTOL.
Why, then, lament therefore.

SHALLOW.
Give me pardon, sir:—if, sir, you come with news
from the court, I take it there's but two ways,—
either to utter them, or to conceal them. I am, sir,
under the king, in some authority.

PISTOL.
Under which king, Besonian? speak, or die.

SHALLOW.
Under King Harry.

PISTOL.
Harry the Fourth? or Fifth?

SHALLOW.
Harry the Fourth.

PISTOL.
A foutre for thine office!—
Sir John, thy tender lambkin now is king;
Harry the Fifth's the man. I speak the truth:
When Pistol lies, do this; and fig me, like
The bragging Spaniard.

FALSTAFF.
What, is the old king dead?

PISTOL.
As nail in door: the things I speak are just.

FALSTAFF.
Away, Bardolph! saddle my horse.—Master
Robert Shallow, choose what office thou wilt in
the land, 'tis thine.—Pistol, I will double-charge
thee with dignities.

BARDOLPH.
O joyful day!—
I would not take a knighthood for my fortune.

PISTOL.
What, I do bring good news?

FALSTAFF.
Carry Master Silence to bed.—Master Shallow,
my Lord Shallow, be what thou wilt; I am fortune's steward. Get on thy boots: we'll ride all
night.—O sweet Pistol!—Away, Bardolph! [Exit
BARDOLPH.]—Come, Pistol, utter more to me;
and, withal, devise something to do thyself good.
—Boot, boot, Master Shallow! I know the young
king is sick for me. Let us take any man's horses;
the laws of England are at my commandment.
Blessed are they that have been my friends; and
woe to my lord chief justice!

PISTOL.
Let vultures vile seize on his lungs also!
'Where is the life that late I led?' say they:
Why, here it is;—welcome this pleasant day!
[Exeunt.

SCENE IV.

London. A street.

Enter HOSTESS QUICKLY, DOLL TEARSHEET,
and BEADLES.

HOSTESS.
NO, thou arrant knave: I would to God that I
might die, that I might have thee hang'd:
thou hast drawn my shoulder out of joint.

FIRST BEADLE.
The constables have deliver'd her over to me;
and she shall have whipping-cheer enough, I
warrant her: there hath been a man or two lately
kill'd about her.

DOLL TEARSHEET.
Nut-hook, nut-hook, you lie. Come on; I'll tell

thee what, thou damn'd tripe-visaged rascal, an
the child I go with do miscarry, thou wert better
thou hadst struck thy mother, thou paper-faced
villain.

HOSTESS.
O the Lord, that Sir John were come! he would
make this a bloody day to somebody. But I pray
God the fruit of her womb miscarry!

FIRST BEADLE.
If it do, you shall have a dozen of cushions again;
you have but eleven now. Come, I charge you
both go with me; for the man is dead that you and
Pistol beat amongst you.

DOLL TEARSHEET.
I'll tell thee what, thou thin man in a censer, I
will have you as soundly swinged for this,—you
blue-bottle rogue, you filthy famisht correc-
tioner, if you be not swinged, I'll forswear half-
kirtles.

FIRST BEADLE.
Come, come, you she knight-errant, come.

HOSTESS.
O God, that right should thus overcome might!
Well, of sufferance comes ease.

DOLL TEARSHEET.
Come, you rogue, come; bring me to a justice.

HOSTESS.
Ay, come, you starved bloodhound.

DOLL TEARSHEET.
Goodman death, goodman bones!

HOSTESS.
Thou atomy, thou!

DOLL TEARSHEET.
Come, you thin thing; come, you rascal.

FIRST BEADLE.
Very well. [Exeunt

SCENE V.

A public place near Westminster Abbey.

Enter two GROOMS, strewing rushes.

FIRST GROOM.
MORE rushes, more rushes.

SECOND GROOM.
The trumpets have sounded twice.

FIRST GROOM.
'Twill be two o'clock ere they come from the
coronation. Dispatch, dispatch. [Exeunt.

Enter FALSTAFF, SHALLOW, PISTOL, BAR-
DOLPH, and PAGE.

FALSTAFF.
Stand here by me, Master Robert Shallow; I will
make the king do you grace: I will leer upon him
as a' comes by; and do but mark the countenance
that he will give me.

PISTOL.
God bless thy lungs, good knight.

FALSTAFF.
Come here, Pistol; stand behind me!—[to SHAL-
LOW] O, if I had had time to have made new
liveries, I would have bestow'd the thousand
pound I borrow'd of you. But 'tis no matter; this
poor show doth better: this doth infer the zeal I
had to see him;—

SHALLOW.
It doth so.

FALSTAFF.
It shows my earnestness of affection,—
SHALLOW.
It doth so.
FALSTAFF.
My devotion,—
SHALLOW.
It doth, it doth, it doth.
FALSTAFF.
As it were, to ride day and night; and not to de-
liberate, not to remember, not to have patience to
shift me,—
SHALLOW.
It is best, certain.
FALSTAFF.
But to stand stain'd with travel, and sweating
with desire to see him; thinking of nothing else,
putting all affairs else in oblivion, as if there were
nothing else to be done but to see him.
PISTOL.
'Tis *semper idem*, for *obsque hoc nihil est:* 'tis all in
every part.
SHALLOW.
'Tis so, indeed.
PISTOL.
My knight, I will inflame thy noble liver,
And make thee rage.
Thy Doll, and Helen of thy noble thoughts,
Is in base durance and contagious prison;
Haled thither
By most mechanical and dirty hand:—
Rouse up revenge from ebon den with fell Alec-
to's snake,
For Doll is in. Pistol speaks naught but truth.
FALSTAFF.
I will deliver her.
[*Shouts within, and the trumpets sound.*
PISTOL.
There roar'd the sea, and trumpet-clangor
sounds.
Enter the KING *and his* TRAIN, *the* LORD
CHIEF JUSTICE *among them.*
FALSTAFF.
God save thy Grace, King Hal! my royal Hal!
PISTOL.
The heavens thee guard and keep, most royal imp
of fame!
FALSTAFF.
God save thee, my sweet boy!
KING HENRY THE FIFTH.
My lord chief justice, speak to that vain man.
LORD CHIEF JUSTICE.
Have you your wits? know you what 'tis you
speak?
FALSTAFF.
My king! my Jove! I speak to thee, my heart!
KING HENRY THE FIFTH.
I know thee not, old man: fall to thy prayers;
How ill white hairs become a fool and jester!
I have long dream'd of such a kind of man,
So surfeit-swell'd, so old, and so profane;
But, being awaked, I do despise my dream.
Make less thy body hence, and more thy grace;
Leave gormandizing; know the grave doth gape
For thee thrice wider than for other men.—
Reply not to me with a fool-born jest:

Presume not that I am the thing I was;
For God doth know, so shall the world perceive,
That I have turn'd away my former self;
So will I those that kept me company.
When thou dost hear I am as I have been,
Approach me, and thou shalt be as thou wast,
The tutor and the feeder of my riots:
Till then, I banish thee, on pain of death,—
As I have done the rest of my misleaders,—
Not to come near our person by ten mile.
For competence of life I will allow you,
That lack of means enforce you not to evil:
And, as we hear you do reform yourselves,
We will, according to your strength and quali-
ties,
Give you advancement.—Be it your charge, my
lord,
To see perform'd the tenour of our word.—
Set on.   [*Exeunt* KING *and his* TRAIN.
FALSTAFF.
Master Shallow, I owe you a thousand pound.
SHALLOW.
Yea, marry, Sir John; which I beseech you to let
me have home with me.
FALSTAFF.
That can hardly be, Master Shallow. Do not you
grieve at this; I shall be sent for in private to him:
look you, he must seem thus to the world: fear
not your advancements; I will be the man yet that
shall make you great.
SHALLOW.
I cannot well perceive how,—unless you should
give me your doublet, and stuff me out with
straw. I beseech you, good Sir John, let me have
five hundred of my thousand.
FALSTAFF.
Sir, I will be as good as my word: this that you
heard was but a colour.
SHALLOW.
A colour that I fear you will die in, Sir John.
FALSTAFF.
Fear no colours: go with me to dinner:—come,
Lieutenant Pistol;—come, Bardolph:—I shall be
sent for soon at night.
Enter PRINCE JOHN OF LANCASTER, *the* LORD
CHIEF JUSTICE, OFFICERS, &c.
LORD CHIEF JUSTICE.
Go, carry Sir John Falstaff to the Fleet;
Take all his company along with him.
FALSTAFF.
My lord, my lord,—
LORD CHIEF JUSTICE.
I cannot now speak: I will hear you soon.—
Take them away.
PISTOL.
Si fortuna me tormenta, spero contenta.
[*Exeunt all but* PRINCE JOHN *and* CHIEF
JUSTICE.
PRINCE JOHN OF LANCASTER.
I like this fair proceeding of the king's:
He hath intent his wonted followers
Shall all be very well provided for;
But all are banisht till their conversations
Appear more wise and modest to the world.
LORD CHIEF JUSTICE.
And so they are.

PRINCE JOHN OF LANCASTER.
The king hath call'd his parliament, my lord.
LORD CHIEF JUSTICE.
He hath.
PRINCE JOHN OF LANCASTER.
I will lay odds that, ere this year expire,
We bear our civil swords and native fire
As far as France: I heard a bird so sing,
Whose music, to my thinking, pleased the king.
Come, will you hence?   [*Exeunt.*

EPILOGUE.

Spoken by a DANCER.

FIRST my fear; then my court'sy; last my speech.
My fear is, your displeasure; my court'sy,
my duty; and my speech, to beg your pardons.
If you look for a good speech now, you undo me:
for what I have to say is of mine own making; and
what indeed I should say will, I doubt, prove
mine own marring. But to the purpose, and so to
the venture.—Be it known to you,—as it is very
well,—I was lately here in the end of a displeasing play, to pray your patience for it, and to
promise you a better. I meant, indeed, to pay you
with this; which, if, like an ill venture, it come
unluckily home, I break, and you, my gentle
creditors, lose. Here I promised you I would be,
and here I commit my body to your mercies: bate
me some, and I will pay you some, and, as most
debtors do, promise you infinitely.

If my tongue cannot entreat you to acquit me,
will you command me to use my legs? and yet
that were but light payment,—to dance out of
your debt. But a good conscience will make any
possible satisfaction, and so would I. All the
gentlewomen here have forgiven me: if the
gentlemen will not, then the gentlemen do not
agree with the gentlewomen, which was never
seen before in such an assembly.

One word more, I beseech you. If you be not
too much cloy'd with fat meat, our humble
author will continue the story, with Sir John in
it, and make you merry with fair Katharine of
France: where, for any thing I know, Falstaff
shall die of a sweat, unless already a' be kill'd
with your hard .opinions; for Oldcastle died a
martyr, and this is not the man. My tongue is
weary; when my legs are too, I will bid you good
night; and so kneel down before you;—but, indeed, to pray for the queen.

KING HENRY THE FIFTH

DRAMATIS PERSONAE

KING HENRY THE FIFTH.
DUKE OF GLOSTER, ⎫ *brothers to the King.*
DUKE OF BEDFORD, ⎭
DUKE OF EXETER, *uncle to the King.*
DUKE OF YORK, *cousin to the King.*
EARL OF SALISBURY.
EARL OF WESTMORELAND.
EARL OF WARWICK.
ARCHBISHOP OF CANTERBURY.
BISHOP OF ELY.
EARL OF CAMBRIDGE.
LORD SCROOP.
SIR THOMAS GREY.
SIR THOMAS ERPINGHAM, GOWER, FLUELLEN,
  MACMORRIS, JAMY, *officers in King Henry's
  army.*
JOHN BATES, ALEXANDER COURT, MICHAEL
  WILLIAMS, *soldiers in the same.*
PISTOL.
NYM.
BARDOLPH.
BOY.
A HERALD.

CHARLES THE SIXTH, *King of France.*
LOUIS, *the Dauphin.*
DUKE OF BURGUNDY.
DUKE OF ORLEANS.
DUKE OF BOURBON.
THE CONSTABLE OF FRANCE.
RAMBURES, GRANDPRÉ, *French lords.*
GOVERNOR OF HARFLEUR.
MONTJOY, *a French herald.*
AMBASSADORS to the King of England.

ISABEL, *Queen of France.*
KATHARINE, *daughter to Charles and Isabel.*
ALICE, *a lady attending on her.*
HOSTESS *of a tavern in Eastcheap (formerly
  Mistress Quickly, and now married to Pistol).*

LORDS, LADIES, OFFICERS, SOLDIERS,
CITIZENS, MESSENGERS, *and* ATTENDANTS.

CHORUS.

SCENE—*England; afterwards France.*

PROLOGUE.

Enter CHORUS.

CHORUS.

O FOR a Muse of fire, that would ascend
  The brightest heaven of invention,—
A kingdom for a stage, princes to act,
And monarchs to behold the swelling scene!
Then should the warlike Harry, like himself,
Assume the port of Mars; and at his heels,
Leasht-in like hounds, should famine, sword, and
  fire,
Crouch for employment. But pardon, gentles all,
The flat unraised spirits that have dared
On this unworthy scaffold to bring forth
So great an object: can this cockpit hold
The vasty fields of France? or may we cram
Within this wooden O the very casques
That did affright the air at Agincourt?
O, pardon! since a crooked figure may
Attest in little place a million;
And let us, ciphers to this great accompt,
On your imaginary forces work.
Suppose within the girdle of these walls
Are now confined two mighty monarchies,
Whose high-upreared and abutting fronts
The perilous narrow ocean parts asunder:
Piece-out our imperfections with your thoughts;
Into a thousand parts divide one man,
And make imaginary puissance;
Think, when we talk of horses, that you see them
Printing their proud hoofs i'th'receiving earth;—
For 'tis your thoughts that now must deck our
  kings,
Carry them here and there; jumping o'er times,
Turning th'accomplishment of many years
Into an hour-glass: for the which supply,

Admit me Chorus to this history;
Who, prologue-like, your humble patience pray,
Gently to hear, kindly to judge, our play.   [*Exit.*

ACT I. SCENE I.

London.   An ante-chamber in the KING'S
palace.

Enter the ARCHBISHOP OF CANTERBURY
and the BISHOP OF ELY.

ARCHBISHOP OF CANTERBURY.

MY lord, I'll tell you,—that self bill is
  urged,
Which in th'eleventh year of the last king's
  reign
Was like, and had indeed against us past,
But that the scambling and unquiet time
Did push it out of further question.

BISHOP OF ELY.

But how, my lord, shall we resist it now?

ARCHBISHOP OF CANTERBURY.

It must be thought on. If it pass against us,
We lose the better half of our possession;
For all the temporal lands, which men devout
By testament have given to the church,
Would they strip from us; being valued thus,—
As much as would maintain, to the king's honour,
Full fifteen earls and fifteen hundred knights,
Six thousand and two hundred good esquires;
And, to relief of lazars and weak age,
Of indigent faint souls past corporal toil,
A hundred almshouses right well supplied;
And to the coffers of the king, beside,
A thousand pounds by th'year: thus runs the bill.

BISHOP OF ELY.

This would drink deep.

265

ARCHBISHOP OF CANTERBURY.
'Twould drink the cup and all.
BISHOP OF ELY.
But what prevention?
ARCHBISHOP OF CANTERBURY.
The king is full of grace and fair regard.
BISHOP OF ELY.
And a true lover of the holy church.
ARCHBISHOP OF CANTERBURY.
The courses of his youth promised it not.
The breath no sooner left his father's body,
But that his wildness, mortified in him,
Seem'd to die too; yea, at that very moment,
Consideration, like an angel, came,
And whipt th'offending Adam out of him,
Leaving his body as a paradise,
T'envelop and contain celestial spirits.
Never was such a sudden scholar made;
Never came reformation in a flood,
With such a heady current, scouring faults;
Nor never Hydra-headed wilfulness
So soon did lose his seat, and all at once,
As in this king.
BISHOP OF ELY.
We are blessed in the change.
ARCHBISHOP OF CANTERBURY.
Hear him but reason in divinity,
And, all-admiring, with an inward wish
You would desire the king were made a prelate:
Hear him debate of commonwealth affairs,
You would say it hath been all-in-all his study:
List his discourse of war, and you shall hear
A fearful battle render'd you in music:
Turn him to any cause of policy,
The Gordian knot of it he will unloose,
Familiar as his garter:—that, when he speaks,
The air, a charter'd libertine, is still,
And the mute wonder lurketh in men's ears,
To steal his sweet and honey'd sentences;
So that the art and practic part of life
Must be the mistress to this theoric:
Which is a wonder how his Grace should glean
  it,
Since his addiction was to courses vain;
His companies unletter'd, rude, and shallow;
His hours fill'd up with riots, banquets, sports;
And never noted in him any study,
Any retirement, any sequestration
From open haunts and popularity.
BISHOP OF ELY.
The strawberry grows underneath the nettle,
And wholesome berries thrive and ripen best
Neighbour'd by fruit of baser quality:
And so the prince obscured his contemplation
Under the veil of wildness; which, no doubt,
Grew like the summer grass, fastest by night,
Unseen, yet crescive in his faculty.
ARCHBISHOP OF CANTERBURY.
It must be so; for miracles are ceased;
And therefore we must needs admit the means
How things are perfected.
BISHOP OF ELY.
But, my good lord,
How now for mitigation of this bill
Urged by the commons? Doth his majesty
Incline to it, or no?

ARCHBISHOP OF CANTERBURY.
He seems indifferent;
Or, rather, swaying more upon our part
Than cherishing th'exhibiters against us:
For I have made an offer to his majesty,—
Upon our spiritual convocation,
And in regard of causes now in hand,
Which I have open'd to his Grace at large,
As touching France,—to give a greater sum
Than ever at one time the clergy yet
Did to his predecessors part withal.
BISHOP OF ELY.
How did this offer seem received, my lord?
ARCHBISHOP OF CANTERBURY.
With good acceptance of his majesty;
Save that there was not time enough to hear—
As, I perceived, his Grace would fain have done—
The severals and unhidden passages
Of his true titles to some certain dukedoms,
And, generally, to the crown and seat of France,
Derived from Edward, his great-grandfather.
BISHOP OF ELY.
What was th'impediment that broke this off?
ARCHBISHOP OF CANTERBURY.
The French ambassador upon that instant
Craved audience;—and the hour, I think, is come
To give him hearing: is it four o'clock?
BISHOP OF ELY.
It is.
ARCHBISHOP OF CANTERBURY.
Then go we in, to know his embassy;
Which I could, with a ready guess, declare,
Before the Frenchman speak a word of it.
BISHOP OF ELY.
I'll wait upon you; and I long to hear it.
[*Exeunt.*

SCENE II.

The same.   The Presence-chamber.

Enter KING HENRY, GLOSTER, BEDFORD,
EXETER, WARWICK, WESTMORELAND, *and*
ATTENDANTS.

KING HENRY.
WHERE is my gracious Lord of Canterbury?
DUKE OF EXETER.
Not here in presence.
KING HENRY.
Send for him, good uncle.
EARL OF WESTMORELAND.
Shall we call in th'ambassador, my liege?
KING HENRY.
Not yet, my cousin: we would be resolved,
Before we hear him, of some things of weight,
That task our thoughts, concerning us and
France.
Enter the ARCHBISHOP OF CANTERBURY *and*
the BISHOP OF ELY.
ARCHBISHOP OF CANTERBURY.
God and his angels guard your sacred throne,
And make you long become it!
KING HENRY.
Sure, we thank you.
My learned lord, we pray you to proceed,
And justly and religiously unfold
Why the law Salique, that they have in France,
Or should, or should not, bar us in our claim:

And God forbid, my dear and faithful lord,
That you should fashion, wrest, or bow your
    reading,
Or nicely charge your understanding soul
With opening titles miscreate, whose right
Suits not in native colours with the truth;
For God doth know how many, now in health,
Shall drop their blood in approbation
Of what your reverence shall incite us to.
Therefore take heed how you impawn our person,
How you awake the sleeping sword of war:
We charge you, in the name of God, take heed;
For never two such kingdoms did contend
Without much fall of blood; whose guiltless drops
Are every one a woe, a sore complaint
'Gainst him whose wrongs give edge unto the
    swords
That make such waste in brief mortality.
Under this conjuration, speak, my lord;
For we will hear, note, and believe in heart
That what you speak is in your conscience washt
As pure as sin with baptism.

ARCHBISHOP OF CANTERBURY.
Then hear me, gracious sovereign,—and you
    peers,
That owe yourselves, your lives, and services
To this imperial throne.—There is no bar
To make against your highness' claim to France
But this, which they produce from Pharamond,—
In terram Salicam mulieres ne succedant,
'No woman shall succeed in Salique land:'
Which Salique land the French unjustly gloze
To be the realm of France, and Pharamond
The founder of this law and female bar.
Yet their own authors faithfully affirm
That the land Salique is in Germany,
Between the floods of Sala and of Elbe;
Where Charles the Great, having subdued the
    Saxons,
There left behind and settled certain French;
Who, holding in disdain the German women
For some dishonest manners of their life,
Establisht then this law,—to wit, no female
Should be inheritrix in Salique land:
Which Salique, as I said, 'twixt Elbe and Sala,
Is at this day in Germany call'd Meisen.
Then doth it well appear, the Salique law
Was not devised for the realm of France:
Nor did the French possess the Salique land
Until four hundred one and twenty years
After defunction of King Pharamond,
Idly supposed the founder of this law;
Who died within the year of our redemption
Four hundred twenty-six; and Charles the Great
Subdued the Saxons, and did seat the French
Beyond the river Sala, in the year
Eight hundred five. Besides, their writers say,
King Pepin, which deposed Childeric,
Did, as heir general, being descended
Of Blithild, which was daughter to King Clothair,
Make claim and title to the crown of France.
Hugh Capet also,—who usurpt the crown
Of Charles the duke of Lorraine, sole heir male
Of the true line and stock of Charles the Great,—
To find his title with some shows of truth,
Though, in pure truth, it was corrupt and naught,

Convey'd himself as heir to th'Lady Lingare,
Daughter to Charlemain, who was the son
To Louis the emperor, and Louis the son
Of Charles the Great. Also King Louis the
    Tenth,
Who was sole heir to the usurper Capet,
Could not keep quiet in his conscience,
Wearing the crown of France, till satisfied
That fair Queen Isabel, his grandmother,
Was lineal of the Lady Ermengare,
Daughter to Charles the foresaid duke of Lor-
    raine:
By the which marriage the line of Charles the
    Great
Was re-united to the crown of France.
So that, as clear as is the summer's sun,
King Pepin's title, and Hugh Capet's claim,
King Louis his satisfaction, all appear
To hold in right and title of the female:
So do the kings of France unto this day;
Howbeit they would hold up this Salique law
To bar your highness claiming from the female;
And rather choose to hide them in a net
Than amply to imbar their crooked titles
Usurpt from you and your progenitors.

KING HENRY.
May I with right and conscience make this
    claim?

ARCHBISHOP OF CANTERBURY.
The sin upon my head, dread sovereign!
For in the Book of Numbers is it writ,—
When the man dies, let the inheritance
Descend unto the daughter. Gracious lord,
Stand for your own; unwind your bloody flag;
Look back into your mighty ancestors:
Go, my dread lord, to your great-grandsire's
    tomb,
From whom you claim; invoke his warlike spirit,
And your great-uncle's, Edward the Black
    Prince,
Who on the French ground play'd a tragedy,
Making defeat on the full power of France,
Whiles his most mighty father on a hill
Stood smiling to behold his lion's whelp
Forage in blood of French nobility.
O noble English, that could entertain
With half their forces the full pride of France,
And let another half stand laughing by,
All out of work and cold for action!

BISHOP OF ELY.
Awake remembrance of these valiant dead,
And with your puissant arm renew their feats:
You are their heir; you sit upon their throne;
The blood and courage that renowned them
Runs in your veins; and my thrice-puissant liege
Is in the very May-morn of his youth,
Ripe for exploits and mighty enterprises.

DUKE OF EXETER.
Your brother kings and monarchs of the earth
Do all expect that you should rouse yourself,
As did the former lions of your blood.

EARL OF WESTMORELAND.
They know your Grace hath cause and means
    and might;
So hath your highness; never king of England
Had nobles richer and more loyal subjects,

Whose hearts have left their bodies here in England,
And lie pavilion'd in the fields of France.

ARCHBISHOP OF CANTERBURY.

O, let their bodies follow, my dear liege,
With blood and sword and fire to win your right:
In aid whereof we of the spirituality
Will raise your highness such a mighty sum
As never did the clergy at one time
Bring in to any of your ancestors.

KING HENRY.

We must not only arm t'invade the French,
But lay down our proportions to defend
Against the Scot, who will make road upon us
With all advantages.

ARCHBISHOP OF CANTERBURY.

They of those marches, gracious sovereign,
Shall be a wall sufficient to defend
Our inland from the pilfering borderers.

KING HENRY.

We do not mean the coursing snatchers only,
But fear the main intendment of the Scot,
Who hath been still a giddy neighbour to us;
For you shall read that my great-grandfather
Never went with his forces into France,
But that the Scot on his unfurnisht kingdom
Came pouring, like the tide into a breach,
With ample and brim fullness of his force;
Galling the gleaned land with hot assays,
Girding with grievous siege castles and towns;
That England, being empty of defence,
Hath shook and trembled at th'ill neighbourhood.

ARCHBISHOP OF CANTERBURY.

She hath been then more fear'd than harm'd, my liege;
For hear her but exampled by herself:—
When all her chivalry hath been in France,
And she a mourning widow of her nobles,
She hath herself not only well defended
But taken, and impounded as a stray,
The King of Scots; whom she did send to France,
To fill King Edward's fame with prisoner kings,
And make her chronicle as rich with praise
As is the ooze and bottom of the sea
With sunken wrack and sumless treasuries.

EARL OF WESTMORELAND.

But there's a saying, very old and true,—
   'If that you will France win,
   Then with Scotland first begin:'
For once the eagle England being in prey,
To her unguarded nest the weasel Scot
Comes sneaking, and so sucks her princely eggs;
Playing the mouse in absence of the cat,
To spoil and havoc more than she can eat.

DUKE OF EXETER.

It follows, then, the cat must stay at home:
Yet that is but a curst necessity,
Since we have locks to safeguard necessaries,
And pretty traps to catch the petty thieves.
While that the armed hand doth fight abroad,
Th'advised head defends itself at home;
For government, though high, and low, and lower,
Put into parts, doth keep in one concert,
Congreeing in a full and natural close,
Like music.

ARCHBISHOP OF CANTERBURY.

Therefore doth heaven divide
The state of man in divers functions,
Setting endeavour in continual motion;
To which is fixed, as an aim or butt,
Obedience: for so work the honey-bees,
Creatures that, by a rule in nature, teach
The art of order to a peopled kingdom.
They have a king, and officers of sorts:
Where some, like magistrates, correct at home;
Others, like merchants, venture trade abroad;
Others, like soldiers, armed in their stings,
Make boot upon the summer's velvet buds;
Which pillage they with merry march bring home
To the tent-royal of their emperor:
Who, busied in his majesty, surveys
The singing masons building roofs of gold;
The civil citizens kneading-up the honey;
The poor mechanic porters crowding in
Their heavy burdens at his narrow gate;
The sad-eyed justice, with his surly hum,
Delivering o'er to executors pale
The lazy yawning drone. I this infer,—
That many things, having full reference
To one concent, may work contrariously:
As many arrows, loosed several ways,
Fly to one mark;
As many several ways meet in one town;
As many fresh streams run in one self sea;
As many lines close in the dial's centre;
So may a thousand actions, once afoot,
End in one purpose, and be all well borne
Without defeat. Therefore to France, my liege.
Divide your happy England into four;
Whereof take you one quarter into France,
And you withal shall make all Gallia shake.
If we, with thrice such powers left at home,
Cannot defend our own doors from the dog,
Let us be worried, and our nation lose
The name of hardiness and policy.

KING HENRY.

Call in the messengers sent from the Dauphin.
   [*Exeunt some* ATTENDANTS.
Now are we well resolved; and, by God's help,
And yours, the noble sinews of our power,
France being ours, we'll bend it to our awe,
Or break it all to pieces: or there we'll sit,
Ruling in large and ample empery
O'er France and all her almost kingly dukedoms,
Or lay these bones in an unworthy urn,
Tombless, with no remembrance over them:
Either our history shall with full mouth
Speak freely of our acts, or else our grave,
Like Turkish mute, shall have a tongueless mouth,
Not worshipt with a waxen epitaph.
   Enter AMBASSADORS *of France, attended.*
Now are we well prepared to know the pleasure
Of our fair cousin Dauphin; for we hear
Your greeting is from him, not from the king.

FIRST AMBASSADOR.

May't please your majesty to give us leave
Freely to render what we have in charge;
Or shall we sparingly show you far off
The Dauphin's meaning and our embassy?

KING HENRY.
We are no tyrant, but a Christian king;
Unto whose grace our passion is as subject
As are our wretches fetter'd in our prisons:
Therefore with frank and with uncurbed plainness
Tell us the Dauphin's mind.
　　　　FIRST AMBASSADOR.
　　　　　　　　Thus, then, in few.
Your highness, lately sending into France,
Did claim some certain dukedoms, in the right
Of your great predecessor, King Edward the
　　Third.
In answer of which claim, the prince our master
Says, that you savour too much of your youth;
And bids you be advised, there's naught in
　　France
That can be with a nimble galliard won;—
You cannot revel into dukedoms there.
He therefore sends you, meeter for your spirit,
This tun of treasure; and, in lieu of this,
Desires you let the dukedoms that you claim
Hear no more of you. This the Dauphin speaks.
　　　　KING HENRY.
What treasure, uncle?
　　　　DUKE OF EXETER.
　　　　　Tennis-balls, my liege.
　　　　KING HENRY.
We are glad the Dauphin is so pleasant with us;
His present and your pains we thank you for:
When we have matcht our rackets to these balls,
We will, in France, by God's grace, play a set
Shall strike his father's crown into the hazard.
Tell him he hath made a match with such a
　　wrangler
That all the courts of France will be disturb'd
With chases. And we understand him well,
How he comes o'er us with our wilder days,
Not measuring what use we made of them.
We never valued this poor seat of England;
And therefore, living hence, did give ourself
To barbarous licence; as 'tis ever common
That men are merriest when they are from home.
But tell the Dauphin, I will keep my state,
Be like a king, and show my sail of greatness,
When I do rouse me in my throne of France:
For that I have laid by my majesty,
And plodded like a man for working-days;
But I will rise there with so full a glory,
That I will dazzle all the eyes of France,
Yea, strike the Dauphin blind to look on us.
And tell the pleasant prince, this mock of his
Hath turn'd his balls to gun-stones; and his soul
Shall stand sore charged for the wasteful vengeance
That shall fly with them: for many a thousand
　　widows
Shall this his mock mock out of their dear husbands;
Mock mothers from their sons, mock castles
　　down;
And some are yet ungotten and unborn
That shall have cause to curse the Dauphin's
　　scorn.
But this lies all within the will of God,
To whom I do appeal; and in whose name,

Tell you the Dauphin, I am coming on,
To venge me as I may, and to put forth
My rightful hand in a well-hallow'd cause.
So, get you hence in peace; and tell the Dauphin,
His jest will savour but of shallow wit,
When thousands weep, more than did laugh at
　　it.—
Convey them with safe conduct.—Fare you well.
　　　　　　　[Exeunt AMBASSADORS.
　　　　DUKE OF EXETER.
This was a merry message.
　　　　KING HENRY.
We hope to make the sender blush at it.
Therefore, my lords, omit no happy hour
That may give furtherance to our expedition;
For we have now no thought in us but France,
Save those to God, that run before our business.
Therefore let our proportions for these wars
Be soon collected, and all things thought upon
That may with reasonable swiftness add
More feathers to our wings; for, God before,
We'll chide this Dauphin at his father's door.
Therefore let every man now task his thought,
That this fair action may on foot be brought.
　　　　　　　[Flourish. Exeunt.

ACT II.
PROLOGUE.
Enter CHORUS.
CHORUS.
NOW all the youth of England are on fire,
And silken dalliance in the wardrobe lies:
Now thrive the armourers, and honour's thought
Reigns solely in the breast of every man:
They sell the pasture now to buy the horse;
Following the mirror of all Christian kings,
With winged heels, as English Mercuries.
For now sits Expectation in the air,
And hides a sword from hilts unto the point
With crowns imperial, crowns, and coronets,
Promised to Harry and his followers.
The French, advised by good intelligence
Of this most dreadful preparation,
Shake in their fear; and with pale policy
Seek to divert the English purposes.
O England!—model to thy inward greatness,
Like little body with a mighty heart,—
What mightst thou do, that honour would thee
　　do,
Were all thy children kind and natural!
But see thy fault! France hath in thee found out
A nest of hollow bosoms, which he fills
With treacherous crowns; and three corrupted
　　men,—
One, Richard earl of Cambridge; and the second,
Henry Lord Scroop of Masham; and the third,
Sir Thomas Grey, knight, of Northumberland,—
Have, for the gilt of France—O guilt indeed!—
Confirm'd conspiracy with fearful France;
And by their hands this grace of kings must die,
If hell and treason hold their promises,
Ere he take ship for France, and in Southampton.
Linger your patience on; and we'll digest
Th'abuse of distance; force a play.
The sum is paid; the traitors are agreed;

The king is set from London; and the scene
Is now transported, gentles, to Southampton,—
There is the playhouse now, there must you sit:
And thence to France shall we convey you safe,
And bring you back, charming the narrow seas
To give you gentle pass; for, if we may,
We'll not offend one stomach with our play.
But, till the king come forth, and not till then,
Unto Southampton do we shift our scene. [*Exit.*

SCENE I.

London. Before the Boar's Head Tavern,
Eastcheap.

Enter CORPORAL NYM *and* LIEUTENANT BAR-
DOLPH.

BARDOLPH.

WELL met, Corporal Nym.
NYM.
Good morrow, Lieutenant Bardolph.
BARDOLPH.
What, are Ancient Pistol and you friends yet?
NYM.
For my part, I care not: I say little; but when
time shall serve, there shall be smites;—but that
shall be as it may. I dare not fight; but I will wink,
and hold out mine iron: it is a simple one; but
what though? it will toast cheese, and it will en-
dure cold as another man's sword will: and there's
the humour of it.
BARDOLPH.
I will bestow a breakfast to make you friends; and
we'll be all three sworn brothers to France: let's
be so, good Corporal Nym.
NYM.
Faith, I will live so long as I may, that's the certain of it; and when I cannot live any longer, I
will do as I may: that is my rest, that is the rendezvous of it.
BARDOLPH.
It is certain, corporal, that he is married to Nell
Quickly: and, certainly, she did you wrong; for
you were troth-plight to her.
NYM.
I cannot tell:—things must be as they may: men
may sleep, and they may have their throats about
them at that time; and, some say, knives have
edges. It must be as it may: though patience be
a tired mare, yet she will plod. There must be
conclusions. Well, I cannot tell.
BARDOLPH.
Here comes Ancient Pistol and his wife:—good
corporal, be patient here.
Enter PISTOL *and* HOSTESS.
How now, mine host Pistol!
PISTOL.
Base tike, call'st thou me host?
Now, by this hand, I swear, I scorn the term;
Nor shall my Nell keep lodgers.
HOSTESS.
No, by my troth, not long; for we cannot lodge
and board a dozen or fourteen gentlewomen that
live honestly by the prick of their needles, but it
will be thought we keep a bawdy-house straight.
[NYM *and* PISTOL *draw.*] O well-a-day, Lady, if

he be not drawn now! We shall see wilful adultery
and murder committed.
BARDOLPH.
Good lieutenant,—good corporal,—offer nothing
here.
NYM.
Pish!
PISTOL.
Pish for thee, Iceland dog! thou prick-ear'd cur of
Iceland!
HOSTESS.
Good Corporal Nym, show thy valour, and put up
your sword.
NYM.
Will you shog off? I would have you *solus.*
PISTOL.
Solus, egregious dog? O viper vile!
The *solus* in thy most mervailous face;
The *solus* in thy teeth, and in thy throat,
And in thy hateful lungs, yea, in thy maw, perdy,
And, which is worse, within thy nasty mouth!
I do retort the *solus* in thy bowels;
For I can take, and Pistol's cock is up,
And flashing fire will follow.
NYM.
I am not Barbason; you cannot conjure me. I
have an humour to knock you indifferently well.
If you grow foul with me, Pistol, I will scour you
with my rapier, as I may, in fair terms: if you
would walk off, I would prick your guts a little,
in good terms, as I may: and that's the humour
of it.
PISTOL.
O braggart vile, and damned furious wight!
The grave doth gape, and doting death is near;
Therefore exhale.
BARDOLPH.
Hear me, hear me what I say:—he that strikes the
first stroke, I'll run him up to the hilts, as I am a
soldier.   [*Draws.*
PISTOL.
An oath of mickle might; and fury shall abate.—
Give me thy fist, thy fore-foot to me give:
Thy spirits are most tall.
[*They sheath their swords.*
NYM.
I will cut thy throat, one time or other, in fair
terms: that is the humour of it.
PISTOL.
Couple a gorge!
That is the word. I thee defy again.
O hound of Crete, think'st thou my spouse to get?
No; to the spital go,
And from the powdering-tub of infamy
Fetch forth the lazar kite of Cressid's kind,
Doll Tearsheet she by name, and her espouse:
I have, and I will hold, the *quondam* Quickly
For the only she; and—*pauca,* there's enough.
Go to.
Enter BOY.
BOY.
Mine host Pistol, you must come to my master,—
and you, hostess:—he is very sick, and would to
bed.—Good Bardolph, put thy face between his
sheets, and do the office of a warming-pan.—
Faith, he's very ill.

BARDOLPH.
Away, you rogue!

HOSTESS.
By my troth, he'll yield the crow a pudding one of these days: the king has kill'd his heart.—Good husband, come home presently.

[*Exeunt* HOSTESS *and* BOY.

BARDOLPH.
Come, shall I make you two friends? We must to France together: why the devil should we keep knives to cut one another's throats?

PISTOL.
Let floods o'erswell, and fiends for food howl on!

NYM.
You'll pay me the eight shillings I won of you at betting?

PISTOL.
Base is the slave that pays.

NYM.
That now I will have: that's the humour of it.

PISTOL.
As manhood shall compound: push home.

[*They draw.*

BARDOLPH.
By this sword, he that makes the first thrust, I'll kill him; by this sword, I will.   [*Draws.*

PISTOL.
Sword is an oath, and oaths must have their course.

BARDOLPH.
Corporal Nym, an thou wilt be friends, be friends: an thou wilt not, why, then be enemies with me too. Prithee, put up.

NYM.
I shall have my eight shillings I won of you at betting?

PISTOL.
A noble shalt thou have, and present pay;
And liquor likewise will I give to thee,
And friendship shall combine and brotherhood;
I'll live by Nym, and Nym shall live by me;—
Is not this just?—for I shall sutler be
Unto the camp, and profits will accrue.
Give me thy hand.   [*They sheathe their swords.*

NYM.
I shall have my noble?

PISTOL.
In cash most justly paid.

NYM.
Well, then, that's the humour of it.

Enter HOSTESS.

HOSTESS.
As ever you came of women, come in quickly to Sir John. Ah, poor heart! he is so shaked of a burning quotidian tertian, that it is most lamentable to behold. Sweet men, come to him.

NYM.
The king hath run bad humours on the knight, that's the even of it.

PISTOL.
Nym, thou hast spoke the right;
His heart is fracted and corroborate.

NYM.
The king is a good king: but it must be as it may; he passes some humours and careers.

PISTOL.
Let us condole the knight; for, lambkins, we will live.   [*Exeunt.*

SCENE II.

Southampton. A council-chamber.

Enter EXETER, BEDFORD, *and* WESTMORE-LAND.

DUKE OF BEDFORD.
'FORE God, his Grace is bold, to trust these traitors.

DUKE OF EXETER.
They shall be apprehended by and by.

EARL OF WESTMORELAND.
How smooth and even they do bear themselves!
As if allegiance in their bosoms sat,
Crowned with faith and constant loyalty.

DUKE OF BEDFORD.
The king hath note of all that they intend,
By interception which they dream not of.

DUKE OF EXETER.
Nay, but the man that was his bedfellow,
Whom he hath dull'd and cloy'd with gracious favours,
That he should, for a foreign purse, so sell
His sovereign's life to death and treachery.

Trumpets sound. Enter KING HENRY, CAMBRIDGE, SCROOP, GREY, LORDS, *and* ATTENDANTS.

KING HENRY.
Now sits the wind fair, and we will aboard.
My Lord of Cambridge,—and my kind Lord of Masham,—
And you, my gentle knight,—give me your thoughts:
Think you not that the powers we bear with us
Will cut their passage through the force of France,
Doing the execution and the act
For which we have in head assembled them?

LORD SCROOP.
No doubt, my liege, if each man do his best.

KING HENRY.
I doubt not that; since we are well persuaded
We carry not a heart with us from hence
That grows not in a fair consent with ours,
Nor leave not one behind that doth not wish
Success and conquest to attend on us.

EARL OF CAMBRIDGE.
Never was monarch better fear'd and loved
Than is your majesty: there's not, I think, a subject
That sits in heart-grief and uneasiness
Under the sweet shade of your government.

SIR THOMAS GREY.
True: those that were your father's enemies
Have steept their galls in honey, and do serve you
With hearts create of duty and of zeal.

KING HENRY.
We therefore have great cause of thankfulness;
And shall forget the office of our hand,
Sooner than quittance of desert and merit
According to the weight and worthiness.

LORD SCROOP.
So service shall with steeled sinews toil,
And labour shall refresh itself with hope,
To do your Grace incessant services.

271

KING HENRY.
We judge no less.—Uncle of Exeter,
Enlarge the man committed yesterday,
That rail'd against our person: we consider
It was excess of wine that set him on;
And, on his more advice, we pardon him.

LORD SCROOP.
That's mercy, but too much security:
Let him be punisht, sovereign; lest example
Breed, by his sufferance, more of such a kind.

KING HENRY.
O, let us yet be merciful.

EARL OF CAMBRIDGE.
So may your highness, and yet punish too.

SIR THOMAS GREY.
Sir, you show great mercy, if you give him life,
After the taste of much correction.

KING HENRY.
Alas, your too much love and care of me
Are heavy orisons 'gainst this poor wretch!
If little faults, proceeding on distemper,
Shall not be winkt at, how shall we stretch our
    eye
When capital crimes, chew'd, swallow'd, and
    digested,
Appear before us?—We'll yet enlarge that man,
Though Cambridge, Scroop, and Grey, in their
    dear care
And tender preservation of our person,
Would have him punisht. And now to our French
    causes:
Who are the late commissioners?

EARL OF CAMBRIDGE.
I one, my lord:
Your highness bade me ask for it to-day.

LORD SCROOP.
So did you me, my liege.

SIR THOMAS GREY.
And me, my royal sovereign.

KING HENRY.
Then, Richard earl of Cambridge, there is
    yours;—
There yours, Lord Scroop of Masham;—and, sir
    knight,
Grey of Northumberland, this same is yours:—
Read them; and know, I know your worthiness.—
My Lord of Westmoreland, and uncle Exeter,
We will aboard to-night.—Why, how now, gentle-
    men!
What see you in those papers, that you lose
So much complexion?—Look ye, how they
    change!
Their cheeks are paper.—Why, what read you
    there,
That hath so cowarded and chased your blood
Out of appearance?

EARL OF CAMBRIDGE.
                I do confess my fault;
And do submit me to your highness' mercy.

SIR THOMAS GREY and LORD SCROOP.
To which we all appeal.

KING HENRY.
The mercy that was quick in us but late,
By your own counsel is supprest and kill'd:
You must not dare, for shame, to talk of mercy;
For your own reasons turn into your bosoms,

As dogs upon their masters, worrying you.—
See you, my princes and my noble peers, [here,—
These English monsters! My Lord of Cambridge
You know how apt our love was to accord
To furnish him with all appertinents
Belonging to his honour; and this man
Hath, for a few light crowns, lightly conspired,
And sworn unto the practices of France,
To kill us here in Hampton: to the which
This knight, no less for bounty bound to us
Than Cambridge is, hath likewise sworn.—But, O,
What shall I say to thee, Lord Scroop? thou cruel,
Ingrateful, savage, and inhuman creature!
Thou that didst bear the key of all my counsels,
That knew'st the very bottom of my soul,
That almost mightst have coin'd me into gold,
Wouldst thou have practised on me for thy use,—
May it be possible, that foreign hire
Could out of thee extract one spark of evil
That might annoy my finger? 'tis so strange,
That, though the truth of it stands off as gross
As black from white, my eye will scarcely see it.
Treason and murder ever kept together,
As two yoke-devils sworn to either's purpose,
Working so grossly in a natural cause,
That admiration did not whoop at them:
But thou, 'gainst all proportion, didst bring in
Wonder to wait on treason and on murder:
And whatsoever cunning fiend it was
That wrought upon thee so preposterously,
Hath got the voice in hell for excellence:
And other devils, that suggest by treasons,
Do botch and bungle up damnation
With patches, colours, and with forms being fetcht
From glistering semblances of piety;
But he that temper'd thee bade thee stand up,
Gave thee no instance why thou shouldst do
    treason,
Unless to dub thee with the name of traitor.
If that same demon that hath gull'd thee thus
Should with his lion-gait walk the whole world,
He might return to vasty Tartar back,
And tell the legions, 'I can never win
A soul so easy as that Englishman's.'
O, how hast thou with jealousy infected
The sweetness of affiance! Show men dutiful?
Why, so didst thou: seem they grave and learned?
Why, so didst thou: come they of noble family?
Why, so didst thou: seem they religious?
Why, so didst thou: or are they spare in diet;
Free from gross passion, or of mirth or anger;
Constant in spirit, not swerving with the blood;
Garnisht and deckt in modest complement;
Not working with the eye without the ear,
And but in purged judgement trusting neither?
Such and so finely bolted didst thou seem:
And thus thy fall hath left a kind of blot,
To mark the full-fraught man and best indued
With some suspicion. I will weep for thee;
For this revolt of thine, methinks, is like
Another fall of man.—Their faults are open:
Arrest them to the answer of the law;—
And God acquit them of their practices!

DUKE OF EXETER.
I arrest thee of high treason, by the name of
Richard earl of Cambridge.

I arrest thee of high treason, by the name of Henry Lord Scroop of Masham.
I arrest thee of high treason, by the name of Thomas Grey, knight, of Northumberland.

LORD SCROOP.

Our purposes God justly hath discover'd;
And I repent my fault more than my death;
Which I beseech your highness to forgive,
Although my body pay the price of it.

EARL OF CAMBRIDGE.

For me,—the gold of France did not seduce;
Although I did admit it as a motive
The sooner to effect what I intended:
But God be thanked for prevention;
Which I in sufferance heartily will rejoice,
Beseeching God and you to pardon me.

SIR THOMAS GREY.

Never did faithful subject more rejoice
At the discovery of most dangerous treason
Than I do at this hour joy o'er myself,
Prevented from a damned enterprise:
My fault, but not my body, pardon, sovereign.

KING HENRY.

God quit you in his mercy! Hear your sentence.
You have conspired against our royal person,
Join'd with an enemy proclaim'd, and from his
   coffers
Received the golden earnest of our death;
Wherein you would have sold your king to
His princes and his peers to servitude, [slaughter,
His subjects to oppression and contempt,
And his whole kingdom into desolation.
Touching our person, seek we no revenge;
But we our kingdom's safety must so tender,
Whose ruin you have sought, that to her laws
We do deliver you. Get you, therefore, hence,
Poor miserable wretches, to your death:
The taste whereof, God of his mercy give
You patience to endure, and true repentance
Of all your dear offences!—Bear them hence.

   [*Exeunt* CAMBRIDGE, SCROOP, *and* GREY,
      guarded.
Now, lords, for France; the enterprise whereof
Shall be to you as us like glorious.
We doubt not of a fair and lucky war,
Since God so graciously hath brought to light
This dangerous treason, lurking in our way
To hinder our beginnings; we doubt not now
But every rub is smoothed on our way.
Then, forth, dear countrymen: let us deliver
Our puissance into the hand of God,
Putting it straight in expedition.
Cheerly to sea; the signs of war advance:
No king of England, if not king of France.

                 [*Exeunt.*

SCENE III.

London. Before the Boar's-Head Tavern, Eastcheap.

Enter PISTOL, HOSTESS, NYM, BARDOLPH, *and* BOY.

HOSTESS.

PRITHEE, honey-sweet husband, let me bring thee to Staines.

PISTOL.

No; for my manly heart doth yearn.—

Bardolph, be blithe;—Nym, rouse thy vaunting
   veins;—
Boy, bristle thy courage up;—for Falstaff he is
   dead,
And we must yearn therefore.

BARDOLPH.

Would I were with him, wheresome'er he is, either in heaven or in hell!

HOSTESS.

Nay, sure, he's not in hell: he's in Arthur's bosom, if ever man went to Arthur's bosom. A' made a finer end, and went away, an it had been any christom child; a' parted ev'n just between twelve and one, ev'n at the turning o' th' tide: for after I saw him fumble with the sheets, and play with flowers, and smile upon his fingers' ends, I knew there was but one way; for his nose was as sharp as a pen, and a' babbled of green fields. 'How now, Sir John!' quoth I: ' what, man! be o' good cheer.' So a' cried out 'God, God, God!' three or four times. Now I, to comfort him, bid him a' should not think of God; I hoped there was no need to trouble himself with any such thoughts yet. So a' bade me lay more clothes on his feet: I put my hand into the bed and felt them, and they were as cold as any stone; then I felt to his knees, and they were as cold as any stone; and so upward and upward, and all was as cold as any stone.

NYM.

They say he cried out of sack.

HOSTESS.

Ay, that a' did.

BARDOLPH.

And of women.

HOSTESS

Nay, that a' did not.

BOY.

Yes, that a' did; and said they were devils incarnate.

HOSTESS.

A' could never abide carnation; 'twas a colour he never liked.

BOY.

A' said once, the devil would have him about women.

HOSTESS.

A' did in some sort, indeed, handle women; but then he was rheumatic, and talkt of the whore of Babylon.

BOY.

Do you not remember, a' saw a flea stick upon Bardolph's nose, and a' said it was a black soul burning in hell-fire?

BARDOLPH.

Well, the fuel is gone that maintain'd that fire: that's all the riches I got in his service.

NYM.

Shall we shog? the king will be gone from Southampton.

PISTOL.

Come, let's away.—My love, give me thy lips.
Look to my chattels and my movables:
Let senses rule; the word is 'Pitch and pay;'
Trust none;
For oaths are straws, men's faiths are wafer-cakes,

And hold-fast is the only dog, my duck:
Therefore, *caveto* be thy counsellor.
Go, clear thy crystals.—Yoke-fellows in arms,
Let us to France; like horse-leeches, my boys,
To suck, to suck, the very blood to suck!

BOY.
And that's but unwholesome food, they say.

PISTOL.
Touch her soft mouth, and march.

BARDOLPH.
Farewell, hostess.　　　　　　　[*Kissing her.*

NYM.
I cannot kiss, that is the humour of it; but, adieu.

PISTOL.
Let housewifery appear: keep close, I thee command.

HOSTESS.
Farewell; adieu.　　　　　　　　　[*Exeunt.*

SCENE IV.

France. A room in the French KING'S *palace.*

Flourish. Enter the French KING, *the* DAUPHIN,
the DUKE OF BURGUNDY, *the* CONSTABLE,
and others.

FRENCH KING.
THUS comes the English with full power upon
us;
And more than carefully it us concerns
To answer royally in our defences.
Therefore the Dukes of Berri and of Bretagne,
Of Brabant and of Orleans, shall make forth,—
And you, Prince Dauphin,—with all swift dispatch,
To line and new repair our towns of war
With men of courage and with means defendant;
For England his approaches makes as fierce
As waters to the sucking of a gulf.
It fits us, then, to be as provident
As fear may teach us, out of late examples
Left by the fatal and neglected English
Upon our fields.

DAUPHIN.
　　　　My most redoubted father,
It is most meet we arm us 'gainst the foe;
For peace itself should not so dull a kingdom,
Though war nor no known quarrel were in question,
But that defences, musters, preparations,
Should be maintain'd, assembled, and collected,
As were a war in expectation.
Therefore, I say 'tis meet we all go forth
To view the sick and feeble parts of France:
And let us do it with no show of fear;
No, with no more than if we heard that England
Were busied with a Whitsun morris-dance:
For, my good liege, she is so idly king'd,
He sceptre so fantastically borne
By a vain, giddy, shallow, humorous youth,
That fear attends her not.

CONSTABLE OF FRANCE.
　　　　　　　O peace, Prince Dauphin!
You are too much mistaken in this king:
Question your Grace the late ambassadors,—
With what great state he heard their embassy,
How well supplied with noble counsellors,

How modest in exception, and withal
How terrible in constant resolution,—
And you shall find his vanities forespent
Were but the outside of the Roman Brutus,
Covering discretion with a coat of folly;
As gardeners do with ordure hide those roots
That shall first spring and be most delicate.

DAUPHIN.
Well, 'tis not so, my lord high-constable;
But though we think it so, it is no matter:
In cases of defence 'tis best to weigh
The enemy more mighty than he seems:
So the proportions of defence are fill'd;
Which, of a weak and niggardly projection,
Doth, like a miser, spoil his coat with scanting
A little cloth.

FRENCH KING.
　　　Think we King Harry strong;
And princes, look you strongly arm to meet him.
The kindred of him hath been flesht upon us;
And he is bred out of that bloody strain
That haunted us in our familiar paths:
Witness our too-much memorable shame
When Cressy battle fatally was struck,
And all our princes captived by the hand
Of that black name, Edward, Black Prince of
Wales;
Whiles that his mountain sire,—on mountain
standing,
Up in the air, crown'd with the golden sun,—
Saw his heroical seed, and smiled to see him,
Mangle the work of nature, and deface
The patterns that by God and by French fathers
Had twenty years been made. This is a stem
Of that victorious stock; and let us fear
The native mightiness and fate of him.

Enter a MESSENGER.

MESSENGER.
Ambassadors from Harry king of England
Do crave admittance to your majesty.

FRENCH KING.
We'll give them present audience. Go, and bring
them.
　　　[*Exeunt* MESSENGER *and certain* LORDS.
You see this chase is hotly follow'd, friends.

DAUPHIN.
Turn head, and stop pursuit; for coward dogs
Most spend their mouths, when what they seem
to threaten
Runs far before them. Good my sovereign,
Take up the English short; and let them know
Of what a monarchy you are the head:
Self-love, my liege, is not so vile a sin
As self-neglecting.

Enter LORDS, *with* EXETER *and* TRAIN.

FRENCH KING.
　　　　From our brother England?

DUKE OF EXETER.
From him; and thus he greets your majesty.
He wills you, in the name of God Almighty,
That you divest yourself, and lay apart
The borrow'd glories, that, by gift of heaven,
By law of nature and of nations, 'longs
To him and to his heirs; namely, the crown,
And all wide-stretched honours that pertain,
By custom and the ordinance of times,

Unto the crown of France. That you may know
'Tis no sinister nor no awkward claim,
Pickt from the worm-holes of long-vanisht days,
Nor from the dust of old oblivion raked,
He sends you this most memorable line,
                                    [Gives a paper.
In every branch truly demonstrative;
Willing you overlook this pedigree:
And when you find him evenly derived
From his most famed of famous ancestors,
Edward the Third, he bids you then resign
Your crown and kingdom, indirectly held
From him the native and true challenger.

FRENCH KING.
Or else what follows?

DUKE OF EXETER.
Bloody constraint; for if you hide the crown
Even in your hearts, there will he rake for it:
Therefore in fierce tempest is he coming,
In thunder and in earthquake, like a Jove,
That, if requiring fail, he will compel;
And bids you, in the bowels of the Lord,
Deliver up the crown; and to take mercy
On the poor souls for whom this hungry war
Opens his vasty jaws: and on your head
Turns he the widows' tears, the orphans' cries,
The dead men's blood, the pining maidens'
    groans,
For husbands, fathers, and betrothed lovers,
That shall be swallow'd in this controversy.
This is his claim, his threatening, and my message;
Unless the Dauphin be in presence here,
To whom expressly I bring greeting too.

FRENCH KING.
For us, we will consider of this further:
To-morrow shall you bear our full intent
Back to our brother England.

DAUPHIN.
                        For the Dauphin,
I stand here for him: what to him from England?

DUKE OF EXETER.
Scorn and defiance; slight regard, contempt,
And any thing that may not misbecome
The mighty sender, doth he prize you at.
Thus says my king: an if your father's highness
Do not, in grant of all demands at large,
Sweeten the bitter mock you sent his majesty,
He'll call you to so hot an answer of it,
That caves and womby vaultages of France
Shall chide your trespass, and return your mock
In second accent of his ordnance.

DAUPHIN.
Say, if my father render fair return,
It is against my will; for I desire
Nothing but odds with England: to that end,
As matching to his youth and vanity,
I did present him with the Paris balls.

DUKE OF EXETER.
He'll make your Paris Louvre shake for it,
Were it the mistress-court of mighty Europe:
And, be assured, you'll find a difference,
As we, his subjects, have in wonder found,
Between the promise of his greener days
And these he masters now: now he weighs time,
Even to the utmost grain:—that you shall read
In your own losses, if he stay in France.

FRENCH KING.
To-morrow shall you know our mind at full.

DUKE OF EXETER.
Dispatch us with all speed, lest that our king
Come here himself to question our delay;
For he is footed in this land already.

FRENCH KING.
You shall be soon dispatcht with fair conditions:
A night is but small breath and little pause
To answer matters of this consequence.
                            [Flourish. Exeunt.

ACT III.
PROLOGUE.

Enter CHORUS.

CHORUS.
THUS with imagined wing our swift scene flies,
    In motion of no less celerity
Than that of thought. Suppose that you have seen
The well-appointed king at Hampton pier
Embark his royalty; and his brave fleet
With silken streamers the young Phœbus fanning:
Play with your fancies; and in them behold
Upon the hempen tackle ship-boys climbing;
Hear the shrill whistle which doth order give
To sounds confused; behold the threaden sails,
Borne with th'invisible and creeping wind,
Draw the huge bottoms through the furrow'd sea,
Breasting the lofty surge: O, do but think
You stand upon the rivage, and behold
A city on th'inconstant billows dancing;
For so appears this fleet majestical,
Holding due course to Harfleur. Follow, follow!
Grapple your minds to sternage of this navy;
And leave your England, as dead midnight still,
Guarded with grandsires, babies, and old women,
Either past, or not arrived to, pith and puissance;
For who is he, whose chin is but enricht
With one appearing hair, that will not follow
These cull'd and choice-drawn cavaliers to
    France?
Work, work your thoughts, and therein see a siege;
Behold the ordnance on their carriages,
With fatal mouths gaping on girded Harfleur.
Suppose th'ambassador from the French comes
    back;
Tells Harry that the king doth offer him
Katharine his daughter; and with her, to dowry,
Some petty and unprofitable dukedoms.
The offer likes not: and the nimble gunner
With linstock now the devilish cannon touches,
                [Alarum, and chambers go off, within.
And down goes all before them. Still be kind,
And eke out our performance with your mind.
                                        [Exit.

SCENE I.

France. Before Harfleur.

Alarums. Enter KING HENRY, EXETER, BED-
    FORD, GLOSTER, and SOLDIERS, with scaling-
    ladders.

KING HENRY.
ONCE more unto the breach, dear friends,
    once more;
Or close the wall up with our English dead!

In peace there's nothing so becomes a man
As modest stillness and humility:
But when the blast of war blows in our ears,
Then imitate the action of the tiger;
Stiffen the sinews, summon up the blood,
Disguise fair nature with hard-favour'd rage:
Then lend the eye a terrible aspect;
Let it pry through the portage of the head
Like the brass cannon; let the brow o'erwhelm it
As fearfully as doth a galled rock
O'erhang and jutty his confounded base,
Swill'd with the wild and wasteful ocean.
Now set the teeth, and stretch the nostril wide;
Hold hard the breath, and bend up every spirit
To his full height!—On, on, you noble English,
Whose blood is fet from fathers of war-proof!—
Fathers that, like so many Alexanders,
Have in these parts from morn till even fought,
And sheathed their swords for lack of argu-
    ment:—
Dishonour not your mothers; now attest
That those whom you call'd fathers did beget
    you!
Be copy now to men of grosser blood,
And teach them how to war!—And you, good
    yeomen,
Whose limbs were made in England, show us here
The mettle of your pasture; let us swear
That you are worth your breeding: which I doubt
    not;
For there is none of you so mean and base,
That hath not noble lustre in your eyes.
I see you stand like greyhounds in the slips,
Straining upon the start. The game's afoot:
Follow your spirit; and, upon this charge,
Cry 'God for Harry, England, and Saint George!'
    [*Exeunt. Alarum, and chambers go off, within.*

SCENE II.

The same.

Enter NYM, BARDOLPH, PISTOL, *and* BOY.

BARDOLPH.

ON, on, on, on, on! to the breach, to the
breach!

NYM.

Pray thee, corporal, stay: the knocks are too hot;
and, for mine own part, I have not a case of lives:
the humour of it is too hot, that is the very plain-
song of it.

PISTOL.

The plain-song is most just; for humours do a-
    bound;
Knocks go and come; God's vassals drop and die;
        And sword and shield,
        In bloody field,
    Doth win immortal fame.

BOY.

Would I were in an alehouse in London! I would
give all my fame for a pot of ale and safety.

PISTOL.

And I:
    If wishes would prevail with me,
    My purpose should not fail with me,
        But thither would I hie.

BOY.
    As duly, but not as truly,
        As bird doth sing on bough.

Enter FLUELLEN.

FLUELLEN.

Got's plood!—Up to the preaches, you rascals!
will you not up to the preaches?
    [*Driving them forward.*

PISTOL.

Be merciful, great duke, to men of mould!
Abate thy rage, abate thy manly rage!
Abate thy rage, great duke!
Good bawcock, bate thy rage! use lenity, sweet
    chuck!

NYM.

These be good humours!—your honour runs bad
humours.
    [*Exeunt* NYM, BARDOLPH, *and* PISTOL
        driven in by FLUELLEN.

BOY.

As young as I am, I have observed these three
swashers. I am boy to them all three: but all they
three, though they would serve me, could not be
man to me; for, indeed, three such antics do not
amount to a man. For Bardolph,—he is white-
liver'd and red-faced; by the means whereof a'
faces it out, but fights not. For Pistol,—he hath a
killing tongue and a quiet sword; by the means
whereof a' breaks words, and keeps whole
weapons. For Nym,—he hath heard that men of
few words are the best men; and therefore he
scorns to say his prayers, lest a' should be thought
a coward: but his few bad words are matcht with
as few good deeds; for a' never broke any man's
head but his own, and that was against a post
when he was drunk. They will steal any thing, and
call it purchase. Bardolph stole a lute-case, bore
it twelve leagues, and sold it for three-half-pence.
Nym and Bardolph are sworn brothers in filching; and in Calais they stole a fire-shovel: I knew
by that piece of service the men would carry coals.
They would have me as familiar with men's
pockets as their gloves or their handkerchers:
which makes much against my manhood, if I
should take from another's pocket to put into
mine; for it is plain pocketing-up of wrongs. I
must leave them, and seek some better service:
their villainy goes against my weak stomach, and
therefore I must cast it up.   [*Exit.*

Enter FLUELLEN, GOWER *following.*

GOWER.

Captain Fluellen, you must come presently to the
mines; the Duke of Gloster would speak with you.

FLUELLEN.

To the mines! tell you the duke, it is not so goot to
come to the mines; for, look you, the mines is not
according to the disciplines of the war: the con-
cavities of it is not sufficient; for, look you, th'athversary—you may discuss unto the duke, look
you—is digt himself four yard under the counter-
mines: by Cheshu, I think a' will plow up all, if
there is not petter directions.

GOWER.

The Duke of Gloster, to whom the order of the
siege is given, is altogether directed by an Irish-
man,—a very valiant gentleman, i'faith.

FLUELLEN.

It is Captain Macmorris, is it not?

GOWER.

I think it be.

FLUELLEN.

By Cheshu, he is an ass, as in the 'orld: I will verify as much in his peard: he has no more directions in the true disciplines of the wars, look you, of the Roman disciplines, than is a puppy-dog.

GOWER.

Here a' comes; and the Scots captain, Captain Jamy, with him.

FLUELLEN.

Captain Jamy is a marvellous falorous gentleman, that is certain; and of great expedition and knowledge in th'auncient wars, upon my particular knowledge of his directions: by Cheshu, he will maintain his argument as well as any military man in the 'orld, in the disciplines of the pristine wars of the Romans.

Enter MACMORRIS *and* JAMY.

JAMY.

I say gude-day, Captain Fluellen.

FLUELLEN.

Got-den to your worship, goot Captain Jamy.

GOWER.

How now, Captain Macmorris! have you quit the mines? have the pioners given o'er?

MACMORRIS.

By Chrish, la, tish ill done; the work ish give over, the trompet sound the retreat. By my hand, I swear, and my father's soul, the work ish ill done; it ish give over: I would have blow'd up the town, so Chrish save me, la, in an hour: O, tish ill done, tish ill done; by my hand, tish ill done!

FLUELLEN.

Captain Macmorris, I peseech you now, will you voutsafe me, look you, a few disputations with you, as partly touching or concerning the disciplines of the war, the Roman wars, in the way of argument, look you, and friendly communication; partly to satisfy my opinion, and partly for the satisfaction, look you, of my mind, as touching the direction of the military discipline; that is the point.

JAMY.

It sall be vary gude, gude feith, gude captains baith: and I sall quit you with gude leve, as I may pick occasion; that sall I, marry.

MACMORRIS.

It is no time to discourse, so Chrish save me: the day is hot, and the weather, and the wars, and the king, and the dukes: it is no time to discourse. The town is beseecht, and the trompet call us to the breach; and we talk, and, be Chrish, do nothing: 'tis shame for us all: so God sa' me, 'tis shame to stand still; it is shame, by my hand: and there is throats to be cut, and works to be done; and there ish nothing done, so Chrish sa' me, la.

JAMY.

By the mess, ere theise eyes of mine take themselves to slomber, ay'll de gude service, or ay'll ligg i'th' grund for it; ay, or go to death; and ay'll pay't as valorously as I may, that sall I suerly do, that is the breff and the long. Marry, I wad full fain heard some question 'tween you tway.

FLUELLEN.

Captain Macmorris, I think, look you, under your correction, there is not many of your nation—

MACMORRIS.

Of my nation! What ish my nation? Ish a villain, and a bastard, and a knave, and a rascal. What ish my nation? Who talks of my nation?

FLUELLEN.

Look you, if you take the matter otherwise than is meant, Captain Macmorris, peradventure I shall think you do not use me with that affability as in discretion you ought to use me, look you; being as goot a man as yourself, both in the disciplines of war, and in the derivation of my birth, and in other particularities.

MACMORRIS.

I do not know you so good a man as myself: so Chrish save me, I will cut off your head.

GOWER.

Gentlemen both, you will mistake each other.

JAMY.

A! that's a foul fault.   [*A parley sounded.*

GOWER.

The town sounds a parley.

FLUELLEN.

Captain Macmorris, when there is more petter opportunity to be required, look you, I will be so pold as to tell you I know the disciplines of war; and there is an end.   [*Exeunt.*

SCENE III.

The same.

The GOVERNOR *and some* CITIZENS *on the walls; the English forces below.* *Enter* KING HENRY *and his* TRAIN *before the Gates.*

KING HENRY.

HOW yet resolves the governor of the town?
This is the latest parle we will admit:
Therefore, to our best mercy give yourselves;
Or, like to men proud of destruction,
Defy us to our worst: for, as I am a soldier,
A name that, in my thoughts, becomes me best,
If I begin the battery once again,
I will not leave the half-achieved Harfleur
Till in her ashes she lie buried.
The gates of mercy shall be all shut up;
And the flesht soldier,—rough and hard of heart,—
In liberty of bloody hand shall range
With conscience wide as hell; mowing like grass
Your fresh-fair virgins and your flowering infants.
What is it then to me, if impious war,—
Array'd in flames, like to the prince of fiends,—
Do, with his smircht complexion, all fell feats
Enlinkt to waste and desolation?
What is't to me, when you yourselves are cause,
If your pure maidens fall into the hand
Of hot and forcing violation?
What rein can hold licentious wickedness
When down the hill he holds his fierce career?
We may as bootless spend our vain command
Upon th'enraged soldiers in their spoil,
As send precepts to the leviathan
To come ashore. Therefore, you men of Harfleur
Take pity of your town and of your people,

Whiles yet my soldiers are in my command;
Whiles yet the cool and temperate wind of grace
O'erblows the filthy and contagious clouds
Of heady murder, spoil, and villainy.
If not, why, in a moment, look to see
The blind and bloody soldier with foul hand
Defile the locks of your shrill-shrieking daughters;
Your fathers taken by the silver beards,
And their most reverend heads dasht to the walls;
Your naked infants spitted upon pikes,
Whiles the mad mothers with their howls confused
Do break the clouds, as did the wives of Jewry
At Herod's bloody-hunting slaughtermen.
What say you? will you yield, and this avoid?
Or, guilty in defence, be thus destroy'd?

GOVERNOR OF HARFLEUR.

Our expectation hath this day an end:
The Dauphin, whom of succour we entreated,
Returns us, that his powers are yet not ready
To raise so great a siege. Therefore, dread king,
We yield our town and lives to thy soft mercy.
Enter our gates; dispose of us and ours;
For we no longer are defensible.

KING HENRY.

Open your gates.—Come, uncle Exeter,
Go you and enter Harfleur; there remain,
And fortify it strongly 'gainst the French:
Use mercy to them all. For us, dear uncle,—
The winter coming on, and sickness growing
Upon our soldiers,—we will retire to Calais.
To-night in Harfleur will we be your guest;
To-morrow for the march are we addrest.

[*Flourish, and enter the town.*

SCENE IV.

The French KING'S *palace.*

Enter KATHARINE *and* ALICE.

KATHARINE.

A LICE, *tu as été en Angleterre, et tu parles
bien le langage.*

ALICE.

Un peu, madame.

KATHARINE.

*Je te prie m'enseignez; il faut que j'apprenne à
parler. Comment appelez-vous la main en Anglois?*

ALICE.

La main? elle est appelée de hand.

KATHARINE.

De hand. *Et les doigts?*

ALICE.

*Les doigts? ma foi, j'oublie les doigts; mais je me
souviendrai. Les doigts? je pense qu'ils sont appelés
de* fingres; *oui, de* fingres.

KATHARINE.

La main, de hand; *les doigts, de* fingres. *Je pense
que je suis le bon écolier; j'ai gagné deux mots
d'Anglois vitement. Comment appelez-vous les
ongles?*

ALICE.

Les ongles? nous les appelons de nails.

KATHARINE.

De nails. *Ecoutez; dites-moi, si je parle bien: de*
hand, de fingres, *et de* nails.

ALICE.

C'est bien dit, madame; il est fort bon Anglois.

KATHARINE.

Dites-moi l'Anglois pour le bras.

ALICE.

De arm, *madame.*

KATHARINE.

Et le coude?

ALICE.

D'elbow.

KATHARINE.

D'elbow. *Je m'en fais la répétition de tous les mots
que vous m'avez appris dès à présent.*

ALICE.

Il est trop difficile, madame, comme je pense.

KATHARINE.

Excusez-moi, Alice; écoutez: d'hand, de fingres,
de nails, d'arm, de bilbow.

ALICE.

D'elbow, *madame.*

KATHARINE.

O Seigneur Dieu, je m'en oublie! d'elbow. *Comment appelez-vous le* col?

ALICE.

De neck, *madame.*

KATHARINE.

De nick. *Et le* menton?

ALICE.

De chin.

KATHARINE.

De sin. *Le col,* de nick; *le menton,* de sin.

ALICE.

*Oui. Sauf votre honneur, en vérité, vous prononcez
les mots aussi droit que les natifs d'Angleterre.*

KATHARINE.

*Je ne doute point d'apprendre, par la grace de Dieu,
et en peu de temps.*

ALICE.

N'avez-vous pas déjà oublié ce que je vous ai enseigné?

KATHARINE.

Non, je réciterai à vous promptement: d'hand, de
fingres, de mails,—

ALICE.

De nails, *madame.*

KATHARINE.

De nails, de arm, de ilbow.

ALICE.

Sauf votre honneur, d'elbow.

KATHARINE.

Ainsi dis-je; d'elbow, de nick, *et de* sin. *Comment
appelez-vous le pied et la robe?*

ALICE.

De foot, *madame; et de* coun.

KATHARINE.

De foot *et de* coun! *O Seigneur Dieu! ce sont mots
de son mauvais, corruptible, gros, et impudique, et
non pour les dames d'honneur d'user: je ne voudrais
prononcer ces mots devant les seigneurs de France
pour tout le monde. Foh! le* foot *et le* coun! *Néanmoins, je réciterai une autre fois ma leçon ensemble:*
d'hand, de fingres, de nails, d'arm, d'elbow,
de nick, de sin, de foot, de coun.

ALICE.

Excellent, madame!

KATHARINE.

C'est assez pour une fois: allons-nous à diner.

[*Exeunt.*

SCENE V.

The same.

Enter the KING OF FRANCE, *the* DAUPHIN,
BOURBON, *the* CONSTABLE OF FRANCE, *and
others.*

FRENCH KING.

'TIS certain he hath past the river Somme.

THE CONSTABLE OF FRANCE.

And if he be not fought withal, my lord,
Let us not live in France; let us quit all,
And give our vineyards to a barbarous people.

DAUPHIN.

O Dieu vivant! shall a few sprays of us,
The emptying of our fathers' luxury,
Our scions, put in wild and savage stock,
Spirt up so suddenly into the clouds,
And overlook their grafters?

DUKE OF BOURBON.

Normans, but bastard Normans, Norman bas-
    tards!
Mort de ma vie! if they march along
Unfought withal, but I will sell my dukedom,
To buy a slobbery and a dirty farm
In that nook-shotten isle of Albion.

THE CONSTABLE OF FRANCE.

Dieu de batailles! where have they this mettle?
Is not their climate foggy, raw, and dull;
On whom, as in despite, the sun looks pale,
Killing their fruit with frowns? Can sodden
    water,
A drench for sur-rein'd jades, their barley-broth,
Decoct their cold blood to such valiant heat?
And shall our quick blood, spirited with wine,
Seem frosty? O, for honour of our land,
Let us not hang like roping icicles
Upon our houses' thatch, whiles a more frosty
    people
Sweat drops of gallant youth in our rich fields,—
Poor we may call them in their native lords!

DAUPHIN.

By faith and honour,
Our madams mock at us, and plainly say
Our mettle is bred out, and they will give
Their bodies to the lust of English youth
To new-store France with bastard warriors.

DUKE OF BOURBON.

They bid us to the English dancing-schools,
And teach lavoltas high and swift corantos;
Saying our grace is only in our heels,
And that we are most lofty runaways.

FRENCH KING.

Where is Montjoy the herald? speed him hence;
Let him greet England with our sharp defiance.—
Up, princes! and, with spirit of honour edged
More sharper than your swords, hie to the field:
Charles Delabreth, high-Constable of France;
You Dukes of Orleans, Bourbon, and of Berri,
Alençon, Brabant, Bar, and Burgundy;
Jaques Chatillon, Rambures, Vaudemont,
Beaumont, Grandpré, Roussi, and Fauconberg,
Foix, Lestrale, Bouciqualt, and Charolois;
High dukes, great princes, barons, lords, and
    knights,
For your great seats now quit you of great shames.
Bar Harry England, that sweeps through our land

With pennons painted in the blood of Harfleur:
Rush on his host, as doth the melted snow
Upon the valleys, whose low vassal seat
The Alps doth spit and void his rheum upon:
Go down upon him,—you have power enough,—
And in a captive chariot into Rouen
Bring him our prisoner.

THE CONSTABLE OF FRANCE.

             This becomes the great.
Sorry am I his numbers are so few,
His soldiers sick, and famisht in their march;
For I am sure, when he shall see our army,
He'll drop his heart into the sink of fear,
And for achievement offer us his ransom.

FRENCH KING.

Therefore, lord Constable, haste on Montjoy;
And let him say to England, that we send
To know what willing ransom he will give.—
Prince Dauphin, you shall stay with us in Rouen.

DAUPHIN.

Not so, I do beseech your majesty.

FRENCH KING.

Be patient; for you shall remain with us.
Now forth, lord Constable, and princes all,
And quickly bring us word of England's fall.

                        [Exeunt.

SCENE VI.

The English camp in Picardy.

Enter GOWER *and* FLUELLEN, *meeting.*

GOWER.

HOW now, Captain Fluellen! come you from
the bridge?

FLUELLEN.

I assure you, there is very excellent services committed at the pridge.

GOWER.

Is the Duke of Exeter safe?

FLUELLEN.

The Duke of Exeter is as magnanimous as Agamemnon; and a man that I love and honour with
my soul, and my heart, and my duty, and my life,
and my living, and my uttermost power: he is not
—Got be praised and plest!—any hurt in the
'orld; but keeps the pridge most valiantly, with
excellent discipline. There is an aunchient there at
the pridge,—I think in my very conscience he is
as valiant a man as Mark Antony; and he is a man
of no estimation in the 'orld; but I did see him do
gallant service.

GOWER.

What do you call him?

FLUELLEN.

He is called Aunchient Pistol.

GOWER.

I know him not.

FLUELLEN.

Here is the man.

Enter PISTOL.

PISTOL.

Captain, I thee beseech to do me favours:
The Duke of Exeter doth love thee well.

FLUELLEN.

Ay, I praise Got; and I have merited some love
at his hands.

PISTOL.

Bardolph, a soldier, firm and sound of heart,
And of buxom valour, hath, by cruel fate,
And giddy Fortune's furious fickle wheel,—
That goddess blind,
That stands upon the rolling restless stone,—

FLUELLEN.

By your patience, Auncient Pistol. Fortune is
painted plind, with a muffler afore her eyes, to
signify to you that Fortune is plind; and she is
painted also with a wheel, to signify to you, which
is the moral of it, that she is turning, and inconstant, and mutability, and variation: and her foot,
look you, is fixt upon a spherical stone, which
rolls, and rolls, and rolls:—in good truth, the poet
makes a most excellent description of it: Fortune
is an excellent moral.

PISTOL.

Fortune is Bardolph's foe, and frowns on him;
For he hath stoln a pax, and hanged must a'
   be,—
A damned death!
Let gallows gape for dog; let man go free,
And let not hemp his windpipe suffocate:
But Exeter hath given the doom of death
For pax of little price.
Therefore, go speak,—the duke will hear thy
   voice;
And let not Bardolph's vital thread be cut
With edge of penny cord and vile reproach:
Speak, captain, for his life, and I will thee re-
   quite.

FLUELLEN.

Auncient Pistol, I do partly understand your
meaning.

PISTOL.

Why, then, rejoice therefore.

FLUELLEN.

Certainly, auncient, it is not a thing to rejoice at:
for if, look you, he were my prother, I would desire the duke to use his goot pleasure, and put him
to execution; for discipline ought to be used.

PISTOL.

Die and be damn'd! and figo for thy friendship!

FLUELLEN.

It is well.

PISTOL.

The fig of Spain!   [Exit.

FLUELLEN.

Very goot.

GOWER.

Why, this is an arrant counterfeit rascal; I remember him now; a bawd, a cutpurse.

FLUELLEN.

I'll assure you, a' utter'd as prave 'ords at the
pridge as you shall see in a summer's day. But it
is very well; what he has spoke to me, that is well,
I warrant you, when time is serve.

GOWER.

Why, 'tis a gull, a fool, a rogue, that now and then
goes to the wars, to grace himself, at his return
into London, under the form of a soldier. And
such fellows are perfect in the great commanders'
names: and they will learn you by rote where services were done;—at such and such a sconce, at
such a breach, at such a convoy; who came off

bravely, who was shot, who disgraced, what terms
the enemy stood on; and this they con perfectly
in the phrase of war, which they trick up with
new-turn'd oaths: and what a beard of the
general's cut, and a horrid suit of the camp, will
do among foaming bottles and ale-washt wits, is
wonderful to be thought on. But you must learn
to know such slanders of the age, or else you may
be marvellously mistook.

FLUELLEN.

I tell you what, Captain Gower;—I do perceive
he is not the man that he would gladly make show
to the 'orld he is: if I find a hole in his coat, I will
tell him my mind. [Drum within.] Hark you, the
king is coming; and I must speak with him from
the pridge.

Drum and colours.   Enter KING HENRY, GLOS-
           TER, and his poor SOLDIERS.

Got pless your majesty!

KING HENRY.

How now, Fluellen! camest thou from the
   bridge?

FLUELLEN.

Ay, so please your majesty. The Duke of Exeter
has very gallantly maintain'd the pridge: the
French is gone off, look you; and there is gallant
and most prave passages: marry, th'athversary
was have possession of the pridge; but he is enforced to retire, and the Duke of Exeter is master
of the pridge: I can tell your majesty, the duke is
a prave man.

KING HENRY.

What men have you lost, Fluellen?

FLUELLEN.

The perdition of th'athversary hath been very
great, reasonable great: marry, for my part, I
think the duke hath lost never a man, but one
that is like to be executed for robbing a church,—
one Bardolph, if your majesty know the man: his
face is all bubukles, and whelks, and knobs, and
flames o' fire: and his lips plows at his nose, and
it is like a coal of fire, sometimes plue and sometimes red; but his nose is executed, and his fire's
out.

KING HENRY.

We would have all such offenders so cut off:—
and we give express charge that, in our marches
through the country, there be nothing compell'd
from the villages, nothing taken but paid for,
none of the French upbraided or abused in disdainful language; for when lenity and cruelty play
for a kingdom, the gentler gamester is the soonest
winner.

Tucket.   Enter MONTJOY.

MONTJOY.

You know me by my habit.

KING HENRY.

Well, then, I know thee: what shall I know of thee?

MONTJOY.

My master's mind.

KING HENRY.

Unfold it.

MONTJOY.

Thus says my king:—Say thou to Harry of
England: Though we seem'd dead, we did but
sleep; advantage is a better soldier than rashness.

Tell him, we could have rebuked him at Harfleur,
but that we thought not good to bruise an injury
till it were full ripe:—now we speak upon our
cue, and our voice is imperial: England shall repent his folly, see his weakness, and admire our
sufferance. Bid him, therefore, consider of his
ransom; which must proportion the losses we
have borne, the subjects we have lost, the disgrace we have digested; which, in weight to re-
answer, his pettiness would bow under. For our
losses, his exchequer is too poor; for th'effusion
of our blood, the muster of his kingdom too faint
a number; and for our disgrace, his own person,
kneeling at our feet, but a weak and worthless
satisfaction. To this add defiance: and tell him,
for conclusion, he hath betray'd his followers,
whose condemnation is pronounced. So far my
king and master; so much my office.

KING HENRY.

What is thy name? I know thy quality.

MONTJOY.

Montjoy.

KING HENRY.

Thou dost thy office fairly. Turn thee back,
And tell thy king,—I do not seek him now;
But could be willing to march on to Calais
Without impeachment: for, to say the sooth,—
Though 'tis no wisdom to confess so much
Unto an enemy of craft and vantage,—
My people are with sickness much enfeebled;
My numbers lessen'd; and those few I have,
Almost no better than so many French;
Who when they were in health, I tell thee, herald,
I thought upon one pair of English legs
Did march three Frenchmen.—Yet, forgive me,
    God,
That I do brag thus!—this your air of France
Hath blown that vice in me; I must repent.
Go, therefore, tell thy master here I am;
My ransom is this frail and worthless trunk;
My army but a weak and sickly guard:
Yet, God before, tell him we will come on,
Though France himself, and such another
    neighbour,
Stand in our way. There's for thy labour, Mont-
joy.   [Gives a purse.
Go, bid thy master well advise himself:
If we may pass, we will; if we be hinder'd,
We shall your tawny ground with your red blood
Discolour: and so, Montjoy, fare you well.
The sum of all our answer is but this:
We would not seek a battle, as we are;
Nor, as we are, we say, we will not shun it:
So tell your master.

MONTJOY.

I shall deliver so. Thanks to your highness.
                         [Exit.

DUKE OF GLOSTER.

I hope they will not come upon us now.

KING HENRY.

We are in God's hand, brother, not in theirs.
March to the bridge; it now draws toward
    night:—
Beyond the river we'll encamp ourselves;
And on to-morrow bid them march away.
                        [Exeunt.

SCENE VII.

The French camp near Agincourt.

Enter the CONSTABLE OF FRANCE, *the* LORD
RAMBURES, ORLEANS, *the* DAUPHIN, *and
others.*

THE CONSTABLE OF FRANCE.

Tut! I have the best armour of the world.—
Would it were day!

DUKE OF ORLEANS.

You have an excellent armour; but let my horse
have his due.

THE CONSTABLE OF FRANCE.

It is the best horse of Europe.

DUKE OF ORLEANS.

Will it never be morning?

DAUPHIN.

My Lord of Orleans, and my lord high-Constable, you talk of horse and armour?

DUKE OF ORLEANS.

You are as well provided of both as any prince in
the world.

DAUPHIN.

What a long night is this!—I will not change my
horse with any that treads but on four pasterns.
Ça, ha! he bounds from the earth, as if his entrails were hairs; *le cheval volant,* the Pegasus, *qui
a les narines de feu!* When I bestride him, I soar,
I am a hawk: he trots the air; the earth sings when
he touches it; the basest horn of his hoof is more
musical than the pipe of Hermes.

DUKE OF ORLEANS.

He's of the colour of the nutmeg.

DAUPHIN.

And of the heat of the ginger. It is a beast for
Perseus: he is pure air and fire; and the dull elements of earth and water never appear in him, but
only in patient stillness while his rider mounts
him: he is, indeed, a horse; and all other jades you
may call beasts.

THE CONSTABLE OF FRANCE.

Indeed, my lord, it is a most absolute and excellent horse.

DAUPHIN.

It is the prince of palfreys; his neigh is like the
bidding of a monarch, and his countenance enforces homage.

DUKE OF ORLEANS.

No more, cousin.

DAUPHIN.

Nay, the man hath no wit that cannot, from the
rising of the lark to the lodging of the lamb, vary
deserved praise on my palfrey: it is a theme as
fluent as the sea; turn the sands into eloquent
tongues, and my horse is argument for them all:
'tis a subject for a sovereign to reason on, and for
a sovereign's sovereign to ride on; and for the
world, familiar to us and unknown, to lay apart
their particular functions, and wonder at him.
I once writ a sonnet in his praise, and began
thus: 'Wonder of nature,'—

DUKE OF ORLEANS.

I have heard a sonnet begin so to one's mistress.

DAUPHIN.

Then did they imitate that which I composed to
my courser; for my horse is my mistress.

DUKE OF ORLEANS.

Your mistress bears well.

DAUPHIN.

Me well; which is the prescript praise and perfection of a good and particular mistress.

THE CONSTABLE OF FRANCE.

Ma foi, methought yesterday your mistress shrewdly shook your back.

DAUPHIN.

So, perhaps, did yours.

THE CONSTABLE OF FRANCE.

Mine was not bridled.

DAUPHIN.

O, then, belike she was old and gentle; and you rode, like a kern of Ireland, your French hose off, and in your strait strossers.

THE CONSTABLE OF FRANCE.

You have good judgement in horsemanship.

DAUPHIN.

Be warn'd by me, then: they that ride so, and ride not warily, fall into foul bogs. I had rather have my horse to my mistress.

THE CONSTABLE OF FRANCE.

I had as lief have my mistress a jade.

DAUPHIN.

I tell thee, constable, my mistress wears her own hair.

THE CONSTABLE OF FRANCE.

I could make as true a boast as that, if I had a sow to my mistress.

DAUPHIN.

Le chien est retourné à son propre vomissement, et la truie lavée au bourbier: thou makest use of any thing.

THE CONSTABLE OF FRANCE.

Yet do I not use my horse for my mistress; or any such proverb, so little kin to the purpose.

RAMBURES.

My lord constable, the armour that I saw in your tent to-night,—are those stars or suns upon it?

THE CONSTABLE OF FRANCE.

Stars, my lord.

DAUPHIN.

Some of them will fall to-morrow, I hope.

THE CONSTABLE OF FRANCE.

And yet my sky shall not want.

DAUPHIN.

That may be, for you bear a many superfluously, and 'twere more honour some were away.

THE CONSTABLE OF FRANCE.

Even as your horse bears your praises; who would trot as well, were some of your brags dismounted.

DAUPHIN.

Would I were able to load him with his desert!— Will it never be day?—I will trot to-morrow a mile, and my way shall be paved with English faces.

THE CONSTABLE OF FRANCE.

I will not say so, for fear I should be faced out of my way: but I would it were morning; for I would fain be about the ears of the English.

RAMBURES.

Who will go to hazard with me for twenty prisoners?

THE CONSTABLE OF FRANCE.

You must first go yourself to hazard, ere you have them.

DAUPHIN.

'Tis midnight; I'll go arm myself.   [*Exit.*

DUKE OF ORLEANS.

The Dauphin longs for morning.

RAMBURES.

He longs to eat the English.

THE CONSTABLE OF FRANCE.

I think he will eat all he kills.

DUKE OF ORLEANS.

By the white hand of my lady, he's a gallant prince.

THE CONSTABLE OF FRANCE.

Swear by her foot, that she may tread out the oath.

DUKE OF ORLEANS.

He is, simply, the most active gentleman of France.

THE CONSTABLE OF FRANCE.

Doing is activity: and he will still be doing.

DUKE OF ORLEANS.

He never did harm, that I heard of.

THE CONSTABLE OF FRANCE.

Nor will do none to-morrow: he will keep that good name still.

DUKE OF ORLEANS.

I know him to be valiant.

THE CONSTABLE OF FRANCE.

I was told that by one that knows him better than you.

DUKE OF ORLEANS.

What's he?

THE CONSTABLE OF FRANCE.

Marry, he told me so himself; and he said he cared not who knew it.

DUKE OF ORLEANS.

He needs not; it is no hidden virtue in him.

THE CONSTABLE OF FRANCE.

By my faith, sir, but it is; never any body saw it but his lackey: 'tis a hooded valour; and when it appears, it will bate.

DUKE OF ORLEANS.

Ill-will never said well.

THE CONSTABLE OF FRANCE.

I will cap that proverb with—There is flattery in friendship.

DUKE OF ORLEANS.

And I will take up that with—Give the devil his due.

THE CONSTABLE OF FRANCE.

Well placed: there stands your friend for the devil: have at the very eye of that proverb, with— A pox of the devil.

DUKE OF ORLEANS.

You are the better by proverbs, by how much—A fool's bolt is soon shot.

THE CONSTABLE OF FRANCE.

You have shot over.

DUKE OF ORLEANS.

'Tis not the first time you were overshot.

Enter a MESSENGER.

MESSENGER.

My lord high-Constable, the English lie within fifteen hundred paces of your tents.

THE CONSTABLE OF FRANCE.

Who hath measured the ground?

MESSENGER.

The Lord Grandpré.

THE CONSTABLE OF FRANCE.
A valiant and most expert gentleman.—Would it
were day!—Alas, poor Harry of England! he longs
not for the dawning, as we do.

DUKE OF ORLEANS.
What a wretched and peevish fellow is this King
of England, to mope with his fat-brain'd followers
so far out of his knowledge!

THE CONSTABLE OF FRANCE.
If the English had any apprehension, they would
run away.

DUKE OF ORLEANS.
That they lack; for if their heads had any intel-
lectual armour, they could never wear such heavy
head-pieces.

RAMBURES.
That island of England breeds very valiant
creatures; their mastiffs are of unmatchable
courage.

DUKE OF ORLEANS.
Foolish curs, that run winking into the mouth of
a Russian bear, and have their heads crusht like
rotten apples! You may as well say, that's a valiant
flea that dare eat his breakfast on the lip of a lion.

THE CONSTABLE OF FRANCE.
Just, just; and the men do sympathize with the
mastiffs in robustious and rough coming-on, leaving their wits with their wives: and then give them
great meals of beef, and iron and steel, they will
eat like wolves, and fight like devils.

DUKE OF ORLEANS.
Ay, but these English are shrewdly out of beef.

THE CONSTABLE OF FRANCE.
Then shall we find to-morrow they have only
stomachs to eat, and none to fight. Now is it time
to arm; come, shall we about it?

DUKE OF ORLEANS.
It is now two o'clock: but, let me see,—by ten
We shall have each a hundred Englishmen.
[*Exeunt.*

ACT IV.
PROLOGUE.

Enter CHORUS.

CHORUS.
NOW entertain conjecture of a time
When creeping murmur and the poring dark
Fills the wide vessel of the universe.
From camp to camp, through the foul womb of
    night,
The hum of either army stilly sounds,
That the fixt sentinels almost receive
The secret whispers of each other's watch:
Fire answers fire; and through their paly flames
Each battle sees the other's umber'd face:
Steed threatens steed, in high and boastful neighs
Piercing the night's dull ear; and from the tents,
The armourers, accomplishing the knights,
With busy hammers closing rivets up,
Give dreadful note of preparation:
The country cocks do crow, the clocks do toll,
And the third hour of drowsy morning name.
Proud of their numbers, and secure in soul,
The confident and over-lusty French
Do the low-rated English play at dice;

And chide the cripple tardy-gaited night,
Who, like a foul and ugly witch, doth limp
So tediously away. The poor condemned English,
Like sacrifices, by their watchful fires
Sit patiently, and inly ruminate
The morning's danger; and their gesture sad
Investing lank-lean cheeks, and war-worn coats,
Presenteth them unto the gazing moon
So many horrid ghosts. O, now, who will behold
The royal captain of this ruin'd band
Walking from watch to watch, from tent to tent,
Let him cry, 'Praise and glory on his head!'
For forth he goes and visits all his host;
Bids them good morrow with a modest smile,
And calls them brothers, friends, and country-
    men.
Upon his royal face there is no note
How dread an army hath enrounded him;
Nor doth he dedicate one jot of colour
Unto the weary and all-watched night;
But freshly looks, and over-bears attaint
With cheerful semblance and sweet majesty;
That every wretch, pining and pale before,
Beholding him, plucks comfort from his looks:
A largess universal, like the sun,
His liberal eye doth give to every one,
Thawing cold fear. Then, mean and gentle all,
Behold, as may unworthiness define,
A little touch of Harry in the night:
And so our scene must to the battle fly;
Where—O for pity!—we shall much disgrace
With four or five most vile and ragged foils,
Right ill-disposed, in brawl ridiculous,
The name of Agincourt. Yet, sit and see;
Minding true things by what their mockeries be.
[*Exit.*

SCENE I.

The English camp at Agincourt.

Enter KING HENRY, BEDFORD, *and* GLOSTER.

KING HENRY.
GLOSTER, 'tis true that we are in great dan-
    ger;
The greater therefore should our courage be.—
Good morrow, brother Bedford.—God Al-
    mighty!
There is some soul of goodness in things evil,
Would men observingly distil it out;
For our bad neighbour makes us early stirrers,
Which is both healthful and good husbandry:
Besides, they are our outward consciences,
And preachers to us all; admonishing
That we should dress us fairly for our end.
Thus may we gather honey from the weed,
And make a moral of the devil himself.

Enter ERPINGHAM.
Good morrow, old Sir Thomas Erpingham:
A good soft pillow for that good white head
Were better than a churlish turf of France.

SIR THOMAS ERPINGHAM.
Not so, my liege: this lodging likes me better,
Since I may say, 'Now lie I like a king.'

KING HENRY.
'Tis good for men to love their present pains
Upon example; so the spirit is eased:

And when the mind is quicken'd, out of doubt
The organs, though defunct and dead before,
Break up their drowsy grave, and newly move
With casted slough and fresh legerity.
Lend me thy cloak, Sir Thomas.—Brothers both,
Commend me to the princes in our camp;
Do my good morrow to them; and anon
Desire them all to my pavilion.

DUKE OF GLOSTER.
We shall, my liege.

SIR THOMAS ERPINGHAM.
Shall I attend your Grace?

KING HENRY.
                    No, my good knight;
Go with my brothers to my lords of England:
I and my bosom must debate awhile,
And then I would no other company.

SIR THOMAS ERPINGHAM.
The Lord in heaven bless thee, noble Harry!
          [Exeunt GLOSTER, BEDFORD, and
          ERPINGHAM.

KING HENRY.
God-a-mercy, old heart! thou speak'st cheerfully.
          Enter PISTOL.

PISTOL.
Qui va là?

KING HENRY.
A friend.

PISTOL.
Discuss unto me; art thou officer?
Or art thou base, common, and popular?

KING HENRY.
I am a gentleman of a company.

PISTOL.
Trail'st thou the puissant pike?

KING HENRY.
Even so. What are you?

PISTOL.
As good a gentleman as the emperor.

KING HENRY.
Then you are a better than the king.

PISTOL.
The king's a bawcock, and a heart of gold,
A lad of life, an imp of fame;
Of parents good, of fist most valiant:
I kiss his dirty shoe, and from heart-string
I love the lovely bully.—What is thy name?

KING HENRY.
Harry le Roy.

PISTOL.
Le Roy!
A Cornish name: art thou of Cornish crew?

KING HENRY.
No, I am a Welshman.

PISTOL.
Know'st thou Fluellen?

KING HENRY.
Yes.

PISTOL.
Tell him, I'll knock his leek about his pate
Upon Saint Davy's day.

KING HENRY.
Do not you wear your dagger in your cap that
day, lest he knock that about yours.

PISTOL.
Art thou his friend?

KING HENRY.
And his kinsman too.

PISTOL.
The figo for thee, then!

KING HENRY.
I thank you: God be with you!

PISTOL.
My name is Pistol call'd.   [Exit.

KING HENRY.
It sorts well with your fierceness.
          Enter FLUELLEN and GOWER, severally.

GOWER.
Captain Fluellen!

FLUELLEN.
So! in the name of Cheshu Christ, speak lower. It
is the greatest admiration in the universal 'orld,
when the true and auncient prerogatifs and laws
of the wars is not kept: if you would take the
pains but to examine the wars of Pompey the
Great, you shall find, I warrant you, that there is
no tiddle-taddle nor pibble-pabble in Pompey's
camp; I warrant you, you shall find the ceremonies of the wars, and the cares of it, and the
forms of it, and the sobriety of it, and the modesty
of it, to be otherwise.

GOWER.
Why, the enemy is loud; you heard him all night.

FLUELLEN.
If the enemy is an ass, and a fool, and a prating
coxcomb, is it meet, think you, that we should
also, look you, be an ass, and a fool, and a prating
coxcomb,—in your own conscience, now?

GOWER.
I will speak lower.

FLUELLEN.
I pray you, and peseech you, that you will.
          [Exeunt GOWER and FLUELLEN.

KING HENRY.
Though it appear a little out of fashion,
There is much care and valour in this Welshman.
Enter three SOLDIERS, JOHN BATES, ALEXAN-
DER COURT, and MICHAEL WILLIAMS.

ALEXANDER COURT.
Brother John Bates, is not that the morning
which breaks yonder?

JOHN BATES.
I think it be: but we have no great cause to desire
the approach of day.

MICHAEL WILLIAMS.
We see yonder the beginning of the day, but I
think we shall never see the end of it.—Who goes
there?

KING HENRY.
A friend.

MICHAEL WILLIAMS.
Under what captain serve you?

KING HENRY.
Under Sir Thomas Erpingham.

MICHAEL WILLIAMS.
A good old commander and a most kind gentleman: I pray you, what thinks he of our estate?

KING HENRY.
Even as men wrackt upon a sand, that look to be
washt off the next tide.

JOHN BATES.
He hath not told his thought to the king?

KING HENRY.

No; nor it is meet he should. For, though I speak it to you, I think the king is but a man, as I am: the violet smells to him as it doth to me; the element shows to him as it doth to me; all his senses have but human conditions: his ceremonies laid by, in his nakedness he appears but a man; and though his affections are higher mounted than ours, yet, when they stoop, they stoop with the like wing. Therefore when he sees reason of fears, as we do, his fears, out of doubt, be of the same relish as ours are: yet, in reason, no man should possess him with any appearance of fear, lest he, by showing it, should dishearten his army.

JOHN BATES.

He may show what outward courage he will; but I believe, as cold a night as 'tis, he could wish himself in Thames up to the neck;—and so I would he were, and I by him, at all adventures, so we were quit here.

KING HENRY.

By my troth, I will speak my conscience of the king: I think he would not wish himself any where but where he is.

JOHN BATES.

Then I would he were here alone; so should he be sure to be ransom'd, and a many poor men's lives saved.

KING HENRY.

I dare say you love him not so ill, to wish him here alone, howsoever you speak this, to feel other men's minds: methinks I could not die any where so contented as in the king's company,—his cause being just, and his quarrel honourable.

MICHAEL WILLIAMS.

That's more than we know.

JOHN BATES.

Ay, or more than we should seek after; for we know enough, if we know we are the king's subjects: if his cause be wrong, our obedience to the king wipes the crime of it out of us.

MICHAEL WILLIAMS.

But if the cause be not good, the king himself hath a heavy reckoning to make, when all those legs and arms and heads, chopt off in battle, shall join together at the latter day, and cry all, 'We died at such a place;' some swearing; some crying for a surgeon; some, upon their wives left poor behind them; some, upon the debts they owe; some, upon their children rawly left. I am afeard there are few die well that die in battle, for how can they charitably dispose of any thing, when blood is their argument? Now, if these men do not die well, it will be a black matter for the king that led them to it; who to disobey were against all proportion of subjection.

KING HENRY.

So, if a son, that is by his father sent about merchandise, do sinfully miscarry upon the sea, the imputation of his wickedness, by your rule, should be imposed upon his father that sent him: or if a servant, under his master's command transporting a sum of money, be assail'd by robbers, and die in many irreconciled iniquities, you may call the business of the master the author of the servant's damnation:—but this is not so: the king is not bound to answer the particular endings of his soldiers, the father of his son, nor the master of his servant; for they purpose not their death, when they purpose their services. Besides, there is no king, be his cause never so spotless, if it come to the arbitrement of swords, can try it out with all unspotted soldiers: some peradventure have on them the guilt of premeditated and contrived murder; some, of beguiling virgins with the broken seals of perjury; some, making the wars their bulwark, that have before gored the gentle bosom of peace with pillage and robbery. Now, if these men have defeated the law and outrun native punishment, though they can outstrip men, they have no wings to fly from God: war is His beadle, war is His vengeance; so that here men are punisht for before-breach of the king's laws in now the king's quarrel: where they fear'd the death, they have bòrne life away; and where they would be safe, they perish: then if they die unprovided, no more is the king guilty of their damnation, than he was before guilty of those impieties for the which they are now visited. Every subject's duty is the king's; but every subject's soul is his own. Therefore should every soldier in the wars do as every sick man in his bed,—wash every mote out of his conscience: and dying so, death is to him advantage; or not dying, the time was blessedly lost wherein such preparation was gain'd: and in him that escapes, it were not sin to think that, making God so free an offer, He let him outlive that day to see His greatness, and to teach others how they should prepare.

MICHAEL WILLIAMS.

'Tis certain, every man that dies ill, the ill upon his own head,—the king is not to answer it.

JOHN BATES.

I do not desire he should answer for me; and yet I determine to fight lustily for him.

KING HENRY.

I myself heard the king say he would not be ransom'd.

MICHAEL WILLIAMS.

Ay, he said so, to make us fight cheerfully: but when our throats are cut, he may be ransom'd, and we ne'er the wiser.

KING HENRY.

If I live to see it, I will never trust his word after.

MICHAEL WILLIAMS.

'Mass, you'll pay him then! That's a perilous shot out of an elder-gun, that a poor and a private displeasure can do against a monarch! you may as well go about to turn the sun to ice with fanning in his face with a peacock's feather. You'll never trust his word after! come, 'tis a foolish saying.

KING HENRY.

Your reproof is something too round: I should be angry with you, if the time were convenient.

MICHAEL WILLIAMS.

Let it be a quarrel between us, if you live.

KING HENRY.

I embrace it.

MICHAEL WILLIAMS.

How shall I know thee again?

KING HENRY.

Give me any gage of thine, and I will wear it in

my bonnet: then, if ever thou darest acknowledge
it, I will make it my quarrel.

MICHAEL WILLIAMS.

Here's my glove: give me another of thine.

KING HENRY.

There.

MICHAEL WILLIAMS.

This will I also wear in my cap: if ever thou come to
me and say, after to-morrow, 'This is my glove,'
by this hand, I will take thee a box on the ear.

KING HENRY.

If ever I live to see it, I will challenge it.

MICHAEL WILLIAMS.

Thou darest as well be hang'd.

KING HENRY.

Well, I will do it, though I take thee in the king's
company.

MICHAEL WILLIAMS.

Keep thy word: fare thee well.

JOHN BATES.

Be friends, you English fools, be friends: we have
French quarrels enow, if you could tell how to
reckon.

KING HENRY.

Indeed, the French may lay twenty French
crowns to one, they will beat us; for they bear
them on their shoulders: but it is no English
treason to cut French crowns; and to-morrow the
king himself will be a clipper. [*Exeunt* SOLDIERS.
Upon the king!—let us our lives, our souls,
Our debts, our careful wives,
Our children, and our sins, lay on the king!
We must bear all. O hard condition,
Twin-born with greatness, subject to the breath
Of every fool, whose sense no more can feel
But his own wringing!
What infinite heart's-ease must kings neglect,
That private men enjoy!
And what have kings, that privates have not too,
Save ceremony,—save general ceremony?
And what art thou, thou idol ceremony?
What kind of god art thou, that suffer'st more
Of mortal griefs than do thy worshippers?
What are thy rents? what are thy comings-in?
O ceremony, show me but thy worth!
What is thy soul, O adoration?
Art thou aught else but place, degree, and form,
Creating awe and fear in other men?
Wherein thou art less happy being fear'd
Than they in fearing.
What drink'st thou oft, instead of homage sweet,
But poison'd flattery? O, be sick, great greatness,
And bid thy ceremony give thee cure!
Think'st thou the fiery fever will go out
With titles blown from adulation?
Will it give place to flexure and low bending?
Canst thou, when thou command'st the beggar's
  knee,
Command the health of it? No, thou proud dream,
That play'st so subtly with a king's repose:
I am a king that find thee; and I know
'Tis not the balm, the sceptre, and the ball,
The sword, the mace, the crown imperial,
The intertissued robe of gold and pearl,
The farced title running 'fore the king,
The throne he sits on, nor the tide of pomp

That beats upon the high shore of this world,—
No, not all these, thrice-gorgeous ceremony,
Not all these, laid in bed majestical,
Can sleep so soundly as the wretched slave,
Who, with a body fill'd and vacant mind,
Gets him to rest, cramm'd with distressful bread;
Never sees horrid night, the child of hell;
But, like a lackey, from the rise to set,
Sweats in the eye of Phœbus, and all night
Sleeps in Elysium; next day, after dawn,
Doth rise, and help Hyperion to his horse;
And follows so the ever-running year,
With profitable labour, to his grave:
And, but for ceremony, such a wretch,
Winding up days with toil and nights with sleep,
Had the fore-hand and vantage of a king.
The slave, a member of the country's peace,
Enjoys it; but in gross brain little wots
What watch the king keeps to maintain the peace,
Whose hours the peasant best advantages.

Enter ERPINGHAM.

SIR THOMAS ERPINGHAM.

My lord, your nobles, jealous of your absence,
Seek through your camp to find you.

KING HENRY.

             Good old knight,
Collect them all together at my tent:
I'll be before thee.

SIR THOMAS ERPINGHAM.

        I shall do't, my lord.   [*Exit.*

KING HENRY.

O God of battles! steel my soldiers' hearts;
Possess them not with fear; take from them now
The sense of reckoning, if th'opposed numbers
Pluck their hearts from them!—Not to-day, O
  Lord,
O, not to-day, think not upon the fault
My father made in compassing the crown!
I Richard's body have interred new;
And on it have bestow'd more contrite tears
Than from it issued forced drops of blood:
Five hundred poor I have in yearly pay,
Who twice a-day their wither'd hands hold up
Toward heaven, to pardon blood; and I have built
Two chantries, where the sad and solemn priests
Sing still for Richard's soul. More will I do;
Though all that I can do is nothing worth,
Since that my penitence comes after all,
Imploring pardon.

Enter GLOSTER.

DUKE OF GLOSTER.

My liege!

KING HENRY.

    My brother Gloster's voice?—Ay;
I know thy errand, I will go with thee:—
The day, my friends, and all things stay for me.
                      [*Exeunt.*

SCENE II.

The French camp.

Enter the DAUPHIN, ORLEANS, RAMBURES,
and others.

DUKE OF ORLEANS.

THE sun doth gild our armour; up, my lords!

DAUPHIN.

Montez à cheval!—My horse! *varlet, laquais!* ha!

DUKE OF ORLEANS.
O brave spirit!

DAUPHIN.
Via!—les eaux et la terre,—

DUKE OF ORLEANS.
Rien puis? l'air et le feu,—

DAUPHIN.
Ciel! cousin Orleans.

Enter CONSTABLE.
Now, my lord Constable!

THE CONSTABLE OF FRANCE.
Hark, how our steeds for present service neigh!

DAUPHIN.
Mount them, and make incision in their hides,
That their hot blood may spin in English eyes,
And dout them with superfluous courage, ha!

RAMBURES.
What, will you have them weep our horses' blood?
How shall we, then, behold their natural tears?

Enter a MESSENGER.

MESSENGER.
The English are embattled, you French peers.

THE CONSTABLE OF FRANCE.
To horse, you gallant princes! straight to horse!
Do but behold yond poor and starved band,
And your fair show shall suck away their souls,
Leaving them but the shales and husks of men.
There is not work enough for all our hands;
Scarce blood enough in all their sickly veins
To give each naked curtle-axe a stain,
That our French gallants shall to-day draw out,
And sheathe for lack of sport: let us but blow on
them,
The vapour of our valour will o'erturn them.
'Tis positive 'gainst all exceptions, lords,
That our superfluous lackeys and our peasants,—
Who in unnecessary action swarm
About our squares of battle,—were enow
To purge this field of such a hilding foe;
Though we upon this mountain's basis by
Took stand for idle speculation,—
But that our honour must not. What's to say?
A very little little let us do, ·
And all is done. Then let the trumpets sound
The tucket-sonance and the note to mount:
For our approach shall so much dare the field,
That England shall couch down in fear, and yield.

Enter GRANDPRÉ.

GRANDPRÉ.
Why do you stay so long, my lords of France?
Yond island carrions, desperate of their bones,
Ill-favoured become the morning field:
Their ragged curtains poorly are let loose,
And our air shakes them passing scornfully:
Big Mars seems bankrout in their beggar'd host,
And faintly through a rusty beaver peeps:
The horsemen sit like fixed candlesticks,
With torch-staves in their hand; and their poor
jades
Lob down their heads, dropping the hides and
hips,
The gum down-roping from their pale-dead eyes,
And in their pale dull mouths the gimmal-bit
Lies foul with chew'd grass, still and motionless;
And their executors, the knavish crows,
Fly o'er them, all impatient for their hour.

Description cannot suit itself in words
To demonstrate the life of such a battle
In life so lifeless as it shows itself.

THE CONSTABLE OF FRANCE.
They have said their prayers, and they stay for
death.

DAUPHIN.
Shall we go send them dinners and fresh suits,
And give their fasting horses provender,
And after fight with them?

THE CONSTABLE OF FRANCE.
I stay but for my guidon:—to the field!—
I will the banner from a trumpet take,
And use it for my haste. Come, come, away!
The sun is high, and we outwear the day.
[Exeunt.

SCENE III.

The English camp.

Enter GLOSTER, BEDFORD, EXETER, ERPING-
HAM, with all his host; SALISBURY, and WEST-
MORELAND.

DUKE OF GLOSTER.
WHERE is the king?

DUKE OF BEDFORD.
The king himself is rode to view the battle.

EARL OF WESTMORELAND.
Of fighting-men they have full three-score thousand.

DUKE OF EXETER.
There's five to one; besides, they all are fresh.

EARL OF SALISBURY.
God's arm strike with us! 'tis a fearful odds.
God b' wi' you, princes all; I'll to my charge:
If we no more meet till we meet in heaven,
Then, joyfully,—my noble Lord of Bedford,—
My dear Lord Gloster,—and my good Lord
Exeter,—
And my kind kinsman,—warriors all, adieu!

DUKE OF BEDFORD.
Farewell, good Salisbury; and good luck go with
thee!

DUKE OF EXETER.
Farewell, kind lord; fight valiantly to-day:
And yet I do thee wrong to mind thee of it,
For thou art framed of the firm truth of valour.
[Exit SALISBURY.

DUKE OF BEDFORD.
He is as full of valour as of kindness;
Princely in both.

Enter KING HENRY.

EARL OF WESTMORELAND.
O, that we now had here
But one ten thousand of those men in England
That do no work to-day!

KING HENRY.
What's he that wishes so?
My cousin Westmoreland?—No, my fair cousin:
If we are markt to die, we are enow
To do our country loss; and if to live,
The fewer men, the greater share of honour.
God's will! I pray thee, wish not one man more.
By Jove, I am not covetous for gold;
Nor care I who doth feed upon my cost;
It yearns me not if men my garments wear;

Such outward things dwell not in my desires:
But if it be a sin to covet honour,
I am the most offending soul alive.
No, faith, my coz, wish not a man from England:
God's peace! I would not lose so great an honour,
As one man more, methinks, would share from
     me,
For the best hope I have. O, do not wish one
     more!
Rather proclaim it, Westmoreland, through my
     host,
That he which hath no stomach to this fight,
Let him depart; his passport shall be made,
And crowns for convoy put into his purse:
We would not die in that man's company
That fears his fellowship to die with us.
This day is call'd the feast of Crispian:
He that outlives this day, and comes safe home,
Will stand a tip-toe when this day is named,
And rouse him at the name of Crispian.
He that shall live this day, and see old age,
Will yearly on the vigil feast his neighbours,
And say, 'To-morrow is Saint Crispian:'
Then will he strip his sleeve and show his scars,
And say, 'These wounds I had on Crispin's day.'
Old men forget; yet all shall be forgot,
But he'll remember with advantages
What feats he did that day: then shall our names,
Familiar in their mouths as household words,—
Harry the king, Bedford and Exeter,
Warwick and Talbot, Salisbury and Gloster,—
Be in their flowing cups freshly remember'd.
This story shall the good man teach his son;
And Crispin Crispian shall ne'er go by,
From this day to the ending of the world,
But we in it shall be remembered,—
We few, we happy few, we band of brothers;
For he to-day that sheds his blood with me
Shall be my brother; be he ne'er so vile,
This day shall gentle his condition:
And gentlemen in England now a-bed
Shall think themselves accurst they were not here;
And hold their manhoods cheap whiles any speaks
That fought with us upon Saint Crispin's day.

Enter SALISBURY.

EARL OF SALISBURY.
My sovereign lord, bestow yourself with speed:
The French are bravely in their battles set,
And will with all expedience charge on us.

KING HENRY.
All things are ready, if our minds be so.

EARL OF WESTMORELAND.
Perish the man whose mind is backward now!

KING HENRY.
Thou dost not wish more help from England, coz?

EARL OF WESTMORELAND.
God's will! my liege, would you and I alone,
Without more help, might fight this battle out!

KING HENRY.
Why, now thou hast unwisht five thousand men;
Which likes me better than to wish us one.—
You know your places: God be with you all!

Tucket. Enter MONTJOY.

MONTJOY.
Once more I come to know of thee, King Harry,
If for thy ransom thou wilt now compound,

Before thy most assured overthrow:
For certainly thou art so near the gulf,
Thou needs must be englutted. Besides, in
     mercy,
The Constable desires thee thou wilt mind
Thy followers of repentance; that their souls
May make a peaceful and a sweet retire
From off these fields, where, wretches, their poor
     bodies
Must lie and fester.

KING HENRY.
     Who hath sent thee now?

MONTJOY.
The Constable of France.

KING HENRY.
I pray thee, bear my former answer back:
Bid them achieve me, and then sell my bones.
Good God! why should they mock poor fellows
     thus?
The man that once did sell the lion's skin
While the beast lived, was kill'd with hunting
     him.
A many of our bodies shall no doubt
Find native graves; upon the which, I trust,
Shall witness live in brass of this day's work:
And those that leave their valiant bones in
     France,
Dying like men, though buried in your dunghills,
They shall be famed; for there the sun shall greet
     them,
And draw their honours reeking up to heaven;
Leaving their earthly parts to choke your clime,
The smell whereof shall breed a plague in France.
Mark, then, abounding valour in our English;
That, being dead, like to the bullet's grazing,
Break out into a second course of mischief,
Killing in relapse of mortality.
Let me speak proudly:—tell the Constable
We are but warriors for the working-day;
Our gayness and our gilt are all besmirch
With rainy marching in the painful field;
There's not a piece of feather in our host,—
Good argument, I hope, we will not fly,—
And time hath worn us into slovenry:
But, by the mass, our hearts are in the trim;
And my poor soldiers tell me, yet ere night
They'll be in fresher robes; or they will pluck
The gay new coats o'er the French soldiers'
     heads,
And turn them out of service. If they do this,—
As, if God please, they shall,—my ransom then
Will soon be levied. Herald, save thou thy labour;
Come thou no more for ransom, gentle herald:
They shall have none, I swear, but these my
     joints,—
Which if they have as I will leave 'em them,
Shall yield them little, tell the Constable.

MONTJOY.
I shall, King Harry. And so, fare thee well:
Thou never shalt hear herald any more.   [*Exit.*

KING HENRY.
I fear thou'lt once more come again for ransom.

Enter YORK.

DUKE OF YORK.
My lord, most humbly on my knee I beg
The leading of the vaward.

288

KING HENRY.
Take it, brave York.—Now, soldiers, march
  away:—
And how thou pleasest, God, dispose the day!
                               [Exeunt.

SCENE IV.
The field of battle.
Alarum: excursions. Enter PISTOL, *French*
SOLDIER, *and* BOY.
PISTOL.
YIELD, cur!
          FRENCH SOLDIER.
*Je pense que vous êtes le gentilhomme de bonne
qualité.*
PISTOL.
Qualtitie calmie custure me! Art thou a gentleman?
what is thy name? discuss.
        FRENCH SOLDIER.
O Seigneur Dieu!
PISTOL.
O, Signieur Dew should be a gentleman:—
Perpend my words, O Signieur Dew, and
  mark;—
O Signieur Dew, thou diest on point of fox,
Except, O signieur, thou do give to me
Egregious ransom.
        FRENCH SOLDIER.
O, prenez miséricorde! ayez pitié de moy!
        PISTOL.
Moy shall not serve; I will have forty moys;
Or I will fetch thy rim out at thy throat
In drops of crimson blood.
        FRENCH SOLDIER.
Est-il impossible d'échapper la force de ton bras?
        PISTOL.
Brass, cur!
Thou damned and luxurious mountain-goat,
Offer'st me brass?
        FRENCH SOLDIER.
O, pardonnez-moy!
        PISTOL.
Say'st thou me so? is that a ton of moys?—
Come hither, boy: ask me this slave in French
What is his name.
        BOY.
Écoutez: comment êtes-vous appelé?
        FRENCH SOLDIER.
Monsieur le Fer.
        BOY.
He says his name is Master Fer.
        PISTOL.
Master Fer! I'll fer him, and firk him, and ferret
him:—discuss the same in French unto him.
        BOY.
I do not know the French for fer, and ferret, and
firk.
        PISTOL.
Bid him prepare; for I will cut his throat.
        FRENCH SOLDIER.
Que dit-il, monsieur?
        BOY.
*Il me commande de vous dire que vous faites vous
prêt; car ce soldat ici est disposé tout à cette heure de
couper votre gorge.*

PISTOL.
Owy, cuppele gorge, permafoy,
Peasant, unless thou give me crowns, brave
  crowns;
Or mangled shalt thou be by this my sword.
        FRENCH SOLDIER.
*O, je vous supplie, pour l'amour de Dieu, me par-
donner! Je suis gentilhomme de bonne maison: gar-
dez ma vie, et je vous donnerai deux cents écus.*
        PISTOL.
What are his words?
        BOY.
He prays you to save his life: he is a gentleman of
a good house; and for his ransom he will give you
two hundred crowns.
        PISTOL.
Tell him my fury shall abate, and I
The crowns will take.
        FRENCH SOLDIER.
Petit monsieur, que dit-il?
        BOY.
*Encore qu'il est contre son jurement de pardonner
aucun prisonnier, néanmoins, pour les écus que vous
l'avez promis, il est content de vous donner la liberté,
le franchisement.*
        FRENCH SOLDIER.
*Sur mes genoux je vous donne mille remercimens; et
je m'estime heureux que je suis tombé entre les mains
d'un chevalier, je pense, le plus brave, vaillant, et
très distingué seigneur d'Angleterre.*
        PISTOL.
Expound unto me, boy.
        BOY.
He gives you, upon his knees, a thousand thanks;
and he esteems himself happy that he hath faln
into the hands of one, as he thinks, the most brave,
valorous, and thrice-worthy signieur of England.
        PISTOL.
As I suck blood, I will some mercy show.—Follow me, cur.   [Exit.
        BOY.
Suivez-vous le grand capitaine. [Exit FRENCH
SOLDIER.] I did never know so full a voice issue
from so empty a heart: but the saying is true,—
The empty vessel makes the greatest sound. Bardolph and Nym had ten times more valour than
this roaring devil i'th'old play, that every one
may pare his nails with a wooden dagger; and
they are both hang'd; and so would this be, if he
durst steal any thing adventurously. I must stay
with the lackeys, with the luggage of our camp:
the French might have a good prey of us, if he
knew of it; for there is none to guard it but boys.
                                 [Exit.

SCENE V.
Another part of the field.
Enter CONSTABLE, ORLEANS, BOURBON,
DAUPHIN, RAMBURES, *and others.*
THE CONSTABLE OF FRANCE.
O DIABLE!
        DUKE OF ORLEANS.
O Seigneur!—le jour est perdu, tout est perdu!
        DAUPHIN.
Mort de ma vie! all is confounded, all!

Reproach and everlasting shame
Sit mocking in our plumes.—*O méchante for-
tune!*—
Do not run away.   [*A short alarum.*
THE CONSTABLE OF FRANCE.
Why, all our ranks are broke.
DAUPHIN.
O perdurable shame!—let's stab ourselves.
Be these the wretches that we play'd at dice for?
DUKE OF ORLEANS.
Is this the king we sent to for his ransom?
DUKE OF BOURBON.
Shame, and eternal shame, nothing but shame!
Let's die in honour: once more back again;
And he that will not follow Bourbon now,
Let him go hence, and with his cap in hand,
Like a base pandar, hold the chamber-door
Whilst by a slave, no gentler than my dog,
His fairest daughter is contaminate.
THE CONSTABLE OF FRANCE.
Disorder, that hath spoil'd us, friend us now!
Let us on heaps go offer up our lives.
DUKE OF ORLEANS.
We are enow, yet living in the field,
To smother up the English in our throngs,
If any order might be thought upon.
DUKE OF BOURBON.
The devil take order now! I'll to the throng:
Let life be short; else shame will be too long.
                                    [*Exeunt.*

SCENE VI.

Another part of the field.

Alarum.   Enter KING HENRY *and* FORCES,
EXETER, *and others.*

KING HENRY.
WELL have we done, thrice-valiant country-
men:
But all's not done; yet keep the French the field.
DUKE OF EXETER.
The Duke of York commends him to your ma-
jesty.
KING HENRY.
Lives he, good uncle? thrice within this hour
I saw him down; thrice up again, and fighting;
From helmet to the spur all blood he was.
DUKE OF EXETER.
In which array, brave soldier, doth he lie,
Larding the plain; and by his bloody side,
Yoke-fellow to his honour-owing wounds,
The noble Earl of Suffolk also lies.
Suffolk first died: and York, all haggled over,
Comes to him, where in gore he lay insteept,
And takes him by the beard; kisses the gashes
That bloodily did yawn upon his face;
And cries aloud, 'Tarry, dear cousin Suffolk!
My soul shall thine keep company to heaven;
Tarry, sweet soul, for mine, then fly abreast;
As in this glorious and well-foughten field
We kept together in our chivalry!'
Upon these words I came, and cheer'd him up:
He smiled me in the face, raught me his hand,
And, with a feeble gripe, says, 'Dear my lord,
Commend my service to my sovereign.'
So did he turn, and over Suffolk's neck

He threw his wounded arm, and kist his lips;
And so, espoused to death, with blood he seal'd
A testament of noble-ending love.
The pretty and sweet manner of it forced
Those waters from me which I would have stopt;
But I had not so much of man in me,
And all my mother came into mine eyes,
And gave me up to tears.
KING HENRY.
I blame you not;
For, hearing this, I must perforce compound
With mistful eyes, or they will issue too.—
                                    [*Alarum.*
But, hark! what new alarum is this same?—
The French have reinforced their scatter'd
men:—
Then every soldier kill his prisoners;
Give the word through.   [*Exeunt.*

SCENE VII.

Another part of the field.

Enter FLUELLEN *and* GOWER.

FLUELLEN.
KILL the poys and the luggage! 'tis expressly
against the law of arms: 'tis as arrant a piece
of knavery, mark you now, as can be offert; in
your conscience, now, is it not?
GOWER.
'Tis certain there's not a boy left alive; and the
cowardly rascals that ran from the battle ha' done
this slaughter: besides, they have burn'd and
carried away all that was in the king's tent; wherefore the king, most worthily, hath caused every
soldier to cut his prisoner's throat.   O, 'tis a gallant king!
FLUELLEN.
Ay, he was porn at Monmouth, Captain Gower.
What call you the town's name where Alexander
the Pig was porn?
GOWER.
Alexander the Great.
FLUELLEN.
Why, I pray you, is not pig great? the pig, or the
great, or the mighty, or the huge, or the magnanimous, are all one reckonings, save the phrase is a
little variations.
GOWER.
I think Alexander the Great was born in Macedon:
his father was call'd Philip of Macedon, as I take
it.
FLUELLEN.
I think it is in Macedon where Alexander is porn.
I tell you, captain, if you look in the maps of the
'orld, I warrant you sall find, in the comparisons
between Macedon and Monmouth, that the situ-
ations, look you, is both alike. There is a river in
Macedon; and there is also moreover a river at
Monmouth: it is called Wye at Monmouth; but
it is out of my prains what is the name of the
other river; but 'tis all one, 'tis alike as my fingers
is to my fingers, and there is salmons in both. If
you mark Alexander's life well, Harry of Monmouth's life is come after it indifferent well; fo
there is figures in all things. Alexander,—Go

knows, and you know,—in his rages, and his furies,
and his wraths, and his cholers, and his moods,
and his displeasures, and his indignations, and
also being a little intoxicates in his prains, did, in
his ales and his angers, look you, kill his pest
friend, Cleitus.

GOWER.

Our king is not like him in that: he never kill'd
any of his friends.

FLUELLEN.

It is not well done, mark you now, to take the
tales out of my mouth, ere it is made and finisht. I
speak but in the figures and comparisons of it: as
Alexander kill'd his friend Cleitus, being in his
ales and his cups; so also Harry Monmouth, being
in his right wits and his goot judgements, turn'd
away the fat knight with the great-pelly doublet:
he was full of jests, and gipes, and knaveries, and
mocks; I have forgot his name.

GOWER.

Sir John Falstaff.

FLUELLEN.

That is he:—I'll tell you there is goot men porn
at Monmouth.

GOWER.

Here comes his majesty.

Alarum. *Enter* KING HENRY *and* FORCES;
WARWICK, GLOSTER, EXETER, *and others.*

KING HENRY.

I was not angry since I came to France
Until this instant.—Take a trumpet, herald;
Ride thou unto the horsemen on yond hill:
If they will fight with us, bid them come down,
Or void the field; they do offend our sight:
If they'll do neither, we will come to them,
And make them skirr away, as swift as stones
Enforced from the old Assyrian slings:
Besides, we'll cut the throats of those we have;
And not a man of them that we shall take
Shall taste our mercy:—go, and tell them so.

DUKE OF EXETER.

Here comes the herald of the French, my liege.

DUKE OF GLOSTER.

His eyes are humbler than they used to be.

Enter MONTJOY.

KING HENRY.

How now! what means this, herald? know'st thou
not
That I have fined these bones of mine for ransom?
Comest thou again for ransom?

MONTJOY.

No, great king:
I come to thee for charitable licence
That we may wander o'er this bloody field
To look our dead, and then to bury them;
To sort our nobles from our common men;
For many of our princes—woe the while—
Lie drown'd and soakt in mercenary blood;
So do our vulgar drench their peasant limbs
In blood of princes; and their wounded steeds
Fret fetlock deep in gore, and with wild rage
Yerk out their armed heels at their dead masters,
Killing them twice. O, give us leave, great king,
To view the field in safety, and dispose
Of their dead bodies!

KING HENRY.

I tell thee truly, herald,
I know not if the day be ours or no;
For yet a many of your horsemen peer
And gallop o'er the field.

MONTJOY.

The day is yours.

KING HENRY.

Praised be God, and not our strength, for it!—
What is this castle call'd that stands hard by?

MONTJOY.

They call it Agincourt.

KING HENRY.

Then call we this the field of Agincourt,
Fought on the day of Crispin Crispianus.

FLUELLEN.

Your grandfather of famous memory, an't please
your majesty, and your great-uncle Edward the
Plack Prince of Wales, as I have read in the chronicles, fought a most prave pattle here in France.

KING HENRY.

They did, Fluellen.

FLUELLEN.

Your majesty says very true: if your majesties is
remember'd of it, the Welshmen did goot service
in a garden where leeks did grow, wearing leeks
in their Monmouth caps; which, your majesty
knows, to this hour is an honourable padge of the
service; and I do pelieve your majesty takes no
scorn to wear the leek upon Saint Tavy's day.

KING HENRY.

I wear it for a memorable honour;
For I am Welsh, you know, good countryman.

FLUELLEN.

All the water in Wye cannot wash your majesty's
Welsh plood out of your pody, I can tell you that:
Got pless it, and preserve it, as long as it pleases
his grace, and his majesty too!

KING HENRY.

Thanks, good my countryman.

FLUELLEN.

By Cheshu, I am your majesty's countryman, I
care not who know it; I will confess it to all the
'orld: I need not to be ashamed of your majesty,
praised be Got, so long as your majesty is an
honest man.

KING HENRY.

God keep me so!—Our heralds go with him:
Bring me just notice of the numbers dead
On both our parts.—Call yonder fellow hither.

[*Points to* WILLIAMS. *Exeunt* HERALDS
with MONTJOY.

DUKE OF EXETER.

Soldier, you must come to the king.

KING HENRY.

Soldier, why wear'st thou that glove in thy cap?

MICHAEL WILLIAMS.

An't please your majesty, 'tis the gage of one that
I should fight withal, if he be alive.

KING HENRY.

An Englishman?

MICHAEL WILLIAMS.

An't please your majesty, a rascal that swagger'd
with me last night; who, if alive, and ever dare to
challenge this glove, I have sworn to take him a
box o'th'ear: or if I can see my glove in his cap,

which he swore, as he was a soldier, he would wear if alive, I will strike it out soundly.

KING HENRY.

What think you, Captain Fluellen? is it fit this soldier keep his oath?

FLUELLEN.

He is a craven and a villain else, an't please your majesty, in my conscience.

KING HENRY.

It may be his enemy is a gentleman of great sort, quite from the answer of his degree.

FLUELLEN.

Though he be as goot a gentleman as the tevil is, as Lucifer and Belzebub himself, it is necessary, look your Grace, that he keep his vow and his oath: if he be perjured, see you now, his reputation is as arrant a villain and a Jack-sauce, as ever his plack shoe trod upon Got's ground and his earth, in my conscience, la.

KING HENRY.

Then keep thy vow, sirrah, when thou meet'st the fellow.

MICHAEL WILLIAMS.

So I will, my liege, as I live.

KING HENRY.

Who servest thou under?

MICHAEL WILLIAMS.

Under Captain Gower, my liege.

FLUELLEN.

Gower is a goot captain, and is goot knowledge and literatured in the wars.

KING HENRY.

Call him hither to me, soldier.

MICHAEL WILLIAMS.

I will, my liege.   [Exit.

KING HENRY.

Here, Fluellen; wear thou this favour for me, and stick it in thy cap: when Alençon and myself were down together, I pluckt this glove from his helm: if any man challenge this, he is a friend to Alençon, and an enemy to our person; if thou encounter any such, apprehend him, an thou dost me love.

FLUELLEN.

Your Grace does me as great honours as can be desired in the hearts of his subjects: I would fain see the man, that has but two legs, that shall find himself aggriefed at this glove; that is all; but I would fain see it once, an please Got of his grace that I might see.

KING HENRY.

Know'st thou Gower?

FLUELLEN.

He is my dear friend, an please you.

KING HENRY.

Pray thee, go seek him, and bring him to my tent.

FLUELLEN.

I will fetch him.

KING HENRY.

My Lord of Warwick, and my brother Gloster, Follow Fluellen closely at the heels: The glove which I have given him for a favour May haply purchase him a box o'th'ear; It is the soldier's; I, by bargain, should Wear it myself. Follow, good cousin Warwick: If that the soldier strike him,—as I judge

By his blunt bearing, he will keep his word,— Some sudden mischief may arise of it; For I do know Fluellen valiant, And, toucht with choler, hot as gunpowder, And quickly will return an injury: Follow, and see there be no harm between them.— Go you with me, uncle of Exeter.   [Exeunt.

SCENE VIII.

Before KING HENRY'S pavilion.

Enter GOWER and WILLIAMS.

MICHAEL WILLIAMS.

I WARRANT it is to knight you, captain.

Enter FLUELLEN.

FLUELLEN.

Got's will and his pleasure, captain, I peseech you now, come apace to the king: there is more goot toward you peradventure than is in your knowledge to dream of.

MICHAEL WILLIAMS.

Sir, know you this glove?

FLUELLEN.

Know the glove! I know the glove is a glove.

MICHAEL WILLIAMS.

I know this; and thus I challenge it.   [Strikes him.

FLUELLEN.

'Splood, an arrant traitor as any's in the universal 'orld, or in France, or in England!

GOWER.

How now, sir! you villain!

MICHAEL WILLIAMS.

Do you think I'll be forsworn?

FLUELLEN.

Stand away, Captain Gower; I will give treason his payment into plows, I warrant you.

MICHAEL WILLIAMS.

I am no traitor.

FLUELLEN.

That's a lie in thy throat.—I charge you in his majesty's name, apprehend him: he's a friend of the Duke Alençon's.

Enter WARWICK and GLOSTER.

EARL OF WARWICK.

How now, how now! what's the matter?

FLUELLEN.

My Lord of Warwick, here is—praised be Got for it!—a most contagious treason come to light, look you, as you shall desire in a summer's day.— Here is his majesty.

Enter KING HENRY and EXETER.

KING HENRY.

How now! what's the matter?

FLUELLEN.

My liege, here is a villain and a traitor, that, look your Grace, has struck the glove which your majesty is take out of the helmet of Alençon.

MICHAEL WILLIAMS.

My liege, this was my glove; here is the fellow of it; and he that I gave it to in change promised to wear it in his cap: I promised to strike him, if he did: I met this man with my glove in his cap, and I have been as good as my word.

FLUELLEN.

Your majesty hear now, saving your majesty's manhood, what an arrant, rascally, beggarly, lousy

knave it is: I hope your majesty is pear me testi-
mony, and witness, and will avouchment, that
this is the glove of Alençon, that your majesty is
give me, in your conscience, now.

KING HENRY.
Give me thy glove, soldier: look, here is the
fellow of it.
'Twas I, indeed, thou promised'st to strike;
And thou hast given me most bitter terms.

FLUELLEN.
An please your majesty, let his neck answer for it,
if there is any martial law in the 'orld.

KING HENRY.
How canst thou make me satisfaction?

MICHAEL WILLIAMS.
All offences, my liege, come from the heart: never
came any from mine that might offend your majesty.

KING HENRY.
It was ourself thou didst abuse.

MICHAEL WILLIAMS.
Your majesty came not like yourself: you appear'd to me but as a common man; witness the
night, your garments, your lowliness; and what
your highness suffer'd under that shape, I beseech you take it for your own fault, and not
mine: for had you been as I took you for, I made
no offence; therefore, I beseech your highness,
pardon me.

KING HENRY.
Here, uncle Exeter, fill this glove with crowns,
And give it to this fellow.—Keep it, fellow;
And wear it for an honour in thy cap
Till I do challenge it.—Give him the crowns:—
And, captain, you must needs be friends with him.

FLUELLEN.
By this day and this light, the fellow has mettle
enough in his pelly.—Hold, there is twelve pence
for you; and I pray you to serve Got, and keep you
out of prawls, and prabbles, and quarrels, and
dissensions, and, I warrant you, it is the petter
for you.

MICHAEL WILLIAMS.
I will none of your money.

FLUELLEN.
It is with a goot will; I can tell you, it will serve
you to mend your shoes: come, wherefore should
you be so pashful? your shoes is not so goot: 'tis
a goot silling, I warrant you, or I will change it.
Enter an English HERALD.

KING HENRY.
Now, herald,—are the dead number'd?

HERALD.
Here is the number of the slaughter'd French.
[*Delivers a paper.*

KING HENRY.
What prisoners of good sort are taken, uncle?

DUKE OF EXETER.
Charles duke of Orleans, nephew to the king;
John duke of Bourbon, and Lord Bouciqualt:
Of other lords and barons, knights and squires,
Full fifteen hundred, besides common men.

KING HENRY.
This note doth tell me of ten thousand French
That in the field lie slain: of princes, in this
number,

And nobles bearing banners, there lie dead
One hundred twenty-six: added to these,
Of knights, esquires, and gallant gentlemen,
Eight thousand and four hundred; of the which,
Five hundred were but yesterday dubb'd knights:
So that, in these ten thousand they have lost,
There are but sixteen hundred mercenaries;
The rest are princes, barons, lords, knights,
    squires,
And gentlemen of blood and quality.
The names of those their nobles that lie dead,—
Charles Delabreth, high-Constable of France;
Jaques of Chatillon, admiral of France;
The master of the cross-bows, Lord Rambures;
Great-master of France, the brave Sir Guiscard
    Dauphin;
John duke of Alençon; Antony duke of Brabant,
The brother to the Duke of Burgundy;
And Edward duke of Bar: of lusty earls,
Grandpré and Roussi, Fauconberg and Foix,
Beaumont and Marle, Vaudemont and Lestrale.
Here was a royal fellowship of death!—
Where is the number of our English dead?—
[HERALD *presents another paper.*
Edward the duke of York, the Earl of Suffolk,
Sir Richard Ketly, Davy Gam, esquire;
None else of name; and of all other men
But five and twenty.—O God, Thy arm was here;
And not to us, but to Thy arm alone,
Ascribe we all!—When, without stratagem,
But in plain shock and even play of battle,
Was ever known so great and little loss
On one part and on th'other?—Take it, God,
For it is only Thine!

DUKE OF EXETER.
'Tis wonderful!

KING HENRY.
Come, go we in procession to the village:
And be it death proclaimed through our host
To boast of this, or take that praise from God
Which is His only.

FLUELLEN.
Is it not lawful, an please your majesty, to tell how
many is kill'd?

KING HENRY.
Yes, captain; but with this acknowledgement,
That God fought for us.

FLUELLEN.
Yes, my conscience, He did us great goot.

KING HENRY.
Do we all holy rites:
Let there be sung *Non nobis* and *Te Deum.*
The dead with charity enclosed in clay,
We'll then to Calais; and to England then;
Where ne'er from France arrived more happy
    men.   [*Exeunt.*

ACT V.

PROLOGUE.

Enter CHORUS.

CHORUS.
VOUCHSAFE to those that have not read the
    story,
That I may prompt them: and of such as have,
I humbly pray them to admit th'excuse

V. Prol. 4–I. 14   KING HENRY THE FIFTH   V. I. 15–60

Of time, of numbers, and due course of things,
Which cannot in their huge and proper life
Be here presented. Now we bear the king
Towards Calais: grant him there; there seen,
Heave him away upon your winged thoughts
Athwart the sea. Behold, the English beach
Pales in the flood with men, with wives, and boys,
Whose shouts and claps out-voice the deep-
     mouth'd sea,
Which, like a mighty whiffler 'fore the king,
Seems to prepare his way: so let him land;
And solemnly see him set on to London.
So swift a pace hath thought, that even now
You may imagine him upon Blackheath;
Where that his lords desire him to have borne
His bruised helmet and his bended sword
Before him through the city: he forbids it,
Being free from vainness and self-glorious pride;
Giving full trophy, signal, and ostent,
Quite from himself to God. But now behold,
In the quick forge and working-house of thought,
How London doth pour out her citizens!
The mayor, and all his brethren, in best sort,—
Like to the senators of th'antique Rome,
With the plebeians swarming at their heels,—
Go forth, and fetch their conquering Cæsar in:
As, by a lower but loving likelihood,
Were now the general of our gracious empress—
As in good time he may—from Ireland coming.
Bringing rebellion broached on his sword,
How many would the peaceful city quit,
To welcome him! much more, and much more
     cause,
Did they this Harry. Now in London place him;—
As yet the lamentation of the French
Invites the King of England's stay at home;—
The emperor coming in behalf of France,
To order peace between them;—and omit
All the occurrences, whatever chanced,
Till Harry's back-return again to France:
There must we bring him; and myself have play'd
The interim, by remembering you 'tis past.
Then brook abridgement; and your eyes advance,
After your thoughts, straight back again to France.
                                        [*Exit.*

SCENE I.

France. The English camp.

Enter FLUELLEN *and* GOWER.

GOWER.

NAY, that's right; but why wear you your
     leek to-day? Saint Davy's day is past.

FLUELLEN.

There is occasions and causes why and wherefore in all things: I will tell you, asse my friend,
Captain Gower:—the rascally, scald, peggarly,
lousy, pragging knave, Pistol,—which you and
yourself, and all the 'orld, know to be no petter
than a fellow, look you now, of no merits,—he is
come to me, and prings me pread and salt yesterday, look you, and pid me eat my leek: it was in a
place where I could not preed no contention with
him; but I will be so pold as to wear it in my cap
till I see him once again, and then I will tell him a
little piece of my desires.

GOWER.
Why, here he comes, swelling like a turkeycock.

FLUELLEN.
'Tis no matter for his swellings nor his turkey-
cocks.

Enter PISTOL.

Got pless you, Auncient Pistol! you scurvy, lousy
knave, Got pless you!

PISTOL.
Ha! art thou bedlam? dost thou thirst, base Tro-
jan,
To have me fold up Parca's fatal web?
Hence! I am qualmish at the smell of leek.

FLUELLEN.
I peseech you heartily, scurvy, lousy knave, at
my desires, and my requests, and my petitions, to
eat, look you, this leek: because, look you, you do
not love it, nor your affections, and your appetites,
and your disgestions, does not agree with it, I
would desire you to eat it.

PISTOL.
Not for Cadwallader and all his goats.

FLUELLEN.
There is one goat for you. [*Strikes him.*] Will you
be so goot, scald knave, as eat it?

PISTOL.
Base Trojan, thou shalt die.

FLUELLEN.
You say very true, scald knave,—when Got's will
is: I will desire you to live in the mean time, and
eat your victuals: come, there is sauce for it.
[*Strikes him again.*] You call'd me yesterday
mountain-squire; but I will make you to-day a
squire of low degree. I pray you, fall to: if you can
mock a leek, you can eat a leek.

GOWER.
Enough, captain: you have astonisht him.

FLUELLEN.
I say, I will make him eat some part of my leek,
or I will peat his pate four days.—Pite, I pray you;
it is goot for your green wound and your ploody
coxcomb.

PISTOL.
Must I bite?

FLUELLEN.
Yes, certainly, and out of doubt, and out of question too, and ambiguities.

PISTOL.
By this leek, I will most horribly revenge:
I eat and eat, I swear—

FLUELLEN.
Eat, I pray you: will you have some more sauce to
your leek? there is not enough leek to swear by.

PISTOL.
Quiet thy cudgel; thou dost see I eat.

FLUELLEN.
Much goot do you, scald knave, heartily. Nay,
pray you, throw none away; the skin is goot for
your proken coxcomb. When you take occasions
to see leeks hereafter, I pray you, mock at 'em;
that is all.

PISTOL.
Good.

FLUELLEN.
Ay, leeks is goot:—hold you, there is a groat to
heal your pate.

294

PISTOL.

Me a groat!

FLUELLEN.

Yes, verily and in truth, you shall take it; or I have another leek in my pocket, which you shall eat.

PISTOL.

I take thy groat in earnest of revenge.

FLUELLEN.

If I owe you any thing, I will pay you in cudgels; you shall be a woodmonger, and buy nothing of me but cudgels. Got b' wi' you, and keep you, and heal your pate.   [Exit.

PISTOL.

All hell shall stir for this.

GOWER.

Go, go; you are a counterfeit cowardly knave. Will you mock at an ancient tradition,—begun upon an honourable respect, and worn as a memorable trophy of predeceased valour,—and dare not avouch in your deeds any of your words? I have seen you gleeking and galling at this gentleman twice or thrice. You thought, because he could not speak English in the native garb, he could not therefore handle an English cudgel: you find it otherwise; and henceforth let a Welsh correction teach you a good English condition. Fare ye well.   [Exit.

PISTOL.

Doth Fortune play the huswife with me now? News have I, that my Nell is dead i'th'spital Of malady of France; And there my rendezvous is quite cut off. Old I do wax; and from my weary limbs Honour is cudgell'd. Well, bawd will I turn, And something lean to cutpurse of quick hand. To England will I steal, and there I'll steal: And patches will I get unto these scars, And swear I got them in the Gallia wars.   [Exit.

SCENE II.

France.   The French KING's palace.

Enter, at one door, KING HENRY, BEDFORD, GLOSTER, EXETER, WARWICK, WESTMORELAND, *and other* LORDS; *at another, the* French KING, QUEEN ISABEL, *the* PRINCESS KATHARINE, ALICE, *other* LADIES, *and* LORDS; *the* DUKE OF BURGUNDY, *and his* TRAIN.

KING HENRY.

PEACE to this meeting, wherefore we are met! Unto our brother France, and to our sister, Health and fair time of day;—joy and good wishes To our most fair and princely cousin Katharine;— And, as a branch and member of this royalty, By whom this great assembly is contrived, We do salute you, Duke of Burgundy;— And, princes French, and peers, health to you all!

FRENCH KING.

Right joyous are we to behold your face, Most worthy brother England; fairly met:— So are you, princes English, every one.

QUEEN ISABEL.

So happy be the issue, brother England, Of this good day and of this gracious meeting,

As we are now glad to behold your eyes; Yours eyes, which hitherto have borne in them Against the French, that met them in their bent, The fatal balls of murdering basilisks: The venom of such looks, we fairly hope, Have lost their quality; and that this day Shall change all griefs and quarrels into love.

KING HENRY.

To cry amen to that, thus we appear.

QUEEN ISABEL.

You English princes all, I do salute you.

DUKE OF BURGUNDY.

My duty to you both, on equal love, Great Kings of France and England! That I have labour'd, With all my wits, my pains, and strong endeavours, To bring your most imperial majesties Unto this bar and royal interview, Your mightiness on both parts best can witness. Since, then, my office hath so far prevail'd, That, face to face and royal eye to eye, You have congreeted, let it not disgrace me, If I demand, before this royal view, What rub or what impediment there is, Why that the naked, poor, and mangled Peace, Dear nurse of arts, plenties, and joyful births, Should not, in this best garden of the world, Our fertile France, put up her lovely visage? Alas, she hath from France too long been chased! And all her husbandry doth lie on heaps, Corrupting in its own fertility. Her vine, the merry cheerer of the heart, Unpruned dies; her hedges even-pleacht, Like prisoners wildly overgrown with hair, Put forth disorder'd twigs; her fallow leas The darnel, hemlock, and rank fumitory, Do root upon, while that the coulter rusts, That should deracinate such savagery; The even mead, that erst brought sweetly forth The freckled cowslip, burnet, and green clover, Wanting the scythe, all uncorrected, rank, Conceives by idleness, and nothing teems But hateful docks, rough thistles, kecksies, burs, Losing both beauty and utility. And as our vineyards, fallows, meads, and hedges, Defective in their natures, grow to wildness, Even so our houses, and ourselves and children, Have lost, or do not learn for want of time, The sciences that should become our country; But grow, like savages,—as soldiers will, That nothing do but meditate on blood,— To swearing, and stern looks, diffused attire, And every thing that seems unnatural. Which to reduce into our former favour, You are assembled: and my speech entreats That I may know the let, why gentle Peace Should not expel these inconveniences, And bless us with her former qualities.

KING HENRY.

If, Duke of Burgundy, you would the peace, Whose want gives growth to th'imperfections Which you have cited, you must buy that peace With full accord to all our just demands; Whose tenours and particular effects You have, enscheduled briefly, in your hands.

DUKE OF BURGUNDY.
The king hath heard them; to the which as yet
There is no answer made.
KING HENRY.
　　　　　　Well, then, the peace,
Which you before so urged, lies in his answer.
FRENCH KING.
I have but with a cursorary eye
O'erglanced the articles: pleaseth your Grace
To appoint some of your council presently
To sit with us once more, with better heed
To re-survey them, we will suddenly
Pass our accept and peremptory answer.
KING HENRY.
Brother, we shall.—Go, uncle Exeter,— [ter,—
And brother Clarence,—and you, brother Glos-
Warwick,—and Huntingdon,—go with the king;
And take with you free power to ratify,
Augment, or alter, as your wisdoms best
Shall see advantageable for our dignity,
Any thing in or out of our demands;
And we'll consign thereto.—Will you, fair sister,
Go with the princes, or stay here with us?
QUEEN ISABEL.
Our gracious brother, I will go with them:
Haply a woman's voice may do some good,
When articles too nicely urged be stood on.
KING HENRY.
Yet leave our cousin Katharine here with us:
She is our capital demand, comprised
Within the fore-rank of our articles.
QUEEN ISABEL.
She hath good leave.
　　　[Exeunt all except KING HENRY, KATH-
　　　ARINE, and ALICE.
KING HENRY.
　　　　　　Fair Katharine, and most fair!
Will you vouchsafe to teach a soldier terms
Such as will enter at a lady's ear,
And plead his love-suit to her gentle heart?
KATHARINE.
Your majesty shall mock at me; I cannot speak
your England.
KING HENRY.
O fair Katharine, if you will love me soundly with
your French heart, I will be glad to hear you con-
fess it brokenly with your English tongue. Do
you like me, Kate?
KATHARINE.
Pardonnez-moi, I cannot tell vat is 'like me.'
KING HENRY.
An angel is like you, Kate, and you are like an
angel.
KATHARINE.
Que dit-il? que je suis semblable à les anges?
ALICE.
Oui, vraiment, sauf votre grace, ainsi dit-il.
KING HENRY.
I said so, dear Katharine; and I must not blush to
affirm it.
KATHARINE.
O bon Dieu! les langues des hommes sont pleines de
tromperies.
KING HENRY.
What says she, fair one? that the tongues of men
are full of deceits?

ALICE.
Oui, dat de tongues of de mans is be full of deceits
—dat is de princess.
KING HENRY.
The princess is the better Englishwoman. I'faith,
Kate, my wooing is fit for thy understanding:
I am glad thou canst speak no better English; for,
if thou couldst, thou wouldst find me such a plain
king, that thou wouldst think I had sold my farm
to buy my crown. I know no ways to mince it in
love, but directly to say, 'I love you:' then, if you
urge me further than to say, 'Do you in faith?'
I wear out my suit. Give me your answer; i'faith,
do; and so clap hands and a bargain: how say you,
lady?
KATHARINE.
Sauf votre honneur, me understand vell.
KING HENRY.
Marry, if you would put me to verses or to dance
for your sake, Kate, why, you undid me: for the
one, I have neither words nor measure; and for
the other, I have no strength in measure, yet a
reasonable measure in strength. If I could win a
lady at leap-frog, or by vaulting into my saddle
with my armour on my back, under the correction
of bragging be it spoken, I should quickly leap into a wife. Or if I might buffet for my love, or
bound my horse for her favours, I could lay on
like a butcher, and sit like a jack-an-apes, never
off. But, before God, Kate, I cannot look greenly,
nor gasp out my eloquence, nor I have no cunning in protestation; only downright oaths, which
I never use till urged, nor never break for urging.
If thou canst love a fellow of this temper, Kate,
whose face is not worth sun-burning, that never
looks in his glass for love of any thing he sees
there,—let thine eye be thy cook. I speak to thee
plain soldier: if thou canst love me for this, take
me; if not, to say to thee that I shall die, is true,—
but for thy love, by the Lord, no; yet I love thee
too. And while thou livest, dear Kate, take a fellow of plain and uncoin'd constancy; for he perforce must do thee right, because he hath not the
gift to woo in other places: for these fellows of infinite tongue, that can rime themselves into ladies'
favours, they do always reason themselves out
again. What! a speaker is but a prater; a rime is
but a ballad. A good leg will fail; a straight back
will stoop; a black beard will turn white; a curl'd
pate will grow bald; a fair face will wither; a full
eye will wax hollow: but a good heart, Kate, is the
sun and the moon; or, rather, the sun, and not the
moon,—for it shines bright, and never changes,
but keeps his course truly. If thou would have
such a one, take me: and take me, take a soldier;
take a soldier, take a king: and what say'st thou,
then, to my love? speak, my fair, and fairly, I pray
thee.
KATHARINE.
Is it possible dat I sould love de enemy of France?
KING HENRY.
No; it is not possible you should love the enemy
of France, Kate: but, in loving me, you should
love the friend of France; for I love France so well,
that I will not part with a village of it; I will have
it all mine: and, Kate, when France is mine and

I am yours, then yours is France and you are mine.

KATHARINE.

I cannot tell vat is dat.

KING HENRY.

No, Kate? I will tell thee in French; which I am sure will hang upon my tongue like a new-married wife about her husband's neck, hardly to be shook off. *Je quand sur le possession de France, et quand vous avez le possession de moi*,—let me see, what then? Saint Denis be my speed!—*donc votre est France et vous êtes mienne.* It is as easy for me, Kate, to conquer the kingdom, as to speak so much more French: I shall never move thee in French, unless it be to laugh at me.

KATHARINE.

Sauf votre honneur, le Français que vous parlez, il est meilleur que l'Anglais lequel je parle.

KING HENRY.

No, faith, is't not, Kate: but thy speaking of my tongue, and I thine, most truly-falsely, must needs be granted to be much at one. But, Kate, dost thou understand thus much English,— Canst thou love me?

KATHARINE.

I cannot tell.

KING HENRY.

Can any of your neighbours tell, Kate? I'll ask them. Come, I know thou lovest me: and at night, when you come into your closet, you'll question this gentlewoman about me; and I know, Kate, you will to her dispraise those parts in me that you love with your heart: but, good Kate, mock me mercifully; the rather, gentle princess, because I love thee cruelly. If ever thou beest mine, Kate, —as I have a saving faith within me tells me thou shalt,—I get thee with scambling, and thou must therefore needs prove a good soldier-breeder: shall not thou and I, between Saint Denis and Saint George, compound a boy, half French, half English, that shall go to Constantinople and take the Turk by the beard? shall we not? what say'st thou, my fair flower-de-luce?

KATHARINE.

I do not know dat.

KING HENRY.

No; 'tis hereafter to know, but now to promise: do but now promise, Kate, you will endeavour for your French part of such a boy; and for my English moiety take the word of a king and a bachelor. How answer you, *la plus belle Katharine du monde, mon très-chère et devin déesse?*

KATHARINE.

Your majestee ave *fausse* French enough to deceive de most *sage demoiselle* dat is *en France.*

KING HENRY.

Now, fie upon my false French! By mine honour, in true English, I love thee, Kate: by which honour I dare not swear thou lovest me; yet my blood begins to flatter me that thou dost, notwithstanding the poor and untempering effect of my visage. Now, beshrew my father's ambition! he was thinking of civil wars when he got me: therefore was I created with a stubborn outside, with an aspect of iron, that, when I come to woo ladies, I fright them. But, in faith, Kate, the elder I wax, the better I shall appear: my comfort is, that old age, that ill layer-up of beauty, can do no more spoil upon my face: thou hast me, if thou hast me, at the worst; and thou shalt wear me, if thou wear me, better and better:—and therefore tell me, most fair Katharine, will you have me? Put off your maiden blushes; avouch the thoughts of your heart with the looks of an empress; take me by the hand, and say, 'Harry of England, I am thine:' which word thou shalt no sooner bless mine ear withal, but I will tell thee aloud, 'England is thine, Ireland is thine, France is thine, and Henry Plantagenet is thine;' who, though I speak it before his face, if he be not fellow with the best king, thou shalt find the best king of good fellows. Come, your answer in broken music,—for thy voice is music, and thy English broken; therefore, queen of all Katharines, break thy mind to me in broken English,—wilt thou have me?

KATHARINE.

Dat is as it sall please de *roi mon père.*

KING HENRY.

Nay, it will please him well, Kate,—it shall please him, Kate.

KATHARINE.

Den it sall also content me.

KING HENRY.

Upon that I kiss your hand, and I call you my queen.

KATHARINE.

Laissez, mon seigneur, laissez, laissez: ma foi, je ne veux point que vous abaissiez votre grandeur en baisant la main d'une votre indigne serviteur; excusez-moi, je vous supplie, mon très-puissant seigneur.

KING HENRY.

Then I will kiss your lips, Kate.

KATHARINE.

Les dames et demoiselles pour être baisées devant leur noces, il n'est pas la coutume de France.

KING HENRY.

Madam my interpreter, what says she?

ALICE.

Dat it is not be de fashion *pour les* ladies of France,—I cannot tell vat is *baiser en* Anglish.

KING HENRY.

To kiss.

ALICE.

Your majestee *entendre* bettre *que moi.*

KING HENRY.

It is not a fashion for the maids in France to kiss before they are married, would she say?

ALICE.

Oui, vraiment.

KING HENRY.

O Kate, nice customs court'sy to great kings. Dear Kate, you and I cannot be confined within the weak list of a country's fashion: we are the makers of manners, Kate; and the liberty that follows our places stops the mouth of all find-faults, —as I will do yours for upholding the nice fashion of your country in denying me a kiss: therefore, patiently and yielding. [*Kissing her.*] You have witchcraft in your lips, Kate: there is more eloquence in a sugar touch of them than in the tongues of the French council; and they should sooner persuade Harry of England than a general petition of monarchs.—Here comes your father.

Enter the French KING *and* QUEEN, BURGUNDY, BEDFORD, GLOSTER, EXETER, WESTMORELAND, WARWICK, &c.

DUKE OF BURGUNDY.
God save your majesty! my royal cousin,
Teach you our princess English?

KING HENRY.
I would have her learn, my fair cousin, how perfectly I love her; and that is good English.

DUKE OF BURGUNDY.
Is she not apt?

KING HENRY.
Our tongue is rough, coz, and my condition is not smooth; so that, having neither the voice nor the heart of flattery about me, I cannot so conjure up the spirit of love in her, that he will appear in his true likeness.

DUKE OF BURGUNDY.
Pardon the frankness of my mirth, if I answer you for that. If you would conjure in her, you must make a circle; if conjure up love in her in his true likeness, he must appear naked and blind. Can you blame her, then, being a maid yet rosed-over with the virgin crimson of modesty, if she deny the appearance of a naked blind boy in her naked seeing self? It were, my lord, a hard condition for a maid to consign to.

KING HENRY.
Yet they do wink and yield,—as love is blind and enforces.

DUKE OF BURGUNDY.
They are then excused, my lord, when they see not what they do.

KING HENRY.
Then, good my lord, teach your cousin to consent winking.

DUKE OF BURGUNDY.
I will wink on her to consent, my lord, if you will teach her to know my meaning: for maids, well summer'd and warm kept, are like flies at Bartholomew-tide, blind, though they have their eyes; and then they will endure handling, which before would not abide looking on.

KING HENRY.
This moral ties me over to time and a hot summer; and so I shall catch the fly, your cousin, in the latter end, and she must be blind too.

DUKE OF BURGUNDY.
As love is, my lord, before it loves.

KING HENRY.
It is so: and you may, some of you, thank love for my blindness, who cannot see many a fair French city for one fair French maid that stands in my way.

FRENCH KING.
Yes, my lord, you see them perspectively, the cities turn'd into a maid; for they are all girdled with maiden walls that war hath never enter'd.

KING HENRY.
Shall Kate be my wife?

FRENCH KING.
So please you.

KING HENRY.
I am content; so the maiden cities you talk of may wait on her: so the maid that stood in the way for my wish shall show me the way to my will.

FRENCH KING.
We have consented to all terms of reason.

KING HENRY.
Is't so, my lords of England?

EARL OF WESTMORELAND.
The king hath granted every article:—
His daughter first; and then, in sequel, all,
According to their firm proposed natures.

DUKE OF EXETER.
Only, he hath not yet subscribed this:
Where your majesty demands, that the King of France, having any occasion to write for matter of grant, shall name your highness in this form and with this addition, in French, *Notre très-cher fils Henri, roi d'Angleterre, héritier de France;* and thus in Latin, *Præclarissimus filius noster Henricus, rex Angliæ, et hæres Franciæ.*

FRENCH KING.
Nor this I have not, brother, so denied,
But your request shall make me let it pass.

KING HENRY.
I pray you, then, in love and dear alliance,
Let that one article rank with the rest;
And thereupon give me your daughter.

FRENCH KING.
Take her, fair son; and from her blood raise up
Issue to me; that the contending kingdoms
Of France and England, whose very shores look pale
With envy of each other's happiness,
May cease their hatred; and this dear conjunction
Plant neighbourhood and Christian-like accord
In their sweet bosoms, that never war advance
His bleeding sword 'twixt England and fair France.

ALL.
Amen!

KING HENRY.
Now, welcome, Kate;—and bear me witness all,
That here I kiss her as my sovereign queen.
[*Flourish.*

QUEEN ISABEL.
God, the best maker of all marriages,
Combine your hearts in one, your realms in one!
As man and wife, being two, are one in love,
So be there 'twixt your kingdoms such a spousal,
That never may ill office, or fell jealousy,
Which troubles oft the bed of blessed marriage,
Thrust in between the paction of these kingdoms,
To make divorce of their incorporate league;
That English may as French, French Englishmen,
Receive each other!—God speak this Amen!

ALL.
Amen!

KING HENRY.
Prepare we for our marriage:—on which day,
My lord of Burgundy, we'll take your oath,
And all the peers', for surety of our leagues.
Then shall I swear to Kate, and you to me;
And may our oaths well kept and prosperous be!
[*Sennet. Exeunt.*

EPILOGUE.

Enter CHORUS.

CHORUS.

Thus far, with rough and all unable pen,
  Our bending author hath pursued the story;
In little room confining mighty men,
  Mangling by starts the full course of their glory.
Small time, but in that small, most greatly liv'd
  This star of England: fortune made his sword;
By which the world's best garden he achieved,
  And of it left his son imperial lord.
Henry the Sixth, in infant bands crown'd king
  Of France and England, did this king succeed;
Whose state so many had the managing,
  That they lost France, and made his England bleed:
Which oft our stage hath shown; and for their sake,
  In your fair minds let this acceptance take.

                             [*Exit.*

KING HENRY THE EIGHTH

DRAMATIS PERSONAE

KING HENRY THE EIGHTH.
CARDINAL WOLSEY.
CARDINAL CAMPEIUS.
CAPUCIUS, *Ambassador from the Emperor Charles V.*
CRANMER, *Archbishop of Canterbury.*
DUKE OF NORFOLK.
DUKE OF BUCKINGHAM.
DUKE OF SUFFOLK.
EARL OF SURREY.
LORD CHAMBERLAIN.
LORD CHANCELLOR.
GARDINER, *Bishop of Winchester.*
BISHOP OF LINCOLN.
LORD ABERGAVENNY.
LORD SANDS.
SIR HENRY GUILDFORD.
SIR THOMAS LOVELL.
SIR ANTHONY DENNY.
SIR NICHOLAS VAUX.
SECRETARIES *to Wolsey.*
CROMWELL, *servant to Wolsey.*
GRIFFITH, *gentleman-usher to Queen Katharine.*

THREE GENTLEMEN.
DOCTOR BUTTS, *Physician to the King.*
GARTER KING-AT-ARMS.
SURVEYOR *to the Duke of Buckingham.*
BRANDON, *and a* SERGEANT-AT-ARMS.
DOORKEEPER *of the Council chamber.* PORTER, *and his* MAN.
PAGE *to Gardiner.* A CRIER.

QUEEN KATHARINE, *wife to King Henry, afterwards divorced.*
ANNE BULLEN, *her maid of honour, afterwards Queen.*
AN OLD LADY, *friend to Anne Bullen.*
PATIENCE, *woman to Queen Katharine.*

Several BISHOPS, LORDS, *and* LADIES *in the Dumb-shows;* WOMEN *attending upon the Queen;* SCRIBES, OFFICERS, GUARDS, *and other* ATTENDANTS.

SPIRITS.

SCENE—*Chiefly in London and Westminster; once at Kimbolton.*

PROLOGUE.

I COME no more to make you laugh: things now,
That bear a weighty and a serious brow,
Sad, high, and working, full of state and woe,
Such noble scenes as draw the eye to flow,
We now present. Those that can pity, here
May, if they think it well, let fall a tear;
The subject will deserve it. Such as give
Their money out of hope they may believe,
May here find truth too. Those that come to see
Only a show or two, and so agree
The play may pass, if they be still and willing,
I'll undertake may see away their shilling
Richly in two short hours. Only they
That come to hear a merry bawdy play,
A noise of targets, or to see a fellow
In a long motley coat guarded with yellow,
Will be deceived; for, gentle hearers, know,
To rank our chosen truth with such a show
As fool and fight is, beside forfeiting
Our own brains, and the opinion that we bring,
To make that only true we now intend,
Will leave us ne'er an understanding friend.
Therefore, for goodness' sake, and as you are known
The first and happiest hearers of the town,
Be sad, as we would make ye: think ye see
The very persons of our noble story
As they were living; think you see them great,
And follow'd with the general throng and sweat
Of thousand friends; then, in a moment, see
How soon this mightiness meets misery:
And, if you can be merry then, I'll say
A man may weep upon his wedding-day.

ACT I. SCENE I.

London. An ante-chamber in the palace.

Enter the DUKE OF NORFOLK *at one door; at the other, the* DUKE OF BUCKINGHAM *and the* LORD ABERGAVENNY.

DUKE OF BUCKINGHAM.
GOOD morrow, and well met. How have ye done
Since last we saw in France?

DUKE OF NORFOLK.
     I thank your Grace,
Healthful; and ever since a fresh admirer
Of what I saw there.

DUKE OF BUCKINGHAM.
     An untimely ague
Stay'd me a prisoner in my chamber, when
Those suns of glory, those two lights of men,
Met in the vale of Andren.

DUKE OF NORFOLK.
     'Twixt Guines and Arde:
I was then present, saw them salute on horseback;
Beheld them, when they lighted, how they clung
In their embracement, as they grew together;
Which had they, what four throned ones could have weigh'd
Such a compounded one?

DUKE OF BUCKINGHAM.
     All the whole time
I was my chamber's prisoner.

DUKE OF NORFOLK.
     Then you lost
The view of earthly glory: men might say,
Till this time pomp was single, but now married
To one above itself. Each following day

Became the next day's master, till the last
Made former wonders its: to-day, the French,
All clinquant, all in gold, like heathen gods,
Shone down the English; and, to-morrow, they
Made Britain India; every man that stood
Show'd like a mine. Their dwarfish pages were
As cherubins, all gilt: the madams too,
Not used to toil, did almost sweat to bear
The pride upon them, that their very labour
Was to them as a painting: now this mask
Was cried incomparable; and the ensuing night
Made it a fool and beggar. The two kings,
Equal in lustre, were now best, now worst,
As presence did present them; him in eye,
Still him in praise: and, being present both,
'Twas said they saw but one; and no discerner
Durst wag his tongue in censure. When these
  suns—
For so they phrase 'em—by their heralds chal-
  lenged
The noble spirits to arms, they did perform
Beyond thought's compass; that former fabulous
  story,
Being now seen possible enough, got credit,
That Bevis was believed.

           DUKE OF DUCKINGHAM.
               O, you go far.

           DUKE OF NORFOLK.
As I belong to worship, and affect
In honour honesty, the tract of every thing
Would by a good discourser lose some life,
Which action's self was tongue to. All was royal;
To the disposing of it naught rebell'd.
Order gave each thing view; the office did
Distinctly his full function.

           DUKE OF BUCKINGHAM.
               Who did guide,
I mean, who set the body and the limbs
Of this great sport together, as you guess?

           DUKE OF NORFOLK.
One, certes, that promises no element
In such a business.

           DUKE OF BUCKINGHAM.
           I pray you, who, my lord?

           DUKE OF NORFOLK.
All this was order'd by the good discretion
Of the right-reverend Cardinal of York.

           DUKE OF BUCKINGHAM.
The devil speed him! no man's pie is freed
From his ambitious finger. What had he
To do in these fierce vanities? I wonder
That such a keech can with his very bulk
Take up the rays o'the beneficial sun,
And keep it from the earth.

           DUKE OF NORFOLK.
               Surely, sir,
There's in him stuff that puts him to these ends;
For, being not propt by ancestry, whose grace
Chalks successors their way; nor call'd upon
For high feats done to the crown; neither allied
To eminent assistants; but, spider-like,
Out of his self-drawing web, he gives us note
The force of his own merit makes his way;
A gift that heaven gives; which buys for him
A place next to the king.

           LORD ABERGAVENNY.
               I cannot tell
What heaven hath given him,—let some graver
  eye
Pierce into that; but I can see his pride
Peep through each part of him: whence has he
  that?
If not from hell, the devil is a niggard;
Or has given all before, and he begins
A new hell in himself.

           DUKE OF BUCKINGHAM.
               Why the devil,
Upon this French going-out, took he upon him,
Without the privity o'the king, t'appoint
Who should attend on him? He makes up the file
Of all the gentry; for the most part such
To whom as great a charge as little honour
He meant to lay upon; and his own letter,
The honourable board of council out,
Must fetch him in the papers.

           LORD ABERGAVENNY.
               I do know
Kinsmen of mine, three at the least, that have
By this so sicken'd their estates, that never
They shall abound as formerly.

           DUKE OF BUCKINGHAM.
               O, many
Have broke their backs with laying manors on 'em
For this great journey. What did this vanity
But minister communication of
A most poor issue?

           DUKE OF NORFOLK.
               Grievingly I think,
The peace between the French and us not values
The cost that did conclude it.

           DUKE OF BUCKINGHAM.
               Every man,
After the hideous storm that follow'd, was
A thing inspired; and, not consulting, broke
Into a general prophecy,—That this tempest,
Dashing the garment of this peace, aboded
The sudden breach on't.

           DUKE OF NORFOLK.
               Which is budded out;
For France hath flaw'd the league, and hath attacht
Our merchants' goods at Bourdeaux.

           LORD ABERGAVENNY.
               Is it therefore
The ambassador is silenced?

           DUKE OF NORFOLK.
               Marry, is't.

           LORD ABERGAVENNY.
A proper title of a peace; and purchased
At a superfluous rate!

           DUKE OF BUCKINGHAM.
               Why, all this business
Our reverend cardinal carried.

           DUKE OF NORFOLK.
               Like it your Grace,
The state takes notice of the private difference
Betwixt you and the cardinal. I advise you,—
And take it from a heart that wishes towards you
Honour and plenteous safety,—that you read
The cardinal's malice and his potency
Together; to consider further, that
What his high hatred would effect wants not

A minister in his power. You know his nature,
That he's revengeful; and I know his sword
Hath a sharp edge: it's long, and, 't may be said,
It reaches far; and where 'twill not extend,
Thither he darts it. Bosom up my counsel,   [rock
You'll find it wholesome.—Lo, where comes that
That I advise your shunning.

Enter CARDINAL WOLSEY, *the purse borne before
him; certain of the* GUARD, *and two* SECRETAR-
IES *with papers. The* CARDINAL *in his passage
fixeth his eye on* BUCKINGHAM, *and* BUCKING-
HAM *on him, both full of disdain.*

CARDINAL WOLSEY.
The Duke of Buckingham's surveyor, ha?
Where's his examination?
                    FIRST SECRETARY.
                              Here, so please you.
                    CARDINAL WOLSEY.
Is he in person ready?
                    FIRST SECRETARY.
                              Ay, please your Grace.
                    CARDINAL WOLSEY.
Well, we shall then know more; and Buckingham
Shall lessen this big look.
                    [*Exeunt* WOLSEY *and his* TRAIN.
                    DUKE OF BUCKINGHAM.
This butcher's cur is venom-mouth'd, and I
Have not the power to muzzle him; therefore best
Not wake him in his slumber. A beggar's book
Outworths a noble's blood.
                    DUKE OF NORFOLK.
                              What, are you chafed?
Ask God for temperance; that's the appliance only
Which your disease requires.
                    DUKE OF BUCKINGHAM.
                              I read in's looks
Matter against me; and his eye reviled
Me, as his abject object: at this instant
He bores me with some trick: he's gone to the king;
I'll follow, and outstare him.
                    DUKE OF NORFOLK.
                              Stay, my lord,
And let your reason with your choler question
What 'tis you go about: to climb steep hills
Requires slow pace at first: anger is like
A full-hot horse, who being allow'd his way,
Self-mettle tires him. Not a man in England
Can advise me like you: be to yourself
As you would to your friend.
                    DUKE OF BUCKINGHAM.
                              I'll to the king;
And from a mouth of honour quite cry down
This Ipswich fellow's insolence; or proclaim
There's difference in no persons.
                    DUKE OF NORFOLK.
                              Be advised;
Heat not a furnace for your foe so hot
That it do singe yourself: we may outrun,
By violent swiftness, that which we run at,
And lose by over-running. Know you not,
The fire that mounts the liquor till't run o'er,
In seeming t'augment it wastes it? Be advised:
I say again, there is no English soul
More stronger to direct you than yourself,
If with the sap of reason you would quench,
Or but allay, the fire of passion.

                    DUKE OF BUCKINGHAM.
                              Sir,
I'm thankful to you; and I'll go along
By your prescription: but this top-proud fellow,—
Whom from the flow of gall I name not, but
From sincere motions,—by intelligence,
And proofs as clear as founts in July, when
We see each grain of gravel, I do know
To be corrupt and treasonous.
                    DUKE OF NORFOLK.
                              Say not, treasonous.
                    DUKE OF BUCKINGHAM.
To the king I'll say't; and make my vouch as
    strong
As shore of rock. Attend. This holy fox,
Or wolf, or both,—for he is equal ravenous
As he is subtle, and as prone to mischief
As able to perform't; his mind and place
Infecting one another, yea, reciprocally,—
Only to show his pomp as well in France
As here at home, suggests the king our master
To this last costly treaty, the interview,
That swallow'd so much treasure, and like a glass
Did break i'the rinsing.
                    DUKE OF NORFOLK.
                              Faith, and so it did.
                    DUKE OF BUCKINGHAM.
Pray, give me favour, sir. This cunning cardinal
The articles o'the combination drew
As himself pleased; and they were ratified
As he cried, 'Thus let be:' to as much end
As give a crutch to the dead: but our count-
    cardinal
Has done this, and 'tis well; for worthy Wolsey
Who cannot err, he did it. Now this follows,—
Which, as I take it, is a kind of puppy
To the old dam, treason,—Charles the emperor,
Under pretence to see the queen his aunt,—
For 'twas indeed his colour, but he came
To whisper Wolsey,—here makes visitation:
His fears were, that the interview betwixt
England and France might, through their amity,
Breed him some prejudice; for from this league
Peept harms that menaced him: he privily
Deals with our cardinal; and, as I trow,—
Which I do well; for, I am sure, the emperor
Paid ere he promised; whereby his suit was granted
Ere it was askt;—but when the way was made,
And paved with gold, the emperor thus desired,—
That he would please to alter the king's course,
And break the foresaid peace. Let the king know—
As soon he shall by me—that thus the cardinal
Does buy and sell his honour as he pleases,
And for his own advantage.
                    DUKE OF NORFOLK.
                              I am sorry
To hear this of him; and could wish he were
Something mistaken in't.
                    DUKE OF BUCKINGHAM.
                              No, not a syllable:
I do pronounce him in that very shape
He shall appear in proof.

Enter BRANDON, *a* SERGEANT-AT-ARMS *before
him, and two or three of the* GUARD.

                    BRANDON.
Your office, sergeant; execute it.

SERGEANT.
Sir,
My lord the Duke of Buckingham and Earl
Of Hereford, Stafford, and Northampton, I
Arrest thee of high treason, in the name
Of our most sovereign king.
DUKE OF BUCKINGHAM.
Lo, you, my lord,
The net has fal'n upon me! I shall perish
Under device and practice.
BRANDON.
I am sorry
To see you ta'en from liberty, to look on
The business present: 'tis his highness' pleasure
You shall to the Tower.
DUKE OF BUCKINGHAM.
It will help me nothing
To plead mine innocence; for that dye is on me
Which makes my whitest part black. The will of
heaven
Be done in this and all things!—I obey.—
O my Lord Aberga'ny, fare you well!
BRANDON.
Nay, he must bear you company.—[to ABERGA-
VENNY] The king
Is pleased you shall to the Tower, till you know
How he determines further.
LORD ABERGAVENNY.
As the duke said,
The will of heaven be done, and the king's pleasure
By me obey'd!
BRANDON.
Here is a warrant from
The king t'attach Lord Montacute; and the bodies
Of the duke's confessor, John de la Car,
One Gilbert Peck, his chancellor,—
DUKE OF BUCKINGHAM.
So, so;
These are the limbs o'the plot:—no more, I hope.
BRANDON.
A monk o'the Chartreux.
DUKE OF BUCKINGHAM.
O, Nicholas Hopkins?
BRANDON.
He.
DUKE OF BUCKINGHAM.
My surveyor is false; the o'er-great cardinal
Hath show'd him gold; my life is spann'd already:
I am the shadow of poor Buckingham,
Whose figure even this instant cloud puts on,
By darkening my clear sun.—My lord, farewell.
[Exeunt.

SCENE II.

The same. The council-chamber.

Cornets. Enter KING HENRY, leaning on the
CARDINAL's shoulder; the NOBLES and SIR
THOMAS LOVELL: the CARDINAL places him-
self under the KING's feet on his right side.
KING HENRY.
MY life itself, and the best heart of it,
Thanks you for this great care: I stood i'the
level
Of a full-charged confederacy, and give thanks
To you that choked it. Let be call'd before us
That gentleman of Buckingham's: in person

I'll hear him his confessions justify;
And point by point the treasons of his master
He shall again relate.
A noise within, crying 'Room for the Queen!'
Enter QUEEN KATHARINE, usher'd by the
DUKES OF NORFOLK and SUFFOLK: she kneels.
The KING riseth from his state, takes her up,
kisses and placeth her by him.
QUEEN KATHARINE.
Nay, we must longer kneel: I am a suitor.
KING HENRY.
Arise, and take place by us:—half your suit
Never name to us; you have half our power:
The other moiety, ere you ask, is given;
Repeat your will, and take it.
QUEEN KATHARINE.
Thank your majesty.
That you would love yourself, and in that love
Not unconsider'd leave your honour, nor
The dignity of your office, is the point
Of my petition.
KING HENRY.
Lady mine, proceed.
QUEEN KATHARINE.
I am solicited, not by a few,
And those of true condition, that your subjects
Are in great grievance: there have been commis-
sions
Sent down among 'em, which hath flaw'd the
heart
Of all their loyalties: wherein, although,
My good lord cardinal, they vent reproaches
Most bitterly on you, as putter-on
Of these exactions, yet the king our master,—
Whose honour heaven shield from soil!—even he
escapes not
Language unmannerly, yea, such which breaks
The sides of loyalty, and almost appears
In loud rebellion.
DUKE OF NORFOLK.
Not almost appears;
It doth appear; for, upon these taxations,
The clothiers all, not able to maintain
The many to them longing, have put off
The spinsters, carders, fullers, weavers, who,
Unfit for other life, compell'd by hunger
And lack of other means, in desperate manner
Daring the event to the teeth, are all in uproar,
And danger serves among them.
KING HENRY.
Taxation!
Wherein? and what taxation?—My lord Cardinal,
You that are blamed for it alike with us,
Know you of this taxation?
CARDINAL WOLSEY.
Please you, sir,
I know but of a single part, in aught
Pertains to the state; and front but in that file
Where others tell steps with me.
QUEEN KATHARINE.
No, my lord,
You know no more than others: but you frame
Things that are known alike; which are not
wholesome
To those which would not know them, and yet
must

Perforce be their acquaintance. These exactions,
Whereof my sovereign would have note, they are
Most pestilent to the hearing; and, to bear 'em,
The back is sacrifice to the load. They say
They are devised by you; or else you suffer
Too hard an exclamation.

KING HENRY.

Still exaction!
The nature of it? in what kind, let's know,
Is this exaction?

QUEEN KATHARINE.

I am much too venturous
In tempting of your patience; but am bolden'd
Under your promised pardon. The subjects'
  grief
Comes through commissions, which compel from
  each
The sixth part of his substance, to be levied
Without delay; and the pretence for this
Is named, your wars in France: this makes bold
  mouths:
Tongues spit their duties out, and cold hearts
  freeze
Allegiance in them; their curses now
Live where their prayers did: and it's come to
  pass,
That tractable obedience is a slave
To each incensed will. I would your highness
Would give it quick consideration, for
There is no primer business.

KING HENRY.

By my life,
This is against our pleasure.

CARDINAL WOLSEY.

And for me,
I have no further gone in this than by
A single voice; and that not past me but
By learned approbation of the judges. If I am
Traduced by ignorant tongues, which neither
  know
My faculties nor person, yet will be
The chronicles of my doing,—let me say
'Tis but the fate of place, and the rough brake
That virtue must go through. We must not stint
Our necessary actions, in the fear
To cope malicious censurers; which ever,
As ravenous fishes, do a vessel follow
That is new-trimm'd, but benefit no further
Than vainly longing. What we oft do best,
By sick interpreters, once weak ones, is
Not ours, or not allow'd; what worst, as oft,
Hitting a grosser quality, is cried up
For our best action. If we shall stand still,
In fear our motion will be mockt or carpt at,
We should take root here where we sit, or sit
State-statues only.

KING HENRY.

Things done well,
And with a care, exempt themselves from fear;
Things done without example, in their issue
Are to be fear'd. Have you a precedent
Of this commission? I believe, not any.
We must not rend our subjects from our laws,
And stick them in our will. Sixth part of each?
A trembling contribution! Why, we take
From every tree lop, bark, and part o' the timber;
And, though we leave it with a root, thus hackt,
The air will drink the sap. To every county
Where this is question'd send our letters, with
Free pardon to each man that has denied
The force of this commission: pray, look to't;
I put it to your care.

CARDINAL WOLSEY [to the SECRETARY].

A word with you.
Let there be letters writ to every shire,
Of the king's grace and pardon. The grieved
  commons
Hardly conceive of me; let it be noised
That through our intercession this revokement
And pardon comes: I shall anon advise you
Further in the proceeding.   [Exit SECRETARY.

Enter SURVEYOR.

QUEEN KATHARINE.

I am sorry that the Duke of Buckingham
Is run in your displeasure.

KING HENRY.

It grieves many:
The gentleman is learn'd, and a most rare
  speaker;
To nature none more bound; his training such,
That he may furnish and instruct great teachers,
And never seek for aid out of himself.
Yet see,
When these so noble benefits shall prove
Not well disposed, the mind growing once cor-
  rupt,
They turn to vicious forms, ten times more ugly
Than ever they were fair. This man so complete,
Who was enroll'd 'mongst wonders, and when we,
Almost with ravisht listening, could not find
His hour of speech a minute; he, my lady,
Hath into monstrous habits put the graces
That once were his, and is become as black
As if besmear'd in hell. Sit by us; you shall
  hear—
This was his gentleman in trust—of him
Things to strike honour sad. Bid him recount
The fore-recited practices; whereof
We cannot feel too little, hear too much.

CARDINAL WOLSEY.

Stand forth, and with bold spirit relate what you,
Most like a careful subject, have collected
Out of the Duke of Buckingham.

KING HENRY.

Speak freely.

SURVEYOR.

First, it was usual with him, every day
It would infect his speech,—that if the king
Should without issue die, he'll carry it so
To make the sceptre his: these very words
I've heard him utter to his son-in-law,
Lord Aberga'ny; to whom by oath he menaced
Revenge upon the cardinal.

CARDINAL WOLSEY.

Please your highness, note
His dangerous conception in this point.
Not friended by his wish, to your high person
His will is most malignant; and it stretches
Beyond you, to your friends.

QUEEN KATHARINE.

My learn'd lord Cardinal,
Deliver all with charity.

KING HENRY.
                    Speak on:
How grounded he his title to the crown,
Upon our fail? to this point hast thou heard him
At any time speak aught?
          SURVEYOR.
                    He was brought to this
By a vain prophecy of Nicholas Henton.
          KING HENRY.
What was that Henton?
          SURVEYOR.
                    Sir, a Chartreux friar,
His confessor; who fed him every minute
With words of sovereignty.
          KING HENRY.
                    How know'st thou this?
          SURVEYOR.
Not long before your highness sped to France,
The duke being at the Rose, within the parish
Saint Lawrence Poultney, did of me demand
What was the speech among the Londoners
Concerning the French journey: I replied,
Men fear'd the French would prove perfidious,
To the king's danger. Presently the duke
Said, 'twas the fear, indeed; and that he doubted
'Twould prove the verity of certain words
Spoke by a holy monk; 'that oft,' says he,
'Hath sent to me, wishing me to permit
John de la Car, my chaplain, a choice hour
To hear from him a matter of some moment:
Whom after, under the confession's seal,
He solemnly had sworn, that what he spoke
My chaplain to no creature living but
To me should utter, with demure confidence
This pausingly ensued,—'Neither the king nor's
     heirs,
Tell you the duke, shall prosper: bid him strive
To gain the love o'the commonalty: the duke
Shall govern England.'
          QUEEN KATHARINE.
                    If I know you well,
You were the duke's surveyor, and lost your
     office
On the complaint o'the tenants: take good heed
You charge not in your spleen a noble person,
And spoil your nobler soul: I say, take heed;
Yes, heartily beseech you.
          KING HENRY.
                    Let him on.
Go forward.
          SURVEYOR.
          On my soul, I'll speak but truth.
I told my lord the duke, by the devil's illusions
The monk might be deceived; and that 'twas dan-
     gerous for him
To ruminate on this so far. until
It forged him some design, which, being believed,
It was much like to do: he answer'd, 'Tush,
It can do me no damage;' adding further,
That, had the king in his last sickness fail'd,
The Cardinal's and Sir Thomas Lovell's heads
Should have gone off.
          KING HENRY.
                    Ha! what, so rank? Ah-ha!
There's mischief in this man:—canst thou say
further?

          SURVEYOR.
I can, my liege.
          KING HENRY.
          Proceed.
          SURVEYOR.
                    Being at Greenwich,
After your highness had reproved the duke
About Sir William Blomer,—
          KING HENRY.
                    I remember
Of such a time:—being my sworn servant,
The duke retain'd him his.—But on; what hence?
          SURVEYOR.
'If,' quoth he, 'I for this had been committed,
As, to the Tower, I thought, I would have play'd
The part my father meant to act upon
The usurper Richard; who, being at Salisbury,
Made suit to come in's presence; which if granted,
As he made semblance of his duty, would
Have put his knife into him.'
          KING HENRY.
                    A giant traitor!
          CARDINAL WOLSEY.
Now, madam, may his highness live in freedom,
And this man out of prison?
          QUEEN KATHARINE.
                    God mend all!
          KING HENRY.
There's something more would out of thee; what
     say'st?
          SURVEYOR.
After 'the duke his father,' with 'the knife,'
He stretch him, and, with one hand on his dagger,
Another spread on's breast, mounting his eyes,
He did discharge a horrible oath; whose tenour
Was,—were he evil used, he would outgo
His father by as much as a performance
Does an irresolute purpose.
          KING HENRY.
                    There's his period,
To sheathe his knife in us. He is attacht;
Call him to present trial: if he may
Find mercy in the law, 'tis his; if none,
Let him not seek't of us: by day and night!
He's traitor to the height.   [Exeunt.

                    SCENE III.
          An antechamber in the palace.

Enter the LORD CHAMBERLAIN and LORD
                    SANDS.
          LORD CHAMBERLAIN.
IS'T possible the spells of France should juggle
Men into such strange mysteries?
          LORD SANDS.
                    New customs,
Though they be never so ridiculous,
Nay, let 'em be unmanly, yet are follow'd.
          LORD CHAMBERLAIN.
As far as I see, all the good our English
Have got by the late voyage is but merely
A fit or two o'the face; but they are shrewd ones;
For when they hold 'em, you would swear
     directly
Their very noses had been counsellors
To Pepin or Clotharius, they keep state so.

                    305

LORD SANDS.

They have all new legs, and lame ones: one would take it,
That never saw 'em pace before, the spavin
Or springhalt reign'd among 'em.

LORD CHAMBERLAIN.

Death! my lord,
Their clothes are after such a pagan cut too,
That, sure, th'have worn out Christendom.

Enter SIR THOMAS LOVELL.

How now!
What news, Sir Thomas Lovell?

SIR THOMAS LOVELL.

Faith, my lord,
I hear of none, but the new proclamation
That's clapt upon the court-gate.

LORD CHAMBERLAIN.

What is't for?

SIR THOMAS LOVELL.

The reformation of our travell'd gallants,
That fill the court with quarrels, talk, and tailors.

LORD CHAMBERLAIN.

I'm glad 'tis there: now I would pray our monsieurs
To think an English courtier may be wise,
And never see the Louvre.

SIR THOMAS LOVELL.

They must either—
For so run the conditions—leave those remnants
Of fool and feather, that they got in France,
With all their honourable points of ignorance
Pertaining thereunto,—as fights and fireworks;
Abusing better men than they can be,
Out of a foreign wisdom,—renouncing clean
The faith they have in tennis, and tall stockings,
Short blister'd breeches, and those types of travel,
And understand again like honest men;
Or pack to their old playfellows: there, I take it,
They may, *cum privilegio*, wear away
The lag end of their lewdness, and be laugh'd at.

LORD SANDS.

'Tis time to give 'em physic, their diseases
Are grown so catching.

LORD CHAMBERLAIN.

What a loss our ladies
Will have of these trim vanities!

SIR THOMAS LOVELL.

Ay, marry,
There will be woe indeed, lords: the sly whoresons
Have got a speeding trick to lay down ladies;
A French song and a fiddle has no fellow.

LORD SANDS.

The devil fiddle 'em! I am glad they are going;
For, sure, there's no converting of 'em: now
An honest country lord, as I am, beaten
A long time out of play, may bring his plain-song,
And have an hour of hearing; and, by'r lady,
Held current music too.

LORD CHAMBERLAIN.

Well said, Lord Sands;
Your colt's tooth is not cast yet.

LORD SANDS.

No, my lord;
Nor shall not, while I have a stump.

LORD CHAMBERLAIN.

Sir Thomas,
Whither were you a-going?

SIR THOMAS LOVELL.

To the cardinal's:
Your lordship is a guest too.

LORD CHAMBERLAIN.

O, 'tis true:
This night he makes a supper, and a great one,
To many lords and ladies; there will be
The beauty of this kingdom, I'll assure you.

SIR THOMAS LOVELL.

That churchman bears a bounteous mind indeed,
A hand as fruitful as the land that feeds us;
His dews fall every where.

LORD CHAMBERLAIN.

No doubt he's noble;
He had a black mouth that said other of him.

LORD SANDS.

He may, my lord,—'has wherewithal; in him
Sparing would show a worse sin than ill doctrine:
Men of his way should be most liberal;
They are set here for examples.

LORD CHAMBERLAIN.

True, they are so;
But few now give so great ones. My barge stays;
Your lordship shall along.—Come, good Sir Thomas,
We shall be late else; which I would not be,
For I was spoke to, with Sir Henry Guildford,
This night to be comptrollers.

LORD SANDS.

I'm your lordship's. [*Exeunt.*

SCENE IV.

The presence-chamber in York-Place.

Hautboys.   A small table under a state for the
CARDINAL, *a longer table for the guests.   Then
enter* ANNE BULLEN *and divers other* LADIES
and GENTLEWOMEN, *as guests, at one door; at
another door, enter* SIR HENRY GUILDFORD.

SIR HENRY GUILDFORD.

LADIES, a general welcome from his Grace
Salutes ye all; this night he dedicates
To fair content and you: none here, he hopes,
In all this noble bevy, has brought with her
One care abroad; he would have all as merry
As, first, good company, good wine, good welcome,
Can make good people—

Enter LORD CHAMBERLAIN, LORD SANDS,
and SIR THOMAS LOVELL.

O, my lord, y'are tardy.
The very thought of this fair company
Clapt wings to me.

LORD CHAMBERLAIN.

You are young, Sir Harry Guildford.

LORD SANDS.

Sir Thomas Lovell, had the cardinal
But half my lay thoughts in him, some of these
Should find a running banquet ere they rested,
I think would better please 'em: by my life,
They are a sweet society of fair ones.

SIR THOMAS LOVELL.

O, that your lordship were but now confessor
To one or two of these!

LORD SANDS.
　　　　　I would I were;
They should find easy penance.
　　　SIR THOMAS LOVELL.
　　　　　　　Faith, how easy?
　　　LORD SANDS.
As easy as a down-bed would afford it.
　　　LORD CHAMBERLAIN.
Sweet ladies, will it please you sit?—Sir Harry,
Place you that side; I'll take the charge of this:
His Grace is entering.—Nay, you must not
　　freeze;
Two women placed together makes cold
　　weather:—
My Lord Sands, you are one will keep 'em
　waking;
Pray, sit between these ladies.
　　　LORD SANDS.
　　　　　　　　By my faith,
And thank your lordship.—By your leave, sweet
　ladies:
If I chance to talk a little wild, forgive me;
I had it from my father.
　　　ANNE BULLEN.
　　　　　　Was he mad, sir?
　　　LORD SANDS.
O, very mad, exceeding mad, in love too:
But he would bite none; just as I do now,—
He would kiss you twenty with a breath.
　　　　　　　　　　　　[Kisses her.
　　　LORD CHAMBERLAIN.
　　　　　　　Well said, my lord.—
So, now y'are fairly seated.—Gentlemen,
The penance lies on you, if these fair ladies
Pass away frowning.
　　　LORD SANDS..
　　　　　　For my little cure,
Let me alone.
Hautboys. Enter CARDINAL WOLSEY, attended,
　　and takes his state.
　　　CARDINAL WOLSEY.
Y'are welcome, my fair guests: that noble lady,
Or gentleman, that is not freely merry,
Is not my friend: this, to confirm my welcome;
And to you all, good health.　　　　[Drinks.
　　　LORD SANDS.
　　　　　　　Your Grace is noble:—
Let me have such a bowl may hold my thanks,
And save me so much talking.
　　　CARDINAL WOLSEY.
　　　　　　　My Lord Sands,
I am beholding to you: cheer your neighbours.—
Ladies, you are not merry:—gentlemen,
Whose fault is this?
　　　LORD SANDS.
　　　　　　The red wine first must rise
In their fair cheeks, my lord; then we shall have
　'em
Talk us to silence.
　　　ANNE BULLEN.
　　　　　　You are a merry gamester,
My Lord Sands.
　　　LORD SANDS.
Yes, if I make my play.
Here's to your ladyship: and pledge it, madam,
For 'tis to such a thing,—

　　　ANNE BULLEN.
　　　　　　You cannot show me.
　　　LORD SANDS.
I told your Grace they would talk anon.
　　　[Drum and trumpet; chambers discharged.
　　　CARDINAL WOLSEY.
　　　　　　　　What's that?
　　　LORD CHAMBERLAIN.
Look out there, some of ye.　　[Exit a SERVANT.
　　　CARDINAL WOLSEY.
　　　　　　　What warlike voice,
And to what end, is this?—Nay, ladies, fear not;
By all the laws of war y'are privileged.
　　　Enter SERVANT.
　　　LORD CHAMBERLAIN.
How now! what is't?
　　　SERVANT.
　　　　　　A noble troop of strangers,—
For so they seem: th'have left their barge, and
　landed;
And hither make, as great ambassadors
From foreign princes.
　　　CARDINAL WOLSEY.
　　　　　　Good lord chamberlain,
Go, give 'em welcome; you can speak the French
　tongue;
And, pray, receive 'em nobly, and conduct 'em
Into our presence, where this heaven of beauty
Shall shine at full upon them.—Some attend him.
　　　[Exit CHAMBERLAIN, attended. All rise,
　　　　and tables removed.
You have now a broken banquet; but we'll mend
　it.
A good digestion to you all: and once more
I shower a welcome on ye;—welcome all.
Hautboys. Enter KING and others, as MASKERS,
　　habited like shepherds, usher'd by the LORD
　　CHAMBERLAIN. They pass directly before the
　　CARDINAL, and gracefully salute him.
A noble company! what are their pleasures?
　　　LORD CHAMBERLAIN.
Because they speak no English, thus they pray'd
To tell your Grace,—that, having heard by fame
Of this so noble and so fair assembly
This night to meet here, they could do no less,
Out of the great respect they bear to beauty,
But leave their flocks; and, under your fair con-
　duct,
Crave leave to view these ladies, and entreat
An hour of revels with 'em.
　　　CARDINAL WOLSEY.
　　　　　　Say, lord chamberlain,
They have done my poor house grace; for which I
　pay 'em
A thousand thanks, and pray 'em take their
　pleasures.
　　　[They choose LADIES. The KING chooses
　　　ANNE BULLEN.
　　　KING HENRY.
The fairest hand I ever toucht! O beauty,
Till now I never knew thee!　　Music. Dance.
　　　CARDINAL WOLSEY.
My lord,—
　　　LORD CHAMBERLAIN.
　　　　Your Grace?

307

CARDINAL WOLSEY.
Pray, tell 'em thus much from me:—
There should be one amongst 'em, by his person,
More worthy this place than myself; to whom,
If I but knew him, with my love and duty
I would surrender it.
LORD CHAMBERLAIN.
I will, my lord.
[*Whispers the* MASKERS.
CARDINAL WOLSEY.
What say they?
LORD CHAMBERLAIN.
Such a one, they all confess,
There is indeed; which they would have your
Grace
Find out, and he will take it.
CARDINAL WOLSEY.
Let me see, then.
[*Comes from his state.*
By all your good leaves, gentlemen;—here I'll
make
My royal choice.
·KING HENRY.
Ye have found him, Cardinal:
[*Unmasking.*
You hold a fair assembly; you do well, lord:
You are a churchman, or, I'll tell you, Cardinal,
I should judge now unhappily.
CARDINAL WOLSEY.
I am glad
Your Grace is grown so pleasant.
KING HENRY.
My lord chamberlain,
Prithee, come hither: what fair lady's that?
LORD CHAMBERLAIN.
An't please your Grace, Sir Thomas Bullen's
daughter,—
The Viscount Rochford,—one of her highness'
women.
KING HENRY.
By heaven, she is a dainty one.—Sweetheart,
I were unmannerly, to take you out,
And not to kiss you [*kisses her*].—A health, gentle-
men!
Let it go round.
CARDINAL WOLSEY.
Sir Thomas Lovell, is the banquet ready
I'the privy chamber?
SIR THOMAS LOVELL.
Yes, my lord.
CARDINAL WOLSEY.
Your Grace,
I fear, with dancing is a little heated.
KING HENRY.
I fear, too much.
CARDINAL WOLSEY.
There's fresher air, my lord,
In the next chamber.
KING HENRY.
Lead in your ladies, every one: sweet partner,
I must not yet forsake you: let's be merry:
Good my lord Cardinal, I have half a dozen healths
To drink to these fair ladies, and a measure
To lead 'em once again; and then let's dream
Who's best in favour.—Let the music knock it.
[*Exeunt with trumpets.*

ACT II. SCENE I.
London.   A street.
Enter two GENTLEMEN, *at several doors.*
FIRST GENTLEMAN.
WHITHER away so fast?
SECOND GENTLEMAN.
O,—'God save ye!
Ev'n to the hall, to hear what shall become
Of the great Duke of Buckingham.
FIRST GENTLEMAN.
I'll save you
That labour, sir. All's now done, but the ceremony
Of bringing back the prisoner.
SECOND GENTLEMAN.
Were you there?
FIRST GENTLEMAN.
Yes, indeed, was I.
SECOND GENTLEMAN.
Pray, speak what has happen'd.
FIRST GENTLEMAN.
You may guess quickly what.
SECOND GENTLEMAN.
Is he found guilty?
FIRST GENTLEMAN.
Yes, truly is he, and condemn'd upon't.
SECOND GENTLEMAN.
I am sorry for't.
FIRST GENTLEMAN.
So are a number more.
SECOND GENTLEMAN.
But, pray, how past it?
FIRST GENTLEMAN.
I'll tell you in a little. The great duke
Came to the bar; where to his accusations
He pleaded still, not guilty, and alleged
Many sharp reasons to defeat the law.
The king's attorney, on the contrary,
Urged on the examinations, proofs, confessions
Of divers witnesses; which the duke desired
To have brought, *viva voce*, to his face:
At which appear'd against him his surveyor;
Sir Gilbert Peck his chancellor; and John Car,
Confessor to him; with that devil-monk,
Hopkins, that made this mischief.
SECOND GENTLEMAN.
That was he
That fed him with his prophecies?
FIRST GENTLEMAN.
The same.
All these accused him strongly; which he fain
Would have flung from him, but, indeed, he
could not:
And so his peers, upon this evidence,
Have found him guilty of high treason. Much
He spoke, and learnedly, for life; but all
Was either pitied in him or forgotten.
SECOND GENTLEMAN.
After all this, how did he bear himself?
FIRST GENTLEMAN.
When he was brought again to the bar, to hear
His knell rung out, his judgement,—he was stirr'd
With an agony, he sweat extremely,
And something spoke in choler, ill, and hasty:
But he fell to himself again, and sweetly
In all the rest show'd a most noble patience.

SECOND GENTLEMAN.
I do not think he fears death.
FIRST GENTLEMAN.
Sure, he does not,—
He never was so womanish; the cause
He may a little grieve at.
SECOND GENTLEMAN.
Certainly
The cardinal is the end of this.
FIRST GENTLEMAN.
'Tis likely,
By all conjectures: first, Kildare's attainder,
Then deputy of Ireland; who removed,
Earl Surrey was sent thither, and in haste too,
Lest he should help his father.
SECOND GENTLEMAN.
That trick of state
Was a deep envious one.
FIRST GENTLEMAN.
At his return
No doubt he will requite it. This is noted,
And generally,—whoever the king favours,
The cardinal instantly will find employment,
And far enough from court too.
SECOND GENTLEMAN.
All the commons
Hate him perniciously, and, o'my conscience,
Wish him ten fadom deep: this duke as much
They love and dote on; call him bounteous
Buckingham,
The mirror of all courtesy,—
FIRST GENTLEMAN.
Stay there, sir,
And see the noble ruin'd man you speak of.
Enter BUCKINGHAM *from his arraignment; tip-
staves before him; the axe with the edge towards
him; halberds on each side: accompanied with* SIR
THOMAS LOVELL, SIR NICHOLAS VAUX,
SIR WILLIAM SANDS, *and common People,
&c.*
SECOND GENTLEMAN.
Let's stand close, and behold him.
DUKE OF BUCKINGHAM.
All good people,
You that thus far have come to pity me, ·
Hear what I say, and then go home and lose me.
I have this day received a traitor's judgement,
And by that name must die: yet, heaven bear
witness,
And if I have a conscience, let it sink me,
Even as the axe falls, if I be not faithful!
The law I bear no malice for my death;
'T has done, upon the premises, but justice:
But those that sought it I could wish more
Christians:
Be what they will, I heartily forgive 'em:
Yet let 'em look they glory not in mischief,
Nor build their evils on the graves of great men;
For then my guiltless blood must cry against 'em.
For further life in this world I ne'er hope,
Nor will I sue, although the king have mercies
More than I dare make faults. You few that loved
me,
And dare be bold to weep for Buckingham,
His noble friends and fellows, whom to leave
Is only bitter to him, only dying,

Go with me, like good angels, to my end;
And, as the long divorce of steel falls on me,
Make of your prayers one sweet sacrifice,
And lift my soul to heaven.—Lead on, o'God's
name.
SIR THOMAS LOVELL.
I do beseech your Grace, for charity,
If ever any malice in your heart
Were hid against me, now to forgive me frankly.
DUKE OF BUCKINGHAM.
Sir Thomas Lovell, I as free forgive you
As I would be forgiven: I forgive all;
There cannot be those numberless offences
'Gainst me that I cannot take peace with: no black
envy
Shall mark my grave.—Commend me to his
Grace;
And, if he speak of Buckingham, pray, tell him
You met him half in heaven: my vows and
prayers
Yet are the king's; and, till my soul forsake,
Shall cry for blessings on him: may he live
Longer than I have time to tell his years!
Ever beloved and loving may his rule be!
And when old time shall lead him to his end,
Goodness and he fill up one monument!
SIR THOMAS LOVELL.
To the water-side I must conduct your Grace;
Then give my charge up to Sir Nicholas Vaux,
Who undertakes you to your end.
SIR NICHOLAS VAUX.
Prepare there,
The duke is coming: see the barge be ready;
And fit it with such furniture as suits
The greatness of his person.
DUKE OF BUCKINGHAM.
Nay, Sir Nicholas,
Let it alone; my state now will but mock me.
When I came hither, I was lord high constable
And Duke of Buckingham; now, poor Edward
Bohun:
Yet I am richer than my base accusers,
That never knew what truth meant: I now seal it;
And with that blood will make 'em one day groan
for't.
My noble father, Henry of Buckingham,
Who first raised head against usurping Richard,
Flying for succour to his servant Banister,
Being distrest, was by that wretch betray'd,
And without trial fell; God's peace be with him!
Henry the Seventh succeeding, truly pitying
My father's loss, like a most royal prince,
Restored me to my honours, and, out of ruins,
Made my name once more noble. Now his son,
Henry the Eighth, life, honour, name, and all
That made me happy, at one stroke has taken
For ever from the world. I had my trial,
And, must needs say, a noble one; which makes
me
A little happier than my wretched father:
Yet thus far we are one in fortunes,—both
Fell by our servants, by those men we loved most;
A most unnatural and faithless service!
Heaven has an end in all: yet, you that hear me,
This from a dying man receive as certain:—
Where you are liberal of your loves and counsels

Be sure you be not loose; for those you make friends
And give your hearts to, when they once perceive
The least rub in your fortunes, fall away
Like water from ye, never found again
But where they mean to sink ye. All good people,
Pray for me! I must now forsake ye: the last hour
Of my long weary life is come upon me.
Farewell: and when you would say something that is sad,
Speak how I fell.—I have done; and God forgive me!   [*Exeunt* BUCKINGHAM *and* TRAIN.

FIRST GENTLEMAN.
O, this is full of pity!—Sir, it calls,
I fear, too many curses on their heads
That were the authors.

SECOND GENTLEMAN.
                    If the duke be guiltless,
'Tis full of woe: yet I can give you inkling
Of an ensuing evil, if it fall,
Greater than this.

FIRST GENTLEMAN.
                    Good angels keep it from us!
What may it be? You do not doubt my faith, sir?

SECOND GENTLEMAN.
This secret is so weighty, 'twill require
A strong faith to conceal it.

FIRST GENTLEMAN.
                    Let me have it;
I do not talk much.

SECOND GENTLEMAN.
                    I am confident;
You shall, sir: did you not of late days hear
A buzzing of a separation
Between the king and Katharine?

FIRST GENTLEMAN.
                    Yes, but it held not:
For when the king once heard it, out of anger
He sent command to the lord mayor straight
To stop the rumour, and allay those tongues
That durst disperse it.

SECOND GENTLEMAN.
                    But that slander, sir,
Is found a truth now: for it grows again
Fresher than e'er it was; and held for certain
The king will venture at it. Either the cardinal,
Or some about him near, have, out of malice
To the good queen, possest him with a scruple
That will undo her: to confirm this too,
Cardinal Campeius is arrived, and lately;
As all think, for this business.

FIRST GENTLEMAN.
                    'Tis the cardinal;
And merely to revenge him on the emperor
For not bestowing on him, at his asking,
The archbishopric of Toledo, this is purposed.

SECOND GENTLEMAN.
I think you have hit the mark: but is 't not cruel
That she should feel the smart of this? The cardinal
Will have his will, and she must fall.

FIRST GENTLEMAN.
                    'Tis woful.
We are too open here to argue this;
Let's think in private more.   [*Exeunt.*

SCENE II.

An ante-chamber in the palace.

Enter the LORD CHAMBERLAIN, *reading this letter.*

LORD CHAMBERLAIN.
'MY lord, the horses your lordship sent for, with all the care I had, I saw well chosen, ridden, and furnisht. They were young and handsome, and of the best breed in the north. When they were ready to set out for London, a man of my lord Cardinal's, by commission and main power, took 'em from me; with this reason,—His master would be served before a subject, if not before the king; which stopt our mouths, sir.'
I fear he will indeed: well, let him have them:
He will have all, I think.

Enter to the LORD CHAMBERLAIN *the* DUKES OF NORFOLK *and* SUFFOLK.

DUKE OF NORFOLK.
Well met, my lord chamberlain.

LORD CHAMBERLAIN.
Good day to you both, your Graces.

DUKE OF SUFFOLK.
How is the king employ'd?

LORD CHAMBERLAIN.
                    I left him private,
Full of sad thoughts and troubles.

DUKE OF NORFOLK.
                    What's the cause?

LORD CHAMBERLAIN.
It seems the marriage with his brother's wife
Has crept too near his conscience.

DUKE OF SUFFOLK.
                    No, his conscience
Has crept too near another lady.

DUKE OF NORFOLK.
                    'Tis so:
This is the cardinal's doing, the king-cardinal:
That blind priest, like the eldest son of fortune,
Turns what he list. The king will know him one day.

DUKE OF SUFFOLK.
Pray God he do! he'll never know himself else.

DUKE OF NORFOLK.
How holily he works in all his business!
And with what zeal! for, now he has crackt the league
'Tween us and the emperor, the queen's great nephew,
He dives into the king's soul, and there scatters
Dangers, doubts, wringing of the conscience,
Fears, and despairs,—and all these for his marriage:
And out of all these to restore the king,
He counsels a divorce; a loss of her
That, like a jewel, has hung twenty years
About his neck, yet never lost her lustre;
Of her that loves him with that excellence
That angels love good men with; even of her
That, when the greatest stroke of fortune falls,
Will bless the king: and is not this course pious?

LORD CHAMBERLAIN.
Heaven keep me from such counsel! 'Tis most true
These news are everywhere; every tongue speaks 'em,

And every true heart weeps for't: all that dare
Look into these affairs see this main end,—
The French king's sister. Heaven will one day open
The king's eyes, that so long have slept upon
This bold bad man.
     DUKE OF SUFFOLK.
          And free us from his slavery.
     DUKE OF NORFOLK.
We had need pray,
And heartily, for our deliverance;
Or this imperious man will work us all
From princes into pages: all men's honours
Lie like one lump before him, to be fashion'd
Into what pitch he please.
     DUKE OF SUFFOLK.
          For me, my lords,
I love him not, nor fear him; there's my creed:
As I am made without him, so I'll stand,
If the king please; his curses and his blessings
Touch me alike, th'are breath I not believe in.
I knew him, and I know him; so I leave him
To him that made him proud, the Pope.
     DUKE OF NORFOLK.
          Let's in;
And with some other business put the king
From these sad thoughts, that work too much upon him:—
My lord, you'll bear us company?
     LORD CHAMBERLAIN.
          Excuse me;
The king has sent me otherwhere: besides,
You'll find a most unfit time to disturb him:
Health to your lordships!
     DUKE OF NORFOLK.
         Thanks, my good lord chamberlain.
[Exit LORD CHAMBERLAIN; and the KING
draws the curtain and sits reading pensively.
     DUKE OF SUFFOLK.
How sad he looks! sure, he is much afflicted.
     KING HENRY.
Who's there, ha?
     DUKE OF NORFOLK.
         Pray God he be not angry.
     KING HENRY.
Who's there, I say? How dare you thrust yourselves
Into my private meditations?
Who am I, ha?
     DUKE OF NORFOLK.
A gracious king that pardons all offences
Malice ne'er meant: our breach of duty this way
Is business of estate; in which we come
To know your royal pleasure.
     KING HENRY.
         Ye are too bold:
Go to; I'll make ye know your times of business:
Is this an hour for temporal affairs, ha?
     Enter WOLSEY and CAMPEIUS, with a commission.
Who's there? my good lord Cardinal?—O my Wolsey,
The quiet of my wounded conscience;
Thou art a cure fit for a king.—[to CAMPEIUS] You're welcome,
Most learned reverend sir, into our kingdom:

Use us and it.—[to WOLSEY] My good lord, have great care
I be not found a talker.
     CARDINAL WOLSEY.
         Sir, you cannot.
I would your Grace would give us but an hour
Of private conference.
     KING HENRY [to DUKES OF NORFOLK and SUFFOLK].
         We are busy; go.
     DUKE OF NORFOLK [aside to DUKE OF SUFFOLK].
This priest has no pride in him!
     DUKE OF SUFFOLK [aside to DUKE OF NORFOLK].
         Not to speak of:
I would not be so sick though for his place:
But this cannot continue.
     DUKE OF NORFOLK [aside to DUKE OF SUFFOLK].
         If it do,
I'll venture one have-at-him.
     DUKE OF SUFFOLK [aside to DUKE OF NORFOLK].
         I another.
     [Exeunt NORFOLK and SUFFOLK.
     CARDINAL WOLSEY.
Your Grace has given a precedent of wisdom
Above all princes, in committing freely
Your scruple to the voice of Christendom:
Who can be angry now? what envy reach you?
The Spaniard, tied by blood and favour to her,
Must now confess, if they have any goodness,
The trial just and noble. All the clerks,
I mean the learned ones, in Christian kingdoms
Have their free voices: Rome, the nurse of judge-
Invited by your noble self, hath sent   [ment,
One general tongue unto us, this good man,
This just and learned priest, Cardinal Cam-
  peius,—
Whom once more I present unto your highness.
     KING HENRY.
And once more in mine arms I bid him welcome,
And thank the holy conclave for their loves:
They have sent me such a man I would have wisht for.
     CARDINAL CAMPEIUS.
Your Grace must needs deserve all strangers' loves,
You are so noble. To your highness' hand
I tender my commission; by whose virtue,
The court of Rome commanding, you, my lord
Cardinal of York, are join'd with me their servant
In the unpartial judging of this business.
     KING HENRY.
Two equal men. The queen shall be acquainted
Forthwith for what you come. Where's Gardiner?
     CARDINAL WOLSEY.
I know your majesty has always loved her
So dear in heart, not to deny her that
A woman of less place might ask by law,—
Scholars allow'd freely to argue for her.
     KING HENRY.
Ay, and the best she shall have; and my favour
To him that does best: God forbid else. Cardinal,
Prithee, call Gardiner to me, my new secretary:
I find him a fit fellow.   [Exit WOLSEY.

Enter WOLSEY, *with* GARDINER.
CARDINAL WOLSEY [*aside to* GARDINER].
Give me your hand: much joy and favour to you;
You are the king's now.
GARDINER [*aside to* CARDINAL WOLSEY].
                          But to be commanded
For ever by your Grace, whose hand has raised me.
          KING HENRY.
Come hither, Gardiner.   [*Walks and whispers.*
          CARDINAL CAMPEIUS.
My Lord of York, was not one Doctor Pace
In this man's place before him?
          CARDINAL WOLSEY.
                          Yes, he was.
          CARDINAL CAMPEIUS.
Was he not held a learned man?
          CARDINAL WOLSEY.
                          Yes, surely.
          CARDINAL CAMPEIUS.
Believe me, there's an ill opinion spread, then,
Even of yourself, lord Cardinal.
          CARDINAL WOLSEY.
                          How! of me?
          CARDINAL CAMPEIUS.
They will not stick to say you envied him;
And fearing he would rise, he was so virtuous,
Kept him a foreign man still; which so grieved
    him,
That he ran mad and died.
          CARDINAL WOLSEY.
                          Heaven's peace be with him!
That's Christian care enough: for living mur-
    murers
There's places of rebuke. He was a fool;
For he would needs be virtuous: that good fellow,
If I command him, follows my appointment:
I will have none so near else. Learn this, brother,
We live not to be griped by meaner persons.
          KING HENRY.
Deliver this with modesty to the queen.
                          [*Exit* GARDINER.
The most convenient place that I can think of
For such receipt of learning is Black-Friars;
There ye shall meet about this weighty busi-
    ness:—
My Wolsey, see it furnisht.—O, my lord
Would it not grieve an able man to leave
So sweet a bedfellow? But, conscience, con-
    science,—
O, 'tis a tender place! and I must leave her.
                          [*Exeunt.*

SCENE III.

An ante-chamber in the QUEEN'S *apartments.*
Enter ANNE BULLEN *and an old* LADY.
          ANNE BULLEN.
NOT for that neither: here's the pang that
      pinches:—
His highness having lived so long with her, and she
So good a lady that no tongue could ever
Pronounce dishonour of her,—by my life,
She never knew harm-doing;—O, now, after
So many courses of the sun enthroned,
Still growing in a majesty and pomp,—the which
To leave a thousand-fold more bitter than

'Tis sweet at first t'acquire,—after this process,
To give her the avaunt! it is a pity
Would move a monster.
          OLD LADY.
                          Hearts of most hard temper
Melt and lament for her.
          ANNE BULLEN.
                          O, God's will! much better
She ne'er had known pomp: though't be temporal
Yet, if that quarrel, fortune, do divorce
It from the bearer, 'tis a sufferance panging
As soul and body's severing.
          OLD LADY.
                          Alas, poor lady!
She's a stranger now again.
          ANNE BULLEN.
                          So much the more
Must pity drop upon her. Verily,
I swear, 'tis better to be lowly born,
And range with humble livers in content,
Than to be perkt up in a glistering grief,
And wear a golden sorrow.
          OLD LADY.
                          Our content
Is our best having.
          ANNE BULLEN.
                          By my troth and maidenhead,
I would not be a queen.
          OLD LADY.
                          Beshrew me, I would,
And venture maidenhead for't; and so would you,
For all this spice of your hypocrisy:
You, that have so fair parts of woman on you,
Have too a woman's heart; which ever yet
Affected eminence, wealth, sovereignty;
Which, to say sooth, are blessings; and which
    gifts—
Saving your mincing—the capacity
Of your soft cheveril conscience would receive,
If you might please to stretch it.
          ANNE BULLEN.
                          Nay, good troth,—
          OLD LADY.
Yes, troth, and troth;—you would not be a queen?
          ANNE BULLEN.
No, not for all the riches under heaven.
          OLD LADY.
'Tis strange; a three-pence bow'd would hire me,
Old as I am, to queen it: but, I pray you,
What think you of a duchess? have you limbs
To bear that load of title?
          ANNE BULLEN.
                          No, in truth.
          OLD LADY.
Then you are weakly made: pluck off a little;
I would not be a young count in your way,
For more than blushing comes to: if your back
Cannot vouchsafe this burden, 'tis too weak
Ever to get a boy.
          ANNE BULLEN.
                          How you do talk!
I swear again, I would not be a queen
For all the world.
          OLD LADY.
                          In faith, for little England
You'ld venture an embālling: I myself

312

Would for Carnarvonshire, although there long'd
No more to the crown but that.—Lo, who comes
here?

Enter the LORD CHAMBERLAIN.
LORD CHAMBERLAIN.
Good morrow, ladies. What were't worth to know
The secret of your conference?
ANNE BULLEN.
My good lord,
Not your demand; it values not your asking:
Our mistress' sorrows we were pitying.
LORD CHAMBERLAIN.
It was a gentle business, and becoming
The action of good women: there is hope
All will be well.
ANNE BULLEN.
Now, I pray God, amen!
LORD CHAMBERLAIN.
You bear a gentle mind, and heavenly blessings
Follow such creatures. That you may, fair lady,
Perceive I speak sincerely, and high note's
Ta'en of your many virtues, the king's majesty
Commends his good opinion to you, and
Does purpose honour to you no less flowing
Than Marchioness of Pembroke; to which title
A thousand pound a year, annual support,
Out of his grace he adds.
ANNE BULLEN.
I do not know
What kind of my obedience I should tender;
More than my all is nothing: nor my prayers
Are not words duly hallow'd, nor my wishes
More worth than empty vanities; yet prayers and
wishes
Are all I can return. Beseech your lordship,
Vouchsafe to speak my thanks and my obedience,
As from a blushing handmaid, to his highness;
Whose health and royalty I pray for.
LORD CHAMBERLAIN.
Lady,
I shall not fail t'approve the fair conceit
The king hath of you.—[*aside*] I have perused her
well;
Beauty and honour in her are so mingled,
That they have caught the king: and who knows yet
But from this lady may proceed a gem
To lighten all the isle?—I'll to the king,
And say I spoke with you.
ANNE BULLEN.
My honour'd lord.
[*Exit* LORD CHAMBERLAIN.
OLD LADY.
Why, this it is; see, see!
I have been begging sixteen years in court,—
Am yet a courtier beggarly,—nor could
Come pat betwixt too early and too late
For any suit of pounds; and you, O fate!
A very fresh-fish here,—fie, fie, fie upon
This compell'd fortune!—have your mouth fill'd
up
Before you open it.
ANNE BULLEN.
This is strange to me.
OLD LADY.
How tastes it? is it bitter? forty pence, no.
There was a lady once—'tis an old story—

That would not be a queen, that would she not,
For all the mud in Egypt: have you heard it?
ANNE BULLEN.
Come, you are pleasant.
OLD LADY.
With your theme, I could
O'ermount the lark. The Marchioness of Pem-
broke!
A thousand pounds a year—for pure respect!
No other obligation! By my life,
That promises moe thousands: honour's train
Is longer than his foreskirt. By this time
I know your back will bear a duchess:—say,
Are you not stronger than you were?
ANNE BULLEN.
Good lady,
Make yourself mirth with your particular fancy,
And leave me out on't. Would I had no being,
If this salute my blood a jot: it faints me,
To think what follows.
The queen is comfortless, and we forgetful
In our long absence: pray, do not deliver
What here y'have heard to her.
OLD LADY.
What do you think me?
[*Exeunt.*

SCENE IV.

A hall in Black-Friars.

Trumpets, sennet, and cornets. Enter two VERGERS,
with short silver wands; next them, two SCRIBES,
in the habit of doctors; after them, the ARCH-
BISHOP OF CANTERBURY *alone; after him, the*
BISHOPS OF LINCOLN, ELY, ROCHESTER, *and*
SAINT ASAPH; *next them, with some small dis-*
tance, follows a GENTLEMAN *bearing the purse,*
with the great seal, and a cardinal's hat; then
two PRIESTS, *bearing each a silver cross; then a*
GENTLEMAN-USHER *bare-headed, accompanied*
with a SERGEANT-AT-ARMS *bearing a silver*
mace; then two GENTLEMEN *bearing two great*
silver pillars; after them, side by side, the two
CARDINALS; *two* NOBLEMEN *with the sword*
and mace. The KING *takes place under the cloth*
of state; the two CARDINALS *sit under him as*
judges. The QUEEN *takes place some distance*
from the KING. *The* BISHOPS *place themselves*
on each side the court, in manner of a consistory;
below them, the SCRIBES. *The* LORDS *sit next*
the BISHOPS. *The rest of the* ATTENDANTS
stand in convenient order about the hall.

CARDINAL WOLSEY.
WHILST our commission from Rome is read,
Let silence be commanded.
KING HENRY.
What's the need?
It hath already publicly been read,
And on all sides the authority allow'd;
You may, then, spare that time.
CARDINAL WOLSEY.
Be't so.—Proceed.
SCRIBE.
Say, Henry King of England, come into the court.
CRIER.
King Henry of England, &c.

KING HENRY.

Here.

SCRIBE.

Say, Katharine Queen of England, come into the court.

.CRIER.

Katharine Queen of England, &c.

[*The* QUEEN *makes no answer, rises out of her chair, goes about the court, comes to the* KING, *and kneels at his feet; then speaks.*

QUEEN KATHARINE.

Sir, I desire you do me right and justice;
And to bestow your pity on me: for
I am a most poor woman, and a stranger,
Born out of your dominions; having here
No judge indifferent, nor no more assurance
Of equal friendship and proceeding. Alas, sir,
In what have I offended you? what cause
Hath my behaviour given to your displeasure,
That thus you should proceed to put me off,
And take your good grace from me? Heaven witness,
I have been to you a true and humble wife,
At all times to your will conformable;
Ever in fear to kindle your dislike,
Yea, subject to your countenance,—glad or sorry,
As I saw it inclined. When was the hour
I ever contradicted your desire,
Or made it not mine too? Or which of your friends
Have I not strove to love, although I knew
He were mine enemy? what friend of mine
That had to him derived your anger, did I
Continue in my liking? nay, gave notice
He was from thence discharged? Sir, call to mind
That I have been your wife, in this obedience,
Upward of twenty years, and have been blest
With many children by you: if, in the course
And process of this time, you can report,
And prove it too, against mine honour aught,
My bond to wedlock, or my love and duty,
Against your sacred person, in God's name,
Turn me away; and let the foul'st contempt
Shut door upon me, and so give me up
To the sharp'st kind of justice. Please you, sir,
The king, your father, was reputed for
A prince most prudent, of an excellent
And unmatcht wit and judgement: Ferdinand,
My father, king of Spain, was reckon'd one
The wisest prince that there had reign'd by many
A year before: it is not to be question'd
That they had gather'd a wise council to them
Of every realm, that did debate this business,
Who deem'd our marriage lawful. Wherefore I humbly
Beseech you, sir, to spare me, till I may
Be by my friends in Spain advised; whose counsel
I will implore: if not, i'the name of God,
Your pleasure be fulfill'd!

CARDINAL WOLSEY.

　　　　You have here, lady,—
And of your choice,—these reverend fathers; men
Of singular integrity and learning,
Yea, the elect o'the land, who are assembled
To plead your cause: it shall be therefore bootless
That longer you defer the court; as well

For your own quiet, as to rectify
What is unsettled in the king.

CARDINAL CAMPEIUS.

　　　　　　His Grace
Hath spoken well and justly: therefore, madam,
It's fit this royal session do proceed;
And that, without delay, their arguments
Be now produced and heard.

QUEEN KATHARINE.

　　　　Lord Cardinal,—
To you I speak.

CARDINAL WOLSEY.

　　　Your pleasure, madam?

QUEEN KATHARINE.

　　　　　　　　Sir,
I am about to weep; but, thinking that
We are a queen,—or long have dream'd so,—certain
The daughter of a king, my drops of tears
I'll turn to sparks of fire.

CARDINAL WOLSEY.

　　　Be patient yet.

QUEEN KATHARINE.

I will, when you are humble; nay, before,
Or God will punish me. I do believe,
Induced by potent circumstances, that
You are mine enemy; and make my challenge
You shall not be my judge: for it is you
Have blown this coal betwixt my lord and me,—
Which God's dew quench! Therefore I say again,
I utterly abhor, yea, from my soul
Refuse you for my judge; whom, yet once more,
I hold my most malicious foe, and think not
At all a friend to truth.

CARDINAL WOLSEY.

　　　I do profess
You speak not like yourself; who ever yet
Have stood to charity, and display'd the effects
Of disposition gentle, and of wisdom
O'ertopping woman's power. Madam, you do me wrong:
I have no spleen against you; nor injustice
For you or any: how far I have proceeded,
Or how far further shall, is warranted
By a commission from the consistory,
Yea, the whole consistory of Rome. You charge me
That I have blown this coal: I do deny it:
The king is present: if it be known to him
That I gainsay my deed, how may he wound,
And worthily, my falsehood! yea, as much
As you have done my truth. But if he know
That I am free of your report, he knows
I am not of your wrong. Therefore in him
It lies to cure me: and the cure is, to
Remove these thoughts from you: the which before
His highness shall speak in, I do beseech
You, gracious madam, to unthink your speaking,
And to say no more.

QUEEN KATHARINE.

　　　My lord, my lord,
I am a simple woman, much too weak
T'oppose your cunning. Y'are meek and humble-mouth'd,
You sign your place and calling, in full seeming,
With meekness and humility: but your heart

Is cramm'd with arrogancy, spleen, and pride.
You have, by fortune, and his highness' favours,
Gone slightly o'er low steps, and now are mounted
Where powers are your retainers, and your wards
(Domestics to you); serve your will as't please
Yourself pronounce their office. I must tell you,
You tender more your person's honour than
Your high profession spiritual: that again
I do refuse you for my judge; and here,
Before you all, appeal unto the Pope,
To bring my whole cause 'fore his holiness,
And to be judged by him.

[*She curtsies to the* KING, *and offers to depart.*

CARDINAL CAMPEIUS.
           The queen is obstinate,
Stubborn to justice, apt to accuse it, and
Disdainful to be tried by't: 'tis not well.
She's going away.

KING HENRY.
Call her again.

CRIER.
Katharine Queen of England, come into the court.

GENTLEMAN USHER.
Madam, you are call'd back.

QUEEN KATHARINE.
What need you note it? pray you, keep your way:
When you are call'd, return.—Now, the Lord
   help,
They vex me past my patience!—Pray you, pass
  on:
I will not tarry; no, nor ever more
Upon this business my appearance make
In any of their courts.

[*Exeunt* QUEEN *and her* ATTENDANTS.

KING HENRY.
           Go thy ways, Kate:
That man i'the world who shall report he has
A better wife, let him in naught be trusted,
For speaking false in that: thou art, alone—
If thy rare qualities, sweet gentleness,
Thy meekness saint-like, wife-like government,
Obeying in commanding, and thy parts
Sovereign and pious else, could speak thee out—
The queen of earthly queens:—she's noble born;
And, like her true nobility, she has
Carried herself towards me.

CARDINAL WOLSEY.
           Most gracious sir,
In humblest manner I require your highness,
That it shall please you to declare, in hearing
Of all these ears,—for where I am robb'd and
  bound,
There must I be unloosed; although not there
At once and fully satisfied,—whether ever I
Did broach this business to your highness; or
Laid any scruple in your way, which might
Induce you to the question on't? or ever
Have to you—but with thanks to God for such
A royal lady—spake one the least word that might
Be to the prejudice of her present state,
Or touch of her good person?

KING HENRY.
           My lord Cardinal,
I do excuse you; yea, upon mine honour,
I free you from't. You are not to be taught
That you have many enemies, that know not

Why they are so, but, like to village-curs,
Bark when their fellows do: by some of these
The queen is put in anger. Y'are excused:
But will you be more justified? you ever
Have wisht the sleeping of this business; never
Desired it to be stirr'd; but oft have hinder'd, oft,
The passages made toward it:—on my honour,
I speak my good lord Cardinal to this point,
And thus far clear him. Now, what moved me to't,
I will be bold with time and your attention:—
Then mark the inducement. Thus it came;—give
  head to't:—
My conscience first received a tenderness,
Scruple, and prick, on certain speeches utter'd
By the Bishop of Bayonne, then French ambas-
  sador;
Who had been hither sent on the debating
A marriage 'twixt the Duke of Orleans and
Our daughter Mary: i'the progress of this business,
Ere a determinate resolution, he—
I mean the bishop—did require a respite;
Wherein he might the king his lord advertise
Whether our daughter were legitimate,
Respecting this our marriage with the dowager,
Sometimes our brother's wife. This respite shook
The bottom of my conscience, enter'd me,
Yea, with a splitting power, and made to tremble
The region of my breast; which forced such way,
That many mazed considerings did throng,
And prest in with this caution. First, methought
I stood not in the smile of heaven; who had
Commanded nature, that my lady's womb,
If it conceived a male child by me, should
Do no more offices of life to't than
The grave does to the dead; for her male issue
Or died where they were made, or shortly after
This world had air'd them: hence I took a thought,
This was a judgement on me; that my kingdom,
Well worthy the best heir o'the world, should not
Be gladded in't by me: then follows, that
I weigh'd the danger which my realms stood in
By this my issue's fail; and that gave to me
Many a groaning throe. Thus hulling in
The wild sea of my conscience, I did steer
Toward this remedy, whereupon we are
Now present here together; that's to say,
I meant to rectify my conscience—which
I then did feel full sick, and yet not well—
By all the reverend fathers of the land
And doctors learn'd. First I began in private
With you, my Lord of Lincoln; you remember
How under my oppression I did reek,
When I first moved you.

BISHOP OF LINCOLN.
           Very well, my liege.

KING HENRY.
I have spoke long: be pleased yourself to say
How far you satisfied me.

BISHOP OF LINCOLN.
           So please your highness,
The question did at first so stagger me,—
Bearing a state of mighty moment in't,
And consequence of dread,—that I committed
The daring'st counsel which I had to doubt;
And did entreat your highness to this course
Which you are running here.

315

KING HENRY.
                        I then moved you,
My Lord of Canterbury; and got your leave
To make this present summons:—unsolicited
I left no reverend person in this court;
But by particular consent proceeded
Under your hands and seals: therefore, go on;
For no dislike i'the world against the person
Of the good queen, but the sharp thorny points
Of my alleged reasons, drive this forward:
Prove but our marriage lawful, by my life
And kingly dignity, we are contented
To wear our mortal state to come with her,
Katharine our queen, before the primest creature
That's paragon'd o'the world.
            CARDINAL CAMPEIUS.
                        So please you highness,
The queen being absent, 'tis a needful fitness
That we adjourn this court till further day:
Meanwhile must be an earnest motion
Made to the queen, to call back her appeal
She intends unto his holiness. [They rise to depart.
            KING HENRY [aside].
                        I may perceive
These cardinals trifle with me: I abhor
This dilatory sloth and tricks of Rome.
My learn'd and well-beloved servant, Cranmer,
Prithee, return: with thy approach, I know,
My comfort comes along.—Break up the court:
I say, set on.   [Exeunt in manner as they enter'd.

ACT III. SCENE I.

London.   The QUEEN'S *apartments.*

Enter QUEEN *and her* WOMEN *as at work.*

QUEEN KATHARINE.

TAKE thy lute, wench: my soul grows sad with
    troubles;
Sing, and disperse 'em, if thou canst: leave work-
    ing.

            Song.
    Orpheus with his lute made trees,
    And the mountain-tops that freeze,
        Bow themselves, when he did sing:
    To his music plants and flowers
    Ever sprung; as sun and showers
        There had made a lasting spring.

    Every thing that heard him play,
    Even the billows of the sea,
        Hung their heads, and then lay by.
    In sweet music is such art,
    Killing care and grief of heart
        Fall asleep, or hearing, die.

            Enter a GENTLEMAN.
            QUEEN KATHARINE.
How now!

            GENTLEMAN.
An't please your Grace, the two great cardinals
Wait in the presence.
            QUEEN KATHARINE.
                Would they speak with me?
            GENTLEMAN.
They will'd me say so, madam.

QUEEN KATHARINE.
                        Pray their Graces
To come near. [*Exit* GENTLEMAN.] What can be
    their business
With me, a poor weak woman, faln from favour?
I do not like their coming, now I think on't.
They should be good men; their affairs as right-
    eous:
But all hoods make not monks.
        Enter the two CARDINALS, WOLSEY *and*
                    CAMPEIUS.
            CARDINAL WOLSEY.
                        Peace to your highness!
            QUEEN KATHARINE.
Your Graces find me here part of a housewife:
I would be all, against the worst may happen.
What are your pleasures with me, reverend lords?
            CARDINAL WOLSEY.
May it please you, noble madam, to withdraw
Into your private chamber, we shall give you
The full cause of our coming.
            QUEEN KATHARINE.
                        Speak it here;
There's nothing I have done yet, o'my conscience,
Deserves a corner: would all other women
Could speak this with as free a soul as I do!
My lords, I care not,—so much I am happy
Above a number,—if my actions
Were tried by every tongue, every eye saw 'em,
Envy and base opinion set against 'em,
I know my life so even. If your business
Seek me out, and that way I am wise in,
Out with it boldly: truth loves open dealing.
            CARDINAL WOLSEY.
*Tanta est erga te mentis integritas, regina serenis-
sima,*—
            QUEEN KATHARINE.
O, good my lord, no Latin;
I am not such a truant since my coming,
As not to know the language I have lived in:
A strange tongue makes my cause more strange,
    suspicious;
Pray, speak in English: here are some will thank
    you,
If you speak truth, for their poor mistress' sake,—
Believe me, she has had much wrong: lord Cardinal,
The willing'st sin I ever yet committed
May be absolved in English.
            CARDINAL WOLSEY.
                        Noble lady,
I am sorry my integrity should breed—
And service to his majesty and you—
So deep suspicion, where all faith was meant.
We come not by the way of accusation,
To taint that honour every good tongue blesses,
Nor to betray you any way to sorrow,—
You have too much, good lady; but to know
How you stand minded in the weighty difference
Between the king and you; and to deliver,
Like free and honest men, our just opinions,
And comforts to your cause.
            CARDINAL CAMPEIUS.
                        Most honour'd madam,
My Lord of York,—out of his noble nature,
Zeal and obedience he still bore your Grace,—
Forgetting, like a good man, your late censure

Both of his truth and him, which was too far,—
Offers, as I do, in a sign of peace,
His service and his counsel.

QUEEN KATHARINE [aside].
               To betray me.
My lords, I thank you both for your good wills;
Ye speak like honest men,—pray God, ye prove
    so!—
But how to make ye suddenly an answer,
In such a point of weight, so near mine honour,—
More near my life, I fear,— with my weak wit,
And to such men of gravity and learning,
In truth, I know not. I was set at work
Among my maids; full little, God knows, looking
Either for such men or such business.
For her sake that I have been,— for I feel
The last fit of my greatness,—good your Graces,
Let me have time and counsel for my cause:
Alas, I am a woman, friendless, hopeless!

CARDINAL WOLSEY.
Madam, you wrong the king's love with these fears:
Your hopes and friends are infinite.

QUEEN KATHARINE.
               In England
But little for my profit: can you think, lords,
That any Englishman dare give me counsel?
Or be a known friend, 'gainst his highness'
    pleasure,—
Though he be grown so desperate to be honest,—
And live a subject? Nay, forsooth, my friends,
They that must weigh out my afflictions,
They that my trust must grow to, live not here:
They are, as all my other comforts are, far hence,
In mine own country, lords.

CARDINAL CAMPEIUS.
            I would your Grace
Would leave your griefs, and take my counsel.

QUEEN KATHARINE.
               How, sir?

CARDINAL CAMPEIUS.
Put your main cause into the king's protection;
He's loving and most gracious: 'twill be much
Both for your honour better and your cause;
For if the trial of the law o'ertake ye,
You'll part away disgraced.

CARDINAL WOLSEY.
           He tells you rightly.

QUEEN KATHARINE.
Ye tell me what ye wish for both, my ruin:
Is this your Christian counsel? out upon ye!
Heaven is above all yet; there sits a Judge
That no king can corrupt.

CARDINAL CAMPEIUS.
          Your rage mistakes us.

QUEEN KATHARINE.
The more shame for ye: holy men I thought ye,
Upon my soul, two reverend cardinal virtues;
But cardinal sins and hollow hearts I fear ye;
Mend 'em, for shame, my lords. Is this your com-
    fort?
The cordial that ye bring a wretched lady,—
A woman lost among ye, laugh'd at, scorn'd?
I will not wish ye half my miseries;
I have more charity: but say, I warn'd ye;
Take heed, for heaven's sake, take heed, lest at once
The burden of my sorrows fall upon ye.

CARDINAL WOLSEY.
Madam, this is a mere distraction;
You turn the good we offer into envy.

QUEEN KATHARINE.
Ye turn me into nothing: woe upon ye,
And all such false professors! Would you have
    me—
If you have any justice, any pity,
If ye be any thing but churchmen's habits—
Put my sick cause into his hands that hates me?
Alas, has banisht me his bed already,—
His love, too long ago! I am old, my lords,
And all the fellowship I hold now with him
Is only my obedience. What can happen
To me above this wretchedness? all your studies
Make me a curse like this.

CARDINAL CAMPEIUS.
          Your fears are worse.

QUEEN KATHARINE.
Have I lived thus long—let me speak myself,
Since virtue finds no friends—a wife, a true one?
A woman—I dare say, without vain-glory—
Never yet branded with suspicion?
Have I with all my full affections
Still met the king? loved him next heaven? obey'd
    him?
Been, out of fondness, superstitious to him?
Almost forgot my prayers to content him?
And am I thus rewarded? 'tis not well, lords.
Bring me a constant woman to her husband,
One that ne'er dream'd a joy beyond his pleasure;
And to that woman, when she has done most,
Yet will I add an honour,—a great patience.

CARDINAL WOLSEY.
Madam, you wander from the good we aim at.

QUEEN KATHARINE.
My lord, I dare not make myself so guilty,
To give up willingly that noble title
Your master wed me to: nothing but death
Shall e'er divorce my dignities.

CARDINAL WOLSEY.
           Pray, hear me.

QUEEN KATHARINE.
Would I had never trod this English earth,
Or felt the flatteries that grow upon it!
Ye have angels' faces, but heaven knows your
    hearts.
What will become of me now, wretched lady!
I am the most unhappy woman living.—
[to her WOMEN] Alas, poor wenches, where are
    now your fortunes!
Shipwrackt upon a kingdom, where no pity,
No friends, no hope; no kindred weep for me;
Almost no grave allow'd me:—like the lily,
That once was mistress of the field and flourisht,
I'll hang my head and perish.

CARDINAL WOLSEY.
           If your Grace
Could but be brought to know our ends are honest,
You'ld feel more comfort. Why should we, good
    lady,
Upon what cause, wrong you? alas, our places,
The way of our profession is against it:
We are to cure such sorrows, not to sow 'em.
For goodness' sake, consider what you do;
How you may hurt yourself, ay, utterly

Grow from the king's acquaintance, by this car-
    riage.
The hearts of princes kiss obedience,
So much they love it; but to stubborn spirits
They swell, and grow as terrible as storms.
I know you have a gentle, noble temper,
A soul as even as a calm: pray, think us
Those we profess, peace-makers, friends, and
    servants.

CARDINAL CAMPEIUS.
Madam, you'll find it so. You wrong your virtues
With these weak women's fears: a noble spirit,
As yours was put into you, ever casts
Such doubts, as false coin, from it. The king
    loves you;
Beware you lose it not: for us, if please you
To trust us in your business, we are ready
To use our utmost studies in your service.

QUEEN KATHARINE.
Do what ye will, my lords: and, pray, forgive me,
If I have used myself unmannerly;
You know I am a woman, lacking wit
To make a seemly answer to such persons.
Pray, do my service to his majesty:
He has my heart yet; and shall have my prayers
While I shall have my life. Come, reverend fathers,
Bestow your counsels on me: she now begs,
That little thought, when she set footing here,
She should have bought her dignities so dear.
                          [Exeunt.

SCENE II.

Ante-chamber to the KING'S *apartment.*

Enter the DUKE OF NORFOLK, *the* DUKE OF
SUFFOLK, *the* EARL OF SURREY, *and the*
LORD CHAMBERLAIN.

DUKE OF NORFOLK.
IF you will now unite in your complaints,
  And force them with a constancy, the cardinal
Cannot stand under them: if you omit
The offer of this time, I cannot promise
But that you shall sustain more new disgraces,
With these you bear already.

EARL OF SURREY.
                  I am joyful
To meet the least occasion that may give me
Remembrance of my father-in-law, the duke,
To be revenged on him.

DUKE OF SUFFOLK.
              Which of the peers
Have uncontemn'd gone by him, or at least
Strangely neglected? when did he regard
The stamp of nobleness in any person
Out of himself?

LORD CHAMBERLAIN.
           My lords, you speak your pleasures:
What he deserves of you and me I know;
What we can do to him,—though now the time
Gives way to us,—I much fear. If you cannot
Bar his access to the king, never attempt
Any thing on him; for he hath a witchcraft
Over the king in's tongue.

DUKE OF NORFOLK.
             O, fear him not;
His spell in that is out: the king hath found

Matter against him that for ever mars
The honey of his language. No, he's settled,
Not to come off, in his displeasure.

EARL OF SURREY.
                    Sir,
I should be glad to hear such news as this
Once every hour.

DUKE OF NORFOLK.
             Believe it, this is true:
In the divorce his contrary proceedings
Are all unfolded; wherein he appears
As I would wish mine enemy.

EARL OF SURREY.
               How came
His practices to light?

DUKE OF SUFFOLK.
           Most strangely.

EARL OF SURREY.
                O, how, how?

DUKE OF SUFFOLK.
The cardinal's letters to the Pope miscarried,
And came to the eye o'the king: wherein was
    read,
How that the cardinal did entreat his holiness
To stay the judgement o'the divorce; for if
It did take place, 'I do,' quoth he, 'perceive
My king is tangled in affection to
A creature of the queen's, Lady Anne Bullen.'

EARL OF SURREY.
Has the king this?

DUKE OF SUFFOLK.
        Believe it.

EARL OF SURREY.
           Will this work?

LORD CHAMBERLAIN.
The king in this perceives him, how he coasts
And hedges his own way. But in this point
All his tricks founder, and he brings his physic
After his patient's death: the king already
Hath married the fair lady.

EARL OF SURREY.
           Would he had!

DUKE OF SUFFOLK.
May you be happy in your wish, my lord!
For, I profess, you have it.

EARL OF SURREY.
           Now, all my joy
Trace the conjunction!

DUKE OF SUFFOLK.
        My amen to't!

DUKE OF NORFOLK.
          All men's!

DUKE OF SUFFOLK.
There's order given for her coronation:
Marry, this is yet but young, and may be left
To some ears unrecounted.—But, my lords,
She is a gallant creature, and complete
In mind and feature: I persuade me, from her
Will fall some blessing to this land, which shall
In it be memorized.

EARL OF SURREY.
        But, will the king
Digest this letter of the cardinal's?
The Lord forbid!

DUKE OF NORFOLK.
        Marry, amen!

DUKE OF SUFFOLK.
No, no;
There be more wasps that buzz about his nose
Will make this sting the sooner. Cardinal Cam-
peius
Is stoln away to Rome; hath ta'en no leave;
Has left the cause o'the king unhandled; and
Is posted, as the agent of our cardinal,
To second all his plot. I do assure you
The king cried 'Ha!' at this.
LORD CHAMBERLAIN.
Now, God incense him,
And let him cry 'Ha!' louder!
DUKE OF NORFOLK.
But, my lord,
When returns Cranmer?
DUKE OF SUFFOLK.
He is return'd in his opinions; which
Have satisfied the king for his divorce,
Together with all famous colleges
Almost in Christendom: shortly, I believe,
His second marriage shall be publisht, and
Her coronation. Katharine no more
Shall be call'd queen, but princess dowager
And widow to Prince Arthur.
DUKE OF NORFOLK.
This same Cranmer's
A worthy fellow, and hath ta'en much pain
In the king's business.
DUKE OF SUFFOLK.
He has; and we shall see him
For it an archbishop.
DUKE OF NORFOLK.
So I hear.
DUKE OF SUFFOLK.
'Tis so.—
The cardinal!
Enter WOLSEY *and* CROMWELL.
DUKE OF NORFOLK.
Observe, observe, he's moody.
CARDINAL WOLSEY.
The packet, Cromwell,
Gave't you the king?
CROMWELL.
To his own hand, in's bedchamber.
CARDINAL WOLSEY.
Lookt he o'the inside of the papers?
CROMWELL.
Presently
He did unseal them: and the first he view'd,
He did it with a serious mind; a heed
Was in his countenance. You he bade
Attend him here this morning.
CARDINAL WOLSEY.
Is he ready
To come abroad?
CROMWELL.
I think, by this he is.
CARDINAL WOLSEY.
Leave me awhile.   [*Exit* CROMWELL.
It shall be to the Duchess of Alençon,
The French king's sister: he shall marry her.—
Anne Bullen! No; I'll no Anne Bullens for him:
There's more in't than fair visage.—Bullen!
No, we'll no Bullens.—Speedily I wish   [broke!
To hear from Rome.—The Marchioness of Pem-

DUKE OF NORFOLK.
He's discontented.
DUKE OF SUFFOLK.
May be, he hears the king
Does whet his anger to him.
EARL OF SURREY.
Sharp enough,
Lord, for thy justice!
CARDINAL WOLSEY.
The late queen's gentlewoman, a knight's
daughter,
To be her mistress' mistress! the queen's queen!—
This candle burns not clear: 'tis I must snuff it;
Then out it goes.—What though I know her vir-
tuous
And well deserving? yet I know her for
A spleeny Lutheran; and not wholesome to
Our cause, that she should lie i'the bosom of
Our hard-ruled king. Again there is sprung up
An heretic, an arch one, Cranmer; one
Hath crawl'd into the favour of the king,
And is his oracle.
DUKE OF NORFOLK.
He's vext at something.
EARL OF SURREY.
I would 'twere something that would fret the
string,
The master-cord on's heart!
DUKE OF SUFFOLK.
The king, the king!
Enter KING, *reading of a schedule, and* LOVELL.
KING HENRY.
What piles of wealth hath he accumulated
To his own portion! and what expense by the
hour
Seems to flow from him! How, i'the name of
thrift,
Does he rake this together?—Now, my lords,—
Saw you the cardinal?
DUKE OF NORFOLK.
My lord, we have
Stood here observing him: some strange com-
motion
Is in his brain: he bites his lip, and starts;
Stops on a sudden, looks upon the ground,
Then lays his finger on his temple; straight
Springs out into fast gait; then stops again,
Strikes his breast hard; and anon he casts
His eye against the moon: in most strange pos-
tures
We have seen him set himself.
KING HENRY.
It may well be;
There is a mutiny in's mind. This morning
Papers of state he sent me to peruse,
As I required: and wot you what I found
There,—on my conscience, put unwittingly?
Forsooth, an inventory, thus importing,—
The several parcels of his plate, his treasure,
Rich stuffs, and ornaments of household; which
I find at such proud rate, that it out-speaks
Possession of a subject.
DUKE OF NORFOLK.
It's heaven's will:
Some spirit put this paper in the packet,
To bless your eye withal.

KING HENRY.
                    If we did think
His contemplation were above the earth,
And fixt on spiritual objects, he should still
Dwell in his musings: but I am afraid
His thinkings are below the moon, not worth
His serious considering.
          [KING *takes his seat; whispers* LOVELL,
               who goes to the CARDINAL.
CARDINAL WOLSEY.
                    Heaven forgive me!—
Ever God bless your highness!
          KING HENRY.
                    Good my lord,
You are full of heavenly stuff, and bear the in-
     ventory
Of your best graces in your mind; the which
You were now running o'er: you have scarce time
To steal from spiritual leisure a brief span
To keep your earthly audit: sure, in that
I deem you an ill husband, and am glad
To have you therein my companion.
          CARDINAL WOLSEY.
                    Sir,
For holy offices I have a time; a time
To think upon the part of business which
I bear i'the state; and nature does require
Her times of preservation, which perforce
I, her frail son, amongst my brethren mortal,
Must give my tendance to.
          KING HENRY.
                    You have said well.
          CARDINAL WOLSEY.
And ever may your highness yoke together,
As I will lend you cause, my doing well
With my well saying!
          KING HENRY.
                    'Tis well said again;
And 'tis a kind of good deed to say well:
And yet words are no deeds. My father loved you:
He said he did; and with his deed did crown
His word upon you. Since I had my office,
I have kept you next my heart; have not alone
Employ'd you where high profits might come
     home,
But pared my present havings, to bestow
My bounties upon you.
          CARDINAL WOLSEY [aside].
                    What should this mean?
          EARL OF SURREY [aside].
The Lord increase this business!
          KING HENRY.
                    Have I not made you
The prime man of the state? I pray you, tell me,
If what I now pronounce you have found true:
And, if you may confess it, say withal,
If you are bound to us or no. What say you?
          CARDINAL WOLSEY.
My sovereign, I confess your royal graces,
Shower'd on me daily, have been more than could
My studied purposes requite; which went
Beyond all man's endeavours:—my endeavours
Have ever come too short of my desires,
Yet filed with my abilities: mine own ends
Have been mine so, that evermore they pointed
To the good of your most sacred person and

The profit of the state. For your great graces
Heapt upon me, poor undeserver, I
Can nothing render but allegiant thanks;
My prayers to heaven for you; my loyalty,
Which ever has and ever shall be growing,
Till death, that winter, kill it.
          KING HENRY.
                    Fairly answer'd;
A loyal and obedient subject is
Therein illustrated: the honour of it
Does pay the act of it; as, i'the contrary,
The foulness is the punishment. I presume
That, as my hand has open'd bounty to you,
My heart dropt love, my power rain'd honour,
     more
On you than any; so your hand and heart,
Your brain, and every function of your power,
Should, notwithstanding that your bond of duty,
As 'twere in love's particular, be more
To me, your friend, than any.
          CARDINAL WOLSEY.
                    I do profess
That for your highness' good I ever labour'd
More than mine own; that am, have, and will be,—
Though all the world should crack their duty to
     you,
And throw it from their soul; though perils did
Abound, as thick as thought could make 'em, and
Appear in forms more horrid,—yet my duty,
As doth a rock against the chiding flood,
Should the approach of this wild river break,
And stand unshaken yours.
          KING HENRY.
                    'Tis nobly spoken.—
Take notice, lords, he has a loyal breast,
For you have seen him open't.—Read o'er this;
          [*Giving him papers.*
And after, this: and then to breakfast with
What appetite you have.
          [*Exit* KING, *frowning upon* WOLSEY: *the*
          NOBLES *throng after him, smiling and*
          whispering.
          CARDINAL WOLSEY.
                    What should this mean?
What sudden anger's this? how have I reapt it?
He parted frowning from me, as if ruin
Leapt from his eyes: so looks the chafed lion
Upon the daring huntsman that has gall'd him;
Then makes him nothing. I must read this paper;
I fear, the story of his anger.—'Tis so;
This paper has undone me:—'tis the account
Of all that world of wealth I have drawn together
For mine own ends; indeed, to gain the Popedom,
And fee my friends in Rome. O negligence,
Fit for a fool to fall by! what cross devil
Made me put this main secret in the packet
I sent the king?—Is there no way to cure this?
No new device to beat this from his brains?
I know 'twill stir him strongly; yet I know
A way, if it take right, in spite of fortune,
Will bring me off again.—What's this?—'To the
     Pope'!
The letter, as I live, with all the business
I writ to's holiness. Nay, then, farewell!
I have toucht the highest point of all my great-
     ness;

And, from that full meridian of my glory,
I haste now to my setting: I shall fall
Like a bright exhalation in the evening,
And no man see me more.

Enter to WOLSEY *the* DUKES OF NORFOLK *and*
SUFFOLK, *the* EARL OF SURREY, *and the* LORD
CHAMBERLAIN.

DUKE OF NORFOLK.
Hear the king's pleasure, Cardinal; who com-
  mands you
To render up the great seal presently
Into our hands; and to confine yourself
To Asher-house, my Lord of Winchester's,
Till you hear further from his highness.

CARDINAL WOLSEY.
                       Stay,—
Where's your commission, lords? words cannot
  carry
Authority so weighty.

DUKE OF SUFFOLK.
             Who dare cross 'em,
Bearing the king's will from his mouth expressly?

CARDINAL WOLSEY.
Till I find more than will or words to do it,—
I mean your malice,—know, officious lords,
I dare and must deny it. Now I feel
Of what coarse metal ye are moulded,—envy:
How eagerly ye follow my disgraces,
As if it fed ye! and how sleek and wanton
Ye appear in every thing may bring my ruin!
Follow your envious courses, men of malice;
You have Christian warrant for 'em, and, no
  doubt,
In time will find their fit rewards. That seal,
You ask with such a violence, the king—
Mine and your master—with his own hand gave
  me;
Bade me enjoy it, with the place and honours,
During my life; and, to confirm his goodness,
Tied it by letters-patents:—now, who'll take it?

EARL OF SURREY.
The king, that gave it.

CARDINAL WOLSEY.
           It must be himself, then.

EARL OF SURREY.
Thou art a proud traitor, priest.

CARDINAL WOLSEY.
           Proud lord, thou liest:
Within these forty hours Surrey durst better
Have burnt that tongue than said so.

EARL OF SURREY.
              Thy ambition,
Thou scarlet sin, robb'd this bewailing land
Of noble Buckingham, my father-in-law:
The heads of all thy brother cardinals—
With thee and all thy best parts bound together—
Weigh'd not a hair of his. Plague of your policy!
You sent me deputy for Ireland;
Far from his succour, from the king, from all
That might have mercy on the fault thou gavest
  him;
Whilst your great goodness, out of holy pity,
Absolved him with an axe.

CARDINAL WOLSEY.
           This, and all else
This talking lord can lay upon my credit,

I answer is most false. The duke by law
Found his deserts: how innocent I was
From any private malice in his end,
His noble jury and foul cause can witness.
If I loved many words, lord, I should tell you
You have as little honesty as honour;
That I in the way of loyalty and truth
Toward the king, my ever royal master,
Dare mate a sounder man than Surrey can be,
And all that love his follies.

EARL OF SURREY.
              By my soul,
Your long coat, priest, protects you; thou shouldst
  feel
My sword i'the life-blood of thee else.—My lords,
Can ye endure to hear this arrogance?
And from this fellow? If we live thus tamely,
To be thus jaded by a piece of scarlet,
Farewell nobility; let his Grace go forward,
And dare us with his cap like larks.

CARDINAL WOLSEY.
              All goodness
Is poison to thy stomach.

EARL OF SURREY.
            Yes, that goodness
Of gleaning all the land's wealth into one,
Into your own hands, Cardinal, by extortion;
The goodness of your intercepted packets
You writ to the Pope against the king: your good-
  ness,
Since you provoke me, shall be most notorious.—
My Lord of Norfolk,—as you are truly noble,
As you respect the common good, the state
Of our despised nobility, our issues,
Whom, if he live, will scarce be gentlemen,—
Produce the grand sum of his sins, the articles
Collected from his life:—I'll startle you
Worse than the sacring bell, when the brown
  wench
Lay kissing in your arms, lord Cardinal.

CARDINAL WOLSEY.
How much, methinks, I could despise this man,
But that I'm bound in charity against it!

DUKE OF NORFOLK.
Those articles, my lord, are in the king's hand:
But, thus much, they are foul ones.

CARDINAL WOLSEY.
           So much fairer
And spotless shall mine innocence arise,
When the king knows my truth.

EARL OF SURREY.
          This cannot save you:
I thank my memory, I yet remember
Some of these articles; and out they shall.
Now, if you can blush, and cry guilty, Cardinal,
You'll show a little honesty.

CARDINAL WOLSEY.
           Speak on, sir;
I dare your worst objections: if I blush,
It is to see a nobleman want manners.

EARL OF SURREY.
I had rather want those than my head.—Have at
  you!
First, that, without the king's assent or knowledge,
You wrought to be a legate; by which power
You maim'd the jurisdiction of all bishops.

321

DUKE OF NORFOLK.

Then, that in all you writ to Rome, or else
To foreign princes, *Ego et Rex meus*
Was still inscribed; in which you brought the king
To be your servant.

DUKE OF SUFFOLK.

         Then, that, without the knowledge
Either of king or council, when you went
Ambassador to the emperor, you made bold
To carry into Flanders the great seal.

EARL OF SURREY.

Item, you sent a large commission
To Gregory de Cassalis, to conclude,
Without the king's will or the state's allowance,
A league between his highness and Ferrara.

DUKE OF SUFFOLK.

That, out of mere ambition, you have caused
Your holy hat to be stampt on the king's coin.

EARL OF SURREY.

Then, that you have sent innumerable sub-
    stance—
By what means got, I leave to your own con-
    science—
To furnish Rome, and to prepare the ways
You have for dignities; to the mere undoing
Of all the kingdom. Many more there are;
Which, since they are of you, and odious,
I will not taint my mouth with.

LORD CHAMBERLAIN.

         O my lord,
Press not a falling man too far! 'tis virtue:
His faults lie open to the laws; let them,
Not you, correct him. My heart weeps to see him
So little of his great self.

EARL OF SURREY.

         I forgive him.

DUKE OF SUFFOLK.

Lord Cardinal, the king's further pleasure is,—
Because all those things you have done of late,
By your power legatine, within this kingdom,
Fall into the compass of a *præmunire*,—
That therefore such a writ be sued against you;
To forfeit all your goods, lands, tenements,
Chattels, and whatsoever, and to be
Out of the king's protection:—this is my charge.

DUKE OF NORFOLK.

And so we'll leave you to your meditations
How to live better. For your stubborn answer
About the giving back the great seal to us,
The king shall know it, and, no doubt, shall thank
    you.
So fare you well, my little good lord Cardinal.

         [*Exeunt all but* WOLSEY.

CARDINAL WOLSEY.

So farewell to the little good you bear me.
Farewell, a long farewell, to all my greatness!
This is the state of man: to-day he puts forth
The tender leaves of hope; to-morrow blossoms,
And bears his blushing honours thick upon him;
The third day comes a frost, a killing frost,
And—when he thinks, good easy man, full surely
His greatness is a-ripening—nips his root,
And then he falls, as I do. I have ventured,
Like little wanton boys that swim on bladders,
This many summers in a sea of glory;
But far beyond my depth: my high-blown pride

At length broke under me; and now has left me,
Weary and old with service, to the mercy
Of a rude stream, that must for ever hide me.
Vain pomp and glory of this world, I hate ye:
I feel my heart new open'd. O, how wretched
Is that poor man that hangs on princes' favours!
There is, betwixt that smile we would aspire to,
That sweet aspect of princes, and their ruin,
More pangs and fears than wars or women have;
And when he falls, he falls like Lucifer,
Never to hope again.

         Enter CROMWELL, *standing amazed.*
         Why, how now, Cromwell!

CROMWELL.

I have no power to speak, sir.

CARDINAL WOLSEY.

         What, amazed
At my misfortunes? can thy spirit wonder
A great man should decline? Nay, an you weep,
I am faln indeed.

CROMWELL.

         How does your Grace?

CARDINAL WOLSEY.

         Why, well;
Never so truly happy, my good Cromwell.
I know myself now; and I feel within me
A peace above all earthly dignities,
A still and quiet conscience. The king has cured
    me,
I humbly thank his Grace; and from these shoul-
    ders,
These ruin'd pillars, out of pity, taken
A load would sink a navy,—too much honour:
O, 'tis a burden, Cromwell, 'tis a burden
Too heavy for a man that hopes for heaven!

CROMWELL.

I am glad your Grace has made that right use of it.

CARDINAL WOLSEY.

I hope I have: I am able now, methinks—
Out of a fortitude of soul I feel—
To endure more miseries and greater far
Than my weak-hearted enemies dare offer.—
What news abroad?

CROMWELL.

         The heaviest and the worst
Is your displeasure with the king.

CARDINAL WOLSEY.

         God bless him!

CROMWELL.

The next is, that Sir Thomas More is chosen
Lord Chancellor in your place.

CARDINAL WOLSEY.

         That's somewhat sudden:
But he's a learned man. May he continue
Long in his highness' favour, and do justice
For truth's sake and his conscience; that his
    bones,
When he has run his course and sleeps in bless-
    ings,
May have a tomb of orphans' tears wept on 'em!—
What more?

CROMWELL.

         That Cranmer is return'd with welcome,
Install'd lord archbishop of Canterbury.

CARDINAL WOLSEY.

That's news indeed.

CROMWELL.
Last, that the Lady Anne,
Whom the king hath in secrecy long married,
This day was view'd in open as his queen,
Going to chapel; and the voice is now
Only about her coronation.

CARDINAL WOLSEY.
There was the weight that pull'd me down. O
Cromwell,
The king has gone beyond me: all my glories
In that one woman I have lost for ever:
No sun shall ever usher forth mine honours,
Or gild again the noble troops that waited
Upon my smiles. Go, get thee from me, Crom-
well;
I am a poor faln man, unworthy now
To be thy lord and master: seek the king;
That sun, I pray, may never set! I have told him
What and how true thou art: he will advance thee;
Some little memory of me will stir him—
I know his noble nature—not to let
Thy hopeful service perish too: good Cromwell,
Neglect him not; make use now, and provide
For thine own future safety.

CROMWELL.
O my lord,
Must I, then, leave you? must I needs forgo
So good, so noble, and so true a master?
Bear witness, all that have not hearts of iron,
With what a sorrow Cromwell leaves his lord.
The king shall have my service; but my prayers
For ever and for ever shall be yours.

CARDINAL WOLSEY.
Cromwell, I did not think to shed a tear
In all my miseries; but thou hast forced me,
Out of thy honest truth, to play the woman.
Let's dry our eyes: and thus far hear me, Crom-
well;
And—when I am forgotten, as I shall be,
And sleep in dull cold marble, where no mention
Of me more must be heard of—say, I taught thee,
Say, Wolsey—that once trod the ways of glory,
And sounded all the depths and shoals of honour—
Found thee a way, out of his wrack, to rise in;
A sure and safe one, though thy master mist it.
Mark but my fall, and that that ruin'd me.
Cromwell, I charge thee, fling away ambition:
By that sin fell the angels; how can man, then,
The image of his Maker, hope to win by it?
Love thyself last; cherish those hearts that hate
thee;
Corruption wins not more than honesty.
Still in thy right hand carry gentle peace,
To silence envious tongues. Be just, and fear not:
Let all the ends thou aim'st at be thy country's,
Thy God's, and truth's: then if thou fall'st, O
Cromwell,
Thou fall'st a blessed martyr! Serve the king;
And,—prithee, lead me in:
There take an inventory of all I have,
To the last penny; 'tis the king's: my robe,
And my integrity to heaven, is all
I dare now call mine own. O Cromwell, Cromwell!
Had I but served my God with half the zeal
I served my king, He would not in mine age
Have left me naked to mine enemies.

CROMWELL.
Good sir, have patience.

CARDINAL WOLSEY.
So I have. Farewell
The hopes of court! my hopes in heaven do dwell.
[Exeunt.

ACT IV. SCENE I.

A street in Westminster.

Enter two GENTLEMEN, *meeting one another.*

FIRST GENTLEMAN.
Y'ARE well met once again.

SECOND GENTLEMAN.
So are you.

FIRST GENTLEMAN.
You come to take your stand here, and behold
The Lady Anne pass from her coronation?

SECOND GENTLEMAN.
'Tis all my business. At our last encounter
The Duke of Buckingham came from his trial.

FIRST GENTLEMAN.
'Tis very true: but that time offer'd sorrow;
This, general joy.

SECOND GENTLEMAN.
'Tis well: the citizens,
I am sure, have shown at full their royal minds—
As, let 'em have their rights, they are ever for-
ward—
In celebration of this day with shows,
Pageants, and sights of honour.

FIRST GENTLEMAN.
Never greater,
Nor, I'll assure you, better taken, sir.

SECOND GENTLEMAN.
May I be bold to ask what that contains,
That paper in your hand?

FIRST GENTLEMAN.
Yes; 'tis the list
Of those that claim their offices this day
By custom of the coronation.
The Duke of Suffolk is the first, and claims
To be high-steward; next, the Duke of Norfolk,
He to be earl marshal: you may read the rest.

SECOND GENTLEMAN.
I thank you, sir: had I not known those customs,
I should have been beholding to your paper.
But, I beseech you, what's become of Katharine,
The princess dowager? how goes her business?

FIRST GENTLEMAN.
That I can tell you too. The archbishop
Of Canterbury, accompanied with other
Learned and reverend fathers of his order,
Held a late court at Dunstable, six miles off
From Ampthill, where the princess lay; to which
She was often cited by them, but appear'd not:
And, to be short, for not appearance and
The king's late scruple, by the main assent
Of all these learned men she was divorced,
And the late marriage made of none effect:
Since which she was removed to Kimbolton,
Where she remains now sick.

SECOND GENTLEMAN.
Alas, good lady!— [Trumpets.
The trumpets sound: stand close, the queen is
coming.

323

THE ORDER OF THE CORONATION.

A lively flourish of trumpets.　Then enter,

1. *Two* JUDGES.
2. LORD CHANCELLOR, *with the purse and mace before him.*
3. CHORISTERS, *singing.*　　　　　[*Music.*
4. MAYOR OF LONDON, *bearing the mace.　Then* GARTER, *in his coat of arms, and on his head he wore a gilt copper crown.*
5. MARQUESS DORSET, *bearing a sceptre of gold, on his head a demi-coronal of gold.　With him, the* EARL OF SURREY, *bearing the rod of silver with the dove, crown'd with an earl's coronet.　Collars of SS.*
6. DUKE OF SUFFOLK, *in his robe of estate, his coronet on his head, bearing a long white wand, as high-steward.　With him, the* DUKE OF NORFOLK, *with the rod of marshalship, a coronet on his head.　Collars of SS.*
7. *A canopy borne by four of the* CINQUE-PORTS; *under it, the* QUEEN *in her robe, in her hair richly adorn'd with pearl, crown'd.　On each side of her, the* BISHOPS OF LONDON *and* WINCHESTER.
8. *The old* DUCHESS OF NORFOLK, *in a coronal of gold, wrought with flowers, bearing the* QUEEN'S *train.*
9. *Certain* LADIES *or* COUNTESSES, *with plain circlets of gold without flowers.*
　　　[*Exeunt, first passing over the stage in order and state; and then a great flourish of trumpets.*

A royal train, believe me.—These I know:—
Who's that that bears the sceptre?

FIRST GENTLEMAN.
　　　　　　　　　Marquess Dorset:
And that the Earl of Surrey, with the rod.

SECOND GENTLEMAN.
A bold brave gentleman.—That should be
The Duke of Suffolk?

FIRST GENTLEMAN.　　　　　　·
　　　　'Tis the same,—high-steward.

SECOND GENTLEMAN.
And that my Lord of Norfolk?

FIRST GENTLEMAN.
　　　　　Yes.

SECOND GENTLEMAN [*looking on the* QUEEN].
　　　　　Heaven bless thee!
Thou hast the sweetest face I ever lookt on.—
Sir, as I have a soul, she is an angel;
Our king has all the Indies in his arms,
And more and richer, when he strains that lady:
I cannot blame his conscience.

FIRST GENTLEMAN.
　　　　　　　　They that bear
The cloth of honour over her are four barons
Of the Cinque-ports.

SECOND GENTLEMAN.
Those men are happy; and so are all are near her.
I take it, she that carries up the train
Is that old noble lady, Duchess of Norfolk.

FIRST GENTLEMAN.
It is; and all the rest are countesses.

SECOND GENTLEMAN.
Their coronets say so.　These are stars indeed;
And sometimes falling ones.

FIRST GENTLEMAN.
　　　　　No more of that.
　　　Enter a third GENTLEMAN.
God save you, sir! where have you been broiling?

THIRD GENTLEMAN.
Among the crowd i'the abbey; where a finger
Could not be wedged in more : I am stifled
With the mere rankness of their joy.

SECOND GENTLEMAN.
　　　　　　　　You saw
The ceremony?

THIRD GENTLEMAN.
　　　That I did.

FIRST GENTLEMAN.
　　　　　　How was it?

THIRD GENTLEMAN.
Well worth the seeing.

SECOND GENTLEMAN.
　　　　　Good sir, speak it to us.

THIRD GENTLEMAN.
As well as I am able.　The rich stream
Of lords and ladies, having brought the queen
To a prepared place in the choir, fell off
A distance from her; while her Grace sat down
To rest awhile, some half an hour or so,
In a rich chair of state, opposing freely
The beauty of her person to the people.
Believe me, sir, she is the goodliest woman
That ever lay by man: which when the people
Had the full view of, such a noise arose
As the shrouds make at sea in a stiff tempest,
As loud, and to as many tunes: hats, cloaks,—
Doublets, I think,—flew up; and had their faces
Been loose, this day they had been lost.　Such joy
I never saw before.　Great-bellied women,
That had not half a week to go, like rams
In the old time of war, would shake the press,
And make 'em reel before 'em.　No man living
Could say, 'This is my wife,' there; all were woven
So strangely in one piece.

SECOND GENTLEMAN.
　　　　　　　But what follow'd?

THIRD GENTLEMAN.
At length her Grace rose, and with modest paces
Came to the altar; where she kneel'd, and, saint-like,
Cast her fair eyes to heaven, and pray'd devoutly:
Then rose again, and bow'd her to the people:
When by the archbishop of Canterbury
She had all the royal makings of a queen;
As holy oil, Edward Confessor's crown,
The rod, and bird of peace, and all such emblems
Laid nobly on her: which perform'd, the choir,
With all the choicest music of the kingdom,
Together sung *Te Deum.*　So she parted,
And with the same full state paced back again
To York-place, where the feast is held.

FIRST GENTLEMAN.
　　　　　　　　Sir,
You must no more call it York-place, that's past;
For, since the cardinal fell, that title's lost:
'Tis now the king's, and call'd Whitehall.

THIRD GENTLEMAN.
                    I know it;
But 'tis so lately alter'd, that the old name
Is fresh about me.

SECOND GENTLEMAN.
                    What two reverend bishops
Were those that went on each side of the queen?

THIRD GENTLEMAN.
Stokesly and Gardiner; the one of Winchester,
Newly preferr'd from the king's secretary;
The other, London.

SECOND GENTLEMAN.
                    He of Winchester
Is held no great good lover of the archbishop's,
The virtuous Cranmer.

THIRD GENTLEMAN.
                    All the land knows that:
However, yet there is no great breach; when it
    comes,
Cranmer will find a friend will not shrink from him.

SECOND GENTLEMAN.
Who may that be, I pray you?

THIRD GENTLEMAN.
                    Thomas Cromwell;
A man in much esteem with the king, and truly
A worthy friend. The king
Has made him master o'the jewel-house,
And one, already, of the privy-council.

SECOND GENTLEMAN.
He will deserve more.

THIRD GENTLEMAN.
                    Yes, without all doubt.—
Come, gentlemen, ye shall go my way, which
Is to the court, and there ye shall be my guests:
Something I can command. As I walk thither,
I'll tell ye more.

BOTH.
You may command us, sir. [Exeunt.

SCENE II.
Kimbolton.

Enter KATHARINE, *dowager, sick; led between*
GRIFFITH, *her gentleman-usher, and* PATIENCE,
her woman.

GRIFFITH.
How does your Grace?
KATHARINE.
                    O Griffith, sick to death!
My legs, like loaden branches, bow to the earth,
Willing to leave their burden. Reach a chair:—
So,—now, methinks, I feel a little ease.
Didst thou not tell me, Griffith, as thou ledd'st me,
That the great child of honour, Cardinal Wolsey,
Was dead?

GRIFFITH.
                    Yes, madam; but I think your Grace,
Out of the pain you suffer'd, gave no ear to't.

KATHARINE.
Prithee, good Griffith, tell me how he died:
If well, he stept before me, happily,
For my example.

GRIFFITH.
                    Well, the voice goes, madam:
For after the stout Earl Northumberland

Arrested him at York, and trought him forward—
As a man sorely tainted—to his answer,
He fell sick suddenly, and grew so ill
He could not sit his mule.

KATHARINE.
                    Alas, poor man!

GRIFFITH.
At last, with easy roads, he came to Leicester,
Lodged in the abbey; where the reverend abbot,
With all his covent, honourably received him;
To whom he gave these words,—'O father abbot,
An old man, broken with the storms of state,
Is come to lay his weary bones among ye;
Give him a little earth for charity!'
So went to bed; where eagerly his sickness
Pursued him still: and, three nights after this,
About the hour of eight,—which he himself
Foretold should be his last,—full of repentance,
Continual meditations, tears, and sorrows,
He gave his honours to the world again,
His blessed part to heaven, and slept in peace.

KATHARINE.
So may he rest; his faults lie gently on him!
Yet thus far, Griffith, give me leave to speak
    him,
And yet with charity. He was a man
Of an unbounded stomach, ever ranking
Himself with princes; one that by suggestion
Tithed all the kingdom: simony was fair-play;
His own opinion was his law: i'the presence
He would say untruths; and be ever double
Both in his words and meaning: he was never,
But where he meant to ruin, pitiful:
His promises were, as he then was, mighty;
But his performance, as he is now, nothing:
Of his own body he was ill, and gave
The clergy ill example.

GRIFFITH.
                    Noble madam,
Men's evil manners live in brass; their virtues
We write in water. May it please your highness
To hear me speak his good now?

KATHARINE.
                    Yes, good Griffith;
I were malicious else.

GRIFFITH.
                    This cardinal,
Though from an humble stock, undoubtedly
Was fashion'd to much honour from his cradle.
He was a scholar, and a ripe and good one;
Exceeding wise, fair-spoken, and persuading:
Lofty and sour to them that lov'd him not;
But to those men that sought him sweet as
    summer.
And though he were unsatisfied in getting,—
Which was a sin,—yet in bestowing, madam,
He was most princely: ever witness for him
Those twins of learning that he raised in you,
Ipswich and Oxford! one of which fell with him,
Unwilling to outlive the good that did it;
The other, though unfinisht, yet so famous,
So excellent in art, and still so rising,
That Christendom shall ever speak his virtue.
His overthrow heapt happiness upon him;
For then, and not till then, he felt himself,
And found the blessedness of being little:

And, to add greater honours to his age
Than man could give him, he died fearing God.
KATHARINE.
After my death I wish no other herald,
No other speaker of my living actions,
To keep mine honour from corruption,
But such an honest chronicler as Griffith.
Whom I most hated living, thou hast made me,
With thy religious truth and modesty,
Now in his ashes honour: peace be with him!—
Patience, be near me still; and set me lower:
I have not long to trouble thee.—Good Griffith,
Cause the musicians play me that sad note
I named my knell, whilst I sit meditating
On that celestial harmony I go to.
                          [Sad and solemn music.
GRIFFITH.
She is asleep: good wench, let's sit down quiet,
For fear we wake her:—softly, gentle Patience.
The vision. Enter, solemnly tripping one after another, six personages, clad in white robes, wearing
on their heads garlands of bays, and golden vizards on their faces; branches of bays or palm in
their hands. They first congee unto her, then
dance; and, at certain changes, the first two hold
a spare garland over her head; at which the other
four make reverent curtsies; then the two that
held the garland deliver the same to the other
next two, who observe the same order in their
changes, and holding the garland over her head:
which done, they deliver the same garland to the
last two, who likewise observe the same order; at
which (as it were by inspiration) she makes in her
sleep signs of rejoicing, and holdeth up her hands
to heaven: and so in their dancing they vanish,
carrying the garland with them. The music con-
tinues.
KATHARINE.
Spirits of peace, where are ye? are ye all gone,
And leave me here in wretchedness behind ye?
GRIFFITH.
Madam, we are here.
KATHARINE.
             It is not you I call for:
Saw ye none enter since I slept?
GRIFFITH.
                      None, madam.
KATHARINE.
No? Saw you not, even now, a blessed troop
Invite me to a banquet; whose bright faces
Cast thousand beams upon me, like the sun?
They promised me eternal happiness;
And brought me garlands, Griffith, which I feel
I am not worthy yet to wear: I shall,
Assuredly.
GRIFFITH.
I am most joyful, madam, such good dreams
Possess your fancy.
KATHARINE.
             Bid the music leave;
They are harsh and heavy to me.   [Music ceases.
PATIENCE [aside].
                      Do you note
How much her Grace is alter'd on the sudden?
How long her face is drawn? how pale she looks,
And of an earthy colour? Mark her eyes!

GRIFFITH [aside].
She is going, wench: pray, pray.
PATIENCE [aside].
                 Heaven comfort her!
Enter a MESSENGER.
MESSENGER.
An't like your Grace,—
KATHARINE.
                 You are a saucy fellow:
Deserve we no more reverence?
GRIFFITH.
                 You are to blame,
Knowing she will not lose her wonted greatness,
To use so rude behaviour: go to, kneel.
MESSENGER.
I humbly do entreat your highness' pardon;
My haste made me unmannerly. There's staying
A gentleman, sent from the king, to see you.
KATHARINE.
Admit him entrance, Griffith: but this fellow
Let me ne'er see again.
          [Exeunt GRIFFITH and MESSENGER.
Enter GRIFFITH, with CAPUCIUS.
                 If my sight fail not,
You should be lord ambassador from the em-
peror,
My royal nephew, and your name Capucius.
CAPUCIUS.
Madam, the same,—your servant.
KATHARINE.
                 O my lord,
The times and titles now are alter'd strangely
With me since first you knew me. But, I pray you,
What is your pleasure with me?
CAPUCIUS.
                 Noble lady,
First, mine own service to your Grace; the next,
The king's request that I would visit you:
Who grieves much for your weakness, and by me
Sends you his princely commendations,
And heartily entreats you take good comfort.
KATHARINE.
O my good lord, that comfort comes too late;
'Tis like a pardon after execution:
That gentle physic, given in time, had cured me;
But now I am past all comforts here, but prayers.
How does his highness?
CAPUCIUS.
             Madam, in good health.
KATHARINE.
So may he ever do! and ever flourish,
When I shall dwell with worms, and my poor name
Banisht the kingdom!—Patience, is that letter
I caused you write, yet sent away?
PATIENCE.
                 No, madam,
             [Giving it to KATHARINE.
KATHARINE.
Sir, I most humbly pray you to deliver
This to my lord the king;—
CAPUCIUS.
                 Most willing, madam.
KATHARINE.
In which I have commended to his goodness
The model of our chaste loves, his young
    daughter,—

The dews of heaven fall thick in blessings on
    her!—
Beseeching him to give her virtuous breeding;—
She is young, and of a noble modest nature;
I hope she will deserve well;—and a little
To love her for her mother's sake, that loved him,
Heaven knows how dearly. My next poor petition
Is, that his noble Grace would have some pity
Upon my wretched women, that so long
Have follow'd both my fortunes faithfully:
Of which there is not one, I dare avow,—
And now I should not lie,—but will deserve,
For virtue and true beauty of the soul,
For honesty and decent carriage,
A right good husband, let him be a noble;
And, sure, those men are happy that shall have
    'em.
The last is, for my men;—they are the poorest,
But poverty could never draw 'em from me,
That they may have their wages duly paid 'em,
And something over to remember me by:
If heaven had pleased to have given me longer life
And able means, we had not parted thus.
These are the whole contents:—and, good my lord,
By that you love the dearest in this world,
As you wish Christian peace to souls departed,
Stand these poor people's friend, and urge the king
To do me this last right.

CAPUCIUS.
              By heaven, I will,
Or let me lose the fashion of a man!

KATHARINE.
I thank you, honest lord. Remember me
In all humility unto his highness:
Say his long trouble now is passing
Out of this world; tell him, in death I blest him,
For so I will.—Mine eyes grow dim.—Farewell,
My lord.—Griffith, farewell.—Nay, Patience,
You must not leave me yet: I must to bed;
Call in more women.—When I'm dead, good
    wench,
Let me be used with honour: strew me over
With maiden flowers, that all the world may know
I was a chaste wife to my grave: embalm me,
Then lay me forth; although unqueen'd, yet like
A queen, and daughter to a king, inter me.
I can no more.   [Exeunt, leading KATHARINE.

ACT V. SCENE I.

London.   *A gallery in the palace.*

Enter GARDINER, *bishop of Winchester, a* PAGE
with a torch before him, met by SIR THOMAS
LOVELL.

GARDINER.
IT'S one o'clock, boy, is't not?
BOY.
              It hath struck.
GARDINER.
These should be hours for necessities,
Not for delights; times to repair our nature
With comforting repose, and not for us
To waste these times.—Good hour of night, Sir
    Thomas!
Whither so late?

SIR THOMAS LOVELL.
          Came you from the king, my lord?
GARDINER.
I did, Sir Thomas; and left him at primero
With the Duke of Suffolk.
SIR THOMAS LOVELL.
          I must to him too,
Before he go to bed. I'll take my leave.
GARDINER.
Not yet, Sir Thomas Lovell. What's the matter?
It seems you are in haste: an if there be
No great offence belongs to't, give your friend
Some touch of your late business: affairs that
    walk—
As they say spirits do—at midnight have
In them a wilder nature than the business
That seeks dispatch by day.
SIR THOMAS LOVELL.
          My lord, I love you;
And durst commend a secret to your ear
Much weightier than this work. The queen's in
    labour,
They say, in great extremity; and fear'd
She'll with the labour end.
GARDINER.
            The fruit she goes with
I pray for heartily, that it may find
Good time, and live: but for the stock, Sir Thomas,
I wish it grubb'd up now.
SIR THOMAS LOVELL.
          Methinks I could
Cry the amen; and yet my conscience says
She's a good creature, and, sweet lady, does
Deserve our better wishes.
GARDINER.
          But, sir, sir,—
Hear me, Sir Thomas: y'are a gentleman
Of mine own way; I know you wise, religious;
And, let me tell you, it will ne'er be well,—
'Twill not, Sir Thomas Lovell, take't of me,—
Till Cranmer, Cromwell, her two hands, and she,
Sleep in their graves.
SIR THOMAS LOVELL.
          Now, sir, you speak of two
The most remarkt i'the kingdom. As for Crom-
    well,—
Beside that of the jewel-house, is made master
O'the rolls, and the king's secretary; further, sir,
Stands in the gap and trade of moe preferments,
With which the time will load him. The arch-
    bishop
Is the king's hand and tongue; and who dare speak
One syllable against him?
GARDINER.
          Yes, yes, Sir Thomas,
There are that dare; and I myself have ventured
To speak my mind of him: and, indeed, this day—
Sir, I may tell it you, I think—I have
Incensed the lords o'the council that he is—
For so I know he is, they know he is—
A most arch heretic, a pestilence
That does infect the land: with which they moved,
Have broken with the king; who hath so far
Given ear to our complaint,—of his great grace
And princely care, foreseeing those fell mischiefs
Our reasons laid before him,—hath commanded

To-morrow morning to the council-board
He be convented. He's a rank weed, Sir Thomas,
And we must root him out. From your affairs
I hinder you too long: good night, Sir Thomas.
SIR THOMAS LOVELL.
Many good nights, my lord: I rest your servant.
[Exeunt GARDINER and PAGE.
Enter KING and SUFFOLK.
KING HENRY.
Charles, I will play no more to-night;
My mind's not on't; you are too hard for me.
DUKE OF SUFFOLK.
Sir, I did never win of you before.
KING HENRY.
But little, Charles;
Nor shall not, when my fancy's on my play.—
Now, Lovell, from the queen what is the news?
SIR THOMAS LOVELL.
I could not personally deliver to her
What you commanded me, but by her woman
I sent your message; who return'd her thanks
In the great'st humbleness, and desired your
     highness
Most heartily to pray for her.
KING HENRY.
                    What say'st thou, ha?
To pray for her? what, is she crying out?
SIR THOMAS LOVELL.
So said her woman; and that her suff'rance made
Almost each pang a death.
KING HENRY.
                    Alas, good lady!
DUKE OF SUFFOLK.
God safely quit her of her burden, and
With gentle travail, to the gladding of
Your highness with an heir!
KING HENRY.
                    'Tis midnight, Charles;
Prithee, to bed; and in thy prayers remember
The estate of my poor queen. Leave me alone;
For I must think of that which company
Would not be friendly to.
DUKE OF SUFFOLK.
                    I wish your highness
A quiet night; and my good mistress will
Remember in my prayers.
KING HENRY.
          Charles, good night. [Exit SUFFOLK.
Enter SIR ANTHONY DENNY.
Well, sir, what follows?
SIR ANTHONY DENNY.
Sir, I have brought my lord the archbishop
As you commanded me.
KING HENRY.
                    Ha! Canterbury?
SIR ANTHONY DENNY.
Ay, my good lord.
KING HENRY.
               'Tis true: where is he, Denny?
SIR ANTHONY DENNY.
He attends your highness' pleasure.
KING HENRY.
               Bring him to us. [Exit DENNY.
SIR THOMAS LOVELL [aside].
This is about that which the bishop spake:
I am happily come hither.

Enter CRANMER and DENNY.
KING HENRY.
Avoid the gallery. [LOVELL seems to stay]. Ha! I
have said. Be gone.
What!   [Exeunt LOVELL and DENNY.
CRANMER [aside].
I am fearful:—wherefore frowns he thus?
'Tis his aspect of terror. All's not well.
KING HENRY.
How now, my lord! you do desire to know
Wherefore I sent for you.
CRANMER [kneeling].
                    It is my duty
T'attend your highness' pleasure.
KING HENRY.
                    Pray you, arise,
My good and gracious Lord of Canterbury.
                    [CRANMER rises.
Come, you and I must walk a turn together;
I have news to tell you: come, come, give me
     your hand.
Ah, my good lord, I grieve at what I speak,
And am right sorry to repeat what follows:
I have, and most unwillingly, of late
Heard many grievous, I do say, my lord,
Grievous complaints of you; which, being con-
     sider'd,
Have moved us and our council, that you shall
This morning come before us; where, I know,
You cannot with such freedom purge yourself,
But that, till further trial in those charges
Which will require your answer, you must take
Your patience to you, and be well contented
To make your house our Tower: you a brother of
     us,
It fits we thus proceed, or else no witness
Would come against you.
CRANMER [kneeling].
                    I humbly thank your highness;
And am right glad to catch this good occasion
Most thoroughly to be winnowed, where my
     chaff
And corn shall fly asunder: for, I know,
There's none stands under more calumnious
     tongues
Than I myself, poor man.
KING HENRY.
                    Stand up, good Canterbury:
Thy truth and thy integrity is rooted
In us, thy friend: give me thy hand, stand up:
Prithee, let's walk. Now, by my holy-dame,
                    [CRANMER rises.
What manner of man are you! My lord, I lookt
You would have given me your petition, that
I should have ta'en some pains to bring together
Yourselves and your accusers: and to have heard
     you,
Without indurance, further.
CRANMER.
                    Most dread liege,
The good I stand on is my truth and honesty:
If they shall fail, I, with mine enemies,
Will triumph o'er my person; which I weigh not,
Being of those virtues vacant. I fear nothing
What can be said against me.

KING HENRY.
　　　　　　　　Know you not
How your state stands i'the world, with the
　　whole world?
Your enemies are many, and not small; their
　　practices
Must bear the same proportion; and not ever
The justice and the truth o'the question carries
The due o'the verdict with it: at what ease
Might corrupt minds procure knaves as corrupt
To swear against you! such things have been
　　done.
You are potently opposed; and with a malice
Of as great size. Ween you of better luck,
I mean, in perjured witness, than your Master,
Whose minister you are, whiles here He lived
Upon this naughty earth? Go to, go to;
You take a precipice for no leap of danger,
And woo your own destruction.
CRANMER.
　　　　　　　　God and your majesty
Protect mine innocence, or I fall into
The trap is laid for me!
KING HENRY.
　　　　　　　　Be of good cheer;
They shall no more prevail than we give way to.
Keep comfort to you; and this morning see
You do appear before them. If they shall chance,
In charging you with matters, to commit you,
The best persuasions to the contrary
Fail not to use, and with what vehemency
The occasion shall instruct you: if entreaties
Will render you no remedy, this ring
Deliver them, and your appeal to us
There make before them.—Look, the good man
　　weeps!
He's honest, on mine honour. God's blest
　　mother!
I swear he is true-hearted; and a soul
None better in my kingdom.—Get you gone,
And do as I have bid you. [Exit CRANMER.] He
　　has strangled
His language in his tears.
Enter OLD LADY.
GENTLEMAN [within].
Come back: what mean you?
OLD LADY.
I'll not come back; the tidings that I bring
Will make my boldness manners.—Now, good
　　angels
Fly o'er thy royal head, and shade thy person
Under their blessed wings!
KING HENRY.
　　　　　　　　Now, by thy looks
I guess thy message. Is the queen deliver'd?
Say ay; and of a boy.
OLD LADY.
　　　　　　　　Ay, ay, my liege;
And of a lovely boy: the God of heaven
Both now and ever bless her!—'tis a girl,—
Promises boys hereafter. Sir, your queen
Desires your visitation, and to be
Acquainted with this stranger: 'tis as like you
As cherry is to cherry.
KING HENRY.
　　　　　　　　Lovell!

Enter LOVELL.
SIR THOMAS LOVELL.
　　　　　　　　Sir?
KING HENRY.
Give her an hundred marks. I'll to the queen.
　　　　　　　　　　　　　　　　　　[Exit.
OLD LADY.
An hundred marks! By this light, I'll ha' more.
An ordinary groom is for such payment.
I will have more, or scold it out of him.
Said I for this, the girl was like to him?
I will have more, or else unsay't; and now,
While it is hot, I'll put it to the issue.　　[Exeunt.

SCENE II.

Before the council-chamber.

Enter CRANMER; PURSUIVANTS, PAGES, *and*
FOOTBOYS.

CRANMER.
I HOPE I am not too late; and yet the gentleman,
That was sent to me from the council, pray'd
　　me
To make great haste.—All fast? what means this?—
Ho!
Who waits there?—Sure, you know me?
Enter KEEPER.
KEEPER.
　　　　　　　　　　　　　　Yes, my lord;
But yet I cannot help you.
CRANMER.
Why?
KEEPER.
Your Grace must wait till you be call'd for.
Enter DOCTOR BUTTS.
CRANMER.
　　　　　　　　　　　　　　So.
DOCTOR BUTTS [aside].
This is a piece of malice. I am glad
I came this way so happily: the king
Shall understand it presently.　　　　　[Exit.
CRANMER [aside].
　　　　　　　　　　　　　'Tis Butts,
The king's physician: as he past along,
How earnestly he cast his eyes upon me!
Pray heaven, he sound not my disgrace! For cer-
　　tain,
This is of purpose laid by some that hate me—
God turn their hearts! I never sought their
　　malice—
To quench mine honour: they would shame to
　　make me
Wait else at door, a fellow-counsellor,
Among boys, grooms, and lackeys. But their
　　pleasures
Must be fulfill'd, and I attend with patience.
Enter the KING *and* BUTTS *at a window above.*
DOCTOR BUTTS.
I'll show your Grace the strangest sight—
KING HENRY.
　　　　　　　　　　What's that, Butts?
DOCTOR BUTTS.
I think your highness saw this many a day.
KING HENRY.
Body o'me, where is it?

DOCTOR BUTTS.
There, my lord:
The high promotion of his Grace of Canterbury;
Who holds his state at door, 'mongst pursuivants,
Pages, and footboys.
KING HENRY.
Ha! 'tis he, indeed:
Is this the honour they do one another?
'Tis well there's one above 'em yet. I had thought
They had parted so much honesty among 'em—
At least, good manners—as not thus to suffer
A man of his place, and so near our favour,
To dance attendance on their lordships' pleasures,
And at the door too, like a post with packets.
By holy Mary, Butts, there's knavery:
Let 'em alone, and draw the curtain close;
We shall hear more anon.   [Curtain drawn.
A council-table brought in with chairs and stools
and placed under the state. Enter LORD CHAN-
CELLOR, places himself at the upper end of the
table on the left hand; a seat being left void above
him, as for CANTERBURY'S seat; DUKE OF
SUFFOLK, DUKE OF NORFOLK, SURREY,
LORD CHAMBERLAIN, GARDINER, seat
themselves in order on each side. CROMWELL
at lower end, as secretary.
LORD CHANCELLOR.
Speak to the business, master secretary:
Why are we met in council?
CROMWELL.
Please your honours,
The chief cause concerns his Grace of Canterbury.
GARDINER.
Has he had knowledge of it?
CROMWELL.
Yes.
DUKE OF NORFOLK.
Who waits there?
KEEPER.
Without, my noble lords?
GARDINER.
Yes.
KEEPER.
My lord archbishop;
And has done half an hour, to know your pleas-
ures.
LORD CHANCELLOR.
Let him come in.
KEEPER.
Your Grace may enter now.
[CRANMER approaches the council-table.
LORD CHANCELLOR.
My good lord archbishop, I'm very sorry
To sit here at this present, and behold
That chair stand empty: but we all are men,
In our own natures frail and culpable;
Of one flesh; few are angels: out of which frailty
And want of wisdom, you, that best should teach
us,
Have misdemean'd yourself, and not a little,
Toward the king first, then his laws, in filling
The whole realm, by your teaching and your
chaplains,—
For so we are inform'd,—with new opinions,
Divers and dangerous; which are heresies,
And, not reform'd, may prove pernicious.

GARDINER.
Which reformation must be sudden too,
My noble lords; for those that tame wild horses
Pace 'em not in their hands to make 'em gentle,
But stop their mouths with stubborn bits, and
spur 'em,
Till they obey the manage. If we suffer—
Out of our easiness, and childish pity
To one man's honour—this contagious sickness,
Farewell all physic: and what follows then?
Commotions, uproars, with a general taint
Of the whole state: as, of late days, our neigh-
bours,
The upper Germany, can dearly witness,
Yet freshly pitied in our memories.
CRANMER.
My good lords, hitherto, in all the progress
Both of my life and office, I have labour'd,
And with no little study, that my teaching
And the strong course of my authority
Might go one way, and safely; and the end
Was ever, to do well: nor is there living—
I speak it with a single heart, my lords—
A man that more detests, more stirs against,
Both in his private conscience and his place,
Defacers of a public peace, than I do.
Pray heaven, the king may never find a heart
With less allegiance in it! Men that make
Envy and crooked malice nourishment
Dare bite the best. I do beseech your lordships
That, in this case of justice, my accusers,
Be what they will, may stand forth face to face,
And freely urge against me.
DUKE OF SUFFOLK.
Nay, my lord,
That cannot be: you are a counsellor,
And, by that virtue, no man dare accuse you.
GARDINER.
My lord, because we have business of more mo-
ment,
We will be short with you. 'Tis his highness'
pleasure,
And our consent, for better trial of you,
From hence you be committed to the Tower;
Where, being but a private man again,
You shall know many dare accuse you boldly,
More than, I fear, you are provided for.
CRANMER.
Ah, my good Lord of Winchester, I thank you;
You are always my good friend; if your will pass,
I shall both find your lordship judge and juror,
You are so merciful: I see your end,—
Tis my undoing: love and meekness, lord,
Become a churchman better than ambition:
Win straying souls with modesty again,
Cast none away. That I shall clear myself,
Lay all the weight ye can upon my patience,
I make as little doubt, as you do conscience
In doing daily wrongs. I could say more,
But reverence to your calling makes me modest.
GARDINER.
My lord, my lord, you are a sectary,
That's the plain truth: your painted gloss dis-
covers,
To men that understand you, words and weak-
ness.

CROMWELL.
My Lord of Winchester, you are a little,
By your good favour, too sharp; men so noble,
However faulty, yet should find respect
For what they have been: 'tis a cruelty
To load a falling man.
GARDINER.
             Good master secretary,
I cry your honour mercy; you may, worst
Of all this table, say so.
CROMWELL.
             Why, my lord?
GARDINER.
Do not I know you for a favourer
Of this new sect? ye are not sound.
CROMWELL.
             Not sound?
GARDINER.
Not sound, I say.
CROMWELL.
             Would you were half so honest!
Men's prayers then would seek you, not their
    fears.
GARDINER.
I shall remember this bold language.
CROMWELL.
             Do.
Remember your bold life too.
LORD CHANCELLOR.
             This is too much;
Forbear, for shame, my lords.
GARDINER.
             I have done.
CROMWELL.
             And I.
LORD CHANCELLOR.
Then thus for you, my lord:—it stands agreed,
I take it, by all voices, that forthwith
You be convey'd to the Tower a prisoner;
There to remain till the king's further pleasure
Be known unto us:—are you all agreed, lords?
ALL.
We are.
CRANMER.
Is there no other way of mercy,
But I must needs to the Tower, my lords?
GARDINER.
             What other
Would you expect? you are strangely trouble-
    some.—
Let some o'the guard be ready there!
Enter GUARD.
CRANMER.
             For me?
Must I go like a traitor thither?
GARDINER.
             Receive him,
And see him safe i'the Tower.
CRANMER.
             Stay, good my lords,
I have a little yet to say. Look there, my lords;
By virtue of that ring I take my cause
Out of the gripes of cruel men, and give it
To a most noble judge, the king my master.
LORD CHANCELLOR.
This is the king's ring.

EARL OF SURREY.
             'Tis no counterfeit.
DUKE OF SUFFOLK.
'Tis the right ring, by heaven: I told ye all,
When we first put this dangerous stone a-rolling,
'Twould fall upon ourselves.
DUKE OF NORFOLK.
             Do you think, my lords,
The king will suffer but the little finger
Of this man to be vext?
LORD CHANCELLOR.
             'Tis now too certain:
How much more is his life in value with him!
Would I were fairly out on't!
CROMWELL.
             My mind gave me,
In seeking tales and informations
Against this man,—whose honesty the devil
And his disciples only envy at,—
Ye blew the fire that burns ye: now have at ye!
Enter KING, *frowning on them; takes his seat.*
GARDINER.
Dread sovereign, how much are we bound to
    heaven
In daily thanks, that gave us such a prince;
Not only good and wise, but most religious:
One that, in all obedience, makes the church
The chief aim of his honour; and, to strengthen
That holy duty, out of dear respect,
His royal self in judgement comes to hear
The cause betwixt her and this great offender.
KING HENRY.
You were ever good at sudden commendations,
Bishop of Winchester. But know, I come not
To hear such flatteries now, and in my presence;
They are too thin and bare to hide offences.
To me, you cannot reach, you play the spaniel,
And think with wagging of your tongue to win me;
But, whatsoe'er thou takest me for, I'm sure
Thou hast a cruel nature and a bloody.—
[*to* CRANMER] Good man, sit down. Now let me
    see the proudest
He, that dares most, but wag his finger at thee:
By all that's holy, he had better starve
Than but once think this place becomes thee not.
EARL OF SURREY.
May it please your Grace,—
KING HENRY.
             No, sir, it does not please me.
I had thought I had had men of some understand-
    ing
And wisdom of my council; but I find none.
Was it discretion, lords, to let this man,
This good man,—few of you deserve that title,—
This honest man, wait like a lousy footboy
At chamber-door? and one as great as you are?
Why, what a shame was this! Did my commission
Bid ye so far forget yourselves? I gave ye
Power as he was a counsellor to try him,
Not as a groom: there's some of ye, I see,
More out of malice than integrity,
Would try him to the utmost, had ye mean;
Which ye shall never have while I live.
LORD CHANCELLOR.
             Thus far,
My most dread sovereign, may it like your Grace

To let my tongue excuse all. What was purposed
Concerning his imprisonment, was rather—
If there be faith in men—meant for his trial,
And fair purgation to the world, than malice,—
I'm sure, in me.

KING HENRY.
            Well, well, my lords, respect him;
Take him, and use him well, he's worthy of it.
I will say thus much for him,—if a prince
May be beholding to a subject, I
Am, for his love and service, so to him.
Make me no more ado, but all embrace him:
Be friends, for shame, my lords!—My Lord of
    Canterbury,
I have a suit which you must not deny me;
That is, a fair young maid that yet wants bap-
    tism,
You must be godfather, and answer for her.

CRANMER.
The greatest monarch now alive may glory
In such an honour: how may I deserve it,
That am a poor and humble subject to you?

KING HENRY.
Come, come, my lord, you'ld spare your spoons:
you shall have two noble partners with you; the
old Duchess of Norfolk, and Lady Marquess
Dorset: will these please you?—
Once more, my Lord of Winchester, I charge
    you,
Embrace and love this man.

GARDINER.
            With a true heart
And brother-love I do it.

CRANMER.
            And let heaven
Witness, how dear I hold this confirmation.

KING HENRY.
Good man, those joyful tears show thy true heart:
The common voice, I see, is verified
Of thee, which says thus, 'Do my Lord of Canter-
    bury
A shrewd turn, and he is your friend for ever.'—
Come, lords, we trifle time away; I long
To have this young one made a Christian.
As I have made ye one, lords, one remain;
So I grow stronger, you more honour gain.
                   [*Exeunt.*

SCENE III.
The palace-yard.

Noise and tumult within. Enter PORTER *and his*
MAN.

PORTER.
YOU'LL leave your noise anon, ye rascals: do
you take the court for Parish-garden? ye rude
slaves, leave your gaping.
[*within*] Good master porter, I belong to the
larder.

PORTER.
Belong to the gallows, and be hang'd, ye rogue! is
this a place to roar in?—Fetch me a dozen crab-
tree staves, and strong ones: these are but
switches to 'em.—I'll scratch your heads: you
must be seeing christenings! do you look for ale
and cakes here, you rude rascals?

MAN.
Pray, sir, be patient: 'tis as much impossible—
Unless we sweep 'em from the door with can-
    nons—
To scatter 'em, as 'tis to make 'em sleep
On May-day morning; which will never be:
We may as well push against Powle's as stir 'em.

PORTER.
How got they in, and be hang'd?

MAN.
Alas, I know not; how gets the tide in?
As much as one sound cudgel of four foot—
You see the poor remainder—could distribute,
I made no spare, sir.

PORTER.
            You did nothing, sir.

MAN.
I am not Samson, nor Sir Guy, nor Colbrand,
To mow 'em down before me: but if I spared any
That had a head to hit, either young or old,
He or she, cuckold or cuckold-maker,
Let me ne'er hope to see a chine again;
And that I would not for a cow, God save her!
[*within*] Do you hear, master porter?

PORTER.
I shall be with you presently, good master puppy.
—Keep the door close, sirrah.

MAN.
What would you have me do?

PORTER.
What should you do, but knock 'em down by the
dozens? Is this Moorfields to muster in? or have
we some strange Indian with the great tool come
to court, the women so besiege us? Bless me,
what a fry of fornication is at door! On my Christian conscience, this one christening will beget a
thousand; here will be father, godfather, and all
together.

MAN.
The spoons will be the bigger, sir. There is a
fellow somewhat near the door,—he should be a
brazier by his face, for, o'my conscience, twenty
of the dog-days now reign in's nose; all that stand
about him are under the line, they need no other
penance: that fire-drake did I hit three times on
the head, and three times was his nose discharged
against me: he stands there, like a mortar-piece,
to blow us. There was a haberdasher's wife of
small wit near him, that rail'd upon me, till her
pinkt porringer fell off her head, for kindling such
a combustion in the state. I mist the meteor once,
and hit that woman, who cried out 'Clubs!' when
I might see from far some forty truncheoners
draw to her succour, which were the hope o'the
Strond, where she was quarter'd. They fell on; I
made good my place: at length they came to the
broomstaff to me; I defied 'em still: when suddenly a file of boys behind 'em, loose shot, deliver'd such a shower of pebbles, that I was fain
to draw mine honour in, and let 'em win the work:
the devil was amongst 'em, I think, surely.

PORTER.
These are the youths that thunder at a playhouse,
and fight for bitten apples; that no audience, but
the Tribulation of Tower-hill, or the Limbs of
Limehouse, their dear brothers, are able to en-

dure. I have some of 'em in *Limbo Patrum*, and there they are like to dance these three days; besides the running banquet of two beadles that is to come.

Enter the LORD CHAMBERLAIN.

LORD CHAMBERLAIN.

Mercy o'me, what a multitude are here!
They grow still too: from all parts they are coming,
As if we kept a fair here! Where are these porters,
These lazy knaves?—Y'have made a fine hand,
      fellows:
There's a trim rabble let in: are all these
Your faithful friends o'the suburbs? We shall
      have
Great store of room, no doubt, left for the ladies,
When they pass back from the christening.

PORTER.
            An't please your honour,
We are but men; and what so many may do,
Not being torn a-pieces, we have done:
An army cannot rule 'em.

LORD CHAMBERLAIN.
            As I live,
If the king blame me for't, I'll lay ye all
By the heels, and suddenly; and on your heads
Clap round fines for neglect: y'are lazy knaves;
And here ye lie baiting of bombards, when
Ye should do service. Hark! the trumpets sound;
Th'are come already from the christening:
Go, break among the press, and find a way out
To let the troop pass fairly; or I'll find
A Marshalsea shall hold ye play these two months.

PORTER.
Make way there for the princess!

MAN.
            You great fellow,
Stand close up, or I'll make your head ache!

PORTER.
You i'the chamblet,
Get up o'the rail; I'll peck you o'er the pales else!
            [*Exeunt.*

SCENE IV.

The palace.

Enter trumpets, sounding; then two ALDERMEN,
LORD MAYOR, GARTER, CRANMER, DUKE
OF NORFOLK, *with his marshal's staff,* DUKE
OF SUFFOLK, *two* NOBLEMEN *bearing great
standing-bowls for the christening-gifts; then four*
NOBLEMEN *bearing a canopy, under which the*
DUCHESS OF NORFOLK, *godmother, bearing
the* CHILD *richly habited in a mantle, etc., train
borne by a* LADY; *then follows the* MARCHION-
ESS OF DORSET, *the other godmother, and*
LADIES. *The* TROOP *pass once about the stage
and* GARTER *speaks.*

GARTER.

HEAVEN, from thy endless goodness, send
      prosperous life, long, and ever happy, to the
high and mighty princess of England, Elizabeth!

Flourish. Enter KING *and* GUARD.

CRANMER [*kneeling*].

And to your royal Grace, and the good queen,
My noble partners and myself thus pray;—
All comfort, joy, in this most gracious lady,

Heaven ever laid up to make parents happy,
May hourly fall upon ye!

KING HENRY.
            Thank you, good lord Archbishop:
What is her name?

CRANMER.
Elizabeth.

KING HENRY.
            Stand up, lord.—
            [*The* KING *kisses the* CHILD.
With this kiss take my blessing: God protect thee!
Into whose hand I give thy life.

CRANMER.
            Amen.

KING HENRY.
My noble gossips, y'have been too prodigal:
I thank ye heartily; so shall this lady,
When she has so much English.

CRANMER.
            Let me speak, sir,
For heaven now bids me; and the words I utter
Let none think flattery, for they'll find 'em truth.
This royal infant—heaven still move about her!—
Though in her cradle, yet now promises
Upon this land a thousand thousand blessings,
Which time shall bring to ripeness: she shall be—
But few now living can behold that goodness—
A pattern to all princes living with her,
And all that shall succeed: Saba was never
More covetous of wisdom and fair virtue
Than this pure soul shall be: all princely graces,
That mould up such a mighty piece as this is,
With all the virtues that attend the good,
Shall still be doubled on her: truth shall nurse her,
Holy and heavenly thoughts still counsel her:
She shall be loved and fear'd: her own shall bless
      her;
Her foes shake like a field of beaten corn,
And hang their heads with sorrow: good grows
      with her:
In her days every man shall eat in safety,
Under his own vine, what he plants; and sing
The merry songs of peace to all his neighbours:
God shall be truly known; and those about her
From her shall read the perfect ways of honour,
And by those claim their greatness, not by blood.
Nor shall this peace sleep with her: but as when
The bird of wonder dies, the maiden phœnix,
Her ashes new create another heir,
As great in admiration as herself;
So shall she leave her blessedness to one,
When heaven shall call her from this cloud of
      darkness,
Who from the sacred ashes of her honour
Shall star-like rise, as great in fame as she was,
And so stand fixt: peace, plenty, love, truth,
      terror,
That were the servants to this chosen infant,
Shall then be his, and like a vine grow to him:
Wherever the bright sun of heaven shall shine,
His honour and the greatness of his name
Shall be, and make new nations: he shall flourish,
And, like a mountain cedar, reach his branches
To all the plains about him:—our children's chil-
      dren
Shall see this, and bless heaven.

KING HENRY.
                    Thou speakest wonders.
          CRANMER.
She shall be, to the happiness of England,
An aged princess; many days shall see her,
And yet no day without a deed to crown it.
Would I had known no more! but she must die,—
She must, the saints must have her,—yet a virgin;
A most unspotted lily shall she pass
To the ground, and all the world shall mourn her.
          KING HENRY.
O lord Archbishop,
Thou hast made me now a man! never before
This happy child did I get any thing:
This oracle of comfort has so pleased me,
That when I am in heaven I shall desire
To see what this child does, and praise my
  Maker.—
I thank ye all.—To you, my good lord mayor,
And your good brethren, I am much beholding;
I have received much honour by your presence,
And ye shall find me thankful.—Lead the way,
  lords:—

Ye must all see the queen, and she must thank ye;
She will be sick else. This day no man think
'Has business at his house; for all shall stay:
This little one shall make it holiday.   [*Exeunt*.

EPILOGUE.

'TIS ten to one this play can never please
    All that are here: some come to take their
        ease,
And sleep an act or two; but those, we fear,
W'have frighted with our trumpets; so, 'tis clear,
They'll say 'tis naught: others, to hear the city
Abused extremely, and to cry, 'That's witty!'
Which we have not done neither: that, I fear,
All the expected good w'are like to hear
For this play at this time, is only in
The merciful construction of good women;
For such a one we show'd 'em: if they smile,
And say 'twill do, I know, within a while
All the best men are ours; for 'tis ill hap,
If they hold when their ladies bid 'em clap.

VENUS AND ADONIS

Vilia miretur vulgus : mihi flavus Apollo
Pocula Castalia plena ministret aqua.

TO THE RIGHT HONOURABLE HENRY WRIOTHESLEY,
EARL OF SOUTHAMPTON, AND BARON OF TITCHFIELD.

RIGHT HONOURABLE,

I KNOW not how I shall offend in dedicating my unpolisht lines to your Lordship, nor how the world will censure me for choosing so strong a prop to support so weak a burthen: only if your Honour seem but pleased, I account myself highly praised, and vow to take advantage of all idle hours, till I have honour'd you with some graver labour. But if the first heir of my invention prove deform'd, I shall be sorry it had so noble a godfather: and never after ear so barren a land, for fear it yield me still so bad a harvest. I leave it to your honourable survey, and your Honour to your heart's content which I wish may always answer your own wish, and the world's hopeful expectation.

Your Honour's in all duty,
WILLIAM SHAKESPEARE.

EVEN as the sun with purple-colour'd face
Had ta'en his last leave of the weeping morn,
Rose cheekt Adonis hied him to the chase;
Hunting he loved, but love he laught to scorn:
  Sick-thoughted Venus makes amain unto him,
  And like a bold-faced suitor gins to woo him.

'Thrice-fairer than myself,' thus she began,
'The field's chief flower, sweet above compare,
Stain to all nymphs, more lovely than a man,
More white and red than doves or roses are;
  Nature that made thee, with herself at strife,
  Saith that the world hath ending with thy life.

'Vouchsafe, thou wonder, to alight thy steed,
And rein his proud head to the saddle-bow;
If thou wilt deign this favour, for thy meed
A thousand honey secrets shalt thou know:
  Here come and sit, where never serpent hisses,
  And being set, I'll smother thee with kisses;

'And yet not cloy thy lips with loath'd satiety,
But rather famish them amid their plenty,
Making them red and pale with fresh variety;
Ten kisses short as one, one long as twenty:
  A summer's day will seem an hour but short,
  Being wasted in such time-beguiling sport.'

With this she seizeth on his sweating palm,
The precedent of pith and livelihood,
And, trembling in her passion, calls it balm,
Earth's sovereign salve to do a goddess good:
  Being so enraged, desire doth lend her force
  Courageously to pluck him from his horse.

Over one arm the lusty courser's rein,
Under her other was the tender boy,
Who blusht and pouted in a dull disdain,
With leaden appetite, unapt to toy;
  She red and hot as coals of glowing fire,
  He red for shame, but frosty in desire.

The studded bridle on a ragged bough
Nimbly she fastens:—O, how quick is love!—
The steed is stalled up, and even now

To tie the rider she begins to prove:
  Backward she pusht him, as she would be thrust,
  And govern'd him in strength, though not in lust.

So soon was she along as he was down,
Each leaning on their elbows and their hips:
Now doth she stroke his cheek, now doth he frown,
And gins to chide, but soon she stops his lips;
  And kissing speaks, with lustful language broken,
  'If thou wilt chide, thy lips shall never open.'

He burns with bashful shame; she with her tears
Doth quench the maiden burning of his cheeks;
Then with her windy sighs and golden hairs
To fan and blow them dry again she seeks:
  He saith she is immodest, blames her miss;
  What follows more she murders with a kiss.

Even as an empty eagle, sharp by fast,
Tires with her beak on feathers, flesh, and bone,
Shaking her wings, devouring all in haste,
Till either gorge be stuft, or prey be gone;
  Even so she kist his brow, his cheek, his chin,
  And where she ends she doth anew begin.

Forced to content, but never to obey,
Panting he lies, and breatheth in her face;
She feedeth on the steam as on a prey,
And calls it heavenly moisture, air of grace;
  Wishing her cheeks were gardens full of flowers,
  So they were dew'd with such distilling showers.

Look how a bird lies tangled in a net,
So fasten'd in her arms Adonis lies;
Pure shame and awed resistance made him fret,
Which bred more beauty in his angry eyes:
  Rain added to a river that is rank
  Perforce will force it overflow the bank.

335

Still she entreats, and prettily entreats,
And to a pretty ear she tunes her tale;
Still is he sullen, still he lours and frets,
'Twixt crimson shame and anger ashy-pale;
     Being red, she loves him best; and being white,
     Her best is better'd with a more delight.

Look how he can, she cannot choose but love;
And by her fair immortal hand she swears,
From his soft bosom never to remove,
Till he take truce with her contending tears,
     Which long have rain'd, making her cheeks all
          wet;
     And one sweet kiss shall pay this comptless
     debt.

Upon this promise did he raise his chin,
Like a dive-dapper peering through a wave,
Who, being lookt on, ducks as quickly in;
So offers he to give what she did crave;
     But when her lips were ready for his pay,
     He winks, and turns his lips another way.

Never did passenger in summer's heat
More thirst for drink than she for this good turn.
Her help she sees, but help she cannot get;
She bathes in water, yet her fire must burn:
     'O, pity,' gan she cry, 'flint-hearted boy!
     'Tis but a kiss I beg; why art thou coy?

'I have been woo'd, as I entreat thee now,
Even by the stern and direful god of war,
Whose sinewy neck in battle ne'er did bow,
Who conquers where he comes in every jar;
     Yet hath he been my captive and my slave,
     And begg'd for that which thou unaskt shalt
     have.

'Over my altars hath he hung his lance,
His batter'd shield, his uncontrolled crest,
And for my sake hath learnt to sport and dance,
To toy, to wanton, dally, smile, and jest;
     Scorning his churlish drum and ensign red,
     Making my arms his field, his tent my bed.

'Thus he that overruled I overswayed,
Leading him prisoner in a red-rose chain:
Strong-temper'd steel his stronger strength
     obeyed,
Yet was he servile to my coy disdain.
     O, be not proud, nor brag not of thy might,
     For mast'ring her that foil'd the god of fight!

'Touch but my lips with those fair lips of thine,—
Though mine be not so fair, yet are they red,—
The kiss shall be thine own as well as mine:—
What see'st thou in the ground? hold up thy head:
     Look in mine eyeballs, there thy beauty lies;
     Then why not lips on lips, since eyes in eyes?

'Art thou ashamed to kiss? then wink again,
And I will wink; so shall the day seem night;
Love keeps his revels where there are but twain;
Be bold to play, our sport is not in sight:
     These blue-vein'd violets whereon we lean
     Never can blab, nor know not what we mean.

'The tender spring upon thy tempting lip
Shows thee unripe; yet mayst thou well be tasted:
Make use of time, let not advantage slip;
Beauty within itself should not be wasted:
     Fair flowers that are not gather'd in their prime
     Rot and consume themselves in little time.

'Were I hard-favour'd, foul, or wrinkled-old,
Ill-nurtured, crooked, churlish, harsh in voice,
O'erworn, despised, rheumatic, and cold,
Thick-sighted, barren, lean, and lacking juice,
     Then mightst thou pause, for then I were not
     for thee;
     But having no defects, why dost abhor me?

'Thou canst not see one wrinkle in my brow;
Mine eyes are gray, and bright, and quick in
     turning;
My beauty as the spring doth yearly grow,
My flesh is soft and plump, my marrow burning;
     My smooth moist hand, were it with thy hand
     felt,
     Would in thy palm dissolve, or seem to melt.

'Bid me discourse, I will enchant thine ear,
Or, like a fairy, trip upon the green,
Or, like a nymph, with long dishevell'd hair,
Dance on the sands, and yet no footing seen:
     Love is a spirit all compact of fire,
     Not gross to sink, but light, and will aspire.

'Witness this primrose bank whereon I lie;
These forceless flowers like sturdy trees support
     me;
Two strengthless doves will draw me through the
     sky,
From morn till night, even where I list to sport me:
     Is love so light, sweet boy, and may it be
     That thou should think it heavy unto thee?

'Is thine own heart to thine own face affected?
Can thy right hand seize love upon thy left?
Then woo thyself, be of thyself rejected,
Steal thine own freedom, and complain on theft.
     Narcissus so himself himself forsook,
     And died to kiss his shadow in the brook.

'Torches are made to light, jewels to wear,
Dainties to taste, fresh beauty for the use,
Herbs for their smell, and sappy plants to bear;
Things growing to themselves are growth's abuse:
     Seeds spring from seeds, and beauty breedeth
     beauty;
     Thou wast begot; to get it is thy duty.

'Upon the earth's increase why shouldst thou feed,
Unless the earth with thy increase be fed?
By law of nature thou art bound to breed,
That thine may live when thou thyself art dead;
     And so, in spite of death, thou dost survive,
     In that thy likeness still is left alive.'

By this, the love-sick queen began to sweat,
For, where they lay, the shadow had forsook them,
And Titan, tired in the mid-day heat,
With burning eye did hotly overlook them;
     Wishing Adonis had his team to guide
     So he were like him, and by Venus' side.

And now Adonis, with a lazy sprite,
And with a heavy, dark, disliking eye,
His louring brows o'erwhelming his fair sight,
Like misty vapours when they blot the sky,—
　　Souring his cheeks, cries, 'Fie, no more of love!
　　The sun doth burn my face; I must remove.'

'Ay me,' quoth Venus, 'young, and so unkind?
What bare excuses makest thou to be gone!
I'll sigh celestial breath, whose gentle wind
Shall cool the heat of this descending sun:
　　I'll make a shadow for thee of my hairs;
　　If they burn too, I'll quench them with my
　　　　tears.

'The sun that shines from heaven shines but warm,
And, lo, I lie between that sun and thee:
The heat I have from thence doth little harm,
Thine eye darts forth the fire that burneth me;
　　And were I not immortal, life were done
　　Between this heavenly and earthly sun.

'Art thou obdurate, flinty, hard as steel,
Nay, more than flint, for stone at rain relenteth?
Art thou a woman's son, and canst not feel
What 'tis to love? how want of love tormenteth?
　　O, had thy mother borne so hard a mind,
　　She had not brought forth thee, but died un-
　　　　kind.

'What am I, that thou shouldst contemn me this?
Or what great danger dwells upon my suit?
What were thy lips the worse for one poor kiss?
Speak, fair; but speak fair words, or else be mute:
　　Give me one kiss, I'll give it thee again,
　　And one for interest, if thou wilt have twain.

'Fie, lifeless picture, cold and senseless stone,
Well-painted idol, image dull and dead,
Statue contenting but the eye alone,
Thing like a man, but of no woman bred!
　　Thou art no man, though of a man's com-
　　　　plexion,
　　For men will kiss even by their own direction.'

This said, impatience chokes her pleading tongue,
And swelling passion doth provoke a pause;
Red cheeks and fiery eyes blaze forth her wrong;
Being judge in love, she cannot right her cause:
　　And now she weeps, and now she fain would
　　　　speak,
　　And now her sobs do her intendments break.

Sometime she shakes her head, and then his hand,
Now gazeth she on him, now on the ground;
Sometime her arms infold him like a band:
She would, he will not in her arms be bound;
　　And when from thence he struggles to be gone,
　　She locks her lily fingers one in one.

'Fondling,' she saith, 'since I have hemm'd thee
　　here
Within the circuit of this ivory pale,
I'll be a park, and thou shalt be my deer:
Feed where thou wilt, on mountain or in dale:
　　Graze on my lips; and if those hills be dry,
　　Stray lower, where the pleasant fountains lie.

'Within this limit is relief enough,
Sweet bottom-grass, and high delightful plain,
Round rising hillocks, brakes obscure and rough,
To shelter thee from tempest and from rain:
　　Then be my deer, since I am such a park;
　　No dog shall rouse thee, though a thousand
　　　　bark.'

At this Adonis smiles as in disdain,
That in each cheek appears a pretty dimple:
Love made those hollows, if himself were slain,
He might be buried in a tomb so simple;
　　Foreknowing well, if there he came to lie,
　　Why, there Love lived, and there he could not
　　　　die.

These lovely caves, these round enchanting pits,
Open'd their mouths to swallow Venus' liking.
Being mad before, how doth she now for wits?
Struck dead at first, what needs a second striking?
　　Poor queen of love, in thine own law forlorn,
　　To love a cheek that smiles at thee in scorn!

Now which way shall she turn? what shall she say?
Her words are done, her woes the more increas-
　　ing;
The time is spent, her object will away,
And from her twining arms doth urge releasing.
　　'Pity,' she cries, 'some favour, some remorse!'
　　Away he springs, and hasteth to his horse.

But, lo, from forth a copse that neighbours by,
A breeding jennet, lusty, young, and proud,
Adonis' trampling courser doth espy,
And forth she rushes, snorts, and neighs aloud:
　　The strong neckt steed, being tied unto a tree,
　　Breaketh his rein, and to her straight goes he.

Imperiously he leaps, he neighs, he bounds,
And now his woven girths he breaks asunder;
The bearing earth with his hard hoof he wounds,
Whose hollow womb resounds like heaven's
　　thunder;
　　The iron bit he crusheth 'tween his teeth,
　　Controlling what he was controlled with.

His ears up-prickt; his braided hanging mane
Upon his compass crest now stand on end;
His nostrils drink the air, and forth again,
As from a furnace, vapours doth he send;
　　His eye, which scornfully glisters like fire,
　　Shows his hot courage and his high desire.

Sometime he trots, as if he told the steps,
With gentle majesty and modest pride;
Anon he rears upright, curvets and leaps,
As who should say, 'Lo, thus my strength is tried;
　　And this I do to captivate the eye
　　Of the fair breeder that is standing by.'

What recketh he his rider's angry stir,
His flattering 'Holla' or his 'Stand, I say'?
What cares he now for curb or pricking spur?
For rich caparisons or trapping gay?
　　He sees his love, and nothing else he sees,
　　For nothing else with his proud sight agrees.

Look, when a painter would surpass the life
In limning out a well-proportion'd steed,
His art with nature's workmanship at strife,
As if the dead the living should exceed;
  So did this horse excel a common one
  In shape, in courage, colour, pace, and bone.

Round-hooft, short-jointed, fetlocks shag and
  long,
Broad breast, full eye, small head, and nostril wide,
High crest, short ears, straight legs, and passing
  strong,
Thin mane, thick tail, broad buttock, tender hide:
  Look, what a horse should have he did not lack,
  Save a proud rider on so proud a back.

Sometime he scuds far off, and there he stares;
Anon he starts at stirring of a feather;
To bid the wind a base he now prepares,
And whe'r he run or fly they know not whether;
  For through his mane and tail the high wind
    sings,
  Fanning the hairs, who wave like feath'red
    wings.

He looks upon his love, and neighs unto her;
She answers him, as if she knew his mind:
Being proud, as females are, to see him woo her,
She puts on outward strangeness, seems unkind;
  Spurns at his love, and scorns the heat he feels,
  Beating his kind embracements with her heels.

Then, like a melancholy malcontent,
He vails his tail, that, like a falling plume,
Cool shadow to his melting buttock lent:
He stamps, and bites the poor flies in his fume.
  His love, perceiving how he is enraged,
  Grew kinder, and his fury was assuaged.

His testy master goeth about to take him;
When, lo, the unbackt breeder, full of fear,
Jealous of catching, swiftly doth forsake him,
With her the horse, and left Adonis there:
  As they were mad, unto the wood they hie them,
  Out-stripping crows that strive to over-fly them.

All swoln with chafing, down Adonis sits,
Banning his boist'rous and unruly beast:
And now the happy season once more fits,
That love-sick Love by pleading may be blest;
  For lovers say, the heart hath treble wrong
  When it is barr'd the aidance of the tongue.

An oven that is stopt, or river stay'd,
Burneth more hotly, swelleth with more rage:
So of concealed sorrow may be said;
Free vent of words love's fire doth assuage;
  But when the heart's attorney once is mute,
  The client breaks, as desperate in his suit.

He sees her coming, and begins to glow,
Even as a dying coal revives with wind,
And with his bonnet hides his angry brow;
Looks on the dull earth with disturbed mind;
  Taking no notice that she is so nigh,
  For all askance he holds her in his eye.

O, what a sight it was, wistly to view
How she came stealing to the wayward boy!
To note the fighting conflict of her hue,
How white and red each other did destroy!
  But now her cheek was pale, and by and by
  It flasht forth fire, as lightning from the sky.

Now she was just before him as he sat,
And like a lowly lover down she kneels;
With one fair hand she heaveth up his hat,
Her other tender hand his fair cheek feels:
  His tenderer cheek receives her soft hand's print,
  As apt as new-faln snow takes any dint.

O, what a war of looks was then between them!
Her eyes petitioners to his eyes suing;
His eyes saw her eyes as they had not seen them;
Her eyes woo'd still, his eyes disdain'd the wooing:
  And all this dumb-play had his acts made plain
  With tears, which, chorus-like, her eyes did
    rain.

Full gently now she takes him by the hand,
A lily prison'd in a goal of snow,
Or ivory in an alabaster band;
So white a friend engirts so white a foe:
  This beauteous combat, wilful and unwilling,
  Show'd like two silver doves that sit a-billing.

Once more the engine of her thoughts began:
'O fairest mover on this mortal round,
Would thou wert as I am, and I a man,
My heart all whole as thine, thy heart my wound;
  For one sweet look thy help I would assure thee,
  Though nothing but my body's bane would
    cure thee.'

'Give me my hand,' saith he; 'why dost thou feel
  it?'
'Give me my heart,' saith she, 'and thou shalt
  have it;
O, give it me, lest thy hard heart do steel it,
And being steel'd, soft sighs can never grave it:
  Then love's deep groans I never shall regard,
  Because Adonis' heart hath made mine hard.'

'For shame,' he cries, 'let go, and let me go;
My day's delight is past, my horse is gone,
And 'tis your fault I am bereft him so:
I pray you hence, and leave me here alone;
  For all my mind, my thought, my busy care
  Is how to get my palfrey from the mare.'

Thus she replies: 'Thy palfrey, as he should,
Welcomes the warm approach of sweet desire:
Affection is a coal that must be cool'd;
Else, suffer'd, it will set the heart on fire:
  The sea hath bounds, but deep desire hath none;
  Therefore no marvel though thy horse be gone.

'How like a jade he stood, tied to the tree,
Servilely master'd with a leathern rein!
But when he saw his love, his youth's fair fee,
He held such petty bondage in disdain;
  Throwing the base thong from his bending crest,
  Enfranchising his mouth, his back, his breast.

'Who sees his true-love in her naked bed,
Teaching the sheets a whiter hue than white,
But, when his glutton eye so full hath fed,
His other agents aim at like delight?
  Who is so faint, that dares not be so bold
  To touch the fire, the weather being cold?

'Let me excuse thy courser, gentle boy;
And learn of him, I heartily beseech thee,
To take advantage on presented joy;
Though I were dumb, yet his proceedings teach
   thee:
  O, learn to love; the lesson is but plain,
  And once made perfect, never lost again.'

'I know not love,' quoth he, 'nor will not know it,
Unless it be a boar, and then I chase it;
'Tis much to borrow, and I will not owe it;
My love to love is love but to disgrace it;
  For I have heard it is a life in death,
  That laughs, and weeps, and all but with a
   breath.

'Who wears a garment shapeless and unfinisht?
Who plucks the bud before one leaf put forth?
If springing things be any jot diminisht,
They wither in their prime, prove nothing worth:
  The colt that's backt and burden'd being
   young
  Loseth his pride, and never waxeth strong.

'You hurt my hand with wringing; let us part,
And leave this idle theme, this bootless chat:
Remove your siege from my unyielding heart;
To love's alarms it will not ope the gate:
  Dismiss your vows, your feigned tears, your
   flatt'ry;
  For where a heart is hard they make no batt'ry.'

'What! canst thou talk?' quoth she, 'hast thou a
  tongue?
O, would thou hadst not, or I had no hearing!
Thy mermaid's voice hath done me double
  wrong;
I had my load before, now prest with bearing:
  Melodious discord, heavenly tune harsh-
   sounding,
  Ear's deep-sweet music, and heart's deep-sore
   wounding.

'Had I no eyes but ears, my ears would love
That inward beauty and invisible;
Or were I deaf, thy outward parts would move
Each part in me that were but sensible:
  Though neither eyes nor ears, to hear nor see,
  Yet should I be in love by touching thee.

'Say, that the sense of feeling were bereft me,
And that I could not see, nor hear, nor touch,
And nothing but the very smell were left me,
Yet would my love to thee be still as much;
  For from the stillitory of thy face excelling
  Comes breath perfumed, that breedeth love by
   smelling.

'But, O, what banquet wert thou to the taste,
Being nurse and feeder of the other four!
Would they not wish the feast might ever last,
And bid Suspicion double-lock the door,
  Lest Jealousy, that sour unwelcome guest,
  Should, by his stealing in, disturb the feast?'

Once more the ruby-colour'd portal open'd,
Which to his speech did honey passage yield;
Like a red morn, that ever yet betoken'd
Wrack to the seaman, tempest to the field,
  Sorrow to shepherds, woe unto the birds,
  Gusts and foul flaws to herdmen and to herds.

This ill presage advisedly she marketh:
Even as the wind is husht before it raineth,
Or as the wolf doth grin before he barketh,
Or as the berry breaks before it staineth,
  Or like the deadly bullet of a gun,
  His meaning struck her ere his words begun.

And at his look she flatly falleth down,
For looks kill love, and love by looks reviveth:
A smile recures the wounding of a frown;
But blessed bankrout, that by love so thriveth!
  The silly boy, believing she is dead,
  Claps her pale cheek, till clapping makes it
   red;

And all-amazed brake off his late intent,
For sharply he did think to reprehend her,
Which cunning love did wittily prevent:
Fair fall the wit that can so well defend her!
  For on the grass she lies as she were slain,
  Till his breath breatheth life in her again.

He wrings her nose, he strikes her on the cheeks,
He bends her fingers, holds her pulses hard,
He chafes her lips; a thousand ways he seeks
To mend the hurt that his unkindness marr'd:
  He kisses her; and she, by her good will,
  Will never rise, so he will kiss her still.

The night of sorrow now is turn'd to day:
Her two blue windows faintly she up-heaveth.
Like the fair sun, when in his fresh array
He cheers the morn, and all the earth relieveth:
  And as the bright sun glorifies the sky,
  So is her face illumined with her eye;

Whose beams upon his hairless face are fixt,
As if from thence they borrow'd all their shine.
Were never four such lamps together mixt,
Had not his clouded with his brow's repine;
  But hers, which through the crystal tears gave
   light,
  Shone like the moon in water seen by night.

'O, where am I?' quoth she; 'in earth or heaven,
Or in the ocean drencht, or in the fire?
What hour is this? or morn or weary even?
Do I delight to die, or life desire?
  But now I lived, and life was death's annoy;
  But now I died, and death was lively joy.

'O, thou didst kill me: kill me once again:
Thy eyes' shrewd tutor, that hard heart of thine,
Hath taught them scornful tricks, and such dis-
    dain,
That they have murder'd this poor heart of mine;
    And these mine eyes, true leaders to their queen,
    But for thy piteous lips no more had seen.

'Long may they kiss each other, for this cure!
O, never let their crimson liveries wear!
And as they last, their verdure still endure,
To drive infection from the dangerous year!
    That the star-gazers, having writ on death,
    May say, the plague is banisht by thy breath.

'Pure lips, sweet seals in my soft lips imprinted,
What bargains may I make, still to be sealing?
To sell myself I can be well contented,
So thou wilt buy, and pay, and use good dealing;
    Which purchase if thou make, for fear of slips
    Set thy seal-manual on my wax-red lips.

'A thousand kisses buys my heart from me;
And pay them at thy leisure, one by one.
What is ten hundred touches unto thee?
Are they not quickly told and quickly gone?
    Say, for non-payment that the debt should
        double,
    Is twenty hundred kisses such a trouble?'

'Fair queen,' quoth he, 'if any love you owe me,
Measure my strangeness with my unripe years:
Before I know myself, seek not to know me;
No fisher but the ungrown fry forbears:
    The mellow plum doth fall, the green sticks fast,
    Or being early pluckt is sour to taste.

'Look, the world's comforter, with weary gait,
His day's hot task hath ended in the west;
The owl, night's herald, shrieks; 'tis very late;
The sheep are gone to fold, birds to their nest,
    And coal black clouds that shadow heaven's
        light
    Do summon us to part and bid good night.

'Now let me say "Good night," and so say you;
If you will say so, you shall have a kiss.'
'Good night,' quoth she; and, ere he says 'Adieu,'
The honey fee of parting tender'd is:
    Her arms do lend his neck a sweet embrace;
    Incorporate then they seem; face grows to face:

Till, breathless, he disjoin'd, and backward drew
The heavenly moisture, that sweet coral mouth,
Whose precious taste her thirsty lips well knew,
Whereon they surfeit, yet complain on drouth:
    He with her plenty prest, she faint with dearth,
    Their lips together glued, fall to the earth.

Now quick desire hath caught the yielding prey,
And glutton-like she feeds, yet never filleth;
Her lips are conquerors, his lips obey,
Paying what ransom the insulter willeth;
    Whose vulture thought doth pitch the price so
        high,
    That she will draw his lips' rich treasure dry:

And having felt the sweetness of the spoil,
With blindfold fury she begins to forage;
Her face doth reek and smoke, her blood doth boil,
And careless lust stirs up a desperate courage;
    Planting oblivion, beating reason back,
    Forgetting shame's pure blush and honour's
        wrack.

Hot, faint, and weary with her hard embracing,
Like a wild bird being tamed with too much
    handling,
Or as the fleet-foot roe that's tired with chasing,
Or like the froward infant still'd with dandling,
    He now obeys, and now no more resisteth,
    While she takes all she can, not all she listeth.

What wax so frozen but dissolves with temp'ring,
And yields at last to every light impression?
Things out of hope are compast oft with vent'ring,
Chiefly in love, whose leave exceeds commission:
    Affection faints not like a pale-faced coward,
    But then woos best when most his choice is
        froward.

When he did frown, O, had she then gave over,
Such nectar from his lips she had not suckt.
Foul words and frowns must not repel a lover;
What though the rose have prickles, yet 'tis pluckt,
    Were beauty under twenty locks kept fast,
    Yet love breaks through and picks them all at last.

For pity now she can no more detain him;
The poor fool prays her that he may depart:
She is resolved no longer to restrain him;
Bids him farewell, and look well to her heart,
    The which, by Cupid's bow she doth protest,
    He carries thence incaged in his breast.

'Sweet boy,' she says, 'this night I'll waste in
    sorrow,
For my sick heart commands mine eyes to watch.
Tell me, Love's master, shall we meet to-morrow?
Say, shall we? shall we? wilt thou make the match?'
    He tells her, no; to-morrow he intends
    To hunt the boar with certain of his friends.

'The boar!' quoth she; whereat a sudden pale,
Like lawn being spread upon the blushing rose,
Usurps her cheek; she trembles at his tale,
And on his neck her yoking arms she throws:
    She sinketh down, still hanging by his neck,
    He on her belly falls, she on her back.

Now is she in the very lists of love,
Her champion mounted for the hot encounter:
All is imaginary she doth prove,
He will not manage her, although he mount her;
    That worse than Tantalus' is her annoy,
    To clip Elysium, and to lack her joy.

Even so poor birds, deceived with painted grapes,
Do surfeit by the eye and pine the maw:
Even so she languisheth in her mishaps
As those poor birds that helpless berries saw.
    The warm effects which she in him finds missing
    She seeks to kindle with continual kissing.

But all in vain; good queen, it will not be:
She hath assay'd as much as may be proved;
Her pleading hath deserved a greater fee;
She's Love, she loves, and yet she is not loved.
　'Fie, fie,' he says, 'you crush me; let me go;
　You have no reason to withhold me so.'

'Thou hadst been gone,' quoth she, 'sweet boy,
　ere this,
But that thou told'st me thou wouldst hunt the
　boar.
O, be advised! thou know'st not what it is
With javelin's point a churlish swine to gore,
　Whose tushes never-sheathed he whetteth still,
　Like to a mortal butcher bent to kill.

'On his bow-back he hath a battle set
Of bristly pikes, that ever threat his foes;
His eyes, like glow-worms, shine when he doth fret;
His snout digs sepulchres where'er he goes;
　Being moved, he strikes whate'er is in his way,
　And whom he strikes his crooked tushes slay.

'His brawny sides, with hairy bristles armed,
Are better proof than thy spear's point can enter;
His short thick neck cannot be easily harmed;
Being ireful, on the lion he will venter:
　The thorny brambles and embracing bushes,
　As fearful of him, part; through whom he rushes.

'Alas, he naught esteems that face of thine,
To which Love's eyes pays tributary gazes;
Nor thy soft hands, sweet lips, and crystal eyne,
Whose full perfection all the world amazes;
　But having thee at vantage,—wondrous dread!—
　Would root these beauties as he roots the mead.

'O, let him keep his loathsome cabin still;
Beauty hath naught to do with such foul fiends:
Come not within his danger by thy will;
They that thrive well take counsel of their friends.
　When thou didst name the boar, not to dis-
　semble,
　I fear'd thy fortune, and my joints did tremble.

'Didst thou not mark my face? was it not white?
Saw'st thou not signs of fear lurk in mine eye?
Grew I not faint? and fell I not downright?
Within my bosom, whereon thou dost lie,
　My boding heart pants, beats, and takes no rest,
　But, like an earthquake, shakes thee on my
　breast.

'For where Love reigns, disturbing Jealousy
Doth call himself Affection's sentinel;
Gives false alarms, suggesteth mutiny,
And in a peaceful hour doth cry "Kill, kill!"
　Distemp'ring gentle Love in his desire,
　As air and water do abate the fire.

'This sour informer, this bate-breeding spy,
This canker that eats up Love's tender spring,
This carry-tale, dissentious Jealousy,
That sometime true news, sometime false doth
　bring,
　Knocks at my heart, and whispers in mine ear,
　That if I love thee, I thy death should fear:

'And more than so, presenteth to mine eye
The picture of an angry-chafing boar,
Under whose sharp fangs on his back doth lie
An image like thyself, all stain'd with gore;
　Whose blood upon the fresh flowers being shed
　Doth make them droop with grief and hang the
　head.

'What should I do, seeing thee so indeed,
That tremble at the imagination?
The thought of it doth make my faint heart bleed,
And fear doth teach it divination:
　I prophesy thy death, my living sorrow,
　If thou encounter with the boar to-morrow.

'But if thou needs wilt hunt, be ruled by me;
Uncouple at the timorous flying hare,
Or at the fox which lives by subtlety,
Or at the roe which no encounter dare:
　Pursue these fearful creatures o'er the downs,
　And on thy well-breathed horse keep with thy
　hounds.

'And when thou hast on foot the purblind hare,
Mark the poor wretch, to overshoot his troubles
How he outruns the wind, and with what care
He cranks and crosses with a thousand doubles:
　The many musets through the which he goes
　Are like a labyrinth to amaze his foes.

'Sometime he runs among a flock of sheep,
To make the cunning hounds mistake their smell,
And sometime where earth-delving conies keep,
To stop the loud pursuers in their yell;
　And sometime sorteth with a herd of deer:
　Danger deviseth shifts; wit waits on fear:

'For there his smell with others being mingled,
The hot scent-snuffing hounds are driven to
　doubt,
Ceasing their clamorous cry till they have singled
With much ado the cold fault cleanly out;
　Then do they spend their mouths: Echo replies,
　As if another chase were in the skies.

'By this, poor Wat, far off upon a hill,
Stands on his hinder legs with list'ning ear,
To hearken if his foes pursue him still:
Anon their loud alarums he doth hear;
　And now his grief may be compared well
　To one sore sick that hears the passing-bell.

'Then shalt thou see the dew-bedabbled wretch
Turn, and return, indenting with the way;
Each envious brier his weary legs doth scratch,
Each shadow makes him stop, each murmur stay;
　For misery is trodden on by many,
　And being low never relieved by any.

'Lie quietly, and hear a little more;
Nay, do not struggle, for thou shalt not rise:
To make thee hate the hunting of the boar,
Unlike myself thou hear'st me moralize,
　Applying this to that, and so to so;
　For love can comment upon every woe.

'Where did I leave?' 'No matter where,' quoth he;
' Leave me, and then the story aptly ends:
The night is spent.' 'Why, what of that?' quoth
   she.
'I am,' quoth he, 'expected of my friends; ℞
   And now 'tis dark, and going I shall fall.'
   'In night,' quoth she, 'desire sees best of all.

'But if thou fall, O, then imagine this,
The earth, in love with thee, thy footing trips,
And all is but to rob thee of a kiss.
Rich preys make true-men thieves; so do thy lips
   Make modest Dian cloudy and forlorn,
   Lest she should steal a kiss, and die forsworn.

'Now of this dark night I perceive the reason:
Cynthia for shame obscures her silver shine,
Till forging Nature be condemn'd of treason,
For stealing moulds from heaven that were divine;
   Wherein she framed thee, in high heaven's
     despite,
   To shame the sun by day, and her by night.

'And therefore hath she bribed the Destinies
To cross the curious workmanship of Nature,
To mingle beauty with infirmities,
And pure perfection with impure defeature;
   Making it subject to the tyranny
   Of mad mischances and much misery;

'As burning fevers, agues pale and faint,
Life-poisoning pestilence, and frenzies wood,
The marrow-eating sickness, whose attaint
Disorder breeds by heating of the blood:
   Surfeits, imposthumes, grief, and damn'd
     despair,
   Swear Nature's death for framing thee so fair.

'And not the least of all these maladies
But in one minute's fight brings beauty under:
Both favour, savour, hue, and qualities,
Whereat the impartial gazer late did wonder,
   Are on the sudden wasted, thaw'd, and done,
   As mountain snow melts with the midday sun.

'Therefore, despite of fruitless chastity,
L ove-lacking vestals, and self-loving nuns,
That on the earth would breed a scarcity
And barren dearth of daughters and of sons,
   Be prodigal: the lamp that burns by night
   Dries up his oil to lend the world his light.

'What is thy body but a swallowing grave,
Seeming to bury that posterity
Which by the rights of time thou needs must have,
If thou destroy them not in dark obscurity?
   If so, the world will hold thee in disdain,
   Sith in thy pride so fair a hope is slain.

'So in thy self thyself art made away;
A mischief worse than civil home-bred strife,
Or theirs whose desperate hands themselves do
   slay,
Or butcher-sire that reaves his son of life.
   Foul-cank'ring rust the hidden treasure frets,
   But gold that's put to use more gold begets.'

'Nay, then,' quoth Adon, 'you will fall again
Into your idle over-handled theme:
The kiss I gave you is bestow'd in vain,
And all in vain you strive against the stream;
   For, by this black-faced night, desire's foul
     nurse,
   Your treatise makes me like you worse and
     worse.

'If love have lent you twenty thousand tongues,
And every tongue more moving than your own,
Bewitching like the wanton mermaid's songs,
Yet from mine ear the tempting tune is blown;
   For know, my heart stands armed in mine ear,
   And will not let a false sound enter there;

'Lest the deceiving harmony should run
Into the quiet closure of my breast;
And then my little heart were quite undone,
In his bedchamber to be barr'd of rest.
   No, lady, no; my heart longs not to groan,
   But soundly sleeps, while now it sleeps alone.

'What have you urged that I cannot reprove?
The path is smooth that leadeth on to danger:
I hate not love, but your device in love,
That lends embracements unto every stranger.
   You do it for increase: O strange excuse,
   When reason is the bawd to lust's abuse!

'Call it not love, for Love to heaven is fled,
Since sweating Lust on earth usurpt his name;
Under whose simple semblance he hath fed
Upon fresh beauty, blotting it with blame;
   Which the hot tyrant stains and soon bereaves,
   As caterpillars do the tender leaves.

'Love comforteth like sunshine after rain,
But Lust's effect is tempest after sun;
Love's gentle spring doth always fresh remain,
Lust's winter comes ere summer half be done;
   Love surfeits not, Lust like a glutton dies;
   Love is all truth, Lust full of forged lies.

'More I could tell, but more I dare not say;
The text is old, the orator too green.
Therefore, in sadness, now I will away;
My face is full of shame, my heart of teen:
   Mine ears, that to your wanton talk attended,
   Do burn themselves for having so offended.'

With this, he breaketh from the sweet embrace
Of those fair arms which bound him to her breast,
And homeward through the dark laund runs apace;
Leaves Love upon her back deeply distrest.
   Look, how a bright star shooteth from the sky,
   So glides he in the night from Venus' eye;

Which after him she darts, as one on shore
Gazing upon a late-embarked friend,
Till the wild waves will have him see no more,
Whose ridges with the meeting clouds contend:
   So did the merciless and pitchy night
   Fold-in the object that did feed her sight.

Whereat amazed, as one that unaware
Hath dropt a precious jewel in the flood,
Or stonisht as night-wanderers often are,
Their light blown out in some mistrustful wood;
    Even so confounded in the dark she lay,
    Having lost the fair discovery of her way.

And now she beats her heart, whereat it groans,
That all the neighbour caves, as seeming troubled,
Make verbal repetition of her moans;
Passion on passion deeply is redoubled:
    'Ay me!' she cries, and twenty times, 'Woe,
      woe!'
    And twenty echoes twenty times cry so.

She, marking them, begins a wailing note,
And sings extemporally a woeful ditty;
How love makes young men thrall, and old men
    dote;
How love is wise in folly, foolish-witty:
    Her heavy anthem still concludes in woe,
    And still the choir of echoes answer so.

Her song was tedious, and outwore the night,
For lovers' hours are long, though seeming short:
If pleased themselves, others, they think, delight
In such-like circumstance, with such-like sport:
    Their copious stories, oftentimes begun,
    End without audience, and are never done.

For who hath she to spend the night withal,
But idle sounds resembling parasits;
Like shrill-tongued tapsters answering every call,
Soothing the humour of fantastic wits?
    She says "Tis so:' they answer all, "Tis so;'
    And would say after her, if she said 'No.'

Lo, here the gentle lark, weary of rest,
From his moist cabinet mounts up on high,
And wakes the morning, from whose silver breast
The sun ariseth in his majesty;
    Who doth the world so gloriously behold,
    That cedar-tops and hills seem burnisht gold.

Venus salutes him with this fair good-morrow:
'O thou clear god, and patron of all light,
From whom each lamp and shining star doth
    borrow
The beauteous influence that makes him bright,
    There lives a son, that suckt an earthly mother,
    May lend thee light, as thou dost lend to other.'

This said, she hasteth to a myrtle grove,
Musing the morning is so much o'erworn,
And yet she hears no tidings of her love:
She hearkens for his hounds and for his horn:
    Anon she hears them chant it lustily,
    And all in haste she coasteth to the cry.

And as she runs, the bushes in the way
Some catch her by the neck, some kiss her face,
Some twined about her thigh to make her stay:
She wildly breaketh from their strict embrace,
    Like a milch doe, whose swelling dugs do ache,
    Hasting to feed her fawn hid in some brake.

By this, she hears the hounds are at a bay:
Whereat she starts, like one that spies an adder
Wreathed up in fatal folds just in his way,
The fear whereof doth make him shake and
    shudder;
    Even so the timorous yelping of the hounds
    Appals her senses and her spirit confounds.

For now she knows it is no gentle chase,
But the blunt boar, rough bear, or lion proud,
Because the cry remaineth in one place,
Where fearfully the dogs exclaim aloud:
    Finding their enemy to be so curst,
    They all strain court'sy who shall cope him first.

This dismal cry rings sadly in her ear,
Through which it enters to surprise her heart;
Who, overcome by doubt and bloodless fear,
With cold-pale weakness numbs each feeling part:
    Like soldiers, when their captain once doth
      yield,
    They basely fly, and dare not stay the field.

Thus stands she in a trembling ecstasy;
Till, cheering up her senses all dismay'd,
She tells them 'tis a causeless fantasy,
And childish error, that they are afraid;
    Bids them leave quaking, bids them fear no
      more:—
    And with that word she spied the hunted boar;

Whose frothy mouth, bepainted all with red,
Like milk and blood being mingled both togither,
A second fear through all her sinews spread,
Which madly hurries her she knows not whither:
    This way she runs, and now she will no further,
    But back retires to rate the boar for murther.

A thousand spleens bear her a thousand ways;
She treads the path that she untreads again;
Her more than haste is mated with delays,
Like the proceedings of a drunken brain,
    Full of respects, yet naught at all respecting;
    In hand with all things, naught at all effecting.

Here kennell'd in a brake she finds a hound,
And asks the weary caitiff for his master;
And there another licking of his wound,
'Gainst venom'd sores the only sovereign plaster;
    And here she meets another sadly scowling,
    To whom she speaks, and he replies with howl-
      ing.

When he hath ceased his ill-resounding noise,
Another flap-mouth'd mourner, black and grim,
Against the welkin volleys out his voice;
Another and another answer him,
    Clapping their proud tails to the ground below,
    Shaking their scratcht ears, bleeding as they go.

Look how the world's poor people are amazed
At apparitions, signs, and prodigies,
Whereon with fearful eyes they long have gazed,
Infusing them with dreadful prophecies;
    So she at these sad signs draws up her breath,
    And, sighing it again, exclaims on Death.

'Hard-favour'd tyrant, ugly, meagre, lean,
Hateful divorce of love.'—thus chides she
 Death,—
'Grim-grinning ghost, earth's worm, what dost
  thou mean
To stifle beauty and to steal his breath,
 Who when he lived, his breath and beauty set
 Gloss on the rose, smell to the violet?

'If he be dead,—O no, it cannot be,
Seeing his beauty, thou shouldst strike at it;—
O yes, it may; thou hast no eyes to see,
But hatefully at random dost thou hit.
 Thy mark is feeble age; but thy false dart
 Mistakes that aim, and cleaves an infant's heart.

'Hadst thou but bid beware, then he had spoke,
And, hearing him, thy power had lost his power.
The Destinies will curse thee for this stroke;
They bid thee crop a weed, thou pluck'st a flower:
 Love's golden arrow at him should have fled,
 And not Death's ebon dart, to strike him dead.

'Dost thou drink tears, that thou provokest such
  weeping?
What may a heavy groan advantage thee?
Why hast thou cast into eternal sleeping
Those eyes that taught all other eyes to see?
 Now Nature cares not for thy mortal vigour,
 Since her best work is ruin'd with thy rigour.'

Here overcome, as one full of despair,
She vail'd her eyelids, who, like sluices, stopt
The crystal tide that from her two cheeks fair
In the sweet channel of her bosom dropt;
 But through the flood-gates breaks the silver
  rain,
 And with his strong course opens them again.

O, how her eyes and tears did lend and borrow!
Her eye seen in the tears, tears in her eye;
Both crystals, where they view'd each other's
  sorrow,—
Sorrow that friendly sighs sought still to dry;
 But like a stormy day, now wind, now rain,
 Sighs dry her cheeks, tears make them wet
  again.

Variable passions throng her constant woe,
As striving who should best become her grief;
All entertain'd, each passion labours so,
That every present sorrow seemeth chief,
 But none is best: then join they all together,
 Like many clouds consulting for foul weather.

By this, far off she hears some huntsman hollo;
A nurse's song ne'er pleased her babe so well:
The dire imagination she did follow
This sound of hope doth labour to expel;
 For now reviving joy bids her rejoice,
 And flatters her it is Adonis' voice.

Whereat her tears began to turn their tide,
Being prison'd in her eye like pearls in glass;
Yet sometimes falls an orient drop beside,
Which her cheek melts, as scorning it should pass,
 To wash the foul face of the sluttish ground,
 Who is but drunken when she seemeth drown'd.

O hard-believing love, how strange it seems
Not to believe, and yet too credulous!
Thy weal and woe are both of them extremes;
Despair and hope makes thee ridiculous:
 The one doth flatter thee in thoughts unlikely,
 In likely thoughts the other kills thee quickly.

Now she unweaves the web that she hath wrought;
Adonis lives, and Death is not to blame;
It was not she that call'd him all to-naught:
Now she adds honours to his hateful name;
 She clepes him king of graves, and grave for
  kings,
 Imperious supreme of all mortal things.

'No, no,' quoth she, 'sweet Death, I did but jest;
Yet pardon me I felt a kind of fear
Whenas I met the boar, that bloody beast
Which knows no pity, but is still severe:
 Then, gentle shadow,—truth I must confess,—
 I rail'd on thee, fearing my love's decease.

''Tis not my fault: the boar provoked my tongue;
Be wreak on him, invisible commander;
'Tis he, foul creature, that hath done thee wrong;
I did but act, he's author of thy slander:
 Grief hath two tongues; and never woman yet
 Could rule them both without ten women's wit.'

Thus hoping that Adonis is alive,
Her rash suspect she doth extenuate;
And that his beauty may the better thrive,
With Death she humbly doth insinuate;
 Tells him of trophies, statues, tombs, and
  stories
 His victories, his triumphs, and his glories.

'O Jove,' quoth she, 'how much a fool was I
To be of such a weak and silly mind
To wail his death who lives, and must not die
Till mutual overthrow of mortal kind!
 For he being dead, with him is beauty slain,
 And, beauty dead, black chaos comes again.

'Fie, fie, fond love, thou art as full of fear
As one with treasure laden hemm'd with thieves;
Trifles, unwitnessed with eye or ear,
Thy coward heart with false bethinking grieves.'
 Even at this word she hears a merry horn,
 Whereat she leaps that was but late forlorn.

As falcons to the lure, away she flies;
The grass stoops not, she treads on it so light;
And in her haste unfortunately spies
The foul boar's conquest on her fair delight;
 Which seen, her eyes, as murder'd with the
  view,
 Like stars ashamed of day, themselves with-
  drew;

Or as the snail, whose tender horns being hit,
Shrinks backward in his shelly cave with pain,
And there, all smother'd up, in shade doth sit,
Long after fearing to creep forth again;
 So at his bloody view her eyes are fled
 Into the deep-dark cabins of her head:

Where they resign their office and their light
To the disposing of her troubled brain;
Who bids them still consort with ugly night,
And never wound the heart with looks again;
  Who, like a king perplex'd in his throne,
  By their suggestion gives a deadly groan,

Whereat each tributary subject quakes;
As when the wind, imprison'd in the ground,
Struggling for passage, earth's foundation shakes,
Which with cold terror doth men's minds confound.
  This mutiny each part doth so surprise,
  That from their dark beds once more leap her eyes;

And, being open'd, threw unwilling light
Upon the wide wound that the boar had trencht
In his soft flank; whose wonted lily white
With purple tears, that his wound wept, was drencht:
  No flower was nigh, no grass, herb, leaf, or weed,
  But stole his blood, and seem'd with him to bleed.

This solemn sympathy poor Venus noteth;
Over one shoulder doth she hang her head;
Dumbly she passions, franticly she doteth;
She thinks he could not die, he is not dead:
  Her voice is stopt, her joints forget to bow;
  Her eyes are mad that they have wept till now.

Upon his hurt she looks so steadfastly,
That her sight dazzling makes the wound seem three;
And then she reprehends her mangling eye,
That makes more gashes where no breach should be:
  His face seems twain, each several limb is doubled;
  For oft the eye mistakes, the brain being troubled.

'My tongue cannot express my grief for one,
And yet,' quoth she, 'behold two Adons dead!
My sighs are blown away, my salt tears gone,
Mine eyes are turn'd to fire, my heart to lead:
  Heavy heart's lead, melt at mine eyes' red fire!
  So shall I die by drops of hot desire.

'Alas, poor world, what treasure hast thou lost!
What face remains alive that's worth the viewing?
Whose tongue is music now? what canst thou boast
Of things long since, or any thing ensuing?
  The flowers are sweet, their colours fresh and trim;
  But true-sweet beauty lived and died with him.

'Bonnet nor veil henceforth no creature wear!
Nor sun nor wind will ever strive to kiss you:
Having no fair to lose, you need not fear;
The sun doth scorn you, and the wind doth hiss you:
  But when Adonis lived, sun and sharp air
  Lurkt like two thieves, to rob him of his fair:

'And therefore would he put his bonnet on,
Under whose brim the gaudy sun would peep;
The wind would blow it off, and, being gone,
Play with his locks: then would Adonis weep;
  And straight, in pity of his tender years,
  They both would strive who first should dry his tears.

'To see his face the lion walkt along
Behind some hedge, because he would not fear him;
To recreate himself when he hath sung,
The tiger would be tame, and gently hear him;
  If he had spoke, the wolf would leave his prey,
  And never fright the silly lamb that day.

'When he beheld his shadow in the brook,
The fishes spread on it their golden gills;
When he was by, the birds such pleasure took,
That some would sing, some other in their bills
  Would bring him mulberries and ripe-red cherries;
  He fed them with his sight, they him with berries.

'But this foul, grim, and urchin-snouted boar,
Whose downward eye still looketh for a grave,
Ne'er saw the beauteous livery that he wore;
Witness the entertainment that he gave:
  If he did see his face, why then I know
  He thought to kiss him, and hath kill'd him so.

''Tis true, 'tis true; thus was Adonis slain:
He ran upon the boar with his sharp spear,
Who did not whet his teeth at him again,
But by a kiss thought to persuade him there;
  And nuzzling in his flank, the loving swine
  Sheathed, unaware, the tusk in his soft groin.

'Had I been tooth'd like him, I must confess,
With kissing him I should have kill'd him first;
But he is dead, and never did he bless
My youth with his; the more am I accurst.'
  With this, she falleth in the place she stood,
  And stains her face with his congealed blood.

She looks upon his lips, and they are pale;
She takes him by the hand, and that is cold;
She whispers in his ears a heavy tale,
As if they heard the woeful words she told;
  She lifts the coffer-lids that close his eyes,
  Where, lo, two lamps, burnt out, in darkness lies;

Two glasses, where herself herself beheld
A thousand times, and now no more reflect;
Their virtue lost, wherein they late excell'd,
And every beauty robb'd of his effect:
  'Wonder of time,' quoth she, 'this is my spite,
  That, thou being dead, the day should yet be light.

'Since thou art dead, lo, here I prophesy
Sorrow on love hereafter shall attend:
It shall be waited on with jealousy,
Find sweet beginning, but unsavoury end;
  Ne'er settled equally, but high or low;
  That all love's pleasure shall not match his woe.

'It shall be fickle, false, and full of fraud;
Bud and be blasted in a breathing-while;
The bottom poison, and the top o'erstraw'd
With sweets that shall the truest sight beguile:
    The strongest body shall it make most weak,
    Strike the wise dumb, and teach the fool to
      speak.

'It shall be sparing and too full of riot,
Teaching decrepit age to tread the measures;
The staring ruffian shall it keep in quiet,
Pluck down the rich, enrich the poor with treas-
   ures;
    It shall be raging-mad and silly-mild,
    Make the young old, the old become a child.

'It shall suspect where is no cause of fear;
It shall not fear where it should most mistrust;
It shall be merciful and too severe,
And most deceiving when it seems most just;
    Perverse it shall be where it shows most toward,
    Put fear to valour, courage to the coward.

'It shall be cause of war and dire events,
And set dissension 'twixt the son and sire;
Subject and servile to all discontents,
As dry combustious matter is to fire:
    Sith in his prime Death doth my love destroy,
    They that love best their loves shall not enjoy.'

By this, the boy that by her side lay kill'd
Was melted like a vapour from her sight;
And in his blood, that on the ground lay spill'd,
A purple flower sprung up, chequer'd with white,

Resembling well his pale cheeks, and the blood
Which in round drops upon their whiteness
   stood.

She bows her head the new-sprung flower to
   smell,
Comparing it to her Adonis' breath;
And says within her bosom it shall dwell,
Since he himself is reft from her by Death:
    She crops the stalk, and in the breach appears
    Green-dropping sap, which she compares to
      tears.

'Poor flower,' quoth she, 'this was thy father's
   guise,—
Sweet issue of a more sweet-smelling sire,—
For every little grief to wet his eyes:
To grow unto himself was his desire,
    And so 'tis thine; but know, it is as good
    To wither in my breast as in his blood.

'Here was thy father's bed, here in my breast;
Thou art the next of blood, and 'tis thy right:
Lo, in this hollow cradle take thy rest,
My throbbing heart shall rock thee day and night:
    There shall not be one minute in an hour
    Wherein I will not kiss my sweet love's flower.'

Thus weary of the world away she hies,
And yokes her silver doves; by whose swift aid
Their mistress, mounted, through the empty skies
In her light chariot quickly is convey'd;
    Holding their course to Paphos, where their
      queen
    Means to immure herself and not be seen.

LUCRECE

TO THE RIGHT HONOURABLE HENRY WRIOTHESLEY,

EARL OF SOUTHAMPTON, AND BARON OF TITCHFIELD.

THE love I dedicate to your Lordship is without end; whereof this pamphlet, without beginning, is but a superfluous moiety. The warrant I have of your honourable disposition, not the worth of my untutor'd lines, makes it assured of acceptance. What I have done is yours; what I have to do is yours; being part in all I have, devoted yours. Were my worth greater, my duty would show greater; meantime, as it is, it is bound to your Lordship, to whom I wish long life, still lengthen'd with all happiness.

Your Lordship's in all duty,

WILLIAM SHAKESPEARE.

THE ARGUMENT.

LUCIUS TARQUINIUS (for his excessive pride surnamed Superbus), after he had caused his own father-in-law Servius Tullius to be cruelly murder'd, and, contrary to the Roman laws and customs, not requiring or staying for the people's suffrages, had possest himself of the kingdom, went, accompanied with his sons and other noblemen of Rome, to besiege Ardea. During which siege the principal men of the army meeting one evening at the tent of Sextus Tarquinius, the king's son, in their discourses after supper every one commended the virtues of his own wife; among whom Collatinus extoll'd the incomparable chastity of his wife Lucretia. In that pleasant humour they all posted to Rome; and intending, by their secret and sudden arrival, to make trial of that which every one had before avoucht, only Collatinus finds his wife, though it were late in the night, spinning amongst her maids: the other ladies were all found dancing and revelling, or in several disports. Whereupon the noblemen yielded Collatinus the victory, and his wife the fame. At that time Sextus Tarquinius being inflamed with Lucrece' beauty, yet smothering his passions for the present, departed with the rest back to the camp; from whence he shortly after privily withdrew himself, and was (according to his estate) royally entertain'd and lodged by Lucrece at Collatium. The same night he treacherously stealeth into her chamber, violently ravisht her, and early in the morning speedeth away. Lucrece, in this lamentable plight, hastily dispatcheth messengers, one to Rome for her father, another to the camp for Collatine. They came, the one accompanied with Junius Brutus, the other with Publius Valerius; and finding Lucrece attired in mourning habit, demanded the cause of her sorrow. She, first taking an oath of them for her revenge, reveal'd the actor, and whole manner of his dealing, and withal suddenly stabb'd herself. Which done, with one consent they all vow'd to root out the whole hated family of the Tarquins; and bearing the dead body to Rome, Brutus acquainted the people with the doer and manner of the vile deed, with a bitter invective against the tyranny of the king: wherewith the people were so moved, that with one consent and a general acclamation the Tarquins were all exiled, and the state government changed from kings to consuls.

FROM the besieged Ardea all in post,
Borne by the trustless wings of false desire,
Lust-breathed Tarquin leaves the Roman host,
And to Collatium bears the lightless fire
Which, in pale embers hid, lurks to aspire
  And girdle with embracing flames the waist
  Of Collatine's fair love, Lucrece the chaste.

Haply that name of 'chaste' unhap'ly set
This bateless edge on his keen appetite;
When Collatine unwisely did not let
To praise the clear unmatched red and white
Which triumpht in that sky of his delight,
  Where mortal stars, as bright as heaven's
    beauties,
  With pure aspects did him peculiar duties.

For he the night before, in Tarquin's tent,
Unlockt the treasure of his happy state;
What priceless wealth the heavens had him lent
In the possession of his beauteous mate;
Reckoning his fortune at such high-proud rate,
  That kings might be espoused to more fame,
  But king nor peer to such a peerless dame.

O happiness enjoy'd but of a few!
And, if possest, as soon decay'd and done
As is the morning's silver-melting dew
Against the golden splendour of the sun!
An expired date, cancell'd ere well begun:
  Honour and beauty, in the owner's arms,
  Are weakly fortrest from a world of harms.

Beauty itself doth of itself persuade
The eyes of men without an orator;
What needeth, then, apologies be made,
To set forth that which is so singular?
Or why is Collatine the publisher
  Of that rich jewel he should keep unknown
  From thievish ears, because it is his own?

Perchance his boast of Lucrece' sovereignty
Suggested this proud issue of a king;
For by our ears our hearts oft tainted be:
Perchance that envy of so rich a thing,
Braving compare, disdainfully did sting
  His high-pitcht thoughts, that meaner men
    should vaunt
  That golden hap which their superiors want.

347

But some untimely thought did instigate
His all-too-timeless speed, if none of those:
His honour, his affairs, his friends, his state,
Neglected all, with swift intent he goes
To quench the coal which in his liver glows.
    O rash-false heat, wrapt in repentant cold,
    Thy hasty spring still blasts, and ne'er grows old!

When at Collatium this false lord arrived,
Well was he welcomed by the Roman dame,
Within whose face Beauty and Virtue strived
Which of them both should underprop her fame:
When Virtue bragg'd, Beauty would blush for
    shame,
    When Beauty boasted blushes, in despite
    Virtue would stain that o'er with silver white.

But Beauty, in that white intituled,
From Venus' doves doth challenge that fair field:
Then Virtue claims from Beauty Beauty's red,
Which Virtue gave the golden age to gild
Their silver cheeks, and call'd it then their shield;
    Teaching them thus to use it in the fight,—
    When shame assail'd, the red should fence the
    white.

This heraldry in Lucrece' face was seen,
Argued by Beauty's red and Virtue's white:
Of either's colour was the other queen,
Proving from world's minority their right:
Yet their ambition makes them still to fight;
    The sovereignty of either being so great,
    That oft they interchange each other's seat.

This silent war of lilies and of roses,
Which Tarquin view'd in her fair face's field,
In their pure ranks his traitor eye encloses;
Where, lest between them both it should be kill'd,
The coward captive vanquished doth yield
    To those two armies that would let him go,
    Rather than triumph in so false a foe.

Now thinks he that her husband's shallow
    tongue,—
The niggard prodigal that praised her so,—
In that high task hath done her beauty wrong,
Which far exceeds his barren skill to show:
Therefore that praise which Collatine doth owe
    Enchanted Tarquin answers with surmise,
    In silent wonder of still-gazing eyes.

This earthly saint, adored by this devil,
Little suspecteth the false worshipper;
For unstain'd thoughts do seldom dream on evil;
Birds never limed no secret bushes fear:
So guiltless she securely gives good cheer
    And reverend welcome to her princely guest,
    Whose inward ill no outward harm exprest:

For that he colour'd with his high estate,
Hiding base sin in plaits of majesty;
That nothing in him seem'd inordinate,
Save sometime too much wonder of his eye,
Which, having all, all could not satisfy;
    But, poorly rich, so wanteth in his store,
    That, cloy'd with much, he pineth still for more.

But she, that never coped with stranger eyes,
Could pick no meaning from their parling looks,
Nor read the subtle-shining secrecies
Writ in the glassy margents of such books:
She toucht no unknown baits, nor fear'd no hooks;
    Nor could she moralize his wanton sight,
    More than his eyes were open'd to the light.

He stories to her ears her husband's fame,
Won in the fields of fruitful Italy;
And decks with praises Collatine's high name,
Made glorious by his manly chivalry
With bruised arms and wreaths of victory:
    Her joy with heaved-up hand she doth express,
    And, wordless, so greets heaven for his success.

Far from the purpose of his coming thither,
He makes excuses for his being there:
No cloudy show of stormy blustering weather
Doth yet in his fair welkin once appear;
Till sable Night, mother of dread and fear,
    Upon the world dim darkness doth display,
    And in her vaulty prison stows the Day.

For then is Tarquin brought unto his bed,
Intending weariness with heavy sprite;
For, after supper, long he questioned
With modest Lucrece, and wore out the night:
Now leaden slumber with life's strength doth fight;
    And every one to rest themselves betake,
    Save thieves, and cares, and troubled minds,
    that wake.

As one of which doth Tarquin lie revolving
The sundry dangers of his will's obtaining;
Yet ever to obtain his will resolving,
Though weak-built hopes persuade him to ab-
    staining:
    Despair to gain doth traffic oft for gaining;
    And when great treasure is the meed proposed,
    Though death be adjunct, there's no death sup-
    posed.

Those that much covet are with gain so fond,
That what they have not, that which they possess,
They scatter and unloose it from their bond,
And so, by hoping more, they have but less;
Or, gaining more, the profit of excess
    Is but to surfeit, and such griefs sustain,
    That they prove bankrout in this poor-rich gain.

The aim of all is but to nurse the life
With honour, wealth, and ease, in waning age;
And in this aim there is such thwarting strife,
That one for all, or all for one we gage;
As life for honour in fell battle's rage;
    Honour for wealth; and oft that wealth doth cost
    The death of all, and all together lost.

So that in vent'ring ill we leave to be
The things we are for that which we expect;
And this ambitious foul infirmity,
In having much, torments us with defect
Of that we have: so then we do neglect
    The thing we have; and, all for want of wit,
    Make something nothing by augmenting it.

Such hazard now must doting Tarquin make,
Pawning his honour to obtain his lust;
And for himself himself he must forsake:
Then where is truth, if there be no self-trust?
When shall he think to find a stranger just,
    When he himself himself confounds, betrays
      To slanderous tongues and wretched hateful
      days?

Now stole upon the time the dead of night,
When heavy sleep had closed up mortal eyes:
No comfortable star did lend his light,
No noise but owls' and wolves' death-boding cries;
Now serves the season that they may surprise
    The silly lambs: pure thoughts are dead and
      still,
    While lust and murder wakes to stain and kill.

And now this lustful lord leapt from his bed,
Throwing his mantle rudely o'er his arm;
Is madly tost between desire and dread;
Th'one sweetly flatters, th'other feareth harm;
But honest fear, bewitcht with lust's foul charm,
    Doth too-too oft betake him to retire,
    Beaten away by brain-sick rude desire.

His falchion on a flint he softly smiteth,
That from the cold stone sparks of fire do fly;
Whereat a waxen torch forthwith he lighteth,
Which must be lode-star to his lustful eye;
And to the flame thus speaks advisedly,
    'As from this cold flint I enforced this fire,
    So Lucrece must I force to my desire.'

Here pale with fear he doth premeditate
The dangers of his loathsome enterprise,
And in his inward mind he doth debate
What following sorrow may on this arise:
Then looking scornfully, he doth despise
    His naked armour of still-slaughter'd lust,
    And justly thus controls his thoughts unjust:

'Fair torch, burn out thy light, and lend it not
To darken her whose light excelleth thine:
And die, unhallow'd thoughts, before you blot
With your uncleanness that which is divine;
Offer pure incense to so pure a shrine:
    Let fair humanity abhor the deed
    That spots and stains love's modest snow-
      white weed.

'O shame to knighthood and to shining arms!
O foul dishonour to my household's grave!
O impious act, including all foul harms!
A martial man to be soft fancy's slave!
True valour still a true respect should have;
    Then my digression is so vile, so base,
    That it will live engraven in my face.

'Yea, though I die, the scandal will survive,
And be an eye-sore in my golden coat;
Some loathsome dash the herald will contrive,
To cipher me how fondly I did dote;
That my posterity, shamed with the note,
    Shall curse my bones, and hold it for no sin
    To wish that I their father had not bin.

'What win I, if I gain the thing I seek?
A dream, a breath, a froth of fleeting joy.
Who buys a minute's mirth to wail a week?
Or sells eternity to get a toy?
For one sweet grape who will the vine destroy?
    Or what fond begger, but to touch the crown,
    Would with the sceptre straight be strucken
      down?

'If Collatinus dream of my intent,
Will he not wake, and in a desperate rage
Post hither, this vile purpose to prevent?
This siege that hath engirt his marriage,
This blur to youth, this sorrow to the sage,
    This dying virtue, this surviving shame,
    Whose crime will bear an ever-during blame?

'O, what excuse can my invention make,
When thou shalt charge me with so black a deed?
Will not my tongue be mute, my frail joints shake,
Mine eyes forgo their light, my false heart bleed?
The guilt being great, the fear doth still exceed;
    And extreme fear can neither fight nor fly,
    But coward-like with trembling terror die.

'Had Collatinus kill'd my son or sire,
Or lain in ambush to betray my life,
Or were he not my dear friend, this desire
Might have excuse to work upon his wife,
As in revenge or quittal of such strife:
    But as he is my kinsman, my dear friend,
    The shame and fault finds no excuse nor end.

'Shameful it is;—ay, if the fact be known:
Hateful it is;—there is no hate in loving:
I'll beg her love;—but she is not her own:
The worst is but denial and reproving:
My will is strong, past reason's weak removing.
    Who fears a sentence or an old man's saw
    Shall by a painted cloth be kept in awe.'

Thus, graceless, holds he disputation
'Tween frozen conscience and hot burning will,
And with good thoughts makes dispensation,
Urging the worser sense for vantage still;
Which in a moment doth confound and kill
    All pure effects, and doth so far proceed,
    That what is vile shows like a virtuous deed.

Quoth he, 'She took me kindly by the hand,
And gazed for tidings in my eager eyes,
Fearing some hard news from the warlike band,
Where her beloved Collatinus lies.
O, how her fear did make her colour rise!
    First red as roses that on lawn we lay,
    Then white as lawn, the roses took away.

'And how her hand, in my hand being lockt,
Forced it to tremble with her loyal fear!
Which struck her sad, and then it faster rockt,
Until her husband's welfare she did hear;
Whereat she smiled with so sweet a cheer,
    That had Narcissus seen her as she stood,
    Self-love had never drown'd him in the flood.

'Why hunt I, then, for colour or excuses?
All orators are dumb when beauty pleadeth;
Poor wretches have remorse in poor abuses;
Love thrives not in the heart that shadows dread-
   eth:
Affection is my captain, and he leadeth;
   And when his gaudy banner is display'd,
   The coward fights, and will not be dismay'd.

'Then, childish fear avaunt! debating die!
Respect and reason wait on wrinkled age!
My heart shall never countermand mine eye:
Sad pause and deep regard beseems the sage;
My part is youth, and beats these from the stage:
   Desire my pilot is, beauty my prize;
   Then who fears sinking where such treasure
     lies?'

As corn o'ergrown by weeds, so heedful fear
Is almost choked by unresisted lust.
Away he steals with open listening ear,
Full of foul hope and full of fond mistrust;
Both which, as servitors to the unjust,
   So cross him with their opposite persuasion,
   That now he vows a league, and now invasion.

Within his thought her heavenly image sits,
And in the self-same seat sits Collatine:
That eye which looks on her confounds his wits;
That eye which him beholds, as more divine,
Unto a view so false will not incline;
   But with a pure appeal seeks to the heart,
   Which once corrupted takes the worser part;

And therein heartens up his servile powers,
Who, flatter'd by their leader's jocund show,
Stuff up his lust, as minutes fill up hours;
And as their captain, so their pride doth grow,
Paying more slavish tribute than they owe.
   By reprobate desire thus madly led,
   The Roman lord marcheth to Lucrece' bed.

The locks between her chamber and his will,
Each one by him enforced, retires his ward;
But, as they open, they all rate his ill,
Which drives the creeping thief to some regard:
The threshold grates the door to have him heard;
   Night-wandering weasels shriek to see him
     there;
   They fright him, yet he still pursues his fear.

As each unwilling portal yields him way,
Through little vents and crannies of the place
The wind wars with his torch to make him stay,
And blows the smoke of it into his face,
Extinguishing his conduct in this case;
   But his hot heart, which fond desire doth scorch,
   Puffs forth another wind that fires the torch:

And being lighted, by the light he spies
Lucretia's glove, wherein her needle sticks:
He takes it from the rushes where it lies,
And griping it, the needle his finger pricks;
As who should say, 'This glove to wanton tricks
   Is not inured; return again in haste;
   Thou see'st our mistress' ornaments are chaste.'

But all these poor forbiddings could not stay him;
He in the worst sense consters their denial:
The doors, the wind, the glove, that did delay him,
He takes for accidental things of trial;
Or as those bars which stop the hourly dial,
   Who with a lingering stay his course doth let,
   Till every minute pays the hour his debt.

'So, so,' quoth he, 'these lets attend the time,
Like little frosts that sometime threat the spring,
To add a more rejoicing to the prime,
And give the sneaped birds more cause to sing.
Pain pays the income of each precious thing;
   Huge rocks, high winds, strong pirates, shelves
     and sands,
   The merchant fears, ere rich at home he lands.'

Now is he come unto the chamber-door
That shuts him from the heaven of his thought,
Which with a yielding latch, and with no more,
Hath barr'd him from the blessed thing he sought.
So from himself impiety hath wrought,
   That for his prey to pray he doth begin,
   As if the heavens should countenance his sin.

But in the midst of his unfruitful prayer,
Having solicited th'eternal power
That his foul thoughts might compass his fair fair,
And they would stand auspicious to the hour,
Even there he starts:—quoth he, 'I must deflower:
   The powers to whom I pray abhor this fact,
   How can they, then, assist me in the act?

'Then Love and Fortune be my gods, my guide!
My will is backt with resolution:
Thoughts are but dreams till their effects be tried;
The blackest sin is clear'd with absolution;
Against love's fire fear's frost hath dissolution.
   The eye of heaven is out, and misty night
   Covers the shame that follows sweet delight.'

This said, his guilty hand pluckt up the latch,
And with his knee the door he opens wide.
The dove sleeps fast that this night-owl will catch:
Thus treason works ere traitors be espied.
Who sees the lurking serpent steps aside;
   But she, sound sleeping, fearing no such thing,
   Lies at the mercy of his mortal sting.

Into the chamber wickedly he stalks,
And gazeth on her yet-unstained bed.
The curtains being close, about he walks,
Rolling his greedy eyeballs in his head:
By their high treason is his heart misled;
   Which gives the watch-word to his hand full
     soon
   To draw the cloud that hides the silver moon.

Look, as the fair and fiery-pointed sun,
Rushing from forth a cloud, bereaves our sight;
Even so, the curtain drawn, his eyes begun
To wink, being blinded with a greater light:
Whether it is that she reflects so bright,
   That dazzleth them, or else some shame sup-
     posed;
   But blind they are, and keep themselves en-
     closed.

O, had they in that darksome prison died!
Then had they seen the period of their ill;
Then Collatine again, by Lucrece' side,
In his clear bed might have reposed still:
  But they must ope, this blessed league to kill;
    And holy-thoughted Lucrece to their sight
    Must sell her joy, her life, her world's delight.

Her lily hand her rosy cheek lies under,
Cozening the pillow of a lawful kiss;
Who, therefore angry, seems to part in sunder,
Swelling on either side to want his bliss;
  Between whose hills her head entombed is:
    Where, like a virtuous monument, she lies,
    To be admired of lewd unhallow'd eyes.

Without the bed her other fair hand was,
On the green coverlet; whose perfect white
Show'd like an April daisy on the grass,
With pearly sweat, resembling dew of night.
  Her eyes, like marigolds, had sheathed their light,
    And canopied in darkness sweetly lay,
    Till they might open to adorn the day.

Her hair, like golden threads, play'd with her
  breath;
O modest wantons! wanton modesty!
Showing life's triumph in the map of death,
And death's dim look in life's mortality:
  Each in her sleep themselves so beautify,
    As if between them twain there were no strife,
    But that life lived in death, and death in life.

Her breasts, like ivory globes circled with blue,
A pair of maiden worlds unconquered,
Save of their lord no bearing yoke they knew,
And him by oath they truly honoured.
  These worlds in Tarquin new ambition bred;
    Who, like a foul usurper, went about
    From this fair throne to heave the owner out.

What could he see but mightily he noted?
What did he note but strongly he desired?
What he beheld, on that he firmly doted,
And in his will his wilful eye he tired.
  With more than admiration he admired
    Her azure veins, her alabaster skin,
    Her coral lips, her snow-white dimpled chin.

As the grim lion fawneth o'er his prey,
Sharp hunger by the conquest satisfied,
So o'er this sleeping soul doth Tarquin stay,
His rage of lust by gazing qualified;
  Slackt, not supprest; for standing by her side,
    His eye, which late this mutiny restrains,
    Unto a greater uproar tempts his veins:

And they, like straggling slaves for pillage fighting,
Obdurate vassals fell exploits effecting,
In bloody death and ravishment delighting,
Nor children's tears nor mothers' groans respect-
  ing,
  Swell in their pride, the onset still expecting:
    Anon his beating heart, alarum striking,
    Gives the hot charge, and bids them do their
    liking.

His drumming heart cheers up his burning eye,
His eye commends the leading to his hand;
His hand, as proud of such a dignity,
Smoking with pride, marcht on to make his stand
On her bare breast, the heart of all her land;
  Whose ranks of blue veins, as his hand did scale,
  Left their round turrets destitute and pale.

They, mustering to the quiet cabinet
Where their dear governess and lady lies,
Do tell her she is dreadfully beset,
And fright her with confusion of their cries:
  She, much amazed, breaks ope her lockt-up eyes,
  Who, peeping forth this tumult to behold,
  Are by his flaming torch dimm'd and controll'd.

Imagine her as one in dead of night
From forth dull sleep by dreadful fancy waking,
That thinks she hath beheld some ghastly sprite,
Whose grim aspect sets every joint a-shaking;
  What terror 'tis! but she, in worser taking,
  From sleep disturbed, heedfully doth view
  The sight which makes supposed terror true.

Wrapt and confounded in a thousand fears,
Like to a new-kill'd bird she trembling lies;
She dares not look; yet, winking, there appears
Quick-shifting antics, ugly in her eyes:
  Such shadows are the weak brain's forgeries;
  Who, angry that the eyes fly from their lights,
  In darkness daunts them with more dreadful
    sights.

His hand, that yet remains upon her breast,—
Rude ram, to batter such an ivory wall!—
May feel her heart—poor citizen!—distrest,
Wounding itself to death, rise up and fall,
Beating her bulk, that his hand shakes withal.
  This moves in him more rage, and lesser pity,
  To make the breach, and enter this sweet city.

First, like a trumpet, doth his tongue begin
To sound a parley to his heartless foe;
Who o'er the white sheet peers her whiter chin,
The reason of this rash alarm to know,
Which he by dumb demeanour seeks to show;
  But she with vehement prayers urgeth still
  Under what colour he commits this ill.

Thus he replies: 'The colour in thy face—
That even for anger makes the lily pale,
And the red rose blush at her own disgrace—
Shall plead for me and tell my loving tale:
Under that colour am I come to scale
  Thy never-conquer'd fort: the fault is thine,
  For those thine eyes betray thee unto mine.

'Thus I forestall thee, if thou mean to chide:
Thy beauty hath ensnared thee to this night,
Where thou with patience must my will abide;
My will that marks thee for my earth's delight,
Which I to conquer sought with all my might;
  But as reproof and reason beat it dead,
  By thy bright beauty was it newly bred.

'I see what crosses my attempt will bring;
I know what thorns the growing rose defends;
I think the honey guarded with a sting;
All this beforehand counsel comprehends:
But will is deaf, and hears no heedful friends;
    Only he hath an eye to gaze on beauty,
    And dotes on what he looks, 'gainst law or duty.

'I have debated, even in my soul,
What wrong, what shame, what sorrow I shall breed;
But nothing can affection's course control,
Or stop the headlong fury of his speed.
I know repentant tears ensue the deed,
    Reproach, disdain, and deadly enmity;
    Yet strive I to embrace mine infamy.'

This said, he shakes aloft his Roman blade,
Which, like a falcon towering in the skies,
Coucheth the fowl below with his wings' shade,
Whose crooked beak threats if he mount he dies:
So under his insulting falchion lies
    Harmless Lucretia, marking what he tells
    With trembling fear, as fowl hear falcon's bells.

'Lucrece,' quoth he, 'this night I must enjoy thee:
If thou deny, then force must work my way,
For in thy bed I purpose to destroy thee:
That done, some worthless slave of thine I'll slay,
To kill thine honour with thy life's decay;
    And in thy dead arms do I mean to place him,
    Swearing I slew him, seeing thee embrace him.

'So thy surviving husband shall remain
The scornful mark of every open eye;
Thy kinsmen hang their heads at this disdain,
Thy issue blurr'd with nameless bastardy:
And thou, the author of their obloquy,
    Shalt have thy trespass cited up in rimes,
    And sung by children in succeeding times.

'But if thou yield, I rest thy secret friend:
The fault unknown is as a thought unacted;
A little harm done to a great good end
For lawful policy remains enacted.
The poisonous simple sometime is compacted
    In a pure compound; being so applied,
    His venom in effect is purified.

'Then, for thy husband and thy children's sake,
Tender my suit: bequeath not to their lot
The shame that from them no device can take,
The blemish that will never be forgot;
Worse than a slavish wipe or birth-hour's blot:
    For marks descried in men's nativity
    Are nature's faults, not their own infamy.'

Here with a cockatrice' dead-killing eye
He rouseth up himself, and makes a pause;
While she, the picture of true piety,
Like a white hind under the gripe's sharp claws,
Pleads, in a wilderness where are no laws,
    To the rough beast that knows no gentle right,
    Nor aught obeys but his foul appetite.

But when a black-faced cloud the world doth threat,
In his dim mist the aspiring mountains hiding,
From earth's dark womb some gentle gust doth get,
Which blows these pitchy vapours from their biding,
Hindering their present fall by this dividing;
    So his unhallow'd haste her words delays,
    And moody Pluto winks while Orpheus plays.

Yet, foul night-waking cat, he doth but dally,
While in his hold-fast foot the weak mouse panteth:
Her sad behaviour feeds his vulture folly,
A swallowing gulf that even in plenty wanteth:
His ear her prayers admits, but his heart granteth
    No penetrable entrance to her plaining:
    Tears harden lust, though marble wear with raining.

Her pity-pleading eyes are sadly fixed
In the remorseless wrinkles of his face;
Her modest eloquence with sighs is mixed,
Which to her oratory adds more grace.
She puts the period often from his place;
    And midst the sentence so her accent breaks,
    That twice she doth begin ere once she speaks.

She conjures him by high almighty Jove,
By knighthood, gentry, and sweet friendship's oath,
By her untimely tears, her husband's love,
By holy human law, and common troth,
By heaven and earth, and all the power of both,
    That to his borrow'd bed he make retire,
    And stoop to honour, not to foul desire.

Quoth she, 'Reward not hospitality
With such black payment as thou hast pretended;
Mud not the fountain that gave drink to thee;
Mar not the thing that cannot be amended;
End thy ill aim before thy shoot be ended;
    He is no woodman that doth bend his bow
    To strike a poor unseasonable doe.

'My husband is thy friend,—for his sake spare me;
Thyself art mighty,—for thine own sake leave me;
Myself a weakling,—do not, then, ensnare me;
Thou look'st not like deceit,—do not deceive me.
My sighs, like whirlwinds, labour hence to heave thee:
    If ever man were moved with woman's moans,
    Be moved with my tears, my sighs, my groans:

'All which together, like a troubled ocean,
Beat at thy rocky and wrack-threatening heart,
To soften it with their continual motion;
For stones dissolved to water do convert.
O, if no harder than a stone thou art,
    Melt at my tears, and be compassionate!
    Soft pity enters at an iron gate.

'In Tarquin's likeness I did entertain thee:
Hast thou put on his shape to do him shame?
To all the host of heaven I complain me,
Thou wrong'st his honour, wound'st his princely
name.
Thou art not what thou seem'st; and if the same,
  Thou seem'st not what thou art, a god, a king;
  For kings like gods should govern every thing.

'How will thy shame be seeded in thine age,
When thus thy vices bud before thy spring!
If in thy hope thou darest do such outrage,
What darest thou not when once thou art a king?
O, be remember'd, no outrageous thing
  From vassal actors can be wiped away;
  Then kings' misdeeds cannot be hid in clay.

'This deed will make thee only loved for fear;
But happy monarchs still are fear'd for love:
With foul offenders thou perforce must bear,
When they in thee the like offences prove:
If but for fear of this, thy will remove;
  For princes are the glass, the school, the book,
  Where subjects' eyes do learn, do read, do look.

'And wilt thou be the school where Lust shall learn?
Must he in thee read lectures of such shame?
Wilt thou be glass wherein it shall discern
Authority for sin, warrant for blame,
To privilege dishonour in thy name?
  Thou back'st reproach against long-living laud,
  And makest fair reputation but a bawd.

'Hast thou command? by him that gave it thee,
From a pure heart command thy rebel will:
Draw not thy sword to guard iniquity,
For it was lent thee all that brood to kill.
Thy princely office how canst thou fulfil,
  When, pattern'd by thy fault, foul Sin may say,
  He learnt to sin, and thou didst teach the way?

'Think but how vile a spectacle it were,
To view thy present trespass in another.
Men's faults do seldom to themselves appear;
Their own transgressions partially they smother:
This guilt would seem death-worthy in thy
brother.
  O, how are they wrapt in with infamies
  That from their own misdeeds askance their
eyes!

'To thee, to thee, my heaved-up hands appeal,
Not to seducing lust, thy rash relier:
I sue for exiled majesty's repeal;
Let him return, and flattering thoughts retire:
His true respect will prison false desire,
  And wipe the dim mist from thy doting eyne,
  That thou shalt see thy state, and pity mine.'

'Have done,' quoth he: 'my uncontrolled tide
Turns not, but swells the higher by this let.
Small lights are soon blown out, huge fires abide,
And with the wind in greater fury fret:
The petty streams that pay a daily debt
  To their salt sovereign, with their fresh falls'
haste
  Add to his flow, but alter not his taste.'

'Thou art,' quoth she, 'a sea, a sovereign king;
And, lo, there falls into thy boundless flood
Black lust, dishonour, shame, misgoverning,
Who seek to stain the ocean of thy blood.
If all these petty ills shall change thy good,
  Thy sea within a puddle's womb is hearsed,
  And not the puddle in thy sea dispersed.

'So shall these slaves be king, and thou their slave;
Thou nobly base, they basely dignified;
Thou their fair life, and they thy fouler grave:
Thou loathed in their shame, they in thy pride:
The lesser thing should not the greater hide;
  The cedar stoops not to the base shrub's foot,
  But low shrubs wither at the cedar's root.

'So let thy thoughts, low vassals to thy state'—
'No more,' quoth he; 'by heaven, I will not hear
thee:
Yield to my love; if not, enforced hate,
Instead of love's coy touch, shall rudely tear thee;
That done, despitefully I mean to bear thee
  Unto the base bed of some rascal groom,
  To be thy partner in this shameful doom.'

This said, he sets his foot upon the light,
For light and lust are deadly enemies:
Shame folded up in blind-concealing night,
When most unseen, then most doth tyrannize.
The wolf hath seized his prey, the poor lamb
cries;
  Till with her own white fleece her voice con-
troll'd
  Entombs her outcry in her lips' sweet fold:

For with the nightly linen that she wears
He pens her piteous clamours in her head;
Cooling his hot face in the chastest tears
That ever modest eyes with sorrow shed.
O, that prone lust should stain so pure a bed!
  The spots whereof could weeping purify,
  Her tears should drop on them perpetually.

But she hath lost a dearer thing than life,
And he hath won what he would lose again:
This forced league doth force a further strife;
This momentary joy breeds months of pain;
This hot desire converts to cold disdain:
  Pure Chastity is rifled of her store,
  And Lust, the thief, far poorer than before.

Look, as the full-fed hound or gorged hawk,
Unapt for tender smell or speedy flight,
Make slow pursuit, or altogether balk
The prey wherein by nature they delight;
So surfeit-taking Tarquin fares this night:
  His taste delicious, in digestion souring,
  Devours his will, that lived by foul devouring.

O, deeper sin than bottomless conceit
Can comprehend in still imagination!
Drunken Desire must vomit his receipt,
Ere he can see his own abomination.
While Lust is in his pride, no exclamation
  Can curb his heat, or rein his rash desire,
  Till, like a jade, Self-will himself doth tire.

And then with lank and lean discolour'd cheek,
With heavy eye, knit brow, and strengthless pace,
Feeble Desire, all recreant, poor, and meek,
Like to a bankrout beggar wails his case:
   The flesh being proud, Desire doth fight with
      Grace,
     For there it revels; and when that decays,
     The guilty rebel for remission prays.

So fares it with this faultful lord of Rome,
Who this accomplishment so hotly chased;
For now against himself he sounds this doom,—
That through the length of times he stands dis-
   graced:
Besides, his soul's fair temple is defaced;
     To whose weak ruins muster troops of cares,
     To ask the spotted princess how she fares.

She says, her subjects with foul insurrection
Have batter'd down her consecrated wall,
And by their mortal fault brought in subjection
Her immortality, and made her thrall
To living death and pain perpetual:
     Which in her prescience she controlled still,
     But her foresight could not forestall their will.

Even in this thought through the dark night he
   stealeth,
A captive victor that hath lost in gain;
Bearing away the wound that nothing healeth,
The scar that will, despite of cure, remain;
Leaving his spoil perplext in greater pain.
     She bears the load of lust he left behind,
     And he the burthen of a guilty mind.

He like a thievish dog creeps sadly thence;
She like a wearied lamb lies panting there;
He scowls, and hates himself for his offence;
She, desperate, with her nails her flesh doth tear;
He faintly flies, sweating with guilty fear;
     She stays, exclaiming on the direful night;
     He runs, and chides his vanisht, loathed
      delight.

He thence departs a heavy convertite;
She there remains a hopeless castaway;
He in his speed looks for the morning light;
She prays she never may behold the day,
'For day,' quoth she, 'night's scapes doth open lay,
     And my true eyes have never practised how
     To cloak offences with a cunning brow.

'They think not but that every eye can see
The same disgrace which they themselves behold;
And therefore would they still in darkness be,
To have their unseen sin remain untold;
For they their guilt with weeping will unfold,
     And grave, like water that doth eat in steel,
     Upon my cheeks what helpless shame I feel.'

Here she exclaims against repose and rest,
And bids her eyes hereafter still be blind.
She wakes her heart by beating on her breast,
And bids it leap from thence, where it may find
Some purer chest to close so pure a mind.
     Frantic with grief thus breathes she forth her
      spite
     Against the unseen secrecy of night:

'O comfort-killing Night, image of hell!
Dim register and notary of shame!
Black stage for tragedies and murders fell!
Vast sin-concealing chaos! nurse of blame!
Blind muffled bawd! dark harbour for defame!
     Grim cave of death! whispering conspirator
     With close-tongued treason and the ravisher!

'O hateful, vaporous, and foggy Night!
Since thou art guilty of my cureless crime,
Muster thy mists to meet the eastern light,
Make war against proportion'd course of time;
Or if thou wilt permit the sun to climb
     His wonted height, yet ere he go to bed,
     Knit poisonous clouds about his golden head.

'With rotten damps ravish the morning air;
Let their exhaled unwholesome breaths make sick
The life of purity, the supreme fair,
Ere he arrive his weary noon-tide prick;
And let thy misty vapours march so thick,
     That in their smoky ranks his smother'd light
     May set at noon, and make perpetual night.

'Were Tarquin Night, as he is but Night's child,
The silver-shining queen he would distain;
Her twinkling handmaids too, by him defiled,
Through Night's black bosom should not peep
   again:
So should I have co-partners in my pain;
     And fellowship in woe doth woe assuage,
     As palmers' chat makes short their pilgrimage.

'Where now I have no one to blush with me,
To cross their arms, and hang their heads with
   mine,
To mask their brows, and hide their infamy;
But I alone alone must sit and pine,
Seasoning the earth with showers of silver brine,
     Mingling my talk with tears, my grief with
      groans,
     Poor wasting monuments of lasting moans.

'O Night, thou furnace of foul-reeking smoke,
Let not the jealous Day behold that face
Which underneath thy black all-hiding cloak
Immodestly lies martyr'd with disgrace!
Keep still possession of thy gloomy place,
     That all the faults which in thy reign are made
     May likewise be sepulchred in thy shade!

'Make me not object to the tell-tale Day!
The light will show, character'd in my brow,
The story of sweet chastity's decay,
The impious breach of holy wedlock vow:
Yea, the illiterate, that know not how
     To cipher what is writ in learned books,
     Will quote my loathsome trespass in my looks.

'The nurse, to still her child, will tell my story,
And fright her crying babe with Tarquin's name;
The orator, to deck his oratory,
Will couple my reproach to Tarquin's shame;
Feast-finding minstrels, tuning my defame,
     Will tie the hearers to attend each line,
     How Tarquin wronged me, I Collatine.

'Let my good name, that senseless reputation,
For Collatine's dear love be kept unspotted:
If that be made a theme for disputation,
The branches of another root are rotted,
And undeserved reproach to him allotted
    That is as clear from this attaint of mine
    As I, ere this, was pure to Collatine.

'O unseen shame! invisible disgrace!
O unfelt sore! crest-wounding, private scar!
Reproach is stampt in Collatinus' face,
And Tarquin's eye may read the mot afar,
How he in peace is wounded, not in war.
    Alas, how many bear such shameful blows,
    Which not themselves, but he that gives them
      knows!

'If, Collatine, thine honour lay in me,
From me by strong assault it is bereft.
My honey lost, and I, a drone-like bee,
Have no perfection of my summer left,
But robb'd and ransackt by injurious theft:
    In thy weak hive a wandering wasp hath crept,
    And suckt the honey which thy chaste bee kept.

'Yet am I guilty of thy honour's wrack,—
Yet for thy honour did I entertain him;
Coming from thee, I could not put him back,
For it had been dishonour to disdain him:
Besides, of weariness he did complain him,
    And talkt of virtue:—O unlookt-for evil,
    When virtue is profaned in such a devil!

'Why should the worm intrude the maiden bud?
Or hateful cuckoos hatch in sparrows' nests?
Or toads infect fair founts with venom mud?
Or tyrant folly lurk in gentle breasts?
Or kings be breakers of their own behests?
    But no perfection is so absolute,
    That some impurity doth not pollute.

'The aged man that coffers-up his gold
Is plagued with cramps and gouts and painful fits;
And scarce hath eyes his treasure to behold,
And like still-pining Tantalus he sits,
And useless barns the harvest of his wits;
    Having no other pleasure of his gain!
    But torment that it cannot cure his pain.

'So then he hath it when he cannot use it,
And leaves it to be master'd by his young;
Who in their pride do presently abuse it:
Their father was too weak, and they too strong,
To hold their cursed-blessed fortune long.
    The sweets we wish for turn to loathed sours
    Even in the moment that we call them ours.

'Unruly blasts wait on the tender spring;
Unwholesome weeds take root with precious
    flowers;
The adder hisses where the sweet birds sing;
What virtue breeds iniquity devours:
We have no good that we can say is ours,
    But ill-annexed Opportunity
    Or kills his life or else his quality.

'O Opportunity, thy guilt is great!
'Tis thou that executest the traitor's treason;
Thou sett'st the wolf where he the lamb may get;
Whoever plots the sin, thou point'st the season;
'Tis thou that spurn'st at right, at law, at reason;
    And in thy shady cell, where none may spy him,
    Sits Sin, to seize the souls that wander by him.

'Thou makest the vestal violate her oath;
Thou blow'st the fire when temperance is thaw'd;
Thou smother'st honesty, thou murder'st troth;
Thou foul abettor! thou notorious bawd!
Thou plantest scandal, and displacest laud:
    Thou ravisher, thou traitor, thou false thief,
    Thy honey turns to gall, thy joy to grief!

'Thy secret pleasure turns to open shame,
Thy private feasting to a public fast,
Thy smoothing titles to a ragged name,
Thy sugar'd tongue to bitter wormwood taste:
Thy violent vanities can never last.
    How comes it, then, vile Opportunity,
    Being so bad, such numbers seek for thee?

'When wilt thou be the humble suppliant's friend,
And bring him where his suit may be obtained?
When wilt thou sort an hour great strifes to end?
Or free that soul which wretchedness hath
    chained?
Give physic to the sick, ease to the pained?
    The poor, lame, blind, halt, creep, cry out for
      thee;
    But they ne'er meet with Opportunity.

'The patient dies while the physician sleeps;
The orphan pines while the oppressor feeds;
Justice is feasting while the widow weeps;
Advice is sporting while infection breeds:
Thou grant'st no time for charitable deeds:
    Wrath, envy, treason, rape, and murder's rages,
    Thy heinous hours wait on them as their pages.

'When Truth and Virtue have to do with thee,
A thousand crosses keep them from thy aid:
They buy thy help; but Sin ne'er gives a fee,
He gratis comes; and thou art well appaid
As well to hear as grant what he hath said.
    My Collatine would else have come to me
    When Tarquin did, but he was stay'd by thee.

'Guilty thou art of murder and of theft,
Guilty of perjury and subornation,
Guilty of treason, forgery, and shift,
Guilty of incest, that abomination;
An accessary by thine inclination
    To all sins past, and all that are to come,
    From the creation to the general doom.

'Mis-shapen Time, copesmate of ugly Night,
Swift subtle post, carrier of grisly care,
Eater of youth, false slave to false delight,
Base watch of woes, sin's pack-horse, virtue's
    snare;
Thou nursest all, and murder'st all that are:
    O, hear me, then, injurious, shifting Time!
    Be guilty of my death, since of my crime.

'Why hath thy servant Opportunity
Betray'd the hours thou gavest me to repose,
Cancell'd my fortunes, and enchained me
To endless date of never-ending woes?
Time's office is to fine the hate of foes;
    To eat up errors by opinion bred,
    Not spend the dowry of a lawful bed.

'Time's glory is to calm contending kings,
To unmask falsehood, and bring truth to light,
To stamp the seal of time in aged things,
To wake the morn, and sentinel the night,
To wrong the wronger till he render right,
    To ruinate proud buildings with thy hours,
    And smear with dust their glittering golden
      towers;

'To fill with worm-holes stately monuments,
To feed oblivion with decay of things,
To blot old books and alter their contents,
To pluck the quills from ancient ravens' wings,
To dry the old oak's sap, and cherish springs,
    To spoil antiquities of hammer'd steel,
    And turn the giddy round of Fortune's wheel;

'To show the beldam daughters of her daughter,
To make the child a man, the man a child,
To slay the tiger that doth live by slaughter,
To tame the unicorn and lion wild,
To mock the subtle in themselves beguiled,
    To cheer the ploughman with increaseful crops,
    And waste huge stones with little water-drops.

'Why work'st thou mischief in thy pilgrimage,
Unless thou couldst return to make amends?
One poor retiring minute in an age
Would purchase thee a thousand thousand friends,
Lending him wit that to bad debtors lends:
    O, this dread night, wouldst thou one hour
      come back,
    I could prevent this storm, and shun thy wrack!

'Thou ceaseless lackey to eternity,
With some mischance cross Tarquin in his flight:
Devise extremes beyond extremity,
To make him curse this cursed crimeful night:
Let ghastly shadows his lewd eyes affright;
    And the dire thought of his committed evil
    Shape every bush a hideous shapeless devil.

'Disturb his hours of rest with restless trances,
Afflict him in his bed with bedrid groans;
Let there bechance him pitiful mischances,
To make him moan; but pity not his moans:
Stone him with harden'd hearts, harder than
    stones;
    And let mild women to him lose their mildness,
    Wilder to him than tigers in their wildness.

'Let him have time to tear his curled hair,
Let him have time against himself to rave,
Let him have time of Time's help to despair,
Let him have time to live a loathed slave,
Let him have time a beggar's orts to crave,
    And time to see one that by alms doth live
    Disdain to him disdained scraps to give.

'Let him have time to see his friends his foes,
And merry fools to mock at him resort;
Let him have time to mark how slow time goes
In time of sorrow, and how swift and short
His time of folly and his time of sport;
    And ever let his unrecalling crime
    Have time to wail th' abusing of his time.

'O Time, thou tutor both to good and bad,
Teach me to curse him that thou taught'st this ill!
At his own shadow let the thief run mad,
Himself himself seek every hour to kill!
Such wretched hands such wretched blood should
    spill;
    For who so base would such an office have
    As slanderous death's-man to so base a slave?

'The baser is he, coming from a king,
To shame his hope with deeds degenerate:
The mightier man, the mightier is the thing
That makes him honour'd, or begets him hate;
For greatest scandal waits on greatest state.
    The moon being clouded presently is mist,
    But little stars may hide them when they list.

'The crow may bathe his coal-black wings in mire,
And unperceived fly with the filth away;
But if the like the snow-white swan desire,
The stain upon his silver down will stay.
Poor grooms are sightless night, kings glorious
    day:
    Gnats are unnoted wheresoe'er they fly,
    But eagles gazed upon with every eye.

'Out, idle words, servants to shallow fools!
Unprofitable sounds, weak arbitrators!
Busy yourselves in skill-contending schools;
Debate where leisure serves with dull debaters;
To trembling clients be you mediators:
    For me, I force not argument a straw,
    Since that my case is past the help of law.

'In vain I rail at Opportunity,
At Time, at Tarquin, and uncheerful Night;
In vain I cavil with mine infamy,
In vain I spurn at my confirm'd despite:
This helpless smoke of words doth me no right.
    The remedy indeed to do me good
    Is to let forth my foul defiled blood.

'Poor hand, why quiver'st thou at this decree?
Honour thyself to rid me of this shame;
For if I die, my honour lives in thee;
But if I live, thou livest in my defame:
Since thou couldst not defend thy loyal dame,
    And wast afeard to scratch her wicked foe,
    Kill both thyself and her for yielding so.'

This said, from her betumbled couch she starteth,
To find some desperate instrument of death:
But this no slaughter-house no tool imparteth
To make more vent for passage of her breath;
Which, thronging through her lips, so vanisheth
    As smoke from Aetna, that in air consumes,
    Or that which from discharged cannon fumes.

'In vain,' quoth she, 'I live, and seek in vain
Some happy mean to end a hapless life.
I fear'd by Tarquin's falchion to be slain,
Yet for the self-same purpose seek a knife:
But when I fear'd I was a loyal wife:
   So am I now:—O no, that cannot be;
   Of that true type hath Tarquin rifled me.

'O, that is gone for which I sought to live,
And therefore now I need not fear to die.
To clear this spot by death, at least I give
A badge of fame to slander's livery;
A dying life to living infamy:
   Poor helpless help, the treasure stoln away,
   To burn the guiltless casket where it lay!

'Well, well, dear Collatine, thou shalt not know
The stained taste of violated troth;
I will not wrong thy true affection so,
To flatter thee with an infringed oath;
This bastard graff shall never come to growth:
   He shall not boast who did thy stock pollute
   That thou art doting father of his fruit.

'Nor shall he smile at thee in secret thought,
Nor laugh with his companions at thy state;
But thou shalt know thy interest was not bought
Basely with gold, but stoln from forth thy gate.
For me, I am the mistress of my fate,
   And with my trespass never will dispense,
   Till life to death acquit my forced offence.

'I will not poison thee with my attaint,
Nor fold my fault in cleanly-coin'd excuses;
My sable ground of sin I will not paint,
To hide the truth of this false night's abuses:
My tongue shall utter all; mine eyes, like sluices,
   As from a mountain-spring that feeds a dale,
   Shall gush pure streams to purge my impure
     tale.'

By this, lamenting Philomel had ended
The well-tuned warble of her nightly sorrow,
And solemn night with slow sad gait descended
To ugly hell; when, lo, the blushing morrow
Lends light to all fair eyes that light will borrow:
   But cloudy Lucrece shames herself to see,
   And therefore still in night would cloister'd be.

Revealing day through every cranny spies,
And seems to point her out where she sits weeping;
To whom she sobbing speaks: 'O eye of eyes,
Why pry'st thou through my window? leave thy
   peeping:
Mock with thy tickling beams eyes that are sleep-
   ing:
   Brand not my forehead with thy piercing light,
   For day hath naught to do what's done by night.'

Thus cavils she with every thing she sees:
True grief is fond and testy as a child,
Who wayward once, his mood with naught agrees:
Old woes, not infant sorrows, bear them mild;
Continuance tames the one; the other wild,
   Like an unpractised swimmer plunging still,
   With too much labour drowns for want of skill.

So she, deep-drenched in a sea of care,
Holds disputation with each thing she views,
And to herself all sorrow doth compare;
No object but her passion's strength renews;
And as one shifts, another straight ensues:
   Sometime her grief is dumb, and hath no words;
   Sometime 'tis mad, and too much talk affords.

The little birds that tune their morning's joy
Make her moans mad with their sweet melody:
For mirth doth search the bottom of annoy;
Sad souls are slain in merry company;
Grief best is pleased with grief's society:
   True sorrow then is feelingly sufficed
   When with like semblance it is sympathized.

''Tis double death to drown in ken of shore;
He ten times pines that pines beholding food;
To see the salve doth make the wound ache more;
Great grief grieves most at that would do it good;
Deep woes roll forward like a gentle flood,
   Who, being stopt, the bounding banks o'erflows;
   Grief dallied with nor law nor limit knows.

'You mocking birds,' quoth she, 'your tunes en-
   tomb
Within your hollow swelling feather'd breasts,
And in my hearing be you mute and dumb:
My restless discord loves no stops nor rests;
A woeful hostess brooks not merry guests:
   Relish your nimble notes to pleasing ears;
   Distress likes dumps when time is kept with
     tears.

'Come, Philomel, that sing'st of ravishment,
Make thy sad grove in my dishevell'd hair:
As the dank earth weeps at thy languishment,
So I at each sad strain will strain a tear,
And with deep groans the diapason bear;
   For burthen-wise I'll hum on Tarquin still,
   While thou on Tereus descant'st better skill.

'And whiles against a thorn thou bear'st thy part,
To keep thy sharp woes waking, wretched I,
To imitate thee well, against my heart
Will fix a sharp knife, to affright mine eye;
Who, if it wink, shall thereon fall and die.
   These means, as frets upon an instrument,
   Shall tune our heart-strings to true languish-
     ment.

'And for, poor bird, thou sing'st not in the day,
As shaming any eye should thee behold,
Some dark-deep desert, seated from the way,
That knows not parching heat nor freezing cold,
Will we find out; and there we will unfold
   To creatures stern sad tunes, to change their
     kinds:
   Since men prove beasts, let beasts bear gentle
     minds.'

As the poor frighted deer, that stands at gaze,
Wildly determining which way to fly,
Or one encompast with a winding maze,
That cannot tread the way out readily;
So with herself is she in mutiny,
   To live or die, which of the twain were better,
   When life is shamed, and death reproach's
     debtor.

'To kill myself,' quoth she, 'alack, what were it,
But with my body my poor soul's pollution?
They that lose half with greater patience bear it
Than they whose whole is swallow'd in confusion.
That mother tries a merciless conclusion
    Who, having two sweet babes, when death takes
      one,
    Will slay the other, and be nurse to none.

'My body or my soul, which was the dearer,
When the one pure, the other made divine?
Whose love of either to myself was nearer,
When both were kept for heaven and Collatine?
Ay me! the bark pill'd from the lofty pine,
    His leaves will wither, and his sap decay;
    So must my soul, her bark being pill'd away.

'Her house is sackt, her quiet interrupted,
Her mansion batter'd by the enemy;
Her sacred temple spotted, spoil'd, corrupted,
Grossly engirt with daring infamy:
Then let it not be call'd impiety,
    If in this blemisht fort I make some hole
    Through which I may convey this troubled
      soul.

'Yet die I will not till my Collatine
Have heard the cause of my untimely death;
That he may vow, in that sad hour of mine,
Revenge on him that made me stop my breath.
My stained blood to Tarquin I'll bequeath,
    Which by him tainted shall for him be spent,
    And as his due writ in my testament.

'My honour I'll bequeath unto the knife
That wounds my body, so dishonoured.
'Tis honour to deprive dishonour'd life;
The one will live, the other being dead:
So of shame's ashes shall my fame be bred;
    For in my death I murder shameful scorn:
    My shame so dead, mine honour is new-born.

'Dear lord of that dear jewel I have lost,
What legacy shall I bequeath to thee?
My resolution, love, shall be thy boast,
By whose example thou revenged mayst be.
How Tarquin must be used, read it in me:
    Myself, thy friend, will kill myself, thy foe,
    And, for my sake, serve thou false Tarquin so.

'This brief abridgement of my will I make:—
My soul and body to the skies and ground;
My resolution, husband, do thou take;
Mine honour be the knife's that makes my
    wound;
My shame be his that did my fame confound;
    And all my fame that lives disbursed be
    To those that live, and think no shame of me.

'Thou, Collatine, shalt oversee this will;
How was I overseen that thou shalt see it!
My blood shall wash the slander of mine ill;
My life's foul deed, my life's fair end shall free it.
Faint not, faint heart, but stoutly say "So be it:"
    Yield to my hand; my hand shall conquer thee:
    Thou dead, both die and both shall victors be.'

This plot of death when sadly she had laid,
And wiped the brinish pearl from her bright
    eyes,
With untuned tongue she hoarsely calls her maid,
Whose swift obedience to her mistress hies;
For fleet-wing'd duty with thought's feathers
    flies.
    Poor Lucrece' cheeks unto her maid seem so
    As winter meads when sun doth melt their
      snow.

Her mistress she doth give demure good-morrow,
With soft-slow tongue, true mark of modesty,
And sorts a sad look to her lady's sorrow,
For why her face wore sorrow's livery;
But durst not ask of her audaciously
    Why her two suns were cloud-eclipsed so,
    Nor why her fair cheeks overwasht with woe.

But as the earth doth weep, the sun being set,
Each flower moisten'd like a melting eye,
Even so the maid with swelling drops gan wet
Her circled eyne, enforced by sympathy
Of those fair suns set in her mistress' sky,
    Who in a salt-waved ocean quench their light,
    Which makes the maid weep like the dewy
      night.

A pretty while these pretty creatures stand,
Like ivory conduits coral cisterns filling:
One justly weeps; the other takes in hand
No cause, but company, of her drops spilling:
Their gentle sex to weep are often willing;
    Grieving themselves to guess at others' smarts,
    And then they drown their eyes, or break their
      hearts.

For men have marble, women waxen, minds,
And therefore are they form'd as marble will;
The weak opprest, the impression of strange
    kinds
Is form'd in them by force, by fraud, or skill:
    Then call them not the authors of their ill,
    No more than wax shall be accounted evil
    Wherein is stampt the semblance of a devil.

Their smoothness, like a goodly champaign plain,
Lays open all the little worms that creep;
In men, as in a rough-grown grove, remain
Cave-keeping evils that obscurely sleep:
Through crystal walls each little mote will peep:
    Though men can cover crimes with bold stern
      looks,
    Poor women's faces are their own faults' books.

No man inveigh against the wither'd flower,
But chide rough winter that the flower hath kill'd:
Not that devour'd, but that which doth devour,
Is worthy blame. O, let it not be hild
Poor women's faults, that they are so fulfill'd
    With men's abuses: those proud lords, to
      blame,
    Make weak-made women tenants to their
      shame.

The precedent whereof in Lucrece view,
Assail'd by night with circumstances strong
Of present death, and shame that might ensue
By that her death, to do her husband wrong:
Such danger to resistance did belong,
    That dying fear through all her body spread;
    And who cannot abuse a body dead?

By this, mild patience bid fair Lucrece speak
To the poor counterfeit of her complaining:
'My girl,' quoth she, 'on what occasion break
Those tears from thee, that down thy cheeks are
    raining?
If thou dost weep for grief of my sustaining,
    Know, gentle wench, it small avails my mood:
    If tears could help, mine own would do me
    good.

'But tell me, girl, when went'—and there she
    stay'd
Till after a deep groan—'Tarquin from hence?'
'Madam, ere I was up,' replied the maid,
'The more to blame my sluggard negligence:
Yet with the fault I thus far can dispense,—
    Myself was stirring ere the break of day,
    And ere I rose was Tarquin gone away.

'But, lady, if your maid may be so bold,
She would request to know your heaviness.'
'O, peace!' quoth Lucrece: 'if it should be told,
The repetition cannot make it less,
For more it is than I can well express:
    And that deep torture may be call'd a hell
    When more is felt than one hath power to tell.

'Go, get me hither paper, ink, and pen,—
Yet save that labour, for I have them here.
What should I say?—One of my husband's men
Bid thou be ready, by and by, to bear
A letter to my lord, my love, my dear:
    Bid him with speed prepare to carry it;
    The cause craves haste, and it will soon be writ.'

Her maid is gone, and she prepares to write,
First hovering o'er the paper with her quill:
Conceit and grief an eager combat fight;
What wit sets down is blotted straight with will;
This is too curious-good, this blunt and ill:
    Much like a press of people at a door,
    Throng her inventions, which shall go before.

At last she thus begins: 'Thou worthy lord
Of that unworthy wife that greeteth thee,
Health to thy person! next vouchsafe t'afford—
If ever, love, thy Lucrece thou wilt see—
Some present speed to come and visit me.
    So, I commend me from our house in grief:
    My woes are tedious, though my words are
    brief.'

Here folds she up the tenour of her woe,
Her certain sorrow writ uncertainly.
By this short schedule Collatine may know
Her grief, but not her grief's true quality:
She dares not thereof make discovery,
    Lest he should hold it her own gross abuse,
    Ere she with blood had stain'd her stain'd
    excuse.

Besides, the life and feeling of her passion
She hoards, to spend when he is by to hear her;
When sighs and groans and tears may grace the
    fashion
Of her disgrace, the better so to clear her
From that suspicion which the world might bear
    her.
    To shun this blot, she would not blot the letter
    With words, till action might become them
    better.

To see sad sights moves more than hear them
    told;
For then the eye interprets to the ear
The heavy motion that it doth behold,
When every part a part of woe doth bear.
'Tis but a part of sorrow that we hear:
    Deep sounds make lesser noise than shallow
    fords,
    And sorrow ebbs, being blown with wind of
    words.

Her letter now is seal'd, and on it writ,
'At Ardea to my lord with more than haste.'
The post attends, and she delivers it,
Charging the sour-faced groom to hie as fast
As lagging fowls before the northern blast:
    Speed more than speed but dull and slow she
    deems:
    Extremity still urgeth such extremes.

The homely villain court'sies to her low;
And, blushing on her, with a steadfast eye
Receives the scroll without or yea or no,
And forth with bashful innocence doth hie.
But they whose guilt within their bosoms lie
    Imagine every eye beholds their blame;
    For Lucrece thought he blusht to see her
    shame:

When, silly groom! God wot, it was defect
Of spirit, life, and bold audacity.
Such harmless creatures have a true respect
To talk in deeds, while others saucily
Promise more speed, but do it leisurely:
    Even so this pattern of the worn-out age
    Pawn'd honest looks, but laid no words to gage.

His kindled duty kindled her mistrust,
That two red fires in both their faces blazed;
She thought he blusht, as knowing Tarquin's
    lust,
And, blushing with him, wistly on him gazed;
Her earnest eye did make him more amazed:
    The more she saw the blood his cheeks re-
    plenish,
    The more she thought he spied in her some
    blemish.

But long she thinks till he return again,
And yet the duteous vassal scarce is gone.
The weary time she cannot entertain,
For now 'tis stale to sigh, to weep, and groan:
So woe hath wearied woe, moan tired moan,
    That she her plaints a little while doth stay,
    Pausing for means to mourn some newer way.

At last she calls to mind where hangs a piece
Of skilful painting, made for Priam's Troy;
Before the which is drawn the power of Greece,
For Helen's rape the city to destroy,
Threatening cloud-kissing Ilion with annoy;
   Which the conceited painter drew so proud,
   As heaven, it seem'd, to kiss the turrets bow'd.

A thousand lamentable objects there,
In scorn of nature, art gave lifeless life:
Many a dry drop seem'd a weeping tear,
Shed for the slaughter'd husband by the wife:
The red blood reekt, to show the painter's strife;
   And dying eyes gleam'd forth their ashy lights,
   Like dying coals burnt out in tedious nights.

There might you see the labouring pioner
Begrimed with sweat, and smeared all with dust;
And from the towers of Troy there would appear
The very eyes of men through loop-holes thrust,
Gazing upon the Greeks with little lust:
   Such sweet observance in this work was had,
   That one might see those far-off eyes look sad.

In great commanders grace and majesty
You might behold, triumphing in their faces;
In youth, quick bearing and dexterity;
And here and there the painter interlaces
Pale cowards, marching on with trembling paces;
   Which heartless peasants did so well resemble
   That one would swear he saw them quake and
    tremble.

In Ajax and Ulysses, O, what art
Of physiognomy might one behold!
The face of either cipher'd either's heart;
Their face their manners most expressly told:
In Ajax' eyes blunt rage and rigour roll'd;
   But the mild glance that sly Ulysses lent
   Show'd deep regard and smiling government.

There pleading might you see grave Nestor stand,
As 'twere encouraging the Greeks to fight:
Making such sober action with his hand,
That it beguiled attention, charm'd the sight:
In speech, it seem'd, his beard, all silver white,
   Wagg'd up and down, and from his lips did fly
   Thin winding breath, which purl'd up to the
   sky.

About him were a press of gaping faces,
Which seem'd to swallow up his sound advice;
All jointly listening, but with several graces,
As if some mermaid did their ears entice,
Some high, some low,—the painter was so nice;
   The scalps of many, almost hid behind,
   To jump up higher seem'd, to mock the mind.

Here one man's hand lean'd on another's head,
His nose being shadow'd by his neighbour's ear;
Here one, being throng'd, bears back, all boln and
   red;
Another, smother'd, seems to pelt and swear;
And in their rage such signs of rage they bear,
   As, but for loss of Nestor's golden words,
   It seem'd they would debate with angry swords.

For much imaginary work was there;
Conceit deceitful, so compact, so kind,
That for Achilles' image stood his spear,
Griped in an armed hand; himself, behind,
Was left unseen, save to the eye of mind:
   A hand, a foot, a face, a leg, a head,
   Stood for the whole to be imagined.

And from the walls of strong-besieged Troy
When their brave hope, bold Hector, marcht to
   field,
Stood many Trojan mothers, sharing joy
To see their youthful sons bright weapons wield;
And to their hope they such odd action yield,
   That through their light joy seemed to appear,
   Like bright things stain'd, a kind of heavy
   fear.

And from the strond of Dardan, where they
   fought,
To Simois' reedy banks the red blood ran,
Whose waves to imitate the battle sought
With swelling ridges; and their ranks began
To break upon the galled shore, and than
   Retire again, till meeting greater ranks,
   They join, and shoot their foam at Simois'
   banks.

To this well-painted piece is Lucrece come,
To find a face where all distress is stell'd.
Many she sees where cares have carved some,
But none where all distress and dolour dwell'd,
Till she despairing Hecuba beheld,
   Staring on Priam's wounds with her old eyes,
   Which bleeding under Pyrrhus' proud foot
   lies.

In her the painter had anatomized
Time's ruin, beauty's wrack, and grim care's
   reign:
Her cheeks with chops and wrinkles were dis-
   guised;
Of what she was no semblance did remain:
Her blue blood changed to black in every vein,
   Wanting the spring that those shrunk pipes
   had fed,
   Show'd life imprison'd in a body dead.

On this sad shadow Lucrece spends her eyes,
And shapes her sorrow to the beldam's woes,
Who nothing wants to answer her but cries,
And bitter words to ban her cruel foes:
The painter was no god to lend her those;
   And therefore Lucrece swears he did her
   wrong,
   To give her so much grief, and not a tongue.

'Poor instrument,' quoth she, 'without a sound,
I'll tune thy woes with my lamenting tongue;
And drop sweet balm in Priam's painted wound,
And rail on Pyrrhus that hath done him wrong;
And with my tears quench Troy that burns so
   long;
   And with my knife scratch out the angry eyes
   Of all the Greeks that are thine enemies.

'Show me the strumpet that began this stir,
That with my nails her beauty I may tear.
Thy heat of lust, fond Paris, did incur
This load of wrath that burning Troy doth bear:
Thy eye kindled the fire that burneth here;
    And here in Troy, for trespass of thine eye,
    The sire, the son, the dame, and daughter die.

'Why should the private pleasure of some one
Become the public plague of many moe?
Let sin, alone committed, light alone
Upon his head that hath transgressed so;
Let guiltless souls be freed from guilty woe:
    For one's offence why should so many fall,
    To plague a private sin in general?

'Lo, here weeps Hecuba, here Priam dies,
Here manly Hector faints, here Troilus swounds,
Here friend by friend in bloody channel lies,
And friend to friend gives unadvised wounds,
And one man's lust these many lives confounds:
    Had doting Priam checkt his son's desire,
    Troy had been bright with fame, and not with
        fire.'

Here feelingly she weeps Troy's painted woes:
For sorrow, like a heavy-hanging bell,
Once set on ringing, with his own weight goes;
Then little strength rings out the doleful knell:
So Lucrece, set a-work, sad tales doth tell
    To pencill'd pensiveness and colour'd sorrow;
    She lends them words, and she their looks doth
        borrow.

She throws her eyes about the painting round,
And who she finds forlorn she doth lament.
At last she sees a wretched image bound,
That piteous looks to Phrygian shepherds lent:
His face, though full of cares, yet show'd content;
    Onward to Troy with the blunt swains he goes,
    So mild that Patience seem'd to scorn his woes.

In him the painter labour'd with his skill
To hide deceit, and give the harmless show
An humble gait, calm looks, eyes wailing still,
A brow unbent, that seem'd to welcome woe;
Cheeks neither red nor pale, but mingled so
    That blushing red no guilty instance gave,
    Nor ashy pale the fear that false hearts have.

But, like a constant and confirmed devil,
He entertain'd a show so seeming just,
And therein so ensconced his secret evil,
That jealousy itself could not mistrust
False-creeping craft and perjury should thrust
    Into so bright a day such black-faced storms,
    Or blot with hell-born sin such saint-like forms.

The well-skill'd workman this mild image drew
For perjured Sinon, whose enchanting story
The credulous old Priam after slew;
Whose words, like wildfire, burnt the shining glory
Of rich-built Ilion, that the skies were sorry,
    And little stars shot from their fixed places,
    When their glass fell wherein they view'd their
        faces.

This picture she advisedly perused,
And chid the painter for his wondrous skill,
Saying, some shape in Sinon's was abused;
So fair a form lodged not a mind so ill:
And still on him she gazed; and gazing still,
    Such signs of truth in his plain face she spied,
    That she concludes the picture was belied.

'It cannot be,' quoth she, 'that so much guile'—
She would have said 'can lurk in such a look;'
But Tarquin's shape came in her mind the while,
And from her tongue 'can lurk' from 'cannot'
        took:
'It cannot be' she in that sense forsook,
    And turn'd it thus, 'It cannot be, I find,
    But such a face should bear a wicked mind:

'For even as subtle Sinon here is painted,
So sober-sad, so weary, and so mild,
As if with grief or travail he had fainted,
To me came Tarquin armed; so beguiled
With outward honesty, but yet defiled
    With inward vice: as Priam him did cherish,
    So did I Tarquin; so my Troy did perish.

'Look, look, how listening Priam wets his eyes,
To see those borrow'd tears that Sinon sheeds!
Priam, why art thou old, and yet not wise?
For every tear he falls a Trojan bleeds:
His eye drops fire, no water thence proceeds;
    Those round clear pearls of his, that move thy
        pity,
    Are balls of quenchless fire to burn thy city.

'Such devils steal effects from lightless hell;
For Sinon in his fire doth quake with cold,
And in that cold hot-burning fire doth dwell;
These contraries such unity do hold,
Only to flatter fools, and make them bold:
    So Priam's trust false Sinon's tears doth
        flatter,
    That he finds means to burn his Troy with
        water.'

Here, all enraged, such passion her assails,
That patience is quite beaten from her breast.
She tears the senseless Sinon with her nails,
Comparing him to that unhappy guest
Whose deed hath made herself herself detest:
    At last she smilingly with this gives o'er;
    'Fool, fool!' quoth she, 'his wounds will not be
        sore.'

Thus ebbs and flows the current of her sorrow,
And time doth weary time with her complaining
She looks for night, and then she longs for
        morrow,
And both she thinks too long with her remain-
        ing;
Short time seems long in sorrow's sharp sustain-
        ing:
    Though woe be heavy, yet it seldom sleeps;
    And they that watch see time how slow it
        creeps.

Which all this time hath overslipt her thought,
That she with painted images hath spent;
Being from the feeling of her own grief brought
By deep surmise of others' detriment;
Losing her woes in shows of discontent.
　　It easeth some, though none it ever cured,
　　To think their dolour others have endured.

But now the mindful messenger, come back,
Brings home his lord and other company:
Who finds his Lucrece clad in mourning black;
And round about her tear-distained eye
Blue circles stream'd, like rainbows in the sky:
　　These water-galls in her dim element
　　Foretell new storms to those already spent.

Which when her sad-beholding husband saw,
Amazedly in her sad face he stares:
Her eyes, though sod in tears, lookt red and raw,
Her lively colour kill'd with deadly cares.
He hath no power to ask her how she fares;
　　Both stood, like old acquaintance in a trance,
　　Met far from home, wondering each other's
　　chance.

At last he takes her by the bloodless hand,
And thus begins: 'What uncouth ill event
Hath thee befaln, that thou dost trembling
　　stand?
Sweet love, what spite hath thy fair colour spent?
Why art thou thus attired in discontent?
　　Unmask, dear dear, this moody heaviness,
　　And tell thy grief, that we may give redress.'

Three times with sighs she gives her sorrow fire,
Ere once she can discharge one word of woe:
At length addrest to answer his desire,
She modestly prepares to let them know
Her honour is ta'en prisoner by the foe;
　　While Collatine and his consorted lords
　　With sad attention long to hear her words.

And now this pale swan in her watery nest
Begins the sad dirge of her certain ending:
'Few words,' quoth she, 'shall fit the trespass best,
Where no excuse can give the fault amending:
In me moe woes than words are now depending;
　　And my laments would be drawn out too long,
　　To tell them all with one poor tired tongue.

'Then be this all the task it hath to say:
Dear husband, in the interest of thy bed
A stranger came, and on that pillow lay
Where thou wast wont to rest thy weary head;
And what wrong else may be imagined
　　By foul enforcement might be done to me,
　　From that, alas, thy Lucrece is not free.

'For in the dreadful dead of dark midnight,
With shining falchion in my chamber came
A creeping creature, with a flaming light,
And softly cried, "Awake, thou Roman dame,
And entertain my love; else lasting shame
　　On thee and thine this night I will inflict,
　　If thou my love's desire do contradict.

' "For some hard-favour'd groom of thine,"
　　quoth he,
"Unless thou yoke thy liking to my will,
I'll murder straight, and then I'll slaughter thee,
And swear I found you where you did fulfil
The loathsome act of lust, and so did kill
　　The lechers in their deed: this act will be
　　My fame, and thy perpetual infamy."

'With this, I did begin to start and cry;
And then against my heart he set his sword,
Swearing, unless I took all patiently,
I should not live to speak another word;
So should my shame still rest upon record,
　　And never be forgot in mighty Rome
　　Th' adulterate death of Lucrece and her groom.

'Mine enemy was strong, my poor self weak,
And far the weaker with so strong a fear:
My bloody judge forbade my tongue to speak;
No rightful plea might plead for justice there:
His scarlet lust came evidence to swear
　　That my poor beauty had purloin'd his eyes;
　　And when the judge is robb'd, the prisoner dies.

'O, teach me how to make mine own excuse!
Or, at the least, this refuge let me find,—
Though my gross blood be stain'd with this abuse,
Immaculate and spotless is my mind;
That was not forced; that never was inclined
　　To accessary yieldings, but still pure
　　Doth in her poison'd closet yet endure.'

Lo, here, the hopeless merchant of this loss,
With head declined, and voice damm'd up with
　　woe,
With sad-set eyes, and wretched arms across,
From lips new-waxen pale begins to blow
The grief away that stops his answer so:
　　But, wretched as he is, he strives in vain;
　　What he breathes out his breath drinks up again.

As through an arch the violent roaring tide
Outruns the eye that doth behold his haste,
Yet in the eddy boundeth in his pride
Back to the strait that forced him on so fast;
In rage sent out, recall'd in rage, being past:
　　Even so his sighs, his sorrows, make a saw,
　　To push grief on, and back the same grief draw.

Which speechless woe of his poor she attendeth,
And his untimely frenzy thus awaketh:
'Dear lord, thy sorrow to my sorrow lendeth
Another power; no flood by raining slaketh.
My woe too sensible thy passion maketh
　　More feeling-painful: let it, then, suffice
　　To drown one woe, one pair of weeping eyes.

'And for my sake, when I might charm thee so,
For she that was thy Lucrece,—now attend me:
Be suddenly revenged on my foe,
Thine, mine, his own: suppose thou dost defend
　　me
From what is past: the help that thou shalt lend me
　　Comes all too late, yet let the traitor die;
　　For sparing justice feeds iniquity.

'But ere I name him, you fair lords,' quoth she,
Speaking to those that came with Collatine,
'Shall plight your honourable faiths to me,
With swift pursuit to venge this wrong of mine;
For 'tis a meritorious fair design
    To chase injustice with revengeful arms:
    Knights, by their oaths, should right poor
      ladies' harms.'

At this request, with noble disposition
Each present lord began to promise aid,
As bound in knighthood to her imposition,
Longing to hear the hateful foe bewray'd.
But she, that yet her sad task hath not said,
    The protestation stops. 'O, speak,' quoth she,
    'How may this forced stain be wiped from me?

'What is the quality of mine offence,
Being constrain'd with dreadful circumstance?
May my pure mind with the foul act dispense,
My low-declined honour to advance?
May any terms acquit me from this chance?
    The poison'd fountain clears itself again;
    And why not I from this compelled stain?'

With this, they all at once began to say,
Her body's stain her mind untainted clears;
While with a joyless smile she turns away
The face, that map which deep impression bears
Of hard misfortune, carved in it with tears.
    'No, no,' quoth she, 'no dame, hereafter living,
    By my excuse shall claim excuse's giving.'

Here with a sigh, as if her heart would break,
She throws forth Tarquin's name: 'He, he,' she
    says,
But more than 'he' her poor tongue could not
    speak;
Till after many accents and delays,
Untimely breathings, sick and short assays,
    She utters this, 'He, he, fair lords, 'tis he
    That guides this hand to give this wound to me.'

Even here she sheathed in her harmless breast
A harmful knife, that thence her soul unsheathed:
That blow did bail it from the deep unrest
Of that polluted prison where it breathed:
Her contrite sighs unto the clouds bequeathed
    Her winged sprite, and through her wounds
      doth fly
    Life's lasting date from cancell'd destiny.

Stone-still, astonisht with this deadly deed,
Stood Collatine and all his lordly crew;
Till Lucrece' father, that beholds her bleed,
Himself on her self-slaughter'd body threw;
And from the purple fountain Brutus drew
    The murderous knife, and, as it left the place,
    Her blood, in poor revenge, held it in chase;

And bubbling from her breast, it doth divide
In two slow rivers, that the crimson blood
Circles her body in on every side,
Who, like a late-sackt island, vastly stood
Bare and unpeopled in this fearful flood.
    Some of her blood still pure and red remain'd,
    And some lookt black, and that false Tarquin
      stain'd.

About the mourning and congealed face
Of that black blood a watery rigol goes,
Which seems to weep upon the tainted place:
And ever since, as pitying Lucrece' woes,
Corrupted blood some watery token shows;
    And blood untainted still doth red abide,
    Blushing at that which is so putrefied.

'Daughter, dear daughter,' old Lucretius cries,
'That life was mine which thou hast here de-
    prived.
If in the child the father's image lies,
Where shall I live now Lucrece is unlived?
Thou wast not to this end from me derived.
    If children pre-decease progenitors,
    We are their offspring, and they none of ours.

'Poor broken glass, I often did behold
In thy sweet semblance my old age new born;
But now that fair fresh mirror, dim and old,
Shows me a bare-boned death by time outworn:
O, from thy cheeks my image thou hast torn,
    And shiver'd all the beauty of my glass,
    That I no more can see what once I was.

'O time, cease thou thy course, and last no longer,
If they surcease to be that should survive.
Shall rotten death make conquest of the stronger,
And leave the faltering feeble souls alive?
The old bees die, the young possess their hive:
    Then live, sweet Lucrece, live again, and see
    Thy father die, and not thy father thee.'

By this, starts Collatine as from a dream,
And bids Lucretius give his sorrow place;
And then in key-cold Lucrece' bleeding stream
He falls, and bathes the pale fear in his face,
And counterfeits to die with her a space;
    Till manly shame bids him possess his breath,
    And live to be revenged on her death.

The deep vexation of his inward soul
Hath served a dumb arrest upon his tongue;
Who, mad that sorrow should his use control,
Or keep him from heart-easing words so long,
Begins to talk; but through his lips do throng
    Weak words, so thick come in his poor heart's
      aid,
    That no man could distinguish what he said.

Yet sometime 'Tarquin' was pronounced plain,
But through his teeth, as if the name he tore.
This windy tempest, till it blow up rain,
Held back his sorrow's tide, to make it more;
At last it rains, and busy winds give o'er:
    The son and father weep with equal strife
    Who should weep most, for daughter or for
      wife.

The one doth call her his, the other his,
Yet neither may possess the claim they lay.
The father says 'She's mine.' 'O, mine she is,'
Replies her husband: 'do not take away
My sorrow's interest; let no mourner say
    He weeps for her, for she was only mine,
    And only must be wail'd by Collatine.'

'O,' quoth Lucretius, 'I did give that life
Which she too early and too late hath spill'd.'
'Woe, woe,' quoth Collatine, 'she was my wife,
I owed her, and 'tis mine that she hath kill'd.'
'My daughter' and 'my wife' with clamours fill'd
    The dispersed air, who, holding Lucrece' life,
    Answer'd their cries, 'my daughter ' and 'my
        wife.'

Brutus, who pluckt the knife from Lucrece' side,
Seeing such emulation in their woe,
Began to clothe his wit in state and pride,
Burying in Lucrece' wound his folly's show.
He with the Romans was esteemed so
    As silly-jeering idiots are with kings,
    For sportive words and uttering foolish things:

But now he throws that shallow habit by,
Wherein deep policy did him disguise;
And arm'd his long-hid wits advisedly,
To check the tears in Collatinus' eyes.
'Thou wronged lord of Rome,' quoth he, 'arise:
    Let my unsounded self, supposed a fool,
    Now set thy long-experienced wit to school.

'Why, Collatine, is woe the cure for woe?
Do wounds help wounds, or grief help grievous
    deeds?
Is it revenge to give thyself a blow
For his foul act by whom thy fair wife bleeds?
Such childish humour from weak minds pro-
    ceeds:
    Thy wretched wife mistook the matter so,
    To slay herself, that should have slain her foe.

'Courageous Roman, do not steep thy heart
In such relenting dew of lamentations;
But kneel with me, and help to bear thy part,
To rouse our Roman gods with invocations,
That they will suffer these abominations,
    Since Rome herself in them doth stand dis-
        graced,
    By our strong arms from forth her fair streets
        chased.

'Now, by the Capitol that we adore,
And by this chaste blood so unjustly stained,
By heaven's fair sun that breeds the fat earth's
    store,
By all our country rights in Rome maintained,
And by chaste Lucrece' soul that late complained
    Her wrongs to us, and by this bloody knife,
    We will revenge the death of this true wife.'

This said, he struck his hand upon his breast,
And kist the fatal knife, to end his vow;
And to his protestation urged the rest,
Who, wondering at him, did his words allow:
Then jointly to the ground their knees they bow;
    And that deep vow, which Brutus made before,
    He doth again repeat, and that they swore.

When they had sworn to this advised doom,
They did conclude to bear dead Lucrece thence,
To show her bleeding body thorough Rome,
And so to publish Tarquin's foul offence:
Which being done with speedy diligence,
    The Romans plausibly did give consent
    To Tarquin's everlasting banishment.

SONNETS

To the Onlie Begetter of
These Insving Sonnets
Mr. W. H. All Happinesse
and that Eternitie
Promised by
Ovr Ever-Living Poet
Wisheth
The Well-Wishing
Adventvrer in
Setting
Forth

T. T.

1.

FROM fairest creatures we desire increase,
That thereby beauty's Rose might never die,
But as the riper should by time decease,
His tender heir might bear his memory:
But thou, contracted to thine own bright eyes,
Feed'st thy light's flame with self-substantial fuel,
Making a famine where abundance lies,
Thyself thy foe, to thy sweet self too cruel.
Thou that art now the world's fresh ornament,
And only herald to the gaudy spring,
Within thine own bud buriest thy content,
And, tender churl, makest waste in niggarding.
    Pity the world, or else this glutton be,
    To eat the world's due, by the grave and thee.

2.

When forty winters shall besiege thy brow,
And dig deep trenches in thy beauty's field,
Thy youth's proud livery, so gazed on now,
Will be a totter'd weed, of small worth held:
Then being askt where all thy beauty lies,
Where all the treasure of thy lusty days;
To say, within thine own deep-sunken eyes,
Were an all-eating shame and thriftless praise.
How much more praise deserved thy beauty's use,
If thou couldst answer, 'This fair child of mine
Shall sum my count, and make my old excuse,'
Proving his beauty by succession thine!
    This were to be new made when thou art old,
    And see thy blood warm when thou feel'st it
    cold.

3.

Look in thy glass, and tell the face thou viewest
Now is the time that face should form another;
Whose fresh repair if now thou not renewest,
Thou dost beguile the world, unbless some
    mother.
For where is she so fair whose unear'd womb
Disdains the tillage of thy husbandry?
Or who is he so fond will be the tomb
Of his self-love, to stop posterity?
Thou art thy mother's glass, and she in thee
Calls back the lovely April of her prime:
So thou through windows of thine age shalt see,
Despite of wrinkles, this thy golden time.
    But if thou live, remember'd not to be,
    Die single, and thine image dies with thee.

4.

Unthrifty loveliness, why dost thou spend
Upon thyself thy beauty's legacy?
Nature's bequest gives nothing, but doth lend;
And, being frank, she lends to those are free.
Then, beauteous niggard, why dost thou abuse
The bounteous largess given thee to give?
Profitless usurer, why dost thou use
So great a sum of sums, yet canst not live?
For having traffic with thyself alone,
Thou of thyself thy sweet self dost deceive.
Then how, when nature calls thee to be gone,
What acceptable audit canst thou leave?
    Thy unused beauty must be tomb'd with thee,
    Which, used, lives th' executor to be.

5.

Those hours, that with gentle work did frame
The lovely gaze where every eye doth dwell,
Will play the tyrants to the very same,
And that unfair which fairly doth excel:
For never-resting time leads summer on
To hideous winter and confounds him there;
Sap checkt with frost, and lusty leaves quite gone,
Beauty o'ersnow'd, and bareness every where:
Then, were not summer's distillation left,
A liquid prisoner pent in walls of glass,
Beauty's effect with beauty were bereft,
Nor it, nor no remembrance what it was:
    But flowers distill'd, though they with winter
    meet,
    Leese but their show; their substance still lives
    sweet.

6.

Then let not winter's ragged hand deface
In thee thy summer, ere thou be distill'd:
Make sweet some vial; treasure thou some place
With beauty's treasure, ere it be self-kill'd.
That use is not forbidden usury,
Which happies those that pay the willing loan;
That's for thyself to breed another thee,
Or ten times happier, be it ten for one;
Ten times thyself were happier than thou art,
If ten of thine ten times refigured thee:
Then what could death do, if thou shouldst depart,
Leaving thee living in posterity?
    Be not self-will'd, for thou art much too fair
    To be death's conquest and make worms thine
    heir.

365

7.

Lo, in the orient when the gracious light
Lifts up his burning head, each under eye
Doth homage to his new-appearing sight,
Serving with looks his sacred majesty;
And having climb'd the steep-up heavenly hill,
Resembling strong youth in his middle age,
Yet mortal looks adore his beauty still,
Attending on his golden pilgrimage;
But when from highmost pitch, with weary car,
Like feeble age, he reeleth from the day,
The eyes, 'fore duteous, now converted are
From his low tract and look another way:
  So thou, thyself outgoing in thy noon,
  Unlookt on diest, unless thou get a son.

8.

Music to hear, why hear'st thou music sadly?
Sweets with sweets war not, joy delights in joy.
Why lovest thou that which thou receivest not
  gladly,
Or else receivest with pleasure thine annoy?
If the true concord of well-tuned sounds,
By unions married, do offend thine ear,
They do but sweetly chide thee, who confounds
In singleness the parts that thou shouldst bear.
Mark how one string, sweet husband to another,
Strikes each in each by mutual ordering;
Resembling sire and child and happy mother,
Who, all in one, one pleasing note do sing:
  Whose speechless song, being many, seeming
    one,
  Sings this to thee, 'Thou single wilt prove none.'

9.

Is it for fear to wet a widow's eye
That thou consumest thyself in single life?
Ah! if thou issueless shalt hap to die,
The world will wail thee, like a makeless wife;
The world will be thy widow, and still weep
That thou no form of thee hast left behind,
When every private widow well may keep
By children's eyes her husband's shape in mind.
Look, what an unthrift in the world doth spend
Shifts but his place, for still the world enjoys it;
But beauty's waste hath in the world an end,
And kept unused, the user so destroys it.
  No love toward others in that bosom sits
  That on himself such murd'rous shame com-
    mits.

10.

For shame deny that thou bear'st love to any,
Who for thyself art so unprovident.
Grant, if thou wilt, thou art beloved of many,
But that thou none lovest is most evident;
For thou art so possest with murd'rous hate,
That 'gainst thyself thou stick'st not to conspire,
Seeking that beauteous roof to ruinate,
Which to repair should be thy chief desire.
O, change thy thought, that I may change my
  mind!
Shall hate be fairer lodged than gentle love?
Be, as thy presence is, gracious and kind,
Or to thyself, at least, kind-hearted prove:
  Make thee another self, for love of me,
  That beauty still may live in thine or thee.

11.

As fast as thou shalt wane, so fast thou grow'st
In one of thine, from that which thou departest;
And that fresh blood which youngly thou be-
  stow'st
Thou mayst call thine when thou from youth con-
  vertest.
Herein lives wisdom, beauty, and increase;
Without this, folly, age, and cold decay:
If all were minded so, the times should cease,
And threescore year would make the world away.
Let those whom Nature hath not made for store,
Harsh, featureless, and rude, barrenly perish:
Look, whom she best endow'd she gave the more;
Which bounteous gift thou shouldst in bounty
  cherish:
  She carved thee for her seal, and meant thereby
  Thou shouldst print more, not let that copy die.

12.

When I do count the clock that tells the time,
And see the brave day sunk in hideous night;
When I behold the violet past prime,
And sable curls all silver'd o'er with white;
When lofty trees I see barren of leaves,
Which erst from heat did canopy the herd,
And summer's green, all girded up in sheaves,
Borne on the bier with white and bristly beard;
Then of thy beauty do I question make,
That thou among the wastes of time must go,
Since sweets and beauties do themselves forsake,
And die as fast as they see others grow;
  And nothing 'gainst Time's scythe can make
    defence
  Save breed, to brave him when he takes thee
    hence.

13.

O that you were yourself! but, love, you are
No longer yours than you yourself here live:
Against this coming end you should prepare,
And your sweet semblance to some other give.
So should that beauty which you hold in lease
Find no determination; then you were
Yourself again, after yourself's decease,   [bear.
When your sweet issue your sweet form should
Who lets so fair a house fall to decay,
Which husbandry in honour might uphold
Against the stormy gusts of winter's day
And barren rage of death's eternal cold?
  O, none but unthrifts: dear my love, you know
  You had a father; let your son say so.

14.

Not from the stars do I my judgement pluck;
And yet methinks I have astronomy,
But not to tell of good or evil luck,
Of plagues, of dearths, or seasons' quality;
Nor can I fortune to brief minutes tell,
Pointing to each his thunder, rain, and wind,
Or say with princes if it shall go well,
By oft predict that I in heaven find:
But from thine eyes my knowledge I derive,
And, constant stars, in them I read such art,
As truth and beauty shall together thrive,
If from thyself to store thou wouldst convert;
  Or else of thee this I prognosticate:
  Thy end is truth's and beauty's doom and date.

15.

When I consider every thing that grows
Holds in perfection but a little moment,
That this huge stage presenteth naught but shows
Whereon the stars in secret influence comment;
When I perceive that men as plants increase,
Cheered and checkt even by the self-same sky,
Vaunt in their youthful sap, at height decrease,
And wear their brave state out of memory;
Then the conceit of this inconstant stay
Sets you most rich in youth before my sight,
Where wasteful Time debateth with Decay,
To change your day of youth to sullied night;
   And, all in war with Time, for love of you,
   As he takes from you, I engraft you new.

16.

But wherefore do not you a mightier way
Make war upon this bloody tyrant, Time?
And fortify yourself in your decay
With means more blessed than my barren rime?
Now stand you on the top of happy hours;
And many maiden gardens, yet unset,
With virtuous wish would bear your living flowers,
Much liker than your painted counterfeit:
So should the lines of life that life repair,
Which this, Time's pencil, or my pupil pen,
Neither in inward worth nor outward fair,
Can make you live yourself in eyes of men.
   To give away yourself keeps yourself still;
   And you must live, drawn by your own sweet
     skill.

17.

Who will believe my verse in time to come,
If it were fill'd with your most high deserts?
Though yet, heaven knows, it is but as a tomb
Which hides your life, and shows not half your
   parts.
If I could write the beauty of your eyes,
And in fresh numbers number all your graces,
The age to come would say, 'This poet lies,
Such heavenly touches ne'er toucht earthly faces.'
So should my papers, yellow'd with their age,
Be scorn'd, like old men of less truth than tongue;
And your true rights be term'd a poet's rage,
And stretched metre of an antique song;
   But were some child of yours alive that time,
   You should live twice, in it and in my rime.

18.

Shall I compare thee to a summer's day?
Thou art more lovely and more temperate:
Rough winds do shake the darling buds of May,
And summer's lease hath all too short a date:
Sometime too hot the eye of heaven shines,
And often is his gold complexion dimm'd;
And every fair from fair sometime declines,
By chance, or nature's changing course, un-
   trimm'd;
But thy eternal summer shall not fade,
Nor lose possession of that fair thou ow'st;
Nor shall Death brag thou wander'st in his shade,
When in eternal lines to time thou grow'st:
   So long as men can breathe, or eyes can see,
   So long lives this, and this gives life to thee.

19.

Devouring Time, blunt thou the lion's paws,
And make the earth devour her own sweet brood;
Pluck the keen teeth from the fierce tiger's jaws,
And burn the long-lived phœnix in her blood;
Make glad and sorry seasons as thou fleets,
And do whate'er thou wilt, swift-footed Time,
To the wide world and all her fading sweets;
But I forbid thee one most heinous crime:
O, carve not with thy hours my love's fair brow,
Nor draw no lines there with thine antique pen;
Him in thy course untainted do allow
For beauty's pattern to succeeding men.
   Yet, do thy worst, old Time: despite thy wrong,
   My love shall in my verse ever live young.

20.

A woman's face, with Nature's own hand painted,
Hast thou, the master-mistress of my passion;
A woman's gentle heart, but not acquainted
With shifting change, as is false women's fashion;
An eye more bright than theirs, less false in rolling,
Gilding the object whereupon it gazeth;
A man in hew all *Hews* in his controlling,
Which steals men's eyes, and women's souls
   amazeth.
And for a woman wert thou first created;
Till Nature, as she wrought thee, fell a-doting,
And by addition me of thee defeated,
By adding one thing to my purpose nothing.
   But since she prickt thee out for women's
     pleasure,
   Mine be thy love, and thy love's use their
     treasure.

21.

So is it not with me as with that Muse
Stirr'd by a painted beauty to his verse,
Who heaven itself for ornament doth use,
And every fair with his fair doth rehearse;
Making a couplement of proud compare,
With sun and moon, with earth and sea's rich gems,
With April's first-born flowers, and all things rare
That heaven's air in this huge rondure hems.
O, let me, true in love, but truly write,
And then believe me, my love is as fair
As any mother's child, though not so bright
As those gold candles fixt in heaven's air:
   Let them say more that like of hearsay well;
   I will not praise that purpose not to sell.

22.

My glass shall not persuade me I am old,
So long as youth and thou are of one date;
But when in thee time's furrows I behold,
Then look I death my days should expiate.
For all that beauty that doth cover thee
Is but the seemly raiment of my heart,
Which in my breast doth live, as thine in me:
How can I, then, be elder than thou art?
O, therefore, love, be of thyself so wary
As I, not for myself, but for thee will;
Bearing thy heart, which I will keep so chary
As tender nurse her babe from faring ill.
   Presume not on thy heart when mine is slain;
   Thou gavest me thine, not to give back again.

23.

As an unperfect actor on the stage,
Who, with his fear is put besides his part,
Or some fierce thing replete with too much rage,
Whose strength's abundance weakens his own
So I, for fear of trust, forget to say   [heart;
The perfect ceremony of love's rite,
And in mine own love's strength seem to decay,
O'ercharged with burthen of mine own love's
   might.
O, let my books be, then, the eloquence
And dumb presagers of my speaking breast;
Who plead for love, and look for recompense,
More than that tongue that more hath more ex-
   prest.
   O, learn to read what silent love hath writ:
   To hear with eyes belongs to love's fine wit.

24.

Mine eye hath play'd the painter, and hath stell'd
Thy beauty's form in table of my heart;
My body is the frame wherein 'tis held,
And perspective it is best painter's art.
For through the painter must you see his skill,
To find where your true image pictured lies;
Which in my bosom's shop is hanging still,
That hath his windows glazed with thine eyes.
Now see what good turns eyes for eyes have done:
Mine eyes have drawn thy shape, and thine for me
Are windows to my breast, where-through the sun
Delights to peep, to gaze therein on thee;
   Yet eyes this cunning want to grace their art,
   They draw but what they see, know not the heart.

25.

Let those who are in favour with their stars
Of public honour and proud titles boast,
Whilst I, whom fortune of such triumph bars,
Unlookt for joy in that I honour most.
Great princes' favourites their fair leaves spread
But as the marigold at the sun's eye;
And in themselves their pride lies buried,
For at a frown they in their glory die.
The painful warrior famoused for fight,
After a thousand victories once foil'd,
Is from the book of honour razed quite,
And all the rest forgot for which he toil'd:
   Then happy I, that love and am beloved
   Where I may not remove nor be removed.

26.

Lord of my love, to whom in vassalage
Thy merit hath my duty strongly knit,
To thee I send this written ambassage,
To witness duty, not to show my wit:
Duty so great, which wit so poor as mine
May make seem bare, in wanting words to show it,
But that I hope some good conceit of thine
In thy soul's thought, all naked, will bestow it;
Till whatsoever star that guides my moving,
Points on me graciously with fair aspect,
And puts apparel on my totter'd loving,
To show me worthy of thy sweet respect:
   Then may I dare to boast how I do love thee;
   Till then not show my head where thou mayst
   prove me.

27.

Weary with toil, I haste me to my bed,
The dear repose for limbs with travel tired;
But then begins a journey in my head,
To work my mind, when body's work's expired:
For then my thoughts, from far where I abide,
Intend a zealous pilgrimage to thee,
And keep my drooping eyelids open wide,
Looking on darkness which the blind do see:
Save that my soul's imaginary sight
Presents thy shadow to my sightless view,
Which, like a jewel hung in ghastly night,
Makes black night beauteous, and her old face new.
   Lo, thus, by day my limbs, by night my mind,
   For thee and for myself no quiet find

28.

How can I, then, return in happy plight,
That am debarr'd the benefit of rest?
When day's oppression is not eased by night,
But day by night, and night by day, opprest?
And each, though enemies to either's reign,
Do in consent shake hands to torture me;
The one by toil, the other to complain
How far I toil, still farther off from thee.
I tell the day, to please him thou art bright,
And dost him grace when clouds do blot the
   heaven:
So flatter I the swart-complexion'd night,
When sparkling stars twire not thou gild'st the
   even.
   But day doth daily draw my sorrows longer,
   And night doth nightly make grief's strength
   seem stronger.

29.

When, in disgrace with fortune and men's eyes,
I all alone beweep my outcast state,
And trouble deaf heaven with my bootless cries,
And look upon myself, and curse my fate,
Wishing me like to one more rich in hope,
Featured like him, like him with friends possest,
Desiring this man's art, and that man's scope,
With what I most enjoy contented least;
Yet in these thoughts myself almost despising,
Haply I think on thee,—and then my state,
Like to the lark at break of day arising
From sullen earth, sings hymns at heaven's gate;
   For thy sweet love remember'd such wealth
   brings,
   That then I scorn to change my state with kings.

30.

When to the sessions of sweet silent thought
I summon up remembrance of things past,
I sigh the lack of many a thing I sought,
And with old woes new wail my dear time's waste:
Then can I drown an eye, unused to flow,
For precious friends hid in death's dateless night,
And weep afresh love's long-since-cancell'd woe,
And moan the expense of many a vanisht sight:
Then can I grieve at grievances foregone,
And heavily from woe to woe tell o'er
The sad account of fore-bemoaned moan,
Which I new pay as if not paid before.
   But if the while I think on thee, dear friend,
   All losses are restored, and sorrows end.

31.

Thy bosom is endeared with all hearts,
Which I by lacking have supposed dead;
And there reigns love, and all love's loving parts,
And all those friends which I thought buried.
How many a holy and obsequious tear
Hath dear religious love stoln from mine eye,
As interest of the dead, which now appear
But things removed, that hidden in thee lie!
Thou art the grave where buried love doth live,
Hung with the trophies of my lovers gone,
Who all their parts of me to thee did give;
That due of many now is thine alone:
    Their images I loved I view in thee,
    And thou, all they, hast all the all of me.

32.

If thou survive my well-contented day,
When that churl Death my bones with dust shall
    cover,
And shalt by fortune once more re-survey
These poor rude lines of thy deceased lover:
Compare them with the bettering of the time,
And though they be outstript by every pen,
Reserve them for my love, not for their rime,
Exceeded by the height of happier men.
O, then vouchsafe me but this loving thought:
'Had my friend's Muse grown with this growing
    age,
A dearer birth than this his love had brought,
To march in ranks of better equipage:
    But since he died, and poets better prove,
    Theirs for their style I'll read, his for his love.'

33.

Full many a glorious morning have I seen
Flatter the mountain-tops with sovereign eye,
Kissing with golden face the meadows green,
Gilding pale streams with heavenly alchemy;
Anon permit the basest clouds to ride
With ugly rack on his celestial face,
And from the forlorn world his visage hide,
Stealing unseen to west with this disgrace:
Even so my sun one early morn did shine
With all-triumphant splendour on my brow;
But, out, alack! he was but one hour mine,
The region cloud hath maskt him from me now.
    Yet him for this my love no whit disdaineth;
    Suns of the world may stain when heaven's sun
      staineth.

34.

Why didst thou promise such a beauteous day,
And make me travel forth without my cloak,
To let base clouds o'ertake me in my way,
Hiding thy bravery in their rotten smoke?
'Tis not enough that through the cloud thou break,
To dry the rain on my storm-beaten face,
For no man well of such a salve can speak
That heals the wound, and cures not the disgrace:
Nor can thy shame give physic to my grief;
Though thou repent, yet I have still the loss:
The offender's sorrow lends but weak relief
To him that bears the strong offence's cross.
    Ah, but those tears are pearl which thy love
      sheeds,
    And they are rich, and ransom all ill deeds.

35.

No more be grieved at that which thou hast done:
Roses have thorns, and silver fountains mud;
Clouds and eclipses stain both moon and sun,
And loathsome canker lives in sweetest bud.
All men make faults, and even I in this,
Authorizing thy trespass with compare,
Myself corrupting, salving thy amiss,
Excusing 'their sins more than thy sins are';
For to thy sensual fault I bring in sense,—
Thy adverse party is thy advocate,—
And 'gainst myself a lawful plea commence:
Such civil war is in my love and hate,
    That I an accessary needs must be
    To that sweet thief which sourly robs from me.

36.

Let me confess that we two must be twain,
Although our undivided loves are one:
So shall those blots that do with me remain,
Without thy help, by me be borne alone.
In our two loves there is but one respect,
Though in our lives a separable spite,
Which though it alter not love's sole effect,
Yet doth it steal sweet hours from love's delight.
I may not evermore acknowledge thee,
Lest my bewailed guilt should do thee shame;
Nor thou with public kindness honour me,
Unless thou take that honour from thy name:
    But do not so; I love thee in such sort,
    As, thou being mine, mine is thy good report.

37.

As a decrepit father takes delight
To see his active child do deeds of youth,
So I, made lame by Fortune's dearest spite,
Take all my comfort of thy worth and truth;
For whether beauty, birth, or wealth, or wit,
Or any of these all, or all, or more,
Entitled in their parts do crowned sit,
I make my love engrafted to this store:
So then I am not lame, poor, nor despised,
Whilst that this shadow doth such substance give
That I in thy abundance am sufficed,
And by a part of all thy glory live.
    Look, what is best, that best I wish in thee:
    This wish I have; then ten times happy me!

38.

How can my Muse want subject to invent,
While thou dost breathe, that pour'st into my
    verse
Thine own sweet argument, too excellent
For every vulgar paper to rehearse?
O, give thyself the thanks, if aught in me
Worthy perusal stand against thy sight;
For who's so dumb that cannot write to thee,
When thou thyself dost give invention light?
Be thou the tenth Muse, ten times more in worth
Than those old nine which rimers invocate;
And he that calls on thee, let him bring forth
Eternal numbers to outlive long date.
    If my slight Muse do please these curious days,
    The pain be mine, but thine shall be the praise.

39.

O, how thy worth with manners may I sing,
When thou art all the better part of me?
What can mine own praise to mine own self bring?
And what is't but mine own when I praise thee?
Even for this let us divided live,
And our dear love lose name of single one,
That by this separation I may give
That due to thee which thou deservest alone.
O absence, what a torment wouldst thou prove,
Were it not thy sour leisure gave sweet leave
To entertain the time with thoughts of love,
Which time and thoughts so sweetly doth deceive,
    And that thou teachest how to make one twain,
    By praising him here who doth hence remain!

40.

Take all my loves, my love, yea, take them all;
What hast thou then more than thou hadst before?
No love, my love, that thou mayst true love call;
All mine was thine before thou hadst this more.
Then, if for my love thou my love receivest,
I cannot blame thee for my love thou usest;
But yet be blamed, if thou this self deceivest
By wilful taste of what thyself refusest.
I do forgive thy robbery, gentle thief,
Although thou steal thee all my poverty;
And yet, love knows, it is a greater grief
To bear love's wrong than hate's known injury.
    Lascivious grace, in whom all ill well shows,
    Kill me with spites; yet we must not be foes.

41.

Those pretty wrongs that liberty commits,
When I am sometime absent from thy heart,
Thy beauty and thy years full well befits,
For still temptation follows where thou art.
Gentle thou art, and therefore to be won,
Beauteous thou art, therefore to be assailed;
And when a woman woos, what woman's son
Will sourly leave her till she have prevailed?
Ay me! but yet thou mightst my seat forbear,
And chide thy beauty and thy straying youth,
Who lead thee in their riot even there
Where thou art forced to break a twofold truth,—
    Hers, by thy beauty tempting her to thee,
    Thine, by thy beauty being false to me.

42.

That thou hast her, it is not all my grief,
And yet it may be said I loved her dearly;
That she hath thee, is of my wailing chief,
A loss in love that touches me more nearly.
Loving offenders, thus I will excuse ye:—
Thou dost love her, because thou know'st I love her;
And for my sake even so doth she abuse me,
Suff'ring my friend for my sake to approve her.
If I lose thee, my loss is my love's gain,
And losing her, my friend hath found that loss;
Both find each other, and I lose both twain,
And both for my sake lay on me this cross:
    But here's the joy; my friend and I are one;
    Sweet flattery! then she loves but me alone.

43.

When most I wink, then do mine eyes best see,
For all the day they view things unrespected;
But when I sleep, in dreams they look on thee,
And, darkly bright, are bright in dark directed.
Then thou, whose shadow shadows doth make bright,
How would thy shadow's form form happy show
To the clear day with thy much clearer light,
When to unseeing eyes thy shade shines so!
How would, I say, mine eyes be blessed made
By looking on thee in the living day,
When in dead night thy fair imperfect shade
Through heavy sleep on sightless eyes doth stay!
    All days are nights to see till I see thee,
    And nights bright days when dreams do show thee me.

44.

If the dull substance of my flesh were thought,
Injurious distance should not stop my way;
For then, despite of space, I would be brought,
From limits far remote, where thou dost stay.
No matter then although my foot did stand
Upon the farthest earth removed from thee;
For nimble thought can jump both sea and land,
As soon as think the place where he would be.
But, ah, thought kills me, that I am not thought,
To leap large lengths of miles when thou art gone,
But that, so much of earth and water wrought,
I must attend time's leisure with my moan;
    Receiving naught by elements so slow
    But heavy tears, badges of either's woe.

45.

The other two, slight air and purging fire,
Are both with thee, wherever I abide;
The first my thought, the other my desire,
These present-absent with swift motion slide.
For when these quicker elements are gone
In tender embassy of love to thee,
My life, being made of four, with two alone
Sinks down to death, opprest with melancholy;
Until life's composition be recured
By those swift messengers return'd from thee,
Who even but now come back again, assured
Of thy fair health, recounting it to me:
    This told, I joy; but then no longer glad,
    I send them back again, and straight grow sad.

46.

Mine eye and heart are at a mortal war,
How to divide the conquest of thy sight;
Mine eye my heart thy picture's sight would bar,
My heart mine eye the freedom of that right.
My heart doth plead that thou in him dost lie—
A closet never pierced with crystal eyes—
But the defendant doth that plea deny,
And says in him thy fair appearance lies.
To cide this title is impanneled
A quest of thoughts, all tenants to the heart;
And by their verdict is determined
The clear eye's moiety and the dear heart's part:
    As thus; mine eye's due is thy outward part,
    And my heart's right thy inward love of heart.

47.

Betwixt mine eye and heart a league is took,
And each doth good turns now unto the other:
When that mine eye is famisht for a look,
Or heart in love with sighs himself doth smother,
With my love's picture then my eye doth feast,
And to the painted banquet bids my heart;
Another time mine eye is my heart's guest,
And in his thoughts of love doth share a part:
So, either by thy picture or my love,
Thyself away art present still with me;
For thou not farther than my thoughts canst move,
And I am still with them, and they with thee;
    Or, if they sleep, thy picture in my sight
    Awakes my heart to heart's and eye's delight.

48.

How careful was I, when I took my way,
Each trifle under truest bars to thrust,
That to my use it might unused stay
From hands of falsehood, in sure wards of trust!
But thou, to whom my jewels trifles are,
Most worthy comfort, now my greatest grief,
Thou, best of dearest, and mine only care,
Art left the prey of every vulgar thief.
Thee have I not lockt up in any chest,
Save where thou art not, though I feel thou art,
Within the gentle closure of my breast,
From whence at pleasure thou mayst come and
    part;
    And even thence thou wilt be stoln, I fear,
    For truth proves thievish for a prize so dear.

49.

Against that time, if ever that time come,
When I shall see thee frown on my defects,
Whenas thy love hath cast his utmost sum,
Call'd to that audit by advised respects;
Against that time when thou shalt strangely pass,
And scarcely greet me with that sun, thine eye,
When love, converted from the thing it was,
Shall reasons find of settled gravity;
Against that time do I ensconce me here
Within the knowledge of mine own desert,
And this my hand against myself uprear,
To guard the lawful reasons on thy part:
    To leave poor me thou hast the strength of laws,
    Since why to love I can allege no cause.

50.

How heavy do I journey on the way,
When what I seek—my weary travel's end—
Doth teach that ease and that repose to say,
'Thus far the miles are measured from thy
    friend!'
The beast that bears me, tired with my woe,
Plods dully on, to bear that weight in me,
As if by some instinct the wretch did know
His rider loved not speed, being made from thee:
The bloody spur cannot provoke him on
That sometimes anger thrusts into his hide;
Which heavily he answers with a groan,
More sharp to me than spurring to his side;
    For that same groan doth put this in my mind;
    My grief lies onward, and my joy behind.

51.

Thus can my love excuse the slow offence
Of my dull bearer when from thee I speed:
From where thou art why should I haste me
    thence?
Till I return, of posting is no need.
O, what excuse will my poor beast then find,
When swift extremity can seem but slow?
Then should I spur, though mounted on the wind,
In winged speed no motion shall I know:
Then can no horse with my desire keep pace;
Therefore desire, of perfect'st love being made,
Shall neigh, no dull flesh in his fiery race;
But love, for love, thus shall excuse my jade,—
    Since from thee going he went wilful-slow,
    Towards thee I'll run, and give him leave to go.

52.

So am I as the rich, whose blessed key
Can bring him to his sweet up-locked treasure,
The which he will not every hour survey,
For blunting the fine point of seldom pleasure.
Therefore are feasts so solemn and so rare,
Since, seldom coming, in the long year set,
Like stones of worth they thinly placed are,
Or captain jewels in the carcanet.
So is the time that keeps you, as my chest,
Or as the wardrobe which the robe doth hide,
To make some special instant special blest,
By new unfolding his imprison'd pride.
    Blessed are you, whose worthiness gives scope,
    Being had, to triumph, being lackt, to hope.

53.

What is your substance, whereof are you made,
That millions of strange shadows on you tend?
Since every one hath, every one, one shade,
And you, but one, can every shadow lend.
Describe Adonis, and the counterfeit
Is poorly imitated after you;
On Helen's cheek all art of beauty set,
And you in Grecian tires are painted new:
Speak of the spring, and foison of the year;
The one doth shadow of your beauty show,
The other as your bounty doth appear;
And you in every blessed shape we know.
    In all external grace you have some part,
    But you like none, none you, for constant heart.

54.

O, how much more doth beauty beauteous seem
By that sweet ornament which truth doth give!
The rose looks fair, but fairer we it deem
For that sweet odour which doth in it live.
The canker-blooms have full as deep a dye
As the perfumed tincture of the roses,
Hang on such thorns, and play as wantonly
When summer's breath their masked buds dis-
    closes:
But, for their virtue only is their show,
They live unwoo'd, and unrespected fade;
Die to themselves. Sweet roses do not so;
Of their sweet deaths are sweetest odours made:
    And so of you, beauteous and lovely youth,
    When that shall vade, my verse distils your
    truth.

55.

Not marble, nor the gilded monuments
Of princes, shall outlive this powerful rime;
But you shall shine more bright in these contents
Than unswept stone, besmear'd with sluttish time.
When wasteful war shall statues overturn,
And broils root out the work of masonry,
Nor Mars his sword nor war's quick fire shall burn
The living record of your memory.
'Gainst death and all-oblivious enmity
Shall you pace forth; your praise shall still find
    room
Even in the eyes of all posterity
That wears this world out to the ending doom.
    So, till the judgement that yourself arise,
    You live in this, and dwell in lovers' eyes.

56.

Sweet love, renew thy force; be it not said
Thy edge should blunter be than appetite,
Which but to-day by feeding is allay'd,
To-morrow sharpen'd in his former might:
So, love, be thou; although to-day thou fill
Thy hungry eyes even till they wink with fullness,
To-morrow see again, and do not kill
The spirit of love with a perpetual dullness.
Let this sad int'rim like the ocean be
Which parts the shore, where two contracted new
Come daily to the banks, that, when they see
Return of love, more blest may be the view;
    Or call it winter, which, being full of care,
    Makes summer's welcome thrice more wisht,
        more rare.

57.

Being your slave, what should I do but tend
Upon the hours and times of your desire?
I have no precious time at all to spend,
Nor services to do, till you require.
Nor dare I chide the world-without-end hour
Whilst I, my sovereign, watch the clock for you,
Nor think the bitterness of absence sour
When you have bid your servant once adieu;
Nor dare I question with my jealous thought
Where you may be, or your affairs suppose,
But, like a sad slave, stay and think of nought
Save, where you are how happy you make those.
    So true a fool is love, that in your Will,
    Though you do any thing, he thinks no ill.

58.

That god forbid that made me first your slave,
I should in thought control your times of
    pleasure,
Or at your hand the account of hours to crave,
Being your vassal, bound to stay your leisure!
O, let me suffer, being at your beck,
The imprison'd absence of your liberty;
And patience, tame to sufferance, bide each check,
Without accusing you of injury.
Be where you list, your charter is so strong,
That you yourself may privilege your time
To what you will; to you it doth belong
Yourself to pardon of self-doing crime.
    I am to wait, though waiting so be hell;
    Not blame your pleasure, be it ill or well.

59.

If there be nothing new, but that which is
Hath been before, how are our brains beguiled,
Which, labouring for invention, bear amiss
The second burden of a former child!
O, that record could with a backward look,
Even of five hundred courses of the sun,
Show me your image in some antique book,
Since mind at first in character was done!
That I might see what the old world could say
To this composed wonder of your frame;
Whether we are mended, or whe'r better they,
Or whether revolution be the same.
    O, sure I am, the wits of former days
    To subjects worse have given admiring praise.

60.

Like as the waves make towards the pebbled shore,
So do our minutes hasten to their end;
Each changing place with that which goes before,
In sequent toil all forwards do contend.
Nativity, once in the main of light,
Crawls to maturity, wherewith being crown'd,
Crooked eclipses 'gainst his glory fight,
And Time that gave doth now his gift confound.
Time doth transfix the flourish set on youth,
And delves the parallels in beauty's brow;
Feeds on the rarities of nature's truth,
And nothing stands but for his scythe to mow:
    And yet, to times in hope my verse shall stand,
    Praising thy worth, despite his cruel hand.

61.

Is it thy will thy image should keep open
My heavy eyelids to the weary night?
Dost thou desire my slumbers should be broken,
While shadows like to thee do mock my sight?
Is it thy spirit that thou send'st from thee
So far from home into my deeds to pry,
To find out shames and idle hours in me,
The scope and tenour of thy jealousy?
O, no! thy love, though much, is not so great:
It is my love that keeps mine eye awake;
Mine own true love that doth my rest defeat,
To play the watchman ever for thy sake:
    For thee watch I whilst thou dost wake else-
        where,
    From me far off, with others all too near.

62.

Sin of self-love possesseth all mine eye,
And all my soul, and all my every part;
And for this sin there is no remedy,
It is so grounded inward in my heart.
Methinks no face so gracious is as mine,
No shape so true, no truth of such account;
And for myself mine own worth do define,
As I all other in all worths surmount.
But when my glass shows me myself indeed,
Beated and chopt with tann'd antiquity,
Mine own self-love quite contrary I read;
Self so self-loving were iniquity.
    'Tis thee, myself, that for myself I praise,
    Painting my age with beauty of thy days.

63.

Against my love shall be, as I am now,
With Time's injurious hand crusht and o'erworn;
When hours have drain'd his blood, and fill'd his
brow
With lines and wrinkles; when his youthful morn
Hath travell'd on to age's steepy night;
And all those beauties whereof now he's king
Are vanishing or vanisht out of sight,
Stealing away the treasure of his spring;
For such a time do I now fortify
Against confounding age's cruel knife,
That he shall never cut from memory
My sweet love's beauty, though my lover's life:
 His beauty shall in these black lines be seen,
 And they shall live, and he in them still green.

64.

When I have seen by Time's fell hand defaced
The rich proud cost of outworn buried age;
When sometime lofty towers I see down-razed,
And brass eternal slave to mortal rage;
When I have seen the hungry ocean gain
Advantage on the kingdom of the shore,
And the firm soil win of the watery main,
Increasing store with loss, and loss with store;
When I have seen such interchange of state,
Or state itself confounded to decay;
Ruin hath taught me thus to ruminate,—
That Time will come and take my love away.
 This thought is as a death, which cannot choose
 But weep to have that which it fears to lose.

65.

Since brass, nor stone, nor earth, nor boundless
sea,
But sad mortality o'ersways their power,
How with this rage shall beauty hold a plea,
Whose action is no stronger than a flower?
O, how shall summer's honey breath hold out
Against the wrackful siege of battering days,
When rocks impregnable are not so stout,
Nor gates of steel so strong, but Time decays?
O fearful meditation! where, alack,
Shall Time's best jewel from Time's chest lie hid?
Or what strong hand can hold his swift foot back?
Or who his spoil of beauty can forbid?
 O, none, unless this miracle have might,
 That in black ink my love may still shine bright.

66.

Tired with all these, for restful death I cry,—
As, to behold Desert a beggar born,
And needy Nothing trimm'd in jollity,
And purest Faith unhappily forsworn,
And gilded Honour shamefully misplaced,
And maiden Virtue rudely strumpeted,
And right Perfection wrongfully disgraced,
And Strength by limping Sway disabled,
And Art made tongue-tied by Authority,
And Folly, doctor-like, controlling Skill,
And simple Truth miscall'd Simplicity,
And captive Good attending captain Ill:
 Tired with all these, from these would I be gone,
 Save that, to die, I leave my love alone.

67.

Ah, wherefore with infection should he live,
And with his presence grace impiety,
That sin by him advantage should achieve,
And lace itself with his society?
Why should false painting imitate his cheek,
And steal dead seeing of his living hue?
Why should poor beauty indirectly seek
Roses of shadow, since his rose is true?
Why should he live, now Nature bankrout is,
Beggar'd of blood to blush through lively veins?
For she hath no exchequer now but his,
And, proud of many, lives upon his gains.
 O, him she stores, to show what wealth she had
 In days long since, before these last so bad.

68.

Thus is his cheek the map of days outworn,
When beauty lived and died as flowers do now,
Before these bastard signs of fair were born,
Or durst inhabit on a living brow;
Before the golden tresses of the dead,
The right of sepulchres, were shorn away,
To live a second life on second head;
Ere beauty's dead fleece made another gay:
In him those holy antique hours are seen,
Without all ornament, itself, and true,
Making no summer of another's green,
Robbing no old to dress his beauty new;
 And him as for a map doth Nature store,
 To show false Art what beauty was of yore.

69.

Those parts of thee that the world's eye doth view
Want nothing that the thought of hearts can mend;
All tongues, the voice of souls, give thee that due,
Uttering bare truth, even so as foes commend.
Thy outward thus with outward praise is crown'd;
But those same tongues, that give thee so thine
own,
In other accents do this praise confound
By seeing farther than the eye hath shown.
They look into the beauty of thy mind,
And that, in guess, they measure by thy deeds;
Then, churls, their thoughts, although their eyes
were kind,
To thy fair flower add the rank smell of weeds:
 But why thy odour matcheth not thy show,
 The soil is this, that thou dost common grow.

70.

That thou art blamed shall not be thy defect,
For slander's mark was ever yet the fair;
The ornament of beauty is suspect,
A crow that flies in heaven's sweetest air.
So thou be good, slander doth but approve
Thy worth the greater, being woo'd of time;
For canker vice the sweetest buds doth love,
And thou present'st a pure unstained prime.
Thou hast past by the ambush of young days,
Either not assail'd, or victor being charged;
Yet this thy praise cannot be so thy praise,
To tie up envy evermore enlarged:
 If some suspect of ill maskt not thy show,
 Then thou alone kingdoms of hearts shouldst
 owe.

71.

No longer mourn for me when I am dead
Than you shall hear the surly sullen bell
Give warning to the world that I am fled
From this vile world, with vilest worms to dwell:
Nay, if you read this line, remember not
The hand that writ it; for I love you so,
That I in your sweet thoughts would be forgot,
If thinking on me then should make you woe.
O, if, I say, you look upon this verse
When I perhaps compounded am with clay,
Do not so much as my poor name rehearse;
But let your love even with my life decay;
 Lest the wise world should look into your moan,
 And mock you with me after I am gone.

72.

O, lest the world should task you to recite
What merit lived in me, that you should love,
After my death, dear love, forget me quite,
For you in me can nothing worthy prove;
Unless you would devise some virtuous lie,
To do more for me than mine own desert,
And hang more praise upon deceased I
Than niggard truth would willingly impart:
O, lest your true love may seem false in this,
That you for love speak well of me untrue,
My name be buried where my body is,
And live no more to shame nor me nor you.
 For I am shamed by that which I bring forth,
 And so should you, to love things nothing
  worth.

73.

That time of year thou mayst in me behold
When yellow leaves, or none, or few, do hang
Upon those boughs which shake against the cold,
Bare ruin'd choirs, where late the sweet birds sang.
In me thou see'st the twilight of such day
As after sunset fadeth in the west;
Which by and by black night doth take away,
Death's second self, that seals up all in rest.
In me thou see'st the glowing of such fire,
That on the ashes of his youth doth lie,
As the death-bed whereon it must expire,
Consumed with that which it was nourisht by.
 This thou perceivest, which makes thy love
  more strong,
 To love that well which thou must leave ere
  long.

74.

But be contented: when that fell arrest
Without all bail shall carry me away,
My life hath in this line some interest,
Which for memorial still with thee shall stay.
When thou reviewest this, thou dost review
The very part was consecrate to thee:
The earth can have but earth, which is his due;
My spirit is thine, the better part of me:
So, then, thou hast but lost the dregs of life,
The prey of worms, my body being dead;
The coward conquest of a wretch's knife,
Too base of thee to be remembered.
 The worth of that is that which it contains,
 And that is this, and this with thee remains.

75.

So are you to my thoughts as food to life,
Or as sweet-season'd showers are to the ground;
And for the peace of you I hold such strife
As 'twixt a miser and his wealth is found;
Now proud as an enjoyer, and anon
Doubting the filching age will steal his treasure;
Now counting best to be with you alone,
Then better'd that the world may see my pleasure:
Sometime all full with feasting on your sight,
And by and by clean starved for a look;
Possessing or pursuing no delight,
Save what is had or must from you be took.
 Thus do I pine and surfeit day by day,
 Or gluttoning on all, or all away.

76.

Why is my verse so barren of new pride,
So far from variation or quick change?
Why, with the time, do I not glance aside
To new-found methods and to compounds
 strange?
Why write I still all one, ever the same,
And keep invention in a noted weed,
That every word doth almost tell my name,
Showing their birth, and where they did proceed?
O, know, sweet love, I always write of you,
And you and love are still my argument;
So all my best is dressing old words new,
Spending again what is already spent:
 For as the sun is daily new and old,
 So is my love still telling what is told.

77.

Thy glass will show thee how thy beauties wear,
Thy dial how thy precious minutes waste;
The vacant leaves thy mind's imprint will bear,
And of this book this learning mayst thou taste.
The wrinkles which thy glass will truly show,
Of mouthed graves will give thee memory;
Thou by thy dial's shady stealth mayst know
Time's thievish progress to eternity.
Look, what thy memory cannot contain,
Commit to these waste blanks, and thou shalt find
Those children nursed, deliver'd from thy brain,
To take a new acquaintance of thy mind.
 These offices, so oft as thou wilt look,
 Shall profit thee, and much enrich thy book.

78.

So oft have I invoked thee for my Muse,
And found such fair assistance in my verse,
As every alien pen hath got my use,
And under thee their poesy disperse.
Thine eyes, that taught the dumb on high to sing,
And heavy ignorance aloft to fly,
Have added feathers to the learned's wing,
And given grace a double majesty.
Yet be most proud of that which I compile,
Whose influence is thine, and born of thee:
In others' works thou dost but mend the style,
And arts with thy sweet graces graced be;
 But thou art all my art, and dost advance
 As high as learning my rude ignorance.

79.

Whilst I alone did call upon thy aid,
My verse alone had all thy gentle grace;
But now my gracious numbers are decay'd,
And my sick Muse doth give another place.
I grant, sweet love, thy lovely argument
Deserves the travail of a worthier pen;
Yet what of thee thy poet doth invent
He robs thee of, and pays it thee again.
He lends thee virtue, and he stole that word
From thy behaviour; beauty doth he give,
And found it in thy cheek; he can afford
No praise to thee but what in thee doth live.
    Then thank him not for that which he doth say,
    Since what he owes thee thou thyself dost pay.

80.

O, how I faint when I of you do write,
Knowing a better spirit doth use your name,
And in the praise thereof spends all his might,
To make me tongue-tied, speaking of your fame!
But since your worth, wide as the ocean is,
The humble as the proudest sail doth bear,
My saucy bark, inferior far to his,
On your broad main doth wilfully appear.
Your shallowest help will hold me up afloat,
While he upon your soundless deep doth ride;
Or, being wrackt, I am a worthless boat,
He of tall building and of goodly pride:
    Then if he thrive, and I be cast away,
    The worst was this; my love was my decay.

81.

Or I shall live your epitaph to make,
Or you survive when I in earth am rotten;
From hence your memory death cannot take,
Although in me each part will be forgotten.
Your name from hence immortal life shall have,
Though I, once gone, to all the world must die:
The earth can yield me but a common grave,
When you entombed in men's eyes shall lie.
Your monument shall be my gentle verse,
Which eyes not yet created shall o'er-read;
And tongues to be your being shall rehearse,
When all the breathers of this world are dead;
    You still shall live—such virtue hath my pen—
    Where breath most breathes, even in the mouths
    of men.

82.

I grant thou wert not married to my Muse,
And therefore mayst without attaint o'erlook
The dedicated words which writers use
Of their fair subject, blessing every book.
Thou art as fair in knowledge as in hue,
Finding thy worth a limit past my praise;
And therefore art enforced to seek anew
Some fresher stamp of the time-bettering days.
And do so, love; yet when they have devised
What strained touches rhetoric can lend,
Thou truly fair wert truly sympathized
In true plain words by thy true-telling friend;
    And their gross painting might be better used
    Where cheeks need blood; in thee it is abused.

83.

I never saw that you did painting need,
And therefore to your fair no painting set;
I found, or thought I found, you did exceed
The barren tender of a poet's debt:
And therefore have I slept in your report,
That you yourself, being extant, well might show
How far a modern quill doth come too short,
Speaking of worth, what worth in you doth grow.
This silence for my sin you did impute,
Which shall be most my glory, being dumb;
For I impair not beauty, being mute,
When others would give life, and bring a tomb.
    There lives more life in one of your fair eyes
    Than both your poets can in praise devise.

84.

Who is it that says most? which can say more
Than this rich praise, that you alone are you?
In whose confine immured is the store
Which should example where your equal grew.
Lean penury within that pen doth dwell
That to his subject lends not some small glory;
But he that writes of you, if he can tell
That you are you, so dignifies his story:
Let him but copy what in you is writ,
Not making worse what nature made so clear,
And such a counterpart shall fame his wit,
Making his style admired everywhere.
    You to your beauteous blessings add a curse,
    Being fond on praise, which makes your praises
    worse.

85.

My tongue-tied Muse in manners holds her still,
While comments of your praise, richly compiled,
Reserve their character with golden quill,
And precious phrase by all the Muses filed.
I think good thoughts, whilst other write good
    words,
And, like unletter'd clerk, still cry 'Amen'
To every hymn that able spirit affords
In polisht form of well-refined pen.
Hearing you praised, I say ''Tis so, 'tis true,'
And to the most of praise add something more;
But that is in my thought, whose love to you,
Though words come hindmost, holds his rank
    before.
    Then others for the breath of words respect,
    Me for my dumb thoughts, speaking in effect.

86.

Was it the proud full sail of his great verse,
Bound for the prize of all-too-precious you,
That did my ripe thoughts in my brain inhearse,
Making their tomb the womb wherein they grew?
Was it his spirit, by spirits taught to write
Above a mortal pitch, that struck me dead?
No, neither he, nor his compeers by night
Giving him aid, my verse astonished.
He, nor that affable familiar ghost
Which nightly gulls him with intelligence,
As victors, of my silence cannot boast;
I was not sick of any fear from thence:
    But when your countenance fill'd up his line,
    Then lackt I matter; that enfeebled mine.

87.

Farewell! thou art too dear for my possessing,
And like enough thou know'st thy estimate:
The charter of thy worth gives thee releasing;
My bonds in thee are all determinate.
For how do I hold thee but by thy granting?
And for that riches where is my deserving?
The cause of this fair gift in me is wanting,
And so my patent back again is swerving.
Thyself thou gavest, thy own worth then not
    knowing,
Or me, to whom thou gavest it, else mistaking;
So thy great gift, upon misprision growing,
Comes home again, on better judgement making.
    Thus have I had thee, as a dream doth flatter,
    In sleep a king, but waking no such matter.

88.

When thou shalt be disposed to set me light,
And place my merit in the eye of scorn,
Upon thy side against myself I'll fight,
And prove thee virtuous, though thou art forsworn.
With mine own weakness being best acquainted,
Upon thy part I can set down a story
Of faults conceal'd, wherein I am attainted;
That thou, in losing me, shalt win much glory:
And I by this will be a gainer too;
For bending all my loving thoughts on thee,
The injuries that to myself I do,
Doing thee vantage, double-vantage me.
    Such is my love, to thee I so belong,
    That for thy right myself will bear all wrong.

89.

Say that thou didst forsake me for some fault,
And I will comment upon that offence:
Speak of my lameness, and I straight will halt,
Against thy reasons making no defence.
Thou canst not, love, disgrace me half so ill,
To set a form upon desired change,
As I'll myself disgrace: knowing thy will,
I will acquaintance strangle, and look strange;
Be absent from thy walks; and in my tongue
Thy sweet beloved name no more shall dwell,
Lest I, too much profane, should do it wrong,
And haply of our old acquaintance tell.
    For thee, against myself I'll vow debate,
    For I must ne'er love him whom thou dost
    hate.

90.

Then hate me when thou wilt; if ever, now;
Now, while the world is bent my deeds to cross,
Join with the spite of fortune, make me bow,
And do not drop in for an after-loss:
Ah, do not, when my heart hath scaped this
    sorrow,
Come in the rearward of a conquer'd woe;
Give not a windy night a rainy morrow,
To linger out a purposed overthrow.
If thou wilt leave me, do not leave me last,
When other petty griefs have done their spite,
But in the onset come: so shall I taste
At first the very worst of fortune's might;
    And other strains of woe, which now seem woe,
    Compared with loss of thee will not seem so.

91.

Some glory in their birth, some in their skill,
Some in their wealth, some in their bodies' force;
Some in their garments, though new-fangled ill;
Some in their hawks and hounds, some in their
    horse;
And every humour hath his adjunct pleasure,
Wherein it finds a joy above the rest:
But these particulars are not my measure;
All these I better in one general best.
Thy love is better than high birth to me,
Richer than wealth, prouder than garments' cost,
Of more delight than hawks or horses be;
And having thee, of all men's pride I boast:
    Wretched in this alone, that thou mayst take
    All this away, and me most wretched make.

92.

But do thy worst to steal thyself away,
For term of life thou art assured mine;
And life no longer than thy love will stay,
For it depends upon that love of thine.
Then need I not to fear the worst of wrongs,
When in the least of them my life hath end.
I see a better state to me belongs
Than that which on thy humour doth depend:
Thou canst not vex me with inconstant mind,
Since that my life on thy revolt doth lie.
O, what a happy title do I find,
Happy to have thy love, happy to die!
    But what's so blessed-fair that fears no blot?
    Thou mayst be false, and yet I know it not.

93.

So shall I live, supposing thou art true,
Like a deceived husband; so love's face
May still seem love to me, though alter'd new;
Thy looks with me, thy heart in other place:
For there can live no hatred in thine eye,
Therefore in that I cannot know thy change.
In many's looks the false heart's history
Is writ in moods and frowns and wrinkles strange;
But heaven in thy creation did decree
That in thy face sweet love should ever dwell;
Whate'er thy thoughts or thy heart's workings be,
Thy looks should nothing thence but sweetness
    tell.
    How like Eve's apple doth thy beauty grow.
    If thy sweet virtue answer not thy show!

94.

They that have power to hurt and will do none,
That do not do the thing they most do show,
Who, moving others, are themselves as stone,
Unmoved, cold, and to temptation slow;
They rightly do inherit heaven's graces,
And husband nature's riches from expense;
They are the lords and owners of their faces,
Others but stewards of their excellence.
The summer's flower is to the summer sweet,
Though to itself it only live and die;
But if that flower with base infection meet,
The basest weed outbraves his dignity:
    For sweetest things turn sourest by their deeds;
    Lilies that fester smell far worse than weeds.

95.

How sweet and lovely dost thou make the shame
Which, like a canker in the fragrant rose,
Doth spot the beauty of thy budding name!
O, in what sweets dost thou thy sins enclose!
That tongue that tells the story of thy days,
Making lascivious comments on thy sport,
Cannot dispraise but in a kind of praise;
Naming thy name blesses an ill report.
O, what a mansion have those vices got
Which for their habitation chose out thee,
Where beauty's veil doth cover every blot,
And all things turn to fair that eyes can see!
    Take heed, dear heart, of this large privilege;
    The hardest knife ill-used doth lose his edge.

96.

Some say, thy fault is youth, some wantonness;
Some say, thy grace is youth and gentle sport;
Both grace and faults are loved of more and less:
Thou makest faults graces that to thee resort.
As on the finger of a throned queen
The basest jewel will be well esteem'd,
So are those errors that in thee are seen
To truths translated, and for true things deem'd.
How many lambs might the stern wolf betray,
If like a lamb he could his looks translate!
How many gazers mightst thou lead away,
If thou wouldst use the strength of all thy state!
    But do not so; I love thee in such sort,
    As thou being mine, mine is thy good report.

97.

How like a winter hath my absence been
From thee, the pleasure of the fleeting year!
What freezings have I felt, what dark days seen!
What old December's bareness every where!
And yet this time removed was summer's time;
The teeming autumn, big with rich increase,
Bearing the wanton burden of the prime,
Like widow'd wombs after their lords' decease:
Yet this abundant issue seem'd to me
But hope of orphans and unfather'd fruit;
For summer and his pleasures wait on thee,
And, thou away, the very birds are mute;
    Or, if they sing, 'tis with so dull a cheer,
    That leaves look pale, dreading the winter's
      near.

98.

From you have I been absent in the spring,
When proud-pied April, drest in all his trim,
Hath put a spirit of youth in every thing,
That heavy Saturn laught and leapt with him.
Yet nor the lays of birds, nor the sweet smell
Of different flowers in odour and in hue,
Could make me any summer's story tell,
Or from their proud lap pluck them where they
    grew:
Nor did I wonder at the lily's white,
Nor praise the deep vermilion in the rose;
They were but sweet, but figures of delight,
Drawn after you,—you pattern of all those.
    Yet seem'd it winter still, and, you away,
    As with your shadow I with these did play.

99.

The forward violet thus did I chide:
Sweet thief, whence didst thou steal thy sweet
    that smells,
If not from my love's breath? The purple pride
Which on thy soft cheek for complexion dwells
In my love's veins thou hast too grossly dyed.
The lily I condemned for thy hand;
And buds of marjoram had stoln thy hair:
The roses fearfully on thorns did stand,
One blushing shame, another white despair;
A third, nor red nor white, had stoln of both,
And to his robbery had annext thy breath;
But, for his theft, in pride of all his growth
A vengeful canker eat him up to death.
    More flowers I noted, yet I none could see
    But sweet or colour it had stoln from thee.

100.

Where art thou, Muse, that thou forgett'st so long
To speak of that which gives thee all thy might?
Spend'st thou thy fury on some worthless song,
Dark'ning thy power to lend base subjects light?
Return, forgetful Muse, and straight redeem
In gentle numbers time so idly spent;
Sing to the ear that doth thy lays esteem,
And gives thy pen both skill and argument.
Rise, resty Muse, my love's sweet face survey,
If Time have any wrinkle graven there;
If any, be a satire to decay,
And make Time's spoils despised everywhere.
    Give my love fame faster than Time wastes life;
    So thou prevent'st his scythe and crooked knife.

101.

O truant Muse, what shall be thy amends
For thy neglect of truth in beauty dyed?
Both truth and beauty on my love depends;
So dost thou too, and therein dignified.
Make answer, Muse: wilt thou not haply say,
'Truth needs no colour, with his colour fixt;
Beauty no pencil, beauty's truth to lay;
But best is best, if never intermixt'?
Because he needs no praise, wilt thou be dumb?
Excuse not silence so: for't lies in thee
To make him much outlive a gilded tomb,
And to be praised of ages yet to be.
    Then do thy office, Muse; I teach thee how
    To make him seem long hence as he shows now.

102.

My love is strengthen'd, though more weak in
    seeming;
I love not less, though less the show appear:
That love is merchandized whose rich esteeming
The owner's tongue doth publish everywhere.
Our love was new, and then but in the spring,
When I was wont to greet it with my lays,
As Philomel in summer's front doth sing,
And stops her pipe in growth of riper days:
Not that the summer is less pleasant now
Than when her mournful hymns did hush the
    night,
But that wild music burdens every bough,
And sweets grown common lose their dear delight.
    Therefore, like her, I sometime hold my tongue,
    Because I would not dull you with my song.

103.

Alack, what poverty my Muse brings forth,
That having such a scope to show her pride,
The argument, all bare, is of more worth
Than when it hath my added praise beside!
O, blame me not, if I no more can write!
Look in your glass, and there appears a face
That overgoes my blunt invention quite,
Dulling my lines, and doing me disgrace.
Were it not sinful, then, striving to mend,
To mar the subject that before was well?
For to no other pass my verses tend
Than of your graces and your gifts to tell;
    And more, much more, than in my verse can sit,
    Your own glass shows you when you look in it.

104.

To me, fair friend, you never can be old,
For as you were when first your eye I eyed,
Such seems your beauty still. Three winters' cold
Have from the forests shook three summers' pride;
Three beauteous springs to yellow autumn turn'd
In process of the seasons have I seen,
Three April perfumes in three hot Junes burn'd,
Since first I saw you fresh, which yet are green.
Ah, yet doth beauty, like a dial-hand,
Steal from his figure, and no pace perceived;
So your sweet hue, which methinks still doth stand,
Hath motion, and mine eye may be deceived:
    For fear of which, hear this, thou age unbred,—
    Ere you were born was beauty's summer dead.

105.

Let not my love be call'd idolatry,
Nor my beloved as an idol show,
Since all alike my songs and praises be
To one, of one, still such, and ever so.
Kind is my love to-day, to-morrow kind,
Still constant in a wondrous excellence;
Therefore my verse to constancy confined,
One thing expressing, leaves out difference.
Fair, kind, and true, is all my argument,—
Fair, kind, and true, varying to other words;
And in this change is my invention spent,
Three themes in one, which wondrous scope
    affords.
    Fair, kind, and true, have often lived alone,
    Which three till now never kept seat in one.

106.

When in the chronicle of wasted time
I see descriptions of the fairest wights,
And beauty making beautiful old rime
In praise of ladies dead and lovely knights,
Then, in the blazon of sweet beauty's best,
Of hand, of foot, of lip, of eye, of brow,
I see their antique pen would have exprest
Even such a beauty as you master now.
So all their praises are but prophecies
Of this our time, all you prefiguring;
And, for they lookt but with divining eyes,
They had not skill enough your worth to sing:
    For we, which now behold these present days,
    Have eyes to wonder, but lack tongues to
    praise.

107.

Not mine own fears, nor the prophetic soul
Of the wide world dreaming on things to come,
Can yet the lease of my true love control,
Supposed as forfeit to a confined doom.
The mortal moon hath her eclipse endured,
And the sad augurs mock their own presage;
Incertainties now crown themselves assured,
And peace proclaims olives of endless age.
Now with the drops of this most balmy time
My love looks fresh, and Death to me subscribes,
Since, spite of him, I'll live in this poor rime,
While he insults o'er dull and speechless tribes:
    And thou in this shalt find thy monument,
    When tyrants' crests and tombs of brass are
    spent.

108.

What's in the brain, that ink may character,
Which hath not figured to thee my true spirit?
What's new to speak, what new to register,
That may express my love, or thy dear merit?
Nothing, sweet boy; but yet, like prayers divine,
I must each day say o'er the very same;
Counting no old thing old, thou mine, I thine,
Even as when first I hallow'd thy fair name.
So that eternal love in love's fresh case
Weighs not the dust and injury of age,
Nor gives to necessary wrinkles place,
But makes antiquity for aye his page;
    Finding the first conceit of love there bred,
    Where time and outward form would show it
    dead.

109.

O, never say that I was false of heart,
Though absence seem'd my flame to qualify.
As easy might I from myself depart
As from my soul, which in thy breast doth lie:
That is my home of love: if I have ranged,
Like him that travels I return again,
Just to the time, not with the time exchanged,
So that myself bring water for my stain.
Never believe, though in my nature reign'd
All frailties that besiege all kinds of blood,
That it could so preposterously be stain'd,
To leave for nothing all thy sum of good;
    For nothing this wide universe I call,
    Save thou, my Rose; in it thou art my all.

110.

Alas, 'tis true I have gone here and there,
And made myself a motley to the view,
Gored mine own thoughts, sold cheap what is
    most dear,
Made old offences of affections new;
Most true it is that I have lookt on truth
Askance and strangely: but, by all above,
These blenches gave my heart another youth,
And worse essays proved thee my best of love.
Now all is done, have what shall have no end:
Mine appetite I never more will grind
On newer proof, to try an older friend,
A god in love, to whom I am confined.
    Then give me welcome, next my heaven the
    best,
    Even to thy pure and most most loving breast.

III.

O, for my sake do you with Fortune chide,
The guilty goddess of my harmful deeds,
That did not better for my life provide
Than public means which public manners breeds.
Thence comes it that my name receives a brand;
And almost thence my nature is subdued
To what it works in, like the dyer's hand:
Pity me, then, and wish I were renew'd;
Whilst, like a willing patient, I will drink
Potions of eisel 'gainst my strong infection;
No bitterness that I will bitter think,
Nor double penance, to correct correction.
  Pity me, then, dear friend, and I assure ye
  Even that your pity is enough to cure me.

112.

Your love and pity doth the impression fill
Which vulgar scandal stampt upon my brow;
For what care I who calls me well or ill,
So you o'er-green my bad, my good allow?
You are my all-the-world, and I must strive
To know my shames and praises from your
  tongue;
None else to me, nor I to none alive,
That my steel'd sense or changes right or wrong.
In so profound abysm I throw all care
Of others' voices, that my adder's sense
To critic and to flatterer stopped are.
Mark how with my neglect I do dispense:
  You are so strongly in my purpose bred,
  That all the world besides methinks are dead.

113.

Since I left you, mine eye is in my mind;
And that which governs me to go about
Doth part his function, and is partly blind,
Seems seeing, but effectually is out;
For it no form delivers to the heart
Of bird, of flower, or shape, which it doth latch:
Of his quick objects hath the mind no part,
Nor his own vision holds what it doth catch;
For if it see the rudest or gentlest sight,
The most sweet favour or deformed'st creature,
The mountain or the sea, the day or night,
The crow or dove, it shapes them to your feature:
  Incapable of more, replete with you,
  My most true mind thus maketh mine untrue.

114.

Or whether doth my mind, being crown'd with
  you,
Drink up the monarch's plague, this flattery?
Or whether shall I say, mine eye saith true,
And that your love taught it this alchemy,
To make of monsters and things indigest
Such cherubins as your sweet self resemble,
Creating every bad a perfect best,
As fast as objects to his beams assemble?
O, 'tis the first; 'tis flatt'ry in my seeing,
And my great mind most kingly drinks it up:
Mine eye well knows what with his gust is greeing,
And to his palate doth prepare the cup:
  If it be poison'd, 'tis the lesser sin
  That mine eye loves it, and doth first begin.

115.

Those lines that I before have writ do lie,
Even those that said I could not love you dearer:
Yet then my judgement knew no reason why
My most full flame should afterwards burn clearer.
But reckoning Time, whose million'd accidents
Creep in 'twixt vows, and change decrees of kings,
Tan sacred beauty, blunt the sharp'st intents,
Divert strong minds to the course of alt'ring things;
Alas, why, fearing of Time's tyranny,
Might I not then say, 'Now I love you best,'
When I was certain o'er incertainty,
Crowning the present, doubting of the rest?
  Love is a babe; then might I not say so,
  To give full growth to that which still doth
    grow.

116.

Let me not to the marriage of true minds
Admit impediments. Love is not love
Which alters when it alteration finds,
Or bends with the remover to remove:
O, no! it is an ever-fixed mark,
That looks on tempests, and is never shaken,
It is the star to every wandering bark,
Whose worth's unknown, although his height be
  taken.
Love's not Time's fool, though rosy lips and cheeks
Within his bending sickle's compass come;
Love alters not with his brief hours and weeks,
But bears it out even to the edge of doom.
  If this be error, and upon me proved,
  I never writ, nor no man ever loved.

117.

Accuse me thus: that I have scanted all
Wherein I should your great deserts repay;
Forgot upon your dearest love to call,
Whereto all bonds do tie me day by day;
That I have frequent been with unknown minds,
And given to time your own dear-purchased right;
That I have hoisted sail to all the winds
Which should transport me farthest from your
  sight.
Book both my wilfulness and errors down,
And on just proof surmise accumulate;
Bring me within the level of your frown,
But shoot not at me in your waken'd hate;
  Since my appeal says I did strive to prove
  The constancy and virtue of your love.

118.

Like as, to make our appetites more keen,
With eager compounds we our palate urge;
As, to prevent our maladies unseen,
We sicken to shun sickness when we purge;
Even so, being full of your ne'er-cloying sweetness,
To bitter sauces did I frame my feeding;
And, sick of welfare, found a kind of meetness
To be diseased, ere that there was true needing.
Thus policy in love, t'anticipate
The ills that were not, grew to faults assured,
And brought to medicine a healthful state,
Which, rank of goodness, would by ill be cured:
  But thence I learn, and find the lesson true,
  Drugs poison him that so fell sick of you.

119.

What potions have I drunk of Siren tears,
Distill'd from limbecks foul as hell within,
Applying fears to hopes, and hopes to fears,
Still losing when I saw myself to win!
What wretched errors hath my heart committed,
Whilst it hath thought itself so blessed never!
How have mine eyes out of their spheres been
    fitted
In the distraction of this madding fever!
O benefit of ill! now I find true
That better is by evil still made better;
And ruin'd love, when it is built anew,
Grows fairer than at first, more strong, far greater.
    So I return rebuked to my content,
    And gain by ill thrice more than I have spent.

120.

That you were once unkind befriends me now,
And for that sorrow which I then did feel
Needs must I under my transgression bow,
Unless my nerves were brass or hammer'd steel.
For if you were by my unkindness shaken,
As I by yours, y'have past a hell of time;
And I, a tyrant, have no leisure taken
To weigh how once I suffer'd in your crime.
O, that our night of woe might have remember'd
My deepest sense, how hard true sorrow hits,
And soon to you, as you to me then, tender'd
The humble salve which wounded bosoms fits!
    But that, your trespass, now becomes a fee;
    Mine ransoms yours, and yours must ransom
    me.

121.

'Tis better to be vile than vile esteemed,
When not to be receives reproach of being;
And the just pleasure lost, which is so deemed
Not by our feeling, but by others' seeing:
For why should others' false adulterate eyes
Give salutation to my sportive blood?
Or on my frailties why are frailer spies,
Which in their wills count bad what I think good?
No, I am that I am; and they that level
At my abuses reckon up their own:
I may be straight, though they themselves be bevel;
By their rank thoughts my deeds must not be
    shown;
    Unless this general evil they maintain—
    All men are bad, and in their badness reign.

122.

Thy gift, thy tables, are within my brain
Full character'd with lasting memory,
Which shall above that idle rank remain,
Beyond all date, even to eternity:
Or, at the least, so long as brain and heart
Have faculty by nature to subsist;
Till each to razed oblivion yield his part
Of thee, thy record never can be mist.
That poor retention could not so much hold,
Nor need I tallies thy dear love to score;
Therefore to give them from me was I bold,
To trust those tables that receive thee more:
    To keep an adjunct to remember thee
    Were to import forgetfulness in me.

123.

No, Time, thou shalt not boast that I do change:
Thy pyramids built up with newer might
To me are nothing novel, nothing strange;
They are but dressings of a former sight.
Our dates are brief, and therefore we admire
What thou dost foist upon us that is old;
And rather make them born to our desire
Than think that we before have heard them told.
Thy registers and thee I both defy,
Not wondering at the present nor the past;
For thy records and what we see doth lie,
Made more or less by thy continual haste.
    This I do vow, and this shall ever be,
    I will be true, despite thy scythe and thee.

124.

If my dear love were but the child of state,
It might for Fortune's bastard be unfather'd,
As subject to Time's love or to Time's hate,
Weeds among weeds, or flowers with flowers
    gather'd.
No, it was builded far from accident;
It suffers not in smiling pomp, nor falls
Under the blow of thralled discontent,
Whereto the inviting time our fashion calls:
It fears not policy, that heretic,
Which works on leases of short-number'd hours,
But all alone stands hugely politic,
That it nor grows with heat nor drowns with
    showers.
    To this I witness call the fools of Time,
    Which die for goodness, who have lived for
    crime.

125.

Were't aught to me I bore the canopy,
With my extern the outward honouring,
Or laid great bases for eternity,
Which proves more short than waste or ruining?
Have I not seen dwellers on form and favour
Lose all, and more, by paying too much rent,
For compound sweet foregoing simple savour,
Pitiful thrivers, in their gazing spent?
No, let me be obsequious in thy heart,
And take thou my oblation, poor but free,
Which is not mixt with seconds, knows no art,
But mutual render, only me for thee.
    Hence, thou suborn'd informer! a true soul
    When most impeacht stands least in thy control.

126.

O thou, my lovely boy, who in thy power
Dost hold Time's fickle glass, his sickle-hour;
Who hast by waning grown, and therein show'st
Thy lovers withering, as thy sweet self grow'st;
If Nature, sovereign mistress over wrack,
As thou goest onwards, still will pluck thee back,
She keeps thee to this purpose, that her skill
May Time disgrace, and wretched minutes kill.
Yet fear her, O thou minion of her pleasure!
She may detain, but not still keep, her treasure:
Her audit, though delay'd, answer'd must be,
And her quietus is to render thee.

127.

In the old age black was not counted fair,
Or if it were, it bore not beauty's name;
But now is black beauty's successive heir,
And beauty slander'd with a bastard shame:
For since each hand hath put on nature's power,
Fairing the foul with art's false borrow'd face,
Sweet beauty hath no name, no holy bower,
But is profaned, if not lives in disgrace.
Therefore my mistress' eyes are raven black,
Her eyes so suited, and they mourners seem
At such who, not born fair, no beauty lack,
Slandering creation with a false esteem:
    Yet so they mourn, becoming of their woe,
    That every tongue says beauty should look so.

128.

How oft, when thou, my music, music play'st,
Upon that blessed wood whose motion sounds
With thy sweet fingers, when thou gently sway'st
The wiry concord that mine ear confounds,
Do I envy those jacks that nimble leap
To kiss the tender inward of thy hand,
Whilst my poor lips, which should that harvest reap,
At the wood's boldness by thee blushing stand!
To be so tickled, they would change their state
And situation with those dancing chips,
O'er whom thy fingers walk with gentle gait,
Making dead wood more blest than living lips.
    Since saucy jacks so happy are in this,
    Give them thy fingers, me thy lips to kiss.

129.

The expense of spirit in a waste of shame
Is lust in action; and till action, lust
Is perjured, murd'rous, bloody, full of blame,
Savage, extreme, rude, cruel, not to trust;
Enjoy'd no sooner but despised straight;
Past reason hunted; and no sooner had,
Past reason hated, as a swallow'd bait,
On purpose laid to make the taker mad:
Mad in pursuit, and in possession so;
Had, having, and in quest to have, extreme;
A bliss in proof, and proved, a very woe;
Before, a joy proposed; behind, a dream.
    All this the world well knows; yet none knows well
    To shun the heaven that leads men to this hell.

130.

My mistress' eyes are nothing like the sun;
Coral is far more red than her lips' red;
If snow be white, why then her breasts are dun;
If hairs be wires, black wires grow on her head.
I have seen roses damaskt, red and white,
But no such roses see I in her cheeks;
And in some perfumes is there more delight
Than in the breath that from my mistress reeks.
I love to hear her speak, yet well I know
That music hath a far more pleasing sound:
I grant I never saw a goddess go;
My mistress, when she walks, treads on the ground.
    And yet, by heaven, I think my love as rare
    As any she belied with false compare.

131.

Thou art as tyrannous, so as thou art,
As those whose beauties proudly make them cruel;
For well thou know'st to my dear doting heart
Thou art the fairest and most precious jewel.
Yet, in good faith, some say that thee behold,
Thy face hath not the power to make love groan.
To say they err I dare not be so bold,
Although I swear it to myself alone.
And, to be sure that is not false I swear,
A thousand groans, but thinking on thy face,
One on another's neck, do witness bear
Thy black is fairest in my judgement's place.
    In nothing art thou black save in thy deeds,
    And thence this slander, as I think, proceeds.

132.

Thine eyes I love, and they, as pitying me,
Knowing thy heart torments me with disdain,
Have put on black, and loving mourners be,
Looking with pretty ruth upon my pain.
And truly not the morning sun of heaven
Better becomes the gray cheeks of the east,
Nor that full star that ushers in the even
Doth half that glory to the sober west,
As those two mourning eyes become thy face:
O, let it, then, as well beseem thy heart
To mourn for me, since mourning doth thee grace,
And suit thy pity like in every part.
    Then will I swear Beauty herself is black,
    And all they foul that thy complexion lack.

133.

Beshrew that heart that makes my heart to groan
For that deep wound it gives my friend and me!
Is't not enough to torture me alone,
But slave to slavery my sweet'st friend must be?
Me from myself thy cruel eye hath taken,
And my next self thou harder hast engrossed:
Of him, myself, and thee, I am forsaken;
A torment thrice threefold thus to be crossed.
Prison my heart in thy steel bosom's ward,
But then my friend's heart let my poor heart bail;
Whoe'er keeps me, let my heart be his guard;
Thou canst not then use rigour in my jail:
    And yet thou wilt; for I, being pent in thee,
    Perforce am thine, and all that is in me.

134.

So, now I have confest that he is thine,
And I myself am mortgaged to thy will,
Myself I'll forfeit, so that other mine
Thou wilt restore, to be my comfort still:
But thou wilt not, nor he will not be free,
For thou art covetous, and he is kind;
He learn'd but, surety-like, to write for me,
Under that bond that him as fast doth bind.
The statute of thy beauty thou wilt take,
Thou usurer, that putt'st forth all to use,
And sue a friend came debtor for my sake;
So him I lose through my unkind abuse.
    Him have I lost; thou hast both him and me:
    He pays the whole, and yet am I not free.

135.

Whoever hath her wish, thou hast thy *Will*,
And *Will* to boot, and *Will* in overplus;
More than enough am I that vex thee still,
To thy sweet will making addition thus.
Wilt thou, whose will is large and spacious,
Not once vouchsafe to hide my will in thine?
Shall will in others seem right gracious,
And in my will no fair acceptance shine?
The sea, all water, yet receives rain still,
And in abundance addeth to his store;
So thou, being rich in *Will*, add to thy *Will*
One will of mine, to make thy large *Will* more.
   Let no unkind, no fair beseechers kill;
   Think all but one, and me in that one *Will*.

136.

If thy soul check thee that I come so near,
Swear to thy blind soul that I was thy *Will*,
And will, thy soul knows, is admitted there;
Thus far for love my love-suit, sweet, fulfil.
Will will fulfil the treasure of thy love,
Ay, fill it full with wills, and my will one.
In things of great receipt with ease we prove
Among a number one is reckon'd none:
Then in the number let me pass untold,
Though in thy store's account I one must be;
For nothing hold me, so it please thee hold
That nothing me, a something, sweet, to thee:
   Make but my name thy love, and love that still,
   And then thou lovest me, for my name is *Will*.

137.

Thou blind fool, Love, what dost thou to mine
   eyes,
That they behold, and see not what they see?
They know what beauty is, see where it lies,
Yet what the best is take the worst to be.
If eyes, corrupt by over-partial looks,
Be anchor'd in the bay where all men ride,
Why of eyes' falsehood hast thou forged hooks,
Whereto the judgement of my heart is tied?
Why should my heart think that a several plot
Which my heart knows the wide world's common
   place?
Or mine eyes seeing this, say this is not,
To put fair truth upon so foul a face?
   In things right-true my heart and eyes have
     erred,
   And to this false plague are they now trans-
     ferred.

138.

When my love swears that she is made of truth,
I do believe her, though I know she lies,
That she might think me some untutor'd youth,
Unlearned in the world's false subtleties.
Thus vainly thinking that she thinks me young,
Although she knows my days are past the best,
Simply I credit her false-speaking tongue:
On both sides thus is simple truth supprest.
But wherefore says she not she is unjust?
And wherefore say not I that I am old?
O, love's best habit is in seeming trust,
And age in love loves not to have years told:
   Therefore I lie with her and she with me,
   And in our faults by lies we flatter'd be.

139.

O, call not me to justify the wrong
That thy unkindness lays upon my heart;
Wound me not with thine eye, but with thy tongue;
Use power with power, and slay me not by art.
Tell me thou lovest elsewhere; but in my sight,
Dear heart, forbear to glance thine eye-aside:
What need'st thou wound with cunning, when
   thy might
Is more than my o'erprest defence can bide?
Let me excuse thee: ah, my love well knows
Her pretty looks have been mine enemies;
And therefore from my face she turns my foes,
That they elsewhere might dart their injuries:
   Yet do not so; but since I am near slain,
   Kill me outright with looks, and rid my pain.

140.

Be wise as thou art cruel; do not press
My tongue-tied patience with too much disdain;
Lest sorrow lend me words, and words express
The manner of my pity-wanting pain.
If I might teach thee wit, better it were,
Though not to love, yet, love, to tell me so;
As testy sick men, when their deaths be near,
No news but health from their physicians know;
For, if I should despair, I should grow mad,
And in my madness might speak ill of thee:
Now this ill-wresting world is grown so bad,
Mad slanderers by mad ears believed be.
   That I may not be so, nor thou belied,
   Bear thine eyes straight, though thy proud
     heart go wide.

141.

In faith, I do not love thee with mine eyes,
For they in thee a thousand errors note;
But 'tis my heart that loves what they despise,
Who, in despite of view, is pleased to dote;
Nor are mine ears with thy tongue's tune de-
   lighted;
Nor tender feeling to base touches prone,
Nor taste, nor smell, desire to be invited
To any sensual feast with thee alone:
But my five wits nor my five senses can
Dissuade one foolish heart from serving thee,
Who leaves unsway'd the likeness of a man,
Thy proud heart's slave and vassal wretch to be:
   Only my plague thus far I count my gain,
   That she that makes me sin awards me pain.

142.

Love is my sin, and thy dear virtue hate,
Hate of my sin, grounded on sinful loving:
O, but with mine compare thou thine own state,
And thou shalt find it merits not reproving;
Or, if it do, not from those lips of thine,
That have profaned their scarlet ornaments
And seal'd false bonds of love as oft as mine,
Robb'd others' beds' revenues of their rents.
Be it lawful I love thee, as thou lovest those
Whom thine eyes woo as mine importune thee:
Root pity in thy heart, that, when it grows,
Thy pity may deserve to pitied be.
   If thou dost seek to have what thou dost hide,
   By self-example mayst thou be denied!

143.

Lo, as a careful housewife runs to catch
One of her feather'd creatures broke away,
Sets down her babe, and makes all swift dispatch
In pursuit of the thing she would have stay;
Whilst her neglected child holds her in chase,
Cries to catch her whose busy care is bent
To follow that which flies before her face,
Not prizing her poor infant's discontent:
So runn'st thou after that which flies from thee,
Whilst I thy babe chase thee afar behind;
But if thou catch thy hope, turn back to me,
And play the mother's part, kiss me, be kind:
    So will I pray that thou mayst have thy *Will*,
    If thou turn back, and my loud crying still.

144.

Two loves I have of comfort and despair,
Which like two spirits do suggest me still:
The better angel is a man right fair,
The worser spirit a woman colour'd ill.
To win me soon to hell, my female evil
Tempteth my better angel from my side,
And would corrupt my saint to be a devil,
Wooing his purity with her foul pride.
And whether that my angel be turn'd fiend
Suspect I may, yet not directly tell;
But being both from me, both to each friend,
I guess one angel in another's hell:
    Yet this shall I ne'er know, but live in doubt,
    Till my bad angel fire my good one out.

145.

Those lips that Love's own hand did make
Breathed forth the sound that said 'I hate'
To me that languisht for her sake:
But when she saw my woeful state,
Straight in her heart did mercy come,
Chiding that tongue that ever sweet
Was used in giving gentle doom;
And taught it thus anew to greet;
'I hate' she alter'd with an end,
That follow'd it as gentle day
Doth follow night, who like a fiend
From heaven to hell is flown away;
    'I hate' from hate away she threw,
    And saved my life, saying—'Not you.'

146.

Poor soul, the centre of my sinful earth—
My sinful earth these rebel powers array—
Why dost thou pine within and suffer dearth,
Painting thy outward walls so costly gay?
Why so large cost, having so short a lease,
Dost thou upon thy fading mansion spend?
Shall worms, inheritors of this excess,
Eat up thy charge? is this thy body's end?
Then, soul, live thou upon thy servant's loss,
And let that pine to aggravate thy store;
Buy terms divine in selling hours of dross;
Within be fed, without be rich no more:
    So shalt thou feed on Death, that feeds on men,
    And Death once dead, there's no more dying
      then.

147.

My love is as a fever, longing still
For that which longer nurseth the disease;
Feeding on that which doth preserve the ill,
The uncertain sickly appetite to please.
My reason, the physician to my love,
Angry that his prescriptions are not kept,
Hath left me, and I desperate now approve
Desire is death, which physic did except.
Past cure I am, now reason is past care,
And frantic-mad with evermore unrest;
My thoughts and my discourse as madmen's are,
At random from the truth vainly exprest;
    For I have sworn thee fair, and thought thee
      bright,
    Who art as black as hell, as dark as night.

148.

O me, what eyes hath Love put in my head,
Which have no correspondence with true sight!
Or, if they have, where is my judgement fled,
That censures falsely what they see aright?
If that be fair whereon my false eyes dote,
What means the world to say it is not so?
If it be not, then love doth well denote
Love's eye is not so true as all men's: no.
How can it? O, how can Love's eye be true,
That is so vext with watching and with tears?
No marvel, then, though I mistake my view;
The sun itself sees not till heaven clears.
    O cunning Love! with tears thou keep'st me
      blind,
    Lest eyes well-seeing thy foul faults should find.

149.

Canst thou, O cruel! say I love thee not,
When I, against myself, with thee partake?
Do I not think on thee, when I forgot
Am of myself, all tyrant for thy sake?
Who hateth thee that I do call my friend?
On whom frown'st thou that I do fawn upon?
Nay, if thou lour'st on me, do I not spend
Revenge upon myself with present moan?
What merit do I in myself respect,
That is so proud thy service to despise,
When all my best doth worship thy defect,
Commanded by the motion of thine eyes?
    But, love, hate on, for now I know thy mind;
    Those that can see thou lovest, and I am blind.

150.

O, from what power hast thou this powerful might
With insufficiency my heart to sway?
To make me give the lie to my true sight,
And swear that brightness doth not grace the day?
Whence hast thou this becoming of things ill,
That in the very refuse of thy deeds
There is such strength and warrantise of skill,
That, in my mind, thy worst all best exceeds?
Who taught thee how to make me love thee more,
The more I hear and see just cause of hate?
O, though I love what others do abhor,
With others thou shouldst not abhor my state:
    If thy unworthiness raised love in me,
    More worthy I to be beloved of thee.

151.

Love is too young to know what conscience is;
Yet who knows not conscience is born of love?
Then, gentle cheater, urge not my amiss,
Lest guilty of my faults thy sweet self prove:
For, thou betraying me, I do betray
My nobler part to my gross body's treason;
My soul doth tell my body that he may
Triumph in love; flesh stays no farther reason;
But, rising at thy name, doth point out thee
As his triumphant prize. Proud of this pride,
He is contented thy poor drudge to be,
To stand in thy affairs, fall by thy side.
   No want of conscience hold it that I call
   Her 'love' for whose dear love I rise and fall.

152.

In loving thee thou know'st I am forsworn,
But thou art twice forsworn, to me love swearing;
In act thy bed-vow broke, and new faith torn
In vowing new hate after new love bearing.
But why of two oaths' breach do I accuse thee,
When I break twenty? I am perjured most;
For all my vows are oaths but to misuse thee,
And all my honest faith in thee is lost:
For I have sworn deep oaths of thy deep kindness,
Oaths of thy love, thy truth, thy constancy;
And, to enlighten thee, gave eyes to blindness,
Or made them swear against the thing they see;
   For I have sworn thee fair; more perjured I,
   To swear against the truth so foul a lie!

153.

Cupid laid by his brand, and fell asleep:
A maid of Dian's this advantage found,
And his love-kindling fire did quickly steep
In a cold valley-fountain of that ground;
Which borrow'd from this holy fire of Love
A dateless lively heat, still to endure,
And grew a seething bath, which yet men prove
Against strange maladies a sovereign cure.
But at my mistress' eye Love's brand new-fired,
The boy for trial needs would touch my breast;
I, sick withal, the help of bath desired,
And thither hied, a sad distemper'd guest,
   But found no cure: the bath for my help lies
   Where Cupid got new fire,—my mistress' eyes.

154.

The little Love-god lying once asleep
Laid by his side his heart-inflaming brand,
Whilst many nymphs that vow'd chaste life to keep
Came tripping by; but in her maiden hand
The fairest votary took up that fire
Which many legions of true hearts had warm'd;
And so the general of hot desire
Was sleeping by a virgin hand disarm'd.
This brand she quenched in a cool well by,
Which from Love's fire took heat perpetual,
Growing a bath and healthful remedy
For men diseased; but I, my mistress' thrall,
   Came there for cure, and this by that I prove,
   Love's fire heats water, water cools not love.

A LOVER'S COMPLAINT

FROM off a hill whose concave womb re-worded
A plaintful story from a sistering vale,
My spirits t'attend this double voice accorded,
And down I laid to list the sad-tuned tale;
Ere long espied a fickle maid full pale,
Tearing of papers, breaking rings a-twain,
Storming her world with sorrow's wind and rain.

Upon her head a platted hive of straw,
Which fortified her visage from the sun,
Whereon the thought might think sometime it saw
The carcass of a beauty spent and done:
Time had not scythed all that youth begun,
Nor youth all quit; but, spite of heaven's fell rage,
Some beauty peept through lattice of sear'd age.

Oft did she heave her napkin to her eyne,
Which on it had conceited characters,
Laundering the silken figures in the brine
That season'd woe had pelleted in tears,
And often reading what contents it bears;
As often shrieking undistinguisht woe,
In clamours of all size, both high and low.

Sometimes her levell'd eyes their carriage ride,
As they did battery to the spheres intend;
Sometime diverted their poor balls are tied
To th' orbed earth; sometimes they do extend
Their view right on; anon their gazes lend
To every place at once, and, nowhere fixt,
The mind and sight distractedly commixt.

Her hair, nor loose nor tied in formal plat,
Proclaim'd in her a careless hand of pride;
For some, untuckt, descended her sheaved hat,
Hanging her pale and pined cheek beside;
Some in her threaden fillet still did bide,
And, true to bondage, would not break from
   thence,
Though slackly braided in loose negligence.

A thousand favours from a maund she drew
Of amber, crystal, and of beaded jet,
Which one by one she in a river threw,
Upon whose weeping margent she was set;
Like usury, applying wet to wet,
Or monarch's hands that lets not bounty fall
Where want cries some, but where excess begs all.

Of folded schedules had she many a one,
Which she perused, sigh'd, tore, and gave the
   flood;
Crackt many a ring of posied gold and bone,
Bidding them find their sepulchres in mud;
Found yet moe letters sadly penn'd in blood,
With sleided silk feat and affectedly
Enswathed, and seal'd to curious secrecy.

These often bathed she in her fluxive eyes,
And often kist, and often gan to tear;
Cried, 'O false blood, thou register of lies,
What unapproved witness dost thou bear!

Ink would have seem'd more black and damned
   here!'
This said, in top of rage the lines she rents,
Big discontent so breaking their contents.

A reverend man that grazed his cattle nigh—
Sometime a blusterer, that the ruffle knew
Of court, of city, and had let go by
The swiftest hours, observed as they flew—
Towards this afflicted fancy fastly drew,
And, privileged by age, desires to know
In brief the grounds and motives of her woe.

So slides he down upon his grained bat,
And comely-distant sits he by her side;
When he again desires her, being sat,
Her grievance with his hearing to divide:
If that from him there may be aught applied
Which may her suffering ecstasy assuage,
'Tis promised in the charity of age.

'Father,' she says, 'though in me you behold
The injury of many a blasting hour,
Let it not tell your judgement I am old;
Not age, but sorrow, over me hath power:
I might as yet have been a spreading flower,
Fresh to myself, if I had self-applied
Love to myself, and to no love beside.

'But, woe is me! too early I attended
A youthful suit—it was to gain my grace—
Of one by nature's outwards so commended,
That maidens' eyes stuck over all his face:
Love lackt a dwelling, and made him her place;
And when in his fair parts she did abide,
She was new lodged, and newly deified.

'His browny locks did hang in crooked curls;
And every light occasion of the wind
Upon his lips their silken parcels hurls.
What's sweet to do, to do will aptly find:
Each eye that saw him did enchant the mind;
For on his visage was in little drawn
What largeness thinks in Paradise was sawn.

'Small show of man was yet upon his chin;
His phœnix down began but to appear,
Like unshorn velvet, on that termless skin,
Whose bare out-bragg'd the web it seem'd to
   wear:
Yet show'd his visage by that cost more dear;
And nice affections wavering stood in doubt
If best were as it was, or best without.

'His qualities were beauteous as his form,
For maiden-tongued he was, and thereof free;
Yet, if men moved him, was he such a storm
As oft 'twixt May and April is to see,
When winds breathe sweet, unruly though they
   be.
His rudeness so with his authorized youth
   Did livery falseness in a pride of truth.

'Well could he ride, and often men would say,
"That horse his mettle from his rider takes:
Proud of subjection, noble by the sway,
What rounds, what bounds, what course, what
     stop he makes!"
And controversy hence a question takes,
Whether the horse by him became his deed,
Or he his manage by the well-doing steed.

'But quickly on this side the verdict went:
His real habitude gave life and grace
To appertainings and to ornament,
Accomplisht in himself, not in his case:
All aids, themselves made fairer by their place,
Came for additions; yet their purposed trim
Pieced not his grace, but were all graced by him.

'So on the tip of his subduing tongue
All kind of arguments and question deep,
All replication prompt, and reason strong,
For his advantage still did wake and sleep:
To make the weeper laugh, the laugher weep,
He had the dialect and different skill,
Catching all passions in his craft of will:

'That he did in the general bosom reign
Of young, of old; and sexes both enchanted,
To dwell with him in thoughts, or to remain
In personal duty, following where he haunted:
Consents bewitcht, ere he desire, have granted;
And dialogued for him what he would say,
Askt their own wills, and made their wills obey.

'Many there were that did his picture get,
To serve their eyes, and in it put their mind;
Like fools that in th' imagination set
The goodly objects which abroad they find
Of lands and mansions, theirs in thought assign'd;
And labouring in moe pleasures to bestow them
Than the true gouty landlord which doth owe
     them:

'So many have, that never toucht his hand,
Sweetly supposed them mistress of his heart.
My woeful self, that did in freedom stand,
And was my own fee-simple, not in part,
What with his art in youth, and youth in art,
Threw my affections in his charmed power,
Reserved the stalk, and gave him all my flower.

'Yet did I not, as some my equals did,
Demand of him, nor being desired yielded;
Finding myself in honour so forbid,
With safest distance I mine honour shielded:
Experience for me many bulwarks builded
Of proofs new-bleeding, which remain'd the foil
Of this false jewel, and his amorous spoil.

'But, ah, who ever shunn'd by precedent
The destined ill she must herself assay?
Or forced examples, 'gainst her own content,
To put the by-past perils in her way?
Counsel may stop awhile what will not stay;
For when we rage, advice is often seen
By blunting us to make our wits more keen.

'Nor gives it satisfaction to our blood,
That we must curb it upon others' proof;
To be forbod the sweets that seem so good,
For fear of harms that preach in our behoof.
O appetite, from judgement stand aloof!
The one a palate hath that needs will taste,
Though Reason weep, and cry, "It is thy last."

'For further I could say, "This man's untrue,"
And knew the patterns of his foul beguiling;
Heard where his plants in others' orchards grew,
Saw how deceits were gilded in his smiling;
Knew vows were ever brokers to defiling;
Thought characters and words merely but art,
And bastards of his foul adulterate heart.

'And long upon these terms I held my city,
Till thus he gan besiege me: "Gentle maid,
Have of my suffering youth some feeling pity,
And be not of my holy vows afraid:
That's to ye sworn to none was ever said;
For feasts of love I have been call'd unto,
Till now did ne'er invite, nor never woo.

' "All my offences that abroad you see
Are errors of the blood, none of the mind;
Love made them not; with acture they may be,
Where neither party is nor true nor kind:
They sought their shame that so their shame did
     find;
And so much less of shame in me remains,
But how much of me their reproach contains.

' "Among the many that mine eyes have seen,
Not one whose flame my heart so much as warmed,
Or my affection put to the smallest teen,
Or any of my leisures ever charmed:
Harm have I done to them, but ne'er was harmed;
Kept hearts in liveries, but mine own was free,
And reign'd, commanding in his monarchy.

' "Look here, what tributes wounded fancies sent
     me,
Of paled pearls and rubies red as blood;
Figuring that they their passions likewise lent me
Of grief and blushes, aptly understood
In bloodless white and the encrimson'd mood;
Effects of terror and dear modesty,
Encampt in hearts, but fighting outwardly.

' "And, lo, behold these talents of their hair,
With twisted metal amorously impleacht,
I have received from many a several fair—,
Their kind acceptance weepingly beseecht,—
With the annexions of fair gems enricht,
And deep-brain'd sonnets that did amplify
Each stone's dear nature, worth, and quality.

' "The diamond,—why, 'twas beautiful and hard,
Whereto his invised properties did tend;
The deep-green emerald, in whose fresh regard
Weak sights their sickly radiance do amend;
The heaven-hued sapphire, and the opal blend
With objects manifold: each several stone,
With wit well blazon'd, smiled or made some
     moan.

' "Lo, all these trophies of affections hot,
Of pensived and subdued desires the tender,
Nature hath charged me that I hoard them not,
But yield them up where I myself must render,
That is, to you, my origin and ender;
For these, of force, must your oblations be,
Since I their altar, you enpatron me.

' "O, then, advance of yours that phraseless hand,
Whose white weighs down the airy scale of praise;
Take all these similes to your own command,
Hallow'd with sighs that burning lungs did raise;
What me your minister, for you obeys,
Works under you; and to your audit comes
Their distract parcels in combined-sums.

' "Lo, this device was sent me from a nun,
A sister sanctified, of holiest note;
Which late her noble suit in court did shun,
Whose rarest havings made the blossoms dote;
For she was sought by spirits of richest coat,
But kept cold distance, and did thence remove,
To spend her living in eternal love.

' "But, O my sweet, what labour is't to leave
The thing we have not, mastering what not
    strives,—
Paling the place which did no form receive,
Playing patient sports in unconstrained gyves?
She that her fame so to herself contrives,
The scars of battle scapeth by the flight,
And makes her absence valiant, not her might.

' "O, pardon me, in that my boast is true:
The accident which brought me to her eye
Upon the moment did her force subdue,
And now she would the caged cloister fly:
Religious love put out Religion's eye:
Not to be tempted, would she be immured,
And now, to tempt all, liberty procured.

' "How mighty, then, you are, O, hear me tell!
The broken bosoms that to me belong
Have emptied all their fountains in my well,
And mine I pour your ocean all among:
I strong o'er them, and you o'er me being strong,
Must for your victory us all congest,
As compound love to physic your cold breast.

' "My parts had power to charm a sacred nun,
Who, disciplined, ay, dieted in grace,
Believed her eyes when they t'assail begun,
All vows and consecrations giving place:
O most potential love! vow, bond, nor space,
In thee hath neither sting, knot, nor confine,
For thou art all, and all things else are thine.

' "When thou impressest, what are precepts worth
Of stale example? When thou wilt inflame,
How coldly those impediments stand forth
Of wealth, of filial fear, law, kindred, fame!
Love's arms are peace, 'gainst rule, 'gainst sense,
    'gainst shame:
And sweetens, in the suffering pangs it bears,
The aloes of all forces, shocks, and fears.

' "Now all these hearts that do on mine depend,
Feeling it break, with bleeding groans they pine;
And supplicant their sighs to you extend,
To leave the battery that you make 'gainst mine,
Lending soft audience to my sweet design;
And credent soul to that strong-bonded oath
That shall prefer and undertake my troth."

'This said, his watery eyes he did dismount,
Whose sights till then were levell'd on my face;
Each cheek a river running from a fount
With brinish current downward flow'd apace:
O, how the channel to the stream gave grace!
Who glazed with crystal gate the glowing roses
That flame through water which their hue en-
    closes.

'O father, what a hell of witchcraft lies
In the small orb of one particular tear!
But with the inundation of the eyes
What rocky heart to water will not wear?
What breast so cold that is not warmed here?
O cleft effect! cold modesty, hot wrath,
Both fire from hence and chill extincture hath.

'For, lo, his passion, but an art of craft,
Even there resolved my reason into tears;
There my white stole of chastity I daft,
Shook off my sober guards and civil fears;
Appear to him, as he to me appears,
All melting; though our drops this difference bore,
His poison'd me, and mine did him restore.

'In him a plenitude of subtle matter,
Applied to cautels, all strange forms receives,
Of burning blushes, or of weeping water,
Or swounding paleness; and he takes and leaves,
In either's aptness, as it best deceives,
To blush at speeches rank, to weep at woes,
Or to turn white and swound at tragic shows:

'That not a heart which in his level came
Could scape the hail of his all-hurting aim,
Showing fair nature is both kind and tame;
And, veil'd in them, did win whom he would
    maim:
Against the thing he sought he would exclaim;
When he most burnt in heart-wisht luxury,
He preacht pure maid, and praised cold chastity.

'Thus merely with the garment of a Grace
The naked and concealed fiend he cover'd;
That th' unexperient gave the tempter place,
Which, like a cherubin, above them hover'd.
Who, young and simple, would not be so lover'd?
Ay me! I fell; and yet do question make
What I should do again for such a sake.

'O, that infected moisture of his eye,
O, that false fire which in his cheek so glow'd,
O, that forced thunder from his heart did fly,
O, that sad breath his spongy lungs bestow'd,
O, all that borrow'd motion seeming ow'd,
Would yet again betray the fore-betray'd,
And new pervert a reconciled maid!'

THE PASSIONATE PILGRIM

1.

WHEN my love swears that she is made of
    truth,
I do believe her, though I know she lies,
That she might think me some untutor'd youth,
Unskilful in the world's false forgeries.
Thus vainly thinking that she thinks me young,
Although I know my years be past the best,
I smiling credit her false-speaking tongue,
Outfacing faults in love with love's ill rest.
But wherefore says my love that she is young?
And wherefore say not I that I am old?
O, love's best habit is a soothing tongue,
And age, in love, loves not to have years told.
    Therefore I'll lie with love, and love with me,
    Since that our faults in love thus smother'd be.

2.

Two loves I have, of comfort and despair,
That like two spirits do suggest me still;
My better angel is a man right fair,
My worser spirit a woman colour'd ill.
To win me soon to hell, my female evil
Tempteth my better angel from my side,
And would corrupt my saint to be a devil,
Wooing his purity with her fair pride.
And whether that my angel be turn'd fiend,
Suspect I may, yet not directly tell:
For being both to me, both to each friend,
I guess one angel in another's hell:
    The truth I shall not know, but live in doubt,
    Till my bad angel fire my good one out.

3.

Did not the heavenly rhetoric of thine eye,
'Gainst whom the world could not hold argument,
Persuade my heart to this false perjury?
Vows for thee broke deserve not punishment.
A woman I forswore; but I will prove,
Thou being a goddess, I forswore not thee:
My vow was earthly, thou a heavenly love;
Thy grace being gain'd cures all disgrace in me.
My vow was breath, and breath a vapour is;
Then, thou fair sun, that on this earth doth shine,
Exhale this vapour vow; in thee it is:
If broken, then it is no fault of mine.
    If by me broke, what fool is not so wise
    To break an oath, to win a paradise?

4.

Sweet Cytherea, sitting by a brook
With young Adonis, lovely, fresh and green,
Did court the lad with many a lovely look,
Such looks as none could look but beauty's queen.
She told him stories to delight his ear,
She show'd him favours to allure his eye;
To win his heart, she toucht him here and there;
Touches so soft still conquer chastity.
But whether unripe years did want conceit,
Or he refused to take her figured proffer,
The tender nibbler would not touch the bait,
But smile and jest at every gentle offer:
    Then fell she on her back, fair queen, and to-
      ward:
    He rose and ran away; ah, fool too froward.

5.

If love make me forsworn, how shall I swear to
    love?
O never faith could hold, if not to beauty vowed:
Though to myself forsworn, to thee I'll constant
    prove;
Those thoughts, to me like oaks, to thee like osiers
    bowed.
Study his bias leaves, and makes his book thine
    eyes,
Where all those pleasures live that art can com-
    prehend.
If knowledge be the mark, to know thee shall
    suffice;
Well learned is that tongue that well can thee
    commend:
All ignorant that soul that sees thee without
    wonder;
Which is to me some praise, that I thy parts admire;
Thine eye Jove's lightning seems, thy voice his
    dreadful thunder,
Which, not to anger bent, is music and sweet fire.
    Celestial as thou art, O do not love that wrong,
    To sing heaven's praise with such an earthly
      tongue.

6.

Scarce had the sun dried up the dewy morn,
And scarce the herd gone to the hedge for shade,
When Cytherea, all in love forlorn,
A longing tarriance for Adonis made
Under an osier growing by a brook,
A brook where Adon used to cool his spleen:
Hot was the day; she hotter that did look
For his approach, that often there had been.
Anon he comes, and throws his mantle by,
And stood stark naked on the brook's green brim:
The sun lookt on the world with glorious eye,
Yet not so wistly as this queen on him.
    He, spying her, bounced in, whereas he stood:
    'O Jove,' quoth she, 'why was not I a flood!'

7.

Fair is my love, but not so fair as fickle,
Mild as a dove, but neither true nor trusty,
Brighter than glass and yet, as glass is, brittle,
Softer than wax and yet as iron rusty:
    A lily pale, with damask dye to grace her,
    None fairer, nor none falser to deface her.

Her lips to mine how often hath she joined,
Between each kiss her oaths of true love swearing!
How many tales to please me hath she coined,
Dreading my love, the loss whereof still fearing!
    Yet in the midst of all her pure protestings,
    Her faith, her oaths, her tears, and all were
      jestings.

She burnt with love, as straw with fire flameth;
She burnt out love, as soon as straw out-burneth;
She framed the love, and yet she foil'd the fram-
    ing;
She bade love last, and yet she fell a-turning.
    Was this a lover, or a lecher whether?
    Bad in the best, though excellent in neither.

8.

If music and sweet poetry agree,
As they must needs, the sister and the brother,
Then must the love be great 'twixt thee and me,
Because thou lovest the one and I the other.
Dowland to thee is dear, whose heavenly touch
Upon the lute doth ravish human sense;
Spenser to me, whose deep conceit is such
As passing all conceit needs no defence.
Thou lovest to hear the sweet melodious sound
That Phœbus' lute, the queen of music, makes;
And I in deep delight am chiefly drown'd
Whenas himself to singing he betakes.
    One god is god of both, as poets feign;
    One knight loves both, and both in thee remain.

9.

Fair was the morn when the fair queen of love,
. . . . . .
Paler for sorrow than her milk-white dove,
For Adon's sake, a youngster proud and wild;
Her stand she takes upon a steep-up hill:
Anon Adonis comes with horn and hounds;
She, silly queen, with more than love's good will,
Forbade the boy he should not pass those grounds:
'Once,' quoth she, 'did I see a fair sweet youth
Here in these brakes deep-wounded with a boar,
Deep in the thigh, a spectacle of ruth!
See, in my thigh,' quoth she, 'here was the sore.'
    She showed hers: he saw more wounds than
        one,
    And blushing fled, and left her all alone.

10.

Sweet rose, fair flower, untimely pluckt, soon
    vaded,
Pluckt in the bud and vaded in the spring!
Bright orient pearl, alack, too timely shaded!
Fair creature, kill'd too soon by death's sharp
    sting!
    Like a green plum that hangs upon a tree,
    And falls through wind before the fall should be.

I weep for thee and yet no cause I have;
For why thou left'st me nothing in thy will:
And yet thou left'st me more than I did crave;
For why I craved nothing of thee still:
    O yes, dear friend, I pardon crave of thee,
    Thy discontent thou didst bequeath to me.

11.

Venus, with young Adonis sitting by her
Under a myrtle shade, began to woo him:
She told the youngling how god Mars did try her,
And as he fell to her, so fell she to him.
'Even thus,' quoth she, 'the warlike god em-
        braced me,'
And then she clipt Adonis in her arms;
'Even thus,' quoth she, 'the warlike god unlaced
        me,'
As if the boy should use like loving charms;
'Even thus,' quoth she, 'he seized on my lips,'
And with her lips on his did act the seizure:
And as she fetched breath, away he skips,
And would not take her meaning nor her pleasure.
    Ah, that I had my lady at this bay,
    To kiss and clip me till I run away!

12.

Crabbed age and youth cannot live together:
Youth is full of pleasance, age is full of care;
Youth like summer morn, age like winter weather;
Youth like summer brave, age like winter bare.
Youth is full of sport, age's breath is short;
    Youth is nimble, age is lame;
Youth is hot and bold, age is weak and cold;
    Youth is wild, and age is tame.
Age, I do abhor thee; youth, I do adore thee;
    O, my love, my love is young!
Age, I do defy thee: O, sweet shepherd, hie thee,
    For methinks thou stay'st too long.

13.

Beauty is but a vain and doubtful good;
A shining gloss that vadeth suddenly;
A flower that dies when first it gins to bud;
A brittle glass that's broken presently:
    A doubtful good, a gloss, a glass, a flower,
    Lost, vaded, broken, dead within an hour.

And as goods lost are seld or never found,
As vaded gloss no rubbing will refresh,
As flowers dead lie wither'd on the ground,
As broken glass no cement can redress,
    So beauty blemisht once for ever lost,
    In spite of physic, painting, pain and cost.

14.

Good night, good rest. Ah, neither be my share:
She bade good night that kept my rest away;
And daft me to a cabin hang'd with care,
To descant on the doubts of my decay. [morrow:'
    'Farewell,' quoth she, 'and come again to-
    Fare well I could not, for I supt with sorrow.

Yet at my parting sweetly did she smile,
In scorn or friendship, nill I conster whether:
'T may be, she joy'd to jest at my exile,
'T may be, again to make me wander thither:
    'Wander,' a word for shadows like myself,
    As take the pain, but cannot pluck the pelf.

15.

Lord, how mine eyes throw gazes to the east!
My heart doth charge the watch; the morning rise
Doth cite each moving sense from idle rest.
Not daring trust the office of mine eyes,
    While Philomela sits and sings, I sit and mark,
    And wish her lays were tuned like the lark;

For she doth welcome daylight with her ditty,
And drives away dark dreaming night:
The night so packt, I post unto my pretty;
Heart hath his hope and eyes their wished sight;
    Sorrow changed to solace and solace mixt with
        sorrow;   [morrow.
    For why she sigh'd, and bade me come to-

Were I with her, the night would post too soon;
But now are minutes added to the hours;
To spite me now, each minute seems a moon;
Yet not for me, shine sun to succour flowers!
    Pack night, peep day; good day, of night now
        borrow:
    Short, night, to-night, and length thyself to-
        morrow.

SONNETS TO SUNDRY NOTES
OF MUSIC.

1.

IT was a lording's daughter, the fairest one of
  three,
That liked of her master as well as well might be,
Till looking on an Englishman, the fair'st that eye
  could see,
  Her fancy fell a-turning.
Long was the combat doubtful that love with love
  did fight,
To leave the master loveless, or kill the gallant
  knight:
To put in practice either, alas, it was a spite
  Unto the silly damsel!
But one must be refused; more mickle was the
  pain
That nothing could be used to turn them both to
  gain,
For of the two the trusty knight was wounded
  with disdain:
  Alas, she could not help it!
Thus art with arms contending was victor of the
  day,
Which by a gift of learning did bear the maid away:
Then, lullaby, the learned man hath got the lady
  gay;
  For now my song is ended.

2.

On a day, alack the day!
Love, whose month was ever May,
Spied a blossom passing fair,
Playing in the wanton air:
Through the velvet leaves the wind
All unseen gan passage find;
That the lover, sick to death,
Wisht himself the heaven's breath,
'Air,' quoth he, 'thy cheeks may blow;
Air, would I might triumph so!
But, alas! my hand hath sworn
Ne'er to pluck thee from thy thorn:
Vow, alack! for youth unmeet:
Youth, so apt to pluck a sweet.
Thou for whom Jove would swear
Juno but an Ethiope were;
And deny himself for Jove,
Turning mortal for thy love.'

3.

My flocks feed not,
My ewes breed not,
My rams speed not;
  All is amiss:
Love's denying,
Faith's defying,
Heart's renying,
  Causer of this.
All my merry jigs are quite forgot,
All my lady's love is lost, God wot:
Where her faith was firmly fixt in love,
There a nay is placed without remove.
  One silly cross
  Wrought all my loss;

O frowning Fortune, cursed, fickle dame!
  For now I see
  Inconstancy
More in women than in men remain.

  In black mourn I,
  All fears scorn I,
  Love hath forlorn me,
    Living in thrall:
  Heart is bleeding,
  All help needing,
  O cruel speeding,
    Fraughted with gall.
My shepherd's pipe can sound no deal:
My wether's bell rings doleful knell;
My curtal dog, that wont to have play'd,
Plays not at all, but seems afraid;
  My sighs so deep
  Procure to weep,
In howling wise, to see my doleful plight.
  How sighs resound
  Through heartless ground,
Like a thousand vanquisht men in bloody fight!

  Clear wells spring not,
  Sweet birds sing not,
  Green plants bring not
    Forth their dye;
  Herds stand weeping,
  Flocks all sleeping,
  Nymphs back peeping
    Fearfully:
All our pleasure known to us poor swains,
All our merry meetings on the plains,
All our evening sport from us is fled,
All our love is lost, for Love is dead.
  Farewell, sweet lass,
  Thy like ne'er was
For a sweet content, the cause of all my moan:
  Poor Corydon
  Must live alone;
Other help for him I see that there is none.

4.

Whenas thine eye hath chose the dame,
And stall'd the deer that thou shouldst strike,
Let reason rule things worthy blame,
As well as fancy partial like:
  Take counsel of some wiser head,
  Neither too young nor yet unwed.

And when thou comest thy tale to tell,
Smooth not thy tongue with filed talk,
Lest she some subtle practice smell,—
A cripple soon can find a halt;—
  But plainly say thou lovest her well,
  And set thy person forth to sell.

What though her frowning brows be bent,
Her cloudy looks will calm ere night:
And then too late she will repent
That thus dissembled her delight;
  And twice desire, ere it be day,
  That which with scorn she put away.

What though she strive to try her strength,
And ban and brawl, and say thee nay,
Her feeble force will yield at length,
When craft hath taught her thus to say:
  'Had women been so strong as men,
  In faith, you had not had it then.'

And to her will frame all thy ways;
Spare not to spend, and chiefly there
Where thy desert may merit praise,
By ringing in thy lady's ear:
  The strongest castle, tower and town,
  The golden bullet beats it down.

Serve always with assured trust,
And in thy suit be humble true;
Unless thy lady prove unjust,
Press never thou to choose anew:
  When time shall serve, be thou not slack
  To proffer, though she put thee back.

The wiles and guiles that women work,
Dissembled with an outward show,
The tricks and toys that in them lurk,
The cock that treads them shall not know.
  Have you not heard it said full oft,
  A woman's nay doth stand for nought?

Think women still to strive with men,
To sin and never for to saint:
There is no heaven, by holy then,
When time with age shall them attaint.
  Were kisses all the joys in bed,
  One woman would another wed.

But, soft! enough—too much, I fear—
Lest that my mistress hear my song:
She will not stick to round me on the ear,
To teach my tongue to be so long:
  Yet will she blush, here be it said,
  To hear her secrets so bewray'd.

5.

Live with me, and be my love,
And we will all the pleasures prove
That hills and valleys, dales and fields,
And all the craggy mountains yields.

There will we sit upon the rocks,
And see the shepherds feed their flocks,
By shallow rivers, by whose falls
Melodious birds sing madrigals.

There will I make thee a bed of roses,
With a thousand fragrant posies,
A cap of flowers, and a kirtle
Embroider'd all with leaves of myrtle.

A belt of straw and ivy buds,
With coral clasps and amber studs;
And if these pleasures may thee move,
Then live with me and be my love.

LOVE'S ANSWER.

If that the world and love were young,
And truth in every shepherd's tongue,
These pretty pleasures might me move
To live with thee and be thy love.

6.

As it fell upon a day
In the merry month of May,
Sitting in a pleasant shade
Which a grove of myrtles made,
Beasts did leap and birds did sing,
Trees did grow and plants did spring;
Every thing did banish moan,
Save the nightingale alone:
She, poor bird, as all forlorn,
Lean'd her breast up-till a thorn,
And there sung the dolefull'st ditty,
That to hear it was great pity:
'Fie, fie, fie,' now would she cry;
'Tereu, Tereu!' by and by;
That to hear her so complain,
Scarce I could from tears refrain;
For her griefs so lively shown
Made me think upon mine own.
Ah, thought I, thou mourn'st in vain!
None takes pity on thy pain:
Senseless trees they cannot hear thee;
Ruthless beasts they will not cheer thee:
King Pandion he is dead;
All thy friends are lapt in lead;
All thy fellow birds do sing,
Careless of thy sorrowing.
Even so, poor bird, like thee,
None alive will pity me.
Whilst as fickle Fortune smiled,
Thou and I were both beguiled.

Every one that flatters thee
Is no friend in misery.
Words are easy, like the wind;
Faithful friends are hard to find:
Every man will be thy friend
Whilst thou hast wherewith to spend;
But if store of crowns be scant,
No man will supply thy want.
If that one be prodigal,
Bountiful they will him call,
And with such-like flattering,
'Pity but he were a king;'
If he be addict to vice,
Quickly him they will entice;
If to women he be bent,
They have at commandement:
But if Fortune once do frown,
Then farewell his great renown;
They that fawn'd on him before
Use his company no more.
He that is thy friend indeed,
He will help thee in thy need:
If thou sorrow, he will weep;
If thou wake, he cannot sleep;
Thus of every grief in heart
He with thee doth bear a part.
These are certain signs to know
Faithful friend from flattering foe.

THE PHOENIX AND TURTLE

LET the bird of loudest lay,
  On the sole Arabian tree,
Herald sad and trumpet be,
To whose sound chaste wings obey.

But thou shrieking harbinger,
Foul precurrer of the fiend,
Augur of the fever's end,
To this troop come thou not near!

From this session interdict
Every fowl of tyrant wing,
Save the eagle, feather'd king:
Keep the obsequy so strict.

Let the priest in surplice white,
That defunctive music can,
Be the death-divining swan,
Lest the requiem lack his right.

And thou treble-dated crow,
That thy sable gender makest
With the breath thou givest and takest,
'Mongst our mourners shalt thou go.

Here the anthem doth commence:
Love and constancy is dead;
Phœnix and the turtle fled
In a mutual flame from hence.

So they loved, as love in twain
Had the essence but in one;
Two distincts, division none:
Number there in love was slain.

Hearts remote, yet not asunder;
Distance, and no space was seen
'Twixt the turtle and his queen:
But in them it were a wonder.

So between them love did shine,
That the turtle saw his right
Flaming in the phœnix' sight;
Either was the other's mine.

Property was thus appalled,
That the self was not the same;
Single nature's double name
Neither two nor one was called.

Reason, in itself confounded,
Saw division grow together,
To themselves yet either neither,
Simple were so well compounded,

That it cried, How true a twain
Seemeth this concordant one!
Love hath reason, reason none,
If what parts can so remain.

Whereupon it made this threne
To the phœnix and the dove,
Co-supremes and stars of love,
As chorus to their tragic scene.

THRENOS.

Beauty, truth, and rarity,
Grace in all simplicity,
Here enclosed in cinders lie.

Death is now the phœnix' nest;
And the turtle's loyal breast
To eternity doth rest,

Leaving no posterity:
'Twas not their infirmity,
It was married chastity.

Truth may seem, but cannot be;
Beauty brag, but 'tis not she;
Truth and beauty buried be.

To this urn let those repair
That are either true or fair;
For these dead birds sigh a prayer.